This book is dedicated to

Jackie Isabell

(October 14, 1936–March 11, 2010)

Jackie was a pioneer co-author of the original edition of Weimaraner Ways. Without her friendship and organizational skills there would have never been a first Weimaraner Ways.

The Weimaraner Ways Trophy

(7 × 11-inch cold cast bronze by T. Acevedo)

Proceeds from the sale of this book will provide the Weimaraner Ways Trophy, pictured above, which is awarded to the Best of Breed winner at the Weimaraner Club of America's annual National Specialty. Proceeds will also benefit rescue and the Weimaraner Foundation Field Fund by supporting annual scholarships to the 1st and 2nd place winners at the National Derby.

Well over three years after the death of author Virginia Alexander's husband, Mark his faithful service dog Rio still loyal and devoted to duty, regularly finds special time to wait by his master's favorite chair. Photograph by Gene LaFollette.

ACKNOWLEDGEMENTS

My heartfelt thanks go to my late husband, Mark, for giving me the encouragement and financial aid to support the printing of the first edition of *Weimaraner Ways,* over 20 long years ago. Mark freed me from the restrictions of publishers and contracts, which gave me control over distribution and editing, thus saving at least seven chapters of the original work that reviewing editors felt were unnecessarily detailed for a breed that was "only 29th" on the doggie popularity list. Mark's continued support also gave me a vehicle to freely champion Weimaraner causes in the areas of health research, field advancement, and rescue support.

I also owe many, many thanks to savvy Weimaraner owners who by word of mouth quickly devoured the first printing of 3000 copies. Without the aid of any professional publishers, promotion or special advertising techniques *Weimaraner Ways* became the book Weimaraner and many sporting dog breeders required a new puppy owner to purchase.

No project of this scope is completed by a single person. Without the assistance of a small army this second edition would have been no more than a simple update of names and dates. The first *Weimaraner Ways* had became known as the Weimaraner Bible for some, and secondary market prices soared to over $500, even for a dented or chewed copy. So, when the first edition sold out I considered re-publishing, but with my husband's health problems as well as those of prior co-author Jackie Isabell, I was unable to focus on such a feat. Still I collected new photos and updated information.

Enter Brett Cosar, who single-handedly turned me on to computers. For that I will always be grateful. Looking back on 20 years worth of countless legal yellow pads of notes and handwritten manuscript, it is hard to imagine how the first *Weimaraner Ways* was produced without a home computer. He supplied me with "super-powered assistance" in a Mac5 computer and the confidence to go beyond the simple update of facts and figures that was originally envisioned. Whenever there were technical glitches my own personal "Mr. Geek Squad" appeared. Because of his can-do attitude, frequent technical support, and a computer push, my world will never be the same.

Thanks to Deborah Andrews for her contributions of international coordination and research and the liaison work required. Without her assistance, most especially *In the Beginning, The German Weimaraner Today,* and *The Influence of American Imports and Exports* would not provide the rich tapestry of photographs and details now available to Weimaraner fanciers.

Shirley Nilsson provided *The Obedient Weimaraner,* but was also always available to supply fact checking, photographs on short notice, as well as contacts, historical information, and details on Canadian Weimaraner activities, not to mention her ever-optimistic attitude.

Thanks go to Joe Strop *(Weimaraners and NAVHDA),* Sharon Sturm *(Best of Field),* Nick Ambulos *(Best in Show),* and Lori Barbee *(The Dance of Dog Agility)* for their patience and flexibility in meeting my needs, and for turning in their contributions so promptly several long years ago. Then when the final deadlines approached they cheerfully made the necessary revisions to ensure that *Weimaraner Ways* was as up-to-date as possible regarding additional titles dogs had earned in the intervening years.

When it came to information from other countries or organizations, I could not have finished this project without the special help of Maria Bondi and NAVHDA. They generously provided historical reports and updates on Weimaraners in NAVHDA. The Federation Cynologique Internationale, provided specialists and review of the material in *The Influence of American Imports and Exports* regarding the FCI and their activities Also, Rafael de Santiago provided his technical expertise to get the details just right. Shelly Shorrock gave an invaluable amount of information on the accomplishments of Canadian Weimaraners and put me in touch with their owners. Birgitta Guggolz, as is so typical of her, never failed to provide a helping hand when it came to information or support regarding her German homeland and Weimaraner activities there. Liz Harding was my primary source of information from Australia.

Highest praise also goes to Alan Patunoff and Sandra West for their tireless and relentless electronic record keeping of Weimaraner statistics. No other sporting breed is so blessed.

Grateful thanks go to Deborah Patton of the American Society for Indexing. After reviewing this manuscript, with the knowledge that this volume is primarily a vehicle for Weimaraner education and rescue support, Deborah offered it to her students as a training project. I thank each of the talented and courageous members of the Mid- and South-Atlantic Chapter of the American Society for Indexing that accepted the *Weimaraner Ways* challenge, and whose only remuneration will be a finished copy of the book to show as an example of their three-month project.

The late Dorothy Derr, Grand Master bridge player and Executive Secretary of the WCA for over 20 years, provided extensive knowledge and personal memory of past events that was simply irreplaceable, for both the first and second editions. Ellen Dodge, our excellent WCA secretary, has been consistently amazing in her willingness and ability to locate missing information and dates, as well as providing total access to the historical volumes of the WCA Magazine and records.

The visuals in *Weimaraner Ways* are key to its appeal. My friend William Wegman contributed over forty new original photographic works to highlight this volume. Thanks are not enough for his ongoing friendship and support. I'd also like to extend my appreciation to Jason Burch for his artistic consultations and for helping select that "just right" Wegman to suit each occasion. Gene LaFollette was Mr. Fix-it, and whenever the call for help went out he responded. Without Gene's creativity and profound patience many technical photos, often taken under the most arduous field conditions, would never have been captured. He has my deepest thanks, especially for the photo of Rio included in the dedication to my husband Mark, which opens this volume. Harry Giglio generously donated his own works for our use, and his artistic attention to detail provided a unique view of the Weimaraner.

Rodney Moon, Leslie Like, Shirley Nilsson, Louis Bonilla, Marek Bejna, and Barney Riley, talented amateur photographers, provided a nearly unending supply of photographs to fill special orders, often on short notice or under bizarre circumstances. Thanks to them and their cheerful assistants, friends (parents of children and owners of dogs), and models.

A select group of volunteers have aided me by proofreading chapters over the years and providing critical feedback. Their input helped to clarify content, correct errors, and locate the inevitable bloopers. Many of these people provided the missing link that put me in touch with long-lost or missing people, dogs, and dates. Judy Eddy, in particular, has proofed the entire book, including the appendices. A special salute goes to her tenacity and attention to detail. Also Rob Riley came in at the end of this project, and on a moment's notice was willing to spend hours verifying details and names.

While many volunteered time and contributed their knowledge over the years, special thanks go to Teresa Borman. She stuck with me through thick and thin, until the last photograph and biography was found or written. Through her efforts it was possible to locate every one of the Top-Producing Dams (65) and Sires (70), and even down to the final days she assisted in locating dogs and their owners in foreign countries. Each of her two chapters could have been a separate volume in their own right.

One of the most valuable assets to any publication is a gifted proofreader and editor. Heidi Orcutt-Gachiri accomplished this and then some, with her finely-tuned ability to turn a phrase in a heartbeat. Her eye for detail helped us to maintain consistency of style throughout this volume.

Producing such a volume as this one cannot be accomplished without the support of close friends and family. How would I have gotten by without the support of Maria Tanhueco, my good friend, handling the organization and processing of book pre-orders? She has been the voice of balance in the face of challenge. Of course my son Lyle, his wife Mindy and my granddaughter Grace always believed in the book. They cheered me on and were never too busy to help, no matter what the need.

Finally, there are three amazing friends without whom this volume simply would not exist, and to whom I will be forever grateful.

The efforts of Karen Millan leave me almost without words. Her ever-present calm, organization, and creative genius pulled me through innumerable revisions of chapters with unpredictable but dependable humor. Even her family joined in to help, including husband Bob, children Nick and Chris, mother-in-law Carol, and their faithful Gray Ghost, Oski. Without their understanding and support I could never have finished. If the reader finds this book to be a visual pleasure it is the result of Karen's gift for artistic page layout.

When it comes to the illustrations in this book Colleen Dugan is without equal. Whether it was scanning pictures from magazines and books, "repairing" old or damaged photographs, or improving candid snapshots, she provided the pictures that explain ideas or do justice to achievements. When I decided to go with full color Colleen patiently managed to get most photographs rescanned, so Colleen's touch is present in nearly every figure in this book. Also an excellent photographer in her own right, *Appendix C* includes her own Weimaraner's Snow Story.

And finally, words would never be adequate to thank Trish Riley, whose positive you-can-do-it attitude has never changed since the first day she called me from Alaska over 25 long years ago. Trish is a true friend with a treasure trove of vocabulary gems, even without a thesaurus. She was forever willing to be challenged by special research needs and remained unflappable and optimistic down to the publication wire. Without her acting as my second, third, and fourth voice and without our day-to-day sessions over several years that allowed me to enlarge and rewrite entire chapters, the book that you read today would still be a dream. Trish is like a dear daughter to me.

In closing, I am sad to report that Jackie Isabell, my close friend and co-author of the first edition, passed away when this volume was just completed. She missed the pleasure of seeing the second edition in print. It's never easy to lose a dear friend—and Jackie was a true friend—to both humans and her beloved Gray Ones. She will be greatly missed. Without Jackie there would have never been a first *Weimaraner Ways*. Jackie, this one honors your memory!

Lovingly,

Virginia Alexander

TABLE OF CONTENTS

THE FAMILY COMPANION AND ITS CARE

A MOST VERSATILE BREED

BREEDING WEIMARANERS

The Great Ones

Beyond These Borders

APPENDICES

Figure I-1. *Bed wrestling begins with just a glance.* Photograph by Gene LaFollette.

INTRODUCTION: WEIMARANER WAYS

Many consider the Weimaraner's role as a family companion the breed's most important one, for dependence on human companionship is exceptionally strong in this sporting breed. Weimaraners give unconditional love and affection. They give children a feeling that somebody cares without imposing demands. Their expressions and mannerisms bring laughter, even when none seems possible, but the amiable clowns become staunch protectors when the need arises.

Weimaraners are a breed for those who enjoy a dog that is intensely devoted and responsive to attention—they demand attention. They follow owners from room to room, usually lying down with body contact when owners sit down. People who are distressed when their dog shoves open the bathroom door to stay near will not enjoy life with Weimaraners. This is a breed for those with a good sense of humor and the willingness to invest the time and effort needed to teach active, imaginative puppies the good manners needed by every family companion. This is a breed with unlimited learning potential—be it bad or good. Anyone who expects their dog to live in a dog run or backyard will regret buying a Weimaraner, as neither dog nor owner will be happy.

Weimaraners get along with cats and other pets if introduced to them at an early age. Although the Germans enhanced the instinct to pursue furred animals through selective breeding, puppies learn to accept most family pets. In general, Weimaraners can be trained to accept cats very easily, and rabbits with a little more difficulty.

In closing, an exposé on bed wrestling is in order. Weimaraner owner Susan Thau has some words of warning for new owners:

The age-old sport of bed wrestling has been practiced between dogs and humans for centuries. It is very subtle, slow-moving, and can take all night, so it isn't much of a spectator sport. To the combatants, however, it is very intense.

It starts out with one or two humans placed lengthwise in a bed, with a dog curled up at the bottom near their feet. For a human to win, all he or she has to do is stay in the same spot until morning. This is not as easy as it seems.

For the dog to win, it takes cunning, persistence, patience and the agility of an eel. The dog has won the wrestling match when it has worked its way from the bot-

tom of the bed to the top, with its head on the pillow and its body under the covers, stretched out to its utmost length but crosswise in the bed. The dog must do this without actually waking the humans, who will have nightmares about being crushed, and will find themselves in the morning desperately clutching the edge of the mattress to keep from falling on the floor.

No reliable statistics on the incidence of bed wrestling could be found, but in an unofficial survey, about half of the owners questioned admitted to sharing their beds with one or more gray ones. After all, this Forester's Dog has apparently been sleeping with owners for almost 500 years.

Figure I-2: *All ready and waiting* for some bed wrestling. Photograph by Gene LaFollette.

Figure 1-1: *The famous trophy collection* in the great banquet hall of Castle Moritzburg, Dresden, Germany. Courtesy of Staatliche Schlösser, Burgen und Gärten Sachsen, Schloss Moritzburg und Fasanenschlösschen. Photograph by Werner Lieberknecht, Dresden.

CHAPTER 1

IN THE BEGINNING

by Deborah Andrews

Histories of the *Weimaraner Vorstehhund* (Weimaraner Pointer) usually open with the Grand Duke Carl August (1757–1828) and noblemen of his brilliant court at Weimar, capital of Thuringia, a principality in central Germany. There, many believed, Carl August—"the hunter among kings and king among hunters"—and his noblemen first developed the silver-gray breed for hunting in Thuringia's great forests. According to one tradition, the German aristocrats deliberately concealed the secret of the breed's origin so that it would remain unique and exclusive to the court of Weimar. Another tradition, however, asserts that Prince Esterhazy introduced Carl August to the breed on his estates in Bohemia and that the Duke imported the gray dogs from "the land of Wenzels Krone"—an old term for Bohemia.

Did the Grand Duke really "create" the breed, or did he start work with an already established breed that he obtained from Prince Esterhazy? Scattered comments in dog literature refer to the Weimaraner as an ancient breed, one portrayed in medieval tapestries. Occasional writers mention the Gray Hounds of Saint Louis and their striking resemblance to modern Weimaraners, and the theory that Weimaraners are a fairly direct descendant of the medieval French breed has gained growing acceptance among European fanciers.

Before beginning the search for the Weimaraner's roots, the historical sleuth must identify specific traits that develop the evidence and build the case. The silver-gray coat of varying shades is the Weimaraner's hallmark, but color alone cannot be considered sufficient evidence. Fortunately, the breed has several other distinctive traits that distinguish it from other pointing breeds. The silver-gray color plus these traits—*markings, head, ears, tail, temperament, and working style*—provides valuable clues.

The silver-gray color occasionally appears in many breeds. Because it is a recessive trait, art depicting a large number of gray dogs indicates selective mating of a specific strain or breed. The peculiar dark stripe down the back—*eel stripe*—that occurs in modern Weimaraners is mentioned in early descriptions of the gray dogs. From the earliest descriptions of the silver-gray hunting dog to the first Weimaraner standard, the occurrence of reddish yellow markings on the legs is mentioned as a breed characteristic by a variety of terms—the so called dobe markings, burning fur, mark of the hound, and bicolored tan markings. Failure to mention these markings in the American breed standard does not alter the fact that they continue to crop up on occasion.

The Weimaraner's flat cheeks (fleshy regions at the side of the head) are a subtle but consistently unique trait. Somewhat less unusual but also consistent are the rather deep median line of the forehead and the pronounced occipital bone.

No other sporting breed has ears quite like the Weimaraner's long, thin, high-set ears. Holding the ear away from the head, the first inch of upward curve of the front edge folds back until beginning a gentle curve toward the tip, which forms a gently rounded triangle.

Karl Brandt (a noted late-19th-century breeder, writer, and one of the founders of the German Weimaraner Club) pointed out that the Weimaraner's undocked tail is so unique that even if dyed brown the breed could be identified by its tail. About one-third of the distance from the base of the tail, the vertebral diameter abruptly decreases, and ideally, the tail is docked one vertebra past the "nick" to obtain an attractive taper. The two-thirds from the neck to the tip tapers gradually and is covered with coarse longer hairs. The undocked tail also has a distinctive curve, more like Salukis than setters; to obtain the setter-type tail in longhairs, it is necessary to dock the last two vertebrae.

The Weimaraner's noteworthy devotion to owners is a consistent motif in the literature. The breed's exceptional tracking ability is almost as much a hallmark as the distinctive color, and this talent has always been considered valid evidence of a fairly direct descent from ancient scent-tracking hounds.

Figure 1-2: *Central and Western Europe 1815 with German Confederation outlined in red.* The Congress of Vienna (1814–15), convened after Napoleon's defeat, sought to restore order to a Europe disrupted by revolutionary and imperial France. Its members' objective was a constellation of states and a balance of power that would ensure peace and stability after a quarter-century of revolution and war. In addition to the delegates of many small states, the congress included representatives of five large European states: Austria, Prussia, Russia, Britain, and France. After months of deliberations, the congress established an international political order that was to endure for nearly 100 years and that brought Europe a measure of peace.

A Breed of Very Old Origins

Our search for Weimaraners in early art and literature led even deeper into the past, and the fascinating story begins in the 13th-century French court.

The 13th Century

Louis IX of France (1226–1270), better known as Saint Louis, became acquainted with a breed of gray hounds in about 1248 when on his first crusade, apparently during his captivity in Egypt. After his return to France, the king obtained a pack of these dogs, which became known as the *Chien Gris de Saint Louis*—the Gray Hound of Saint Louis. What did these dogs look like? The most detailed description is given by Ludwig Beckmann, a late-19th-century dog authority and writer:

These dogs cannot really be considered beautiful, their hair is rather coarse and wiry, especially at the belly, the ears are very long, thin, curled and seemingly soft and fine.

As seen from the front, the head is remarkably slim and pressed in at the sides [flat cheeks], the strong tail is

curved over the back and full of rather coarse hair. The hair on the legs, on the other hand, is less short. Good illustrations of these dogs can be found on the antique Gobelin tapestries in Castle Pau and in the series of twelve tapestries entitled the Hunts of Emperor Maximilian I [Belles Chasses de Guise]....

The color of these dogs is a dark-gray, flecked with a reddish color that melts into the yellowish color of the hair at the legs, on the back is blackish [eel stripe] and the legs red-yellow flecked.

There are also those of a complete silver-gray. They are described as being very attached to their master, whose voice and horn they can distinguish; they need no encouragement during hunting and are equally energetic in the cold as in the heat.[1]

Thus, these hounds possessed many of the identifying criteria—flat cheeks, distinctive ears, eel stripe, distinctive tail, color solid gray or with bicolored tan markings, keen scenting aptitude, and strong bonding with owners.

The 14th Century

By the end of the 14th century, most French noblemen owned some of the royal gray hounds. This is not surprising because good hunting dogs made appropriate gifts for all occasions, and in a similar manner, the *Chien Gris de Saint Louis* undoubtedly spread to other European courts. The favorite pastime of medieval knights was hunting because (or so they claimed) it kept them mentally and physically fit for combat. Nobles waxed poetic when lauding the virtues of the hunt.

The most famous of all medieval hunting treatises is *Le Livre de la Chasse*, written by Gaston III, count of Foix (1331–1391)—called Gaston Phoebus—and completed shortly before his death. Illuminated manuscript copies portray the hunting dogs of the time and provide the earliest portraits of the *Chien Gris de Saint Louis.*

Medieval big-game hunting dogs fall into three basic types—*alaunt, levrier,* and *chien courant.* The term *alaunt* referred to any large, swift, fierce dog capable of seizing and bringing down any type of game (the Great Dane is considered the closest modern equivalent). The *levriers* are typical greyhounds—white with patches of color, slim head, rose ears—used for insight pursuit of game. The *chiens courants,* or running hounds, hunted by scent; they had full muzzles, blunt noses, well-shaped square heads, rather pendulous lips, and hanging ears—the larger ones resemble the modern Bloodhound.

Of the three types, the *chiens courants* were the most prized, and Gaston considered hunting by strength of hounds (*par force* hunting) from horses the finest of all sports. He wrote, "With greyhounds and other dogs, good as they may be, a beast is taken or lost immediately, but the running-hound must hunt till the day's end, talking and drying in its own tongue, reviling the beast it pursues; so I prefer them to any other breed of dog, for they have more virtue in them, it seems to me, than any other animal."[2]

The most elite of the running hounds were those used as *lymers* (onlead trackers trained and handled by lymerers); the German term for *lymer* is *Leithund*—that is, a hound

Figure 1-3: *Manuscript illuminations* from *Le Livre de la Chasse.* The famous hunting treatise by Gaston III, count of Foix—Gaston Phoebus—was completed shortly before his death in 1391. The illuminations (this page and next) are probably the earliest portraits of the silver-gray *Chien Gris de Saint Louis,* which bears a strong resemblance to the modern Weimaraner. **(a) The** *lymer* (a *chien courant* or lead dog with excellent tracking ability) leads the others to the selected game. Courtesy of the Pierpont Morgan Library (copyright 1994), New York City.

that tracks on a lead. While the participants assembled for a hunt breakfast, the handlers with the *lymers* on lead spread through the forest, each taking a selected area, to locate the resting quarry (wild boar or red stag) without disturbing them and then reported the size and location of the game to the assembly.

Figure 1-3: (continued) ***Manuscript illuminations*** from *Le Livre de la Chasse*. **(b)** *The hart* (a red-deer stag) is flushed, and the hounds are loosed. Courtesy of the Pierpont Morgan Library (copyright 1994), New York City.

Hunting accounts of the French royal pack in the 1390s show that although the total number of dogs fluctuated from year to year, the ratio remained rather consistent. One year, for example, food was purchased for 32 *levriers*, 96 *chiens courants*, and 10 *lymers*.[3]

Avid medieval sportsmen practiced selective breeding to perpetuate their favorite strains. Leather straps with protruding spikes and placed like belts around the bitch's loin effectively prevented unplanned matings. Surprisingly, Baston recommended spaying bitches that would not be bred, "for a spayed bitch will last in her worth and her hunting half again or twice as long as an unspayed bitch."[4]

Par force hunting was the sport of aristocrats, but hunting with nets brought food to the tables of all levels of society, even nobles, in times of scarcity. All kennel pages learned to weave nets of many types, to be used to capture game ranging from hare to wild boar, usually with the aid of dogs.

With spears, nets, knives, and bows and arrows, a rich variety of game was hunted, most in specified seasons. Deer (red, fallow, and roe), ibex, chamois, bear, and boar (the archetype of unrelenting ferocity) provided meat for the table, as did the ubiquitous hare (prized for their speed and cleverness at outwitting pursuit). Predator control was also important: the fox, a clever villain; the otter, a brazen thief of domestic pond fish; and the wolf, a vile beast and symbol of evil.

The 15th Century

The bronze hound in front of the Las Palmas Cathedral in the Canary Islands is frequently mentioned in European breed literature because the dog's head and ears bear a striking resemblance to the modern Weimaraner, although German literature refers to the statue as a *Canis segusius* of a type resembling the *Saint Hubertus Bracke*.

According to Andre Harmand, the bronze (Figure 1-7) commemorates Jean de Bethencourt (1360–1425), the Norman baron who began the conquest and colonization of the Canary Islands in 1402. The expedition's history mentions dogs only once in a passing reference to a hunting foray.[5] Although the evidence is hardly conclusive, it has a certain degree of credibility, for what other breed than a *Chien Gris de Saint Louis* would be owned by a French baron who served as counselor to Charles VI and Charles VII?

The *lymers* were housed separately from the other hounds, usually in the handlers' homes. Thus, the modern Weimaraner's dependence on humans and need to be an intimate family member have their roots in the close bonding between the medieval silver-gray *lymers* and their handlers.

The best packs, according to medieval authorities, had a blend of the running hounds; one sort hunted by scenting the air, the other with its nose to the ground. Those that hunted with high heads tracked the prey through heavy woodland cover where prey brushed the undergrowth, whereas the ground trackers took the lead in open fields and meadows.

Figure 1-4: *Manuscript illumination* from *Le Livre de la Chasse.* Medieval hunting dogs. Courtesy of the Pierpont Morgan Library (copyright 1994), New York City.

The 1320s produced two items of interest. A brightly colored illumination in the *Hours of Marguerite d'Orléans* (circa 1425) portrays women hunting on horseback, with a smooth-coated silver-gray hound leading the pack. The Gothic Playing Cards (circa 1428), thought to be the oldest in Europe, were used by royalty. The hand-painted cards are decorated with game, such as falcons, stags, and ducks, as well as hunting dogs, including the short-haired silver-gray royal hounds.

The best evidence of the continued popularity of the *Chien Gris de Saint Louis* with royalty at the end of the 15th century is the *Hunt of the Unicorn,* seven magnificent French tapestries tentatively dated 1500 (Figures 1-10 through 1-12). According to old inventories, they were originally 15 feet high, but it is believed that they were cut down and mutilated during the French Revolution (only two fragments remain of one). Some authorities believe they commemorate the marriage of Anne of Brittany and Louis XII in 1499. Slight variations in style suggest that more than one artist designed the set, especially the 7th panel, in which the wounded unicorn is chained to a tree and resting in a fenced enclosure.

Although portraying a mythical prey, the tapestries illustrate the ritualized medieval hunting technique known as *par force de chiens*—by strength of hounds. The major-

Unfortunately, no one gives information about the artist or date, and further information has proved elusive. The only clue to the bronze's date is the nearby bronze of an earcropped dog that may have been done by the same artist; that dog is probably a *Perro de Presa Canario* (Canary Dog), a breed developed by 19th-century English immigrants who crossed Mastiffs and Bulldogs with the indigenous tulip-eared breed, the Perro de Pastor Mallorquin.

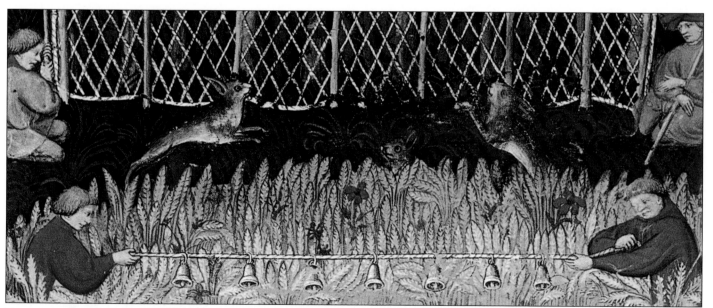

Figure 1-5: *Gaston Phoebus already recommended to his students to kill game with nobleness and a distinguished manner,* because then they had good entertainment and more animals were left over. The hunt for common hares required some effort; only a net and some beaters, who held a rope provided with small bells tightened between each other. The hares were driven into the nets. Photograph courtesy of the Jagd- und Fischereimuseums in München, as well as, H. F. Ullmann in der Tandem Verlag GmbH, Germany.

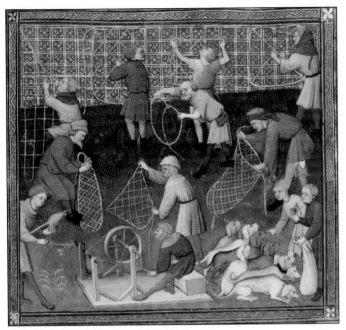

Figure 1-6: *Manuscript illumination* from *Le Livre de la Chasse.* Medieval hunter making net traps for foxes and hares. Courtesy of the Pierpont Morgan Library, New York City.

ity of the running hounds are shorthaired and gray, and although rather crudely executed, they exhibit the flat cheeks and peculiar ear fold of the modern Weimaraner, as well as the curled, bristle-haired tail.

The 16th Century

The hunting exploits of the Emperor Maximilian I (1493–1519) were immortalized in the 12 tapestries known as the *Belles Chasses de Guise* or the *Hunts of Emperor Maximilian I* (Figure 1-13). Designed after the emperor's death by Bertrand Van Orley and his school for Emperor Charles V and woven in the workshops of Jean Gheteels of Brussels, they set the Renaissance style for tapestries. Each representing a month of the year, the tapestries show accurate views of the Forest of Soignes outside Brussels, and alterations of the ducal palace in the background indicate that Van Orley designed the tapestries in 1521 or 1522. Panels 1 through 8 are devoted to the stag hunt; panels 9 through 11 depict boar hunting. Panel 12 shows homage being paid to King Modus (Method) and Queen Ratio (Reason), which refers to the late-14th-century hunting text, *Les Livres du Roy Modus et de la Royne Ratio*, which inspired Van Orley's designs.

Unlike the smooth-coated hounds depicted in earlier art, the hounds in the Maximilian tapestries display the wiry coat described by Beckmann, raising the question whether a wire-haired variety also occurred in the breed. Supporting evidence of the second coat is found with the modern *Griffon Nivernais* (Figure 1-14), a wire-haired French scent hound that

resembles the hounds in the tapestries and is considered a descendant of the *Chien Gris de Saint Louis*. Interestingly, the *Griffon Nivernais* is also used for hunting birds, but it works like a flushing spaniel rather than a pointer.

Later in the century in *La Chasse Royale*, Charles IX (1560–1574) not only mentions the gray running hounds of earlier times (for their popularity in France was waning) but also states that King Louis IX had heard of a breed of excellent deer-hunting hounds in Tartary (central Asia) while in the Holy Land and had had a pack brought to France. He also commented that these silver-gray hounds were somewhat wilder, bigger, and longer legged than the black or white breeds.

The earliest evidence of the *Chien Gris de Saint Louis* in Germany is found in *Wild Boar Hunt*, the watercolor by Jost Amman (1539–1591). The pen and sepia watercolor (Figure 1-1) shows three silver-gray hounds similar to those in the tapestries among a pack attacking a wild boar, which tradition identifies as the Weimaraner's earliest use. The Swiss-born artist was a long-time resident of Nuremberg, which suggests that painting's locale might be Germany.

The 17th Century

Early in the 17th century, the silver-gray breed's place in the royal pack was usurped by the *Chien Blanc*, the ancestor of the modern French hound called the *Billy*, which resembles a white Weimaraner. Evidence that other nobles continued to breed the *Chien Gris de Saint Louis* comes from the 1632 Anthony Van Dyck (1599–1641) portrait *Prince Rupert of the Palatinate*, which shows the prince with a favorite hunting dog that resembles the modern Weimaraner (Figure 1-16). The silver-gray dog's head has an exaggerated stop, but the ear is distinctive. Written references identify the dog as a *Huehnerhund* (literal translation, partridge dog), an old German term for pointers and setters.

Figure 1-7: *The bronze* in front of the Las Palmas Cathedral in the Canary Islands. Reprinted, by permission, from Klaus Hartmann, *Der Weimaraner Vorstehhund,* 1972.

Figure 1-8: *Illumination* from the *Hours of Marguerite d'Orléans* (circa 1425). Courtesy of the Bibliothèque Nationale, Paris, France.

A Pure and Independent Breed

Medieval bird dogs were "setter," which dropped to the ground and crept toward the birds, flushing them into nets on command. Those that indicated the birds' location while standing—"pointers"—were undesirable. The introduction of firearms for bird hunting around the middle of the 18th century created the need for a new type of hunting dog—a "pointer" with intense interest in birds and a lighter build for speed. While the British developed specialized breeds for pointing and retrieving birds, the Continental Europeans developed versatile hunting breeds that could be used for many types of game—deer, wild boar, wolf, fox, rabbit, hare, and various birds. They also developed new training methods to strengthen each dog's natural abilities. The versatile dogs had to track, search, and indicate the

The 18th Century

Evidence that the *Chien Gris de Saint Louis* still existed in France in the 18th century comes from the paintings of Jean Baptiste Oudry (1686–1755). This great French painter and tapestry designer was the court artist of Louis XV (1715–1774). He is one of the most famous of all animal artists, and it is not surprising that several of his paintings portray the silver-gray hunting dogs that were once the hallmark of the French royal pack.

Although the painting of *Blanche* (Figure 1-18) is identified as a Weimaraner in some American breed literature, the bitch is a *Braque d'Arrêt Francais* (Shorthaired French Pointer). The elegant breed was characterized by a white coat with sparse, dark markings, a light build, long ears, and a straight, slender tail. The painting is considered historically significant because it portrays the 18th-century transition from the heavy hound type to the lighter pointer type.

Although the muzzle is somewhat snippy and the stop exaggerated, Oudry's *Weimaraner* (Figure 1-19) clearly shows the breed's typical ears.

The 19th Century

Evidence of the breed in the early 19th century is scant. An 1805 book by aus dem Winckell (1762–1839) mentioned that purebred dogs of solid gray or yellow had been observed, identifying both as the same breed and as Weimaraners.

Weimaraners continued to appear in occasional art. The back of a portrait by Joesph Kidd (1808–1889) bears a note that it was painted in Geneva in 1850 (Figure 1-20). A fine stock pin with what appears to be a Weimaraner head belonged to an English manufacturer (Figure 1-21). Other evidence that the silver-gray dogs had crossed the Channel comes from a white porcelain statue of Queen Victoria (1837–1901) with a dog resembling a Weimaraner lying at her feet.[6]

Figure 1-9: *One of the most famous Gothic Playing Cards* (circa 1428). Forty-nine of the hand-painted cards remain in good condition. Each is identified by a special watermark. Courtesy of the Wurttembergisches Landesmuseum, Stuttgart, Germany.

Figure 1-10: *The Hunt of the Unicorn* (circa 1500). *The Unicorn Dips His Horn into the Stream to Rid It of Poison.* A silver-gray running hound just behind the unicorn's hocks leans forward with an expression of curiosity. The head displays a fold in the high-set, slightly pointed ear that is similar to the modern Weimaraner's. Courtesy of the Metropolitan Museum of Art, Gift of John D. Rockefeller, Jr., the Cloisters Collection, 1937. (37.80.2) Copyright 1988 by the Metropolitan Museum of Art, New York City.

location of various types of game; they had to retrieve anything they could carry and show the handler the location of the larger game.

This is when Grand Duke Carl August entered the Weimaraner's story. Art and literature provide evidence that scattered Continental aristocrats had maintained a fairly pure strain of the old French royal breed—the *Chien Gris de Saint Louis*—although Carl August might well have obtained fresh bloodlines from Prince Esterhazy. Both Strebel and Friess, turn-of-the-century authors of dog books, commented that Weimaraners had excellent hunting abilities and that *large numbers appeared in Thuringia.*[7]

Like most other sportsmen of the period, the Grand Duke sought to expand the old running-hound's function to include feathered game by selecting crosses with the bird-hunting strains, and one or more of these crosses probably introduced the longhaired trait. Because of the Weimaraner's more houndlike working qualities, many believe that the process occurred at a later date and with fewer pointer crosses, certainly not enough to alter its distinctive physical traits—color, flat cheeks, ear shape, and unique tail.

Dr. Paul Kleemann, a noted German Shorthaired Pointer authority whose grandfather had bred Weima-

Figure 1-11: ***The Hunt of the Unicorn*** (circa 1500). *The Unicorn Leaps the Stream.* In the water and just above the unicorn's back, a light gray running hound appears to be taking a drink. Courtesy of the Metropolitan Museum of Art, Gift of John D. Rockefeller, Jr., the Cloisters Collection, 1937. (37.80.3) Copyright 1982 by the Metropolitan Museum of Art, New York City.

raners, proclaimed that by "the beginning of the 1880's the Weimaraner was known as the king of hunting dogs and an ornament of classical hunting." Sporting writers of the time, however, described the dog as "very timid and the slightest mistreatment can spoil him, especially if he is of a fearful disposition. It is an accepted rule to treat him well and lovingly and to speak softly to him as often as possible."[8] Despite the softness in response to training, an inherent sharpness and protectiveness made the Weimaraner a favorite of professional hunters and forest wardens, earning it the honorary title of "Forester's Dog."

The earliest known document of pure Weimaraner breeding mentions that the father of Baron von Wintzingerode-Knorr bred Weimaraners near Weimar around 1850. The Baron also owned and hunted the breed. A photograph dated 1871 shows Wintzingerode as a young boy, sitting beside his Weimaraner, Nimrod.

An 1882 report of a show held by the Thuringia Club for Breeding Purebred Dogs indicates that Weimaraners were "strongly represented." The same report discouraged the practice of crossing with other German pointers because it produced an unattractive mixture of type (usually coarse) and color (usually reddish brindle to brown).

Karl Link of Apolda (Thuringia) describes Weimaraners that might have appeared at that 1882 show, as well as changes that occurred in the following decades:

Figure 1-12: ***The Hunt of the Unicorn*** (circa 1500). *Unicorn Defends Himself.* The silver-gray running hound just above the unicorn's back looks at the white Greyhound at its right. The forward edge of the ear appears to have a line representing a fold, and although more relaxed, the tail shows a typical houndlike curl. The light-colored hound to its right could represent either a deergray *Chien Gris de Saint Louis* or a *Chien Blanc,* a closely related white breed. A second silver-gray hound is located to the right of the unicorn's horn, and a third is located just to the left of the forelegs. Courtesy of The Metropolitan Museum of Art, Gift of John D. Rockefeller, Jr., The Cloisters Collection, 1937. (37.80.4) Copyright 1982 by The Metropolitan Museum of Art, New York City.

I was an enthusiastic dog lover even as a young boy and have visited the dog market at Apolda since the early 1870's. I always found there a collection of Weimaraners coming from Apolda or its nearest neighborhood....I have seen Weimaraners follow the trend of the German Hunting Dog. The Weimaraner has undergone changes. In my younger years I saw it look like a "German Blood Dog" with hanging lips and watering eyes, but now it has arrived at the form of the German Shorthair and so it has certainly changed for the better. There can be no notion that the Weimaraner might stem from the Pointer. I and others believe the Weimaraner to be exclusively German, a "German Short Hair." As to color, the light silver-gray will probably remain the ideal color, but a good-looking dark gray dog is not to be despised either.[9]

In addition to Karl Brandt and von Wintzingerode, early breed literature frequently mentions F. Pitschke, L. Lindblohm, and P. Wittekop. All were influential breeders and active in achieving the Weimaraner's recognition by the German Delegate Commission.

Figure 1-13: *Hunts of Emperor Maximilian I* (circa 1500). Details from 2 of the 12 tapestries that celebrate the hunting exploits of the emperor. Courtesy of Service Photo-graphique de la Réunion des Musées Nationaux, Paris, France.

(a) (left) *January–Aquarius (How the Wild Boar Were Singed)*. This detail portrays both varieties of the silver-gray *Chien Gris de Saint Louis* described by Beckmann: the dog in the lower left is solid colored like the modern Weimaraner, whereas the head of the one just to the left has the tan facial marking typical of the modern *Griffon Nivernais*. Their shaggy appearance suggests they had *Stockhaarig* coats.

(b) (below) *October–Scorpio (Rewarding of the Hounds)*. This black-and-tan hound might be a *Saint Hubertus Bracke*. Note the royal brand on its side.

Pitschke, a lawyer and county official, is considered the earliest breeder of "pure" Weimaraners. He followed the breeding and traditions of his father, who had used Weimaraners for hunting. In 1881, Pitschke and an old hunting friend acquired the pair of Weimaraners that founded the Sandersleben line. In the 1890s, Sandersleben Weimaraners competed at the first Erfurt show.

The three Sandersleben Weimaraners in Figure 1-24 won many prizes during the late 1800s. Treff (born 1891) had excellent conformation and type, except for his head, which looked too much like that of the German Setter. Bella (born 1892) had a much better head. Juno (born 1894), the daughter of Treff and Bella, inherited the best qualities of both parents and was considered the best of the three.

Wittekop, a writer, showed his Rüdemanns line at Apolda in 1896 and at Kiel in 1899. Rüdemanns Held, the winner at

Figure 1-14: *Griffon Nivernais.* These modern descendants of the *Chien Gris de Saint Louis* resemble the rough-coated dogs in the Maximilian tapestries. Courtesy of Ann Gammard.

Figure 1-15: *A 16th-century nobleman* with his falcon and a bird dog in a woodcut by Jost Amman. Reprinted from Ludwig Beckmann, *Geschichte und Beschreibung der Rassen des Hundes*, 1894.

Figure 1-16: *Prince Rupert of the Palatinate* by Anthony Van Dyck, an oil painted at the Hague, Netherlands, in 1632. Courtesy of the Kunsthistorisches Museum, Vienna, Austria.

Figure 1-17: *A bronze of two hounds.* The dogs represent *lymers* of the royal French deer pack during the middle of the French Empire (circa 1589–1789), descendants of the 13th-century *Chien Gris de Saint Louis*. The base bears the inscription "A. Cain 1880" and was probably done by August Nicholas Cain (1822–1894), a prolific sculptor of birds and animals. These July 1990 photographs were taken in front of the Bourbonenschloss in Chantilly, France. Courtesy of Deborah Andrews.

(a) *The front hound* is identified as Brillador, the other as Farfaru. Note the triangular brand; valuable *lymers* were often identified with the kennel-owner's brand.

(b) *Brillador's head* (bottom) shows the deep median line typical of the modern Weimaraner, and Farfaru's expression (top) is familiar to every Weimaraner owner.

(c) *The shape and folds*—particularly the deep fold on the front—of the thin, high-set ear closely resemble that of the Weimaraner. The coat's texture suggests that the model had the hound's coarse *Stockhaarig* coat, a type that occurs rarely in modern Weimaraners.

Figure 1-18: *Blanche, a Bitch in Louis XV's Pack of Hounds* by Jean Baptiste Oudry, an oil painted about 1727. Courtesy of Photographie Giraudin, Paris, France.

Figure 1-19: *Weimaraner* by Jean Baptiste Oudry, an oil painted about 1750. Courtesy of Dr. Sigrid Krieger-Huber, Neuburg/Inn, Germany.

Kiel, was described as quite an elegant dog—deep chested, well standing, with very good color. Wittekop crossed his dark gray strain with the Sandersleben line.

The dogs in Lindblohm's paintings always appeared smaller with softer coats, compared with those found in hunting scenes by other artists of the time.

A request submitted to the German Delegate Commission (established in 1880) for official recognition of the Weimaraner as a pure and independent breed aroused considerable opposition. Many authorities considered the Weimaraner a sub-breed of the German Shorthaired Pointer. However, Strebel, Brandt, and others maintained that color and structural differences proved the Weimaraner was a distinct breed. Their opinion prevailed, and the commission granted official recognition in 1896.

The first breed standard, crude and vague, was published in 1894 (Appendix A), before official recognition. It is of interest because it not only describes Weimaraners of over a century ago, it also identifies traits that, although no longer common, were once typical of the breed. For example: "white markings in small measure, mostly on the chest, are neither ugly nor faulty since also characteristic of the breed. Neither is the reddish-yellow shade on the head or legs, which nowadays seldom occurs, to be regarded as a fault."

The Club for Pure Breeding of the Silver-Gray Weimaraner Pointer was founded on 20 June 1897. The name, however, was altered to Club for Breeding of the Weimaraner Pointer a short time later. The purpose of the

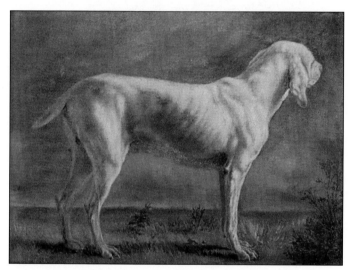

Figure 1-20: *Weimaraner* by Joseph Kidd (founding member of the Royal Scottish Academy of Painting, Sculpture, and Architecture). An oil painted in Geneva in 1850. Courtesy of John and Deborah Kenney.

Figure 1-21: *A late-19th-century stock* or tie pin. The pin is 3½ inches long. The case with the portrait (¾-inch diameter) has a thin backing of gold sheet, with a circular area of white enamel on which is inscribed "W. B. Ford 1873," a manufacturer who lived in Manchester, England. The miniature painting appears to be enamel on china or opaque glass. Courtesy of the Canterbury Museum, Christchurch, New Zealand.

Figure 1-22: *A classic, old photo of 4 hunters calling themselves "four old hares".* They surely knew many tricks. [l-r:] Friedrich Wilhelm Worz, Farmer and Borough Council Member, Ludwig Heinrich Pflugfelder, Master Carpenter, Friedrich Wilhelm Pflugfelder, Innkeeper, Friedrich Wilhelm Kuder, a Fish Baron. The four hunters lived in Neckergartach (Heilbronn-Neckargartach) when this photograph was made in 1895. Photograph courtesy of the Jagd- und Fischereimuseums in München, as well as, H. F. Ullmann in der Tandem Verlag GmbH, Germany.

club was the advancement of the breed, with emphasis on its field utility. Major Robert a. d. Herber (1867–1946, President of the German Weimaraner Club from 1921 to 1946) coined the German club's motto: "It is not the breed, but the breeder's selection that guarantees highest quality of conformation and best performance!"

In 1908, the Weimaraner club survived a bitter conflict over coat color. One group favored silver-gray, allowing a small amount of white; the other group favored the dark-gray shade with yellow, claiming they were better hunters. One effect of the compromise was the change of the club's name to the German Weimaraner Club. At the time, new breeders relied upon the foundation bloodlines of Lindblohm (Lindblohm), Pitschke (Sandersleben), and Wittekop (Rüdemanns).

Despite the rigorously enforced breeding restrictions and selective membership, purebred Weimaraners apparently spread quickly to other European countries. Illustrated standards of France, England, Germany, and the Netherlands published in 1904 document many differences between early and modern Weimaraners.

World War I decimated the Weimaraner population, and according to Fritz Kullmer, fewer than a dozen German Weimaraners survived.[10]

The breed fared little better in World War II, and postwar recovery was hampered by the division of Germany and the occupation. American occupation regulations forbade hunting and possession of firearms except when

Figure 1-24: ***Carl August with His Two Dogs in a Park at Weimar*** by Carl August Schwerdgeburth, mezzotint made in 1824. The dog on the left is a Bengalese Bracke; the one on the right is a *Saint Hubertus Bracke*. Courtesy of the Goethe Museum, Düsseldorf, Germany.

Figure 1-23: ***Carl August Returning from the Hunt*** by Carl August Schwerdgeburth, etching made in 1831. The light, unicolored dog riding in the carriage is believed to be a Weimaraner; the black-and-white dog near the center is a Bengalese Bracke; and the dark dog near the rear is a *Saint Hubertus Bracke*. Courtesy of the Goethe Museum, Düsseldorf, Germany.

accompanied by military personnel. The vital performance tests to select for breeding could not be held for years, and many Weimaraners were sold for export.

The German Weimaraner Club was re-established in West Germany in October 1951, and the original high goals and standards were reaffirmed. The modern German Weimaraner is discussed at length in Chapter 35.

Theories of the Weimaraner's Origin

Belief that the Weimaraner originated with and was the deliberate creation of Carl August led to many theories of the breeds used in its development, and of themselves, these theories have become part of the breed's history. Scholars have attempted to prove that the Weimaraner originated from various crosses of the English Pointer, Spanish Pointer, German Shorthaired Pointer, Great Dane, *Saint Hubertus Bracke, Lei-*

Figure 1-25: *Weimaraners of Herren Oberamtsmann F. Pitschke and O. Andreae, Sandersleben:* *Treff von Sandersleben, Bella von Sandersleben, Juno von Roda.* Drawing by Richard Strebel. Courtesy of the German Weimaraner Club.

thund, Schweisshund, and Bloodhound. The controversy was liveliest during the first decades of the 20th century, before geneticists discovered the inheritance of canine coat color—a factor that must be taken into consideration.

The Spanish Pointer and English Pointer

The Spanish Pointer, of legendary pointing talent, figures prominently in the heritage of modern pointing breeds. The breed was first named and mentioned by Selincourt in 1683, who described Spanish Pointers as "big dogs in robust form, which stood before any wild prey and guarded or hunted with a high nose" (air scenting).[11] They had the light-colored eyes typical of the Weimaraner and occasionally seen in (but not typical of) other modern pointers.

Once considered extinct, the breed was restored early in this century in Navarra and Alava (Basque country), where it is known as the *Perdiguero de Navarro* (Old Spanish Pointer). They come in shorthaired and longhaired varieties.[12]

The Spanish breed is considered the direct ancestor of the English Pointer, and Beckmann describes the traditional lore about the origin of the English Pointer:

> *The old Spanish dog of England is described as very intelligent; good nose but heavily built and slow.*

> *That's why they tried to improve him by crossing him with a Foxhound. A Colonel Thornton was supposed to be the first to have tried this crossbreeding successfully in the year 1795. His new pointer "Dash," dark brown and white, slender throat, incomparable shoulders, back and rear, soon became very famous.[13]*

In 1902, Dr. August Stroese, a noted German sporting dog authority and writer, stated that "the silver Weimaraner is said to have descended from a yellow and white, smooth-haired English Pointer bitch, imported into Germany in the 1820s by the Duke of Weimar and crossbred with German dogs." According to Brandt, Carl August bred a German Shorthaired Pointer bitch to an English Pointer, which produced a gray dog that was the foundation of the breed.[14]

Despite this evidence, the English Pointer theory of the Weimaraner's origin has never been widely accepted. However, it is generally accepted that the direct or indirect pointer crosses in the 19th century contributed to the Weimaraner's transition from a trailing hound to a bird-

Figure 1-26: *The love between 2-year-old Heide and Mia Bella Mara* might not have been anticipated by her father Karl Hildebrand when he acquired Mara in 1939 but is a perfect example of the intense desire Weimaraners have to bond with their humans. It is easy to see why this photograph taken by Dorothea Hildebrand, won first place in a Berlin exhibition in 1941. Photograph courtesy of Heide Hildebrand-Fandreyer.

hunting breed and that the Weimaraner's size, substance, and light eye color support a cross with the Spanish rather than the English Pointer.

The German Shorthaired Pointer

It is reasonable to assume from geographic proximity alone that there should be a close relationship between the German Shorthaired Pointer and the Weimaraner. This, however, is regarded as doubtful because of the marked differences in the bony structure of the skull, the shape and twist of the ears, and the eye color.

In 1939, an individual identified only as "R. F." (believed to be Rudolf Friess) published his theory that Weimaraners are degenerate descendants of the brown German Shorthaired Pointers. He believed that continued breeding of brown-colored dogs for many generations led to silver-brown and gray and that a Vitamin D deficiency caused the silver-gray shades in all breeds that had previously been purely brown. R. F. pointed to the silver-gray puppies born in litters of Doberman Pinschers and brown pointers as examples. In one of his many articles about the breed's origin, Major Robert a. d. Herber not only pointed out the flaws of R. F.'s theory, but also commented that the Weimaraner is the older of the two breeds.

The Blue Dane

Kleemann became convinced that the Weimaraner descended from the blue Great Dane. Kleemann based this theory on the occasional very large Weimaraner, the blue-gray color, the less glossy quality of the coat, and the flat cheeks. Critics argued that the incidence of unusually large Weimaraners was no greater than that observed among other pointing breeds, the color of the blue Dane was quite different from that of the Weimaraner, and the coat glossiness related more to nutrition than to heredity; only the flatness of the cheeks could not be discounted. The Weimaraner, however, has far more pronounced jowl muscles than the Dane. Moreover, the typical blue Dane has dark eyes, whereas the typical Weimaraner (even the blue Weimaraner) does not. Weimaraner fanciers overwhelmingly rejected Kleeman's theory, but they believed that the publicity increased the breed's popularity.

The Saint Hubertus Bracke

Most American breed literature mentions the theories that the Weimaraner is descended from or related to the *Saint Hubertus Bracke,* the *Leithund,* and the *Schweisshund.*

All long-eared scent hounds of Europe descend from a common ancestor, the *Segusierhund (Canis segusius),* a collective name for the group of Gallic-Celtic running hounds revered for their blood-tracking ability and described as having the facial expression of a street beggar—sad and haggard, with many wrinkles. These well-balanced, deliberate dogs were capable of extraordinary tracking feats. Of note, they did not give voice while tracking or searching. By the 4th century, hounds of this type were distributed throughout Europe.

The *Saint Hubertus Bracke,* which became extinct in the 19th century, is among the earliest to be recognized as a pure breed—*Bracke* (plural *Bracken)* is a generic German term for any dog that searches the forest floor, driving game and barking on the trail.

The hounds, famous for their keen tracking ability and melodious voices, were bred by the monks of Saint Hubert's Abbey in Ardennes (France), founded early in the 8th century. Historians believe that most of the hounds in the packs of Charlemagne (768–814) were *Saint Hubertus Bracken.* Although typically black with tan markings, a 16th-century writer commented that the breed at that time came in all colors.

Beckmann described the *Saint Hubertus Bracke* in vivid detail:

> *The color of the original Saint Hubertus hounds was a reddish black, with red-yellow distinguishing marks at eyes and paws, long ears, well-formed but long back, legs less long than the Norman dog and with the same hunting characteristics. A magnificent bark, very refined nose, a lot of body, not much speed, very snappish and audacious toward game.... There was also a white variety, from which Louis XII (1498–15[15]) bred the Greffiers through a crossing with an Italian bitch (braque). The Saint Hubertus hounds were very tenacious and not susceptible to cold and wetness, but difficult to handle.*

Figure 1-27: *Nidung,* an example of Weimaraner type circa 1896. Courtesy of Deborah Andrews.

Figure 1-28: *Early Weimaraners.* The white feet on several of what are probably the best Weimaraners of the time suggest that this modern fault was quite prevalent. Reprinted from Comte Henri de Bylandt, *Dogs of All Nations,* 1904.

(a) Blitz.

(b) Hektor v. d. Wolfsschlucht.

(c) Lore v. Achersleben.

(d) Roland.

Charles IX (1560–1574) found them too slow and writes in his essay La Chasse Royale: "all in all they are good for people who suffer from the gout, but not for those whose occupation it is to take the stag's life."

The Saint Hubertus hounds were often used as lead dogs for black game [wild boar], and the dogs from the abbey of Saint Hubertus in the Ardennes that, in former times, used to be sent to the king annually, were mostly trained for that purpose and were good lead dogs

for the royal pack until 1789. Toward the end of the reign of Louis XIV (1643–1715), they could be seen only with some aristocrats from the north of France who preferred them to all other breeds, because they would hunt every type of game.... (There should be no doubt that the English Bloodhound originally was a black Saint Hubertus hound that was brought into England by the Normans and there, in the course of time, developed the awkward shape of its head.)[15]

Figure 1-29: *Pointers.* Reprinted from Ludwig Beckmann, *Geschichte und Beschreibung der Rassen des Hundes,* 1894.

(a) The Spanish Pointer.   **(b)** The English Pointer.

Leithund and Schweisshund

The German term *Leithund* causes considerable confusion because it has two quite different meanings. The first is synonymous with the French *lymer,* a hound that tracks on lead. The second refers to the 11th-century *German Leithund,* a breed that stemmed from the ancient *Segusierhund* and existed, without a name change, until the early 19th century.

The related *Schweisshund* theory is based on an old German hunting book by a writer known only as "Fama," who wrote,

> *The ideal hunting dog in old times was the so-called Leithund (Leading Dog). This dog was set on the scent of a chosen, not wounded, stag or other deer in the herd and was able to lead the hunter to this single animal. For this purpose they developed the 'Schweisshund,' brown of color.*
>
> *Then they had Pointers for smaller game, for birds, rabbits, and so forth. Then came the idea to cross these races to meld the hunting qualities of both. The 'Weimaraner' was the result of this noble experiment, a dog that points, with exceedingly good nose.*[16]

Fama's brown *Schweisshund* probably refers to the *Hannovarian Schweisshund,* bred at the famous court at Hannover at the beginning of the 19th century, a breed that bears a remarkable similarity to the 16th-century *German Leithund.* The *Schweisshund,* an exquisitely cold-nosed blood trailing hound, is often erroneously referred to as a Bloodhound. (The *Rote Schweisshund* mentioned in some American literature is not discussed in any of the hunting classics.)

Before the late 19th century, the term *purebred* should be interpreted as *relatively purebred.* Deliberate crossbreeding to improve a particular strain occurred all the time, and it is remarkable that specific breed types retained distinguishing traits over many centuries. A shared ancestry between the Weimaraner and other European hound breeds must be assumed because occasional crosses through the centuries are probable.

Nevertheless, it is important to remember that the *Chien Gris de Saint Louis* was brought to Europe from somewhere in central Asia in the 13th century and managed to survive for centuries as an identifiable breed in its own right. Canine historians even debate whether early art depicts the Weimaraner or *Segusierhund.*

A Most Controversial Question

The scope and nature of the controversy over the Weimaraner's origin are fascinatingly evident in this excerpt from a 1939 article by Major Robert a. d. Herber. Herber begins with his general views of the breed's origin:

> *As I have achieved the title "father of the Weimaraners" after seventeen years of activity for the gray breed,…I suppose I may express my opinion.…*
>
> *As the Weimaraner was not found in old literature, it did not exist as a breed. However, such short-haired light-gray dogs could have possibly existed in small numbers in that period.… But they were unknown or disregarded by these sporting writers. In their opinion they were unvalued results of crossbreeding. But as it has been proved that two black animals can produce gray ones, it seems best to look for black ancestors in the old period. There was one black breed, the St. Hubertus Brachen [sic], among the dogs used for hunting in the old days. As the characteristics of both breeds are almost the same, it is possible that the Weimaraner is a mutation within the Brache breed, which is more or less the ancestor of all Vorstehhunde (Pointers). At the time a dog-breeder seemed to like these gray mutations, he paired them and gradually these dogs appeared in larger numbers here in Thuringia. As this gray dog was not identical with any other Vorstehhund breed, especially not the German Shorthair, the Weimaraner was accepted as a breed by the Delegate Commission. The Delegate Commission would surely*

Table 1-1: *Evolution of European hound breeds.*

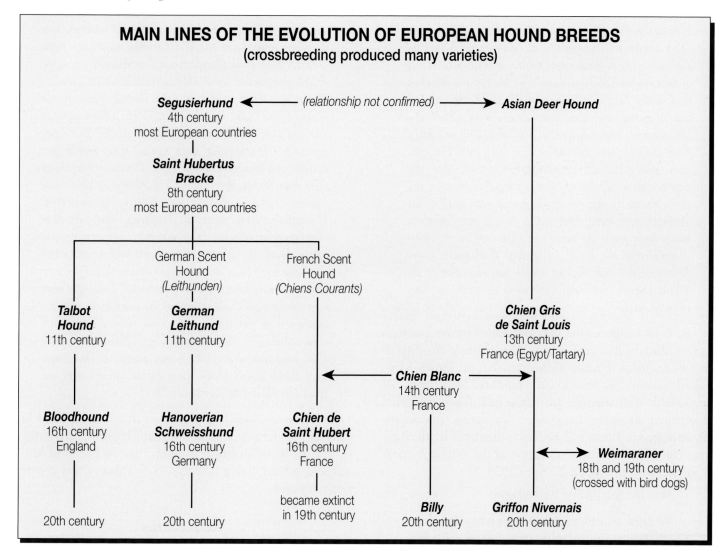

MAIN LINES OF THE EVOLUTION OF EUROPEAN HOUND BREEDS
(crossbreeding produced many varieties)

Segusierhund ← (relationship not confirmed) → **Asian Deer Hound**	
4th century	
most European countries	

Saint Hubertus Bracke
8th century
most European countries

German Scent Hound (*Leithunden*) — French Scent Hound (*Chiens Courants*)

| **Talbot Hound** 11th century | **German Leithund** 11th century | | **Chien Gris de Saint Louis** 13th century France (Egypt/Tartary) |

Chien Blanc ← → 14th century France

| **Bloodhound** 16th century England | **Hanoverian Schweisshund** 16th century Germany | **Chien de Saint Hubert** 16th century France | **Weimaraner** 18th and 19th century (crossed with bird dogs) |

| 20th century | 20th century | became extinct in 19th century | **Billy** 20th century | **Griffon Nivernais** 20th century |

have named this gray dog a gray German Shorthair if they could have proven any connection between the two breeds.

Our Member of Honor, Mr. Winztingerode [sic] auf Adelsborn, knows the Weimaraner since 1869 and asserts that they gave voice on trail, which indicated an inheritance from the Brache and not from the German Shorthair; furthermore, that black parents produced grays.[17]

R. F.'s theory that the Weimaraner is a German Shorthaired Pointer with a degenerate color is firmly refuted:

If R. F. can produce gray dogs from brown German Shorthairs by withdrawing vitamins, then he can do the same with black ones; therefore, this is no proof for stating that the Weimaraner originates from German shorthairs. The Weimaraner color is simply a faded (degenerated) brown, says R. F. Yes, that would be very simple, if it were true, but this opinion is false. If you

Figure 1-30: *French Hounds Used for Hunting from Horseback.*
A *Saint Hubertus Bracke* stands behind a Norman Hound. Note that the short coat shown here differs from the long-coated *Saint Hubertus Bracken* in the illustrations of the Grand Duke Carl August. Reprinted from *Geschichte und Beschreibung der Rassen des Hundes*, Ludwig Beckmann, 1894.

can show me one brown spot on a Weimaraner I will have to destroy the whole Weimaraner pedigree. The Weimaraner is of a gray-reddish-yellow, shimmering color, which we incorrectly call "deer-gray." Now and then there are Weimaraners with a reddish-yellow hue or markings on the jowls and legs, such as the Brachen had, never brown or a tint of the same. Brown was not wanted by the Brache breeders. Has the Weimaraner inherited these reddish-yellow markings from the German shorthair? R. F. goes on: "The eyes, nose and nails are automatically drawn into this degeneration (process of color fading)." Naturally, yes, if his theory of degeneration were correct. Half of my Weimaraners have dark nails, just a part of them posses light ones; the noses are according to the characteristics of the breed, of a dark flesh color, never light-colored; and the eyes which suit the color of the Weimaraner's coat have nothing to do with the German Shorhair.[18]

R. F. had commented that longhaired brown pointers had produced silver-gray longhairs, suggesting crossbreeding. In response, Herber points out that no brown long-haired pointer is considered purebred and that all longhaired Weimaraners are descended from registered shorthaired ancestors. Longhaired Weimaraners occasionally appeared in litters and had been registered by the Austrian club. The German club approved the longhaired coat at the annual meeting on 27 April 1935.

Now the long-haired Weimaraner:

We know that the pure brown long-hair breeds can possess Weimaraner colors, but this does not occur here. We have no brown German Longhairs and do not intend to borrow any. Our Long-haired Weimaraners have been bred from short-haired ones, which has been proved. We, therefore protest against the expression "German Longhairs with Weimaraner color;" they are just as much not German Longhairs, as our short-haired Weimaraners are not German Shorthairs. As they are being listed as long-haired Weimaraners, every registered long-haired Vorstehhund (Pointer) is a long-haired Weimaraner; and as gray German long-haired Pointers are not allowed to be registered. We did not intend to establish a new breed with the long-haired Weimaraner, we have only gratefully acknowledged and accepted this gift of nature, which we had formerly stupidly rejected. Who can reproach us for this action?[19]

Herber goes on to clarify these significant differences between the Weimaraner and the German Shorthaired Pointer:

In conclusion, Mr. R. F. mentions the hunting qualities of the Weimaraner, the best of which are scenting, retrieving and his sharpness. However, this does not prove that the Weimaraner originates from the Brache or from the German Shorthair. Every other breed can claim these characteristics as its own.... When von Otto and I trained Weimaraners at the World Exhibition, Frankfurt in 1935, a man came to our training stand and politely asked the following question: "If the color were not as it is, would you believe the Weimaraner to be a Deutsche Kurzhaar [German Shorthair]?" Von Otto, always ready to give information even during ardent activities, answered: "Certainly, there exists a similarity, but just look closely, the color is not so important. Look at the shape of the head, the longer fangs of all present seventeen dogs, the muscles of the jowls, the different, longer, and slightly pointed ears, the longer back." I did not hear everything von Otto said, but he continued the discussion. The questioner, who had listened attentively then asked: "Are they German dogs?" Von Otto replied: "Yes, probably of very old origin, but we do not know very much about them. They by no means originate from the Deutsche Kurzhaar."[20]

Herber concluded by graciously thanking R. F. for his attempt "to develop a clear statement regarding the origin of our noble, beautiful, gray dogs," but on behalf of himself and other notable breeders, R. F.'s theory was courteously rejected.[21]

Reflections

The evidence in art and literature strongly supports the theory that the Weimaraner traces directly to the *Chien Gris de Saint Louis*. Written descriptions and tradition link them to the silver-gray dogs brought from Egypt (or Tartary) about 1248, and from the end of the 14th century, the evidence in art provides an almost uninterrupted record of the breed.

Although it is the unique color that first commands attention, close examination of structural traits (broad skull, flat cheeks, ear length and curl, bent tail) reveals a striking resemblance to the modern Weimaraner, a combination of hereditary traits that cannot be found in any other breed. Finally, the blackish back and red-yellow legs of the 13th-century hound can still occasionally be seen in the modern Weimaraner. The *eel stripe* is a dark-gray stripe along the back of the Weimaraner; it is always apparent in some dogs, and appears only when shedding in many others. Despite an effort to completely eliminate the trait, the reddish yellow legs (dobe markings) continue to appear occasionally in modern Weimaraners.

The Grand Duke Carl August certainly played an important role in breeding and establishing Weimaraners as the special prerogative of the German aristocracy. His interest in the breed coincided with the introduction of firearms to bird hunting, and several authorities mention that he crossed English Pointers with German dogs; thus, it is possible that Carl August played a role in the transition of the Weimaraner from a trailing hound to a pointer.

There is little doubt that pointers (English, Spanish, or German) were crossed with the Weimaraner to develop its bird-hunting traits. The strongest evidence that such crosses were very sparing is the persistence of the unique structural traits that characterized the gray French hounds; the only physical trait that suggests the pointer cross is the shorter, thicker ear seen in many modern Weimaraners. In addition, the strong tracking and retrieving abilities, eagerness to pursue furred game, and inherent protective desire are traits that continue to distinguish the Weimaraner from other pointing breeds.

Figure 1-31: *On the occasion of Duke Karl von Wuerttemberg's (1737–1793) wedding festivities* with Elisabeth Friederike Sophia, born Marquise zu Brandenburg-Bayreuth on October 8, 1748. This hunting spectacle was organized in Leonberg, which is located approximately 15 km west of Stuttgart. The colored copperplate engraving by Jakob Wagner captured the lavishly produced spectacle. As the contemporary description of the festivities reports, more than 800 red deer and wild boar were driven together already weeks before. When the bloody entertainment was finally called off, half was killed, the rest got away with a scare this time. Photograph courtesy of the Jagd- und Fischereimuseums in München, as well as, H. F. Ullmann in der Tandem Verlag GmbH, Germany.

Figure 2-1: *Breed publicity* began in 1950 with a beautiful photograph on the cover of *Look* (3 January 1950). Highly publicized as a "wonder dog" with near-human intelligence, AKC registrations soared from 419 in 1949 to an incredible 10,000 in 1957.

CHAPTER 2

AMERICA'S WONDER DOG

by Jackie Isabell

The first few Weimaraners reaching the United States just before the outbreak of World War II roused no unusual public interest. Following the war, however, the Weimaraners that were brought home by returning servicemen initiated a wave of publicity for the wonder dogs with near-human intelligence.

America Welcomes Weimaraners

Howard Knight

American Howard Knight learned of Weimaraners through fellow sportsman Fritz Grossman, who later sponsored Knight's membership in the German Weimaraner Club, the prerequisite for ownership. Knight imported the first pair of Weimaraners, Cosack v. Kiebitzstein and Lotte v. Bangstede, to the United States in October 1929. Impressively trained, they hunted with Knight for about 9 years. Unbeknownst to Grossman, who had selected the pair, they had been sterilized by radiation before leaving Germany.

Knight renewed his efforts to import foundation stock. In 1938, Knight imported several 3-month-old puppies, but all except Mars a. d. Wulfsriede died of distemper. Knight then imported Aura v. Gaiberg, Adda v. Schwarzen Kamp, and Dorle v. Schwarzen Kamp. Mars was bred to only four bitches before his early death: Aura v. Gaiberg, Import, CD, BROM; Adda v. Schwarzen Kamp, Import; CH Grafmar's Venus, CD; CH Grafmar's Diana.

When Knight decided to give up hunting in 1939, he gave Mars, Aura, and Adda to Gus and Margaret Horn, already well known for their German Shepherds. Their capable management developed the famous Grafmar Weimaraners, foundation of American bloodlines.

Early Developments and Achievements

The Weimaraner's formal acceptance by the American Kennel Club (AKC), a milestone for every newly introduced breed, came on 8 December 1942, and the first breed standard was published in February 1943 (Appendix A). The Weimaraner Club of America (WCA) held its first annual national meeting in Boston on 21 February 1943. Howard Knight became the first president and a lifetime honorary president.

No history is complete without mention of the "firsts." Activities focused on show and obedience competition, probably because few field events could be held during the war years.

The public met the first class of Weimaraners at Madison Square Garden in 1943. The points and best of breed went to Grafmar's Kreutz, CD (Aura v. Gaiberg, Import, CD, BROM × Grafmar's Silver Knight, CD), and the distaff honors went to his litter sister, Grafmar's Diana. They went on to become the breed's first champions: Kreutz finished on 17 April 1943, and Diana finished the following day.

Figure 2-2: ***Howard Knight imported the first pair*** of Weimaraners to the United States in 1929. When the WCA held its first annual national meeting in 1943, Howard Knight became the first president and a lifetime honorary president. Photograph from William W. Denlinger, *The Complete Weimaraner,* 1954.

Figure 2-3: *Aura v. Gaiberg, Import, CD, BROM.* Imported and owned by Howard Knight. Later given to Gus and Margaret Horn, she became the breed's first great dam. Aura was also the first Weimaraner to earn a CD. Courtesy of the WCA.

Figure 2-4: *Mars a. d. Wulfsriede, Import.* Brought to the United States by Howard Knight as a 3-month-old puppy in 1938 to establish American breeding stock. Courtesy of the WCA.

Aura v. Gaiberg became the first to hold an obedience title, earning her Companion Dog (CD) title in three trials. Through the incredible feat of competing in three obedience trials in 2 days, Grafmar's Ador, CD, BROM, earned his title at 6 months, 2 days, becoming the youngest of all breeds to hold a CD. CH Grafmar's Jupiter, UDT, became the breed's first Utility Dog (UD).

In addition to her other achievements, Aura v. Gaiberg proved to be the breed's first great dam, with four champions in her second litter and one in her third, all sired by Grafmar's Silver Knight, CD; additionally, eight of the nine puppies in her second litter finished their obedience titles. Aura's daughter, Grafmar's Silver Dusk, CDX, BROM, produced the breed's first group winner, CH Forever Silver Dawn (sired by Adventure of Mortgaged Acres, CD, BROM), who won Best of Breed at Westminster in 1948 and 1949 and became the first to place in that show's group with a fourth place.

The Postwar Imports

Until the postwar imports began to arrive in 1948, all American Weimaraners descended from Mars, Aura, Adda, Dorle, and the "refugee," Suzanne v. Aspern, brought from Austria in 1940. So many Weimaraners left Germany during the early postwar years that the German Club began to limit foreign sales of puppies to no more than half a litter. In 1949, for example, about half of the 99 puppies registered by the club went to American soldiers.[1]

There is no way to do justice to the many fine German and Austrian Weimaraners that began to reach the United States after the war. Although many never finished American

Figure 2-5: *When Howard Knight decided to give up hunting* in 1939, he gave his dogs, including Aura and Mars, to Gus and Margaret Horn. The Horns' Grafmar Kennel was destined to become an influential contributor to the early development of the Weimaraner. Courtesy of the WCA.

championships, one measure of their quality is the fact of their American registration; at that time, the AKC gave imports a foreign listing number and registered them only after they had won 10 points toward their championships.

Many of the postwar imports had a lasting influence on the breed. The exceptional talent of the progeny of the legendary CH Dido v. Lechsteinhof, for example, gave rise to the maxim, "You can't win big in the field unless Dido is in the pedigree." Others—like CH Flott v. Haimberg, CH Enno v. d. Berg, Casar v. Reiningen, and CH Apoll Treu Hauentwiete—earned distinction as sires of show and field achievers.

No other German strain, however, had quite the impact of the imports from the Harrasburg Kennel. Few—if any—American Weimaraners do not have one, or more, of the Harrasburg dogs in their heritage, often appearing many times in extended 12- to 15-generation pedigrees. They were not only exceptional individuals, they were also the sires of great sires, particularly when crossed with the Grafmar line.

Alto v. d. Harrasburg arrived first, in 1948, with returning serviceman Owen Gent. Alto sired seven champions, and most American Weimaraners trace back to Alto through his outstanding son, CH Count Von Houghton, SD, BROM (18 champions). The Count was only shown long enough to finish his championship because his owner valued him more as a field competitor and hunting companion. The Count passed on this dual nature, siring many progeny who succeeded in the field and the show ring. Perhaps his most well-known

son is CH Val Knight Ranck, BROM. Val sired 34 champions and held the record for many, many years for the most Best in Show wins (9). He was a pivotal sire in the development of the modern American breed type and field potential.

The first of the Harrasburg B litter imports arrived in 1949. CH Bert v. d. Harrasburg, SDX, BROM (21 champions), finished his show championship quickly and then entered field competition. The big, rangy, hard-running dog became the first Weimaraner to win an open All-Age stake in an all-breed competition; in 1951, Bert defeated an entry of

Figure 2-7: *The first Weimaraner to finish an AKC Championship* and earn Best of Breed at Westminster in 1943, CH Grafmar's Kreutz, CD, is shown here with his owner, Howard Noel, and Grafmar's Gay Spirit, CD. Courtesy of the WCA.

Figure 2-6: *CH Dido v. Lechsteinhof, Import;* owned by Clarence H. Schukei. In the early 1950s, Weimaraners competed in American Field events. Dido is the sire of 19 winners of 84 American Field stakes, with two field champions. In addition, American Field ranked both Dido and seven of his sons in their list of outstanding Weimaraner sires. Courtesy of the WCA.

Figure 2-8: *CH Flott v. Haimberg, Import, RDX, SDX, BROM;* owned by Mr. and Mrs. Adolf Haussermann. Imported from Germany in 1951, Flott demonstrated his hunting talent by earning the WCA's RDX and SDX ratings. He not only finished his show championship with ease, but also went on to 96 Best of Breed wins and to sire 16 champions. Many of his offspring were multi-talented, excelling in the field as well as in conformation. Courtesy of the WCA.

Figure 2-9: *CH Enno v. d. Burg, Import, BROM;* owned by Robert Hoffman. A companion gundog, group-placed Enno is the sire of 18 champions, including Dual CH Patmar's Silver Countess, RD. Courtesy of the WCA.

nine English Pointers, two English Setters, and three Weimaraners. A year later, he won the breed's national amateur All-Age championship. Most Weimaraners trace to Bert through his son, CH Deal's Sporting True Aim II, BROM (23 champions), and True Aim's sons—CH Debar's Platinum Specter, BROM (29 champions), and CH Ann's Rickey Boy, CD, BROM (28 champions).

CH Burt v. d. Harrasburg, BROM (19 champions), was the first Weimaraner to capture an all-breed Best in Show, winning at the Alaska Kennel Club in April 1952. Burt appears in many American pedigrees, although not as often as littermate Bert. Although highly desirable for his outstanding conformation and field talent, Burt was often overshadowed by brother Bert, as his residence in Alaska made him less accessible to potential mates.

Sporting-group winner CH Boddy v. d. Harrasburg, BROM, sired 11 champions. CH Cuno v. d. Harrasburg sired the great FC Fritz von Wehmann aus Rocklege, RDX, SDX, an influential sire of many great field competitors. The imports from the Harrasburg C (Calvin, Cherry) and D litters (Dago, Dick, Droll, Dux) are rarely found in American pedigrees.

By the end of the 1950s, the wave of imports had slowed to a mere trickle, and the only subsequent import that had a major impact on the breed was Bella v. d. Reiteralm, CD, BROM, imported in the early 1960s. Bred twice to CH Val Knight Ranck, BROM (grandson of Alto v. d. Harrasburg), to produce a record, at the time, of 11 champions, Bella provided a superb infusion of true moving structural soundness and field performance. By virtue of having 10 puppies finish in a single year, Bella was awarded the title of Kennel Review's national all-breed, top-producing dam. It is primarily through her son,

CH Maximilian v. d. Reiteralm, NSD, BROM (sire of 63 champions from just 21 dams, including two duals), that Bella appears in the pedigree of most of today's Weimaraners.

The "Crazy Years"
Jack Denton Scott, Publicist

Many newly introduced breeds enjoy a surge of popularity, but it is doubtful that any can match the Weimaraner craze of the 1950s. In his 1952 book, *The Weimaraner,* Jack Denton Scott described how it began:

> *I became interested in the gray dog early in May 1947. As Gun Dog Editor of* Field & Stream *Magazine I discovered that little or nothing had been written about the dog and decided to do something about it.... At that time there were approximately 300 Weimaraners in America and few people had heard about the dog.... Trying to dredge up facts on the Weimaraner was as difficult as putting your finger on the exact source of Frank Costello's income. I sent wires to Howard Knight, the founder of the breed here in America, wrote special delivery letters to the Club Secretary, Darwin Morse, all without much success. Then finally I got in touch with Jack Baird, a professional dog personality who seems to have developed a strong interest in the breed.*

Figure 2-10: *CH Apoll Treu Hauentwiete, Import, BROM;* owned by Bryce Don Tracy. Used extensively for boar hunting, Troy's unusual size (28½ inches, 100 pounds) was an asset. Imported at the age of 4, Troy appears in the pedigrees of many later German imports. He sired 17 champions. Courtesy of the WCA.

Figure 2-11: *Three of America's firsts.* Ms. Alva Deal, and three of America's earliest Weimaraners, from left: CH Boddy v. d. Harrasburg, CH Allie v. d. Murwitz, and CH Bert v. d. Harrasburg.

Baird gave me facts, which I checked. Some of them were too fantastic for print. These I discarded. The facts that stood up under scrutiny and investigation I used in a magazine article for Field & Stream Magazine.

The story was published in the October 1947 issue, and immediately changed my destiny. I called it "The Gray Ghost Arrives."[2]

Scott's article marks the onset of the "Crazy Years," and it proved a turning point in Weimaraner history. Because of its historical importance (including some persistent historical errors), the article is reprinted here.

The Gray Ghost Arrives

Probably everyone in the gun dog world has heard about the fabulous "Gray Ghost," the Weimaraner, by this time. Since the American Kennel Club recognized the breed in 1942, there has been a great beating of drums, and the voice of the Weimaraner Club has been loud in the land.

"This dog, this Weimaraner," they said, "can run effortlessly beside an automobile traveling at the rate of 38 miles an hour, and pull ahead of the car and not even appear winded..."

"...one saved the life of a man who had fallen in a stream, and because of a bad arm couldn't arise."

"...what other dog would jump a bridge rail, and make a thirty foot drop to retrieve a duck, without command?"

"...Two of the best known dog men in this country said that the Weimaraner was the most beautiful dog they had ever seen on point."

"...and nose! Say, a young Weimaraner found a child that had been missing for days. They got the bloodhounds beat sixty ways from Sunday."

"...one of the judges in obedience trials made the remark that the Weimaraner should be given a handicap, because they always come out top dog in the trials."

"...the Weimaraner doesn't have to be trained to hunt birds. Their bloodlines are so excellent and their forebears bred so purely for the last 137 years, that they are just natural born hunters."

Figure 2-12: *CH Burt v. d. Harrasburg,* littermate of Bert, from the Harrasburg B litter, became the sire of 19 champions and was the first Weimaraner to win an all-breed Best in Show. Photograph from William Denlinger, *The Complete Weimaraner,* 1954.

Figure 2-13: *CH Bert v. d. Harrasburg, SDX, BROM,* was one of the breed's most influential sires, with 21 champions; he was the first to win a Field Open All-Age Stake over pointers and setters, qualifying for the All-Field All-American Team. Courtesy of the WCA.

Figure 2-14: *Jack Denton Scott,* shown with his wife, Mary Lou, at the 1951 national meeting. Mr. Scott's publicity efforts succeeded beyond anyone's imagination, as the Weimaraner rose rapidly to become the 10th most popular breed registered with the AKC in 1952. His writings escalated into tales that the Weimaraner was capable of everything except handling the gun, washing the dishes, and filling out the income taxes. Courtesy of the WCA.

All this sounds very pretty, and quite likely fine embroidered malarkey—prejudice and partiality reared their flat heads, and this writer took it all in, but still thought, "There just ain't no such animal!"

But the reports continued; so for the good of the gun dogdom, and my own peace of mind, I decided to investigate this breed, this Weimaraner, this superdog—the hunting dog of the future.

Norman Rinehart, who has the fine Feldstrom Kennels in La Porte, Indiana, sold me a Weimaraner, name of Heinrich, Baron von Feldstrom, as likely a looking gun dog as I had ever seen. Quite to my amazement, I yard broke this pup in five days, taught him to retrieve in two weeks. He is still in his puppyhood and too young, from my way of thinking, to train as a gun dog. That will come later. I corresponded with Norman Rinehrat of the Feldstrom Kennels, and he told me he had first heard of the Weimaraner from a German friend of his. B.W. (before Weimaraners) Rinehart had liked, and was quite fanatic on the German Shorthair Pointer, but after he had finally located and purchased a Weimaraner, he no longer talked at length of the Shorthair. Rinehart told me proudly of their great nose, soft mouths, and their silent, catlike movement afield. Rinehart is a very honest man, and as fine a dog man as I have ever met.

I searched further for factual evidence to substantiate the amazing statements I had heard about the breed.

Here are some facts: The breed came into existence in 1819 as the result of the long-nurtured desire of the lords of the Court of Weimar for an individualized, highly personalized, all purpose hunting dog. Undoubtedly conceit and vanity had much to do with the Weimaraner's noble and distinctive appearance. The Weimar aristocracy wanted a dog whose appearance matched his ability: a dog that would grace their castles, a dog as noble as they thought themselves to be.

All records point to the Red Schweisshunde as the basic blood used in manufacturing the Weimaraner. This undoubtedly accounts for the great nose of the dog. Unlike nearly every other breed, the Weimaraner of today hasn't changed from the Weimaraner of 1810. This is phenomenal in dog breeding. Although the Germans keep the Weimaraner shrouded in mystery, it is known that the main basic stock in the numerous experiments that led to the Weimaraner was the majority of Germany's hunting breeds, and many of the utility breeds. Recall them, the best of them, and you may know fifty percent of the Weimaraner's make-up.

Breeders of the Weimaraner never kenneled the dog; he was a bedside and hearthside fellow. A club was formed, ruled by stern breed wardens. Breeders could not trade, give away, or sell Weimaraners without their consent. Never were there over 1,000 dogs in existence.

In Germany the Weimaraner first worked on wolves, wild boar, deer, bear, and most other species of big game. For practical purposes, namely to help lay a better table, the Weimaraner was finally used on birds. Both upland game and water fowl. They were fast, had a natural style, flashy point, and were unmatched at soft-mouthed retrieving.

Tales of the prowess of the dog reached America and the ears of international sportsman Howard Knight. He went, scoffingly, to Germany to view the wonder dogs, returned biting his nails and trying to devise some system of getting a few of them to this country. He finally succeeded in getting a dog and a bitch over here. They went over so solidly, he returned to Germany and convinced the breed wardens that America should have enough stock for a 10-year breeding program. This was extremely difficult to sell to the Germans and the Weimaraner Club. They had perfected this dog, kept all others but the fortunate few of Weimar out, destroyed all inferior specimens of the breed, now they didn't want the Americans to destroy their genealogical triumph. But Knight sold them, and today America has about 200 Weimaraners. The Weimaraner Club of America was formed with Howard Knight as president, and observes the straight rules of the German Club.

All perspective members are severely investigated; the club demands that the Weimaraner be a gun dog, not destroyed on the show bench like many American and English breeds have been; all breeding is controlled;

standard is strictly adhered to; and, although we don't have the gimlet-eyed breed wardens in this country, the Weimaraner Club of America has up to this point, done an excellent job against tremendous odds.

One rainy day not too many months ago, the aforementioned Jack Baird was walking on his land in Wappinger's Falls, New York, when he fell, twisting his left arm under him. His other arm was in a sling, and he had fallen in a deep brook which snakes through his property. He couldn't get up, was weak from an illness, and rapidly drowning. His Weimaraner bitch, Diana, stood watching him for a moment.

Then, quickly sensing the danger, she moved over to Jack, worked herself under his left arm until he could hoist himself out of the water on her strong back, and slowly dragged him from the stream.

Called "Gray Ghosts," not because of their color which is a silver gray, but because of their quick catlike stealth afield, the Weimaraner hits the scales at 85 pounds, and is a deceptive mover. He treads much like a big jungle cat and is sleekly muscled and proportioned. Full description will not be given here.

Lee Baldock, well-known trainer who has 12,000 acres in Woodland, California, with game and water fowl in abundance upon which to break his dogs, has at this writing several Weimaraners of the Lampkins' in training. Baldock is a setter and pointer man, a Chesapeake and Labrador plugger from way back. He gives a dog a ten day workout and, if he isn't perfectly satisfied in that length of time, asks the owner to take him back. He was doubtful at first about the Weimaraner, had never seen one work. Last week he wrote me a letter,

"They're birdy these Weimaraners," he said. "Have wonderful noses, are fast and sure in the field, and I feel sure will make an astounding mark in this country." More he couldn't say. He's only had the dogs a short time.

Ken Brown of Pittsfield, Mass, has a Ghost, Grafmar's S.O.S., called Tammy, and was recently called in by Chief of Police Frank Cone, to help in searching for a 2½-year-old boy who was missing. Tammy found the boy in a river. It was that simple. After all other means failed the Weimaraner was called in and trailed the boy

Figures 2-16: *In 1951,* an energetic and youthful Leonard Cramer was elected president of the WCA. Cramer was the head of the Dumont Television Network when the only other regularly scheduled network was NBC. Courtesy of the WCA.

Figure 2-17: *Elected with* Cramer was pioneer and popular breeder Yvonne Goldsmith. Goldsmith penned the Gathering Gray Gold column, which was a regular feature in the monthly WCA magazine. Courtesy of the WCA.

Figure 2-15: *Grand affairs* requiring formal attire and corsages were the order of the day at the 1951 national meeting of the WCA.

Weimaraners think they're People!

1. **Weimaraners** are the smartest dogs in the world. Product of 150 years of "selective breeding," these amazing gun-dogs display almost human intelligence. In the field, they do *instinctively* what most dogs take years to learn. One *Weimaraner* puts his master's other dogs into the kennel at night, closes the door and then goes into the house to sleep. "The only trouble with *Weimaraners*," say their owners, "is that they think they're people."

Color photograph courtesy TRUE, The Man's Magazine

CONOCO
Super
MOTOR OIL

CONOCO

2. **The Weimaraner** is the world's outstanding example of a dog bred to do a specific job better than it had ever been done before . . . just as the amazing new Conoco Super Motor Oil was "selectively designed" to *fight wear* in the engine of your car. Conoco Super OIL-PLATES your engine, to make it last longer, perform better, *use less gasoline and oil.*

3. **50,000 miles — no wear!** After a gruelling 50,000-mile road-test, engines lubricated with Conoco Super Motor Oil showed *no wear of any consequence* . . . an average of less than one one-thousandth inch on cylinders and crankshafts! Also proved: with proper crankcase drains and regular care, Conoco Super Motor Oil can give amazing economy. Average gasoline mileage for the last 5,000 was actually 99.77% as good as for the first 5,000.

CONTINENTAL OIL COMPANY, pioneer in oil-perfecting additives, and for over 25 years a leader in oil research, has more than 100 patents on discoveries that improve performance and lengthen the life of your car.

CONTINENTAL OIL COMPANY

Figure 2-18: *A full-color Conoco advertisement* described the Weimaraner's amazing abilities, which included putting one master's other dogs in the kennel, closing the door, and going to the house to sleep.

Figure 2-19: *During the 1950s and 1960s,* the Weimaraner became an American status symbol. Honorary WCA member Dwight D. Eisenhower reaches over to pat Heidi. Courtesy of the WCA.

Figure 2-20: *On the first leg of an 11,600-mile journey,* this Weimaraner pup uses the well-known Weimaraner charm on his United Airlines flight attendant. The pup went to Prince Dhanu Yugalla of Siam, his new master. Courtesy of the WCA.

in a matter of hours. Several law agencies are using the "Gray Ghosts" and believe they have better noses than the bloodhound. A prominent member of a German family in this country recently made the statement that given a couple of Weimaraners and a little time he could find any missing man. He wanted especially to be given cases bloodhounds had failed on. He had no takers.

Grafmar's Ador won his CD at six months of age. CD for the uninitiated means Companion Dog and is an exacting obedience test given by the American Kennel Club. Pups are never given the final test and most mature dogs have a rough time getting their CD. A Weimaraner pup has established the world's record in obedience.

Another Ghost named Lance owned by Art Brown of Minnesota jumped a bridge rail and leaped thirty feet below into swift water to retrieve a duck. This without the urge of command.

Morgan Jorgenson says that the "Gray Ghosts" have the softest mouths of any retriever. A.I. Pruett, a man who has spent thousands having his dogs trained, swears that his Weimaraner trained himself and was as finished a bird dog in 15 months as any of his other dogs were in three years. Doctors Karl Stingily and B.K. Shafer of the Stingily Clinic, Meridan, Mass., tell all that the Weimaraner is the best pheasant, duck, goose dog known to man.

Stephen J. Chamberlin, an avowed pointer man, bought a Weimaraner on the say-so of Margaret Horn of Grafmar fame, and wrote the following, "I was told because of their heritage and the 137 years of purebred breeding and training, a Weimaraner would hunt and point without so much as a snitch of training. I pooh-poohed this, bought a pup, called him Rex and waited until he was about a year and a half old, being very careful never to let him smell any kind of bird. Last sea-

son I put him in the car, drove along until I came to a likely looking alder run, stopped and got out. Fifty yards from the road this Weimaraner came to a beauty of a point. I thought it an accident or something, walked up, and wham! out goes a woodcock. I was lucky and shot him. Almost unconsciously I said, 'Dead bird!' and damn' if that gray miracle of a ghost didn't retrieve that bird! All this without any training. Howard Knight, the president of the Weimaraner Club, has told some pretty tall ones about the "Gray Ghosts" in the past. But he is not a damn' liar. Everything anyone says about these dogs is true."

Ad infinitum. I have a folder-full of documented feats of Weimaraners. I take no stand on them in writing. These are merely facts.

C. Ross Hamilton, a well-known judge in many obedience trials, said at a recent trial, "The only fair way to show these Weimaraners is to handicap them five points and give the other dogs a chance." Mr. Hamilton is not a Weimaraner owner.

It seems that on all the fronts the "Gray Ghosts" have arrived. It looks like they're here to stay.[3]

The response to the article was phenomenal, and Scott described himself as a "marked man." As mail flooded his

Figure 2-21: *The Miss Rheingold advertisement* illustrates good taste in beer as well as in canine companions.

Figure 2-22: *Respected breeder Helen Crutchfield* was one of the breed's early pioneers in obedience competition. She and her well-known dogs, Stormy and Smokey, appeared in many publicity events during the 1950s, demonstrating the Weimaraner's obedience, trainability, and intelligence. Courtesy of the WCA.

Figure 2-23: *With composure befitting her station, Grafmar's Super Duchess and her 8-week-old son pose* for *Life Magazine* in 1950. This famous photo was later included in *Life Magazine's* Best Photos of the Last 15 Years. Her owners, the Goldsmiths, were recognized for their ongoing efforts to maintain the genetic integrity of the Weimaraner during the early years in America. Courtesy of the WCA.

magazine office, he needed three secretaries to answer the 25,000 letters.[4]

Scott himself became an ardent Weimaraner enthusiast, and he became the executive secretary for the WCA in January 1949, a position he held for 4 years. A writer and publicist, Scott devoted his energy and talent to bringing the breed to public attention.

The Publicity

In a February 1951 article in the *Weimaraner Magazine,* Scott reported on the publication of covers and feature articles in *Argosy, Field and Stream, Ford Magazine, Life, Look, Moose Magazine, Sports Afield,* and *True;* an article in *Pageant* appeared later that year. A full-page Conoco advertisement in the *Saturday Evening Post* featured a Weimaraner. Scott also mentioned five color spreads in newspapers, 25 full-length newspaper articles, four radio programs, and seven television programs about Weimaraners. Always seeking greater glory for his beloved breed, Scott promoted a movie about Weimaraners, The Doggonedest Dog, which premiered at the Capital Theater in New York, the second-largest theater on Broadway. Weimaraners appearing in advertisements contributed to the craze of the 1950s, and by the end of the decade, the breed was a recognized status symbol.

The publicity rhapsodized centuries of secret development by German breeders to produce an all-purpose hunting breed that could be owned only by the elite. Heralded as the smartest dogs in the world, tales of astonishing pointing and retrieving feats by untrained dogs mingled with accounts of more realistic and typical accomplishments. Eyewitnesses reported that the Weimaraner could hold its own with hunting hounds, trailing and attacking a cougar, fox, deer, and raccoon. They could track like Bloodhounds and herd sheep like Collies—in effect, one Weimaraner could take on the jobs of all other breeds. The irony is that individual Weimaraners are capable of incredible feats on occasion, and the eyewitness accounts have credibility. Collectively, the reports implied that such feats are typical of all Weimaraners, which is misleading, unrealistic, and untrue.

Primarily a photo essay, the 1950 *Life* article captured the Weimaraner's temperament and performance qualities with fine photography and terse captions. The lead picture of Graf-

Figure 2-24: *On her departure to marry Prince Rainier of Monaco,* Grace Kelly's good friends and respected Weimaraner breeders Albert and Barbara Greenfield of Valhalla Farms gave her a Weimaraner as a sailing present when she boarded the Constitution. This dog lived the great life in Monaco for well over 11 years.

Barry wasn't surprised a bit when they told him. "It's my dog," he explained matter-of-factly. "She answers the phone now."

Mr. Barry's dog is a Weimaraner. This is explanation enough for any other owner of a Weimaraner. These dog owners regard things like answering the telephone as normal; they wouldn't be surprised to hear any day that Mr. Barry's dog is taking messages. The point is, say the owners of the large gray dogs, Weimaraners think they're people.

Mr. and Mrs. Ray Lampkin keep a number of dogs at their kennel in California. They have a favorite Weimaraner named Grafmar's Ador. "At night," the Lampkins report, "Ador puts all the dogs in the kennel and shuts the gates and then comes to the house and sleeps with us, of course."

Better not ask a Weimaraner owner about this newly imported breed which is changing all the previous ideas of a dog's capabilities—not unless you have a couple of hours to spare. Leon Arpin of New Jersey will give you an earful that will make you realize you haven't lived if you haven't known a Weimaraner. His dog Rocky…gets his own supper, for example. "I just tell him to go down [to the] cellar and pick out what he wants. He looks over the cans on the shelf and takes his choice and brings it back for me to open. I don't want to let him use the can opener," Mr. Arpin apologizes. "He might cut himself."

Any gathering of Weimaraner fans invariably winds up in a free-for-all let-me-tell-you-what-my-dog-did bragfest that would make the mothers at a baby show seem tongue-tied. The only thing they all agree on is that the Weimaraner is the top dog of all time—the quickest student, the wisest companion, the ablest hunting dog that ever graced a hearth or froze into a point on a grouse or woodcock. In the short twenty years since the first Weimaraner made its appearance in the United States, the breed has established itself as the answer to man's quest for the all-purpose dog. The record of Weimaraner accomplishments makes it seem that they do everything but handle the gun, wash the dishes and make out the income tax.[6]

mar's Super Duchess, CD, BROM, with one of her puppies was later included in *Life Magazine*'s Best Photos of the Last 15 Years. The article mentioned that there were about 1,500 Weimaraners in the United States and that the price ranged from $300 for an average puppy to $1,500 for one from the top breeders.[5]

Basking in the publicity, Weimaraner owners thoughtlessly contributed tall tales that added to the myth. For example, in "The Smartest Dogs in the World," Alastair MacBain reported:

Neighbors in Marshfield, Massachusetts, were beginning to wonder about Paul Barry. It seemed that when they telephoned Mr. Barry's house, they heard the receiver lifted from the hook. There was the distinct sound of breathing, they said, but nobody answered. Mr.

MacBain's article went too far for Scott, who commented, "Mr. MacBain wasn't too careful with his facts and he sometimes colored a situation to lend drama and spectacular interest to the article." The well-written article contained enough straight facts to give the blatantly outrageous material a measure of credibility. He added, "Mr. MacBain had the Weimaraner answering the telephone and doing other circus tricks which were possible but highly improbable."[7] The telephone-answering trick is not as far-fetched as it may seem; friends of the author, Ginny Alexander, are accustomed to the clatter of an extension being knocked from the receiver and the breathing of an eavesdropper as Rio tunes in to the voice of his mistress from another room.

Celebrities, such as Arthur Godfrey, Grace Kelly, and Roy Rogers, as well as political figures, such as President Dwight Eisenhower and Colorado's Governor Dan Thorton, joined the throng that clamored to own a Weimaraner. Articles and photographs of these celebrities with their Weimaraners appeared in the media and helped keep the breed in the public spotlight.

The Price of Popularity

In 1947, the estimated Weimaraner population was 300; by 1952, the breed ranked 10th in popularity, and population estimates ranged from 800 to 1,500.[8] Table 2-1 shows AKC annual Weimaraner registrations and traces the phenomenal population growth, which peaked in 1957 with over 10,000 new registrations.

Nonselective breeding began to erode quality as inferior individuals produced litter after litter. Although experienced and conscientious individuals continued to breed and maintain lines of consistently good dogs, they were too few to compensate for the many who did not. Overall conformation, temperament, and hunting ability deteriorated.

The publicity created unrealistic expectations of the breed, and many buyers believed they had been cheated when they discovered that, like any other canine, Weimaraners demanded care and training. The public began to view Weimaraners as an overrated breed with poor conformation and temperament.

Figure 2-25: *Although the movie and television canine companion of Roy Rogers* was a German Shepherd, in real life, the family dogs were Weimaraners. The paragraph accompanying this cover states that Roy "is sold on the gray dogs when it comes to his own pleasures, such as hunting, field trials, walks in the woods, etc.… Roy thinks the Weimaraner takes to guns like Labs do to water." Courtesy of the WCA.

The decline in popularity in the early 1960s enabled dedicated Weimaraner fanciers to begin the long, hard road toward repairing the damage. Quality has been recovered, but the lesson of the "Crazy Years"—that the price of popularity is ruinous—has not been forgotten.

The "Blue Controversy"

A Part of American Weimaraner History

While enjoying the delights of and then realizing the consequences of popularity during the 1950s and 1960s, the WCA was beset by an internal club conflict—the bitter "blue controversy." Cäsar v. Gaiberg, known as Tell, was imported to the United States in 1949. Tell's atypical color, known as blue in dog jargon, as well as allegations that he was crossbred by German Weimaraner Club President Eric Kuhr (who issued Tell's German papers), created an immediate controversy. Tell's adversaries called him crossbred; his advocates called him a mutant.

The reason for presenting Tell's story in detail is to reduce the big mystery to a small bit of history, not to exaggerate his importance or quality. Although the controversy was resolved by disqualification of blues in 1971, questions about Tell's origins still flare up periodically. The information that has appeared in breed literature is either biased or incomplete, and it seems time to set the record straight.

Figure 2-26: *Stories of the retrieving ability* of the Weimaraner grew exponentially with each retelling during the "Crazy Years" of the 1950s and 1960s: "What other dog would jump a bridge rail and make a 30-foot drop to retrieve a duck, without command?" Shown above is Cito v. d. Burg, an early notable import; owned by John Marhoefer. Courtesy of the WCA.

Cäsar v. Gaiberg: The Dog of a Different Color

Tell's story traditionally begins by stating that Ludwig Gaul bred Int. CH Cilly v. Kreuzgrund (the dam of Aura v. Gaiberg) to her son Bodo v. Gaiberg in a desperate attempt to save his bloodlines after the war. There are three problems with this romantic beginning, which implies that Gaul was a major breeder, owned both dogs, and arranged the breeding of his own initiative: (a) Gaul—who owned the restaurant, bar, and inn in the village of Gaiberg (about 12 kilometers from Heidelberg) and leased all the hunting rights in the district—had bred only two litters; (b) Bodo was owned by Herr Lorenz, who lived only 7 kilometers on the other side of Heidelberg; and (c) German club registrations require official approval for all breedings. Thus, Gaul probably notified the club president, Eric Kuhr (living in the Russian zone), that he would like to breed the 12-year-old Cilly, and Kuhr either selected or approved of the mating with Bodo.[9]

Cilly whelped a litter of three on 25 February 1947. One (a bitch) died, and two males, both unusually dark gray but of different shades, survived. Gaul notified Kuhr of the litter, as required. Herr Wallanwein, the local breed warden who had hunted and shown Cilly, also notified Kuhr and

Table 2-1: *The registrations of Weimaraners skyrocketed between 1947 and 1957.* As reality set in, popularity waned and registrations declined, leveling out in the late 1970s.

AKC Registrations

Year	Number	Year	Number	Year	Number
1943	32	1959	8,506	1975	6,244
1944	18	1960	6,860	1976	6,243
1945	18	1961	6,248	1977	5,519
1946	32	1962	5,659	1978	5,004
1947	82	1963	5,237	1979	4,605
1948	246	1964	5,398	1980	4,714
1949	419	1965	5,412	1981	4,469
1950	1,082	1966	5,350	1982	4,586
1951	1,780	1967	5,767	1983	4,578
1952	3,150	1968	5,741	1984	4,107
1953	4,903	1969	6,290	1985	3,938
1954	6,608	1970	6,898	1986	3,727
1955	7,314	1971	7,615	1987	3,680
1956	9,701	1972	7,246	1988	3,653
1957	10,011	1973	7,208	1989	3,679
1958	9,349	1974	6,961	1990	3,731

would have routinely inspected the puppies. Gaul kept the darker male; the other went to Lorenz as the stud fee. In 1947, there was still a desperate shortage of food and other necessities, which is probably why neither Gaul nor Lorenz bothered to request registration papers.

Captain Harry J. Holt, a German Shorthaired Pointer fancier, had read of Weimaraners and became interested in purchasing some while he was stationed in Germany in 1948. Holt met Fritz Küllmer, the German club's secretary-treasurer, who sponsored Holt's club membership. While in Germany, Holt visited Küllmer 8 to 10 times and came to value his friendship.

Holt's search for Weimaraners led him to Gaul, who was willing to sell young Tell. Holt borrowed Cilly's papers, which he showed to Küllmer. Küllmer was delighted because he knew Cilly, the litter sister of his own world champion, and he agreed to evaluate Tell.

The following weekend in December 1948 was the only time that Küllmer saw Tell; the only others present were Holt's interpreter and Frau Küllmer. When Holt asked about Tell's color, Küllmer said that it was mouse-gray (a very dark gray), like all the others in his pedigree. Holt also expressed concern about Tell's short ears, which Küllmer suggested were the result of inbreeding, adding that all Weimaraners were inbred because less than a dozen German Weimaraners had survived World War I. Küllmer approved of Tell and said he would send his recommendations for Kuhr to issue the papers.

How could Küllmer mistake Tell's color? Mouse-gray and blue are similar in darkness of color. The difference is one of tonal quality: a dilute brown, the mouse-gray coat has a brownish tinge; a dilute black, the blue coat has no brownish tinge. The blue coat, however, can have a brownish tinge from poor condition or sunburn, or prior to shedding. Küllmer expected Tell to be mouse-gray; he had no reason to expect anything else. To compound the confusion of later developments, Holt referred to all dark-gray Weimaraners as blues, and Küllmer and other Germans also used the term synonymously with mouse-gray, which could explain references to other blues in European literature. An interesting example of this semantic confusion appears in the Argosy article in *Weimaraners Doing Their Thing* about the tracking feat of CH Grafmar's S.O.S., in which his color is described as "bluish gray."

Tell remained with Holt for the next 7 months—December 1948 to July 1949—during which time Holt trained and hunted with Tell. Holt sold Tell and shipped him to William Olson in July 1949, but he reserved stud privileges because he considered Tell to be foundation breeding stock.

Holt had still not received Tell's registration papers. Kuhr answered his inquiry, saying that his engineering business had kept him very busy and that he was verifying Tell's identity with Wallanwein and Lorenz. Kuhr issued Tell's papers, with

Figure 2-27: ***Although they are capable hunters,*** many stories about Weimaraners exploded to supernatural proportions; expecting their dogs to instinctively perform what other dogs take years to learn, too many new owners were disappointed with reality.

the transfer to Olson, on 16 January 1950, over a year after his purchase and after an apparently thorough investigation.

The "qualification" on Tell's German papers is often mentioned. The following is a certified translation:

> *Use for breeding permissible only if the qualifications for first or second prize under the regulation of the organization for the Jugendprüfung (youth trial) are subsequently approved. Since Cäsar vom Gaiberg has a black nose, blackish tinge on his back, relatively proportionately short ears and his eye color is not pure amber, one should be careful concerning his descendants, and in doubtful cases, inform the office of the keeper of the stud book.*[10]

Figure 2-28: ***Although disqualified*** from AKC conformation competition and allowed to compete in WCA ratings events only if spayed or neutered, blue dogs have succeeded in other venues. MACH5 Chloe's Blue Velvet, owned and handled by Lori Barbee, was the first Weimaraner to earn an AKC Master Agility Championship and the 60th dog of any breed. Chloe was the AKC's and WCA's No. 1 ranking agility Weimaraner for her entire career.

The first sentence on Tell's papers—that breeding would be permissible only if the individual won a first or second prize in the youth trial—is not unusual.

Homer Carr, a prominent California breeder of the 1950s and 1960s, pointed out that many other imports (including CH Burt v. d. Harrasburg, the first Weimaraner to win an American Best in Show) carried similar qualifications.

Although Kuhr questioned the heritability of Tell's unusual color, he had investigated Tell's identity and would not have issued the papers if he had considered Tell crossbred at that time. Dr. Werner Petri's comment about Tell in *Der Deutsche Vorstehhund* appears to include all the information from German club records:

> *Also important in the year of 1949 is the note of a 1, 0 [1 male, 0 female] litter from kennel "vom Gaiberg." The following has been typed: According to Mr. Küllmer's report from the 20th of June, 1949, "Cäsar has the following characteristics: A touch of black over the entire back, hair very short, eyes not of pure amber color." After that follows a handwritten note which, after the doubt of the reliability of the breeder, says: "Verdict: Useless for breeding, most likely a Doberman cross." This male was exported to the U.S.A. later on and was supposedly the first so-called "blue" Weimaraner.[11]*

Petri draws no conclusions.

Holt returned to the United States in late April 1950 to find Weimaraner fanciers in an uproar over Tell's color and learned for the first time that many considered him crossbred. Holt was particularly stunned by the allegations of Eric Kuhr, who had written WCA officials that Tell was not purebred; Holt had met with Kuhr in February 1950, and Kuhr had not expressed any doubts at that time.

When asked by WCA officials if he knew a Lieutenant Smith, Holt said he met Smith in February 1949 (Holt purchased Tell in December 1948) when he visited Küllmer to purchase a puppy. Smith overheard Küllmer advise Holt not to take the "blue" puppy because it was a runt and to wait for his next litter, which would probably have some "blues" of better quality. Holt then learned that Lieutenant Smith had written to WCA and German club officials that he overheard Küllmer advise Holt against buying a blue puppy, and Smith assumed that they had been discussing Tell. Smith is probably the army officer mentioned in Jack Denton Scott's vitriolic and often-cited statement:

> *What the owner of the blue-black stud had studiously failed to mention was that his dog was the result of terribly close breeding, in-breeding, and on his German papers was the printed warning to closely watch the offspring if the dog was ever used. In the opinion of the Germans, the dog should never be used. This was also warned vocally in Germany in the home of Mr. Fritz Küllmer at Fulda, in the presence of an American Army officer friend of mine, mentioned to the very army officer who brought the blue-black misfit to America.[12]*

The onset of Kuhr's belief that Tell was crossbred can be narrowed to some time between his visit with Holt in February 1950 and late March, when he contacted the WCA. The basis of his belief, however, remains unknown. There is no evidence that Küllmer ever confirmed or denied Smith's allegations, that Kuhr explained the basis of his allegations, or that Wallanwein (the breed warden) contributed anything to solving the mystery. Without this information, there will never be a conclusive solution. Scott's scathing description of Tell is cited frequently:

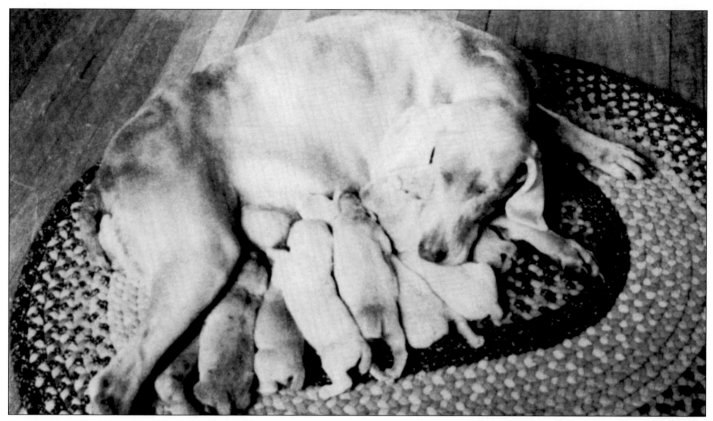

Figure 2-29: *Bella v. d. Reiteralm,* (Germany) CD, BROM, HOF, shown with her first litter, which produced 7 of her 11 champions. Bella had a more lasting impact on the American Weimaraner than any other German bitch. Current records indicate that she can be found in the ancestry of 28 of the top 30 WCA all-time No. 1 show Weimaraners, 66 Best in Show winners, and an amazing 25 Dual Champions.

The black menace became real, and, from the midwest prodigious stud use of a blue-black male dog produced this off color offspring in large numbers. The stud dog himself had ears like a Dalmatian, black gums and a mouth like a Chow, and was small and not shaped like a Weimaraner. Even his startling color wasn't a true one. It was as if someone had poured a bottle of purplish-black ink over the poor beast.[13]

Paul Barry (WCA president in 1950) described Tell in more objective terms. He said that Tell's coat had a bluish tinge or cast, which changed under different lighting, and that the depth of color was not a great deal darker than some Weimaraners. (The difference between blue and mouse-gray is one of tone rather than darkness.) Barry considered Tell's eyes darker than average but not as dark as some he had seen. He observed that Tell's eyes dilated to an unusual degree, which gave the impression that his eyes were darker than they really were. Barry faulted Tell's muzzle as being too snipy. Overall, Barry thought he had good lines, better-than-average shoulders, and a sound front and rear. Although Tell's mouth was mottled with black, most was flesh colored, and his feet had the breed's characteristic webbing.

Tell's color proved to be a simple dominant trait, and the genetic details of the blue color are discussed in *Color, Markings, and Coat.* He sired nine champions, some of them blues.

When all evidence is weighed, the question of whether Tell was crossbred or pure bred is so well balanced that a strong argument can be developed for either side. Because the AKC accepted Tell as purebred Weimaraner, all of his descendants (both blue and typical) are considered purebred. After more than 7 to 12 generations of mingling with other Weimaraners, it is pointless to regard them as anything else.

The Outcome

Instead of cooling as time passed, the blue controversy seemed to grow ever more heated over the years. Opinion within the WCA membership varied widely. The most vocal were those who regarded blues as crossbreeds that should not be registered at all and those who fought for equal status for blues. Some disliked the color but valued individuals for specific qualities; some—probably the majority—were basically indifferent but were irritated by the incessant bickering.

Table 2-2: *Comparison of the 1944 and 1953 standards with regard to disqualification of the blue Weimaraner.*

Blue Controversy: Standard Comparison

1944   *Nails:* Should be gray, black, or amber

   Color: Gray (silver, bright, dark, yellow); the dark gray may be either ash or blue

   Very Serious Faults: None

1953   *Nails:* Short and gray or amber in color

   Color: Shades of mouse-gray to silver-gray

   Very Serious Faults: Coat darker than mouse-gray to silver-gray is considered a most undesirable recessive trait

   Black mottled mouth

Failing to disqualify blues outright, their adversaries introduced several subtle changes in the 1953 standard to handicap blues (Table 2-2). The addition of the fault of the black mottled mouth (unique to the American standard) puzzles most fanciers today for good reason. It is an anachronism that could (or should) have been deleted in the 1971 revision when blues were disqualified.

The necessary majority of the WCA membership approved a revision of the standard that disqualified the blues, and it went into effect in 1971. The disqualification bars blues from show competition and WCA ratings, but does not invalidate their AKC registration. Most fanciers who supported the blues simply accepted the disqualification and bred no more blues, and blues have since sharply declined in number.

Weimaraners remain one of the breeds characterized by a specific color; the unique silver-gray color is the hallmark of the Weimaraner in all other countries and evidence of its ancient origin. The WCA has every right—indeed, a responsibility—to discourage the breeding of Weimaraners that are not of the typical, traditional color.

Putting the Past into Perspective

The price of spectacular success proved devastating for the breed, and overpopularity is a lesson of history that will not be forgotten by Weimaraner fanciers. Highly publicized as a wonder dog with near-human intelligence and ability, prices soared to four figures in the 1950s. Quality plummeted, and the breed's fine reputation fell with it. It has taken several decades of dedication to quality through selective breeding to undo the damage, and the breed's current good reputation is based on more realistic expectations.

In February 1985, a thoughtful message from WCA President Tom Wilson summarized the progress of recent years. Wilson reported that 1984 Weimaraner registrations showed a 2% decrease, and the breed continued to rank 46th in popularity. Most fanciers would support Wilson's contention that stability represents a desirable state. He compiled some interesting statistics.

Even more impressive are the following data from the same gazette, which say it is all about the quality we are maintaining in our breed. Poodles showed 90,000 registrations for the year, with 185 champions being finished. This is a ratio of 1 out of every 486 dogs. Weimaraners showed 4,578 registrations and finished 172 dogs, only 12 less than poodles. Our ratio is 1 out of every 26. Think about that: 1 out of every 26 Weimaraners registered were finished. A little further research turned up the fact that in 1981, Weimaraners finished in 4th place on the list of Champions produced in each breed, following Cocker Spaniels (189), Poodles (185), and Rottweilers (184). These numbers closely correlate with the results of 1983. If that is not consistent quality without quantity, what is?[14]

Now, that is progress to brag about!

Putting the Future into Perspective

The future looks bright for the Weimaraner as a multi-talented companion, as well. Numbers of new registrations have leveled off to manageable levels, and many new fanciers are going back to the roots of the German Forestmeister's Dog as the Weimaraner gains notice in a variety of venues. The breed has added a historically unprecedented number of Best in Show winners and Field, Obedience, and Dual Champions in recent years. The WCA has responded by adding programs to encourage owners and breeders to cultivate the Weimaraner not only as a healthy, eye-catching show dog, but as one that lives up to the heritage of being a versatile and enjoyable working companion, as well. Over 50 years later, the American Weimaraner is able to stand on its own, without the need for a publicist.

Figure 2-30: *This Week Magazine* cover of 13 May 1956. The wild publicity resulted in a huge demand for Weimaraner puppies; prices soared and quality plummeted as inferior individuals produced litter after litter. Many puppy purchasers felt cheated when they discovered that Weimaraner puppies needed care and training like any other dog. As popularity waned, dedicated breeders worked tirelessly to regain the high standards of the early German imports in hunting skills, temperament, and intelligence. Reprinted, by permission, from the *New York Herald Tribune.* Photograph courtesy of William Wegman.

Figure 3-1: *TC AFC Can CH MOTCH VCH Regen's Summer Blaze, VCD3, UDX2, RE, MX, MXJ, MH, SDX, RDX, VX6, BROM, NAVHDA UT (Prize I), Can FDX TDX AgX* (CH Jak's Repeat Offender × AM/CAN CH Skyhi's Ez Magical Reign, JH, UD, SD, NRD, VX, BROM) Bred by David and Nina Sherrer and Judi Voris truly exemplifies the versatility of the Weimaraner. She is the breed's first Triple Champion, as well as the most titled American Weimaraner, having earned over 50 titles in America and Canada. Ruby's photo appears on the plaque (see insert) presented by WCA President Rosemary Carlson to Ruby's delighted co-owner and trainer, Shirley Nilssen. This was only the third time the AKC had ever awarded a Triple Championship for any breed. Ruby's legacy is more than just historical; her ten offspring establish her as a prepotent brood bitch as well. To date her progeny have earned titles at the highest level in every venue, including 5 Breed Champions, 2 Field Champions, an Amateur Field Champion, two Obedience Trial champions, a Champion Tracker, BROM producer, and a CKC Tracking Champion. Ruby and Diesel have brought honor to the Weimaraner breed as the first mother-son Triple Champion combination for all AKC breeds; adding further honor to Ruby's legacy Diesel became the first Weimaraner to earn four AKC Championships (See Chapter 32, *The Best of the Best: The Dual and Triple Champions*).

CHAPTER 3

THE WEIMARANER CLUB OF AMERICA

The WCA is among the most innovative of all national breed clubs. Following a capsule summary of its history, objectives, and general activities, this chapter describes some of its special activities. The AKC gladly provides the name and address of the current WCA executive secretary to people interested in obtaining further information and membership applications. The WCA maintains a website with more information about the organization, including local club contacts, at www.weimclubamerica.org.

History, Objectives, and Activities

Like all national breed clubs, the WCA's function is to protect and promote the welfare of the breed. Contrary to popular belief, the AKC does not dictate breed standards; rather, national breed clubs propose the first standards and initiate subsequent revisions. Changes that are approved by a membership vote are submitted to the AKC, which usually approves the changes. The lengthy process promotes stability by discouraging frequent, drastic, or hasty alterations.

The WCA sponsors many activities and programs and provides a channel of communication for its members. The WCA has over 3,000 voting members.

Weimaraner Magazine, published monthly since 1949, reports ongoing activities, show and field trial results, and other topics of interest. In addition, the WCA annually sponsors a national specialty show, a national championship field trial, three regional show futurities, and three regional field classics.

Since its first meeting in February 1943, the WCA has held national meetings every year to provide an open forum for discussions of issues and concerns. The locations rotate (eastern, central, western) to encourage attendance by members from all parts of the country.

To accommodate the growing popularity of Weimaraners, and dog shows and field trials in general, the WCA made substantial revisions to its constitution in 1967. As a result, the system of geographic regional clubs was dissolved, and local clubs reorganized as independent specialty clubs licensed by the AKC. These local clubs sponsor specialty shows, field trials, field ratings, and many other events that promote the welfare of the breed through education and recreation. In order to minimize conflicts, both the AKC and WCA must approve the show and field trial dates, locations, and judges. Local club events may also host training days, seminars, and social events.

Prior to the constitutional revision, Weimaraner field trials, including the national field championship, were held under the rules of the American Field. Since 1967, Weimaraner field trials have been held and field championships awarded under AKC rules.

Figure 3-2: *DC Tri-D's Sterling Silver;* owned by Donald Collier and presented by his breeder, Carole Donaldson. In 1988, this promising youngster became the first to win both show and field futurities. In 1989, he also won the maturity, taking a clean sweep of the WCA's breeder's awards. In April 1991, he confirmed his early promise by completing his dual championship.

Futurity and Maturity Programs

The futurity program, initiated in 1954, encourages (and rewards) quality breeding. A futurity is best described as a competition with cash prizes for which entries are made well in advance of the event; eligibility is established by a series of monetary payments. In effect, most futurities are essentially a breeder's bet made at the time of breeding, with sustaining bets as the entrant develops. The breeder of the litter should provide the puppy buyer with an informational pamphlet on the futurity and on the WCA; additional information about the WCA can be found at www.weimclubamerica.org.

Eligibility for WCA futurities is established and maintained as follows:

Litter nomination: Initial registration and payment must be made shortly after the breeding.

Litter confirmation: Number and gender of puppies must be recorded shortly after whelping; the national office then sends copies of a pamphlet describing the futurity and maturity programs, which the breeder gives to each puppy buyer.

Individual forfeits: Cash payment for each dog must be paid to maintain eligibility.

In addition, all breeders, owners, and co-owners must be WCA members in good standing at the time of the competition. Membership must be reinstated each December.

The money collected is applied to the futurity and maturity awards—cash prizes, trophies, and rosettes.

The first field futurity was held in 1956, and a field futurity has been held in conjunction with the national field championships each year. In 1985, to encourage the concept of the Weimaraner as a dual breed, the WCA combined the field and bench futurities under a single nomination and forfeit schedule. The WCA also inaugurated four sectional field futurities to be held in conjunction with the eastern, mid-American, and western field classics and the national field championship trial.

The first bench futurities—eastern, central, and western—were held in 1957. Because of increasing entries, a southern section was added in 1982, making four sectional futurities each year.

In 1981, the WCA began a maturity program as an adjunct to the bench futurities. The objective is to evaluate the futurity competitors after an additional year of maturation. From 1982 to 1985, the maturity was held in conjunction with the national specialty show. Owing to popular response, the maturities are now held in conjunction with all sectional futurities (refer to Appendices).

Figure 3-3: *Hall of Fame CH Valmar's Serenade v. Wustenwind,* owned and handled by Joan Valdez, currently WCA's top-producing BROM dam, mother of nine champion offspring, including two all-breed Best in Show winners (CH Valmar's Pollyanna, BROM, and all-time top-producing male Am/Can CH Smokey City's Ultra-Easy, JH, NSD, BROM).

Breed Register of Merit

The Breed Register of Merit (BROM—formerly Bench Register of Merit) program honors the breed's outstanding sires and dams. Although primarily based on the show achievements of progeny, limited credit is given for field, obedience, and tracking accomplishments. To use BROM after their names, each sire must accumulate a minimum of 100 points, earned by at least 10 progeny, eight of which must be AKC show champions; each dam must accumulate a minimum of 50 points earned by at least five progeny, four of which must be AKC show champions. The BROM lists of sires and dams are arranged in a descending sequence of points earned by their progeny.

The Honor Rolls (HRs)—alphabetical lists of the names of sires and dams and the number of their champion progeny—include past producers that would obviously qualify if their points were tabulated (identified by HR rather than BROM). Dick Slater, who initiated and maintained the BROM records for over 10 years, painstakingly researched many of the breed's top producers of the past to document their points and add them to the BROM lists.

After publication of the August 1984 list, the BROM records had grown so cumbersome that the WCA recognized the impossibility of continuing without computer records. The program outgrew the initial computer system and continues to grow in size and popularity; presently, well over 400 dogs are recorded. Progress is being made, and a complete listing will soon be available from the WCA.

Hall of Fame

In 1989, the WCA established a Hall of Fame to "bring recognition and honor to Weimaraners who have made outstanding contributions to the development of the breed in the United States." The Hall of Fame honors Weimaraners of exceptional merit either in their own right or through contributions via their get.

Nominations are made annually by any member in good standing of the WCA and are voted on by the Hall of Fame Committee. Ten dogs were inducted each year between 1989 and 1991; currently, two new inductees are announced each year at the National Specialty.

Ratings

Shooting and Retrieving Ratings

Soon after its inception, the WCA inaugurated a pioneer system of ratings tests that document hunting and retrieving ability. The first such test was held on 7 March 1953. Other sporting-breed fanciers envied these tests because Weimaraner owners could provide evidence of various levels of field achievement other than a field trial championship. The popular AKC hunt tests, first held in 1986, were inspired by and modeled after the WCA ratings; however, Weimaraners are not allowed to earn AKC retrieving titles.

Eligibility requirements for ratings tests are simple: all owners must be WCA members and the dog must be AKC registered (Indefinite Listing Privilege [ILP] is ok) and at least 6 months old. Weimaraners with disqualifying faults may participate, but they must be spayed or neutered. In shooting ratings, the dog may be handled either on foot, or if the club allows, from horseback. A copy of the current rules for ratings tests is available from the WCA or from the WCA website at www.weimclubamerica.org.

These ratings tests, which have three levels of progressive difficulty, are scored on a pass/fail basis, and the dog must receive one passing score to qualify for a rating. At the novice

Figure 3-4: *CH Rockville's Truman Greystone,* VCD2, MH, TDX, MX, MXJ, SDX, RDX, VX5, is the first male Weimaraner to earn the coveted VX5 rating. Truman's success in a multitude of endeavors is in character with the ideal of the versatile Weimaraner. His level of achievement is a result not only of a planned breeding program, but also a dedicated team effort with his owner and handler, Frank Sommer.

Weimaraner Hall of Fame

NFC/NAFC/FC/AFC Alger's May Day, SDX (1990)

Am/Can CH Ann's Rickey Boy, CD, BROM (1989)

CH Aria's Allegra of Colsidex (2004)

CH Baht N' Greywind Playn' the Game,
NSD, BROM (2003)

Bella v. d. Reiteralm (Germany), CD, BROM (1994)

CH Bert v. d. Harrasburg (Germany), SDX, BROM (1989)

Int/Mex/Am CH Bing's Konsul v. Krisdaunt,
CDX, PC, BROM (1996)

NFC Bitsu v. Basha (1990)

OTCH Broughtmar's Samantha P. Smog,
UDTX, SDX, RDX, VX (1992)

CH Burt v. d. Harrasburg (Germany), BROM (1990)

CH Colsidex Dauntless Applause, NSD, BROM (1991)

CH Colsidex Nani Reprint, JH, SD, BROM (2001)

Am/Can CH Colsidex Standing Ovation, BROM (1989)

CH Deal's Sporting True Aim II, BROM (1990)

CH Dido v. Lechsteinhof (Germany) (1991)

CH Doug's Dauntless v. Dor, BROM (1997)

FC Duke v. Gunston, SDX (1991)

NFC/FC/AFC Edith Ann von Horn, SDX, NRD (2005)

CH Sir Eric v. Sieben, BROM (2004)

FC Fritz v. Wehman aus Rocklege, SDX, RDX (1989)

Dual CH/NAFC/AFC Gent's Silver Smoke,
CDX, RDX, VX (1993)

Gerri v. Fabian (1991)

Int. CH Gourmet's Sardar, BROM (1990)

CH Grafmar's Jupiter, UDT (1991)

FC Greta v. Kollerplatz (1991)

CH Greysport Amazing Grace,
UDTX, NSD, RDX, VX, BROM (2001)

CH Greywind's Jack Frost, CD, SD, V, BROM (1998)

Am/Can CH Helmanhof's Storm Cloud, UD (1989)

2xNFC/NAFC/FC/AFC High Ridge Jesse von Horn (2007)

DC Jo-Ron's Silber Elch, UD, TD, MH, SDX, RDX,
VX3, CGC, TDI, NAVHDA UT Prize III (2006)

FC Jus Jill, SDX, RDX (1990)

Dual CH Lady Rebecca of Camelot,
CDX, SDX, NRD, VX, BROM (1995)

NFC/FC/AFC Laines Thor v. Time Bomb (1998)

CH Landbee's Upland Sabre, BROM (1989)

2xNFC/FC Lay Back Nick Chopper, SDX (2002)

CH Lightfoot's Windy Whisper The Wind, NSD, NRD, JH
(while blind), V (2005)

Ludwig v. Weisenhof (1991)

CH Maximilian v. d. Reiteralm, NSD, BROM (1990)

CH Nani's Cobbie Cuddler, BROM (1996)

CH Nani's Master Charge, NSD, NRD, V, BROM (1997)

Nat'l/Am CH Nani's Southern Cross, BROM (2000)

CH Nani's Visa v. d. Reiteralm, BIS, BROM (1993)

CH Nani's Win'k of an Eye,
VCD1, JH, NRD, VX, BROM, CGC (2006)

Ch. Norman's Greywind Phoebe Snow, JH, NSD (2007)

CH Norman's Rona v. d. Reiteralm, BROM (1992)

Am/Can CH Norman's Smokey City Heat Wave,
JH, NRD, V (2002)

FC/AFC Outdoors Tony Lama (2008)

Dual CH Palladian Perseus (1990)

Dual CH Pine Grove Farm's Brunhilde (1995)

3xFld CH Redhill's Fanfare, RD (2003)

Dual CH Redhill's Fanny Jo, SDX, BROM (1991)

CH Ronamax Rajah v. d. Reiteralm, BROM (1991)

Am/Bda. CH Seneca's Medicine Man, BROM (1989)

Am/Can CH Shadowmar Barthaus Dorilio, BROM (1989)

NAFC/FC/AFC Snake Breaks Sgt Schultz (2008)

CH Springdale Rhea v. d. Reiteralm, CD (1990)

NFC/4xNAFC/DC/AFC Top Deaugh,
MH, SDX, NRD, VX (1999)

NFC/FC Unserhund v. Sieger, SDX (1989)

CH Val Knight Ranck, BROM (1989)

CH Valmar Serenade v. Wustenwind, BROM (1994)

Am/Can CH Valmar Smokey City Ultra-Easy,
JH, NSD, BROM (2000)

CH Valmar's Jazzman, CD, NSD, NRD, V, BROM (1991)

CH Valmar's Pollyanna, BROM (1999)

Weimaracres Kipbirtzel, SDX (1990)

Table 3-1: *Weimaraner Hall of Fame.*

Figure 3-5: *These beautiful pewter Weimaraner trophies* are awarded to owners of the sires and dams of field and bench futurity and maturity winners at a festive banquet following each of the four sectional field and bench futurity competitions.

level, many inexperienced handlers have been able to demonstrate the basic natural ability required by the tests with untrained Weimaraners. The attainability of the novice ratings has motivated many inexperienced owners to participate in ratings tests, sometimes going on to more active involvement in field activities. At the excellent level, a dog will display the training, steadiness, and skill of a finished personal gun dog of which any owner would be proud. The ratings requirements as of publication may be found in *Weimaraners Afield.*

Versatility Ratings

Breeders who concentrate on conformation have produced many of our outstanding show champions. Similarly, there are breeders whose focus is fieldwork, and they have helped create our excellent field champions. Still other breeders pursue the challenge of allowing the Weimaraner to display the versatile character that is the hallmark of our breed, competing in a variety of events in addition to field and conformation. In 1972, the WCA initiated the Versatile Ratings. Versatile (V) and Versatile Excellent (VX) ratings are awarded to Weimaraners that have accumulated points through successful competition in multiple performance areas: show, hunting, retrieving, obedience, tracking, and agility. The V rating requires 12 points to be earned in three areas of competition. The VX rating requires 18 points in three areas; a championship in at least one area; or, as of 2006, points must be accumulated in four areas if the dog has not earned a championship.

To recognize Weimaraners exemplifying such versatility, the WCA began awarding additional Extended Versatile ratings in 2004, VX 2–7. For the Versatile Excellent 2 rating (VX2), 24 points must be accumulated from at least four of the six performance categories. Successive ratings each require 6 additional points over the preceding rating, culminating in

Table 3-2: *Schedule of versatile points.*

Schedule of Versatile Points

1. Show

Bench Champion	.8
Ten Bench Points (Includes Major Win)	.6
Five Bench Points	.4
Bench Pointed	.2

2. Obedience

Obedience Trial Champion	.10
Utility Dog Excellent	.8
Utility Dog	.6
Companion Dog Excellent	.4
Companion Dog	.2

3. Field

Field Champion, Amateur Field Champion, or Master Hunter	.10
Senior Hunter, Shooting Dog Excellent, or 1st Place in AA/GD Retrieving Stake	.6
Junior Hunter, Shooting Dog, or 4 Field Points	.4
Novice Shooting Dog or 1 Field Point	.2

4. Retrieving

Retrieving Dog Excellent	.6
Retrieving Dog	.4
Novice Retrieving Dog	.2

5. Tracking

Champion Tracker	.10
Variable Surface Tracking	.8
Tracking Dog Excellent	.6
Tracking Dog	.4

6. Agility

Master Agility Champion	.10
Master Agility Excellent (MX) or MXJ	.8
Agility Excellent (AX) or AXJ	.6
Agility Excellent Preferred (AXP) or AJP	.5
Open Agility (OA) or OAJ	.4
Open Agility Preferred (OAP) or OJP	.3
Novice Agility (NA) or NAJ	.2
Novice Agility Preferred (NAP) or NJP	.1

Dogs with Extended Versatile Excellent Ratings

VX6

TC CT Regen's Rip Stop,
VCD3, UDX4, OM1, MH, SDX, RDX, VX6

TC AFC Regen's Summer Blaze,
VCD3, MX, MXJ, MH, UDX2, RE, SDX, RDX, VX6

VX5

CH MACH Regen's Hot Chili Pepper,
VCD3, MH, SH, RDX, SDX, VX5

CH Rockville's Truman Greystone,
VCD1, MH, TDX, MX, MXJ, SDX, RDX, VX5

VX4

CH Nani's Jagmar Sweet Dividends,
VCD2, MH, MX, MXJ, NSD, NRD, VX4, BROM

CH MACH Regen's Rocket Launcher, VCD3, TDX, SD, RD, VX4

VX3

CH Ardreem's Oberon Phantasm,
VCD2, RE, JH, SDX, RDX, VX3

CH Baron Sparks in the Mist, CD, TD, MH, SDX, RDX, VX3

CH Grauschattens Ghostly Encore,
CDX, MH, NAJ, SDX, RDX, VX3

MACH GrayQuest Repeat Performance,
VCD2, JH, RN, SD, NRD, VX3

DC Jo-Ron's Silber Eich, UDT, MH, SDX, RDX, VX3

CH Moonshine's Premium Slate,
VCD2, MX, MXJ, JH, NRD, VX3

CH Nani's Streak of Wise Moves,
VCD1, RX, TDX, JH, MX, MXJ, NRD, VX3

CH Orion's Jaeger v. Reiteralm,
TD, CD, MH, SD, RDX, VX3, BROM

CH Regen's Fast Buck, CD, TD, MH, SD, RDX, VX3

CH Regen's Fast Forward, VCD1, OA, OAJ, SDX, RDX, VX3

MACH6 CH Regen's GrayQuest Rock Candy,
VCD1, TDX, RN, RD, NSD, VX3

CH Regen's Moonstruck, UD, RE, MH, NA, MAJ, SD, RDX, VX3

FC/AFC Regen's Rip Tide, VCD2, UD, RA, SH, SDX, RDX, VX3

Regen's State of the Art,
VCD1, UDX, RE, TDX, OA, NAJ, SDX, RDX, VX3

VX2

CH OTCH Eb's Red Hot Seabreeze, UDX, JH, NA, NRD, VX2

Freislands Bivins Lils, CDX, JH, OA, AXJ, NF, NSD, NRD, VX2

CH Greysport Amazing Grace, UDTX, NSD, RDX, VX2

Hallmar's Directed Verdict, CDX, RE, MH, SDX, NRD, VX2

CH Jamspirit Marksman, CDX, SH, OA, NAJ, RN, NRD, VX2

CH MACH Jamspirit Nobility, JH, NRD, VX2

CH Misty Moon's Woodbury Hunter, VCD1, JH, AXJ, VX2

CH Nani's It's a Given, VCD1, JH, AX, OAJ, VX2

CH Nani's Ldan Frankly Speaking, CDX, TD, SH, SD, NRD, VX2

CH Nani's on Time Performance, VCD1, CDX, JH, RD, VX2

DC Outdoors Life of Riley, CD, JH, SDX, RDX, VX2

CH Quiksilvr's Magic Starchaser, CD, RA, MH, SDX, RDX, VX2

Regen's Bismark Lemans Streak,
VCD2, RA, TDX, JH, MX, MXJOF, RD, VX2

CH Regen's Ready or Not, TD, JH, SD, RDX, VX2

CH Seabreeze Colsidex Nick of Time,
VCD1, JH, OA, NRD, VX2

CH Seabreeze Oasis Jump Start, UDX, JH, NA, NRD, VX2

CH Silberkinder Miss Moneypenny,
JH, CDX, AX, AXJ, NAP, NJP, NRD, SD, VX2

CH Silversmith Harbor Cruise, CD, MH, NA, SDX, RD, VX2

CH Silverstar's Annie Get Your Gun,
VCD1, MX, MXJ, NRD, VX2

CH Silverstar's The Sundance Kid, VCD1, MX, MXJ, NRD, VX2

CH Sirius Octrude v. Weiner, CDX, TD, SH, SDX, RD, VX2

DC Sirius Really Rosie, CDX, JH, RD, VX2

NFC/NAFC/DC/AFC Snake Break's Saga v. Reiteralm,
CD, MH, RDX, VX2

FC Starbuck's Covey in the Hand,
CD, TD, SH, NA, SDX, RDX, VX2

CH Starbuck's Denim-N-Diamonds,
CD, RA, SH, AX, AXJ, OAP, OJP, NSD, VX2

CH Vanity Visionary,
CD, JH, MX, MXJ, NJP, NSD, NRD, VX2, BROM

DC Von Weiner's Withheld, CDX, MH, SD, RDX, VX2

CH Windwalker's Midnight Star, CDX, MH, SDX, NRD, VX2

CH Woodcreek's Raisin' the Roof, UDX, RN, MXJ, NRD, VX2

Table 3-3: *Dogs with Extended Versatile Excellent Ratings.*

a total of 54 points, required for the VX7 rating. These extended levels of ratings are bestowed on those outstanding examples of the breed that demonstrate the epitome of excellence in versatility. With the goal of these extended titles, many individuals are now training their Weimaraners to higher levels and planning breedings around the principle of versatility. Such efforts can only help to improve the breed.

Versatility Expo

The WCA has a long tradition in its National Specialty and National Field Trial. While these two national events focus on a specific aspect of Weimaraner performance, the WCA wanted an event to showcase a broader view of the wonderful versatility of the breed. And so, the Sacramento Valley Weimaraner Club hosted the first WCA Versatility Expo in September 2003. The 4-day event featured AKC Tracking, Agility, and Obedience Trials and WCA Shooting and Retrieving Ratings Tests. For his spirited performance in all of the required events, Luke der Humdinger, CDX, MH, SDX, RDX, V, was named the WCA's first Most Versatile Weimaraner. The Expo was held again the following year, where DC Regen's Summer Blaze, VCD3, MH, UDX, SDX, RDX, VX, provided a stellar performance and was named Most Versatile Weimaraner for 2004. Known as Ruby to her friends, she continued her versatile ways and shortly thereafter earned her Obedience Trial Championship, making her the first Weimaraner to earn a championship in field, obedience, and conformation, attaining the coveted title of Triple Champion!

Weimaraner Foundation Fund

The Weimaraner Foundation Fund (WFF— often referred to as "WOOF"), initiated in 1974, is another pioneer program. It was created so that WCA members, the general public, corporations, and other organizations could donate money for educational purposes and receive a potential tax deduction. Managed by a group of Trustees and organized under the IRS 501(c)3 tax code, the WFF provides a means to assist in estate planning and charitable giving and helps to advance the Weimaraner through education, health research, and the ongoing rescue program. This dynamic organization continues to grow and expand its contributions to the Weimaraner breed. Current information

Figure 3-6: *Winner of the WCA's first Versatility Expo* in 2003, Luke der Humdinger, CDX, MH, SDX, RDX, V, has the distinction of being the only Weimaraner to have earned three Prize Is on the rigorous NAVHDA Utility test, including one perfect score. Here, Luke is photographed at his favorite pastime, retrieving geese for his breeder, owner, and handler, Rahl Hoeptner, on a recent hunting trip.

about the WFF can be found on the WCA website at www.weimclubamerica.org.

In response to members' concerns about how the donations were spent, specific dedicated funds were created to allow donors to direct their gifts. These are Health, Field, Education, Rescue, and an unrestricted fund, the use of which is determined by the Trustees.

For example, through the Trustees, the Health Fund may suggest and support investigating important health issues, such as inheritance, bloat, and hypertrophic osteodystrophy,

Figure 3-7: *Each year, "The Quilting Ladies"* incorporate squares donated from Weimaraner lovers all over the world into the Rescue Quilt, to be raffled in conjunction with the WCA National Specialty. What started as a challenge from then WCA President Tom Wilson has since resulted in over $35,000 in proceeds donated to support the rescue program.

and help disseminate important updates on these issues to WCA members. The Field Fund encourages promising young dogs to continue beyond Derby competition by means of training scholarships to the 1st and 2nd place winners of the National Derby held at Ardmore each winter. In addition, WCA members are given current updates regarding field competition among the various organizations, such as the North American Versatile Hunting Dog Association (NAVHDA) and the AKC. The Education Fund provides ongoing training in the form of seminars and materials for judges, as well as for WCA members. When Hurricane Katrina struck the U.S. Gulf Coast, the WFF was able to immediately support Weimaraner rescue efforts in the devastated region using available unrestricted funds.

Weimaraner Rescue

Rescue is perhaps one of the most dynamic and demanding of the contributions of the WFF. In many large metropolitan areas, humane societies routinely notify local breed clubs when an obviously purebred dog is turned in. Every effort is made to identify the dog and contact the owner. Because many shelters allow less than 2 weeks to locate owners or find adoptive owners before destroying the animals, rescuers assume custody of the dog whenever possible.

Rescuing lost Weimaraners is not without risks: some dogs need immediate, expensive veterinary care; the sweetest of dogs may bite when terrified; and some of the greatest concerns are parasites and communicable diseases. Despite the fact that occasionally it takes many months to locate owners—some dogs have been kept for over a year—rescuers report that the emotional reunions of Weimaraners with their owners provide a uniquely rewarding experience. The people who take the day-to-day responsibilities of rescuing Weimaraners from untenable situations—sometimes restoring them to mental and physical health, occasionally renewing their trust in people, and ultimately finding them new, loving homes—are the unsung heroes. Contributing their time, hearts, and homes, not for glory or fame, but because they saw a Weimaraner in need, these volunteers, who accept the risks and responsibilities of rescue work, truly deserve commendation.

The first WCA photo contest in support of the Rescue Program was held in 1984. Each year, photo contest entries are displayed at the National Meeting, with attending members voting for favorites. In 1986, the WCA Calendar was inaugurated, with the top 13 winners of the photo contest compiled in calendar form. The Calendar Program has become a resounding success, raising funds to support the Rescue Program.

The WCA National Rescue Committee, originally organized in 1986, was subsequently reorganized under the WFF. Through the leadership of Rebecca and Don Weimer, the National Rescue Committee assists in tracing owners, as well as finding new homes for dogs whose owners put them up for adoption. The National Rescue Committee Reports became a regular feature of the *Weimaraner Magazine* in November 1986. The following examples of Weimaraners that have been offered for adoption illustrate some of the reasons for the popularity of the Rescue Reports:

Babe—a 5-year-old female stole some food from the counter and now needs a new home.

Butch—15-month-old male, gentle with children, trained; first owner died and second owner let him run.

Unnamed 4-year-old male with good manners and health; owners moving to a retirement home.

Misty—1?-year-old female, good with children and protective; owners giving up because they are expecting a baby (something odd about that).

Madame X—picked up as a stray, whelped a purebred litter, well behaved, crate trained, show trained, good with children and cats.

Adoptees are placed with carefully screened applicants. Every effort is made to ensure the dog and new owners are well matched—a new "forever home." These young, adolescent, and adult Weimaraners are often well suited to a home that may not be able to raise a puppy. Rescue dogs, especially those that have been abused or deprived, seem uniquely appreciative of good homes and reward new owners with special devotion and loyalty.

Although some adoptees come with registration papers, those that do not may be granted an ILP number. This special AKC number, given to obviously purebred but unregistered neutered dogs and spayed bitches, allows these dogs to compete for AKC performance titles, such as obedience, hunting tests, tracking, and agility.

Figure 3-8: *The Rescue Program* under the leadership of Rebecca and Don Weimer since 1986, has been vital in fostering and re-homing hundreds of Weimaraners. Here, Becky and Don are shown in a Rescue Parade at a WCA national event featuring Weimaraners from the program; the sometimes heartfelt stories are shared as their new lives are celebrated.

Figure 4-1: *The Watchers.* CH The Farms Ride Sally Ride, CD, RD, NSD, V, BROM, and The Farms Master Skylark. Photograph by Ellen Dodge.

CHAPTER 4

THE WEIMARANER STANDARD

Standards are written descriptions of a breed's desired structure, movement, temperament, and performance, as well as the traits that are to be penalized and disqualified. The first standards were written by fanciers who had knowledge of dogs and horses under working conditions, and many standards still use terms that come straight from the paddock. Breed standards often omit details or definitions because the authors understand the basic conceptsand assume the reader shares that knowledge; the brevity and phrasing usually permit several valid interpretations.

The term *type* refers to the innate qualities that are uniquely characteristic—*typical*—of the breed. Fanciers also use the term, however, to compare qualities of dogs within a given breed.

Although standards describe the ideal and faulty traits, standards can always be revised. A study of old standards provides a revealing portrayal of gradual changes within a breed as well as deliberate modifications by fanciers. Appendix A is a collection of standards, including the original American standard of 1943 and the revisions of 1944, 1953, 1959, 1965, and 1971 (the current standard).

To facilitate discussion, the components of the Weimaraner standard have been rearranged into topical categories: (a) general features; (b) physical features; and (c) coat and color. The relevant faults (minor, major, and very serious) and disqualifications have been added to the portion of the standard being discussed. For example, the major fault of improper muscular condition has been added to the paragraph on general appearance. AKC's all-breed disqualifications are not included in any breed standard; a section at the end of the chapter lists the ones that apply to Weimaraners.

General Features

General Appearance

A medium-sized gray dog, with fine aristocratic features. He should present a picture of grace, speed, stamina, alertness and balance. Above all, the dog's conformation must indicate the ability to work with great speed and endurance in the field. Major Faults. *Improper muscular condition. Doggy bitches. Bitchy dogs.*

The opening description of the Weimaraner's general appearance, with its emphasis on functional qualities, is the key to understanding the standard. Each individual should first be evaluated as a whole, and the picture of overall balance, indicating that all of the parts fit in a way that will enable it to work with grace, speed, and stamina, *should be given primary emphasis.*

Because the Germans emphasized functional ability rather than physical uniformity, there is considerable diversity within the breed. The height-length proportions of the breed, as well as substance, have always varied widely. In general, the height-length proportions should convey an impression of pleasing balance that is confirmed by smooth coordination of the front and rear strides.

Specific physical characteristics and typical physical traits should be weighed by their effect on functional ability. For example, a Weimaraner with muscles so soft that it "rolls" around the ring exhibits the major fault *improper muscular condition.* A Weimaraner whose rough coat is also a major fault—*faulty coat*—but whose rock-hard muscles suggest that the coat is damaged because of exposure to weather while working in the field should be given preference because it is functionally fit to work with speed and stamina.

Many exhibitors are reluctant to run their Weimaraners in the field, at least until they finish their bench championships, because of the risk of injuries and scars, which they fear judges will penalize too harshly. Judges should differentiate between a typical field injury such as a severed toe tendon and an inborn structural fault such as a splayed foot or shallow pad; Weimaraner fanciers tend to view field injuries as badges of honor to be penalized far more lightly than inborn structural faults.

The major faults *doggy bitches* and *bitchy dogs* are a good example of omitted details, because the standard fails to mention that a Weimaraner's gender should be easily recognized by its overall appearance. In addition to being smaller than a *dog* (male), a *bitch* (female) is typically lighter boned, with less muscle mass than a dog. Thus, a *doggy bitch* is one that has the heavier bone and muscle mass of a dog; a *bitchy dog* is one that has the lighter bone and muscle mass of a bitch.

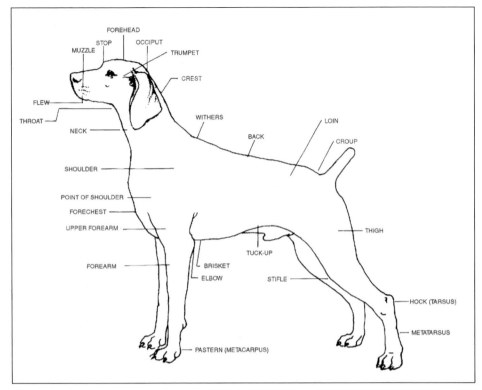

Figure 4-2: *Canine anatomical terms:* parts of the Weimaraner.

Height

Height at the withers: dogs, 25 to 27 inches; bitches, 23 to 25 inches. One inch over or under the specified height of each sex is allowable but should be penalized. Dogs measuring less than 24 inches or more than 28 inches and bitches measuring less than 22 or more than 26 inches shall be disqualified.

When measuring, *height at the withers* means the highest point of the shoulders immediately behind the neck. Anatomically, however, *withers* are defined as the seven vertebrae to which the shoulder muscles are attached.

There has always been a wide range in the height and weight of the Weimaraner. In an effort to encourage standardization within this range, the size disqualification was incorporated into the 1965 revision. The success of the height disqualification in standardizing size has become more apparent over time, as fewer individuals are so close to the extremes that they must be measured.

The ideal height, which allows a 2-inch range, is made even more generous by permitting an additional inch over and under. This has ensured that many outstanding individuals close to either extreme of the desired height suffer little prejudice in the show ring and in breeding. Each Weimaraner that is within the standard should be judged by its overall quality. Where quality is equal, the individual that falls within the desired 2-inch range should be given preference.

Most Weimaraners grow slowly, reaching their mature height sometime between 12 and 24 months. Because early ring experience is so valuable, owners sometimes show 6- to 9-month-old puppies that might be a little below the required height, assuming that judges realize that there is little cause to disqualify a puppy for a fault that will be outgrown in a few weeks or months.

Temperament

The temperament should be friendly, fearless, alert, and obedient. Very Serious Faults. *Dogs exhibiting strong fear, shyness, or extreme nervousness.*

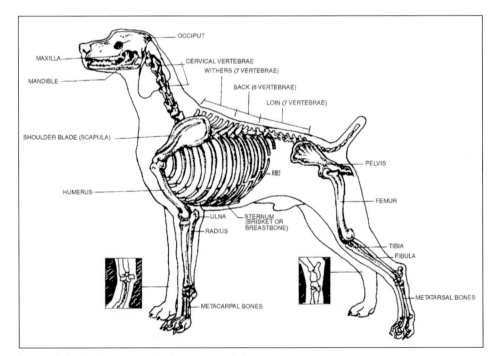

Figure 4-3: *Canine anatomical terms:* the skeleton.

One of the most attractive traits of the Weimaraner is its friendly, outgoing attitude toward people. The typical, desired adult Weimaraner temperament is characterized by the following:

- Boldly self-confident in unfamiliar situations, exhibiting a friendly attitude toward strange people and dogs, and clearly expecting admiration from one and all

- Views training situations as an opportunity to please and enjoys showing off accomplishments

- Gives an alerting bark when strangers arrive, offering a friendly greeting but becoming protective if owner is threatened

When presented in the show ring, the Weimaraner's tail is a gauge of its temperament. A tail carried at a 45-degree angle demonstrates the desired friendly, self-confident temperament.

A young or inexperienced Weimaraner may express uncertainty by resisting examination of the bite or genitalia, which should not be regarded as evidence of shyness. It should be assumed, however, that a Weimaraner entered in open class or as a special has enough experience to permit examination without fear or resentment.

The Germans cultivated the Weimaraner's protective instinct, which is more highly developed than in other pointing breeds. This protectiveness should be exhibited only under appropriate circumstances—protection of the home, the owners, and the owners' property. Even a highly protective dog should never exhibit viciousness.

The standards of 1944, 1953, and 1959 listed viciousness as a very serious fault, but it was deleted in the 1965 revision, leaving the breeder, exhibitor, and judge in limbo. Nevertheless, the current standard clearly states that the correct temperament *should be friendly, fearless, alert, and obedient;* therefore, common sense dictates that any indication of viciousness must be considered atypical and undesirable. Furthermore, AKC dog show rules specifically state that judges shall excuse any dog that threatens to bite them and shall disqualify any dog that attacks a person in the ring.[1]

Like all hunting breeds, Weimaraners work in the company of other dogs; any Weimaraner that exhibits unprovoked aggressiveness toward other dogs of the same or opposite gender or around the show ring should be faulted as one that would not be trustworthy in a hunting situation. The rules for AKC hunting tests permanently disqualify dogs that demonstrate repeated aggressiveness toward other dogs.

Some young Weimaraners (both dogs and bitches) just reaching maturity go through an aggressive phase, but most quickly learn to curb the behavior if the owners apply immediate and consistent correction. Aggression itself is normal, but failure to respond to correction is neither typical nor desirable. In our unofficial survey, the majority of owners considered *unprovoked* aggressiveness toward other dogs so undesirable that they considered it a very serious fault.

Gait

The gait should be effortless and should indicate smooth co-ordination. When seen from the rear, the hind feet should be parallel to the front feet. When viewed from the side, the topline should remain strong and level. Major Fault. *Poor gait.*

No two Weimaraner fanciers, it seems, can agree on how the description of gait should be interpreted. Our initial attempts to write an interpretation for this chapter provoked strong disagreement. After repeated drafts and requests for feedback, most WCA members who were questioned agreed that the following description was compatible with their own interpretation of correct Weimaraner gait:

The gait is reaching, elastic, seemingly without effort, and covers the maximum amount of ground with the minimum number of strides. Viewed from the rear, the hind legs move in a straight line from the hip joint to the pad, with no inward or outward deviation of the hocks. Viewed from the front, the forelegs move in a straight line from the shoulder joint to the pad. The front and rear feet track on parallel lines, never deviating to the side in a crabwise fashion. Although the lines converge slightly inward when trotting in order to maintain balance, the feet do not strike or cross over. When viewed from the side, the topline should remain strong and level.

Interpretation of the fault *poor gait* varies greatly. Owners questioned about which movement faults they considered major ones listed the following, which are defined in Chapter 5: crabbing, crossing over (front and rear), in or out at the hocks, interference, out at the elbows, and paddling.

Gait as well as its relationship to structure is discussed further in Chapter 5.

Physical Features

Head and Neck

Moderately long and aristocratic, with moderate stop and slight median line extending back over the forehead. Rather prominent occipital bone and trumpets well set back, beginning at the back of the eye sockets. Measurement from tip of the nose to stop equals that from stop to occipital bone. The flews should be straight, delicate at the nostrils. Skin drawn tightly. Neck clean-cut and moderately long. Expression kind, keen, and intelligent. Major Faults. *Snipy muzzle. Neck too short, thick, or throaty.*

Figure 4-4: *Typical feminine heads.*

There is great variety in Weimaraner head types (more obvious than any other trait), and all that meet the loose, general description of the standard should be regarded as typical. The best criterion for assessing head type is whether it is appropriate for the individual's gender and overall structural type. The head should be neither too large nor too small in proportion to the rest of the body and should contribute to the overall appearance of beauty and balance.

The prominent occipital bone is more noticeable in puppies. It tends to recede with bony maturation of the skull and, today, is rarely prominent in adults.

The *trumpet* is defined as the slight depression or hollow on either side of the skull just behind the orbit or eye socket; this region is comparable to the human temple.

Although the standard specifies that the neck should be moderately long, it does not define what this means. There is no doubt that a short, thick, heavily muscled neck seriously

Figure 4-5: *A snipy muzzle,* the only head fault specified in the standard, is usually accompanied by a lack of stop. In addition, the planes of the muzzle and skull are not parallel, which contributes to the lack of pleasing balance.

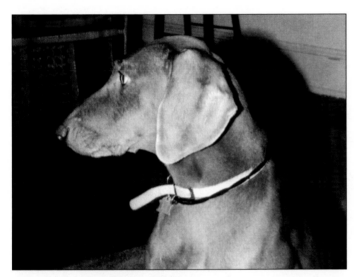

Figure 4-6: *A non-typical head* with a lack of stop plus a slight Roman nose.

Figure 4-7: *The prominent occipital bone in puppies* is rarely pronounced in adults.

detracts from the appearance. Rare Weimaraners have goose-like necks that simply do not fit the dog's other proportions. Thus, a correct neck is clean, well arched, and enhances a Weimaraner's elegance, and the line of the neck blends smoothly into the line of the shoulders, creating an eye-pleasing, balanced profile.

Be aware, however, that a Weimaraner's neck length can be deceptive. The neck may disappear, sinking between the shoulders when the Weimaraner is relaxed, but exhibit startling length when gaiting or when watching something of interest.

Figure 4-8: *An attractive neck* enhances the overall appearance of elegance.

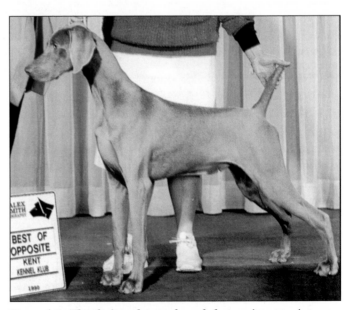

Figure 4-9: *This dog's neck is moderately long* under normal circumstances. When the photographer tossed a toy just before snapping this photograph, the dog's neck suddenly "grew" inches.

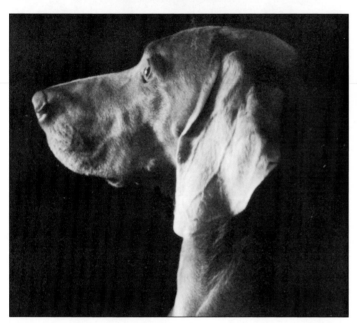

Figure 4-10: *Typical masculine heads.*

Ears

Long and lobular, slightly folded and set high. The ear when drawn snugly alongside the jaw should end approximately 2 inches from the point of the nose. Major Fault. Short ears.

There is considerable variation in ear length, placement, and texture, but most Weimaraners' ears exhibit the breed's typical shape and folds.

The description of ear length implies that the ear should end approximately 2 inches from the point of the nose. In fact, 2 inches is the *minimum* length. Short ears are any ears that end more than 2 inches from the point of the nose when drawn snugly alongside the jaw.

By 6 months, all Weimaraner ears are full grown; the skull continues to grow for at least another year, and continued minor maturation after the age of 2 is not unusual. In other words, puppies grow into their ears, which become progressively shorter in proportion to the skull.

The leather of the longer type of ear is usually softer and thinner than that of the shorter ear. In addition to the typical range in texture, the leather tends to grow thicker and tougher with age and exposure to weather and hunting conditions.

Ear injuries are common in working Weimaraners, and scars or old tears in the ears should not be penalized.

Figure 4-11: ***The Weimaraner's expressive ears*** show surprising variation in placement, depending on the emotions. **(a)** High when alert or curious. **(b)** Low when relaxed. Note her round eyes.

Figure 4-12: ***The tightly curled ears*** express disgust or guilt. Note the almond-shaped eyes.

Figure 4-13: ***The so-called broken or folded ears*** are a typical breed trait and are unrelated to mood expression.

Figure 4-14: *A third eyelid* shows in the inner corners of the eye. This is also a common and acceptable shade of eye color in this adult Weimaraner.

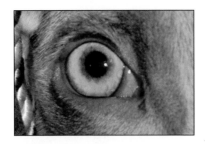

Eyes

In shades of light amber, gray, or blue-gray, set well enough apart to indicate good disposition and intelligence. When dilated under excitement the eyes may appear almost black. Very Serious Fault. Eyes other than gray, blue-gray, or light amber.

Sadly, the appealing, intense blue eye color of the puppy usually begins to fade by 10–12 weeks. After the blue fades, orange-yellow spikes appear and slowly widen. The yellow pigmentation spreads and sometimes deepens to dark amber. The changes are gradual, and color stabilizes when the Weimaraner is about a year old, although there is wide variation. The complete color change does not occur in all individuals: some retain the bluish color, some remain very light, some progress to dark amber, and some have eyes of different colors (Figures 4-15 and 4-16).

Depth of eye color is unrelated to coat color. A light silver Weimaraner may have dark amber eyes, and vice versa. Both are typical.

There is great diversity in the shape of the eye. They range from round (Bulldog) to almond (Doberman), although most fall between these extremes. The question is often raised about the correct shape of the eyes. This point has never been included in any American standard, but the German standard states, "Round, but sometimes slightly almond shaped."

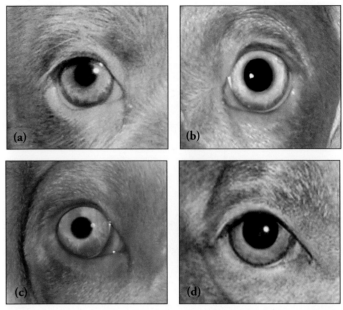

Figure 4-15: *Eye color:* puppies. **(a)** All begin with a brilliant sapphire blue. **(b)** The inner iris begins to lighten by about 10 weeks. **(c)** Orange-yellow pigment spikes appear as the blue continues to fade. **(d)** The spikes merge to form a uniform color that is typical in the adult Weimaraner.

All Weimaraners have a third eyelid, or nictitating membrane, on the inside corner of the eye that is normally retracted and visible only when needed for protection. Weimaraners that hunt a great deal or are exposed to irritating substances for an extended period of time develop thicker, more visible third eyelids. Although these provide important eye protection, more than a few owners have reported that veterinarians have insisted on their removal; some innocent owners have permitted this mutilating surgery.

Figure 4-14: *Eye Spy....* These pictures were all taken on the same sunny day at a club water event where all the dogs were between 3 and 12 months. The shape, color, and pigment will vary even among puppies from the same litter. Pupil size may vary depending not only on the amount of sunlight, but also on the level of the dog's excitement. Try to spy the single 3-month-old puppy. Photographs by Gene LaFollette.

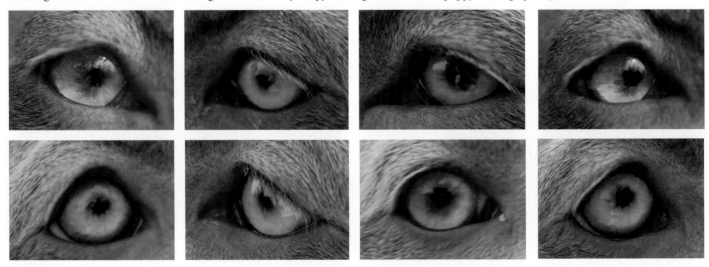

Teeth

Well set, strong, and even; well-developed and proportionate to jaw with correct scissors bite, the upper teeth protruding slightly over the lower teeth but not more than 1/16 of an inch. Complete dentition is greatly to be desired. Major Faults. *Badly affected teeth. More than four teeth missing. Badly overshot, or undershot bite.*

The *scissors bite,* in which part of the inner surface of the upper incisors meet and engage part of the outer surface of the lower incisors, is typical of most purebred dogs. *Wry mouth* (laterally displaced jaw) and misaligned incisors (much like a child who needs braces) occur occasionally. Because of the standard's phrasing, a wry mouth and misaligned incisors are penalized only as type faults—that is, not typical.

Missing molars are considered a hereditary trait; fortunately, Weimaraners today very rarely have more than four missing. Missing canines and incisors are usually caused by trauma. If the dog is being shown, the stump of the damaged tooth (especially a canine) should be saved, if possible, as evidence that it is not a congenital defect.

Judges are not the only ones who find the vague description of the major fault *badly affected teeth* puzzling. The consensus of breeders questioned is that it refers to the following: (a) the discoloration characteristic of dead teeth; (b) the discoloration and pitting associated with distemper and other febrile diseases—the so-called distemper teeth; or (c) the discoloration or banding caused by some drugs, such as tetracycline. There is considerable disagreement over whether the phrase should apply to teeth that are badly stained from plaque, which merely reflects careless grooming.

Nose

Gray. Minor Fault. *Pink nose.*

The shade of the nose is usually but not always similar to the overall color of the dog—dark, medium, or light. Some strains have deeper pigmentation of the nose, which is associated with darker pigmentation around the eyes. Although the very light gray Weimaraner typically has a lightly pigmented nose, it should never be bright pink.

Lips and Gums

Pinkish flesh shades. Very Serious Fault. *Black mottled mouth.*

Today, the very serious fault *black mottled mouth* is one of the most puzzling points of the American standard, particularly because the standard of no other country mentions it. After failing to initiate a move to disqualify blue Weimaraners, opponents settled for adding several changes that would handicap blues, including the very serious fault of the black mottled mouth, which is typical of the blue color (Table 2-2). An extensive survey by one

Figure 4-17: *Dentition and bite.* Complete dentition: each side of upper jaw—3 incisors, 1 canine, 3 premolars, 1 carnassial (4th premolar), and 2 molars: each side of lower jaw—3 incisors, 1 canine, 3 premolars, 1 carnassial, and 3 molars.

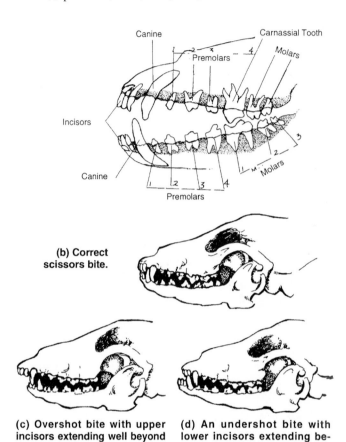

(b) Correct scissors bite.

(c) Overshot bite with upper incisors extending well beyond the lower ones.

(d) An undershot bite with lower incisors extending beyond upper ones.

(e) A level or pincer bite. Although not specified faulty in the standard, it is not a correct scissors bite. Many breeders regard it as a form of undershot, with a higher than average probability of undershot bites in offspring.

(f) Wry mouth (laterally displaced jaw) and misaligned incisors (much like a child who needs braces) occur occasionally. Because of the standard's phrasing, a wry mouth is penalized only as type faults—that is, not typical.

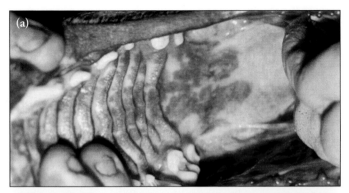

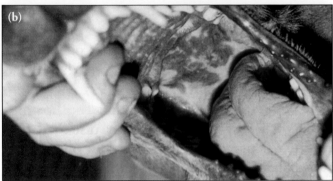

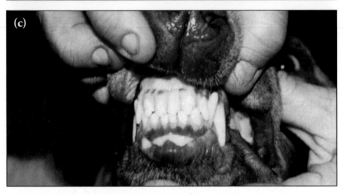

Figure 4-18: *Normal mottling of the mouth.* (a) Pigmentation of the palate and of the upper gum and lip. (b) The same mouth about a year later, showing increased depth and slight extension of pigmentation. (c) The dark-gray Weimaraner shows corresponding dark-gray pigment along the gum line.

author failed to reveal a single silver-gray Weimaraner with black mottling, and our conclusion is that the fault is an anachronism that should have been deleted when blues were disqualified in 1971.

Although the phrasing implies that the lips and gums should be solidly pink, the survey disclosed that approximately 90% of the breed develops *gray mottling* of a shade similar to the coat and skin on the palate, gums, and inside the flews as well as some on the eyelids as the dogs age. Thus, gray mottling is typical and appears to be related to the aging process.

Body

The back should be moderate in length, set in a straight line, strong, and should slope slightly from the withers. The chest should be well developed and deep with shoulders well laid back. Ribs well sprung and long. Abdomen firmly held; moderately tucked up flank. The brisket should extend to the elbow. Major Faults. Back too long or too short. Faulty backs, either roached or sway.

The topline is subdivided into withers (seven vertebrae), the back (the next six), the loin (the next seven), and the croup (from the last vertebrae of the loin to the first of the tail) (Figure 4-3). *Back length,* therefore, refers to the six back vertebrae, which should be moderately long.

The 13 vertebrae of the withers and the back form the thoracic spine. The long spinous processes of the first four are almost straight. From the 5th to the 9th vertebrae, the spinous processes successively decrease in length and begin to slant. The spinous processes of the last three are shorter, thicker, and relatively straight. The change in length and slant between the 9th and 10th vertebrae is responsible for the dip behind the withers. This normal dip is more pronounced with excessive development of the shoulder muscles and is common in dogs used extensively in the field.

The seven loin vertebrae function as a bridge between the front and rear assemblies. An *arched loin* is the slight arching of the seven vertebrae of the loin; a *roached back* is the arching of the loin and all or part of the back.

Immature Weimaraners often appear to have a roached back for several reasons: (a) anxiety over a new experience; (b) resisting the handler's attempts to stack it; and (c) being in the stage of growth in which the rear legs are markedly longer than the front. To identify a true skeletal roach, gait the dog; a Weimaraner that does not have a skeletal fault usually moves with a level topline. (A transient roached back at any age often indicates a health problem such as full anal glands or abdominal pain.)

When the Weimaraner stands in a balanced position with the hocks perpendicular to the ground, the topline should show a slight slope from the withers to the croup. A mature Weimaraner may be *high in the rear* (the croup higher than the withers) for several reasons: (a) the front legs may be too short in relation to the head, neck, and chest; (b) the stifles may be too straight; or (c) the rear legs may be incorrectly positioned (too far under the body).

At maturity, the brisket should be level with the elbows. Chest depth and rib spring are the last to mature, sometimes not until the Weimaraner is 2 or 3 years old.

Shoulder angulation (layback) is closely related to rear angulation and movement and is discussed in Chapter 5, *Movement and Structure.*

Figure 4-19: *Toplines.* **(a)** Straight topline. **(b)** Dip behind the withers. **(c)** Roached back. **(d)** Swayback.

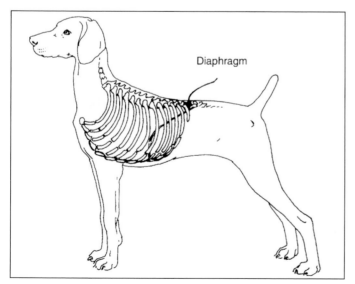

Figure 4-20: *The brisket line* should be parallel to the ground, beginning its upward sweep at the 8th or 9th rib so that the horizontal sternum allows ample space for the heart and lungs. The tuck up (the curve of the abdominal line) should begin at the point of the sternum.

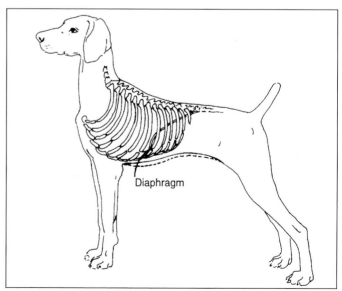

Figure 4-21: *With a herring gut,* the brisket is not parallel to the ground, beginning its upward sweep not far behind the elbows. The reduced area for the heart and lungs is a handicap in the sporting dog.

Figure 4-22: *Comparison of frontal structure and faults.* **(a)** Correct front. **(b)** Narrow front lacking good brisket depth. **(c)** East-west front with inward rotation of elbows and outward rotation of feet. **(d)** Front too wide with toeing in (pigeon toed). **(e)** Fiddle front (French front) with forelegs out at the elbows.

Forelegs

Straight and strong, with the measurement from the elbow to the ground approximately equaling the distance from the elbow to the top of the withers. Major faults. *Elbows in or out. Feet east and west.*

Although a Weimaraner that is *out* at the elbows may be stacked to disguise this fault, rocking the dog from side to side at the shoulders causes the front leg to pivot to its natural stance. It is also evident in the freestanding position.

East-west describes a common front problem in which the front feet point outward. It is usually, but not always, associated with a narrow rib cage or lack of forechest.

Young Weimaraners often have an east-west front because of immature chest development. To a certain degree, an east-west front is desirable in an immature Weimaraner because the chest normally deepens and widens with maturity. Therefore, a slightly east-west immature front is less likely to be too wide, out at the elbows, or pigeon toed at maturity.

Hindquarters

Well-angulated stifles and straight hocks. Musculation well developed. Major Fault. *Cow hocks.*

A well-angulated rear provides the long, ground-covering stride desired in the hunting dog (see Chapter 5, *Movement and Structure,* for the relationship between angulation and movement). The muscles of the hindquarters should be firm, both standing and moving, indicating great driving power.

Straight stifles are structurally stronger than those with greater angulation, which require greater muscle mass and tone for comparable strength. Thus, *cow hocks* (hocks that point inward) are more common in dogs with greater angulation. Puppies with the degree of angulation needed for a ground-covering stride often go through a cow-hocked stage as muscle development lags behind bone growth; maturity alone often corrects the problem.

Because cow hocks are so closely related to musculation, the inward turning characteristically affects both legs. When only one leg turns inward, a traumatic injury should be suspected.

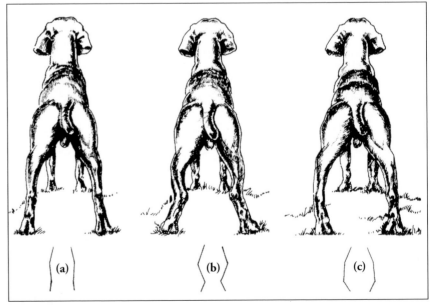

Figure 4-23: *Comparison of rear* structure and faults. **(a)** Correct rear. **(b)** Cow hocks. **(c)** Barrel or spread hocks.

Feet

Firm and compact, webbed, toes well arched, pads closed and thick, nails short and gray or amber in color. Major Fault. *Poor feet.*

The brevity of this section reflects the development of dog standards by fanciers familiar with field and paddock, for the horseman's adage "no feet, no horse" is just as true of dogs. Leon Whitney, author and sportsman, regarded splayed feet as fatal to any hunting dog: "Those of us who have tried to use such dogs as hunters soon learn that the feet become cut and sore, rendering the dogs useless except as pets."[2] Flat feet cannot grip the ground when it is slippery or when the dog must climb. *Paper feet* are characterized by thin pads and appear flat because the heel pad does not elevate the third digital bone. Their shallow pads are easily bruised and injured or *slip* (peel off) entirely on rocky terrain. Therefore, a modification of the horseman's adage to "no feet, no field dog" is appropriate.

The *cat foot* is characterized by short third digital bones, whereas the *hare foot* is characterized by long third digital bones (the longer bones of the hare foot provide leverage and, thus, greater speed). Most Weimaraner feet fall somewhat between a hare and a cat foot. However, the third digital bones of the front feet are typically shorter than those of the rear feet.

When judging, each foot should be picked up to check the thickness of the pad and be allowed to drop to its natural position; note the straightness of the pastern and compactness of the foot.

Working Weimaraners are at risk for injuries to the feet—even perfect feet. The most common injuries are broken toes and severed tendons, which cause the toe to appear completely flattened. Traumatic damage is easily identified because it rarely affects more than one toe or several toes on one foot.

Correct pasterns have a slight bend for balance, spring, and shock absorption. Their vertical line of support is from the front of the foreleg through the metacarpals to the rear of the pad.

Nails vary in color. Dark-gray (almost black) nails occur in the breed, usually with the very dark-gray (mouse-gray)

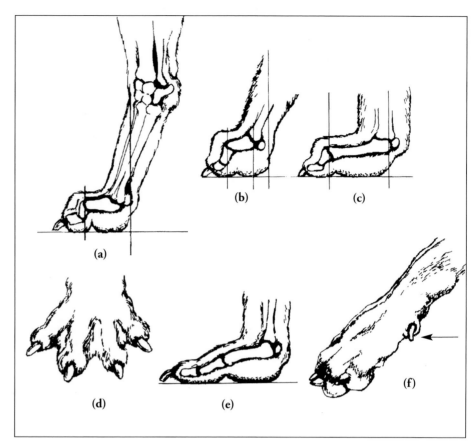

Figure 4-24: *Feet and pasterns.* (a) Correct pastern with slight bend. (b) Cat foot. (c) Hare foot. (d) Splayed foot, spread to show the typical webbing. (e) Paper foot. (f) Dewclaw.

coat color. Lightly pigmented nails rapidly grow to remarkable lengths unless they are trimmed regularly. It is no wonder that some breeders prize the mouse-gray color because the highly pigmented nails grow at a slower rate, wear down more evenly, require less trimming and care, and rarely break.

Dewclaws

Should be removed.

Dewclaws are vestigial toes located on the inner aspect of the pasterns and hocks; the length and placement are hereditary. Although rear dewclaws occur in some breeds, they do not in Weimaraners. Because the dewclaw's nail does not touch the ground to wear down, it grows to great length, often in a complete circle. In addition, dewclaws are so vulnerable to injury under hunting conditions that their removal is required by most American sport-breed standards. However, dewclaws are not routinely removed in England and Germany, and they are often present on imports from these countries. Note that the standard does not penalize unremoved dewclaws.

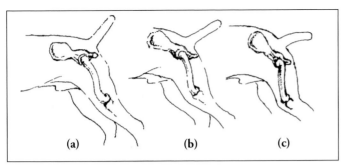

Figure 4-25: *Croup and tail set.* (a) 1 o'clock. (b) 2 o'clock. (c) 3 o'clock.

Figure 4-26: *The banana tail is not a genetic trait.* The downward curving banana tail is most commonly caused by leftover bone chips or a tail tip that is sutured too tightly after docking. This should not be confused with a tail that is clamped against the body from croup to tip which may indicate poor temperament or a dog that is frightened or hurt.

Figure 4-28: *This American-bred Weimaraner* was whelped in Italy, where tail docking is prohibited. The carriage of his intact tail exaggerates the combination of the high placement of his tail on a flat croup, limiting his show-ring potential.

Figure 4-27: *Overweight Weimaraners* have a pad of fat at the end of the croup, usually with a dimple, causing the tail to appear low set.

Tail

Docked. At maturity it should measure approximately 6 inches with a tendency to be light rather than heavy and should be carried in a manner expressing confidence and sound temperament. A non-docked tail shall be penalized. Minor Fault. *Tail too short or too long.* Major Fault. *Low-set tail.* Very Serious Fault. *Non-docked tail.*

Faults of tail docking are entirely human made; thus, incorrect length is only a minor fault. Nothing can be done, of course, if the tail is too short, but exhibitors often redock a tail that is too long. Redocking is risky and may lead to the following complications: (a) the normal, confident tail carriage may never be recovered; (b) the dog may become hypersensitive about the tail being touched; (c) nerve damage can cause a total lack of feeling in the tail; and (d) the procedure may leave a tail that curls either upward or downward ("banana tail"). Because of the risks, some owners choose not to redock a tail that is too long, especially if it is attractively shaped and expresses the Weimaraner's merry temperament.

Tail set refers to skeletal placement and is determined by the angle of the croup: a low tail set indicates a steeply angled croup; a high tail set indicates a flat-angled croup. *Tail carriage* refers to the muscular control and reflects the dog's attitude.

Hairless spots on the upper surface of the tail may be caused by the following: (a) habitually tucking the tail under when sitting; (b) constant licking or biting of a spot that is irritated by bone fragments; and (c) constant rubbing of the tail against the back of the crate or other objects.

Coat and Color

Short, smooth and sleek, solid color, in shades of mouse-gray to silver-gray, usually blending to lighter shades on the head and ears. A small white marking on the chest is permitted, but should be penalized on any other portion of the body. White spots resulting from injury should not be penalized. A distinctly long coat is a disqualification. A distinctly blue or black coat is a disqualification. Major Faults. *Faulty coat.* Very Serious Faults. *White, other than a spot on the chest.*

Few aspects of the standard are more controversial or present greater difficulties of interpretation than coat and color. This section discusses coat length, color, and markings. The genetics of coat length and color are discussed in Chapter 6, *Color, Markings, and Coat.*

Length

Analysis of the Weimaraner's shorthaired coat reveals surprising differences in specific qualities:

- The texture ranges from satin smoothness to harsh coarseness

- The hair is usually thicker and somewhat longer over the shoulders and sometimes toward the end of the tail

- The overall length varies (longest on the shoulders and back, shortest on head and feet)

- The soft, lighter-colored hairs of the abdominal area range from a sparse covering to areas with no hair at all

- Some have a sparse, soft undercoat; most have no undercoat

- Exposure to cold weather may increase the hair length and density; prolonged exposure produces an area of particularly dense hair of slightly different color and texture over the kidneys

All variations must be considered characteristic of the breed.

A longhaired coat is a disqualification. The recessive longhaired trait has apparently always existed in Weimaraners, and the heredity is discussed in Chapter 6.

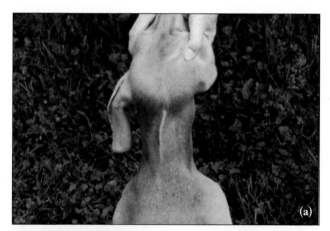

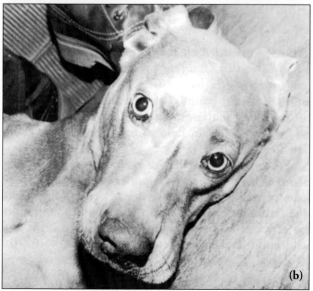

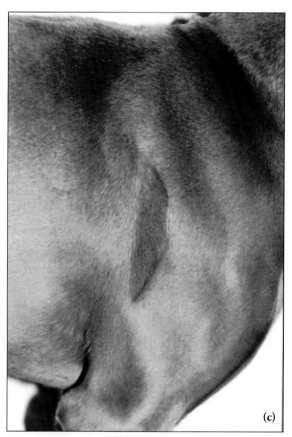

Figure 4-29: *Typical locations of cowlicks.* (**a**) Back of neck. (**b**) Face. (**c**) Shoulder.

Color

Weimaraner colors range from very light to very dark gray. The Germans identify three shades: *deer-gray* (very light gray), *silver-gray* (medium gray), and *mouse-gray* (very dark gray). Attempts to describe differences between the typical color and the disqualified blue color immediately encountered semantic difficulties; the difference is easier to visualize with an understanding of the genetic basis, which is discussed and illustrated in Chapter 6.

The gray color is never of uniform shade. The ears are noticeably lighter than the overall body color. The back half of the skull is often lighter (the *Weimaraner cap*); the difference may be more pronounced if the Weimaraner has been out in the sun, and the cap usually lightens with age. A dark *eel stripe* down the back is mentioned in many standards. In some Weimaraners, the stripe is noticeable at all times; in others, it is apparent only when shedding. This is typical of the breed and should not be regarded as faulty.

Coat color is easily affected by exposure to sun, causing a rather typical sunburned yellowish tone. The coat also becomes lighter or yellowish just before shedding, especially along the chest and legs, where the coat is less dense.

The coat usually sheds twice a year. Shedding begins at the topline, and the contrast between the darker new coat and the fading old coat produces a noticeable dark-gray stripe. Occasionally, Weimaraners shed in patches; the new coat appears in dark-gray patches interspersed with the lighter, duller old coat that is not quite ready to shed, often producing a startling buckshot effect.

Some Weimaraner strains develop frosting on the muzzle and over the eyes as early as 2 years. With age, many Weimaraners develop a salt-and-pepper coat with white hairs scattered throughout. White hairs may begin to appear near the pads, eventually extending upward to cover the toes.

Weimaraners that carry the *agouti* (banded pigment) gene typically have a scattering of agouti hairs with little if any dark pigment at the tips, which makes them look white. The number of these white hairs changes each time the coat sheds, increasing or decreasing randomly. Some adolescents with the agouti color factor go through a stage in which they have an unusual number of white hairs—rather like they have been sprinkled with powdered sugar. Typically, when the coat sheds, the new coat is normal.

The standard states that white spots resulting from injury should not be penalized. Injured hair follicles produce white hairs that may or may not return to gray when the coat is shed. If a cut requires sutures, follicular damage may be minimized by careful shaving and microscopic sutures. White hairs are commonly seen on the face as a result of thorn and briar scratches. The causes of white hairs include vaccine injections, abscesses, cat bites, and sores from casts. Traumatic removal of adhesive tape from unshaven skin also causes follicular damage and may cover an extensive area.

Tail docking always causes follicular trauma, which leads to some white hairs. If a tourniquet is used to control bleeding, the portion beyond the tourniquet usually becomes heavily sprinkled with white hairs. The white hairs upset buyers who think their puppy has developed a very serious fault; fortunately, the white often disappears later. White hairs on the tail are to be regarded as the result of injury and should not be penalized.

In conclusion, although the standard describes the coat as solid in color, the eel stripe, lighter areas on the head and ears, grizzling from age, and scattered white agouti hairs are breed traits. In addition, the coat is easily discolored and injured under working conditions.

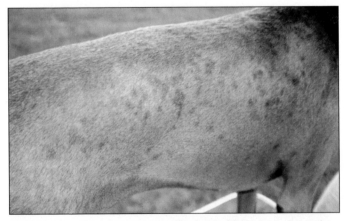

Figure 4-30: *Most Weimaraners begin shedding* along the topline, exhibiting a widening eel strip of darker new hair. Occasionally, the coat is shed in patches, producing a startling "buckshot" effect. This Weimaraner exhibits both shedding patterns at once.

Figure 4-31: *The owners of this bitch* decided she was not breeding quality because of so many white hairs, and they spayed the otherwise show-quality puppy. The white hairs disappeared the next time she shed.

Figure 4-32: *A 3-year-old Weimaraner* with grizzling of the muzzle.

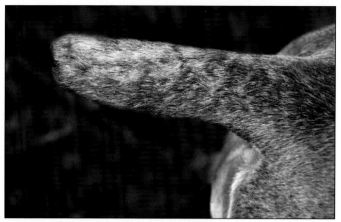

Figure 4-33: *Dogs may have a surprising amount of white suddenly appear on the tail as they mature.* New owners may frantically call the breeder concerned their puppy may no longer be show quality. **(a)** In puppies, this appears spontaneously as a band in the middle of the tail and is the result of trauma from the docking procedure. It normally disappears with the next shedding. **(b)** However, when this occurs in adults, it is often the result of continuing damage to the hair on the top of the tail; the silver tip of each hair gets broken off, for example by the tail banging against the inside of the crate, consistently tucking the wagging tail underneath when sitting, or excessive self-grooming, which then exposes the second white color band on the hair (refer to *Color, Markings, and Coat*). This issue can be corrected by identifying the behavior that is causing the damage. A knowledgeable conformation judge should not penalize this "fault," as white caused by an injury is not penalized in the American standard.

Markings

Bicolored Tan

It is common knowledge that the breed carries recessive genes that produce *bicolored tan markings,* also referred to as *dobe markings* or the *mark of the hound,* which are light beige or orange hairs above each eye and on the muzzle, throat, forechest, feet, and inner aspect of the legs and under the tail in the typical Black-and-Tan Hound or Doberman pattern (Figure 6-8). This hereditary trait is unrelated to changes caused by sun damage or shedding, and most breeders regard the markings as extremely undesirable.

Tan markings, unfortunately, are not mentioned in the American standard, probably because it would be difficult to give a clear description that would not penalize sunburned coats. Failure to mention bicolored tan markings in the standard means that judges cannot penalize dogs with this recessive trait; however, judges can (and should) fault them as an atypical color, that is, bicolored rather than solid gray.

The tan markings are less distinct on a dobe-marked Weimaraner than on a fawn Doberman. If the area over the Weimaraner's eyes appears tan, the other typical pattern areas should be carefully examined. *All areas are not always marked,* and it is more difficult to detect the markings on the lighter shades of gray. The faint markings may be detectable only in bright sunlight. They are less apparent, for some reason, in the late fall and winter and are intensified during the summer months (Figure 6-8).

White

White markings, other than those caused by injury, are one of the most controversial issues in the breed. They are a trait that can be identified by anyone, whereas the ability to assess desirable qualities of structure and movement requires considerable study and experience. Because many fanciers consider white markings a near-disqualifying fault, a rather extensive discussion is warranted here.

Despite the prevalent opinion that white spots on the chest are increasing in frequency, historical evidence discloses a somewhat different trend. According to the first German standard in 1894 (Appendix A), white markings on the chest and toes were common, although it was hoped that selective breeding would eliminate them. The 1935 German standard (Appendix A) states, "White markings in small measure, mostly on the chest, are neither ugly nor faulty since also characteristic." White markings, it seems, have always been a breed trait.

A review of contemporary standards from several countries disclosed that all allow a *small* white mark on the chest but none define it. This is so consistent that it suggests a deliberate policy to avoid definition. It also suggests a worldwide belief that the Weimaraner is first and foremost a hunting breed and that the presence or absence of white on the chest, pasterns, and body has no effect on the breed's performance ability.

So many American judges and exhibitors requested a definition of a small white spot that the WCA Board of Directors wrote the following definition at their December 1985 meeting: "One white marking of not greater than four square inches, confined to the fore chest of the dog, is allowable but not desirable."[3]

The very serious fault of white on any part of the body except the chest refers primarily to white spots on the throat, neck, and abdominal areas, which are genetic extensions of white spots on the chest.

It is often pointed out that many Weimaraners have white on the back of the pasterns and that this should be penalized. In practice, this presents two problems. First, the hairs on the back of the pastern are typically less dense and of a lighter shade than overall body color, similar to the lighter shades of the ears with which the color of the pasterns is genetically linked. Because the hairs on the back of the pasterns are often mixed with beige, yellowish, or white hairs, it is almost impossible to draw a clear distinction between light shading and a white marking. Second, the trait is so common that it is almost typical of the breed.

White pastern markings are not mentioned in any of the standards, either old or new, and only one historical reference

Figure 4-36: *Judges should note* that the standard does not penalize white marks resulting from injuries. The white markings on this show champion's neck are the result of scar tissue from an abscess. White marks or scarring from injuries is not uncommon on field dogs and is most often found on the extremities and sides.

to the trait was found: Brandt reported that in 1899, Pitschke commented that white on the pasterns was so common that he would even consider it a breed trait.

From 1981 to 1990, one author surveyed the incidence of Weimaraners with white or light-colored pasterns. Between attending shows in many parts of the country and information gathered by friends, the sample represents most bloodlines and geographical areas. Of the 562 Weimaraners observed from ringside and on the bench, the pasterns of 394 appeared obviously light colored. In other words, the trait was seen in 70% of American Weimaraners observed, which tends to support Pitschke's observation.

No Weimaraner breeder deliberately breeds for more white or selects show and field prospects because they have white markings. Rather, Weimaraners that happen to have white markings are selected for competition and retained for breeding because of other undeniably outstanding qualities.

In a 1984 WCA survey about white markings, the overwhelming feeling expressed was that *all other things being equal,* the Weimaraner without white on the chest should be preferred, but until they are equal, no Weimaraner with inferior conformation or movement should be preferred for the sole virtue of having no white.

Figure 4-35: *A white spot* on the throat is a very serious fault.

All-Breed Disqualifications

To avoid unnecessary repetition, the all-breed disqualifications are not included in any AKC breed standard. Because of the omission, there is a tendency to forget they are an integral part of *every* AKC standard. The following disqualifications are applicable to Weimaraners:

A dog which is blind, deaf, castrated, spayed, or which has changed in appearance by artificial means except as specified in the standard for its breed, or a male which does not have two normal testicles normally located in the scrotum, may not compete at any show and will be disqualified except that a castrated male may be entered as Stud Dog in the Stud Dog Class, and a spayed bitch may be entered as Brood Bitch in the Brood Bitch Class. A dog will not be considered to have been changed by artificial means because of removal of dewclaws or docking of a tail, if it is of a breed in which such removal or docking is a regularly approved practice which is not contrary to the standard. [Note: Spayed bitches and monorchid or cryptorchid dogs may compete in obedience trials.]....

A dog that in the opinion of the judge attacks any person in the ring shall be disqualified....

A dog that is lame in any class may not compete in that class. It is the judge's responsibility to determine whether a dog is lame.

No dog shall be eligible to compete at any show, and no dog shall receive any award at any show in the event the natural color or shade of natural color or the natural markings of the dog have been altered or changed by the use of any substance whether such substances may have been used for cleaning purposes or for any other reason. Such cleaning substances are to be removed before the dog enters the ring.[4]

Conclusions

Dog fanciers often refer to *The Breed Standard* in tones of awe and reverence usually reserved for Scriptures. It is more appropriate to regard standards as civil statutes, subject to amendment by majority vote. The present Weimaraner standard has been in effect since 1971, a longevity record for the breed; since the first standard in 1943, revisions followed in 1944, 1953, 1959, 1965, and 1971. Clearly, breed standards are not static; they change to meet the needs and desires of fanciers.

Figure 4-37: *There is no perfect dog.* Photograph courtesy of Nancy McKord.

Figure 5-1: *Britta vom Auhofer Gut,* an Austrian-bred longhaired Weimaraner, is the foundation bitch of Dr. Hans Schmidt's Zum Laubwald Kennel in Ostfriesland, Germany. Photograph by Hans Schmidt.

CHAPTER 5

COLOR, MARKINGS, AND COAT

by Jackie Isabell

Color is the most easily identifiable and predictable of all hereditary traits, and it has been the key to the discovery of many genetic principles. The purpose of this chapter is twofold: (a) define some basic terms used here and in later chapters; and (b) describe the heredity of Weimaraner color, markings, and coat.

Basic Terms

In any discussion of genetics, an understanding of basic terms is essential. Although the terms are defined in the glossary contained in this chapter for easy reference, some need clarification.

A *gene* is most simply defined as the basic unit of heredity. Genes are often described as beads on a string, with the string being the *chromosome,* a rod-shaped, microscopic cellular body composed of genes. Chromosomes are paired, and the number of pairs varies in different species. Humans have 46 chromosomes arranged in 23 pairs; dogs and many other canine species have 78 chromosomes in 39 pairs.

In mammals, the pair of chromosomes that determines gender is distinctive. In females, the largest pair of chromosomes appears X shaped, and these chromosomes are, logically, called the X chromosomes. In males, one of the paired chromosomes is smaller and contains fewer genes; it is called the Y chromosome. All other chromosomes are called *autosomes;* an *autosomal trait* is one that is determined by a gene located on any chromosome other than the X or Y chromosomes.

Every observable and measurable trait of every individual is his or her *phenotype.* However, every individual also possesses units of heredity that cannot be directly measured but that may be transmitted to the next generation. The visible and invisible hereditary units are collectively referred to as *genotype.*

If paired genes are identical, they are called *homozygous.* This means that all offspring receive an identical gene for that trait. Therefore, in terms of genetic predictability, homozygosity ensures that all progeny will carry one of those genes. If the genes are beneficial, homozygous pairs are desirable. Some genes produce undesirable traits, in which case homozygosity is detrimental. If paired genes are not identical, they are called *heterozygous,* and the probability of a particular gene's being passed to offspring is also halved.

The simplest genetic relationship is that in which one of a genetic pair is *dominant*—that is, it masks the presence of an unlike gene; the phenotype is governed by the dominant gene. A *recessive* gene, on the other hand, has a visible effect only when paired with a like recessive gene. The phenotype expressed by a dominant gene provides no clue about whether it is homozygous or heterozygous. The phenotype expressed by a recessive gene can only be homozygous.

An *allele* is any one of two or more alternative forms of gene that occupy the same position on a particular chromosome. The term is synonymous with "gene" but is usually used when referring to a specific gene.

Locus (plural, *loci*) refers to the site or location an allele occupies on a chromosome. Every individual with two chromosomes has two slots available at a given locus. For many traits, however, there are more than two alleles that can fill that particular slot. The slot for the black-brown pair of alleles is called Locus *B,* and dogs have only two alleles for that locus. Cats, however, have an additional allele at Locus *B* that produces light brown and is designated *bˡ*. In other words, three different alleles can occupy the two slots, which complicates matters considerably.

Multiple alleles usually vary in dominance, and the sequence of relative dominance is called an *allelomorphic series.* Lists of alleles are always ranked from the most dominant to the least dominant in the series. The relative dominance is not always clear, and many are incompletely dominant. In dogs, four different alleles can occupy Locus *S* in the following allelomorphic series: S—solid-colored coat with no white, sʲ—Irish spotting factor, sᵖ—piebald spotting, sʷ—extreme piebald spotting

Glossary of Basic Genetic Terms

allele. Any one of two or more alternative forms of a gene occupying the same position on a particular chromosome; the term is synonymous with gene, but has a more specific meaning.

allelomorphic (or allelic series). The sequence of relative dominance of alleles (genes) that can occupy a locus. For example, Locus *A* or agouti series is a group of pattern factors that controls the regional distribution of dark (black/brown) pigment and light (tan/yellow) pigment.

autosomal trait. A trait determined by a gene located on any chromosome other than the *XY* sex chromosomes.

autosome. Any chromosome except the *XY* sex chromosomes.

blue. The dilute black color produced by the *B-dd* alleles.

chromosome.[1] A rod-shaped microscopic cellular body composed of genes.[2] Each chromosome contains one DNA molecule consisting of hundreds to thousands of genes.

codominance. A heterozygous single-gene trait that produces an intermediate phenotype because both alleles are biochemically active.

dark pigment. See *phaeomelanin*.

dominant.[1] A gene that, when heterozygous, masks the presence of an unlike gene; the phenotype is determined by the dominant gene.[2] A biochemically active gene.

eumelanin. The pigment that produces all yellow shade (which includes all reds); also called *light pigment*.

gene. The basic unit of heredity.

gene frequency. The population's total number of genes at any given locus.

gene pool. See *gene frequency*.

genotype. An individual's collective units of heredity, which cannot be directly measured but which may be transmitted to the next generation.

heterozygote. A heterozygous individual.

heterozygous. Paired genes that are not identical.

homozygote. An individual that is homozygous.

homozygous. Paired genes that are identical.

incomplete dominance. Heterozygous genes that produce an intermediate phenotype. See *incomplete penetrance*.

incomplete penetrance. Heterozygous genes with variable expression; less than 100% of the genotype show the expected phenotype. See *penetrance*.

isabella. The dilute brown color produced by the *bbdd* alleles; in all animals except dogs, the term lilac is preferred.

light pigment. See *eumelanin*.

locus (plural *loci*). The site or location an allele occupies on a chromosome.

major genes. Genes that produce readily identifiable effects on the phenotype and that can be studied by Mendelian methods.

minor genes. Genes that produce such minor effects they cannot be studied individually. See *polygenes*.

modifiers. A group of polygenes that affect the expression of alleles at only one identifiable locus. See *polygenes*.

penetrance. The proportion of individuals of a specified genotype that shows the expected phenotype; for example, if 100% show the phenotype, the gene has 100% penetrance.

phaeomelanin. The pigment that produces black and brown; also called *dark pigment*.

phenotype. The observable and measurable genetic traits.

polygenes. A group of genes (also called *minor genes*) that control a variable phenotype and are characterized by continuous variability, blending in smooth transition from one extreme to the other; also called multifactorial genes because environmental effects often further complicate identification of their expression. It is conventional to regard polygenes as having plus or minus effects.

psuedo-Irish pattern. The most extreme expression of the minus modifiers of the *S* (solid or self) allele, producing a white pattern similar to the most extreme expression of the *s* (Irish spotting pattern).

recessive.[1] A gene that, when heterozygous, is masked by the unlike gene; the phenotype can be expressed only when homozygous.[2] A biochemically inactive allele.

sex-linked trait. A genetic trait in which the genes are located on one of the sex chromosomes, usually the *X* chromosome.

Weimaraner Color and Markings

Clarence Little, the best-known authority in canine color genetics *(The Inheritance of Coat Color in Dogs)*, identified 10 loci and 27 alleles that determine canine coat color. Co-author Jackie Isabell's work, *Genetics*, is also an excellent resource for further study. Research has clarified and modified various aspects of canine color since Little's work. Additional alleles have been identified, and other color traits still remain somewhat theoretical. The symbols in this chapter are those used by Robinson *(Genetics for Dog Breeders)*, which reflect the most recent understanding of allelic series and their relative dominance.

In describing the genetics of Weimaraner color and markings, it is necessary to mention only six loci—*A, B, C, D, S,* and *T*—discussing the simpler pairs before tackling the more complex series.

All canine colors are produced by modifications of only two pigments. All yellow shades (which includes all reds) are produced by *phaeomelanin*—also called *light pigment*. *Eumelanin*—also called *dark pigment*—produces black and brown.

Locus B Pair (Brown/Black Pigment)

The Locus *B* pair *(B* and *b)*, simple dominant-recessive alleles, determines whether the basic coat color is black *(B)* or brown *(b)*. Dog fanciers sometimes refer to brown as liver or chocolate.

The dominant *B* allele produces black pigment with elongated eumelanin granules. In yellow dogs, the dominant *B* allele can always be identified by black noses and eye rims. The paired *bb* alleles produce brown with ovoid or spherical eumelanin granules. In yellow dogs, the *bb* alleles can always be identified by brown noses and eye rims.

Both alleles occur in American Weimaraners. The breed's typical shades are produced by dilution of the recessive brown *(bb)* pigment; the blue Weimaraner shades are produced by dilution of the dominant black *(BB* or *Bb)* pigment. The difference between the two dilute pigments (black and brown) is one of tonal quality rather than darkness of color. Thus, the very dark mouse-gray (dilute brown) shade, which is uncommon in the United States, is often mistaken for blue (dilute black).

Locus D Pair (Pigment Density)

The Locus *D* pair *(D* and *d)* determines the density of dark pigment. The dominant *D* gives full pigment density. Even with full pigment density *(D),* the color pales slightly and appears bluish near the hair's roots. The paler regions are normally hidden by the intensely colored tips but are exposed if the hairs are partially clipped.

The recessive *dd* alleles dilute pigment density by clumping the granules of pigment. The pigment is deposited irregularly in such a way that some sections of hair have more than normal, whereas others may have less or none. In black dogs, the dilute color is known as *blue,* and in brown dogs, the dilute color is silver-gray. The *dd* alleles have little, if any, effect on light (yellow) pigment, and the only clues to their presence are lighter skin and eyes.

Oddly, most breeds that carry the *b* (brown) allele do not carry the *d* (dilution) allele. The Weimaraner is the only breed characterized by the homozygous *bbdd* alleles, although the combination also occurs in Doberman Pinschers and several other breeds. In dogs, the silvery color produced by the *bbdd* combination is called *isabella.* The combination is quite common in other species, and geneticists refer to it as *lilac*—for example, the lilac point Siamese cat.

Dominant-Recessive Genetic Combinations

B = dominant gene for black pigment
b = recessive gene for brown pigment

1. Genotype of Parents: *BB* × *bb*

	B	B
b	Bb	Bb
b	Bb	Bb

Phenotype (Genotype) of Progeny
100% black (*Bb*)

2. Genotype of Parents: *Bb* × *bb*

	B	b
b	Bb	bb
b	Bb	bb

Phenotype (Genotype) of Progeny
50% black (*Bb*)
50% brown (*bb*)

3. Genotype of Parents: *Bb* × *Bb*

	B	b
B	BB	Bb
b	Bb	bb

Phenotype (Genotype) of Progeny
50% black (*Bb*)
25% black (*BB*)
25% brown (*bb*)

4. Genotype of Parents: *BB* × *Bb*

	B	B
B	BB	BB
b	Bb	Bb

Phenotype (Genotype) of Progeny
50% black (*BB*)
50% black (*Bb*)

Table 5-1: *Canine color alleles, effects, and examples.*

Allele	Effects	Examples	Allele	Effects	Examples
Locus A Series: Dark Pigment Pattern				Dark color of puppy gradually lightens to gray	Skye Terrier
A^s	Uniform dark pigment	Labrador Retriever			Yorkshire Terrier
A^y	Restricts expression of dark pigment, producing sable or tan	Basenji Irish Terrier	g	Uniform color throughout life	Most other breeds
			Locus M Pair: Merle		
A	Banded pigment in hair	Norwegian Elkhound	M	Merle or dappled	Merle Collie
a^{sa}	Saddle pattern	Airedale Terrier	m	Uniform pigment	Most other breeds
a^t	Bicolor pattern	Doberman Pinscher	**Locus S Series: White Pattern**		
a	Recessive black	German Shepherd	S	Solid-colored coat	Weimaraner
Locus B Pair: Black/Brown Pigment				Plus-and-minus modifiers cause no white or small white spots on chest and toes	Scottish Terrier
B	Black	Labrador Retriever			Irish Setter
b	Brown	Sussex Spaniel			Irish Setter
Locus C Series: Pigment Depth					Poodle
C	Full pigment depth	Black, liver, yellow	s^i	Irish-spotting pattern	Basenji
c^{ch}	Reduced pigment (chinchilla)	Schnauzer		White on neck, chest, feet, and abdomen	Boston Terrier
c^b	Blue-eyed grayish white	Pekingese	s^p	Piebald spotting	Brittany
c	Albino	Pekingese (rare)	s^w	Extreme piebald spotting	Bull Terrier
Locus D Pair: Pigment Density				Occasional pigmentation of eye, ear, or base of tail in an otherwise all-white coat	Sealyham Terrier
D	Intense pigment density	Newfoundland			Samoyed
d	Dilute pigment density	Weimaraner			
Locus E Series: Extension of Pigment			**Locus T Pair: Ticking**		
E^{br}	Brindle	Brindle Great Dane	T	Ticked coat	English Setter
E	Full-body dark pigment	Sussex Spaniel (liver)			German Shorthaired Pointer
e	Red-yellow pigment	Irish Setter	t	No ticking	Most other breeds
Locus G Pair: Graying with Age					
G	Incomplete dominance	Kerry Blue Terrier			

Figure 5-2: *Although exact color reproduction is impossible,* the different tonal quality imparted by the underlying brown and black pigment is easy to see between the colors of Weimaraners. These three Weimaraners demonstrate the spectrum of coloration from gray, silver-gray, and blue. Although the darkest shade of gray, called mouse-gray by the German Weimaraner Club, may sometimes include dark toenails, the blue variation will exhibit black toenails and usually black mottling inside the mouth as well. Only shades of gray are recognized by Weimaraner standards throughout the world; only the Canadian and American standards mention the blue (as a disqualification) since colors other than the accepted grey shades are uncommon elsewhere. Photographs courtesy of Karis Johnston Photography.

Locus T Pair (Ticking)

The dominant *T* allele produces small pigmented spots or flecks of color in white coat areas. The areas are white at birth, with ticking appearing a little later.

Most breeds are homozygous for the recessive *t* allele, and one would assume that Weimaraners are among this majority. Evidence that the breed carries the dominant *T* allele is shown by Weimaraners with chest markings that are solid white at birth but that develop ticking at a few weeks; some white markings become so heavily ticked that the white almost disappears (Figure 29-4).

Locus C Series (Pigment Depth)

The *C* (chinchilla or albino) series controls the size and number of pigment particles, and each allele in this series produces progressively less pigment. Although the series has been extensively studied in rodents and other mammals, information on dogs is based on observations of phenotype rather than experimental studies.

C confers normal pigmentation, and it is incompletely dominant over c^{ch}, which reduces the size and number of particles. The chinchilla allele, c^{ch}, reduces the size and number of light pigment particles with little, if any, effect on dark pigment.

Weimaraners, obviously, come in a variety of gray shades, and a range of shades occurs with dilute black as well as dilute brown pigment. According to Little, the different Weimaraner shades are produced by three possible combinations: *CC,* mouse-gray; Cc^{ch}, silver-gray; or $c^{ch}c^{ch}$, deer-gray.

The first problem with Little's theory becomes apparent when two silver-gray Weimaraners are mated, because some puppies should then be homozygous, *CC* and $c^{ch}c^{ch}$. However, most American Weimaraners are silver-gray (Cc^{ch}), and they rarely produce deer-gray or mouse-gray puppies. Mating two silver-gray Weimaraners carrying one c^{ch} allele should produce the following color distribution in their progeny: 50% silver-gray, 25% mouse-gray, and 25% deer-gray. The second problem with Little's theory is that the c^{ch} allele has little effect on dark pigment, and all Weimaraners (both blue and gray) have dark pigment. Therefore, all Weimaraners are probably homozygous for the *C* allele; if the c^{ch} does occur in the breed, it should have little effect on color.

Interestingly, Little himself suggests the possibility that variations of color "may be caused by modifying factors act-

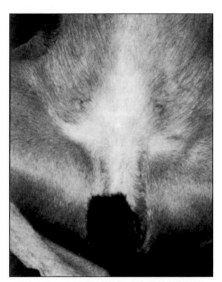

Figure 5-3: *White on the abdomen* (or penile sheath) is not uncommon but is difficult to identify at an early age. The white skin appears as early as 2–3 months, with white hairs following at around 5–7 months.

ing on the *C* gene for degree of pigment depth."[1] These modifiers will be discussed later.

Locus S Series (White Pattern)

The alleles of the Locus *S* series are white pattern factors. All alleles at this locus are influenced by genetic modifiers—minor genes that affect the expression of the alleles at only one locus. Like major genes, minor genes are inherited in pairs. It is conventional to regard modifiers acting in the same direction as having plus and minus effects. At Locus *S,* the modifiers are designated as plus (more dark pigmented area, less white) and minus (less dark pigmented area, more white).

Figure 5-5: *Weimaraner colors.* Weimaraner shades of gray are a continuum from very light to very dark, with no clear transition between the shades recognized by the WCA. The color of individual dogs also varies, being most silvery when the coat is new and developing a yellowish or brownish hue with exposure to sunlight and just before shedding. Photographs courtesy of Karis Johnston Photography.

(a) *Gray,* the most common color in Weimaraners, with the greatest shade variation, usually exhibiting lighter shades on the ears.

(b) *Silver gray.* Silver-gray, lightest shade, is most often subject to sun damage, appearing bleached out or burnt orange if the dog is frequently kenneled outside.

(c) *Blue.* No matter how light the shade blue, reflects the dilution of black pigment in the overall color. Blue is a disqualification in the AKC Weimaraner Standard.

All Weimaraners are homozygous *SS*—the factors for a solid coat. The plus and minus modifiers produce the occasional white markings on the Weimaraner's throat, neck, chest, toes, abdomen, and penile sheath.

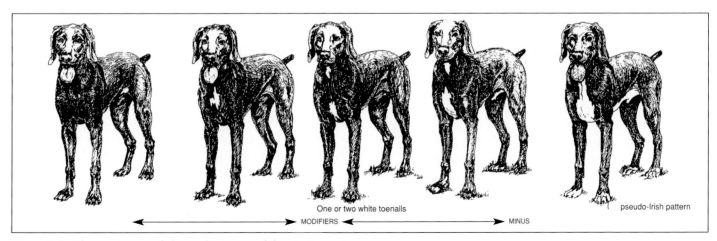

One or two white toenails

MODIFIERS   MINUS

pseudo-Irish pattern

Figure 5-4: *The continuum of plus and minus modifiers in Locus S.*

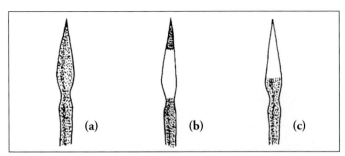

Figure 5-6: *The agouti factor* produces a terminal or sub-terminal band of light pigment in otherwise dark hairs. **(a)** Normal hair. **(b)** Sub-terminal bank of light pigment. **(c)** Terminal band of light pigment.

Figure 5-7: *The dark tips and light bands* of agouti hairs are easily seen in this photograph, taken when shaving a tail for redocking.

With paired *S* alleles, the most extreme expression of the minus modifiers—that is, the greatest amount of white—is known as the *pseudo-Irish pattern.* Weimaraners, Irish Setters, and other solid-colored breeds do not carry the Irish spotting allele (*s^i*), and it is genetically impossible for them to have more white than the pseudo-Irish pattern shown in Figure 6-7.

The *S* modifiers are *multifactorial,* meaning that their expression is influenced by environmental factors, and the *S* modifiers appear to be particularly sensitive to prenatal environmental factors, such as the age of the dam, the uterine environment, and even the season of the year. The most vivid example of the sensitivity of the *S* modifiers to the uterine environment is found with identical twins having nonidentical spotting. Because identical twins are from a single fertilized ovum, they have identical genes and normally an identical phenotype. Cattle also have Locus *S* alleles, and identical twins are easily confirmed because of the single massive placenta. In Holstein cattle, the variable spotting of identical twins is well documented. Canine identical twins are rarely identified because it is almost impossible to accurately determine the number of placentas except with cesarean births. Whitney illustrates this phenomenon with pictures of the identical twin particolored Cocker Spaniels Idahurst Twin Su and Idahurst Twin So, which do not have identical spots.[2]

The Locus *S* modifiers, then, have genetic characteristics, and environmental factors influence their expression. In breeds that require a solid color, selective breeding can reduce the incidence and area of white, but at best, it is a very slow process. The Weimaraner's first standard (1894) states, "White markings are common on most dogs—on chest and toes." Nowadays, white on the toes is extremely rare, and over 90 years of selective breeding have obviously reduced the incidence, which suggests that further gradual reduction may be anticipated.

None of the *S* alleles explain the white on the back of the pasterns that occurs on so many Weimaraners. The hairs are always lighter, showing a range from the light shades on the ears to very light silver, champagne-silver, platinum-silver, and pure white, and the underlying skin may be gray or white. Although no formal studies have been done, its expression appears to be unrelated to *S* modifiers that produce white on the chest and toes, and it may be an entirely different genetic factor.

Locus A Series (Dark-Pigment Pattern)

Locus *A,* named for the agouti (a rodent), is considered the most complex of all color loci. The four alleles identified by Little have grown to six. They are all pattern factors that control the amount and regional distribution of dark (black/brown) pigment and light (tan/yellow) pigment.

A^s—dominant black (uniform dark pigment)

A^y—dominant yellow (uniform light pigment)

A—agouti (original wild allele)

a^{sa}—saddle pattern

a^t—bicolored pattern (tan point)

a—recessive black

Three of the alleles in this series occur in Weimaraners—*A^s,* *A,* and *a^t.*

The complex interaction of the agouti alleles continues to baffle geneticists. The alleles have intricate dynamics, and the usual dominant-recessive relationships do not apply in that one allele is not necessarily dominant over others for all body regions. In addition, environmental differences appear to influence pigment production.

The *A^s* allele permits uniform distribution of dark pigment over the entire body. The action is expressed in all dogs with uniformly black or brown coats. It is almost completely dominant over others in the series. Although Little classifies Weimaraners as homozygous *A^s,* most have banded (agouti) hairs, indicating the presence of the *A* allele.

The *A* (agouti or wolf-color) allele is considered the normal or wild allele in the series, as it is the basic color of wild canines. The allele produces a terminal or subterminal band of light pigment on otherwise dark hair. The location of the band varies, and the dorsal (back) regions are usually darker than the ventral (abdomen). The wolf and Norwegian Elkhound are considered homozygous for this allele.

Figure 5-8: *Clear tan markings like this are produced by homozygous alleles.*

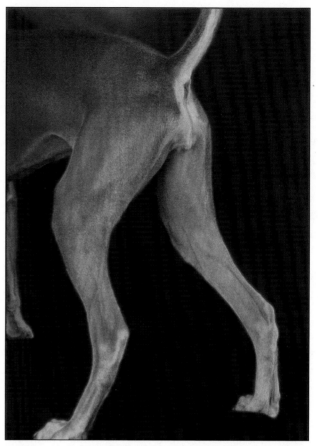

(a) Whether the markings are this distinct, or only visible in very bright light, both are carriers of this trait. Obviously a dog with markings this distinct would not be considered for breeding; less distinct markings should be carefully weighed against the dog's other positive qualities before breeding.

(b) Tan on the underside of the tail and the perineum are usually the most obvious identifications of carriers of this homozygous allele. Note that the tan also extends from the rear feet up the inner thigh; when markings are found on the back legs, they will also appear on the front legs.

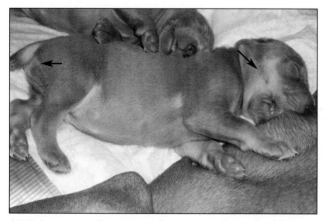

(c) Doberman markings are evident even on this week-old puppy. Since markings may take several days to become apparent, sometimes the first time the breeder notices less clearly marked puppies may be when the underside of the tail is exposed under the bright examination lights of the vet's office when the tails are docked.

(d) Carried as a genetic dilution factor, "Doberman" markings may range from very clear to a slight brownish cast visible only in very bright light. Less distinct markings may be concealed at the base of any whiskers on the face, such as the muzzle and eyeblinkers as well as the legs and underside of the tail.

Figure 5-9: *Although disqualified in the U.S.,* most countries, including the Weimaraner parent country, Germany, accept the long hair and value the trait for hunting in cold weather. This German bitch, Dorle zum Laubwald, exhibits correct coat type and thick, soft body hair that is not excessively long (1–2 inches), with only slight feathering on the legs. Longer hair is allowed only on the ears, neck, and the plume of the tail.

Although no studies of canines could be found, studies of other species indicate that in general, the width of the band is influenced by pairing with other alleles in the series, and the number and width of bands can be modified by factors at other loci. This variation in band width can be observed in the Weimaraner coat, especially the scattered, apparently white hairs, which are really agouti hairs with terminal bands of light pigment.

The a^t allele produces the characteristic tan-point pattern in dogs such as the Doberman Pinscher, Rottweiler, and Gordon Setter. The tan points are typically located above each eye, each cheek, lips, and lower jaw, extending under the throat, two spots on the forechest, below the tail, and from the feet to the pasterns and hocks, extending up the inner sides of the legs.

In the Weimaraner, the a^t factor produces the so-called dobe markings. There is a remarkable color similarity between the Weimaraner and the fawn Doberman, which also has the paired brown and dilution factors *(bb/dd)*, although that lack of variable shading may reflect an absence of the A or c^{ch} factors. The marks are more distinct in the fawn Doberman, and the pattern shows considerable variation. Weimaraners that carry only one a^t allele sometimes show a reddish or lighter tinge in the areas that would be tan if the dog had paired alleles. In some, this slight color difference can be seen only under certain conditions—age, light, and time of year.

The pattern shows greater variation than Little could explain, which is why an interaction with another factor is suspected. Even when paired, the depth of pigmentation varies, the typical tan points are not always marked, and the color contrast is not always distinct. In some, the areas of tan are so reduced that without careful examination, the animal might be classed as solid. Little admitted, *"Sometimes the spots actually disappear."*[5] Therefore, a dog that shows identifiable markings should be considered homozygous for a^t.

Other Color Factors

Other canine color factors have been identified, but they have not been assigned a specific locus.

Table 5-2: *Weimaraner coat traits.*

Trait	Mode	Expression
Density	Not consistent, probably polygenic In general, sparse coat dominant over dense	A very sparse coat is considered polygenic evidence that all longhaired modifiers are absent Some evidence that sparse coat is linked with thyroid deficiency in Weimaraners
Undercoat	Undercoat recessive to lack of undercoat	Associated with longhaired and *Stockhaarig* coats Shorthaired Weimaraners with undercoat are suspected longhaired Carriers—undercoat often disappears by 6–18 months
Straight/ Wavy	Straight tends to be dominant over wavy	Wavy coat associated with longhairs Shorthaired Weimaraners with wavy hair on the ears and back are suspected longhair carriers
Texture	Not consistent, probably polygenic In general, coarse hair dominant over silky	Silky hair characteristic of longhairs Silky-coated shorthairs are suspected longhair carriers, especially if associated with other signs
Feathering	Tends to be dominant over nonfeathering in longhairs	Associated with longhaired and *Stockhaarig* coats

Intensity Series

The chinchilla-like *Intensity (Int)* series was postulated by Iljin in *Wolf-Dog Genetics* with wolf-dog hybrids. A dilution factor, it differs from the c^{ch} allele in that the dominance sequence is from the greatest dilution to the least dilution—that is, lightest to darkest. The presence of c^{ch} is difficult to confirm, and in most cases the *Intensity* alleles are considered equally probable. Despite the similarities, there are enough subtle differences to support the belief that two different series are involved. Carver confirmed the influence of an intensity factor in the German Shepherd, and it is certainly a possibility in other breeds.[4]

The *Intensity* alleles modify agouti banding in the following ways:

- *Int*—dilutes the light band to a dirty white; overall color appears white or dirty gray
- *int^m*—produces a yellowish brown band; overall color appears wolf-gray
- *int*—no dilution, broad, bright yellow band; overall color appears reddish

Iljin's wolf-dog hybrids carried the bicolor pattern, and when combined with the *Intensity* alleles, he observed grayish-white *(Int)*, light yellow *(int^m)*, and rust *(int)* shades at the normally tan points, although the rust was lighter than that in Doberman Pinschers.[5]

The *Intensity* alleles could occur in Weimaraners. They would contribute to the variable visibility of the bicolored tan markings, for example, and they might influence different shades.

Dilution Modifiers

The plus (darker) and minus (lighter) dilution modifiers produce varying shades of dilute dark pigment. It is not clear whether they are a distinct group or act with other groups. In the United States, the prevalent Weimaraner shades of intermediate silver-gray tend to be stable from one generation to the next, and the extreme light and dark shades are not common. This hereditary pattern is consistent with what would be expected with dilution modifiers.

Weimaraner Coat

Background

New Weimaraner owners are often surprised to learn that some purebred Weimaraners are not shorthaired. In an article that appeared in an Australian all-breed magazine, Wally Finch quipped that longhairs "can appear at any time…, and ironically in the only country that rejects longhaired Weimaraners it happens more frequently than anyone will admit."[6] He is correct on both points: the United States is the only country that disqualifies longhaired Weimaraners, and they appear more often than breeders admit.

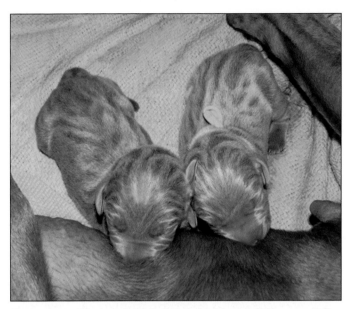

Figure 5-10: ***The stripes of the longhaired puppy*** (left) are no different than its one-day old shorthaired littermate (right). The yarn collar of the longhaired puppy is more difficult to see, covered by the thicker and slightly longer hair. Photograph by William Redmond.

Historically, the longhaired trait occurred in the Weimaraner long before its recognition in 1896. Initially excluded from the studbook, the German Weimaraner Club changed this policy in 1935.

According to Helen Schulz (WCA liaison to Germany for many years), the decision was influenced, in part, by several negative traits that began appearing in Weimaraners in which all of the modifiers linked with the longhaired recessive had been eliminated: (a) the coat was very short, sparse, and brittle; (b) the sparse coat provided little protection from cold, insect bites, and injuries while hunting; and (c) the skin was more sensitive to allergens. The most disturbing problem, however, was a high incidence of thyroid deficiency, which appeared to have been genetically linked with the shorthaired coat. Therefore, the Germans decided to stop trying to eliminate the longhaired trait from the breed and to accept longhaired Weimaraners in the studbook.

Despite official recognition, longhairs remain a minority in Germany. Since 1965, the German club has encouraged separation of the two coat types: longhaired males may be bred *only* to longhaired bitches; the mating of longhaired bitches to shorthaired and *Stockhaarig* males is permitted.

Types and Heredity

Superficially simple, the heredity of canine coats is so complex that very little is known. The shorthaired coat is consistently dominant over the longhaired coat. The very complexity of coat genetics seems to discourage research, and Whitney appears to be the only one to have attempted any analysis at all. Some of the traits associated with Weimaraner coats are described in Table 6-2.

The three Weimaraner coat types—shorthair, longhair, and *Stockhaarig*—can be further subdivided:

Short, fine, no undercoat

Short, fine, with undercoat

Short, coarse, no undercoat

Short, coarse, with undercoat

Long, smooth, no undercoat

Long, smooth, with undercoat

Long, wavy, no undercoat

Long, wavy, with undercoat

Stockhaarig

The *Stockhaarig* coat is associated with progeny from longhair-shorthair matings. The coat is described in the German standard as "guard hair or topcoat medium long, dense, straight and close-fitting, with dense undercoat. Moderately developed feathers and trousers" (Appendix A).

Figure 5-11: *Longhaired coat,* **1 week.**

In an interview conducted by co-author Deborah Andrews, Dr. Hans Schmidt (the leading spokesman for longhaired Weimaraners in Germany) provided some additional information about the *Stockhaarig* coat and its heredity. The ideal coat is similar to that of the Dingo and the shorthaired German Shepherd: it has a "full," symmetrical appearance; the hair is shorter and coarser than the longhaired coat, making it more protective and water repellent; and there is always an undercoat. The tail is full, with no plume. Hair on the ears is shorter than the longhair. It is believed that originally all *Bracken* were *Stockhaarig*.

The *Stockhaarig* coat is recessive to the typical shorthaired Weimaraner coat, and a hypothetical series of three alleles would fit the pattern that Dr. Schmidt described: S, shorthair; s^{st}, *Stockhaarig*; and s^l, longhair. These would produce the following possible combinations:

SS—shorthaired

Ss^{st}—shorthaired

Ss^l—shorthaired

$s^{st}s^{st}$—*Stockhaarig*

$s^{st}s^l$—*Stockhaarig*

s^ls^l—longhaired

(a) Compare the texture.

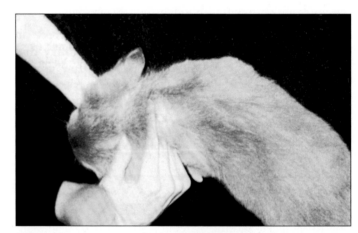

(b) Run fingers crosswise through the hair on the neck.

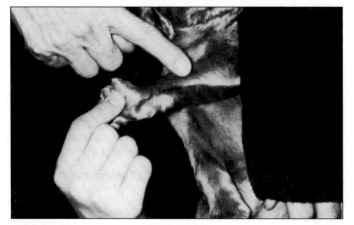

(c) The feathering line shows a cowlick.

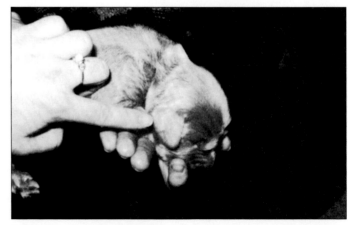

(d) The ear has slightly wavy hair.

The *Stockhaarig* coat is rare in Germany and is not mentioned in any other Weimaraner standard.

American breeders have reported a coat that they refer to as a *scruffy coat*. It is characterized by a slight marcel (wave) on the ears and along the back, and the hair is usually somewhat longer than the typical coat.

The Longhaired Coat

Many shorthaired Weimaraners are carriers of the recessive longhaired trait. The only foolproof way to identify carriers is by appearance of longhaired puppies in litters from shorthaired parents.

Puppy Coat

The longhaired coat is very difficult to identify before a puppy is 7–8 days old, even for experienced breeders. The following information here should help fanciers everywhere to identify possible longhaired puppies before docking tails at 3–5 days.

At whelping. There are very few observable differences between longhaired and shorthaired puppies. Longhaired puppies do have the typical striped (ripple) coat at birth,

contrary to popular breed lore. The only visible clue is that the hair over the nape of the neck is often thicker and is slightly longer. The most distinctive trait is the overall soft, velvety feeling when the longhaired puppy is held in the hand, especially when compared with a clearly shorthaired sibling.

One week old. If longhairs are suspected, docking can be safely deferred until the puppies are at least 7–9 days old. At 7 days, more differences can be identified. Select an obviously shorthaired puppy as gauge for comparison with suspected longhairs. Note the crisp, bristly hardness of the shorthaired coat and the iridescent quality of individual hairs. The most distinctive longhaired trait continues to be the overall thicker, silkier feeling of the longhaired coat—texture is the vital clue. Cradle the suspected longhair in your hands to feel the overall plushness of coat—the shorthair feels naked in comparison. Run your fingers crosswise through the hairs at the nape of the neck to evaluate the thickness and length—this is often the only area in which the longer hairs can be observed at this age. Feel the ears between the thumb and the forefinger and compare the two. The ears

Figure 5-12: *Longhaired coat,* **3 weeks.**

(a) Compare the puppies.

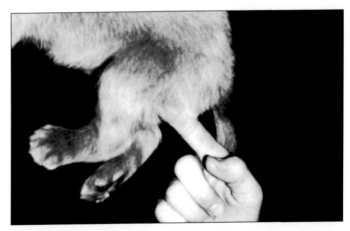

(b) Thigh feathering.

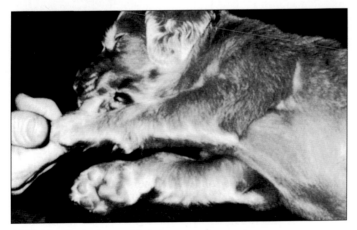

(c) Foreleg feathering and hair between the toes.

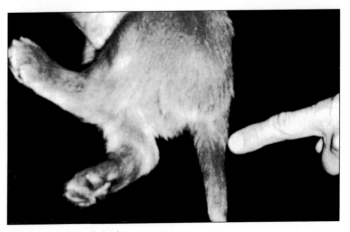

(d) Base of the tail thickens.

Figure 5-13: *Longhaired coat, 7–8 weeks.*

(a) The straight, plush puppy coat usually develops into the Setter-type adult coat.

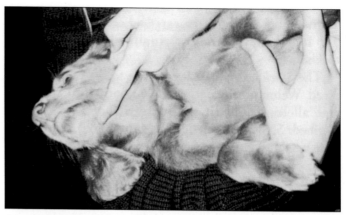

(b) Longhair on the underside of the neck, forechest, and back of legs. Long hair on ears may be curly.

(c) The curly puppy coat usually develops into the Golden Retriever–type adult coat.

(d) Telltale hair between the toes.

of a longhaired puppy feel thicker and the hair feels denser, and slightly wavy ear hair begins to appear at this time. Hair along the back of the thigh and leg may be slightly longer than that of a shorthaired littermate, and it may also show a sheen. Examine front legs along the feathering line, especially the upper half, for the earliest definite clue. The longhair appears to have a distinct cowlick, and the line is more pronounced than in the shorthair; the cowlick looks lighter and brighter. The longhaired puppy "looks" larger and heavier than its actual weight, and it will weigh several ounces less than the shorthaired littermates that appear to be the same size.

Longhaired puppies are less dependent on environmental warmth, and they begin to avoid sleeping in a pile. However, the shorthairs may follow longhairs, seeking their cozy warmth.

Ten days. One breeder reported that the first clue that she might have a longhaired puppy was when she trimmed toenails at 10 days. She noticed that the hair was beginning to cover the nails, and the puppy was indeed a longhair.

Three weeks. By three weeks, the differences between the shorthaired and longhaired coats are obvious. Wavy hair appears over the shoulders. Flat, shining, silky, longer hair encircles the neck. The hair on the ears begins to curl. The feathering along the back of the thigh becomes more obvious, and the foreleg shows definite feathering. Hair covers the toenails, and when looking at the underside of the paw, there is more hair between the toes. The tip of the tail remains unchanged, whereas the hair at the base of the tail begins to thicken.

Seven to eight weeks. At 7–8 weeks, longhaired puppies exhibit a rich, plush coat, and the body is covered with longer straight or curly hair. The hair is especially thick over the shoulders, and it encircles the neck. The ears have abundant wavy or curly furnishings. The tail still tapers, but the tip has a swirl of excess hair. Thigh and rear leg furnishings are sparse, compared with the long feathers of the lower forearm. The feet have long hair on top as well as between the toes. This is the age of the maximum longhaired puppy coat.

Figure 5-14: *Longhaired coat,* 10–12 weeks.

(a) Overall loss of topcoat.

(b) Foreleg feathering disappears, but the leg retains fullness. The hair between the toes increases in density.

(c) The longest hair remains on the ears, although curly ear hair is often replaced by straight (longhair on left).

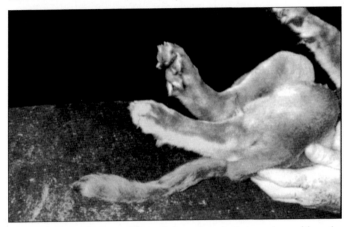

(d) The hair at the base of the tail thins, but the hair at the end lengthens—forerunner of the adult plume.

Ten to twelve weeks. One of the most surprising developments of the longhaired coat is the loss of feathering and overall body hair at about 10–12 weeks, when there is no longer a dramatic difference from the shorthaired puppy's coat. The hair over the shoulders thins out. Foreleg furnishings almost completely disappear, but the overall leg still looks fuller than in the shorthaired puppy's coat. The ears retain their feathering but often lose their curl, and there is still hair between the toes. However, the tail exhibits the most striking change, as the base thins and the tip thickens to a club-like shape.

Adult Coat

The longhaired Weimaraner's coat shows little development in the months that follow, often not until the puppy is more than 8 months old. Then, it gradually begins to lengthen and thicken. Adult length is often not achieved until the age of 2 years. The overall adult coat is highly variable—quite flat with sparse feathering like a Brittany, as luxuriant as a Golden Retriever, or flat with feathering like an Irish Setter in show bloom.

Figure 5-15: *Adolescent longhaired coat.* At 6 months, this longhair's ears are feathered, but the legs are not. The overall sparse, silky body coat lies flat. The tail hair is longer and thicker, but still has no plume. Although undocked, this tail does not curl.

Figure 5-16: *Undocked tails.*

(a) These 7- to 8-week-old longhaired littermates were donated to the German Weimaraner Club. The puppy on the left shows the typical tail carriage and curl of tail of a puppy that has not had the last two vertebrae docked. Note the curly, wooly coat.

(b) Note the curled tail of one of the above puppies at maturity.

When asked to describe the ideal adult longhaired coat, Dr. Schmidt listed the following qualities.

- The top coat lays flat and smooth and is not curly or wavy
- Although the standard does not require it, an undercoat provides greater protection when hunting and is more water repellent (coats are judged when the dogs finish the water work)
- The hair on the ears is long; more velvety hair is permitted on the tip
- The feet have hair between the toes
- The tail is well covered with hair—on top as well as underneath—and has a good plume
- The legs and underside have a good feathering, although not so extreme as to interfere with the dog's hunting function
- Faulty qualities include a curly or excessively wavy coat; too much coat, giving the appearance of a wooly bear; a thin, open coat; and too soft a coat

Dr. Schmidt recommends keeping longhaired dogs outside at night in an area that is cool to maintain conditioning and develop a fuller coat.

The longhaired Weimaraner's tail should be either undocked or (according to some standards) have only one to two vertebrae removed. (The undocked tail has a curve more like a Saluki than a Setter; the Setter-type tail is obtained by docking one to two vertebrae.) The plume of the tail begins 4–5 inches from the base of the tail; if the tail has been docked to the usual 6 inches, the plume resembles a pompom.

The "Fuzzy-Wuzzy" Puppy Coat

Between whelping and 7 weeks, shorthaired Weimaraner coats also exhibit a considerable range in length and texture. Many puppies exhibit a coat that breeders call "fuzzy wuzzy." These are often mistaken for longhairs when there is no genuine longhair in the litter for comparison.

Like longhairs by 7 days, fuzzy wuzzies usually look larger and fluffier than littermates that are clearly shorthaired. Some even appear to have feathers along the back of the forelegs and thighs. Their coats have sparse, longer hairs that stand straight out, unlike the longhaired coat, which usually flattens by 7 days. Although the fuzzy-wuzzy coat is definitely longer, it is never curly over the ears like the longhaired coat. The longer hairs stand straight out; these longer hairs are particularly obvious if the fuzzy wuzzy has a plush undercoat, which is often lighter in color. The fuzzy wuzzy's coat often sports sparse, coarse, dark, wiry hairs, causing one worried breeder to exclaim, "Please, not a wirehaired Weimaraner!"

By 5 weeks, just when the breeder is sure the puppy is a longhair, all signs of feathering suddenly disappear. By 6 weeks, the fuzzy-wuzzy coat becomes progressively coarser, and the longer, wiry hairs shed out. By 7 weeks, it is usually impossible to distinguish a fuzzy wuzzy from its shorthaired littermates.

Differentiating fuzzy wuzzies from longhairs is even more difficult when there is a noticeable difference between the fuzzy wuzzies. At 2 weeks, Figure 6-17 shows that the puppy on the right—clearly shorthaired—had a short, smooth, firm coat. The coat of the puppy on the left was longer, silkier, and fluffier than three others in the litter with typical fuzzy-wuzzy coats, and the inexperienced breeders assumed he would be a longhair, docking only two vertebrae from his tail. (The veterinarian said that even docking only two vertebrae inhibits nerve and blood vessel development and that it would be less traumatic if redocking proved necessary.) However, the coat never exhibited any curl.

By 7 weeks, the puppy still had a distinctly long, full coat, compared with his littermates. However, the long hairs on the ears and back of the legs had disappeared, and the overall texture felt coarser every day. Meanwhile, the puppy had been promised to a German Forester, who still wanted the puppy when told that he would not be a longhair. The German Weimaraner Club officially classified him as a shorthair, and his tail has since been redocked.

Figure 5-17: *The "fuzzy-wuzzy" puppy.* Even at 2 weeks, it is easy to see why Ash could have been mistaken for a longhair. His coat, and that of his littermate in front of him, are long, straight, thick, and dense to the touch, but without the telltale "marcel," or curl, on the ears. A close look shows that the guardhairs, although long, are not curled either. Usually by 8–9 weeks, these longer hairs will have disappeared, leaving behind a full, particularly dense, insect- and water-resistant adult coat. Photograph by Brett Cosar.

Figure 5-18: *German breeder Pavi Schmidt* returns from her customary outing with a litter of 2-month-old longhaired puppies. These walks typically begin shortly after weaning the litter, regardless of the weather, and provide an opportunity for puppies to experience increasing environmental challenges as their mother leads the way through obstacles such as tall grass and small streams, as well as the chance to encounter a variety of wildlife. Photograph by Hans Schmidt.

Figure 6-1: *CH Johmar Misty Splendor,* NRD, SD, V; owned by Marvin and Karen Berlin. On her first retrieving lesson, 10-week-old Misty demonstrates the breed's strong, instinctive aptitude. Photograph courtesy of Jan Harding.

CHAPTER 6

MOVEMENT AND STRUCTURE

by Jackie Isabell

It is said that a properly constructed dog always moves correctly, and lack of harmony between parts shows up in the gait—especially a show-ring trot. Thus, incorrect movement helps the judge identify specific structural flaws. Exhibitors should be familiar with the basic principles of movement, as well as with the terms used in standards and judging.

It is not surprising that videotapes have proven themselves the best media for understanding the complexities of canine movement. *The Weimaraner—Structure and Gait* is an outstanding videotape that can be obtained from the WCA. In addition, Rachel Page Elliott's *Dogsteps—A Study of Canine Structure and Movement* and its companion video, *Canine Cineradiography*, are highly recommended. The AKC's video *Gait, Observing Dogs in Motion* is also very popular.

The Canine Gaits

The term *gait* refers to any of several patterns of leg movement used by four-legged animals—walk, trot, pace, and gallop. In dog show jargon, however, *gait* refers to the trot, which is the gait judged in the show ring. More than any other gait, the trot reveals faults in the dog's structure.

The *walk* is a four-beat gait—all four feet strike the ground at different times. The feet on the right and left sides follow two parallel tracks.

The *trot* is a two-beat gait, with the *diagonal* front and rear legs moving forward and back in unison. The trot is timed so that the front foot strikes the ground a split second before the hind foot, which allows it to lift out of the way before the hind foot strikes. As speed increases, the stride lengthens and timing becomes more critical.

The *pace* is also a two-beat gait, with the *lateral* front and rear legs moving forward and backward in unison. As in the trot, the front foot strikes a split second ahead of the coordinating back foot. Pacing is comfortable for the animal, especially when tired. The pace is a normal, even desirable, gait in some four-legged species; it is a normal *but not typical gait* in canines, and it is regarded as unattractive and undesirable in the show ring.

There are three distinct variations of the gallop. The *sustained gallop* (canter) is a three-beat gait; the *normal gallop* is a four-beat gait; and the *double suspension gallop* is a four-beat

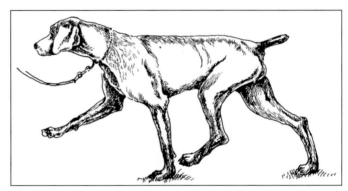

Figure 6-2: *The trot.* The *diagonal* feet strike the ground simultaneously.

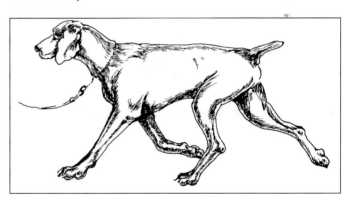

Figure 6-3: *The pace.* The *lateral* feet strike the ground simultaneously.

gait characteristic of gazehounds—hounds that hunt by sight rather than scent. The sustained and normal gallops are the characteristic hunting gaits of the Weimaraner.

Some Basic Terms and Principles

Single tracking is the convergence of all four feet toward a single line or track to maintain the center of balance. As the dog moves forward at a walk, the right and left legs move along parallel tracks that are fairly far apart. To maintain balance as forward momentum increases, the parallel tracks *converge* toward a single line but never actually meet, falling slightly to the right and left of the center of lateral balance. The best example of this principle is a bicycle; although balance cannot be achieved at a halt or a slow speed, the ten-

Table 6-1: *Movement faults.*

Glossary of Movement Faults

brushing. The front (or rear) legs move so close that they touch or brush in passing.

clipping. See *interference*.

crabbing. Moving with the body at an angle to the line of travel. A dog employs this sidestepping movement and twists its body to avoid interference (clipping) at the trot. It is an indication that the dog's coupling is too short in relationship to the length of the rear stride. However, crabbing may also be an acquired bad habit or the result of poor conditioning. Also called *side wheeling, side winding,* and *yawing.*

crossing over. The crossing of the front (or rear) feet in front of one another, over the center line of travel. Also called *dishing, weaving,* and *knitting and purling.*

dishing. See *crossing over.*

hackney action. The high, exaggerated lifting of the front feet (and to some degree the rear), like that of a hackney horse. The term is often used to describe the movement caused by raising the dog's head too high with the lead or by simple restraint of forward momentum, converting the long reach of the forelegs into a short-striding, high action.

in at the hocks. The hocks incline inward instead of being parallel and tend to brush in passing.

interference. The back foot strikes the front foot. Caused by overreaching. Also called *clipping.*

knitting and purling. See *crossing over.*

moving close. The front (or rear) legs are insufficiently well separated, sometimes leading to brushing.

out at the elbows. Moving with the elbows protruding from the body or natural line from the shoulder to the foot, indicating a lack of lateral balance; it is associated with wide chests, tight shoulders, or overdeveloped shoulder muscles—common in Weimaraners conditioned for field trials.

out at the hocks. A waddling-type gait associated with outward bowing of the hocks.

overreaching. A gait fault caused by greater angulation and drive from the rear assembly than length of the forward reach, causing the rear feet to be placed to one side of the forefeet to avoid *interference* or *clipping.*

pacing. Although a normal gait of four-legged animals, the pace, with its side-to-side sway and rolling topline, is an unattractive gait and is penalized in the show ring. Pacing may be the result of several factors or a combination of them. First, the pace is considered a fatigue gait—that is, a gait that reflects muscular weakness or fatigue. Foals and puppies often pace before their muscles become strong enough to trot; in a more mature animal, it is an indication of poor muscular condition. Second, pacing may indicate incorrect balance, and the dog must resort to a pace to avoid interference—for example, a young Weimaraner whose rear legs are longer than the front legs. Third, pacing may merely be a bad habit. Puppies that resorted to pacing to avoid interference may continue to pace after it is no longer a necessity.

paddling. The outward flipping or twisting of one or both paws at the pastern joint is associated with wide or east-west fronts. Also called *winging.*

side wheeling. See *crabbing.*

side winding. See *crabbing.*

snatching hocks. A gaiting fault with a noticeable rocking of the rear quarters characterized by a quick outward snatching of the hock as it passes the supporting legs and twists the rear pastern far beneath the body.

weaving. See *crossing over.*

winging. See *paddling.*

yawing. See *crabbing.*

---

dency to fall to one side or the other decreases as forward speed increases over a single line of travel.

Angulation refers to the angles of the lines and planes of the dog's body, specifically the front and rear assemblies. *Front angulation* is the relationship of angles formed by the shoulder blade, upper forearm, forearm, pasterns, and feet; *rear angulation* is the relationship between the pelvis, upper thigh, lower thigh, hock, metatarsus, and feet. These angles determine the length of the stride. Whether straight or acute, the front and rear angles must balance so that the front and rear strides are equal.

Although less critical than balanced angulation, it is important to note that the steeply angled croup of the quarter horse is the hallmark of the sprinter, whereas the flat croup of the thoroughbred is characteristic of the long, easy stride of the router or distance runner.

A dog's *coupling*—that is, the distance between the front and rear assemblies—is another related factor. Obviously, the bridging structure—the body—must be long enough to prevent interference between the front and rear feet.

The Field Dog in the Show Ring

Judges should be aware that the competing field Weimaraner may exhibit musculature that appears somewhat different from that which is typically seen in the show ring. Most commonly observed is a more pronounced development of the muscles in the shoulder resulting from swim-

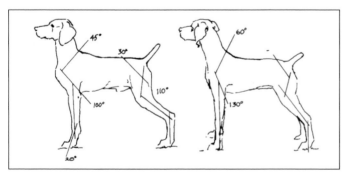

Figure 6-4: *Angulation.* **(a)** Excellent shoulder angulation plus a well-angulated rear give the desired ground-covering stride; the balanced angulation contributes to stamina. **(b)** Straight shoulder angulation gives a short stride that requires more steps to cover the same distance; nevertheless, the balance between the front and rear angulation contributes to stamina.

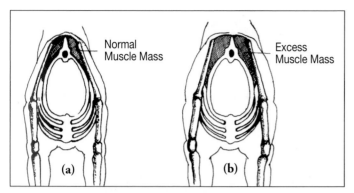

Figure 6-5: *Shoulder alignment.* (a) Normal muscle mass permits the correct vertical alignment. (b) Excessive muscle mass under the shoulders throws the elbow out of vertical alignment, causing the dog to move out at the elbows. This is frequently seen in Weimaraners that have had excessive roading or that have dragged heavy chains for field conditioning.

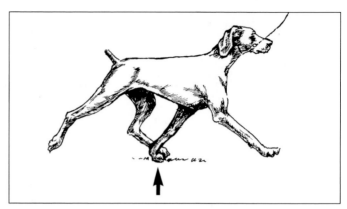

Figure 6-6: *Overreaching.*

ming, pulling in a roading harness, and miles spent galloping rather than trotting; a hands-on examination will often reveal the musculation that has created a dip behind the withers and that may initially appear to be a structurally flawed topline. The hard-worked field dog will often have highly defined muscles in the hind quarters rather than a typically smooth outline; this is not only from the type and amount of work the dog is performing but the resulting generally lower body fat, which may also present a leaner overall appearance. Additionally, the Weimaraner coat is easily burned as a result of the hours spent in the weather; these dogs may also exhibit imperfections resulting from injuries incurred in the field. Most importantly in field competition, balanced structural moderation is the key to a long, healthy working life for this sporting breed; judges should keep in mind that, all things being equal, a smaller muscular dog, as long as he is within the breed standard, should not be penalized.

Summary

The preamble to the WCA's standard is clear: "Above all, the dog's conformation must indicate the ability to work with great speed and endurance in the field." When evaluating gait, the conformation judge is limited to using the show trot to identify the structural faults that create weakness in the working sporting dog, despite the fact that successful hunting dogs will usually be working at a sustained gallop. Fortunately, the trot will still allow judges to identify a dog with well-balanced front and rear angulatation that moves freely from the side, without forgetting the special importance of clean, unencumbered movement coming and going.

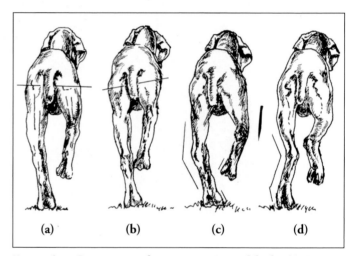

Figure 6-7: *Comparison of rear movement and faults.* (a) Correct. (b) Crossing over (weaving). (c) Out at the hocks and toeing in. (d) In at the hocks and toeing out (cow hocked).

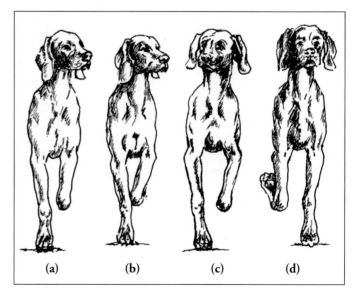

Figure 6-8: *Comparison of frontal movements and faults.* (a) Correct. (b) Crossing over (weaving). (c) Out at the elbows with toeing in. (d) Paddling (winging).

Jahrgang 53
Ausgabe 1/04
April 2004

Weimaraner
Nachrichten

Figure 7-1: *It is never too early* to provide young puppies with a variety of experiences to prepare them for their future endeavors. German hunters know the value of early positive exposure and rarely miss the opportunity to acquaint the future hunting dog with the scent and texture of a fresh kill. While chasing deer is considered a vice in the U.S., in Germany the ability to follow the blood track of a wounded deer is a highly valued skill, and the ability to follow the drag track of furred and feathered game is required to achieve breeding certification. Photograph by Virginia Alexander, courtesy of *Weimaraner Nachrichten*.

CHAPTER 7

GETTING OFF TO THE RIGHT START

The moment is at hand! The new puppy will be arriving soon. Are you ready? Are you sure? Bringing a new puppy home can be exciting and challenging; this chapter provides hints and suggestions to get a jump start on establishing a positive relationship with the new family member and to prepare for the unexpected.

Before the Puppy Comes Home

Ground Rules

It is essential to set consistent limits from the beginning. Decide immediately what limits will be set for the adult Weimaraner. Will the full-grown Weimaraner be allowed on the furniture? To sleep on beds? To be fed from the table? Identify behavior that will be tolerated in the full-grown Weimaraner, and agree to set those limits from the first day of the puppy's arrival.

Make a list of basic command words so that all family members can begin using them consistently from the first day; if someone else will be providing day care or exercise for the puppy, they also should know the agreed- upon vocabulary. A puppy is as confused by different words as a child who is told to go to bed in English, Greek, and Chinese, even though the child may get the general idea from tones, gestures, and context.

Finding a Veterinarian

Select a veterinarian before bringing the puppy home. Ask the breeder, who may be able either to recommend a Weimaraner-oriented veterinarian close to home, or to put the new owner in contact with other Weimaraner fanciers in the area. Find a veterinarian who takes time to answer questions, and do not hesitate to look further if the first one does not inspire confidence. Since most owners spend more time interacting with the staff, be sure they inspire the same sense of confidence and comfort as the veterinarian. It is beneficial if the prac-

tice has experience with Weimaraners and knowledge of the special needs of working sporting dogs. A willingness to be flexible and follow the breeder's guidelines in the vaccine schedule is mandatory. Also inquire whether the veterinarian is current on the most contemporary literature, which encourages delayed sterilization; recent studies show altered growth patterns, increased incontinence, and other health considerations in dogs sterilized before 12 months. Most distressing, impaired muscular development and altered bone structure may leave the canine athlete more prone to hip dysplasia and potential injury. Read Chapter 10, *The Best of Health,* and discuss the particular needs of the Weimaraner with the veterinarian under consideration. If a practice has

Figure 7-2: *Before the puppy arrives,* decide whether or not it will be allowed on the furniture. The habit is easier to prevent than to cure. *Lolita,* by William Wegman.

multiple veterinarians, try to meet as many as possible and establish a "regular" favored doctor for your dog.

The only thing worse than having a crisis with a new puppy is not knowing where to get prompt help. Find out how the veterinarian may be reached at night and on weekends. Is it a group practice in which there is always a veterinarian on call? Is it an independent practice in which the veterinarian shares an answering service and emergency calls with several others? Is there an emergency animal clinic nearby? For some reason, emergency clinics rarely have prominent signs and can be impossible to locate at night. Avoid panic by locating the clinic during the daytime. Precious minutes have saved lives!

Start a basic first-aid kit immediately. Keep the supplies in a sturdy container, such as a toolbox, tackle box, or cosmetic case, that can be tossed into the car when leaving on a trip. If the container is large enough, it can also be used for nail clippers and other grooming aids. *Pet First Aid* by the American Red Cross provides a list of items to include in the kit.

Household Safety

Puppies will explore every nook and cranny they can get to, and anything found will be thoroughly investigated with paws and mouth. Houseplants, electric cords and connections, blind sashes, hanging tablecloths, and small objects, such as children's toys, appear to be novel play objects to the young puppy and present potential dangers. As the puppy grows big enough to investigate tables and counters, make

Table 7-1: *New owner's checklist*

Food—breeder's brand	Quick-release collar
4´–6´ lightweight lead	10´+ lightweight lead
Size 400 plastic crate	Big buddy/stuffed toy
Bottled water, not milk	Pedialyte®
Kaopectate®	Floor and carpet cleaner
Febreze™	30″ × 21″ Quiet Time mat (2)

Table 7-2: *Breeder checklist*

A few days' supply of food	Day's supply of water
Vaccine record and schedule	Health certificate, if needed
Signed copy of contract	Children's pledge, if appropriate
AKC registration paperwork	3- to 4-generation pedigree
WCA membership	(mail it in early, before deadlines)
Piece of fabric or toy from whelping box	Referral for veterinarian or local contact
Referral for puppy kindergarten or field training	Breeder's phone number

sure those surfaces are also cleared of temptation. Because unrewarded behavior does not persist, this curiosity soon passes if the puppy is not rewarded with pencils or other delightful chewables and edibles.

Removable gates can restrict the areas a puppy has access to, but do not forget to carefully secure closet and bedroom doors, as well.

Read the labels on household cleaning products, not only in the house, but the yard and garage, as well. Many common household products are extremely toxic to dogs, such as ethylene glycol (antifreeze), rat poisons, and chocolate. Refer to *The Best of Health* for a list of common dangers.

The typical Weimaraner, like Houdini, views latches as a personal challenge to its ingenuity; few closures foil any Weimaraner with the motivation to open them. Weimaraners have solved the riddle of opening every closure in Figure 7-4. The

Figure 7-3: *From a puppy's point of view* a new home offers many novel and exciting amusements. Before arrival get down on the puppy's level and look for tempting and dangerous opportunities. Check for items that hang down and look behind and under large furniture; a puppy's small size allows access to areas people do not normally see. Photograph by Rodney Moon.

Figure 7-4: *Doors and latches Weimaraners have opened.*

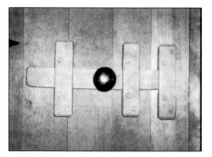

(a) Fay—New York, New York

(b) Rajah—Germantown, Maryland

(c) Bamford—Washington, D.C.

(d) Murphy—Phoenix, Arizona

(e) Astor—Carlyle, Pennsylvania

(f) Saber—West Chester, Pennsylvania

(g) Rio—Germantown, Maryland

(h) Nani—Wilmington, North Carolina

(i) Sook—Los Angeles, California

only missing picture is of a refrigerator, which has been reported. Flip-up gate latches are hardly a challenge unless secured by a snap. The only defense against a Weimaraner's problem-solving talent is to minimize its initial opportunities for rewarding success while it is too young to be adept and can be conditioned into believing obstacles are real. Capitalize on its strong desire for approval versus disapproval for opening things, and never rely on closures of the types pictured in Figure 7-4 to keep a Weimaraner from the object of its desire, such as food or sex.

Kids and Dogs

Young children and puppies should never be left together unsupervised. Remember that puppies are babies, too, and have not had the chance to learn good manners. Very young children need instruction and maturity to be able to interact safely and respectfully with the dog, as well. Young children display behaviors that are very stimulating to puppies and dogs. Running and rapid, unpredictable movement with high-pitched shouts can result in the puppy joining in the play with his new littermates. Unfortunately, this can end up with a puppy being stepped on or a child being unintentionally nipped or scratched. Close supervision will protect both puppy and child; too many such incidents can turn what should be a lifelong friendship sour in a hurry. If there are children in the household, the new owner may refer to *Living with Kids and Dogs* by Colleen Pelar.

It is natural for dogs to use their mouths to communicate, but beginning at 7 weeks, puppies must learn to inhibit their desire to bite when playing with people. Dogs have an amazing ability to control their mouths; when the puppy's teeth make contact with human skin or clothing, a loud yelp from the human, along with ending the play for several minutes, usually teaches the puppy very quickly that mouthing, nipping, or biting humans is undesirable behavior. "Kisses," or licking, at least while the puppy is young, can provide an acceptable alternative behavior from the canine and human perspectives.

When there are small children in the home, it is extremely important, for health reasons, that children not have access to the dog's potty area. Although unusual, it is possible for children to become infected with parasites or become ill from animal waste. Conversely, baby diapers and soiled clothing must be secured against the inquisitive puppy, which may find such items irresistible.

In spite of some popular psychology and children's pledges (see Chapter 29, *Picking the Perfect Puppy*), it is neither reasonable nor fair to expect young children to be responsible for the total care of a pet. Children may gain a sense of pride from the praise of parents for completed tasks, as well as learning responsibility and compassion from these duties; however, while children may have a schedule of chores, parents must always follow up to ensure that the needs of the dog are actually being fulfilled.

The Backyard

Fencing

Many Weimaraners live in urban areas with leash laws and fenced backyards. While Weimaraners are not typically a breed content to be relegated to the status of "yard dog,"

the puppy or dog may occasionally find itself unsupervised in the backyard. A well-fenced yard will contribute to the safety of the dog. There are advantages and disadvantages to every type of fencing. Although a 6-foot fence is generally adequate, it will not stop a Weimaraner that is determined to get out. For the determined fence jumper, there are several options. The first is to build a fenced enclosure with a secure top. If a separate kennel is not financially feasible or is not allowed by neighborhood codes, a second reliable option is to install PVC pipe strung on a strong cable along the top edge of the fence. Since most Weimaraners will not jump cleanly, but rather need a boost on the way over, the PVC pipe will rotate and prevent the dog from gaining purchase on the top of the fence. It is very important to discourage the fence jumper by not placing items that can aid escape, such as a dog house, near the fence.

Not only can an athletic Weimaraner jump over nearly any fence, it is not unusual for a determined escapist to tunnel under the fence, as well. At the first sign of excavation, drop the day's stools in the hole; this will usually curb the behavior. Installing cinder blocks at the base of the fence line can be discouraging for the novice digger. Although it is an investment of effort and money, hardware wire buried 12″–18″ along the base of the fence line will generally stop even the most determined digger. In extreme cases, a livestock fence charger may prove to be an effective deterrent. For the fence jumper, the line can be run across the top, and for diggers, across the bottom. Be sure to follow all safety guidelines.

In general, invisible electronic-type fences do not work well with a sporting breed such as the Weimaraner, although there are always exceptions. A fence also keeps dogs and people out of the yard, which is an important consideration for the safety of all dogs, but especially for those with brood bitches.

Hedges not only enhance the attractiveness of the yard and provide shade, they also eventually transform a modest 4-foot fence into an impregnable 6- to 10-foot barrier. They keep the Weimaraner away from the crumbling concrete at the base of the block fence, the sharp edges of the chain-link fence, and the weak or damaged slats of the wooden fence. The visual disadvantages of the chain-link

Figure 7-5: *Lifelong friendships are established early.* Rob and TC learned from the beginning to respect each other through supervised interaction and instruction. TC joined the family at 7 weeks, when Rob was 2 years old. They had a positive influence on each other growing up; Rob, now college bound, became an Eagle Scout, and TC became the first Weimaraner to earn an AKC agility title, as well as obedience, conformation, and field titles. Photograph by Barney Riley.

Table 7-3: *Advantages and disadvantages of fencing types.*

Advantages	Disadvantages
Block Fencing	
Most safe and secure	Most expensive
Concrete footings prevent digging (footings should extend under gates)	Footings may break off in chunks
No visual stimulus to bark at passing people and dogs	If dog develops a rock-eating habit, pieces must be picked up regularly
Minimizes teasing problems	
Chain-Link Fencing	
Reasonable cost	Dogs can see through it
Easy to maintain	Encourages barking, fence fighting, and teasing
Strong	Easy for dogs to dig out and escape
	Sharp edges at bottom may cause injury during escape efforts
Wood Fencing	
No visual stimulus to bark at passing people and dogs	Less secure
Reasonable cost	Slats may break or work loose
	Broken slats or projecting nails may cause injury
	Easy for dogs to dig out and escape
Invisible Fencing	
Reasonable cost	Highly variable success rate
Option when fencing not allowed by deed restrictions	Professional initial training recommended
Protects view	Regular maintenance training required
	Least secure; does not protect dog from intruders (animal or human)
	Not obvious whether fence is turned off

fence become minimal, and the visual stimulus of activities outside the fence is reduced.

No fence is complete without a secure latch. As mentioned before, Weimaraners are fond of the puzzles humans may pose for them. A Weimaraner can manipulate many types of latches, so be sure that the latch on the gate will prevent the dog from escaping. Additionally, the latch will be ineffective if it does not catch easily and completely each time. Many tears have been shed over the loss of fine Weimaraners that let themselves out to look for some fun in which to join.

Landscaping

The question is not whether any puppy will damage ornamental shrubs and trees, but rather how much. Even older dogs that are considered trustworthy sometimes astonish their owners. Although the trunks of mature trees cannot be chewed through, they will die if enough bark is stripped. Thorns are not enough protection for sweet roses and tasty pyracantha. An investment in chicken wire can contribute to amiable relationships and lovely yards.

Maintaining landscaping can be frustrating with (helpful) Weimaraners, who may view gardening as a family affair. If permitted to accompany the gardener, the dog may imitate the owner, who may later find previous landscaping efforts completely undone and the scoundrel waiting on the porch for the next opportunity to repeat the game.

All dog owners must be cautious regarding mulch and gravel. Some types of mulch can be toxic to dogs. Gravel must be either very tiny or large enough to not be swallowed. Weimaraners love to mouth and carry objects, and ingestion of foreign objects is, unfortunately, all too common a cause of death in our breed. Read *The Best of Health* for the warning signs of intestinal blockage. The Weimaraner-owning gardener must review the labels of all chemicals used around the house and garden, including herbicides, insecticides, fertilizers, and snow melters. Refer to *The Best of Health* for a list of dangerous chemicals and plants. Cheryl Smith has written *Dog Friendly Gardens, Garden Friendly Dogs,* which provides additional information.

Pools

Pools are a marvelous way to keep a dog in good condition, as well as to practice water retrieving; however, unfenced swimming pools are a hazard. A puppy, like a child, should always be supervised around the pool. Pool covers are a special hazard, as most dogs cannot comprehend the difference between pool covers and the water's surface; special care should be taken to secure the pool area when the cover is in place, since escaping from the pool cover, especially the soft type, is nearly impossible for a dog. See *Ages and Stages* for hints on teaching the puppy to swim. After teaching the dog to swim in a shallow pond or stream, be sure that the dog not only knows where to find the steps, but that it can actually get out of the pool. Older dogs and smaller dogs may have difficulty scrambling out from the side. Contact a pool supplier for the latest innovations to allow dogs and other animals to escape more easily from the pool.

Equipment

Buyers usually budget money for the puppy's purchase price and immunizations, but rarely consider the cost of equipment. Although all the following items will not be needed immediately, all contribute to making life with the new family member a lot easier.

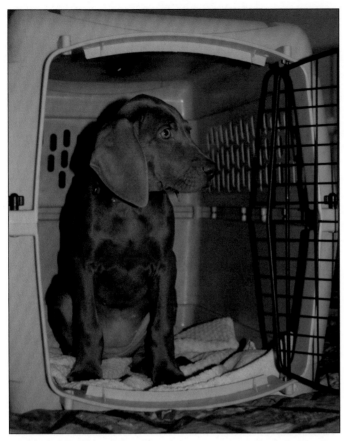

Figure 7-6: *The likelihood of separation anxiety is reduced* if the breeder has conditioned the puppy from an early age to see his open plastic crate, shared with litter mates, as a den, a place of safety and comfort. In the puppy's new home, a similar plastic crate provides a safe and familiar place when the puppy cannot be supervised.

Dog Crates

The most expensive initial equipment purchase is a dog crate. Owners who have never used a dog crate are appalled by the idea of forced confinement in a "cage," and for humans it would indeed be cruel. From the canine perspective, however, a crate serves as a den, fulfilling the instinctive association of darkened enclosures with safety and comfort—a refuge when troubled, frightened, or just sleepy. Wild canines are born in a den, and dogs consistently seek out a dark, confined place for naps. When the crate door is left open, many choose to use the crate—it is not unusual to find two or three Weimaraners snuggled together in a crate. Some dogs, especially those in a busy, noisy household, actually need a den, a place that offers seclusion and privacy from stress. Canine behaviorists have found that some dogs considered "hyperactive," "nervous," or "high strung" showed remarkable improvement when a den-like refuge was provided. Crates are also a wonderful place to stash bones and other treasures. Whenever something is missing, check the puppy's "den."

Crates are invaluable in housetraining a puppy. Just as important, however, having a crate means the puppy is less likely to develop bad habits, such as persistent barking and destructive chewing, and when it becomes an adult, it will be far more trustworthy when mature enough to be left loose in the house in the owner's absence. Other uses and considerations include the following:

- Preventing destructive chewing when the puppy cannot be supervised, at night and during brief absences. Puppies under 5 months should have the opportunity to relieve themselves a minimum of every 4 hours during the day.

- Providing comfort—a crate-trained dog is comforted rather than stressed when boarded or confined at a veterinary clinic.

- Providing protection in moving vehicles—the dog cannot cause accidents and is protected if an accident occurs. When parked, windows can be left open for ventilation; however, be aware that cars heat up very quickly to temperatures that can cause illness or injury, even in the shade or moderate temperatures.

- Providing security—when stopping in motels, the dog feels secure in its "home," while owners can dine without fear of finding panic damage on their return.

The dog crate contributes to the safety of the puppy, the sanity of the owner, and the well-being of the house, and owners who have learned the advantages would not consider raising a puppy without one. Sometimes it is simply necessary to confine the dog while the owner's attention is elsewhere. Doing the laundry and not watching the puppy? A shoe suddenly needs new laces! Paying bills and balancing the checkbook? Crash goes the plant stand! Watching the plumber fix a leaky faucet? His helper may or may not mention that your puppy ran out as he came in the door and is playing in the traffic! Dog crates come in such a variety of types and sizes that something can be found for every need. Currently, there are models available that are as much furniture as dog den, fitting in with even upscale décor. Measure the space available in the car or truck to be sure the crate can be used for transportation; many models open on the side.

It is possible to abuse the use of dog crates. Aside from the need to eliminate, a puppy isolated for long periods of time can develop undesirable behaviors. If the owners will be gone all day, make arrangements to have someone let the puppy out around midday for a bit of play and a chance to go potty, at least until 5 months of age. Select a care provider whom the dog likes and who will agree to guidelines of acceptable manners to avoid confusing the puppy. Alternatively, an exercise pen can provide a bit more room for the puppy. Cover a section of the pen with newspaper, and provide a crate with the door removed on the opposite end.

Plastic polymer crates are lightweight and easy to clean, and dogs enjoy their den-like security. Before the puppy chews it up, use the cardboard floor that comes with the crate as a template to make a permanent floor of quarter-inch tempered pegboard. The pegboard provides a smooth, warm surface and allows hair, dirt, and liquids to drop through, keeping the crate surprisingly clean.

Airlines prefer plastic polymer crates, which provide greater security, and if the buyer expects to ship the dog sometime—to a show handler, a field trainer, or stud owner—the plastic polymer crate is a good choice. The airlines require a size 500 kennel for shipping most adult males and a size 400 kennel for most bitches.

Some people prefer a wire crate for traveling. The wide variety of sizes and shapes (side or end doors, slanted ends for station wagons) should meet every need. Because blankets never stay in place on the cold, slippery bottoms, pegboard floors are also useful here. Be advised, however, that Weimaraners seem more adept at escaping from wire crates than from plastic polymer ones. The open sides stimulate the curiosity and senses of the Weimaraner, instead of creating a den-like feeling,

Figure 7-8: *Although not suitable for an escapist or chewer,* new collapsible nylon mesh crates are lightweight and portable and set up in a snap! Very convenient for traveling to shows, seminars, or vacations, these crates offer superb ventilation, and some include multiple entrance options from two sides as well as the top. Keep in mind that the nylon crate provides less protection for the occupant from aggressive passersby or weather. Photograph by Vicki Lombardi.

which encourages attempts to escape. Cat-like dexterity and insatiable intelligence allow the dog to pull items into the crate, move the crate to a more interesting location, jimmy the latches, and work loose connectors. And when creativity does not work, brute force might. It only takes one escape to convince a Weimaraner that he can escape from anything. Wire crates are a reasonable option for travel, but are not the best choice for home confinement, where a Weimaraner with time on his paws has the opportunity to ponder possibilities.

Exercise Pens

Exercise pens are regarded as a nonessential luxury until they are purchased. Then, everyone wonders how they lived so long without one. The most obvious use, of course, is for dog shows, but most puppy owners find them to be indispensable. A few other uses include camping trips and vacations, an indoor-outdoor pen for 5- to 7-week-old puppies, and a temporary fence to keep the dog on the patio while the garden is being reseeded or the mud is knee deep or to keep the dogs from eating all the peaches on the backyard tree before they are harvested.

Figure 7-7: *Wire crates are not the safest option,* especially for a Weimaraner that has not been crate trained. A dog can pull objects into the crate or chew through the wires, injuring mouth or jaws or breaking teeth. The doors to this type of crate seem to yield readily to the creative and determined escapist Weimaraner.

The 3-foot height is easier to pack into a vehicle and to reach over with a poop scoop than the 4-foot height, which will not deter a Weimaraner that really wants to jump out. For jumpers, purchase extra panels to make a top that provides not only additional security but also good support for a shade-providing cover.

Collars, Leads, and Identification Tags

A 7-week-old Weimaraner needs an inexpensive size 12″ or 14″ strap (leather or stiff nylon) collar immediately; one adjustable size 14″–20″ Quick-Klip® collar will fit until the puppy is full grown. The puppy should wear a collar at all times for control and for the identification tag. A choke collar is not necessary for the young puppy. The author also uses Resco or thick English leads, which have an adjustable loop that is kind to the puppy's neck but still offers control. These leads usually come in bright colors, making them easy to find if dropped in the grass.

Because the odds are high that the puppy will manage to chew a lead or two, get the least expensive one that will serve the purpose—even clothesline or sash cord and snap will do for early lead training. The lead should be small and lightweight with a small snap—about 6 feet long will be sufficient.

A 20-foot nylon cord or clothesline with a lightweight swivel snap, which is less noticeable to the puppy, is useful in teaching the recall.

Retractable Leads

The young puppy on a retractable lead will learn that pulling on the lead is a successful strategy to achieve her goal; this conditions the puppy to expect pressure from the collar, resulting in an adult dog that pulls on the lead. Additionally, retractable leads can also inflict injuries on both dog and owner. When the dog hits the end of the line, a hard jerk can pull either the dog or the owner off her feet. The line easily gets wrapped around dogs and humans, which can quickly inflict minor to severe rope burns. In the author's experience, retractable leads are useful for potty breaks for well-trained adult dogs but are not appropriate for puppies.

Send for an identification tag immediately—round tags are much less likely to get caught on things. Instead of putting the puppy's name on the tag, use the name REWARD—a name that may ensure its immediate return. If the breeder has not already done so, the puppy may be microchipped; microchips inserted after 4 months are less prone to migration. Inquire about licensing requirements, but in general, this can be deferred until the puppy is old enough for rabies immunization at 5–6 months.

Food and Water Bowls

Food and water bowls should not be easy to overturn or to carry. Weimaraners love to pick up their dishes and bring them to the owner when hungry or looking for attention. This can be especially annoying when the bowl is full of water. For home use, a good stainless-steel bowl with a wide base or a heavy ceramic crock type works well, especially for water. Plastic bowls are as likely to be viewed as a chew toy as they are to be viewed as a water or food container. Purchase more than one bowl for food and water so that they can be washed frequently. For traveling, a wide-based plastic dish is convenient and inexpensive enough to keep in the car at all times.

When there is no danger of freezing, a Lixit™ attached to an outside faucet provides a constant source of fresh, clean drinking water. Puppies learn to use a Lixit™ quickly, as soon as they can reach it. To train the puppy, empty the water dish. When the puppy begins to fuss at the water dish, indicating thirst, smear some honey on the Lixit™ and encourage the puppy to lick the sweet. The licking produces water for the thirsty puppy, and a second lesson is often unnecessary.

Things to Chew

Canine behaviorists recommend that only one or two generic types of chew toys should be selected because learn-

Figure 7-9: *Even 8-week-old Smiley* can pull 8-year-old Lola off her feet. Retractable leads cannot only cause injury—rope burns or entanglement—but they also condition young puppies to pull on the lead.

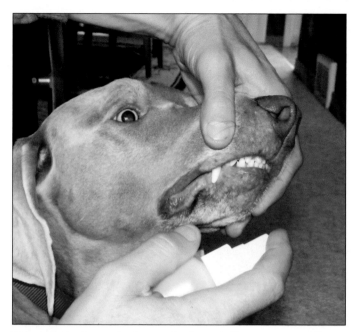

Figure 7-10: *Bitter Apple™ and other repellents* are more effective when the puppy is first conditioned to associate the odor with a generous sample of the disgusting taste. Photograph by Bob Millan.

ing to discriminate between what is allowed and what is forbidden is difficult for puppies, and offering variety encourages generalization of chewing behavior. Toys and games that encourage tug-of-war may result in problems for the future hunter and retriever. Toys that can be dissected or torn apart or that have small parts should be saved for supervised play. Only toys designed to withstand the sharp, determined teeth of a small puppy should be left unattended. Even then, all toys should be inspected and cleaned on a regular basis.

Shank (marrow) bones are safe and appealing to Weimaraners of all ages. The bones, which should be at least 2–3 inches long, can be purchased from most butchers. Keep a supply in the freezer, handing them out on appropriate occasions, such as leaving the puppy in a crate while running errands. Kong® toys can be used this way as well: fill the hole with peanut butter or small treats; although freezing is not necessary, the frozen "stuffing" will take a bit longer to consume. The cold sensation of the frozen bone or Kong® is soothing to a teething youngster. The Weimaraner will treasure them, and there will usually be quite a pile in its crate or favorite corner. Cow's toes, with or without filling, may also be treated in this same manner to provide variety. As with all toys, bones and cow's toes should be inspected regularly and should be discarded when small enough to be swallowed.

All dogs adore rawhide and pig's ears, but it is advisable to avoid these entirely. Behaviorists warn they may stimulate generalized chewing; they may also contribute to intestinal upset. Rawhide and pig's ears manufactured outside the United

States are often not well regulated and may contain chemicals that could be hazardous to the dog's health. An adult Weimaraner can consume an entire medium-sized rawhide bone in a few hours, or a pig's ear in minutes. Weimaraner owners have reported that their dogs have swallowed the large pieces, which lodged in the throat or intestines, requiring emergency life-saving surgery.

Nylabones® are almost indestructible and are safer than rawhide. Some owners complain that the dogs do not like Nylabones® and simply ignore them; some dogs dislike the slickness of a new bone, and it can be made more appealing by using a rasp on the ends to roughen them up. Several manufacturers have developed puppy toys made from softer materials, which puppies seem to enjoy chewing. These toys are not only extremely durable, but are also interactive, providing crevices and holes for hiding treats to keep puppies amused. Often made in irregular shapes, these toys are very easy for the puppy to pick up and carry, a most desirable feature.

Old socks, slippers, and shoes make delightful puppy toys; so do new ones! Puppies quickly identify the generic characteristics, but discrimination between old and new is simply beyond their comprehension. It is easier to teach puppies that all socks, slippers, and shoes are forbidden, and it is cheaper to keep a generous supply of shank bones and appropriate toys on hand.

Figure 7-11: *Weimaraners love to carry dishes.* For some reason, those filled with water are especially appealing. Photograph by Wayne Cowles.

Figure 7-12 (a) and **(b)**: *A dog door that leads to a safe, secure area* provides an opportunity for exercise without requiring a human valet. Newer models have a special collar that allows only the dog through, preventing unwelcome guests. For the budget minded, this Italian fancier uses an economical cloth flap, as have generations of his family in Europe. Photograph by Telma Tucci.

When the object of desire cannot be moved out of reach, protect it with a repellent. Bitter Apple® (the lotion lasts longer) is the traditional repellent, and it is effective for most puppies. Tabasco® sauce broke one puppy of chewing woodwork, but other puppies like it. A Farnam product called Dog-Away® which is best described as "essence of evil," is proving to be the most effective of all products. In addition to chewing, it has been used for discouraging repeat accidents on carpeting.

Big Buddy

Most Weimaraner puppies love to have a "big buddy." Especially valuable when arriving at a new home, an oversized plush toy offers comfort for the puppy away from littermates for the first time. If possible, the new owner can drop the toy off with the breeder a couple of days before picking up the puppy so it will offer familiar scents, as well as a comforting presence. The toy should be of a good size, but small enough to go through the washing machine, since it will get soiled.

Nail Clippers

Weimaraner nails should be trimmed every 1–2 weeks, starting shortly after birth. It is easiest to get the puppy used to the procedure while it is small enough to control, and it is easier to prevent the growth of a long quick than to drive it back. Many types of clippers (scissors and guillotine) are satisfactory, but for a young puppy, a pair of strong kitchen scissors will work. A dremel tool or nail grinder can be effective, as well. Liberal use of treats and short sessions early on can create a more positive experience for the puppy and encourage cooperation instead of resistance. Remember, it is not a requirement that all nails be completed in one session; it is all right to do one or two at a time, and then progress to all the nails on a single paw.

No matter how carefully the nails are trimmed, the quick is occasionally cut. The amount of blood and the difficulty of stopping the bleeding can be alarming. Many owners become so frightened the first time they cut the quick that they refuse to trim the nails again. Be prepared! The smallest container of Kwik-Stop™—almost a lifetime supply—should be kept on hand. Pour some powder into the cap before trimming the nails, and dip the nail into the powder if the quick is cut. Kwik-Stop™ is also an effective cauterizing agent in other emergencies, such as cut ears, which produce an unbelievable amount of blood that is difficult to stop. The technique for trimming nails is illustrated in Chapter 25, *Raising the Litter,* and in Chapter 15, *Showing the Weimaraner.*

Sanitation

Although stools can be picked up with a shovel, a puppy is a 15-year commitment to scooping poop, and the chore can be accomplished in a fraction of the time with a pooper scooper.

The droppings should be placed in a sturdy plastic bag inside a garbage container with a locking lid. The lid minimizes fly problems, and the locking feature makes it fairly dog proof.

Most municipalities do not object to collecting the remains if they are securely contained in plastic bags. Avoid using fly bait, which sometimes has a sweet taste and may be toxic.

When out walking, every responsible owner will be prepared to pick up dog waste. Picking up dog waste is not only a health consideration, it is simply good manners, and in many areas, it is the law. Certainly, no one likes to step in what the dog left behind, and since not everyone likes dogs, leaving "landmines" is a surefire way to encourage more anti-dog legislation. Special bags are available, in either decorator or discreet designs, with dispensers that can attach to belt or leash. For the environmentally conscious, biodegradable bags are also available; for the cost conscious, recycled bread, newspaper, or grocery bags are equally effective. See Figure 7-13 to see how to turn the bag inside out on the hand, use it like a glove to pick up, and then turn the bag right side out. Tie a knot in the top and dispose of it in a waste receptacle. It is easy to keep a couple in a pocket, or a roll in the vehicle.

Kitchen Garbage Container

One of the most frequent sources of irritation with the Weimaraner puppy (and of quarrels with family members who did not want a puppy) is cleaning up kitchen garbage. A low wastebasket lined with a paper bag invites investigation and eating of attractive items. The most foolproof method is to keep the container in a cupboard or closet, but this is often inconvenient. A compromise is to invest in a tall container with a swinging lid that is hinged in the middle. The height and the lid make the garbage less accessible to the puppy and prevent the garbage habit while the puppy is developing behavioral patterns. Adults that have not developed the habit as puppies will usually not bother a tall, covered container later. However, overfull and deliciously aromatic containers invite the novice and tempt the reformed sinner. Aside from

Figure 7-14: *A good trick for keeping a crated puppy amused* for hours is to stuff a clean, cooked marrowbone, or a Kong® toy, with peanut butter or cream cheese. Prepare several at a time and store them in the freezer. Photograph by Zachary Hohenzy.

the mess, trash can treasures can easily result in an expensive trip to the veterinarian.

Grooming Table

A grooming table for a breed that hardly needs any grooming? Although the grooming table makes the minor needed grooming easier, 'training table' would be a more descriptive term. This is another of those things that seem like frivolous luxuries until you buy them, and then you wonder how you lived without them. For those on a budget, the top of a size 400 or 500 crate converts into a decent substitute with a heavy skid-proof mat; textured vinyl shelf liners will work very well. Some mail-order catalogs offer a special legless grooming tabletop that fits securely on the crate.

For show training, there is no substitute for a grooming table; refer to *Showing the Weimaraner* and *Picking the Perfect Puppy*. When the puppy is on the ground, you are theoretically on equal terms, but the puppy usually wins. When the puppy is on a grooming table, you are in complete control. A puppy that is trained to pose on a grooming table is steadier and more reliable. When a dog that has been trained on a grooming table is turned over to a professional handler, the handler can apply his or her skills to the best advantage and usually starts winning sooner and more consistently. It only takes a few wins to more than pay for the expense of a grooming table.

Interior Gates

Like crates, interior gates contribute to peace of mind, as well as household well-being, by restricting the puppy's unsupervised access to some parts of the house. Moveable gates, such as those used for toddlers, are useful until the puppy is housebroken and past the age of indiscriminate chewing.

Many owners consider permanently mounted interior gates more a necessity than a luxury— for example, to keep bitches in

Figure 7-13: *Picking up after a dog* is not only polite, in some areas it is the law. Slip the plastic bag inside out over the hand like a glove, pick up the waste, turn the bag right side out, knot, and dispose of properly.

season or young puppies off carpeted areas. The securely mounted custom wrought-iron gate in Figure 7-15 is attractive as well as useful, although the bars are so wide apart that it is not an effective barrier for puppies under 10 weeks—hindsight is 20/20. The wall plate is held so securely in place by toggle bolts that three adult bitches simultaneously hitting the gate have not disturbed it. Opening the sliding latch, however, is child's play to a typical Weimaraner, and the kennel matriarch figured it out in less than 5 minutes. After being caught in the act and given a firm lecture, she agreed to respect the symbolic barrier. The younger bitches learned to accept the barrier as puppies, before they became clever enough to reach the latch.

Feeding Your Puppy

The puppy should continue on the same brand of food and the breeder's feeding program for at least the first few weeks. Most breeders provide enough food to feed the puppy for several days. It is also a good idea to ask the breeder for a gallon of water; if this is not available, use bottled or cooled boiled water for the first week. All changes in diet and water should be gradual; a sudden change in water can cause digestive upsets, and a change in diet can cause a puppy to go down in the pasterns, develop flat feet, and become temporarily very unpromising in a short time, almost overnight. If the puppy is still eating gruel, a considerate breeder will provide instructions. Soak the dry food thoroughly with boiled and cooled

Figure 7-15: *Weimaraners can be taught to respect* the symbolic nature of indoor barriers. Since their athletic nature makes it a relatively simple matter to jump most fences or gates, such training must start at a young age to avoid reinforcing escape behavior.

Figure 7-16: *Even the best-fitting lid* will not stop a determined dog like the unrepentant Misty. Better to make garbage and trash inaccessible behind a tightly latched cabinet or pantry door. The enticing dangers of the garbage have sent many a Weimaraner to the vet. Photograph by Carol Parron.

Figure 7-17: *Although securing trash* behind a firmly latched door is best, if you must leave a container out, the best type of lid for a Weimaraner is hinged in the middle. Photograph by Karen Millan.

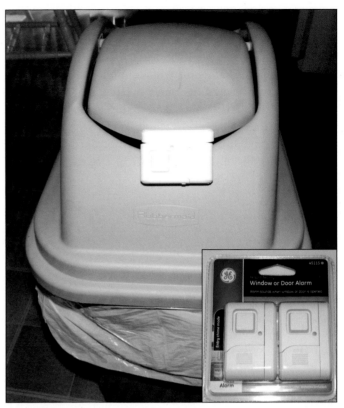

Figure 7-18: *Dumpster diving* can be adverted by the shrill sound of an inexpensive window/door alarm that can be found at almost any home supply or hardware store. Installation requires no tools and takes less than a minute using either two-sided tape or Velcro®.

water. Do not moisten the food with cow's milk! This is the most common cause of diarrhea in puppies. Puppies around 6 weeks will usually soon tire of the gruel and be ready to move on to a diet of dry food.

Food should be offered to the puppy in the crate; any food not consumed in about 5 minutes should be removed. When the puppy begins to leave most of the midday feeding almost untouched, it is time to reduce the number of daily meals. In general, a Weimaraner puppy will be on a schedule of three meals a day by 7 weeks and two meals a day by 12 weeks; a minimum twice-daily feeding is recommended for all Weimaraners after this time. However, most Weimaraners of any age welcome a small, latenight snack, such as a crunchy biscuit; for puppies, this will help them sleep through the night sooner, and it establishes a bedtime routine.

Selecting a Food

Current foods are formulated to meet nutritional requirements; large-breed formulas are designed for the special needs of larger dogs like Weimaraners. A quality food may be more expensive, but since they are more easily and completely digested, the owner will find that the dog eats less of the quality food than one of inferior quality—less food in, less waste out, saving pickup time in the yard.

Look for at least two animal protein sources named by species listed in the first five ingredients. For example, an ingredient panel that included "turkey" and "chicken meal" in the first five ingredients would be preferred over one that listed "poultry" and "poultry meal." By-products and fractions (beef by-products, wheat middlings, and rice bran, for example) are often leftovers or waste products from human food production; typically, these items are less nutritious and digestible than their whole counterparts (beef or beef meal, whole wheat, or rice). Some manufacturers add sugar to make a food more palatable, but as with humans, added sugar is just empty calories and may cause digestive upset or behavior problems. Artificial colors and flavors are added for the benefit of the human; look for a food that concentrates on nutrition, not marketing. The point must be made that there is no single perfect dog food for every dog. While one dog may thrive on a particular food, another may not. A dog's needs also change throughout its life; the food that was perfect for the adolescent may not work as well for the performance dog or the mature dog. If a food does not provide the appearance and condition expected in the dog, try a different food for at least 8 weeks; these days, there are plenty of quality foods out there to choose from.

Speaking of condition, just like for humans, extra weight is not good for your dog; this is especially true for the very young Weimaraner and the older Weimaraner. Roly-poly puppies are photogenic, but that much extra weight is hard on growing joints, bones, and muscles. Even puppies should have the ribs easily felt, but not readily visible, without any obvious fat deposits.

Supplementation

If a few vitamins and minerals are good, more must be better. Wrong! Fat-soluble Vitamins A and D are stored in the body, and excessive amounts will accumulate and can cause serious health problems; too much calcium is associated with anomalies of the bones, joints, and teeth. Dog food manufacturers maintain extensive research programs to develop completely balanced rations to meet all nutritional requirements at different ages and levels of activity. Adding such things as meat, eggs, milk, and table scraps alters the nutrient amounts and defeats the purpose of the balanced rations.

Some Weimaraner puppies have periods of extremely rapid growth during their first 18 months; at these times, consult a veterinarian for advice on proper supplementation.

Tummy Upset

It is not uncommon for a puppy to develop loose stools due to the stress of changing food, water, or environment, sometimes after vaccinations, or to develop the occasional gas-

Figure 7-19: *There is no single perfect food for every dog.* Photograph by William Wegman and the *New York Times*.

tric indiscretion. If the puppy has a fever in conjunction with diarrhea, a visit to the veterinarian is in order. If the puppy does not have a fever, Kaopectate® (original flavor) and Pedialyte® will help the puppy regain bowel control more quickly. Three to 5 tablespoons of Kaopectate® at the first episode and a subsequent dose several hours later will usually resolve the problem. Fortunately, most dogs eagerly accept original flavor Kaopectate® offered in a turkey baster; a special oversized dosing syringe for offering oral medication to small children works well for the puppy, too. Unflavored Pedialyte® should be offered instead of water; allow only $1/2-3/4$ cup at a time, at intervals of $1/2$ hour, as drinking too much may cause vomiting. For the dog reluctant to drink fluids, mix the yolk of a hard-boiled egg or a small amount of strained meat baby food in a cup of Pedialyte® to encourage fluid consumption. Should the condition not respond after $3-4$ doses of Kaopectate® and $4-5$ cups of Pedialyte®, continue offering Pedialyte® and consult a veterinarian. Be prepared to describe the frequency and consistency of the stool (custard-like, soup-like, or projectile) to the veterinarian; take a refrigerated sample of the stool, if possible.

Housetraining

One of the leading reasons dogs are given up for adoption is housetraining problems; the owner who is patient, persistent, and observant can avoid most of the stress of the housebreaking process and start the new relationship off on a positive footing. A puppy's natural instinct is to keep its sleeping or "den" area clean. A wise breeder uses this instinct to start the housetraining process as soon as the puppies are able to move around easily.

Most Weimaraner puppies will try early on to get out of the whelping box, or at least move to one end, to relieve themselves. Allowing puppies free access to a toileting area is important for maintaining the instinct to keep this area clean; puppies raised under circumstances that force them to soil the whelping box or a crate—conditions often found in puppy mills and pet shops—will usually be more difficult to housetrain. Feeding the litter outside will encourage the puppies to become accustomed to "going" outdoors, since the puppy will need to relieve itself almost immediately after eating.

The most important rule to remember is that if the puppy has an accident inside, it is the owner's fault, so use that rolled-up newspaper on the owner, not the puppy. The young puppy has very little control over the need to eliminate; the necessary physiological maturity is simply not fully developed. Early on, the puppy is actually training the owner to take her out on a regular basis. In the case of housetraining, success begets success; the more opportunities the owner provides for successful, appropriate elimination, the faster the puppy learns what is appropriate. Additionally, the odor of housetraining lapses is hard to completely remove—to the dog's sensitive nose anyway—and will encourage the puppy to seek out the same spot in the future.

Figure 7-20: *These puppies are already responding* to the natural instinct to keep the den area clean; once they have relieved themselves they can be counted on to howl for the owner's assistance to rejoin littermates. **Clip on heat lamps, such as the one in the corner of this box, are an invitation to severe injury** and should never be used, but rather should be suspended from the ceiling or otherwise secured out of reach.

Keys to Success

The keys to successful housetraining are a leash, a schedule, supervision, and a crate. A puppy is pretty predictable in certain things. Puppies need to relieve themselves on a regular basis, they avoid soiling the den or sleeping area, and they will seek out areas that have been used before. At 7–10 weeks, a puppy typically needs to relieve itself after waking, after playing and after eating or drinking, but at a minimum every 2–3 hours. Feeding the puppy in the crate encourages her to eat without distraction and allows the owner to be sure that the puppy is eating well; it is an added deterrent from using the crate as a toileting area. To establish a successful pattern of housetraining, ideally, water should be freely available only at meals for the 7- to 12-week-old puppy; in the event of excessive thirst, or in warmer climates, puppies may need water more frequently. However, removing water in the early evening will reduce nighttime toileting calls. Offering a snack—a crunchy dog biscuit, for example—late in the evening will also help the puppy sleep through the night sooner.

The Schedule and the Leash

After each of these events, take advantage of these predictable behaviors by snapping on the leash—very young puppies may be carried to avoid accidents—using the same door each time, going to the same spot, and standing still and being quiet. Using the same door consistently will help the puppy learn where to go when she needs to "ask" to go outside. Using the same spot reinforces the puppies' need to "go." A dog's sense of smell is extremely keen, so even the odor of the feces that were promptly removed last time will linger, communicating that this is a "good" place to go. Promptly picking up feces encourages cleanliness in the dog and prevents bad habits—such as stool eating—as well as preventing the potential spread of parasites. Standing quietly in the same spot quickly becomes boring for the puppy; she will be less distracted from the business at hand and will more promptly perform the necessary behavior. The lightweight long line will allow a more self-conscious puppy to move to a more comfortable distance but still allow the owner a degree of control. Hopefully, the breeder started the puppy out with beginning leash training, so the puppy is accustomed to the leash already. If this is not the case, or in the rare case of a puppy that may be uncomfortable or suspicious of a person standing too close when relieving herself, an alternative is necessary. If the puppy repeatedly refuses to urinate while on leash, find a small area that can be enclosed until housetraining is well established. Eventually, the owner will want to teach the puppy to walk on lead and that it is all right to relieve herself on lead, but housetraining takes priority early on. The owner must still watch the puppy to be sure that the job is done, but can do so from a distance more comfortable for the puppy. It is not sufficient to just turn a young puppy loose in the backyard alone; it will be impossible to know for sure whether the puppy has taken care of business, a sure set-up for an indoor accident.

The Cue

A cue can quickly be established by using the same prompt ("go potty," "hurry up," "go now," and "get busy" are common) as soon as the puppy squats—very handy when traveling, time is short, or the weather is inclement! When the job is done, a quiet word of praise is in order. Move to another area of the yard and then play with the puppy for a bit. If there is simply no time for play, at the very least give a word of praise and a small treat. A common error of new dog owners is to take the dog for a walk to relieve herself, but as soon as the dog performs the necessary duties, the walk is over. Weimaraners are pretty smart—it does not take long to figure out that the longer the dog waits to go, the longer the walk. This can be quite frustrating when time is of the essence. When the dog eliminates off the owner's property, it is important to always pick up after the dog with plastic bags that are carried for that purpose.

Supervision

If the puppy has emptied her bladder, there is a 20- to 30-minute window of relative "safety" in which the puppy can, under supervision, explore, play, and enjoy limited freedom without worry of accidents. If the puppy has an accident shortly after coming back in the house, then allow a little more time for her to completely empty her bladder; some dogs prefer several small puddles. If the puppy did not urinate, it is a good idea to put her back in the crate for 10 or 20 minutes and then try again before allowing playtime inside. If you see the puppy begin to circle or sniff intently, it is time for a potty break. Once the puppy has the idea, the puppy may begin to look worried and head for the door when the need arises, often looking back over the shoulder. If that does not work, the puppy may tip-toe off to a quiet spot behind the sofa or into another room. If the owner missed all the signs and the puppy begins to squat, a loud "No!" or "Ack!" will usually interrupt the process momentarily. If not, just wait it out and then clean up the spot immediately; moving the puppy midstream just makes a bigger area to clean. "No!" is meant only to startle the puppy, not to punish it. No scolding! Especially not as you are carrying the puppy outside. Gently pick the puppy up, grab the leash, and head for the "right spot;" praise the puppy as soon as she squats. If the puppy repeatedly has an accident shortly after going potty, it is possible that the puppy's habit is to make to more than one puddle or pile. Next time, wait a few minutes longer and see whether the puppy has actually completed the job.

A Handy Trick

At this time, it is not difficult to teach the puppy to ring a bell or other signal (scratching at the door will result in damaged doors and walls when the puppy grows to be an adult). When the puppy is routinely heading towards the door when the urge strikes, if it is not an "emergency exit," smear a bit of peanut butter on the bell. When the puppy noses or licks the bell, praise the puppy and take her out to the right spot. It will not take long! Be prepared for the dog to also learn to use this same signal when the urge is to go out to play; if this is not a desirable behavior, be sure to always put the puppy on lead and go to the exercise area when the puppy signals. If the puppy does not "produce," go back inside without any interaction—no punishment, but no praise.

When Accidents Happen

Remember, just because the puppy has not made any mistakes in a few days does not mean the puppy is housetrained,

Figure 7-21: *A longer lead* allows the self-conscious puppy to find a comfortable distance with which to take care of business while still giving the owner control. By waiting patiently and quietly and offering praise and play after the job is done, the owner encourages the puppy to perform promptly and to not procrastinate.

only that the owner has been diligent. Use barriers and gates to keep the puppy in areas of easy supervision. If the puppy has passed the window of "safety," a leash can tether the puppy close enough for the owner to be aware if the need to go outside arises, without having to keep an eagle eye on the puppy.

When a housetraining lapse occurs, it is completely useless, and perhaps detrimental, to scold or punish the puppy after the fact. Dogs simply do not have the same perceptions as humans and are unable to connect the puddle from 5 minutes ago to the owner's angry behavior. It is quite possible for a puppy to learn that punishment occurs not for soiling the house, but when the owner and a puddle are in the same room. Such a puppy may decide it is unsafe to eliminate in the owner's presence (so there is no opportunity to praise the puppy for appropriate elimination) or may decide it is all right when the owner is in another room.

If an accident does occur, either in the crate or elsewhere in the house, it is essential to clean it up immediately and thoroughly. As mentioned before, completely removing the odor is difficult, and the lingering odor will encourage the puppy to return to the same area later. Scrape up feces as thoroughly as possible; blot urine with a thick pad of paper towels (after the initial paper towels are coming away dry, try standing on several folded over to soak up even more). Urine will soak through to any padding underneath, so if possible, try to lift the carpet or rug and clean underneath, as well. Use a quality cleaning agent designed to remove pet odors. Keep the puppy away from the area until it is completely dry. Just because the odor is covered up with perfumes does not mean the dog cannot smell it, so be thorough; hard surfaces must be cleaned as thoroughly as carpeted areas.

If brown spots occur in grassy areas used to exercise the puppy, keep a hose or sprinkler can of water nearby. Thoroughly watering the urine spot will not only prevent the brown spots, but it actually results in greener grass as the diluted urine provides nitrogen.

If a puppy seems to be urinating more frequently, or despite close supervision it has many accidents, a trip to the veterinarian may be in order, as a urinary tract infection is a possibility.

Crate Training

Learning to accept the crate will be important to your puppy for many reasons. A dog will likely have to spend the night at the vet at some time during its lifetime; sometimes a sick or injured dog may need to be confined at home, as well. A dog that is familiar with the crate can get down to the business of getting well sooner. Sometimes it is simply necessary to keep the dog safely out of the way. Providing a crate gives the dog a place to "escape" to when the chaos of the household gets to be too much; children can be instructed that the crate is the dog's private space and should

Figure 7-22: *Get off to the right start* with current household residents—introduce the very young puppy to other pets in the house under close supervision, and the puppy may become accustomed to even unusual housemates. Photography by J. D. Studios.

not be disturbed. Car travel is safer with a crated dog, and specific types of crates are mandatory for air travel by cargo.

Most puppies, especially if the breeder provided early opportunities, will accept a crate fairly quickly if the crate is not overused. A wise breeder has provided the litter of puppies with a doorless crate, so the puppy has probably spent some time napping in a crate with his littermates. As the puppies became a little older, the breeder hopefully put the puppy in the crate with a littermate the first couple of times the door was closed. If the breeder provided these early experiences, the crate has already become associated with a positive experience. If this is the case, then providing a tired puppy with a toy as company will usually result in the puppy's falling asleep in the crate in short order—after a minimum of fussing. Some breeders will provide a piece of material from the whelping box. Do not wash it, even if it is a bit soiled; the odors of the mother and littermates will linger and provide a sense of comfort to a lonely puppy. Expect that anything put into a crate with a puppy will be completely dissected, so choose toys and bedding carefully; for now, choose a durable toy and old towels or shredded paper, not an expensive pet bed. Starting crate training with a young, healthy puppy is a better idea than trying to convince a strong, uncooperative adult dog. Each time the puppy enters the crate, repeat a chosen word, such as "kennel" or "go to bed." Here is where the crate truly comes in handy. Remember that one key to success is avoiding indoor accidents. If the puppy cannot be supervised, the crate will help prevent accidents from occurring, since the puppy will avoid soiling the crate whenever possible. An overly large crate for the young puppy may inad-

Figure 7-23: *If the puppy is unwilling to enter the crate* head first, try putting him in tail first! A properly sized crate is important; growing pups quickly outgrow their first crate, as is the case pictured above. The dog should be able to sit or stand with the head in a normal position; this is especially important for the older dog, who may suffer neck injury from being confined in a crate that is not tall enough. Photograph by Rodney Moon.

vertently sabotage housetraining efforts by allowing her to soil the crate and still move away from the mess, so be sure the crate is just large enough for comfort, but too small to encourage this undesirable behavior; a size 400 crate is usually the largest the new puppy needs. It is possible that at some point the puppy will have an accident in the crate. When this happens, remove the soiled bedding immediately, scrupulously clean the crate—remember how sensitive a dog's nose is—and replace the old bedding with clean bedding. Since bedding must be thoroughly washed when it gets soiled, resist the temptation to buy an expensive crate mat until the puppy is mature; the best choices are easily washed towels or disposable shredded paper. It is likely that a tired puppy will seek out the crate for a nap, but when the young puppy is not necessarily ready to settle down but must be crated anyway, toss a few treats in to entice the puppy—and use the cue word. A frozen marrowbone or Kong® stuffed with peanut butter or other special and appropriate toys will keep a puppy occupied until she is ready to settle down. Save a couple of special toys for crate training and rotate them each day to keep them "special." If the puppy protests confinement, do not release the puppy until she is quiet. Pitiful cries and shrill howls may be hard to bear, but if the owner yields, the puppy quickly learns that this unruly behavior results in release. Repeat the mantra, "Behavior that is not reinforced does not persist.... Behavior that is not reinforced does not persist...." It might not hurt to turn on a radio with some soothing music—for the owner and the puppy. If the owner allows the puppy to cry and then eventually gives in, the puppy learns to be even more persistent in its protests. Most puppy tantrums do not last too long, and soon it will settle down to work on the Kong® or marrowbone or will fall asleep. If nothing else, the puppy has to stop to take a breath sometime.

A new puppy comes with a host of new responsibilities. These tasks can be onerous, or they can be an opportunity to begin establishing a positive relationship from the beginning. This is the time to set the precedent that enjoyable things happen when the puppy is with the owner. Owners who have fun while teaching the puppy will teach more, and more often; and just like people, puppies learn more quickly when lessons are presented in short, fun experiences. Remember to stop while the puppy is still enjoying the action and before she is tired or bored. An optimistic and humorous outlook on the everyday tasks will not only help the puppy get off to the right start, but perhaps will even provide fond memories.

A Special Sound. Every puppy needs to learn a word or signal that means to stop whatever she is doing immediately. Forget the folded newspaper or can of pennies; it probably will not be handy when it is needed. The word can be any sound that is loud and irritating. No! Ack! Eeeeek! Ahnk! or any other sound agreed on by the family; everyone will need to practice so the sound is the same. The author makes a ritual of having the family choose and practice this sound before the puppy goes to its new home. This special signal is a warning to the puppy to STOP! Right now! Or the sky will fall! With the exception of housetraining, if the puppy does not respond immediately, the sound should be followed by a swift and convincing correction, such as a sharp (but not abusive) slap on the behind or strong leash correction. Handy in housetraining, the sound can also tell the dog to not take an object, to stop sniffing at something dangerous, to drop whatever is in its mouth, to not get on the counter, or to stop any other potentially dangerous or objectionable behavior. Once the puppy learns this sound, it can be used in a variety of ways, such as teaching the puppy not to pull on the lead. This signal has saved many a dog's life, both literally and figuratively.

Figure 7-24: ***Getting off to the right start*** should include introducing puppies to the smell and taste of feathers from a live bird between 5 and 6 weeks to help build the drive needed to become competitive hunters as adults. Chapter 8, *Weimaraner Kindergarten,* discusses this in more detail. Photograph by Rodney Moon.

Figure 8-1: *He may look like an angel now,* but without a well-planned training program, be assured that this innocent puppy will develop his own plan for you! Like a baby elephant, the Weimaraner possesses a tenacious memory, even at this early age. Sadly, many new owners have found out how difficult it can be to redirect a once-spoiled puppy to the responsibilities of an adult dog. Photograph by John Suttle.

CHAPTER 8

WEIMARANER KINDERGARTEN

All Weimaraners, to fulfill their potential as companions, must understand basic obedience commands, and training this intelligent, imaginative breed is easiest and most effective in the period from 2–4 months old. The techniques in this chapter are based on kindergarten puppy training, with modifications for Weimaraners. The goals are to establish communication, human leadership, and desirable behavior patterns that provide a solid foundation for later show, field, and obedience work.

Ideally, the new owner begins with a puppy from a breeder who understands the importance of psychosocial development and who has given the youngster a head start using the techniques described in *Ages and Stages* and *Testing Natural Aptitude*.

Establishing Leadership

The typical Weimaraner is a very manipulative creature. By 10 weeks, con artist techniques can be highly developed, and a Weimaraner puppy can have an entire household dancing to its tune. Training cannot be accomplished when there is any question about who is in charge, and the puppy must learn who is boss at an early age. Dog trainers call this boss the "leader of the pack."

"Top Dog" is an exercise that uses canine body language to communicate dominance. When interacting with older canines, a puppy avoids injury by dropping to the ground to expose its throat and abdomen. Adult dogs assume the juvenile posture to demonstrate submission to the pack leader—the top dog—and all other dominant pack members. The first stage of this exercise is to hold the very young puppy on its back in your arms. Refer to *Evaluating Natural Aptitude* for more information on this subject. For older puppies, gently but firmly place the puppy on its side while stroking it all over. The puppy that relaxes and submits to this control is acknowledging the pack hierarchy. The exercise can be practiced daily, not only as a gentle reminder of who is in charge, but also as a great opportunity to check your puppy for

Figure 8-2: *Puppy games or puppy problems?* **(a)** This innocent human is having fun; the canine is testing his playmate's strength and dominance. Better to develop positive rapport and leadership with less stressful games, such as retrieving and hide and seek. **(b)** Uncontrolled tugging and pulling can lead to problems such as hard mouthing or game release issues. However, some experienced top level obedience, agility and tracking trainers use tug as a reward, and so use such games to teach self control and obedience in high arousal circumstances. Tug is only played by strictly enforced rules; break the rules (tooth on skin, grabbing and not releasing or tugging on inappropriate object) and the game ends. It can easily be started at a low level and raised to very high levels of arousal. Children or inexperienced trainers should never participate in such games of strength or control, as the pup or young dog may learn that humans may be vulnerable or intimidated. Photographs by Shirley Nilsson.

Figure 8-3: ***Communicating leadership.*** **(a)** This puppy is learning to submit to his mother's discipline. **(b)** The "top dog" exercise uses similar canine body language to clarify who is the pack leader, with the added opportunity to check for fleas and ticks.

injuries and parasites. Puppies who experience this regular practice soon come to appreciate the attention.

The exercise called "Mother doesn't want you any more" will teach the puppy that even though she may be left alone for a little while, she is not abandoned, and that if she waits patiently and quietly, her owner will return. Tether the puppy to something sturdy—a stake or post—that allows her to move around freely but not escape. Secure the lead or rope—never a chain—close to the ground, using a flat collar—never a choke chain. Then, turn around and walk a distance away; initially, the owner will remain in view, but after a couple of successful lessons, the owner may disappear for a couple of minutes. Most puppies will begin to bark and complain. As soon as the puppy quiets down, the owner returns with low-key praise, and playtime ensues. After a few repetitions, the puppy's complaints should diminish as she comes to understand that she has not been abandoned and that barking and complaining will not get her owner to return. For the rare puppy that becomes seriously entangled or completely hysterical, obviously it would be necessary to return; a whistle or sharp clap should distract the puppy from her complaints long enough for the owner to return while she is quiet. However, the exercise should be repeated on another day, perhaps when she is a bit tired—not overtired—or with a calm older dog nearby to keep her company and set a good example. Routine practice for the puppy that does become hysterical should start with the owner a shorter distance away and should continue at a much slower pace, but the puppy must learn that she can be left alone and that she has not been truly abandoned. Some successful obedience trainers consider how quickly the puppy learns to wait calmly as an early measure of a puppy's future trainability.

Lead Training

Begin lead training as soon as the puppy is brought home. If already started by the breeder, training must be continued in the new environment. A strap or buckle collar (leather or nylon) is used for all early training. It gives adequate control until the puppy is 4–5 months old, and a puppy that receives early training rarely requires severe correction with a choke collar when older.

The best time for lessons is when the puppy needs to eliminate, again to establish a desirable association. Plus, a puppy that has no opportunity to eliminate on a lead grows into an adult that will not do so—a considerable inconvenience when traveling.

If the weather is bad, practice loose leash walking in the house. The puppy can learn a lot while going through the rooms of the house, just having the best time in the world strutting down the hall. If the breeder has not done any training, begin by attaching a lead or a rope with a knot in the end to the collar, and let the puppy get used to dragging something about. The puppy must be supervised because the dragging lead will get caught up in many things. Initially, the puppy resents this violation of freedom, and the objective is to avoid any unpleasant association with a human on the end of the lead. By the time the human has picked up the lead, the puppy has struggled with the door, the chair, and the bush, and the tug on the neck is old hat.

When the lead no longer disturbs the puppy, pick up the end and gently encourage the puppy to follow. Bend down for better eye contact, and use a coaxing tone to communicate encouragement and approval. Most Weimaraners are so eager for loving attention that they adore the new game; food treats, delivered while the puppy is in the proper heeling position, may encourage the reluctant student that this new game is fun and rewarding. If, however, the puppy fails to respond readily, go back to lead dragging for a while, or follow the puppy wherever it goes while you hold the lead.

Many Weimaraner puppies start out by grabbing the lead in play. They prance proudly, head and tail up, so very pleased with themselves. Never discourage this behavior. These puppies associate the lead with marvelous fun. Moreover, they cannot pull on the lead while carrying it, and they begin to learn to gait on a loose lead. The lead-carrying behavior is soon outgrown; hopefully, the happy, self-confident attitude toward on-lead work will not change. Even if the puppy will eventually be trained for obedience trials, this happy experience with lead training promotes a positive attitude toward later on-lead work.

As soon as the youngster follows willingly, begin conditioning the puppy to walk on the handler's left side. Instead of using the lead to move the puppy into the desired position, the trainer should turn with the puppy's moves so that it always ends up on the handler's left. This may require some fancy footwork, but in a surprisingly short time, the puppy becomes so accustomed to his position on the handler's left that any other position "feels" wrong. In other words, the puppy is easily conditioned to always move in the approximate heel position, convinced that this position is the one most likely to result in treats, and obedience heeling is then just a matter of a little polish.

Make lead work a pleasant occasion with lots of happy talk to keep the tail up and wagging. Happy chatter and frequent changes of pace will help keep the puppy's attention. Add interest by changing the location—a walk to the mailbox or the neighbor's house. Offer frequent treats when the puppy is on the left side, at least near the heel position. Keep the session brief, making a trip anywhere an exciting occasion that is associated with lots of praise and happiness.

Once the puppy has the basics, take the show on the road to expose the puppy to new noises and sights. Visit parks, shopping malls, and other locations with friendly people who can praise and offer treats the owner provides. Avoid dog parks and areas frequented by other dogs until after 3 months of age.

Figure 8-5: ***Condition the puppy to accept the lead*** by attaching a long sash cord line to the puppy's collar when outside. The puppy will learn to "give" to the pressure of the lead when it catches on obstructions; the owner can also step on the line to keep the puppy from straying too far.

Never let the puppy pull on the lead, an unpleasant habit that is easily avoided during early lead training; retractable leads encourage and reward puppies for pulling. Use a narrow leather or nylon lead—1/8″ is usually sufficient for 2- to 4-month-old puppies—with a lightweight snap. As soon as the lead becomes taut, give a sharp warning sound (see the boxed text, "A Special Sound," in *Getting Off to the Right Start*) followed by a quick tug if the puppy does not immediately respond, to communicate that this is unacceptable. The tug should be quick—as soon as the lead tightens—and be released immediately; it should be firm enough that the

Figure 8-4: ***Accepting the lead.*** **(a)** Well before the puppies leave for home many breeders begin pre-conditioning lead work. Closely supervised, and for very short periods of time, evenly matched pups (so neither has an advantage) begin to accept the restraint of the collar and lead. **(b)** Combined with early collar and lead conditioning, this pup's desire to be with his person will result in a puppy that will gait with a loose lead, or even a dropped lead.

puppy is aware of the correction. Again, a puppy that never learns to pull on the lead quickly becomes one that cannot imagine anything but a loose lead.

Lead pulling is minimized by frequent changes of direction and about-turns. When the puppy charges ahead, get its attention by saying, "Puppy, heel!" and turn in the opposite direction. This initiates the habit of being aware of the trainer's position and anticipating a change in direction.

If started early on lead work, there is a remarkable difference in the Weimaraner's attitude when gaiting in the show ring. To have a puppy with a happy tail carriage, one that gets out and looks good whether going around the block or the show ring, make the act of putting the lead on be an important and exciting event that signals going outdoors and having fun. Always put the lead on inside the house. Take the puppy outside and parade up and down for just a few minutes on a loose lead. Then, drop the end of the lead and let the puppy play. It is essential to put the lead on consistently before going outside to produce the consistently stylish response.

Figure 8-6: *A dog focused on its handler* will be more receptive to direction and less vulnerable to distractions. Teaching the "watch me" command is indispensable for everyday life, but it is also valuable in achieving top scores in obedience trials or in directional retrieving. To begin "watch me," Dennis, with his hands behind his back, drops a treat from his mouth to Miss Kitty.

All Done!

The puppy needs to learn a release command to indicate when an exercise has been completed. The dog cannot be under control at all times, and without a release command, the dog is left unsure about when attention and strict obedience are required. When the exercise is completed, the release command indicates that playtime is forthcoming and that focused attention is no longer required. "Okay" is common, but because it is frequently used in normal conversations and the puppy may be inadvertently released, another signal may be preferred, such as "all done," "break," "thank you," or even a sharp clap of the hands. With the puppy on lead in a boring environment, when the puppy is not engaged in play or focused on something else, say, "All done!" in an excited voice, then take several moments to engage in play with the puppy. It is important not to use a toy or game that could be confused in formal training or future competition in order to avoid having the puppy learn bad habits. Once the puppy understands the "All done!" command, it will then be clear during training that the exercise is finished. Playtime also offers the opportunity to relieve mental and physical stress and pressure, similar to a coffee break for a person. Giving the chance to "blow off steam" between exercises allows the trainer to work more frequently for longer periods of time and to practice more repetitions while maintaining the enthusiasm of the dog.

Watch Me

Having a dog that will look at the handler on command is valuable in many venues of competition, as well as in everyday life. The dog can be stopped and given directions where to search for a fallen bird. For the dog that loves to chase squirrels, the "watch me" command can abort the chase before it begins.

Teaching the basics of "watch me" is quite simple. Start with the puppy in front of the handler, with the handler's hands behind his back—this avoids having the puppy focus on the hands as a possible source for treats—and treats in the handler's mouth. Call the puppy, ask for a sit, and lean over to allow the puppy to get the smell of the treats in the handler's mouth. Give the "watch me" command; most puppies will automatically look up at the handler in anticipation of the forthcoming reward for the sit, and the odor of the treats will encourage the puppy's attention. When the puppy is looking up, the handler spits a treat out directly to the puppy from a very short distance away. Treats can be items such as small pieces of hot dog, liver, cheese, or chicken, or any small, tasty tidbit that is not objectionable to the handler. After a few repetitions, it will no longer be necessary to lean over; the puppy's attention will be riveted on the handler's face each time the "watch me" command is given in anticipation of treats flying through the air.

Not all commands are given with the puppy directly in front of the handler, so the handler needs to teach the puppy "watch me" from various positions. Once the puppy is responding immediately when the command is given with the puppy directly in front, try giving the command with the puppy at the handler's side or a short distance away. For the obedience prospect, "watch me" will aid in garnering the highest possible scores in the competition ring; in the show ring, "watch me" creates an eye-catching animation during the free-stack; and for the hunting Weimaraner, "watch me" is indispensable for directional retrieving performance.

Stand and Stay

The stand and stand-stay commands are combined with mealtimes to develop a conditioned association between food (pleasure and love) and the behavior. If done with only one meal a day, within a surprisingly short time, the puppy should not only master the commands but also be well started in show training and relaxed about being touched in every way. Practicing for three meals a day brings even faster results. Keep the lessons short and always pleasurable.

A grooming table is ideal but not inexpensive. A stiff outdoor welcome mat with a rough surface for good traction converts any dog crate into a training table.

At mealtime, place the puppy on the crate and hold the food dish about chest level. While the puppy eats, say, "Stand-stay!" and move one leg at a time into a comfortable, balanced standing position. If the puppy tries to sit, place a hand under the abdomen, then move the legs back again (see *Raising the Litter*). Touch the puppy all over, stroking the back and moving the feet. Pay particular attention to the tail, stroking the underside frequently to encourage the puppy to hold the tail erect, occasionally grasping the tail and pulling playfully. Weimaraners are typically shy about having their tails handled, and overcoming this tendency by developing an association between tail touching and pleasure pays dividends in the field (styling up), as well as in the show ring.

When the puppy finishes the food, set the dish aside and continue the stroking and handling for a short time while giving lots of praise.

To finish the lesson, gently touch the puppy's muzzle and say, "Let me see your teeth." Stroke the muzzle and gently raise the lips to check the bite. Being touched this way by a veterinarian, by you, or by a judge needs to be acceptable in the future.

Figure 8-7: *A table gives the trainer added control* while teaching many exercises; the training table (or NAVHDA retrieve table) shown here is preferred by field trial trainers and can be substituted for the grooming table. The ramp allows the puppy to climb on and off the table safely and be at eye-level with the trainer. Three-month-old Sarge showed great promise on the "whoa" command until the live bird appeared at eye level; with time and patience table training will help Sarge safely develop steadiness despite programmed increases of distraction and temptation.

Give lots of praise, lift the puppy from the crate, and go outdoors, ending on a happy note.

If the puppy tries to jump from the crate, allow a partial fall by holding the collar, letting the hind legs hang off, and encouraging it to scramble back onto the crate to get out of the uncomfortable predicament. The object of the lesson is that the handler is always in control, jumping off the crate is uncomfortable and ineffective, and the only way off the table is to be lifted down. If the puppy learns always to wait until being lifted off the table, the adult Weimaraner will, too.

Once the puppy understands the commands and seems confident while on the table, do the training before meals. Very gradually, begin to move away from the table while the puppy is on the stand-stay command. Step back to the table to touch the puppy, play with the tail, and walk away again. Give the puppy a release command. When the puppy is reasonably steady while you walk around the crate several times in either direction, move the mat to the floor. Only the perspective has changed. The handler is still in control, and the procedure is the same. Give the command, "Stand-stay!" while stroking and praising the puppy. If the puppy misbehaves and the transition is not smooth, merely go back to the top of the crate until the puppy is steadier and ready to make a smooth transition to the new situation. Again, keep the lessons short and happy. Short, frequent sessions are the

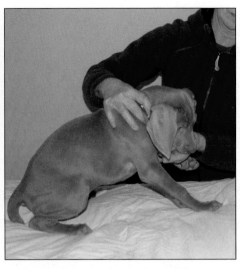

Figure 8-8: *with a very young puppy,* and should be fun and rewarding. Use a treat to coax the puppy into a down position, and reward profusely. A puppy that has been given this early conditioning will be less resistant to learning the down command when he is larger and stronger. Don't forget to teach a release command to make the end of the exercise clear. Photographs by Shirley Nilsson.

secret of successful training with any young puppy. The "stand-stay" is not only the beginning of the show career, it can also serve as the foundation for early field training, as well. In fieldwork, the command "whoa" is most commonly used. Trainers competing in fieldwork often use a specially constructed training table, shown in Figure 8-7, for this exercise.

To develop more advanced skills for the show ring—a longer stand and baiting—find a place where the lead can be tied to something, such as a doorknob. Tell the puppy, "Stand-stay," and move slightly away in front of the puppy. Toss a small treat to the attentive, motionless, standing puppy; discourage the tendency to sit by using a foot to gently raise the puppy back to a standing position and rewarding the puppy only while it is standing. In the beginning, the treat must be tossed a short distance and directly to the dog's mouth; catching treats is a learned skill. As training progresses, delay the reward. Place the treat on a chair; as the handler goes over the dog, as a judge would, the dog remains focused on the treat. Start with the familiar mat, but later, practice with a variety of surfaces. A dog with a steady "stand-stay" looks quite impressive in the show ring, allowing the handler to step away, leaving the statuesque presentation unobstructed by the handler's presence. The Weimaraner puppy properly trained to "whoa" on the table will be much easier to steady to wing and shot as a personal hunting companion or future field trial competitor.

Down and Stay

The "down" can be taught next. Say, "Down!" ("Platz," if the German command is preferred) and place the puppy in a "down" position. At this age, it is quite easy to force a down

position on the table by pressing down and back on the shoulders. Or, a tidbit can be used to coax the little one into a down position. Give the puppy the release command to indicate that the exercise is complete. Repeat, "Down-stay!" several times.

The "down-stay" progresses in the same manner as the "stand-stay," by slowly extending the time and circling the table as the puppy remains in the "down" position. If the puppy gets up, place the puppy back in the "down" and remain close by, asking for a shorter duration. Increase only time or distance, not both at the same time; do not extend the time or distance until the puppy is reliable at the current time and distance. The extended "down-stay" can be started on the table for up to several minutes; as the puppy becomes reliable, transition to the floor. "Down-stay" can be practiced in two contexts: the formal "down-stay" and the informal "place." For the formal "down-stay," progress in the same manner as the "stand-stay," above. This will be useful for the future obedience prospect, but also vital for other more controlled conditions outside the home, as well. The dog will be more comfortable on a "down-stay" for an extended period and will be more controlled while the owner's attention is diverted, perhaps while chatting with a neighbor, or writing a check at the veterinarian's.

Place

A marvelous behavior to teach your Weimaraner is the informal, relaxed stay or "place" command. It offers the option of keeping the dog from being underfoot without crating; he is still part of the family, but is just "hanging out," observing affairs without being in the way. If the dog is obnoxiously soliciting attention or is simply underfoot, the ability to send the dog to a specific place is invaluable. It provides a comfortable spot where the dog may rest, out of the way, and still be in the company of its "pack." Learning to accept this mild form of separation and control may also help forestall the possible development of separation anxiety, establish the leadership position of humans, and increase frustration tolerance in a dog on the way to being spoiled or overindulged.

The dog should have a bed or mat that marks his own place, much like a person's favorite chair. The author prefers the Quiet Time® pet beds (30" × 21" size works for all Weimaraners; a smaller size may be more convenient when the puppy first comes home) because they are comfortable for the dog and small enough to be easily machine washed; buy several so the dog has a "place" in each room in which he will be spending a lot of time.

Teaching "Place"

Place a pet bed near a favorite chair; choose a relatively quiet time during the household routine, such as watching TV or reading a book. Place the puppy on the pet bed and push him into a "down" position using the word "place" or "rest." For very young puppies, a leash can be used to secure the puppy to the chair; it may be convenient to temporarily "install" a leash for this purpose by looping the leash around the leg of the chair. If the puppy attempts to chew the leash, correct the puppy gently but firmly. If the puppy gets up, simply push the puppy back into position and repeat the command. Gradually increase the time the puppy is expected to stay in its place. Provide a favorite toy or chew so the time becomes a pleasant experience. Occasionally reach down to stroke the puppy and offer quiet—not stimulating—praise or a small treat; as an added incentive, the puppy may occasionally find a treat or toy waiting for him on the bed when he comes into the room. When the exercise is over, unsnap the leash and give the release cue to let the puppy know the exercise is over.

When the puppy is reliably staying on the mat for several minutes, practice with the owner standing up; if the puppy gets up, push him back into position. As the puppy learns his responsibility in the "place" game, move farther from the chair, and eventually the dog will stay in "place" until released, even when the owner is moving around the room or when the puppy is left alone in the room. When the puppy stays quietly without any reminders from the owner, the leash can be

(b) (right) Fearing her discipline, the puppies remain on the mat even after Lena leaves to fetch a new toy for the puppies to play with. Photographs by Virginia Alexander.

Figure 8-9: *Place.* (a) Another example of the strong tendency to mimic, young puppies may learn to wait quietly on a mat by imitating the mother or a responsible older mentor. The location of "place" will depend on what is convenient for the owner; in Germany, "place" is usually a small rug in the center of the kitchen area (left). Here, mother Lena is teaching her puppies to respect the "place" command, learned from her dam mother, who learned it from her mother....

Figure 8-10: ***To build a reliable recall response,*** practice with distractions. Have one person restrain the puppy while another builds enthusiasm with an inviting posture, treats, toys, and praise until the puppy's desire rockets him past the distraction. Start with simple distractions and slowly increase temptation and distance.

unsnapped from the collar, but it should be left on the chair for a while longer in case of a relapse. If the puppy approaches the pad on his own, quietly praise the puppy.

Many dogs come to think of the "place" as their favorite spot in the room; if the practice becomes routine, the puppy will quickly learn that when the people in the room are sitting and relaxed, the puppy should be playing or resting quietly on in his "place," too. This exercise can be started as early as 6 weeks, or when the puppy arrives in its new home; the sooner this exercise begins, the more automatic the behavior becomes. As the dog matures, he can be expected to remain in "place" for a longer time and when the owner leaves the room.

Sit

Most owners teach their puppy to sit before anything else—probably because this is the easiest of all commands. This gives the owners a feeling of achievement and fulfills a human need for control of the puppy. The "place" command serves the same purpose, with far greater long-term benefits.

The "sit" command may create confusion for the puppy being trained for the show ring or field. The show prospect must then be taught not to sit when being baited—considerably more difficult than teaching the show stance—and not to sit when the judge presses on the hindquarters. The "sit" causes even greater difficulties in the field trial prospect—sitting when being "styled up," or even when looking for praise. It is, however, invaluable in teaching the puppy an alternate behavior to jumping up on people.

Although countless dogs have been trained to sit by simply pushing on the hindquarters, field and obedience training experts consider this to be the least effective technique. Many trainers favor the "tuck" technique (Figure 8-11), which reduces the potential for confusion in the show ring or in field training.

Recall

If the Weimaraner knows no other command, the "recall" is the single most important; this command has saved the life of many a dog and the sanity of many an owner. The patterned behavior of coming without hesitation on cue should be started by the breeder, calling the puppies to come for food during the weaning process. These early experiences will be reinforced during playtime and then formal training sessions. As long as the owner maintains the positive associations, later in life, the dog will happily respond, reflexively, without even thinking.

There are several exercises the owner can use to teach the "recall;" this combination of exercises will help the puppy to generalize the behavior and respond under many different circumstances. For all the exercises, there are some basic guidelines. The puppy always succeeds; early in training, conditions are set up so the puppy cannot fail to respond appropriately. The owner must consciously appear to be inviting, kneeling down on the puppy's level, never looming or charging aggressively forward. The puppy is always rewarded, with no unpleasant consequences. Practice often, throughout the dog's life. For every "real" recall, when it is necessary for the dog to come, practice five or six times for fun.

Calling at Snack Times

Make wonderful reward associations for the puppy by calling the puppy for snacks. Have a helper hold the puppy a short distance away while the owner makes a big deal about getting out a treat. Call the puppy's name and "Come!" The helper releases the puppy on the word "come." Initially, reward the puppy as soon as it reaches the owner. Once the puppy is eagerly coming, the owner can ask for a specific behavior when the puppy arrives. If training for the show ring or field trial, reward the puppy for standing attentively in front of the owner; for the obedience prospect, lure the puppy into a sit with the treat. As the puppy begins to respond to the "come," the distance can be increased.

Restrained Recall

Similar to calling at snack time is the restrained recall. A helper holds the puppy while the owner entices the puppy with a toy or treats. While the puppy is focused on the treat, the owner runs away, encouraging the puppy by calling, "Puppy, puppy, puppy!" or other phrases. When 40 or 50 feet away from the puppy, the owner stops and turns, presenting the puppy with an inviting posture, and calls, "Rio, come!" in a pleasant and welcoming voice. The helper releases the puppy on the word "come," and the puppy races to the owner for treats, praise, and play. This is a very good exercise to use to help a puppy run past distractions—the bigger the distance to the owner, the more easily the pup will be able to resist the distraction. End this recall exercise before tiring the puppy out, while the game is still fun and the puppy is still fresh and eager.

Puppy Relays

A great way to get in many repetitions of the "recall" is the puppy relay. Have two people sit a short distance apart, 10–15 feet; each person has very small, especially enticing treats. While one person holds the puppy, the other calls, "Rio, come!" The helper releases the puppy on the word "come." The puppy runs the short distance; the helper quickly offers the small treat and then gently grasps the puppy's collar while the puppy is eating the treat. After the puppy has consumed the treat but before the puppy begins to squirm or stops paying attention, the other helper will call, "Rio, come!" Again, the puppy is released on the word

Figure 8-12: *Runaway puppy.* **(a)** Never chase after a puppy that refuses to come; better not to call the puppy if the odds are likely he won't respond. **(b)** But no puppy can resist a game of chase…turn and pretend to run away. When the puppy follows and arrives offer pets and treats. Best to practice recalls often in a safe place and release the puppy back to play.

"come," and the puppy races over to gobble the treat again. This game can be repeated several times, again ending the game before the puppy tires. Distance can be increased as the puppy gets older, even moving to different rooms. Make a habit of holding the collar in this exercise because it conditions the puppy to this action and reduces the possibility of the puppy's becoming hand shy.

With the young Weimaraner puppy, these exercises seem to create a much more enthusiastic recall than the commonly used "reel 'em in and grab 'em" technique.

In early training, call the puppy only when obedience is reasonable—for example, not when chasing a squirrel! It is advisable that very early lessons be conducted indoors, with minimal distractions.

Figure 8-11: *Adam avoids miscommunication with his the future field and show dog* by teaching Juno the tuck sit rather than pressing down on her rear. **(a)** With the collar behind the ears, tenderly "lift" with the right hand while gently applying pressure behind the stifles with the left hand. **(b)** Praise as the rump touches the ground. Photographs by Gene LaFollette.

Figure 8-13: *Lonely puppy?* Consider a feline friend. If another dog is out of the question, a cat may be the answer. When introduced as puppies and kittens usually they will become fast friends.

Practice the recall in a variety of locations, indoors and out, within the abilities of the puppy. Change the situation and change the circumstances.

Once the puppy is eagerly responding, offer variety in the rewards—belly rub, chest scratch, play with a toy, or the opportunity to return to play. The puppy will never know just what reward will be forthcoming and will be even more eager to come when called, even if it knows the owner does not have any food.

There are few things more exasperating than a puppy that responds with eye contact after a recall and then runs away. If the puppy likes to ride in the car and it is nearby, opening the door and calling, "Let's go bye-bye," usually brings the culprit on the run. Opening the house door might work as well. Never run after a puppy that is not responding. Movement toward the puppy communicates anger and aggression, whereas movement away from the puppy communicates lack of aggression and arouses the desire for pursuit and contact. Get the puppy's attention and start to move away from it. The puppy will begin to run after the trainer, who can turn around when the puppy catches up and make a big fuss about how good it is. Outside of training scenarios, when the owner may not be in complete control of the circumstances, it may be advisable to attach a long light line to the puppy's collar to ensure a prompt response to the first command.

Never punish the puppy when it eventually comes. The puppy understands only that it is being punished for coming. The puppy must always be received with praise for coming, no matter how great the urge to punish the animal, and it is better to omit all discipline than to diminish the puppy's response to the recall.

Separation Anxiety
What it is, what it is not

The canine evolved as a pack animal, with an inborn need to be near family; understandably, isolation can create distress for some dogs. Separation anxiety can occur in all breeds, mixed breeds, too. The Weimaraner tends to be unusually social with humans, bonding closely with its owners; as a result, it may be predisposed to suffer from separation anxiety. First of all, do not confuse separation anxiety with boredom or a lack of training. Many dogs can be destructive while their owner is away and not suffer the least pangs of fear or desperation. Nearly any dog, especially the young or old, may experience housetraining lapses if left in the house for long hours; canine operas may be a way to while away the lonely hours. The dog of any breed that truly suffers from separation anxiety is a different game altogether; while the dog may display destructive chewing or digging, excessive barking or howling, or housetraining lapses, the motivation is completely different. The barking is frantic in nature. The destruction is desperate, often displaying attempts to escape from the confinement that is separating the dog from its human companions. Physical symptoms of distress often accompany the behavioral signs—dilated pupils, panting, trembling, diarrhea, and excessive drooling—and may even begin before the owner leaves, perhaps while the owner is preparing breakfast or reading the newspaper. While rare, and ranging in degree from mild to extreme, true separation anxiety causes a dog to genuinely suffer emotionally and physiologically—and many compassionate owners suffer with them.

It is likely there are multiple reasons why dogs develop separation anxiety, perhaps a frightening or painful experience while home alone, a low tolerance for frustration, or maybe just a more dependent or nervous personality. Onset of separation anxiety may begin in puppyhood, where poor crate manners can create an escalating cycle of hysteria; however, it can also occur in mature dogs. It may begin all at once, full-blown, from a frightening event, or progress slowly after the death of a household companion. Sometimes an abrupt change in schedule or location can trigger the beginning of separation anxiety in a previously well-trained and reliable dog. Regardless, some thoughtful precautions on the part of the owner may help control or forestall the development of problems.

Prevention

Housetraining and crate training should be a basic for all dogs; read *Getting Off to the Right Start* for guidelines. Many Weimaraners seem to prefer the den-like quality of solid plastic crates over open wire crates. A wise breeder will have given the puppy a good head start by providing a doorless, den-like crate for the litter in the puppy pen. Puppies will often be found napping in a pile inside the crate. In the week or so before puppies leave for their new homes, a puppy and a littermate can be placed in the crate together for a short time with the door closed. Each puppy will then graduate to learning to spend a brief period of time alone in the crate with a special toy, such as a stuffed frozen Kong® or marrowbone or other interactive, entertaining prize. Remember that puppies are often indiscriminate chewers, so in the beginning it is unwise to offer the puppy an expensive crate cushion, as it may well end up shredded. Old towels or clean shredded paper offer a soft bed and can be easily washed or disposed of when soiled. The crate should be a place with positive associations, not a prison; puppies and adults who spend more time in a crate than out are at high risk for behavioral problems resulting from lack of mental and physical stimulation. If behavioral problems seem to be developing, consider doggie day care, or hire someone to come let the dog out during the day for a play period.

It is very important to routinely check the crate for "security breaches;" ensure that all bolts are tight and the door fits securely. Should the Weimaraner accidentally discover a slightly loosened bolt or door that can be worked free to provide escape, future efforts will be more sincere, and the likelihood of creating an "escape artist" increases with each successful breakout. The emancipation process itself can cause serious injuries, such as broken teeth, jaws, or toes, as well as lacerations, not to mention the cost of replacing crates and hardware.

Teach all dogs, regardless of age, appropriate items to chew on; chewing can actually help relieve stress and forestall a panic attack. Rotating a selection of special items helps keep them novel and interesting. Stuffing and freezing a Kong® or similar toy with peanut butter or canned dog food will keep the dog interested for even longer.

Exercise for dogs, like people, produces a sense of well-being and relaxation, and if a dog is a bit tired, she is more likely to take a nap than to worry about when the owner is coming home. The point of the exercise is to take the "edge" off an active dog and produce a sense of relaxation; the dog that is completely exhausted may become even more grumpy and irritable, just as a person would after unusual or extended exercise. An owner who has clearly defined the social rank of the members of the "pack" will help reduce the dog's overall stress level. Basic obedience exercises, such as retrieving, recalls, and walking on a loose leash, when conducted in a positive and fun manner, help clarify social rank and may help increase

Figure 8-14: *It's never too early.* Given a jumpstart from 6–12 weeks, with the right training and opportunities, develops a solid foundation for an exceptional future. **(a)** At 7 weeks, Pearl is full of promise. **(b)** Pearl would eventually be known as FC AFC Regen's Rip Tide, VCD2, TDX, UDX, RE, SH, SDX, RDX, VX3 Canadian titles OTCH, FDX, TDX, UTD, AgI, AgNJ

Figure 8-15: *Early exposure to wild birds* is vital to getting off to the right start. Here, Sage (CH Nani's Streak of Wise Moves, VCD1, RE, TDX, JH, MX, MXJ, NRD, VX3) meets her first bird at 10 weeks and gives solid notice of her future potential. Photograph by Terrie Borman.

the dog's frustration tolerance, as well, by teaching that "good things come to those who wait patiently and politely."

As much as possible, try to maintain a regular schedule for the dog's activities. A brief visit by a neighbor or friend can help if an unexpected schedule change prevents the owner from returning at the usual time.

One of the strongest cautions is to keep the emotional level of the owner's comings and goings low-key. Dramatic stroking and heart-rending monologues, intended to reassure, will actually increase the stress level for the dog. When arriving home, over-emotional, high-energy reunions convince most canines that the owner barely escaped the jaws of death. Instead, when departing, make it matter-of-fact, leaving the puppy secure in a crate or ex-pen with a wonderful toy, stuffed with a tasty filling—a reward for calm behavior and a distraction from the worrisome ponderings. While it may bruise human feelings, a dog may actually look forward to the tasty treats and some quiet time to enjoy them, a small price to pay for a dog that is comfortable and happy home alone. Upon the owner's return, a simple pat on the head and a hello are sufficient for the adult dog, and the puppy can wait patiently for a few moments, at least, before being escorted quietly out for a potty break. Save the playtime until the emotional level of homecoming has abated.

Treatment

While prevention is a far better course of action, treatment is most successful through early intervention. In mild cases, the dog may benefit from a companion, such as another dog or a cat; there is, however, the possibility that

the new housemate may imitate the distressed dog's behavior, so take all the appropriate precautions to prevent separation anxiety for the new dog. This is not a reason to purchase two puppies of the same age, which will simply result in the two puppies' learning bad habits from each other. It may seem contrary to human perception, but some dogs would actually rather not be "responsible" for having free access to an entire house and may be happier if confined to a portion of the house, a single room, or even a crate. The decision when to allow a dog more freedom is very much dependent on the dog, but any time there is a lapse of house manners, such as housetraining issues, inappropriate chewing, or excessive barking, immediate action, returning to the crate or restricting access to a small area, may forestall escalation. Dog-appeasing pheromones may be useful in preventing or treating the mildest cases. In some cases, doggie daycare may be an option, as well.

I'll Be Home Soon, by Dr. Patricia McConnell, is a great resource not only for preventing this distressing problem, but for offering a treatment program, as well. Separation anxiety is a situation in which prevention is immeasurably better than attempting to treat the problem. In some cases, the owner may wish to consult a professional behaviorist experienced in treating separation anxiety. Treatment should include a well-planned program of behavior modification, desensitization, and positive motivation; separation anxiety will never be cured by punishment or coercion. Medications may be used in the initial stages, but they are only a stopgap measure, not a cure. Medications should be proven to reduce anxiety, not to simply sedate the dog. Owners who are committed to helping their dog overcome separation anxiety will usually see at least some improvement.

For the Fun of It

It is no surprise that the easiest and best time to train Weimaraners is between the ages of 2 and 4 months, taking advantage of the breed's unusual dependency on humans during this stage. Habits—good and bad—a Weimaraner learns at this time tend to be lifelong. The blank slate of the kindergarten puppy offers the perfect opportunity to introduce vital skills needed for the future. Two of the most important—and fun—are the ability to use his nose and to pick up and carry a variety of objects.

It is common practice in early training for German hunters to hide, encouraging the young pup to use his nose to locate the owner. This early training sharpens the olfactory potential of the puppy as a working hunter in the field and may help the grown dog find his way back to the hunter should he become lost. There are many different opportunities to learn that using his nose can be fun and exciting. Finding people, treats, or toys will all pique the puppy's interest and desire: hidden treats under pillows, a toy tossed behind a bush, or discovering people who reward or play with the puppy while walking in the woods or fields. Most importantly, expose your young puppy to birds at this time to awaken the natural instinct to hunt through fun, positive experiences. Although the polished performance may require training when the pup has matured, these early experiences make a lifelong impression.

Although the Weimaraner is a natural retriever, reinforcing the puppy while young and anxious to please will help develop a Weimaraner that retrieves with joy and style. Give the young puppy the opportunity to fetch and carry a variety of objects in a fun and positive environment. Toss a small retrieving bumper into tall—but not too tall—grass, a toy behind a chair, and especially provide the puppy with the opportunity to fetch and carry birds. Experiencing the taste and feel of feathers as a youngster increases the likelihood of an adult dog that loves retrieving birds. It is important to stop the retrieving games while the puppy is still eager to avoid tiring the puppy, which wold take the fun out of the entertaining pastime.

A Weimaraner puppy is adorable and craves your attention and company. Problems are more easily prevented than cured; if the puppy is not supervised, provide a safe, secure place to stay where they cannot get into trouble. But, when things go wrong, remember that good manners are not inherent; a puppy—like a toddler—needs to be closely supervised to learn what is acceptable. Household manners are best learned through close supervision and firm, consistent management. The necessary obedience can be taught in short, fun lessons of 5 minutes or so, several times a day. This way the puppy comes to think of the time spent with the owner as the best part of the day, instead of dreading the time together if it is boring or uncomfortable. The kindergarten stage is one of rapid mental and physical growth and has some of the cutest and most rewarding days in the life of your puppy—make those memories fun and positive ones for puppy and handler.

Figure 8-16: *Encourage the puppy to pick up and carry* a variety of objects. Fun challenges lay the groundwork for demanding future performance. Here, 10-week-old Axel gives a hint of the VX title in his future. Photograph by Jurs Decker (Netherlands).

WILLIAM WEGMAN
Man's Best Friend

Figure 9-1: *Sport.* 2001 photograph by William Wegman.

CHAPTER 9

LIFE WITH WEIMARANERS

The Well-traveled Weimaraner

Car Care

The typical Weimaraner is crazy about riding in cars. Fortunately, car sickness is rare. For the first few trips, avoid feeding for 2–3 hours before departure, give the puppy a chance to eliminate just before leaving, and take along some paper towels in case of an accident. Dramamine® or ginger cookies before traveling can help alleviate travel misery.

A loose puppy in a moving vehicle is an accident waiting to happen. The puppy can cause the driver to swerve or lose control of the vehicle, and accidents have occurred because the puppy stood on the accelerator. For the safety of the puppy, the passengers, and all other vehicles on the road, the puppy must be restrained while the vehicle is moving. A dog crate is ideal for cars and mandatory if the dog must ride in the back of a pickup.

In vehicles that cannot accommodate a Weimaraner-sized dog crate, other measures must be employed until the puppy learns to ride quietly. Currently, traveling harnesses are available that secure the dog using the seat belt. Be sure to arrange the seat belt to prevent your Weimaraner from getting access to buttons or handles that could lock or unlock the doors. In an emergency, if no crate or harness is available, place the puppy in the back seat of the vehicle with a lead or rope (sturdy enough that it cannot be chewed through before the driver notices) attached to the strap collar. Secure the lead by closing a back door on the end of the lead (tie a knot to prevent slippage) or in some other manner that keeps the puppy from jumping into the front seat with the driver. Leave enough slack for the puppy to move around and climb to the seat from the floor, but not enough to jump into the front. An old blanket or mat helps the puppy identify its special place in the car and also minimizes soiling the interior with wet or muddy feet.

When the car is parked, release the puppy to prevent accidental injury while it is alone. Invariably, the puppy will jump into the front seat, usually sitting behind the steering wheel.

Car windows can be opened all the way if the puppy is in a crate, but even this may not ensure enough ventilation on a hot day. If a dog's body temperature reaches 107°F–108°F, irreversible brain damage occurs within minutes.

- When the outdoor temperature is 85°F, the interior of a car parked in the sun reaches 102°F within 10 minutes if the window is cracked, less if not cracked.
- When the outdoor temperature is 105°F, the car interior reaches 215°F within 2 minutes.[1]

It is far better to leave the Weimaraner at home when running summer errands than to join the ranks of heart-broken owners who have thoughtlessly killed their beloved pets by leaving them in a car.

Figure 9-2: *Puppies often feel safe in a small comforting space,* but a den-like plastic crate is probably a safer choice for traveling home with your new puppy. A positive experience on what may be his first car ride could prevent a problem with carsickness in the future. The same is true once you arrive home, the cave-like airline crate is more reassuring than the open wire crates for your puppy's "safe space" at home. Photograph by Williams Wegman.

Figure 9-3: ***Car control without a crate.*** Car harnesses have now become available and can control a dog in the car. A harness does no good if the dog is not buckled in. If neither harness nor crate is available, a knotted leash secured by shutting the door on it can be a temporary substitute. Photograph by Karen Millan.

if it barks when alone—leave the dog in the car (parked away from the rooms) while eating, or eat in the room; and (c) pick up the dog's droppings.

Air Travel

In general, when shipping a Weimaraner by air, expect the unexpected, and be prepared for last-minute changes of plans.

The Reservation

Begin making travel arrangements as early as possible. The United States Department of Agriculture requires all dogs being transported by air to have a health certificate issued no more than 10 days prior to the trip. Without a health certificate, the dog is not going anywhere. The shot or health record is not sufficient. Be sure to have the veterinarian include a phrase indicating that the dog is accustomed to the range of temperatures to be expected during transportation; without this phrase, the dog may be denied travel in spite of the health certificate. Be sure to have more than one copy of the health certificate in case the original becomes lost, or if it becomes necessary to present a copy of the certificate upon arrival.

Shop as many airlines as possible; there may be a tremendous difference in price and schedules. Have the exact dimensions of the crate and the dog's weight when asking for prices. A direct flight is preferred, even if it costs more; if a

Travel Tips

Some Weimaraners do not tolerate changes of water, and a sick dog can ruin a vacation. When traveling a long distance, try to carry enough water for the entire trip. If this is impossible, mix the home water with small amounts of new water along the way—as little as possible. Purchasing bottled water along the way is also an option.

When making room reservations, ask whether dogs are welcome and request a secluded ground-level room; many motels that seem reluctant when asked will accept the reservation if assured that the dog will be crated while in the room. Frequent travelers can invest in *Touring with Towser*, a directory of hotels and motels that welcome pets.[2] Many hotels are denying travelers with pets due to the carelessness or the lack of consideration of a few. Good motel manners for dog owners include the following: (a) never leave an uncrated Weimaraner alone in the room; (b) never leave the dog in the room

Figure 9-4: ***Rosie rides comfortably*** in the back seat of her owner's car while wearing a stylish padded harness that attaches to the seat belt. You will find that after being released when the car is parked, Rosie, like most Weimaraners, sits confidently behind the steering wheel.

Figure 9-5: *A crate is preferred* for the well-traveled Weimaraner in the United States. Young Argon von Walhalla, however, recently imported from Germany by Debbie Andrews, has already learned a customary method of transportation in a country where car space is at a premium and crates are not as common. Puppies are taught self-control as early as 5 or 6 weeks, learning to wait quietly on command, resulting in dogs that are welcomed in nearly all public places, including stores and restaurants. *The German Weimaraner Today* gives other illustrations and explains more of these training practices. Photograph by Debbie Andrews.

direct flight is not possible, be sure there is adequate time for the plane change. When shopping flights, consider that it may be less expensive for a person to fly with the dog as excess baggage than to ship the dog as cargo, especially when shipping more than one dog; verify that the airline will charge only as excess baggage and not charge cargo rates if considering this option. The prospect of a free round trip to preferred locations will likely produce volunteers eager to escort the dog to its destination.

Some airlines will accept only a certain number of dogs for shipment on a single flight; verify whether this is the case. Make reservations well in advance, and be sure to arrive early; this is especially important if the dog is traveling as excess baggage.

Locate the drop-off location well before the actual shipping date; the shipping offices are often hard to locate. Arrive at least 2 hours prior to departure time. Some airlines also offer an online tracking service. Many airlines restrict travel during the hottest and coldest months of the year, or based on the predicted temperatures for the cities the dog is stopping in; on the day of travel, verify with the airline before leaving for the shipping office that temperatures will be within the allowable range, and confirm the reservation. Currently, air travel regulations are in a state of flux and are always subject to change. Be sure to check with the particular airline for the most up-to-date regulations and requirements. Consider purchasing additional insurance, at least double the purchase price of the dog.

If planning to travel with the dog as excess baggage, make a reservation for the dog when buying the tickets—some airlines limit the number of animals on each flight. Only very young Weimaraner puppies can meet the airlines' requirement that carry-on pets be confined in a container able to fit under the passenger's seat during take-off and landing.

The Crate

The crate-trained Weimaraner—adult and puppy—experiences minimal stress when being shipped in the security of its personal den. A favorite blanket, a bone, and a few toys also help to reduce stress. Wire crates do not meet airline regulations. Shipping crates must meet all the following specifications. The crate must:

Figure 9-6: *The spring latches of fiberglass crates* sometimes break during shipping, so for extra insurance, firmly fasten a lead across the front. Current security measures require that the bedding and the interior of the crate be inspected, and perhaps even the dog itself, so be sure to have an extra collar and lead handy. Consider replacing the standard nuts and bolts with heavy zip ties for additional security. Zip ties can also be used through the door grate and postholes.

- Be sturdy, leak-proof, properly ventilated, and large enough for the dog to be able to stand with head erect, turn around, and lie down in a normal, comfortable position
- Have ventilation on all four sides; it will be necessary to drill holes on the back side of most plastic crates
- Close securely with a latch that requires no special tools to open
- Have an empty water dish accessible from the outside.
- Contain absorbent material (shredded newspapers will do)
- Display feeding instructions, even instructions stating that the dog is to receive neither food nor water; attach a day's supply of food and water firmly to the crate in case of emergency

For your dog's comfort in the crate, take away all food at least 4 hours before travel begins. Dogs are less stressed by hunger and thirst during shipping than from the need to eliminate. The last thing before leaving the dog with the airline is give the dog the chance to relieve himself; if necessary, use the "match trick" discussed in *Showing the Weimaraner*. Most airlines will not accept animals under sedation. Make sure the dog is accustomed to the crate well before traveling so that the crate provides the dog with a sense of comfort and security.

The size 400 kennel is usually adequate for most Weimaraners, except the largest males. However, be sure to

have the larger size 500 crate available at the time of drop-off; if at the time of shipment the cargo personnel determine a larger crate is necessary, it will be very expensive to purchase one from the airline. At the time of reservation, verify that the airline equipment will accept both the size 400 and 500 kennel if there is a possibility that the larger crate will be necessary.

Crate latches can be damaged in transit, and securing the crate door with a lead (or elastic cord), as shown in Figure 9-6, may prevent your dog from getting loose at the airport. Except for very young puppies, dogs should always wear a strap collar with an identification tag in case of escape, as well as for attaching a lead when opening the crate.

On Arrival

The shipper should wait until the plane has actually departed and check to be sure that the dog was actually placed on the flight. Be sure the person picking up the dog has the waybill number and flight information, as well as a method to contact the shipper at any time during the trip. A call as soon as possible upon arrival will minimize stress to the shipper.

Picking up a strange Weimaraner at an airport can be particularly hazardous if the Weimaraner is more than a few months old. Even one accustomed to crates may not behave rationally, and if possible, the dog should be left in the crate until it can be brought into the house or fenced yard.

If it is necessary to release the dog from the crate at the airport, do so only in an enclosed area, anticipating that the dog might bolt. To remove the dog from the crate, open the door just enough to snap a lead to the strap collar.

Form a noose by pulling a length of the lead through the handle and slip it over the head just behind the ears as the dog steps out; this also prevents the collar from slipping off if the dog pulls back.

The typical Weimaraner has enough self-confidence to step out of the crate and attach itself to the first friendly face it sees, but always anticipate and be prepared for the worst possible scenario.

Many airlines insist that the person receiving the dog sign a statement that it arrived in good health before releasing it. At least insist that the dog is standing up in the crate before signing. Otherwise, there is not much that can be done except to check the dog more carefully before leaving and start a riot (get some witnesses) if the dog appears ill.

"In-Cabin" Travel with a Puppy

For very young puppies, in-cabin travel should be considered. Some breeders will insist on meeting the purchaser in person, allowing the puppy to accompany the buyer in the cabin for the return trip. Make travel arrangements as early as possible. Many airlines limit the number of in-cabin animals, so be sure to inform the airline that the puppy will be traveling home. Special pre-travel arrangements will make the trip easier. Feed the puppy a larger-than-normal meal the night before and a small snack of its regular food and a brief drink the morning of travel—no food within 4 hours of travel. Do everything possible to get the puppy to have a bowel movement before leaving home; use the "match trick" in *Showing the Weimaraner,* if necessary. Give the puppy the opportunity to urinate right before going to the airline gate.

Carry a small bag of the puppy's regular food to offer a restless or very hungry puppy during travel. For the very thirsty puppy, offer only a very small amount of water; ice is preferred. If possible, request a small bottle of water from airline staff; save the remainder of the bottle to offer the puppy shortly after landing. If during travel the puppy becomes restless, indicating the need to urinate, securely hold the puppy over the toilet or spread a very heavy layer of newspaper on the lavatory floor; the elimination reflex may be stimulated by wiping the puppy's genitals, mommy-style, with a warm, moistened paper towel.

Purchase a special Sherpa soft-sided carrying case designed specifically for air travel to ensure it will fit under the seat—because of variations in seating among airlines, occasionally, the under-seat hard-sided crates do not fit. A carrier with top and side zippers will provide the greatest comfort and convenience for the traveler and the puppy. A few essentials can increase comfort during the trip: a medium-sized towel so the puppy can sit comfortably in the owner's lap, chew toys, a small bag of food, newspapers, and a collar and leash. Indicate contact information on the carrier. Be a polite passenger by boarding as discretely as possible; puppies can be a big distraction to other boarding passengers, and you want to minimize potential hassles from airline staff regarding the size and weight of the puppy in relation to the carrier. Keep the puppy and carrier in your possession until after take-off; handing the puppy off to airline staff may result in the puppy's being stowed in baggage.

Lost Weimaraner

The repairman left the front door open, the meter reader left the back gate open, a tree knocked down the fence, a rabbit chase lured the dog too far—these are only a few of the many ways in which Weimaraners can get lost. A lost or roaming Weimaraner risks injury or death from many sources; an effective plan can help get a dog home sooner.

When the author's bitch, Chanty, escaped from her handler at an interstate rest area in another state, she contacted John Keane, who has a professional pet-finding business, "Sherlock Bones." Keane feels a search should focus on two goals: (a) making people aware the dog is lost; and (b) motivating people to find and return the dog. Keane divides people into two groups—those who love animals and those who are indifferent. Since he believes only about 3% of people fall into the animal lover category, search efforts must motivate the other 97% to take an interest.

Flyers should be printed in black and red on white paper to be attention grabbing and easy to read. The flyer should clearly state that a reward will be paid "for information leading to the return of" the pet. This will help motivate the 97% to view the dog seen running down the street or raiding garbage cans as potentially profitable instead of just a nuisance.

If a good photograph of the dog is not available, any breed photo will suffice. Weimaraner owners have found the description "gray ghosts about the size of a Labrador Retriever, long ears, short tail" to be effective. In addition, stating the dog must receive medication decreases the attraction to anyone who might think about keeping the lost Weimaraner.

Keane suggests the following information about how and where to post flyers:

- Staple them to telephone and light poles (where permitted) low enough that they can be read by passing motorists—especially at stop lights
- Post them in grocery stores—everybody buys food
- Distribute them at schools—kids are wonderful at finding lost dogs
- Veterinary clinics—if the dog is injured, someone might take it in for treatment
- Place an advertisement in local papers

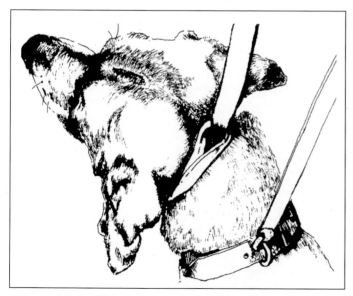

Figure 9-7: *To safely remove a strange, possibly frightened, dog* from a crate, draw the lead through the handle to make a noose that can be quickly slipped over the dog's head before snapping the lead to the collar's ring. This will not only ensure control of the dog but also will prevent a loose collar from slipping over the dog's head if the dog pulls back hard.

Steps and Strategies of an Effective Search

Phase 1. *When the dog disappears, move quickly, before the dog has time to go far. Remember, 90% of lost dogs are found less than 2 miles away. Mobilize help—family, friends, neighbors, and breed-club members—and assign different tasks.*

- Leave the dog's crate—with the door open—at the spot it was last seen, with articles of clothing bearing your scent.
- Walk and drive through the neighborhood calling the dog.
- If the dog is friendly with strangers, check parks and schools.
- If the dog is shy, frightened, or might be injured, check places that offer seclusion.
- Notify all residents in the immediate area to be on the lookout for the lost dog, leaving a written description, name, veterinarian's name, and phone numbers (to make copies quickly, type the information about eight times on an 8 1/2" × 11" master that can be photocopied and cut into smaller pieces).
- Try to locate someone with a trained tracking dog; if you do not know anyone, contact the local Search-and-Rescue organization or pet finder.
- Contact emergency animal hospitals, leaving information and stating that you will be responsible for any medical care your dog might need.

Phase 2. *If the dog is not found within a few hours, begin more organized measures.*

- Notify county animal control officials and all local animal shelters; policies vary, so ask questions and keep a record of each one—some maintain lost-dog reports with the description and contact owners if it is brought in; some only contact owners of dogs with license tags; others must be contacted daily.
- Notify all law-enforcement agencies—police, highway patrol, and sheriffs cover different areas.
- Place advertisements offering a reward for information leading to the dog's recovery in all local papers.
- Ask the newspapers for names of delivery people in the area and notify them.
- Check with radio and television stations—some broadcast news about missing pets.
- Notify local dog clubs—all-breed as well as specialty.
- Print and distribute flyers—most people use about 2,000.
- If you do not already have an answering machine, consider buying one so no calls are missed.
- Check out all leads, no matter how remote they seem.
- Consider consulting a professional.
- A psychic might be able to describe what the dog can see and hear—and confirm that it is still alive.

Phase 3. *If the dog is not recovered within several days or a week, it might have left the immediate area or the finder might have kept it. Remember, lost dogs have been recovered after more than 6 months.*

- Pets have been recovered 300 miles or more from where they disappeared, so expand the search—newspaper ads, all-breed and specialty dog clubs, law enforcement agencies, animal shelters, national park officials, veterinarians, and veterinary schools.
- Notify regional organizations that alert places that use dogs for experimentation, giving a description and tattoo number.
- Pray a lot, and do not give up hope!

Once your dog is lost, a collar, tags, tattoo, and microchip could be your dog's ticket home. Keep the registration information current! If the information has lapsed, call the registry as soon as the dog goes missing. Most registries are determined to reunite dogs with owners. One Weimaraner owner received a call from a registry asking if the dog was missing. It turned out that a male Weimaraner had been injured while roaming and the microchip had been damaged, offering only a partial number. The registry was calling every contact for male Weimaraners that had numbers matching the partial number. The author includes a collar and tag with the name "Reward" with the placement of every adult dog; this has resulted in the return of many a lost dog. Be sure that the phone number on the tag is manned or has a reliable answering machine while the search is underway. If a dog is covered by pet health insurance, be sure to indicate the agency on the tag; not only does this increase the possibility of getting care if the dog is injured, it also offers a means of contact with the owner.

Call all the local animal shelters and animal control centers within at least a 50-mile radius. Visit in person as often as possible; many shelter workers are not familiar with different or unusual breeds. Notify the Weimaraner

Figure 9-8: *A two-color flyer* illustrates the design John Keane has found most eye-catching—"REWARD" and "For information leading to the return of this lost pet" in red, with the balance in black on white paper.

Foundation and local breed-rescue groups, and post the notice on Internet lists to marshal volunteers in the area who may be able to help; sometimes, shelters contact rescue groups as soon as a Weimaraner arrives. Contact your veterinarian in case someone calls the number on the rabies tag.

On the 9th day of Chanty's misadventure, someone saw the flyer, realized the starving dog hanging around was worth some money, and called. John Keane was right about the importance of monetary motivation in the recovery of lost pets, but a friend who cared posted the flyer.

Most important, never give up; some dogs have been reunited with their owners as much as a year later.

Tattoos and Other Identification

A flank tattoo is without question the best single method of identifying a dog. One type of tattoo employs a multiple needle punch on the dog's ear. In addition to horror stories of ears cut off to remove tattoos, this is not recommended for Weimaraners because injury to the ear's vascular network seems to predispose long-eared breeds to hematomas later in life. Therefore, the procedure of choice is done with a standard tattoo needle on the inner thigh.

Although the ideal time to tattoo a dog is when it is anesthetized for any other reason, such as hip X-rays, a puppy can be tattooed any time after 6 months. Waiting until after 6 months will avoid the tattoo's "stretching" and becoming unsightly or unreadable as the tattoo grows with the puppy. Local dog clubs often host tattoo clinics.

Any tattoo is better than none. Owners debate the advantages of using the dog's AKC number, the owner's social security, or a national registry number. The author highly recommends using the letters "AKC" and the dog's registration number for several reasons:

- The tattoo does not require any special equipment to read
- The dog is uniquely identified even if the collar is lost

Figure 9-9: ***The best name on a dog's tag is "REWARD."*** Along with an 800 number, this simple inscription has reunited many dogs with the owner. This author gives a collar and tag with this inscription whenever placing an adult dog or rescue dog in a new home. While searching for a lost dog, be sure there is someone to answer the phone or that you have a reliable message machine.

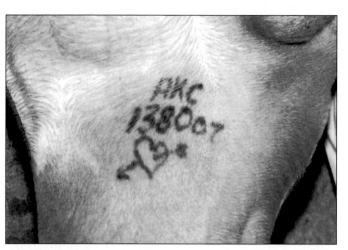

Figure 9-10: ***Tattoo.*** Often omitted, the letters "AKC" are a necessary clue to reunite a dog and owner. The letters "AKC" with the registration number are the most effective tattoo when applied to the inner thigh.

- The AKC will contact the registered owner or breeder and give them the name and phone number of someone who has found a dog tattooed with an AKC registration number
- The AKC is well known, and it is easier to locate a phone number for the AKC than to figure out how to contact a national registry
- When an owner dies, is incapacitated, or is absent, a tattoo with the AKC number is often the only way to prove the dog's identity if the owner has several of the same breed

The latest development in animal identification (dogs, cats, horses, exotics) is the microchip. Each chip contains a unique number that is registered to identify the animal carrying the microchip. The owner's name and contact information are registered, as well as alternate contact information. Microchips, tattoos, or other permanent identification are required by OFA before X-rays can be submitted.

The procedure is simple. Using a disposable, preloaded syringe, the chip is inserted under the skin between the shoulder blades of the dog—the procedure is no more uncomfortable than any other injection. It is vitally important that the owner register the chip after implantation; otherwise, the chip will be valueless. The wise breeder can purchase the chips at a special rate, with a prepaid registration fee (www.revivalanimal.com), and have them inserted by the veterinarian at the final health check before the puppies leave for new homes. The breeder thus ensures that if the new owner fails to re-register the chip, the puppy can at least be reunited with the breeder, who was identified at the original chip registration.

The chips are virtually impossible to remove, even under special conditions and using the most advanced technology.

Once injected, the chip becomes encased in a thin layer of protein that anchors it in place for the animal's lifetime. On occasion, chips can "migrate" from the original injection site, so it is advisable to verify the chip's location when the dog is in for its annual health check-up.

Special readers recover the information on the chip. At this time, there are two major manufacturers of microchips in the United States, Avid and Home Again. Information regarding the purchase of scanners and chips may be obtained from a veterinarian.

Even with tattoos and microchips, owners should not overlook basic identification methods. Every Weimaraner should wear a strap collar with an identification tag—the best name is REWARD—and a license tag at all times. If a neighbor checks the tag of a stray Weimaraner, she can bring the wanderer directly home. Keep a record of the dog's current license number in an easy-to-find location, and report that number to rabies control when the dog disappears; they may be able to refer a finder who calls in and save you a trip to the shelter.

To strangers, all Weimaraners look alike. The owner with 20/20 foresight who can provide a clear description of the ways in which her dog is unlike others of the same breed is far more likely to recover it. Everybody takes pictures of their pets, so be sure that the photo album includes several of the dog's distinctive physical features—all markings, scars, cowlicks—and a head shot showing the ear set and shape. Keep a written record of other physical features, such as white on the back of the pasterns, white hairs or pigment on the abdomen, tail length, normal weight, and bite abnormalities, such as missing or broken teeth.

Problem Behaviors

Forbidden Territory

Soon after a puppy is big enough to climb on furniture, it will be smart enough to stay off of forbidden furniture as long as the family is around, but will sneak up as soon as no one is watching. Counter-surfing is also an easily acquired and self-reinforcing habit. It may also be desirable to keep the Weimaraner out of particular rooms. Many training aids are available in dog catalogs to discourage dogs from furniture or other undesired areas: scat mats, ultrasonic noisemakers, and snappy traps (oversized mousetraps with protective bales), for example. All these items depend on the diligence of the owner to set them in place every single time the owner will be away. Prevention is easier than untraining this habit, but no plan will be successful without total compliance from all members of the household.

Barking

Excessive barking is the second most common reason dogs are surrendered to shelters. As more and more dog owners live in multiple-family dwellings or smaller city lots, the possibility of a dog creating a noise issue increases with reduced exercise opportunities and increased proximity to neighbors. Excessive barking leaves the owner with few choices, often boiling down to choosing between relocating, surrendering the pet, or committing to a training program.

Sometimes all the dog needs is more exercise while the owners are at home, combined with engaging toys and activities to amuse the bored canine when home alone. A regular routine also helps reduce barking. Pet-sitting videos are available and may be popular with less-active breeds, but some Weimaraners may consider these to be interactive and decide to give chase to the interesting critters or participate in the apparently enjoyable activities, causing destruction to the electronic equipment. Many times just leaving the television on and tuned to a music station or non-stimulating regular programming—perhaps the dog will become a soap opera fan—gives the dog the sense of human activity. If a secure outside area is available, a doggie door may provide the Weimaraner with alternate distractions while the owner is away. An owner may decide to invest in a pet-sitting service or doggie daycare.

Bark collars can be successful, but they do have limitations. The collar is a training tool and should not be left on the dog for more than 8 hours at a time. Many different types of collars are available. Most give a warning tone and allow single or alarm barking, but correct repeated barking.

Figure 9-11: *A simple carpet runner,* turned bottom side up, makes a soft couch much less desirable to a Weimaraner. Electronic mats are available from most pet suppliers to discourage the truly determined Weimaraner. Just do not forget to remove these training aids when people want to sit on the couch! Photograph by Shirley Nilsson.

Figure 9-12: *The best way to prevent the habit of jumping up* on people is to start very young, by teaching the puppy to sit. As the puppy approaches, it is cued to sit before jumping up. A puppy in this position cannot jump up, and sitting becomes more rewarding than jumping up. Photograph by Shirley Nilsson.

Newer models have a wide range of adjustments to accommodate both very soft and very hard dogs; some even adapt to the bark pattern of the dog, increasing the correction if the barking persists—these types seem to be most successful for extreme cases. Currently, collars use three different methods for correcting the dogs: electronic correction, noise correction, and citronella spray. Electronic corrections appear to be more effective than the alternatives. It is very important to follow the manufacturers' instructions in the training program for greatest success; continued maintenance training is usually necessary. For the very smart Weimaraner, it is sometimes sufficient to simply leave the collar in plain sight after the initial training period. Collars can provide a humane and consistent approach to eliminating a barking problem with a Weimaraner.

Should all else fail, an owner may decide to confine the dog to an area of the house to minimize the neighbors' perception of annoying barking. Teaching the puppy good manners from the beginning can avert the need to deal with this challenging problem. Never let the young puppy learn that the owner will give in to continued barking; never allow the puppy out of a crate or back into the house while it is barking; wait until the dog is quiet.

Jumping

All friendly dogs jump up on people in greeting and excitement, but Weimaraners also jump to get a closer view

Figure 9-13: *When the Weimaraner jumps up,* catch his paws and hold the paws for 2–3 minutes while turning your face away to deny him the pleasure of seeing the person's face.

of facial expressions. Some people do not mind the small puppy greeting people with this behavior, and after all, what harm can a small puppy do? If sharp puppy toenails are not enough to make the owner want to discourage this habit, imagining the 50-pound adolescent jumping up on Grandma should be persuasive. Teaching a puppy not to jump up in greeting is far easier than teaching a strong adult dog in which this habit has become ingrained.

With puppies, minimize situations that stimulate jumping and habit formation. When possible, simply crouch when the puppy approaches, so there is no need to jump up in greeting, then pet the puppy and move away.

Teach "Sit"

A classic method of problem control is to teach the animal to do something incompatible with the undesired behavior; a puppy that is sitting is not jumping up. Teach the puppy to sit by luring the puppy into a sit position with a treat or by using the method illustrated in *Weimaraner Kindergarten.* Once the puppy is sitting reliably on cue, when

Figure 9-14: *Waiting at the door* is an important safety precaution for dogs as well as people; door manners are essential in multiple-dog households. Slate has learned since puppyhood to wait politely for permission to go through the door. Habits learned while young remain strong with regular reinforcement throughout life. Photograph by Nick Ambulos.

the puppy comes running to greet someone, the cue to sit can be given before the puppy jumps up in greeting. Watch for the rump to drop as the puppy shifts the weight to the hind legs, so the puppy is already halfway to the sit. When the puppy is sitting quietly, praise it and offer a treat. If everyone who meets the puppy consistently follows this program, it will not be long before the puppy greets new people with a polite sit instead of jumping up.

Knee Bumping

If the opportunity to give the sit cue has passed, and the puppy already has its front feet off the ground, an effective technique, especially when used consistently, is lifting one knee so that the leaping dog strikes the person's leg with the force of its own momentum. Consistent correction by all members of the family and a few strangers during the first few weeks establishes a lifelong pattern of behavior. Warning: with this technique, there is danger that a strong blow on the chest can cause internal injuries, such as a diaphragmatic hernia. Be sure the dog strikes the front part of the person's leg and not the knee.

Holding the Paws

When all else has failed and the dog has already gotten his feet up on the person, another corrective technique works well with Weimaraners. When the dog jumps, catch the paws while turning your face away to deny the dog's desire to view facial expressions. The Weimaraner's initial pleasure at not being rebuffed quickly turns to dismay at being unable to get down, and the struggle begins. Be prepared to hold the dog for 2–3 minutes to make sure that the dog is thoroughly disgusted with the situation.

Door Dashing

Dashing out the door as it opens is dangerous for people and dogs on either side of the door; furthermore, the dog may become lost or run into the street and be struck by a car. Additionally, altercations between dogs passing through doorways are one of the most common problem points in multiple-dog families, as emotions spiral upward in the excitement of going somewhere.

Every dog should therefore learn to sit and wait politely for the leash to be attached or for permission to pass through. The owner should pass through the door while the dog is waiting to be released and vary the amount of time the dog must wait to develop reliability. This easy-to-learn exercise is second in importance only to teaching the dog to come when called.

Young Weimaraners are most responsive to the following technique:

- With the puppy on lead, open the door a few inches
- When the puppy starts through the door, try to close the door so that it catches the puppy at the neck
- Hold the door firmly enough that the puppy struggles and panics
- Release the puppy, move well away from the door, and give lots of comfort, communicating that the puppy's fear is justified, that it has survived a very dangerous experience
- Repeat the exercise until the puppy no longer tries to go through the door—once is sometimes enough
- Reinforce the impression of danger by approaching the door and slamming it loudly as the puppy comes close
- When the puppy is convinced that the door is dangerous, the owner appears to be the protector who will escort the puppy through the dangerous area
- When the puppy is reliably waiting at the door for permission to go out, introduce the sit command before reaching for the doorknob. If the same routine is followed each time, the puppy will learn to automatically sit and wait for permission at the door

- Practice frequently—throughout the dog's life— and from both sides of the door, varying the time before the puppy is released

Begging

Weimaraners are intelligent creatures, and it does not take them long to figure out that the dinner table is a potential bonanza. Decide from the beginning whether the dog will be allowed to participate in family meals. If this behavior will be allowed, be prepared to have dinner stolen right off the table, to be the subject of an intense and soulful gaze, and to drown in copious puddles of dog drool. These behaviors are easy enough to avoid by crating the dog during mealtimes or teaching the dog to leave the dining room while the family is eating. If the dog is never fed from the table, the idea is less likely to develop.

Pawing

"High five" and "shake hands" are among the most commonly taught tricks for a Weimaraner because the behavior occurs so naturally. The catlike use of paws is a typical Weimaraner mannerism, and "high five" and shaking hands reinforce the inherent tendency to demand attention with the paw. Very cute in the puppy, in an adult this habit can quickly become more than an annoyance. Long or short, being raked by a Weimaraner's nails hurts! It also tears pockets and rips clothing. If the "shake" or "high five" has already been learned, be sure to put the behavior on strong stimulus control by never rewarding the behavior unless the cue is given first. If the behavior persists or degenerates to pawing or clawing, give the dog a cue to perform an alternate behavior, like "place" or "roll over." If the same cue is given consistently, the dog will soon learn to offer the alternate behavior to solicit attention instead of pawing. The dog may also be distracted from the pawing with a noise—because even an angry response is perceived as rewarding attention.

Separation Anxiety

The worst possible thing that can happen to a Weimaraner is to be completely ignored, and leaving it alone is another form of ignoring it. For a few Weimaraners, this feeling of isolation may escalate into a difficult problem called separation anxiety. There is a big difference between a bored, untrained dog and one suffering from separation anxiety; this issue is addressed in *Weimaraner Kindergarten*.

Dr. Patricia McConnell's *I'll Be Home Soon!* can help diagnose, prevent, and treat separation anxiety.

Children

Kids and dogs can establish lifelong relationships that are emotionally beneficial to both; however, fostering good relations may take some prior planning and good management. Parents adding a Weimaraner to the household may consult *Living with Kids and Dogs*, by Colleen Pelar, in order to be well prepared.

Child Chasing

The instinctive juvenile behavior of both humans and canines leads to "child chasing," with potentially serious consequences for both unless the behavior is nipped in the bud. Children, especially those under 6 years of age, often initiate games with puppies by squealing and running away. Many puppies instinctively respond to this clear invitation to play by chasing, jumping, and biting at the new playmate. Naive parents smile indulgently at this sign that the youngsters are bonding: "They're going to be such good friends."

As the Weimaraner rapidly gains size and coordination, the puppy collides with greater force. Puppy teeth and nails catch and tear clothes, sometimes even tender skin. Children cannot discriminate between a scratch and a bite, but they understand that the puppy is no longer such a nice playmate. The inexperienced parents who allowed the game to develop are often equally unprepared to find a solution, other than

Figure 9-15: The "high five," offered to another canine, presents minimal hazard, but the behavior can degenerate into pawing, which can result in painful scratches and torn clothing for humans. Photograph by Virginia Alexander.

getting rid of the puppy. Prevention begins with the child. Most children can grasp the concept that the puppy is not smart enough to understand that chasing is a bad game; because they, the children, are smarter, they must promise to protect the puppy by refusing to play the game and by teaching their friends the same. Neighborhood children invited over to play must also be introduced to the puppy and learn the appropriate response to puppy chasing.

The author provides the following learning opportunity for new owners with small children before they leave with the new puppy. The child—be sure the child has the ability to follow simple instructions and is wearing denim for protection from puppy teeth and nails—teases the puppy into a chase and runs past the adult, who shouts "No!" and slaps the puppy smartly on the rump as it passes. The child also stops, which ends pursuit, and shouts at the puppy. Repeat this one more time to reinforce the lesson for both puppy and child.

Figure 9-17: *Chasing.* The child on the left teaches the puppy a bad habit—chasing. The twin on the right follows instructions and stops running—ending the exciting chase.

Parents must supervise play and repeat the lesson whenever the puppy shows willingness to chase. Most puppies soon respond to a loud "No!," repeating the slap only when necessary. Have the child practice shouting, "No!" in a voice pitched low enough for the puppy to identify it as a reprimand. If the child shouts, "No!" in the high-pitched voice common to children, the puppy may become more agitated. Vary the procedure using two children. Even 3-year-olds respond to the idea of playing trainer and quickly get the idea that it is time to give that dumb puppy another lesson.

Children should be instructed that if the puppy begins to chase or nip during play, the child should immediately stop and give the same low-pitched command, "No!," as was practiced earlier.

With Weimaraner puppies, the pursuit instinct appears to taper off at about 3 months unless reinforced by getting away with child chasing. Interestingly, about half of Weimaraner puppies do not have a strong pursuit instinct, although given enough opportunity, all have the aptitude for learning to chase.

New Baby

A new baby in the household is an exciting and stressful event for everyone, including the family dog. Initial introductions are a valuable opportunity to establish a positive and workable relationship with the Weimaraner and the new baby. Babies make all sorts of interesting noises and smells; excluding the dog from interacting with the baby will arouse a sense of anxiety and curiosity in any dog, but especially the highly people-oriented Weimaraner. Allow the Weimaraner, from the moment of the baby's arrival, to thoroughly inves-

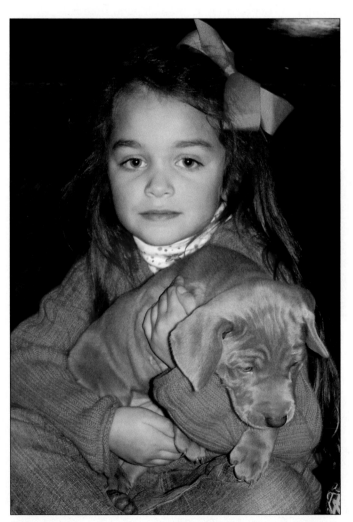

Figure 9-16: *For the safety and comfort* of both puppy and child, children should be seated comfortably on the floor before the puppy is placed in the child's lap.

tigate every part of the baby, from head to toe. In a relaxed, low-key manner, inform the Weimaraner, "This is the new puppy we are planning to keep." This will foster the sense that the baby is simply a new pack member, not an intruder or replacement.

Be sure to continue to share individual time with your Weimaraner with and without the baby, and try to maintain as much as possible the dog's regular routine. Owners should be aware of behavior changes in their Weimaraner; it is common for this watchful, family-oriented breed to alert parents to the baby's behavior, such as when the baby awakens from a nap. Numerous new parents report having been roused from a sound sleep with the news of a dirty diaper.

While their easy-care coat and clean nature make them an ideal family companion, the athletic and mysterious guard dog–like appearance makes the devoted Weimaraner an effective protector for the infant.

Food and Object Guarding

Under no circumstances should any Weimaraner ever show hesitation about giving up an object—the first challenge to pack leadership. The owner of a Weimaraner must surely be the best hunter in the pack (think how the results of a trip to the grocery store must look to the dog) and is surely deserving of the ability to control the pack's resources. Social status is determined by who has the most access to preferred resources; by controlling access to the "good stuff," the owner becomes the de facto highest-ranking pack member. When control of resources is in doubt, the owner can simply remove access to a preferred object by putting it away until the owner returns to dole it out. Practice taking objects from the puppy from the beginning, but at the first sign of reluctance about surrendering any "prize," additional training becomes mandatory.

Two Toys

One method of teaching the dog to relinquish resources, such as toys or food, is the "two toys" game. The object does not have to be a ball, but any object the dog finds desirable. Have two identical items; offer one to the puppy. Once the puppy has possession and interaction with the toy, show the puppy the other one. If the puppy shows no interest, make a big deal over the toy, tossing it in the air, cuddling it, etc. As soon as the puppy is interested, say, "Give!" or "Out!" and let the puppy have the new toy, or toss it a very short distance. The puppy is rewarded for relinquishing the object it has by possession of the new toy.

The same principle can apply with different toys or food objects, with a slight twist. The puppy is given a "ho-hum" item, while the owner has something really valued; the puppy "trades up" by relinquishing the ho-hum item on cue for the really good one—self-reinforcing.

From the time the puppy comes home, controlling the food resource will prevent many problems. It is not always necessary to feed the puppy its entire meal in one sitting; serve the meal in small portions, feeding a small amount initially. When that is gone, the owner picks up the bowl, adds more food, and replaces the bowl; repeat this until the meal is consumed. Make a habit of removing the food bowl from the puppy while there is still food left, putting a small, special goodie in, and returning the bowl. Alternatively, reach into the bowl while the puppy is eating and drop in a small, tasty treat.

Give Me the Bone

At some point during the puppy's adolescence, the puppy may directly challenge the owner for possession of an object or food. Often, these are the dogs that will excel in the future if provided with clear leadership. If the dog is allowed to be successful in possessing the prized object, the behavior may progress to an aggression issue as the puppy matures. Press on the lips, forcing the puppy to release the object, and command, "Give!" Reward compliance with praise, and give the object back immediately. Repeat the exercise to help the puppy understand.

Then, set the puppy up with the type of object that is most likely to provoke an objection. With most, a piece of marrowbone with scraps of meat works, but some are even

Figure 9-18: *When an adolescent Weimaraner displays aggression* in refusing to relinquish an object and discipline is clearly appropriate, grasping the loose skin of the neck and back and giving a few shakes is similar to the way the dam disciplines puppies. Although the challenge may be distressing to the new owner, puppies expressing a strong personality and desire to possess objects will often develop into outstanding companions and performers if the leadership issue is clearly resolved early on.

more possessive of a special toy. Have the puppy on lead and allow the dog ample time to relax and fully savor the treasure before taking it away using the same technique as before.

If the puppy should growl or express active resentment in any way, pick it up by the loose skin of the back and neck, as the mother would discipline a puppy, and drop it down, giving a sharp "No!" Return the prize again.

All family members should practice taking items away from the puppy; training should continue for a lifetime, but extra diligence may be required during adolescence. Always be alert for the opportunity to reinforce positive and willing exchanges—an acknowledgement of who is truly in charge of resources.

Nooking

Nooking, or adult nursing behavior, is not considered a problem behavior, but the habit of sucking on an object (often there is a favored object) may be fairly unique to the Weimaraner breed. Dogs who "nook" are almost never destructive in the behavior; in fact, the favored object is treasured and well cared for. This behavior usually starts very early in life and seems to be similar to thumb sucking, providing comfort in times of stress or boredom. This endearing behavior is rumored to have a strong genetic component, as nookers seem to produce nookers, who themselves produce nookers.

The Multiple-Weimaraner Family

Despite the breed's size and active nature, multiple-Weimaraner families are surprisingly common. Two Weimaraners can be twice as much fun and little more work than one, because they expend a lot of their energy in play; but, for some reason, three Weimaraners seem to require twice as much attention as two.

Wild canines depend on a social structure of pack dynamics for survival. Higher-ranking individuals get priority access to resources first, and other pack members defer to them. In the wild, actual fights are uncommon; after all, an injury to a pack member reduces the survival chances of the entire pack. Conflict is reduced by using body language to communicate submission to higher-ranking individuals. Books by Turid Rugaas *(On Talking Terms with Dogs)* and Brenda Aloff *(Canine Body Language: A Photographic Guide)* will help humans learn how to interpret this canine language. Understanding this language can help owners defuse escalating situations through early recognition of potential problems.

Figure 9-19: *Taking time out* from a busy show schedule, Dharma and Chili relax with a bit of serious nooking in their hotel room.

Figure 9-20: *This pack is congenial,* even though Oscar, Otto, and Oliver are all intact males, as a result of good household management and well-spaced ages. While one dog is away from home at shows or training, there is still a pack mate for company.

Maintaining harmony in a multiple-dog family depends primarily on maintaining control—establishing obedience control first with one dog, and then in a group. Teach the concept "reward comes to he who waits politely and patiently." Once the dogs learn to wait to access doors or treats, to wait politely to be greeted, "off" or "back," tension levels and conflicts will decrease. Every dog in a multiple-dog family really needs to understand the "place" command (see *Weimaraner Kindergarten*) and should be comfortable if one dog is loose while the other dogs are crated or isolated. Dr. Patricia McConnell offers great solutions and techniques in *Feeling Outnumbered?*

If the owner is spending the time training each dog, then one of the common issues of a multiple-dog family can be easily avoided. Each canine member of the family needs to have some individual time with its owner, one-on-one, a trip to the store or park. This simple act is important for the dog, the human, and the pack; the time spent together reinforces the bond between the dog and people, as well as establishing control. If dogs never spend time interacting with the humans, the bond between dog and human deteriorates. It is so much easier for dogs to communicate with dogs; the

amount of effort the dogs put forth in interacting with people declines unless the human-dog relationship is cultivated on a regular basis.

Twice the Fun?
Twice the Trouble

Many prospective puppy purchasers are tempted to get two puppies at once, thinking that the two will provide company and amusement for each other. The authors strongly feel that any breeder that would allow two puppies to go to a new home together should arouse a sense of wariness in the purchaser. It is important for the emotional development of a puppy that it be separated from its littermates around 7–8 weeks of age. If puppies stay together past about 8 weeks, they bond very closely with each other, sometimes to the exclusion of developing relationships with humans, not to mention that keeping up with two puppies is akin to having two tornadoes loose in the house. While one is getting into the trash, the other is in another room chewing on the dining room table, and once they put their heads together to find mischief, the humans are likely to come out on the short end of the stick. Finally, finding the time to provide the proper individual attention and training for two puppies is quite demanding.

Introducing the New Packmate

The most common addition is a puppy when the family Weimaraner is getting up in years. Unless the puppy is given too much attention, older Weimaraners enjoy the newcomer, and some even seem to regard a youngster as a personal pet and special responsibility. With Weimaraners, dominance relationships established at an early age appear to be lifelong; in one case reported to the author, for over 10 years a tiny teacup poodle dominated an adult Weimaraner that had been brought into the household as a puppy.

While initial introductions usually go quite smoothly, the owner can take several steps to ensure a positive experience for all involved. In particular with an adult dog, and especially when the animals are of the same gender, initial introductions should take place on neutral ground. Each canine should be introduced individually if there is already more than one dog in the household.

Have both dogs on lead, and let them size each other up to determine which is more aggressive. Sometimes it is less a question of aggression than that the bolder dog, in its friendliness, may simply overwhelm and frighten the less dominant or under-socialized dog or puppy. Drop the lead from the less aggressive dog, allowing it the freedom to approach and initiate the play when ready.

Keeping the lead attached to the more aggressive dog will allow the owner to maintain control and distract the more

Figure 9-21: *CH Vanity Visionary,* CD, JH, MX, MXJ, NJP, NSD, NRD, BROM, VX2 and his son, CH MACH4 JamSpirit Nobility, JH, NRD, VX2. Rock and Jag show that multiple-dog families, even those of the same sex, can be harmonious; the older dog provides a role model for the younger. Be proactive and prevent conflicts over resources—such as toys—before they begin. Photograph by Melissa Chandler.

dominant dog, giving the puppy the opportunity to back out and regroup if it is frightened. When they seem to be getting along well, the lead may be dropped, but supervision should be continued for some time, especially in the presence of valued resources, such as toys, treats, or human attention. After a week or so of one-on-one interaction, dogs may be allowed to interact in a small group; group play should be restricted and closely monitored for some time in families of more than two dogs.

Dogs and bitches accept each other easily, usually enthusiastically. Normally, the bitch is dominant in the relationship. The touchiest introductions are between adults of the same sex, and they should be introduced on neutral territory to minimize the territorial instinct to attack an intruder. Contrary to popular belief, conflicts between bitches are as common as those between males. In general, however, Weimaraners get along very well. Give adults time to become used to each other. For the first few days at least, keep one in a dog run or crate while the other is loose, letting them get better acquainted in a controlled situation until they are no longer excited by each other's presence.

Be proactive and avoid conflicts over preferred items, such as special toys, juicy treats, food, or a bitch in season. Be alert for signs of aggression, and immediately play alpha (dominant) wolf, making aggressive noises and cuffs to distract the dogs. Crate the aggressor, or both if the behavior was mutual.

Family Rivalry

In multiple-Weimaraner families, most fights and lasting feuds are initiated by owner carelessness in situations that stimulate confrontations, such as feeding and returning home. Grumbles and growls are a common canine method of communication, and an owner should not be distressed over occasional sparring or snapping between housemates. However, it is unusual for frequent or repeated conflicts to occur that result in actual injury or serious bloodshed. The use of an electronic collar is rarely successful in mediating household aggression between packmates; seek professional assistance as soon as possible, since the longer the problems continue, the more difficult they will be to resolve once the dogs have established a history or pattern of behavior.

Food confrontations are easily avoided by feeding the dogs in their crates. This is a prudent practice, for even dogs that behave well when the owner is around may decide to challenge each other when fed by someone else.

Weimaraners are always wildly excited by the owners' return home. If loose, they leap and bump one another. Occasionally, this precipitates a lightning slash, so swift that it seems a reflex response; most often, it is between dogs that are normally very devoted to each other and occurs when more than two Weimaraners are involved. The prevention is to leave no more than one or two Weimaraners loose in the house when gone.

Returning home with a Weimaraner that has been away from home, even for a short time, such as to a show, after breeding, or even to the veterinarian, requires common sense and proactive management by the owner. If a bitch in heat is present in the household, males will be more volatile, and extra vigilance is required of the owner. Avoid confrontations at the door by first crating the one at home. After a run around the yard, crate the returnee. Then, release the first one and make a fuss over it, making it the center of exclusive attention for a few minutes. Allow time for both to calm down. The length of time the dogs should be separated depends on their temperaments and on the length of time they have been separated—for example, 15 minutes after a trip to the vet, 60 minutes after a dog-show weekend, 1 day after longer separations. The dogs quickly settle down again if confrontations are avoided.

If a fight does occur, never try to grab hold of the dogs. When fighting, a dog's reflexes cause it to whirl and slash at every touch. Owners who attempt to catch hold of the dogs frequently require expensive hand surgery, and tendon repairs are not always successful.

Any measure that gets the antagonists' attention is legitimate, and strong distractions are required. A loud voice, combined with water from a hose, a garden tool, a broom, or even feet, may work—anything but your hands. One owner recalled the time she carried three bowls of food into the backyard and two bitches began fighting. She dropped one bowl when she "bopped" them on their heads with the other two, which got their attention long enough to discover the spilled food and begin eating. The owner bought some crates for feeding, but she still has the dented metal bowls.

If the suggested measures to avoid situations that stimulate fighting seem unnecessary and a little silly, remember that dogfights really are dangerous. It is a lot easier to avoid setting the dogs up for confrontation than it is to restore affection and trusting relationships.

Mating Moods

The most common combination in a multiple-Weimaraner family is a dog and a bitch. Owners must be prepared to separate them when the bitch comes in season, because even if a mating is planned, it should be supervised.

The Weimaraner male's reaction to a bitch in season varies considerably. Many owners have been fooled by the male that does not seem to notice the bitch is in season until it is the right moment for conception or no one is looking. At the other extreme is the male that starts chomping a week before the bitch comes in season and drives everyone crazy by his nonstop whining or howling. Compassionate veterinarians dispense tranquilizers (for the males, of course), but sometimes the only way to avoid a nervous breakdown is to board one of the dogs. Most males fall between these extremes.

Many a young dog—way too young—figures things out before the owner has any idea that Romeo is considerably more mature than was thought; Weimaraners as young as 7 months have successfully sired a litter.

In multiple-bitch families, there is no danger of mis-matings, but there are other problems. When one bitch comes into season, the others usually follow within a few weeks, and eventually their cycles tend to become almost simultaneous.

Some bitches show a marked change of behavior when in season, such as becoming flighty and disobedient; this behavior may begin a couple of weeks prior to the onset of estrus. Other bitches may give no easily observed indication of their season; these ladies must be watched most carefully as the expected time approaches. Some are so fastidiously clean that the most obvious signs are missed.

Occasionally, the season precipitates alpha (dominant) behavior in a normally non-aggressive bitch as she attempts to prove herself worthy of mating by fighting with the other bitches. At the first sign of alpha behavior, the bitch should be isolated for the remainder of her season. Behavior usually returns to normal when the urge to mate passes if she has not had an opportunity to establish a pattern of fighting. Alpha behavior during season appears to be more pronounced in maiden bitches; after a litter, the drive to dominate seems less intense. Curiously, alpha Weimaraner bitches usually have submissive dams, and daughters of alpha bitches rarely exhibit this behavior.

Weimaraner males are typically congenial, but may become somewhat edgy and protective while a family

Figure 9-22: *The signs of a bitch in season* are usually obvious and annoying. Stylish and convenient apparel is now available in most pet catalogs that will minimize the inconvenience; in a pinch, a disposable diaper or a little boy's underwear will work. For safety, such articles should be removed if the dog is unsupervised or crated. These are also useful for the older dog that has become incontinent. Photograph by Rodney Moon.

Figure 9-23: ***The Weimaraner is a very social, highly intelligent animal.*** They have problem-solving skills well above average, as well as the ability to learn by observation. The Weimaraner owner should be prepared to be one step ahead in order to use these traits to their best advantage and avoid the acquisition of undesirable habits. Gretchen displays typical Weimaraner intelligence and creativity to quench her thirst. Photograph by Marc Jonas.

bitch is in season, even if she is kept isolated from them. While some males seem oblivious to what is going on—until the owner's vigilance strays for just a moment—other dogs become extremely vocal, agitated, or single-minded. If a bitch is brought in for breeding, the male should be bathed afterward, and they should be kept separated for several hours or longer if still excited. Boarding the males will reduce the stress and tension levels for the dogs, as well as for the owners. Alternatively, stress levels may reach the point that the choice boils down to neutering or spaying one of the dogs.

Monkey See, Monkey Do

Weimaraners have a strong aptitude for learning by mimicking the behavior of both humans and other dogs; this is called allelomimetic behavior. The characteristic is more pronounced in submissive personalities, and most puppies are submissive to adults.

Mimicking undesirable behavior is a problem. Do not hope that the puppy will not learn bad habits, such as digging, jumping, chronic barking, table begging, stealing food from counters, and so forth. Count on the puppy learning all undesirable behavior from the dominant dog! The only way to avoid having two or more Weimaraners with the same bad habits is to have the first well trained before adding another dog. Puppies raised with an obedience-trained, well-behaved adult usually respond more quickly to training and develop socially desirable behavior. Nevertheless, there is always some risk that the adult may acquire some bad habits from a puppy or an older adult that misbehaves.

Be alert for the first signs that the older dog is learning bad habits. Although canine behaviorists flatly assert that dogs have no sense of morals, novice sinners often appear to be aware of their transgressions and to respond more quickly to prompt correction.

Most often this copycat behavior is helpful. For example, a puppy will follow an older dog out the dog door and is quickly housebroken; if the first dog has an outgoing and confident temperament, the puppy will usually become outgoing.

This trait can be invaluable in the training arena. It is not uncommon for the Weimaraner's keen observation skills to allow them to figure out how to open doors and gates on the first try after seeing the latch opened by the owner. It is common practice for field trainers to use this trait to their advantage by staking out inexperienced Weimaraners and allowing them to watch other dogs in training, such as swimming, obedience, and many other aspects of field training.

Whatever Works

Owning a Weimaraner should be a pleasure, not a trial. The most important thing to remember is that each owner should find a way to maintain a lifestyle that suits him or her. There are no hard-and-fast rules about what makes a harmonious multiple-dog household. For example, while one owner may teach the dogs to ring a bell to go out, another may prefer the dogs to ring the bell to come in. In the end, do what works.

Figure 9-24: *The common tendency of Weimaraners to mimic* observed behaviors is an invaluable tool in training. Experienced trainers never miss the opportunity to allow young puppies to watch well-trained older dogs perform. Here, a young recruit is staked out and given the opportunity to watch an experienced dog complete a retrieve. Photograph by Shirley Nilsson.

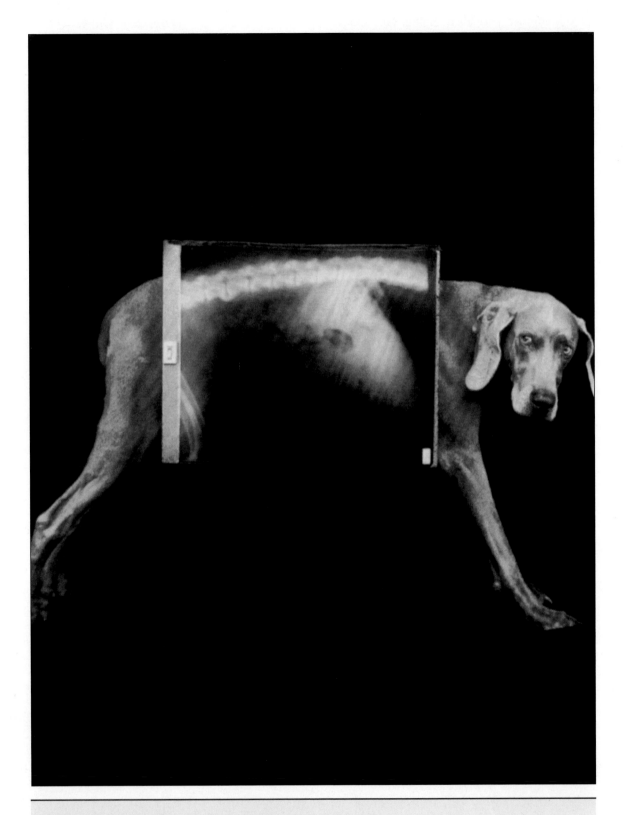

Figure 10-1: *Fay Ray X-Ray.* 1993 photograph by William Wegman.

CHAPTER 10

THE BEST OF HEALTH

by Jackie Isabell

This chapter provides brief, descriptive information that Weimaraner owners are most likely to need for quick reference. For more detailed information, the *Weimaraner Magazine* publishes many health-related articles of both general and specific interest for the breed, and there are whole libraries of information available on the topic of canine health. In an informal survey, the reference that received the most votes for personal libraries was *Dog Owner's Home Veterinary Handbook,* by Carlson and Giffin. The Merck *Veterinary Manual* is the gold standard for veterinary reference and can be found on the shelf of every veterinarian and most serious dog fanciers, providing background technical reference and guidance for nearly all canine health care issues.

First Aid

When at home or within reach of a phone, the dog owner's first resource is a veterinarian. Remember, first-aid instructions are generalizations, so call for professional help whenever possible before using the generic instructions given here. In addition, if the dog needs immediate veterinary care, the veterinarian can set up equipment, defer routine surgery, or even keep the clinic open if forewarned. Keep the phone numbers of the veterinarian, emergency clinic, and poison control center next to the phone, where a frantic owner or dog sitter can find it immediately. Be prepared to provide the veterinarian with the dog's vital signs. The following are normal:

Temperature: 100.5°F–102.5°F
Pulse: 80–140 beats per minute
Respiration: 10–30 breaths per minute

First-Aid Kit

A well-stocked first-aid kit is vital for emergencies and handy for routine care. Take it along whenever traveling with a dog. If the dog is in severe pain, apply a muzzle before attempting first-aid measures. Soft cloth muzzles store easily in a small space, but an improvised muzzle—shown in *Mating Games*—can be made from a strip of cloth or a stocking. An easy

reference guide for emergency first aid, such as *The American Red Cross Pet First Aid,* is a must for any complete first-aid kit. Some local veterinarians and Red Cross chapters offer pet first-aid classes, a worthwhile investment of any dog lover's time. These classes usually teach emergency care, as well as CPR and Heimlich maneuver for dogs.

Tourniquets are now considered extremely dangerous. They should be used only when firm pressure on the arterial pressure point (Figure 10-2) fails to control the bleeding and when the choice is between loss of life and loss of the limb. Contrary to earlier practices, it is now advised that once a tourniquet is applied, it should not be released to allow blood flow to the limb. It is now known that the resulting blood flow carries life-threatening blood clots, as well as toxins pro-

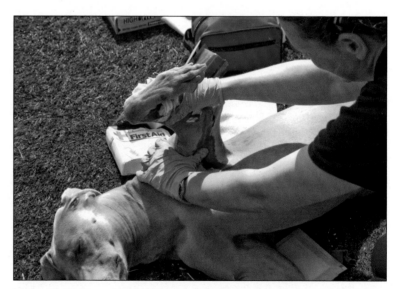

Figure 10-2: *Severe bleeding is best controlled by direct pressure.* Firmly press absorbent material over the wound. No peeking! If material becomes soaked, add more material on top to avoid disturbing blood clotting. If necessary a pressure bandage can be used to hold material in place; the bandage should only be tight enough to hold material firmly without restricting blood flow below the injury. If bleeding is spurting with the heart beat, or continues for more than five minutes, or otherwise seems excessive, use the heel of the palm to apply pressure to an arterial pressure point (see Figure 10-6). A tourniquet should only be applied when the decision is between life and death, or when the loss of the limb is either likely or acceptable. Since toxins will be released into the bloodstream, once applied, a tourniquet should only be removed or loosened by a veterinarian!

Table 10-1: *First aid for common emergencies.*

First Aid for Common Emergencies

Allergic Reaction (Acute)
Causes: Vaccines, medications
Signs: Shock, collapse, swollen face and ears, hives
Care: Contact veterinarian immediately

Allergic Reaction (Insects)
Causes: Bees, wasps, scorpions
Signs: Pawing at the site (usually muzzle, tongue, or near eyes; site red, hot, swollen)
Care: If stinger is visible, remove with tweezers or edge of credit card
Apply paste of baking soda or meat tenderizer and water
Give antihistamine, apply cold compress, contact veterinarian

Bleeding, Ear Wound
Causes: Dog fight, barbed wire, thorns
Care: Apply firm pressure until bleeding stops
Apply styptic or EMT gel
Prevent head shaking until blood coagulates
Transport to clinic if sutures necessary

Bleeding, Major Wound
Care: Apply firm pressure to arterial pressure point and directly to wound with absorbent material; additional material is added on top of soaked material to avoid disturbing clotting
Use tourniquets only when choosing between loss of life and loss of the limb
Once applied, only a veterinarian should release tourniquet
Transport to clinic immediately

Bloat—Life threatening! See text.

Burns
Signs: Burned hair; red, blistered area
Care: Chemical burn—flush with cold water
Electrical burn—pull plug before touching dog
Contact veterinarian for further directions

Cardiac Arrest
Causes: Chest trauma, drugs, poisons, burn, bloat
Signs: Collapse, pulse weak, irregular, or absent, gums blue/white
Care: Check throat, remove obstructions
It is best to take a CPR class before this skill is needed. With dog on its side, place hands one on top of the other behind dog's left elbow. With elbows straight, compress chest 1–3 inches
Repeat every second, while assistant treats respiratory arrest
Continue CPR for 20–30 minutes while transporting to clinic

Convulsions/Seizures
Do not attempt to "end" seizure by slapping, splashing with water, or startling
Note beginning and ending times
Keep hands away from dog's mouth
Make area safe (remove objects, pets, and unnecessary people)
Contact vet (transport immediately if lasting more than 5 minutes)

Dog Bite
Signs: Puncture or tear wound
Care: Minor, superficial—clip hair around wound, clean with sterile saline or Betadine twice daily
Major: Transport to clinic

Ear Disorders
Causes: Insects (ticks, mites); foreign objects
Signs: Shaking head, digging at ear with paw, red, inflamed ear canal, foul-smelling ears, sometimes with pus
Care: Contact veterinarian and treat as directed

Fracture
Signs: Lameness, swelling, heat, places no weight on limb
Care: Muzzle dog before handling
Cover open wounds with gauze, immobilize limb with splint
Transport to clinic

Heat Stroke
Causes: Confinement in closed crate or car (90%); overexercise on a hot day
Signs: Sudden collapse, heavy gasping, panting, foaming at mouth, drooling, blank, staring expression, muscle twitching, seizures, gums brick red, temperature over 104°F
Care: Prompt treatment may prevent death
Wet down or immerse in cold water until temperature reaches 103°F, give sips of cool water
Contact veterinarian immediately

Internal Injury
Signs: Shock, collapse, rapid, shallow breathing, bleeding from mouth, rectum, or bladder
Care: Keep warm and immobilize while transporting to clinic

Poison
Causes: Insecticides, fertilizers, antifreeze, ornamental plants (see Table 10-5)
Signs: Vary with toxic agent
Typical Signs: Salivation, vomiting with diarrhea, tremors, staggering, seizures, depression, weakness, collapse, bleeding problems
Care: Identify toxic agent, if possible
Contact poison control center for correct treatment (inducing vomiting is often dangerous)
Transport to clinic if necessary

Respiratory Arrest
Causes: Drowning, asphyxiation, foreign object blocking throat, congestive heart failure
Signs: Breathing slow, shallow, gasping, or absent, gums bluish to dark red
Care: Remove collar, check for and remove foreign objects
If drowning, grab rear legs, hold upside down for 15–30 seconds
Lay dog on side, extend head and neck, grasp tongue with cloth and pull to clear airway
Hold dog's mouth and lips closed, place your mouth over dog's nose, blow firmly for 3 seconds, relax for 2 seconds, repeat
Transport to clinic immediately

Shock
Causes: Blood loss; trauma; hypo-/hyperthermia; bloat; poison
Signs: Collapse, gums pale or brick red, weak, rapid pulse
Care: Keep warm and quiet while transporting to clinic

Snakebite (Venomous)
Signs: Paired puncture wounds (usually face or legs), shock
Care: Do not cut or suck wound
Transport to clinic immediately

Vomiting
Causes: Food change; fatty foods; garbage; parasites; infection; organ failure/disease
Signs: Sometimes accompanied by fever, diarrhea, dehydration
Care: No food for 24 hours (12 hours if puppy)
No water for 4–6 hours, then offer small sips of water or ice cubes
If no more vomiting after 12–24 hours, offer small amounts of rice boiled with equal chicken (no broth or grease) 3–4 times a day
Contact veterinarian

Figure 10-3: ***For liquid medication*** use a needle-less syringe for liquid medication and as an extreme measure to offer liquids to support a dog before going to the veterinarian. Slip the syringe into the corner of the mouth with the tip close to the base of the tongue; express small amounts that the dog can swallow without choking.

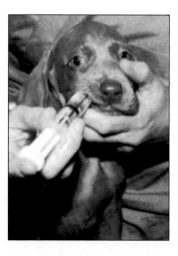

Figure 10-4: ***To apply eye drops*** or ointment, cradle the dog's head and hold it steady—sweet talk helps. Gently pull the skin under the eye downward so the lid forms a pouch, and insert the medication into the pouch without touching the eye.

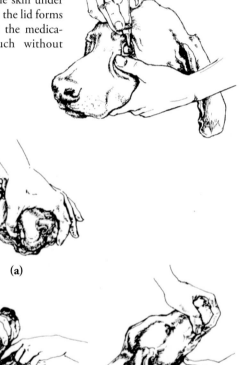

(a)

(b)   (c)

Figure 10-5: ***Giving pills.***
(a) Gently roll or tuck the dog's lip against the teeth and apply pressure against the teeth until the dog opens its mouth.
(b) Holding the pill with the thumb and forefinger, slide it into the mouth and deposit it as far past the base of the tongue as possible.
(c) Quickly grasp the dog's muzzle to hold the mouth closed, tilt it upward, and stroke the throat to induce swallowing. Some Weimaraners become as crafty as humans about holding a pill in the corner of their mouths until they are able to slip away and spit it out, so watch carefully for a few minutes.

Table 10-2: ***First-aid kit.***

A First-Aid Kit

Keep first-aid instructions with the first-aid supplies (such as **The American Red Cross Pet First Aid***)*

Equipment

Thermometer (rectal)	Tweezers/forceps
Bandage scissors	Watch with second hand
Flashlight	Wire cutters
Muzzle	Needle-nosed pliers

General Supplies

Adhesive and elastic tape	Self-adhesive gauze rolls
Alcohol	Flea and tick preventive
Artificial tears	EMT gel (www.emtgel.com)
Kwik-Stop®	Pedialyte®
New Skin (for cut pads)	Bandages
Q-tips®	Betadine® or sterile saline (eyewash)
Stretchable gauze rolls, nonstick gauze squares, elastic bandage (i.e., Ace®)	Sterile syringes and needles (refer to local restrictions)

Nonprescription Medication

Antibiotic ointment	Glycerine suppositories
Aspirin (1/2–2 tablets twice daily with food)	Hydrocortisone ointment
	Syrup of ipecac
Kaopectate® original flavor (1 tsp or 5 cc per 5 lb of dog weight every 4–6 hrs)	Dramamine® (25–50 mg 1 hour before travel to prevent motion sickness)
Diphenhydramine (Benadryl®)	Hydrogen peroxide
Lubricating gel	

Phone Numbers

Veterinarian   Poison control   24-hour emergency clinic

Check and replace items with expiration dates on a regular basis.

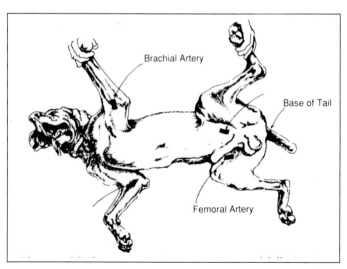

Brachial Artery

Base of Tail

Femoral Artery

Figure 10-6: ***If direct pressure on a wound fails*** to stop bleeding, apply firm pressure where the artery crosses a bone—pressure must be maintained until you reach a clinic.

duced by damaged tissue. Once applied, therefore, a tourniquet should be released only by a veterinarian.

Give liquid medications with a syringe (needle removed), slipping the tip in at the corner of the mouth and between the teeth and expressing the medication at the base of the tongue; refer to Figure 10-3.

Most Weimaraners eagerly gulp down pills that are hidden inside a ball of canned dog food or hamburger. For the geniuses that realize it contains medicine, try two balls without pills and then try again. If this fails, use the technique outlined in Figure 10-5, and reward them with praise and a treat. A big, strong Weimaraner turning cartwheels to avoid taking medication can turn the procedure into an ordeal, especially if the medication must be given several times a day for several weeks, and the sneaky approach is wonderful when it works.

Medications for the eye can be intimidating; a calming presence and patience will make the process easier. Figure 10-4 shows how to apply ointments or drops.

Regular grooming sessions provide an opportunity for "practice runs" to acclimate the dog to these procedures. The owner goes through the motions without actually giving the medication, rewarding the dog for calm acceptance of the process with treats and praise. When the time comes for the "real thing," the dog will be used to the process and will be much more cooperative.

Bloat and Gastric Torsion

Bloat (gastric dilation) is the abnormal distension of the stomach with gas. If not relieved, it can progress to gastric torsion (the rotation of the stomach on its axis), with obstruction of the blood supply, which leads quickly to shock and death.

Table 10-3: *Bloat.*

Precipitating Factor	Preventive Measure
Difficulty digesting food	Soak food in water until completely expanded (about 1/2 hr)
Eating too rapidly	Free-feed dry kibble, or slowly hand feed
Overfilling stomach	Feed twice daily
Overdrinking	Have water available at all times Limit water after exercise to 1 cup every 10 minutes Do not allow water after meals
Exercise after eating	Avoid vigorous exercise for 2 hours after eating
Change in dog food	Change foods gradually
Parasites	Routine stool examination and treatment as needed
Eating a foreign object	Pick up toys and other tempting objects
Stress	Crate 30–60 minutes before eating Avoid food conflicts in multiple-dog households

Figure 10-7: *Do not worry if the ice trays are empty* when ice is needed to treat heat stroke. Large bags of small frozen vegetables, such as peas or corn, make excellent ice packs, too.

Gastric torsion can also occur as a primary condition, as well, with the stomach twisting on its axis, followed by bloat. Bloat and/or torsion are often sudden, and the symptoms are dramatic, especially the abdominal distension; however, symptoms may also progress slowly at the initial onset (perhaps hours after eating or exercise) and then suddenly progress quickly. *The dog becomes excessively agitated, panting and salivating excessively, with nonproductive retching, often circling and looking back at or biting at the abdomen. Symptoms may progress as rapidly as 10–20 minutes to shock, with pale gums, cold ears, and collapse. Bloat is always a medical emergency, and immediate surgery is usually mandatory if a tube cannot be passed.* Even if a tube can be passed and the emergency is temporarily averted, bloat usually recurs; discuss the need for preventive "tacking" surgery with the dog's regular veterinarian.

The Morris Animal Foundation estimates that gastric torsion kills 18,000–36,000 dogs each year. The incidence is highest in the large, deep-chested breeds—Great Danes, German Shepherds, Irish Setters, Weimaraners, and so forth. Dogs that survive bloat are at high risk for recurrence.[1] Desperate dog owners are turning to prophylactic surgery in which the stomach is stabilized so that it cannot rotate. This procedure prevents torsion but not bloat; a dog can die of bloat without torsion. The owner must continue to employ proactive measures to reduce the likelihood of recurrence.

Although bloat and torsion are the subject of extensive research and many theories, there is no definitive explanation of the cause of bloat and torsion, and until the disorders are fully understood, owners can only use the suggested measures listed in Table 10-3. Be aware of the symptoms. When bloat strikes, take the dog to the veterinary clinic immediately. In this emergency, minutes make the difference between life and death.

Intestinal Obstructions

All dog owners are occasionally stunned by the poor judgment—not to mention depraved taste—their pets can exhibit. Unfortunately, the occurrence of intestinal obstructions is all too common in Weimaraners. Their curiosity and tendency to mouth and carry all too often result in their swallowing inappropriate objects. Some have a rock fetish; others cannot resist children's toys, bar soap, pantyhose, sanitary napkins, or squeakers from squeaky toys.

If the dog is observed to have swallowed such an inappropriate object, consult a veterinarian without delay. Veterinarians commonly recommend immediately inducing vomiting by giving the dog two teaspoons of hydrogen peroxide by mouth every three minutes while continuously walking the dog in circles. Repeat until the dog regurgitates the object; a healthy, mature Weimaraner may ingest up to 2 cups of hydrogen peroxide without ill effects. Any vomitus should be saved for inspection by the vet.

New expanding polyurethane glues (Gorilla Glue™, among others) pose an unsuspected hazard because even ingesting a very small amount can be life-threatening as the mass expands in the stomach or intestines. The American Society for the Prevention of Cruelty to Animals (ASPCA) has reported a 740% increase since 2002 in the number of reported cases of dogs needing treatment for this life-threatening problem. All foreign objects are dangerous and potentially lethal if lodged in the intestinal tract.

The following measures are recommended:

- Crate puppies and young dogs when they cannot be supervised to control the behavior and prevent the habit
- Assume that puppies and young dogs will eat everything, and keep all ingestible objects out of reach
- Use Bitter Apple® on any object to which the puppy returns
- Use a repellent spray, such as Farnam Dog Away®, to discourage extensive exploration of problem areas
- Confine rock eaters in concrete-surfaced runs; if a rock eater stays in a gravel run or has access to it in the backyard, note whether one spot seems particularly attractive and spray the area with Farnam Dog-Away® or Bitter Apple®

Owners and veterinarians all too easily misdiagnose the signs and symptoms of intestinal blockage. Signs of intestinal blockage include lethargy, pacing, vomiting, retching, and loss of interest in food or water. Early detection is vital; a veterinary consult is indicated when a foreign object is even remotely suspected. A skilled veterinarian can sometimes pal-

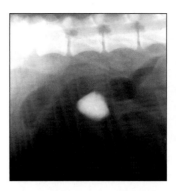

Figure 10-8: *Intestinal blockage.* (a) Intestinal blockages, such as this rock, may need to be surgically removed; if left untreated, these blockages may prove fatal. **(b)** X-rays are often needed to diagnose intestinal blockages. In this case, the rock is clearly visible; however, sometimes barium X-rays may be required.

The Disappearing Sock...

If you have seen your dog swallow an object, and are unable to reach a vet, it is possible to induce vomiting by using a turkey baster to place 1/4 cup of 3% hydrogen peroxide well down the dog's throat. Repeat every 10–20 minutes, up to three times, while on the way to the vet.

---

pate the object or a pocket of air on either side of a suspect blockage in the intestines.

Although some items will not show up on an X-ray (cloth, for example), pockets of air or gas may be revealed. If an object is not visible but the condition is still problematic, then a barium X-ray is in order. If a blockage is not indicated by the barium X-ray, it is possible that an equally dangerous condition, called telescoped intestine, may be revealed. Either condition demands immediate emergency surgery.

Poisoning

Poisons are a particular problem with Weimaraners because of the breed's fondness for nibbling on plants, instinct to pick up and carry everything, and aptitude for opening doors. Common causes of poison in dogs include human and pet prescriptions, household chemicals, plants, and some food items that, while safe for humans, are toxic to pets.

First Aid for Poisoning

Prevention is the best first step where poisoning is concerned. Medications, chemicals, and certain food items should be kept behind secured cabinets. Also teach pets the "leave it" command to avoid exposure resulting from dropped medication, a food item, or a potentially dangerous item, such as a dead mouse or contaminated rag. Symptoms of poisoning vary widely, depending on the substance, but may include drooling, diarrhea, general loss of coordination, tremors, seizures, or bleeding. Be on the lookout for suspicious circumstances—spilled chemicals, dropped or missing medication, chewed-up containers, or any dead rodent remains. Learn whether there are special hazards in your community—in some areas, Colorado River toads pose a danger, for example.

The ASPCA Animal Poison Control Center (APCC), an allied agency of the University of Illinois, is a 24-hour hotline with a professional staff available 7 days a week. These specialists have experience in a wide variety of poisonings involving not only dogs but all species of animals, as well as an extensive database of over 1 million cases. There is a fee for the service; however, consultation is available for both the pet owner and the professional veterinarian.

> ASPCA Animal Poison Control Center
> 888-426-4435
> www.aspca.org/apcc

Always contact a veterinarian or the ASPCA APCC before administering first aid for suspected toxic substances; inducing vomiting or other methods of decontamination may be contraindicated for many poisons. If the substance is known, have the container at hand when calling, and take it to the clinic with the dog. If the dog vomits spontaneously, save a specimen for analysis. Be prepared to give your dog's age, weight, breed, and general health history, as well as a description of the symptoms the dog is experiencing.

In 2005, the APCC responded to more than 100,000 calls. Here is a list of the 10 most common types of calls, in order of frequency[2]:

- Human medications (+46,000 calls)
- Insecticides (+21,000 calls)
- Rodenticides (6,900 calls)
- Veterinary medications (6,200 calls)
- Household cleaners (5,200 calls)
- Herbicides (4,600 calls)
- Plants (4,400 calls)
- Chocolate (2,600 calls)
- Home improvement products—paints, glues, etc. (1,800 calls)
- Fertilizers (1,700 calls)

Medications

Prescription and non-prescription drugs, whether for humans, canines, or other animals, are a common cause of poisonings. Many medications that treat common human health complaints can be extremely toxic for dogs; even non-prescription drugs, such as acetaminophen and ibuprofen, can cause serious, even fatal, complications. The medications given to the dog to treat an illness or injury can be poisonous if the same dog eats all or part of the contents if the container is left on the counter. Also, dogs can eat medications intended for a different dog. Since the dog cannot read, Suzie would have no way of knowing that the vial of Thyroxine was for her canine housemate, Roxie. A medicine vial can be very interesting to a bored Weimaraner, especially since it bears the odor of his owner; even a childproof container is no match for the dexterous paws and jaws of most Weimaraners. Medications may be dropped on the floor, and the curious Weimaraner is likely to anticipate a tasty treat. When taking or giving medications, be sure to account for all tablets or capsules; additionally, leave the dog on a "stay" or outside the room, teach the dog to wait for permission before grabbing objects that fall on the floor, and regularly practice the "leave it" command.

Herbicides, Pesticides, Fertilizers

Herbicides, pesticides, and fertilizers are, unfortunately, part of modern life. Because toxicity is always relative to the amount ingested and to body weight, the literature is often confusing. Roger Yeary estimates that if a dog's diet consisted solely of grass containing the normal application concentration of the herbicide 2,4-D, it would be unlikely to ingest enough to have an observable effect.[3] Most properly applied residential weed killers and insect sprays would not be expected to cause problems once dry.

Regardless of the toxicity rating, follow the manufacturer's directions for dilution and application precisely. Unused products must be stored where children and pets cannot reach them. These toxins are perhaps more likely to be absorbed through the skin or ingested when licked off the feet or fur than to actually be consumed when eating plants. Follow the manufacturer's instructions regarding animal access to areas that have been sprayed. Regardless of brand or safety claims, do not allow access to areas that have been sprayed recently enough that the area is still wet. If a dog accidentally steps into a freshly treated area, wash the dog's feet to remove any product residue. Be aware of the location of animals when sprays are being applied to ensure that over-spray does not contaminate the areas where the dogs are or where they spend a great deal of time.

Rodenticides provide a particular hazard, since there are many different types that can have carrying effects on animals. Since some are made to be attractive to rodents, they may be attractive to dogs, as well. Owners should routinely be on the lookout for dead or dying animals that may present a poisoning hazard, since they may be particularly interesting to the Weimaraner, based on their odd behavior or novel appearance; they may provide a potential risk of disease transmission or gastrointestinal problems from eating dead wildlife.

Once again, look for the least toxic options and consider non-poisonous options, such as barriers and keeping areas free of rodent-attracting debris, and clean up all spills immediately.

Table 10-4: *This list is not entirely exhaustive,* but is intended only to make the owner think about hazards that are commonly found in our homes.

Foods

Alcoholic beverages	Fatty foods
Chocolate (all forms)	Foods containing Xylitol
Coffee (all forms)	Raw yeast dough
Macadamia nuts	Raw fish
Moldy/spoiled foods	Raisins
Mushrooms (some species)	Tea leaves

Objects

Balls	Paper clips
Batteries	Potpourri (solid and natural)
Bread twist ties	Plastic wrap
Buttons and coins	Rubber-bands
Rocks, pebbles, or gravel	Sharp objects (razors, needles, etc.)
Cotton balls and swabs	Small toys or parts
Feminine sanitary items	Soiled paper towels
Fish hooks	Some dog toys
Jewelry	String, yarn, or dental floss
Nylons and socks	

Chemicals

Over-the-counter medications	Liquid potpourri
Prescription medications	Oven cleaner sprays
Pesticides (insect, rodent, snail)	Lime/scale remover
Flea and tick control	Detergents
Bleach	Tobacco products
Disinfectants	Antifreeze/coolant
Fabric softener	De-icing salts
Lighter fluid	Compost
Solvents (paint thinners, etc.)	Fertilizer
Drain cleaners	Mulches (especially cocoa)

Household Cleaners

Fortunately, today there are many more choices of products used to clean homes. All products should be stored in secured cabinets or on shelves out of the reach of an athletic and curious Weimaraner. Although most modern household cleaners can be safely used in the home, provided that label directions are followed, virtually any product is potentially hazardous. Choose products that are the least toxic that accomplish the job. Consider alternatives: products like baking soda and vinegar or mild soaps can be as effective as more expensive commercial products. Sponges, mops, rags, or paper towels used to apply or remove cleaners should be thoroughly rinsed and safely stored or immediately disposed of. Remember when disposing of these materials that the Weimaraner is a curious beast and is likely to wonder what enticing objects have been dropped in the trash or garbage lately; secure lids carefully.

Plant Hazards

All Weimaraners enjoy grazing on greenery. Normally, this is a harmless (albeit sometimes destructive) pastime, but if a pet ingests a toxic plant, it could result in harmful or even fatal consequences. Toxic wild plants may be less of a threat to the urban Weimaraner than the ornamentals growing in the house and garden. In addition, certain toxic herbicides and pesticides could be ingested with normal harmless plants.

Like children, puppies satisfy their curiosity by tasting or eating plants. Moving household plants out of reach and fencing off outdoor plants are the most effective ways to prevent habitual plant eating. Sometimes, well-behaved adults may suddenly begin eating plants. This behavioral change is usually associated with: (a) becoming familiar with a new home; (b) boredom and a sudden decrease in activity; (c) stress; or (d) any change in daily routine. Treatment depends on the specific plant involved and the clinical signs that are present; therefore, identification of the ingested plant helps the veterinarian initiate the correct measures. Common names vary widely, and knowing the scientific name of a plant is vital; for example, the toxic *Poinciana gilliesii* and the nontoxic *Strelitzia reginae* are both called "bird of paradise."

It would be unrealistic to eliminate all plants in Table 10-5 (apple, peach, and so forth), but it is realistic to be aware of potential hazards. Use such plants in areas that can be secured from unsupervised pets. Contact dermatitis is an occasional problem with shorthaired breeds; the sap from the highly poisonous oleander may also cause skin irritation.

Other Toxic Dangers

Other items commonly found around the house can be toxic, too. Unfortunately, some are not only dangerous, they also have an appealing taste—antifreeze and chocolate, for example—so do not count on an obnoxious taste to be a deterrent. Recently, such common items as raisins, grapes, and onions have been implicated in toxic reactions. Owners need to be up to date in a rapidly changing world. Xylitol, a relatively new sweetener on the market, particularly common in sugar-free gums and candies, has been shown to be a hazard to dogs; consuming large amounts can cause a rapid drop in blood sugar, depression, loss of coordination, and even seizures.

Prevention

So many household products are poisonous that no list is exhaustive, so it bears repeating that poison prevention goes a long way. Treating poisonings can be dicey, and some toxins may have long-term effects, even if the dog's life is saved. Additionally, many items are not only toxic to pets but pose

Table 10-5: *Toxic ornamental plants.*

Common name	Scientific Name	Toxic Part	Symptoms
Allamanda	Allamanda cathartica	All	Occasional vomiting, diarrhea, abnormal behavior, contact dermatitis
Aloe	Aloe spp.	Latex	Delayed vomiting, abdominal pain, diarrhea
Amaryllis	Amaryllis spp.	All, esp. bulb	Occasional vomiting, diarrhea
Anemone	Anemone canadensis	All	Salivation, blistering of mucous membranes, delayed vomiting, abdominal pain, diarrhea, death
Angel's trumpet	Datura arborea	All	Convulsions, dilated pupils, fever, abnormal behavior, death
Apple	Malus spp.	Seed	Convulsions, vomiting, aberrant behavior, coma, death
Apricot	Prunus spp.	Kernel of pit	Convulsions, vomiting, aberrant behavior, coma, death
Arrowhead vine	Syngonium podophylum	Leaf	Occasional vomiting, diarrhea, oral pain and inflammation
Asparagus fern	Asparagus spp.	Young stem, berry	Contact dermatitis, possible gastrointestinal upset
Azalea	Rhododendron spp.	Leaf, flower, honey	Convulsions, vomiting, altered cardiac rhythm, abdominal pain, diarrhea, depression, death
Balsam pear	Momordica charantia	Seed, fruit rind	Vomiting, abdominal pain, diarrhea, death
Begonia	Begonia spp.	Leaf	Possible renal damage
Bird of paradise	Poinciana gilliesii	All, esp. seed	Vomiting, abdominal pain, diarrhea
Bittersweet	Celastrus scadens	Leaf, bark, seed	Convulsions, delayed vomiting, abdominal pain, death
Black-eyed Susan	Abrus precatorius	All, esp. seed	Delayed vomiting, abdominal pain, diarrhea, coma, death
Bleeding heart	Dicenta spp.	All	Convulsions, depression, death
Bluebonnet	See lupine		
Brazilian pepper	Schinus terebinthifolious	Flower, fruit	Contact dermatitis, asthma
Buckeye	Aesculus spp.	Twig, leaf, nut	Convulsions, vomiting, abdominal pain, diarrhea, coma, death
Caladium	Caladium spp.	All	Salivation with swelling and irritation of mouth, throat, and esophagus, death
Calla lily	Zantedeschia azedarach	All	Salivation with swelling and irritation of mouth, throat, and esophagus
Cardinal flower	Lobelia spp.	All	Convulsions, salivation, vomiting, rapid pulse
Castor bean	Ricinus communis	All, esp. seed	Convulsions, delayed vomiting, abdominal pain, diarrhea, coma, death
Cherry	Prunus spp.	Kernel of pit	Convulsions, vomiting, aberrant behavior, coma, death
Chinaberry	Melia azedarach	Fruit, bark	Convulsions, vomiting, abnormal behavior, diarrhea, paralysis, death
Clematis	Clematis spp.	All	Salivation, blistering of mucous membranes, delayed vomiting, abdominal pain, diarrhea, death
Climbing lily	See glory lily		
Coral plant	Jatropha mutifida	All, esp. seed, latex	Convulsions, delayed vomiting, abdominal pain, diarrhea, coma, contact dermatitis
Croton	Codiaeum spp.	Leaf	Possible gastrointestinal upset
Crown of thorns	Euphorbia milii	Latex	Local irritation from latex, gastrointestinal upset from ingestion
Daffodil	Narcissus spp.	All, esp. bulb	Occasional vomiting, diarrhea
Delphinium	Delphinium spp.	All	Convulsions, salivation, vomiting, difficulty breathing, collapse, coma, death
Dumb cane	Dieffenbachia spp.	All	Salivation with swelling and irritation of mouth, throat, and esophagus, death
Easter lily	Lilium longiflorum	All	Possible renal damage
Elderberry	Sambucus spp.	All (cooked fruit safe)	Convulsions, vomiting, aberrant behavior, coma
Elephant's ear	Colacasia spp.	All	Salivation with swelling and irritation of mouth, throat, and esophagus
English ivy	Hedera helix	All	Vomiting, abdominal pain, diarrhea, contact dermatitis
English yew	Taxus baccata	All	Vomiting, altered cardiac rhythm, abdominal pain, diarrhea, death
Euonymus	Euonymus spp.	Fruit	Convulsions, vomiting, abdominal pain, diarrhea
Four o'clock	Mirabilis jalapa	Root, seed	Occasional vomiting, diarrhea, contact dermatitis
Foxglove	Digitalis purpurea	All	Vomiting, altered cardiac rhythm, abdominal pain, diarrhea, death
Glory lily	Gloriosa spp.	All	Intense thirst, vomiting; later, abdominal pain, diarrhea, shock, coma, death
Heavenly bamboo	Nandina domestica	All	Vomiting, diarrhea, abnormal cardiac rhythms, convulsions, respiratory failure, death
Holly	Ilex spp.	Leaf, fruit	Vomiting, abdominal pain, diarrhea, death
Honeysuckle	Lonicera spp.	Berry	American varieties of honeysuckle may apparently be eaten safely, but the same species in Europe is highly toxic. Convulsions, delayed vomiting, abdominal pain, diarrhea, coma, death

Table 10-5: *Toxic ornamental plants.*

Common name	Scientific name	Toxic part	Symptoms
Horse chestnut	See Buckeye		
Hyacinth	*Hyacinth orientalis*	All	Occasional vomiting, diarrhea, contact dermatitis
Hydrangea	*Hydrangea macrophylla*	Flower bud	Convulsions, aberrant behavior, coma
Iris	*Iris* spp.	Root	Occasional vomiting, diarrhea
Jack-in-the-pulpit	*Arisaema triphyllum*	All	Salivation with swelling and irritation of mouth, throat, and esophagus
Jasmine	*Cestrum* spp.	All	Convulsions, dilated pupils, fever, abnormal behavior
Jerusalem cherry	*Solarnum psuedo-capsicum*	All	Delayed vomiting, abdominal pain, diarrhea
Jimson weed	*Datura stramonium*	All	Convulsions, dilated pupils, fever, abnormal behavior, death
Lantana	*Lantana camara*	All	Weakness, abdominal pain, diarrhea, circulatory failure, occasional death
Larkspur	See delphinium		
Lily-of-the-valley	*Convalleria magalis*	All	Vomiting, altered cardiac rhythm, abdominal pain, diarrhea, death
Lupine	*Lupinus argenteus*	All	Convulsions, death
Marijuana	*Cannabis sativa*	All	Salivation, abnormal cardiac rhythms, vomiting, diarrhea, convulsions, depression, incoordination, coma
Mistletoe	*Phoradendron* spp.	Leaf, stem, berry	Vomiting, abdominal pain, diarrhea
Mock orange	*Poncirus trifolata*	Fruit	Vomiting, abdominal pain, diarrhea
Morning glory	*Ipomoea* spp.	Seed	Convulsions, abnormal behavior
Narcissus	See daffodil		
Nightshade	*Atropa belladonna*	All	Convulsions, dilated pupils, fever, abnormal behavior, death
Oleander	*Nerium* spp.	All	Contact dermatitis, vomiting, altered cardiac rhythm, abdominal pain, diarrhea, death
Ornamental pepper	*Capsicum annuum*	Fruit, seed	Oral pain and inflammation
Peach	*Prunus* spp.	Kernel of pit	Convulsions, vomiting, aberrant behavior, coma, death
Pencil cactus	*Euphorbia tirucalli*	Latex	Local irritation from latex, gastrointestinal upset from ingestion
Periwinkle	*Vinca rosea*	All	Convulsions, abnormal behavior
Philodendron	*Philodendron* spp.	All	Salivation with swelling and irritation of mouth, throat, and esophagus
Plum	*Prunus* spp.	Kernel of pit	Convulsions, vomiting, aberrant behavior, coma, death
Poinsettia	*Euphorbia pulcherrrima*	All	Local irritation from latex, gastrointestinal upset from ingestion
Pokeweed	*Phytolacca americana*	All, esp. root	Delayed vomiting, abdominal pain, diarrhea, coma, death
Potato	*Solanum tuberosum*	Uncooked sprout, green skin	Delayed vomiting, abdominal pain, diarrhea, depression, death
Pothos	*Epipreminum aureum*	All	Occasional vomiting, diarrhea, salivation with swelling and irritation of mouth, throat, and esophagus
Privet	*Ligustrum* spp.	All	Vomiting, diarrhea, abdominal pain, death
Pyracantha	*Pyracantha* spp.	Berry	Contact dermatitis
Rhododendron	See azalea		
Rhubarb	*Rheum rhaponticum*	Leaf	Delayed vomiting, abdominal pain, diarrhea, coma, death
Rosary pea	See black-eyed Susan		
Rubber plant	*Ficus elastica*	Leaf, stem	Oral pain and inflammation
Sago palm	*Cycas revoluta*	All, esp. seeds	Vomiting, diarrhea, depression, convulsions, liver failure
Schefflera	*Brassaia actinophylla*	All, esp. root	Occasional vomiting, diarrhea, oral pain and inflammation
Snow-on-the-mountain	*Euphorbia marginata*	Latex	Local irritation from latex, gastrointestinal upset from ingestion
Sweet pea	*Latthyrus* spp.	Seed	Convulsions
Tobacco	*Nicotiana* spp.	All	Salivation, vomiting, rapid pulse, death
Tomato	*Lycopersicon esculentum*	Plant, green fruit	Vomiting, abdominal pain, diarrhea
Tulip	*Tulipsa* spp.	Bulb	Contact dermatitis
Weeping fig	*Ficus benjamina*	All	Oral pain and inflammation, dermatitis, vomiting and diarrhea if ingested
Windflower	See anemone		
Wisteria	*Wisteria* spp.	All	Occasional vomiting, diarrhea
Yellow jasmine	*Gelsenium sempervirens*	All	Convulsions, vomiting, abnormal behavior, diarrhea, paralysis, death

a hazard to children, as well. A diligent owner will purchase the least toxic products available to accomplish the job in the smallest quantity needed, to minimize the possibility of poisoning. Check the house and garage periodically to be sure that all chemical products are securely stored. Potential toxins should be kept as high as possible behind a well-secured door; safely discard products that are no longer needed or that have expired. Contaminated containers or rags should be stored securely and disposed of properly as soon as possible. Remember that the Weimaraner's curiosity may entice it into areas that are less commonly frequented by other household members, resulting in the dog's investigating forgotten boxes or chewing on old boards or paint flakes at the back of the closet, which may contain lead paint. Routinely inspect less-frequented areas for potential hazards.

Immunizations

Vaccination and Immunity

All puppies receive a series of inoculations for protection from contagious diseases, and adults should have regular boosters. Table 10-6 summarizes the diseases (except rabies) that can be prevented by immunization.

Passive immunity to communicable diseases is conferred by antibodies from an external source. The immune systems of all newborn mammals are incapable of producing antibodies, and they receive passive immunity from the mother. In canines, 5%–10% of the newborn's immunoglobulin G is obtained through placental transfer. All other maternal antibodies are transmitted in colostrum, the bluish milk produced immediately after giving birth (the puppies' intestines allow absorption of the large protein antibody molecules for about 24 hours after birth).

Active immunity develops through stimulation of the immune system to produce antibodies against specific antigens, either through infection with the organism or through vaccination. Vaccines resemble disease-causing organisms, stimulating the immune system to produce antibodies that attack and destroy the organisms. Modified-live (attenuated) vaccines are developed by laboratory culture of disease-producing organisms until the virulence is reduced and the disease is no longer produced. The living vaccine organisms stimulate an immune response that is almost as effective as an infection, but no living microorganism is foolproof. As the term suggests, killed vaccines are made from killed organisms; they stimulate a weaker, less-lasting immune response, but are safe to give during pregnancy and illness.

One of the most frequent causes of immunization failure is interference from the maternal antibodies that puppies obtain through the dam's colostrum. The maternal antibodies identify vaccines as infectious organisms and destroy them before the vaccines can stimulate an immune response. Thus, maternal antibodies must dissipate before vaccines can stimulate active immunity. When planning a litter, the breeder should try to give the dam's booster at least 6–9 months before breeding, never with the health examination prior to breeding.

On average, maternal distemper antibodies suppress an effective immune response until the puppies are about 14 weeks old. Vaccines are given earlier to protect the puppies at the low end of the spectrum; additionally, at least one parvovirus vaccine should be given after 18 weeks.

Canine parvovirus remains the single most serious threat to the puppy's health; outbreaks are still frequent and widespread. With canine parvovirus, interference from maternal antibodies is an even greater concern, especially if the dam received a booster shot just prior to breeding.

- Complete suppression of the response to canine parvovirus by maternal antibodies has been documented in puppies as old as 18 weeks
- Levels of maternal antibodies that suppress the response to vaccines do not provide protection against infection
- The response to canine parvovirus vaccine is blocked for 2–4 weeks after maternal antibodies are no longer detected
- 3–5 weeks may elapse between the time a puppy becomes susceptible to parvoviral infection and the time immunization with modified-live vaccine stimulates an immune response

A Safe and Effective Immunization Program

The breeder should discuss vaccine protocol with the veterinarian prior to breeding the bitch. Ask whether the vet has or will purchase and administer vaccines that are appropriate to the breed-specific needs of a Weimaraner and whether breeder or litter discounts are available. If not, some breeders may find it necessary to purchase and administer vaccines themselves to minimize costs or when appropriate vaccines are not available through the regular vet. When purchasing vaccines be sure that shipping procedures keep vaccines properly chilled. Also check that expiration dates are well in the future so that excess vaccines can be properly stored and used at a later date.

The vaccination procedure is simple and quite safe, as long as the following precautions are observed:

- Transport vaccines in a refrigerated container and store in a refrigerator—biological products lose potency when warm for even a brief time
- Store vaccines out of direct sunlight
- Discard vaccines after the expiration date—biological products lose their potency over time
- Give the exact dose indicated—the immunizing dosage is the same for Chihuahuas and Saint Bernards

- Allow alcohol to evaporate before giving the injection—vaccines can be inactivated by excessive alcohol
- Use a new, sterile syringe for each shot

The WCA currently has the following statement on its website (www.weimclubamerica.org) regarding vaccinations:

A small percentage of Weimaraner puppies manifest an autoimmune reaction following vaccination. When the immune system of susceptible individuals is challenged by multiple antigens, it becomes hyper-reactive and responds in the same way it would respond to fight off an infection: fever, elevated white blood cell count, and inflammatory reaction of tissues and joints. Although many puppies can be vaccinated with no adverse reaction, there is no way at the present time to determine which puppies may react. Past research has documented reactions occurring between 8–16 weeks of age, with the greatest number of reactions seen in puppies 12—16 weeks of age.

Several of the vaccine manufacturers have assured breeders that immunity in puppies can be achieved with only two vaccines, provided that the second vaccine is given when the puppy is 12 weeks old. Therefore, the Board of Directors of the WCA recommends the following vaccine schedule:

8 weeks: Distemper, Adenovirus Type 2, Parainfluenza, and Parvovirus

12 weeks: Distemper, Adenovirus Type 2, Parainfluenza, and Parvovirus

Recombinant-DNA vaccines have shown a significantly lower incidence of reactions; while this protocol helps in preventing reactions, it does not prevent them in all susceptible individuals. Vaccinations for Corona, Leptospirosis, Bordetella, and Lyme should be considered "elective" and only given to dogs considered "at risk." The occurrence of Leptospirosis is increasing among working dogs, so dogs that hunt regularly or have frequent contact with wild game or rodent feces should be considered at risk. Refer to Appendix F for Dr. Draper's article on this matter. "Elective" vaccines should be given only after the initial puppy series is completed.

However, if a breeder is concerned that autoimmune disorder might be a problem in their dogs' bloodlines, the more aggressive program outlined here might help expose this weakness. The authors believe in a practical vaccination program that will moderately challenge the immune system of a puppy and reveal any susceptibility to auto-immune weakness. A breeder, who suspects the potential for an autoim-

mune susceptibility may wish to delay placing puppies in homes to allow for further evaluation.

6 weeks	Parvovirus vaccine (modified-live): Pfizer's Vanguard +CPV
9 weeks	Canine distemper, Adenovirus Type 2, measles, parainfluenza vaccine (modified-live): Pfizer's Vanguard DA2 MP
12 weeks	Parvo (modified-live): Vanguard +CPV
14 weeks	Canine distemper, Adenovirus Type 2, measles, parainfluenza vaccine (modified-live): Pfizer's Vanguard DA2 MP (this should not occur earlier than 14 weeks)
16 weeks	Parvo (modified-live): Pfizer's Vanguard +CPV (Bordatella vaccine may be given at this time if you may be boarding your dog in the future; although it has not necessarily been proven effective, most reputable kennels require this)
20 weeks	1-year rabies: The initial vaccine is valid for only one year; some states allow subsequent rabies vaccines at 3-year intervals (local laws may require adjustments, but giving rabies in conjunction with other vaccines should be avoided whenever possible)

Leptospirosis, Bordatella, and Lyme vaccinations should only be considered if your veterinarian indicates they are endemic to your area. Since they are "elective," these additional vaccines should be given after the initial puppy series is complete.

No matter what immunization series and vaccines are used, minimize everything that could possibly contribute to the puppy's stress. Only vaccinate normal, active, healthy puppies; never vaccinate a puppy that shows signs of illness, such as fever or diarrhea. Avoid giving worming preparations at the same time as vaccines.

2006 AAHA Vaccine Recommendations

The American Animal Hospital Association (AAHA) issued new recommendations in April 2006. Vaccines are now arranged in core and non-core groupings. Core vaccines, recommended for all dogs, include rabies, distemper, hepatitis, and Parvovirus. Non-core vaccines, those suggested only for "at-risk" dogs, include Bordatella, Leptospirosis, and Lyme. Giardia and Corona are not recommended as part of an immunization program. The guidelines can be reviewed at www.aahanet.org. All

---

Vaccination Education

American Animal Hospital Association 2006 Vaccine recommendations: http://www.aahanet.org/PublicDocuments/VaccineGuidelines06Revised.pdf

American Veterinary Medical Association Vaccine FAQs: http://www.avma.org/animal_health/brochures/vaccination/vaccination_brochure.asp

Table 10-6: *Communicable diseases for which vaccines are available.*

Disease Type	Symptoms	Other Characteristics	Disease Type	Symptoms	Other Characteristics
DISTEMPER			**PARVOVIRUS**		
Subacute	Initial mild symptoms often overlooked	Airborne viral disease	*Acute* *Enteric form*	Strikes all ages Sudden onset 5–10 days after exposure	Often subacute or subclinical Most deaths occur 48–72 hours after exposure
	Onset 6–9 days after exposure	Neurological complications (encephalitis, seizures, residual impairment)		Depression Loss of appetite Elevated temperature	Uncomplicated cases usually recover rapidly after 3–4 days
	Elevated temperature subsides after 1–3 days	Distemper teeth (pitting, brownish discoloration)		Vomiting, diarrhea Severe dehydration	
Acute	Obvious clinical distress Onset 12–16 days after exposure Temperature rises again Reddened mucous membranes and eyes (avoids light) Purulent discharge—eyes, nostrils Loss of appetite Occasional diarrhea		*Myocardial form*	3–4 weeks of age— sudden death, occasionally preceded by brief respiratory difficulty 8 weeks or older— weakness, depression, acute respiratory difficulty	Prenatal placental infection Prenatal placental infection Becoming rare as more dams are vaccinated Mortality rate 90%; many survivors die within a year from residual cardiac impairment
HEPATITIS	Onset 4–6 days after exposure Elevated temperature Loss of appetite and weight Jaundiced (yellow) corneas and mucous membranes	Viral disease related to distemper Not common, but has high mortality	**KENNEL COUGH**	Dry, hacking cough Gagging with occasional vomiting Appetite usually remains normal Elevated temperature rare, unless infection present	Caused by 13 different bacteria and viruses; vaccines for only 3: Parainfluenza, Bordatella, and Adenovirus Type 2 Highly contagious, but rarely serious in healthy adults Secondary infections can be fatal in puppies and aging dogs
LEPTOSPIROSIS			**CORONA VIRUS**	Sudden onset Vomiting, diarrhea	Highly contagious diarrhea Usually self-limiting
Subacute	Loss of energy Dry coat Dull eyes	Affects most warm-blooded species, but most strains prefer specific hosts		Dehydration Elevated temperatures Loss of appetite Depression	Can be fatal to puppies and aging dogs Effectiveness of vaccine debatable, so no longer recommended by AAHA
Acute	Sudden onset Elevated temperature Loss of appetite Dehydration, vomiting Reddened eyes Tense abdominal muscles, arching loin May exhibit pain when urinating	Transmitted by direct contact through cuts, abrasions, and and even unbroken skin Infected animals excrete organism for 2 years after clinical recovery	**LYME DISEASE**—See text		

dog owners should discuss the needs and implications of these recommendations with a trusted veterinarian.

The first adult boosters, as recommended by AAHA, should be given 1 year after the last puppy shot at 16 weeks, not at 1 year of age. After the first adult boosters, core vaccines should be updated on a 3-year rotation, while non-core vaccines are normally recommended to be updated on an annual basis. Annual health checks would still be a wise course of action to forestall other health issues. A trusted veterinarian can provide counsel regarding the vaccines and boosters needed to keep your Weimaraner healthy based on the age, locale, and activities of the individual dog.

Parasites
External Parasites

Fleas and Ticks

Fleas and ticks are more than just a nuisance, they can spread parasites and disease to humans as well as other pets. Fortunately, flea and tick control has progressed a great deal in recent years. In the past, flea and tick control products were often difficult to apply, lasted only a short time, and could be toxic to people and pets if not applied following extremely specific instructions.

Today, new products are available that offer relatively long-lasting protection and are safer and easier to apply. Currently, there are several different products using differing methods of control: some kill only adults, others prevent the pests from reproducing. Basically, once a month, a small amount of liquid is applied to the back of the dog's neck to protect against both fleas and ticks. Two of the most popular products come well recommended by veterinarians— Frontline® and Advantage®. It is still important to consult a veterinarian before using the products and to follow the instructions exactly. Be aware that some flea and tick control products may be fatal to cats; cats that groom their canine housemates are at higher risk. Use of the product should be discontinued in the case of breeding animals, or seasonally as the weather permits.

Use of the product does not mean that an owner should neglect the routine of checking the dog for external parasites (or injury) following excursions to areas where fleas and ticks are known to be present.

Ticks

Disease-carrying ticks are prevalent throughout the United States. Check your pet for ticks when returning home from a run in the woods, the veterinary clinic, or any other place where ticks may have dropped off other dogs. Be sure to carefully check the tick's favored hiding spots—inside the folds of the ears, inside the elbow, at the base of the tail, and between the forelegs and perineal area. Spotting these pests is relatively easy with the short, sleek coat of the Weimaraner.

If the dog has only a few ticks, they may be removed with tweezers or a tick puller. Never remove ticks with your fingers; if the tick ruptures, the organism that causes Rocky Mountain spotted fever and Lyme disease can be transmitted though the skin. Kill ticks by placing in a vial of isopropyl alcohol; remember that crushing the tick may spread disease, and ticks flushed down the toilet can readily crawl back out.

If occasional ticks are detected and removed immediately, the house and yard may not become infested. Professional exterminators use long-acting products that are safer around pets to control ticks. Some breeders consider sonic insect repellents highly effective for ticks as well as fleas.

Tick-borne Diseases

Tick fever is a popular term for any tick-borne disease. If a previously healthy dog begins to display symptoms of fever, sudden lethargy, and swollen joints after being in an area where ticks are endemic, consider having a tick panel run on a blood sample. There are a number of tick-borne diseases that encompass a variety of symptoms. Although some respond better to treatment than others, in all cases, the sooner treatment is initiated, the better the prognosis.

Lyme Disease

Lyme disease is of special concern because it infects humans as well as dogs (especially hunting dogs), cats, cattle, and horses. The organism is spread by ticks and is particularly prevalent in deer ticks.

The disease is characterized by painful swollen joints, lameness, and fever; other symptoms are produced by the organism's invasion of the heart, kidney, liver, and other organs. After diagnosis, Lyme disease usually responds readily to treatment; however, when the disease has progressed to the point of nephrosis, prognosis is more guarded. It should be noted that many dogs will titer-test positive for quite some time even after treatment. Dogs that have been successfully treated for Lyme are NOT immune to future infection and should still be revaccinated under the regular vaccination protocol.

An improved vaccine that became available in 2004, Rlyme® (*Borrelia burgdorferi* bacterial extract) by Merial, has reduced the potential for complications. However, it is not necessary to vaccinate for this disease unless it is endemic to areas the dog frequents.

Canine Erlichiosis

Canine erlichiosis reached the United States around 1962, carried by dogs returning from Vietnam, but no vaccine has been developed. Because of the rapid spread of canine erlichiosis to all parts of the United States, dog owners should be familiar with its symptoms, especially after being exposed to brown dog ticks, which are the primary vector and are found throughout the country. Do not assume that a dog does not have erlichiosis just because the disease has not yet been reported in the area.

The acute phase of erlichiosis occurs 10–14 days after exposure and is characterized by bleeding from the nose or gums, bruising on the skin (caused by low platelets), loss of appetite, weight loss, and intermittent fever. The severity ranges from so mild that it is unnoticeable to life threatening. Untreated survivors become carriers, and they enter one of the two chronic phases—mild chronic/subclinical or severe chronic.

The mild chronic/subclinical phase is characterized by general unthriftiness. Stress, such as pregnancy, surgery, malnutrition, or illness, may precipitate a transition to the severe chronic phase.

The severe chronic phase develops 50–100 days following exposure. The organism inhibits all bone-marrow functions that produce the red and white blood cells and clotting factors. The dog is acutely ill, and treatment at this stage is often unsuccessful.

Several aspects of this disease are particularly alarming: (a) recovery does not confer immunity, and re-infection may occur despite a high antibody level; (b) an infected bitch not only transmits the disease to her puppies but also may hemorrhage during delivery; and (c) a healthy carrier state has been identified.

Rocky Mountain Spotted Fever

Although more common in humans, canines are also susceptible to the organism that causes Rocky Mountain spotted fever. Several species of ticks, known as "hard ticks," are vectors for the spread of this disease, most commonly the deer and wood ticks.

The severity ranges from acute to subclinical. Symptoms vary greatly and include fever, loss of appetite, depression, joint pain, swelling, and neurological abnormalities such as seizures. As with erlichiosis, the clotting mechanism is affected, causing bleeding from the nostrils and certain areas of the skin. Treatment is usually successful, and dogs appear to develop immunity.

Fleas

Fleas are a source of discomfort and annoyance; in addition, they transmit tapeworms, which infest both dogs and cats. Flea collars are minimally effective on dogs as large as Weimaraners. Although sprays, shampoos, and powders kill live fleas, new eggs hatch in 8–10 days. As with ticks, dips provide residual protection for up to 2 weeks; spot-on products may give protection for up to 1 month. Most flea and tick products for dogs are often fatal to cats.

Check with your veterinarian before using flea-killing products on puppies that are less than 2 months old. To rid puppies of fleas, fill a tub with warm water deep enough to reach the puppy's throat and slowly immerse the puppy. The fleas climb to the puppy's head, where they must be removed and killed by hand. Keep the puppy warm until completely dry.

Mange

Mange is diagnosed by microscopic examination of a skin scraping and hair roots. Sarcoptic mange is caused by a mite found in the hair and outer layers of the skin, causing severe itching and thickening of the skin. Although mange is highly contagious, treatment is easy and usually effective. Sarcoptic mange may be transmitted to humans, causing intense itching and small red lesions. A physician or dermatologist should be consulted; treatment is usually as simple and effective for humans as it is for dogs.

Demodectic mange is caused by a mite that most dogs carry, and the onset of skin lesions usually coincides with something that suppresses the immune system, such as stress, illness, vaccinations, or shipping. The mild, localized type of mange begins with loss of hair near the mouth and eyes or the forelegs, which may clear up spontaneously. The serious type of demodectic mange (possibly a severe allergic reaction) is characterized by loss of hair in large areas and red skin, which eventually thickens. Treatment is usually successful, although untreated mange leads to severe debilitation and even death; lack of response to treatment may suggest an underlying autoimmune deficiency. Demodectic mange is not normally transmitted to humans.

Internal Parasites

Gastrointestinal

So many non-prescription anthelmintics (worming products) can be purchased though veterinary supply stores and catalogs that dog owners tend to be complacent about their usage. No anthelmintic is effective against all gastrointestinal parasites, and some products are highly dangerous if improperly used.

Any bitch that has ever had roundworms (most have) can pass them on to puppies despite consistently negative stool examinations. The dormant parasites in her tissues are reactivated by pregnancy and pass through the placental barrier to infest unborn puppies. Despite this shortfall, it is still advisable to worm a bitch several weeks prior to breeding to ensure her optimal health. After whelping, roundworms are transmitted through her milk. Because of this, many breeders routinely worm puppies—Nemex 2 is a safe, easy-to-give

Table 10-7: *Gastrointestinal parasites.*

Roundworms
- Acquired at any age by ingesting of contaminated food, water, and so forth
- Mature roundworms are periodically expelled in the stool; the white, spaghetti-like worms are about 3 inches long and may be straight or curly
- Rarely cause symptoms in adults; larvae that are not excreted migrate and become dormant cysts in the somatic tissues
- Dormant larvae are activated by pregnancy, migrating through the placenta to puppies (check dam's stool before breeding); later, larvae are transmitted through milk
- Infested puppies are characteristically unthrifty, with potbellies, dull coats, and occasional diarrhea; mature roundworms are expelled in vomit and stool

Hookworms
- Serious and potentially fatal at any age
- Acquired at any age by ingestion of contaminated food, water, and so forth; also penetrate skin from contaminated soil, migrating to intestinal tract
- Adult parasites attach to the intestinal lining, suck blood, and cause bleeding into the intestines
- May have foul-smelling, tarry stool; other symptoms include pale gums (from anemia), weakness, emaciation, occasional diarrhea with dehydration, and dull, brittle coat
- Larvae that are not excreted may become dormant in somatic tissues
- Dormant larvae are activated by pregnancy (check dam's stool before breeding); some placental transfer, but most larvae transmitted through milk
- Heavily infested puppies appear acutely ill, with pale gums (severe anemia); may die from anemia before 3 weeks old
- Puppies and older dogs with serious infestations may require blood transfusions before treatment for the parasites

Whipworms
- Small, threadlike worms acquired at any age by ingestion of contaminated food, water, and so forth
- Vague symptoms such as dry coat, poor condition, and a characteristic intermittent diarrhea with mucous and blood
- Expelled at infrequent intervals and often absent in stool specimens; such a common cause of chronic diarrhea in adult dogs that many are treated empirically without a positive stool

Tapeworms
- Flat, segmented worms spread by fleas and lice from infested animals (dogs, cats, rodents)
- Head attaches to intestinal lining; flat, square, whitish segments break off and may be observed in stool or attached to hairs around the anal area
- Often non-symptomatic, but may produce intermittent diarrhea, dry coat, and unthrifty appearance

Coccidia
- Occurs in puppies over 1 month old; not highly pathogenic in adults
- Characterized by weight loss, dehydration, and diarrhea (sometimes bloody)
- Usually associated with other infectious agents, stress, or immunosuppression

Giardia
- Characterized by weight loss and chronic diarrhea (continuous or intermittent) but sometimes non-symptomatic
- Stool soft, poorly formed, pale, and contains mucus

Figure 10-9: *"I told you those puppies had roundworms,"* said the breeder to the veterinarian, who had objected to dispensing the worming product for puppies with negative stool specimens. Stool samples are usually viewed for eggs of parasites; pups can have worms that are too immature to have laid eggs. Many worming products are safe enough to use if there is no other explanation for unthrifty puppies.

liquid. Always be sure that the puppy or adult takes the entire amount of the anthelmintics, whether mixed with very small amounts of very tasty food— fed by hand to be sure the dog consumes all the medication—or given in capsules or pills. If vomiting occurs after worming several dogs, try to identify which one lost all or part of the dose. Check with the veterinarian before re-treating the dog with any product that causes vomiting.

Heartworms

Once limited to the southern and coastal areas, heartworm is now found throughout the United States. The larvae of this insidious killer are transmitted in infected mosquitoes.

Symptoms depend on the severity and duration of the infection. Early symptoms include weight loss, poor appetite, loss of stamina, cough, weakness, and bloody sputum. As the parasites fill the heart chamber and interfere with circulation, cardiac abnormalities develop. Larvae and immunological phenomena may damage the liver and kidneys. Sudden death may occur at any stage of the disease from blockage of blood vessels.

Treatment and prognosis depend on the severity and duration of the infection. Recently introduced products have proven to be far more effective than the older ones, with fewer side effects. Most dog owners now maintain their dogs on preventive medication during mosquito season or year-round. Dogs must first be screened for heartworm because giving the medication to infected dogs may cause serious— sometimes fatal—reactions. Currently, Heartguard® and Interceptor® are the most popular heartworm preventives recommended by veterinarians. Heartguard Plus® and Interceptor® also provide treatment for certain types of intestinal worms as well, for Weimaraners living in areas and participating in activities that expose them to these parasites on a regular basis. For areas in which mosquitoes are seasonal, treatment should be discontinued during the winter months. There is anecdotal evidence suggesting that heartworm preventives potentially cause complications with bitches during breeding, pregnancy, and lactation.

Unfortunate Encounters

Skunks

No Weimaraner owner will ever forget it if their canine companion has ever had a close encounter with a skunk. The thick, gooey, liquid musk seems to stick to anything and unfortunately the thiolacetates (responsible for the foul smell) slowly break down into other thiols, which most people can smell even in small concentrations. Most skunk odor remedies merely mask the odor for a short time, and given the least amount of moisture to refresh the thiols, the odor of skunk is a gift that just keeps on giving. The following remedy has proven to be the most effective (even if not complete) method for reducing skunk odor to manageable levels. The mixture can only be mixed as needed and cannot be stored; the ingredients react to released oxygen molecules, which bind with the thiols, but if enclosed, the mixture may cause the container to explode.

1 quart of peroxide

1/4 cup baking soda

2 tablespoons dishwashing liquid

(double or quadruple recipe as needed for size of dog)

Mix ingredients in an open container. Immediately pour on the dog, being sure to saturate the coat and skin. Avoid getting mixture in eyes, nose, or mouth. Rinse completely with warm water.

WARNING: Do not mix ahead of time or try to store the solution in a closed container.

Recent conversations with owners of skunk-sprayed canines have revealed that the readily available Febreze™ spray effectively removes skunk odors. The ASPCA has given Febreze™ its Seal of Approval when used as directed. This solution may be the most convenient because Febreze™ is easily stored at home or carried in a car.

Porcupines

Encounters with porcupines are some of the most painful wildlife encounters the Weimaraner may experience. Although most porcupines are peace-loving animals and will usually attempt to amble off when confronted by the insistent and curious Weimaraner, they will not hesitate to make their point. The quills of the porcupine can inflict severe and painful injuries; the poor dog only seems to make the situation worse, biting and pawing at the barbs, working them farther in. The actual process of removing the quills is usually not difficult: clip off the end of the hollow barb and draw the quill straight out.

However, because the quills are usually numerous, very painful to remove, and often in very sensitive areas—such as the face and mouth—the services of a veterinarian are usually required to sedate or tranquilize the dog and to prescribe follow-up care to prevent infection, especially if quills are in the mouth or ears, or in or near the eyes.

Figure 10-10: *The natural curiosity of the Weimaraner* may lead it to an unfortunate encounter. Hopefully, Cash has learned his lesson and will stop to reconsider the next time he meets the odd-looking porcupine.

Snakes

Admittedly, not all snakes are poisonous; however, snakebites are notorious for becoming infected. All snakebites should be closely monitored for infection. If the species of snake is not identifiable, it is best to assume that the snake was poisonous. Current veterinary recommendations include:

Do: Keep the dog as quiet and calm as possible
Immobilize the bite area
Keep the bite below the level of the heart
Transport immediately for veterinary care

Do not: Attempt to cut the bite or suction out poison
Do not use ice packs and pressure bandages
Do not apply a tourniquet

A California company—Red Rock Biologics—has recently introduced a vaccine that is reported to stimulate the dog's immune system to create antibodies against the venom of certain species of rattlesnakes commonly found in the western United States. Although the dog would still require veterinary treatment, the company claims that vaccinated dogs experience less pain and fewer complications and that they recover more quickly. The company advertises that it is working to develop vaccines for other species of snakes in other parts of the country, including coral snakes and water moccasins. This vaccine has an especially low rate of allergic responses, but little evidence exists at this time regarding the efficacy of the vaccine in field conditions. If the Weimaraner frequents areas where these species of rattlesnakes are common, discuss the vaccine with your veterinarian. Refer to the current guidelines available through the AAHA website regarding this vaccine.

Owners and trainers of dogs that are trained or that run regularly in areas where snakes may be a threat should consider the option of snake aversion training; consult a professional for this service.

Juvenile Acne

Juvenile acne is quite common in young Weimaraners up to about 9 weeks, and is not unusual up to about 10 months. It is characterized by small pimples, commonly on the upper and lower lips and occasionally on the back, legs, or feet; in areas where the fur is denser, the pimples will not be easily visible but may be inferred by the area of raised fur. The acne is caused by a low-grade *Staphylococcus* infection. However, it appears there may be a connection between recurring episodes of juvenile acne and a weak or compromised immune system; owners of these pups should have titers performed before routine vaccinations to avoid unnecessary immune challenges.

Cleanliness of the puppy's play and sleeping areas is the first step in controlling puppy acne. For very young puppies, sponge on a 1:100 Betadine® solution, which appears the color of weak tea. For older puppies, the dog can simply stand in the solution to soak only the feet, with the owner sponging on additional solution. Allow the solution to dry for approximately 10 minutes and then rinse with clean water. It is important not to get the solution in the eyes or to frighten the puppy during the procedure to avoid creating a fear of bathing or water; make the experience a positive one for the future water retriever with treats, praise, and play.

Should the problem persist or become widespread, with swelling over the head and neck area, a veterinarian should be consulted, as it is possible that the infection, left untreated, could advance to a serious condition called puppy strangles. Typical treatment requires more rigorous cleaning procedures and antibiotic therapy.

Figure 10-11: *Snakebite.* This 8-month-old Weimaraner puppy was bitten in the face by a rattlesnake that got into his dog run. The ice pack, improvised from a 6 × 24-inch rag with the ends torn into four tails that could be criss-crossed over the ears, slowed the spread of venom during the frantic drive to the veterinarian's.

Gynecological Disorders

Vaginitis, the inflammation of the vagina, is usually caused by a bacterial infection. It is characterized by a vaginal discharge that ranges from clear to blood-tinged. Many puppy bitches have vaginitis, and some veterinarians consider treatment unnecessary because the problem usually clears up spontaneously with the first heat. The absence of fever, generalized illness, and abnormal laboratory tests helps to differentiate vaginitis from uterine disorders in an older dog. The usual treatment of this condition in adult dogs is antibiotics.

Metritis is an acute or chronic bacterial infection of the uterus that can occur anytime the cervix is open: (a) during season; (b) at the time of breeding, being introduced to the stud; and (c) at whelping. It is most common after whelping that has been complicated by dystocia and retained placental material, but it can also follow an uncomplicated pregnancy and delivery.

Acute metritis is characterized by an elevated temperature, increased thirst, loss of appetite, depression, vomiting, occasional diarrhea, and a purulent vaginal discharge; however, not all metritis is open and draining.

The symptoms of chronic metritis are highly variable. There may be persistent or intermittent vaginal discharge. Chronic infection may be suggested by failure to conceive and by stillborn or weak puppies that die soon after birth.

Pyometra is the accumulation of pus in the uterus, with or without concurrent bacterial infection, and is associated with increased progesterone production. It is more common in bitches over 5 years old.

The first sign is usually loss of appetite, followed by depression, excessive thirst, and excessive urination; vomiting often occurs after drinking a large amount of water. Initially, the temperature may be elevated, but later, the temperature drops to subnormal. Other signs include progressive weakness, distended abdomen, enlarged vulva, and vaginal discharge. Recently, new treatments have been developed that may be successful in treating the early stages of this problem; find a veterinarian who will provide testing and cultures if pyometra is suspected in order to protect the reproductive potential of the bitch. Testing and treatment may prove quite costly; for animals not reserved for a breeding program, spaying may be the preferred course. Unless diagnosed and treated early, pyometra often progresses rapidly to an acute, life-threatening emergency in which the only way to save the bitch's life is to spay her immediately.

Lick Granulomas

Lick granulomas—skin ulcers caused by obsessive licking—are common in Weimaraners, especially in the fall. The typical causes of the behavior are isolation, boredom, and changes in the environment. The most frequent site is the anterior surface of the pastern or foot, so convenient to lick while lying down.

Unless the behavior is changed, treatment is frustrating. The best way to alter the behavior is to introduce change in the dog's daily routine; reduce crate time, enroll the dog in doggie daycare or have playtime at the dog park 1 or 2 days a week, take more frequent walks, or even give the dog some new, different toys to play with.

If caught when the spot is bald and before the skin surface is broken, spraying the skin with Bitter Apple® or other foul-tasting product may discourage the behavior. The author has had good results with EMT Wound Care Gel,® allowed to air dry, and alternated with a product called Sulfodene® by Farnam Pet products, applied 3 or 4 times daily to the irritated area. Bandaging the opposite paw maybe also be sufficient to distract the dog; if not, both front legs and feet should be treated several times a day for 3–4 days or longer if necessary, because the Weimaraner determined to lick tends to start on a different spot. Once the surface of the skin is broken and ulcerations appear, treatment of a lick granuloma becomes more difficult. The ulcer must be protected from licking; try EMT Wound Care Gel,® with or without a dressing, secured firmly with adhesive tape or even duct tape and thoroughly sprayed with Bitter Apple.® Dressings must be changed daily. Some Weimaraners are not deterred by this, and an Elizabethan collar is the only way to stop licking long enough to permit healing. In addition, the collar offends the Weimaraner's dignity and pride, which sometimes helps to discourage the behavior. In extreme cases, steroids may be indicated; accupuncture has also been successful as an alternative treatment.

Hot Spots

Weimaraners are not typically prone to "hot spots," which are more frequently associated with breeds with longer hair, but they can occasionally occur in this breed. Hot spots, left

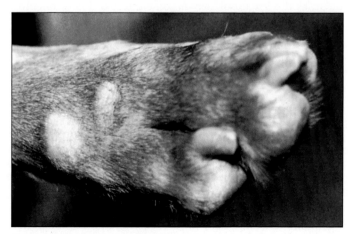

Figure 10-12: *Lick granulomas.*

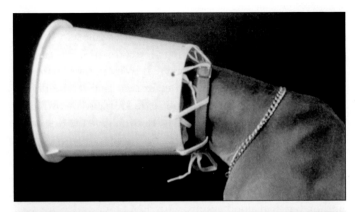

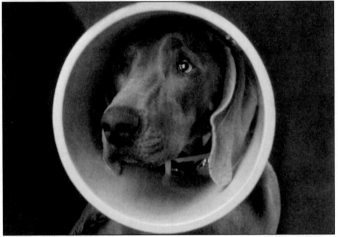

Figure 10-13: *An inexpensive substitute for an Elizabethan collar* can be made from a small, round, plastic wastebasket (99¢). It has the additional advantage of not gouging holes in walls. **(a)** Cut off the bottom, punch holes every 3–4 inches, and lace the basket onto the collar. **(b)** Annie enjoyed showing off her "bucket head."

untreated, can quickly become large and infected. If noticed quickly, apple cider vinegar and tea tree oil may be effective in reducing the hot spot immediately. For larger or more irritated areas, the above-mentioned EMT and Sulfodene will normally reduce the discomfort without further treatment. Large, oozing hot spots may require veterinary treatment, as the irritations may become infected due to ongoing scratching. Once again, an Elizabethan collar may be required to stop the dog from further exacerbating the irritation.

Hygromas

A hygroma is a cyst-like, subcutaneous swelling of the joint capsule caused by repeated bruising against a hard surface; the swelling comes from the joint's bursa—a fibrous sac lined with a membrane that secretes fluid.

In dogs, hygromas (sometimes the size of a golf ball) typically occur on the elbow, and prevention is easier than cure. When questioned, owners may recall that the dog habitually rests on a hard surface, such as ceramic tile in hot weather, and often lies down with a "flop," striking the surface forcefully. When this behavior is observed, immediately place a thick rug on the dog's usual resting place, or provide an invitingly den-like dog crate with a padded bottom. Even after a hygroma begins, elimination of the cause improves the prognosis.

In Weimaraners, unfortunately, breeders have observed a higher incidence in some families, suggesting a hereditary predisposition to elbow hygromas. To some degree, this appears to be age related, often starting at just over 6 months. If the hard surfaces habitually used when the dog lies down are eliminated, the hygromas often disappear spontaneously and without medical treatment by the time the dog is 12–18 months old. A cushioned bandage designed specifically for dogs is made by DogLeggs® (www.dogleggs.com) and is covered by some pet health insurance companies.

For extreme or resistant cases, therapy consists of draining the fluid and injecting a steroid into the joint. This is not always successful, particularly if the cause has not been eliminated; it also carries some risk of introducing infection, especially if done repeatedly, as is usually necessary with this treatment. If the hygroma continues to recur, the problem can be cured by surgical removal of the bursa. However, this is an expensive and somewhat risky major surgical procedure; oftentimes this procedure may alter the dog's front end movement. Reports of the most successful treatment have included a multi-pronged approach: using a pressure bandage to protect and cushion the joint and to reduce swelling; providing a cushioned surface in the dog's favored resting areas; and having a healthy dose of patience and time.

Coprophagia

Coprophagia means stool eating, and many canines shock and shame their owners with the extremely offensive behavior. Eating cat and horse feces is often considered normal canine behavior. Eating the stool of mature canines is the most distressing and difficult-to-control type and is considered a behavior vice.

The incidence of coprophagia is difficult to assess because few owners admit to the problem, but coprophagia is mentioned often enough in the literature to suggest that it is fairly prevalent. Owners suffer silently, too embarrassed to ask for help. If they find the courage to admit to the problem, they receive little compassion, receive assurances there is no harmful effect on the dog, and—above all—receive no help!

In fact, coprophagia is far from harmless:

- It is almost impossible to keep coprophagics free of intestinal parasites
- Coprophagia is the primary mode of transmission of lungworm in dogs

Figure 10-14: *A new treatment for hygromas.* **(a)** The result of constant pressure or frequent "banging," the joint becomes filled with fluid, but hygromas are usually not painful. Treatment usually involves time and patience, and prevention is far easier than a cure. **(b)** Resolution requires not only treatment of the dog, but removing the circumstances that caused the problem in the first place. To avoid surgery, a new treatment has recently been developed; a clever wrap-around Velcro garment, Dogleggs,® protect joints from a variety of ailments and have been very successful in treating hygromas. Photograph courtesy of Adriana Carolina Kubes.

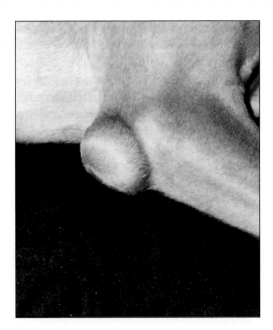

- Coprophagia is a symptom of chronic pancreatic insufficiency
- Severe thiamine deficiency is associated with loss of appetite and coprophagia

The most harmful effect is probably the damage to the owner's love for his or her pet. Many coprophagics are banished to the backyard; when they are taken to the dog pound, the disorder must be considered life threatening.

An intensive search of veterinary literature reveals that no formal, systematic research has been done. Except when the cause is a disease, theories of the causes boil down to vague guesses. Some of the suggestions include boredom, stress, confinement to a dog run, lack of human companionship, and so forth.

Treatment is generally unsuccessful. Suggested measures include making the stool unpalatable by sprinkling it with Bitter Apple®, Tabasco,® or red pepper. The literature also recommends a change in environment and dog food, as well as alleviating boredom and stress.

Two products are currently available on the market to treat this problem: For-Bid® and Dis-taste.® They are only moderately effective and must be used shortly after the onset of the behavior. For-Bid® is slightly more effective; however, it is too expensive for long-term use—the active ingredient for this product is MSG, which is also the active ingredient in the meat tenderizer Accent.® Furthermore, coprophagics prefer the stool of kennelmates, which means that all dogs must be maintained on the product indefinitely. Upon inquiry and with assurance of confidentiality, a number of Weimaraner owners confessed to their dog's shameful vice and provided information. With only five exceptions, the onset of coprophagia followed confirmed association with another coprophagic! In Weimaraners, coprophagia appears

to be another expression of the breed's copycat trait, and the primary cause is learning the behavior from another dog.

The following pattern appeared consistently:

- All five exceptions to association with another coprophagics were bitches between the ages of 3 and 6 months, and they were the least responsive to corrective measures
- The younger the bitch, the more quickly she copied the behavior
- Males were slowest to copy the behavior and the most responsive to corrective measures

Three hard-core adult coprophagic bitches were used to discover which corrective measures—if any—were effective. They were first wormed—despite regular wormings, all had hookworms, whipworms, and tapeworms because of their vice. All were negative for pancreatitis.

Figure 10-15: *Long before being inducted into the Hall of Fame,* this Best in Show Weimaraner became famous for his artwork, produced from recycled dog food. Although not a cure, MSG and Vitamin B, added daily to the food of all dogs in the household, may reduce the temptation to snack on such artistic creations.

- MSG. Using gradual increments, the addition of 1 1/2 tablespoons per 2 cups of dog food inhibited but did not halt the behavior; increasing the amount of MSG produced no further effect. (For-Bid® was not tested because the recommended amount cost more than $3 per day per dog.)

- Brewer's yeast. To test whether the addition of a rich source of B vitamins might decrease their craving, brewer's yeast was added to the MSG. This proved to be the most effective nutritional measure, as the least determined of the three stopped eating the stool.

- Asparaginase. Literature for nutritional supplements that contain the enzyme asparaginase claims that coprophagics cease the behavior after a few weeks on the products (K-zyme®, Pro-zyme®), and it certainly seemed worth trying. The only response observed was that they seemed to find the stool tastier.

- Electric shock. As a last resort, an electric shock collar was used, and this proved to be highly effective.

Interestingly, the response to electric shock supported the theory of mimicry and behavioral reinforcement of coprophagia. As each received the shock treatment and observed that the other bitches no longer regarded the stool as desirable, she seemed to exhibit a certain relief, as if to say, "I never really liked it, and the only reason I ever ate it was because the others seemed to know something I didn't."

The more quickly corrective measures are initiated after the onset of the behavior, the better the response. Like all habitual behaviors, the longer it persists, the harder it is to correct. Immediately isolate the perpetrator from the view of other Weimaraners whenever the opportunity to indulge in this vice may occur. Worm the dogs immediately, add MSG and brewer's yeast to the dog food, and pick up all droppings immediately. Alleviating boredom as recommended may not cure the vice in Weimaraners, but when combined with other measures, it certainly may help to start going to obedience class or spending extra time in play. Above all, remember that controlling behavior is the only way to prevent spreading the vice.

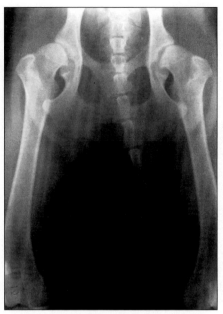

Figure 10-16: *This 1968 X-ray illustrates HD* in a Weimaraner whose owner chose to defer euthanasia until the dog became symptomatic. By age 11, the dog did not exhibit any disability other than what would be considered typical of most dogs in their teens. The dog showed no signs of pain but did develop difficulty handling slippery surfaces, which was minimized by carpeting the kitchen. This Weimaraner died of natural causes at age 13.

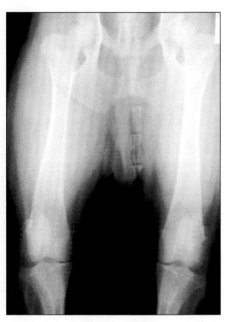

Figure 10-17: *This X-ray displays an acceptable position* of the dog's right femoral head. The tilting of the pelvis, however, forces the left femoral head out from the acetabular rim, leaving less than half the femoral head seated. Additionally, the right patella is not fully rotated into an upward-facing position. When X-rayed in the correct position, such as the one shown in Figure 10-18, and using the procedure recommended in the text, this dog received a good rating for both hips.

Diaphragmatic Hernia or Split Diaphragm?

Trauma-induced split diaphragm should never be confused with the congenital defect diaphragmatic hernia. In years past, diaphragmatic hernia was not an uncommon genetic occurrence; as affected dogs rarely lived to maturity, it is quite rare in the Weimaraner today. Owners of highly active dogs should be especially diligent about monitoring a dog after a serious collision, fall, or other impact trauma. A seemingly uninjured dog, especially one with a high pain tolerance, may seem unaffected but may in time develop complications. The small initial tear of the diaphragm may expand and allow the intestines to enter the thorax; symptoms may develop slowly or rapidly and are usually exacerbated by very active dogs or extreme physical activity. Symptoms include reduced stamina and shallow breathing, progressing to physical collapse and difficulty breathing; symptoms may or may not include fever. If diagnosed in time, surgical treatment will likely allow the dog, after recovery, to pursue a normal lifestyle.

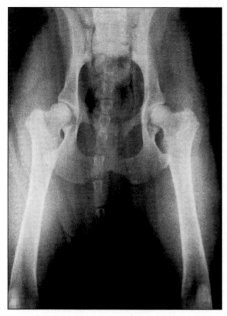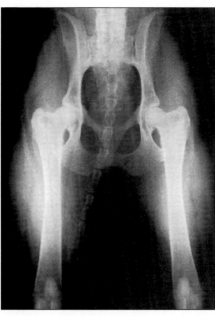

Figure 10-18: *Correct positioning for the X-ray is of critical importance.* If the first X-ray is a disaster, do not hesitate to have another done, even if it means finding a more skillful veterinarian. **(a)** The owner was understandably distressed by this incorrectly positioned hip X-ray. The first thing that stands out is that the femurs are not parallel. Looking closer, it can be seen that the patellas are not centered, indicating that the femurs have too much outward rotation, which contributes to the shallow appearance. Notice the flattened area on the hip to the left, which might be mistaken for dysplasia. This is the place where the tendon attaches to the femoral head, and it is visible only because of the extreme outward rotation. The tilted pelvis makes the hips appear asymmetrical and of uneven depth. **(b)** The owner took the bitch to a veterinarian recommended by other Weimaraner owners. When correctly positioned, the hips appear entirely different, and the X-ray received an OFA rating of "good." The hips are symmetrical, with deep sockets and smoothly rounded femoral heads.

Hip Dysplasia
History and Control Program

Hip dysplasia (HD), first described in dogs in 1935, is a malformation of the hip joint of variable severity: subluxation is the slight displacement of the joint; luxation is the total dislocation of the joint. The hip is a ball-and-socket type joint, with the head of the femur (ball) fitting snugly into the acetabulum (socket). A shallow socket does not allow for a snug fit, which leads to abnormal friction and secondary damage to the joint. The symptoms range from none to severe crippling, and the condition can be diagnosed only by X-rays.

The Orthopedic Foundation for Animals (OFA) (www.offa.org), founded in 1966, evolved from a dysplasia control program organized in 1960 by the Golden Retriever Club of America. From 1966 to 1973, OFA examined and certified hip X-rays of dogs over 12 months and classified them as normal, near normal, or dysplastic; in 1974, the age of examination and certification was raised to 24 months, and classifications changed to excellent, good, fair, borderline, mild dysplasia, moderate dysplasia, or severe dysplasia. (All OFA statistics are for radiographic HD, and a diagnosis of radiographic

HD does not necessarily mean that the dog will ever have clinical HD; unfortunately, there are no statistics for clinical HD.)

OFA offered dog breeders a national registry for dysplasia-free dogs and a way to rid dogdom of this hereditary scourge. In a nationwide frenzy of enthusiasm, breeders jumped on the bandwagon with a wave of wholesale euthanasia of animals that failed to receive OFA certification.

Fortunately, the majority of Weimaraner owners took a diagnosis of HD in stride and refused to end their pets' lives until they developed symptoms. Most of these dysplastic Weimaraners hunted and competed in obedience trials until other health problems ended their activities, and they died of old age.

Clinical (symptomatic) HD has always been relatively rare in Weimaraners, but radiographic HD has not. From 1966 to 1973, 18% of the X-rays submitted to OFA showed HD. The consistent practice of breeding only Weimaraners with certified normal hips has paid dividends. From 1974 to 1986, the percentage of radiographic HD dropped to 11.7%, a decrease of 35% and the greatest improvement of all sporting breeds.[4]

Choose a veterinarian who takes hip X-rays with great care. Correct positioning for the X-ray is of vital importance; accurate demonstration of good hip depth and fit requires considerable skill. If the hips appear questionable and there is no evidence of bony spurs or arthritis, many owners have learned that finding a more skillful veterinarian often makes a critical difference in the OFA classification and is well worth the additional expense.

With general anesthesia, there is some risk of too much relaxation, which makes even the best hips appear too loose. Some veterinarians have perfected the technique of taking excellent X-rays without any anesthesia or tranquilizers. For more than 10 years, Peachtree Animal Clinic has found that using acepromezine for the X-ray produces the most consistently accurate results.

Naturally, everyone hoped for a way to identify HD in puppies. Palpation of the hip joints under anesthesia at the age of 8–12 weeks identified varying degrees of joint laxity, which was thought to predict the quality of hips at maturity. During the heyday of hip palpation, conscientious breeders put down many puppies, even entire litters, before the correlation was found to be inconsistent.

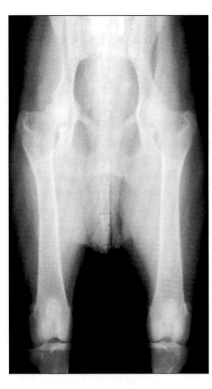

Figure 10-19: *A prudent breeder rechecks the hips* of OFA-certified dogs that are important producers. The absence of arthritic changes at an older age contributes to an active and comfortable old age, a desirable trait to pass on. Rated OFA excellent at 2, this Weimaraner's hips look as good at the age of 5 (shown) and at nearly 8. Its offspring had consistently good hips, as well.

its more attention. Riser points out that HD is "not one disease, but many diseases that result in common degenerative lesions of the hip joints" and that "many genetic and environmental factors can secondarily trigger events that bring about the condition." He concludes that HD: (a) "occurs only if hip joint instability and joint incongruity are present in the young child or animal;" and (b) "can be prevented if hip joint congruity can be maintained until ossification (bone formation) makes the acetabulum less elastic and the abductor muscles and supporting soft tissues become sufficiently strong and functional to recent femoral head subluxation."[6]

In humans, the role of mechanical congruity—that is, harmony between the parts—is well established. HD can be identified in newborns by manipulating the joint to elicit the characteristic click or a popping sensation (Ortolini's click). Treatment is to apply a Frejka splint, which consists of a pillow that is belted between the legs to maintain continuous contact (congruity) between the acetabulum and hip joint until the acetabulum deepens.

In other words, early treatment actually cures HD in humans by mechanical means.

Willis pooled the results of three palpation studies. Puppies were palpated at about 2 months and were later X-rayed. From 90 puppies diagnosed as normal on palpation, 25.6% were diagnosed as dysplastic when X-rayed. From 108 puppies diagnosed as dysplastic on palpation, only 66.7% were diagnosed as dysplastic when X-rayed.[5]

When the initial belief that HD was a simple Mendelian recessive gene fell before evidence that more factors were involved, new theories of the cause popped up with regularity. Theories of a neuromuscular disorder of the pectineus muscle and of a hormone imbalance attracted a substantial following. For a while, many breeders gave megadoses of Vitamin C as an HD preventive.

Genetic and Environmental Interactions

It is now well established that HD is a polygenic trait, which means that it is influenced by a combination of genetic and environmental factors. Control programs in many countries with many breeds have proven that using normal × normal or normal × near-normal matings significantly increases the percentage of normal hips. The more severely the parents are affected, the higher the frequency and severity in the offspring; the higher the proportion of normal ancestors and siblings of the parents, the higher the proportion of normal offspring. The genetic modifiers appear to be additive—that is, when breeders stack the deck in favor of good hips, they produce a higher percentage of puppies with good hips.

There has been a tendency to ignore the fact that environmental factors influence the expression of polygenic traits, and the interaction between genetic and environmental factors mer-

Recommended Procedure for Hip X-Rays

- No food after supper the night before the procedure.
- Remember to take along the registration certificate.
- Upon the dog's arrival at the clinic, the veterinarian gives the dog intramuscular acepromezine. The dosage is based in weight:
     60-pound bitch—about 1 cc (maximum total 3 cc)
     80-pound male—about 1¼ cc (maximum total 4 cc)
- The owner and dog wait for 30 minutes in a quiet environment. The time can be used to fill out the OFA application, set up the equipment, and so forth.
- Check the dog's third eyelids. If they do not cover at least one-third of the eye, give a second dose of acepromezine, half the amount of the first, and wait another 30 minutes.
- Most Weimaraners are relaxed enough at this point, but if necessary, give another half dose of acepromezine and wait 15 minutes.
- In addition to visible haws, signs of readiness to watch for are shivering and (usually) an extended, somewhat rigid tail.
- Walk or carry the dog quietly to the radiology area with a minimum of talking and clattering noises.
- The X-ray is taken in the standard positioning and manner. If the first two exposures (one for the veterinarian and one for OFA) do not yield one that is perfectly positioned, take a third one immediately and a fourth one if necessary. Ideally, the owner should remain with the dog during the procedure.
- By the time three or four X-rays have been taken, developed, and dried, most Weimaraners are beginning to recover from the tranquilizer. If not, this is a good time to trim the nails, which brings them out of it rapidly, and they can walk out of the clinic.

The secret of success with this procedure is a quiet, stress-free environment and the calming presence of the trusted owner. Any strong stimuli, such as dropping a metallic object, can overcome acepromezine's effect and break the spell. Giving the medication in gradual stages avoids the danger of overdose while ensuring that the X-ray is obtained at the optimum level of relaxation.

In dogs, the hip joints are always normal at birth, when the acetabulum and femoral head are composed of soft hyaline cartilage. Stress begins when the puppy pushes itself to nurse. The most critical period of development of HD is from birth to 60 days. The newborn's hip joints are soft and elastic, and according to Riser, "any changes in biomechanical balance, stress, compression, traction, muscle pull, lubrication, or congruity between the femoral head and acetabulum affect the programmed pattern of normal hip joint development."[7] He states:

> The changes that occur seem to correlate with the degree and length of time of the biomechanical imbalance. If the imbalance is corrected and congruity (harmony) is reestablished before a certain stage in the development of the hip, progression of the dysplasia stops and the hip returns to normal development. If full congruity can be maintained until the muscles and nerves are fully functional, muscle power is sufficient to maintain biomechanical balance so that full congruity between the parts is maintained.[8]

The hereditary factors are clearly multiple in nature—some major, some minor. The critical genetic traits that determine whether dogs have a high or low risk of developing HD are related to body size, body type, and growth pattern, as well as pelvic muscle mass. Minor factors include weight, movement, and temperament.[9] If temperament seems a bit far-fetched, remember that eager eaters get more food, weigh more, and grow faster, which places them at higher risk.

The incidence of HD is about the same in a number of breeds with similar structure, even though there is no genetic exchange between the breeds. When Riser ranked 38 medium to giant breeds according to the prevalence of HD, he found a gradual transition of type—highest in breeds characterized by poor muscles and coordination to lowest in breeds characterized by good muscles and coordination.[10]

The positive correlation between the pelvic muscle index and the incidence of HD further substantiates the importance of the relationship between height, weight, and muscle. Riser found that the probability of HD could be predicted by this index: HD rarely occurs in dogs with an index over 10.89 and always occurs in dogs with an index below 9.0. Furthermore, he also determined that pelvic muscle mass is more dependent on heredity than exercise.[11]

Overweight puppies run a high risk of stressing and injuring the muscles that maintain correct contact within the joint. In general, the age of onset and severity of symptoms is higher in heavier, more rapidly growing puppies.[12] Restricted feeding during periods of rapid growth can reduce the development and severity of hip dysplasia. Therefore, during the period of rapid growth, puppies should be kept slightly underweight, with the ribs just barely showing.

Figure 10-20: *Excess body weight and heavy exercise prior to physical maturity can harm growing joints and muscles,* even contributing greatly to acquired HD. However, many Weimaraner owners have found ingenious ways to provide sufficient exercise and conditioning even under urban and suburban circumstances. City-dweller Brett finds his Segway ideal to provide his buddy Lew with a good daily workout, now that he is over 11 months old.

Limiting exercise during periods of rapid growth also decreases trauma and stress to vulnerable, rapidly growing hips, especially between 4 and 6 months old. This does not mean confinement to a crate or dog run. It does mean no playing Frisbee, no treadmills, controlling wild jumping, leaving the puppy home when jogging, and limiting the amount of running when training for the field. Self-exercise in a roomy, fenced yard is all a growing puppy needs. This is a good age to work on water retrieving because swimming provides exercise without being a weight-bearing activity. Watch for those thigh muscles to develop enough strength and mass to hold the head of the femur firmly in the acetabulum. Even then, avoiding strenuous exercise and field conditioning until the puppy is over 1 year may ensure a lifetime without lameness—which is the whole idea, is it not? As with most things, moderation and common sense help.

Riser suggests that HD is so rare in wolves because they grow slowly, remain fairly underweight, and do not begin hunting until between 6 and 10 months old, all of which minimizes stress and injury to their immature joints.[13]

How many breeders and owners take great pride in feeding puppies well to speed their growth or to make them appear more mature in the show ring? How many enjoy long walks, jogging, or early field training with their young puppies? Those who do run a high risk of creating the environmental conditions that can precipitate HD in a puppy that might have developed normal hips if it had been given a sensible amount of food and exercise.

Exercise

Many owners find that a well-exercised Weimaraner is a happy Weimaraner and that with exercise, problem behaviors are often reduced or eliminated. Additionally, a well-conditioned Weimaraner is a requirement for success in competition, field, conformation, agility, and other athletic pursuits. Regular exercise helps maintain good health, a strong immune system, and structural health. Many areas prohibit dogs from running free, and the urban owner may be especially challenged; but necessity is the mother of invention, and solutions can usually be found that meet the needs of both Weimaraner and owner. Although moderate exercise is necessary for all growing puppies, young dogs should not get heavy exercise before they are 6–8 months old, and they should not be roadworked prior to reaching 1 year old.

Hypertrophic Osteodystrophy

Hypertrophic osteodystrophy (HOD) is a group of signs and symptoms characterized by lameness with warm, painful swelling of the epiphyses (growth plates) of the long bones (usually above the pasterns, though it can also affect the rear legs), and puppies are reluctant to stand or move. When reviewed by a specialist, X-rays of the affected joints may reveal a thin band of necrotic bone next to the periosteum. The disorder may also be accompanied by an elevated temperature, lethargy, depression, and loss of appetite. However, HOD may be easily confused with a less severe growing pains syndrome; although initially presenting with similar symptoms, treatment for each varies.

Growing Pains

In general, and except in conjunction with an immunodeficiency, the causes of osteodystrophies in all species are associated with nutritional imbalances of calcium, phosphorus, and Vitamin D; excessive calcium is implicated in HOD. (Once again, the dangers of giving calcium-phosphorus supplements, except on veterinary prescription, are clear.) In dogs, HOD of this type usually strikes actively growing youngsters of the large and giant breeds at 3–7 months old and often shortly after a vaccine. Weimaraner breeders have commented on a high incidence in puppies fed extremely high vitamin-mineral products, but the highest number of cases is associated with changing from an ultra-rich product to one less concentrated. Thus, it seems wise to avoid the richest puppy foods entirely. Currently, special diet formulations are available for large-breed puppies, designed for appropriate growth rather than maximal growth.

So far, the most effective treatment for non-autoimmune HOD includes correcting dietary or excessive exercise issues and adding ascriptin. Some veterinarians may prescribe non-steroidal anti-inflammatories (NSAIDs), such as Rimadyl®; when NSAIDs are used for more than a few weeks, regular blood work must be performed to monitor kidney and liver function. Steroids should be avoided at this point in order to evaluate whether the problem is simply growing pains or more severe auto-immune related HOD. Antibiotics may be prescribed if the dog presents with a fever. It is beneficial to encourage additional fluids by offering Pedialyte® in measured amounts up to 4 cups per day to maintain hydration.

The prognosis is excellent. The disease typically runs its course in 2–3 weeks, although on occasion, a single recurrence has been noted, if treatment is discontinued too early. It would be wise to evaluate the puppy's environment for the possibility of overexercise or unusual physical demands—such as excess weight, running on very hard surfaces, or excessive exercise encouraged by an older playmate. Unless symptoms recur regularly, the owner may assume that the issue was the result of nutritional or environmental complications and is of little consequence; if problems do recur—often on a cyclical basis and with increasing severity—the likelihood is that the disease is the result of autoimmune complications.

Immune-Mediated HOD

The same group of symptoms is associated with immunodeficiency and post-vaccinal problems. The HOD symptoms are more severe and are frequently accompanied by other symptoms of immune system impairment including extreme sensitivity to touch, diarrhea, high fever, or extreme, debilitating lethargy, and often elevated white blood cell counts. The age of onset is usually earlier, typically 7–10 days after vaccination.

The prognosis is not as good. Should symptoms recur on a cyclical basis, an autoimmune problem should be considered. Treatment includes steroids, such as cortisone, more powerful antibiotics and pain-control medications; hydration should be closely monitored. In the long term, most dogs out grow the symptoms, episodes recur less frequently and decrease in severity and duration. While it is unwise to rush to judgment in diagnosing immune-related HOD, with cyclical recurrence and/or escalating symptoms, the dog should not be used in a breeding program.

Hypothyroidism

Although hypothyroidism is not terribly common in the breed, it does occasionally occur. Symptoms include general unthriftiness—characterized by brittle coat (especially bilateral discoloration or loss of coat over the kidney area)—infertility, low libido, and lack of stamina. A complete thyroid panel should be routinely performed to determine thyroid function, especially in dogs over the age of 8. This panel should include T3, T4, Free T3, free T4, and TGAA levels. Refer to *Prenatal Care* for additional information.

Wobbler Syndrome

The symptoms of wobbler syndrome (cervical malformation-malarticulation or cervical spondylomyelopathy) are produced by spinal-cord compression and are characterized by an awkward swaying of the hindquarters when walking. This genetic condition may often be confused with the results of repeated trauma caused by activity or lifestyle. The diagnosis is based on clinical symptoms and X-rays, and it is vital to differentiate wobbler syndrome from other skeletal disorders. The cause is unknown, and some suggested factors include nutrition, growth rate, heredity, and mechanical factors. Interestingly, the dogs often have a history of being well fed or given a generous calcium supplement as puppies, another reason to avoid feeding puppies too rich a diet and giving mineral supplements.[14]

In Weimaraners, the symptoms of wobbler syndrome have been observed in older dogs that spend a lot of time in crates in which they must lower their heads to peer out. Excess weight may also contribute to the problem. The symptoms, if caused by trauma and not genetic predisposition, often disappear or are alleviated by not crating the dog at all or by using an oversized (Great Dane) crate or an exercise pen. Swimming therapy may prove beneficial.

Valley Fever

Valley Fever (coccidioidomycosis) is caused by a fungus found in the desert dust of the southwestern United States. Veterinarians and dog owners who live in these areas routinely test dogs that show any of the varied symptoms, which commonly include coughing, lethargy, fever, or loss of appetite or weight. Symptoms may also include skin abscesses that do not respond to antibiotics, lameness, back or neck pain, or seizures. Since seizure disorders are uncommon in this breed, any Weimaraner that has been to the Southwest and experiences a seizure should be tested for Valley Fever.

Early diagnosis and treatment are the keys to complete recovery. Usually, Valley Fever is easily detected with a simple blood test—part of the desert disease profile—which checks for several tick-borne diseases with similar symptoms, as well. If initial tests are negative but Valley Fever is suspected, tests should be repeated in 3–4 weeks, since the disease may sometimes produces false negatives early on.

Despite the fact that Valley Fever is endemic in the Southwest—more than 80% of the people who live in the highest-risk areas test positive in skin-test reaction tests—most never knew they had it and never displayed symptoms. Dogs are as likely to contract the disease as people, and it is likely that, as with people, most will never show symptoms. Valley Fever is only transmitted through direct contact with the spores; it cannot be transmitted from dog to dog, dog to human, or human to dog.

Currently, research is progressing on a vaccine. Exposure can be reduced by avoiding dusty areas that may harbor the fungal spores, especially during the highest-risk months of June through July and October through November. Reduce dust in areas where the dog spends the most time with grass, gravel, or appropriate mulch surfaces.

An infected dog may not display all symptoms. Symptoms normally appear within 1–3 weeks; however, dogs may not begin to show symptoms for a year or more. Dogs at greatest risk are obviously those participating in any activity where dust is likely to be stirred up and inhaled—field trials, hunting, tracking, hiking in natural areas, etc. Owners of Weimaraners that have been in the endemic region need only be aware of possible exposure and bring this to the attention of their veterinarian if their dogs develop Valley Fever symptoms, unexplained illness, or illness that does not respond to treatment. Valley Fever is primarily a disease of the lungs, and X-rays may be helpful if Valley Fever is suspected. In some cases, the disease may progress (disseminate) and become systemic, involving complications of the bones, skin, and central nervous system.

Dogs in which the disease has disseminated require more extensive treatment, and the prognosis is guarded, especially when the central nervous system is affected. The good news however, is that although treatment is prolonged—averaging 6–12 months on antifungals—prognosis for dogs in which the disease is confined to the lungs is very good, resulting in a return to the normal good health most Weimaraners enjoy.

Ketoconazole® (Nizoral) and Fluconazole® (Diflucan) are the most common drugs of choice for dogs. Ketoconazole® is somewhat less expensive; however, it is more prone to inducing side effects. Fluconazole® is more expensive, but side effects are rare; it is currently the best option for dogs in which the disease has disseminated. Research is progressing on this disease, and new treatment options are being developed. Currently, there is no vaccine available, but fortunately research continues, since this disease also affects humans, and there is hope that a vaccine may be developed in the near future.

The Valley Fever Center for Excellence provides extensive information at their website, www.vfce.arizona.edu.

Redocking

Historically, redocking was not a common procedure. However, increasing numbers of Weimaraners are being imported from countries where tail docking is prohibited. Redocking is necessary for these imports to be competitive in the U.S. conformation ring. Bear in mind that redocking a tail is a major surgical procedure. When considering redocking, ask other Weimaraner owners to recommend a veterinarian who is experienced in the procedure, and if possible, see examples of his or her work. It is extremely important to be aware that if the tail must be redocked, it is vital that all bone chips be removed and that a

Figure 10-21: *Measuring and marking a tail for redocking.*

(a) Place a ruler firmly under the base of the tail, above the anus, being sure that the tail is straight out and aligned with the dog's spine.

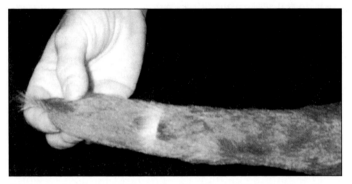

(b) Make the first mark by cutting the hair at 6½ inches (maximum length) to indicate where the veterinarian will make the first incision.

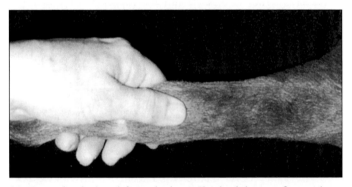

(c) Grasp the dog's tail from the base. Slowly slide your fingers down the tail to the taper point, where the diameter suddenly becomes thinner. Continue past for the distance of one vertebra.

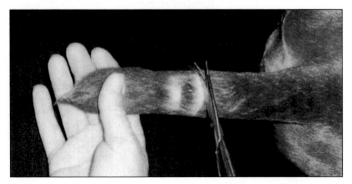

(d) Cut the hairs to make the second clear mark.

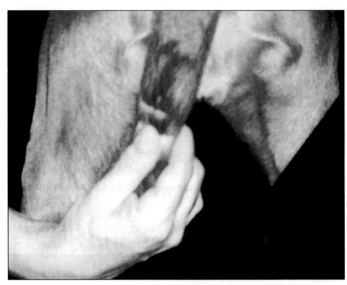

(e) For a final test, be sure that the 6½-inch mark completely covers the vulva or scrotal sac, and adjust as necessary.

generous pocket of skin over the end of the redocked tail be allowed in order to ensure unrestricted and confident tail carriage.

The owner of 8-month-old Asta decided her 9-inch tail needed redocking. In addition to length, the tail was too thick and heavy, and although the tail was high set, the bitch did not carry it attractively. An appointment was made with the veterinarian who had redocked other Weimaraners with excellent results.

The night before surgery, Asta was fed only a half ration and then no further food or fluids until after surgery. The place to redock her tail was carefully studied and marked in the manner shown in Figure 10-21 (a)–(e).

At the clinic the next morning, the veterinarian began by shaving the end of Asta's tail. Everyone was surprised when this revealed the typical dark tips and light base of the agouti coat factor so clearly that the photograph was selected to illustrate the trait (Figure 6-6).

With Asta safely asleep, a tourniquet was placed at the base of the tail to control bleeding, the skin was scrubbed, and the tail was draped with sterile towels. Starting from the top of the tail at the 6½-inch mark (maximum length), the veterinarian made a diagonal cut halfway down the side toward the base of the tail and made a matching cut on the other side. Matching cuts were made from the bottom to create two V-shaped flaps—one on the top and one on the bottom. The bone was completely severed. The remainder of the severed tail vertebrae were removed. Then, pulling the skin toward the base of the tail, the veterinarian removed one additional vertebra at the joint; when the remaining flaps were sutured, the skin over the tip was loose so that there was no pressure to restrict Asta's ability to wag her tail. After stitching the blood vessels to stop bleeding, the end of the tail was neatly sutured and bandaged.

Figure 10-22: *Preoperative preparation.*

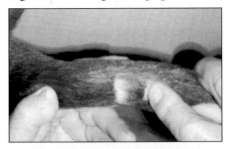

(a) The veterinarian palpates the vertebra.

(b) Agreeing with the measurements, he marks them with ink.

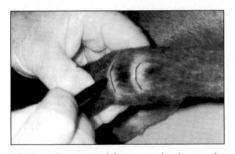

(c) The tail is prepared for surgery by shaving the hair. Normally, the entire tail is shaved. With Weimaraners, the regrowth is often disfigured by many white hairs, so the veterinarian only trimmed as much as necessary.

Figure 10-23: *Day after surgery.*

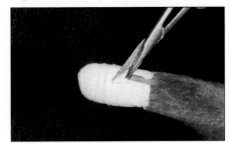

(a) The bandage is removed.

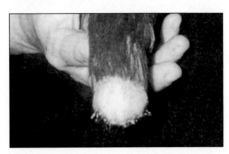

(b) The veterinarian palpates the vertebra.

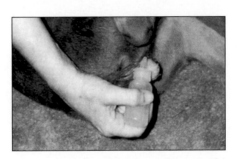

(c) Asta observes with interest as Bitter Apple® is applied to the shaved skin.

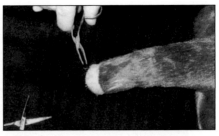

Figure 10-24: *To remove sutures,* grasp an end firmly with a pair of tweezers, pull on the suture until there is enough slack to slip the tip of a sharp pair of manicure scissors into the loop and snip, and gently draw the suture out.

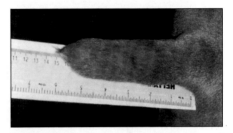

Figure 10-25: *With hair regrown,* the tail looks great!

Figure 10-26: *The white spot on the end of the tail* is the end of a vertebra. In this case, redocking was done for humanitarian reasons rather than cosmetic reasons.

Asta's owner removed the bandage the next morning and applied Bitter Apple® frequently in the days that followed. The Bitter Apple® was effective until the 4th day after surgery, when the itching caused Asta to begin licking and chewing on the sutures. Observation became more intensive—her owner took her along to work. In addition, she gave Asta the tranquilizer that the veterinarian had dispensed after surgery. Bandaging Asta's front feet distracted her attention from her tail and gave her something safer to work on.

The sutures were removed 10 days after surgery. As soon as the tail healed, Asta began carrying her tail with confidence and style. The hair regrew within 4 months with no unsightly white hairs.

In addition to there being too long a tail, it is occasionally necessary to redock to remove irritating bone splinters that were not removed with the original docking. The Weimaraner often indicates discomfort by chewing on the tail and may also habitually tuck the tail under when sitting, developing bald spots on the anterior surface.

Malingering

To close on a lighter note, any discussion of breed-typical problems would be incomplete without mentioning malingering. One veterinarian textbook commented, "Most practitioners will agree that canine hypochondriacs and malingerers exist. Real injury or illness at home may bring such a showering of affection and choice food that the dog will, in the future, repeatedly feign illness to obtain these benefits."[15] Indeed, the author might well have been thinking of Weimaraners, who are quick to add malingering to their repertoire of con-artist tricks. So beware!

Figure 11-1: *Home for the Holidays* by Harry Giglio. CH Smoky City Riverboat Gambler, CH Smoky City Hail Mary, CH Smoky City Devil May Care, CH Smoky City Toy Story Cowgirl, CH Smoky City Treasure Trove, CH Smoky City Pure Elation, CH Smoky City Ava Gabor, CH Smoky City Wallstreet Wizard, CH Smoky City Harbor West Encore, CH Smoky City Hell-fighter, CH Smoky City D'Nunder Lazer Beam, Daisy, the Jack Russell Terrier, and, of course, Tom Wilson. Photograph by Harry Giglio.

CHAPTER 11

OLD AS WELL AS GRAY

Healthy Lifestyle

Maintaining a healthy lifestyle is the single most important consideration in maintaining a healthy older Weimaraner. Exercise, nutrition, and medical consideration are the cornerstones to prolonging the life and well-being of the senior companion.

Exercise and Condition

Allowing the Weimaraner to continue to participate in customary activities will not only keep the dog interested in life but will also help maintain fitness. Maintenance of muscle tone will help support aging joints, and mild exercise produces endorphins, which create a positive mental state. However, as the dog ages, the owner must take several factors into consideration to protect the older dog from himself, limiting the duration or exertion in spite of the dog's willingness to continue. The spirit is willing, but the body simply cannot keep up. Excessive or extreme physical efforts may not only produce soreness but can contribute to chronic ailments or even create additional problems, such as orthopedic injury.

Swimming is ideal for older dogs—it encourages physical activity while limiting stressful weight-bearing exercise. Older dogs are less tolerant of extreme water and air temperatures, so care must be taken to protect the dog from chills and heat. As with any exercise, the owner should be alert to signs of overexertion: oftentimes the thrill of the retrieve may override both the owner's and the dog's awareness of his condition. Animal spas are becoming more common, offering indoor heated pools and hydrotherapy; look for facilities catering to canine or equine interests. If areas are not available for swimming, walking in calm waters is great exercise, too.

Physical Limitations

The older dog will need some consideration to accommodate progressive physical limitations. Much like people, the older dog needs a comfortable and quiet place to rest; provide well-cushioned bedding out of the way of the hustle and bustle of the household but not isolated from the family, perhaps in an out-of-the-way corner in the family room or under

Figure 11-2: *Swimming improves muscle tone* and overall body condition without the disadvantage of a stressful weight-bearing activity. Rosemary Carlson's constant companion, CH Daroca's Pop Up, JH, CD, RD, NSD, VX, shows excellent form in completing the final retrieve for his WCA RD rating at the ripe old age of 11.

the desk in the office; in some cases, it may be necessary to separate the dogs using an oversized crate or exercise pen. The mature dog needs a place to escape from the invasion and obnoxious attentions of younger, overactive housemates. Younger dogs may inadvertently abuse the older dog by persistently pestering or physically knocking the dog over. Check regularly to be sure that temperature ranges are adequate; older dogs may lose the ability to regulate their body temperature or to respond to excessive heat or cold. It goes without saying not to leave the dog in the car in extreme heat, but it is just as important not to leave the older dog in the car when temperatures are quite cold.

Stairs and vehicle access may challenge the senior dog. Provide water on each level of a multiple-level home or restrict access to stairs. Ramps are easily available now to provide access to higher SUVs and trucks. Older dogs should always be assisted down from high places such as beds or vehicles; old joints and muscles can be too easily injured jumping up or down. For the debilitated dog, a support sling or large towel allows the owner to aid the dog while walking, climbing stairs, or relieving itself without excessive strain or embarrassment to the dog or owner.

In some cases, the older dog may benefit from using a non-restrictive harness when walking on leash to reduce stress on the neck and back. However, older dogs may sometimes lose their bearings and wander off; be sure to keep the dog's collar and tags on at all times. A wider collar may be more comfortable.

With aging, sometimes hearing and vision loss may also occur. Keep this in mind when the older dog seems less obedient—he simply may not be able to hear or understand what is being asked. Be alert for signs that the dog's vision might be deteriorating. Vision loss is uncommon in Weimaraners, but should be considered if the older dog begins to stumble or bump into people or objects, seems confused or hesitates in unfamiliar environments, or displays reluctance to move into dark areas.

Diet

One of the most important contributions to a healthy older Weimaraner is to maintain the dog at a healthy weight. Weight maintenance can become challenging with reduced activity, reduced metabolism resulting from sterilization or increasing age, or chemical imbalances due to diabetes, thyroid, or impending heart complications. When medical complications have been ruled out, one of the first areas to consider is reducing access to snacks or changing to a food designed for reduced activity. When a dog is at a healthy weight, the ribs should be easily felt but not easily visible; there should be an obvious waistline and no obvious pads of fat, particularly at the base of the tail or over the ribs (see Figure 4-28 in *The Weimaraner Standard*).

As knowledge of nutrition advances, canine diets are becoming more suited to maintaining dogs under a variety of conditions. Special diets are now available to meet the nutritional needs not only of the senior dog but also those experiencing health challenges, such as kidney and heart problems. Special attention may be needed for the nutritional requirements of older canine athletes; if the dog's appearance, performance, or condition is unsatisfactory, consult a veterinarian for nutritional guidance. Most Weimaraners over the age of 8 or 9 benefit from glucosamine/chondroitin supplementation for joint maintenance and health.

Every dog should have an annual health check-up, but it is especially important for dogs over the age of 7 or 8. These "health reviews" can identify potential problems before they become serious conditions. For dogs used as a stud, a semen analysis should be performed every 6 months; this is useful not only for determining the presence of an infection or prostate problems but also because the old saying "use it or lose it" has proven to be quite true in the case of stud dogs.

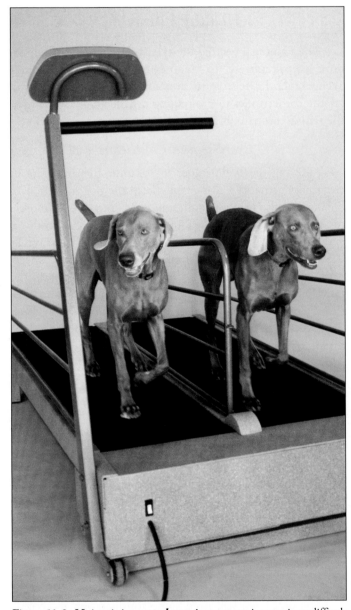

Figure 11-3: *Maintaining a good exercise program* is sometimes difficult as the older dog's tolerance for extreme temperatures is reduced. These two half-brothers, Derich and Galan, both AKC Master Hunters, regularly volunteer to work out, barking at their owner, Luis Bonilla, demanding that he turn on the treadmill so they can exercise in air-conditioned comfort, given the intense Arizona summer heat outside.

Medical Considerations

Skin

Benign skin tumors of fatty (lipoma) or fibrous (fibroma) tissue are fairly common in Weimaraners. They are characterized by slow growth and encapsulation, and the hard nodules are freely moveable. These tumors are not serious and are usually removed only for cosmetic reasons.

Malignant skin tumors, which are not common in the breed, are characterized by ulceration, bleeding, and rapid growth, and the spongy masses do not move freely under the skin. Surgical excision is very successful unless the malignancy has extended to the underlying tissue.

Eyes

The Canine Eye Registration Foundation (CERF) provides a certification for eye health for many breeds. In some breeds, eye problems such as progressive retinal atrophy are common enough to warrant this certification before using an animal for a breeding program. Eye diseases are very uncommon in the Weimaraner; however, the certification process can identify other eye troubles as well, such as scratches to the cornea. The process is extremely safe, and clinics are often available at conformation shows or other canine events for a very reasonable fee. Taking the mature Weimaraner in for a CERF exam can do no harm and may identify potential problems.

Epiphora—the overflow of tears—is fairly common in the old Weimaraner and is usually the result of an irritation that stimulates excess tears—such as allergies, distichiasis, trichiasis, entropion, or ectropion. In older dogs, epiphora is also caused by blockage of the tear-draining canals. The obstruction may respond to medical treatment, or the veterinarian may need to open the duct under anesthesia.

Nuclear sclerosis—a loss of translucency of the lens of the eye, characterized by a blue-gray cloudiness—is far more common than cataracts in Weimaraners. With aging, the lens fibers increase in density, owing to a decrease in fluid, and some of the light entering the eye is reflected back. Despite the resemblance to a cataract, nuclear sclerosis has little effect on vision.

Glaucoma—increased intraocular pressure—though uncommon, requires prompt attention to prevent blindness. Glaucoma is characterized by periodic episodes of increased pressure, rather than a sustained increase in pressure. The warning signs are subtle, but alert owners sometimes observe them in time to save their dog's vision. The dog shows signs of pain by rubbing the eye against a rug, furniture, or the owner. The Weimaraner, with its typical catlike use of the paws, may rub the eye with the paw.

Ears

Weimaraners do not seem to develop a significant loss of hearing until they reach 12–14 years, and it is rare even then.

Figure 11-4: *CH Colsidex Standing Ovation, BROM, HOF,* the No. 1 BROM producer for over 24 years, was a legendary stud dog well into his senior years as a result of breeder/owner Judy Colan's loving care, which included regular veterinary attention, appropriate diet, mental and physical exercise, and companionship. "Joga" is shown here handled, as always, by Judy, winning his second WCA National Specialty in 1984, this time from the Veteran's class. To learn more about Joga's spectacular career see Figure 34-18.

Detection is difficult because, like humans, old (and young) Weimaraners often pretend they cannot hear.

Sometimes owners observe a slight change in behavior, signs of confusion, and decreased response to verbal commands. The dog's response to sound can be tested by clapping the hands when it is looking the other way.

An old dog that is deaf can be managed quite well. The greatest concern is safety, and a fenced yard is usually ample protection. Whether or not the dog should be hunted or be permitted to run off-lead depends on the degree of hearing impairment and how far the dog tends to range. Running it with another Weimaraner that responds to recall is helpful.

The almost inevitable problem in this breed occurs when the small blood vessels of the ears become fragile with age. The Weimaraner's long, flapping ears are particularly vulnerable to hematomas—blood-filled cysts that may be the size of small hot dogs. Hard shaking of the head is the most common precipitating cause of spontaneous hematomas. The long Weimaraner ears fly wildly, often striking walls, furniture, crates, and even heavy metal rings on the collar. In both young and old Weimaraners—head shaking provoked

Figure 11-5: *Hearing loss.* Sue Czajka has been deaf since birth; Pike is Sue's third hearing dog, alerting her to the sound of the TDD phone, doorbell, fire alarms, and more. Although it is unusual in Weimaraners, as his 13th birthday approached, Pike began to lose his hearing. Duchess joined the family, and Sue and Pike began training her as a hearing dog. Sue is pictured above with the new trainee, Duchess, and her mentor, Pike.

by an ear infection is a common cause of hematomas; keeping the ears clean and free of ear mites or infection is the most effective way to prevent excessive ear shaking. Frequent shaking of the head and carrying it slightly lopsided, one ear lower than the other, are common warning signs of incipient hematomas.

Teeth

Good nutrition throughout life is the best guarantee of health and vitality in old age, and healthy teeth promote good nutrition. If dental problems become painful, the old dog may be unable to eat.

Dry dog biscuits and kibble decrease the build-up of scalar. When scalar build-up leads to swollen, painful, bleeding gums, it must be removed by the veterinarian. This is a simple procedure but must be done under anesthesia, which is always a risk with an old dog. The decision to have the teeth cleaned under anesthesia must be based on the dog's general health and the severity of the problem. Loose or decaying teeth can be extracted at this time.

Regular care of the teeth reduces plaque and bad breath. It is helpful to simply wipe the dog's teeth and gums once or twice a week with a dry washcloth. If asked, many dentists are happy to give away an old scaling tool that is ready to be discarded. Weimaraners will often lie quietly and permit the yellow scale to be removed with the tool—in fact, some seem to enjoy the attention.

Infrequent Complications

Diabetes and thyroid and heart problems are not uncommon occurrences in old age. A complete blood panel at the annual health exam will identify impending problems before they jeopardize the dog's general health.

Consult a veterinarian with regard to the merit of booster shots, which could challenge the aging Weimaraner's immune system.

Neutering

The typical male Weimaraner is born with little concept of the birds and the bees and is generally graced with a congenial, even personality. Neutering for temperament issues, such as social or sexual misbehavior, is rarely necessary and should never be considered prior to full muscular and skeletal maturity—usually over 1 year old—except when the dog's health is endangered. Prostate and testicular cancer, common justifications routinely stressed by veterinarians for sterilization, are extremely rare in this breed. The benefits of neutering any dog, especially the older dog, should be thoroughly questioned and weighed against any potential complications. Refer to "Finding a Veterinarian" in *Getting off to the Right Start.*

Spaying

Many breeders routinely spay older bitches that they no longer wish to breed simply to avoid the inconvenience of seasons and the risk of pyometra. Few veterinarians inform owners of the short- and long-term complications of the surgery.

The short-term risk is that Weimaraner bitches should not be left unattended the night after surgery. A disproportionately high number of Weimaraner bitches that come out of anesthe-

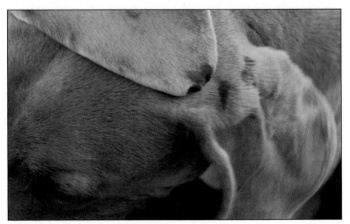

Figure 11-6: *Hard head shaking* can lead to ear injuries like this. The owner may first notice telltale spots of blood on the head. In an older dog, head shaking can be symptomatic of other potential problems, so a visit to the vet may be in order, as continued head shaking can lead to further complications, such as hematomas on the ear. Refer to Appendix F for additional information on hematoma repair.

sia alone and unsupervised remove their stitches in stress and confusion. If they are too sick to go home, they should spend the night in an emergency facility under close supervision.

The long-term concern is the high incidence of urinary incontinence in spayed bitches. In a study of 412 spayed bitches, 30.9% weighing over 44 pounds developed urinary incontinence. The onset ranged from immediately after surgery to 12 years, with an average of 2.9 years. In general, treatment with ephedrine produced good results in 73.7% and some improvement in 23.7%.[1]

These statistics indicate that one friend's experience is far from unique. Less than 6 months after routine spaying of a healthy brood bitch, she lost total urinary control and did not respond to treatment. Wherever she rested, the bitch was constantly soaked and chilled in her own urine, and setting up special quarters to control where this occurred did not alter her misery. Putting the otherwise healthy 7-year-old bitch to sleep still distresses her owner 10 years later.

In most cases, there is little choice about spaying a bitch. But, when there is a choice, as with neutering, the benefits should be carefully weighed against the potential consequences.

Incontinence

Not unusual in older spayed females, incontinence can also occur in the older male dog as well. When a dog suddenly develops incontinence, the first step is a veterinary evaluation—be sure to collect a fresh urine sample before the visit. Often, simple antibiotic therapy will clear up the problem; however, it may occasionally be a sign of a larger or more serious problem. Incontinence is a treatable condition in most cases to a greater or lesser degree.

Figure 11-8: *Older dogs sometimes experience a decrease in mobility* and coordination and need a little bit of help getting around. A car travel harness can serve double duty—the seat belt loop provides a handle to help guide and support the older dog, as well as providing safety and control while traveling. Other products specifically designed for mobility support are also available.

Figure 11-7: *Older dogs often tolerate* a surprising amount of abuse from puppies before making it clear just who the pack leader is. When dominance patterns are established at this age, the youngster will continue to defer to the older dog. Photograph by Barney Riley.

For the dog that has become incontinent, the owner can take several steps to maintain sanity and dignity. Dog accessories are available for both males and females to protect the home décor; however, these should not be left on unsupervised animals. The older dog should be provided with comfortable, easily washed bedding when confined. In favored resting areas or when confined to an exercise pen, a tarp can be placed on the floor and covered with blankets or other absorbent material, which will also provide additional traction.

The dog should be routinely examined for potential skin irritations.

Maintaining Interest in Life

The measures discussed in "Healthy Lifestyle" will help support the dog's mental and physical well-being; the thoughtful owner can help maintain a simple zest for life with a few other actions, as well. Keep the Weimaraner involved in all the

Figure 11-10: *VC, DC, AFC Magnum Gunnar Silvershot,* MH, SDX, RDX, VX. Still part of the action years after his retirement, Gunnar became a well-known fixture at NAVHDA tests, at his perch in the driver's seat of owner Judy Balog's truck, where he could oversee the performance of his many offspring.

usual aspects of family life, but understand and respect the limitations imposed by his advancing age. Many older dogs find a new lease on life by starting a new career. There are many activities suited to the less agile and athletic dog, such as tracking, rally obedience, and therapy work. These new activities provide both dog and owner with interesting new experiences and the opportunity to spend more time together. Do keep in mind that the dog may not learn new skills with the same alacrity as when he was younger, however.

A new companion can also provide a spark of life for the older dog. While a new puppy is certainly an option, not all owners will be ready or willing to add another Weimaraner to the household pack, and other options, such as adopting a smaller breed of dog or a cat, may be considered; very small prey-type animals may not be a good choice for most Weimaraners. It is often hard to resist the temptation of raising the offspring of a beloved companion. If the owner wishes to add a new puppy, be sure not to wait until the older dog is too infirm to enjoy a new companion; elderly or ill dogs may become depressed by the constant activity or attention or may be overwhelmed by the responsibility of training a new puppy. Remember that the whole point is to provide a companion, not a replacement; be sure that the older dog continues to get a fair share of the owner's attention. The copycat tendencies of the Weimaraner breed often result in the young dog's mimicking the endearing personality characteristics of its mentor; sometimes, the added responsibility and activity stimulated by the new puppy may add several years to the older dog's life.

Figure 11-9: *Who says you can't teach an old dog new tricks?* CH Kasamar Amberly, JH, NSD, NRD, V, BROM, is the foundation dam of Kasamar Kennel and mother of eight champions. Amber completed the requirements for her Novice Retrieving Dog title a few weeks before her 13th birthday. She is shown here with breeder/owner Karen Sandvold.

Figure 11-11: *Am/Can CH Skyhi's Delta Nonstop Delite,* CD, AX, MXJ, NSD, NRD, VX. "Scully" began a new career at 7 years of age, earning advanced titles after her 11th birthday. Competing at this level and advanced age required some good luck, good genetics, and responsible care to meet the physical demands.

Coping with Loss

Most old Weimaraners die suddenly, passing away quietly in their sleep. But sometimes owners face the painful decision of whether or not to put the dog to sleep. They must ask many questions: "Should I keep the dog on chemotherapy for an inoperable tumor?" "Can I carry the dog up and down the stairs or in and out of the house when it cannot walk?" "Is prolonging life fair to the dog?" Perhaps the key question is, "What is the true quality of life for this dog?"

The decision is always painful. If it is thoughtful and made with love, the grief and guilt may not be as hard to bear. It also helps if the veterinarian comes to your home so that the dog's last moments are in the peaceful comfort of familiar surroundings.

Grief is normal, and grief over the loss of any beloved companion—canine, feline, equine, and human—can be devastating. Psychologists recognize a grieving process that must be resolved after such loss.

The death of a dog is hardest if it is the only one in the household. There is nothing quite so dreadful as coming home to a silent house with no joyous tail-wagging greeting. This experience can be avoided by bringing in a puppy as the old dog's companion. Timing often works out well to keep the grandpup of a favored dam or sire; sometimes, the added responsibility of a puppy to mentor may prolong the older dog's active years. Watching the younger generation grow in the image of a cherished grandparent seems to ease the eventual loss of a special companion. Owners may be surprised when the younger dog also grieves the loss of the older companion—this is not unusual. The youngster shares in the grieving process and aids resolution.

An experience shared by a friend offers a comforting closing message:

> News of my dog's death came on Thanksgiving morning as I was leaving for church. I grabbed a box of Kleenex and went anyway, and all through the service, tears quietly flowed. After the service, the pastor stopped me at the door. He knew of my dog's illness and said, "He died, didn't he?"
>
> Unable to speak, I nodded.
>
> "You'll see him in Heaven you know," he said kindly.
>
> I looked up, startled by the rather unorthodox statement.
>
> He explained, "Of course dogs go to heaven. How could anyone who has known a dog ever doubt it?"[2]

Figure 11-12: *Am/Can CH Skyhi's EZ Magical Reign,* UD, JH, Can, CDX, SD, NRD, BROM. In 1994, Reign earned High in Trial and Best of Breed at the same Specialty event. She completed her UD just 2 weeks shy of her 12th birthday and continued to compete in obedience, conformation, and ratings tests. Granny Reign's offspring carry on her legacy; many have earned Versatile 2–6 ratings. Reign is also the mother of the breed's first Triple Champion and the grandmother of the second.

Figure 11-13: *Man Ray Contemplating the Bust of Man Ray.* We chose our 6-week-old Weimaraner puppy from a litter in Long Beach, California. Sitting there in the dining room in a ray of light, he looked like a little old man. Except for a big case of chewy-itis, there was nothing puppylike about him. I named him Man Ray....But Man Ray had some problems, he followed me everywhere. Everywhere. Outside, inside, in the kitchen, to the bathroom, to the bedroom...and to the studio....Only in the studio, when I let him work with me, was Man Ray well behaved. No high-pitched whining there. He was calm and attentive while posing for pictures and performing in live video pieces.... "This stuff must be important to Bill," thought Man Ray. Then and there, Ray changed the way I thought about my work. In his eleventh year, Man Ray became gravely ill.... I thought I could prepare for the inevitable by looking it straight on. The Polaroids from that year, which included Dusted and the life-size portrait heads of Man Ray, are to me the most profound works our photographic relationship summoned. However, this work would not prepare me for the loss I was to experience. Man Ray died late in his 11th year. I was devastated. I vowed I would never get another dog." William Wegman—1982

Figure 11-14: *FC/AFC Outdoors Tony Lama* is a legend in our breed. She maintained an incredible field trial career for more than 12 years, was named WCA's No. 1 All-Age Gun Dog for 1991 and 1992, and successfully competed in all-breed field trials well into her teens. Tony is shown here winning an all-breed gun dog stake at the tender age of 13. Not only a top field competitor, she also established herself as the all-time top field trial–producing bitch, with her offspring earning 10 championships in the field. Tony enjoyed her life as a hunting and traveling companion with Gorden and Shirley Hanson until her passing at the respectable age of 17 years.

Figure 11-15: *It is not unusual in Germany for a seasoned companion* that is otherwise healthy to be included in the day's hunt, even at 13 or 14 years old. Senior dogs are often given tasks that make allowances for their mature limitations but still allow the dog to maintain dignity. Not so for Catja vom Kohlwald; old as well as gray, she refused to be relegated to guarding game or equipment. She is shown here at age 16 with a trophy *roe-buck* [Rehbock] she tracked; Catja enjoyed the hunt, with more than 66 registered deer tracks to her credit, until she passed away from complications of an automobile accident at age 18. Photograph courtesy of Peter Reichert, Germany.

Figure 12-1: *A wild bird solution....* At one of his innumerable seminars, the legendary Charlie Williams demonstrates with an Irish Setter the advantage of using an all-terrain vehicle (ATV) to facilitate training of a field Weimaraner. Charlie often recommended the ATV as transport during field training; it is faster than moving on foot but is easier to mount, ride, and dismount than a horse. Charlie firmly believed in the importance of running dogs on wild birds, and the ATV encouraged dogs to run with the wide range typical of a field trial competitor in the open terrain of the Midwest. Once the dog located a bird, Charlie could approach, style, and steady the dog. He could maintain control while the bird was flushed to prevent the green dog from breaking point, then easily signal the gunner also along for the ride (often a disabled veteran friend of Charlie's), and either ask the dog for the retrieve or send it on to hunt more birds, depending on the training level and expected performance of the individual dog.

CHAPTER 12

STARTING THE GUN DOG

Field Dog Nursery School:

The Breeder's Obligation

Hopefully, the breeder of the field dog prospect has provided a solid nursery school education to create an attitude of willingness and acceptance of novel events, a valuable trait in any dog and of particular importance in a hunting dog. If plans include hunting the pup for personal pleasure, ratings, or field trials, begin with a puppy whose breeder provided a strong start. True hunting ability begins with a genetic jump-start endowed by hundreds of years of selective breeding; however, since its introduction to America, the Weimaraner has become highly valued as a family companion, and the dual nature of the breed has many times been neglected, sometimes resulting in a tendency to drift away from its original German hunting heritage. The task of creating the ideal hunting companion will be immensely easier with a puppy with the genetic blueprint of hunting instinct and skills. The casual guarantee from the breeder that the dogs are hunters is not enough. Look for a sire and/or dam who have acquired titles in the field, whether ratings, tests, or trials, or take the opportunity to hunt over the prospective parents.

A thoughtful breeder will provide early acculturation for the potential hunting partner. *Raising the Litter* and *Ages and Stages* explain practices that will help establish a strong mental and physical foundation. This breeder takes advantage of the early learning potential of the puppy and offers many experiences before the puppy ever leaves its first home, exposing the puppy to good socialization, fur and feathers, and pick-up-and-carry skills. The chapter *Testing Natural Aptitude* not only helps identify puppies with strong natural skills but provides the entire litter with exposure to valuable opportunities to develop confidence. The introduction to water and crate training are an added plus, as well.

If, when you visit the breeder's premises, these opportunities appear to be lacking, suggest the breeder provide enrichment, as in the above-referenced chapters, or consider whether another litter might be more appropriate. If you are still convinced this is the right pup—because of an outstanding pedigree, for example—take the puppy home as soon as possible, as early as 7 weeks, and begin a head start program

right away. A puppy's mind is a terrible thing to waste. Lost time is difficult to recover, and the longer the puppy goes without opportunities to learn, the harder it will be; at some point, remedial action may be too late, and the wide-open window of acceptance may be lost. Working with a dog that has not "learned to learn" can be a challenge.

Pick Up and Carry

As part of the Rule of Sevens (see *Ages and Stages*), puppies should have had the opportunity to play with different toys even while in the whelping box. To encourage very young puppies to begin to pick up and carry sooner, look for toys designed especially for them, such as Pet Stages®; they are small and soft enough to entice a puppy just learning to walk to grab, hold, and carry and are also washable. The breeder of the future field Weimaraner should go well beyond that, however, providing not only a variety of opportunities

Figure 12-2: *It is never too early.* If the puppy's health and pedigree seem just right for the owner's needs but the breeder is unable to provide an early head start for the highest potential, take the puppy home as soon as possible and begin an enrichment program before boredom leads a precocious pup to acquire such bad habits as raiding the garden for entertainment. Refer to *Ages and Stages* and *Testing Natural Aptitude* for opportunities to develop the pups natural talents. Photograph by Colleen Dugan.

but plenty of encouragement and reinforcement whenever the Weimaraner puppy displays the desire and aptitude for picking up and carrying anything from fuzzy toys to flattened plastic bottles. Since the Weimaraner, as a personal gun dog or trial competitor, must be a happy, willing retriever, having the puppy pick up and carry a variety of items goes far toward developing the typical Weimaraner attitude that anything that can be carried should be carried, especially birds or game the owner has thoughtfully provided.

Figure 12-3: *Learning about life.* (a) Lena's German owners have provided her with furred game to share with her puppies. Much like wild canids, she entices the puppies by shaking and running away with the prey; when the puppies' prey drive is fully aroused, she releases the game and the puppies are rewarded with the taste and feel of the fur. This process is the first step in awakening the natural instinct to chase, catch, and possess game. (b) In Texas, future field trial prospects are evaluated by encouraging entire litters to explore and range freely in grassy fields as early as 6 to 7 weeks of age. (c) Winter or summer, early exposure to the taste and feel of a goose or pheasant wing encourages the beginning of the much-needed prey drive in aspiring gun dogs. (d) For puppies born mid-winter, swimming lessons may begin (and continue) in a warm bathtub. (e) Digging can be a family affair; Mother started the hole, and once the puppies became interested, left them to discover the naturally exciting new scents and textures. (f) This innocent pup is about to learn that "Cats rule!" Many breeders have or borrow a cat to teach this lesson to 4- to 6-week-old puppies, since the sooner this lesson is learned, the greater the impression it will make, although it may sometimes apply only to cats in their own family.

Developing Independence

The field dog must have the opportunity to develop a sense of confidence and personal identity. This will result only from a puppy's having been given plenty of chances to explore his surroundings. Puppies should ideally be divided by emotional and physical development; smaller, weaker, or less bold puppies need the chance to explore and interact without the oppressive presence of stronger, pushier littermates. Conversely, these pushy pups should not be learning the habit of bullying others and should get as much as they give from their equally precocious littermates and be challenged to develop good socialization skills. Starting at 5 weeks, all puppies should also have the chance to explore new areas one at a time, without the emotional support of littermates, to encourage independent confidence and to help the puppy discover his individual identity. The sooner puppies are provided with these individual learning experiences, the greater the likelihood of developing a confident, bold attitude toward exploring the new world. These first weeks with the breeder are also the ideal time to kindle the puppy's prey drive by providing stimulating objects of fur and feathers to drag and carry, as well as the chance to chase these objects. If it appears that puppies will not be provided with these opportunities before leaving the breeder's home, the new owner should provide them as soon and as often as possible.

Field Dog Kindergarten

Socialization

Once the puppy goes to its new home, the owner has the responsibility to begin building a strong socialization foundation or better yet, to carry on building the strong foundation begun by the breeder. Initiate a second round of the "Rule of Sevens" by introducing the puppy to as many new places, people, footing, sights, sounds, and events as is safely possible. Never force the puppy into a position that is frightening; rather, provide the opportunity and then back off, letting the pup approach at his own pace. For example, when entering a dark, spooky room from a well-lit area, provide supportive leadership presence and confidence but do not coddle or reinforce frightened behavior. Take the pup to new places, but use common sense—a heavily used dog park is no place for a puppy that has not completed its initial vaccination series, and pushy or aggressive adult dogs can have a lifelong negative impact on an impressionable pup.

Any dog that is going to grow up to be a good hunting companion needs to be well accustomed to car travel. If the pup has not established good traveling habits, start now. Read *Life with Weimaraners* for some car safety and travel tips.

The new owner should take the puppy on short walks, as determined by the age and stamina of the puppy, where he can take rest breaks as often as needed. Remember that the bones and joints are gristly and still soft up to 4–6 months, and overexercise before physical maturity can cause soreness or even permanent damage, particularly to the hips and shoulders, regardless of the puppy's genetic heritage. These outings will give the puppy the opportunity to learn to cope with different surfaces, to climb over and under natural obstructions such as rocks and branches, to feel different types of vegetation against his face and legs, and to meet new people. The puppy quickly learns that the world is full of interesting sights and even more exciting scents. These outings encourage the puppy to explore independently. The puppy also learns that his leader will not allow anything bad to happen to him.

Developing the Point

Paintings and photographs of a dog on point usually portray a breathtaking classic point, with a raised forefoot as the dog stares intently in the direction of the bird. A point is actually any body language used by the dog to tell its handler, "I've found game, and if you follow the direction I'm looking, you will find it, too."

The stalking nature of the point is most evident when a dog scents the prey, crouches, and creeps toward the scent until the prey is located. Any frozen posture that indicates the location of game is a valid point. The dog may have all feet on the ground or a rear leg raised in mid-stride, which Germans consider quite typical of Weimaraners. Even lying down to point is quite acceptable under European standards but not under AKC standards. Some American field-trial rules also fault a point in which there is any movement of the body, tail, or head while the dog is on point. Many Weimaraners indicate the presence of game with a high-speed wag of the tail just before locking on point. Some dogs will tremble all over with excitement when on point, and for others, the excitement of scenting the bird will cause the hairs on their tail to puff up like a bottle brush.

For the typical Weimaraner puppy, pointing begins with stalking and creeping into a sight point—that is, a point stimulated by the sight of the prey, which can be anything. Birds feeding on the lawn, butterflies, and even littermates may prompt the first stalking and pointing behavior. Because of the Weimaraner's strong fur-hunting heritage, the sight of a cat is often a powerful stimulus to the pointing reflex; many times, the unexpected sight of a cat half-hidden in the bushes will trigger a point long before the puppy demonstrates the same response to the sight or scent of birds.

Rod and Wing

The goal of early training is to strengthen the puppy's interest in prey and to develop the pointing instinct by facilitating the discovery that a bird or wing cannot be caught

Figure 12-4: (a) *A stylish point* with a raised hind leg. FC NFC Rynmichel Sir Knight Von Horn was the winner of the 1992 National Open All-Age Championship.

(b) *Some points are not classically graceful* because of terrain or sudden wind shifts. CH Quiksilvr's Magic StarChaser, CD, RE, MH, SDX, RDX, VX2, comes to a rapid halt and freezes when catching the scent of a bird.

by chasing. The rod and wing technique is ideal because it requires little equipment, it can be done in a small backyard, and—most importantly—it is fun for both puppy and trainer.

A 4-foot pole or short fishing rod (with or without a casting reel) and a game bird wing (or toy) are the only equipment needed. Tie the object securely to the end of about 6 feet of nylon fishing line, which has low visibility and therefore does not distract the puppy from the wing.

Attract the puppy's attention by flipping the wing in front of its nose and teasing it into chasing. Whenever the puppy pounces to catch the wing, flip it up over the puppy's head to a new location, giving the puppy another opportunity to stalk and point. Do not let the puppy get too close.

Not only is a close point undesirable in a finished dog, but also a puppy can leap and catch the object with incredible speed; flipping the wing out of the puppy's reach to prevent a catch is far preferable to waiting too long to see whether the puppy will indeed point.

Keep such training sessions very short, a few minutes at most—whether the puppy points or not—in order to maximize the excitement level associated with "bird" contact. Short, frequent opportunities to "play the game" keep each lesson exciting and build enthusiasm.

Ideally, each lesson ends when the puppy has established a stalk or point. When the puppy breaks, end the lesson by flipping the wing or toy into the air and catching and hiding it. The objective is to teach the puppy that the fun ends when it breaks point and the "bird" escapes.

If the puppy should happen to catch the wing—and a fast, crafty puppy will likely catch it sooner or later—take it away as quietly as possible. No praise is given to reward catching the wing nor any scolding when it is removed from the puppy's mouth. Reprimands or roughness would be unfair and confuse the puppy; because the pup had first been encouraged to chase and catch the wing, scolding would only be punishing success. Remember, the objectives of this exercise are twofold; first, to create an interest in live game, and second, to teach the puppy that birds cannot be caught. The wonderful, exciting game simply ends, and the trainer will be more alert next time.

Bird on a String

Puppies will usually respond to the rod and wing right from the beginning or after a few sessions; although most puppies will at least stalk or chase, it is important to remember that late onset of the pointing reflex is a not uncommon

Figure 12-5: *A stylish point* to the rod and wing at the early age of 7–8 weeks is a reliable indicator of adult potential; however, a puppy that chases, stalks, and pounces should not be discounted, as the pointing instinct often develops later in this breed. Do not forget to develop the sporting nature of your Weimaraner puppy. Photograph by Elena Smith.

Figure 12-6: *Because the puppy begins by sight pointing*, a small, bouncy toy can substitute until a bird wing can be obtained. For Lexy, the sudden appearance of a tossed toy may initially be more exciting than an unusual bird wing, stimulating this striking point. Photograph by Mark Benja.

Figure 12-7: *The stronger scent of a live bird* on a string and the sight of its fluttering and then suddenly landing where the puppy can both see and smell the bird will nearly always incite a sudden point. Now, Eve will begin to develop the magical association between the scent of the bird and the point. Photograph by Shirley Nilsson.

characteristic in the breed. For the "late bloomers," who may or may not be interested in just a wing or toy, it may help to make the situation more realistic. Start with a freshly killed quail on a string (previously frozen and thawed quail will do but are second best). Allow the puppy to inspect the bird and get a good smell. If the puppy is still with its littermates, allow the boldest puppy to make a grab at the dead bird and to stalk, chase, catch, and carry it off for a few proud moments; the experience of the scent and taste of feathers can make an indelible impression on the young puppy. The success of the first puppy will make a reluctant littermate more keen to possess this mysterious new toy; allow the second puppy to make an attempt to grab the prize. Since the first pup has already demonstrated his natural aptitude, he is held so that he can only watch. Allow the less bold puppy to stalk, creep, and try to carry off the non-threatening dead bird; this greed will increase the puppy's prey drive and possessiveness of this feathered object.

Once the puppy has been introduced to a dead bird and is eager to chase and grab it, switch to a live bird on a harness and string, and follow the same procedure as with the wing on a rod. Quail are ideal game birds for this purpose as they are small and do not intimidate a small puppy. The stronger scent of a live bird and the sight of its fluttering in the air will invariably create a pup that will stalk and chase. Most pups will initially attempt to pounce, but if the quail continues to fly away and land again (with the help of the rod), in time, the pup will become more cautious in his attempts to catch the bird. As he learns that the quail always escapes his efforts, he will begin to stalk and finally to point. As the puppy begins to associate breaking point with the bird's escape and the end of fun, it becomes more intent on the bird and less easily distracted.

Figure 12-8: *To encourage the puppy to point by scent,* begin by hiding the birds in cover, giving the bird a better opportunity to flush and escape if Eve pushes too close. Although catching the bird intensifies Eve's desire to search more widely using her nose, it also decreases the mystique and need to point—a signal that Eve is ready to switch from the more easily caught pen-raised quail to the more strongly flying homing pigeons. Photograph by Holly Palmer.

Once the dog has begun to point, catching the bird is undesirable as it decreases the mystique and the need to point; it increases the likelihood of breaking on wing or shot when the dog realizes that he can catch the bird on his own. In some special cases, an experienced dog may be allowed to catch birds under highly controlled circumstances in order to rekindle enthusiasm and drive in a dog that has been trained too hard or that has otherwise soured on the hunt. However, it should be borne in mind that in solving the problem of lack of desire, a lesser problem of encouraging the habit of chasing and catching live birds may be created. In general, it is advisable to keep an unsteady dog on a check cord if any possibility exists of catching the bird. This dog will benefit from working on more unpredictable wild birds, which are harder to catch.

Running Wild

Every young pup will have the greatest opportunity to fulfill its potential if it is given plenty of opportunity to learn the ways of birds while running in safe areas with natural cover, with plenty of wild birds as teachers. Puppies need the chance to run in these areas on their own; initially, a well-versed mentor or a puppy companion will provide encouragement, but once the puppy is moving out independently, it needs to run without the distraction of a potential playmate or an overly assertive older dog. The youngster will discover the places the birds hide and see how easily the bird can be bumped by a pushy puppy. The pup learns to accept grass and brush in the face and to run on uneven terrain, all at its own pace. These experiences will be invaluable in helping the developing Weimaraner puppy mature into an independent and sensible hunter.

Reinforcing the Retrieving Instinct

Related to retrieving, pick-up-and-carry behavior is easily reinforced at an early age simply by providing puppies with soft toys that are not too heavy to carry; tasty toys such as beef ribs may encourage early enthusiasm. The behavior is so strongly instinctive, however, that the problem is not getting a puppy to carry things but teaching discrimination between desirable and undesirable objects, such as rocks, pillows, shoes, and clothing. It is better to keep such objects out of reach, especially when the puppy is playing with other dogs, as the pup is more likely to swallow an object when trying to keep it away from a playmate.

Begin play retrieving at the earliest possible age. It is best if the same person initiates the early training to ensure consistent expectation. Get down on the floor with the puppy. Use a special toy that the puppy can pick up easily and really likes and gets only during play retrieving. Stimulate interest in the article by moving it about, teasing, and enticing. When the puppy is completely engaged, toss the toy a few feet away; remember that very young puppies have limited peripheral vision and may lose interest if the toy is tossed too far away or not directly in front of the pup.

When the puppy picks up the article, call coaxingly and avoid looming over the top of the puppy as he approaches; rather, crouch invitingly. If the puppy does not bring the object at first, try using a narrow hallway so that options to run off are limited. Block the ends of the hall (a dog crate is handy) and close the doors. As with the recall, never scold or move toward the puppy that fails to come. If the puppy fails to bring the article when called, move away, stimulating the chase instinct, and catch the culprit while passing.

Figure 12-9: *Where's the boss?* Keep perspective in mind when calling the small puppy. If all he sees is a pair of boots like this, he may have no idea where his owner is; be sure to get down on his level, where he can see a friendly face and welcoming posture. Photograph by Jay Fleming.

Figure 12-10: *The Shirley Nilsson technique* teaches very young puppies like Gretta to reliably retrieve. Very special treats, such as cat food, are inserted in a plastic film container, and the puppy is given a taste. Gretta watches as the top is replaced on the canister and it is tossed a short distance. When the toss is consistently accompanied by a clear signal, the puppy will quickly learn to mark the fall and take a directed line. The puppy is rewarded for the retrieve with a taste of the food inside. Puppies as young as 9 weeks have learned to perform directed and double retrieves.

Gently hold the pup's collar and stroke the puppy while praising lavishly. Never pull the toy roughly from the pup's mouth. If the pup is reluctant to surrender the prize, simply continue the praise and stroke until the object begins to get heavy. For the truly possessive pup, a soft puff of air in the ear or a tasty tidbit can be offered in exchange for the object, alternating with praise, but not every time. Be sure to stop after a couple of good retrieves while the puppy is still enthusiastically running after and returning with the object. End on a positive note, before the puppy begins to tire of the game.

Below are some retrieving guidelines:

- Never correct a puppy for bringing anything to the owner, even if it is disgusting or something they "should not" have.

- Use one SPECIAL item to practice retrieving; the puppy gets to play with it only during training.

- Never "fake" throwing an object early on. The dog must get a retrieve if he believes something is out there.

- Initially control the situation so that the puppy has no option other than to bring the item back. Provide an escape-proof area to develop a positive pattern in the response.

- When in doubt that the puppy will return, don't just stand there! Get down on the puppy's level, and if that doesn't work, run away. Be exciting and enticing and encourage the puppy to come to you. DO NOT CHASE!!!! Use a long line in the future.

- Do not tear the item out of the puppy's mouth; take time to admire the puppy for his efforts and wait until the puppy is more willing to relinquish the object. Be gentle.

- When the puppy becomes reliable, begin adding variability one step at a time, such as teaching it to sit before or after the retrieve, introducing new areas, or varying distances and directions.

Figure 12-11: *Teenage independence.* Remember that some young dogs go through a phase in which a previously reliable puppy suddenly begins running away when called or refuses to return the object, and even the welcoming posture may not be enough to incite the puppy to return. Take a few steps back in training and return to using the long line. This reinforces the desired behavior through repetition and prevents undesirable behavior patterns. At this age, Sage's owner may still exchange the object for a tasty treat or reward. Photograph by Gene LaFollette.

- Do not lose your temper. Finish the session with something positive, even if it is ultra-simple, and end the session. Come back in a few days after a break; the puppy will learn he is not allowed the privilege of playing the game unless he plays by the rules.

- Never overdo the retrieve practice. Keep it short. Start when the puppy has picked up something he likes and is carrying it around, and end with the puppy wanting more. Get a couple of good fetches in and call it a day.

Introducing "Whoa"

Every bird dog should understand the "whoa" command, or at least some variation of it, and the pup that goes into bird training with a good understanding of this concept and a positive reinforcement history will already be well along the path to becoming a valued hunting companion. Refer to "Stand and Stay" in *Weimaraner Kindergarten*. A dog that is stressed out or confused will often default to well-known or early behaviors; the sit is frequently the first behavior a puppy learns, and the sit and down are usually practiced most frequently. But a dog that sits or lies down on a point will be heavily penalized. If planning a field career, it is important that the stand-and-stay command be practiced more often and that it be more amply rewarded than the down or sit with a stay. Be consistent in making sure that the puppy maintains the position in which he was left. If asking for a sit-stay, do not allow the puppy to lie down; if practicing the stand, do not allow the puppy to sit. While obedience training is strongly recommended, if you are taking classes, be sure the instructor understands the trainer's goals and does not

Figure 12-13: ***Never too early to "whoa."*** Eight-week-old Streak has learned to "whoa," even to the point of actively resisting being moved. This well-learned command, initially taught by his breeder, Shirley Nilsson, with plenty of treats and without the distraction of birds, is a strong foundation skill for the future hunting companion.

require the puppy to sit every time the handler stops or practices the stay. Plenty of repetition and reward will soon have the puppy happily responding to this steadying command.

Introduction to Water

Love of water, a dominant hereditary trait, is so firmly established in the breed that fear of water can usually be traced either to a total absence of early exposure or to an experience at an early age that may cause lifelong fear. The most common causes are falling or being tossed or dragged into deep water.

Some Weimaraners that have not learned to swim as puppies have difficulty learning later, so to some degree, swimming appears to be as much a learned as an instinctive accomplishment. There is even a clear difference between

Figure 12-12: ***"Whoa" training in the field with birds*** continues on a check cord when the pup is old enough to actually be able to catch the bird. Mary has planted several quail, clearly marked with flags. **(a)** Six-month-old Mister has been sent some distance downwind to hunt, dragging a lightweight 30-foot check cord. Well before Mister reaches a flagged bird, Mary picks up the check cord. **(b)** When his body language indicates that the puppy is in the scent cone and he points, Mary is there to steady and style him and to be sure he does not give chase if the bird flushes. Photograph by Gene LaFollette.

puppies that have been imprinted (see *Testing Natural Aptitude*) sometime between the 6th and 12th weeks and those that are introduced to swimming later. Hopefully, the breeder provided early water experience, as explained in *Raising the Litter* and *Testing Natural Aptitude*. If weather or circumstances have prevented these early experiences, provide similar exposure before attempting the first swimming lesson.

Water's Edge

As soon as conditions permit, plan a water day; continue with tub swimming if the weather is bad. Choose a day when the water will be warm and inviting. Bring favorite toys (with string attached), dead birds, and food—bring along a selection because you will not know what works until you try. Bring waders or be prepared to get wet. Make sure to have towels to dry off the pup after swimming. A wet pup can not only make a mess of the car, but can end up chilled; a crate allows the mess to be contained and provides a place to snuggle up with a warm towel. A human assistant is also necessary. A friendly dog (preferably a littermate or Mom) that already loves to swim can also be a great assistant, not only setting a good example but fetching "escaped" toys. A collar with identification provides a handle and is also important if the puppy wanders off.

Before swimming, make sure the area is safe; scout an area in advance. Submerged branches, stumps, rocks, or broken glass can turn a fun day at the lake into an emergency trip to the vet. Check the temperature of the water; if it is too cold for human comfort, it is much too cold for a puppy's first experience. In the beginning, find an area free of vegetation, such as lily pads or reeds, with low or minimal vegetation on the bank. A small sandy or gravel beach is comfortable and provides sure footing as well as an easy entry. Look for a firm, gradually sloping entry area; a gooey or slippery bottom will reduce confidence. Choose freshwater with minimal current, like a pond or stream; save the ocean or fast-flowing river for the experienced swimmer, as

Figure 12-15: *Never push, pull, or throw* an unwilling puppy into the water. This is a recipe with a high probability of producing a dog that is at best a reluctant swimmer and at worst actually afraid to enter at all.

salt water waves or running currents could result in an unpleasant experience for the novice.

Taking the Plunge

Never push, pull, or throw an unwilling puppy into the water. This is a recipe with a high probability of producing a dog that is at best a reluctant swimmer and at worst actually afraid to enter at all. When the situation can be arranged so that the puppy thinks that entering the water was his own idea, the Weimaraner's instincts will surface. Observing and playing with a water-wise canine companion makes the process simpler and helps the puppy quickly discover that swimming is fun. Before long, he will seek out any opportunity to play or swim in water. Whether the puppy simply splashes in the water or actually swims, end the lesson while he is still enjoying himself and before he is too tired. Make it happy and playful; do not overdo it. A puppy that has had a positive, FUN experience has had solid groundwork laid for the future. Be

Figure 12-14: *First swimming lesson.* Duncan is carried out to a convenient sandbar in a shallow, slow-moving stream. His sister, Dana, waits on the near bank to encourage his return. After pleading for rescue, Duncan decides on his own to swim back across. A dog that chooses to enter the water on his own will most likely develop confidence in the water and enjoyment in water sports. Photograph by Tammy Weiner.

Figure 12-16: *A prized floating toy* can be used to entice a reluctant puppy into the water. The string keeps the toy from floating too far away while the puppy makes up his mind, or from being pushed out of reach by the puppy's splashing. The string can be used to maneuver the toy into the puppy's mouth as he reaches the edge of his comfort zone. When he finally reaches to grab the toy, the puppy will most likely end up automatically swimming as he turns around to bring his prize home.

patient, with no pressure; let the puppy observe other dogs having fun while he is not. The dog must go in of his own choice, even if it means repeating the lesson several times.

Here are just a few ideas to create opportunities for the pup to think up the idea of swimming on his own.

Follow the Pack

If a swimming party can be arranged for littermates or puppies of similar age, "follow the pack" will often get the entire group in the water. Even if the puppy does not swim but merely wades in and splashes at first, that is fine. Carry one puppy to the far bank of a slow-moving, shallow stream and leave him there, with all he knows in the world on the near bank to entice him back over. Once the first puppy has crossed, let another puppy give it try, letting each puppy watch the others. Do not be surprised if the first puppy follows you back over.

Toy on a String

Build up desire for a toy that floats by engaging the puppy in play on land at the water's edge. Tie a string on the toy so it will not float out of reach. Once the pup shows great desire for the toy, toss it a very short distance into the water. The string can be used to pull the toy toward the puppy's mouth when he has gone just as far as he can without swimming, just before he gives up. Since the puppy's splashing will usually push the toy farther away, very often that last final reach throws the balance off just enough that once the puppy actually gets the toy in his mouth, he must swim in order to turn around and return with the prize. The success of reaching the toy will encourage the pup to go just a bit farther the next

Figure 12-17: *Whatever works.* **(a)** These creative owners are using a combination of food and toy bribes, human company, and "monkey see, monkey do" to entice these doubtful Weims into the water. **(b)** Arrange for puppies of similar age to get together for a swimming party. Carry a reluctant puppy to the far bank of a shallow stream with a nice gravel bottom; he will need to cross the stream to rejoin his littermates and owners on the near side. The best-laid plans were foiled, when these confident pups simply waded over to the far side but then proceeded to play and entice the less enthusiastic swimmer into the water with their playful antics. This tactic allowed the pup to develop some confidence and to make the decision to enter the water on his own, an important aspect of developing a self-assured adult swimmer.

Figure 12-18: ***Repeated casual exposure*** to water increases the non-swimmer's comfort level. Eventually, greed and competition for a prized object will result in the dog's deciding to swim on his own. Photograph by Inara Knight.

time, and eventually he will swim on his own. Most puppies are eager to repeat this new game, as long as the distance and swimming requirements are increased slowly. When the puppy returns with the toy, offer lavish praise and allow him time to strut around and display his prize to all admirers. Make sure the puppy is successful!

If there is more than one puppy, this is a good time to allow competition for the toy to inspire greater effort from the bold pup and to encourage even the reluctant puppy. Remember, quit while the puppy is still having a good time and before he is too tired.

Starting the Four-Legged Dog Paddle

Then there is the pup that is confident around the water— unafraid to enter and play—but that simply won't go quite far enough to actually swim. Rather, the dog persists in walking with the back feet remaining on the bottom of the pond. This pup can often be coaxed to a full-fledged four-legged dog paddle; the owner, treats in hand (yes, bribery works before the pup discovers how much fun swimming

actually is), takes the pup out into the water on a leash and buckle collar, just to the spot of no return. The owner continues walking while offering extra-special, delicious treats to coax the pup forward off his back leg perch until the pup must swim in order to turn for home. The leash ensures that the pup does not return to the shore; the owner uses much praise and generous treats to encourage the puppy to repeat the experience, moving back and forth between the shallower and deeper water. As the pup gains confidence on these short forays, the owner will eventually be able to walk with the pup "heeling/swimming" on the deep water side. When the pup is successful, be sure to communicate how wonderful this accomplishment is with plenty of praise and extra treats. Follow this training with rest periods, and plenty of opportunities for unrestricted play on the water's edge and shallows, and the chance to watch strong swimming canine mentors and people confidently playing in the water. More and more such forays will soon have even the most reluctant pup swimming confidently, and then the fun of mucky pond bottoms and varying vegetation begins.

Figure 12-19: ***For the reluctant older dog,*** many times, a toy is not interesting enough to be an enticement; for the experienced field dog; a live bird on a tether may be the perfect lure. With its movement and more enticing scent, a live bird may provide the irresistible impetus to get those first few strokes in. Work the bird just like the toy in Figure 12-16. After the first success in shallow water, the desire to possess the bird will encourage the dog to swim farther to capture the shackled bird. For puppies, a pigeon can be used; a live duck like this is only appropriate for a seasoned field dog, such as Izzy. After a few lessons, Izzy passed the water certification, which is required for all Weimaraners who complete a Field Championship.

Getting Adults in the Water

Greed works well with puppies but is especially effective with an older pup or mature dog. Older dogs will often attempt to steal the toy as the retriever is coming back and eventually work up the courage to swim.

The non-swimmer will wade out as far as he dares, going a bit farther each time as he gains familiarity and becomes more comfortable in the water. Eventually, the prized object is thrown for the "non-swimmer," with the swimmer held in reserve, threatening to retrieve the object if the non-swimmer does not pluck up the courage to take the plunge. Should the non-swimmer fail to go for the object, allow the swimmer to retrieve the toy, and next time, use a prize more highly valued by the dog (such as a dead bird, floating pool toys, such as Fat Cat® or Kyjen® water toys); slowly place it farther and farther into the water for the non-swimmer to retrieve.

Be sure to rinse the dogs off with clear water after swimming; this can help them avoid potential skin irritations and minimize odors the skin may acquire from some bodies of water. Give the dog a once-over to look for injuries, parasites, and sore spots. Avoid squirting the dog with the hose, as this may be cold and frightening, especially for a young dog. Be sure to provide the dog with a warm, dry place to rest until he is dry.

Introduction to Gunfire

Weimaraners are not particularly sensitive to loud noises or thunder; the gun-shy Weimaraner is most often created by poor judgment. The typical story of the gun-shy Weimaraner is that the owner decides to go dove hunting or to shoot birds for retrieving practice with a puppy that has never heard a gun fired, and the puppy's introduction to gunfire is the blast of a 10-gauge shotgun while half-asleep at the owner's side. This is a guaranteed way to create a gun-shy dog. Although it requires considerable time and patience, it is possible to cure gun-shyness; however, this is a case where it is manifestly better to prevent the problem than to try to cure it.

Gun sureness starts long before the first formal exposure to gunfire and is based on common sense. Refer to *Raising the Litter* and *Ages and Stages* for building the foundation. If the breeder has not laid this foundation, or if the new owner suspects the puppy is unprepared, provide this experience before attempting to formally introduce the puppy to gunfire. Expose the puppy to sudden, loud household noises, such as a vacuum cleaner or the clatter of pots and pans. Initially, these noises should start in another room, and the puppy should be distracted by a tasty meal or an exciting game.

Here are important suggestions to keep in mind for the formal introduction of gunfire:

Figure 12-20: ***After early conditioning to gunfire,*** the ideal time for a pup's first field exposure would be the moment when he is committed to chasing the flushed bird. A gun fired in the distance will not be a disturbing experience, as his attention is completely focused on his prey. With future experiences, the assistant gunner can slowly move closer until a blank pistol can be fired within reasonable gun range, as required by the hunt and ratings tests. Photograph by Gene LaFollette.

- Start far away, where the dog shows no reaction
- Start with a smaller caliber and work up
- Provide positive reinforcement with each shot, such as a game or treat that keeps the puppy engaged with the trainer and not the noise
- Move closer slowly; if the puppy startles or shows a negative reaction, go no closer until the puppy is completely relaxed
- If the puppy overreacts, do not reinforce fearful behavior; calmly move away to a point at which the dog no longer reacts at all and start over with better distractions
- Do not assume the previous lesson will be remembered with a young puppy; repeat this process several times from the beginning
- Do not leave the puppy alone; a canine companion confident around gunfire sets a good example during the lesson, and a friendly person to play with and observe puppy's reaction will make the lesson smoother

For the safety and best performance of the dog and handler, confer with an experienced field trainer about the art and etiquette of firing a blank pistol. Remember that at a trial or test, the handler is responsible for firing the blank pistol to demonstrate the dog's gun sureness at bird contact, so practice this scenario ahead of time. Always follow gun safety rules.

Field Dog Elementary School

A Smooth Transition to the Field

If the puppy has been well prepared, the transition from the rod and wing to wild/free birds should be smooth. However, handler error with an introduction to live, pen-raised birds is common and has set back the training of many promising youngsters. The most common errors—letting the puppy catch birds (not uncommon with weak-flying pen-raised birds) or punishing the mishap too harshly—can impair further development.

Pigeons

With this thought in mind, many trainers prefer pigeons for several reasons:

- Pigeons are more readily available and less expensive than quail
- Pigeons fly more strongly and are hardier than quail
- Pigeons are easier and less complicated to raise than game birds

Figure 12-21: *The essential pigeon coop.* Many patterns are available for pigeon coops of various sizes. After a pair or two of healthy birds have had the opportunity to settle into their new home for several months, birds can be used for training. With a little bit of luck, after release the birds will "home" back to the coop, having served their training purpose. A one-way door in this super-sized coop allows the birds to enter but not exit unless released. Young birds will more reliably home back to the coop where they were reared, ready for future training sessions. Photograph by Todd Herrig.

- If a young dog begins to resent lessons, changing to the more exciting game bird is the easiest way to rekindle enthusiasm

Commercially bred pigeons and quail may be purchased for training, but check local game laws first to see whether a permit is required. The best way to ensure a supply of live, healthy pigeons is to trap them or maintain a coop. The birds are hardy and strong and almost always return home. Not so with quail. *The Quail Palace* by Lion Country offers safe, reliable housing for a dozen quail, with a dependable recall ability if sufficient birds remain in the trap to lure the others back. Alternatively, pigeons (as well as chukar) can also be hobbled to limit their flight capability when thrown or placed in a launcher so they can be used several times at the same training session.

Introduce the Pigeon

Fair Game. While pigeons are very useful in training the gun dog, to most dogs the pigeon does not register as "fair game," so the dog must be introduced to pigeons and taught to consider them as such for training purposes. This process is fairly simple and straightforward; introduce the pigeon in a manner similar to the quail on a string. Use a well-conditioned pigeon in a harness and attach a weight, such as a length of garden hose, to the harness to limit flight; the bird can still fly, but not a great distance. An assistant can handle the bird while the handler works the dog on a check cord. The fluttering of the pigeon will attract and excite the young dog, surprising the dog. However, it will usually instinctively point when the assistant tugs the line and drops the pigeon to the ground at a desirable distance in sight of the dog. This lesson need only be repeated a time or two to get the mes-

Figure 12-22: *Ms is introduced to pigeons* as "fair game" at a recent Harmeyer NAVHDA clinic. Traci develops Ms' interest by using a hobbled bird (a quick loop of cord weighted with a length of garden hose). **(a)** The dog is teased with a tethered bird. At the height of excitement, the bird is tossed into the air; the weight of the hobble allows the bird to flutter a short distance and then land. **(b)** A surprised Ms locks into a striking point with her owner stepping discreetly on the 30-foot check cord to prevent an inadvertent chase.

sage across that pointing pigeons is appropriate. Now, the pup is ready to move on to learning the intricacies of pointing birds in the field.

To maintain the mystique of the bird, it is advisable to maintain pigeon and wild bird coops in an area where they will not have regular contact with the dogs. Familiarity with the birds reduces the excitement for the hunt. And, it may confuse a dog to be corrected for "harassing" the cooped birds at home yet be encouraged to hunt them in the field.

Sight Point. With the puppy confined where it cannot see the bird being planted, place the bird in an open area where the puppy will be able to sight it. Remember where the bird is planted to avoid coming close enough for the puppy to catch it. With the puppy on a check cord, approach the bird from downwind so that the puppy can scent as well as sight the bird. If the puppy has been well prepared on the rod and wing, it will point the bird. The handler should flush

the bird as soon as the puppy points or begins to stalk, showing that the bird has been scented. It is helpful to have an assistant hold the check cord to prevent the puppy from breaking when the handler flushes the bird. If the puppy points, give it plenty of praise after the bird has flown away. As with the rod and wing, end the lesson when the puppy has found the bird.

Scent Point. As soon as the puppy seems to be locating birds by scent—showing a response before the bird can be sighted—begin planting the bird, either dizzied or tied, where it cannot be seen. Hide the pigeons in the type of cover preferred by the local game birds. If using grass for cover, plant the bird in vegetation tall enough to provide cover but not so tall that the puppy has difficulty working. Kick a hole in the grass to make a tunnel into which the bird can be slipped. The trainer without an assistant can guarantee that the dog will not make contact by using a mesh Bag-Its™ (available through www.dogsunlimited.com), which ensures that the birds remain in the desired location, as well as preventingthe green-broke dog from consuming the bird if he does grab it. The trainer can plant or toss the bagged birds into likely cover while on the outbound leg of the day's training, unnoticed by the dog ranging in front of him; the dog will find the planted birds on the return trip. As the dog becomes steadier, the snap end of the bag can be opened to allow the bird to wander off or be flushed.

Continue to approach the bird from downwind. There must be some air movement to carry the scent of the bird; a gentle breeze is perfect. In dead calm, the puppy may not locate the bird until he is close enough to dart forward and

Figure 12-23: *Willow starts with sight pointing.* A harnessed pigeon on string is a sturdy, safe bird to point. Photograph by Cindilla Trent.

grab it. In addition, the puppy may develop the bad habit of getting too close to the bird before pointing, which makes it difficult to flush the bird and increases the risk of a successful catch. If the wind is too strong, it can blow the bird into the puppy, which will then break point and often catch it.

Tracking the Planter

The Weimaraner is a superb tracking breed, and it is not unusual for a young genius to figure out that the fastest way to find the bird is to track the bird planter; this often results in a close point or failure to point at all in favor of the dog's just picking up the bird. This is a classic example of the breed's problem-solving aptitude; however, it complicates training situations in which planted birds are vital, and it is troublesome in field-trial competition or any hunting test using planted birds. Using Bag-Its™ is one option, as the trainer can throw the bagged birds into cover without the tell-tale track that is left behind when planting. *Hot on the Track* discusses measures that help the Weimaraner understand when it is expected to hunt and when it is expected to track, and it suggests ways to both prevent and correct tracking of the bird planter.

Enthusiasm

The Weimaraner wants to hunt by instinct; the Weimaraner loves to hunt by training. Since most Weimaraners tend to perceive life as a game, when birds stop being fun, Weimaraners may quickly lose their enthusiasm or even quit. Steady work on the check cord is not fun! Just because it is essential to establish the behavioral patterns so strongly that the dog can be controlled by voice alone when not on a check cord, this does not alter the reality that a drill is a drill. The deep-seated desire to hunt for birds is critical to developing other skills, such as range, pattern, and steadiness. Since the innate urge is constantly being frustrated, lavish praise and the potential of the reward of a fun release activity for correct responses are often necessary to maintain the passion for the hunt and to counter the necessary drill and frustration. The reward will be different for each dog; it is the trainer's responsibility to discover the motivation that is most successful for each Weimaraner. When developing enthusiasm, it is important to quit while the dog is still "into" the game or when he has just performed to the best of his ability, even if it means simplifying the exercise to ensure success.

Figure 12-25: *Determine wind* direction by tossing some fluffy seeds or grass into the air. Photograph by Jacob Schulte.

The Wait

Sometimes, just the thing to increase or restore the dog's desire is to deny him what he thinks he is tired of. Leaving the dog on a stake-out while other dogs work will often remind the dog of the fun he is missing. He not only does not get to hunt, he also does not get the attention of the trainer. If he is allowed to observe the other dogs working, this also takes advantage of the Weimaraner's instinctive "monkey see, monkey do" nature. Eventually, he will get bored with just hanging out and want to play the game too, eagerly demanding his chance to show what he is capable of.

The Chase

Enthusiasm can be built or restored by providing periodic opportunities for the puppy to chase birds. The birds must be healthy, mature, and in good flight condition, of course, because the worst thing that can happen is for the puppy to catch one, whereas an exciting but fruitless chase of a wild bird reinforces the concept that birds cannot be caught. Avoid housing or transporting birds in close contact with the dog or puppy to maintain the mystique of the bird.

Figure 12-24: *Is it my turn yet?* Stake out the dog with several kennelmates and let him simply watch a few training sessions. Follow this with a few sessions where the dog has to wait before getting to work, and most dogs are soon barking and complaining, anxious to be chosen; this is especially effective when the dog can actually see the other dogs working. Photograph by Shirley Nilsson.

Figure 12-26: *An electronic release trap* is a valuable tool throughout the field dog's training. The ability to control the flush and chase will rekindle enthusiasm in the stale dog. For the eager dog well along in training, the launcher can help develop a "long nose." By flushing many birds as soon as the dog's body language, such as stalking, indicates they have entered the scent cone, the likelihood that the dog will catch the released bird is minimized and the dog will learn to point the moment he catches scent instead of crowding the bird. Correct timing of the release avoids having a young dog begin to blink because he is too close to the trap and is startled by the sound or motion when the bird is released. As it is difficult for the handler, well behind his dog, to know exactly where the trap is, this process may be greatly enhanced if an experienced helper, concealed near the trap, can focus on the dog's behavior and operate the trap at just the right moment to most closely simulate the flush of a wild bird.

(a) A handheld transmitter is used to trigger the release of the bird from the launcher. Transmitters can be set up to operate multiple release traps and will trigger the trap from a range of hundreds of yards away. Compared with training with planted birds or wild birds, remote-release traps have the advantage of giving the dog handler total control over the timing of the flush and can therefore be very useful at various stages of training.

(b) The remote-release trap consists of a spring-loaded trampoline into which the bird is placed. The mesh trampoline and large air holes in the box of the launcher facilitate movement of bird scent out of the launcher.

(c) The bird is placed on the trampoline, and the sides of the trampoline are closed over it. Release traps come in various sizes and can be used to launch game birds of any size, up to and including pheasants.

(d) The spring-loaded lever is brought over to secure the bird in the trap. Some trap designs permit variable adjustment of the spring tension; lower tension results in a quieter trap release, and higher tension will launch a heavier bird more quickly up and away from the dog.

(e) Some trainers like to keep one wing of the bird extended out of the trap when it is loaded in order to increase the amount of bird scent available to the dog; this may be of particular benefit on days of light wind or when scenting conditions are otherwise poor.

The unpredictable nature of working an area with plentiful wild birds will go far to instill or rekindle a dog's passion; however, for many owners, such areas are not available. A visit to a bird farm or preserve provides opportunities, but in other circumstances a measure of contrivance is unavoidable—birds are dizzied and planted or placed in a bird releaser. A remote bird launcher is very useful here; however, if it is not properly used, it may create highly undesirable associations. Some models may be quite noisy—particularly older types that are not in good working condition—and the sudden, sharp noise of the launcher being activated can frighten the puppy. Worse yet, a young dog that is too close when the bird is released may be struck by or spooked by the mechanism when the bird is abruptly released in his face. Some newer models more closely simulate a natural flush with smoother, quieter operation. The Natural Flush Remote Bird Launcher™ has proven reliable and is one of the quietest launchers available. Alan and Marcia Davison, dedicated Weimaraner enthusiasts, believe it is the best available and offer it through their website, www.dogsunlimited.com, along with plenty of guidance for the problems a Weimaraner owner may face while training with this equipment in the field.

Since timing is vital for a successful lesson, not only does a launcher require a mechanism that responds reliably and promptly, but the person using the transmitter must release the bird at the right moment, as soon as the puppy indicates scent (not necessarily a point) but before he has approached too closely (certainly no closer than 10–15 feet). An assistant hidden near the launcher with a good view of both the trap and the approaching dog will produce the most effective release. Ideally, the trainer will be able to provide another launcher farther up the course to provide a second, reinforcing experience.

Field Dog High School

Developing Range and Pattern

Developing a puppy's range and hunting pattern requires no special skill, experience, or equipment—except a whistle and a large, safe area in which the dog may run with little risk of chasing birds or rabbits across roads. Ideally, start with open terrain and low cover; vary the terrain later to include denser cover, more obstacles, and trickier footing.

It is, unfortunately, increasingly difficult to find safe places to let a dog run, especially for owners who live in urban areas—it helps to have friends who live in rural areas. When asked permission, farmers usually have no objection to running dogs on their land, especially if they are assured that no gun will be used, that gates will be closed, and that the dogs can be controlled around livestock. Observing these courtesies helps to ensure a future welcome.

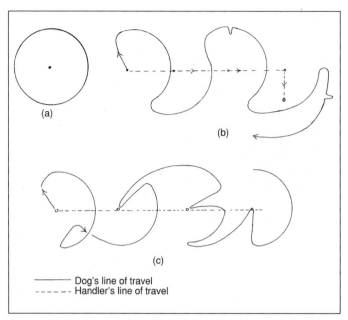

Figure 12-27: *Quartering.* (a) When the handler is at a standstill, the puppy circles at the end of an invisible tether. **(b)** When the handler moves, the puppy runs in an arc ahead of the handler's line of movement, breaking the smooth sweep only to check promising cover more carefully. At the handler's signal, the puppy swings wide and resumes the quartering pattern in the handler's new line of movement. **(c)** In the yo-yo pattern, the puppy's swings are interrupted by frequent swings back to the handler.

Check the area for hazards, such as a trash dump, barbed wire, or a precipice. Be alert for polluted water—some do not have warning signs posted. Finally, be well informed about local gun and hunting regulations; it is also a good idea to check local laws about loose dogs. In most states, livestock owners may legally shoot any loose dog because packs of wild dogs have become such a serious problem.

Initially, a puppy stays close to the handler, and as it gains confidence, the distance gradually increases. After a release command, do not give commands or speak to the puppy. Simply allow the Weimaraner's lively interest in everything to stimulate the desire to range and hunt.

The typical Weimaraner develops an excellent hunting pattern if given the opportunity to run and explore in the places where wild birds would naturally be found, without constant verbalization or signaling from the hunter.

A very young puppy is linked to the handler by an invisible tether that gradually lengthens as the puppy gains confidence. As the handler moves forward, the puppy begins to double back on the part of the circle ahead of the handler in the desired arcs of the quartering pattern. Circular sweeps behind the handler become less frequent as the puppy becomes more independent. Calling the puppy back, even having conversations with a hunting partner, encourages the undesirable yo-yo pattern of frequently checking back with

Figure 12-28: ***A horse's size, noises, and unexpected movements*** may initially awe or even frighten a young puppy. Human supervision is necessary, and a familiar canine will bolster the puppy's confidence, when the first introductions are made. Many a young pup has ruined his chances for the day at a field trial by hunting horse manure instead of birds. Horses at the Alexander farm are accustomed to dogs and routinely help teach puppies how to behave around them and to ignore the magnetic call of manure before entering a trial or test.

the places in which they are most likely to hide—clumps of grass, rows of weeds, bushes, logs, and low-hanging branches. At the same time, the puppy discovers how to use the wind to scent birds from a distance and to come closer with a sneaky stalk from downwind. To prevent the undesirable habit of roading (hunting just the cover along the road), avoid the temptation of taking the easiest route on a path or road, which is especially important when working in woods or heavy cover.

A good bird chase takes the puppy farther away and helps to extend range—that is, distance from the handler. If wild birds are scarce, plant one or two birds (marking the spot) close to the anticipated end of the walk so that the experience ends with excitement and suc-

the handler. Encourage the puppy to go into heavy cover to discover where birds like to hide; plant strong flying birds, if necessary, to be sure the effort is rewarded occasionally.

Fuhrigkeit is the German term that refers to the dog's responsiveness to the handler's leadership, which is, in part, demonstrated by the dog's awareness of the handler's location. This relationship can be encouraged in the young or green dog with judicious use of the whistle. Communicating a change of direction is vital because the puppy assumes that the handler is following. The typical German trainer gives a couple of toots (use any signal as long as it is consistent) and then drops to the ground (disappearing from the pup's sight). The Weimaraner pup should naturally come in search of the handler and is rewarded with lavish praise, then sent back to hunting. This technique should be used sparingly (perhaps once every one or two outings), so as not to restrict the dog's range from fear of abandonment, but should result in an independent dog that checks in when the signal is given. Once the hander has the dog's attention, a change of course (to avoid hazards or search a different area) can be indicated by walking in a new direction. Over-handling, with persistent signals or commands, is considered a fault in both the U.S. and Germany.

While learning to quarter, the youngster encounters bird scent and occasionally flushes birds to chase. This is the world's most wonderful game, and instinct reinforces experience as the puppy begins to look for birds and to figure out

Figure 12-29: ***Learning to take a line.*** First, Argon started by watching from nearby as the bird was planted near the barn (the bird's location is marked by an arrow). He was then cast a short distance to find it. Then, the bird was planted in the same location and Argon, who can no longer see the bird being planted from his position behind the barn, was moved farther and farther back before being sent to find and flush the bird. He was eventually sent quite some distance away, with the objective out of sight. Repeating this process of relocating the dog (but not the bird) in many different training areas will produce a dog that will consistently play the game of casting with confidence, moving long and straight from the line toward realistic objectives. Be sure that the practice birds are planted in places where wild birds would naturally be found. Photograph by Deborah Andrews.

cess. Always quit before the puppy tires, and end the session while the puppy is eager to go on. Vary the location of the training as well as the type of terrain and cover. Avoid a patterned route, occasionally picking the puppy up at the most distant point instead of returning to the starting point.

Take the puppy out in all kinds of weather. Field events are run when scheduled—in rain, sleet, snow, or extreme heat. Fair-weather trainers create fair-weather hunting dogs.

If the handler owns or has access to a horse, so much the better. The puppy soon learns he can see the handler from a greater distance, and this tends to extend range. Handlers, too, are less worried if the puppy can be observed; ideally, the horses should be accustomed to dogs underfoot.

The puppy learns so much when it is simply given the opportunity to develop its basic hunting instincts that the time and effort of going some distance are well rewarded. It cannot be overemphasized that a Weimaraner needs plenty of opportunity to run on its own in natural areas, without correction, with wild birds to develop its full potential. This is so important to developing the Weimaraner as a hunting dog that if the owner is unable to provide these opportunities locally, she should give great consideration to the idea of sending the puppy to a professional trainer's "boot camp," where it can gain range and confidence and the sure knowledge that birds cannot be caught.

Taking a Line

If you are planning to have the dog compete in tests or trials, with or without a horse, teach the young dog to make the best first impression with a fast, determined break from the start line, undistracted by its bracemate or handler. The pro-

Figure 12-31: *When teaching a dog to honor,* a well-trained gun dog is an irreplaceable asset; however, the backing cut-out allows a trainer to teach the honor without the assistance of a second, fully trained dog. The cut-out is strategically placed where the approaching dog will come on it suddenly, without scenting the bird before her arrival. If the dog does not stop naturally, a well-timed "Whoa!" command should stop the dog in her tracks as soon as she sees the pointing dog. With repetition, the visual cue of the pointing dog will become the stimulus for the dog to honor without a verbal command. One advantage of using a pop-up instead of a real dog is that the pop-up can be knocked down (some commercial aids have a transmitter to allow the dog to fall), and the honor dog can be sent to make the retrieve, thus rewarding her for backing. Photograph by Shirley Nilsson.

Figure 12-30: *A properly equipped 4-wheeler* can be a valuable asset when there are no safe areas in which to allow dogs to run free while being transported or when there are many dogs to be conditioned. Steve Reynolds uses roading harnesses encourage the dogs to pull and build muscle; longer, slower trips help build stamina. Do not attempt this without the proper equipment and training for the safety of dogs and driver.

cedure shown in Figure 12-29 outlines the "secret" method frequently used by professionals to pattern this behavior, conditioning the dog through repetition to the idea that the fun of finding the birds begins after a long cast to the treeline, rather than at the start line.

Conditioning

While conditioning is one of the foundation blocks of a successful hunting dog, whether field trial competitor or personal gun dog, it is not for young dogs. Excessive exercise, especially weight-bearing exercise like roading, can damage

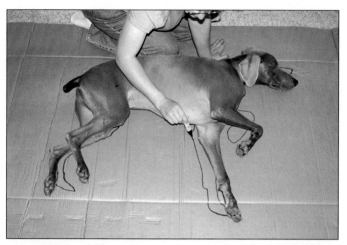

Figure 12-32: *Training pop-up honor dogs* can be purchased commercially, but they can also be constructed inexpensively at home by tracing the outline of your favorite hunting companion on heavier cardboard, waterproof corrugated plastic, or light paneling. Attach metal, rebar struts, or plastic electric fence posts to each leg to position the cutout upright in the ground. An added advantage of the homemade variety is that it can be changed to reflect different breeds; surprisingly, a dog that has been taught to honor a Weimaraner may not necessarily honor other breeds, such as a Pointer or a Brittany. Photograph by Andy Sowers.

growing muscles and joints. Dogs under 15–18 months need free exercise, so the pup can start and stop as needed and set its own pace, without chains or extra weight.

Do not expect a dog to compete well if it has laid off for the summer. A dog is not a seasonal item where the batteries are removed and then stored away for the summer. Keep the hunting dog in condition year-round, so the dog is ready for the season and for his mental and physical well-being. Build up slowly. Watch the tail; when the dog is tired, put it away. With just one dog, an owner can jog or bike; swimming is an excellent conditioning exercise, as well.

Backing/Honoring

Honoring appears to be a mixture of instinctive good manners and learned behavior. Dog that do not honor instinctively at the sight or scent of another dog on point must be taught to honor on command. Backing is a matter of safety to protect the dogs and to ensure that the hunter has a better chance to get a good shot. A dog that steals points will be unwelcome with other hunters (and their dogs), as it is detrimental to the training they have invested in their own animals. Honoring is required at higher levels of competition, such as the Senior and Master Hunter and the Shooting Dog and Shooting Dog Excellent Rating. While it takes some effort to train a dog that does not instinctively back, it is the ultimate sign of a polished personal gun dog that most hunters should be proud to safely hunt over. Training a dog to honor is best accomplished with the assistance of an expe-

rienced mentor and a well-trained gun dog, in order to accomplish the correct timing and manage all the training aids. The steadiness of the second dog is paramount, or the ensuing chaos of a stolen point or wild flush and chase will be detrimental to both dogs (Figure 13-1). Additionally, since there are no cardboard cutouts in competition, the knowledgeable advice of a professional trainer or accomplished amateur competitor and his dog will be invaluable in achieving the performance necessary for higher-level competition.

Choices: Steady to Wing and Shot or Not?

A fully trained, finished bird dog is steady to wing and shot (stands staunchly when the bird is flushed, flies, and is shot) and retrieves the bird to hand on command. In field jargon, the dog is "gun-broke." The objectives of this training are: (a) to give the hunter a chance to shoot the bird without risk of hitting the dog; and (b) to give the dog an opportunity to mark the bird's fall so it is easier to find and retrieve.

Training approaches differ, depending on the owner's ultimate goals. Field trial derby stakes emphasize wide range and stamina; while the dog must locate and point, he gets no extra credit for steadiness to wing and shot. Since the corrections involved in steadying a dog to wing and shot usually shorten its range and dampen enthusiasm, most field trial trainers will defer steadying until the dog is over 2 years old and out of derby age, when it is more mature and its ranging habits and desire for birds are well established. This is less of a concern, however, for the companion gun dog; these dogs are usually steadied as soon as they demonstrate appropriate readiness. With awareness of the potential damage that could be done to the dog's training through poorly executed methods, the authors have not attempted to offer instruction on the process of producing a dog that is steady to wing and shot, but rather have provided all the information through the kindergarten, elementary, and high school sections needed to prepare the young dog for his college education. Owners should determine their personal needs and goals at a fairly early stage and consult a professional or highly experienced mentor on the timing of graduating to the advanced training of steadiness to wing and shot.

The High School Land Retrieve

So far, retrieving has been pretty much a game; now it is time to teach the retrieve under more controlled circumstances. There are many, many ways to teach the formal retrieve. Read extensively the many books that are available or consult experienced trainers to find a method that works for both trainer and Weimaraner. However, some general guidelines apply.

Take advantage of the Weimaraner's tendency to mimic and her natural desire for the owner's attention by allowing the pup to watch experienced dogs retrieving and having fun doing it.

Pointing   →|←   Steady to Flush   →|←   Steady to Wing   →|←   Steady to Shot   →|←   Steady to Fall

Figure 12-33: *Steadiness* is the hallmark of a fully trained gun dog. Steadiness is divided into the following phases; flush—from the handler's approach to the bird's rise into the air; wing—from the bird's rise into the air to the gunshot; shot—from the gunshot to the bird's fall to the ground; and fall—from the bird's fall to the ground to the command to retrieve.

Start on land and teach the basics. The dog should already have a solid foundation of positive reinforcement with pick up and carry. It helps if the dog has a solid recall, as well.

It is recommended that the formal retrieve be taught using objects other than a bird whenever possible. First, there are likely to be some mistakes and corrections involved in getting the formal retrieve to a high level of reliability. It is better if these unpleasant events are not connected with the bird so that retrieving the bird is always exciting and fun. Second, it gives the trainer an ace in the hole. If the dog gets sour or is competing at a trial, the novelty of the bird will rev up the dog's desire.

When introducing the bird to the formal retrieve, avoid allowing the young dog to learn bad habits by using an appropriately sized bird, one big enough to discourage eating the bird but not so large that the dog cannot carry the bird properly if he tries. During the first lessons, a partially frozen bird will also discourage eating or hard mouthing.

Be sure that the puppy becomes convinced that if he is told to retrieve there will be something out there for him to bring back. Be sure to have a spare bumper or bird held in reserve for this purpose.

In the early stages, it is vital to lavish praise on the young student and even "trade" the prized object for a treat. If the young dog is unwilling to relinquish the bird, after much praise and encouragement has been given, calmly grasp the dog's collar, then simply wait until the dog is bored enough to part with his prize.

It is a wise course to have the dummy or the bird on a light cord to prevent the pup from dashing away with the prize and to be able to snatch the object away quickly if the puppy drops it instead of delivering it to hand. Next time, the pup will hold a little tighter lest the prize escape.

Quit while you are ahead and end on a good note after a couple of fetches. Do not wear him out, or the "game" will stop being fun. There is plenty of time for drills in the future.

Play Retrieves

For most Weimaraners, retrieving is intrinsically rewarding. A few play retrieves can be used to take the edge off an overexcited dog before a competition or training session or to rev up the less enthusiastic student. Consistently use the same cue to indicate that you are going to switch to an informal game.

Directed Retrieve

The ability to take a line on a directed retrieve may make the difference between a duck on the table or a title when there are multiple falls. While most dogs can mark the first fall, as the number of targets increases, the time between the fall and the retrieve increases; therefore, wind and current will move the bird from the original position, and the handler must be able to reliably direct the dog to the location of additional birds. Many books, such as the *Tri-tronics Retriever Training Book,* give directions on how to play "doggie baseball," a good way to practice this skill.

Figure 12-34: *Bend down and use a long line* to bring him in if the puppy appears to be planning on not returning the object. Always praise!

Add Water

If a Weimaraner is expected to be an enthusiastic water retriever, a deep history of fun and games in the water will go a long way toward that goal. Provide plenty of playtime in the water before asking for a formal water retrieve. Do not assume that just because a Weimaraner is a grown dog that she can or will swim or retrieve, especially in the water. If starting an adult dog, start with kindergarten. Start with the concept that the dog will have fun, and the new experience will be positive.

As with any time spent working around water, check the area to be sure it is safe—no underwater hazards, rocks, trunks, or branches. The first time you ask for the formal water retrieve, minimize distractions. Avoid areas in which there are other dogs playing, ducks swimming, or other potential activities that might tempt the dog's attention away from the task at hand.

Now is the time to combine all the pieces learned in the lower grade levels.

Figure 12-35: ***Dogs just wanna have fun!*** After the discipline and focus of intense retrieve training, a "fun bumper" allows the dog to blow off steam and enjoy the thrill of the chase as a reward for a job well done. It may also be useful in taking the edge off an overexcited dog before a competition. It is vital to use a clear cue and be consistent so the dog does not become confused between playtime and the formal retrieve when using the same equipment. Photograph by Shirley Nilsson.

But before putting it all together, remember that this is a new game. Review all the pieces individually. Will she willingly enter the water to swim and play? Will the dog pick up and carry an object? Does she retrieve reliably on land? Remember the Rule of Sevens? Apply that here too. Will the dog retrieve seven different items in seven different locations on seven different surfaces?

Bring an assistant dog if possible. Allowing the assistant to play and retrieve to show the new recruit what she will be expected to do will make her more eager to mimic the other dog's behavior when it is her turn. The presence of another dog may go far to allay any reservations on the part of the novice. The assistant provides some motivation (competition) and can pick up "lost" articles if they float out of reach.

An extra human assistant would not hurt either, to restrain a dog while building excitement or to toss the object.

Initially, use something the dog likes to retrieve that floats well. It probably would not hurt to have the article on a string until the dog has displayed a confident, capable water retrieve.

For the first retrieve, look for a place with a short, easy entry. Look for open water with a gently sloping bank and always encourage safe water entry. A dock probably would not be a good choice, but a boat launch might be.

Training the retrieve is not a race. It is easier to avoid problems by going back to kindergarten or separating out problem areas, rather than trying to fix a bad habit.

Start the first lessons by letting the novice dog watch an experienced dog reliably retrieving and having fun before allowing her to join in the fun. The first lessons should end while the dog is still eager to continue. It might only be two or three tosses. Put the dog away for at least a little while before getting her out to try again. Not only does this create motivation, it gives the dog time to "think" about what happened. End each "lesson" on a positive note.

Once the dog is retrieving reliably, vary the training locations. Just because a dog will retrieve in the "home" pond does not necessarily mean she will retrieve from any body of water.

One of the most appealing aspects of a well-trained retrieving dog is that this is an activity that a reasonably talented amateur trainer can accomplish with a very high level of performance without professional assistance. It is also a useful, fun activity with limited equipment requirements. There is no rush, and the pressure levels are low, since most events are pass/fail rather than scored. Retrieving is a great way to keep dogs active and fit well into the mature years, as long as they are otherwise healthy. A dog trained as a polished retriever is often a dog accepted in many family activities and may be a welcome visitor at community centers and nursing homes. Just as the 19th-century Forester's Dog was not only his able hunting assistant but his valued constant companion, today's well-

Figure 12-36: *Teach the formal retrieve on land first.* Luke has learned to retrieve many objects, to wait to mark the fall, and to take a line. Dokken Dead Fowl Trainers™ are useful because they teach balance and because the dog will be more eager for the real thing if the mistakes have been worked out on a training duck. These trainers are less expensive than using real ducks and come in several sizes. Since they are convenient to carry, owners are more likely to practice more often. Photograph by Traci Hoeptner.

trained Weimaraner is not just a hunter but is welcome to just hang out with his family, where his retrieving talent can be both a source of assistance and pleasure.

Decisions, Decisions...

Go with a Pro or Home School?

The typical Weimaraner will be very happy to make a career out of doing what he loves most, just hanging out or providing food for the hunter's table.

But there are other options, as well. If the owner is interested in continuing the training and education of his Weimaraner, there are many careers to consider; consult the *Weimaraners Afield* chapter to learn more about AKC field trials and tests and WCA ratings, and the *North American Versatile Hunting Dog Association* chapter for information on their training and tests.

The training and experiences outlined throughout this chapter will provide the Weimaraner with a fine foundation for the additional training required for advanced levels of competition. If you are considering any type of competition, attend several events to get a better idea of the standard of performance and the procedures and to meet other people with the same interests. This is also a good time to consult the breeder or mentor for a referral to a Weimaraner-oriented

Figure 12-37: *Start the dog with short retrieves,* shallow water, and clear objectives to ensure success; as the dog becomes successful, depth and distance can be increased. Later challenges, such as steep entries, water vegetation, or distractions, can be added one at a time. If the dog "loses" the object, be prepared to sneak a spare bumper in a place where he is sure to find it; Rio is convinced that if he is sent out, there must be something to bring back. Photograph by Gene LaFollette.

field professional who can evaluate the dog's potential; this often requires that the dog be sent to stay for several weeks with the professional at a "bird camp," where the dog will ideally be exposed to many wild birds under a variety of circumstances. Be sure that the trainer uses methods the owner feels comfortable with and that she has experience training Weimaraners for the venue(s) selected.

Although many Weimaraners successfully compete in novice and entry-level classes when owner trained and handled, coaching and advice from a professional often provide that extra edge to fine tune the performance of both handler and dog. Steadiness to wing and shot is the keystone for success in advanced field competition and classes; a professional can accomplish this in the shortest amount of time with the least amount of negative experiences for the dog.

When an owner considers the use of electronic training, advice from like-minded professionals can be invaluable. Electronic training is not easily learned from a book, and the unique character of the Weimaraner requires a deft, experienced touch; poor timing or a fit of temper can set back all the good training that preceded it in a dog with the memory and sensitive nature of the Weimaraner.

Consider also that the professional can continue to be a valuable resource as a mentor to critique and coach the novice handler and his dog, whether the career includes the day-to-day job of hunting for the table or the pursuit of advanced training titles and awards.

Figure 12-39: *"To boldly go…"* Although it is aesthetically pleasing to see a dog leaping boldly into the water, a leap like this landed Axel in the hospital with broken, bruised ribs. Unless the handler is positive that the area is clear of underwater dangers, it is unwise to encourage spectacular water entries. Teaching a dog to enter the water directly and eagerly does not mean teaching him to enter in a foolhardy manner. Photograph by Luis Bonilla.

Figure 12-38: *Be prepared to prevent bad habits.* For the dog inclined to run away with his prize, first remember, DO NOT CHASE! Try using something less special (like a dumbbell) on a long line, and meet the dog at the shoreline. Reward the dog immediately. For the dog that runs away to eat the bird, try using a frozen duck on a long line. For the dog that drops the object at the shoreline for lack of enthusiasm, run backward to get him to move out of water and reward enthusiastically. Build enthusiasm with a review of the land retrieve to hand, get the dog more comfortable in the water, and start a shorter distance from the water's edge so the "reward" is not so far away. Photograph by Gene LaFollette.

Figure 12-40: *Introduce decoys* before a test or hunting season. Give the dog a chance to sniff and explore the decoys on land before placing them for the first time in shallow water. First, toss the retrieve object in front of the decoys, then among them, and then beyond the decoys. Most Weimaraners, once their curiosity is satisfied, will casually ignore the minor nuisance. Photograph by Traci Hoeptner.

Figure 12-41: *On their initial swimming attempts,* some dogs, whether young or old, often attempt to walk on the pond bottom with the back feet instead of swimming, producing a great deal of splashing with the front feet and invariably pushing the retrieve object beyond reach. With experience, especially when given the chance to watch and swim alongside other skillful swimmers, the dog will usually gain a smoother style as she learns to balance herself in the water. Timer (CH Nani's On Time Performance, VCD2, RE, JH, OAP, OJP, RD, VX2) gives picturesque proof that carrying a weighted object counterbalances the front end; for young, inexperienced dogs, this may be all that is needed to help the dog learn a more fluid style. Photograph provided by Terrie Borman.

Figure 13-1: ***When introducing the dogs to the expected terrain and ground cover*** of an upcoming field event, Steve Reynolds also sets up a lesson to emphasize the importance of backing. Early training and preparation are factors that will contribute to success at any field event, but last-minute brushing up (off the trial grounds) can help, too. His canine training assistant, Rudy—a field champion herself and mother of three others—has established a solid point on a planted game bird. If the young dog breaks, veteran Rudy can be counted on to provide a swift, sharp reminder on the finer points of honor, a lesson that the green-broke dog will hopefully remember at the upcoming trial. Photograph by Luis Bonilla.

CHAPTER 13

WEIMARANERS AFIELD

Satisfaction with a dog's performance depends on how well it fulfills the owner's expectations. "Bird dog" means different things to different people, and the key to satisfaction with a Weimaraner is understanding the breed's special aptitudes and knowing how to expand the Weimaraner's versatility as a field dog.

A Unique Hunting Dog

Origins and Hunting Style

The Germans developed the Weimaraner to meet the needs of the 19th-century German forester. To a hound-like, fur-hunting, tracking breed that was aggressive toward predators, the German breeders added the functions of bird-hunting and retrieving needed by the professional forester. The breed they developed had the following qualities:

- Ability to search for and retrieve birds and small, furred game in fields and forest and on land or in water
- Manner of hunting characterized by the thoroughness of search rather than speed and range
- Keen nose for the search and natural tracking ability to find wounded furred and feathered game
- Love of water and the ability to swim tirelessly while searching dense cover
- Temperament that is protective but never vicious
- Easily trainable with problem-solving aptitude

Because the dog was expected to perform these many functions, he shared every part of his master's life.

As a result, the Forester's Dog developed a strong bond with humans and willingly looked to the handler for leadership and direction. European sporting writers of the 1880s commented that it was an accepted rule that the Weimaraners, unlike most hounds, were kept in the home rather than in a kennel; in order to work their best, Weimaraners should be treated with more kindness than many hunting dogs.

By the early 20th century, the qualities the Germans desired had become so well established in the breed that they are still typical of many American Weimaraners today. The WCA's founding members of the 1950s also adhered to the versatile nature of this breed by demanding water tests before allowing the Weimaraner to compete in field trials.

Figure 13-2: *Not just a pointing dog,* despite AKC's categorization, the American Weimaraner's heritage is deeply rooted in the needs of the gentleman hunter, not only to point birds, but also to track and retrieve both furred and feathered game. Dargo vom Blaken. Photograph courtesy of the Weimaraner Klub e. V.

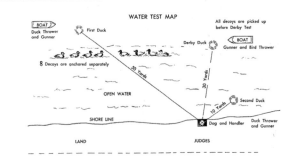

WATER TEST MAP

All decoys are picked up before Derby Test

BOAT
Duck Thrower and Gunner

First Duck

Derby Duck

BOAT
Gunner and Bird Thrower

8 Decoys are anchored separately

30 Yards

30 Yards

10 Yards

Second Duck

OPEN WATER

SHORE LINE

Dog and Handler

Duck Thrower and Gunner

LAND

JUDGES

All spectators and dogs not in test must stay in this area until called to line

The gunner is in the boat with the duck thrower, the shot gun is fired first to attract the dog's attention, then the duck is thrown. The No. 1 duck (the 50 yd. bird through decoys) is first, then the No. 2 duck (the 10 yd. bird which is the diversion bird) is second. After both birds are thrown, the judges send the dog for the retrieve. The dogs can pick up either bird first.

WATER CERTIFICATION RULES FOR 1958

No dog will be eligible to run in the National Gun Dog Trial or any Weimaraner Championship field trial recognized by the Weimaraner Club of America unless he holds a valid water test certificate for the stake entered. A water test certificate shall be valid until July 1st of the year following that in which it is issued.

Judging must be done by competent retriever judges with either Regional Governor, Regional President, or a representative appointed by one of them present.

1. Live shackled, or shot ducks shall be used for all retrieves.

2. All dogs must be shot over on each retrieve, with a 12 gauge shotgun, field or trap load.

3. A dog handled by an amateur handler shall be eligible for both open and amateur stakes. A dog handled by a professional handler shall be eligible for open stakes only.

DERBY DOGS

A derby dog shall be required to make a single retrieve from a distance of 30 yards,

swimming 30 yards each way. Derby dog can be held by collar on the line and is not expected to deliver to hand (within radius of six feet is okay). Dog must hit water within 3 min. after judge gives signal to go or start. Dog can have only one try per event. A maximum of 5 min. swimming time per bird.

ALL-AGE DOGS

An All-Age dog shall be required to make a double retrieve. One retrieve shall be made through decoys (8) and be of a distance of 50 yards. swimming 50 yards each way. The second retrieve shall be a minimum of 10 yards, swimming 10 yards each way. An All-Age dog **must** be steady on line, and must retrieve to hand. Dog cannot be touched by handler after coming on line. Dog must hit water within 1 min. after judge gives signal to go or start. A dog can have only one try per event. A maximum of 5 min. swimming time per bird.

Regions may hold as many water certification tests as required by their region.

Figure 13-3: *The preservation of the unique combination of Weimaraner talents* was important to the early founding members of the WCA. In an effort to maintain the original German character, every dog was required to demonstrate the test described above before competing in WCA-sponsored field trial events; this test closely duplicates the current WCA Retrieving Dog rating test. Even Derby dogs were required to perform the equivalent of the water portion of today's Novice Retrieving Dog rating test.

A Versatile Hunting Breed

The versatile hunting dog is defined as a "dog that is bred and trained to dependably hunt and point game, to retrieve on both land and water, and to track wounded game on both land and water."[1] The Weimaraner is not the only versatile hunting breed developed on the European continent, and in Germany, all are tested by standards established by the German Versatile Hunting Dog Association before the dog may be bred in order to register offspring. The following versatile breeds are recognized by the AKC: Brittany, German Shorthaired Pointer, German Wirehaired Pointer, Spinone Italiano, Vizsla, Weimaraner, and Wirehaired Pointing Griffon. In the United States, those interested in pursuing the more versatile nature of the Weimaraner may be interested in NAVHDA, discussed in the next chapter.

Breed development followed a different pattern in the British Isles, where breeds were expected to excel in only a specific function: the pointer as well as the Irish, English, and Gordon setters pointed feathered game; the Golden, Labrador, Flat Coated, and Curly Coated Retrievers retrieved feathered game; a variety of hounds filled the needs for large- and small-furred-game hunting and blood tracking.

The AKC, established in 1884, developed field trial rules and performance standards for its recognized breeds following the model of the British specialists. Bird dogs either pointed or retrieved, never both. When the versatile breeds arrived later, the AKC classified all as pointers instead of designing a new type of trial to evaluate the diverse talents of the versatile breeds.

Through selective breeding to enhance speed, range, and pointing style, the performance of some versatile breeds has been radically altered for greater competitive success in the typical AKC horseback pointing-breed trials. In general, however, this has been achieved at the expense of their retrieving, tracking, trainability, and interest in furred game, which are desired by many amateur owner/hunters. Fortunately, out of respect for the Weimaraner's original purpose, the WCA has been steadfast in requiring Weimaraners to earn at least 4 points from a retrieving stake, as well as passing a certified water test or earning at least a WCA Novice Retrieving Dog Rating before the title of Field Trial Champion is bestowed.

Owners who lack the time and skill to train their Weimaraners, especially if they believe the dog has competitive potential, must send them to the few professional trainers who understand the Weimaraner's temperament. Field trainers who are accustomed to the hard-headed Pointer often lack the soft touch and the partnership bond required for success with a Weimaraner.

Fortunately, the very quality that frustrates so many professional trainers—the need to treat a Weimaraner gently and lovingly—makes the breed uniquely suitable for the amateur. Some trainers admit that the breed's intelligence and instinctive aptitude are so strong that the best way to train a Weimaraner is to provide an opportunity for the dog to hunt and to observe other dogs hunting. This is, in fact, the approach used by German trainers—to provide guided experience that allows instinctive behavioral patterns to unfold.

The dog's instinct provides the motivation, and its intelligence helps it discover the best way to do it. Moreover, when Weimaraners work with an older, well-trained dog, the breed's copy-cat trait accelerates and reinforces learning.

The Weimaraner is an excellent breed for sportsmen who want a gun dog that will range farther afield when the hunter is mounted on horseback but does not range too far when hunting on foot, that thoroughly covers the terrain, that retrieves birds on land and in water, that is easily trained by a novice, and that is an agreeable companion when not hunting. The Weimaraner thrives on human companionship and must be part of the family. This bonding with humans is linked with its versatile working traits, and if the dog is isolated from household activity, the Weimaraner's hunting aptitude rarely develops properly. Those who desire these traits consider the Weimaraner not only the finest of all bird dogs but the ideal companion for the conservation-minded hunter who also needs a dog capable of tracking injured game.

AKC Field Trials

AKC field trials are sponsored by local breed clubs. There are never too many helpful hands at these events, and novices (even without a dog to run) can quickly learn a great deal by assisting at club trials.

At an AKC field trial, dogs are judged against a standard for each class; classes are divided by age and experience. Unlike WCA Ratings and AKC Hunt Tests, which are judged on a pass/fail basis, at a field trial, points toward a title are only awarded to the first-place dog, and under certain circumstances the second-place dog, in each class, depending on the number of dogs competing.

Standard of Performance for AKC Field Trial Stakes

Puppy Stake *(Open and/or Amateur Walking) for dogs 6 months of age and under 15 months of age on the first advertised day of the trial.*

Puppies must show desire to hunt, boldness, and initiative in covering ground and in searching likely cover. They should indicate the presence of game if the opportunity is presented. Puppies should show reasonable obedience to their handlers' commands, but should not be given additional credit for pointing staunchly. Each dog shall be judged on its actual performance as indicating its future as a high class bird dog. Every premium list for a licensed or member trial shall state whether or not blanks are to be fired in a Puppy Stake. If the premium list states that blanks will be fired, every dog that makes game contact shall be fired over if the handler is within reasonable gun range. At least 15 minutes and not more than 30 minutes shall be allowed for each heat. Championship points will be withheld if a dog has not run for the required time.

Derby Stake *(Open and/or Amateur Walking) for dogs 6 months of age and under 2 years of age on the first advertised day of the trial.*

Derbies must show a keen desire to hunt, be bold and independent, have a fast, yet attractive, style of running, and demonstrate not only intelligence in seeking objectives but also the ability to find game. Derbies must establish point but no additional credit shall be given for steadiness to wing and shot. If the handler is within reasonable gun range of a bird which has been flushed after a point, a shot must be fired. A lack of opportunity for firing over a Derby dog on point shall not constitute reason for nonplacement when it has had game contact in acceptable Derby manner. Derbies must show reasonable obedience to their handlers' commands. Each dog is to be judged on its actual performance as indicating its future promise as a high class bird dog for Gun Dog or All-Age stakes. Preference should not be given to one potential over another. Application is more important than range in a Derby. At least 20 minutes and not more than 30 minutes shall be allowed for each heat. Championship points will be withheld if a dog has not run for the required time. All placed dogs must have established a point.

Gun Dog Stake *(Open and/or Amateur) for dogs 6 months of age and older on the first advertised day of the trial.*

A Gun Dog must give a finished performance and must be under its handler's control at all times. It must handle kindly, with a minimum of noise and hacking by the handler. A Gun Dog must show a keen desire to hunt, must have a bold and attractive style of running, and must demonstrate not only intelligence in quartering and in seeking objectives but also the ability to find game. The dog must hunt for its handler at all times at a suitable Gun Dog range, and should show or check in front of its handler frequently. It must cover adequate ground but never range out of sight for a length of time that would detract from its usefulness as a practical hunting dog. The dog must locate game, must point staunchly, and must be steady to wing and shot. Intelligent use of the wind and terrain in locating game, accurate nose, and style and intensity on point, are essential.

Walking Handler Gun Dog range—In Walking Gun Dog Stakes, the dog's range should be suitable for the walking handler.

Horseback Handler Gun Dog range—In Horseback Handling Gun Dog Stakes, the dog's range should be suitable for a horseback-mounted handler taking into consideration the cover and terrain. A dog that does not point cannot be placed. A dog should not be called back to point after the running of its brace except under the most extreme and unusual circumstances. At least 30 minutes shall be allowed for each heat. Championship points will be withheld if a dog has not run for the required time.

All-Age Stake *(Open and/or Amateur) for dogs 6 months of age and older on the first advertised day of the trial.*

An All-Age Dog must give a finished performance and must be under reasonable control of its handler. It must show a keen desire to hunt, must have a bold and attractive style of running, and must show independence in hunting. It must range well out in a forward moving pattern, seeking the most promising objectives, so as to locate any game on the course. Excessive line-casting and avoiding cover must be penalized. The dog must demonstrate its independent judgment in hunting the course, but must show a willingness to handle when called upon. The dog must find game, must point staunchly, and must be steady to wing and shot. Intelligent use of the wind and terrain in locating game, accurate nose, and style and intensity on point, are essential. A dog that does not point cannot be placed. A dog should not be called back to point after the running of its brace except under the most extreme and unusual circumstances. At least 30 minutes shall be allowed for each heat. Championship points will be withheld if a dog has not run for the required time.

Source: AKC *Field Trial Rules and Standard Procedure for Pointing Breeds.* Revised August 2006.

All AKC field trial stakes are designated either open (entries may be handled by both professionals and amateurs) or amateur (entries may be handled only by amateurs). The AKC defines an amateur handler as "a person who, during the period of 2 years preceding the trial has not accepted remuneration in any form for the training of a hunting dog or the handling of a dog in a field trial."[2] In addition, no household member of a professional can handle in an amateur stake.

Unlike the Winner's class at conformation shows, the number of points for winning a field trial class is the same for all pointing breeds in all parts of the United States. To become a field champion, or an amateur field champion, a dog must win 10 points in at least 3 field trials. Only 2 points won in puppy stakes and 2 in derby stakes may be applied to the total, and the remaining 6 points must be earned in broke (gun dog and all-age) stakes. No more than 4 points won for first place in an amateur stake can be applied toward a regular field championship. At least one stake must be a major—that is, 3 or more points are awarded—in open gun dog or open all-age, including limited. Although amateur championship points are awarded for second and third place in amateur stakes, each must win one first place in a major plus one other first place. For both championships, in recognition of its versatile heritage, Weimaraners must win at least 4 of these points in retrieving stakes.[3]

AKC Schedule of Points		
No. of starters	1st place	2nd place
4–7	1 point	
8–12	2 points	
13–17	3 points	
18–24	4 points	
25+	5 points	2 points

Source: AKC *Field Trial Rules and Standard Procedures for Pointing Breeds.* Revised August 2006.

In addition to the all-breed point requirements, Weimaraners must prove their ability to retrieve from water. In an AKC water test, the dog must retrieve a live or dead game bird about 20 yards from shore, with the handler standing at least 6 feet from the water. The dog must enter the water willingly, swim, and retrieve, but it is not required to deliver the bird into the handler's hand. The AKC accepts a WCA Novice Retrieving Dog Rating in lieu of the water test.[4]

AKC field trials are an exciting activity enjoyed by many Weimaraner enthusiasts; the thrill of breeding, owning, training, or merely watching the dogs is an incomparable experience.

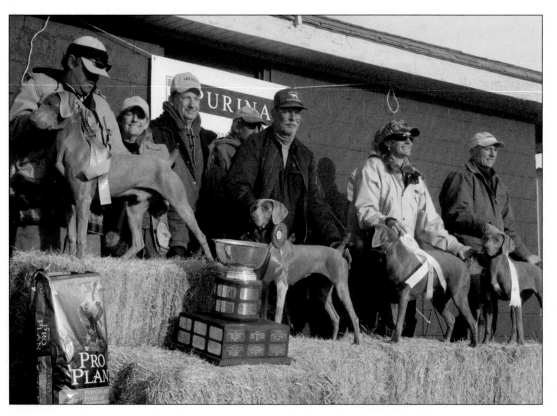

Figure 13-4: *The winners of the WCA's 2006 National Amateur Field Championship.* Each one of these winners was handled by his or her owner or breeder in this prestigious competition. Stakes available only to amateurs encourage the character that allows these dogs to be field trial winners today and to be out hunting for the owner's table the next weekend. From left to right: NAFC Aztec's American Pie (1st place), FC Grau Giest's True Love Ways (10-year-old dam of the 1st place winner), NFC FC AFC Gould's GRB Little Chular, and Jax's Treeline Blitzin' Tilly.

AKC Hunting Tests

Until recently, American pointing-breed fanciers have found it difficult to document their dog's hunting ability except through field trial competition. Buyers looking for a bird dog could evaluate puppies' hunting potential only by the number of field champions in a pedigree and representations by the seller.

In 1986, the AKC inaugurated a system of hunting tests for pointers and retrievers. Like field trials, the tests are sponsored by local specialty breed clubs; unlike field trials, all handling must be done on foot. All AKC-registered dogs of the pointing breeds that are at least 6 months old may be entered in the tests for pointing breeds. In addition, dogs with disqualifying faults may earn titles. Ironically, despite the fact that both the hunting tests for pointers and retrievers are closely modeled on the pre-existing Weimaraner Club Shooting and Retrieving Ratings, the AKC does not consider Weimaraners eligible to compete in Hunting Tests for Retrievers as a result of the AKC's 1884 division of breeds based on the English "specialist" model.

The AKC hunting tests offer three levels of achievement, with three titles—Junior Hunter (JH), Senior Hunter (SH), and Master Hunter (MH)—that will be added after the dog's registered name in show and field trial catalogs and certified pedigrees.

The dogs are given numerical scores from 0 to 10 in the categories of hunting, bird-finding ability, pointing, and trainability, with the addition of retrieving and honoring at the Senior and Master levels. A dog must receive a score of no less than 5 in each category, with an average greater than 7 for all categories to be awarded a qualifying score.

WCA Ratings

Shortly after the WCA began, the need for a noncompetitive venue for Weimaraner owners to display and validate the hunting and retrieving abilities of their dogs was recognized. The inherent quality of hunting within range of the hunter on foot put the typical Weimaraner at a disadvantage when judged against a standard modeled on the wide-ranging pointers and setters when competing at an AKC all-breed field trial. Additionally, the

Figure 13-5: *On continuous courses*—when the next brace starts where the previous left off—the host club provides a dog wagon to transport entries to the start line and back to trial headquarters. A trial official identifies each dog and handler as the dog is presented to run. Successful handlers recognize the importance of mentally connecting with the dog before releasing on the breakaway.

Figure 13-6: *The field trial handler* removes the dog from the wagon and establishes a physical and mental connection with her dog before moving to the start line; it is more efficient for a handler on horseback to have an assistant to actually release the dog from the line. Notice that although Gina has remounted, Chular remains focused on her, not the helper.

Figure 13-7: *After the dogs break from the line,* they are followed by their handlers; the judges will follow behind the handlers. Next, a marshal will ensure that scouts and those observing from the gallery do not interfere with the work of the dogs or the judges. On continuous courses, the gallery will include some of the upcoming handlers, as well as spectators and scouts. Photograph by Leslie Like.

Figure 13-8: *Call-backs* allow dogs under consideration to be individually tested on a planted bird in a designated area called a bird field. The judges can more closely observe the dog's manners and steadiness, as well as the required tender retrieve to hand. Because Rogue remained steady when this bird flushed wild and could not be shot, Tim was offered the choice of testing again immediately on a second bird or waiting until the remaining call-backs had run. Photograph by Gene LaFollette.

AKC Hunting Tests

Test	Desired Performance
Junior Hunter	**Hunting:** demonstrate keen desire to hunt, boldness and independence, and a fast, attractive manner of hunting **Trainability:** show reasonable obedience to commands **Bird-finding ability:** show an intelligent ability to find game **Pointing:** must hold point until handler gets within normal gunshot range No additional points may be awarded for steadiness to wing and shot The handler must fire a blank cartridge if within reasonable range of a flushed bird **Qualifying scores:** a dog that receives a qualifying score in 4 tests is awarded the title JH
Senior Hunter	**Hunting/bird-finding ability:** demonstrate keenness of desire, boldness, speed, and style, as well as the location of game, which are scored with less leniency than for a JH **Pointing:** must be steady to wing and remain in position until the shot has been fired Must honor without command **Trainability:** must be more responsive to commands than a JH **Retrieving:** a shot bird must be retrieved but need not be delivered to hand **Honoring:** must acknowledge its bracemate's point; it may then be verbally cautioned; the SH may be restrained to avoid interference with the flush **Qualifying scores:** A dog that has earned the title of JH and receives a qualifying score in 4 tests or a dog that has no JH title and earns a qualifying score in 5 tests is awarded the title of SH
Master Hunter	**Hunting/bird-finding ability:** demonstrate the attributes of the SH with the finished style of an experienced hunting dog **Pointing:** intense, staunch, and steady to wing and shot Must honor through the flush, shot, and retrieve without command **Trainability:** response to gun, handling, and honoring must be more finished **Retrieving:** prompt, gentle, and to hand **Honoring:** the dog must be steady throughout the honor, with no verbal or physical restraint allowed **Qualifying scores:** a dog that has earned the title of SH and receives a qualifying score in 5 tests or a dog that has not earned the title of SH and receives a qualifying score in 6 tests is awarded the title of MH

Figure 13-9: *The honor is, in essence, a sight point* where the honoring dog freezes instantly upon observing another dog on point. A finished gun dog is expected to remain steady on the honor during all phases of the subsequent birdwork—that is, steady to the shot, fall, and retrieve of the fallen bird.

Figure 13-11: *The Master Hunter* must display perfect manners in the field, including a delivery to hand. Longhairs are eligible to compete in AKC hunt tests. Pella zum Laubwald. Photograph by Gerhard Eiben, Germany.

Figure 13-10: *The Senior and Master Hunters* must display all the required skills while running the course or bird field since there are no call-backs. The dog must not only be steady to wing and shot but must also honor (back) if the opportunity presents itself. Although a great photo opportunity, Lovett is closer than is generally desired for an honor; however, she should not be penalized as long as she remains behind Sgt. Schultz and does not steal his point.

Figure 13-12: *When running as a brace in trials* brightly colored collars makes it easier for the judges to identify the similar-looking Weimaraners by the top dog's red collar and the bottom dog's yellow collar. Be sure that the dog is accustomed to the collar and that it is properly fitted before going to the start line; a collar that is unfamiliar, too tight, or too loose can be a major distraction, even a hazard, by impairing breathing or quality performance. Photograph by Gene LaFollette.

strong inherent retrieving ability of the Weimaraner is a characteristic that sets it apart from many of the Continental pointing breeds. So in 1943, the WCA initiated its revolutionary ratings program, modeled on the German concept of the Weimaraner as an all-around gentleman's hunting companion that both points and retrieves upland birds and waterfowl. This program gives owners the opportunity to showcase their dog's talents and gives breeders the chance to evaluate the abilities of potential breeding stock and the

success of breeding programs in maintaining the skills and heritage of the Weimaraner. Complete requirements may be found in the appendices or on the WCA website (www.weimclubamerica.org).

Since these events are sponsored by the WCA, all owners and co-owners of any dog entered must be members in good standing with the WCA; ratings tests are open to any purebred Weimaraner with either an AKC registration or an ILP number.

Figure 13-13: *A top-producing beauty queen can work in the field, too,* as Colsidex Kaceem Act Two proves while taking time out from a busy career in the conformation ring and the whelping box. Many conformation enthusiasts find that their show dogs can demonstrate their field proficiency at ratings tests without devoting the huge time commitment required of field trial competition.

Figure 13-15: *At hunt tests and ratings,* the two handlers of each brace are on foot while the judges are on horseback. In addition to ensuring that the dog hunts likely cover, each handler should be sure to work in a manner that prevents the dogs from interfering with one another.

Figure 13-14: *The first Weimaraner recorded with the WCA to earn a rating,* Anka die Humdinger, earned an RD on August 31, 1960, handled by Herb Hoeptner. Almost 50 years later, her descendant, Luke der Humdinger, handled by Herb's son, Rahl, would earn the title of Most Versatile Weimaraner at the WCA's first Versatility Expo in 2003 and would become the breed's second NAVHDA Versatile Champion in 2007.

In order to promote the integrity of the breed, dogs with disqualifying faults—as listed in the breed standard—must be spayed or neutered and must receive a disqualification (DQF) number from the WCA before being entered in a ratings test.

Every dog's performance is evaluated by two judges on a pass/fail basis, with no score given. A dog must not only pass a single event in order to earn any title but must pass all phases of each test on the same day. Dogs may be entered at any level and may usually enter in more than one level at a given test; however, a handler should be sure not to "overtest" a dog at an event, which may result in a dog's providing less than optimal performance.

Shooting Dog Ratings

The Novice Shooting Dog (NSD) is required to display a point on bird contact; however, a clear flash point is acceptable. The purpose of this level is for the dog to display a desire and natural aptitude to hunt. A reasonable responsiveness to command is necessary, but strict obedience and control are not required. Extra credit is not awarded for a dog that is steady to wing and shot. A dog that is gun-shy cannot be awarded a title.

The Shooting Dog (SD) must show desire, ability, bird sense, and a degree of training. The dog must exhibit a staunch point before the flush but need not be completely steady to wing and shot. Should the opportunity arise, the dog must display honor to another dog's point; a dog that steals a point will be disqualified. The dog need not retrieve to hand, but serious hard-mouthing will disqualify the dog.

Shooting Dog Excellent (SDX) is awarded to a finished, fully broke gun dog that displays all the manners and skills necessary for a successful day's hunt. As with the SD, the SDX must back if the opportunity arises and will be disqualified for stealing a point. A table-worthy retrieve to hand is required.

Game birds are preferred in all levels, but pigeons are allowed; birds must be capable of flight—wing clipping or hobbling is not permitted. A bird field is permitted, but no more than 8 minutes of the run is allowed in the bird field.

Retrieving Dog Ratings

The retrieving instinct is so strong in the typical Weimaraner that most dogs can pass the land portion of the Novice Retrieving Dogs (NRD) level with little previous training. Many first-time Weimaraner owners who become hooked on field events start out at the NRD and NSD tests. The dog passing the Retrieving Dog Excellent (RDX) test displays a polished performance that any hunter would be proud to shoot over.

Figure 13-16: *Since only a single passing score is required,* some handlers are tempted to enter dogs in ratings tests before they are ready; when entering at lower levels, a dog can learn bad habits from a less well-trained bracemate. Here, a dog on a solid point found that his bracemate flushed his bird, and both have given chase. Many exhibitors with advanced dogs may therefore choose only to enter only at higher-level ratings, tests, or trials. Photograph by Gene LaFollette.

Recognized game birds or pigeons are used in each test. Hard-mouthing at any level may result in disqualification. Dogs are required to pass the land retrieve in order to progress to the water phase and must pass both phases of the test in order to earn a title. No dog may be released to retrieve until all birds for the current phase of the test have fallen. Birds must be shot while in the air. No gun-shy dog may receive an award. The handler must stand within a circle of rope or hose during the test.

The Novice Retrieving Dog (NRD) test is designed to show the natural aptitude of the Weimaraner to retrieve. The NRD need not be steady on the line and may be restrained. The novice dog need not retrieve to hand but must have at least two feet inside the rope/hose circle before the handler takes or picks up the bird.

The Retrieving Dog (RD) must be steady on the line, although a controlled break is allowed—the dog moves before released, stops on its own, or can be stopped with a voice command. The dog must deliver to hand with at least two front feet inside the rope/hose circle.

The RDX must enter the circle off-leash and under control and must be steady to wing and shot. The dog must deliver each bird to hand with at least two front feet within the rope/hose circle. The dog must enter and re-enter the water without hesitation.

WCA Shooting Dog Ratings

Level	Time	Point Required	Steady	Honor	Retrieve
NSD	20	flash accepted	no	no	no
SD	30	yes	staunch	yes	yes
SDX	30	yes	to wing and shot	yes	yes

WCA Water Retrieve Ratings

Level	Venue	No. of Birds	Steadiness	Decoys	
NRD	Land	single	20–40 yds	not required	n/a
	Water	single	20–40 yds	not required	no
RD	Land	double	1: 20 yds	controlled break	n/a
			2: 50 yds	allowed	
	Water	double	1: 20 yds	controlled break	yes
			2: 50 yds	allowed	
RDX	Land	double	1: 30 yds	to wing and shot	n/a
			2: 60 yds		
	Water	triple	1: 20 yds	to wing and shot	yes
			2: 40 yds		
			3: 60 yds		
	Water	single	1: 50 yds	blind	yes

Figure 13-17: *For WCA retrieving ratings,* the dog must complete a land retrieve before being allowed to attempt the water retrieve. Paloma begins by chatting with the judges to be sure the rules are clear and that they answer any questions she might have. At the NRD level, Samba may be restrained so that he can get a clear mark of the fall. A bird will be thrown from the side to provide a 20- to 40-yard retrieve. While Samba need not retrieve to hand, he must get at least two feet inside the circle before Paloma can take the bird. Photographs by Gene LaFollette.

Plan Early for Success

Training

Equipment needed: Be sure to have all the necessary equipment, that it is in working order, and that the handler knows how to use it.

Blaze orange vest or hat

Comfortable shoes

Briar-proof pants

Blank pistol and ammunition

Whistle

ID collar

Red and yellow brace collars

Long line and walking lead

Stake-out and/or crate

Regular food and water

First-aid kit

- Ensure that dog is properly conditioned for the duration of the test/stake; an exhausted dog will not hunt effectively

- If honoring is required, practice backing with breeds similar to those that can expected in the test/stake (do not do this on the test grounds) (see *Starting the Gun Dog*)

- Find out what kind of birds will be used for each station in the test or trial. If it is a retrieving test, also inquire what their condition will be—dead, live, or shackled. Practice using a bird that has been used multiple times or that is in poor condition

- Practice loading, aiming, and firing the blank pistol

Avoid Entry and Travel Complications

- Select appropriate stake/class; consider how many stakes are to be entered and whether dog and handler will have time to rest in between

- Send in a legible, correct, complete entry, accompanied by the appropriate fee. AKC events require both sides of the entry be completed and signed

- Be sure to use the correct mailing address for entries (the trial secretary is the only person allowed to accept entries). Allow plenty of time; do not wait until the last minute. Send with a tracking number or return receipt (such as FedEx or UPS) and take the receipt to the event, just in case

- Obtain the location and directions ahead of time in case clear instructions do not come with entry confirmation. Websites such as Mapquest (www.mapquest.com) are very useful, but sometimes directions to remote trial locations may not be accurate; if possible, also get directions from a second source, such as a local resident or experienced exhibitor

- Ask for the cell phone number of the trial secretary or day-of-test contact

Trial Day

Before entering the grounds:

- Allow plenty of travel time in case of poor road conditions, detours, inaccurate directions, etc.

- Come rain, shine, or snow, hot or cold, field events are held regardless of the weather. Make sure the dog has experience in these conditions. Come prepared to cope with inclement weather for both dog and handler

- Conduct a brief refresher training on the dog's weakest point

- Provide an opportunity such as fun bumpers or a brief run to either rev the dog up or to blow off steam if needed, depending on the dog's activity level

At the trial:

- Absentees, withdrawals, and pick-ups can alter running times; do not count on a schedule. Be there when the first stake casts off in the morning

- Stake the dog out to give him the opportunity to acclimate and relieve himself

- Do not feed the dog a big meal right before or after running. Provide a bit of water and several hours' rest before feeding

- If it is a mounted trial, make sure a horse is reserved for the handler's brace if needed and arrange for a friend to bring the dog to the line

- Select an earlier brace to follow and become familiar with the course and conditions and to identify potential challenges

- Double check that the handler has water, leash, a loaded blank pistol, and blaze orange vest or hat

- Introduce bracemates

- Do not be late for your brace

Figure 13-18: *The RD rating* requires a double retrieve on land with one shot bird before attempting the water portion. **(a)** Denise may not restrain or touch her dog as she gives Cobe a line for the first bird of the double water retrieve. Photograph by Lisa DeLauder. **(b)** Pete can move around inside the circle to encourage Cobe to get his front feet inside the circle as required for a complete retrieve. **(c)** Charlie neatly completes the hand delivery to Barbara well inside the circle.

Figure 13-19: *The RDX* also requires a double retrieve on land (at a longer distance), but the dog must be absolutely steady on the line. The water test requires a triple retrieve in the water. **(a)** Saga's intelligent use of land, when combined with a prompt return to hand, should not be penalized. **(b)** Mary quickly hands the retrieved bird off to the judges to allow Saga to refocus on the next retrieve. **(c)** Mary must remain inside the circle while she gives Saga a clear signal using a whistle as well as hand and body motions to direct her dog to the widely spaced falls. **(d)** The final test of the RDX is a blind retrieve, an unmarked fall of 50 yards, where the dog must locate the duck hidden behind the decoys and return it to hand. Photographs by Gene LaFollette.

Figure 13-20: *The stake-out* should be familiar to the dog prior to the event. The stake-out allows the dog to work the kinks out of its muscles, become accustomed to local scents and sounds, and relieve itself. Be sure the dog is dry and shaded if necessary, with adequate water. This allows Rio to just be a dog until he needs to be a superdog. Photograph by Gene LaFollette.

Figure 13-21: *Ivana was introduced to horses* ahead of time so she would not be intimidated and could be handled safely, and so she would resist the aroma of fresh horse manure. In nearly every event, the judges are mounted, so the dog needs to be confident and steady on point despite the proximity of the horses. Photograph by Gene LaFollette.

Figure 13-22: *Determine the terrain* and cover of the trial grounds ahead of time. Although AKC rules prohibit training on the grounds the day of the test or trial, it may be possible to train several days or weeks prior to the event or in a similar area nearby. With a little practice, Hailey and Wow will learn where to locate the birds as the cover and terrain varies at trials in different regions around the country; handlers will also have to practice finding and successfully flushing these birds as well. There may be new types of distractions as well—how many dogs have seen an armadillo?

Figure 13-23: *Since training is not allowed* on the test/trial grounds, for the handler's confidence and to be able to remind the dog of the correct response in privacy, practice on your dog's weakest point before entering the trial grounds. Pete reinforces taking a line in preparation for a retrieve. Since Cobe is a "righty" (he has a tendency to veer to the right as he swims or runs out to make a retrieve), Pete compensates for this tendency by setting up the line slightly to the left of the bird's actual location in the blind retrieve.

Figure 13-24: *Give the bracemates a chance to meet* before going to the line. Allow the dogs to sniff while on a loose lead. The handler can then give a couple of basic obedience commands to reinforce the idea that the dog must still obey and must not be distracted by the other dog. Then, allow the dog to return to the ritual greeting. When the time comes to cast off the line, the novelty of the new bracemate will have diminished, and the dog should be focused and responsive.

Figure 13-25: *No chapter on field events would be complete* without a tribute to one of the all-too-often unsung heroes of any field trial, the bird planters. Instead of being the last job assigned to whatever help is left, the responsibility of bird planting should be delegated to a person whose experience and dedication are equal to the hopes and expectations of every handler who has spent not only an entry fee but many hours of preparation and training. Without high-quality bird planting, even the best dogs may be hard pressed to demonstrate their true ability. The appendix includes an article by John Rabidou, respected trainer and judge, called "Give Your Dog a Chance." This article describes not only the best techniques for locating and planting birds, but also the subtle differences between planting birds on the course or in the bird field to give every dog the best opportunity to display their skills. **(a)** Professional trainer Mike Mullineaux demonstrates bird planting on the back course by releasing the birds from horseback to minimize human scent. Mike is careful to choose sites where a bird would naturally conceal itself. **(b)** The bird field requires bird planter Wendy Moon to be on foot and use a "harder" plant so the birds remain in the desired location but will still fly well, to guarantee the best contact for judging. Photograph by Gene LaFollette.

Conclusion

There are many reasons why Weimaraner owners compete in these various sporting events with their dogs. Some people just enjoy the opportunity to work with a well-trained dog, while others appreciate the challenge of training to accomplish a specific standard of performance and the chance to earn titles.

Some fanciers want to compete to determine which dog and handler are best on a given day, while breeders are often driven to prove that their program produces dogs that honor the heritage of their predecessors. Most everyone enjoys the social aspect of meeting others with like interests and the opportunity to exchange new ideas with knowledgeable competitors and judges they would otherwise likely never meet. Hunt tests and trials are great family events, usually with good food, in a pleasant outdoor setting with congenial company, many times with special stakes and activities for youngsters. The hunter and his dog get the chance to work live birds with other people cooperating to create new learning experiences for each dog. The average person can travel to a competition and relatively inexpensively enjoy something similar to the guided hunts of the well-to-do.

In the end, remember that the Weimaraner has no concept of titles, placements, or points; the owner can learn from his dog that the important aspect is the relationship he has with his dog. The pointer hunts because birds are the most important thing in his life; the Weimaraner hunts because hunting is a most wonderful activity that can be shared with the people he loves. At the end of the day, the dog will go home and lie at his owner's feet. His owner, whether basking in the glow of a big win and the accolades of friends, or reflecting on lessons learned, knows there is always another test or trial on another day.

Figure 13-26: ***When dog is on point,*** follow her eyes to the bird's location. If the bird is either too close or between the dog and the handler, flush the bird with care, and nudge it gently until it is far enough away from the dog and in a direction that will reduce the dog's temptation to give chase and that will give the gunners a good shot. While Ivana's bird flushed wildly, Nicole remembered that such bad luck helps to identify weaknesses in training that will lead to future success on another day in another trial. Photograph by Gene LaFollette.

Figure 14-1: *The first* **Weimaraner Ways** *Gunnar Memorial trophy* is awarded by Judy Balog, in memory of her dog, VC DC AFC Magnum Gunnar Silvershot, MH, SDX, RDX, NA I, UPT I, UT I, to Michael Hall and Gunnar's granddaughter, Steele's Mian Beata, MH, SDX, RDX, V, NA I, UT I, at the 2006 WCA Nationals. *Weimaraner Ways* honors the outstanding contributions of Gunnar, not only as a sire, but also as a competitor, and hopes to encourage Weimaraner participation in NAVHDA events. The highlights of Gunnar's career, including being the first Weimaraner to earn the title of NAVHDA Versatile Champion, as well as the qualifications for the trophy, can be found within this chapter.

CHAPTER 14

WEIMARANERS AND THE NORTH AMERICAN VERSATILE HUNTING DOG ASSOCIATION

by Joe Stroup

In 2009, the North American Versatile Hunting Dog Association (NAVHDA) celebrated its 40th anniversary. The Weimaraner, as one of the versatile breeds that is recognized and tested through the NAVHDA organization, shared in this celebration. Throughout the 40-year history of this ultimate versatile hunting breed testing organization the Weimaraner has made great strides in achievement and participation in this system. Ultimately, this participation contributes to the overall betterment of the Weimaraner breed.

NAVHDA was established in the late 1960s by a team of committed versatile dog enthusiasts that included Edward Bailey, John Kegel, and Bodo Winterhelt. NAVHDA is an international, multi-breed, educational organization with the premise of conserving game through the use of well-trained hunting dogs. With 76 chapters and more than 5,000 members in the U.S. and Canada, a local chapter can be found through the NAVHDA website, www.navhda.org.

In order to further the education of dog owners, trainers, and hunters, NAVHDA provides a studbook registry for 27 breeds of versatile dogs (including both the long- and shorthaired varieties of the Weimaraner), along with a breeder recognition program. NAVHDA also hosts hunting tests and training clinics for handlers and a development program for judges that includes an apprenticeship, ongoing training, and an annual performance review. An invitational event is held each year to showcase NAVHDA's best dogs and to award the title of Versatile Champion to dogs that display exceptional skill, ability, and obedience.

Many local chapters offer regularly scheduled training sessions with experienced trainers to provide beginning members and novice dogs with training opportunities. These sessions, typically held early on a weekend morning, provide not only advice but also the often difficult-to-acquire opportunities to work in water and on live birds, to develop in a young pup the manners and skills necessary to be a personal gun dog for the hunter on foot, and to prepare for the challenges of NAVHDA evaluations.

NAVHDA Testing System

In pursuit of the organization's goal of game conservation, NAVHDA created a comprehensive evaluation program for the versatile pointing breeds and held the first test in 1969. The NAVHDA testing system was based partly on test requirements found in the German JGHV testing system, used with German-registered versatile breeds, such as the Deutsch Drahthaar, Deutsch Kurzhaar, and Weimaraner, which had been producing quality hunting dogs for nearly 70 years.

Today, the NAVHDA program is the most comprehensive testing program for versatile dogs bred and registered in North America. More than 30 different breeds of dogs have participated in this system. NAVHDA provides a certificate for each dog that achieves a prize-winning test score, and owners have the opportunity to purchase a commemorative plaque. In return, breeders have gained valuable information to help improve their individual breeds.

Successful test participants are awarded a Natural Ability (NA), Utility Preparatory Test (UPT), or Utility Test (UT) title, with a further designation of Prize I, II, or III. In order

Figure 14-2: *Always return with something:* the cardinal rule for the dedicated NAVHDA dog sent for a retrieve.

Figure 14-3: ***Early socialization will make a difference*** in the puppy's eventual success. Not only is Cora the first German import to earn a Master Hunter title, but her litters by VC DC AFC Magnum Gunnar's Silvershot, MH, SDX, RDX, VX, and DC NFC NAFC AFC Snake Breaks Saga v. Reiteralm, CD, MH, RDX, VX2, have earned her two NAVHDA NA Breeder's Awards. To date, Cora's talented children by these two sires have amassed 19 prizes in NA testing.

This NA test is open to dogs of all ages; however, only dogs younger than 16 months are eligible for prizes. Many owners have found it beneficial to first test a puppy at 7–8 months to gauge its true natural aptitude, as well as to identify areas in which the handler or dog may be weakest. For Weimaraners, who tend to mature more slowly than some of the continental breeds, these early results should be viewed with caution, as in many cases, maturity and a little practice result in improved performance. The average age of natural ability-tested Weimaraners who earned a Prize I score was just shy of 13 months, which endorses not only patience but persistence when working with a young Weimaraner eligible for natural ability testing.

In the field search, dogs are run individually to hunt in a natural environment where game birds (chukar and quail are most common) have been released. The dog's performance is observed by the three judges (and sometimes a gallery); with particular emphasis on the dog's use of nose, pointing ability, search, and cooperation. During the field portion of the test, early in the field search, a gunner will fire a shotgun twice at random intervals to assess the dog for gun sensitivity; the novice handler should be sure to condition the dog to the sound of the shotgun, which is much louder than the blank pistol commonly used in training.

to pass the test and receive a prize, the dog's score must exceed a minimum in each test subset as well as a minimum overall. Because of the minimum score requirement for some test subsets, it is possible to have a very high score yet still receive only a Prize II designation. Dogs that receive a Prize I score have demonstrated superior performance in all aspects of the test and Prize II and III dogs have demonstrated competence in the test but either a somewhat lesser degree of proficiency overall or a major weakness in one aspect of the test.

Three specially trained judges evaluate each dog's performance and agree on a score from 0 (failing) to 4 (superior). This score is then multiplied by a fixed index number that has been assigned to each category as a way of establishing the degree of importance for each area of evaluation. At the end of the test, an overall score is determined for each dog.

A more thorough explanation of the scoring system and minimum requirements for each prize is available in the NAVHDA *Aims, Programs, and Test Rules* book, which is available online at www.navhda.org.

The Natural Ability Test

The NA test is designed to evaluate a dog's fundamental inherited abilities in seven areas related to versatile hunting capability: use of nose, field search, swimming, pointing, tracking, desire to work, and cooperation. The test consists of a field search, swim, and track component; in addition, there is an assessment of physical attributes and temperament that is noted but not given any point value and thus is not reflected in the final score.

Figure 14-4: ***Begin training the NAVHDA candidate*** as soon as possible. Club training sessions are frequently held conveniently on early weekend mornings, often with live birds available for purchase. More advanced club members are often willing to share leftover dead game to give young beginners the opportunity to experience the thrill of the taste, feel, and retrieve of a variety of feathered and furred game. More extensive training is also outlined in Chapter 12, *Starting the Gun Dog*. Photograph by Gene LaFollette.

The tracking portion of the test entails the release of a flightless pheasant or chukar that has been released into cover (such as a tree or brush line), unobserved by the dog or handler. The handler has the option of allowing the dog to see and smell the bird before going to the blind prior to the release of the bird. The track should be of sufficient distance based on cover and the Senior judge's discretion. The dog is then brought to the release point of the bird, where a few soft feathers have been pulled and left on the ground to mark the start; the dog is sent off-lead to follow the track of the bird across the field and to break cover to locate the bird in hiding. This test is designed to simulate the retrieval of a crippled bird in a hunting scenario. However, to receive the maximum score, the dog does not have to locate the released bird—the dog must just demonstrate the willingness and ability to follow its footscent.

In the water portion of the test, the dog is required to demonstrate a willingness and an ability to swim (using all four legs) at least twice. Dogs that actually retrieve the bumper do not receive higher scores; however, if the dog will not swim to retrieve a dummy, it may be called back later for a second chance using a dead bird instead of a bumper. If a game bird is required to induce the dog to swim, the participant can receive only a maximum score of 2.

The physical examination usually occurs after the water portion of the evaluation. The judges note any faults or traits that could affect performance or breeding. This would include such things as missing or extra teeth, alignment of the bite, presence or absence of testicles, coat texture and quality, and temperament problems. It is not a bad idea to practice such examinations in advance to ensure that the dog and handler are comfortable with the procedure.

By the end of this thorough assessment, handlers and breeders have critical feedback regarding their puppies' strengths and weaknesses. By examining the scores of several puppies in a litter, breeders can make better-informed decisions about breeding future litters. If four puppies from the same litter each earn a prize and collectively earn scores totaling over 360 points, the breeder is recognized with the NA Breeder's Award.

THE MOST COMMON ERROR NOVICE OWNERS MAKE...

...is missing the announcement for testing events. Handlers should be aware that unlike AKC trials and hunt tests—which are usually held at predictable times and locations—NAVHDA entries close when the available spots are filled, often within just days of the official announcement of the trial date, which occurs 3–4 months prior to the event. As a result, by the time the announcement appears in the NAVHDA magazine, clubs are placing excess entries on a "reserve list" in the rare event that an entered dog should withdraw. Close contact with a mentor in the local club and establishing good contacts with surrounding clubs will help the new handler to be aware of the official announcement of test dates, the soonest entries can be accepted, and where to send entries during the brief window of opportunity. Sending entries by FedEx makes it possible to document receipt of the entry.

Figure 14-5: *Encourage the puppy to pick up, carry, and deliver* to hand from the earliest age. One method employed by many German trainers is to first teach the puppy to take and hold the owner's fingers in the casual and informal environment of the home and later more formally on the training table as shown. Once the puppy will take and hold the owner's fingers until asked to release, a stuffed, smelly old sock or a bumper can be substituted. When the dog is actively reaching to take the object, then the dog must be trained to reach down to pick it up off the ground; initially, it may be necessary to elevate the bumper or sock on a couple of bricks to make it easier. Only then is a bird substituted.

Figure 14-6: *Field Search.* On the field portion of the NA test, the dog is scored in five categories. A point like this with multiple finds should earn Randy a full mark of 4. But a good point is not enough; search, use of nose, desire to work, and cooperation are awarded separate scores from 1–4. Randy is one of a multiple NA Prize I litter. Not only has he earned his bench championship, but his great start in NAVHDA has also led him to frequent placements in all-age, all-breed gun dog stakes, and in the true NAVHDA spirit, he is a treasured hunting companion.

Figure 14-8: *Tracking.* Eve returns with her prize after following the track of the flightless bird. Eve broke cover into the tree and brush line and located the live bird; although it was not necessary for a maximum score, she earned extra credit in cooperation for returning the bird to her handler.

Figure 14-9: *Physical Exam.* Recognizing that a sound body and protective coat contribute to a long, useful life and efficient performance, after the water work, the judges examine the dog's physical structure for defects that will affect hunting performance, including the coat, teeth, genitals, body condition, and temperament. As in Germany, this information also becomes part of Carly's permanent record, along with her NA and UT Prize I test results. Photograph by Judy Balog.

Figure 14-7: *Swimming.* Dogs must demonstrate ability to swim twice for the NA. **(a)** The dog will earn a higher score for swimming freely for a bumper (whether or not the retrieve is completed). **(b)** If the dog must be enticed with a bird (regardless of whether the retrieve is completed), the dog will lose up to 2 points. Teach your dog to swim with enthusiasm in many different locations and under varying conditions.

Table 14-1: *NAVHDA Natural Ability.*

Field	Performance	Water	Performance
Field search	Rated for use of nose, search, pointing, desire, cooperation, and gunsureness. Hunts for a minimum of 20 minutes in typical hunting cover where game birds have been released. A shotgun is fired at two random points along the course and the dog's reaction is noted as not gun-shy, gun-sensitive (disturbed but resumes hunting willingly), or gun-shy. The judges look for purpose and potential at this level; a mature pattern is not required.	Swimming	Rated for cooperation, desire to work, and water entry. A training bumper is thrown a short distance into water of sufficient depth that the dog is required to swim. A retrieve is not required, as the test is only of willingness to enter water and confidence to swim. The dog must enter the water and swim twice in order to pass. If the dog will not enter the water for the bumper, a game bird can be thrown to entice it, but doing so will reduce the dog's score.
Tracking	Rated for use of nose, desire to work, cooperation, and ability to track a running pheasant or chukar. The dog is taken from a blind to the beginning of a track, where the start is marked by a few pulled feathers. The dog is shown the feathers, encouraged to acquire the track, and then released. This exercise is primarily a test of the dog's ability to use its nose and to concentrate on the track. A retrieve is not necessary in order to achieve a maximum score.	Physical exam	Evaluation of physical traits, including coat and dentition, takes place immediately after the dog completes one of the water exercises, while its coat is still wet. A basic evaluation of temperament is performed at the same time, with judges noting shyness or aggression. As in Germany, this information also becomes part of the dog's permanent record, along with the test results.
Objective	To evaluate the fundamental hereditary characteristics of a versatile hunting dog.		
Scoring	Maximum points, 112: Prize I, 99–112; Prize II, 80–98; Prize III, 58–79		
Source	NAVHDA: *Aims, Programs, Test Rules.* Rev. ed. 2005.		

Table 14-2: *Scoring system for the Natural Ability Test.*

Test	Maximum Score	Index Number	Maximum Points Attainable	Prize I	Prize II	Prize III
Nose	4	6	24	24(4)	18(3)	18(3)
Search	4	5	20	20(4)	15(3)	10(2)
Water	4	5	20	15(3)	15(3)	10(2)
Pointing	4	4	16	12(3)	12(3)	8(2)
Tracking	4	2	8	6(3)	4(2)	2(1)
Desire to work	4	4	16	16(4)	12(3)	8(2)
Cooperation	4	2	8	6(3)	4(2)	2(1)
Total			**112**	**99**	**80**	**58**

Note: Minimum score for each prize classification is indicated in parentheses.

Source: NAVHDA: Aims, Programs, and Test Rules. Rev. ed. 2005.

The Utility Preparatory Test

The UPT is a test of the dog's progress toward becoming a finished hunting dog. The UPT resembles and is modeled much like the UT. However, there are some very subtle differences in the judging because of the level of training a UPT dog requires. The test is composed of two major sections: the field test and the water portion of the exam.

First, in the field portion of the test, the dog is evaluated to determine its steadiness to game, search, retrieve of a shot bird, retrieve by drag, and pointing abilities.

At the water, the dog is expected to walk at heel, either off lead or on a loose lead, on the way to the water. The dog demonstrates steadiness by a duck blind until sent for a single marked retrieve of a dead duck and then performs a blind search of the water for a dead duck that has been thrown in at a location unknown to either handler or dog.

In a UPT, steadiness to wing is required for a maximum steadiness score in the field, while at the water a dog must be steady to the presence of gunfire and while a dead duck is thrown. For a maximum score, the dog must remain by the blind until commanded by the handler to retrieve.

The UPT is very similar to the UT in nearly all other areas; however, the judging is less rigid in each facet. The test should clearly establish that the dog has moved away from the puppy stage and is progressing towards becoming a finely finished hunting dog.

Table 14-3: *Scoring system for the Utility Preparatory Test.*

Test		Maximum Score	Index Number	Maximum Points Attainable	Prize I	Prize II	Prize III
Water	Water search	4	4	16	16(4)	12(3)	8(2)
	Walking at heel	4	2	8	6(3)	4(2)	2(1)
	Steadiness by blind	4	2	8	6(3)	4(2)	2(1)
	Retrieve of duck	4	3	12	9(3)	6(2)	3(1)
Field	Search	4	5	20	15(3)	15(3)	10(2)
	Pointing	4	4	16	16(4)	12(3)	8(2)
	Steadiness on game	4	3	12	9(3)	6(2)	3(1)
	Retrieve of shot bird	4	3	12	9(3)	6(2)	3(1)
	Retrieve by drag	4	3	12	9(3)	6(2)	3(1)
Judged Throughout							
	Use of nose	4	6	24	24(4)	18(3)	18(3)
	Desire to work	4	5	20	20(4)	15(3)	10(2)
	Cooperation	4	3	12	9(3)	6(2)	3(1)
	Obedience	4	3	12	9(3)	6(2)	3(1)
Total				184	157	116	79

Note: Minimum score for each prize classification is indicated in parentheses.
Source: NAVHDA Aims, Programs, and Test Rules. Rev. ed. 2005.

Figure 14-10: *Retrieve of shot bird.* Major is not required to deliver to hand but must bring the bird within a reasonable distance that is accessible to the handler. Find out what kind of birds will be used (chukars are the most common) and be sure the dog has experience with the designated birds for each specific event.

Figure 14-11: *Retrieve of duck.* Baltur demonstrates the UT retrieve. NAVHDA rules state, "The ideal marsh will have swimming depth water and a substantial amount of vegetation so that the dog can demonstrate desire and persistence as it searches for downed game."

Table 14-4: *Utility Preparatory Test summary.*

Field Group	Performance	Water Group	Performance
Field search	Rated for search, use of nose, pointing, desire, obedience, and cooperation. The dog hunts for a minimum of 25 minutes over typical hunting terrain in which game birds have been released. The search should show some maturity at this level. Objectives should be checked and the wind should be used to advantage. Because the UPT dog is not expected to be steady to shot, it is not necessary to fire unless the bird can be safely shot.	*Walking at heel*	The dog is expected to walk at heel either off-lead or on a loose lead for approximately 25 yards to a position by a blind beside the water.
		Steadiness by blind	When a dead duck is thrown, the handler fires a single blank shot with a shotgun. The dog is expected to mark the fall and to remain steady until sent for the retrieve.
Pointing	Points must be intense and productive; however, there is no greater reward for any particular style.	*Retrieve of duck*	The dog must enthusiastically find and bring back the duck to within reach of the handler, who must remain far enough back from the water's edge that the dog must come fully out of the water to complete the retrieve.
Steadiness	The highest score in steadiness is awarded for quiet, confident teamwork between dog and handler with the dog steady to wing. At a minimum, the dog must permit its handler to move in front to begin the flush.	*Water search*	A dead duck is placed into cover in swimming-depth water with both dog and handler positioned so that they cannot see the location of the duck. The handler is signaled to position the dog at the starting area and then to fire a single blank shot in a direction away from the location of the duck before sending the dog in to search. The dog is expected to remain steady until it is sent and then to enter the water willingly and to search diligently for up to 10 minutes without guidance. It is not necessary for the dog to find the duck in order to receive a maximum score as it is primarily its searching capability that is being judged. A retrieve is not necessary unless the dog makes contact with the duck.
Retrieve of shot bird	The dog is expected to happily and promptly retrieve shot game to its handler with minimal commands. If no opportunity to retrieve presents itself, the dog may be held by the collar while a bird is shot in order that a retrieve can be judged. Hardmouthing the bird is penalized and the dog, at a minimum, is expected to bring the bird to within reach of the handler.		
Retrieve by drag	The dog is expected to follow a drag track of approximately 50 yards that ends out of sight of the handler to find a live, shackled game bird and willingly retrieve it to at least within reach of the handler. The dog must demonstrate willingness to find and retrieve the game without direct influence by the handler.		
Objective	To measure the dog's progress toward becoming a complete hunting dog.		
Scoring	Maximum points, 184: Prize I, 157–184; Prize II, 116–156; Prize III, 79–115		
Source	NAVHDA: *Aims, Programs, Test Rules,* Rev. ed. 2005.		

Figure 14-12: *Walking at heel.* This exercise is often overlooked in training, but points can be easily lost by those unprepared for the heeling test. His owner prepared Piezl by training in many different areas, with friends simulating the observing judges, so Piezl was able to focus on the task despite distractions. Photograph by Clyde Vetter.

Figure 14-13: *Steadiness by blind.* It is easy to neglect training for steadiness at blind. Major must remain in position when the bird is thrown and the blank shot is fired by the handler; he must wait calmly until he is released for the retrieve. As in the NA test, after the retrieve is completed, the dog is once again examined by the judges.

The Utility Test

The UT is a test for finished versatile hunting dogs to show their true merit and worth in the field and water. The test is composed of a field and water portion, just as in the UPT.

In the field portion of the test, the dog is expected to search a field actively seeking out game, point the game, remain steady to wing, shot, and fall, and retrieve the game directly to hand. Additionally, the dog is evaluated on its ability to follow the 200-yard dragged track of a dead game animal and its willingness to promptly return to the handler with this game.

On the way to the water, the dog must walk at heel off-lead or on a loose lead and then must stay at the blind while the handler goes out of sight and fires two shots. The dog must remain steady by the blind before being sent for a marked retrieve of a dead duck through decoys, with multiple distraction shots fired prior to the throw of the duck. The dog must also perform a blind search of the water for 10 minutes for a live, flightless duck that has been released in a location unknown to either handler or dog. Should the dog find and retrieve the duck too soon, the dog must be sent back out to continue the search for at least a total of 10 minutes.

Throughout the test, the dog's use of nose, cooperation, desire to work, stamina, and obedience are evaluated. In the end, this test allows the hunter to genuinely assess the abilities of the dog and the training provided to it by performance against this standard. This can be valuable information to the breeder as well, to give an idea not only of the dog's inherited abilities but also the dog's trainability.

Table 14-5: *Scoring system for the Utility Test.*

Test		Maximum Score	Index Number	Maximum Points Attainable	Prize I	Prize II	Prize III
Water	Search for duck	4	4	16	16(4)	12(3)	8(2)
	Walking at heel	4	2	8	6(3)	4(2)	2(1)
	Remaining by blind	4	2	8	6(3)	4(2)	2(1)
	Steadiness by blind	4	2	8	6(3)	4(2)	2(1)
	Retrieve of duck	4	3	12	9(3)	6(2)	3(1)
Field	Search	4	5	20	15(3)	15(3)	10(2)
	Pointing	4	4	16	16(4)	12(3)	8(2)
	Steadiness on game	4	3	12	9(3)	6(2)	6(2)
	Retrieve of shot bird	4	3	12	9(3)	6(2)	3(1)
	Retrieve by dragged game	4	3	12	9(3)	6(2)	3(1)
Judged Throughout	Use of nose	4	6	24	24(4)	18(3)	18(3)
	Desire to work	4	5	20	15(3)	15(3)	10(2)
	Stamina	4	3	12	9(3)	9(3)	6(2)
	Cooperation	4	3	12	9(3)	6(2)	3(1)
	Obedience	4	3	12	9(3)	6(2)	6(2)
Total				**204**	**172**	**129**	**90**

Note: Minimum score for each prize classification is indicated in parentheses.
Source: NAVHDA Aims, Programs, and Test Results. Rev. ed. 2005.

Figure 14-14: *The UT dog* should be a capable and reliable hunting companion that demonstrates teamwork and steadiness to wing, shot, and fall. Bleu Bayou is expected to point staunchly, even in a difficult situation such as this, where the bird will be flushed from directly under his nose.

Figure 14-15: *Retrieve.* Since the earliest German origins of the NAVHDA system included the retrieve of furred as well as feathered game, in the UT, the handler has the option of providing a dead furred or feathered game animal for the 200-yard drag track. Photograph by the Weimaraner Klub e. V. (Petri 2001).

Table 14-6: *Utility Test summary.*

Field Group	Performance	Water Group	Performance
Field search	Rated for use of nose, stamina, desire, obedience, and cooperation. The dog must demonstrate the ability to locate game in varied terrain and cover, adapt range to conditions, maintain contact with the handler, and search the field thoroughly. Objectives should be checked, and the wind should be used to advantage. The dog hunts for a minimum of 30 minutes over typical hunting terrain in which game birds have been released.	*Walking at heel*	The dog is expected to walk at heel either off-lead or on a loose lead along a serpentine course marked by stakes or trees for approximately 25 yards to a position by a blind beside the water.
		Remaining by blind	Handler positions the dog by a blind beside the water and then goes out of sight of the dog and fires two blank shots at 10-second intervals. The dog is expected to remain steady throughout to demonstrate obedience.
Pointing	Points must be intense and productive; however, there is no greater reward for any particular style.	*Steadiness by blind*	When a dead duck is thrown, the handler fires a single blank shot with a shotgun. The dog is expected to mark the fall and remain steady.
Steadiness	The dog is expected to demonstrate quiet, confident, teamwork with its handler and to remain steady to flush, wing, shot, and fall, with the highest score being awarded to the dog that is steady without any commands given by the handler.	*Retrieve of duck*	The dog must swim through or around the decoys and must locate and return promptly with the duck to sit or stand close to the handler until commanded to release the bird to hand. The handler must remain far enough back from the water's edge that the dog must come fully out of the water to complete the retrieve.
Retrieve of shot bird	The dog is expected to mark the fall of each shot bird and to locate and retrieve all shot birds to hand quickly and eagerly, with the highest score being awarded to the dog that retrieves without any commands given by the handler.	*Water search*	A live, flightless duck is released into cover in swimming-depth water with both dog and handler positioned so that they cannot see the location of the duck. The handler is signaled to position the dog at the starting area and then to fire a single blank shot in a direction away from the location of the duck before sending the dog in to search. The dog is expected to remain steady until it is sent and then to enter the water willingly and to search diligently for up to 10 minutes without any guidance or encouragement. It is not necessary for the dog to find or retrieve the duck in order to receive a maximum score as it is primarily its searching capability that is being judged; however, if the opportunity to retrieve presents itself, it must be successfully completed.
Retrieve by drag	The dog is expected to demonstrate its ability as a retriever of furred or feathered game and its ability to track as well as to establish that it is free from retrieving vices. The drag track is 200 yards long, with one sharp turn near the middle of the course. The game is left in cover out of sight of the handler. A dog performs well when it quickly and accurately follows the track, finds the game, and brings it directly and quickly back to the handler.	*Physical exam*	Evaluation of physical traits, including coat and bite, takes place immediately after the dog completes one of the water exercises while its coat is still wet. A basic evaluation of temperament is performed at the same time, with judges noting shyness or aggression.
Objective	To evaluate the dog's usefulness as a finished hunting companion for the on-foot hunter in both field and water.		
Scoring	Maximum points, 204: Prize I, 172–204; Prize II, 129–171; Prize III, 90–128		
Source	NAVHDA: *Aims, Programs, Test Rules.* Rev. ed. 2005.		

Figure 14-16: *Steadiness by the blind.* Astor must demonstrate steadiness by the blind while a dead duck is thrown past the decoys and two shots are fired by the handler. The highest scores are awarded when both the dog and handler are silent and the dog remains motionless until commanded to fetch to complete the retrieve.

Figure 14-17: *Water search.* A flightless duck is released into water with high cover while Zoe waits behind a blind. It is not necessary for her to return with the duck to receive a maximum score, as she is being judged on her searching skills and persistence; however, if she makes contact with the bird, she must retrieve it.

The Invitational Test

The Invitational is a test where NAVHDA's best of the best compete. Only dogs who earn a Prize I UT Score can enter this prestigious event.

During the examination, the entrants will be braced with another dog for a one-hour hunt. The dogs will be expected to handle birds flawlessly in the field and honor each other on point.

At the water, the dogs will be expected to complete a blind retrieve of 100 yards across open water. Additionally, the candidate will be expected to retrieve a shackled duck that has been thrown into the water 76–87 yards from the handler. Finally, the dog must honor the retrieve of another dog while stationed by a blind at the edge of the water.

Overall, this test solidifies the participant's status as an elite versatile hunting dog. Dogs that pass this extremely taxing test are among the best their breed has to offer.

Weimaraners in NAVHDA

Test Results Overview

Between 1969 and 2008, 810 Weimaraners 16 months and older were evaluated in one of the four levels of tests that NAVHDA offers. Three dogs, Ronamax Rumford v. Reit-

Table 14-7: *Scoring system for the Invitational Test.*

Test		Maximum Score	Index Number	Minimum Qualifying Score	Maximum Points	Minimum Points
Field	Search	4	5	3	20	15
	Backing	4	3	3	12	9
	Pointing	4	5	4	20	20
	Steadiness to wing and shot	4	3	3	12	9
	Retrieve of shot bird	4	3	3	12	9
Water	Heeling	4	2	3	8	6
	Steadiness at blind	4	2	3	8	6
	Mark/search/duck retrieve	4	4	3	16	12
	Honoring	4	2	3	8	6
	Blind retrieve	4	4	3	16	12
Overall	Nose	4	6	4	24	24
	Desire to work	4	5	4	20	20
	Cooperation	4	3	3	12	9
	Obedience	4	3	3	12	9
Total					200	166

Source: NAVHDA Aims, Programs, and Test Rules. Rev. ed. 2005.

Figure 14-18: *Fieldwork.* A passing score requires exceptional skill and polish in all phases of work and in a variety of hunting situations. Each of Molly's retrieves should be promptly and gently delivered to hand with minimal commands from her handler.

Figure 14-19: *Honor in the field.* The Invitational competitor must display honor and steadiness at all times without command. Harlie and Zoe demonstrate the type of polished performance that is required to successfully compete at the NAVHDA Invitational.

Table 14-8: *Invitational Test summary.*

Field Group	Performance
Field search	Dogs are run in braces, with handlers hunting together as a team, for a minimum of 60 minutes. Dogs are expected to find and handle game properly. Stop-to-flush situations may be encountered. Dogs may be disqualified for interfering with the bird work of their bracemate.
Backing	Backing will be tested, and a dog is expected to back without command and remain steady throughout the sequence. The backing dog must be off-wind or down-wind a sufficient distance that the judges feel the dog stopped as a result of seeing its bracemate point and not from scenting game.
Pointing	Should both dogs be on point on different birds at the same time, the second dog will be expected to remain on point and steady while the bird of the first dog to establish a point is worked.
Steadiness	On worked birds, the handler will swing a shotgun as if shooting, and dogs are expected to display steadiness through the fall.
Retrieve of shot bird	Birds must be retrieved to hand. Handlers must remain standing and may be penalized for kneeling or crouching.

Water Group	Performance
Heeling	Handlers will carry a shotgun and heel their dog off-lead for 50–100 yards on a clearly defined path to the water's edge. Commands may reduce the score.
Steady at blind	The dog must display steadiness to the fall and remain until the handler sends it for the retrieve.
Mark/search/ duck retrieve	A wing-taped duck is thrown into water cover approximately 70 yards from the dog. While the duck is mid-air, the handler swings the shotgun and fires a blank. The taping of the duck allows it to swim freely but not dive for any distance. The dog must retrieve the duck. Handler commands can reduce the score.
Honoring	A dog other than the one being tested is positioned near the water's edge. The handler of the honoring dog places it sitting or standing 10 feet from the retrieving dog and then stands quietly to the side. The handler of the retrieving dog fires a shot as a dead duck is thrown into open water. The honoring dog must remain steady throughout the retrieving sequence.
Blind retrieve	Prior to the dog's arrival on the scene, a dead duck is placed on land a short distance from the shore's edge across 100 yards of water. The position of the duck is known by the handler. The dog is heeled to the water's edge and sent on the retrieve without a shot being fired. A minimum amount of handling is allowed. The dog must retrieve the duck.

Overall Performance	
Nose	The dog must not only demonstrate the quality of its nose but also that it is able to use its nose to maximum advantage in finding and handling game.
Desire to work	The desire to work must be evident throughout the test. The dog that continues when the going gets rough, in thick cover or cold water, shows the presence of this fundamental quality in the animal. Desire is not demonstrated by speed, nor is aimless running to be confused with desire. It is the firm, determined, yet controlled will to get on with the job that marks the dog possessing this indispensable characteristic.
Cooperation	The dog should at all times demonstrate his willingness to handle and hunt with the purpose of producing game for his master. Cooperation should not be mistaken for overdependence. The cooperative dog is sure of himself and his work and displays eagerness.
Obedience	A good, versatile dog must be in control at all times. The actual success of the hunt can hinge on an obedient dog that will willingly suppress its natural instincts and desires and obey its master's commands.

Figure 14-20: *Blind retrieve.* Baltur is required to take a line from the handler when no shot is fired, swim approximately 100 yards, locate and follow a short drag track of the duck on the opposite shore, and return the bird promptly and gently to hand.

Figure 14-21: *Honor on the retrieve.* Diesel honors as Booster prepares to retrieve. To earn a maximum score, the honoring dog must remain still and quiet until the retrieve to hand is completed. The retrieving dog is not being scored on this exercise.

eralm, Halanns Gustav v. Reiteralm, and Thunder Rocket v. Reiteralm, took this first step together as part of a UT nearly 2 years after the first NAVHDA tests were held.

Although this first appearance did not produce any prize-winning performances, it did mark the beginning of four decades of testing for Weimaraners in the NAVHDA system. From this humble beginning, the Weimaraner's participation in NAVHDA events has grown steadily, while at the same time its performance has dramatically improved.

As evidence of the increased participation, 458 of the 567 (or 81%) of the Weimaraners to have run in NA tests have done so since 1995. In 2008 alone, Weimaraners were evaluated 78 times in one of the four levels of the NAVHDA Testing System. That accounts for nearly 10% of all the Weimaraners ever tested in NAVHDA.

The Weimaraners' improved performance is demonstrated by the recent upswing in NA maximum scores of 112. In 40 years of NAVHDA testing, 60 puppies have earned this distinction. Fifty-three of these maximum score performances, or 88%, have been accomplished since the year 2000. In 2007 alone, 13 Weimaraners earned a maximum score of 112 in a NA test, which represents the most in any single year.

During the 40-year span between 1969 and 2008, 16-month-old or younger Weimaraners have been evaluated 567 times in an NA test, and 68% of the time, the dog has earned a prize. An additional 21 dogs have run in NA tests for evaluation purposes only.

During the first 25 years, only 47% of Weimaraners tested in an NA test qualified for a prize, and less than 1% of these participants earned a Prize I. In comparison, between 1995 and 2008, 73% of all Weimaraners that were tested in NA tests earned a prize, with 21% of these being Prize I performances.

Because of this, today's Weimaraner can boast test success rates rivaled only by some of the more popular Continental breeds. Their 73% prize performance rate between 1995 and 2008 in NA tests would rank behind the all-time rates of only the Pudlepointer, the German Shorthaired Pointer, and the German Wirehaired Pointer, among the other Top 10 tested breeds. The Pudlepointer has a success rate of 78%, the German Shorthaired Pointer, 76%, and the German Wirehaired Pointer, 73% prize percentage in the NA test.

The test success rate average for all breeds in NA tests is 71%, with 22% earning a Prize I. From these statistics, it can be seen that over the past decade and a half, the Weimaraner compares favorably in performance with all other breeds tested in NAVHDA.

Similar increases can be noted in the performance of the Utility dogs in NAVHDA since 1995. The total number of entries in UTs for Weimaraners during that same 40-year period was 189. The UT entries obtained prizes roughly 51% of the time during that span.

Between 1995 and 2009, the prize-earning performance rate for Weimaraners in UTs was 66%. This compares well with the prize-earning percentage of the Top 10 tested breeds. Using this figure, the Weimaraner would trail only the all-time rates of the German Wirehaired (67.8%), the German Short-haired (67.5%), the Pudelpointer (66.6%), and the small Munsterlander (66.2%) in producing a higher percentage of UT prize-winning performers among the top 10 NAVHDA tested breeds.

There have been 23 Prize I performances in UTs for Weimaraners in the history of NAVHDA. Twenty of these Prize I performances have been awarded since 1995, 12 since 2005.

These data clearly illustrate not only that the Weimaraner has been tested more regularly between 1995 and 2008 but that their performances have shown steady improvement as well.

This progress is a tribute to the dedicated breeders and handlers who have devoted many hours to training and testing their dogs to help re-establish the virtues of the breed for which it was created: versatility in the field, forest, and water.

Table 14-9: *Weimaraner NAVHDA prize winners from 1969–2008.*

	Natural Ability Test					Utility Preparatory					Utility Test					Invitational		
	Dogs Tested	Prize I	Prize II	Prize III	None	Dogs Tested	Prize I	Prize II	Prize III	None	Dogs Tested	Prize I	Prize II	Prize III	None	Dogs Tested	Pass	Fail
1969–1984	59	5 8%	5 8%	17 28%	32 54%	N/A	N/A	N/A	N/A	N/A	49	3 6%	5 10%	9 18%	32 65%	0	0 N/A	0 N/A
1985–1994	50	1 2%	10 20%	13 26%	26 52%	8	0 0%	1 13%	5 63%	2 25%	34	0 0%	1 3%	8 24%	25 74%	0	0 N/A	0 N/A
1995–2004	264	53 20%	58 22%	80 30%	73 28%	24	1 4%	1 4%	8 33%	14 58%	63	8 13%	13 21%	16 25%	26 41%	2	1 50%	1 50%
2005–2008	194	41 21%	43 22%	54 28%	52 27%	10	1 10%	0 0%	4 40%	5 50%	43	12 28%	15 35%	6 14%	10 23%	10	2 17%	8 83%
Totals 1969–2008	567	100 18%	116 20%	164 29%	183 32%	42	2 5%	2 5%	17 40%	21 50%	189	23 12%	34 18%	39 21%	93 49%	12	3 25%	9 75%

Top Gun

Along the way, there have been many significant testing firsts that allowed the breed to gain exposure and its breeders to gain vital breeding information, which allowed the breed to have greater success in the NAVHDA system. None of these were of greater significance than Magnum Gunnar Silvershot (Gunnar).

Gunnar and his owner/handler, Judy Balog, entered NAVHDA at a time when the Weimaraner was considered not only a minority breed but an inferior breed. The performances, honors, and awards earned by Gunnar went a long way toward erasing these misconceptions. Today, his progeny continue this legacy and are helping to return the Weimaraner to a status of prominence among NAVHDA enthusiasts.

Prior to Gunnar and Judy's emerging on the NAVHDA scene in 1995, Weimaraners had a less-than-stellar track record in NAVHDA tests. Fewer than 50% of Weimaraner puppies optained prizes in NA tests, and barely 30% earned prizes in the UT. These figures have nearly doubled since Gunnar's emergence on the scene.

Gunnar made several historic firsts for the breed in NAVHDA testing, which sparked not only the breed's popularity with NAVHDA enthusiasts but also proved that the Weimaraner could indeed reach the performance levels of the other breeds.

On 24 August 1998, Gunnar became the first Weimaraner ever to register a Prize I UPT score at the age of 2 years, 2 months with 181 points. It was not until 2008, that another Weimaraner would replicate this feat of earning a Prize I in a UPT.

In the fall of 1997, Gunnar again broke new ground for the breed by becoming the third Weimaraner in history ever to register a Prize I UT score and the very first to do so with a maximum score of 204 points. Since then, five other Weimaraners have earned this distinction, all of them occurring since 2003. In April 1998, Gunnar graced the cover of the Versatile Hunting Dog magazine for this honor.

However, this did not mark the end of Gunnar's stardom. Less than a year later, in September 1998, Gunnar became the first Weimaraner in history to pass the Invitational Test with a score of 187 points. Today, only two other Weimaraners have been able to duplicate this accomplishment.

Gunnar's legacy continues in his offspring. Through 31 December 2008, 31 of his offspring have been NA tested. Thirty-four prizes were awarded to these dogs for their performances. Overall, Gunnar's puppies had an NA test success rate of 97%, with only one individual not earning a prize. Gunnar has sired 11 Prize I–earning NA dogs. Seven of these have earned the maximum score of 112 points. Additionally, Gunnar has sired two dogs that have earned UT Prize I honors and another who earned a Prize II.

Of the 17 Weimaraner litters that have earned an NA Breeder's Award, Gunnar has sired four. A fifth award-winning litter was produced by Steele's Titanium Gun, who is Gunnar's Prize I UT daughter.

Figure 14-22: *VC DC AFC Magnum Gunnar Silvershot,* MH, SDX, RDX, NA1, UPT1, UT1. In NAVHDA, Gunnar was the breed's first Versatile Champion and the leading sire of NA prized puppies.

The prominent role that Gunnar played in the transformation of the Weimaraner cannot be overstated. Gunnar's role in terms of throwing great hunting puppies and genetics is obvious. However, the role he and Judy Balog played in getting other Weimaraner owners to participate in NAVHDA events and the confidence they instilled in other owners that the Weimaraner could indeed be successful at this level will be a far greater legacy.

The April 1998 cover of the *Versatile Hunting Dog* magazine was the spark that ignited the success for the Weimaraner in NAVHDA over the past decade. It is hoped that this legacy will continue and the breed will again excel in our nation's forests, fields, and water.

Weim Time

There have been numerous other memorable performances by Weimaraners in NAVHDA. These are exemplified in the results of all four tests offered by NAVHDA.

The NA test allows puppies younger than 16 months to display the inherited trait that will make them fine hunting companions. During the first 40 years of NAVHDA, 18% of

Figure 14-23: *Weimshadow Sterlinsilverjoy* NAVHDA UT Prize I. Joy with her breeder, owner, trainer and handler, Sally Jo Hoaglund, coming in from a successful NAVHDA UT Test. Sally Jo is just one of many talented women who have enjoyed great success in the NAVHDA arena. Sally Jo and her husband are avid 'real-life hunters,' and Sally Jo breeds Weimaraners under the Weimshadow prefix, with both of the litters she bred since joining the NAVHDA organization being awarded NA Breeder's Awards.

these NA dogs earned a Prize I, while 20% earned a Prize II and 29% earned a Prize III. Recent years have seen progress;in 2005 and 2006, 76% of Weimaraners that took the NA passed with a prize-winning performance.

The maximum score of 112 points in the NA test is the top goal of all NAVHDA enthusiasts for their puppies that are younger than 16 months. Tortuga Paloma's was the first Weimaraner to produce an NA maximum score in 1981. This was nearly eight years after the first Weimaraner, Orkan's Dustin v. Reiteralm, prized in an NA Test and nearly 10 years after the first Weimaraner competed in an NA test. By the start of the 2009 testing season, 60 Weimaraners had earned this distinction. Seven of these puppies were produced by Shirley Nilsson and by Anne Tyson's Regen's Kennel, while Sally Jo Hoaglund and her Weimshadow Kennels, Donnie Steele and Steele's Kennel, and Virginia Alexander and her Reiteralm Kennel each produced five of these maximum score recipients.

To date, 30 males and 30 females have each earned a 112 NA score. VC Magnum Gunnar Silvershot has been the sire of seven of these top-performing puppies. Von Weiner-n-Weimshadow Maxx has also sired a respectable five maximum score recipients. FC/AFC Snake Break Saga v. Reiteralm and Hans von Birdbuster each have produced four maximum-score-earning puppies.

Hans von Birdbuster, owned by Robert Huta, is the only male Weimaraner to both earn the maximum score of 112 and throw offspring that earned this distinction. His partner in this breeding, Steele's Titanium Gun, was the first maximum-score-earning female to throw a 112-scoring puppy as well. She is also the top-producing female of maximum-score puppies, having produced four. Sophie James, owned by Marilyn James, has produced three 112-scoring puppies under the Regen Kennel, as has Shirley Nilsson's Regen's Summer Blaze.

Few Weimaraners have participated in the UPTs over the years. Through 2008, only 42 Weimaraners had entered this event, with 21 (or 50%) of those qualifying for a prize. The number of participants in the UPT is few for two reasons. First, the UPT was not a part of NAVHDA's testing program initially. It was not instituted as a NAVHDA test until 1988. Second, the subtle differences between it and the UT convince many handlers to forego the UPT and wait to test the dog in a UT.

Of the 21 dogs who have earned prizes in the UPT, VC Magnum Gunnar Silvershot is one of only two dogs to ever to earn a Prize I. His score of 181 is three points shy of the maximum UPT score of 184. Axel's Humdinger of Reiteralm became the second dog to accomplish this in 2008. with a score of 178. To date, no Weimaraner has earned a maximum score in a UPT. Only two other dogs have even earned a score as high as a Prize II. A German import by the name of Caesar von der Schelmelach and another male, Herr Gunther Jager Meister, accomplished this with scores of 163 and 175 points, respectively.

Of the 189 Weimaraners that entered UTs between 1969 and 2008, 96 dogs (or 51%) earned a prize. Because of the complexity and variety of tasks required of a dog in a NAVHDA UT, any prize is quite an accomplishment; however, 17 Weimaraners have distinguished themselves as Prize I UT dogs, earning a total of 25 Prize Is between them.

The first to earn this distinction was the Dual Champion Lilith v. Hirschhorn. In 1977, Lilith accomplished this feat twice, with scores of 190 and 187. Ten years later, a male by the name of Shadowmar Hunter Jake accomplished this feat with his 201 score and Prize I performance.

In 1997, VC Magnum Gunnar Silvershot became the first Weimaraner in history to earn the maximum score of 204 and opened the floodgates for the Weimaraner's most recent success. In honor of Gunnar's groundbreaking contributions, *Weimaraner Ways* initiated the Gunnar Memorial Trophy in 2006, to be awarded to Weimaraners earning a maximum score in the NAVHDA UT. Since Gunnar's breakout performance in 1997, 14 other Weimaraners have turned in Prize I performances, with five of those earning a maximum score of 204. Of the 17 UT Prize I Weimaraners (since 1969), the males hold a slight edge having accounted for nine compared with eight for the females.

Superstars of NAVHDA

Six dogs have achieved a maximum score in the NAVHDA UT, including DC VC Magnum Gunnar Silvershot, MH, SDX, RDX, NA1, UPT1, UT1 (see "Top Gun"), and Steele's Mian Beata, MH, SDX, RDX, V, NA1, UT1 (see Figure 14-1). The remaining four are presented here.

Figure 14-24: *Grey Wynn Franklin's Freedom,* UT1, RDX, SDX, owned and trained by Mark Colantuno and bred by Kenneth Miller. After a long day of hunting, Sam loves to rest with the hunting party and be the best friend his family could ever have asked for. Sam's motto is "Feed Me, Love Me & Shoot Straight for Me."

Figure 14-25: *VC Skeeter's Tannerbaum,* MH, SDX, RDX. Tanner's hard work is appreciated not only by his owner/trainer but also by the patients at the Urgent Care Clinic when he accompanies Gerald Gertiser to work. Since Tanner was his first Weimaraner, Gerald credits his success in NAVHDA to his dog's intelligence, work ethic, and natural skills, as well as the support of the Northern Michigan NAVHDA chapter. Tanner was bred by Karla McLeod.

Figure 14-26: *CH Rockville's Truman Greystone,* VCD1, MH, TDX, MX, MXJ, SDX, RDX, VX5, owned by Frank Sommer and bred by Kristina Muratori. Truman earned an abundance of titles in fields outside NAVHDA and was the first male Weimaraner to earn a VX5. His versatility also earned Truman the title of Most Versatile Weimaraner at the 2006 WCA Versatility Expo. To date, Truman is the only Weim to earn two maximum scores in the UT.

Figure 14-27: *VC Luke der Humdinger,* CDX, MH, SDX, RDX, NA2, UT1, bred, owned, and trained by Rahl Hoeptner. Luke has earned an unprecedented four Prize Is in NAVHDA Utility, including his perfect score. The multi-talented Luke was also declared the winner of the WCA's first Versatility Expo.

Table 14-10: *NAVHDA Prize I Natural Ability Awards (maximum scores appear in bold type).*

Dog	Sire/Dam	Owner/Breeder	Date/Score
AK Bella Blue Gun	**Samurai's Gunner/Bella Blue Baroness**	**Cody Anger/Marie Johnson**	**06.13.99/112**
AK Boomer E	Outdoors Spanky Von Hi/Thor Bomba Plains	Cody Anger/Jake Russell	05.01.99/110
Arrowrock Bittersweet LL Gal	**Davison's Orion on the Rise/Wingpoint GBD Alsace Alexis**	**Gerry Snapp**	**09.10.04/112**
Artos vom Wolfsfels	**Cent vom Pfadelsberg/Braca von Lilienthal**	**Piero C. Drouin/Winfried Schupp**	**06.08.02/112**
Baht's Top Gun Salute	Nani's Baht a Pack of Trouble/Baht Our Sophie's Choice	Allison M. Atsiknoudas/Jill Watson	08.10.03/110
Baltur von Hubertus	**Arto vom Nollenwald/Bina von der Letzlinger Heide**	**Chad Gelderloos/Roman Braun**	**05.22.05/112**
BamBam's 007 Weezer Wubble Hill	**TLC Willy Wubbel's Cooper/TLC Outlaw Nickel Hill**	**Pamela Balfanz/John Thompson**	**06.08.08/112**
Bedrock Tess Valkrie	**Bedrock's Aranar No Doubt/Bearden's Lippin Libby**	**Kerry Starin/Greg Bearden**	**05.20.07/112**
Berkley Mtn Ash von Reiteralm	VC Luke der Humdinger/Axel Reiteralms Bina Hubertus	Sharon Clark/Julianne Brooks	04.13.08/110
Billet of Steele	**Hans von Birdbuster/Steele's Titanium Gun**	**Scott Flatt/Donald Steele**	**06.05.04/112**
Camelot's Commander in Chief	**Smokycity Mob Boss/Camelot's Star Attraction**	**Todd MacPhee/Susan Thomas**	**09.07.03/112**
CC's Saskia Snow Daze	Jax's Iron Steele/CC's Rainy Daze Sweet Desire	Anthony Griffore/Christine Conklin	08.25.01/106
Classic Butternut Kaiser	**Grau Geist Lil's Caprock Rev/Camelot's Classic Hot to Trot**	**Lynn Gregorash/Joe Wohlfert**	**07.10.04/112**
Cousin Eddie's Ruby Souix	Jake Mattew Bierl/Ellie's Sitting Dead Red	David Lyon/Trent Eckstaine	05.13.05/108
CR's Timberdoodle Autumn's Aspen	**Sandbar Echoin' Cowboy Colt/Grayangel Kodiak II**	**Kurt Engler/Camille Rice**	**05.19.07/112**
CR's Timberdoodle Black Velvet	**Sandbar Echoin' Cowboy Colt/Grayangel Kodiak II**	**Camille Rice**	**05.19.07/112**
Dietreich vom Heldenhain	**Amboss vom Heldenhain/Banja vom Senftenberg**	**Charles Coulter/Peter Koch**	**12.03.06/112**
Echobar's Queen of Hearts	Arokat's Echobar Riverdance/Echobar's Fan the Fire	Mary McNeil/Barbara Heuman	05.13.07/110
Gemco's Country Gentleman	Ardreem Wolf von Betelgeuse/Gemco's Big Time Belle	Gema Coleman	08.19.00/110
Gould's Truely Cool Falls Fun	Briarmeadow Buck/Gould's Jus Call Me TJ	Bruce McLachlan/David Gould	06.01.03/110
Gray v. Trapp of Camelot	Maximilliam v. Trapp/Lady Leah of Camelot	Alan Sinnett/Steven Capello	09.08.84/107
Gunmettle's Grayt Granite	**Axel Reiteralm of Weimar's Joy/Gunmettle's Song in the Shadow**	**Bonnie Bartlett/Michael O'Donnell**	**09.12.03/112**
Gunmettle's Shot in the Dark	Axel Reiteralm of Weimar's Joy/Gunmettle's Song in the Shadow	Josh Simpson/Michael O'Donnell	09.12.03/101
Hans von Birdbuster	**Gray Shadow Ghostbuster/Doc's SS Lady Silvia Belle**	**Robert Huta/Mark Deming**	**05.20.00/112**
Heidi's Heart of Steele	Hans von Birdbuster/Steele's Titanium Gun	Fred Saber/Donald Steele	06.06.04/110
Heidi's Pearl	Dans Birtzel/Miss Ts Heidi	Mrs. Sal Williams/Ron Cameron	05.08.77/101
Herwig's Komet von Reiteralm	**Sundown Jaeger von Reiteralm/Sanbar's Spirit v. Reiteralm**	**Sal Castaneda/Virginia Alexander**	**04.10.99/112**
Holy Roller Zum Ziel	**Aztec's American Pie/Amor's Amsel Zum Ziel**	**Aline Scharpf**	**10.05.07/112**
Indabas Wipe the Slate Clean	**Grayshar's Royal Valor/Wagner's Bella of Starwood**	**Lisa McGreevy/Kim Harter**	**06.18.00/112**
Indian Creek's Princess Rose	Exuma Hyatt of Norton/High Ridge's Top Choice	Kevin Barndt/John Goldstein	09.28.03/110
JC's Silver Phoenix	**VC Magnum Gunnar Silvershot/Jaycon's Starlite Express**	**Erin Hamrick/Pamela Wenzel**	**09.20.98/112**
Legend's Emma of Reiteralm	Snake Breaks Saga v. Reiteralm/Cora von der Schelmelach	Joseph Stroup/Virginia Alexander	09.18.05/110
Legend's Mister Reiteralm	Snake Breaks Sage v. Reiteralm/Cora von der Schelmelach	Virginia Alexander	04.01.07/110
Legend's Reign von Reiteralm	**Snake Breaks Saga v. Reiteralm/Cora von der Schelmelach**	**Cedar Paddock/Virginia Alexander**	**08.26.06/112**
Legend's Samba von Reiteralm	Snake Breaks Saga v. Reiteralm/Cora von der Schelmelach	Ronald Costa/Virginia Alexander	11.12.06/110
Legend's Silvershot Reiteralm	**VC Magnum Gunnar Silvershot/Cora von der Schelmelach**	**Brad Oleson/Virginia Alexander**	**09.08.02/112**
Legend's Theodore v. Reiteralm	Snake Breaks Saga v. Reiteralm/Cora von der Schelmelach	David Bontrager/Virginia Alexander	10.22.06/110
VC Magnum Gunnar Silvershot	Green Acres Good Grief Colby/Dustivelvet's Spring Rain	Judy Balog/Kathleen Elkins	04.30.95/108
Marshall's Mila Minute	**Stormcrow's Deaugh Blitzen/Treeline's Liza Jane**	**Kirk Marshall/Julie McClellan**	**04.25.98/112**
MGD's N' Lite's Gray Sky's Full Moon Maggie	Sandbar Echoin' Cowboy Colt/N'Lites Stormy Gray Sky	Ryan Miller	10.11.08/110
Misty's Little Spirit	**Jack Genius Snyder/Misty Blue Snyder**	**Scott Roker/Kenny Snyder**	**10.09.05/112**
Northwoods River to Graytsky	**Baht n'Greywind Playin' the Game/Grayhawk Sage v. Silversmith**	**Amy Anderson/Phillip Warren**	**05.11.96/112**
Panu zum Laubwald	Nando von der Wapelburg/Eika vom Schulzenberg	Steve Graham/Hans Schmidt	05.03.02/106 06.10.02/108
PikQwik Silvershot Next Gen	**VC Magnum Gunnar Silvershot/Arimarlisa Rona vom Reiteralm**	**Judy Balog/Cheryl Potter**	**06.01.02/112**
PikQwik Dynamite O'Reiteralm	VC Magnum Gunnar Silvershot/Arimarlisa Rona von Reiteralm	Cheryl Potter	06.01.02/104
PikQwik Jaeger von Reiteralm	VC Magnum Gunnar Silvershot/Arimarlisa Rona von Reiteralm	Cheryl Potter	06.01.02/108
PikQwikLilly v. s Reiteralm	**VC Magnum Gunnar Silvershot/Arimarlisa Rona vom Reiteralm**	**Fritzie Undegrahe/Cheryl Potter**	**09.09.00/112**
PikQwik Magnmandy Reiteralm	**VC Magnum Gunnar Silvershot/Arimarlisa Rona vom Reiteralm**	**Steven Vaness/Cheryl Potter**	**06.01.02/112**
PikQwik Morgen Reiteralm	VC Magnum Gunnar Silvershot/Arimarlisa Rona vom Reiteralm	Anthony Griffore/Cheryl Potter	08.20.00/110
Pine Creek Ivan Rider	**Rocksands Wing Runner/Von Nimrod Lil's Sweet Libby**	**Randy Sorgenfrey/Lynn Moser**	**10.05.08/112**

Table 14-10: *NAVHDA Prize I Natural Ability Awards, continued.*

Dog	Sire/Dam	Owner/Breeder	Date/Score
PM Southern Bernadette Lace Zum Ziel	Aztec's American Pie/Amor's Amsel Zum Ziel	Dawna Miller/Aline Scharpf	10.07.07/112
Point in View AJ	Sir Silver von Bullet/Holly von Ostfriesland	Michael Kuper/Kris Wright	05.07.94/108
PTS Nth Steele Reinforcement	Hans von Birdbuster/Steele's Titanium Gun	Robert Huta/Donald Steele	05.22.04/112
Raintree's Chester Goulds	Westend's Li'l Sage Rider/Goulds Cascade Shasta	Maureen Conley/Greg Dielman	08.26.06/112
Regen Sweet and Sassy	Silver Rain's Rodeo Rider/Regen's Rip Tide	Grace Anne Mengel/Shirley Nilsson	04.05.08/107
Regen's Bismark Lemans Streak	Regen's Rip Stop/Sophie James	Wanda Gunter/Marilyn James	06.02.07/112
Regen's Bismark St Quentin	Regen's Rip Stop/Sophie James	Carmen Spencer/Marilyn James	05.05.07/112
Regen's Bismark Woerth	Regen's Rip Stop/Sophie James	Carol Meshon/Marilyn James	05.06.07/110
Regen's Frederick II Prague	Regen's Rip Roaring Good Time/Sophie James	Marilyn James	09.25.05/112
Regen's Full Speed Ahead	Von Weiner's Withheld/Regen's Fast Forward	Darci Sowers/Judith Voris	10.24.04/108
Regens's Harvest Moon	Dust Storm on the Rise/Regen's Fast N' Furious	Alicia Rae Puckett	05.21.05/112
Regen's Jet Setter	Snake Breaks Saga v. Reiteralm/Regen's Fast n Furious	Judith Voris/Alicia Rae Puckett	05.06.07/112
Regen's Rip Stop	NorthernLights This BudsForU/Regen's Summer Blaze	Anne Tyson/Shirley Nilsson	08.03.03/112
Regen's Rip Tide	NorthernLights This BudsForU/Regen's Summer Blaze	Shirley Nilsson/Judith Voris	08.03.03/112
Regen's Rocket Launcher	Rockville's Truman Greystone/Regen's Hot Chili Pepper	Steven Jenks/Judith Voris	05.15.04/107
Regen's State of The Art	Von Weiner's Withheld/Regen's Summer Blaze	Shirley Nilsson	09.10.04/112
Reiteralms Lucy v. Brooksburg	VC Luke der Humdinger/Axel Reiteralms Bina Hubertus	Noel Querrazzi/Julianne Brooks	04.05.08/110
Reiteralm's Remington v. Brooksburg	VC Luke der Humdinger/Axel Reiteralms Bina Hubertus	Karen Haynes/Julianne Brooks	04.06.08/110 04.13.08/112
Rosaic's Diamonds Out of Dust	Dust Storm on the Rise/Gunmettle Rosaic's Portfolio	Lorna Godsill	09.21.07/112
Rubicon Rose	Stillwater Run Zeus/Wendel's Stormy Angel	Deborah Starin/Dan Wendel	05.20.07/112
Shadow Dancer's Schatzi	Prince Bytor Shadow Runner/Miss Sadie Shadow Dancer	Peter Osentoski/Cort Heimsoth	09.21.03/112
Silberkinder the Next Chance	Snake Breaks Saga v Reiteralm/Silberkinder Miss Money Penny	Susan Wallace	03.04.07/112
Silberkinder the Next Hit	Snake Breaks Saga v Reiteralm/Silberkinder Miss Money Penny	Hugh Reed/Susan Wallace	03.02.07/112
Silberkinder the Next Thing Ya Know	Snake Breaks Saga v Reiteralm/Silberkinder Miss Money Penny	Susan Wallace	03.04.07/110
Silvershot Truely Cool Scout	VC Magnum Gunner Silvershot/Silver Star's Sassy Dancer	Bruce Mclachlan/Brent Miller	06.06.99/112
Silvershot's Lil'Tom Boy	Grau Geist Lil's Gust v. Westend/Gould's Truly Cool Falls Fun	Judy Balog	05.20.07/112
Silvershot's Mirage v. Reiteralm	Snake Breaks Saga v Reiteralm/Reiteralm's Absolute Point	Gerald Gertiser, II/Steven Keene	09.25.05/108
Sirius Single Shot Sako	Westend's Li'l Sage Rider/Sirius Really Rosie	Paul Dryburgh/Helene Moore	05.26.02/105
Sirius Supertanker	VC Magnum Gunnar Silvershot/Sirius Really Rosie	Helene Moore	09.12.99/108
Sirius Sweet Margaret Rose	VC Magnum Gunnar Silvershot/Sirius Really Rosie	Helene Moore	07.14.02/110
Skeeter's Tannerbaum	Gray Shadow Ghostbuster/McLeod's Unser Shatze	Gerald Gertiser, II/Karla McLeod	06.01.02/112
Spectrum Once in a Blue Moon	Spectrum Spudnick v. Aalto/Grete Bridge the Gap Blue	Anne Taguchi/Christa Johnson	08.10.02/112
Steele's Mian Beata	Hans von Birdbuster/Steele's Titanium Gun	Michael Hall/Donald Steele	06.05.04/112
Steele's Precious Gem	Hans von Birdbuster/Steele's Titanium Gun	Donald Steele	06.05.04/112
Steele's Silver Fox Fawn	Hans von Birdbuster/Steele's Titanium Gun	Cary Armbruster/Donald Steele	06.05.04/108
Steele's Titanium Gun	VC Magnum Gunnar Silvershot/Steele's Shooting Star	Donald Steele	05.07.00/112
Strike it Rich Millertime Welm	Wyndom Garth the Great/Gerorge and Julie's Gem	Joseph Delaney/Michael Cimaroli	05.03.08/105
Taga v. Nimrod's Radreiter	Efer v Nimrod's Cruxrad/Kipud v Nimrod's Radreiter	Harry Hirschhorn/Susan Wagner	04.14.84/112
Timberdoodle Black Velvet	Sandbar Echoin' Cowboy Colt/Grayangel Kodiak II	Camille Rice	05.19.07/112
Tortuga Paloma	Shadowmar Excalibur/Redhill's Ad Lib of Tortuga	Molly Vitale/Robert Sanchez	09.12.81/112
Trax Thunder Thighs	Starfire Cash Flow Trouble/Regen's Rip Tide	Shirley Nilsson	09.14.08/106
Weatherrun Automatic Overdrive	Weatherrun Just Do It V Stealyka/Weatherrun ClassicalJaz Kelco	Robert McLeod	08.04.06/112
Weimshadow Cross the Rockies	Von Weiner-N-Weimshadow Maxx/Little Edith Ann von Mac	Jack Scullion/Sally Jo Hoaglund	06.09.02/112 09.22.02/112
Weimshadow Drake of the North	Von Weiner-N-Weimshadow Maxx/Weimshadow SterlinsilverJoy	Mike Kostelecky/Sally Jo Hoaglund	04.24.04/112
Weimshadow Huntsabird	Von Weiner-N-Weimshadow Maxx/Little Edith Ann von Mac	Sally Jo Hoaglund	09.22.02/112
Weimshadow's Hunting Spree	Von Weiner-N-Weimshadow Maxx/Weimshadow SterlinsilverJoy	Sally Jo Hoaglund	09.21.03/112
Westend's Coolest Lite	Northernlights This BudsForU/Grau Geist's My Tmaus B Westwind	Debra Meifert/Myron Meifert	05.29.05/107
Westend's Jetson	Grau Geist Lil's Gust v. Westend/Abigail vom Blocksberg	Katrina Neufeld/ Debra Meifert	08.23.08/112

Several Weimaraners performed at the Prize I level on multiple occasions. Often times, this was done as an attempt to re-qualify for the Invitational. VC Luke der Humdinger leads the way, having turned in four Prize I performances. VC Skeeter's Tannerbaum sits in second place, having been a three-time Prize I performer. Both Lilith v. Hirschorn and Silvershot's Mirage both have accomplished this twice.

Steele's Mian Beata's (Bea) performance and maximum score of 204 in 2005 led to a couple of other remarkable firsts for the Weimaraner breed. First, Bea became the first and only female to date to earn the honor of a maximum UT score. Second, she became the first Weimaraner to earn a maximum score in both the NA test and the UT.

Over the past 40 years, Weimaraners have participated in the Invitational Test on 12 occasions. Three were able to successfully complete this strenuous evaluation. VC Magnum Gunnar Silvershot was the first to accomplish this in 1998. In 2007, VC Luke der Humdinger, owned and handled by Rahl Hoeptner, joined Gunnar among the NAVHDA elite with his score of 187. Most recently, Gerald Geister and his

Table 14-11: *NAVHDA Utility Prize Is 1969–2008 (maximum scores appear in bold type).*

Dog	Sire/Dam	Owner/Breeder	Date/Score
Grey Wynn Franklin's Freedom	**Grey Wynn Slick Chipper** **Grey Wynn Total Eclipse**	**Mark Colantuno** **Kenneth Miller**	**09.21.03/204**
Leaping Leopold Garnett	Casper Musick Stormy VI	Derrick Garnett Donna Musick	08.26.01/198
Lilith v. Hirschhorn	Braunhildes Silver Blaze Crook N Nanny's Tosca	Ellen Hirschorn Marie Seidelman	09.05.77/187
VC Luke der Humdinger	**Kugel vom Blum** **Jill die Humdinger**	**Rahl Hoeptner** **Herbert Hoeptner**	03.01.03/190 02.24.06/197 **02.26.06/204** 03.04.07/199
VC Magnum Gunnar Silvershot	**Green Acres Good Grief Colby** **Dustivelvet's Spring Rain**	**Judy Balog** **Kathleen Elkins**	**09.20.97/204**
PikQwik Morgen Reiteralm	VC Magnum Gunnar Silvershot Arimarlisa Rona von Reiteralm	Anthony Griffore Cheryl Potter	08.23.03/192
Regen's Summer Blaze	Jak's Repeat Offender SkyHi's EZ Magical Reign	Shirley Nilsson Judith Voris	09.10.04/195
Rockville's Truman Greystone	**Windwalkers Graeagle** **Windwalker's Felicity v. Gaul**	**Frank Sommer** **Kristina Muratori**	**11.12.06/204** **10.27.07/204**
Shadowmar Hunter Jake	Reichenstadt's Majestic Dauntmar's Silver Splendoress	Allen Rapp D. Remensnyder	04.08.78/201
Silvershot's Mirage v. Reiteralm	Snake Breaks Saga v. Reiteralm Reiteralm's Absolute Point	Gerald Gertiser, II Steven Keene	07.29.07/199 10.04.08/197
Skeeter's Tannerbaum	**Gray Shadow Ghostbuster** **McLeod's Unser Shatze**	**Gerald Gertiser, II** **Karla McLeod**	**06.06.04/204** 10.02.05/201 08.25/07/201
Steele's Mian Beata	**Hans von Birdbuster** **Steele's Titanium Gun**	**Michael Hall** **Donald Steele**	**06.04.05/204**
Steele's Precious Gem	Hans von Birdbuster Steele's Titanium Gun	Donald Steele	06.04.05/196
Steele's Titanium Gun	VC Magnum Gunnar Silvershot Steele's Shooting Star	Donald Steele	08.24.02/190
Weatherrun's Perfect Storm	Weatherrun Arokat Spindrifter Weatherrun Lady in Red	Robert McLeod Christine Richey	09.09.07/195
Weimshadow SterlinsilverJoy	Weimshadow's Double-D Dillon Little Edith Ann von Mac	Sally Jo Hoaglund	05.14.05/195
Windancers Jota v. Reiteralm	Westend's Li'l Sage Rider Reiteralms Sandbar Snake Break	Brian Wayson Sandy West	05.03.08/201

Figure 14-28: *Hans von Birdbuster* earned an NAVHDA NA perfect score and a UT II. His litter by Steele's Titanium Gun (also an NA perfect score and UT I) produced nine NA prizes, of which six were Prize Is, including four perfect scores.

VC Skeeter's Tannerbaum accomplished this with a score of 198 in 2008. Although nine other times Weimaraners participated unsuccessfully in the Invitational Test, the dogs and their handlers deserve a lot of credit just for rising to this challenge. Among the other Invitational participants were Silvershot's Mirage, Weatherun's Perfect Storm, Rockville's Truman Greystone, Steele's Mian Beata, and Steele's Precious Gem.

Two other Weimaraners, in addition to Magnum Gunnar Silvershot, were honored by having their pictures appear on the cover of the *Versatile Hunting Dog* magazine in 2005. Steve Graham's Panu zum Laubwald, a longhaired Weimaraner, graced the cover in April, and in October, it was Mark Colantuna's Grey Wynn Franklin's Freedom. These appearances marked only the second and third times that Weimaraners appeared on the cover of the *Versatile Hunting Dog* magazine.

The German Connection

While NAVHDA tests were modeled on German tests, there are some major differences between the two systems. Primarily, the German tests highly value the dog's skills in the recovery of wounded or downed game, placing tracking skills in high esteem. While working furred game is optional in NAVHDA, most German tests require work on furred game in addition to upland game birds and waterfowl.

The organization that is responsible for testing and keeping records for all versatile pointing breeds in Europe is the Jagdgebrauchshund-Verband (JGHV), or German Versatile Hunting Dog Association (www.jghv.de/). Under this umbrella organization are the various European breed clubs, including the Weimaraner Klub e. V., as well as a North American affiliate, the Jagdgebrauchshund Verein (JGV-

Figure 14-29: *Steele's Mian Beata,* MH, SDX, RDX, V, NA1, UT1, owned, trained, and handled by Michael Hall, was the first Weimaraner to earn maximum scores in both the NA test and UT. Her mother, Steele's Titanium Gun, and her sister Steele's Precious Gem also earned NA and UT Prize Is. A special salute is given to her breeder, Donald Steele, for his efforts in producing these talented NAVHDA competitors.

Figure 14-30: *The Weimaraner Ways Gunnar Memorial Trophy* is awarded to any Weimaraner that earns her first maximum score of 204 in the NAVHDA UT. It is hoped that such recognition will encourage Weimaraner owners to not only participate in NAVHDA activities at the NA level but to continue to strive for excellence in the advanced level as well.

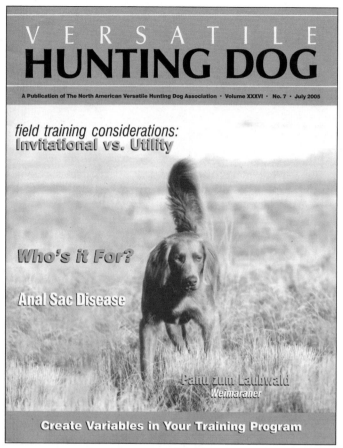

Figure 14-31: *Panu zum Laubwald,* JH, NA1, UPT3, UT3, VJP, HZP, owned, trained, and handled by Steve Graham, bred by Dr. Hans Schmidt (Germany). Piezl tested not only in NAVHDA but also in the US-JGHV. Piezl is one of only three Weimaraners to appear on the NAVHDA cover and the only longhair to do so.

USA), that offer the JGHV tests in North America and report the results of those tests back to Germany.

In order to participate in JGHV tests, Weimaraners must be registered with the Federation Cynologique Internationale (FCI), not necessarily an easy task unless the dog is imported from Europe; dogs with only AKC or CKC registration are not eligible to participate even if the test is held in North America.

A few Americans have taken advantage of the opportunity to test their German-import Weimaraners in the JGHV test system by traveling to Europe to compete there; others have participated in the JGHV tests held in the United States.

The Verbands-Jugend-Prüfung (VJP) is similar to the NAVHDA NA test. It is designed to evaluate the inherited hunting attributes of young dogs. It is held in the spring for puppies born in the previous year or the last 3 months of the previous year. The dog is scored on nose, field search, pointing, tracking, cooperation, gun sensitivity, and desire to work, as well as being examined for physical deficiencies and temperament faults.

The Verbands-Herbstzucht-Prüfung (HZP) is a more advanced test of natural ability, and in the test the dog is also expected to show that it has had some formal training. The HZP is taken in the fall of the year in which the dog is eligible for the VJP. The dog is scored on all the elements of the VJP and, in addition, is rated on desire and water work, including tracking a swimming duck and the blind retrieve of a duck and 150- and 300-m-long tracks to retrieve feathered and furred game that has been dragged. The dog is expected to demonstrate a good degree of obedience and a formal retrieve in all test categories.

For both of the junior-level tests, each test element is scored as follows: 0 = failing, 1–2 = unsatisfactory, 3–5 = satisfactory, 6–8 = good, 9–11 = very good, 12 = excellent. A score of 11 or 12 can be given only in certain categories and only if the dog has demonstrated excellence despite encountering a particularly difficult situation—a condition that might not present itself in every test. The maximum score available in all obedience areas is 10. For each testing category there is a multiplication factor, ranging from 1 to 3, depending on the relative importance placed on that quality. In the VJP test, a pup that scored 8 in each test category would have an overall score of 56. Due to the added elements in the HZP test, a dog that receives an 8 in each HZP category would receive a total score of 144.

The Verbands-Gebrauchsprüfung (VGP) is a two-day test held each fall that evaluates the abilities of the fully trained versatile hunting dog in 18 different hunting situations. In addition to a more advanced level of field and water work than was required in the VJP and HZP tests, the VGP also entails the retrieve of a dead fox and a 400-m-long blood track that simulates a wounded deer or other large game. The dog is expected to be steady to wing and shot on all birdwork and to successfully work independent of the handler on both land and water. A high value is placed on obedience in the VGP, with the dog expected to be under complete control at all times.

In this test, the dog and handler are judged as a team in a total of 26 test categories. The VGP scoring scheme is a four-point system: 0 = failing, 1 = deficient, 3 = good, 4 = very good, 4h = excellent. The passing scores are designated with both point total and prize classification; for example, VGP II/300 means a Prize II with 300 points. To meet each prize classification, the dog and handler team must achieve a minimum point total and demonstrate qualifying performance in selected essential categories.

The Verbands-Schweißprüfungen (VSwP, or Blood Tracking Test) provides the opportunity to further evaluate a dog on a 20- or 40-hour blood track, with notation made if the dog gives voice on the track.

The testing system for German Weimaraners is completed by breed shows where conformation is more formally evaluated and a written critique provided, X-rays are taken to evaluate the dog's hips for hip dysplasia, and tests are performed of guarding instinct and temperament.

A few North Americans have taken advantage of the opportunity to compete on both sides of the Atlantic in recent years. Chad Gelderloos and his German import, Baltur von Hubertus, have competed in NAVHDA as well as earning a VJP in Germany and an HZP through an American JGHV club.

Sal Casteneda and his dogs have also earned titles in both the American NAVHDA system and the European evaluations. His longhaired Weimarener, Quell, participated in the VJP in Germany and prized in NAVHDA titles in the U.S. In addition to participating in the HZP in Germany, Komet, Casteneda's short coated male, passed the Wasser Prüfung in Austria before returning to the U.S. for the NAVHDA NA and UT.

These owners, and a number of others, have taken advantage of the dual registration of their imported dogs to not only develop the abilities of their dogs, but to foster positive relationships and the exchange of knowledge between Weimaraner enthusiasts in several countries.

The Breeders

The recent success of the Weimaraner in NAVHDA events is attributable to the breeders' use of the system as an evaluation tool. Some Weimaraner breeders have begun breeding specifically for NAVHDA events, while others are using the test results as a cornerstone in their versatile breeding program.

Figure 14-32: *A few of the dual registered (AKC and JGHV) Weimaraners* that have traveled with their owners to Europe to successfully compete in Weimaraner Klub e. V. **(a)** CH Herwig's Komet von Reiteralm, NA (112), HZP, and Sal Castaneda; Kosmo earned his NA in the U.S. and his HZP in Germany. **(b)** Quell zum Laubwald NA, UT, VJP, and Sal Casteneda earned a NAVHDA NA and UT in the U.S. and a VJP in Europe. **(c)** Baltur von Hubertus, NA (112), VJP, HZP, and Chad Gelderloos earned a VJP in Europe, as well as a NAVHDA NA and a JGHV, VGP, and HZP in the U.S.

Figure 14-33: *Although the NAVHDA testing is strongly patterned after the German performance examinations,* one of the major differences at all levels is that the German programs place a strong emphasis on furred game in contrast to the NAVHDA focus on feathered game. In NAVHDA, the UPT and UT tests allow the handler to provide furred game for the drag if desired; in Germany, the dog must be tested on furred game as well as feathered. While NAVHDA does not provide advanced testing for blood or game tracking, such titles are highly prized in Germany. More in-depth information on this subject can be found in Chapter 35, *The German Weimaraner Today.* Photograph by Mimmi Erixon, Sweden, reprinted with permission of Deborah Andrews, *The Weimaraner Memory Book,* 2003.

Helene Moore and her husband Richard have been breeding Weimaraners for this purpose far longer than most other breeders. Their Sirius Kennels produced the first two NAVHDA NA Breeder's Awards and three of the first five of these awards. In all, 15 different dogs out of the Sirius Kennels have competed in NAVHDA events.

Altogether, there have been 17 different litters that have earned the distinction of being a NAVHDA NA Breeder's Award-winning litter. To earn this distinction, four members of a NAVHDA-registered litter must earn prizes in a NA test with an average score of 90 points or higher. Fifteen out of these 17 award-winning litters have been recognized since

2000. The Moores and their Sirius Kennels have earned three Breeder's Awards, while Cheryl Potter and Barbara Walsh's Pikqwik's Kennel and Sally Jo Hoaglund's Weimshadow Kennels have each earned two such awards.

Through 2004, Sally Jo's Weimshadow Kennels has had 14 different dogs examined as a part of the NAVHDA system. In 17 out of 20 (or 85%) of the tests in which they have participated, the Weimshadow dogs have earned a prize. This is a tribute not only to her breeding program but to her ability to find appropriate homes for the type of dogs that she is producing. Although genetics is a major component in any dog's hunting ability or test performance, the exposure they receive is a great and necessary aspect in developing these inherited abilities.

Two extremely experienced Weimaraner enthusiasts earned their first NA Breeders Awards in 2007. It is hoped that this marks the start of a regularly occurring trend for these two breeders.

Judy Balog earned an NA Breeder's Award by pairing Grau Geist Lil's Gust v. Westend with Gould's Truly Cool Falls Fun. The sire, Gus, earned a Prize II on his first UT in 2008 at the age of 11.

Aline Scharpf also received her first Breeder's Award for her litter between Aztec's American Pie and Amor's Amsel Zum Ziel. This litter was arguably one of the greatest-achieving litters ever tested in the NA test. Eight of the puppies from this litter earned prizes in the NA test, with two earning maximum scores. The production from this litter inspired a repeating of this breeding.

By far the most common kennel name found in the test records of NAVHDA-tested dogs has been Virginia Alexander's Reiteralm Kennel. More than 30 dogs have been tested that include her kennel name in the dog's registered name. Additionally, the name appears in the pedigree of dozens of other dogs that have been tested through the NAVHDA system. In 2008, Virginia garnered her fourth NA Breeder's Award, becoming the first and only breeder to accomplish this feat.

Virginia's key to success has been her importation and use of the German bloodlines in her breeding program. These German-bred Weimaraners and their ancestors have participated in the JGHV system, which NAVHDA is loosely based upon, for more than half a century. The JGHV system is a far more restrictive registry system than registration organizations commonly used in North America. The JGHV requires every animal to meet a minimum standard of performance in field events prior to being admitted into the breeding and registration program. This system has helped to instill and maintain the hunting instincts in those dogs that were imported and in their offspring.

In 2002, Virginia earned her first NA Breeder's Award with a litter from her German import Cora Von Der Schelmelach, a Prize III–175 UT dog, and VC Magnum

Table 14-12: *NAVHDA Breeders Awards: Weimaraner Litters*

Breeder	Sire	Dam	Whelp Date
Helene and Richard Moore	Texmara's Jeb the Great	Siruis Sweet Samantha	4/28/94
Helene and Richard Moore	VC Magnum Gunnar Silvershot	Sirius Really Rosie	6/6/98
Kim Harter	Grayshar's Royal Valor	Wagners Bella of Starwood	5/17/99
Cheryl Potter, Barbara Walsh, and Virginia Alexander	VC Magnum Gunnar Silvershot	Arimarlisa Rona von Reiteralm	9/16/99
Helene and Richard Moore	Westend's Little Sage Rider	Sirius Really Rosie	5/3/01
Cheryl Potter, Barbara Walsh, and Virginia Alexander	VC Magnum Gunnar Silvershot	Arimarlisa Rona von Reiteralm	5/14/01
Sally Jo Hoaglund	Von Weiner-n-Weimshadow Maxx	Little Edith Ann von Mac	8/10/01
Joe Stroup and Virginia Alexander	VC Magnum Gunnar Silvershot	Cora von der Schelmelach	12/10/02
Sally Jo Hoaglund	Von Weiner-n-Weimshadow Maxx	Weimshadow Sterlinsilverjoy	1/9/03
Susan K. O'Donnell	Axel Reiteralm of Weimar's Joy	Gunmettle's Song in the Shadows	10/17/02
Donald Steele	Hans von Birdbuster	Steele's Titanium Gun	3/28/03
Mark Caluntuno	Grey Wynn Franklin's Freedom	Westend's Buck'n the Wind	4/4/05
Joe Stroup and Virginia Alexander	Snake Breaks Saga v. Reiteralm	Cora von der Schelmelach	12/14/05
Judy Balog	Grau Geist Lil's Gust v. Westend	Gould's Truly Cool Falls Fun	4/9/2006
Aline Scharpf	Aztec's American Pie	Amor's Amsel Zum Ziel	9/17/06
Susan Wallace	Snake Breaks Saga v. Reiteralm	Silberkinder Miss Money Penny	4/21/06
Julie Brooks and Virginia Alexander	VC Luke Der Humdinger	Axel's Bina von Hubertus	4/08/07

Gunnar Silvershot. This breeding was the first pairing between two UT-prized Weimaraners. The following year, Hans von Birdbuster was bred to Steele's Titanium Gun to replicate this accomplishment.

As of yet, no pair of Prize I–winning NAHVDA dogs have been bred together. In addition, no Weimaraner breeding has earned a UT Breeder's Award. To do this, three individuals from a litter must earn prizes with a score of 190 points or better. Several kennels seem to be on the verge of doing so, but as of yet, it has not been accomplished.

NAVHDA Competitors Branch Out

For some, training for and competing in NAVHDA tests is an entry point into AKC and WCA events, and many of the top NAVHDA-titled dogs have excelled in other competitive venues.

Figure 14-34: *The first time an entire Weimaraner litter* achieved NAVHDA NA Prize Is, the June 2002 event also marked the first time four littermates received Prize Is at the same test, earning Cheryl Potter and Barbara Walsh their second NA Breeder's Award. This was a repeat of the CH Arimarlisa's Rona v. Reiteralm and VC CH Magnum's Gunnar Silvershot breeding, which earned PiqQwik their first NA Breeder's Award.

Three of the Steele NAVHDA stars also hold AKC MH titles and advanced WCA Shooting and Retrieving Ratings: Steele's Mian Beata, Steele's Precious Gem, and Steele's Titanium Gun.

Highly successful Weimshadow NAVHDA competitors have also distinguished themselves in other venues, with Weimshadow Across the Rockies also holding an AKC MH title and a number of Weimshadow NAVHDA competitors having also earned AKC obedience titles.

VC Magnum Gunnar Silvershot earned an AKC Dual Championship and MH title, twice placed second in the WCA National Amateur Field Championship, and earned WCA SDX and RDX level ratings.

The Regen Kennel sets an example that many breeders are striving for, a truly versatile family dog. Not only has Regen produced the only two Triple Champions in the breed (for the story of Ruby and Diesel, see Chapter 3, *The WCA*, and Chapter 32, *Dual and Triple Champions*), the progeny from these lines continually succeed in a variety of other events. In a little more than 12 years, Regen has produced 26 WCA VX dogs (including VX5 and 6), 10 SDX, 16 RDX,

25 AKC Hunting titles, and 18 NAVHDA titles (including eight NA maximum scores). While Regen dogs are successfully competing, they also strive to maintain the heritage of the Weimaraner as a versatile family hunting dog and companion; Regen believes that NAVHDA provides a strong grounding for future success as a personal gun dog as well as other venues.

All of the Sirius dogs descend from Greysport Perfect Peach, who held AKC obedience, tracking, and hunt test titles, and 82% of the Sirius-bred dogs have been NAVHDA tested. Many of the Sirius NAVHDA-titled dogs have also gone on to achieve success in other venues. A remarkable three of those have become AKC Dual Champions: Sirius Really Rosie was the first Dual Champion Weimaraner to produce two Dual Champions: Sirius Peppermint Schnapps and Sirius Mostly Mongo. Rosie also won a WCA Regional Classic Open Gun Dog stake and AKC Obedience and Hunt Test titles. Pepper was a WCA Top 10 Gun Dog. Mongo won his WCA Field Futurity and then broke the bank by winning the WCA Top Open Gun Dog at the tender age of three.

Figure 14-35: *Sirius success.* Dick and Helene Moore with five of their home-bred champions: Polly, Mongo, Pepper, Maggie, and Tanker. The 23 dogs that carry the Sirius prefix have earned 77 working titles from WCA, NAVHDA and AKC, as well as an additional eight Bench CH, three Field CH, and the 2005 National Field Championship, plus honorary titles (such as the V and VX) and three NAVHDA NA Breeder's awards.

Closing Thoughts

The purpose of this chapter was threefold. First and foremost, the chapter was written to celebrate and honor the breeders, owners, and dogs who have turned in memorable and inspiring performances in the NAVHDA testing system.

Second, the information was assembled to help acknowledge NAVHDA's existence and its unrivaled ability to serve as a testing and breed-development program for all versatile hunting breeds in North America. The data clearly demonstrates improved performances from the Weimaraners participating in NAVHDA over the past 40 years. This in turn leads to better, more productive hunting dogs that fulfill the purpose for which the breed was originally created.

Finally, this chapter was written to inspire Weimaraner owners to get involved in NAVHDA events and to continue using the system as a breed development tool. The breed will, no doubt, be better for it. The past 10 years have marked a dramatic upswing for the Weimaraner competing in NAVHDA. The Weimaraner is just one of many versatile hunting breeds that have benefited from having an evaluation system that realistically assesses the majority of the skills that the German Weimaraner was originally bred to undertake. After all, the NAVHDA system best replicates the system under which the Weimaraner was developed and allowed to gain its prominence in Germany.

It is hoped that this information will contribute to the continued growth of participation and the performance of Weimaraners in NAVHDA events in the future. This would ultimately allow the Weimaraner to regain the reputation it once had as a truly outstanding versatile hunting breed. While NAVHDA provides the Weimaraner owner with the opportunity to lay an excellent foundation for a personal gun dog, as well as developing other aspects of the Weimaraner's natural heritage, it also provides a wonderful stepping stone to prepare the Weimaraner and the owner mentally as well as physically for venturing into an ever-increasing variety of field, water, and performance events.

Figure 14-36: ***Celebrating at the 2007 NAVHDA Invitational,*** Luke and Rahl have just completed the demanding search test, to become the breed's second NAVHDA Versatile Champion; when the results were announced, this team had earned 196 out of 200 points. The Hoeptners' Humdinger lines are one of the longest still-active programs in the United States, breeding and training for more than 50 years. Beginning with Anka's becoming the first dog to earn a WCA rating (an RD) in 1960 (see Figure 13-14), the Hoeptners have bred litters A–L, following the German tradition of naming the puppies through an alphabetical progression. Luke, from their most recent litter, and the great-great-great-great-great-grandson of Anka, continues the fine tradition of hunting companions. He is the only Weimaraner to earn four NAVHDA Utility Prize Is before finally ringing the bell to crown his NAVHDA career with a Versatile Championship.

Table 14-13: NAVHDA Chapters in the United States.

Alaska (ANCHORAGE)	GREATLAND	www.greatlandnavhda.org
Arizona (ARIZONA)	GRAND CANYON OF ARIZONA	www.azteclobo.com/navhda/
California (CARLSBAD)	CALIFORNIA BACKCOUNTRY	
California (SACRAMENTO)	GREAT CENTRAL VALLEY	
California (SAN DIEGO)	SAN DIEGO	www.sandiegonavhda.com
California (SOUTHERN)	SOUTHERN CALIFORNIA	www.socalnavhda.com
Colorado (DENVER)	ROCKY MOUNTAIN	www.rmc-navhda.com
Connecticut (CT, MA and RI)	SOUTHERN NEW ENGLAND	www.snenavhda.org
Delaware (CENTRAL)	DELMARVA	www.delmarvanavhda.org
Florida (ORLANDO)	FLORIDA PALMETTO	www.floridapalmettonavhda.org
Idaho (MERIDIAN)	TREASURE VALLEY	
Illinois (NORTH CENTRAL)	ILLINOIS	www.illinoisnavhda.org
Illinois (NORTHERN)	NORTHERN ILLINOIS	www.ninavhda.org
Illinois (CENTRAL ILLINOIS)	SPOON RIVER	www.spoonrivernavhda.org
Indiana (INDIANAPOLIS)	CENTRAL INDIANA	www.centralindiananavhda.com
Iowa (IOWA)	HAWKEYE	www.iowahawkeyenavhda.org
Iowa (QUAD CITIES)	WESTERN ILLINOIS	www.westernillinoisnavhda.org
Maine (UPPER)	SEBASTICOOK	www.sebasticook.com
Maine (NORTHERN NEW ENGLAND)	YANKEE	www.yankeenavhda.org
Maryland (MARYLAND/VIRGINIA)	POTOMAC	www.potomacnavhda.com/
Michigan (KALAMAZOO)	MICHIGAN	www.michigannavhda.com
Michigan (TRAVERSE CITY)	NORTHERN MICHIGAN	www.nmnavhda.org
Michigan (DETROIT)	SOUTHEASTERN MICHIGAN	www.seminavhda.com
Minnesota (MINNEAPOLIS-VIRGINIA)	MINNESOTA	www.mnnavhda.com
Minnesota (SOUTHERN)	SOUTHERN MINNESOTA	www.somnnavhda.com
Minnesota (ST CROIX VALLEY MN and WI)	ST CROIX	www.scnavhda.org
Missouri (NW MO, NE KANSAS)	BIG MUDDY	www.bigmuddynavhda.org
Missouri (COLUMBIA)	MISSOURI UPLANDS	www.mouplands.org
Montana (MONTANA)	BIG SKY	www.bigskynavhda.com
Nebraska (OMAHA, NE)	HEARTLAND	www.heartlandnavhda.com
Nebraska (NEBRASKA)	SANDHILLS	www.nebraskasandhillschapter.com
New Hampshire (LONDONBERRY)	MERRIMACK VALLEY	www.mvnavhda.org
New Jersey (JACKSON)	DELAWARE VALLEY	www.delvalnavhda.com
New Mexico (NEW MEXICO)	ZIA	www.navhda-zia.com/
New York (BUFFALO-ROCHESTER)	FINGER LAKES	www.flnavhda.com
New York (MID HUDSON RIVER)	HUDSON VALLEY	www.hvnavhda.org
New York (ROCK TAVERN)	ROCK TAVERN	www.rocktavernnavhda.com/
New York (S. ADIRONDACK and E VT)	SOUTHERN ADIRONDACK	www.sacnavhda.com
New York (GREENE)	SOUTHERN TIER OF NEW YORK	www.southerntier-navhda.org
North Carolina (CHARLOTTE)	CAROLINAS	www.carolinas-navhda.com/index.html
North Dakota (BISMARCK,MANDAN)	CENTRAL DAKOTA	www.centradakotanavhda.com
North Dakota (FARGO)	RED RIVER VALLEY	www.rrvnavhda.org
Ohio (E OH, W PA)	BUCKEYE	www.buckeye-chapter-navhda.com
Ohio (CENTRAL OHIO)	MID-OHIO	www.midohionavhda.com
Ohio (W PA,E OHIO, WEST VA)	SHENANGO	www.shenangonavhda.com/
Oklahoma (TULSA)	OK-NAVHDA	www.oknavhda.com
Oregon (WASHINGTON, OREGON)	PACIFIC NORTHWEST	www.pnwnavhda.com
Oregon (EUGENE)	WILLAMETTE VALLEY	www.wvnavhda.com
Pennsylvania (EASTERN)	BUSHKILL - EASTERN PA	www.bushkillnavhda.com
Pennsylvania (LEHIGH VALLEY/POCONO)	HICKORY RUN	www.hickoryrunnavhda.com
Pennsylvania (HARRISBURG)	KEYSTONE	www.keystonenavhda.com
Pennsylvania (CENTRAL)	NITTANY	
Pennsylvania (CENTRAL PA)	SUSQUEHANNA	www.susquehannanavhda.com
South Carolina (COLUMBIA)	SOUTH CAROLINA	
South Dakota (NEBRASKA and MINNESOTA)	MIDWEST TRI STATE	www.midwesttristatenavhda.org
South Dakota (SIOUX FALLS and SE, SD)	SOUTH DAKOTA	
Tennessee (TN, KY, AL, AR, MS, GA, TX)	MID SOUTH	www.home.comcast.net/~midsouthnavhda/
Texas (HOUSTON)	LONE STAR	www.lonestarnavhda.org/
Utah (PROVO)	WASATCH MOUNTAIN	
Virginia (WARSAW)	RAPPAHANNOCK	
West Virginia (WV, KY and SOUTHERN OHIO)	APPALACHIAN VALLEY	www.avc-navhda.com
Wisconsin (WEST BEND)	KETTLE MORAINE	www.kmnavhda.com
Wisconsin (WISCONSIN RAPIDS)	NORTH CENTRAL WISCONSIN	www.ncwnavhda.com
Wisconsin (MILWAUKEE-MADISON)	WISCONSIN	www.winavhda.com
Wisconsin (MADISON)	WISCONSIN RIVER	www.wrcnavhda.com
Wyoming (CHEYENNE)	FRONTIER	

Remember that NAVDHA restricts NA Prize awards to dogs between 6 and 16 months. Therefore, it is necessary for the owner to plan well in advance; NAVHDA rules restrict the number of dogs that can be tested at an event, so opportunities are limited. Available slots fill quickly as soon as the entries open, and within days dogs are being placed on the "reserve list." It might not be a bad idea to plan for several tests as soon as the puppy comes of age! Contact the NAVHDA Office for advance information and establish contacts with nearby clubs for planned tests.

For more information about NAVHDA:
P.O. Box 520,
Arlington Heights, IL 60006
Phone: (847) 253-6488
Email: navoffice@aol.com
Website: www.navhda.org

If there is not a chapter in your area, consider starting one!

Figure 14-37: *VC Skeeter's Tannerbaum became the third Weimaraner* ever to successfully complete the Invitational Test in the fall of 2008 with a score of 198 points. Skeeter is owned, trained, and handled by Gerald Geister. The pair spends hours together in the forests of Michigan hunting grouse and woodcock. They also spend hours at work together at the urgent care facility Gerald operates. This is another great example of the versatility of the Weimaraner breed. Next year, Gerald hopes to become the first handler to have two dogs successfully pass the Invitational Test, as his female, Silvershot's Mirage v. Reiteralm, is eligible for the 2009 Invitational. Photograph by Judy Balog.

Figure 15-1: *Since Carole Donaldson's untimely passing in 2006, the Carole Donaldson Memorial Trophy* has been awarded each year to the Best Bred by Exhibitor entry at the WCA National Specialty. Win or lose, always the consummate sportswoman, Carole was a role model to aspiring breeders and believed there was no greater thrill than to be the breeder, owner, AND handler of a winning dog. Large specialty classes may often come down to the final evaluation, where the judge asks that all the remaining dogs be free-baited; Carole (in red) and Allie (BIS CH Tri-D's Grand Finale) exemplify their belief that showmanship and soundness can be presented on its own four feet without the hands-on assistance of a handler. Photograph by Ginger Spreen.

CHAPTER 15

SHOWING THE WEIMARANER

Dog showing is an exciting—and addictive—sport, and many owners enjoy handling their own Weimaraners. Even those who lack the athletic coordination to handle well can participate in all phases of preparation, and professional handlers appreciate a dog that is ready to win at its first show.

Except for the fortunate few who grow up in families that show dogs, most dog owners are in their twenties or thirties before going to their first dog shows. Therefore, rest assured that most exhibitors and bystanders are sympathetic and willing to help the novice. It is not necessary to preface each query with, "I know this is a dumb question, but...." This chapter presents basic information about dog shows, training, and ring procedures that will, hopefully, provide many of the answers.

About Dog Shows

Champions

To become an AKC champion, a dog must win a minimum of 15 points under at least three different judges. From 1–5 points (based on the number competing) are awarded at a show. The points schedule, which is annually revised by the AKC, varies between breeds and between geographic areas. It is based on the number of dogs and bitches of the breed that competed at shows during the preceding 3 years. To ensure that every champion has competed against large entries, each must win at least two majors (shows awarding 3–5 points) under two different judges.

Types of Shows and Classes

The most common type of show is the all-breed show, which is open to all AKC-registered dogs. An all-breed dog club may sponsor two shows a year, selecting the judges and grounds and managing all physical aspects. Most clubs elect to use the services of licensed show superintendents, who send out premium lists, compile show catalogs, and complete the records required by the AKC.

A dog show proceeds in a quiet, orderly fashion with dogs entering the ring, being judged, and leaving. A show catalog is the only way for spectators to identify the competitors and follow the judging.

ORGANIZATION OF DOG SHOWS

DOG CLASSES
Puppy 6–9 months
Puppy 9–12 months
Puppy 12–18 months
Novice
Bred by Exhibitor
American Bred
Open

BITCH CLASSES
Puppy 6–9 months
Puppy 9–12 months
Puppy 12–18 months
Novice
Bred by Exhibitor
American Bred
Open

WINNERS CLASS
(Class Winners)

WINNERS CLASS
(Class Winners)

Reserve Winners Dog

WINNERS DOG

WINNERS BITCH

Reserve Winners Dog

BEST OF BREED CLASS
Specials (champions)
Winners Dog
Winners Bitch

Best of Winners

Best of Opposite Sex

GROUP CLASSES
(All Breed Winners)

Sporting	Hound
Working	Terrier
Toy	Herding
Non-Sporting	

BEST IN SHOW CLASS
(All Group Winners)

BEST IN SHOW WINNER

Figure 15-2: *Non-regular classes* are becoming more frequent at specialty shows. Chris Grisell (to the judge's right) of Nani's Weimaraners is shown taking the breeder's class, offered for the first time at the Weimaraner National Specialty in 2006. Differing from the more common stud or brood bitch class, where the progeny of a single parent are judged, this class requires that at least three or more different parents be represented among the three to five dogs presented. Destined to become popular among fanciers, this class gives breeders the opportunity to showcase the direction of their breeding program. Photograph by Suzanne Mayhew.

Class dogs and bitches are those that have not finished championships; they are shown in puppy (6–9, 9–12, and 12–18 months), novice, bred-by-exhibitor, American-bred, and open classes. All classes are offered at every show, but some classes may have no entries. Specials are AKC champions that compete only for best of breed and best of opposite sex.

The dog (male) classes are judged first. Then, the winners of each class compete in winners class for winners dog (WD) and the championship points, which are determined by the number of males defeated. After the winners dog leaves the ring, the dog that placed second in that class returns to the ring and competes against the other class winners for reserve winners dog (RWD). Very rarely, the AKC later disqualifies the winners dog (for example, because of an irregularity in ownership or registration); the points are then transferred to the RWD. The bitch classes are judged in the same manner.

Judging for best of breed commences when all of the champions have entered the ring, followed by winners dog and winners bitch. The judge selects best of breed and best of opposite sex. The best-of-breed winner goes on to com-

pete in the sporting group and, winning that, may then compete against other group winners for best in show.

While judging the best-of-breed class, the judge also selects either the winners dog or winners bitch as best of winners. Best of winners can be an extremely important award. The number of points awarded to winners dog and winners bitch is often different, and the best of winners may win additional points if the number won by the opposite sex is greater. For example, if winners dog wins 1 point and winners bitch wins 3 points, the male may win 2 additional points by being best of winners.

A specialty show is one that is sponsored by an independent breed club. The specialty may be either independent or in conjunction with an all-breed show. If the specialty is independent, the highest award is best of breed. Specialties attract large entries because clubs offer trophies for all classes, sometimes for all placements. In addition to regular classes, specialty shows offer non-regular classes for stud dog, brood bitch, field-trial dog and bitch, and veteran dog and bitch.

A sweepstakes is a group of irregular classes in which a portion of the entry fees is awarded to the winners. Although

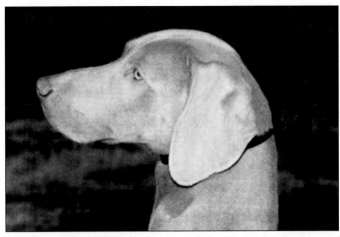

Figure 15-3: *Skillful collar and leash placement* can hide many faults. **(a)** A short neck and wet throat like this are a fault. **(b)** Careful placement of the lead disguises it effectively.

traditionally held for puppies and sometimes adults up to 24 months old, most clubs now offer sweepstakes for veterans, as well.

An AKC-sanctioned (licensed) all-breed match is an informal show sponsored by an all-breed club, in which dogs, handlers, and judges practice and develop their skills. No points are awarded. Entries are usually taken the day of the match, but many all-breed matches have become so large that some clubs require advance entries. The usual dog and bitch classes are 3- to 6-month puppy, 6- to 9-month puppy, 9- to 12-month puppy, and adult; many matches do not allow dogs with 3 or more points to compete. Puppy and adult best-of-breed winners compete in puppy and adult groups and ultimately for best puppy and best adult in match.

Independent breed clubs also sponsor sanctioned matches, and many enjoy nonlicensed fun matches, which are even less formal. These "grassroots" dog shows provide an opportunity to practice handling skills, train puppies, and hold a picnic.

Show Training

Getting Started

Early show training produces rewarding results in the mastery of stacking (the show stance) and gaiting (the show trot). A show Weimaraner should be a well-behaved dog that is a pleasure to live and travel with; the early training techniques described in *Weimaraner Kindergarten* provide a solid foundation.

Whenever possible, the puppy and handler should enroll in show handling classes. The puppy learns to associate handling with an exciting car ride, and practice is far less tedious with company. Most all-breed clubs either offer classes or know where they can be found.

The type of collar and lead to buy varies with the dog's age and the amount of control needed while gaiting. Puppies usually begin with a Resco show lead, which has a sliding clip and loop that eliminate the need for a collar. When additional control is needed, change to a nylon choke collar or a fine-link choke chain, which should be just large enough to slip over the dog's head. Nylon choke collars should be a neutral color (white, gray, black, brown)—bright collars are the hallmark of novices. Nylon leads should match nylon collars. Fine leather leads are preferred by many exhibitors. Show leads should be fairly short because excess length is gathered and hidden in the

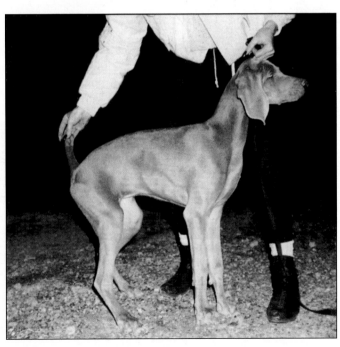

Figure 15-4: *Pressing on its hindquarters* to teach a show or field prospect puppy may lead to problems like this.

Figure 15-5: *Stacking the Weimaraner.*

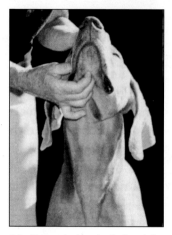

(a) Control the dog's head by grasping the jaw firmly.

(b) Grasping the head with the left hand, shift the dog's weight slightly to the left and pick up the foreleg by the elbow. Rotate the elbow out and place the front leg in a straight position.

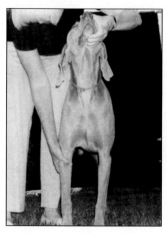

(c) Shift the dog's weight to the right to hold it there.

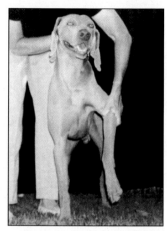

(d) Transfer control of the head to the right hand, reach over the shoulder, and grasp the elbow.

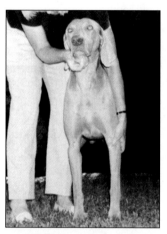

(e) Position the left foreleg.

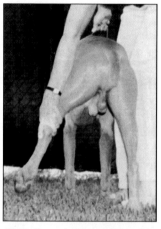

(f) Still reaching over the dog, grasp the left hock.

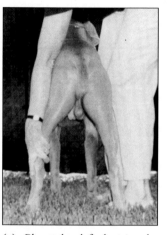

(g) Place the left leg in the desired position.

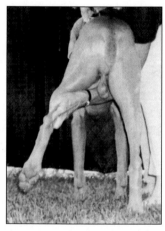

(h) Some handlers prefer reaching under the dog to grasp the left hock.

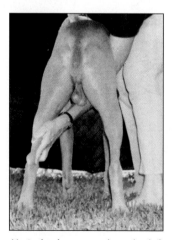

(i) A third way to place the left leg in the desired position.

(j) Lift the dog's head, rocking the dog forward.

(k) Gently raise the tail to a 45-degree angle.

fist while gaiting. (If training a Weimaraner for obedience at the same time as show, using a different collar and lead helps the dog to understand when a different response is expected.)

The correct collar and lead for showing a Weimaraner are any combination that is comfortable for the dog while providing good control for the handler. Weimaraners are highly individual, and the type of collar and the best placement while stacking and gaiting must be discovered by trial and error; there is no convenient formula.

Stacking

Training Tips

Control of the stacked dog begins by controlling the head. The dog's left side always faces the judge, and the head is controlled by the right hand. Place four fingers into the groove of the lower jaw and grasp firmly. If the dog is throaty (has a lot of loose skin on the neck), scoop all of the extra skin into the right hand and present the dog with a tight, lean neck.

Cultivate speed and smoothness by always following the same sequence when placing the feet until little conscious thought is needed. Practice in front of a mirror to get the feel of the most flattering silhouette.

Although the goal is a "plastic" dog that will allow the feet to be placed in any position, do not expect instant cooperation from the puppy! If the puppy has had preliminary training and understands the stand-stay command, the task will be far easier. Remember, Weimaraners tend to grow in sections, and faults come and go until maturity. Concentrate on perfecting steadiness in the show stack; fret about correcting faults when certain they will still be there next month.

As the puppy becomes steady on the stand-stay, vary the routine. Stand in front of the dog for a minute. Walk around and step over the youngster. Teach the puppy that a little stroke of the finger while stacked is a caress. Most Weimaraners do not mind if they think stacking is a big game and that they are having a lot of fun.

The puppy must learn to stand in a stack while being touched all over by strangers, which is another advantage of handling classes. Practice having friends and strangers approach the stacked puppy quietly, offer a hand to sniff, feed the dog a tidbit, and run their hands gently but firmly over the dog.

When stacking has become smooth and automatic, start polishing the routine. When walking into the ring, the Weimaraner often stops with two or three legs correctly placed. The novice begins stacking the dog from scratch, one leg at a time. Experienced handlers know that the judge first looks over the class as a whole, seeing only the dog's profile. They quickly place the legs that are not in correct position for a profile view and have their dogs posed while the novice is still trying to hide flat feet instead of showing off a smashing topline.

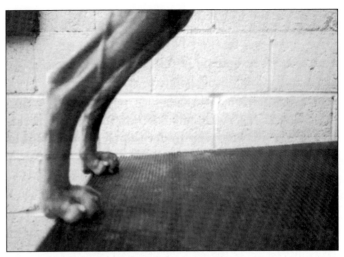

Figure 15-6: *Avoid the habit of rocking back* and teach the dog to lean forward into the stack by placing the pads of the back feet over the edge of the table and giving the command, "Stretch!"

Figure 15-7: *Many successful amateur/owner and professional handlers get started early.* At a recent national specialty, 7-year-old Jakob Randlett Hinman presented 10-year-old CH Graenit's Rushin' Roulette, JH, SD, in the Veteran's class. Although his arms were too short to properly present his dog, Jakob and Kaiya won the hearts of spectators and exhibitors alike. While Junior Showmanship classes require youngsters to be at least 9 years old, younger children may compete in the regular conformation classes. Information on age limits and the rules for Junior Showmanship can be found at www.AKC.org.

Preventing and Correcting Problems

The most frequent stacking problem with Weimaraners is rocking back, an unattractive stance that is often combined with arching the back like a camel. Rocking back expresses passive resistance to being stacked.

The best way to prevent habitual rocking back is to keep the lessons short and interesting. Training in the boring backyard triggers rebellious behavior, which can be minimized by training in a variety of locations. When lessons are preceded by an exciting walk or ride to a park, the puppy may feel less abused and more cooperative. If the puppy does not respond to shorter training sessions and a more interesting environment, return to the basic stand-stay exercise.

Training on a grooming table before moving to the ground teaches the Weimaraner to push forward with the rear legs when stacking, and the same technique is useful for correcting habitual rocking back. Place the pads of the back feet over the edge of the table and give the command, "Stretch!" The Weimaraner quickly discovers that moving a foot or rocking back causes the rear legs to fall off the table. At a show, a curb makes a handy substitute table if a reminder is needed.

For the camel trick, stack the puppy, give the command, and stand back. Even the most stubborn Weimaraner cannot maintain the arched back and braced legs indefinitely, and the teacher must be more stubborn than the student. As soon as the puppy relaxes, release from the command, praise lavishly, and end the lesson. After a few marathon stand-stays, most puppies become more cooperative.

Some Weimaraners are leaners. If the dog leans to the side while stacking, use its own stubbornness to correct the behavior by applying pressure on the opposite side of the body, encouraging the lean. A typical Weimaraner thinks, "Oh! Gee! That's not what I had in mind," and leans the other way. The same principle sometimes works for rocking back; instead of trying to pull the dog forward, pull backward on the tail.

If the Weimaraner's height is close to either end of the standard, practice using the measuring wicket. If small, teach the Weimaraner to stand on tiptoe while being measured. If tall, practice stacking slightly flat-footed and not stretching up while being measured.

Baiting

Bait is anything that encourages a dog to demonstrate alert, happy enthusiasm. Bait is usually food, but some dogs respond better to a squeaky toy or a feather. Baiting is the technique of using bait skillfully to enhance the dog's ring performance.

Beef liver is the traditional tidbit used for show dogs, and preparation can be almost ceremonial. However, many other tidbits work just as well. Most Weimaraners just love Snausages®; they are not greasy, do not soak a pocket, and have no strong odor, and the dogs will absolutely KILL for a taste. Other Weimaraners go wild over Alpo Beef Bites® and Jerky Bits®. The important thing is to use whatever the dog will go mad over and is convenient. Liver, however, is economical and remains the most popular bait.

The two methods of baiting are stacked baiting and free baiting (free stacking). With stacked baiting, the handler places the dog's feet in position, and the lure is used to keep the dog alert when stacked and to encourage an attractive stance when standing free before the judge. Stacked baiting is used by most Weimaraner exhibitors and is easier for both

Figure 15-8: *Practice baiting on a crate or grooming table.* (a) If the puppy refuses to cooperate or will not lean into the bait, arrange a controlled fall.

(b) After the scare, the puppy appreciates the greater security of the crate top and is attentive to the bait.

dog and handler to learn. With free baiting, the dog is guided into a show stance without touching. Although free baiting is an advanced handling skill, training should start at an early age. Free baiting is spectacular on a loose lead, for the judge usually thinks the dog is marvelous, even if he or she recognizes the trained, controlled stance. This is the plan and the strategy! Another advantage is that the dog is not under as much pressure when the stance has become second nature.

The choice of method may be determined by the dog's conformation. If the dog does not have a strong rear, for example, stacked baiting is the most effective presentation. Free baiting is flattering to the sound and balanced individual, especially one that poses well in the front and rear.

The dog is not really fed when being baited. It only looks as if the dog is going to get the treat. This is done with ceremony, moving a hand to the mouth or fumbling in a pocket. The movements are slow and teasing, heightening the anticipation. The dog must work very hard just to get a few nibbles.

Begin teaching the puppy to bait while practicing the stand-stay on top of the crate or grooming table. Command, "Stand-stay!" while moving the treat from side to side. Teach the puppy to watch the bait, not the handler. When the lure moves away, the puppy is not allowed to move its head. In all fairness, however, do not move the bait out of visual range. Touch the tail, come to the front, and give the reward. When the puppy is steady on the crate, transfer to a mat on the floor and loop the lead on a doorknob.

Pick up all dropped bait and never let an on-lead dog eat food from the floor or ground. The dog must associate treats only with the handler's hands and respond to the handler's movements. A dog that expects to find treats elsewhere becomes less attentive to the handler. It is sometimes difficult to teach a Weimaraner to gait with its head up, and the task is complicated if the puppy begins looking for dropped bait.

Never use bait when gaiting. The dog begins to anticipate treats, holding the head to one side and tracking awkwardly in front—prancing, throwing an elbow out, or giving a half hop.

Gaiting

Training Tips

Lead training should begin as early as possible and should always be associated with something enjoyable. When the puppy is accustomed to walking on the left side, begin to jog with the puppy trotting alongside on a loose lead, in the heel position or slightly ahead of the handler. Practice jogging very smoothly, taking long strides and moving in circles to the right and left, as well as smooth turns. Talk to the puppy to give encouragement and keep its attention. An attentive youngster anticipates turns and is less apt to cut in front and trip the handler.

Figure 15-9: *How to photograph a dog standing free.*

(a) Rocking back is especially difficult to correct.

(b) The right bait to correct the problem comes in a surprising form—in this case, a cat.

(c) Pick up the "bait" and raise it until the dog rocks forward into a perfect show pose.

Many Weimaraners initially gait with their heads a few inches from the ground. Do not use the lead to support or suspend the dog's head. Practice giving a quick snap on the lead every time the head drops until the dog learns to hold its head at the desired level. Another way to keep the dog's attention off the ground is to make an about-turn.

When moving freely and happily on a loose lead, the puppy is ready for additional control. Bring the collar as high as possible on the neck (just behind the ears and jaw), smoothing the skin so that the collar will not pinch, and exert just enough tension to keep the collar in that position. (Some Weimaraners have unusually

Figure 15-11: *The lead should be a vertical line* from the puppy's neck to the handler's hand, neither **(a)** too wide, nor **(b)** too close.

sensitive ears and shake their heads to indicate discomfort when the lead touches their ears; these dogs must be trained to respond to voice control.)

Hold the lead in the left hand and gather the excess length into the fist. Keep the left elbow close to the side, with the forearm over the dog's shoulder, and concentrate on keeping the left arm and hand steady to avoid interfering with the dog's movement, which leads to weaving, swerving, and uneven speed. Keep the right arm close to the side, mov-

ing it only enough for balance. In other words, do not "flap" your elbow while gaiting.

When gaiting, the waist and shoulders should turn slightly toward the center of the circle. Practice watching the instructor (judge), the ground, and the dog ahead.

Although dogs are gaited counterclockwise (to the left) in the ring, practice in both directions.

Provide opportunities for the puppy to become familiar with a wide variety of underfoot textures. The greater the variety, the better the learning experience.

Practice gaiting on rugs, mats, concrete, asphalt, linoleum, and plastic. If the puppy is not accustomed to the tactile sensation of a particular surface, unexpected textures can be unnerving. Do not wait until the puppy goes to a match, show, or futurity to encounter strange surfaces for the first time. The puppy may not only blow the event but could

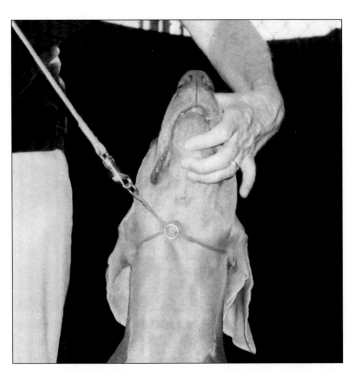

Figure 15-10: *Place the collar snugly,* just behind the jaw.

Figure 15-12: *A distraction can change a dog* with **(a)** correct front movement to **(b)** one that appears to move out at the elbows.

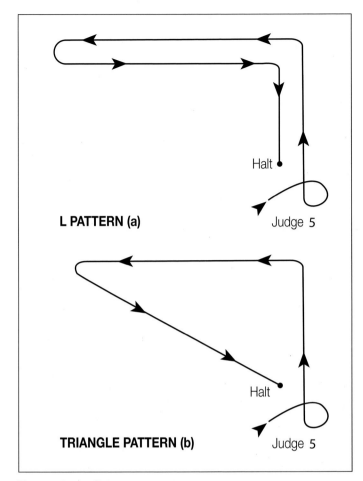

Figure 15-13: *Gaiting patterns.*

also have a terrifying ring experience that, with foresight and planning, could have been avoided.

Gaiting Patterns

Gaiting patterns usually begin with a courtesy turn—that is, the dog is walked in front of the judge and then turned toward the judge in a smooth circle to begin the pattern. This moving start is smoother, and the puppy is less likely to take off with a leap or a pace.

To move in a straight line, focus on an object in or near the ring as a sight mark and move straight toward it. Do not weave. Make the turns smoothly, look up, and aim the dog at the judge. The dog—not the handler—must come straight toward the judge. Stop the dog directly in front of the judge, about 4–6 feet away, and stand in front of the dog, not to the side.

The judge observes the dog's natural stance at this time. Use bait to encourage an alert expression, and try to work the dog into a balanced, square position by moving the bait. With bait, the dog can be twisted and turned in any direction. When baiting in front of the judge, do not assume the dog is properly posed; make sure the dog is standing correctly. If not,

Figure 15-14: *Gait the dog on the runner!* The judge needs to see the dog's movement, not the handler's.

Figure 15-15: *Great differences in type* create a serious problem for the Weimaraner that is one of a kind. Sometimes, the only solution is to send the dog to another part of the country, where Weimaraners of a similar type are being shown.

use the bait and the lead to create the most beautiful image. It takes a lot of practice, a lot of trial and error, playing with the lead and the dog's balance to use the bait and pull on the lead simultaneously. But, how stylish the result!

Preventing and Correcting Problems

Early lead training prevents or minimizes many problems, such as lunging, hopping, pacing, and sidewinding, that are commonly seen in the Weimaraner ring. A puppy that is at ease on a lead and has learned to heel at different speeds usually grows into a show dog that moves well.

If you are aware that the dog has a tendency to pace, make the courtesy turn before the judge slowly. Then, snap the lead and start off suddenly and rather fast. The swift transition usually starts the dog at a trot. Practice and, if necessary, seek assistance from a professional handler. Many judges forgive a dog that has paced if the handler can straighten it out on a second try.

Dogs sidewind for many reasons: immaturity with transient loss of balance; mechanical overexercise; expecting bait while gaiting; anticipating a left turn; poor muscle tone; poor conformation; or simply a bad habit. Sidewinding as a bad habit is easier to prevent by early lead training than to cure. When all else fails, "unwinding" the dog in a clockwise circle just before going into the ring sometimes works like magic. Another seemingly magical technique is to practice gaiting the dog on the right side—this gets attention.

Loose Lead

A dog that is ready for open class should trot on a loose lead with just enough tension on the lead to keep the collar in position and to signal for turns. Also practice gaiting on a slack lead. A Weimaraner that is supported by the lead or forges into it may appear to have faulty movement, such as a hackneyed gait or throwing front feet in every direction; a judge may ask for a slack lead to differentiate between the structural fault and the handling fault. Sometimes, changing to a different type of collar may allow you to regain some control. It may be helpful to let the dog run a bit before the show to take the edge off its excitement. These are simply temporary measures to get through the day; the problem of gaiting in the ring needs to be addressed in training outside the ring.

A Happy Attitude

If the preliminary training steps have been faithfully followed, the puppy will be well

Figure 15-16: *Teach the young show prospect* to stack and focus on the bait. With training, the slow movement of the treat will not only keep the dog's attention riveted on the delicacy, but is useful in maintaining that perfect pose. Showmanship like this, combined with great movement, won the 2003 National Specialty for CH Dakota Ridge Carousels Ola, Lola!

prepared for the first show. The most important thing is to develop style and confidence. Teach the dog that showing is a great way to get good food and have fun. The dog with the happy attitude and the pleasant, free-moving gait will often win over the Weimaraner with fewer faults but an unhappy attitude.

Preparing for Dog Shows

Long-Term Planning

Take a careful look at the show hopeful, checking with the breeder or professional handler if uncertain. Many factors influence competitive success and the decision whether to enter a particular show. Is the planned judge kindly, known to have an easy hand with novice or soft dogs? Geographic location or the judge's known preference (elegant, chunky, small, large) may influence the type or size of dogs most likely to enter. Some dogs may show better at outdoor shows or at indoor shows.

In addition to basic show training, other preparations begin long before entries are mailed. Does the dog need to gain or lose weight? Are the muscles firm, or do they bounce like jelly when moving? Is the coat sleek and shining? Evaluate the dog periodically, because none of these can be corrected after the entries are sent. The traits of top-winning strains or individuals fluctuate, and type variations are most easily observed over decades. However, the most consistently successful long-term qualities will always be basic soundness when standing or gaiting and charisma.

Boot Camp

Professional handler Peggy Kepler Roush likes to spend 7–10 days with each dog for what she calls boot camp. She is optimistic about Weimaraners that demonstrate the following:

- Contented and relaxed in a crate
- Eats eagerly in a dog run or crate
- Rests quietly in a moving vehicle
- Eliminates when on a lead
- Accustomed to a bathtub, grooming table, and all grooming procedures
- Relaxed when all parts of the body are touched and examined, including mouth and tail.

Returning home from boot camp reassures the dog that it has not been abandoned, and the dog will be happier and more confident the next time. While at home, the owners and dogs continue mental as well as physical preparation for competition. The dog returns to Peggy about a week before the shows for final training and polish.

The weeks before a show are the one exception to wearing a strap collar and identification tag at all times. Leaving the collar off allows the hair to lie smooth and flat, creating a smooth line from the neck to the withers.

Whether the owner or a professional handler will show the Weimaraner, Peggy's routine offers many helpful hints. Careful, long-term planning and attention to many details are typical of winners.

Many urban show Weimaraners enjoy pampered lives and do not get enough exercise to stay in good muscular condition. A few highly active individuals can maintain fairly good muscle tone by simply running around the backyard and roughhousing with other dogs, but even these show improvement after regular exercise.

Take walks regularly, with the dog running loose in traffic-free rural areas or on a long line in urban areas. Running up and down stairs, as well as swimming, does wonders for muscle tone. In addition to overall firmness, conditioning improves movement and strengthens toplines and rears.

Do not begin any mechanically assisted conditioning routine (bicycles, gaiting machines) until the puppy is at least 10 months old, and even then, owners should be careful not to stress immature joints. Begin with no more than one-half mile and increase the distance a little each week to no more than 5 miles. Consistent exercise two or three times a week is far more productive than a frantic effort 2 weeks before the show.

Grooming

As with other aspects of preparing for shows, walking into the ring with a perfectly turned out Weimaraner begins months before the show. Peggy has graciously shared her professional techniques and demonstrated them for the photographs.

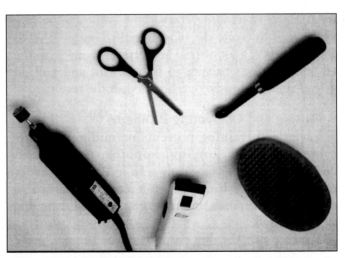

Figure 15-17: *Weimaraner grooming equipment.* Beginning at the upper left, Peggy uses a rubber curry brush, cordless electric clipper, nail grinder, thinning shears, and magnetic shedding blade.

Figure 15-18: *Good nail care is vital.*

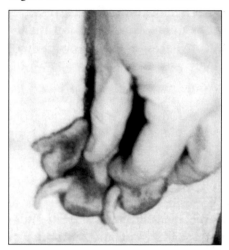

(a) Without regular trimming, Weimaraner nails quickly grow to a length that is painful and prone to injury.

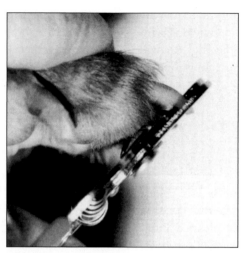

(b) Using scissors-type nail trimmers, grasp the foot firmly for control and clip the hooked tip. Squeezing the toe extends the nail for a better view.

15-19: *Nail care with an electric sander or "grinder."*

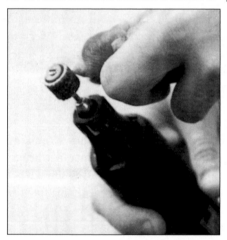

(a) With an assistant to hold the dog on the grooming table, Peggy demonstrates how to hold the foot.

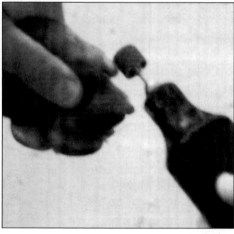

(b) Pulling the leg forward, Peggy smooths the top, bottom, and sides. She moves the grinder from one spot to another to avoid friction heat.

Feet and Nails

Proper care of the feet and nails is one of the most important and most neglected aspects of general care. Concrete dog runs can be deadly because they cause flattening of the arch and splaying of the toes; gravel runs strengthen foot tendons and develop tighter, more compact feet. However, puppies' feet often flatten during periods of physical stress such as teething; indeed, feet can be a barometer of health, and flat feet are an early warning sign of an infection or parasite infestation.

Whether or not the Weimaraner will be shown, nails should be trimmed at least every 2 weeks, starting a few days after birth. Long toenails lead to irreparable damage, causing growing feet to permanently flatten and splay. Long nails split—even tear off entirely—in a concrete run, in the field, and even on the carpet. Some Weimaraners indicate the discomfort of long nails by chewing on them. If your Weimaraner protests nail trimming, visualizing torn or infected nails and deformed feet fortifies faltering determination. When nails are trimmed regularly, however, Weimaraners become accustomed to the task surprisingly quickly, and some seem to enjoy the special attention.

Split nails should be trimmed and smoothed as much as possible. Dirt packed in the split may cause an infection, so if the split cannot be smoothed completely, soak the foot daily in diluted hydrogen peroxide (this may bleach the foot) until the damage grows out. Badly torn and infected nails cause obvious lameness; they should be examined and treated by a veterinarian. Severely damaged nails may never grow back.

When held in front of a light, the quick—the soft, highly sensitive, pinkish flesh under the horny exterior nail tissue—looks like a shadow inside the light gray nail. Trimming the nail to the soft part of the quick causes the exposed area to harden and the vein to retreat. The squeezing pressure of nail clippers seems to cause as much or more discomfort as nipping the quick, particularly in a dry climate, which hardens the nail, requiring greater pressure to clip it. Although experience helps, occasional nipping of the vein is unavoidable. Therefore, always have Kwik-Stop® (a styptic powder) or silver nitrate sticks within reach when trimming nails; in an emergency, cornstarch helps. If nothing is available, simply wrap the toe in a paper towel and apply firm pressure for at least 5 minutes, then confine the dog to a crate and observe it closely for 1 hour.

It is easiest to trim nails on a grooming table, but many owners trim nails while sitting on the floor with the dog lying down. Good light is essential.

A nail grinder makes routine care even easier and is vital for rehabilitating neglected or injured nails. Unlike the clipper, the grinder causes no painful pressure on the quick, and Weimaraners quickly become accustomed to the noise and vibration. The abrasive tip allows gradual removal of the outer

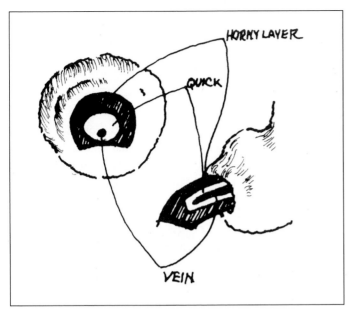

Figure 15-20: *The parts of a canine toenail.*

layer and exposes the soft quick with little risk of injury. Within a few days, the exposed tissue becomes horny and the vein recedes. For overlong nails, this is repeated every few days to shorten the quick.

Ears

Do not plan on cleaning ears the day of the show; rather, clean them on a regular basis using cotton balls, tissue, a soft washcloth, or baby wipes. Use Q-tips® only in places that can be visualized (the outer ear) because of the risk of puncturing the eardrum. Panalog® salve soothes sore, irritated ears. To remove hard, crusty wax, use a wax-softening solution, which can be purchased in any drugstore. Pour the solution into the ear and massage gently, then remove the excess solution and wax with tissue.

Teeth

Teeth should be checked regularly and kept free of tartar—dry dog biscuits and kibble decrease the build-up of plaque and promote dental health. Good dental care prevents bad breath and tooth decay, whereas neglect leads to scalar build-up and swollen, painful, bleeding gums, as well as tooth decay.

Figure 15-21 shows a technique for removing tartar if it does occur. Dental scalers are carried by medical suppliers, but if asked, many dentists are happy to give away an old scaling tool that is ready to be discarded. The edge of a dime is also effective. The back molars are difficult to reach and not as vital as the ones the judge sees when checking the bite, but keeping them free of tartar prevents tooth decay and bad breath.

Weimaraners often learn to lie quietly and permit the yellow scale to be removed—in fact, some seem to enjoy the attention. This is a good time to practice examining the molars and palate, for some judges insist on doing this.

Coat

A shining silver coat is the Weimaraner's hallmark and glory. Unlike most shorthaired coats, the Weimaraner's is surprisingly vulnerable to damage, which alters the color and dulls the sheen.

A beautiful coat begins internally, with good nutrition and parasite control. A high-fat diet enables oil glands in the skin to produce natural oils that prevent coat damage and healthy skin that does not flake and that is more resistant to allergens. Most owners have a favorite additive, such as corn oil, peanut oil, coconut oil, or commercial preparations. Adding coat conditioners after damage occurs is less effective, but the coat usually shows improvement in 3–4 weeks.

House dogs always have the best coats. Outdoor kenneling (even for a few hours a day) is hard on the Weimaraner's coat: in summer, the sun burns the coat to yellow, brown, or even orange shades; in winter, a heavy undercoat grows, which sheds unevenly and unattractively for months.

A low-fat diet and dry climate also contribute to a dry, brittle coat. Other causes of coat problems include thyroid deficiency, allergies, hives, insect bites, and skin infections such as juvenile acne. In each case, the cause must be identified and treated.

Weimaraners typically begin shedding along the topline and then the sides of the body, but some shed in spots that produce a startling buckshot appearance (see Figure 4-30). Other causes of dark spots that sometimes appear overnight include insect bites, hives, and infections. The only thing that can be done for the spots is to accelerate the shedding process by adding coat conditioners to the diet and engaging

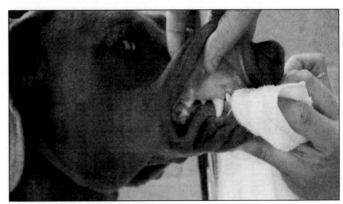

Figure 15-21: *Clean the upper and lower canines* with a dry washcloth and use the edge of a newly minted dime or professional dental scalers to remove tartar.

in frequent bathing and brushing. Hot oil treatments for dry coats also hasten shedding.

Hot oil treatments (use any product for human hair) provide external first aid for dry coats. The dog is first given a bath. Following directions on the product, heat the oil, pour it over the dog, and work it into the coat. Then, follow the steps shown in Figure 15-22. When the plastic is removed, Peggy works a generous amount of Kolestral® (Wella Balsam®) into the coat, but any other high-lanolin product would also be effective. Place the dog in a crate for an hour or so while the oil finishes soaking into the hair. The procedure should be done several days before a show. If time permits, the procedure can be done once a week.

When the hair loosens just before shedding, removing it seems to stimulate growth of the new coat. A pumice stone is safe and effective. A hacksaw blade removes a lot of hair but can injure the skin and hair. A rubber currycomb removes loose hair that is ready to fall without damaging the others. It also stimulates circulation and the oil glands of the skin, enhancing the sheen of the coat.

Magnetic shedding blades should be used carefully, pulling the skin taut to avoid cutting into wrinkles and using a light stroke. Learn the technique from someone who is familiar with it, such as a handler or groomer.

Before the Show

A complete grooming procedure should be done 1–2 days before the show. After a bath, Peggy's grooming routine includes nails, teeth, ears, eyes, and anal glands, as well as trimming fur. Wipe off crusty matter in the corner of the eye with a moistened cotton ball. If the matter is not easily removed, soften it with saline eye drops.

The anal glands just inside the rectum produce a strong-smelling, thick to liquid lubricant. They normally empty from pressure as the dog expels feces, but any swelling or irritation interferes with the process. The dog may indicate the discomfort of full anal glands by sliding its rear on the floor, which sometimes empties the glands. Peggy says that she can identify full anal glands by lifting the tail: if the tail comes up like a feather, with no feeling of heaviness, it is probably fine. Dogs with full anal glands dislike having the area

Figure 15-22: *Hot oil treatment.*

(a) The plastic coat is made by cutting a hole in the end of a leaf bag, which is then slipped over the head of this rather surprised-looking Weimaraner.

(b) Peggy gathers the excess wrap to one side.

(c) Bringing the excess wrap under the body, Peggy makes a snug coat that holds the heat and helps the oils penetrate the hair. This bag is large enough to cover the tail.

(d) Peggy keeps the oil warm for 10–15 minutes by moving a hair dryer over all parts of the wrap. She usually has an assistant with another dryer for this step.

Figure 15-23: *Demonstrating the technique* (without tissue for illustration purposes only).

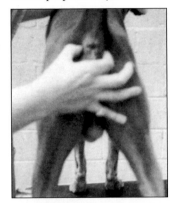 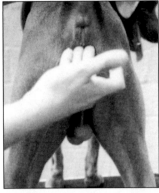

(a) Holding the tail up with the left hand, Peggy grasps both sides of the base of the rectum with her thumb and one or two fingers. When the fingers meet, she empties the gland with an outward, squeezing movement.

(b) Although this is usually effective, Peggy makes doubly sure the glands are empty by placing three fingers under the rectum and giving an upward, outward scoop.

touched and jump or pull back when the judge tries to examine them. Therefore, emptying the anal glands is a routine part of Peggy's grooming.

When emptying anal glands, Peggy always uses the grooming table so that the dog does not associate the somewhat uncomfortable procedure with the judge's examination of its rear. (Always have a generous wad of soft, absorbent tissue in the palm of the hand when using the techniques demonstrated in Figure 15-23.)

Whiskers were traditionally trimmed well into the 1990s; however, research has shown the value of the whisker as a sensory organ. Consequently, many sporting breed fanciers protested their removal, and as a result, the trimming of whiskers has become optional. Using scissors can be tricky. If the puppy jerks its head just as a whisker is snipped, it can receive a painful pinch or even a cut. A few traumatic experiences will create a head-shy dog, so use special blunt-tipped whisker scissors, which can be purchased at most pet stores.

A cordless clipper with a quiet motor is ideal for trimming whiskers. With the Weimaraner on the grooming table with its head held high and secure by the adjustable arm, lay the humming clippers on the dog's neck to get it used to the vibration and noise. Wait until the dog no longer twitches at its touch before trimming. Trim the muzzle, lip, and chin whiskers against the grain to make the whiskers stand up. A dog tightens its lips as they are trimmed, and it is difficult to locate all of the finer ones, which usually show up later, when the dog relaxes or is in a different light.

For the final touches, thinning shears produce a softer, more natural appearance than the sharp line of regular scissors, which also expose the white agouti band. If the dog has cowlicks on the neck or shoulders, careful trimming with the thinning shears minimizes their eye-catching quality. Grooming can also do wonders for a tail that is too long. After trimming the hair as close to the tip as possible, use thinning shears to obtain a natural-looking taper.

The aura of the well-groomed Weimaraner sometimes makes the difference between first and second place.

Organizing for the Show

Plan the show outfit ahead of time. Although informal apparel is acceptable at matches, it is a good idea to practice in the clothes that will be worn at point shows.

Women should dress conservatively to avoid drawing attention away from their dogs. Choose a contrasting color to emphasize a strong topline, or a blending color to avoid drawing attention to a poor one. Wear shoes that are neither large nor clumsy and with heels that are comfortable and do not cause an awkward, mincing stride. Select a skirt that is full enough to gait the dog and, at the same time, to bend over without being unintentionally revealing. The outfit should be "bend-over proof" and tested in front of a mirror. Remember, the objective is to show off the dog, not the handler's anatomy.

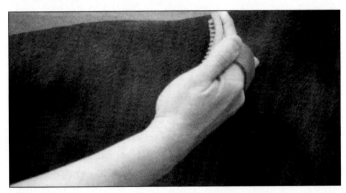

Figure 15-24: *A rubber currycomb* fits smoothly in the palm of Peggy's hand as she uses a firm stroke in the direction of the hair.

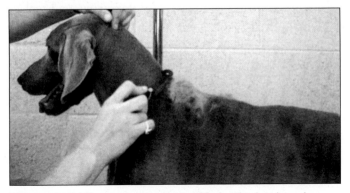

Figure 15-25: *The magnetic stripping blade.* This handy tool removes loose hair most effectively.

Figure 15-26: Peggy enhances the dog's clean lines with electric clippers. (a) Lightly trim the fringe of soft hairs on the flank with an upward stroke. **(b)** To remove any white hairs, the penile sheath is trimmed with a forward stroke. **(c)** The abdominal line is trimmed with a backward stroke.

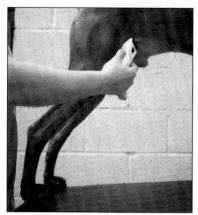
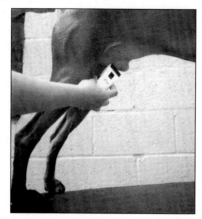
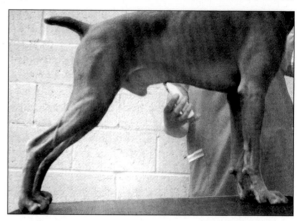

Figure 15-27: *Peggy adds the final touches with thinning shears.* (a) Hair growing in different directions forms a ridge on the Weimaraner's neck. Grasping the dog's muzzle, Peggy trims this with the thinning scissors to enhance the clean lines of the neck. **(b)** Peggy trims the hair spike at the end of the tail for a smoothly rounded appearance. **(c)** If the hair is thick, or the tail looks fat, careful trimming on the underside with the thinning shears will improve the taper and appearance.

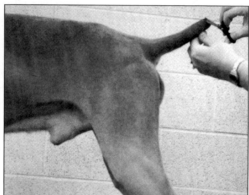
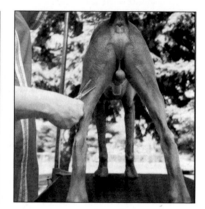

A sports coat and slacks are the proper attire for men. Note whether the judge is wearing a jacket. If not, protocol allows handlers to remove their jackets.

A tack box is any kind of sturdy box, usually with a handle, used for dog show equipment such as leads (exercise and show), shampoo, towels, baby wipes, nail clippers, a spray bottle for water, and other indispensable odds and ends. If large enough, the tack box can also hold the first-aid kit. Check the contents several days before leaving, and replace worn or missing items. The rest of the show equipment depends on personal preference and budget. Dog crates, exercise pens, first-aid kits (dog and human), cooler coats, bait, dog food, food and water bowls, chairs, ice chest, and refreshments are typical items on the dog show checklist.

Always carry water, even if only going to a match. Some dogs tolerate changes in water without any problems; others become quite ill. When necessary, carry enough drinking water for an entire trip.

Off to the Shows

Showmanship

A common misconception novices have about dog shows is that the judge will identify the best dog in the ring. Sorry! A more realistic conception is that each handler shows the judge the beauty and worthiness of her dog. A few judges can and will find the best dog, especially if the class is small, but it is unjust to expect the judge to identify a great dog in a class of 30 or even 10 very good ones if the best features are obscured by poor handling.

Remember, amateur does not mean unskilled, and amateur handlers do well with Weimaraners. With experience, there are definite advantages in making skilled amateur handling appear to be novice blundering—something the professionals are far less likely to get away with.

Evaluate the Weimaraner objectively. What are its best features? Its poorest? Plan the strategy that presents the dog in the most flattering way. A skilled handler fades into the background and presents the dog as a priceless art object.

Figure 15-28: *This young handler stays in the background* as she presents her entry to the judge as if it were a prized possession.

Strategy

Experienced exhibitors arrive at shows long before they are due in the ring. This allows time to relax, locate the ring, pick up armbands, check ground conditions, and so forth. Some Weimaraners show better if rested before showing; others need exercise to slow down. If the Weimaraner has never been shown indoors or gaited on a runner (mat), allow time for some practice. Either the evening before the show or before classes start in the morning, take the dog into the arena to become accustomed to the strange, echoing sounds and practice stacking and gaiting on the runners. Remember, the dog, not the handler, gaits on the runner.

Give the dog's grooming a final check before going to the ring. Snip stray whiskers that have appeared as if by magic. Wipe matter from the corner of the eye. If a bitch is in season, clean her perineal area and hocks, and slip a baby wipe into a pocket for a last-minute touch-up at ringside. In hot weather, keep the dog comfortable with a cooler coat or water spray.

Walk the dog for about 15 minutes before you are due in the ring to give it a last chance to eliminate. (Many Weimaraners refuse to defecate away from home or on a lead. If the suppositories were forgotten, the slightly irritating chemicals on the tips of wet matches make an effective emergency substitute.) Accidents in the ring are humiliating, and an uncomfortable dog cannot give its best performance.

Arrive at ringside early enough to observe the judge's ring procedure. Which side of the ring are the entries stacked on? Are they gaited as a group before individual examination? What pattern is used for individual gaiting? Most judges use the same pattern throughout the day, even from show to show, modifying the pattern only for special conditions, such as to avoid a hole in the ground or to have exhibitors stand in the shade when not being examined.

It is the judge's option to permit the exhibitors either to enter the ring in any order or to ask them to enter in catalog order—that is, in the numerical sequence of armband numbers. If the judge does not request catalog order, the astute handler has several strategic options.

Evaluate the dogs at ringside, and try to enter the ring, if possible, behind a poorer dog. For example, if showing a dog with a good rear, walk into the ring behind a dog with a poor one so that the judge cannot overlook this admirable trait after just examining the preceding dog: it is more likely to make a memorable impression. The same might go for heads and toplines. With a Weimaraner that is close to the minimum or maximum size, put as much distance as possible between an entry of the opposite extreme. Try to stay close to other dogs of the same basic size and type—littermates are ideal.

Being first in the ring has definite advantages. It demonstrates confidence, and it conveys the impression that the

Figure 15-29: *To ensure the best performance on a hot day,* remember to take a spray bottle of water and a small cooler filled with ice to ringside. Grooming and a light mist of water can be applied without penalty while the handler and dog remain in the shade during the judge's examination of other entries in a large class. The cooler can be used to hold ice and cooler coats. Photograph by Cindy Martin.

dog belongs in first place; it is particularly important if the dog has driving movement and needs room to move out. On the other hand, if the dog does not set up quickly, twists when stacked unless it can watch another dog ahead, or moves better when following another, being first in line can be deadly.

Walk the dog into line, stop when it is straight in line at the desired distance behind the preceding dog, and move only those legs that are incorrectly placed. As the judge takes the first look at the class, the initial impressions are made. This is not the time to fiddle with the dog's flaw. If the front is slightly east-west, do not spend too much time trying to stack it perfectly; it only calls attention to the fault. After the initial appraisal, the judge either asks the class to gait or begins individual examinations.

During individual examinations, judges periodically glance up and down the line, often exposing the dog's most unflattering trait and stance. A skillful handler always watches the judge and does not permit the dog to display itself awkwardly, even when relaxing. Does the dog have a poor topline? Stand between the judge and the topline. A poor front? Turn the dog slightly out of line, hiding the front so that when the judge glances over, the lovely topline or strong rear is in view. Be ready to move the dog into position and stack it to perfection while the judge examines or gaits the preceding entry.

Figure 15-31: *Arrive early* to observe the judge's ring procedure; equally important, it gives dog and handler a chance to compose themselves before entering the ring. At ringside, a small cooler will keep the spray bottle and drinking water cold. Photograph by Barney Riley.

Figure 15-30: *Jennifer ensures the judge gets the best view* of Dharma's movement by **(a)** gaiting the dog, not the handler, directly in front of the judge on the down and back. **(b)** The judge only has a few moments to see the dog's side movement, so Jennifer is sure to give the best view by allowing the dog in front to get far enough ahead not to impede Dharma's reach and drive, permitting a smooth sweep around the ring. Photographs by Cindy Martin and Lisa Croft-Elliot.

Figure 15-32: *The match trick.* A dog with a full bladder or bowel will rarely move with style or enthusiasm. While not a disqualification in conformation, the judge's ring procedure will be disrupted and delayed, and the dog certainly will not be seen in its most flattering light. If the dog has not relieved itself before entering the ring, the tips of a few moistened paper matches will often stimulate a bowel movement within moments.

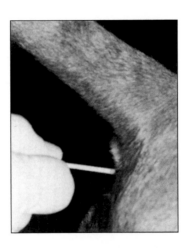

When the judge examines the head, offer to lift the lips to show the bite. Many judges (especially if they have been bitten) appreciate this. Drop the tail and pivot to the dog's front as the judge examines shoulders, topline, and rear. As the judge steps for a final look, pivot back to the dog's side and raise the tail.

If the dog starts to rock back while in the ring, three things may help:

(a) offer bait to induce a forward stretch;

(b) press the thumb and finger behind the shoulder blades and push forward; or

(c) pull backward on the tail to induce a reflex move forward.

When a well-trained dog begins to rock back in the ring, it is a sign of fatigue and protest. Ask it to stack only as long as necessary, break whenever the judge looks away, turn in a circle, and stack again only when anticipating the judge's final look at the class.

When the dog starts to lose interest, begin to tease with the bait. The most important thing is for the dog to present an alert and interested appearance, with or without baiting. If the dog shows signs of pressure or stress, ease off. It is less costly to lose that day than to risk an association between the show ring and an unpleasant experience.

Before starting to gait with the class, make sure that the other handlers have their leads attached and are ready to go. Let the preceding dog get a good start to avoid checking your own dog's free stride. A playful slap communicates that it is "fun time" and encourages a lively response and a happy tail. Avoid lagging behind the others, cutting corners rather than pulling on the lead, which draws attention to the problem. On the other hand, with a Weimaraner that moves beautifully at an extended trot, do not let the slow-moving dog in front ruin an opportunity to show this to the judge. Make the biggest possible circle, and if necessary, pass on the inside. As the class gaits, the judge watches only part of the circle. In a small, crowded ring, gauge the pace and allow room to speed up when reaching that part of the circle.

A Parting Thought

The thing to keep in mind again and again is that if the judge has a good class, there is no disgrace in coming in second or third or not even placing in an excellent class. It is important to learn how to lose as well as to win. It is much more graceful (and difficult) to be a good loser than to be a good winner. The dog's natural attributes cannot be changed, but perhaps they can be improved or minimized with proper training, conditioning, or handling. Take every opportunity at a show to learn and observe skills, from grooming to handling. Win or lose, there is always another show, on another day, with a different judge and different competition.

Figure 15-33: *Planning and preparation* before a dog show always pays off, but in the old days it really paid off. A 50-year-old photograph shows CH Klarbert's Ador as he poses with the magnificent Roy Rogers trophy he permanently captured by winning the 1950 National Specialty. Courtesy of the WCA.

Figure 16-1: *OTCH Freder's Gray Velvet v. Elsax, UDT, JH, RDX, VX.*
Owned by Stephanos and Jeanne Popovits, Velvet's vivacious enthusiasm
and precision performance delighted spectators and led to many accolades.
Her forte was the Utility class, and one of her career highlights was winning HIT from the Utility class with an outstanding score of 199. Velvet
was ranked on WCA Obedience Top 10 lists for 6 consecutive years and
was No. 1 in 1988. After earning her championship, Velvet continued to
compete in obedience and amassed 209 OTCH points; her record stood
until 2007 when FC OTCH Regen's Rip Stop, VCD2, UDX3, TDX, AX,
SH, SDX, RDX, V4, claimed the title.

CHAPTER 16

THE OBEDIENT WEIMARANER

by Shirley Nilsson

What Is Obedience?

Distilled to its essence, obedience is when the dog does what its handler wants when the dog would rather do something else. An obedient Weimaraner willingly complies with its owner's requests, even if those requests are contrary to the dog's natural inclinations, for example, sitting still while other dogs are playing energetically nearby, ignoring the pizza set on the coffee table, or heeling politely beside the owner through a park full of pigeons.

Why Obedience Train?

Whether the goal is to gain a measure of control over the dog in everyday situations or to prepare for formal obedience competition, properly conducted obedience training has many potential benefits. Working together strengthens the bond between dog and handler. Basic obedience makes the dog a better companion, one that is more enjoyable for the owner and the owner's neighbors to live with and more pleasant for guests and the general public to meet. A working knowledge of obedience fundamentals, such as "Stay" or "Come," can greatly reduce the likelihood of the dog's suffering accidental injury or death. Having a job to do provides the dog with an outlet by which to reduce mental tension. Many aspects of obedience training are also essential for success in higher-level fieldwork, in agility competition, and for dogs that perform service, therapy, hunting, or Search and Rescue work. Last, but definitely not least, obedience training and competition can be very pleasant pastimes for both dog and handler.

The Foundation for Successful Obedience Training

While every dog can benefit to some degree from obedience training, success is ensured if that training is applied to a sound, healthy dog with a stable temperament that was well socialized as a puppy. Another key prerequisite is that the basic underlying relationship between dog and owner is both positive and healthy. In this type of relationship, the dog trusts and respects its owner and the owner demonstrates good leadership by accepting both his or her own and the

Figure 16-2: *Sassafrass Rita's Lady in Red, UDX.* Because of some hysterical and dramatic behavior at a vet visit when she was 8 weeks old, it was suggested to her owner, Carol Meshon, that "Sadie" attend obedience classes. Soon fully reformed, Sadie now has a UDX title and 60 points toward her OTCH. She has also won HIT and HC awards and was the AKC Top Utility A dog of all breeds in 2003.

dog's innate character and limitations; setting rules for respectful and mannerly conduct and enforcing those rules consistently and fairly; responding to the dog's efforts and successes with heartfelt praise and appreciation; taking the time to learn how dogs think and see the world; and bonding with the dog through play and gestures of social affection, such as petting, greeting, and kind words. In particular, the value of enthusiastic and interactive play in cementing the relationship between dog and handler cannot be overstated. The effort and time invested in developing play games that are fun for both parties, such as hide-and-seek, tug-of-war, fetch, or wrestling, will be reflected in a dog that is attentive and responsive to its handler.

When obedience training is undertaken with a healthy dog-handler relationship as its key underpinning, training progress is steady and the dog performs its work with confidence, competence, and animation. The opposite is also true. While helpful to a degree, no amount of training to "Heel,"

Figure 16-4: *CH Grafmar's Jupiter, UDT,* "Jupiter," owned by Helen Peck, was the breed's first to earn the UDT title. Photograph courtesy of the WCA.

"Stay," or "Come" will fully reform the attitude of a Weimaraner that has been spoiled and allowed to become disrespectful of or dominant over its owner. In that case, the owner's time and effort would be better spent first examining and restructuring the basic relationship she has with the dog and then commencing with formal obedience training.

How Dogs Learn

Learning is a process by which a dog's behavior pattern is changed in a relatively stable way through its experiences. However, in order for that learning to be evident, the dog must be motivated to demonstrate the learned behavior. For instance, a Weimaraner may understand perfectly that the command "Fetch" means to run out and bring back its toy, but if it is distracted or tired, it may choose not to demonstrate that knowledge. Motivation is clearly integral to the successful performance of any learned behaviors!

Dogs are capable of learning in a number of different ways. The most rapid form of learning occurs when a dog is exposed, very often for the first time, to something that is, in the dog's view, either very, very good, or very, very bad. Typically, this type of learning requires just a single event or repetition, and, unfortunately, behaviors that are learned in this manner are not always ones that an owner wishes for the dog to learn. For example, a young Weimaraner that successfully steals and eats a pound of butter off the counter will likely learn, in just that one repetition, exactly how to counter surf and, unless retrained otherwise, will likely be highly motivated to demonstrate that learning at every opportunity. Likewise, a Weimaraner pup that is stepped on and injured by the first horse it meets will likely learn, in that single experience, to fear and avoid horses. Behaviors learned in the context of such highly positively or negatively charged situations tend to be extremely stable over time and are difficult to reverse through subsequent retraining efforts.

Figure 16-3: *Obedience is bonding.* The bond built between handler and dog by working together in obedience is clearly evident in the attentive and willing expression shown by this 6-month-old puppy toward his handler.

Figure 16-5: *Many obedience skills have practical everyday value.* Obedience training readily transfers to carrying packages, searching for lost car keys, and picking up dropped items. Here, "Trader," CH Nani's Jack of all Trades, UDX, RD, NSD, VX, owned by Sally Watson, demonstrates the practical usefulness of a trained retrieve as he performs with pride his daily ritual of collecting the morning paper for his owner.

Dogs can also learn if the positive or negative consequences that occur in response to their actions are less dramatic, although in that case, more repetitions will be required for learning to take place. Pleasant consequences reinforce an action and make the dog more likely to repeat that action in the future. For instance, if a Weimaraner that loves tennis balls brings one to its owner and is rewarded with another throw, the dog will probably bring the ball back over and over again. Rewarding a dog for performing a desired action is the basis of clicker training and all other positive reinforcement training methods, and it is also the method by which dogs teach themselves a wide variety of behaviors. For example, a Weimaraner that jumps up and paws a gate latch, causing the gate to open, and that is then rewarded by an invigorating chase of the neighbor's cat will very likely apply its paws to the gate latch in the future and may soon become a very adept escape artist.

Learning by positive reinforcement typically results in rapid learning and a happy working attitude in the dog. This method can often be successfully employed to remediate entrenched or problem behaviors. However, this method has some disadvantages. Some degree of ongoing reward is required to maintain the learned behaviors. For instance, teaching a Weimaraner pup to come by always giving it a tug-of-war game when it does will generally lead to a rapid, happy recall. However, after a certain point, if the pup is never again given a tug-of-war game for coming, he will continue to come rapidly for a short time after the game is withdrawn but will soon come less enthusiastically and less consistently. In the absence of reinstatement of the tug-of-war reward, the dog will, in time, probably completely ignore recall commands altogether. Another disadvantage is that a lengthy period of slow weaning of the dog from constant or frequent rewards will be required in order for the dog to have a reliable performance with a good attitude for any practical length of time between rewards. A final disadvantage of this method is that both the initial learning phase and long-term reliability of reward-based training hinges on the dog's being more interested in the owner's reward than in anything else occurring in the environment. Because of that, it could prove difficult to teach a Weimaraner the "Down" command by giving it cookies for volunteering to lie down if the training session is taking place in a park filled with squirrels!

Learning through reinforcement can also occur when the reward is simply the removal of something the dog views as unpleasant. For example, a Weimaraner can be taught to lie down by the handler pressing his fingers down on the dog's shoulders, with the movement into the down position leading to the release of the pressure—the action of lying down is rewarded by the removal of the unwanted pressure. This version of reinforcement training is the basis for all training methods based on physical compulsion. It is also the basis of some electronic collar training methods, for example, training the dog to hold some-

Figure 16-6: *Arimar Lisa's Enchantment,* "Chanty," bred and owned by Jackie Isabell and Lisa McClintock, demonstrates the Weimaraner's typical catlike use of a paw to solve a problem as she tries to bring some tempting tidbits within reach.

Figure 16-7: *One of the greatest benefits of obedience training is reliable recall,* and each level of obedience competition contains a recall exercise. At the novice level, it is a simple recall across the ring from a sit-stay. At the Open level, an element of difficulty is added as the dog is required to drop on command into a down position midway through the recall. At the Utility level, pictured here, the dog responds with obvious enthusiasm to a recall command, which must be given by a hand signal alone.

thing in its mouth by applying a low-level shock, presenting the item to be taken, and turning the stimulation off the instant the dog opens its mouth to take the offered item.

Compulsion-based training of any kind can produce a moderately rapid, reliable, and relatively stable performance, but learning in this manner requires a number of repetitions, and care must be taken not to overwhelm, confuse, or intimidate sensitive dogs with a degree of negative pressure that is excessive for their character.

Dogs are also capable of learning through methods that employ various degrees of punishment in response to their actions. The mildest form of punishment is merely to withhold any reward for an unwanted action. For instance, a Weimaraner puppy that begs at the table can be readily taught to give up this behavior if all diners merely avoid ever giving it any tidbits from the table. Punishment-driven learning can also occur though stronger forms of punishment, for example using choke, prong, or electronic collars to dissuade the dog from performing a given action. For example, a pop from a choke chain can be used to punish a dog for leaving the heel position during heeling training. With repetition, the dog learns to remain in the correct position to avoid the correction pop from the choke collar. Similarly, a dog can be taught not to jump up by spraying water in its face or stepping on its back toes when it does, or an electronic shock can be given to a dog for tipping over the neighbor's garbage can.

All training methods that employ active punishment as a response to the dog's actions fall into the category of aversion-based training.

Although often employed as a way to reverse learned bad habits, punishment-based training is not generally as effective for that purpose as are positive reinforcement methods, and doing the bulk of training with aversive methods tends to demotivate and discourage the dog. Therefore, the benefits of training by aversive methods must be weighed against the risks, and caution must be taken not to use a level of punishment that is excessive for the dog's character and the situation at hand. For example, many Weimaraners are highly interested in chasing deer, a habit from which they can generally be readily broken by an appropriately timed and appropriately strong electric collar shock. While the dog will not likely be enamored of that training method, the benefit of keeping the dog safe may outweigh the risk of accidental injury or death that could result from chasing the deer through barbed-wire fences or across busy roads.

Another way dogs can learn is through classical conditioning. This type of learning occurs by sheer repetition of a sequence of two events that are consistently paired. For instance, if the owner of a Weimaraner always puts on his pajamas right before putting his dog in a crate for the night, in time, the dog on its own will head for the crate as soon as the pajamas come out of the dresser. Similarly, if the owner begins heeling training by saying, "Heel!" and then moving forward, the dog will initially lag in response to the handler's movement but will learn that "Heel" signals that the owner is going to start walking; the dog will from then on be prepared to move in concert with the owner upon hearing the command.

It takes about 100 repetitions for classically conditioned learning to be evident through a change in the dog's behavior. Although learning by classical conditioning requires more repetitions than many other methods, behaviors learned in this way tend to become habits that are very stable and require little or no long-term maintenance. Because of that stability, a handler will want to ensure that the habit being formed by this process is the good one!

Which Training Method to Use?

All the training options outlined above have strengths and weaknesses, and rigidly applying training based on only one method to the exclusion of all others does not yield optimum results. It is preferable to think of all the available training strategies as tools in a toolkit. Which is the best "tool" to use for any training job depends on the dog's temperament, the phase of learning, and the situation at hand. For instance, a retrieving-crazy Weimaraner may need to be held by the collar (physical compulsion) to learn to stay while a toy is thrown, but it might best learn not to pull on the lead by being given a cookie the moment the lead becomes loose (positive reinforcement).

Not only can each aspect of training be done by a different method, methods can also be combined to even better effect, much like a painter selecting and blending colors from his palette. For example, it may take 100 repetitions to teach a Weimaraner to sit by commanding, "Sit" and then pushing down on the dog's rear to make him sit (classical conditioning). However, if that dog is given praise and a treat reward after each repetition (classical conditioning + positive reinforcement), the habit will still be formed, but the learning speed will be much faster and the dog more animated. While properly based in science, the art of obedience training lies to a large extent in the trainer's ability to "paint" a beautiful performance using the best training "tools" for the job.

Guidelines for Building a Training Program

The first order of business is to set training or competition goals that are achievable, given the character of both dog and handler and the time available for training. For example, it might involve accepting that a dog with severe separation anxiety might never be able to tolerate out-of-sight stays, or accepting that with only an hour to spare for training time each week, a Companion Dog title might be a more suitable aspiration than an Obedience Trial Championship. Goals for a serious obedience competitor have to be very detailed and specific, for instance, picking up the dumbbell cleanly, maintaining perfect heel position, sitting perfectly straight on a recall, and lying down instantly on a hand signal.

Any obedience training program should balance three types of exercises: those that build motivation and drive, those that teach or reinforce attention, and those that teach or reinforce self-control. As all dogs are born with varying degrees of aptitude for each of these traits, the amount of training time spent on each aspect should be adjusted accordingly. For instance, a Weimaraner that is by nature energetic and lacking focus will require relatively more exercises on focus and self-control; a Weimaraner that is by nature insecure and handler focused will require relatively more exercises geared to enhance motivation and drive.

The rewards and corrections that are used must be effective. Any externally provided reinforcement must be rewarding in the dog's opinion or it is not a reward for that dog. Most Weimaraners consider tug-of-war, chase, fetch, wrestling games, and any kind of commercial or homemade dog tidbit to be excellent rewards, and many appreciate their owner's praise and petting, as well. However, if a Weimaraner does not happen to like to play ball or eat dry cookies, or does not care about the handler saying, "Good boy," then

Figure 16-8: *OTCH Haiku Solar Eclipse, UDT,* "Teak," demonstrates tremendous athleticism in practicing the Retrieve Over the High Jump exercise from the Open program at a time when the obedience jump heights were much higher than they are at present. In the Retrieve Over the High Jump exercise, the dog is instructed to wait, sitting at heel, while the handler throws a dumbbell over the jump. On a single command, the dog must clear the jump, pick up the dumbbell, and return back over the high jump to sit in the recall position in front of its handler. The exercise is completed when the handler takes the dumbbell from the dog and the dog returns on command to the heel position.

those things are not rewards for that dog, and providing them will not facilitate the training process.

In all cases, the reward should be given to the dog after, only after, and always immediately after it has performed the desired behavior. If a trainer holds a cookie in front of his Weimaraner's nose and then commands, "Sit," the cookie is being used primarily as a lure to cause the dog to perform the behavior in the first place rather than as a reward for doing the correct action. Training in this commonly applied fashion typically results in a dog that will only work for cookies.

During the initial stages of learning something new, progress will be accelerated by giving the dog a reward for each successful, small step along the way. However, once the dog understands what is required by a given command, the rewards should not be given for every repetition of that behavior, but instead should be given on a random basis, or selectively, for only those repetitions that are better performed. The unpredictability of random rewards helps to stave off boredom in the dog, and using selective rewards for progressively better and better performance is a powerful method by which to achieve whatever degree of competence is desired.

The training program should be set up to build on success, so that the minimum number of corrections is required. Often, slowing the pace at which training progresses or increasing distractions only once the dog has succeeded in working through lesser distractions will dramatically reduce the need for corrections. When required, corrections should be of a type and firmness that cause the dog to change its behavior but not so strong as to frighten the dog or break its spirit, and they must be consistently applied. For example, a Weimaraner that fully understands the "Down" command should be corrected each and every time it fails to obey that command.

Corrections should be given without any negative emotion, and after the correction, the dog should be given a chance to repeat the task, or a version of the task that has been modified so that the dog can be successful. The first successful performance after the correction should be profusely rewarded.

The optimum number of days to train per week, time to spend per session, and number of repetitions performed depends on the dog's character and drive. Too little time spent and the rate of progress will be very slow, too much time spent and the dog may become stressed or lose enthusiasm. In general, new behaviors should be taught early on in a training session, the training of each exercise in the session should end on a positive note, and short bouts of play should be interspersed between exercises.

With regard to learning non-instinctive behaviors such as heeling or staying, dogs are very location specific. A Weimaraner that is taught to sit only in the backyard or at an obedience class may perform very reliably in those locations, but if it is asked to "Sit" in the park, the dog may meet the request with nothing more than a blank look. Once any command has been trained in about five different locations, the learning becomes generalized and the dog will understand what the command means, no matter where it is given.

Commands

Commands can be given verbally, by hand signals, or by changes in the handler's body language, but dogs tend to attend better to non-verbal commands. In order to avoid confusing the dog, each command should mean one thing and one thing only. Therefore, "Down" should mean either "get down off of me," or "lie down on the ground," but not both. Dogs learn commands most quickly if the command is given immediately before, rather than at the same time as, the handler assists the dog to do the commanded behavior. For example,

Figure 16-9: *For the Drop on Recall.* For one of the more difficult exercises from the Open program, the dog is recalled from a sit-stay and, at the judge's direction, the handler commands the dog in the midst of running in on the recall to drop into a down position. The handler then awaits the judge's instruction to command the dog to complete the last part of the recall. This Weimaraner shows excellent attention to her handler and a very prompt response to the command to drop.

if a Weimaraner is being taught to "Stand" on a verbal command, the command should be given with the handler standing fully upright, arms hanging down; as soon as the command has been given, the handler should immediately lure or position the dog into the stand position.

At all times, the handler's approach to training should be firm, fair, patient, and, above all, consistent. The handler should only give a command once, should only give a command she is prepared to assist with or insist that the dog respond to, should progress at the speed at which the dog is capable of performing, and should alter the training strategy if the dog shows lack of progress or signs of confusion or undue stress.

It was thought many years ago that puppies should not be given any formal training until they were at least 6 months old. However, it is now known that a pup of any age is capable of starting on a program of basic manners and obedience training; therefore, training should begin immediately.

Figure 16-10: *OTCH Jarem's Lightning Storm, UDX7, JH, NRD, VX.* Storm shows excellent jumping technique in performing the Broad Jump exercise in the Open class with his handler Randy Scharich. In the Broad Jump exercise, the dog is told to sit and stay facing the jump while the handler moves into position beside the jump. On a single command, the dog must clear the broad jump and come immediately into the recall position in front of the handler, who pivots to the right while the dog is in the air. The exercise is completed when the dog moves from the recall to the heel position on command.

Training Steps

The steps for training any behavior are the same.

Identify the specific aim of the training.

Break what is to be taught into components.

Teach each component separately.

Combine the components.

Generalize the learning to new locations.

Proof the learning by adding distractions.

Maintain and balance the learning.

Using the recall exercise as an example, the aim of training might be to have the dog perform a Novice recall exercise. The components of the recall are the dog sits and stays while the handler walks away and then turns to face the dog; the dog waits for the handler's command to "Come;" the dog runs to the handler; the dog sits squarely in front of the handler and waits for the finish command; and the dog swings into heel position. The components can be individually taught using whatever training method is best suited to the task, and selective rewards can then be employed to fine tune the performance to achieve the desired level of perfection. Next, the recall exercise should be practiced in a number of new locations in the presence of progressively stronger distractions. Lastly, the training is maintained and balanced to prevent anticipation errors and to optimize motivation by the handler, sometimes leaving the dog and going back to reward the stay, sometimes motivating the speed of the recall by releasing the dog to chase a toy as it is coming in, and sometimes ending the exercise with praise and a treat at the recall position. As the training progresses, the trainer gradually shifts from "assisting" the dog to perform correctly to "insisting" that the dog perform correctly, with the dog gradually assuming all of the responsibility for doing the work correctly.

Figure 16-11: *Am/Mx/Int (FCI) CH Bing's Spring Madness, CDX, JH, NA, SD, NRD, VX.* Madi is shown heeling in style with her owner and handler, Kathy Weber. Madi made quite a splash in her obedience ring debut by winning HIT at the 1999 WCA National Specialty Obedience Trial, and her wonderful work ethic and upbeat attitude also resulted in an all-breed HIT. Now, at age 10, she is preparing to compete in the Utility class.

Trainers wishing to compete in Open obedience will require a high jump and a broad jump, as well as a correctly fitted wooden or plastic dumbbell. For training purposes, the jumps can be made of wood, plastic, or metal and more portable 3- to 4-foot widths, but in competition, they will be 5 feet wide. The dog high jumps its height at the withers and broad jumps twice that measurement.

The dumbbell should be sized so that the bells are big enough to permit space for the lower jaw of the dog to fit under the bar when it picks up the dumbbell, yet not so large as to block the dog's field of vision when it is being carried. The bar of the dumbbell should be long enough that it does not pinch the skin of the dog's muzzle, but not so long that the bar can be seen when the dog is holding it.

Additional useful items for this level or above are a retractable lead that permits a measure of control over the dog when it is

In terms of teaching the mechanics of each particular obedience exercise, a good instructor is invaluable. Choose an instructor whose dogs and whose students' dogs perform with the skill and attitude that you would like to see in your own dog. In addition, or in the absence of a suitable instructor, several good texts covering every stage of obedience, from puppy training to formal competition, are referenced in the bibliography.

Obedience Equipment

The basic required equipment for practical everyday obedience training and for competition at the Novice level consists of a collar and a leash. Collars can be made of leather, fabric, or chain, although it is not recommended to leave any type of collar other than a flat buckle collar on the dog when the dog is unsupervised because of the risk that the collar could catch on something, causing the dog to choke. All buckle collars should be fitted to the dog in order to allow space for two fingers to be inserted sideways between the collar and the dog's neck.

Specialized collars, such as prong or electric collars, if used at all, should only be employed with the guidance of someone well versed in their safe and proper usage.

Leashes can be made of leather or fabric, and for initial training, a 6-foot leash is the most practical, as it gives the trainer enough length to train the recall and stays while offering good control at all times.

Figure 16-12: *A lovely working team* performs the Novice Heel Free exercise. Diesel, who was only 10 months old at the time, displays accuracy and animation in his work. In the Heel Free exercise, the dog must maintain heel position when the handler is moving and must automatically sit any time the handler stops. The handler, under direction of the judge, follows a heeling pattern consisting of brisk walking interspersed with fast- and slow-paced sections, left turns, right turns, about-turns, and halts.

Figure 16-13: *The Group Exercises.* A Weimaraner patiently awaits the return of her handler during the Group Long Down exercise, which is part of the Open level of obedience competition. In Open level stay exercises, up to 12 dogs are in the ring at a time; handlers go out of sight for a period of 3 minutes in the Group Long Sit exercise and for 5 minutes in the Group Long Down exercise.

working at a distance and a short tab collar that provides the handler ready access to collect or correct the dog but does not impede the dog from jumping or fetching.

For Utility level work, the handler will need a set of three white, or predominantly white, cotton gloves, a bar jump, a high jump sized the same as the Open high jump, and at least one set of scent-discrimination articles.

A set of scent articles consists of five leather and five metal articles, and often a few extra practice or spare articles of each type. Most competitors opt to use single- or triple-barred dumbbells for the scent discrimination exercise, in which case the dumbbells should be sized the same as the Open dumbbell. However, the scent articles can be made of any set of identical everyday leather or metal items—baby shoes or biscuit cutters have been used—provided they can be readily picked up by the dog and easily scented by the handler.

AKC Obedience Competition

AKC Obedience consists of three Regular class levels of competition—Novice, Open, and Utility—with each level becoming progressively more difficult. The Novice and Open levels consist of both individual exercises and group stay exercises; the Utility level has individual exercises only.

The Novice class consists of heeling, stay, and recall exercises that are practical for everyday use. At the Novice level, the dog performs some of the individual exercises on lead, the handler is permitted to give a verbal command for each segment of the exercise, and the handler remains in the ring during the group stay exercises. At the Open level, the dog is required to perform much more complicated behaviors, including fetching and jumping exercises, on a single command, and the handlers leave the ring and go out of sight of the dogs during the group stay exercises. At the Utility level,

every individual exercise poses a significant challenge. In many of the Utility exercises, the dog must work independently and at a distance from the handler, making the correct choice despite the presence of a number of incorrect options, and, in one exercise, the dog is commanded to heel, stand, stay, down, sit, recall, and return to heel position entirely by hand signals alone.

Each competition level is divided into A and B classes and consists of 6–7 different exercises that are each assigned a point value. The maximum possible combined point total for all the exercises in each level is 200. Dogs are scored on their precision in performing the exercises, and the dog should ideally work with willingness, accuracy, and enthusiasm.

In order to qualify and earn one of the three 'legs' required for a title from one of the Regular classes, the dog must earn at least 50% of the points available in each exercise and must earn at least 170 points in total, with each leg earned under a different judge.

In each class, the judge will award 1st through 4th placements, with a qualifying score being required for a placement and with any tied scores being resolved by a run-off that consists of an off-leash heeling pattern. At the end of the trial, two further awards are given: High Scoring Dog in the Regular Classes (often shortened to High in Trial or HIT) and

Table 16-1: *AKC Obedience Competition Levels.*

Novice	
Heel on Leash and Figure 8	40 points
Stand for Examination	30 points
Heel Free	40 points
Recall	30 points
Group Long Sit (1 minute)	30 points
Group Long Down (3 minutes)	30 points
Open	
Heel Free and Figure 8	40 points
Drop on Recall	30 points
Retrieve on the Flat	20 points
Retrieve over High Jump	30 points
Broad Jump	20 points
Group Long Sit (3 minutes)	30 points
Group Long Down (5 minutes)	30 points
Utility	
Signal Exercise	40 points
Scent Discrimination Article 1	30 points
Scent Discrimination Article 2	30 points
Directed Retrieve	30 points
Moving Stand and Examination	30 points
Directed Jumping	40 points

Figure 16-14: *CH Silversmith's Rainbow Row, UD.* Scarlet was a tireless retriever, an enthusiastic swimmer, and an effortless jumper, as shown in this broad jump, where she is jumping three times her height at the withers. (Prior to 1989, dogs in Obedience were required to jump much higher and farther than currently.) Not only athletic, Scarlet was beautiful and smart, finishing her show championship with 4 majors and her obedience titles with several HITs, at all times handled by her owner, Pat Gannon. Scarlet also won HIT at the 1984 WCA National Obedience trial and was the No. 1 Weimaraner in Obedience for 1985. She had 74 OTCH points before her untimely death.

Highest Combined Score in Open B and Utility (often shortened to HC), which is the dog with the highest combined point total from the Open B class and either the Utility A or B class. Again, in the event of a tied score for either award, a run-off consisting of an off-leash heeling pattern is used to determine the winner.

A Companion Dog (CD) title is attained by earning three qualifying scores from the Novice A or B class. A Companion Dog Excellent (CDX) title is attained by earning three qualifying scores from the Open A or B class. A Utility Dog (UD) title is attained by earning three qualifying scores from the Utility A or B class. A dog must earn a CD title before entering Open classes and must earn a CDX title before entering Utility classes.

Novice A classes are for dogs that have not yet earned a CD title and are handled by their owner or a member of the owner's family who has never previously put an AKC Obedience title on any dog. Open A and Utility A classes are for dogs that have not yet earned an Open or Utility title, respectively, and whose handler has not previously handled a dog to an Obedience Trial Championship (OTCH) title. In all A classes and in the Novice B class, the exercises are performed as listed in the table. In the Open B and Utility B classes, the order of exercises is varied.

A dog that has earned a CD title from either the Novice A or B class may continue to compete in Novice B for 60 days after earning the Novice title, and after that until the

dog either wins a HIT or until the dog earns a qualifying score in the Open class. A dog that has earned a CDX title from either the Open A or B class may continue to compete in Open B indefinitely. A dog that has earned a UD title from either the Utility A or B class may continue to compete indefinitely in both Utility B and Open B toward the advanced obedience titles—UDX and the highest available obedience title, OTCH.

A UDX title requires 10 legs, each of which is earned by qualifying in both the Utility B class and the Open B class in the same trial on the same day. If a dog holding a UDX title earns another 10 UDX legs, it is awarded a UDX2 title, and that title is upgraded similarly for every additional 10 legs earned.

An OTCH is attained both by accruing championship points and by winning Open B and Utility B classes. A dog must earn 100 OTCH points from either Open B or Utility B classes to earn an OTCH title. Points are accrued by winning, or, if the class is large enough, by placing, in either the Open B or the Utility B class. The number of points awarded is determined by how many dogs are competing in the class, with relatively more points awarded for success in the Utility B class, compared with those given for success in the Open B class. In addition, the dog must also win an Open B class and a Utility B class at least once and must have another win from either an Open B or Utility B class, with the three required wins coming under three different judges. Obedience titles also are part of the recently developed five levels of AKC VCD titles.

At some Obedience Trials, Non-regular classes are offered. These classes are meant to give dogs and handlers ring experience, to be intermediate steps between Regular class levels, and to be fun. While competitors in these classes are scored and given placements, official AKC titles are not awarded for them.

Table 16-2: *AKC Versatile Companion Dog titles.*

VCD1	**Companion Dog** + Tracking Dog + Novice Agility + Novice Agility Jumpers
VCD2	**Companion Dog Excellent** + Tracking Dog + Open Agility + Open Agility Jumpers
VCD3	**Utility Dog** + Tracking Dog Excellent + Agility Excellent + Agility Excellent Jumpers
VCD4	**Utility Dog Excellent** + Variable Surface Tracking + Masters Agility Excellent + Masters Agility + Excellent Jumpers
VCCH	**Obedience Trial Champion** + Champion Tracker + Masters Agility Champion

sisting of 10–20 different stations. At each station, a sign posted to a pylon directs the team to perform a different obedience exercise. The judge designs the Rally course, and competitors are provided with a course map and given the opportunity to walk the course without their dog prior to the start of the class.

During competition, the judge's only command is, 'Forward,' to release the team at the starting line. Handler and dog then move continuously at their own pace but no faster than at a brisk walk through the course, with the dog remaining in heel position unless directed otherwise at a station. The handler is not permitted to touch or harshly verbally correct the dog but is permitted to provide unlimited verbal encouragement and direction and may give multiple signals or commands to the dog without penalty. The degree of precision required for a perfect or passing score in Rally is not as high as that required in Regular obedience competition.

There are three levels of Rally competition—Novice, Advanced, and Excellent—with three legs required to earn a title of Rally Novice (RN), Rally Advanced (RA), or Rally Excellent (RE), respectively. Once the dog has earned the RE title, the team can opt to compete for a Rally Advanced Excellent title (RAE), which is achieved by qualifying in both the RallyA and RE class at the same trial, 10 times. For each additional 10 legs, the title is changed to reflect the accomplishment, so a team with 40 RAE legs would be awarded an RAE4 title.

Each Rally competition level is divided into A and B classes. "A" classes are for dogs that do not have any Regular Obedience titles and hold no Rally titles (Novice A class) or only hold Rally titles below the level at which the

Figure 16-15: *CH MACH Regen's GrayQuest Rock Candy, VCD1, TDX, RN, NSD, RD, VX3.* Roca attentively awaits the next instruction from handler Lori Barbee during a Novice Rally class competition. The Rally ring is full of distracting elements, including a judge, ring stewards, pylons, signs, jumps, and bowls of dog food or toys left on the ground, but the handler is permitted to help the dog resist those distractions through verbal encouragement and by repeating commands as often as necessary.

Typical Non-regular classes include Graduate Novice, where the exercises are intermediate in difficulty between the Novice and Open exercises; Veterans, where dogs over 7 years old perform the Novice class exercises; Team, where four dog and handler pairs perform a mixture of Novice and Open exercises synchronously; Brace, where one handler handles two dogs through the Novice exercises; and Versatility, where, at the judge's random selection, the dog and handler perform two of the individual exercises from each class (Novice, Open, and Utility) level.

AKC Rally

Rally is a new obedience sport in which obedience fundamentals are performed in an agility-style course. Designed at an introductory level of obedience competition, it is an excellent precursor to regular obedience competition. In Rally obedience, handler and dog negotiate a course con-

Figure 16-16: *The new sport of Rally Obedience.* NFC NAFC FC AFC Grau Geist Lil's Gust v. Westend, CD, MH, RA, SDX, RDX, VX. Gus, handled by Debra Meifert, puts to rest the myth that field and obedience do not mix, as they compete successfully toward a RN title.

team is competing (Advanced and Excellent A classes); all "A" class dogs are handled by their owner, who must not have previously earned any Rally or Regular Obedience titles with other dogs.

For each leg toward a Rally title, a passing score of 70 out of the maximum of 100 points is needed, and the team must not miss any stations. At the end of the class, the judge awards 1st through 4th placements. Each competitor's run is timed, and in the event of a tied score, the dog with the fastest time is awarded the higher placement.

At the Novice level, there are 10–15 stations, and all of the exercises are performed with the dog on lead. The stations consist of relatively simple exercises, such as heeling fast, making a right turn, halting and walking around the dog, and weaving through pylons.

RA courses have 12–17 stations and must have at least one station that requires the dog to jump a bar or high or broad jump. The stations can consist of any of the Novice exercises plus any of the more difficult Advanced exercises, such as making a figure 8 around pylons with containers of food or toys on the ground nearby or pivoting 90 or 180 degrees in place.

In RE courses, all of the exercises are done with the dog off-lead except for the honor exercise; in this exercise, the dog must either sit or down in the recall or heel position in the ring while another team completes the course.

RE courses consist of 15–20 stations, and at least two of those stations must be jumps. The stations can be any of the exercises from the Novice or Advanced level plus any of the even more difficult RE exercises, such as heeling backward, having the dog halt, then stand, then sit, or having the dog perform a moving stand with the handler immediately walking around the dog.

Preparing for Competition

Obedience competition is a team event, and in addition to mastering all of the required exercises, both handler and dog will benefit from thorough preparation for the show environment.

Preparation for the handler includes setting realistic and attainable goals and tailoring the training program to achieve those goals. The higher the goal, the more time and preparation you will need prior to showing—a goal of winning HIT may take hours of training each day for months to years, whereas a goal of qualifying in Novice may take only a few minutes of training a day for several weeks to several months.

Figure 16-17: *Non-Regular Classes.* The Team Class is one of the Non-regular classes offered by some clubs. Known as the Ghostbusters, this all-champion team represented the breed at the Phoenix Field and Obedience Club's fall trial in 1989. From left to right, the competitors are: CH Kapp's Scharf vom Reiteralm, CDX, NRD, NSD, with Rebecca Kapp; CH Siblerholm's Adelaide, CD, with Linda Hufford; CH Valmar's Victoria, CDX, with Alice Morgan; and OTCH Freder's Gray Velvet c. Elsax, UDT, JH, RDX, NSD, VX, with Jeanne Popovits.

Whatever the goal, it is very important to be familiar with the obedience rules and regulations that are available from the AKC. Not all of the obedience rules make sense to the casual bystander. For example, sometimes it is permitted to give the dog a second command and sometimes the handler is allowed to use both verbal and hand signals, but other times these aids are not permitted. Knowledge of the rules reduces the likelihood of not qualifying due to an error on the handler's part. It is also extremely helpful to be familiar with obedience trial etiquette and ring procedures. For example, it is expected that competitors will check with the ring steward at their obedience ring as soon as they arrive, be ready on time to go into the ring for the group exercises, maintain control over their dog at all times, and not do anything to disrupt the con-

Figure 16-18: *Regen's Moonstruck, UD, NA, NAJ, JH, SD, RDX, VX.* Nick is directed over the broad jump by handler Pat Gannon in an RE class. Many competitors use Rally competition to build confidence and polish performance en route to Regular obedience class competition, and that is exactly what this team did; after earning all three levels of Rally titles, Nick went on to earn his CD title with ease in three straight legs, with a top score of 198.5.

centration of any team working in the ring. The best ways to learn both trial etiquette and ring procedures are to attend trials without your dog to observe the running of the event, taking particular note of the B classes, where more experienced handlers can be observed, and also to volunteer to act as a ring steward for a trial-hosting club.

The last aspect of preparation for nearly all handlers is to learn how to control or conquer nervousness. One of the best antidotes for competition jitters is for handlers to defer entering a competition until they are very confident that their dog has mastered all of the exercises to be performed and until they are completely familiar with obedience ring procedures. Many handlers put too much pressure on themselves in a competition situation and it often helps to maintain perspective to remember that the love between dog and handler will be just the same no matter what happens in the ring. Making a checklist of items to bring to the trial, arriving at the trial in good time, taking note of the heeling pattern and the judge's routine in running the class, just acknowledging nervousness, and taking a deep breath or a moment to meditate and focus completely on the dog can also help to reduce ring nerves. Some handlers find a drop or two of the herbal flower essence Rescue Remedy on their tongue beneficial and, if nerves are still present, chewing a mint might help to minimize the dog's noticing it. Since nervousness is highly individual, experimentation to find

Figure 16-19: *CH Seabreeze Oasis Jump Start, UDX, NA, NRD, VM.* Speedy lives up to his name by performing all obedience exercises with speed and enthusiasm, as demonstrated here in the Utility Scent Discrimination exercise, in which the dog is required to select the one dumbbell scented by its handler from a group of dumbbells that have been scented by a stranger. Speedy, owned and handled by Louise Brady, won both specialty and all-breed Obedience HIT and HC awards in his obedience career. He competed in the AKC National Obedience Invitational in 2003 with performances that brought talk from judges and handlers alike.

Figure 16-20: *Practice matches.* A great way to prepare for competition. Here, Am/Can CH Regen's Rocket Launcher, TDX, AX, AXJ, CD, SD, RD, VX3, is shown with one of his owners, Laurie Jenks, in training for Rally competition. Amateur-owner handled, Booster's high drive and desire to work have propelled him to many titles, including a VX2 at 2 years old and a VX3 at 3 years old. He has also made his mark in obedience, with a top score of 197.5 in Novice B competition.

Figure 16-21: *Getting prepared for competition.* In all regular obedience classes, there are occasions when the judge will approach the dog from behind, so all obedience dogs should be exposed to and proofed for this potentially distracting or intimidating occurrence in training sessions.

the most effective pre-competition routine to dampen butterflies is a good idea, as a calm, confident handler is a tremendous asset to any dog looking for guidance from its leader in a new situation.

Preparing the dog for obedience competition should include proofing each of the exercises by training in a variety of locations and around distractions, similar to those that will be encountered at the show, as well as proofing the training around general distractions, such as toys or food lying around or loose dogs working or playing nearby. Done correctly, proofing builds confidence in the dog, but if the proofing program is too rapid or the distractions presented lead too often to failure, the dog's confidence will be eroded and the dog will become stressed or shut down.

Another good preparation tool is to have the dog perform "run-throughs" of the obedience exercises in a class setting or in a group of experienced obedience competitors, with participants taking turns acting in the roles of judge, steward, or handler. This assists the dog to be comfortable with the roles and behaviors of the people it will encounter in the ring. A step beyond that are fun or correction matches where the dog has the opportunity to perform the exercises in a setting that mimics the formal trial situation, but where the handler still has the opportunity to encourage, correct, or reward the dog as needed in the ring.

Most dogs fail in obedience trials not because they do not know the exercises but because they have not been properly transitioned from training mode to showing mode. In training, the handler is providing the dog with frequent feedback and motivational support. At a trial, handlers are not permitted to bring food or toys into the ring, and only in Rally classes is the handler permitted to verbally encourage the dog during the exercises. A dog that has never trained under these conditions can easily become confused and stressed in a trial situation. Therefore, once the dog has learned all the exercises, show mode training sessions should be interspersed with regular training sessions. In the show mode sessions, the handler praises the dog between exercises but remains silent during the exercises, and no toys or food rewards are given until the entire program has been completed. At first, the handler will want to perform only one or two exercises in show mode; however, prior to competing, a good rule of thumb would be to have the dog be able to successfully perform an entire class routine twice in row without the need for correction or motivation before sending in an entry form.

Dogs can also experience ring nervousness. The primary cause is handler nervousness, which is readily transmitted down the lead to the dog; if the dog has a nervous handler, it would probably be better to have the dog resting in a crate in a quiet location away from the handler until just before it is time to enter the ring. Dogs can also get ring nerves if they

Figure 16-22: *BISS CH Behringer's Sweet Chablis, CDX, RD, NSD, VX, CGC.* Blis made her mark in the Weimaraner world by being the only dog in the past quarter century to earn a perfect score of 200 in obedience competition. She was Louise Brady's first Weimaraner and she was owner handled to all of her titles, as well as to a Best in Specialty Show conformation win. Blis earned her perfect score of 200 in 1997 while earning the second leg toward her Open A title. Blis also demonstrated great aptitude in all competitive venues, earning a Dual Futurity award from the WCA for placing in both her Show and Field Futurities.

have not been regularly socialized to crowds of people and dogs or if they have had a bad experience at a show in the past. In general, attending a show is exhausting for dogs. It is stress-reducing for all dogs to be taken for a walk everywhere around the immediate area of the obedience ring prior to entering the ring to compete and to have a crate or blanket and water bowl set up in a quiet area away from the crowd as a place to rest when they are not working.

200

The magic number in obedience is 200. A perfect score of 200 signifies that all of the class exercises were performed without even a slight error. That degree of precision is rarely attained by any team at any class level. In the past quarter century, only one Weimaraner has achieved a perfect score of 200 in competition, and that dog is BISS CH Behringer's Sweet Chablis, CDX, RD, NSD, VX, CGC. Blis was owned, trained, and handled by Louise Brady, and she scored 200 while earning the second leg of her CDX title. Blis had other notable career accomplishments, including winning a WCA Dual Futurity award for placing in both her Show and Field Futurities, winning Best of Breed multiple times, and once winning Best in Specialty Show.

Our Perfect Day

It was a beautiful, warm, sunny June day in Southern California and I was competing with Blis at an all-breed trial, to earn her CDX second leg. The individual exercises felt great and I was very happy coming out of the ring. However, as Blis was working through some stay issues and had previously failed the group exercises several times, I was not at all confident of qualifying at that point. Apparently, another exhibitor-friend had happened to see the score sheet as she was checking in for her next class and she knew I was holding a perfect score going into groups. Word of this spread quickly amongst the exhibitors, with everyone careful not to tell me— thankfully. I was stressed enough just trying to keep it together for stays, and the added pressure of knowing I was on the verge of a perfect score would have put me over the edge. Despite my worry, the stays went smoothly. As I was also showing in conformation that day, I had not been able to watch other dogs in the class for any comparison to Blis' performance. In the end, there were only two qualifiers, and the other qualifier was a very, very good working dog, so when the judge started his introduction to the class placements by saying, "Today we have a very rare occurrence in the obedience ring...." I realized he was going to award a score of 200, but assumed he was talking about the other dog. Imagine my thrill and surprise as it was my armband number that was called when the team with the perfect score was announced!

Utility Dog Excellent

CH OTCH Eb's Red Hot Seabreeze, UDX, JH, NA, VX2, CGC—Sherry Cooper and Marge Davis

Greysport's Sparklin' Pewter, UDX2—Leroy Frey

OTCH Jar Em's Lightning Storm, UDX7, JH, NRD, VX—Randy Scharich

CH OTCH Jar Em's Special Sporting Clay, UDX4, JH, VX—Randy Scharich

CH Nani's Jack of All Trades, UDX, NSD, VX—Sally Watson and Christine Grisell

Nani's Tell 'Em Off, UDX, NSD, V—Sally Watson

CT Regen's Rip Stop, VCD3, UDX5, OM1, MH, SDX, RDX, VX6
Owned by Anne Tyson and Judi Voris

OTCH Regen's State of the Art, VCD2, UDX2, RE, TDX, MH, SDX, RDX, VX4
Shirley Nilsson and Judi Voris

TC AFC Regen's Summer Blaze, VCD3, MH, MX, MXJ, RE, SDX, RDX, VX6
Shirley Nilsson and Judi Voris

Sassafras Rita's Lady in Red, UDX—Carol Meshon and Barbara Duckworth

CH Seabreeze Oasis Jump Start, UDX, NA, NRD, VX—Louise Brady

CH Sunnydell's Perseus, UDX, RN—Doris McCullough and Andrea Martin

Valkyries That's My Boy, UDX—R. Cashman and K. Reilly

CH Woodcreek's Raisin the Roof, UDX, MX, MXJ, NRD, VX—Mark and Cynthia Tilly

CH Wynwoods Legend of the Links, UDX4, JH, NRD, VX—Patricia Gannon

The Superstars of Obedience

Excellence at advanced obedience competition is achieved by few, with the highest honors going to those dogs that are able to perform with excellence and consistency.

The UDX title is deceptively difficult, available only to dogs that have already earned a UD title; it is earned by qualifying in both Open B and Utility B on the same day, 10 times. At first glance, it would seem that having already earned CDX and UD titles, it should be a relatively simple matter to merely qualify in both classes on the same day. However, at these class levels, very small errors can result in a non-qualifying score, and it is no easy task to maintain proficiency in the Open and Utility exercises. This difficulty is reflected in the fact that, to date, only 13 Weimaraners have earned the title of UDX.

And the Champions are...

OTCH Freder's Gray Velvet v. Elsax, UDT, JH, RDX, VX (see Figure 16-1)
Owned by Stephanos and Jeanne Popovits
Sire: CH Reichenstadt's Axel v. Gab, CD, TD; Dam: Elsa Von Brandt

HOF CH OTCH Eb's Redhot Seabreeze, UDX, JH, NA, NRD, VX, CGC
Owned by Sherry Cooper and Marge Davis
Sire: CH Greywind's Jack Frost, CD; Dam: CH Seabreeze Autumn Piper, CD

TC CT Regen's Rip Stop, VCD3, UDX4, MH, SDX, RDX, VX6
Owned by Anne Tyson and Judi Voris
Sire: NAFC FC AFC Northern Lights This BudsForU;
Dam: TC AFC Regen's Summer Blaze, VCD3, MH, MX, MXJ, RE, SDX, RDX, VX6

OTCH Jar Em's Lightning Storm, UDX7, JH, NRD, VX
Owned and handled by Randy Scharich
Sire: CH Arnstadt's Wotan von Doblen, CD, TD, JH; Dam: CH Jarem's Casino Roulette

OTCH Heidi v. Falkenberg, UDT
Owned by Booth and Anna Kelley
Sire: Kurt's Krazy Kriss; Dam: Ranah's Royal Lady Priscilla

OTCH CH Jar-em's Special Sporting Clay, UDX5, JH, VX
Owned by Randy Scharich
Sire: CH Hope's Thunder Jack of Diamonds, JH; Dam: CH Jar Em's Casino Roulette

OTCH Haiku Solar Eclipse, UDT
Owned and handled by Marty Fast
Sire: CH Star-N-Tsuru-Tani Majitsu; Dam: CH Star-N-Love Song v. d. Reiteralm

TC AFC Regen's Summer Blaze,
UDX2, MH, TDX, RE, MX, MXJ, SDX, RDX, VX6
Owned by Shirley Nilsson and Judi Voris
Sire: CH Jak's Repeat Offender; Dam: CH Skyhi's EZ Magical Reign, UD, JH, SD, RD, VX

HOF OTCH Brought Mar's Samantha P. Smog, UDTX, SDX, RDX, VX
Owned by Wentworth and Irene Brown
Sire: CH AFC Brought-Mars Game Bandit v. Tor; Dam: Madchen's Blu Phantom

OTCH Regen's State of the Art, VCD2, UDX2, RE, TDX, MH, SDX, RDX, VX4 (see *Index*)
Owned by Shirley Nilsson and Judi Voris
Sire: DC Von Weiner's Withheld, CDX, MH, SD, RDX, VX2;
Dam: TC AFC Regen's Summer Blaze, VCD3, UDX2, RE, MX, MXJ, MH, SDX, RDX, VX6, BROM

The Obedience Trial Champions

An AKC OTCH is arguably the most challanging title to obtain, and that difficulty is reflected in the very small number of Weimaraners that have reached this pinnacle: only nine Weimaraners have earned an OTCH title.

These outstanding obedience competitors are listed above in order of the total OTCH points accrued during their competitive careers. Randy Scharich and Shirley Nilsson are fortunate to have each owned two of these OTCH dogs, with both of Randy's Jar Em champions from the same dam. Shirley's Regen champions are a dam and her offspring. Two of the breed's obedience champions have been inducted into the Hall of Fame, in part because of their achievements in the obedience trial ring.

Figure 16-23: *OTCH Brought Mar's Samantha P. Smog, UDTX, SDX, RDX, VX, HOF.* Owned by Wentworth and Irene Brown, Samantha was the first Weimaraner to earn an OTCH, in 1981. She ranked on the WCA Top 10 Obedience lists for 6 consecutive years, first achieving the No. 1 spot in 1980. After earning exactly the 100 points required for an OTCH title, Samantha retired from obedience and took to the fields, where she went on to earn every AKC Tracking title and WCA Ratings titles available at that time—a remarkable achievement!

Figure 16-24: *TC CT Regen's Rip Stop, VCD3, UDX4, MH, SDX, RDX, VX6.* Owned by Anne Tyson and Judi Voris and trained and handled by Anne Tyson, Diesel earned his OTCH in 2005 at just 3 years old. Diesel was Anne's first obedience dog, and together they earned numerous all-breed HIT and HC awards, as well as three WCA National HIT in Obedience awards, one in 2003, one in 2004, and one in 2006. He was the No. 1 WCA Weimaraner in Obedience for 2005 and attended the AKC National Obedience Invitational that year also, finishing strongly. Diesel's top score in competition is 199.5 in the Open class and 199 in the Utility class. At the time of writing, he was still competing and had 241 OTCH points.

Figure 16-25: *OTCH Jar Em's Lightning Storm, UDX7, JH, NRD, VX.* Owned and handled by Randy Scharich, Storm has proven to be a loyal companion and hard worker over many years, both inside and outside the ring. Storm had only been in the ring 12 times before starting to work toward his UDX, a difficult title that only one Weimaraner had earned before Storm. Showing incredible consistency, on a record 70 different occasions, Storm qualified in both Open and Utility on the same day, earning a UDX7 title, the highest UDX title of any Weimaraner. Storm was the first Weimaraner ever to attend the AKC National Invitational to compete against the top obedience dogs in the country and attended the Invitational 5 out of the 6 years he was invited (1997–2001). His OTCH title was earned in 2000, and Storm was the 6th dog in the breed's history to receive this title and the second male; he retired from competition ranked No. 3 on the all-time OTCH point list, with a total of 137 points.

Figure 16-26: *HOF CH OTCH Eb's Redhot Seabreeze, UDX, JH, NA, NRD, VX, CGC.* Sparky was bred by Marge Davis, Barbara Didjurgis, and Karen Lewis, owned by Sherry Cooper and Marge Davis, and handled by Sherry Cooper. She was the No. 1 Obedience Weimaraner 6 times and Top Obedience Weimaraner in all systems for 5 years. She was the first Champion Weimaraner to earn an OTCH title and also the first Weimaraner to be awarded a UDX title. Sparky was a multiple HIT and HC winner, including winner of the 1994 WCA National Obedience Trial. She earned her OTCH title in 1992, and after retiring from the obedience ring in 1994 with 172 career OTCH points, Sparky was handled by Junior Maggie Bonness for a year. At the age of 10, Sparky earned her Novice Agility title in 3 straight trials, as well as her NRD title. Sparky's greatest honor was being inducted into the WCA Hall of Fame in 2005.

Figure 16-27: *OTCH Heidi v. Falkenberg, UDT.* Owned by Booth and Anna Kelley and handled by Anna, Heidi was Anna's first obedience dog. They learned together, and their efforts were rewarded with an OTCH in 1981. Heidi ranked on the WCA Top 10 Obedience lists for 7 consecutive years, placing No. 1 in 1978, 1979, and 1981; she retired from obedience competition with a total of 128 OTCH points.

Figure 16-28: *OTCH CH Jar Em's Special Sporting Clay, UDX5, JH, VX.* Clay launched his obedience career in August 1999 and received his UD title less than 7 months later. He was the WCA No. 1 Obedience Dog 3 times (2000, 2001, and 2004). Clay earned his OTCH in 2005, the first Champion male Weimaraner to do so. He was invited to the AKC National Obedience Championship 5 times, attending in 2001 and 2004. In 2000, he was the WCA National Specialty winner, with a score of 197 from Utility B, also winning HC. Clay had 108 points at the time of writing and he continues to compete, with his top score in competition thus far 198.5 in both the Utility and Open classes. Randy Scharich is fortunate to be the owner and handler of two OTCH Weimaraners, both from the same dam, CH Jar Em's Casino Roulette.

Figure 16-29: *TC, AFC Regen's Summer Blaze, UDX2, MH, TDX, RE, MX, MXJ, SDX, RDX, VX6.* Ruby, owned by Shirley Nilsson and Judi Voris and handled by Shirley, completed the requirements for an OTCH in 2005, in the process also becoming the first OTCH Weimaraner to also hold Field, Dual, and Triple Champion titles. Along the way, she garnered many HIT and HC awards and was the No. 1 Delaney Weimaraner in 2004. Ruby is the only OTCH Weimaraner to have an OTCH offspring; she retired from obedience with 101 lifetime OTCH points and a top score in obedience competition of 199.5 in the Open class and 198.5 in the Utility class.

Figure 16-30: *OTCH Haiku Solar Eclipse, UDT.* Owned and handled by Martha Fast, Teak started his obedience career in Hawaii, where he was also the first Weimaraner to earn a Tracking Dog title. Despite the limited number of obedience trials available in Hawaii, Teak made the WCA Top 10 Obedience lists and managed to accrue 35 OTCH points before moving, at age 8, to California. Equally successful in the "lower 48," he ranked No. 1 on the WCA Top 10 list in 1989, the same year in which he also won HIT at the WCA National Specialty Obedience Trial. Teak completed his OTCH—the first male Weimaraner to do so—at the age of 10 and retired with 102 lifetime OTCH points and three all-breed HIT awards.

Figure 17-1: *MACH 5 Chloe's Blue Velvet,* "Chloe," was the 60th dog of any breed, the 9th sporting breed dog, and the first Weimaraner to earn the MACH title. Chloe is owned and handled by Lori Barbee of California. She retired from competition in 2004, at 9 years old, and still holds the record for the most lifetime accrued championship double qualifiers (111). Chloe was the AKC and WCA No. 1 ranking Weimaraner throughout her entire career. Photograph by Tien Tran.

CHAPTER 17

THE DANCE OF DOG AGILITY

by Lori Barbee

Watching a Weimaraner working in the field or running at play leaves one with little doubt about the agile qualities of the breed. They possess the intelligence and athleticism needed to excel in sporting endeavors. Since many dog owners seek new ways to challenge the intellect of their canine companions and to strengthen their bonds with them, dog sports such as agility have been created. Agility requires a constant communication between dog and human. It is a dynamic and fluid sport, a dance of sorts, where teamwork is essential to navigate a designated obstacle course. The desire and willingness to work that many Weimaraners possess, combined with the playful nature of the breed, make agility a truly enjoyable sport for both Weimaraner and owner.

Enter Agility

The roots of agility lie in equestrian sports. In England in 1978, the sponsors of the Crufts Dog Show were looking for an event that could fill time in the ring between obedience and the large conformation show. The idea was conceived to use dogs, in the fashion of equestrian jumping, to entertain the spectators. It was fast and exciting, and the seed was planted for a new type of canine performance event. Dog agility came on the scene in the United States in 1986.

Agility combines elements of obedience with challenging jumps and obstacles to create a physically demanding dog sport. Agility interested those who were looking for something beyond traditional obedience, something more athletic to do with their dogs. Agility now has widespread popularity, and participation has exploded, creating the fastest-growing dog sport in this country to date.

What Is It?

Agility is a sport requiring speed, accuracy, and athleticism. It is an obstacle course for dogs.

Dogs are free of leashes and are guided around an obstacle course by verbal commands and physical cues from their human team member. Each team's run is judged on the accuracy of the performance and the speed with which the course is navigated. Obstacles on the agility course consist of open and collapsed tunnels, a variety of

Figure 17-2: *The athletic nature of the breed shines* in the sport of agility. The tail of the Weimaraner is used to assist in balance, as turning and jumping occur simultaneously. Proper timing of commands from the handler gives the dog the needed information to direct him to the next obstacle. This information allows the dog to adjust his stride length and footing for optimum efficiency. CH TopHat's Bad Moon Rising, CDX, RA, OA, OAJ, NJP, NSD, VX. Photograph by Marcy Mantell Photography.

Figure 17-3: *Agility takes its roots* from equestrian jumping events. Dogs are directed through an obstacle course by their human partner. These obstacles include jumps, tunnels, see-saws, dog walks, tables, and A-frames. It is a dynamic sport that uses many talents of the Weimaraner, such as speed, balance, strength, and attention. CH MACH Regen's Rocket Launcher, VCD2, XF, SD, RD, VX4. Photograph by Ken Kennedy.

jumps (including broad, tire, and double- and triple-bar jumps), and a series of vertical weave poles that the dog must slalom through. Obstacles that must be climbed are called contact obstacles, since the dog must make physical contact with painted zones located on the initial portion of the ascending side and the final section of the descending side. These include an A-frame, an elevated dog walk plank, and a see-saw. A pause table, on which the dog must sit or lie down, based on the judges' instructions, is also found on the course.

There are three major organizations that sanction agility events in the United States. They are the AKC, the United States Dog Agility Association (USDAA), and the North American Dog Agility Council (NADAC). As the sport of dog agility has grown, new organizations have begun to form. Rules differ by organization. Information about each of these organizations can be found on their respective websites. The WCA recognizes agility titles awarded by the AKC.

There are three types of courses found at an AKC agility trial. The Standard Agility Class includes a combination of all the above-mentioned obstacles. It is a course designed to challenge a team's speed, control (contact obstacles and

table), and accuracy. The second type of course is called Jumpers with Weaves (JWW). It may consist of any combination of jumps, tunnels, and weave poles, and it tests the team's accuracy and jumping ability at full speed. The newest event in the line-up for AKC agility, which was added in 2007, is called Fifteen and Send Time, or FAST. It is a game that combines the strategy of point accumulation (with every obstacle having a point value) and distance work, as each course contains a short sequence of obstacles that must be performed with the handler at a marked distance away from the dog. Extra points are earned by sending the dog to the designated obstacles while the handler remains behind the distance line. The send portion must be successfully completed to earn a qualifying score.

In competition, each course of obstacles is unique. It is designed by the official who will be judging the dogs for that day. It is this judge who determines the Standard Course Time (SCT) using a measuring wheel along the anticipated path of the dogs and calculating yards per second. Courses are approved for use by the parent organization sanctioning the event. Before competition begins, handlers have an opportunity to view a course map and walk through the courses without their dogs. This provides the handlers with the opportunity to familiarize themselves

Figure 17-4: *Success in agility* requires the blending of many elements of teamwork. Drive and focus are key components in that combination. The dog needs to pay close attention to the handler's cues, both in body language and verbal commands, while executing obstacles on the course at top speed. Weaving through the poles, as shown here, is a complex task that requires skill and concentration. It is but one of the "dance steps" required in a sport called Dog Agility. Can CH Greyghost M. Christie, YMG Oreos, CD. Photograph by Dixon Zalit.

Figure 17-5: *Teaching correct and efficient contact performance* on the see-saw includes the dog touching the yellow "contact zone" on the ascending and descending sides of the board. The dog must safely control the moving see-saw until it touches the ground on the descending side. Agility performance is a mixture of speed and control. The see-saw is an obstacle that requires both of these elements. Photographs by Lori Barbee and Trista Hidalgo.

Figure 17-6: *Weave poles* are one of the more difficult obstacles for the dog to learn. The dog must slalom through a series of 12 poles, always entering the obstacle with the first pole at the dog's left shoulder and then weaving in and out of each pole. Dogs develop their own individual footwork pattern, which may be a single-footed or "swimming" style, as seen in this photo. Photograph by Tien Tran.

with the numbered sequence of obstacles on the course and to analyze how best to handle their dog through the course. During the actual competition, jumps are set at varying heights, according to the height of the dog at the withers. Most Weimaraners are required to jump 24 inches, as 22 inches and over at the withers is the specification for that height division. The occasional Weimaraner will measure 22 inches or less and can compete in the 20-inch division.

Dogs are run on courses that are created for three different levels of difficulty. In AKC agility, these levels are called Novice, Open, and Excellent. As in obedience, Novice is split into Novice A and B classes. The Novice A class is for handlers who have never put an agility title on a dog and for dogs without an agility title. Novice B is for all dogs and handlers who have previously earned an agility title. Excellent-level teams are also designated A or B. Excellent A is for dogs that have not yet earned the Excellent Standard or Excellent Jumpers agility title. Excellent B is for dogs that have completed the requirements for their Excellent titles and that are working toward earning the required number of qualifying runs for the Master Agility titles and the Master Agility Championship (MACH) title. Dogs must start at the Novice level and complete the requirements for each level before advancing to the next.

The AKC also offers a Preferred class in its agility program. Preferred classes are designed as a modified program, allowing a greater number of agility teams a chance to com-

Figure 17-7: *Performance events* such as agility, obedience, tracking, and hunt tests are open to all AKC-registered Weimaraners. This includes blues, long hairs, and ILP-registered Weimaraners. Agility organizations require that a dog be registered prior to competing in agility events. GreyGhost's Hair Apparent, CD, OA, OAJ.

Figure 17-8: *There is no doubt* about the athletic ability of this Weimaraner. He is exhibiting speed, strength, balance, and desire. This perfect combination of skills creates a talented, successful agility dog. A solid foundation built on progressive and consistent training methods will establish a working relationship that can achieve many goals. CH MACH4 JamSpirit Nobility, JH, NRD, VX2. Photograph by V. W. Perry.

pete. This may include young dogs just starting out in agility or the dog–handler team who desire to continue to compete but are no longer able to meet the time and height requirements of the Regular agility classes. The Preferred class provides a less strenuous environment for dog and handler. Dogs are allowed more time on the course, spread jumps are removed, and jump heights are one height lower than would be required in the Regular classes. Many Preferred titles can be earned; however, there is no Championship title in the Preferred program.

In each agility run, a dog can earn a maximum score of 100 points. A perfect score is termed a "clean run," and a qualifying score at the Excellent B level requires a clean run. At all class levels, deductions, or faults, are subtracted from the perfect score for certain performance errors. These faults include failing to complete the course in less than the Standard Course Time, taking extra or out-of-sequence obstacles, or running past or refusing to perform an obstacle. At all levels, knocking a bar down, missing an obstacle completely, or failing to touch the yellow zones of the contact obstacles results in a non-qualifying score for that run.

Agility Titles

Titles are earned in Standard, JWW, and FAST classes at the Novice, Open, and Excellent levels. Earning a qualifying score or "leg" toward an agility title requires a minimum score of 85 out of a possible 100 points, with three legs needed in order to earn a title. No faults are allowed when the dogs are competing at the Excellent B level. Following are the agility titles.

AJP: Excellent Agility Jumpers with Weaves "A" Preferred

AX: Agility Excellent

AXJ: Excellent Agility Jumper

AXP: Agility Excellent "A" Preferred

FTC: FAST Century

Figure 17-10: *Successful completion of the A-frame* obstacle occurs after the dog scales the 5'6" frame and touches the yellow contact zone on the descending side. This requirement constitutes an element of control and is based on safety, so that the dog is not taught or encouraged to leap from the obstacle at an unsafe height. CH MACH3 Jamspirit Nobility, JH, NRD, VX2. Photograph by Woof Wear.

Figure 17-9: *Whether young in years or young at heart,* the AKC offers a Preferred agility program that provides the dog and handler team a less demanding venue in which to compete. Handlers are given more time to navigate their dogs through the course, and the jump heights are lower than those in Regular agility competition. This may be the perfect option for those who are just beginning to compete or who still love to play the game in a less strenuous environment. Princess Cholla, CD, JH, AX, MXJ, NAP, NJP, V, and her 9-year-old handler, Raven Emmons (left), and Kaceem's Devil's Double, VCD2, with Sharlene Kline (right). Photograph by Eric Hedstrom.

Figure 17-11: *This 7-week-old pup* has learned to master a balance board. It teaches a puppy body awareness and balance on a moving surface. These skills are helpful to a dog that must later master the moving see-saw. Safety and fun are concepts that need to be foremost on the agenda when training a puppy. Regen's Gray Quest Callback, CD, TD. Photograph by Lori Barbee.

FTCP: FAST Century Preferred

MACH: Master Agility Champion

MFP: Master Excellent FAST Preferred

MJP: Master Excellent Jumpers with Weaves "B" Preferred

MX: Master Agility Excellent

MXF: Master Excellent FAST

MXJ: Master Excellent Jumpers with Weaves

MXP: Master Agility Excellent "B" Preferred

NA: Novice Agility

NAJ: Novice Agility Jumper

NAP: Novice Agility Preferred

NF: Novice FAST

NFP: Novice FAST Preferred

NJP: Novice Jumpers with Weaves Preferred

OA: Open Agility

OAJ: Open Agility Jumper

OAP: Open Agility Preferred

OF: Open FAST

OFP: Open FAST Preferred

Figure 17-12: *Teamwork on the agility course* is like a dance. With time and training, a dog can become an experienced partner that knows the dance steps and reads the handler's body language clearly and effortlessly. Time spent with a dog while training can create or strengthen the special bond between handler and dog. While achieving goals can be rewarding, the journey in getting to those goals may be even more valuable. CH Vanity's Visionary, CD, JH, MX, MXJ, NJP, NSD, NRD, VX2, BROM. Photograph by Temple Imaging Services.

OJP: Open Jumpers with Weaves Preferred

PAX: Preferred Agility Excellent

XF: Excellent FAST

XFP: Excellent FAST Preferred

At the Masters (Excellent B) level of competition, dogs are run on exactly the same course as in the Excellent A class. These dogs have earned their Excellent titles from the Excellent A class and are now working toward their Master Agility, Master Jumpers, and/or MACH titles. Master Agility and Master Jumpers titles are earned by qualifying 10 times in each respective Excellent B category.

Master Agility Championship

The AKC initiated its agility championship program in February 1999. It is designed to reward and acknowledge those dogs that possess the desired combination of speed and accuracy. To achieve this title, a dog must earn a total of 20 double qualifiers from the Excellent B class. Also termed Double Q's, a double qualifier signifies that the dog has qualified in both a Standard and JWW run on the same day. The dog must also earn a total of 750 Championship points. One Championship point is earned for every full second a dog runs faster than the SCT in the Excellent B class. Points are multiplied if a dog places first or second in their jump height. First-place finishers multiply points by a factor of 2, and second-place finishers by a factor of 1.5. A dog that meets the above requirements earns the prefix title of MACH. The MACH title may be followed by a numeric suffix. This number indicates that the dog has fulfilled the requirements of the MACH title for each number designated (example, 40 Double Q's and 1,500 points = MACH2).

Getting Started

There are many fine books and audiovisual media available that give sound advice and instruction to those interested in starting agility training. Training can begin in the backyard, with attention games and simple drills. Finding a local facility that offers classes can give a handler the advantage of learning from those with experience in the sport of agility.

Puppies should be exposed to many different types of stimulation to enhance their learning experiences. This may include walking and running on different surfaces, climbing on and through safe obstacles that are stationary and moving, and being exposed to many sights, sounds, and people. A variety of stimuli and experiences will help develop a puppy that is accustomed to encountering new, different, and possibly stressful situations.

Through training, a dog will learn to watch, understand, and respond to the body language and verbal commands of the handler. Establishing this communication enables a handler to

Figure 17-14: *Tunnels are safe to begin with,* even for the youngest of pups. Obstacle training should be age appropriate, with jumps placed at ground level and see-saw and dog walk planks placed flat on the ground. Safety and proper technique are primary concerns. When a puppy has a proper foundation in his training program, the results are a dog that is skilled and confident.

Figure 17-13: *Learning to run through a collapsed tunnel* challenges a dog's tactile and visual senses. The dog must run into a barrel and push through the fabric tube at the other end. In doing so, the dog loses sight of his handler as he races through the tunnel. Progressive, safe training can build a dog's confidence and trust in her handler as she learns to navigate obstacles in training. Gray Sky's Broadway Bound, CD, JH, NA, OAJ. Photograph by Steve Surfman.

Figure 17-15: *Can you see the smile* on this Weimaraner's face? Agility is a dynamic sport that enables a Weimaraner to exhibit her individual style and personality. Dogs love the running, jumping, and weaving involved with agility. It is good exercise for both dog and handler and a fun way to spend time together. GreyGhost Fuzzy by Design, CD.

Figure 17-16: *Dogs jump* many different types of obstacles, including the double-bar jump. Also seen on the agility course are the tire jump, broad jump, panel jump, and single- and triple-bar jumps. The jump height required for most Weimaraners is 24 inches. CH Silver Honey's She's the One, CD, RE, OA, OAJ. Photograph by Tien Tran.

direct the dog, without a leash around the agility course. This training consists of foundation work in obstacle performance and flat work (the handling on the ground that takes place between obstacles). Done in small increments and at age- and skill-appropriate levels, both of these concepts can be taught to puppies or to dogs that are older and just beginning agility.

Training actual obstacle performance at competition height requires a dog that is physically mature. Growth plates should be closed before the repetitive stress of full-height jumping is introduced. Prior to initiating any training program, the dog should be fit, flexible, and in good general condition. Safety must be the primary concern until the dog understands how to control his body on each of the obstacles at speed. The obstacle performance that is taught to a young or beginner dog should be appropriate to its age and skill level. This means that jumps are no higher than the elbows (on the ground for puppies), that contact obsta-

cles start flat on the ground, that tables remain low, and that weave poles are laterally spaced off the midline to create a center channel to minimize spinal stress. Tunnels can be safely performed by dogs of all ages and levels.

Although obstacle performance is very important, a larger portion of the time spent on an agility course occurs between obstacles, or "on the flat." Fortunately, it is safe to begin working these skills with any dog, regardless of age or physical maturity. The flat work includes exercises that mimic the handling that occurs on the ground between obstacles. This is done with few or no actual pieces of agility equipment. Flat work includes but is not limited to teaching the dog to run alongside the handler, to understand and respond to handler acceleration and deceleration, to target (nose touch) the handler's hand while running, to turn toward or away from the handler while in motion, to turn left or right on command, and to move away from the handler both forward and laterally.

Keep it Fun

One of the first things to remember with agility, as with most dog sports, is that it is intended to be fun for both dog and handler. A happy working canine partner is eager to learn and play, while a worried dog may find anything more interesting than his handler or the agility course. Keep the training fun and exciting. Keep the training sessions short. If it has been a "bad day" for the human team member, postpone a session until training can be approached in a positive frame of mind.

Learn what motivates the dog. Is it food? Is it that Frisbee or tennis ball? Is happy praise, used together with food and toys, what he likes best? Above all, if the handler is enjoying the time spent training, the dog should enjoy it, too!

Handler vs. Obstacle Focus

Some dogs are very focused on their owners, while others are much more stimulated by what is happening in their environment. Keep in mind that Weimaraners were bred to leave their master's side and to independently hunt and find game. That type of genetic programming can create a dog that is very interested in the sights and smells of his surrounding environment. As agility training begins, be aware of what the dog is focused on. A handler-focused dog may be running into or around obstacles because he is watching the handler, or even tripping the handler because he is reluctant to move beyond what the dog feels is a comfortable distance. In this case, a large portion of training time should be spent on getting the dog to work at a greater distance from the handler. Incrementally increasing the distance from an obstacle, placing a target at the end of a line of jumps, and throwing toys to reward distance all encourage and reinforce the dog for looking and moving ahead or to the side of the trainer.

A dog that is more focused on the obstacles or the environment, as many Weimaraners are, needs training exercises that encourage him to keep his attention on the handler. An example of this might be performing short sequences of handling or obstacle training, followed by a vigorous game of tug. Food and toys can be used to reward the dog for returning to the handler after she has gone out to a tunnel or jump. The key to success for an obstacle- or environment-focused dog is for the handler to become the most exciting and rewarding thing in the environment for that dog.

Figure 17-17: *Training a dog to stay focused* on the handler results in optimum communication throughout the course. A dog is required to remain in a designated position (a sit or down) on the pause table while the judge executes a 5-second count. This dog eagerly awaits a release from the table to continue along the agility course. Photograph by Trista Hidalgo.

Obedience

Many of the skills taught in agility take their start from basic obedience commands. It is prudent, while working on foundation agility skills, to continue to reinforce and proof the basic obedience skills. Sit, stay, down, wait, and come are skills that you will continue to use throughout the dog's agility career. Be aware that the agility environment is one that is highly charged. There is much activity and noise at an agility training center or trial site that may be distracting to a dog. Visiting a training or competition site with the goal of working on the dog's attention and obedience skills will pay off in the long run by developing a dog that is familiar with working and paying attention to her handler in this type of environment.

Enjoy the Process

There are many ways to teach each agility skills. Some ways will be better for a particular dog and handler than others. Be open to trying new ideas. Using a variety of games for teaching skills will keep it fun and interesting for the dog. Discuss the pros and cons of agility concepts with training friends and instructors. It is useful to have multiple training methods, each for use in a different situation or with a different dog. Above all, both dog and handler should enjoy the process of learning and the time spent together.

Figure 17-18: ***An agility dog must learn*** to work away from his handler when directed to do so. He must then check in with the handler for further direction. The peripheral vision of a canine, paired with understanding of verbal commands, assists the dog in following command from a distance. Windson N Mystic High Spirits, OA, AXJ, NAP, NJP. Photograph by Bruce McClelland.

Entering the Ring

The teamwork needed for agility competition should solidify with continued training and practice. Both human and canine should be enjoying the process and the game. Perhaps the idea of competing has begun to take root. What are the next steps toward entering a competition?

- Ask an instructor or friend experienced in agility competition to evaluate the dog–handler team to determine whether the skills and teamwork necessary to safely compete are present.

- Search the Internet and write or call sanctioning organizations to find out what the requirements are for registering a dog. Obtain a rule book and become familiar with the rules. Event calendars may be found on the agility organization's website.

- Attend a competition to observe how it is run. Volunteering to help at an agility event will give you an up-close look at how the event is organized.

- Take the dog along to a competition event, just to watch. Use this time not only to watch but to test the dog's focus and attention in an atmosphere where many distractions are present. Check the rules to be sure this is allowed, as some sanctioned events do not allow unentered dogs on the grounds.

- Attend a fun match or a "Show and Go" to test the dog and handler skills in a practice arena that is different from the usual training grounds.

- Make a list of equipment needed at a trial. This includes but is not limited to a crate or pen to contain the dog while walking the course, leash, toys, treats, water, shade, chair, and registration card.

When it is time to compete, entering an agility trial requires submitting an entry form to the trial secretary. Confirmation will be returned in the mail or by email, acknowledging receipt of the entry and providing important information, such as start time, directions to the site, the number of dogs entered, class running order, etc.

An agility handler who has prepared well for the competitive environment will find confidence in the foundation that has been built and the working relationship developed with his dog. Competition provides the opportunity to identify the strengths and weaknesses of the team, and future training programs can be developed to improve on those weaknesses. The most important thing to remember, whether training or competing, is that agility should be fun for both handler and dog.

Figure 17-19: ***Agility is a sport that can be fun*** for both dog and handler. Running and jumping are intrinsically rewarding to the dog. It is the handler's job to make it fun to work together. Keeping the training fun, interesting, and rewarding will create an eager agility partner. This in turn will pay off with a dog that loves to work with his owner, whether it is in actual competition, a training session, or just a fun day at the park. CH MACH Regen's Hot Chili Pepper, VCD3, SH, RDX, SDX, VX5.

Figure 17-20: ***Prior to the beginning of competition,*** agility handlers have an opportunity to complete a "walk through." This is a short period when handlers walk the agility obstacle course without their dogs, allowing themselves a chance to memorize the sequence of obstacles and to plan a handling strategy for their dog. Photograph by Lori Barbee.

Table 17-1: *Agility organizations.*

United States		Canada	
American Kennel Club 5580 Centerview Drive Raleigh, NC 27606 919.233.9767	www.akc.org	**Agility Association of Canada** 16648 Highway 48 Stouffile, ON L4A 7X4 905.473.3473	www.aac.ca
United States Dog Agility Association P.O. Box 850955 Richardson, TX 75085 972.487.2200	www.usdaa.com	**Canadian Kennel Club** 89 Skyway Avenue, Suite 100 Etobiocoke, ON M9W 6R4 800.250.8040	www.ckc.ca
North American Dog Agility Council 11522 South Highway 3 Cataldo, ID 83810	www.nadac.com	**General Interest**	
United Kennel Club 100 East Kilgore Road Kalamazoo, MI 49002 269.343.7037	www.ukcdogs.com	**Clean Run Productions** Books, videos, monthly magazine	www.cleanrun.com
Canine Performance Events PO Box 805 South Lyon, MI 48179	www.k9cpe.com		

Agility Healing

The AKC's Regulations for Agility Trials (September 2006) state, "The purpose of AKC agility trials is to afford owners the opportunity to demonstrate a dog's physical ability/soundness and willingness to work with its handler under a variety of conditions." Along the way, agility provides fun and recreation for both dog and handler, but many dogs realize a secondary benefit of the sport.

Agility can have a therapeutic effect. It can help to boost the confidence of dogs that are shy, polish those that are lacking in social skills, and heal the wounds of previous abuse and mistrust. Such is the story of Sadie, a rescued Weimaraner whose owner, Sheila Cook, took Sadie from a dog that was labeled "not trainable" to one that now holds the title of Master Agility Champion. The road was not one easily or quickly traveled, but the rewards from the journey have been invaluable for both dog and human.

Sadie was 18 months old when Sheila brought her home. Sadie's previous owners did not have time for her. She was undersocialized and had probably been abused. Sadie had issues facing many rescue dogs. She was fearful of humans and easily frightened by sights and sounds. Her confidence was lacking, and Sheila sought ways to boost her courage. They gave obedience competition a try, but Sadie was always too worried about the judge in the ring with them. Another Weimaraner owner suggested giving agility a try. Sheila began to teach Sadie to have fun and to play with her, which Sheila felt was not allowed in Sadie's previous home. Time and patience were needed in abundance, and Sheila began to use food and lavish praise as prime motivators for Sadie. Slowly, Sadie began to enjoy the new game she was learning. She developed trust in her new owner and found confidence in the new places that they were going. Sheila learned that training had to be accomplished with a very positive attitude and that it must be FUN. It was well over a year before Sheila felt that she and Sadie were ready for the competition agility ring. But love, patience, and praise paid off, and they came home from their first agility trial with a blue ribbon!

According to Sheila, there is no better way to strengthen the bond between an owner and her rescue Weimaraner than the time spent training, showing, and traveling for agility. She wants other owners to know it can be an amazing experience and rewarding journey to see your "shy" rescue dog blossom into a confident, happy agility dog.

Superstars of Agility

MACH5 Chloe's Blue Velvet, "Chloe" was the first Weimaraner to earn the title. To honor her achievements, her picture and story appear on the overleaf to this chapter.

And the Champions are...

MACH5 Chloe's Blue Velvet
Owned by Gene and Lori Barbee (see Figure 17-1)

CH MACH2 Lechsteinhof's Silver Lady, CDX, RN
Owned by Kimberly Budd

CH MACH3 Jamspirit Nobility, JH, NRD, VX2
Owned by Melissa Chandler

MACH2 Wanric Trevor Tracks, CDX, RN, RD, NSD, VX
Owned by Wanda Gunter

MACH GrayQuest Repeat Performance, VCD2, JH, RN, SD, NRD, VX3
Owned by Lori Barbee

CH MACH Regen's Hot Chili Pepper, VCD3, SH, RDX, SDX, VX5
Owned by Judi Voris and Shirley Nilsson

MACH Princess Fallon of Amber Glen, CD, NAP, NJP
Owned by Sheila Cook

MACH August Grub Grau, NSD, NRD, V
Owned by Jennifer Dec DVM

CH MACH Regen's GrayQuest Rock Candy, VCD1, TDX, RN, RD, NSD, VX3
Owned by Lori Barbee and Judi Voris

CH MACH Regen's Rocket Launcher, VCD2, XF, SD, RD, VX4
Owned by Steve and Laurie Jenks (see *Index*)

Figure 17-21: ***CH MACH 2 Lechsteinhof's Silver Lady, CDX, CGC.*** Ayla was handled to her MACH titles by her owner, Kimberly Budd of Iowa. Ayla was the second Weimaraner to earn the MACH title. Ayla amassed 40 Double Q's and 1,819 championship points during her career. She is now retired from agility and remains passionate about hunting. She continues to compete in obedience and rally.

Figure 17-22: ***CH MACH3 Jamspirit Nobility, JH, NRD, VX2.*** Jag was the first male Weimaraner to fulfill the requirements for the MACH title. Owned and handled by Melissa Chandler of Ohio, Jag achieved the AKC/WCA ranking of No. 1 agility Weimaraner in 2004 and 2005. He is still competing at the time of printing and is well on his way to reaching his MACH4 status.

Figure 17-23: *MACH2 Wanric Trevor Tracks, CDX, RN, RD, NSD, VX.* Trevor is owned and handled by Wanda Gunter of Tennessee and earned his MACH title in 2005. Trevor has been consistently ranked in the Top 10 of the WCA agility standings.

Figure 17-24: *MACH GrayQuest Repeat Performance, VCD2, JH, RN, SD, NRD, VX3.* Encore was the 5th Weimaraner to earn the MACH title. Encore follows in Chloe's footsteps, being owned and handled by Lori Barbee. Encore earned her MACH title in 2005. Encore continues to train and compete in agility, obedience, tracking, and field events. Photograph by Tien Tran.

Figure 17-25: *CH MACH Regen's Hot Chili Pepper, VCD3, SH, RDX, SDX, VX5, CGC.* Pepper was bred by and is owned by Judi Voris and Shirley Nilsson. She was guided to her MACH title by Judi Voris of Washington State in 2005. Pepper's first project following her MACH title will be to pursue an MH title. Photograph by Tien Tran.

Figure 17-26: *MACH Princess Fallon of Amber Glen, CD, NAP, NJP.* Sadie is owned and handled by Sheila Cook of Kentucky. She earned her MACH in 2006 at 8 years old. Sadie came into Sheila's life from Weimaraner Rescue. Together, they overcame many hurdles on the road to MACH status, earning Sadie the honor of being the first rescued Weimaraner to do so. Photograph by Arroo Photography.

Figure 17-27: *MACH August Grub Grau, NSD, NRD, CGC, V.* Gus was handled from Novice A to his MACH solely by his owner, Jennifer Dec DVM from Michigan. Since entering the Excellent level of competition, he has consistently been ranked in the Top 10 Weimaraner standings, despite limited competition opportunities while Jennifer was attending veterinary school. In 2006, Gus earned the title of WCA National Agility Champion, in addition to his MACH. Gus remains actively competitive in agility, working toward his MACH 2, and has started Rally competition.

Figure 17-28: *CH MACH Regen's GrayQuest Rock Candy, VCD1, TDX, RN, RD, NSD, VX3.* Roca is owned and handled by Lori Barbee and co-owned by Judi Voris. In 2006, Roca became the youngest Weimaraner to earn the MACH title, at 3¹/2 years old. She is actively training and competing in agility, obedience, tracking, hunting, and retrieving. Photograph by Terry Curtiss.

Figure 18-1: *CT CC's Amaz'n Rainy's Gabriele, CD, RN,* owned by Linda Swanson and bred by Chris Conklin, made history, earning the breed's first Variable Surface Tracking (VST) and Champion Tracker (CT) titles on November 6, 2005. Here is Gabi's story, as told by Linda Swanson.

"Gabi first showed interest in tracking at 9 weeks, and was following scent on hard surfaces, like concrete, from the beginning. Our first AKC tracking experience was in May 2002. Her breeder was putting on a mini-tracking demonstration and invited us to come along. At that time Gabi was 17 weeks old, and I was *hooked!* Chris Conklin, Gabi's breeder and trainer, prepared us for her certification. Actually, Gabi was probably ready from day one, but I needed to gain trust in her and confidence in myself. Gabi passed her Tracking Dog (TD) test after just our second attempt at the age of 9 months. In spring 2003, we entered our first Tracking Dog Excellent (TDX) test, where Gabi passed to become the youngest TDX Weim at the age of 13 months.

"Then the hard work began. Formal tracking on hard surfaces is so different from the fields that held the TD and TDX tests or the games we played around work. Her tracking style changed as she matured, which meant I had to relearn her body language. Most importantly, Gabi and I learned to work as a team. I learned to not influence her by thinking I knew where the track was, to keep my mind focused on my end of the partnership and let her work.

"On November 6, 2005, the hard work and training paid off, and CC's Amaz'n Rainy's Gabriele, CGC, TDI, became the first AKC Champion Tracker Weimaraner at the age of 3½."

See Figure 18-33 for a map of Gabi's actual track and Linda's account of this memorable event.

CHAPTER 18

HOT ON THE TRACK

by Patricia Riley

Dogs are born able to use their sense of smell and in fact use their nose to find their first meal of mother's milk. Canids in the wild depend on their sense of smell to find food, water, and mates, among many other survival needs. Modern *Canis lupus* v. *familiaris* has evolved with incredible variety to meet the needs and desires of humans, and many breeds, including the Weimaraner, were bred specifically for their scenting abilities. While humans have a mere 4–5 cm² of olfactory surface and approximately 5 million olfactory cells, a dog has an olfactory surface of 92–170 cm², with 125–300 million olfactory cells! The wide ranges are due mostly to size and breed variations. A talented and trained dog can discern the presence of some odors in dilutions of up to 1 part in 1 quadrillion; that would be like finding a single penny in a stack as tall as the Empire State Building.

So, What Is Tracking?

A person, animal, or object moving through an area leaves a scent trail, a bouquet believed to be composed of disturbance of the substrate, as well as gases and microscopic debris shed from the body. In its most general sense, tracking is the ability to follow this scent trail. Dogs are born knowing how to track; the sport of tracking, however, requires that the dog learn to follow a specific scent on command, despite other possibly more inviting or conflicting scents, and to indicate articles found along the way that harbor the tracklayer's scent. The handler motivates, directs, and refines the dog's progress through a well-planned, wide-ranging program to develop the complex skills and stamina necessary to accomplish a task akin to playing a concert while simultaneously solving a calculus problem and running a marathon. The handler must also learn to "read" the dog's body language while handling the tracking line and avoid distracting the dog from its work; often, it is harder for the handler to learn the necessary skills than the dog. Tracking comes naturally to most Weimaraners, and their enthusiasm usually makes training enjoyable for both dog and handler.

Getting Started

Equipment

Tracking does not require a great deal of equipment, but a few items are necessary to prepare a dog for AKC tracking tests.

Harness

The AKC requires the dog to be on a harness; the harness must be of a soft, pliable material and designed to minimize restriction of the dog's movement. Each material has advantages and disadvantages, and it is really a personal choice. When starting with a puppy, harnesses that are highly adjustable are necessary, and several may be needed to accommodate the growth of a very young puppy to an adult dog. Nylon harnesses, which come in the widest variety of sizes and have great adjustability, can be purchased at very reasonable prices from many dog catalogs. Leather harnesses are more expensive but can last a handler's lifetime.

Figure 18-2: *CH Greysport Amazing Grace, UDTX, RDX, NSD, VX3, BROM, HOF,* owned by Judy Thompson. Its heritage makes tracking a natural for the Weimaraner. With a well-planned training program and experience, a Weimaraner can become a skilled tracking dog whose accomplishments rival those of any breed. Grace shows the natural ability and drive typical of Weimaraners.

Figure 18-3: *A sport for all....* In September 2003, Gabi (featured in Figure 18-1) became the youngest Weimaraner (at that time) to earn a TDX. To show that tracking tests are not just for the young, but also for the young at heart, at the same test, Gabi's grandmother, Izzy (Sunrise Again Sweet Izabelle, CDX, TDX, NA, NSD, NRD, V), became one of the oldest Weimaraners to earn a TDX.

Tracking Line

AKC tests require a tracking line 20–40 feet long. However, the novice handler and dog may do well with a 6-foot lead early on and progress to a longer line with more experience. A shorter line allows the handler to keep the dog on track early on, to help the dog develop confidence, and to observe the behavior and body language of the dog without the additional task of avoiding entanglement in the excess line. Some experienced handlers even prefer a line closer to 20 feet than 40 feet. It is easier to observe important details of the dog's body language—rate of respiration and more subtle positions of the head—when the handler is closer to the dog; with a shorter line, the excess lead is less likely to get caught in brush or roots, tangle the handler's feet, or get stepped on, all of which might inadvertently result in a disruptive or de-motivating jolt on the hardworking dog.

The line may be of any sturdy, weather-resistant material that is strong enough to restrain the dog. Keep in mind that the line must also be comfortable to grip.

Lines of cotton or nylon webbing are inexpensive but may be hard on the hands if the dog pulls hard, and they tend to collect debris when dragged behind the handler. Cotton leads will also soak up water when the dog is tracking under wet conditions and can become rather heavy; the moisture-retaining potential also makes cotton lines prone to mold and mildew, so be sure the line is dry before storing it. Static climbing rope comes in a variety of widths to accommodate the needs of most handlers; many bright colors are available, making it easier to spot a dropped line in tall grass or brush. Also, the larger diameters rarely tangle or snag.

A well-maintained leather line develops a wonderful "feel" as well as a certain amount of natural "give," which facilitates the communication between dog and handler; additionally, well-maintained leather has a very long service life and rarely tangles or gathers debris. Leather lines can be expensive, however. New synthetic leather materials boast the positive "feel" of leather with virtually no maintenance and with greater strength than nylon or cotton.

Success in the tracking field may depend on being able to "read" a dog through the tracking line, so try as many different lines as possible to find just the right one. The snap should be strong but not act as an anchor on the dog. Regulations require that the handler be holding the line attached to the dog when performing the track; if the line or snap breaks and the dog finishes without the handler, it may not count as a "pass"—a good reason to carry a spare.

Track Markers

In early training, it may be necessary to mark the track to ensure that the dog is on the trail. Maps are necessary, but early on, flagging will be easier for the handler. Tracking stakes can be inexpensive garden stakes with a small piece of surveyor's tape attached, or surveyor's flags from a home or farm supply store.

Clothespins or washers with flagging or sidewalk chalk may be used in areas where flagging is not practical. Be generous when purchasing stakes and track markers, since they tend to disappear.

Gloves

Some handlers may require sturdy gloves to grip the line firmly and to avoid rope burns from the tracking line. Custom LeatherCraft Manuafacturing Company makes the excellent Tradesman™ glove. Although a bit more expensive than standard leather cowhide gloves, these are reinforced with synthetic leather in the areas most prone to wear and will last much longer, and the spandex body may be much more comfortable. The terrycloth sweat patch at the base of the thumb area may be much appreciated, as well. The safety model is also available in bright orange, to make it easier to locate a dropped glove.

Scent Articles

A variety of scent articles will also be necessary. The tracklayer will leave an article at the beginning and end of the track. In the TD test, the articles must be a glove or wallet; advanced titles require the dog to indicate a variety of articles, including leather, fabric, plastic, and metal. Initially, soft articles, such as socks and gloves—items that easily retain scent and are easy for the dog to grab—may be preferred to engage the dog in play and to hide food inside; however, as training progresses, it is necessary for the dog to become accustomed to an assortment of articles. A well-stocked supply of scent articles will be necessary, since it is not unusual for articles to disappear from the track, being carried off by well-meaning passersby, by stray dogs delighted to discover a new toy, or by a wild animal looking for denning material, or they can even be blown away by the wind or dropped on the return to the car.

Figure 18-4: *AKC rules require the dog to wear a harness while tracking.* The harness must be of a soft, pliable material and be designed so there is minimal restriction while the dog is working. Bina shows a nylon harness, relatively inexpensive and easily washable. Rio wears a leather harness with a protective chest plate, which minimizes stress and coat wear for dogs that pull like a freight train.

Treats

Initially, some food treats may be used when laying tracks. Bait should be something odorous that the dog finds appealing, but it can be reasonably nutritious, as well. Some dog food manufacturers produce nutritious food in sausage-like chubs that are easily cut into small portions. Turkey hot dogs, usually lower in fat and additives than beef hot dogs, can be sliced quite thinly, even cut into fourths for small puppies, and most dogs find them very tasty; leftover chicken or beef can be used if it is not highly seasoned. The idea of bait is to tempt the dog to move down the trail, not to feed a five-course meal; it is not difficult to end up with an overweight dog if these calories are not included in the dog's daily requirements, so these tasty tidbits should be small and easy to swallow in one gulp.

Tracking Log

A tracking log is needed to record each training session. These notes will not only allow the handler to identify weaknesses that must be addressed, but to follow the dog's progress and plan future training. Should a handler later decide to become involved in Search and Rescue, a training log is mandatory. Commercial logbooks are available, but it is just as easy to use a three-ring binder and copy log page "blanks." Figure 18-8 shows two common log pages.

Other Handy Items

Other items can be useful when training but are not strictly necessary. For longer and older trails, a handheld global positioning system (GPS) unit can be a great asset,

since flagging has a tendency to disappear in direct proportion to the age of the trail. Some sort of device to keep track of paces may be handy, too; it is easy to get distracted and forget, wondering, "Was that 125 or 225?" A pedometer will work, but a cord with pony beads works well, too. A camcorder can be a wonderful tool, not only to record successes, but also to identify the dog's body language from a perspective otherwise unavailable to the handler and to allow the handler to see deficiencies in line-handling technique.

Pace

A requisite skill for a tracklayer is being able to determine the length of the track or leg of the track while it is being laid; so, learning to calculate pace is a necessary skill. Measure off and mark a 300-foot distance on level ground; a local football field is perfect for this exercise. Starting several strides away, approach the first mark, and at a normal walking speed and stride, walk the distance to the second marker. Do not stop at the marker, but continue several strides past it; only count the steps between the markers. Start before and continue after the markers so that the strides are normal since it is common to start and end with shorter-than-average strides. Count the number of paces—how many times the same foot hits the ground—it takes to cover the 300 feet. Calculate the length of the average pace: distance in feet divided by the number of paces = feet per pace. Repeat the process several times to get a representative average. The tracklayer can either keep track of the distance trav-

Figure 18-5: *Tracking lines.* Cotton cord and nylon or cotton flat leads are lightweight and relatively inexpensive. Static climbing ropes come in variety of sizes and colors and rarely tangle or snag. Leather (or synthetic leather) has an excellent feel and long life. The snap should be strong and reliable; note the lock jaw snap on the two leads on the right. Photograph by Barney Riley.

eled or figure the number of paces necessary for a particular distance. The length of the pace will vary with terrain and vegetation. Practice and experience will help the tracklayer make the needed adjustments.

A Dog, of Course!

Of course, a dog is required! One of the wonderful aspects of tracking is that as long as the dog is in general good health, it is never too late or too early to start tracking with a Weimaraner. Although puppies are not eligible to enter tests until they are over 6 months old, tracking games can begin as early as 5 or 6 weeks, and even very short tracks can be started when puppies are 8 or 9 weeks old. Tracking with puppies develops their olfactory skills and confidence, as well as providing great opportunities for bonding with the handler. The middle-aged dog that has become bored with the same old training routine will enjoy the opportunity to develop a new skill. Older dogs, perhaps a dog whose career in the field, conformation, or obedience is entering its waning years, will appreciate the chance to be back in the limelight and participate in a training routine that is not very stressful on aging joints and muscles, in addition to benefiting from the regular mental and physical exercise.

Training Resources

Sport Tracking

Some how-to books on tracking are included in the bibliography, and several are of particular value to the Weimaraner owner. Any handler planning to participate in tracking should read Betty Mueller's *About Tracking Dog Training—Creating a Problem Solving Relationship;* while not a training book, regardless of the training method used, this book will provide invaluable insights. *Fascinating Scent,* by Susan and Orrin Eldred, the author's favorite, is an excellent resource with some novel suggestions for tracking training. *Tracking from the Ground Up,* by Sandy Ganz and Susan Boyd (with accompanying DVD), and *Enthusiastic Tracking,* by William Sanders, describe their structured methods with exceptional clarity. In *Tracking Dog—Theory and Methods,* Glen Johnson combines basic information about tracking and scent theory with interesting excerpts about his experiences. Modification of Johnson's extremely intense training program has been effective for training Weimaraners. Johnson had many successes with retrieving and advocates this method by preference, but each of the books mentioned above includes instruction using food motivation. Boguslaw Gorny's *Tracking for Search and Rescue* offers an excellent discussion and training plan using the dog's natural desire to hunt and follow scent to train a Search and Rescue dog, but the sport tracking enthusiast may find it useful, as well.

Try Tracking, by Carolyn Krause, and *Bring Your Nose Over Here,* by Wentworth Brown, are inexpensive works with basic information on teaching a dog to track and are a good resource to pique your curiosity or help you decide whether tracking sounds interesting. (Mr. Brown's book has the added advantage of being written by a Weimaraner enthusiast whose dogs were among the first Weimaraners to earn the TDX.) Steve White's *Tracking* DVD was produced specifically for trainers wishing to train with beginning or experienced dogs for the demands of the VST title.

Schutzhund

The bibliography of this book includes a couple of books on the stylized tracking required for Schutzhund work. Although it emphasizes the accuracy and steadiness required for Schutzhund work, many of the principles are equally applicable, and in fact advantageous, to training for AKC tests.

The Nose Knows

Some reading about what is known about scent theory will aid in understanding the dog's work and facilitate training. *K9 Professional Tracking,* by Resi Gerritsen and Ruud Haak, dedicates only a small portion of the book to actual training methods; it has, however, a wealth of information on the canine olfactory system and some of the older research into canine olfaction. Adee Schoon and Ruud Haak also dedicate a large portion of their book, *K9 Suspect Discrimination,* to the canine olfactory system and current research conducted on behalf of the Canine Department of the Netherlands, one of the pre-eminent law enforcement and scent-detection canine programs in the world. It contains some absorbing stories about the use and effectiveness of the canine nose.

Scent Theory

To become proficient in handling a tracking dog, it is necessary to learn at least a little bit about scent theory—how scent moves and changes. Learning how the environment affects scent can give a handler an added advantage in training and handling a tracking dog. Science has not provided the answers regarding exactly what dogs are following, but some effects do seem to be apparent, and many more will become obvious as the handler gains experience.

Although slightly outdated by the more recent work of Schoon and Haak, *Scent and the Scenting Dog,* by William Syrotuck—still considered required reading by many tracking enthusiasts—gives a basic understanding of scent and its movement, as does *Scenting on the Wind,* by Susan Bulanda. Oddly enough, *Fire Weather,* distributed by the U.S. Department of Agriculture, is a developed analysis of meteorological conditions and air currents (and therefore scent movement) that provides an excellent description of where and how scent moves.

Figure 18-6: *Trail markers* can be a variety of items. Surveyor's or agricultural flags are great for grassy or dirt areas. Clothespins or washers with reflective tape are convenient when it is necessary to attach flagging to a variety of objects, fences, or bushes, or to mark areas with dirt or grass less obviously. Sidewalk chalk comes in very handy in urban areas. Gloves may be an essential item for the hard-pulling Weimaraner; although they are not waterproof, these gloves have well-reinforced fingers and palms, as well as a sweat patch on the thumb. Photograph by Barney Riley.

Figure 18-7: *Articles.* Soft items, such as socks or gloves, are good for initial training because they hold scent well, dogs rarely mind picking them up and playing with them, and tasty treats can easily be tucked inside. However, as the dog progresses in training, items should vary in size, shape, weight, and material to prepare for the TDX and VST.

Local Resources

Although it is certainly possible to train a dog for a tracking title on one's own using the processes in these books, it is more fun to train with a friend. In many parts of the country, there are tracking groups or clubs; these are an excellent resource for you to find experienced tracking handlers and instructors. Contact local dog breed clubs, obedience clubs, or working dog groups.

Training Methods

Motivation

The most effective tracking training methods are based primarily on natural drives and instincts. They use positive reinforcement because, unlike obedience, tracking requires the dog to use a great deal of initiative. After all, if the dog does not want to track, it is difficult to force him to do so, and most likely impossible to teach him to excel at tracking. Commonly used methods use four different motivational factors. The desire to retrieve can be used as motivation; it is effective only with a dog (regardless of breed) in which this desire is naturally highly developed. Pack drive, or the dog–handler relationship, may also be used as motivation; in the initial stages of training, the dog tracks the handler and is rewarded by reunion with the person it loves more than any other. The strong desire to chase objects, or prey drive, is the foundation for some training programs. The beginning dog chases the excited, running tracklayer; eventually, the tracklayer moves out of the dog's sight before the dog is released to track, and when the dog arrives at the point where the tracklayer disappeared, the dog will then begin to hunt with its nose for the scent and follow the track to the prey.

Hunt Drive

A fourth method of motivation can be the dog's natural hunt drive—focusing the dog's natural desire to use its nose to follow any interesting scent, which is often combined with and reinforced by the natural instinct to find food using its nose. If food is highly motivating for the dog, it may follow a track that leads from one tasty tidbit to the next; the distance between tidbits is gradually increased, and the food is soon eliminated. Although all Weimaraners are not food motivated, this method gives fast, reliable results with the majority.

The use of hunt drive has proven successful to start the Weimaraner tracking, when consistently combined with a highly desired reward at the end of the track. This method

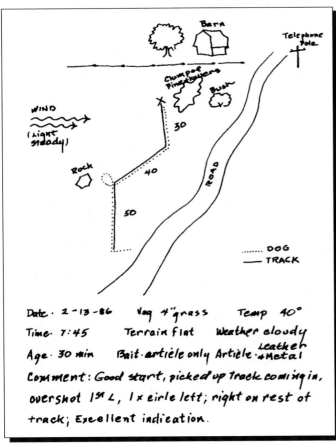

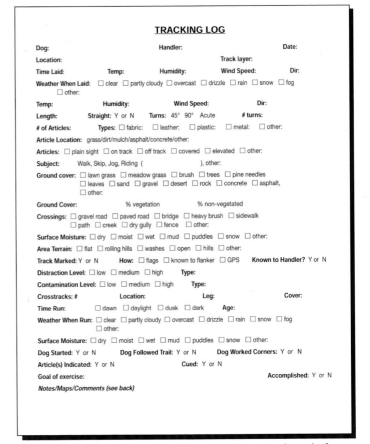

Figure 18-8: *A tracking log* is necessary to record progress and plan future training. **(a)** Simple and concise, this note-taking records easily forgotten details. **(b)** Another style of note-taking records basic information with a minimum of effort.

also develops accuracy in the initial training, which can be vitally important when progressing to the complexities of advanced tracking or Search and Rescue. When properly managed, the motivating factor shifts from food to the articles and the rewards at the track's conclusion; the food is eliminated from the training program rather quickly—food can be reintroduced later in training to aid in problem solving. As the transition occurs, the dog actually begins to ignore food drops, too intent on the track to pause for treats. The track becomes a challenge, a series of problems the dog enjoys solving, and the reward at the end of the track overshadows the desire for treats. Although food may be useful in helping the beginning Weimaraner to focus on the track, the highly evolved hunt drive of Weimaraners often allows the handler to use this drive even without food.

In either case, the basic premise is the same: in the first stages of training, the handler allows the dog to move forward only along the track; should the puppy move off the track or become distracted, the handler stops, gradually shortening the lead, and waits patiently until the puppy is physically and mentally back on the track before moving forward again. Many trainers are choosing to begin puppies on hard surfaces to minimize distractions and prepare for the VST from the beginning.

One advantage of starting a dog in hunt drive is that when a dog is stressed, it will often revert back to its foundational training. If hunt drive (searching for food or a nonmoving person or article) was the foundation, the dog will probably first attempt to solve challenges by using its nose; if the foundation was based on prey drive or retrieving (chasing a moving person or article), the dog may first attempt to solve challenges by using its eyes.

The Training Program

A well-planned training program is essential to developing an enthusiastic, competent tracking Weimaraner.

A Weimaraner often learns to track so quickly that the trainer forgets the dog is only a beginner. As a result, training may progress too quickly and the dog may become confused or discouraged. Or worse, a skill may not be thoroughly learned and may show up as a serious weakness in later, more advanced, training. Keep a record of every track (tests as well as train-

ing) to chart the dog's progress, strengths, and weaknesses. This is also handy for documenting the dog's experience for future reference, problem solving, or bragging.

The program should set short- and long-term training goals, not time limits. Push on only when each goal is achieved. Be flexible enough to allow the dog to progress without becoming bored; true boredom, however, is unusual if the dog is properly motivated and rewarded, so build a strong foundation. Be detailed enough in the training plan that there is a specific goal for each track, with objective goals to continue making progress.

A training program is especially important if the trainee is a puppy. It is not unusual for a 6-month-old Weimaraner to be ready for (and pass) an AKC TD test. It is exciting to see how quickly a puppy grasps the concept of tracking. The puppy is so enthusiastic about this new game that it can make incredible progress! Younger puppies usually cannot concentrate long enough for formal training, but play training (hide-and-seek or find-the-treat games) or VERY short tracks can begin as early as 7–10 weeks. Because of this precocious aptitude, it is very easy to forget that the puppy is just a baby and to push too hard, too long, or too fast. Keep it fun and not too difficult for the little one. Keep the track short, on vegetation, surfaces, and terrain suitable for young muscles, short legs, and short attention spans.

Do not be in a hurry to get out to the full 40-foot length of the lead that is called for in AKC tracking tests. In the

Figure 18-9: *CH Rockville's Truman Greystone,* VCD2, MH, TDX, MX, MXJ, SDX, RDX, VX5, proves that a bird dog can be a tracking dog, too. The Weimaraner is bred to be versatile; if competition is planned in multiple arenas, the handler must be prepared to be one step ahead of the talented and intelligent Weimaraner, whose nose can cut short training plans.

beginning, stay close enough to give the dog confidence, to give help when needed, to observe the dog's body language, and to keep the dog as close to the track as possible. Some handlers prefer to stay at the 20-foot distance because it is easier to observe the dog's body language and even hear the rate and type of the dog's respirations, which provide vital clues about the dog's tracking performance.

A training program outlines the introduction of changes and challenges in tracking conditions—age, length, cross-tracks, roads, moisture, and so forth. Most how-to books provide a program that introduces each of the challenges of a tracking test, but not all incorporate new challenges while simplifying other factors. This is in spite of the fact that it is basic principal of learning theory to only change one variable or criterion at a time. For example, many programs increase distance and age at the same time. By keeping tracks the same distance and increasing age first, then increasing distance while maintaining age, the dog can learn to handle each new aspect of the track. If the new challenge is a road crossing, make the track fresher and in easy terrain, so the dog only has to puzzle out the challenge of the crossing and not both aged track and terrain challenges at the same time. Changing only one variable at a time provides the dog with a better opportunity to learn how the change affects the track and how to solve that challenge without becoming overwhelmed; this also allows the handler to focus on the changes in the dog's behavior caused by the road crossing and not the age of the track or the terrain. Once the dog can solve each challenge separately, they may then be combined.

A well-paced tracking program considers the dog's progress and abilities and always allows the dog to win. It offers new challenges only with the proper preparation, which will develop confidence and the desire to track. Use the Weimaraner's inherent tenacity by motivating it to track for itself, for the challenge of the problem and the reward of solving it. This is an asset when a track is really tough; the dog will keep working because of that stubbornness long after it would have given up if it were merely tracking to please the trainer.

The Weimaraner is a good problem-solver, so let the dog work the problem out by itself. Help the dog along the track only when it becomes obvious that the dog does not understand but before it is totally lost and quits tracking; if it is necessary to actually help the dog finish the track, on the next track back up, make the problem easier, shorter, or smaller to ensure the dog's independent success. This will increase the dog's self-confidence and its perseverance in working a track. If the dog is repeatedly unable to solve the problem, examine the process and find a different way to present the challenge or work on building stronger foundation skills or motivation.

Do not be tempted to try something tough just to see if the dog can do it. Train slowly and follow the training program, concentrating on short-term goals before challenging the dog's knowledge and ability. A Weimaraner loves and trusts people. If told there is a track, it believes there is one; the fault, the Weimaraner believes, lies in its own inability, not the trainer. If the trainer is repeatedly wrong or constantly nags for more speed or accuracy in situations beyond the dog's experience, the dog will begin first to doubt its own ability and then the trainer's. Such doubts ruin the dog–handler relationship and may result in the dog's refusal to track at all.

Practice under every conceivable circumstance—sand, brush, plowed fields, morning, evening, even at night—

Figure 18-10: *One way to maintain the older dog's interest in life is to teach a new skill,* such as tracking. Here, Liz Raiman, well-known tracking enthusiast, is shown with 11-year-old Molly. Since the nose is one of the last things to go on a Weimaraner, training can be tailored to the physical condition of the dog while providing mental challenges.

whatever, wherever, and whenever. Providing variety in training will help dog and handler be prepared to accommodate the unexpected at a test. Always expect the unexpected—tracking tests are the tracking gremlin's favorite playground. Train beyond the level of skills required for the test so that the dog and handler feel confident. If the track is run in a livestock pasture, how will the dog react to fresh manure? How will it respond to birds in a wildlife preserve? What if you stop to offer your dog water in the middle of the track? What about people who want to pet your dog while you are working? Know the answers before the test. Anticipate things that could go wrong; do not complain—train.

Form and Style

Body Language

The ability to read a Weimaraner's body language is critical to success in the tracking field. The clues may be much more subtle than in breeds that have upright ears and long tails. It takes practice and concentration to understand, since each individual will have unique non-verbal communication. One may wag its tail while on the track and raise the tail when off the track; another may track with a raised tail and wag it when off the track. One may pull hard when on the track; another may pull hard only when the track is lost. The rhythm of the dog's breathing may be significant, as may the dog's posture; for instance, "stacked" respirations with the head up often indicate air scenting, while deep respiration with the head low may indicate a change in the character of the track or "crittering." Observing the dog at play or while solving other problems will help, as will having someone else watch while the dog is tracking. Videotaping the dog while tracking will also be very helpful.

In the Right Gear?

Each dog has its own style, and this is difficult to change. A Weimaraner can be an enthusiastic tracker and is sometimes likened to a freight train because it tracks so hard and so fast. This can lead to badly overshot corners and missed articles, and it can tire the dog unnecessarily; additionally, some dogs may work so fast they pose a safety hazard to the handler. Harsh corrections to slow the dog down may cause discouragement and confusion, however. Some handlers have had success teaching the "Easy!" command, but more often than not, this ends up more being nagging than changing the dog's behavior. Running the lead from one hand behind the handler to the opposite hand allows the handler to sit on the line and use body weight as an anchor in situations where safety becomes an issue.

Work in a composed manner, especially early in training, to develop calm, steady working habits. Some dogs are actually working at high speed not because they are confident but

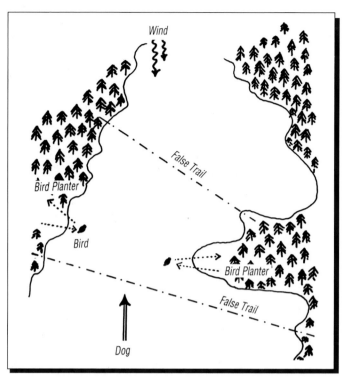

Figure 18-11: *False trails* (broken dotted line) discourage Weimaraners that have learned to follow the human trails into the planted bird by not rewarding the behavior. The dog and handler (arrow) walk into the wind (wavy arrow). The bird planter (dotted lines) minimizes the opportunity for the dog to locate the track.

because they are frantic and unsure; these dogs need to develop conviction and skill, so build a solid foundation, work on easier problems, and maintain a relaxed manner. For the overconfident dog, tone down the praise and motivation just a little; use commands and praise judiciously, just enough to keep the dog motivated. Emphasize the articles by working tracks with multiple articles. Let the dog work out tough parts on its own. The dog may slow down somewhat with additional experience.

The opposite extreme, although not as common among Weimaraners, is the dog that works too slowly. Time is important. As the dog dawdles, the track gets older and more difficult. Encourage the dog to work at a reasonable pace with occasional reminders (not corrections) when attention wanders. Do not emphasize speed by constantly repeating "Find!" or "Hurry!" Find things to stimulate motivation, such as an especially desirable food treat, a favorite toy, a romp at the end of the track, or more praise. Work on shorter tracks until motivation increases.

Remember, some dogs are just more thorough than others; some need more encouragement or self-confidence. The slow, methodical dog that is not goofing off is less likely to miss an article or turn; the dog working slowly because of poor concentration is more likely to be distracted from tracking.

The Article Indication

In AKC tracking, the final key to a passing performance is the indication on the article; without a readable indication, the dog simply will not pass, no matter how talented it is. A good handler, however, probably knows well before the dog gives the final trained indication that the article is close at hand. In general, the ability to read the dog is invaluable in tracking and many other dog activities. By comparison, a bird dog in the field often displays various behaviors as it approaches the hiding bird; at the initial scent, the dog's head often snaps in the direction of the scent and the tail begins to wag in large circles. As the dog approaches close enough to localize the scent, the tail moves in smaller and smaller circles, and as the dog locks onto point, the dog freezes, all muscles locked. The handler, seeing the initial change in the dog's behavior, knows to keep out of the dog's way and to be in a position to steady the dog if necessary.

As the tracking dog and handler progress through training, the handler will begin to notice behaviors that indicate the dog is eager to work, is acquiring or reacquiring the track, or has lost the track. Often these are natural, untrained behaviors or the result of Pavlovian conditioning—the dog responds without conscious effort. When the tracking dog is initially looking for scent, most will breathe in short, sometimes noisy, puffs. This is necessary to force larger amounts of air through the olfactory system for processing. Once the track is found, the dog settles down to breathing in a somewhat longer, more regular pattern so it can follow the trail and still breathe. When the trained dog catches the initial scent of the upcoming article, it realizes that a reward is imminent, so breathing and heart rate may increase. Respiration rate and pattern may also change as the dog once again processes larger amounts of air in order to localize the scent source. The dog knows the article must be found and indicated, so focus and intensity increase, resulting in a change in body carriage and increased muscle tension. The dog does not think about these behaviors, they just happen. When the dog finds and confirms the article, the handler is already prepared for the final trained indication.

For the untrained dog, the handler can use natural behaviors to aid in training. If the dog misses the corner and suddenly stops and lifts its head to air scent, the handler can reward this behavior to create a trained negative indication. The dog is then aided in learning the behaviors necessary to reacquire the track. When the breathing and body carriage return to the normal tracking mode, the handler knows the dog has settled back into the trail and can reward the effort and performance with a soft word of praise. It is normal for a tracking dog to pause if it comes across an article bearing the tracklayer's scent; that momentary pause to investigate gives the handler the opportunity to give a command for the desired trained behavior and then a reward. It will not take long for the article itself to become the cue for the trained indication.

Use the natural body language the dog offers to enhance and improve not only the dog's performance, but the handler's skills, as well.

Figure 18-12: *TinCup's Classic v. Reiteralm, CD.* Owned by Patricia Riley. **(a)** Friday's body language—raised tail, nose to the ground, and pulling well into the harness—shows that she is intent on the track and working well. **(b)** Casting for an air scent, head high, short, rapid sniffing, and tail level, Friday clearly communicates that she has lost the track. A camcorder is an excellent tool to help the handler learn to identify characteristic body language. Photographs by Barney Riley.

Handling Skills

The ability to handle the tracking line has a significant effect on the tracking dog. A handler that is constantly stopping to untangle either himself or the dog may see a decrease in the dog's motivation. Hard jerks on the line may inadvertently convey the message that the dog is in error. An easy way to get perspective on what the dog is experiencing is to play dog and handler with two humans. One person—the dog—holds the snap end of the line. The other person—the handler—holds the opposite end. Have the "dog" run a short trail, pretending to cast and pull as the dog would. Practice having soft hands to allow the line to slide through, slowly increasing the tension to minimize the shock if the dog starts with a lunge down the track or takes off on a corner. Feed out the line or reel it in to encourage the novice dog to stay on the track, or as the experienced dog is casting. Practice as the dog circles to reacquire a trail after overrunning the corner, so the line does not entangle either the dog or the handler. The ability to handle the tracking line to avoid distracting or interfering with the dog while it works is one of the handler's contributions to the tracking team effort.

When the dog has lost the track, another of the handler's contributions to the team is to assist the dog in reacquiring the trail. The idea is not to show the dog where the track is, but to develop a systematic process that allows the handler to put the dog in position to relocate the trail on its own; after all, in a test or the real world of Search and Rescue, the handler is not going to know where the track is. The ability to read the dog and mentally log points where the handler knows the dog is working scent, along with learning to circle the dog back on the track and to analyze environmental conditions, will allow the handler to give the dog the best opportunity to pick the scent back up again.

Some Training Tips

The handler should have a detailed map or an assistant who knows the location of the track, in case the dog has been overmatched by the challenge of the track and needs to be assisted to complete it. Carry a spare article (scented by the tracklayer) to drop when a situation is totally lost. If the handler has no idea where the track is located or the dog is tracking poorly owing to injury or illness, or if weather conditions deteriorate, it is vital to call the track to a halt by dropping the spare article to end the track with a win. Hidden articles may be stolen by the tracking gremlin or carried off by wild animals, birds, stray dogs, people, or other unknown agents.

The dog must (almost) always win, even if it is necessary to cheat occasionally. The track is not finished until the article is found; routinely pulling the dog off a track without a find will teach the dog that it is okay to quit. Do not confuse good handling—putting the dog in the right position to reacquire the track—with actually showing the dog where the track is. However, under some circumstances, it is better to quietly end the track rather than teach the dog that when all else fails, mom will find the track. Some days, the dog may be too distracted, or perhaps the dog has been worked past its physical or mental limits or is ill or injured—in those cases, remove the harness, attach the lead to the collar, and with as little emotion as possible, walk the dog out of the field (no play time, but no corrections). Depending on the circumstances, the handler may wish to try the dog on a less demanding track later in order to rekindle the positive sense of success before ending the training.

Keep in mind that certain medications or health conditions may temporarily alter a dog's scenting ability; the tracking log should record when a dog is ill or injured, or taking medication. If a dog that has previously been working with enthusiasm and proficiency suddenly begins to struggle or lose interest, a visit to the veterinarian may be in order. True anosmia (loss of sense of smell) is rare, but injury or illness can impair a dog's proficiency or concentration. If the dog can find some bits of dry kibble scattered in the grass, the sense of smell is working.

Conditioning is vital for both dog and trainer. Tracking is hard work. Hard panting compromises the dog's scenting ability, altering airflow through the olfactory and respiratory system. A Weimaraner may wear itself out or ignore an injury when intent on its work. It is not fair to the hard-working, enthusiastic dog to have an exhausted trainer dragging back on the line, too tired to watch out for hazardous situations or to provide encouragement, help, and praise.

Progressive training will help condition both dog and handler, but a physical conditioning program will help, too. Using the tracks themselves as a sole conditioning program may cause frustration and a decrease in motivation. After an extended layoff, reduce the track length and difficulty and gradually work back to the previous level.

Tracking knows no limitations on conditions or weather. Practice in all kinds of weather—rain, snow, fog, and heat. Be aware, however, of weather that is potentially dangerous to both dog and handler; for example, warm weather can cause heat exhaustion and stroke, while cold can cause frostbite and hypothermia. Carry plenty of water to working sessions (for dog and trainer) to prevent dehydration, regardless of the weather. Moisture is critical to the optimal functioning of the olfactory system.

Figure 18-13: *The ability to handle the tracking line* well is one of the handler's contributions to the tracking team. Jack Sappenfield teaches handlers how to smoothly shorten the line or let the line slide through the hands to minimize distracting or demoralizing jerks on the tracking line while the dog is working.

Figure 18-14: *Hard surfaces are just a matter of training,* as Jack and CiCi prove, not the nearly impossible undertaking they were thought to represent in the early years of sport tracking in the United States.

Balance challenges with common sense. Do not track under obviously dangerous conditions, such as near broken glass, hazardous chemicals, or cliffs—an intent dog really may not notice such things—or if the dog appears ill or injured. A few not-so-obvious dangers include fire ants (which may swarm to the food dropped on the track), yellow jackets, and foxtail (a special hazard to the tracking dog's eyes and nose). Watch the dog for signs of injury or exhaustion and, if necessary, throw down a spare article (scented by the tracklayer) to end the track with success.

Although judges make every effort to provide a safe test, do not hesitate to withdraw from a test if the conditions appear unsafe, even if it is necessary to stop in the middle of the track. Sometimes circumstances can change after a track is laid; livestock may move into the area, chemicals may be applied to the tracking surface, or temperatures may rise (or drop) to levels for which the dog is not conditioned. No title is worth the endangerment of the dog or the handler's safety

or health. Explain to the judge the reason for withdrawal, or request an alternate track if this is allowed. Inform the authorizing organization of the conditions and the reason for withdrawal by letter, or discuss it with the Trial Secretary.

In early training, know exactly (within inches) where the track is so you know when the dog is on or off the track. If the dog loses the track, the handler must be able to position the dog in the exact spot that will provide the best chance for the dog to relocate the track. Early in training, teaching the dog to be accurate and to follow the strongest scent will contribute to future success on more advanced and difficult tracks. In the beginning, the dog will learn to follow the actual trail quickly if the handler stops when the dog's nose leaves the actual footstep track; the handler simply waits for the dog to get its nose back on the track before moving forward again. Allowing a dog to fringe scent, especially early on, will cause much frustration in the future.

Practice laying tracks, if necessary. Lay the track, wait 10–15 minutes (longer as skill progresses), then go back (without the dog) and walk the track to find the object at the end. Money, car keys, or house keys will provide a good incentive. In the beginning, highly visible flags (garden stakes with a small piece of surveyor's tape, or surveyor's flags, for example) will help to demarcate the track exactly; sidewalk chalk is useful for hard surfaces. Some dogs become flag happy, figuring out that the flags mark the track; for these "caninesteins," put out decoy flags or chalk marks. Many how-to books have explanatory sections on how to properly lay tracks. You may also refer to *Training for Tracklayers,* by Joyce Geier, or *About Track Laying,* by Betty Mueller.

In early training, flags are often used to keep the dog on the trail while it is learning; the handler also needs to know where the track is in order to learn to identify body language that indicates that the dog is on or off the track, or working to reacquire the track. However, the handler will not become truly competent at reading the dog until the flags are removed. The flags can be removed when the dog is eagerly following the track, negotiating turns, and showing the consistent ability to search for and reacquire the trail when it has been lost, without the handler's assistance. Removing the flags before the basic desire and skills are in place will not only reduce the confidence of the dog and the handler, but can encourage bad habits. When the flags are initially removed, reduce the distance and complexity of the track— perhaps even to a simple short track with a single turn—to allow the handler to gain confidence without undue stress.

Remember that training for the handler progresses one step at a time, just as it does for the dog. It is de-motivating to both handler and dog to leave a trail not completed, so if a trail is not flagged, the handler must have an accurate map or flanker who knows where the trail is in case the team is unable to reacquire the trail without assistance.

Obedience training of a tracking dog is controversial. Although some aspects (such as teaching the dog to indicate the articles) are easier with an obedience-trained dog, others are more difficult. As with hunting, training a Weimaraner is usually easier if tracking is introduced prior to obedience. Because of the Weimaraner's strong desire to please, it is often difficult to convince those that have been trained to heel (especially when strong coercive measures have been used) that the trainer really wants them to take the initiative required for tracking, to be out in front and pulling on the lead. This does not mean that a dog that has been obedience trained cannot be trained to track as well, just that the trainer may have to be more patient and, sometimes, more imaginative. It will also require a real finesse in line handling; the handler will need a great deal of practice with the dog and handler game discussed earlier.

It all boils down to working with the experience the dog brings to the training. Teaching the dog the obedience skills required to pass an AKC tracking test should be done separately from the tracking training. The tracking field is not the place to teach the dog to sit, down, or retrieve. It is wise to use positive reinforcement techniques—as opposed to coercion—to teach the indication behavior; a dog that has associated unpleasant corrections with the indication behavior (collar pops or electronic corrections) may avoid indicating the articles in an attempt to avoid the possibility of punishment. Finding an article should always have positive associations for the dog; even if the dog follows every footstep on the track, if it fails to indicate the article lying at the end of a test track, the dog will not pass.

A Few Myths and Misconceptions

When a person walks into the kitchen where dinner is cooking, they might say, "It smells like spaghetti sauce!" Some people would be able to smell some of the component odors, especially the strongest ones, such as garlic and tomatoes. A dog, on the other hand, would smell tomatoes, oregano, basil, garlic, onions, pepper, salt, and all the other ingredients in the sauce. A dog's nose is much more specialized and is therefore able to break down what humans might perceive as a single scent into component parts. It is this skill that makes the dog a valuable asset in many scent-detection tasks, such as narcotics and explosives detection and tracking. It is rather difficult to mask the target odor from the properly trained dog.

Human perceptions have resulted in some myths and misconceptions about limitations in the abilities of tracking dogs.

Early on in sport tracking, some superstitious behaviors became commonly accepted as part of tracking dog abilities and training. One commonly accepted idea was the significance of the footwear of the tracklayer; in particular, it was deemed important that tracklayers wear leather shoes and never rubber boots. Today, common experience has shown that well-trained tracking dogs can work regardless of the type of footwear the tracklayer is wearing. In fact, the well-trained dog may be able to follow the trail of a baby in a stroller or of a cyclist; it is now known that the scent the dog may be following is composed of more than just the scent left by the feet and the disturbance of the ground substrate.

Those training for the TDX, in the early years, would encourage the dog to simply cross hard surfaces—such as roads or sidewalks—and reacquire the trail on the other side of the "barrier" under the assumption that it was too difficult to track across these surfaces. Today, the AKC offers the VST title, which requires the dog to follow a track and negotiate at least one turn on such surfaces. Anecdotal evidence shows that trained dogs can follow even aged tracks on concrete, asphalt, and gravel. Gottfried Dildei (*Tracking* video) and Steve White (*Hydration Intensified Tracking Training* video) actually start dogs on non-vegetated surfaces, based partly on the premise that there are fewer competing scents (human and vegetation) to distract the novice dog from the target scent.

Old movies often showed the quarry taking to a stream to throw the tracking dog off the scent. In real life, a well-trained

Figure 18-15: *A fun beginning.* Using her nose at this early age provides Pearl—who would later earn her TDX—with a solid foundation. Tracking with puppies is exciting because they love to use their nose and they learn so quickly. Remember, they are just babies; plan physical and mental challenges appropriate to the puppy's age and development.

Figure 18-16: *An unusual snowstorm* in Mississippi provides TinCup's Chiarra v. Reiteralm with a refreshing change of pace and introduces the dog to different scenting conditions. Snow keeps the scent tight on the track; bait and articles can be covered with snow to encourage the dog to search harder for them. Training under a wide variety of circumstances will help prepare for the unexpected at the big test. Photograph by Barney Riley.

Figure 18-17: *Tracking is hard work!* A drooping Keya shares a cup of water while Patricia Riley writes up the record of their track before the details are forgotten. Proper hydration is necessary for a dog to be able to scent well. The handler needs to be aware of the dog's health and safety at all times, since the dog may be too intent to be aware of dangers or exhaustion. Even on a relatively cool day, Keya can easily become overheated or mildly dehydrated. Photograph by Barney Riley.

dog would simply continue to follow the trail, as the scent would lie on top of the water and on the vegetation and soil alongside the water. Even the quarry hiding beneath the water would not fool the well-trained dog, since the human body is still giving off skin rafts, exhaling air, sweating, and otherwise still producing the odors that create the total scent picture.

Another common concern is commercially available products to hide or mask scent. Hunters often use them, hoping to hide their scent from prey animals. Again, experience shows that there are many components to the track scent, so these products are unlikely to fool the well-trained dog unless the subject is wearing a completely self-contained suit that prevents the escape of any bodily fluids, solids, or gases.

Early tracking guides indicated that the relative weights of the tracklayer and cross-tracklayers could be a problem in scent discrimination. The myth went that if the track and cross-track were laid by people whose weights were very similar, many dogs had difficulty discriminating. This turned out to be a training issue, not a lack of canine ability. Once again, the complexity of the total scent picture allows the properly trained dog to easily discriminate between people of similar weights, even family members, and in some circumstances, even identical twins.

Aged tracks do bring up a controversial issue. The pass rate for the AKC's VST test is quite low—a trail that is only 3–5 hours old. A tracking team able to consistently follow a blind (unknown) trail that is over several days old would be considered competent indeed; and there are substantiated anecdotes of dogs following trails that are a week old or older. Claims of teams following trails that are over a month old, and even over a year old, should be closely scrutinized.

Also, it is not necessary for the tracking dog to be able to retrieve. The AKC does allow the tracking dog to retrieve the article to the handler. However, this is by no means required; the dog may retrieve or indicate the article. While the sit, down, and retrieve are the most traditional trained indications for articles, the rules do not specify what the indication must be; if the handler can read and articulate the behavior, then it works. A solid point is just as acceptable as a down, as long as the handler is confident that it will be reliably recognizable from the tail end of the dog. In Search and Rescue, it is highly recommended that the dog not disturb any articles that may be found, so the passive indication (sit, stand, down, or even a point) is actually preferred. A few training methods may use the retrieve to build a foundation for tracking or as a reward for the completed track; in these cases, the natural retrieve—as opposed to a trained retrieve—is the basis. Be aware that although the dog may retrieve the article as an indication, tossing the article or playing with the article as a toy is prohibited in the AKC regulations.

Figure 18-18: *Early in training,* leaning the flag to indicate the direction of a turn makes it easier for the handler to pay attention to the dog instead of searching for the next leg. Experienced tracklayers use environmental features to make mapping easier and to remember where the track is. Here, lining up the right hand goalpost and tree indicates the exact location of the track. When selecting environmental markers, be sure to select items that will remain visible for the entire length of the leg and that are far enough apart to maintain a straight line. Select immovable objects; markers such as cars and garbage cans can be easily moved, making relocating the track leg impossible. When mapping, be sure to note unique features of the object; all fence posts will look the same a few hours later. Photograph by Barney Riley.

Tracking Tests and Titles

Tracking tests are sponsored by and titles are awarded by the AKC, as well as other dog registries. There are subtle differences between the rules each organization applies to its tests with regard to dropping articles, their types, the length and laying of the tracks, and so on. Anyone planning to take a test should contact the test organization for complete rules and be thoroughly familiar with the regulations. It would be beneficial to observe a test before entering. Organizations hosting tests always appreciate volunteers, and volunteering provides the best opportunity to see what needs to be done to prepare for a successful test. The AKC Tracking Rulebook states, "Tracking, by nature, is a vigorous, noncompetitive outdoor sport. Tracking tests demonstrate the willingness and enjoyment of the dog in its work, and should always represent the best in sportsmanship and camaraderie by the people involved." Tracking tests are full of good sportsmanship and socializing and are a pleasure to the volunteer, observer, or entrant. Observing the magic of a well-trained, skilled dog following an invisible line of scent across a pasture or parking lot is well worth the time.

The AKC offers three levels of tracking tests and other titles related to tracking. The tests include the TD, TDX, and VST. Dogs may also earn Champion Tracker (CT), which goes before the dog's name, for earning the TD, TDX, and VST. Additionally, the Versatile Companion Dog (VCD) series (VCD1–4 and VCCH) require tracking titles. Between January 1985 and December 2007, 325 Weimaraners earned the TD and 72 earned the TDX. On November 2, 2005, CT CC's Amaz'n Rainey's Gabriele, DC, RN, became the first Weimaraner to earn the VST and highly coveted CT. Two more Weimaraners have also earned the VST and CT.

Before entering into AKC tests, read the Tracking Regulations, published by the AKC. Being familiar with the regulations will help ensure that both handler and dog are completely prepared and will not inadvertently be disqualified. For example, it is now required that all entered dogs be on lead at all times at a tracking event. Having an off-lead dog will result in disqualification or excusal. Also, it is

Figure 18-19: *CH Seabreeze Seraphim, VCD1, TDX,* owned by Richard S. and Jane A. Craig of Jupiter, Florida, was the first dog of any breed to earn a VCD title on January 1, 2001. The VCD1 requires CD, TD, NA, and NAJ titles.

Table 18-1: *AKC tracking tests.*

	TD	TDX	VST
TRACK			
Length	440–500 yards	800–1,000 yards	600–800 yards
Description	3–5 turns	5–7 turns	4–8 turns, at least one on a surface devoid of vegetation
Age	1/2–2 hours	3–5 hours	3–5 hours
Surface	uniform vegetation	vegetated, variable	3 different surfaces, 1/3–2/3 devoid of vegetation
Obstacles/ Challenges	may not cross a body of water no sidewalk or path wider than 6′ no changes in cover no cross-tracks	two sets of cross-tracks and at least two physical obstacles, such as changes in terrain, streams, or human-made obstacles, such as fences, bridges, or lightly traveled roads	no physical obstacles, such as those found in a TDX, but may include stairs or buildings with no closed doors and two or more open sides
ARTICLES			
Number	2	4	4
Location	start and end	one at start, two along track—at least 30 yards from turn or cross-track—one at end	one at start, two along track—at least 20 yards from turn—one at end
Description	start must be fabric, end may be glove or wallet	personal, dissimilar, only last may be glove or wallet	dissimilar, common, one each of fabric, leather, plastic, and metal, first must be fabric or leather
START	marked by two flags, one at start, one 30 yards beyond to indicate direction of track	single flag, which allows direction of track to proceed in a 180° arc	single flag, which allows direction of track to proceed in a 180° arc, at least 20 yards of vegetation
PREREQUISITE	6 months old, certificate of ability	TD	TD
FAILURE	failure to follow track, failure to find and indicate end article, guiding or restraining	failure to follow track, failure to find and indicate articles 2–4, following a cross-track more than 50 yards	Failure to follow track, failure to find and indicate articles 2–4

necessary to have an acceptable harness (non-restrictive), lead, and collar.

AKC tracking tests are open to any qualified AKC-registered dog that is at least 6 months old; dogs with ILPs are also eligible. To qualify for the TD test, the dog must first have a certification of tracking ability from an AKC tracking judge, which entails performing a stand-ard TD track for an AKC judge under conditions similar to those found at a real test, although a waiver may be obtained under unusual circumstances. When the dog and handler are prepared for a TD, contact a nearby tracking judge; the AKC provides a directory of judges at www.akc.org/judges_directory/index.cfm?action=oat. To qualify to enter the TDX or VST, the dog must have earned the TD title.

After receiving 4 original certificates of ability from the certifying judge, a test must be found in which to enter, and this might not be easy. The demands on a club's resources and members when hosting a tracking test and the require-ments of large tracts of suitable land limit the number of tests offered each year. As a result, there are usually far more entrants than there are test tracks available; so in the interest of enhancing success and out of respect for fellow enthusi-asts, enter a test only when fully trained and prepared.

After the closing date of the test, the lucky entrants are selected by lottery to fill the number of test tracks available; the remaining entrants are drawn for an alternate list. So it is not just a matter of training and preparing, a little bit of luck is involved, too. And since the number of TDX tests and espe-cially the VST tests is even further limited, it may take quite some time to actually be successful in entering the test! All-breed pass rates range from an average of 56% for the TD to 6% for the VST. It is therefore considered good form, if one has been lucky enough to be drawn for multiple tests and sub-sequently achieves a title, to notify the Test Secretaries of the remaining tests and to withdraw from those tests if there are untitled alternates wishing to enter. So be a good sport and give another team the chance to earn that coveted title, too.

In all AKC tracking tests, which are judged on a pass/fail basis by two judges, the track is laid by a stranger to the dog. The dog must wear an acceptable harness with an attached 20- to 40-foot lead. The lead must show on the top of the

Tracking Hall of Fame

Arnstadt's Chandu the Magician, TDX

CH Arnstadt's Double Dare Ya, TDX, JH, NSD, VX

Arnstadts F McGee'N Molly, TDX

CT Ardreem's Oberon Phantasm, RE, JH, SDX, RDX, VX2

Arnstadt's Sly Fox, TDX

Baht Chili Pepper, TDX, JH, NSD, NRD, V

CH Bama Belle's Chelsea v. Indenhof, CDX, TDX, RDX, VX

Bama Belle's Csabr v. Indenhof, UDTX, RDX

CH Bama Belle's Kachina, CD, TDX, V

Bama Belle's Kleine Madchen, CD, TDX

CH Bama Belle's Lanzer v. Indenhof, UDTX, RDX, NSD, VX

CH Bama Belle's Schoen II v. Indenhof, UDTX, SD, RDX, VX

CT Beau's Li'l Bird Dawg, CD

Bing's Bundle of Joy, CD, TDX, JH, NSD, NRD, V

CH Bitte Ihre Hoheit von Mart, UDTX, VX

Blue Moon Melody, TDX

Brandy Huntress, UDTX

OTCh Broughtmar's Samantha P. Smog,
UDTX, SDX, RDX, VX, HOF

Broughtmar's Stormy Weather, CD, TDX

Cassiopeia, TDX, RN, CGC, NSD

CT CC's Amaz'n Rainy's Gabriele, CD, RN

CH Colsidex Seabreeze Bet the Farm, TDX

Cynthia de Cimmeron, UDTX

CH Dustivelvet's Fashion Flair, UDTX

Echo's Whitney, TDX, JH

CH Grayshar Easy Radar, TDX

CH Green Acres Cardi Carousel, TDX

CH Green Acres Cash 'N Carry, CD, TDX

CH Green Acres Yesterday's Rima, TDX

CH Greysport Amazing Grace,
UDTX, NSD, RDX, VX, BROM, HOF

Hawthorne's Heidi, UDTX, Can TDX, NRD, V

CH Hoot Hollow's Firefly, CD, TDX, V

CH Hoppy's Nellie von Weiner, TDX, CDX, JH, NRD, VX

CH Jar Em's Bold Venture, CD, TDX, NSD, NRD, VX

JC's Viva Las Vegas, TDX

Kelso, TDX

Luger von Blitzen, UDTX, NSD, NRD, V

Luvleis Challange v. Indenhof, UDTX, SD RDX, VX

Maverick, CD, TDX

CH Nani's Cool Your Jetts, TDX, JH, NSD, NRD, VX

CH Nani's Jett Setter, CD, TDX, V

CT PewterRun's Diamond in the Sky, JH, NRD, VX

CT PewterRun's Papermoon, VCD2, RE, V

CH Picastar's Zeus v. Reiteralm,
TDX, NA, NAJ, NSD, NRD, VXMACH

Regen's Bismarck Lemans Streak, CD, TDX, RA, NRD

CH Regen's GreyQuest Rock Candy,
VCD1, TDX, RN, NSD, RD, VX3

CH MACH Regen's Hot Chili Pepper,
VCD3, SH, SDX, RDX, VX5

CT TC Can OTCH Can VCH Regen's Rip Stop,
VCD3, UDX4, MH, SDX, RDX, VX6, NAVHDA NA (I)

FC AFC Regen's Rip Tide,
VCD2, TDX, UD, SH, RE, SDX, RDX, VX3

Am/Can CH Regen's Rocket Launcher,
VCD2, TDX, AX, MXJ, SD, RD, VX3

OTCh Regen's State of the Art,
VCD2, UDX, MH, TDX RE, SDX, RDX, VX

TC AFC Regen's Summer Blaze, VCD3, UDX2, TDX,
MX, MXJ, MH, RE, SDX, RDX, VX6, BROM

CH Rockville's Truman Greystone,
VCD1, TDX, MH, MX, MXJ, SDX, RDX, VX5

CH Sagenhafts Tosca of Trioaks, TDX, JH, VX

CT Sandstorm's a Lady of the Lake

CH Seabreeze Seraphim, CD, TDX, NRD, V

Shabri's Simon Says, TDX, NA, NAJ

CH Shadowmar Classical Review,
CD, TDX, NRD, NSD, VX

Sir Beauregard Sephus, VCD1, TDX, AX, AXJ, V

Silversmith Crystal Harbor, CD, TDX, NSD, NRD, V

Silver Star's Cherokee Dawn, TDX

Sky's Alene De Couer, TDX

CH HH Smokey City EZ Ramblin Rose,
CD, TDX, SD, NRD, VX

CH Smokey City's EZ Yankee Annie,
UDTX, JH, SD, NRD, VX

Spicey von Aichlburg, TDX

CH Stainless Steel Jelica Joy, CD, Am and Can TDX, V

CH Starbuck's Shimmering Star, CDX, TDX, JH, RD, VX

CH Starbuck's Son of a Gun, TDX, JH

Sunrise Again Sweet Izabelle,
CDX, TDX, NA, NSD, NRD, V

Weick's Tidewater Wonder, CDX, TDX, NSD, NRD, V

CH Weick's Silver Dollar v. Wyvern, CD, TDX, NSD, VX

CH Win' Weim's Show No Mercy v. Arras, TDX

Woodcreek's on the Road Again, CD, TDX

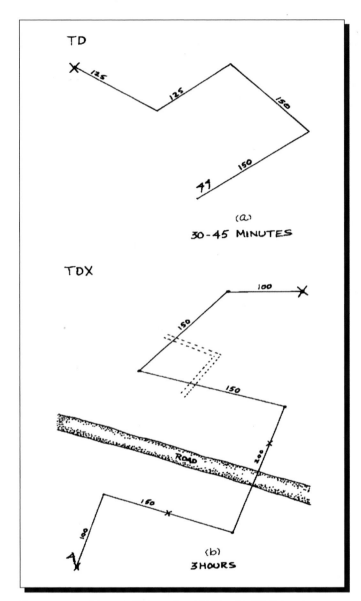

Figure 18-20: Typical AKC tracks. **(a)** TD; **(b)** TDX (see Figure 18-33 for VST track).

harness while tracking and may not be deliberately run beneath the dog. After the start, the handler must stay behind the dog a specified minimum distance (20 feet for the TD and TDX and 10 feet for the VST). The dog must track to one or more articles and must indicate or retrieve the article; other requirements are outlined in Table 18-1. Requirements for tracking tests and titles offered by the Canadian Kennel Club are similar—but not identical—to those of the AKC.

Several all-breed working dog organizations offer tracking titles for Weimaraners, as well. These are usually scored with the dog losing points for such faults as poor starts, impetuous tracking, tracking with a high nose, quartering, circling, excessive handling, poor indication of articles, and any deviation from the track. For the Fahrtenhundprufing 2 (FH2, offered by the United Schutzhund Club of America),

the most advanced and highly prized title offered by these working dog organizations, even the most minor deviations from the track will be penalized. Because of the extreme accuracy demanded, most dogs will track rather slowly (at a walking pace for the handler), steadily, and methodically. Some of these organizations allow the dog to work free (off-lead) or on a 10-m (33-foot, 7-inch) lead attached to a collar or harness.

Tracking with the Bird Dog

Hunting (using airborne scent) and tracking (using ground scent) are two aspects of the same survival instinct—to find food. The Weimaraner is equally proficient in both, using hunting and tracking skills to achieve its goal. The Germans reinforced these traits to produce a versatile hunting dog, and the ability to both hunt and track is one of the breed's most special characteristics. However, it can create a problem for the trainer; the Weimaraner instinctively uses the quickest, most efficient technique, whereas the trainer usually wants the dog to perform one or the other under a given set of circumstances and on command.

A Weimaraner intuitively uses its tracking ability to locate birds and other game, which can cause a problem when competing against the standards set for American field trials. A common problem is that the Weimaraner (even one that has not been trained to track) may figure out that the quickest way to find the bird is to follow the track of the bird

Figure 18-21: *Blood tracking* requires a dog of exceptional talent. In Germany, hunting lessee owners are required to provide a certified blood-tracking dog to locate wounded game that escapes. Esta's (Esta vom Schulzenburg) blood-tracking skill allows her to continue contributing to the hunt even at 14 years old.

planter. To prevent this problem, bring the dog into the field by a different route than the one used by the bird planter and work the dog from a different direction. If the problem develops, it can be helpful to lay false trails that do not lead to a bird (see Figure 18-11). When it becomes evident the dog is tracking either the bird planter or the bird ground scent (pottering), a light correction, coupled with calling the dog in and casting it off again, interrupts the dog's concentration on the ground scent and communicates disapproval of the behavior. Be sure of the tracking before giving a correction so the dog is not confused by unfair corrections. It is better to let the dog get away with a little of this tracking occasionally than to correct unfairly and diminish your dog's trust and confidence.

For the Weimaraner used to tracking game as well as people, use a different command for tracking each and proof the dog, in training, off tracking the inappropriate subject. It is not uncommon to see different body language in the dog when working game vs. people.

Conversely, the Weimaraner's strong, instinctive desire to hunt game can conflict with the trainer's desire when the goal is to track something else. To help the Weimaraner differentiate between hunting and tracking, use a different routine, equipment, and commands for tracking than for bird work, and work in areas that are free of game birds until the "Find!" command is understood. Introduce tracking first to minimize hunting behavior when tracking. Use different training locations for tracking, hunting, and retrieving.

If the dog starts to hunt, stop, shorten the line and repeat the "Find!" command, then wait patiently and quietly for the dog to resume tracking. Should the dog lock up on a valid point, it will probably be necessary to physically move the dog, with as little emotion as possible, past the bird and then restart the dog. If the dog remains focused on the prey, try circling the dog to break its attention and give the command to track; give a light line check only if necessary to break the dog's focus on the scent of the prey. Should the dog be unable to refocus on the task at hand, this is one of the few times when it is advisable to pull the dog from the track; with no admonishment, indeed with as little interaction as possible, remove the harness and line, clip the lead on the dog's collar, and return the dog to its crate. After a short time-out,

Figure 18-22: *Baltur von Hubertus* not only earned the coveted VGP but uses his talent in real life, too, while hunting in Illinois. New laws in some parts of the United States now allow the use of blood-tracking dogs under certain circumstances. Without Baltur's skill as a blood-tracking dog, at least three of these deer would not have been recovered.

offer the dog the opportunity to run a short track in an area devoid of hunting distractions, and conclude with a great deal of praise and rewards.

The attributes that make a good bird dog often result in a Weimaraner that would rather air scent than track. As with tracking the bird, this is excellent canine problem solving and a desirable behavior for a Search and Rescue dog, but not for a competitive tracking dog. In order to please a trainer who demands too much too soon, a dog may resort to air scenting directly to the article. "After all," the dog thinks, "I did find it!" Therefore, to avoid this situation, pay close attention to the wind direction and lay the track so the wind does not blow the scent from the article directly to the dog. Also, keep the line short until the dog understands the "Find!" command thoroughly. Should the dog lift its head and indicate interest in the direction of the articles, the handler should stop and remain quiet and still until the dog puts its head down and resumes tracking. As a last resort, the trainer may teach the dog the "Search!" command and then proof the dog off air scenting: "No search—Find!" Prevention is the easier part of training.

Tracking in the Real World

Sport tracking is an enjoyable pastime, but the Weimaraner was not bred just for the sake of competition or sport. The breed's character and skills were cultivated to defend his master, to provide game and birds for the table, and to locate injured game that might otherwise be lost. Some of the unique talents of the Weimaraner can be used in the real world, where the ability to follow a trail benefits not only his master, but the community, as well.

Blood Tracking

In most parts of Europe and more recently in the United States, the use of a dog to track wounded game has been integral to hunting. Indeed, in Germany, the lessee of a hunting area is required to provide a dog certified by the district's hunting organization in blood tracking. Should an animal be injured but not killed, a skilled dog can make the difference between the needless suffering and waste of an animal and the humane dispatch and recovery of game, deer, chamois, elk, boar, bear, or rabbit. The German Weimaraner Club offers an advanced certification; the dog may either lie down beside the animal and bay to alert the hunter to its location or it may return and lead the hunter back to the game.

In some areas of the United States, new laws allow blood tracking of game with dogs under certain conditions.

Game Tracking

Most Americans are familiar with the Weimaraner as a field dog, but its heritage also includes tracking various species of game, as well. As large game, and consequently hunting of large game, disappeared from most of Europe, the need for this skill became less and less common. However, the German breed worthiness test still includes tracking a rabbit or hare, and the ability of the Weimaraner to follow large game has not been lost. In some countries, it is legal to hunt many varieties of game with tracking dogs for sport, and the Weimaraner's talents have proven to excel in this type of hunting. As the agricultural needs of Europe have changed, the trespass of game into crops, especially corn, has increased. Weimaraners are used frequently to track such nuisance animals; the dogs are not expected to bring the animal down, but to corner or harass it until the hunter arrives. Obviously, this skill requires not only outstanding tracking skills, but strong nerves and a great deal of good sense, as well.

Search and Rescue

The AKC Tracking Regulations state, "The purpose of a tracking test is to demonstrate the dog's ability to recognize and follow human scent, a skill that is useful in the service of Mankind."

Although Weimaraners are not among the breeds usually associated with Search and Rescue work, the breed's remarkable tracking and hunting abilities, as well as its high energy level, general good health, size, and athleticism, make it suited for this highly skilled and demanding specialty. The generally sound conformation, low rate of congenital disease (in particular, hip dysplasia), and tendency toward a long, healthy

Figure 18-23: *The Weimaraner's heritage includes tracking game* as well as hunting birds. Tracking big game requires not only an outstanding nose, but also courage, steady nerves, and good sense. The Weimaraner is not expected to bring the game down, but to harry the game or hold it at bay until the hunter arrives. **(a)** Nine-month-old Axel's Lena von Hubertus develops her tracking talent and courage, starting with young boars. **(b)** One year later, Lena received a prize for her skill at the 12th International Work Contest for Dogs Hunting Wild Boar, held in Podgorna, Poland.

Figure 18-24: *The Weimaraner is well suited for the demands of Search and Rescue* with its heritage as both a tracking and hunting dog and its strong desire to work for a human partner. In addition to finding both live and deceased subjects on land, dogs have proven to be very useful in recovering victims in the water. Joan watches Blitz for changes in behavior and directs the boat handler to work back and forth across the water. In training, when Blitz gives a correct trained indication, a scuba diver may come to the surface and give him his reward.

working life make the Weimaraner a breed worthy of consideration as a Search and Rescue partner.

Canine Search and Rescue can be divided into two broad categories—ground scent and air scent. Ground scent—determining the direction of travel by following scent left as the subject passes through the area—is often called tracking or trailing. Air scent—following scent carried on air currents from the subject to the dog—is subdivided into specialties, including wilderness (area) search, disaster work, and human remains detection. Wilderness or area searches may further specialize in other sub-specialties, such as avalanche work and evidence searching. Weimaraners are, by their heritage, usually naturally talented in both ground and air scent work. Search and Rescue demands a high level of physical and mental stamina from handler and dog. Searches are sometimes long and often cover difficult terrain in all kinds of weather. Search and Rescue is not for every person, or every dog, requiring a dog of exceptional ability and skill. While the most advanced tracking tests require a dog to work a track 6–8 hours old and 2/3 mile long in easy to moderate terrain, many Search and Rescue teams require certification tests on trails 12–24 hours old that are 1 mile long or more in moderate to rough terrain. On a real search, one cannot predict how old or how long the track might be, or where it might lead.

Of course, any candidate for Search and Rescue must not only be a skilled scent-detection dog, but also have strong nerves and impeccable temperament to handle the stressful circumstances of this type of work. It is imperative that a Search and Rescue candidate Weimaraner, as any Search and Rescue

dog, be highly socialized from a very young age. Search and Rescue dogs are sometimes expected to fly in planes or helicopters, be transported in confined spaces, encounter or even work with strange dogs, meet people who behave in an unexpected manner, traverse all types of surfaces, and tolerate loud noises and excited people. They will frequently see, smell, or hear new, unusual, and sometimes startling things. Exposure to all kinds of people, new places, sights, smells, and sounds is necessary to develop an accepting temperament, which may be in conflict with the sometimes protective and reactive nature of the breed. This emotional and social conditioning should continue throughout the dog's life, not just for the first few months.

The handler must be skilled in a wide range of abilities and skills. Land navigation, radio communications, first aid for both canine and human, scent theory, search strategy, survival skills, mantracking, and more are needed. In addition, the handler must be able to perform these skills in all types of weather and terrain, often under very stressful circumstances. Search and Rescue takes a huge commitment of time; it is not just a hobby—it is a lifestyle. Call-outs come at all hours of the day and night, often on holidays, and frequently in inclement weather. In addition to searches, the hours of required training, for both dog and human, are substantial. It takes an investment on the part of many, as other volunteers will commit many hours to train those who are just beginning. It frequently takes 1–2 years, sometimes more, to field a mission-ready team. Time dedicated to the training of a new team that is not fully committed is time that is stolen from preparing other teams for call-outs. On the other hand, there are many skills needed by Search and Rescue teams that do not require one to go afield or work with a dog; base camp and support members are highly valued, as well. Most Search and Rescue teams work on a volunteer basis; food and transportation may or may not be provided. There is also a substantial financial investment for equipment.

Because one never knows what the outcome of a search will be, Search and Rescue work requires a special mental outlook on the part of both handler and dog. A handler must maintain a sense of positive urgency while being prepared for the possibility that a person may never be found or may be found injured or dead.

If one is looking for glorious headlines or media spotlights and TV interviews, know that Search and Rescue is mostly about being out in the dark and the weather with teammates and returning to the car tired and footsore. Being part of a Search and Rescue team requires one to leave personal ego behind and to focus on the mission of finding the

Test Day Arrives

Figure 18-25: *Plan to arrive early.* Do not count on the tracking dog to find the test location; plan to arrive early. The handler should be present for the drawing or an alternate may be given the chance to draw for a track instead. Tracking tests are often held in remote locations; leave extra time to actually find the location and allow for the unexpected. Photograph by Barney Riley.

Figure 18-26: *Track lottery.* The dog and handler passed a lottery drawing to get into the test, but a second lottery drawing is held on test day to determine the running order of the dogs. The handler appearing first in the catalog draws the first number but may draw any track. Although most clubs simply draw numbers written on a piece of paper, some clubs get creative. In this case, the track numbers were on the underside of cute little stuffed Weimaraner puppies! While some competitors prefer to be drawn first, there is no correlation between passing rates and running order. Once the draw is complete, take time to relax and envision the passing performance to come! Photograph by Barney Riley.

Figure 18-27: *The gallery.* Andrew had prepared Zoe for the potential distraction of judges, and possibly a gallery of observers, near the start of her track. Zoe was able to focus on what is often the hardest part of the track and successfully completed her TD with Kyla Smay (provisional judge), Sally Nesbitt (judge), Peter Ho (tracklayer), Alice Keegan (judge), and Betty Withers (AKC Representative) accompanying her at the start.

Figure 18-28: *Test nerves.* Test nerves can be an issue for some competitors. It is important to behave at the test in the same manner in which the dog has been trained; otherwise, the dog may become confused by his handler's odd conduct. At the 2007 WCA Nationals Tracking Test, Kristen demonstrates the same form in casting for a corner as she does when training with Riesa.

Figure 18-30: *The last article.* Barbara knows there will be plenty of time to celebrate later, but she first praises her dog Charlie for a job well done. Be familiar with the rules; the dog may carry the article, but excessive play or fetch games are prohibited. Also, the handler may be asked to present the article to the judges, so keep track of all articles.

Figure 18-29: *Let the celebration begin.* Be considerate of others who may be running or who have yet to run their track. Once all tracks are concluded and the judges have completed their paperwork, they are usually eager to congratulate the passing teams. Judges Phil Gallagher and Dr. Lily Mummert sign the final glove of Jett's TDX at the 2007 WCA National Tracking Test.

For more information about tracking or tracking groups:

American Kennel Club
260 Madison Avenue
New York, NY 10016
212.696.8200 — www.akc.org/index.cfm

Canadian Kennel Club
Commerce Park
89 Skyway Avenue, Suite 100
Etobicoke, Ontario
M9W 6R4
416.675.5511

National Association of Search and Rescue
P.O. Box 232020
Centreville, VA 20120-2020
877.893.0702 — www.nasar.org/nasar

United Schutzhund Club of America
3810 Paule Avenue
St. Louis, MO 63125-1718
314.638.9686

Australian Shepherd Club of America
6091 East State Highway 21
Bryan, TX 77808-9652
979.778.1082 — www.asca.org

http://pets.groups.yahoo.com/group/Tracking_Dog
http://groups.google.com/group/trackingdogs

Figure 18-31: *Search and Rescue is unpredictable.* Axel's natural abilities, trainability, and strong nerves have prepared him well to address whatever challenges may arise—including following this hiker into a cave—as a Search and Rescue volunteer for the Red Cross in Torino, Italy.

lost. There may be times when one can best contribute to the search by fielding without a dog, as support for other teams.

On the other side of the coin, few things are as rewarding as reuniting the lost child, the wandering Alzheimer's patient, or the injured hunter with the family. Sometimes, it is just the knowledge that closure has been provided to a family that provides solace. A motto that has been widely adopted by Search and Rescue groups and personnel is "This we do, so that others may live."

Weimaraner owners interested in Search and Rescue should contact a local Search and Rescue team, often through a county sheriff. The National Association of Search and Rescue may be able to provide contacts in local communities.

A Few Last Words...

The key ingredients to success in tracking with a Weimaraner are true of most dog-training ventures, only more so: patience, perseverance, concern, and respect for the dog. All how-to books are necessarily generic, so learn what is successful for the individual Weimaraner. Make haste slowly, and be willing to discard ineffectual techniques after a fair trial and try something new; there is no single perfect technique for all dogs.

If it involves so much effort, why would anyone want to get involved in tracking? Although it is true that training a tracking dog requires a great deal of time, if the trainer and the trainee enjoy the work, it is no longer work, but fun. Many dogs blossom during tracking training and, as a dog begins to rely on its own ability, a stronger, more self-confident attitude develops that is reflected in other activities. There is the reward of titles from official organizations that recognize the skills, the work, and the training. But there is also a special magic in watching a tracking dog perform a feat far beyond human abilities, a skill that is fascinating but not fully understood.

The limits of a dog's nose have yet to be identified. They can follow tracks days old; follow an individual person for miles, through a busy city intersection, crossed by hundreds of people; follow a particular child on a bike or stroller; and even tell twins apart. Because of the intense nature of the training, tracking creates a strong bond between trainer and dog that few other activities can rival. The dog–handler bond is priceless—a treasure beyond any title. Tracking provides an opportunity to express instincts that the Weimaraner has been carefully bred to possess.

Keep that joyful, positive attitude; tracking is supposed to be fun! Most important, tracking is teamwork. Neither the trainer nor the dog can work or progress without the other. Have fun and revel in the thrill and beauty of watching a Weimaraner display the unique heritage of hundreds of years of careful husbandry.

Figure 18-32: *By virtue of earning the CT title,* Gabi and Linda also secured an invitation to the AKC National Tracking Invitational, held each Fall at the Biltmore Estate. Entrants are drawn by lottery, with preference going to dogs that have not previously had the chance to participate in this auspicious event. Tracks combine features of both the TDX and VST. Like all AKC tracking events, this is a non-competitive event; although no titles are awarded, nevertheless, the attendees are honored by the chance to demonstrate their skills at this special event.

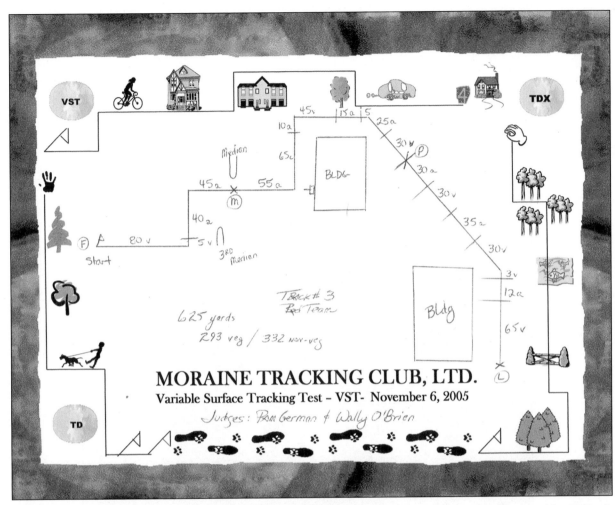

Figure 18-33: *This is not just any VST track,* but a commemorative copy of the track Gabi ran when she earned her VST title and became the breed's first CT.

Gabi and Linda Earn the VST

"Our track was 625 total yards, 293 vegetated surfaces and 332 non-vegetated surfaces (mowed grass, asphalt, concrete). Cloth, metal, plastic, and leather articles were used and the wind was strong with medium to high gusts. I am not sure if it was the longest half hour of my life or the shortest. The first 80 yards of Gabi's track was on sparse grass; as she approached her corner, she slowed down, checking both directions before committing to a left-hand turn. Gabi proceeded a few steps into the leg to enter a large parking lot and moved down a space dividing paint lines 45 yards to her metal article. Whew! Another 55 yards up to a sidewalk next to a building and again I stood back for the moment of truth as Gabi worked a hard surface corner, back and forth, gradually moving less and less in the wrong direction, longer and longer down the leg of her track. After committing to the leg, Gabi paused but a minute to admire the Weimaraner tracking alongside her in the mirrored windows. Out into a driveway entrance and across a grassy area for another turn, this time on the grass. This leg went across another drive entrance into another grassy area to an open-angle turn. Gabi took the angle, but was doing some quartering down this leg. Fortunately, not so much as to cause her to miss her next article and on she went. About 20 yards from the turn, the judges and gallery held tense as Gabi and I reached a grass hill with a stand of pine trees next to it. The leaves were swirling so much that it was distributing the scent of her track every which way; down toward a pond; nope, it didn't go there; back up the hill; off the other direction back on the concrete…not there either; how about the trees? Finally, I quietly asked Gabi if her track didn't go just a bit further? Off we went to complete our second to last leg. We took the last corner out into another paved area. (The judge told me after the test that Gabi was working parallel to the track by a few yards on this pavement.) At this point, the track was up against a multilevel parking garage protecting us from the wind. Gabi moved onto the grass next to the building; jumped up on her hind legs to check that the article hadn't been hidden in the garage and then went back to work down the last grassy 15 yards. She stopped dead and told me with her eyes we had found it—the last article, the coveted No. 4! As the judges gingerly approached and the gallery appeared with not a dry eye in the crowd, they found me kneeling on the ground crying, hugging, and telling my Gabi just how much I loved her and how very proud I was of her. I always knew we could do it, but now the rest of the world knew it, too."

19-1: *Bikini,* by William Wegman.

CHAPTER 19

WEIMARANERS DOING THEIR THING

In developing a breed that would be the German Forester's working companion, the Weimaraner became something very special. The Weimaraner is more than another pointing breed; it is more than another versatile hunting breed. The forester needed an intelligent dog with the ability to solve problems encountered in everyday work, which led to the open-ended, problem-solving aptitude that makes the Weimaraner an enthusiastic participant in virtually every aspect of its owner's life. The lively intelligence, need for people, and desire to share every human activity are as characteristic of the Weimaraner as its silver coat. For Weimaraners, "doing their thing" covers the spectrum of most canine talents.

The Weimaraner in Art and Advertising

The Weimaraner's adaptability, intelligence, and striking good looks make the breed a natural in today's advertising and art world. The work of artists like William Wegman (whose work is featured throughout this volume) has made the Weimaraner recognizable to almost everyone. Wegman quips, "My Weims are the perfect fashion models. Their elegant slinky forms are covered in gray. And gray, as everyone knows, goes with anything." The perspective of such artwork strikes a note that captures the eye as well as the imagination of the art connoisseur, the Weimaraner enthusiast, and the general public. Wegman takes advantage of the dog's distinctive appearance and captures the unique personality of each dog. The dogs take pride in their work and seem to recognize when the "perfect shot" has been taken, reveling in the "Wow!" that echoes through the studio. Some of this may sound familiar between human fashion models and photographers, except the dogs are less demanding…. Wegman says, "My Weimaraners don't need first class tickets or fancy hotels, but really love a good ride in the car."

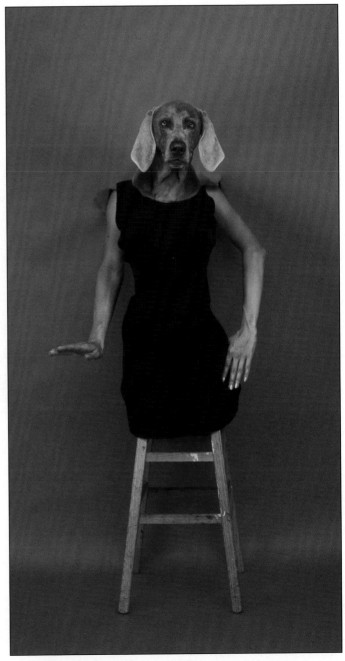

Figure 19-2: *Wegman's photo of Bettina* in a little black dress proves that gray does go with everything; the Weimaraner and art are a perfect combination.

FASHION

Saks Fifth Avenue offered William Wegman and his canine companions free rein of the store in order to produce a fashion series. They traveled through the various departments, from fur to footwear, and the book **Fashion** *resulted.*

Remember, the essence of glamour is fragrance.
What will be Batty's scent du jour? You choose.

"Dress Up Batty." William Wegman (2004).

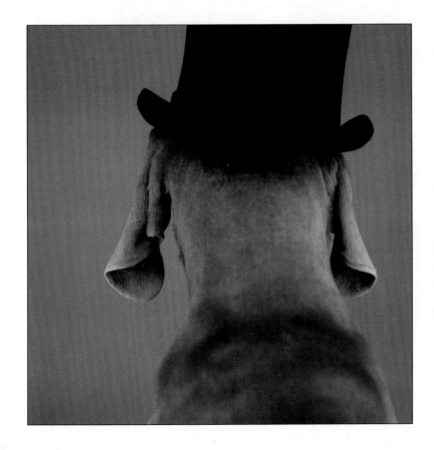

ADVERTISING

The striking appearance of the Weimaraner makes it a natural for advertising as well. Weimaraners have graced a wide variety of advertising campaigns.

Mr. Martin McMartin St Martin III, famous sports car buff, says: "For love or money, you can't beat a Stutz Bearcat for style or stamina. The same thing is true of Springmaid sheets. I used them on my yacht until I lost it in the storms of the recession. But I salvaged the running lights and made seat covers out of the sheets. My driving cape came from the draperies, but my crash helmet was designed in London. You can't go wrong on a Stutz Bearcat."

Figure 19-3: *This advertisement for Springmaid Fabric* appeared over 50 years ago when the Weimaraner was one of the ultimate status symbols, showing the Weimaraner is a classic, even in advertising. (Close examination reveals the true copycat spirit of the Weim, as he too sports a green and red eye).

Figure 19-4: *Zoe is well established in the fame game.* One of her most recent projects was a campaign for Target featuring many different products, including dog food. Photograph courtesy of Target.

Figure 19-6: *The Weimaraner's appeal lasts* season in and season out. This JC Penney campaign appeared over 10 years ago. Photo courtesy of JC Penney.

Figure 19-5: *Posing as July's Uncle Sam* in a calendar, Blitz proclaims, "We want your business!" Photograph courtesy of Lance Fargo, Coastal Printing and Graphics.

Figure 19-7: *The Magic Flute.* The 1996–1997 season catalog for the Houston Grand Opera featured Wegman's Weimaraners depicting each of the season's productions.

MOVIES & TELEVISION

*Their strong desire to please, intelligence, and charming good looks
make them ideal co-stars in the movie and TV studios, as well.*

Figure 19-8: ***Peach graced the silver screen,*** starring in the hit movie *Best in Show,* a
parody of the dog show world. Photograph courtesy of Castle Rock Entertainment.

Figure 19-9: ***Fay Ray was a popular cast member of Sesame Street*** and helped children learn everything from counting to nursery rhymes.

Figure 19-10: *Wegman shows that Weims and movies go together* like movies and popcorn as his dogs show their various reactions to a scary movie.

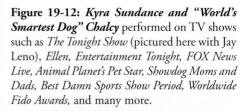

Figure 19-11: *Batty and Crooky lead* the Wegman pack, solving crimes and unraveling mysteries. *Hardly Boys* was screened at film festivals around the world and selected for the 1996 Sundance Film Festival. Available on DVD at www.wegmanworld.com.

Figure 19-12: *Kyra Sundance and "World's Smartest Dog" Chalcy* performed on TV shows such as *The Tonight Show* (pictured here with Jay Leno), *Ellen, Entertainment Tonight, FOX News Live, Animal Planet's Pet Star, Showdog Moms and Dads, Best Damn Sports Show Period, Worldwide Fido Awards,* and many more.

Subtraction, by William Wegman.

CHILDREN'S LITERATURE

Children's books featuring Weimaraners can be not only entertaining but educational.

Figure 19-13: *Chip Wants a Dog,* by William Wegman (2003).

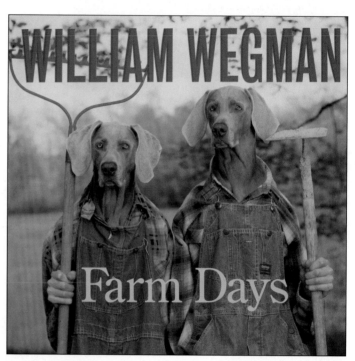

Figure 19-15: *Farm Days,* by William Wegman (1997).

Figure 19-14: *Jack Sprat* could eat no fat, from *Mother Goose,* by William Wegman (1996).

Figure 19-16: *On the Way to the Ball,* from *Cinderella,* by William Wegman (1993).

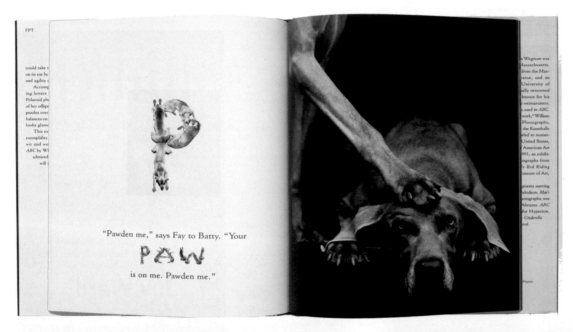

Figure 19-17: *ABC's,* by William Wegman (1994).

Figure 19-18: *What Faust Saw,* by Matt Ottley (1995).

Figure 19-19: *Educational Poster,* by William Wegman.

A GOOD READ

Weimaraners make good reading for adults as well as children.

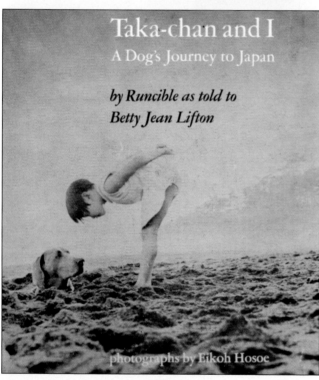

Figure 19-20: *Taka Chan and I,* by Betty Jean Lifton (1967).

Figure 19-22: *Haint: A Tale of Extraterrestrial Intervention and Love Across Time and Space,* by Joy Ward (2006).

Figure 19-23: *Fay,* by William Wegman (1999).

Figure 19-21: *Weimaraners are featured* in a popular fundraising cookbook, www.norcalweimrescue.org.

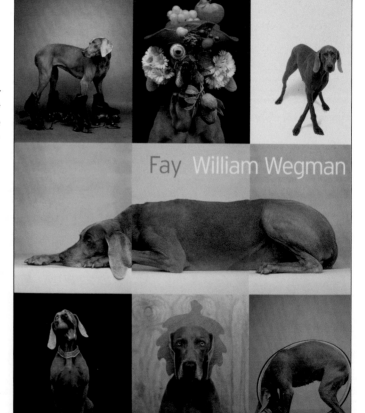

A GOOD LAUGH

The aristocratic and distinguished Weimaraner is not lacking in a sense of humor.

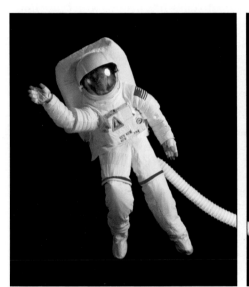  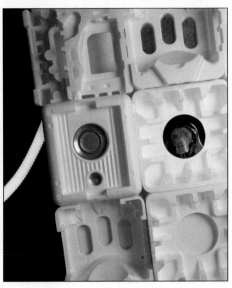

Figure 19-24: *Wegman's Chip* appeared in an ad campaign on the Washington, DC, transit system for the National Air and Space Museum.

Figure 19-26: *Too sexy?* This unusual variety of Weimaraner found in Russia sports a mustache and a thick, wiry, silver-gray coat to fend off the bitter cold while hunting in winter.

Figure 19-25: *Arlo and his friend Indigo,* by Martha Fast.

IN REAL LIFE

The versatile Weimaraner plays hard.

While articles and reports from the "Crazy Years" (see *America's Wonder Dog*) made it seem as if the Weimaraner could walk on water and leap tall buildings, and while these reports were exaggerations, the truth is not exactly mundane. The athletic nature and "ready to go" attitude of Weimaraners make them a natural for a variety of sports as good citizens and family members. There are few AKC activities in which the Weimaraner cannot give it a "good go." Weimaraners excel in the traditional activities, such as obedience and fieldwork, but do not think that their feats can be limited by anything but their owner's (or the dog's) imagination. As good citizens, they can fulfill nearly any role requested of them. As family members, Weimaraners will find ways to integrate into daily life, helping to get the chores done, or providing endless entertainment and companionship. Expect the unexpected and do not let stereotypes create unnecessary restrictions on what might provide an interesting day on the sports field.

Figure 19-27: *Joe and Mia* show that disk competition is not just for Border Collies or Whippets. While dogs may compete in several forms, including multiple catches and freestyle, Mia competes in the Quad competition, where the winning team is the one that catches the longest throw. For more information, check www.skyhoundz.com or www.ufoworldcup.org. Photograph courtesy of Pix n' Pages Photography.

Figure 19-28: *From a Weimaraner's point of view,* what could be more fun than a sport that combines running, jumping, and fetching tennis balls? In flyball, a team of four dogs each retrieve a ball from a special box at the end of a series of hurdles. Each race in a flyball tournament has 3–5 heats. The fastest team in each heat is awarded points determined by their team's time. Currently, the team record for a relay is under 16 seconds. Martha's dogs, Zoey and Arlo, demonstrate the form that earned them Master's titles in flyball. More information on flyball can be found at www.flyball.org.

Figure 19-29: *Weimaraners make great dance partners* in freestyle obedience. The team presents a series of "dance steps" to music that take advantage of the Weimaraner's athletic ability and desire to work as a team. Candy, a familiar sight at the WCA National Specialty, performs at a charity benefit with Travler and Lincoln. More information on freestyle can be found at www.worldcanine-freestyle.org.

Figure 19-31: *On the way to becoming* the only Weimaraner to earn New Zealand's Working Trial Championship, Mac and Meredith had to achieve outstanding performances in a series of competitions involving obedience, agility, and tracking. These exercises challenge not only the dog's trainability and focus, but also his athleticism and willingness.

Figure 19-30: *A breed often known for its "need for speed,"* a Weim will take excitement where he can find it! This German longhair takes a short break from sledding and snowboarding with his family. Photograph courtesy of Weimaraner Klub e. V.

ALL IN THE FAMILY

The strong bond between the Weimaraner and its owner makes it willing to provide whatever service is needed, whether it is a babysitter or a personal assistant.

Figure 19-32: *Personal secretary.* Each morning, Chloe helps read and sort the mail and then plan the day's activities with her owner, writer and lecturer Dr. Maragaret Williams.

Figure 19-34: *The Dutch Yachtsman.* Well-known Winner in Show and Field throughout Europe, Roy's favorite pastime is Chief of Security when his owners', the Theel's, sloop sails into the harbor.

Figure 19-33: *Puppysitter.* In most Weimaraner families, there is usually an adult, as often as not a male, that is surprisingly tolerant of the excesses of the young and is willing to puppysit—up to a point.

Figure 19-35: *Dinner dancer.* The rhythmic clapping of hands is all that is needed to get Tia dancing at Miller family get-togethers.

Figure 19-36: *Transport specialist.* Most Weims are willing to do almost any job as long as it means spending time with the family. Bach happily pulls a cart of groceries and equipment during the Sevieking's recent trip along the Santa Fe Trail.

Figure 19-37: *Isaiah, the night watchman.* The Weimaraner is typically alert and curious; usually a very friendly and relatively quiet breed, they are most always ready to check things out and let the family know when something unusual is afoot. Photo courtesy of Shirley Nilsson.

WORKING FOR A LIVING

The desire to please and willingness to work can go well beyond casual assistance and can be channeled into a full-time job. Some Weimaraners assist their owners in accomplishing daily tasks that are difficult or impossible to perform without the assistance of their partner. Others provide services that benefit society as a whole.

Figure 19-38: *The Weimaraner's typical devotion* to its owner, highly trainable nature, size, and athleticism make it a good candidate as an assistance dog. In addition to her constant companionship, Sadie's skills allow Linda to go places and do things knowing that her partner will be there to help her perform tasks that she cannot do herself. Photograph by Jack Fields.

Figure 19-40: *Raymond and Scnapps* were the first successful guide dog team in the United States. Photograph courtesy of the WCA.

Figure 19-39: *Spook served as a narcotics detection dog* and Search and Rescue dog in the scorching deserts of Arizona. According to his handler, Kent, his 100+ pounds, yellow eyes, and toothy grin were usually sufficient to overcome the objections when searching for drugs.

Figure 19-41: *Tom Knott and his partner, Justice,* made law enforcement history as the first successful cross-trained narcotics/explosives detection dog. Tom and Justice not only worked the streets, but also served as instructors for a variety of national and international law-enforcement agencies.

Figure 19-42: *A girl's got to earn a living too!* When not working the show circuit, Trixie works the fashion circuit as a runway model, among her many credits. Photograph courtesy of Traer Scott.

Figure 19-43: *The world-acclaimed acrobatic stunt dog team* of Kyra Sundance and Chalcy has starred on premier stages such as NBA, MLB, and AFL halftime shows, in Disney's Underdog stage show in Hollywood, and in a command performance in Marrakech for the King of Morocco. Kyra and Chalcy authored several books and DVDs, including the successful *101 Dog Tricks* series and *The Dog Rules.*

DREAM JOBS

Given the chance, Weimaraners might volunteer for jobs their owners never imagined, since in a dog's world they probably would rather be doing what people do anyway.

Figure 19-44: *Sheriff, What Do You Do?* by William Wegman.

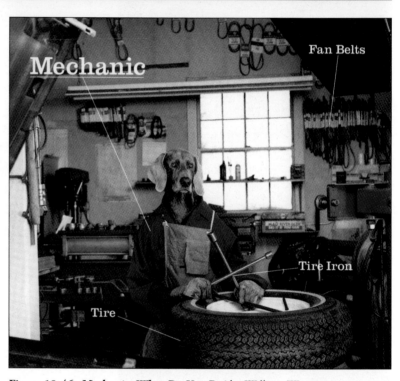

Figure 19-46: *Mechanic, What Do You Do?* by William Wegman.

Figure 19-45: *Drummer, What Do You Do?* by William Wegman.

Figure 19-47: *Farmer, What Do You Do?* by William Wegman.

VOLUNTEERS

Some dogs and their owners volunteer their time to help others.

Figure 19-48: *Gabriel* (the founding dog of Gabriel's Angels) visits abused and at-risk children, providing unconditional love, teaching empathy, and helping the kids feel better about their lives. What started with one girl and one dog has grown to an organization with over 90 teams visiting 80 facilities. Good dog, Gabriel! Visit www.gabrielsangels.org for additional information.

Figure 19-50: *Desdemona visits the elderly*, bringing cheer and entertainment. The skills of a retired but well-trained Weimaraner can be used to benefit others. For more information on therapy dogs, visit www.deltasociety.org.

Figure 19-49: *Günther uses the natural heritage of the Weimaraner,* outstanding olfactory skills, and desire to work for his handler, as well as the natural tendency to work relatively close to his handler to locate human remains as a volunteer Search and Rescue dog.

SEASON'S GREETINGS

Weimaraners never want to be left out and consider themselves to be part of the family, and holidays are no exception. Here are a few holiday greeting cards that include Weimaraners.

Figure 19-51: *The Snyders' Christmas card.*

Peace On Earth

Mark & Jinny Alexander

Figure 19-52: *The Alexanders' holiday card.*

Merry Christmas

May your Holidays go as planned!

The O'Briens

Figure 19-53: *The O'Briens' Christmas card.*

Figure 19-54: *Weimaraners seem to be particularly devoted* to the youngest members of the family. Do Shadow and Zoe just instinctively know that babies get plenty of attention and lots of "good stuff?"

Figure 19-55: *Constant Companions,* Jackie and Fanny.

BEST FRIEND

Although the games may change, the Weimaraner is usually willing to do whatever is asked. A breed that is pretty much willing to do anything, their "thing" is usually the owner's thing, so they can be with you. At the end of the day, their deepest desire is to be a "Constant Companion."

VX5 + VX5 = !!!!

Figure 20-1: *Breeding for versatile excellence.* Now that the WCA is offering the extended versatility program, more breeders are designing matings to showcase a trait that is as much a hallmark of this breed as the shining silver coat. A planned breeding between two of America's most versatile dogs, Truman VX5 and Chili Pepper VX5, certainly produced results; at 3 years old, this talented litter had amassed an impressive array of placements and titles in every venue of AKC and WCA competition. Left to right: Booster (son), CH Regen's Rocket Launcher, VCD1, TDX, AX, AXJ, SD, RD, VX3; Truman (sire), CH Rockville's Truman Greystone, VCD2, TDX, MH, MX, MXJ, SDX, RDX,VX5; Lacey (Granddam), CH Windwalkers Felicity v. Gaul, BROM; Pepper (dam), CH MACH Regen's Hot Chili Pepper, VCD3, SH, SDX, RDX, VX5; Rock-It, Regen's Rock It Man, CD, OAJ, NA, RN; Roca, CH Regen's GrayQuest Rock Candy, MX, MXJ, TD, RN, NSD, NRD, VX2; Roxie, CH Regen's Ready to Rock, CD, TD, NSD, V.

CHAPTER 20

BREEDING BASICS

According to the AKC, the person who owns or leases the bitch at the time of whelping is the breeder, a definition that could include:

- Sentimental Sam, who just wants a puppy from Old Shep
- Model Mother, who wants one litter to teach the kids about birds and bees
- Greedy Gus, who buys a "pair" to make a few bucks
- Careless Connie, who forgot to close the gate between Young Buck and Old Mama

In this chapter, the term breeder means something more, someone who plans a multi-generation series of step-by-step matings (short-term goals) that lead to the perfect Weimaraner (long-term goal).

Identifying Goals

Because there is no perfect Weimaraner, each breeder should create an imaginary picture of what the perfect animal should look like and how it should perform—the ideal dog standing on a faraway hill. This image of the long-term goal is so personal that it is doubtful any two fanciers imagine the same dog. In a similar way, desirable and undesirable traits are essentially a subjective, personal value judgment. When developing a breeding plan, this image of the perfect dog must be sharpened to identify the dog's desired characteristics, including temperament, health, and preferred performance traits, in addition to the dog's structural appearance. Only when the vision has been defined can the traits be identified that must be strengthened or modified in the quest for the perfect dog. Step-by-step short-term goals should be developed to help make the dog on the hill a reality.

Although the purpose of competition is to identify individuals worthy of perpetuating the breed, maintain a realistic perspective about competitive success; remember that winning is merely the exterior gauge of progress, and success is fleeting unless the winning individuals reproduce their good traits. Keep an open mind, and make every effort to consistently strive for something a little bit better with each generation. The breeder of sound, healthy, balanced Weimaraners with good temperament, showmanship, and hunting ability who maintains objective breeding goals and flexibility over the years is bound to be a winner.

Start with the Best Bitch

Give the breeding program a solid foundation by starting out with individuals that are closest to your ideal, beginning with the best dogs available. Why waste years and generations to achieve a level of quality that could have been obtained at the beginning, while the competition is 10 steps

Figure 20-2: Breeders Pat and Connie O'Brien established a well-defined vision of what the ideal Weimaraner head should look like. These four champion littermates out of CH OB's Midnight Serenade, BROM, by BISS CH Camelot's Go for the Gold, BROM, exhibit striking consistency of type.

ahead since they started with the best stock available? Buying a bitch with top breeding potential places the beginner on the same level as the breeder. Where the novice goes with that is entirely a matter of luck and judgment.

When selecting foundation-breeding stock, the competitive records of individuals are a less reliable guide than the overall records of the family and progeny. How many great champions of the past have progeny of comparable merit? Great winners come from great families, so concentrate on the family; evaluate the bad traits as well as the good ones—all aspects (including performance and overall health) of the family. Foundation dogs with sound reproductive potential should, with luck, consistently duplicate these qualities in their offspring; the ease of achieving a breeding and healthy whelping should not be forgotten among the many other important traits in a breeder's plans.

A breeding program begins with a quality brood bitch, the foundation on which to build. The bitch should be from

Figure 20-4: *A quality brood bitch* is not only the foundation for a kennel name but for generations to come. Never forget to consider health and longevity as well as type and talent. CH Sanbars Diva von Sagenhaft, CDX, NRD, BROM, illustrates this concept. More silver than gray, but still proud and active even at the age of 14, Diva was not only the dam of nine conformation champions, she has helped establish the Sagenhaft line as one that produces healthy dogs that can be counted on to excel in performance events as well as the show ring.

Figure 20-3: *Start with the best.* This puppy was purchased from a litter out of a Best in Show sire bred to a show-titled personal gun dog dam. With the goal of developing a dual-oriented breeding program, Rainy was selected for her birdiness and sound conformation. Rainy fulfilled the first goal of her owners by completing a Dual Championship, with style and top wins to spare. Bred to three different studs, Rainy consistently produced quality offspring, with a record of six U.S. field trial champions, three U.S. show champions—two of them Dual Champions—as well as two German-rated International Dual Champions. When her owners made the decision to start with the best, and backed it up with a well-planned training and breeding program, DC Wynwoods Rain on the Rise, SDX, SH, VX, certainly fulfilled the dream of every beginning breeder.

bloodlines of proven quality, preferably but not necessarily a champion. Through the brood bitch, the breeder can select the stud dog that is most likely to produce the desired traits, whereas the stud dog can only hope for discovery by the owner of that "just-right bitch." The real limitation with a bitch is the potential number of litters she can produce, which allows less room for experimentation and testing, and every litter must count.

Because the prospective brood bitch is often acquired as a puppy, she must be objectively evaluated when she reaches maturity. Odds will favor a bitch acquired from a litter of a highly consistent type, from a dam or stud that has established a reputation for prepotency in traits that the prospective breeder values. For her overall qualities, seek (and carefully weigh) the opinions of experienced breed authorities—breeders, judges, handlers—for the likelihood of reproductive potential of specific traits that will contribute to building the image of the individual's vision of the "perfect dog;" the bitch's breeder is usually the best source of information. So many factors must be weighed that no general rule is possible. Nevertheless, culling may need to begin with the brood bitch if she fails to produce progeny that advance the breeding program. If the quality

Figure 20-5: *Purchasing a puppy* as a potential brood bitch involves a great deal of risk. In the case of Spree, the goal was to produce top-level field trial competitors. Although from a famous field champion sire and dam, and displaying great early potential, she never fulfilled her initial promise. Although her physical conformation was superior to her parents, and her great nose found many birds, she consistently lacked the range and independence needed for top field competition. Bred to a dog with great range and conformation, she produced puppies with excellent conformation, but unfortunately also her limited range. The best choice for Spree, in light of goals of the breeder's program, was to place her in a home where she excelled as a personal gun dog and was a cherished pet.

of the first litter is disappointing, it could merely be an unfortunate combination with the stud; select another stud (preferably from different bloodlines) for her second litter. If the same traits show up again, it is usually better to start over with another bitch than to live with those undesired traits for generations to come.

Purchasing a puppy as a potential foundation bitch includes a great deal of inherent risk, not to mention the time and money spent developing a puppy who may or may not achieve her early potential. A sensible option would be to become a team member with an established breeder by leasing a proven brood matron that most closely represents the goals of the prospective breeding program. Alternatively, such a bitch may on rare occasions be available for sale, prior to her final litter, if she is guaranteed a responsible and loving home in her retirement. If the perfect bitch is not available, then it might be worth considering a full littermate or a puppy from a repeat breeding; failing that, consider a half-sister that resembles her the most, in as many ways as possible.

Breeding Principles

Never be in a hurry. Begin by reading everything that can be found on genetics and be familiar with the terms. Few traits fit into neat dominant-recessive categories, but an understanding of genetics helps the observant breeder identify hereditary patterns. *Genetics: An Introduction for Dog Breeders* (Alpine 2003), by *Weimaraner Ways* co-author Jackie Isabell, is an easily understood guide for beginning breeders, offering a practical and comprehensive explanation of Genetics 101.

Prepotency—the ability to predictably transmit specific traits to progeny—is a vital consideration in any breeding plan. The prepotent dog is to possess paired (homozygous) combinations for certain traits, desired or undesired, that are consistently transmitted to his offspring. When genes are not paired (heterozygous) for a trait they are transmitted randomly, resulting in less predictability. A wise breeder selects and tests for dogs that are prepotent in the areas in which improvement is most desirable and may likely be completely different from the choice of a competitor looking only for a certain head type and expression (a headhunter). The "pick" for a wise breeder will be the puppy that exhibits the phenotype for the traits that are most highly valued or difficult to achieve when weighed against the challenge of overcoming the dog's less desirable features through future matings. A breeder, on occasion, must be far-sighted enough to accept certain minor flaws, such as ear set or length of neck, to achieve more complex traits, such as superior nose and range in the field. It is often easier to "fix" structural problems than those of health or performance. *Picking the Perfect Puppy* will be invaluable in helping the breeder identify the structural characteristics of each puppy in the litter, helping to further the goals of a breeding program.

A breeder should strive for genetic reliability and consistency, quality inside and out. Competitive success in the conformation ring is primarily recognition of outstanding phenotype; however, the breeder is equally concerned about traits that cannot be observed and defy genetic analysis. Too often, breeding goals focus only on structure, but realistically they should also include a dog's ability to reproduce desired

Figure 20-6: *Prepotency is a rare and valued trait.* A far-sighted breeder will accept and adjust for minor imperfections of a prepotent dog that do not interfere with the long-term goal; this homozygous genetic pattern allows for a far greater predictability in a breeding program. Bred to only eight bitches in his lifetime, NAFC/FC/AFC Snake Breaks Sgt. Schultz, HOF, produced in nearly all his offspring a strong range, nose, pointing style, and trainability, resulting in at least 13 field champions and 2 duals to date. A posthumous AI litter by FC Briarmeadow's Sunshine Abigail produced a record-setting 6 field championship titles from a single litter.

traits, such as longevity with good health, a long productive life, performance aptitude, and a biddable temperament.

Study the prepotency of both families and individuals. Familial prepotency is evaluated by in-depth study of the pedigree, noting traits (both good and bad) that occur with regularity in individuals and littermates. It is possible to go back surprisingly far by talking with old breed fanciers and reading old magazines. A little detective skill may be required to learn about littermates that never appeared in competition. The beauty of the German pedigree, when dealing with imported dogs, is the availability of records on the sibling's evaluations by the breed warden and competition records as well, which may provide extremely valuable information for the astute breeder. It is also worthwhile to discover more about the non-champions in the pedigree. Although the lack of a title may mean that the individual lacks merit, consider some of the following exceptions, discovered with a little sleuthing:

- A male sired one litter, won two 5-point majors at his first two shows, and was killed by a car
- A pick-of-litter bitch was kicked in the head by a horse, causing loss of an eye and a deformed jaw
- A multiple Best of Breed Winner from the classes retired before finishing because of her owner's divorce

- A bitch that lacks a single point on a Field Trial Championship gets a career-ending illness

Bloodlines are an indicator—not a guarantee—of individual prepotency, which can be identified only through the quality of the progeny. In addition, occasional individuals from unremarkable bloodlines prove to be highly prepotent for desirable traits; however, this is the exception and not the usual occurrence. More often than not, a dog from unremarkable lines will produce unremarkable puppies. Benjamin Franklin's advice in *Poor Richard's Almanac,* offered to young bachelors well over 200 years ago, still applies, *"Marry not the fairest maid from a poor lot; but rather the plainest from the best."* When reading pedigrees, it is not sufficient to look merely at the names and titles of the sire and dam on the AKC registration papers. Further investigation, with an in-depth pedigree of at least five to six generations, may provide a wealth of hidden successes or skeletons in siblings or progeny. A bitch with a fine pedigree but an unremarkable personal career that produces outstanding puppies from multiple studs should not be dismissed without due consideration for her potential genetic value.

Prepotency patterns are easier to identify with popular stud dogs that have many offspring to consider. Study the quality of the bitches bred to a stud; bitches of exceptional quality and prepotency make any stud look good. The progeny of mediocre bitches reveals more of his prepotency for specific traits. Examine progeny from different combinations of bloodlines. Do all of his puppies have their sire's outstanding shoulders or stylish point, or do they have this only when the dam is equally good or comes from a family well known for these traits?

Do not disregard a stud just because he has been lightly used, provided that the quality of pups is consistently high. Sometimes individuals "nick" well and are able to genetically cement a specific characteristic. Bella v. d. Reiteralm was a German import of the late 1950s; solidly built front and rear but quite plain in type, she possessed a powerful, straight, coming-and-going movement that was unusual for her era. Val Knight Ranck was a winner noted for his extended, effortless gait; his record of nine Best in Shows stood for decades, only to be broken by his own descendants. Bella produced two litters by Val Knight. Eleven of her 12 puppies finished and earned many honors. Such a result could never be predicted, but this genetic blueprint for superior movement is still a powerful influence found in the pedigrees of many of today's winning show Weimaraners.

Val Knight Ranck illustrates the hallmark of an outstanding and prepotent sire, despite the fact that he was infrequently used at stud. His Best in Show record reflects the impact of his modern type, but his greatest mark on the breed remains today through generations of his offspring. Bred to only 15 bitches, he produced 34 champions, six of whom won Sporting Groups. Val's son, Maximilian, would soon eclipse his sire's record by producing 62 champions from 26 breedings. Max's son, Rajah, in turn would set new show and production records, with 118 champions from 51 bitches.

And still today, over 50 years later, Val's genetic power can be seen through the influence of his great- and great-great-granddaughters when bred to the legendary contemporary studs Ultra Easy and Standing Ovation, currently the No. 1 and No. 2 Top-Producing Weimaraner sires and 4th and 5th among all breeds with 148 and 147 champion offspring, respectively. It is fortunate indeed for the breed that a few fanciers recognized the genetic promise of Val Knight Ranck.

Mapping Tools of a Breeding Program

Dog fanciers discuss the merits of inbreeding, linebreeding, and out-crossing as if they were mutually exclusive systems of breeding. A more productive approach is to regard each as a tool that breeders employ to achieve the desired results. The choice of method should be determined by the traits the astute breeder realizes the brood bitch is likely to transmit to her progeny and that must be corrected to achieve the long-term goal.

A highly popular technique, inbreeding is the mating of closely related individuals, usually sibling or parent-progeny matings. One of the most successful forms of inbreeding is backcrossing, the mating of an individual to a parent or grandparent. With the recent development of frozen canine semen, more breeders will be able to include backcrossing as a way to achieve their long-term goals.

The purpose is to fix and preserve desirable traits in a strain; the drawback is that extensive inbreeding may do the same for undesired traits as well. Few advocates are aware of or consider the consequences of inbreeding depression—

Figure 20-7: *Breeder's dilemma:* repeat the breeding of CH Chataway's Time to Tattle, TD, JH, NSD, NRD, VX, BROM, to BISS CH Camelot's Go for the Gold, BROM, a third time? Tattle (in the middle) is shown above, winning the Brood Bitch class with just two of the many champions produced from these litters. Unusually successful breedings, called "nicks," are worth repeating. However, resist the temptation to breed the dam to the same sire a third time; rather, choose an unrelated stud so that the dam's excellent genetic material will be available from a different direction for future line breedings.

most often exhibited by poor fertility, associated with increasing homozygosity. This may be fine for swine, when the goal is rapid growth and increased body mass, but is not so when intelligence, longevity, and working instinct are at issue.

Line-breeding is a rather loose term to describe the mating of related individuals. The difference between line-breeding and inbreeding is relatively subjective and varies only in the degree of closeness of a common ancestor. This relationship can be expressed in a mathematical formula; refer to Malcolm Willis' *Genetics of the Dog* (Howell) on the coefficient of inbreeding for a complete explanation.

Line-breeding is a less direct way to fix desirable traits than inbreeding, but provides more options for reducing undesirable ones. One avenue for accomplishing this would be to select two individuals prepotent for the desired trait that share a common grandparent outcrossed to different mates—for example, the proposed sire and the dam share a grandsire, bred to unrelated dams—that possesses the same desired trait, but hopefully does not carry the potential to spark undesirable surprises previously disguised in the genotype. While creating uniformity and consistency of type, it is

necessary to recognize that line-breeding, as well as inbreeding, inherently has the potential to trigger unwanted characteristics that naturally appear in the gene pool, as well.

Those who tout inbreeding as the best way to fix desirable traits tend to regard outcrossing, the mating of relatively unrelated individuals, as a backward step in breeding programs. Used judiciously, however, outcrossing is a useful tool to: (a) acquire desired traits that do not exist in a line; (b) dilute undesired traits; and (c) obtain healthy, hybrid vigor. Granted that outcrossing has the potential to introduce unexpected faults and dilute desired traits, many times the increased hybrid vigor introduced by carefully selected stock will allow the return to a line-breeding program to cement the original type minus the undesirable baggage.

The frequent, repeated use of popular studs will also reduce genetic diversity. Thus, the periodic infusion of totally new bloodlines is not only beneficial, but also vital, when the genetic base of a breed becomes so limited there is no other way to avoid combinations that produce undesired recessive traits.

Unfortunately, type-to-type breeding (the mating of animals with similar but unrelated phenotypes) yields scattered results. However, combined with line-breeding, it reinforces the desired type with less risk of concentrating recessive problems; combined with outcrossing, it minimizes loss of the desired phenotype while perpetuating the desired traits.

Plan for the future. Laying out a 12-generation pedigree is a graphic lesson in how the popularity of inbreeding has narrowed the genetic base of the American Weimaraner. Never underestimate the power of the patterning effect when the same ancestor appears many times in a pedigree. Faults from the distant past are as likely to crop up as the ancestor's better traits—and more likely to be an unpleasant surprise. Sheer distance in generations does not always dilute. By reviewing 10 or 12 generations, a pattern may begin to emerge, with the same combination of bloodlines, or a specific dog, appearing repeatedly. An unpleasant occurrence is sometimes explained when that 12-generation pedigree reveals 20 crosses to old CH Eat 'Em Alive or CH Long-as-a-Freight Train in the 11th and 12th generations. Written history records their glory; only oral history from old-timers recalls their faults. It is vital for the far-sighted breeder to look at a pedigree in more depth than the commonly seen three- or four-generation papers that most breeders provide. It is well worth investigating the true nature and genetic contributions of a frequently appearing dog; although a big winner back in the "good old days," the same dog today may not be considered competitive or even desirable.

Figure 20-8: *A welcome infusion of genetic material in the 1980s.* CH Ladenburg Arco v. Reiteralm, BROM, producer of 23 champions, along with BROM brother and sister Atilla and Anni, as well as BROM sisters Bessie and Bryna, from the equally well-known B litter, produced a welcome infusion of new genetic material in the 1980s. These fortuitous outcrosses, accompanied by their detailed German records of multigenerational structural and performance faults and virtues, when combined with many established American bloodlines, offered a healthy genetic wash that resulted in hybrid vigor and a strong work ethic. See page 768 for more details on this breeding.

The Stud Dog

Choosing the Stud

Set at least one major and several minor objectives for each litter. Although the long-term goals are to eliminate undesired traits and to strengthen desirable ones, this is not always possible in one generation. Choose realistic, achievable, short-term objectives (such as better hips, stronger topline, or a more stylish point) for each mating.

Selecting the stud dog is, obviously, a vital decision. The best-winning dog in show or field is not necessarily the optimum, complementary mate for a particular bitch. However, the stud should be proven in competition, preferably a champion from a breeding that produced littermates that also possessed similar desirable qualities. It is valuable to consider the total number of puppies the sire has produced, compared with the number of his successful progeny, as well as the record of successful second-generation offspring.

When looking for the stud that is most likely to accomplish the major objectives, consider all males in the United States as potential mates—and do not overlook Canadian-owned males that are accessible. Analyze their individual qualities, their bloodlines, and their progeny. See as many studs as possible in person, or obtain videotapes. Talk with people who know the studs and have seen their ancestors. Study their progeny. Consider the big winner's champion litter brother, who may produce the desired traits more consistently, or perhaps it would be better to go back to their sire.

After identifying studs that appear promising, shipping and other factors may then be taken into consideration. The last place to economize is by limiting the choice of stud to one that is local, because the merit of the sire is reflected in the quality of the litter and the salability of the puppies; surprisingly, puppies sired by faraway studs are often in greater demand than those sired by local studs. Occasionally, however, after all factors are studied and carefully weighed, the stud most likely to fulfill the objectives may turn out to be the champion in the breeder's own kennel.

Managing the Stud's Career

An impatient owner can ruin a promising stud career by breeding to an inferior bitch just to see what happens, because faults in the puppies are usually blamed on the sire and could haunt the stud for years to come. However, infe-

Figure 20-9: *Dream Date.* A prudent owner realizes the necessity of initially choosing only quality bitches for the young stud's career, as well as the need to beg, borrow, or lease a truly superior bitch to start him off with a bang. A bitch like Rena would be a "dream date" for any young stud beginning his career. At nearly 7 years old, and after nursing three large litters, BISS CH Northwoods Rena von Reiteralm, NSD, BROM, is shown receiving an Award of Merit at the WCA National Specialty. Photograph by Chuck Tatham, The Standard Image.

rior bitches (especially known producers of undesirable recessive hereditary traits that are culled from the breeding program) are priceless for test breeding a young male that the owner hopes to develop as a stud. Such test breedings require exceptional fortitude because—however stunning—the progeny remain known carriers of undesirable traits, and they should only be given limited papers, prohibiting the registration of their offspring. In so doing, the stud owner gains valuable information that demonstrates the youngster's prepotency—or lack of it—whether the dog should be included in a breeding program at all.

Although the principles of quality and evaluation of the brood bitch are similar, there are some important differences with a stud dog. Until the owner has experience and a reputation, the stud dog that is not a big winner must wait for others to recognize and appreciate his sterling qualities. A prudent owner often realizes the necessity of buying or leasing several suitable bitches to showcase the stud's reproductive potential. The truly wise owner will beg, borrow, steal, or lease a truly superior bitch with a great record in competition and a proven record in the brood box as a "dream date" to showcase the young stud's genetic potential. With luck, this well-planned jump-start will establish the stud's reputation at a very early age as both the owner of the bitch and the stud campaign the offspring of the litter from such a well-known dam.

Figure 20-10: *This almost 50-year-old photograph* shows a modern-looking CH Val Knight Ranck winning the WCA National Specialty way back in 1959. Val would prove to be the pivotal sire for the modern Weimaraner, with a prepotency and a type that would prove timeless. A few prescient breeders were able to use the outstanding genetic type to pass on Val's best traits, without compounding his faults in future generations. As a result of this foresight, Val appears in the pedigrees of 37 of the last 40 National Specialty winners and all but four of the dogs going Best in Show since his offspring first hit the show circuit. A successful breeder must learn to recognize genetic shortcomings (no dog is perfect) and if they are not vital to health or temperament, develop a plan to work around them for the betterment of a future breeding plan. If a fancier feels she has finally found that "dog on the hill," breed to him, even if he is owned by her worst enemy.

Most Valuable Resources

A great deal may be learned by studying the breed's greatest individuals of the past—competitive records, pedigrees, photographs, and breed literature (written and oral)—to identify traits that made them outstanding. However, do not hold great dogs of the past in unrealistic reverence, for the legend may surpass the reality.

What specific qualities must be developed to keep dogs competitive currently?

- Is the current generation mentally and physically superior to their ancestors, and enjoy a longer life span?

- Is the incidence of undesirable genetic traits increasing or decreasing—or have totally different problems emerged?

While many aspects of establishing a breeding program may seem overwhelming, the novice may find that an experienced breeder or mentor may provide a strong head start and an invaluable resource.

Most breeders are less than willing to give up control of a potentially outstanding or established bitch. They may, however, be willing to offer a co-ownership. Do not disregard this potential opportunity, as it may be the best entrance to otherwise unavailable genetic material and hard-won experience. A breeder willing to co-own with a novice is expressing conviction that the bitch in question has value or potential for a head start in a breeding program and will usually offer guidance and moral support during fledgling efforts in breeding.

Patricia Wilkie said it best in *Future Dog: Breeding for Genetic Soundness*:

"The breeder is the first line of awareness. Breeders who raise the flag to help others, help themselves, and the breed they cherish at the same time. Dog breeders are in this together whether they like it or not because the ancestors of a breed are all related to some degree or another. The only recourse in dealing with inherited diseases is careful observation and conscious in competition and breeding."

Dog breeding is a combination of art and science—an endless quest for perfection, an endless challenge with each litter and generation. The study of conformation, movement, genetics, and bloodlines is vital. The breeder designs the genetic potential by selecting the best combination of mates, but there is a threefold challenge of environmental factors that can enhance or sink the best-laid plans. Husbandry must be more than adequate, it should provide the highest level of veterinary care and the appropriate nutrition for the dam and puppies. The breeder must provide canine mentors that set a desirable example so puppies learn positive dog-related behaviors. The breeder must also provide an enriched environment with physical and mental challenges and opportunities tailored to each individual puppy. And the final link in the chain is to find homes where the new owners will create a plan for success for the development of the potential provided by the breeder. However, as long as genes randomly combine, dog breeding will probably remain as much art as science. Experience helps, but there is an undeniable element of luck, since over 2.8 billion coding base pairs found within the canine genome can spice up the outcome of each breeding.

Figure 20-11: *Ideally, a breeding program should start with a bitch* (not a stud) that most closely approaches the fancier's ideal Weimaraner. This trio, CH Nani's Perfect Cadence, CH Nani's Wink of an Eye, and CH Nani's Emma von Derr, have produced 20 conformation champions, 11 hunt titles, eight obedience titles, three tracking titles, and three versatile ratings in the first generation. As breeder and co-owner of all three dogs, Chris Grisell (seated in front) is able to share her experience and expertise while benefiting from the teamwork as the other breeders accomplish their own separate goals. Mentoring and co-ownership builds on the collective effort, allowing each fancier to pursue their own vision of "the perfect dog on the hill."

Figure 20-12: *The breeder has built a solid foundation* by creating a desirable genetic blueprint; now it is necessary to cement the genetic promise created by this careful breeding program with exposure to favorable examples of well-trained and even-tempered canine behavior models, as well as humans willing to patiently guide the earliest experiences of young dogs. Selecting the best genes is the key that unlocks potential, while early environmental exposure and learning opportunities open the door to success.

Figure 21-1: *Extreme diligence* may be required to prevent disruption of the owner's best-laid plans. A Weimaraner bitch may not be too choosy for those 2 or 3 days during her season when Nature's siren calls and may find herself willing to consider even the most unlikely suitor, especially if he is an old family friend. Photograph by Virginia Alexander.

CHAPTER 21

MATING GAMES

After having read *Breeding Basics,* as well as other resources to gain an education in the intricacies of developing a breeding program, the fancier should now be prepared to take the first steps in the pursuit of "the Weimaraner on the hill"—too bad no one told the dogs. As a result, the best-laid plans may be foiled even before they are begun. A surprising variety of factors precede the consummation of the canine marriage, requiring the organized collaboration of the breeder and the stud owner, in consultation with a supportive veterinarian, and hopefully the cooperation of a dog and a bitch—and on occasion, a couple of friends with a good sense of humor.

The Brood Bitch

Preventing Unplanned Breedings

The most important aspect of breeding is to have a bitch to breed; security will ensure the bitch's safety and the integrity of the breeding. Extreme diligence may be required to prevent disruption of the owners' best-laid plans; guard the bride to be as if with a medieval chastity belt! Fences tend to give owners a false sense of security. A Weimaraner that wants to get out—or in—can jump a 6-foot wall with ease or tunnel like a badger. A determined suitor may sneak in and then lie in wait behind a bush until the owner turns the lovely lady out for exercise; always check the area completely, and when in doubt, keep her on a leash. A covered dog run with a concrete floor and chain-link fence may not always work. People who work in boarding kennels report that ties through chain link are not particularly unusual. Keep in mind that if the bitch in season is exercised off the property, any place she urinates will become a party point for neighborhood Romeos, and it is not impossible for them to track the enticing lady to where she lives. Never, never discount the presence of a resident suitor—even a long-time resident male that had shown no previous interest in a bitch. Many a surprised owner has discovered that the previously unsuspected male in the household hid his interest well, until the (in)appropriate moment—and then it was too late. Never underestimate the determined inventiveness and sheer athletic prowess of canine desire!

The old rule of thumb that a bitch is mature enough to breed on her second season does not cover all situations. On average, Weimaraner bitches have their first season at about 12 months, but any time from 8 to 24 months is perfectly normal. In general, it is desirable to have a first litter by the age of 4, after which the birth canal becomes less elastic and there is greater risk of cesarean delivery. However, this is not a hard-and-fast rule, and a good example of a late-starting bitch is CH Kamsou Riptide, who had the first of her three outstanding litters at age 5.

Natural Breeding or Artificial Insemination?

Psychological factors must also be considered, because they affect willingness to mate and conception. A bitch that has little or no contact with other Weimaraners often develops such strong bonds to males of other breeds—those she sees often—that she resists mating with a Weimaraner. The breed's best-known brood matron, Rona, preferred her gentlemen friends to sport a mustache.

It is also advisable to introduce the bitch to all the conditions and environments she could expect during the breeding and whelping process well before the time at which such arrangements are needed. For example, if a bitch is easily stressed and driving to a mutually convenient location is not an option, it does not bode well to introduce her to a crate for the first time when dropping her off at the airport to be shipped to the stud. On occasion, the stress of a long trip has caused a bitch to go out of season; if a bitch has a history of this, artificial insemination (AI) may be a better option. For an extremely valuable bitch, one that may be incompatible with the physical or temperamental attributes of the stud (too large or small for example), or a bitch unused to travel, the breeder may wish to consider the alternative presented in the section on AI. By the time the costs of shipping, pick-up fees, and boarding are added up, the trade-offs of reduced stress and increased safety may well balance out the costs of two shipments of chilled semen and insemination. The ability to immediately go home to a familiar environment also maximizes the chances of conception and implantation of the embryos during the critical 8–10 days after breeding.

A Few Myths

There are many myths and misconceptions that abound regarding dogs and dog breeding. Many are simply old wives' tales that came to be commonly accepted, even entrenched, well before scientific investigation was available to address the issues. A few directly address important issues that affect the bitch and her breeding. First, and most importantly, a litter CAN have more than one sire. As mentioned before, a bitch may not only not be too picky, she can be downright promiscuous, willingly breeding with any and all male dogs that approach at the right time. DNA testing can, with a high degree of certainty, identify the sire of each pup when the potential sires are known and have a DNA profile. Review the current AKC regulations for registering multiple sired litters at www.akc.org/dna/multisire.cfm. A bitch in season must be carefully guarded to avoid the substantial costs of testing and registering a split litter, not to mention the disruption of the breeding program and potentially undesirable genetic combinations.

Another common misconception is that a bitch can be "ruined" by breeding with a dog of another breed or a mixed breed. While any resulting progeny of that breeding will be mixed breed, the sperm are only viable for a few days. After that time, the union has no effect on the genetic integrity of the bitch. However, an unplanned breeding will again disrupt the well-planned breeding program and unnecessarily expose the bitch to communicable disease or injury, as well as the potential for whelping complications from an incompatible sire.

Most American Weimaraner bitches are over 2 when first bred, not just because of OFA certification, but primarily because it takes several years to determine her breed worthiness through testing and competition. Novices sometimes heed advice (usually from someone unfamiliar with the breed) that a litter will improve her chest spring and accelerate a mature appearance that looks better in the ring. Few experienced owners risk breeding before a bitch has finished her championship, having learned that waiting another 6–12 months accomplishes the same objectives without the risk of ruining her topline and underline. A few bitches (only fully mature ones) regain a svelte figure after breeding, but many never recover their trim underline. If bred before full skeletal maturity, a pregnancy can also ruin a topline, and a large litter can ruin a topline at any age.

The Veterinarian

Before planning a breeding, it is essential to first establish a good rapport with a veterinarian with an excellent reputation for supporting and understanding reputable breeders. Ask a lot of questions to discover the veterinarian's views and interest in breeding and whelping, and find out how he or she handles emergencies and after-hours calls. If you are not completely satisfied, consider finding another veterinarian before services are needed.

Before the Season

Physical Considerations

The bitch should be in blooming health—muscles firm, coat sleek, and eyes sparkling with vitality. A flabby Weimaraner bitch is a candidate for cesarean delivery, and she should be brought into good muscular condition well before breeding. Above all, the bitch should not be overweight, as she cannot be placed on a reducing diet after she conceives. Obesity not only decreases fertility and increases delivery complications, but the stud may also have difficulty grasping the bitch around her loin if she is too fat. Begin to increase physical activity and/or decrease the quantity of the daily ration months before breeding to have the bitch slightly underweight as she comes in season.

Figure 21-2: *Start with a healthy bitch.* CH Silberkinder Miss Moneypenny, SH, CDX, AX, AXJ, NAP, NJP, NRD, SD, NA(II), VX2, shows the excellent health, good muscle tone, and condition desired in a prospective brood bitch. Shortly after this picture was taken, she was successfully bred and produced a litter of 10 puppies.

Vaccines and medications

Never give vaccine boosters just before breeding. Few veterinarians warn breeders that such hyperimmunization produces a high maternal antibody level that can inactivate all vaccines given to the puppies for as long as 18 weeks of age.

Quite a few breeders have reported whelping difficulties with bitches on heartworm preventive, and many are discontinuing the medication during pregnancy. These drugs, regardless of the manufacturer, may be indicated in prolonged duration of pregnancy and placental attachment, leading to very large puppies at whelping, profuse bleeding, and retained placentas. Should a breeder discontinue heartworm medications, measures should be taken to protect the bitch from mosquitoes and possible heartworm infection.

Roundworms and hookworms pass through the placental barrier to infest unborn puppies. No worming preparation is effective against parasites that are not in the gastrointestinal phase of their life cycle, but treatment significantly reduces the number transmitted to the puppies. Experienced breeders routinely worm all bitches just before breeding.

Testing

If a bitch has a history of metritis or failed conception, perform a uterine culture a month or so before the bitch is expected to come in season. If required, appropriate antibiotic treatment before the breeding may allow a safe conception and normal pregnancy. If there is a history of streptococcal infection, a streptococcal differential culture should be requested. Some strains of *Streptococcus* are not highly pathogenic and, if treated early in the season, do not necessarily contraindicate breeding. Other types are highly dangerous. *Beta Streptococcus,* for example, is the most common cause of aborted litters, acute metritis, and sterility, and the veterinarian may recommend not breeding until the bitch has a negative culture. Streptococcal infections are also implicated as a cause of neonatal septicemia (fading puppy syndrome), and some authorities suggest that it might be prevented by a preconceptual culture and sensitivity to identify and treat infections.

Canine brucellosis is a highly contagious infection that causes aborted litters and often sterility. Although it is not common, it is occurring in sporadic regional areas, and the potential loss of irreplaceable individuals and bloodlines remains terrifying. Knowledgeable Weimaraner stud owners test their dogs several times a year and require a recent negative report from the bitch's owner before breeding. Have the bitch checked well in advance of the planned breeding, as the test results may take longer than expected.

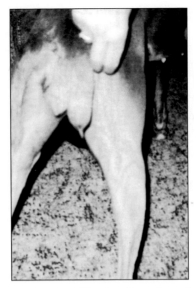 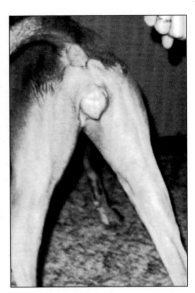

Figure 21-3: *Flagging.* Regardless of the bitch's attitude toward the stud and the whole idea of being bred, she cannot control one involuntary response to the stud's advances. **(a)** Tickling the base of the tail should elicit... **(b)** the telltale arch and straining of the vulva.

Thyroid levels may too often be the hidden clue behind the mystery of failed breedings. If a bitch has failed to conceive with no obvious explanation, thyroid testing should be considered. It is not unusual for a dog that has tested normal to low-normal to successfully conceive when given a low dose of thyroid several weeks or months prior to breeding. Many Weimaraner bitches thought to be barren have conceived and whelped healthy litters on extremely low doses of thyroid supplement. Refer to the *Prenatal Care* chapter for specific tests and considerations. Any other testing, such as X-rays for dysplasia or cardiac or eye testing, should have been completed before determining whether the bitch will even be bred, and the results should be confirmed before she comes in season.

Onset of Season

It is courteous to alert the stud owner that the bitch is coming into season at the first sign of swelling; it is vital to notify the stud owner on the first day of her season.

During the proestrus period, a bitch is unlikely to stand for a male, however; the onset of estrus is impossible to predict without progesterone testing. The wise breeder will not let the bitch out of sight unless she is undoubtedly secure from the amorous attentions of any male.

Plan to ship the bitch at least 4 or 5 days before the expected date of breeding. This not only allows time for her to settle down in the new environment, but also allows some leeway for inclement weather, early ovulation, and the thousand other things that can go wrong at the last minute. See *Life with Weimaraners* for additional information on shipping.

The Stud Dog

Refer to the AKC website for requirements of stud dogs and their owners with respect to the age of a stud, number of bitches serviced in a year, and permanent and/or DNA identification requirements.

The AKC registers litters sired by any stud that is at least 7 months old. Although there are occasional reports of young Weimaraner males impregnating kennelmates as early as 8 months, the typical Weimaraner male is not sexually mature until about 11 months. There are many other considerations as well with this slow-maturing breed. The age of breeding on a dog may vary widely, as some males are more precocious or heavily campaigned early in their careers to establish their ability and breed worthiness. Others may only come to light as the sibling of a successful littermate.

Preconditioning the Young Stud

Although there is a wide normal range, Weimaraner males seem to have a lower libido than many other sporting breeds. It sometimes seems as if the price of the Weimaraner's unusually high intelligence and open-ended learning aptitude has been a slight but observable alteration of what most consider purely instinctive behavior. The Weimaraner is much like a human child devoid of innate carnal knowledge at an early age; early experiences will have an enormous impact on adult behavior, and it is not difficult to completely shut down the instinctive reproductive behavior with only a little punishment or even discouragement of natural sexual curiosity. The Weimaraner male may then have difficulty imagining his role in the reproductive process and may need encouragement or even role models as a youngster in order to develop into a successful stud dog as an adult. Then, too, breeding reluctance is more common in dogs raised without other canine companionship, or those removed from their littermates before 8 weeks old.

The stud dog's career should begin well before he breeds his first bitch; some young males have no idea how to go about breeding when the opportunity finally arises. Supporting the theory of the Weimaraner's unusual learning aptitude is the fact that letting the youngster observe another male service a bitch is often all that is needed. Never punish young stud prospects for sniffing or for sexual curiosity, as this may come back to haunt the breeder later in the dog's career with a negative attitude toward the possibility of actually breeding.

A young stud dog's first sexual encounter can make or break his future attitude toward breeding. It is wisest for stud owners to make special efforts to improve the odds that the youngster gets off to a good start before puberty, with pleasurable encounters, socializing, and romping with easygoing bitches of varying ages to learn the basic protocols of intersex behavior. If a garden party such as the one in Figure 21-4 cannot be arranged, wait a few months and allow the slightly more mature stud prospect to observe another stud dog in action; prior to 6 months the young male will be probably oblivious to the lesson; after about 9 months the active stud may be intimidated or distracted by what he perceives to be a rival male. At this point, it is important to allow the young stud to develop at his own rate. Be sure to select a bitch that is amenable to his advances; a pushy or aggressive bitch would not be the best choice for an inexperienced stud.

It is preferable that a stud's first breeding be a natural one, as it is possible that a young dog can learn bad habits from the artificial collection process; if it is necessary to use AI, ensure that a bitch in season is available as a teaser, and make every effort to make the process as realistic as possible to prepare for a natural breeding in the future. If the first experience must be an AI collection, be sure it is performed with extreme compassion and by an experienced practitioner equipped with the appropriate collection vehicle; do not force him beyond his comfort zone. With time, patience, and a dash of humor, after a few lessons his Sex 101 education will have prepared him for his future career.

The Adult Stud

Being a stud dog sometimes is not all it is cracked up to be. After all, in order to be in demand, a dog must first prove himself worthy of the limited reproductive abilities of the bitch. The successful stud often spends a great deal of time training or campaigning. Such physical demands, extended travel, and competition can take its toll on the physical reproductive ability of a dog and reduce the quality and quantity of sperm, not to mention the logistical demands of arranging a breeding at the most optimal time for conception. Additionally, many owners are concerned that frequent stud use will divert the athlete from his top competitive form, increasing the occurrence of undesirable behaviors in the field and obedience ring, such as marking, dominance posturing, and distractibility. The owner of any dog that is showing great promise or that has proven himself as breed worthy should carefully read the section on AI and consider the options that collected semen may offer. A stud dog should have a routine health check twice a year, not only for his own health, but for the health of the bitches he services as well. It is possible for a male to contract an infection from a bitch as well as to pass it on to subsequent bitches. Problems discovered early provide the veterinarian with a better chance of successfully treating them before they become irreversible. At least annually, a stud should have a semen evaluation to ensure that he is fertile; for a stud that is used infrequently, having a semen evaluation as soon as the bitch comes in season will not only allow for an evaluation of quality and quantity of sperm but will also clear out older material and encourage production of fresh (and often more viable)

The Garden Party

Figure 21-4: ***Host a garden party*** for your prospective stud puppy at about 4 months of age. Invite an older, romantically experienced lady friend, preferably at her most receptive time in her season, so that his potential advances will not be rebuffed. Well-mannered, older matrons make the best guest as they stand more patiently while the youngster muddles through his first advances. His attendance at this social event is bound to increase his enthusiasm and help overcome his lack of experience in the future. Most certainly, both guests will leave the party wiser and in good spirits. Photographs by Virginia Alexander.

sperm. The old wives tale "use it or lose it" bears a slight ring of truth. Usually all the old, lesser-used stud needs is to "clean out his pipes." While the first ejaculate may be "rusty," subsequent material is usually just fine.

The Stud Owner's Obligation

The most successful stud owners realize that the owner of the bitch is the other half of an all-important team—a reciprocal relationship. They are appreciative of the breeder's confidence in the stud, offering close cooperation and flexibility in all financial matters. Without the support and encouragement of the stud owner, many first-time breeders might never raise another litter. The astute stud owner is always interested in the quality and traits his dog produces, is willing to help evaluate the litter, and assists with their sale.

Perfect litters are rare, and occasional puppies cause embarrassment to both sire and dam. With a team approach, however, all problems can be managed. Experienced breeders who mentor those new to the game not only forge friendships, but set an example that those novice breeders will hopefully pass on when the shoe is on the other foot.

General Considerations Before Breeding

The Most Common Problems in Conception

The three most common problems in conception are related to:

- Health (overall health or physical condition)
- Genetics (either of the animal itself or in a genetic combination, such as lethal recessives)
- Inappropriate timing (the most common cause of failure in conception)

The information provided here, along with proper research, planning, and care, can either identify or prevent these issues from disrupting a breeding program.

Physical and Mental Health

It should go without saying that any animal being considered for breeding should be in outstanding health and display a healthy constitution as well. Not only will an unhealthy dog or bitch be less likely to produce a healthy litter, a general lack of a vigorous constitution is not a desirable attribute to pass on to another generation of pups. A bitch that is out of condition or under- or overweight may have more difficulty conceiving and delivering; a bitch should also be parasite free. Refer to *Prenatal Care*. An unhealthy sire or dam will add an unnecessary burden on the breeder as well, in trying to get such pups off to the best start and provide new owners with physically and mentally healthy pups.

Figure 21-5: *Shipping the bitch.* In light of increased expense and regulation of shipping dogs as cargo, many fanciers now find that the safest and easiest (and sometimes the least expensive) option is to fly with the bitch as excess baggage. The owner is more comfortable witnessing the breeding and caring for her own bitch; in turn, the bitch (especially the maiden) is usually more relaxed and easier to manage as well. Many successful stud owners often offer hospitality for the visiting owner choosing to accompany the bitch, in appreciation for not having to assume the responsibility for and care of an unfamiliar animal. Although suitable for car travel, this crate would be too small for air transport. See *Life With Weimaraners*. Photograph by Barney Riley.

Sound physical health in itself is not entirely sufficient for an animal selected to pass on its genetic heritage. The breeding candidate has probably been selected for outstanding physical traits; however, the ability to contribute a healthy mental status should not be underestimated. Ideally, breeding animals should be proven to have a stable temperament, trainability, and talent through evaluation and testing. Refer to *Breeding Basics*.

Screening for Genetic Defects

The WCA considers breeding any dog or bitch that has not been certified free of hip dysplasia to be a violation of the Breeder's Code of Ethics. In Weimaraners, this practice has resulted in one of the greatest reductions in hip dysplasia among the sporting breeds. In most countries around the world, hip dysplasia certifications may be taken at 1 year old; however, in the United States the OFA does not certify any dog until it is over 2 years old. Promising young studs are sometimes bred at an earlier age, but only after screening X-rays have confirmed that there are no indications of hip dysplasia at that time.

LH Levels

Historically, the expensive LH assays had to be performed by specialized veterinary laboratories and had a long wait for results. Synbiotics, Inc., now offers the International Canine Genetics (ICG) Status LH, a serum test, which takes about 20 minutes to determine LH levels. This test can be valuable in bitches with a history of failed conception, so that a breeder can be prepared to begin testing progesterone levels at the appropriate time. But given the cost, it is perhaps more cost effective to skip this test and simply use progesterone testing.

Progesterone Levels

Although knowledge of the relationship between the progesterone level and ovulation is not new, a practical test was not available until late 1980s. In May 1989, ICG pioneered a simple blood test that could be performed at the veterinary clinic. The Ovulation Timing Test identified the progesterone surge that occurs 2 days before ovulation, 5–6 days before the most fertile period. ICG has since been acquired by Synbiotics, Inc., which now offers the Ovucheck Premate test. The test takes about an hour and compares the progesterone level of the sample of serum or plasma with a high and low standard, establishing whether the bitch has or has not ovulated. While this test gives quick results, the gold standard would be a progesterone assay performed by laboratory, which normally takes 24–48 hours for results.

In attempting a breeding in which the quality or quantity of semen may be suboptimal, or with a bitch known to have difficulty conceiving, determining the date of ovulation may be the key to success. The person managing the breeding should discuss these tests with the veterinarian well before the bitch comes in season, allowing ample time to purchase the test kits. The first progesterone test may begin the 6th or 7th day after discharge begins.

If using progesterone testing to establish optimum timing for breeding, keep in mind that it is not unusual for progesterone levels to fluctuate during the early stages of proestrus. Progesterone levels between 4.0 and 10.0 ng/mL (nanograms/milliliter) indicate that ovulation has occurred. Since unfertilized eggs need 2–3 days to "ripen" before fertilization, and fresh sperm can easily survive inside the bitch for several days, natural breedings can take place any time after proges-

terone levels reach 5.0 ng/mL and be repeated every 2–3 days until the bitch is no longer willing to stand. If using an older stud, or when the number of breedings needs to be minimized, breeding should commence when progesterone levels exceed 10 ng/mL; successful breedings have been achieved with levels in excess of 16.0 ng/mL.

The Canine Tie

Practical Considerations

Often territorial, the male dog's sexual behavior will usually be less inhibited in the home environment, so breeding can be expected to occur at the stud's residence. However, practicality sometimes offers opportunities in less "regular" accommodations—with potential locations such as a hotel room on the road, or in the woods after a field trial. Scout out a location ahead of time that will provide security as well as privacy; a little pre-planning might avoid your finding out at an inconvenient moment that the "ideal spot" is actually alongside a jogging path or the shortcut to the park's restroom. Be sure to provide for a safe and successful honeymoon experience with as few distractions as possible.

Regardless of the bride's opinion of her groom, and to ensure the safety of the stud, as well as the handlers, be prepared in advance with a muzzle in case it is needed. Try the muzzle on the bitch well ahead of time to be sure it is reasonably comfortable and fits properly; leave the muzzle on

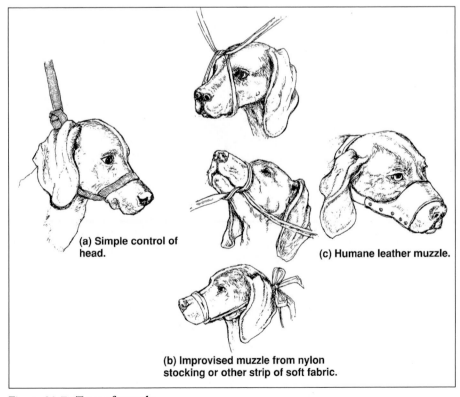

Figure 21-7: *Types of muzzles.*

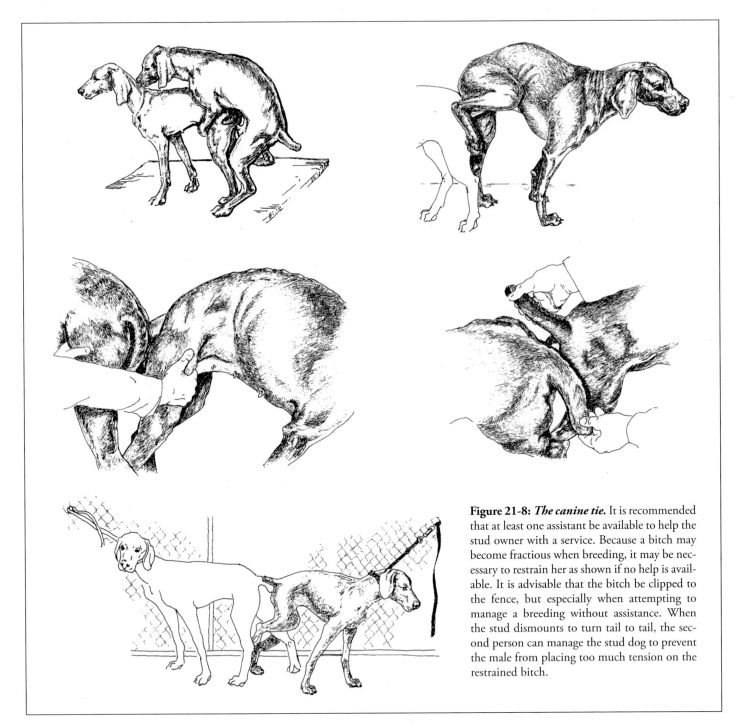

Figure 21-8: *The canine tie.* It is recommended that at least one assistant be available to help the stud owner with a service. Because a bitch may become fractious when breeding, it may be necessary to restrain her as shown if no help is available. It is advisable that the bitch be clipped to the fence, but especially when attempting to manage a breeding without assistance. When the stud dismounts to turn tail to tail, the second person can manage the stud dog to prevent the male from placing too much tension on the restrained bitch.

for several minutes—under supervision—to be sure the bitch cannot remove it at just the wrong moment.

If the possibility exists for a large discrepancy between the sizes of the potential mates, plan to use natural terrain features—such as a small grassy hill or depression. Heavy welcome mats or horse trailer mats placed beneath the mating pair may give a boost to romantic efforts as well as provide more confident footing. Based on past experience, the owner of the stud dog may have some potentially useful materials available. A heavy meal prior to breeding is inadvisable for either dog's health and comfort, but both dogs will

probably appreciate a snack afterward. Bring along comfortable, washable clothing and a low stool. Breeding often necessitates at least one person being in position at a level where it is possible to observe the actual tie and assist if necessary; a well-positioned stool makes this task much more comfortable (see Figure 21-11). When using an experienced stud and matron, breedings usually run into few difficulties; stud owners should, however, arrange to have at least one assistant available at every breeding—preferably one with a good sense of humor and who is not easily embarrassed.

Setting the Mood

The romance of "doing what comes naturally" is considerably more involved than most people realize. Experienced stud owners are usually willing to help novices until they are comfortable handling matings in which Mother Nature is less cooperative. Veterinary assistance may be sought as a last resort; with its slick floors, distressing and distracting odors, previous associations, and often intimidating atmosphere, the veterinary clinic is nearly a sure-fire shut down on a romantic mood.

Between the bitch's desire to choose her own mate and the average Weimaraner male's inherent lack of knowledge of the birds and the bees, canine courtship plays a surprisingly important role in Weimaraner breeding. If possible, early in the bitch's season, introduce the two daily and observe their behavior. If shipping, send the bitch as soon as possible. A bitch that is still under stress from shipping too often tends to take exception to the advances of any male, whereas providing an opportunity for courtship may be all that is needed to win her eager cooperation.

Courtship and mating proceed best in a quiet, private environment with secure footing. A safely fenced area is highly desirable, and, if available, a small, enclosed, chain-link kennel run is ideal. Do not feed the dogs before breeding. Distractions—cats, other dogs, traffic, and pedestrians—are minimized during the late night and early morning hours. Curtail conversations, particularly speaking to either of the mating pair, and leave the phone off the hook. Have any material needed for footing or height adjustment close at hand (not in another building, but inside the kennel run).

Start by placing the bitch in the small, fenced yard. Check her height alongside the fence and place a double-ended swivel clip in the appropriate position on the fence. If while observing the bitch from the outside the male seems unsure or disinterested, take the bitch away after she urinates and let the unleashed stud enter and check out the scents. This is a good time to determine whether there is a height issue and position any footing material. As the male indicates interest in her scent, allow the bitch to flirt from outside the run to further encourage the male. When the male seems aroused, return the bitch to the enclosure to join her prospective mate; at this time additional assistants should also quietly enter. When either mate is inexperienced, the process will go more smoothly by waiting until the bitch has had a chance to flirt and play with the male and finally begins to stand and position herself for the male; the stud should also have the opportunity to court the bitch and finally appear eager to do his duty before clipping the bitch to the fence and attempting the breeding. Should the male be inexperienced or unsure, allow him plenty of time to figure out what he plans to do and develop enough courage to actually make the big move to mount the bitch. When

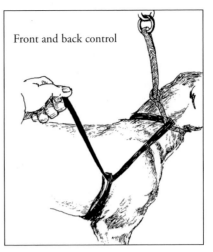

Front and back control

Figure 21-9: *Managing without an assistant.* When trying to control the stud and bitch alone, clip the bitch to the fence and use a leash as shown to control her front end while maintaining a position near her hindquarters to help the stud and prevent the bitch from lying down.

his thrusting becomes more confident and well aimed, carefully and gently move the bitch toward the clip on the fence. With an experienced male, the bitch can be positioned at the fence before he is allowed to enter the enclosure.

It is not unusual for the bitch to be uncooperative. Weimaraner bitches, especially maidens, tend to be skittish, running as the stud mounts, or jumping. After penetration, the bitch may change her mind about the whole idea, jumping sky high, or attempting to roll over. Although bitches rarely attack males, it is not uncommon for them to growl, snap, or simply refuse to stand. Weimaraner bitches have strong opinions about desirable mates, and their ideas often differ from the owners' plans. Bitches are capable of incredible craft and resourcefulness in escaping to consummate a mating with the male they desire. Conversely, they may go to extraordinary lengths to prevent matings with the stud the breeder has chosen.

Getting the Tie

The first phase of canine erection allows penetration of the vagina by thrusting movements, during which the stud makes paddling movements with his rear legs. At this time, if the bulbus begins to swell outside the bitch, the male can be successfully removed without losing a significant amount of sperm. A brief walk and a small drink will usually allow the bulbus to relax, and within a short time the male is usually ready and willing to try again.

The second phase of the tie is characterized by a swelling of the bulbus that locks, or "ties," the dogs into position while sperm pumps into the bitch. If the bulbus is engorged but the penis is not inside the bitch, immediately remove the dog from the area before ejaculation; with luck the male will settle down and a second attempt can be made within half an hour or so. Engorgement has occurred and the tie is secure when the bitch begins to complain and groan—or decides to lie down. The second fraction, which contains the greatest part of the spermatozoa, is ejaculated during this phase, just after the thrusting movement ceases and the tie occurs. Visually check to ensure that the penis is inside the vagina; if so, make every effort to keep the male on top of the bitch for a count of 300. An aged stud should be encouraged to stay on top of the bitch as long as possible. After the count of 300, a vigorous stud may be assisted in dismounting the bitch to assume the more comfortable tail-to-tail position. The tie usually lasts from 10 to 40 minutes. During this time, it is necessary to supervise the pair, and it is very important to avoid distractions. Do not allow the bitch to lie down or roll over; each handler should maintain attentive control of their charge to avoid injury to either animal.

It is important to allow the tie to follow its natural progression. With a physically fit male, a tail-to-tail tie aids conception, as the pressure and tension of the dog's penis against the roof of the vagina stimulates muscular contractions, assisting the movement of sperm down the bitch's reproduc-

Figure 21-10: *Elevate the hindquarters.* If the tie is very short, or when using an older stud dog, elevating the bitch's hindquarters for 5–10 minutes after walking her in circle for 5–15 minutes may enhance the potential for a successful breeding. If a comfortable couch is not available, a stairway will work as well, although it is less comfortable for both the bitch and the helper. If neither is available, the bitch's hindquarters can be manually elevated with her weight on her forequarters, similar to a wheel barrow. Photograph by Virginia Alexander.

tive tract. With an older male, the tie is often shorter and he should be encouraged to remain on top of the bitch as long as possible (at least to a count of 300), since he will be less able to maintain the tension that encourages the muscle contractions in the bitch's vagina. Refer to the section on the Aged Stud for more suggestions.

A third fraction of ejaculate, containing few sperm, is expelled as the tie continues, and further aids conception by propelling the sperm-rich second fraction toward the waiting eggs; it is natural for a small amount of this fraction to gush out as the bulbus relaxes and the dogs separate at the end of the tie.

Inside the bitch, normal, healthy sperm lives 5–7 days, and breeding every other day while the bitch is receptive usually results in conception. The serial ovulation of canines leads to serial conception, and it is not unusual for puppies to be of different gestational ages at whelping—one reason for a wide range in birth weight.

After that Perfect Moment

Aftercare is particularly important with bitches of marginal fertility, a short tie, or an older stud dog.

• Be sure the male has totally retracted, has a drink of cool water, and is allowed to walk off any stiffness from exertion in an enclosed area

• Some breeders will elevate the bitch's hindquarters immediately after the tie breaks for at least 10–15 minutes

• Walk the bitch in circles for at least 5–15 minutes—longer if the tie was less than 10 minutes, as is common in older studs. Choose an area for the bitch's exercise that offers no opportunity for her to urinate, easiest if on a concrete surface

• Crate the bitch for several hours, offering her a small amount of water and the choicest of marrowbones or anything pleasurable to chew on, in a quiet environment—anything to keep her in a prone position for an additional period of time

• If the owner did not accompany the bitch, do not forget to call and give information about the breeding, the date, the time, and the length of the tie

• The bitch and stud owner may wish to discuss the need for additional breedings or make arrangements for the return of the matron.

When What Comes Naturally Does Not; When and How to Help

On the level view

It is necessary to get on a level that allows actually observing the penetration and tie. A side-on view is not possible from a standing position; it does not take long for a person to get uncomfortable trying to maintain the necessary crouched position, so a low stool will be much appreciated. The stud handler can gently assist and encourage the male if needed; particularly with an older dog, or when there is a significant height discrepancy, this person may need to discreetly push the bitch's pelvis to the right or left or reach under the bitch to steady or position the vulva without interfering with the male's intent. As the male is about to mount, check to be sure the bitch's tail is on the same side as the assistant; this will make it more convenient to grasp her tail and help her maintain a level, standing position if she has a tendency to sink as the weight of the stud tires her. Assistance is most successful when the bitch can be discreetly adjusted to accommodate the stud's efforts.

Up and over

The key to a successful tie is for the male to get up and over the top of the bitch's back in order to be able to firmly grasp her waist, adjust his aim, and maintain his position. Several circumstances can occur that thwart the male's efforts, but the most common error is to stand too close to or over the bitch's head. This looming presence may intimidate the male from jumping far enough forward to achieve a secure position. The bitch's handler should kneel or sit in front of the bitch, maintaining control at the most discreet distance possible, and should be sure not to offer any dominating behaviors, such as direct eye contact with the male. This same person has a daunting task and must be ready to steady the bitch should she lunge or lurch forward, attempt to roll over, or turn on the male.

Bitch too short or too tall

A bitch may be too short or too tall for the male to mount successfully. The dog must be able to mount the bitch high enough on her back to get the appropriate position for penetration of the vulva and to grasp her waist firmly. For the male's continued cooperation, it is preferable to adjust the bitch so her vulva is in the proper position rather than trying to adjust the male. Rather than allow the male to exhaust himself, as soon as it becomes apparent that a discrepancy exists, separate the dogs while adjustments are made. Many times, positioning the pair alongside a chain-link fence will be all that is necessary.

Depending on the male's style and the physical discrepancy, it may be necessary to either raise or lower the bitch's front end or her rear end. Stall mats or thick welcome mats can often be used under the bitch's or stud's hindquarters to give a more favorable position. The terrain of a small, grassy hill may be useful; sometimes, it may be easier to put the

Figure 21-11: *Dig a hole.* With a taller or larger bitch, when other efforts have failed, consider digging a shallow hole for the bitch's front or rear end. Depending on the difference in size of the mating pair, this will allow the stud to thrust more easily, as his center of balance is over the bitch rather than back off of her. An older stud will appreciate sturdy fencing to aid him in maintaining his position on top of the bitch more comfortably and for as long as possible (older dogs may often lose contact if turned away from the bitch). A strategically placed stool allows an assistant to observe whether the male has fully penetrated, to more easily assist the older stud if needed, and quickly remove the male if full penetration is not achieved. Photograph by Virginia Alexander.

bitch on the uphill side or perhaps on the downhill side. It is really a matter of trying until a successful solution is found. If unsuccessful after several tries, it may be necessary to break off the attempt and separate the pair until a better adjustment can be found. Continued efforts will tire the male, and he may lose his enthusiasm for the project; his most zealous efforts, those most likely to bring success, will be while he is fresh on "the mission" and well rested.

The stud says yes, but the bitch says no

The stud's nose says yes, but the bitch says no for the entire heat in spite of her progesterone reading, which indicates an immediate service. This is often the result of improper cycling of the bitch; check her thyroid and hormones through a complete cycle.

The bitch says yes, but the stud says no

A progesterone check of the bitch will determine whether she is truly ready, as the experienced stud dog's nose is normally considered the highest authority. Additionally, a smear or culture might be taken to determine whether an infection is present that turns the stud dog off.

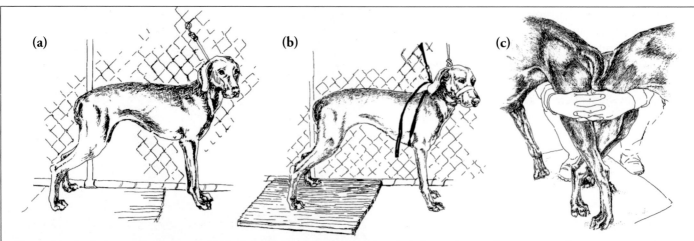

Figure 21-12: *Assisting the aged stud.* **(a)** Bitch is restrained alongside a chain-link fence, along with matting to allow more secure footing and if needed to raise the bitch to a more favorable position for the older male. The fencing provides welcome support for the older male to lean against while he is encouraged to remain on top of the bitch until ejaculation of the first and second fractions are complete (count to at least 300 from the time the bitch begins to complain). Provide as much support as needed to help the stud remain on top of the bitch, preferably until completion of the third phase (see "The Canine Tie"). **(b)** A double-ended swivel clipped to a chain link fence gives control to prevent the bitch from lunging forward, turning, or lying down while the aged stud makes his romantic advances. Two helpers should be on hand to maintain front and rear control. Such assistance should be very discreet, as a person looming over the bitch or stud will inhibit his enthusiasm and efforts to cover as much of the bitch's back as possible and achieve the most effective thrusting. **(c)** If the stud can no longer remain on top of the bitch, the assistants should provide support during the turn to maintain the tie and, after the dismount, lock the stifles as shown to avoid premature withdrawal.

Overweight bitch

An overweight bitch offers no place for the male to securely grip her waist, so he may repeatedly slide off her back. Two scarves or thin dish towels may be tied around the bitch's waist to make "handlebars." This odd arrangement may be off putting to a male, so give him a chance to investigate the addition prior to the actual breeding attempt. Do not tie the towels too tightly as they will be uncomfortable for the bitch; remove the towels after the male dismounts to reduce any pressure on her abdomen, which may discourage the advance of the swimming sperm.

Over-aggressive bitch

A bitch that is so dominant or aggressive that she either intimidates or actually attacks the male must be handled carefully so that the male's libido is not permanently reduced. Determine whether the bitch is simply not at the proper stage of her heat cycle through hormone testing. A muzzle and physical restraint may reduce her dominant or aggressive attitude (see Figure 21-7). For a truly adamant bitch, a visit to the vet might be in order to determine that the bitch does not have an illness or physical defect (such as a vaginal stricture or persistent hymen tissue) that prevents breeding. Finally, if a bitch is so aggressive (whether dominant- or fear-based) that these methods are unsuccessful, it may be necessary to reconsider whether the bitch is suitable for breeding.

The virgin male

When the stud appears to be clueless about what is expected, the stud owner may simply need to offer more encouragement or wait for playful games and courtship of the bitch to boost his confidence. Sometimes a cup of tea for the handlers while the dogs engage in some foreplay will be sufficient. Patience is the key and worth the effort. Do not rush to an artificial collection, as this may create bad habits, such as premature ejaculation. Avoid this situation by reading the section on *Preconditioning the Young Stud.*

When the "giddy up" is gone

Some difficulties occur simply as a result of the age of the stud and resulting physical limitations. The mind is willing, but the body may need a little extra help. Refer to the next section for special handling of the older stud dog.

The Aged Stud

Most studs that are bred several times a year are fertile until the age of 9 or 10, but good healthcare can extend their breeding life for additional years. Then too, it is a pleasure to work with an older dog for, without fail, he appreciates the chance to have fun again and welcomes any extra help that is needed to aid him to achieve his goal.

First, a veterinary examination of the aging Romeo is needed to be sure his kidneys, heart, and total health picture are up to the extra exertion. The aged stud in particular should be examined by the veterinarian every 6 months for a prostate check, sperm evaluation, and semen culture (if needed). Before registering litters sired by studs over 12 years old, the AKC requires a veterinary certificate of fertility (must state that the dog has live sperm of adequate quality and quantity for impregnation).

Check with a veterinarian for a recommendation on one of the many high-powered tonics that are rich in minerals and B vitamins; these have often proven very beneficial to aged studs. The old boys get a spark in their eyes and an arch in their necks, and the sperm counts improve in both number and quality.

Even with certification of fertility, having a veterinarian present at the breeding is well worth the financial investment, as this professional stands as witness to the event if questions about the dog's ability may arise at a later date. In addition, emergencies requiring immediate care are not unheard of. With the veterinarian's approval, one to two regular-strength adult-dose 325-mg ascriptin (aspirin buffered with Maalox) can be given several hours before the attempt at breeding. This medication seems to give some relief from arthritic stiffness and pain so the old guys have a bit more enthusiasm and staying power.

When the proper time to breed the bitch has been established, call the veterinarian and arrange for a house call if at all possible, and plan the breeding arrangements around his or her availability. Be sure to arrange for a helper in case the veterinarian is called away for an emergency.

A clinic is not a first choice due to slick linoleum floors, the cramped space, and a lack of privacy. Many dogs, too, are intimidated the minute they step over the veterinarian's threshold. Few veterinarians are zoned in areas where great breeding adventures, with all to witness, can go on outside the building. Safe, secure footwork is the key to success with the aged dog. The best bet is 6 feet of horse trailer mat; such matting is flexible and washable and can be padded with newspaper underneath to accommodate the height of each dog. Place the mat beside a wall or a chain-link fence in a quiet, secluded location.

A securely fenced enclosure will allow the prospective bride to relieve herself before meeting her intended (which will be an added enticement to the older dog) and permits the breeder to gauge the attitude of the bitch and anticipate potential challenges of the proposed mating. Have a trial run, adding padding (newspapers work best) under the matting to compensate for differences in size before the male enters the enclosure. The secure area increases safety while the older stud works up his enthusiasm for the task at hand, running around and investigating the scents left behind by his lady guest. After relaxation and the veterinarian's arrival, arrange for a period of courtship. Let the dogs romp a bit and

flirt, and when both seem willing and anxious, go back to the planned set-up with great speed so that while the stud is fresh and before the bitch can organize any resistance the breeding is consummated.

It is not uncommon for older dogs to become fully erect prior to penetrating the bitch. If this occurs, gently prevent the dog from mounting and casually walk him around to allow him to regain his composure. When remounting the bitch, it may be beneficial to raise the stud slightly higher on the mats—or use terrain to lower the bitch's front or back end—to allow him to mount higher on the bitch and to aid the thrust and ease the proper penetration.

Bear in mind that many older studs have delayed engorgement due to a diminished blood supply, and they need 2–3 minutes longer to accomplish a tie. Observe the dogs closely to be sure that the penis does not slip out of the vagina during initial engorgement; if it appears that the stud has not made a deep enough penetration—a significant portion of the penis is engorging outside the bitch—quickly remove the male, before his thrusting has ceased if possible, to prevent ejaculation of the second fraction (once thrusting ceases, sperm ejaculation is occurring and cannot be stopped). This problem is not uncommon in older dogs,

Figure 21-13: *Side-by-side tie.* While it looks romantic, the side-by-side tie is not a good idea. The older stud should be encouraged to maintain a "riding tie," while the younger stud should be allowed to turn tail to tail, providing the greatest comfort for the dogs and the maximum opportunity for sperm to reach their destination. A side-by-side tie such as this is less than optimal for even a young dog and may well prove too physically demanding for the older stud to maintain the tie and too challenging for less vigorous sperm. See Figure 21-12 for the best positioning.

Figure 21-14: ***Walk the bitch in circles*** for at least 5 to 15 minutes to dislodge any semen that might be caught up in the vaginal folds. Discourage the bitch from sitting, jumping, or urinating, and encourage her to remain in a prone position for half an hour.

especially those that have been frequently collected for AI. The "outside tie" is the most common breeding problem with aged stud dogs; although not ideal, successful breedings have been accomplished despite this. When the possibility of an outside tie occurs, the stud manager will be forced to make an on-the-spot decision about whether it will be preferable to attempt to try to hold the pair together as long as possible or to risk being able to repeat the effort later. The decision will be based on the stud owner's appraisal of the stud's condition and how long he will need to recover, whether he will be able to repeat his performance within the desired breeding schedule, and the awareness that the current semen may be of greater quality than that subsequently produced in the short period before the next breeding. If the decision to try to maintain the tie is made, as soon as the male withdraws, the bitch's hindquarters should be elevated to try to conserve as much semen as possible.

Unlike the younger dog, the older stud should not necessarily be turned tail-to-tail with the bitch, as mentioned in "The Canine Tie." Experience is valuable at this point because it allows you to know when the dog has finished ejaculation. It is especially important that the pair be physically restrained to maintain the tie (see Figure 21-12). A "riding" tie—with the dog on top of the bitch—is a more comfortable position for the male and allows for a more sustained ejaculation with less risk of breaking the tie. This position is more easily maintained if the bitch is tethered to a chain-link fence, allowing the pair to lean against the fence while the male remains mounted and the bitch is prevented from sitting, rearing up, or turning. If the bitch begins to sink under the male's weight, it is preferable to support her under her chest or by her tail rather than under the abdomen (see Figure 21-8).

After the tie is broken, the bitch should be led in a circle for at least 5–15 minutes to encourage any semen trapped in the folds to move through the vagina and to aid the sometimes lethargic older semen on its way to the waiting eggs. Afterward, she should be confined to prevent her from urinating for several hours; if at all possible, keep the bitch prone or walking (not sitting or jumping up).

The older stud will benefit from a bit of attention as well. Lead him around until his vital equipment has properly retracted. Congratulate him with a few kind words and praise, but give him plenty of time to calm down. Restrict his food and water for several hours (perhaps only a few ice cubes) to reduce the possibility of bloat after all the excitement. As long as the elderly stud feels willing and anxious to perform his job, this alone should be enough to encourage the breeder to continue his use with natural breedings. Lack of interest in sex, coupled with physical health problems, should, of course, mean retirement from natural breedings and the use of AI through fresh or stored semen. There is no greater thrill for the breeder than to be able to help a famous aged stud to score again and provide a genetic improvement of himself. An argument in favor of the aged dog is that it allows use of an animal whose best and poorer points are now

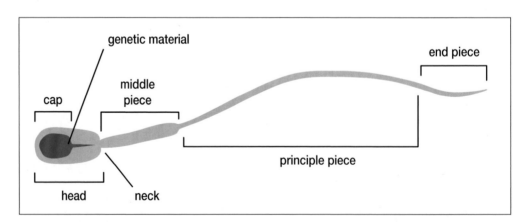

Figure 21-15: ***Sperm evaluation.*** At least 80% of the sperm in the sample should appear acceptably motile, with normal morphology. Ideally there should be at least 10 million sperm/lb of the dog's weight, with a safe pH of 6.2–6.6. For successful insemination, no more than 20% of sperm should be abnormal. Unacceptable sperm may be missing heads or tails or may have slow or erratic movement. These conditions appear more commonly in older dogs, but sometimes also appear in younger or infrequently used studs; such abnormalities often may be significantly reduced in fresh samples taken after the "stale" ejaculate has been flushed out. Courtesy of Dr. Robert Hutchinson.

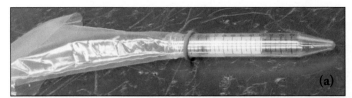

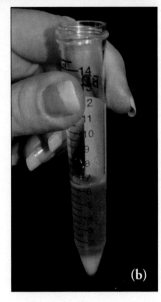

Figure 21-16: *The artificial vagina* **(a)** It directs the ejaculate into a labeled collection tube. The first fraction of the semen is a lubricant. The second fraction contains the sperm. The third fraction, the prostatic fluid, is also a lubricant and helps propel the sperm through the vaginal tract. **(b)** The collection vial is removed and is then centrifuged, unless used immediately. Note: milk-colored sperm appears at the tip of the vial. Photograph by Virginia Alexander.

known to the breeder. It is a treat to be able to have an opportunity to redo the genetic material that he is allowed to leave behind him, to create vehicles for the dilution or total washout of his undesirable recessives and, through several carefully targeted breedings, to provide offspring that will effectively position his best points in homozygous pairs for future use.

Artificial Insemination

Once the realm of large-animal reproduction, science has made great strides in recent years in the field of AI for dogs as well. AI provides many opportunities for potential breedings that might otherwise be difficult or impossible because of a variety of circumstances:

- A physical disability that makes the act of breeding difficult
- Vaginal opening too small or bitch has a stricture
- Uterine infection—even when treated early, the scent may be so altered that a stud will not attempt to breed
- Intractable bitch—time of ovulation does not coincide with receptiveness
- Stud timid after being attacked by a bitch
- Dogs simply dislike each other

- A stud-dog owner may be wary of contact if a bitch has a history of pyometra; AI protects both the stud and bitch from other communicable diseases, such as canine brucellosis
- The exact quantity and quality of semen can be evaluated and adjusted if needed
- Use of frozen assets after the death of a valuable stud dog
- New techniques now allow for the storage and use of bloody semen for both transcervical and intrauterine inseminations

More practical considerations allow the use of semen from a stud that is from a geographically distant area or one in which transportation options are limited by access, climate, or stringent quarantine regulations. Stud dogs that are being heavily campaigned may be severely limited in the number of bitches they can service. Stud owners may be concerned that frequent breeding may distract a male from top-level performance, resulting in marking, aggression, or possible infection. AI allows training and campaigning to continue uninterrupted and with fewer distractions. Additionally, a dog that is being heavily trained or campaigned may have lower sperm count and quality due to stress. Continuous evaluation through routine collections also allows for the regular monitoring of the stud's health and the quality of his sperm.

From the bitch owner's perspective, AI may be preferable to the inconvenience and potential hazards of shipping and turning the care of a valuable bitch over to another. Conversely, many stud owners would rather not be responsible for the care of another dog during such a critical period.

Often-Overlooked Details

Whether or not to collect a dog's semen is a personal decision, of course. Should a stud dog not fulfill his potential, stored semen can always be disposed of; however, if the semen was not collected and the valuable stud dies from an accident or illness, semen collected just prior to or at death is necessarily of limited quantity and often reduced quality. Collecting while the young stud is in his prime allows for collection of a larger quantity and better quality. Waiting until the dog is older not only often results in less and perhaps sperm of insufficient vigor to even attempt freezing.

At this time, collection fees range on either side of $400 in most parts of the country, and storage fees run approximately $80/year. The number of facilities licensed to collect and store semen is growing rapidly; if a local veterinarian is unable to provide the information, contact the AKC (or appropriate national registry of a foreign country) for a list of approved facilities and most recent policies on collection, storage, and registration of litters produced by AI.

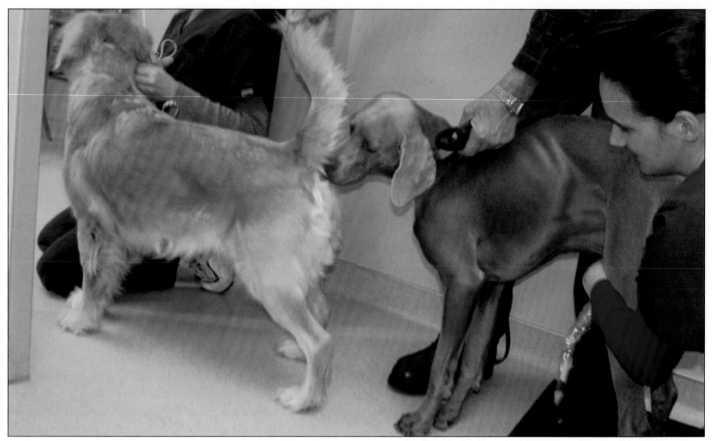

Figure 21-17: *Whatever works.* This 10-year-old male—against all tradition—prefers blonds with long, fluffy tails over short-haired ladies of his own kind. The teamwork of at least two helpers, with a great sense of humor, is vital for a successful collection. Photograph courtesy of Dr. Shauntelle Gallaher.

When conducting an AI breeding, it is very important to determine ahead of time which fees will be paid by each party, how and when they will be paid, and how many collections will be made or straws/vials used. Generally speaking, two collections give the most favorable results when using fresh or fresh-chilled semen for vaginal or transcervical insemination; with surgically implanted semen, only one procedure is necessary.

The breeder should be aware that when using AI, the AKC requires additional documentation; refer to the AKC website for details at www.akc.org/reg/registeralitter. DNA testing is required when using fresh extended or frozen semen. Check the regulations to verify what signatures and certifications are required well in advance of making arrangements for semen collection, storing, shipping, or insemination. Be sure to secure the necessary signatures from the collecting and implanting veterinarian at the time of the action.

Semen shipped to or from a foreign country may be subject to even more scrutiny and may be approved by a specific registry only on a case-by-case basis. Investigate the requirements in detail, both from the customs aspect as well as the registry requirements. For example, some countries require a titer or vaccination to occur within a certain period prior to the collection and shipment of the semen. Other countries may limit the number of breedings allowed from a single shipment.

Semen Collection

The collection process of the semen for AI can ultimately determine success or failure; proper collection and handling will ensure adequate quantity, viability, and longevity of semen upon implantation. Prior to collection, determine how the semen will be dispersed: fresh, on the spot, fresh extended chilled, or frozen. This will affect how the collected semen is handled. Regardless of the insemination method used, correct preparation of the semen is critical to future success.

The collection process itself is obviously subject to the cooperation of the stud dog. Experienced, sympathetic assistance will make the process easier for the dog as well as the support personnel. Ideally, it is best to have a bitch available in standing heat on the premises to put the stud in the mood; keep in mind that some Weimaraners may have less interest in a bitch of another breed. Failing this, many stud owners and canine reproductive specialists keep gauze or Q-tip® swabs on hand collected from the vulva of a bitch in standing season (these can be stored in a Ziploc® bag or collection tube in the freezer); once thawed, they are wiped around the genitals of any cooperative bitch, even one that is spayed. If insufficient swabs are available, consider holding the Ziploc® bag that contained the swabs on the bitch's tail for several minutes to impart an enticing perfume. These will help get the stud dog "in the mood" for his work.

Once aroused, the penis is inserted in an artificial vagina to collect the ejaculate. The appropriate collection vehicle can impact not only the dog's willingness to participate, but current research shows that certain types of materials can adversely affect the survivability of the semen itself. The first fraction is a clear lubricant. The second fraction appears milky and contains the sperm. The third fraction is also a lubricant and helps wash the sperm down the vaginal tract during a natural breeding. After the stud has made his contribution, assign an assistant to see to his comfort, allowing him to have a brief walk, and ensuring that his equipment has properly retracted.

The semen will be evaluated for mobility, quality, and quantity and then centrifuged to separate the fractions. It is important to do so before storing, as the inclusion of the third fraction can be detrimental to the lifespan of the sperm. Upon examination, it may be determined that the sperm lacks the mobility or quantity necessary for a successful

breeding; it may be advisable to attempt a second collection the next day, particularly with older or rarely used studs. Sperm showing abnormal physiology in concentrations of greater than 20% are considered a poor choice for success with the exception of direct surgical implant. Buffers and extenders are necessary for the survival of the semen to be shipped or stored. They increase the volume of the fluid, provide a favorable environment for survival with the correct pH, an energy source for the cells, and protection from the chilling or freezing process during transportation or storage. Buffers usually also contain an antibiotic to protect the semen and the bitch from bacteria.

The semen can be used immediately or placed in vials, straws, or pellets for shipping or storage. It is vital for the semen to be properly packaged to maintain a favorable temperature and protection from damage to the containers during shipping. Double check that all the necessary documentation, signatures, and instructions are included.

Chilled or frozen semen should always be shipped by the fastest means available, at a minimum guaranteed next day service. If it appears that insemination will occur on a Sunday, be sure to make arrangements to receive the shipment on Saturday and that proper storage arrangements are made to hold the semen until implantation.

Figure 21-18: *The fresh semen is evaluated* to determine concentration, morphology, and mobility before use (fresh or chilled) or storage (chilled or frozen); this helps Tracey determine how much semen is needed for each successful breeding. Before storage, the sperm is mixed with a nutrient medium (often a proprietary mixture specific to each veterinarian) to support the semen during the freezing, storing, and thawing processes. Courtesy of Northview Animal Clinic, Inc.

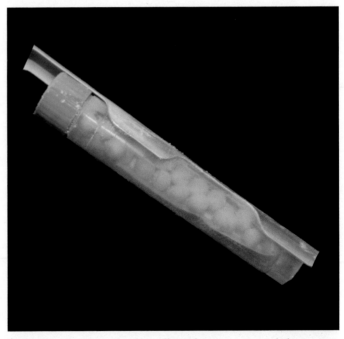

Figure 21-19: *New technology allows the semen,* suspended in a nutrient medium, to be stored as frozen pellets. The pellets are collected in a vial that will provide the optimal amount of sperm for a single breeding. This method gives the stud owner greater conservation and control over the use of the semen, which is particularly important for the older or deceased stud. One vial is intended to provide a single service. Courtesy of Northview Animal Clinic, Inc.

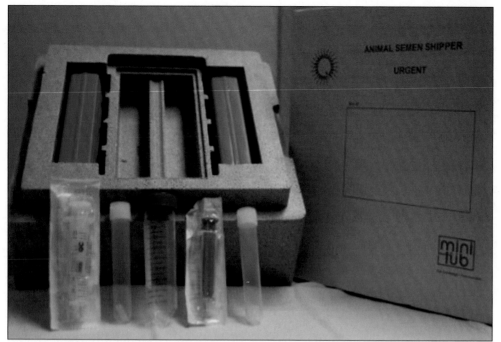

Figure 21-20: ***The chilled semen is shipped*** in a special container provided by the collecting veterinarian; the shipping boxes will vary slightly by provider. Although weekends may be challenging, for maximum results, every effort should be made to ensure delivery within 48 hours. An outer shipping box meets postal guidelines, provides protection, and aids temperature control. An inner Styrofoam package provides the majority of cushioning, protection, and insulation. Photograph by Barney Riley.

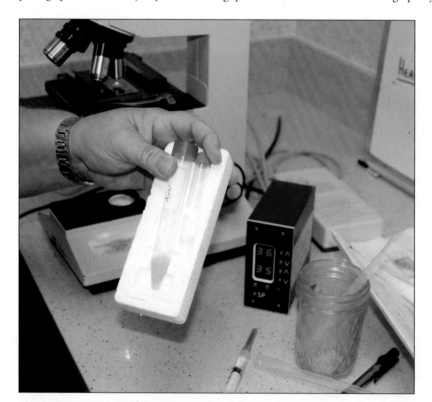

Figure 21-21: ***The chilled sperm arrives*** safely nestled in a temperature-controlled container. Before use, the semen will be microscopically examined on a carefully warmed slide. Once the sperm's viability is determined to be adequate, it will be mixed with the diluents provided and maintained in a warming bath while the bitch is prepared for either transcervical or surgical insemination. Photograph courtesy of Dr. Bill Cortiaus, Campbell Village Veterinary Clinic, Dallas, Texas.

Fresh, extended semen

A breeder may choose to use fresh semen artificially implanted dog-to-dog on the spot for a variety of reasons, such as a temperamental bitch or an injured stud. Semen can be collected from the male and implanted immediately in the bitch in the room next door. The semen is first collected and then analyzed for quality and quantity and is typically inserted using the vaginal insemination method, as shown in Figure 21-22. This is an ideal option for an older stud that may be physically limited in mounting the bitch but is anxious and well able to do the job; he may be more comfortable with an AI procedure. Conception rates for properly collected and deposited, fresh, extended semen are often considered equal to that of natural breeding.

Chilled semen

Chilled semen offers a host of advantages and potentials for breeding programs across the country as well as around the world. While natural breedings or fresh insemination may be limited by geography or transportation, chilled semen overcomes these challenges with the advent of 24-hour overnight delivery for the handling and shipping of chilled semen, while the costs of collection, preparation, and storage are significantly less than that of frozen semen, which also requires surgical implantation for best success. Optimally, chilled semen should be collected just prior to the scheduled pick-up; in other words, if the pick-up is scheduled for the afternoon, the collection would be made in the afternoon, not early in the morning. Chilled semen should be used within 48 hours. Although not recommended, there is documentation of viable puppies produced from semen as old as 4 days; if properly chilled and maintained semen is left over from a previous insemination, no harm could be done by using it for additional insemination, as it may potentially increase litter size.

Frozen semen

In the early 1970s, effective techniques for freezing and storing canine semen were developed. Rapid advances in technology have improved the rate of conception remarkably, and now with proper insemination, when all variables are maximized, leading veterinarians document conception rates almost as good as with natural breeding. Freezing allows long-term storage of semen; extenders are used to maintain pH, protect the semen from cold shock, prevent ice crystals, and provide an energy source for the semen during storage and when thawed for use. It is worth repeating that the best time to collect and freeze semen is when the dog is relatively young and in prime health.

Frozen sperm can be included in future breeding programs after the death of a high-quality producer. One of the most exciting potentials lies in the possibility of "fresh" infusions of older genetic material from an underused stud dog from previous generations, or the backcrossing of a granddaughter to a prepotent stud, something rarely possible in the past. A significant advance is the ability to map genes and identify a stud from a previous generation that may be free from a recently identified genetic flaw that has become common in the current gene pool through the frequently used stud syndrome or convergence of bloodlines.

In the United States, the AKC requires frozen semen to be stored at an approved facility. The list is organized by state

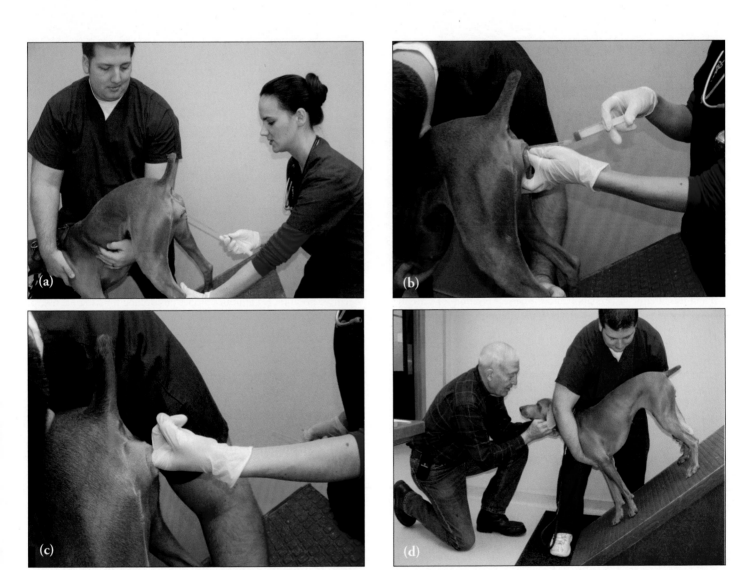

Figure 21-22: *Vaginal or transcervical insemination.* The bitch is placed on a slant board to allow gravity to assist in moving the semen to the awaiting eggs. Notice that the assistant does not apply pressure to the bitch's abdomen to avoid moving organs or occluding the flow of semen. **(a)** A flexible pipette is inserted up and over into the vagina to the ideal position, in order to deposit the semen as close as possible to the cervix, depending on the procedure. **(b)** Once the semen has been injected, the properly placed pipette is removed. **(c)** In an effort to simulate a natural tie, manually stroking the vaginal roof for approximately 5 minutes stimulates muscular contractions and helps propel the semen down the vaginal tract. **(d)** The bitch, with the attending assistant providing comfortable support, is encouraged to remain on the slant board for an additional 5–10 minutes. Courtesy of Dr. Shauntelle Gallaher, Northview Animal Clinic, Inc.

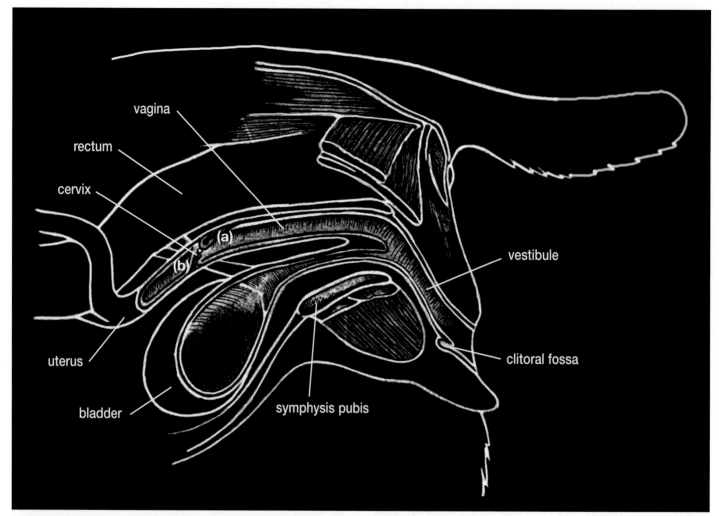

Figure 21-23: *Canine anatomical terms: female reproductive system.* This diagram illustrates the location the pipette or endoscope takes for vaginal and intrauterine insemination and the correct position for placement of the semen. Location **(a)** indicates proper positioning for a vaginal insemination. Location **(b)** represents the ideal positioning for an intrauterine insemination. Diagram courtesy of Dr. Robert Hutchinson, Northview Animal Clinic, Inc.

A back-up plan if a bitch in season is not available for a semen collection is as follows: the vulva of a bitch at her peak of receptivity can be wiped with gauze pads or Q-tips®; these can be stored in a Ziploc® bag in the freezer. When needed, the gauze can be thawed and wiped around the genitals of a bitch, even one that is spayed, or any cooperative male. This is guaranteed to get the stud in the mood for his work and ensure the largest possible collection.

and can be found at www.akc.org/reg/AIstorage.cfm. When using frozen semen, it is preferable to take the bitch to the storage facility for the implantation procedure whenever possible, rather than exposing the more fragile semen to the vagaries of shipping. Alternatively, the semen is shipped to the veterinarian performing the implantation procedure. When shipping semen internationally, add an additional several hundred dollars to the cost of shipping. Since airlines classify liquid nitrogen as a dangerous or hazardous material, frozen semen shipments may be subject to additional handling or freight fees. Despite the additional expense, frozen semen is more likely to reach its destination in a usable condition since differing customs regulations may subject chilled semen to delays or environmental changes that could be detrimental to semen viability.

Methods of Insemination

When considering AI, the owner of the bitch should discuss the procedure with the veterinarian well in advance of the bitch's coming in season. The owner of the mother-to-be should also be well versed in the current registration requirements when using artificial insemination to ensure that resulting progeny are eligible for AKC registration: www.akc.org/reg/registeralitter.cfm.

Vaginal insemination

Since conception rates using vaginal insemination with frozen semen are under 50%, vaginal insemination is more commonly used with fresh or chilled semen, which affords a much higher success rate. For breeders wishing to avoid stud contact with the bitch, semen can also be collected and immediately emplaced using this technique. Semen is placed in the vaginal canal using an insemination pipette, preferably as close as possible to the cervical opening.

In order to duplicate a natural tie, stroke the vaginal roof to stimulate contractions to propel the semen to its target. Elevating the bitch's hindquarters during insemination and for 10 minutes longer will allow the force of gravity to further aid the movement. This can be accomplished by standing the bitch head downward on a stairway or placing her rump on a couch with her forequarters on the floor. Walking the bitch in circles will help move pockets of semen from the vaginal folds toward the cervix. As with natural breedings, it is important to avoid letting the bitch urinate for several hours and encourage her to maintain a prone or standing position (no sitting or jumping) for 3–5 hours (see Figure 21-22).

Intrauterine inseminations

In recent years, improvements in insemination techniques have increased the success rates of AI using chilled or frozen semen through intrauterine techniques, which places the semen directly into the uterus whether by inserting it through the cervical opening using a pipette or by injecting it directly into the uterine horns through a small abdominal incision. The decision about which method to use is determined by several factors, including most importantly the availability of a skilled reproductive veterinarian. The condition of the bitch is also important, as is the type and quality of semen and the willingness of the bitch's owner to place her under general anesthesia.

Transcervical insemination. Fresh or chilled semen may also be placed transcervically (beyond the cervical opening) using a Norwegian pipette or an endoscope. Although this procedure does not generally require anesthesia or sedation, due to the cost of equipment and the requirement of excellent technique and practice for highest success, this procedure should only be performed by a reproductive specialist. Common practice is to perform at least two inseminations using this technique to increase the odds of conception and litter size. This technique may not be possible on very large or overweight bitches, where it may be difficult or impossible to visualize or steady the cervix sufficiently to pass the pipette or catheter; in those cases, surgical implantation may be the only option.

Surgical implantation. Alternatively, semen can be surgically implanted. This is primarily the option when using frozen semen or low-quality chilled semen or when transcervical insemination is not possible. With the bitch under general anesthesia, a small incision is made, exposing the uterine horns.

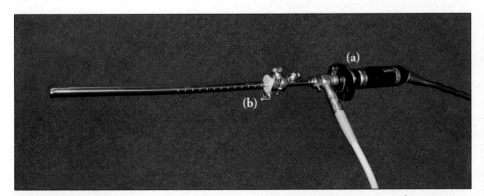
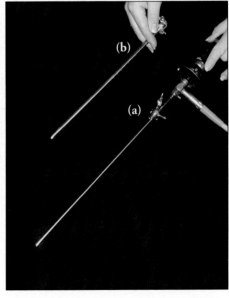

Figure 21-24: ***Intrauterine insemination can be performed without anesthesia*** and with minimal discomfort to the bitch. A carrier tube is inserted into the vagina, which allows a tiny, lighted camera to transmit a picture to a television monitor as it travels along the walls of the vagina and past the cervix. The veterinarian can then view when the carrier moves beyond the cervical opening into the position for optimal placement of the semen—the uterus. The lighted camera **(a)** is then removed while the carrier tube **(b)** remains in place, permitting the semen to be deposited directly into the uterus and the awaiting eggs. Photographs by Virginia Alexander.

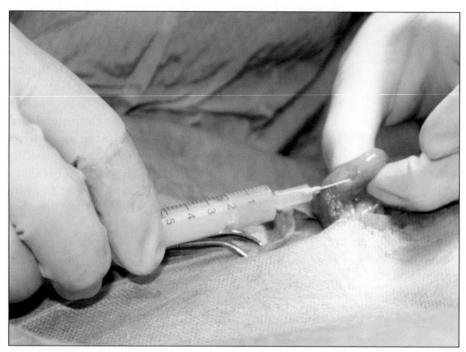

Figure 21-25: *In surgical implantation,* approximately 1¹/₂ cc of premixed, warmed semen is injected in each of the two uterine horns of the anesthetized Weimaraner. Photograph courtesy of Dr. Bill Cortiaus, Campbell Village Veterinary Clinic.

The importance of progesterone testing to determine the optimal time for breeding cannot be overemphasized; counting days or viewing smears is far less reliable than progesterone testing. In fact, no other test is as accurate or reliable as a progesterone assay of the blood; because it must be sent to an outside lab, test results usually take at least one full day. Although progesterone levels may fluctuate, once the 5.0-ng/mL level has been reached, ovulation has occurred, and fertilization of the eggs can begin in about 48 hours. If using vaginal or transcervical insemination, two breedings are recommended to increase the chance of pregnancy and litter size; however, using surgical implantation with frozen semen necessarily limits the breeder to one opportunity for insemination. Considering the significantly reduced life span of frozen semen (12–24 hours), timing remains the most critical issue for success.

It is hoped that the information in this section provides the breeder with guidelines to help avoid these most common causes of failure and disruption of a breeding program. Fanciers considering AI should further educate

A needle is used to inject the sperm into both horns of the uterus, which are then replaced in the abdominal cavity, and the incision is closed. The requirement of general anesthesia and an incision limit this option to one insemination. The cost of this surgery (usually $200–$300) is generally significantly higher than vaginal or transcervical implantation, but offers the highest rate of success with frozen semen, semen with low motility or volume, or highly valuable semen (for example, the last few straws of a deceased stud).

The secret to AI success. In personal correspondence (25 September 2006), Dr. Robert Hutchison commented that when all variables are optimized (health, genetics, and timing), the current state of AI technology achieves success rates that are better than natural breedings. The leading causes of AI conception failure, he believes, are:

- improper placement of semen
- mishandling of semen
- timing of cycle

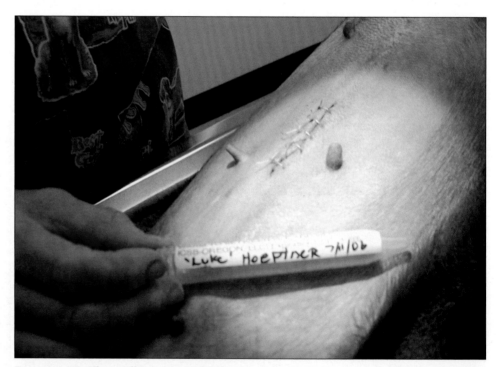

Figure 21-26: *The small incision is closed.* After an antibiotic injection, the dog is sent home as soon as the anesthesia wears off. Photograph courtesy of Dr. Katie Gardener, Meadowlands Veterinary Clinic.

themselves on the subject. The authors recommend Dr. Robert Hutchison's recently released DVD, *Maximizing Conception in the Bitch,* as an excellent resource for the management, collection, and implantation of semen: www.northviewvet.com.

The WCA and the AKC

No discussion of breeding would be complete without at least mentioning the ethics and requirements of breeding pure-bred dogs. The WCA requests that every member sign a Code of Ethics with the membership application. These can also be found at the WCA website: www.weimclubamerica.org. The AKC (www.akc.org) also has requirements and procedures before a litter can be registered. Failure to comply with AKC rules can result in at best frustration and delay and at worst the refusal to register a litter.

What the Future Holds

Thirty years ago, virtually the only exposure veterinary students had to AI was in relation to large agricultural animals; today, most vet schools have at least one professor who specializes in small-animal reproduction. The use of AI will continue to increase in popularity since it allows for the exchange of genetic material between individuals separated by generations or in areas that were previously separated by quarantine laws or distance. As a result of these changes and demands, huge advances have been made in recent years in the field of AI. Since timing of ovulation is the least controllable variable, it is hoped that progesterone assays, or some other techniques, can be made more affordable and accurate, to allow breeders to specifically pinpoint the peak of fertility with less expense and greater convenience for both natural and artificial breedings. Whether a breeding is natural or artificial, no matter the advances in science, timing is, and always will be the key to a successful breeding. Reviewing the progress of the last decade in canine reproduction, it seems highly probable that these difficulties will be overcome in the very near future. Fortunately for the Weimaraner, physiological and psychological impairments are not currently an issue for most breeders. Regardless of the advances that may be made in the field of AI, it is important that breeders keep in mind that, barring prejudicial circumstances, well-timed natural breeding should be the method of choice for long-term success.

Figure 21-27: *Love in the afternoon near Haimberg, Germany.* Sometimes when all the expensive and complicated artificial means have been exhausted, weary breeders have learned that the nose of an experienced Weimaraner stud dog can be notoriously accurate at determining the optimal moment for successful breeding. Routinely, many European Weimaraner breeders prefer to allow the instincts of the potential mates to determine the proceedings, minimizing human involvement and stepping in only after the actual tie has been consummated. Photograph by Dr. Roman Braun.

Figure 22-1: *Day's Outing* (1992), by William Wegman. The mother to be should be in top physical condition before being bred.

CHAPTER 22

PRENATAL CARE

Good prenatal care and organization of the equipment needed for whelping contribute to a smooth, uneventful labor and delivery of the litter. In addition, the breeder who is aware of environmental agents that cause congenital abnormalities can often avoid them.

Conception and Nonconception

Is She Pregnant?

The weeks between a breeding and confirmation of conception are anxious ones. Should an advertisement be sent to the breed magazine? Should a new whelping box be built or the old one repaired? Should time off from work be arranged?

About a week after breeding, a Weimaraner that has conceived often has a slight, thick, odorless, creamy discharge for 3–4 days. This is not a sign of infection. However, any discharge that persists for longer than 4 days and that has a foul odor or strange color should be brought to the veterinarian's attention.

Canine embryos float in "uterine milk" for 18–20 days before implantation and formation of the placenta. In Weimaraners, the embryos are the size and shape of a walnut by the 28th day of gestation. The veterinarian can usually palpate and sometimes count the embryos between the 22nd and 30th day after conception. After the 30th day, the amount of amniotic fluid increases, and the embryos become too soft to differentiate from the abdominal organs. The embryos cannot be palpated again until about the 49th day, by which time the other signs of pregnancy are usually obvious.

Do not lose hope if the veterinarian cannot palpate any puppies. Since keeping records, one author found that 50% of the bitches in which no puppies could be palpated were pregnant, including one with 10 puppies.

The early signs of pregnancy include enlargement of the breasts, frequent urination, changes in behavior, and progressive swelling and softening of the vulva. However, the same signs occur with false pregnancy (pseudocyesis). Embryos can implant in the far ends of the uterine horns under the ribs, however, and there may be little abdominal enlargement. A large Weimaraner bitch can conceal a surprising number of puppies under her ribs, and the only clue to her pregnancy is an easily overlooked expansion of the rib cage, which can often only be seen when she is viewed from above. By the last week, the bitch should have an adequate supply of milk and it is often possible to feel or observe the puppies' bodies moving and kicking while she is at rest.

If a bred bitch shows no signs of pregnancy other than mammary enlargement and milk development about the 56th day, do not assume that she has no puppies; make certain that she has none. An X-ray or sonogram is the only way to confirm whether or not she has any—either living or dead. If the puppies are dead, then the bitch will require antibiotic treatment and close observation to prevent infection.

Eight weeks after a mismating and an abortion shot, one owner had a bitch checked because she was developing milk. Two veterinarians examined her carefully and assured the owner that she had a false pregnancy. They were somewhat embarrassed a week later when the owner walked in with eight tiny blue-black newborn puppies sired by a traveling salesman.

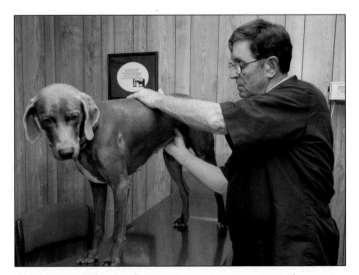

Figure 22-2: *Palpating for puppies* requires a veterinarian's expertise. The proper time for an accurate examination will vary, depending on the specific date of conception. This should be done no earlier than the 25th through the 30th day after fertilization. Be prepared to return within 5 days if no puppies can be felt on the first attempt due to delayed conception. Photograph of Dr. Chet by Gene LaFollette.

If Not, Why Not?

Fertility is, of course, of primary concern in the brood bitch. When a bitch fails to conceive, the potential reasons should be reviewed.

Contraceptives

One of the few hard-and-fast rules in dog breeding is that if you have any plans to ever breed a bitch, avoid the use of any product to alter her heat cycle. Many contraceptives that have been marketed with glowing assurances of their safety have been removed after trusting owners proved they were not safe. At this time, no product currently on the market to keep a bitch from coming in season is foolproof. Before using the next one to come along, first obtain a written guarantee from the pharmaceutical company of product safety and financial liability if the bitch fails to ever produce puppies—we would love to see such a document.

Abortion shots

Despite claims of infallibility and safety, abortion shots do not always work, and complications leading to pyometra are all too commonly reported in Weimaraners. Weigh the consequences carefully. Unless the bitch is so young, so old, or so sick that any pregnancy is dangerous, it is usually better in the long run for her to have the litter, even if it produces crossbred puppies.

Anovulatory seasons

Some seasons are infertile because no ovulation occurs—particularly in late fall and early winter. This is not uncommon when a bitch is drawn into season prematurely as the result of proximity to another bitch in season.

Silent seasons

Some Weimaraner bitches have a very light flow and seem to have a shorter season. Owners typically comment on the bitch's unusually attentive grooming of her hind-quarters. The onset of the season and time of ovulation are particularly difficult to pinpoint. To identify the onset, place a white sheet in the crate or favorite resting place at the first sign of swelling or a male showing interest. The best time to visually check the bitch is when she rises from a resting posi-

Table 22-1: *Estimated whelping dates.*

Bred: January	1 2 3 4 5 6 7 8 9 10 11 12 13 14 15 16 17 18 19 20 21 22 23 24 25 26 27 28 29 30 31
Due: March	5 6 7 8 9 10 11 12 13 14 15 16 17 18 19 20 21 22 23 24 25 26 27 28 29 30 31 April 1 2 3 4
Bred: February	1 2 3 4 5 6 7 8 9 10 11 12 13 14 15 16 17 18 19 20 21 22 23 24 25 26 27 28
Due: April	5 6 7 8 9 10 11 12 13 14 15 16 17 18 19 20 21 22 23 24 25 26 27 28 29 30 May 1 2
Bred: March	1 2 3 4 5 6 7 8 9 10 11 12 13 14 15 16 17 18 19 20 21 22 23 24 25 26 27 28 29 30 31
Due: May	3 4 5 6 7 8 9 10 11 12 13 14 15 16 17 18 19 20 21 22 23 24 25 26 27 28 29 30 31 June 1 2
Bred: April	1 2 3 4 5 6 7 8 9 10 11 12 13 14 15 16 17 18 19 20 21 22 23 24 25 26 27 28 29 30
Due: June	3 4 5 6 7 8 9 10 11 12 13 14 15 16 17 18 19 20 21 22 23 24 25 26 27 28 29 30 July 1 2
Bred: May	1 2 3 4 5 6 7 8 9 10 11 12 13 14 15 16 17 18 19 20 21 22 23 24 25 26 27 28 29 30 31
Due: July	3 4 5 6 7 8 9 10 11 12 13 14 15 16 17 18 19 20 21 22 23 24 25 26 27 28 29 30 31 August 1 2
Bred: June	1 2 3 4 5 6 7 8 9 10 11 12 13 14 15 16 17 18 19 20 21 22 23 24 25 26 27 28 29 30
Due: August	3 4 5 6 7 8 9 10 11 12 13 14 15 16 17 18 19 20 21 22 23 24 25 26 27 28 29 30 31 September 1
Bred: July	1 2 3 4 5 6 7 8 9 10 11 12 13 14 15 16 17 18 19 20 21 22 23 24 25 26 27 28 29 30 31
Due: September	3 4 5 6 7 8 9 10 11 12 13 14 15 16 17 18 19 20 21 22 23 24 25 26 27 28 29 30 31 October 1 2
Bred: August	1 2 3 4 5 6 7 8 9 10 11 12 13 14 15 16 17 18 19 20 21 22 23 24 25 26 27 28 29 30 31
Due: October	3 4 5 6 7 8 9 10 11 12 13 14 15 16 17 18 19 20 21 22 23 24 25 26 27 28 29 30 31 November 1 2
Bred: September	1 2 3 4 5 6 7 8 9 10 11 12 13 14 15 16 17 18 19 20 21 22 23 24 25 26 27 28 29 30
Due: November	3 4 5 6 7 8 9 10 11 12 13 14 15 16 17 18 19 20 21 22 23 24 25 26 27 28 29 30 December 1 2
Bred: October	1 2 3 4 5 6 7 8 9 10 11 12 13 14 15 16 17 18 19 20 21 22 23 24 25 26 27 28 29 30 31
Due: December	3 4 5 6 7 8 9 10 11 12 13 14 15 16 17 18 19 20 21 22 23 24 25 26 27 28 29 30 31 January 1 2
Bred: November	1 2 3 4 5 6 7 8 9 10 11 12 13 14 15 16 17 18 19 20 21 22 23 24 25 26 27 28 29 30
Due: January	3 4 5 6 7 8 9 10 11 12 13 14 15 16 17 18 19 20 21 22 23 24 25 26 27 28 29 30 31 February 1
Bred: December	1 2 3 4 5 6 7 8 9 10 11 12 13 14 15 16 17 18 19 20 21 22 23 24 25 26 27 28 29 30 31
Due: February	2 3 4 5 6 7 8 9 10 11 12 13 14 15 16 17 18 19 20 21 22 23 24 25 26 27 28 March 1 2 3 4

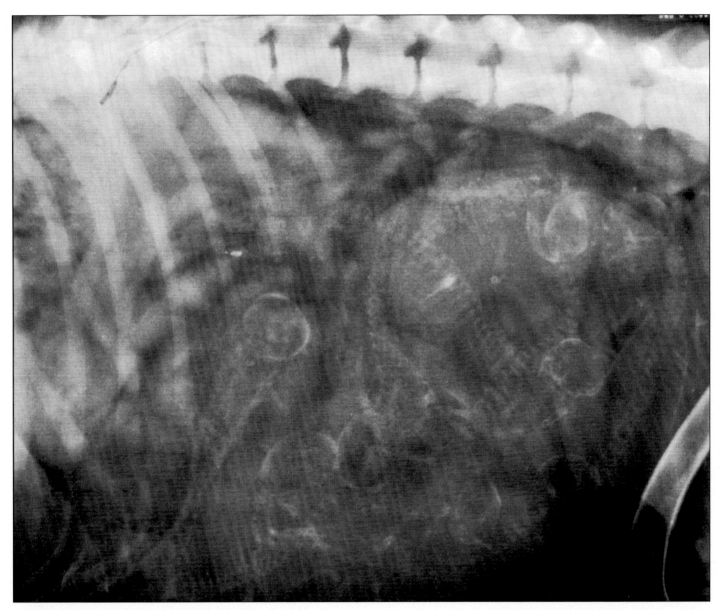

Figure 22-3: *During the final weeks of pregnancy,* the puppies' bones begin to calcify, making it possible to confirm the presence of puppies by a single side-view X-ray. The procedure should be deferred until at least the 55th day after the first mating, because the closer the bitch is to whelping, the easier it is to identify the puppies. Can you find all 10 puppies?

tion. With these bitches, close veterinary monitoring (smears and progesterone levels) is vital.

Metritis and pyometra

Both metritis and pyometra are common causes of non-conception as well as abortion, fetal resorption, stillbirths, and neonatal deaths. (See *Best of Health.*)

Hypothyroidism

Mature Weimaraner bitches that have consistently produced healthy litters and that suddenly stop conceiving should have a complete thyroid panel performed, including T3, T4, Free T3 and T4, T3 and T4 antibodies, TgAA, and Thyroglobulin autoantibodies. Although the number of tests sounds daunting, the complete panel usually runs under $100, and the information provided can be invaluable. In the absence of a predisposition for genetic hypothyroidism, if test results show a low or even a low-normal thyroid function, a minimal-dosage thyroid supplement, given under veterinary direction for several months before breeding, may be all that is needed to help the older bitch conceive. A breeder may wish to reconsider future breeding of a bitch that indicates a positive profile for the T3AA, T4AA, or TgAA tests, indicating the existence of inheritable hypothyroidism.

Figure 22-4: ***The regular exercise and nutrition program*** the bitch enjoyed prior to breeding can usually be maintained up until the 4th week of confirmed pregnancy. Charlene has found rollerblading to be a useful way to safely condition and exercise Tru, despite her urban setting, while avoiding the potential hazards of the local dog park. Although rollerblading on a regular dog collar could teach bad habits, a skijoring or weight-pulling harness, or even a seatbelt harness, cues the dog as to when pulling is appropriate and distributes the dog's weight properly to avoid strain.

Nutrition

Every Weimaraner breeder has firm convictions about what constitutes a proper pregnancy diet, and many have a tendency to add everything, reasoning that if a little is good, more is better. The addition of such things as calcium was once the only way to supplement the regular kibble during pregnancy. Commercial preparations suitable for the pregnant and lactating bitch may be available in the brand she is currently eating, frequently labeled as puppy formula. After the pregnancy is confirmed, a once-daily over-the-counter human prenatal vitamin should supply any additional nutritional needs. It has also been the practice of the authors to include one or two hardboiled eggs, divided among the daily meals, during the last two or three weeks of pregnancy. Three or four days before the expected delivery date, small amounts of liver should be provided daily; the juice from the boiled liver can be used as flavoring for the electrolytic drink, unflavored Pedialyte,® which should be provided at a rate of 1 to 2 cups daily during the last few days and continued during the delivery. Do not use any supplements other than those suggested in this book or prescribed by a veterinarian, as overdoses of some vitamins and minerals are known to cause certain congenital abnormalities.

The bitch should be started on the puppy formula food when bred, but the quantity should not be increased until the pregnancy is confirmed—after the 4th week—when the puppies begin rapid growth from the size of a walnut to birth weight. The bitch's caloric intake should be slowly increased as pregnancy progresses; it may be necessary to divide her meals into three or four portions to accommodate the growing puppies and the pressure on the internal organs. The bitch should be maintaining her body condition; ribs should be easily felt but not seen. If hips and ribs become visible, her ration should be increased.

Exercise

The mother-to-be should be in top physical condition when bred, and regular exercise should be continued throughout pregnancy; it pays dividends during labor and delivery. Proper exercise is probably the most frequently neglected aspect of prenatal care. Some owners are afraid that exercise will stress the bitch and cause her to lose the litter. Do not worry! Nature protects the puppies, and the bitch that is participating in her accustomed daily activity will not lose a normally developing litter. The breeder must use good judgment, however.

After the 4th week, the bitch should not go out for a long day of hunting, practice obedience jumps, roughhouse with other dogs, or play Frisbee. Her regular exercise program should continue—the key is regularity and moderation.

Teratogenic Agents

Conscientious breeders go to great lengths to avoid perpetuating recessive traits that produce congenital disorders, and most are aware of the risks of X-rays during early pregnancy. Few, however, realize that many disorders commonly considered hereditary are often caused by environmental agents.

Congenital disorders are those present at birth; they are caused by teratogens—that is, anything that interferes with normal embryonic development. The two types of teratogens of concern to breeders are (a) hereditary genetic disorders and (b) those caused by teratogenic agents (drugs, chemicals, and infections).

Exposure to teratogenic agents can be minimized if breeders are aware of the common hazards. If congenital defects do occur, knowledge of possible exposure helps to differentiate between genetic and environmental causes.

Cleft palate is a classic example of a disorder once considered exclusively genetic but now known to be caused by many teratogenic agents. It is well established that cleft palate can be produced by Vitamin A deficiency, Vitamin A overdose, aspirin, cortisone, hypothermia, and oxygen insufficiency, as well as many other agents listed in Table 22-3.

Here are a few general guidelines to minimize teratogenic exposure.

- Vaccination boosters should be completed well in advance of breeding the bitch.

- Bitches should also be tested and treatment completed for parasites well before breeding, at the very latest when she first comes into season.

- Avoid the use of any extraneous chemicals as much as possible prior to breeding and during pregnancy and lactation; for example, discontinue heartworm prevention whenever possible.

- Give antibiotics, oral or topical, only by prescription from a veterinarian, who will only offer those that are not contraindicated by pregnancy.

Dog breeders have an overwhelming tendency to assume that all congenital disorders are hereditary. Clearly, both possibilities—genetic and teratogenic agents—must be carefully considered. In other words, review the events that occurred during the pregnancy, such as illness, medications, extreme temperatures, and lawn chemicals, before jumping to conclusions and blaming the parents.

Table 22-2: *Checklist—whelping equipment.*

Alarm clock
Betadine® or alcohol
BIZ®: remove stains
Newspapers
Large blankets for beneath whelping box
Drop cloth for furniture and floor
Notebook and pen
Cot or reclining chair
Overhead heat lamps or other source of warmth
Dog crate (large, sterilized)
Paper towels
Heavy thread or dental floss: tie umbilical cord
Scale: baby scale is best
Scissors: trim umbilical cords, cut identifying patches
Identifying collars: potholder loops or colored yarn
Shot glass: to collect colostrum
Incubator: lidded 15"× 12" storage box with handle openings
Surgical clamps (Kelly forceps)—two for clamping umbilical cord
Insulin syringe (1 cc, with needle removed)—feed newborn puppies
KY® jelly and sterile surgical gloves: free large puppy from birth canal
Cell phone
Rectal thermometer
Terrycloth hand towels
Large plastic trash bags
Kaopectate®
Low stool suitable for sitting in whelping box
Baby monitor
8-hour ThermaCare® heat wrap
Canine milk formula
Pedialyte®—*not* generic brand
NutriCal®: nutritional supplement paste
Hamburger balls
Boiled chicken
Beef liver
Frozen dinners: feed human family

Getting Organized for Whelping

The Whelping Box

Although an inexpensive plastic wading pool or a large plastic dog crate is easily portable and can be used in an emergency, a well-designed whelping box is vital for the safety of the puppies and for the ease of caring for the litter. It is far better to plan ahead and have the whelping box set up 7–10 days before the bitch is due to whelp.

There are many good whelping box designs. A 4 × 4–foot whelping box is perfect for Weimaraners. Figure 22-6 shows a hinged, 12-inch entrance that is ideal during the first few weeks, making it easier for the bitch to see into the box as she enters, minimizing possible injury to puppies. This hinged entrance is raised to 24 inches when the puppies reach 4–5 weeks, are eager to get out of the box, and are less likely to be hurt when the bitch blindly jumps into the box. All square whelping boxes should have a pig rail—an interior railing that protects newborn puppies when the mother lies down. The box rests on a bottom made of a separate sheet of plywood, extending 4–6 inches beyond the edge of the box, so that a blanket can be tightly stretched and secured to provide warmth and avoid a chill from the cold floor. The soft blanket covering the bottom should be used only with this type of whelping box because its weight holds the blanket securely in place. (If a puppy crawls under the blanket, there is great danger that the mother will not see it when she lies down.) The blanket edges can also be taped to the outside of the box to ensure their drum-like tightness. Besides warmth, blankets will make the whelping box more comfortable and encourage the dam to spend more time with her puppies, improving nutrition and helping to maintain body temperature.

The budget whelping box shown in Figure 22-6 is made from one 4 × 8–foot piece of plywood cut into four 2 × 4–foot pieces. Again, instead of a floor, the box rests on larger piece

Table 22-3: *Teratogenic agents.*

Agent	Suspected Teratogenic Effects
Nutrients	
Asparaginase (ProZyme, KZyme)	Skeletal, brain, lung, kidney defects
Calcium excess	Aortic arch defects
Niacin deficiency	Fetal death
Riboflavin deficiency	Cleft palate; short mandibles; skeletal defects; extra toes
Thiamin deficiency	Fetal death
Vitamin A excess	Skeletal, neural tube defects; cleft palate; no eyes; microcephaly
Vitamin A deficiency	Cleft palate; diaphragmatic hernias; heart defects; hydrocephaly; fetal death
Vitamin C deficiency	Fetal death; premature birth
Vitamin D excess	Cleft palate; heart, skeletal, dental defects; mental retardation; increased fetal/neonatal death
Vitamin E deficiency	Hydrocephaly
Vitamin E excess	Cleft palate; growth retardation
Zinc deficiency	Cleft palate; hydrocephaly; defects of skeleton, eyes, lungs, nervous system
Antibiotics	
Acromycin	Cryptorchidism
Antimycin A	Cardiac anomalies
Chloramphenicol (Chloromycetine)	Neural tube defects; diaphragm defects; cleft palate; cryptorchidism
Chlorotetracycline (Aureomycin)	Skeletal defects; hypertension in offspring
Penicillin	Rapid neonatal growth; no defects
Streptomycin	Hearing loss
Tetracycline	Stunting; skeletal anomalies; cleft palate; cataract
Other Drugs	
Aspirin and Other Salicylates	Hydrocephaly; palate, facial clefts; eye, rib, vertebral defects; stillbirths; low birth weight
Corticosteroids	Cleft palate, lip; intrauterine death; umbilical hernias; decreased immunoglobulins
Dilantin	Cleft palate, lip; cardiac, digital anomalies
Phenothiazines	Neonatal respiratory distress; increased neonatal mortality
Phenylbutazone (Butazoladin)	Possible embryotoxicity
Sulfonamides	Skeletal, dental defects

Agent	Suspected Teratogenic Effects
Anthelmintics (Worming Preparations)	
Dichlorvos (task)	Multiple abnormalities
Diethylcarbamazine (Caricide)	No established teratogenic agents (some suspected)
Telmintic	Embryotoxic, teratogenic effects
Piperazines	Safety not established
Nemex	No known teratogenic effects
Vercom paste	Increased abortion; fetal abnormalities
Vermiplex	Cleft palate; growth retardation
Pesticides	
Captan	Crooked tails; hydrocephaly; open fontanelles
Carbaryl (Sevin)	Multiple skeletal, internal organ abnormalities; extra toes
Cyclodiene (Aldrin, Dieldrin)	Multiple defects; webbed feet; cleft palate
Diazinon	Enlarged fontanelles; missing teeth
Dichlorvos (flea collars, wormers)	Multiple abnormalities
Fenthion	Decreased birth weight
Mirex	Decreased litter size
Rotenone	Neural tube defects; growth inhibition
Warfarin	Skeletal anomalies; blindness; fetal death
Oxytetracycline (Terramycin)	Brownish discoloration of teeth; cryptorchidism
Miscellaneous	
Dehydration	Cleft palate (up to 28% of litter)
Hyperthermia (fever)	Central nervous system, skeletal, eye defects; microcephaly; mental retardation
Insufficient oxygen	Structural, functional abnormalities
Parvoviruses	Locomotor incoordination; hydrocephaly; dwarfism; mental retardation; behavioral abnormalities; skeletal, dental defects
Pine needles (ingestion)	Decreased birth weight; fetal death; abortion
Potato blight	Neural tube defects
Vaccines	All modified live viral vaccines are potentially teratogenic

of plywood that extends beyond the sides. One or two sides may be hinged so the mother can easily enter by walking.

Choices of the place to set up the whelping box are often limited, and the most vital factor to consider is being able to provide a uniform temperature of 85°F at all times. Whenever there is a choice of whelping locations (the box can be moved later), other factors may influence the decision: stairs, drafts, privacy, access to an outdoor exit, convenience of monitoring puppies, and controlling access to the rest of the house. Carpeting poses a special problem because the bitch's discharge during and shortly after whelping will permanently stain carpeting, and carpeted areas should be safely covered with heavy newspaper on top of plastic drop cloths.

The temperature of the floor of the whelping box should be a primary deciding factor, especially during the first week and particularly for a winter delivery. To prevent chilling, if the bottom of the whelping box rests on a concrete or tile floor, be sure to provide a thick, insulating layer of plywood or cardboard, with an additional layer of tightly stretched blankets secured outside the edges of the whelping box. Be very, very careful about doors that open directly onto the whelping box. Try sitting in the box to see whether there is a draft. Be especially careful of floor drafts—they are killers. It may be necessary to seal windows with duct or masking tape or to cover them with clear plastic. Little things that may not seem important can make the difference between a live puppy and a dead one.

An environmental temperature of 85°F in the whelping box can be provided in a variety of ways. Heating pads give the most convenient warmth, and they should always be set at the lowest temperature (some controls are very sensitive and can be accidentally turned off or turned to a higher setting, and they should be checked frequently). When a human-grade heating pad is used, the fabric cover should be sewn shut to prevent puppies from crawling inside. The best heating pad for puppies is one designed originally designed for swine and now marketed for canine nurseries, with a preset low temperature, a chewproof cord, and a waterproof heating element impregnated in the plastic.

Infrared heat lamps must be suspended by a chain (never by the electrical cord) at least 4 feet above the whelping box. The heat should be off-center to allow the mother and puppies to move toward or away from the heat. Never mount heat lamps on the side of a whelping box—some breeders have learned through tragedies; they can be dislodged when the bitch gets in and out of the whelping box and start fires. The stability and size of oil-filled radiator-style heaters may be useful alongside the box and provide a more diffuse type of ambient warmth for the entire room. Portable electric heaters may, however, present a hazard—beware of those that do not automatically turn off when tipped over.

Figure 22-5: *Whelping pool.* (a) A plastic wading pool is very inexpensive, easily cleaned, and portable. The round shape is often preferred by the expectant mother. Additionally, since it is so easily relocated, it allows the bitch to spend those early anxious hours, and even delivery time, with her human family. **(b)** Since most Weimaraner bitches expect the puppies to be part of the family also, the wading pool can be easily moved to a location that allows the dam to perform her maternal duties properly and still stay connected to her people. Once the puppies are delivered and the whelping box cleaned, a large blanket can be draped over the pool and a second pool used to snugly hold the excess blanket underneath the first. The second pool also adds some stability to the sides and provides some additional draft protection. However, by 2 or 3 weeks, puppies will easily escape this whelping box.

Other Equipment and Preparations

One of the most important preparations to make is to have a rough idea how many puppies are expected. The breeder should have notified the veterinarian ahead of time and established a rapport and emergency plan around the time of the bitch's breeding; however, an X-ray 5–7 days before delivery will be provide the best opportunity to re-

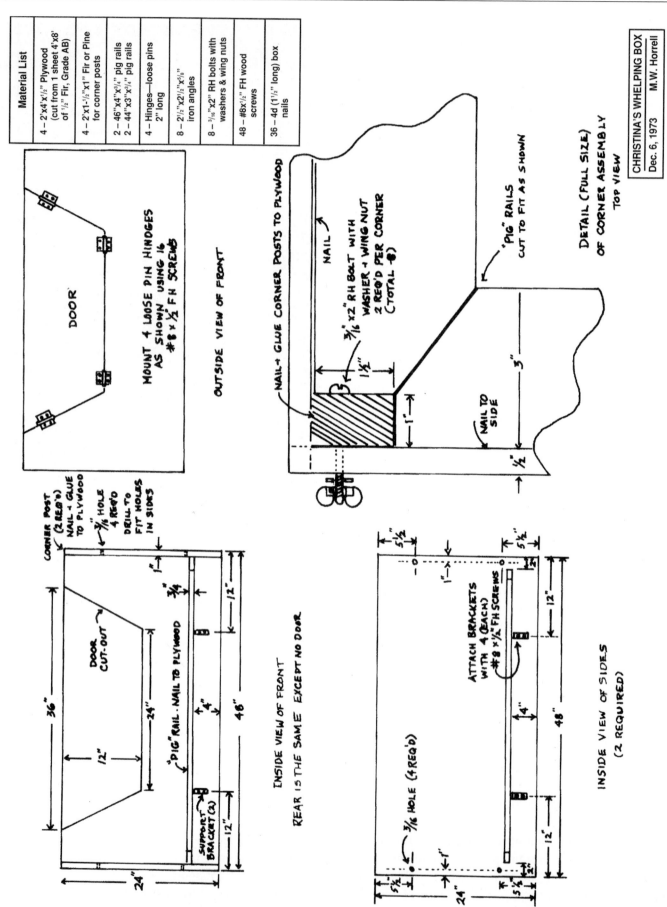

Figure 22-6: *Plans for a deluxe whelping box.*

establish the connection and confirm a contact procedure in case of emergency. A single side-view X-ray will confirm the bitch's pregnancy and give an estimated number and size of puppies. Although many breeders' experiences show that it is not unusual to have more puppies than predicted by X-ray, avoid the temptation to take multiple X-ray views to attempt to get an exact number, as it is an unnecessary additional expense and stress on the mother-to-be. This would be the time to get two pitocin shots, pre-loaded with the appropriate dosage, to have on hand when the breeder's call to the veterinarian mandates their use. Also get some extra 1-cc insulin syringes (needles removed) from the veterinarian to provide fluids to newborn puppies during the first vital 24 hours after birth. Remember to have all necessary supplies on hand a week or more prior to delivery; this is the time to check expiration dates and purchase fresh Nutri-Cal® or Pedialyte®, which will help supply the much-needed fluid intake to facilitate a speedy delivery.

When traveling with the bitch within 4 or 5 days of delivery, it is wise to have an extra person, a drop cloth, and a roll of paper towels in the car in the event that stress or excitement precipitates an emergency delivery.

Soft towels are ideal for catching and stimulating newborn puppies; eight to 10 old Turkish hand towels will probably be sufficient. When it is obvious that whelping is imminent, fill the washing machine with cold water and add a cup of BIZ® and a little laundry detergent. As each towel or blanket becomes soiled, drop it into the machine and turn on the agitator for a few seconds. This prevents permanent stains and leaves the towels fresh and clean for their next use.

Some breeders prefer the disposable convenience of paper towels and have 23 rolls of high-quality, extra-large paper towels on hand for the big event. While waiting for delivery, tear off three or four towels at a time and fold neatly in preparation.

Start saving newspapers as soon as the pregnancy is confirmed. A simple way to avoid messy stacks that fall over is to unfold the newspapers, make a half-inch stack of open sheets, and then fold the stack into quarters, making bundles that can be neatly stacked. Discarding all the unusable flyers and odd-sized pieces substantially reduces the stack, and messy access areas to the whelping box can be changed in a fraction of the time.

Figure 22-7: *Bottomless budget whelping box.* Note that the box itself has no bottom, but is placed over a larger piece of thick, insulating plywood. The layer of blankets, tightly stretched over the oversized plywood base, provides additional insulation from deadly floor drafts and prevents a puppy from getting underneath or inside the folds of the blanket, where it could be smothered or accidentally injured.

A layer of two or three blankets is usually enough to keep the floor under the whelping box warm and cozy; have at least two or three sets in order to keep ahead of the laundry. They may be old and ragged around the edges, but they should not have any holes that a puppy can crawl through. Select blankets that offer some texture to afford puppies a better "grip" for nursing and for learning to crawl. The blankets should be large enough to extend far enough beyond the plywood so the edges can be taped or securely tucked under to prevent the dam from pulling the blanket loose by scratching or digging.

An "incubator" is needed to keep the puppies warm when the bitch is about to deliver another puppy or for the pontoon system referred to in *Whelping.* The best is a cardboard filing box with handling holes on the sides for ventilation; however, old aquariums have also been used by breeders, as long as they have a ventilated top to keep the warmth in and prevent the mother from attempting to join the puppies in the restricted space. A heat source will be needed to provide the necessary warmth. Hot-water bottles must be shielded from direct contact with the puppies by inserting them in a sock or other material. Pedialyte® bottles are especially useful, as their square shape reduces rolling and even allows puppies to perch on top of them for warmth. ThermaCare™ heat wraps, when properly shielded in a knotted sock, are a boon to a weary breeder as they last a full 8 hours without requiring electricity. It is necessary to be sure that whatever heat source is used in the incubator, puppies have an area to which they may crawl that is away from the heat source if they become too warm (panting and reddening of the tongue, ears, and gums are indicators that puppies are too warm).

A spiral notebook ensures that all the information is kept together. The cover is a handy place to jot down the phone numbers of the veterinarian and emergency clinic. Attach a pen to the wires with a string. Begin the log with the dates of breeding and confirmation of pregnancy. As the whelping date nears, add notes about the bitch's temperature and behavior. Whelping notes with description of contractions, time of delivery, and whether or not the placenta was delivered are all items that may be invaluable for a veterinarian if things do not progress normally. Later, the notebook serves as a useful daily log for observations, puppy identification, weights, growth, behavior, and so forth that, no matter how tattered, may be saved as a record for the litter.

Do not forget to sterilize a large plastic crate, which can serve as a portable, emergency whelping box. Its familiarity and seclusion may be comforting during the first stage of labor. Access to a landline phone or cell phone enables the

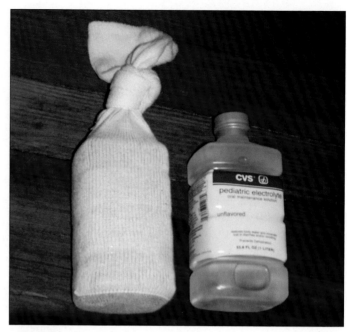

Figure 22-9: *An improvised heat source* is made by filling an empty Pedialyte® bottle with hot water and covering it with a heavy sock. The square shape prevents the bottle from shifting position. These are conveniently available since the breeder will likely have a few empty bottles left over from pre-partum ministrations to the mother.

Figure 22-8: *The maternal instinct of the bitch will draw her to comfort her pups if they cry.* When using a whelping box in conjunction with an incubator in the execution of the "pontoon system" as described in *Newborn Period,* the bitch must be supervised as she may smoother the pups in the incubator if there is not a sturdy ventilated top protecting the whelps not being nursed at that time. The best solution is vigilance or crating and resting the bitch between feedings.

breeder to talk with the veterinarian or mentor without leaving the room. Keeping the cell phone fully charged will ensure that it will be available until the end of a difficult delivery.

Because of the usual loss of appetite and the importance of energy during labor, plan some tempting treats. Have several full tubes of NutriCal®—a highly concentrated and appetizing nutrient formula that comes in a tube—on hand, as well as some raw hamburger or boiled chicken. Pedialyte®, when flavored with Nutri-Cal® or liver or chicken broth, will encourage the fluid intake necessary to keep the dam's energy supply up to the demands of delivery. For the humans involved in the drama, lay in a 5-day supply of frozen dinners.

Figure 22-10: *One breeder's snug solution* for a litter whelped in the kennel in the winter is a large produce box (used to transport watermelons or pumpkins) with one side cut down to give the bitch access. With newborn pups, the floor is lined with a cut-to-fit plywood board, under which the blanket can be safely tucked. After 3 weeks, more convenient bedding material can be used; here, snug-fitting, easily replaced layers of cardboard boxes beneath a soft blanket provide insulation from a cold floor. The handle holes or seams allow the cord to pass through for a kennel-safe warming pad, but otherwise should be taped closed. The door cutout was saved and taped back in place when the puppies got large enough to crawl out. Photograph by Julie Brooks.

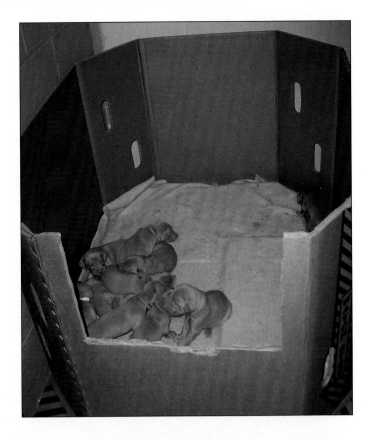

Figure 22-11: *Do not be surprised* if a maiden bitch displays unusual behavior. Some will simply curl up in a ball, refuse to eat, become antisocial, or hide away. Others will race around, shredding any material available, and stealing and nurturing toys. A sudden display of frantic behavior may indicate that delivery is imminent, so it is wise to have all preparations completed well ahead of time. Too often, a bitch with this type of frenzied response, in the absence of a vigilant breeder, may well deliver her first pup unexpectedly, even in the middle of a darkened backyard, without anyone, the bitch or the breeder, ever realizing what has happened. Photograph by Harry Giglio.

Figure 23-1: *Most newborn Weimaraners have ripple coats;* the zebra-like stripes range from faint to crisp, but all disappear within a few days.

CHAPTER 23

WHELPING

Whelping the litter and caring for the puppies through the first 72 hours are the most critical phases of breeding. Going to bed as a bitch goes into labor and getting up to find seven or eight live, gorgeous puppies that are not in trouble is a dream, but unfortunately not a very realistic one.

Those who believe in "natural whelping" and do not give the bitch any assistance often lose several puppies in each litter—and sometimes the bitch.

The natural whelping philosophy makes no allowance for the fearful inexperience of a maiden bitch, a transverse presentation, an oversized puppy, sheer exhaustion toward the end of a large litter, or puppies that may have been in the birth canal a long time and need help to start breathing. Too often, the bitch is blamed for the dead puppy, for having a defective maternal instinct, when the true culprit is an indifferent breeder.

The fancier who has a bitch worthy of breeding and has invested in a proper stud dog is foolish to jeopardize the welfare of the bitch—whether her first or third litter—and the puppies by trusting instinct to cope with every crisis that can arise during whelping. The breeder arranged for the pregnancy; the breeder should stay with the bitch during its consequences. Those not willing or able to put forth this much effort really should not breed dogs.

Care of the Bitch During Labor

Watching and Waiting

Canine gestation averages 63 days, but normal, healthy litters have been whelped from 56 to 70 days after a single mating.[1] The two guidelines for multiple matings are (a) estimate the due date from the first breeding and (b) estimate the date from the breeding preceding a decreased willingness to stand for the stud. Since there is no way to be sure when the eggs were actually fertilized, these dates are just estimates and not hard-and-fast rules. Some breeders report that some bitches are routinely early or late in their deliveries; a bitch that was late on previous litters may be late on future litters. The veterinarian may also be able to provide input on any

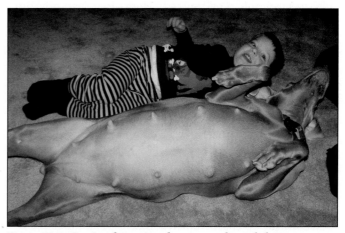

Figure 23-2: ***During the anxious hours preceding whelping,*** expectant mothers expect sympathy and pampering—and usually get it.

possible variation from the estimated date based on the number and size of the pups when the pre-delivery X-ray is taken.

There is no consistently reliable way to predict the onset of labor, but monitoring the bitch's temperature and watching for the characteristic drop usually gives some forewarning. On the 56th day after the first breeding, begin taking the temperature in the morning and evening, as well as any time the bitch will be left alone for more than 2 hours. Although this guideline is not infallible, it may be useful. Sometimes the bitch's temperature may not drop at all, or it may drop so suddenly and labor ensue so quickly that the breeder may be caught off guard. Despite considerable individual variation, the following pattern is quite typical:

- Normal: 101°F–102°F
- Preparatory phase: gradual drop from normal to 99.6°F–100.4°F degrees, where it may fluctuate for as long as 1 week
- Onset of labor—abrupt drop to 97°F–99°F, 2 to 24 hours before the onset of observable contractions

Notify the veterinarian when the temperature drops—this is when good rapport pays off—to find out whether he or she will be available after the clinic closes. If another veterinarian will be taking calls or it is necessary to go to the emergency clinic, a copy of the bitch's detailed health records may be priceless. Use the cover of the notebook to record the phone number and address for the alternate veterinarian and clinic, so it will be quickly available. Be sure that the location of the emergency clinic is known in advance; this is not a time to get lost.

If the temperature has not dropped and there are no signs of active labor by the 63rd day, a veterinarian should be consulted. There are many reasons why a bitch may not go into labor. In most cases, it is simply the fact that delivery dates can only be estimated. More often than not, puppies are just waiting for full development from a late fertilization. Occasionally, only prompt veterinary intervention can save the viable puppies. In all cases, after the 63rd day check with the veterinarian, and if a sonogram is available, determine whether the puppies are just waiting for the right moment or are in need of rescue.

Weimaraner bitches show a wide range of normal response to a whelping box. An experienced mother may avoid it or may hop right in and stay there most of the time until the puppies arrive. Maiden bitches and experienced mothers that avoid the box should not be forced to stay in it—once the puppies arrive, they normally accept the box readily.

Several days before whelping, the bitch may exhibit increased nervousness and carry toys or other objects from one place to another. Nesting behavior is manifested by restless digging, tearing, and rearranging material in the whelping box or any secluded, den-like area. Absence of nervousness or nesting behavior, however, does not mean that whelping is not imminent. Every breeder has at least one tale of the bitch (usually a maiden) who approached them with a worried expression, gave a grunt, and delivered a puppy.

When restlessness and nesting behavior are observed, place newspapers, an old towel, or a piece of blanket in the whelping box and encourage the bitch to "nest" in the whelping box instead of a secluded closet. Covering the top of whelping box with a blanket at this time may make it more appealing to the bitch that is instinctively looking for a dark, enclosed, den-like area.

Most litters are born at night. According to one theory, this is because most breedings are done during the evening hours. The more probable reason, however, is that dogs have some control over labor contractions and, whenever possible, hold them off until the quiet, safety, and privacy of the night.

The appetite may drop sharply, and some bitches do not willingly eat anything for 1 or more days before whelping. Frequent, small meals of low-bulk, concentrated rations, such as boiled chicken and unflavored Pedialyte® with a small amount of chicken or liver broth added, are almost invariably accepted and ensure optimal physical reserves during labor and delivery.

The onset of active labor is preceded by the "breaking of the water," a sudden gush of clear fluid, occasionally confused with incontinence. The breeder can differentiate between incontinence and water breaking by the bitch's response. When the water breaks, the bitch will instinctively begin to groom herself in preparation for the delivery. This attention to her rear end will continue either with grooming, or concerned looks as labor shortly develops. If the fluid is urine, she will not try to groom herself. Although this event may be missed by the breeder, the bitch's behavior is a tell-tale sign that the water has indeed broken. Active labor ensues with panting and then shivering, which gradually spreads over the entire body. After a period ranging from 30 minutes to 8 hours—or even more—observable contractions begin. This is an extremely important phase and in every way be should be a private time for the bitch; while the breeder should keep a sharp eye on the bitch, he or she should keep strange people and other dogs away.

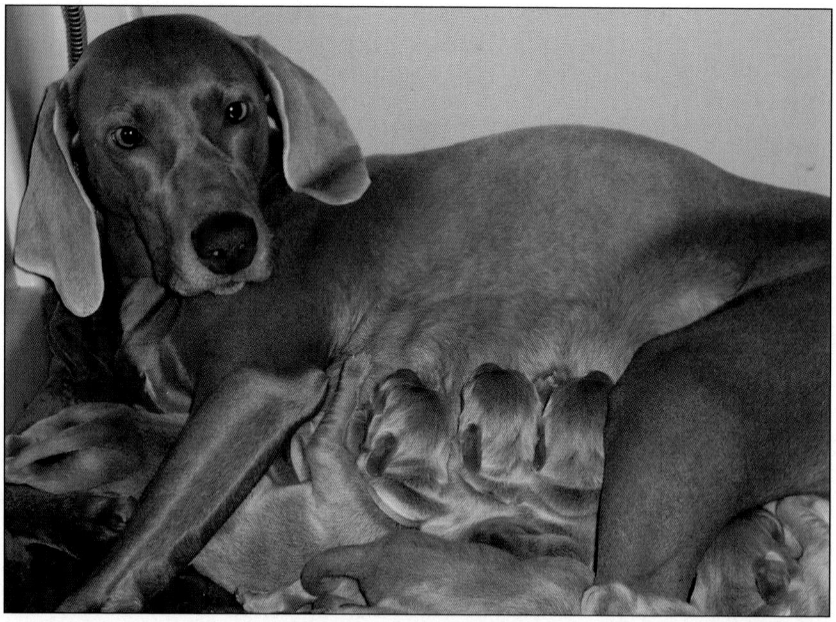

Figure 23-3: *A size 500 crate (400 is too small),* with the door removed, makes a convenient temporary whelping box. For many bitches, the den-like quality offers greater security, while the close sides may make pushing out the first puppy, or a difficult delivery, easier. Be prepared to quickly remove the top portion as soon as the first puppy is about to be delivered. This bitch is not exhibiting genetic strabismus (crossed eyes). Who wouldn't be cross-eyed after delivering 9 fat babies in 6 hours?

The birth canal is fully dilated with the birth of the first puppy, which is usually the one to be most stressed and to have fluid in its lungs; later ones usually arrive more easily. Rest periods between births range from less than 5 minutes to as long as 3 hours. Hard contractions preceding the delivery of a puppy last from 5 to 30 minutes. If hard contractions, with straining and bearing down every couple of minutes, continue for more than 1 hour, contact the veterinarian. Call the veterinarian immediately any time the bitch appears to be in difficulty, or if more than 3 hours elapse without a delivery and it is apparent that there are more puppies. Keep notes that include the time and description of the bitch's behavior because the pattern helps the veterinarian identify impending problems.

Setting the Scene

Labor proceeds best in a private, secluded environment with one or two assistants whom the bitch knows and trusts. As soon as a stranger arrives, the bitch often slows down or stops labor. It is ideal to have two people for assistance in an emergency and so that at least one will be awake through a long night.

Anxiety and distraction not only prolong labor but also inhibit the flow of milk and increase the risk that the bitch will injure the puppies as a result of her nervous behavior.

Privacy does not mean leaving the pregnant bitch alone outdoors when there is the slightest possibility that she is in, or could go into, labor. Go outdoors with the bitch, observe her closely, and walk her on lead, even in a fenced yard.

This is one of the times that a flexi-lead may be necessary, providing the bitch with a greater sense of freedom but allowing the breeder control and contact; the well-prepared breeder will also be armed with a towel and a flashlight—just in case.

When whelping is imminent, Weimaraner bitches, particularly maidens, may refuse to stay in the whelping box until after the first puppy arrives. Simply limit them to the room with the whelping box while allowing them to go in and out of their crate (with the door removed). It is not always obvious that the bitch's water has broken, but the release of the

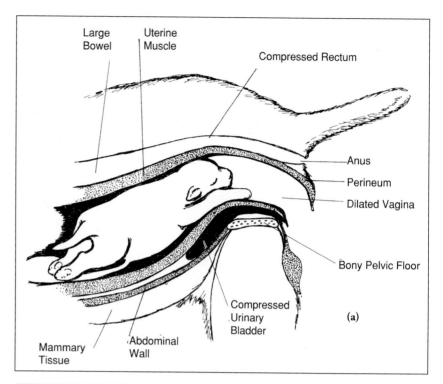

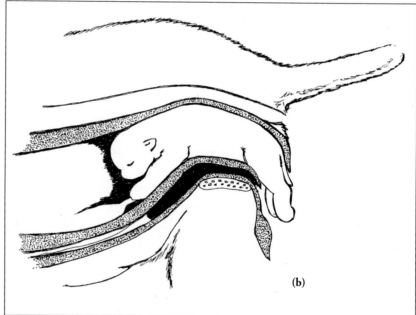

Figure 23-4: *Normal fetal presentations.* (a) head first or **(b)** breach; both are acceptable.

amniotic fluid usually results in the bitch's natural response to frequently look back at her nether regions and groom her genital area more frequently. At this point, never leave the bitch alone. This is when the breeder will appreciate a comfortable chair or cot and a good book. Television or music may mask the subtle sounds of a bitch preparing for delivery; a baby monitor may be tempting at this time, but again, the subtle sounds may not be picked up by the transmitter.

It is convenient if the bitch finds the den-like quality of a plastic crate comforting, especially if she refuses to settle into the regular whelping box.

During the early stages of labor she may feel the confines of a crate gives her better purchase for pushing. Once the first pup has been delivered it takes only a few moments to remove the top section to provide a cramped but adequate delivery area for the bitch that has refused the whelping box. If the bitch avoided the whelping box earlier, after the placenta has been delivered and the puppy cleaned and is attempting to nurse, most bitches will forsake the crate once the puppy is relocated to the whelping box. Later, if the labor seems slow or if she seems to be having a difficult time, move her back into the crate so that she can push against the sides and obtain maximum benefit from each contraction. Be sure to allow a puppy or two in the crate with the dam to provide comfort as well as to stimulate contractions; eagle-eyed observation is necessary so that a puppy can be swiftly removed as soon as hard contractions recommence in order to avoid potential injury to a nursing puppy.

Observation is vital with a maiden bitch because the mothering instinct has not been triggered. Her uncertainty and confusion about what else to do with the strange, wriggling, squeaking object is frequently obvious. One Weimaraner bitch ran from her first puppy, circled the room, whirled, and went on a solid point.

The bearing-down contractions feel like imminent defecation, and fear of an accident in the house or the whelping box can cause a great deal of mental distress. Babe, for example, whelped six of eight puppies outdoors, behind a bush, in the middle of winter, because she was so fastidious and failed to realize that she could bear down in the whelping box. Poor Babe spent nearly her entire labor desperately wanting to go outside where she could let those labor contractions rip.

The breeder's presence, reassurance, and approval of nurturing behavior helps to reinforce the bitch's maternal instinct. The onset of the nurturing instinct can be observed as the scent, movement, and sound of the puppy stimulate curiosity, interest, and desire to lick the wet object. The bitch may flinch and watch suspiciously as the puppy touches her and latches on to nurse, then gradually relax as she realizes it is a pleasant sensation. Rarely, over-possessive behavior develops: "These are mine!" If it is going to occur, it will usually appear during the first 24 hours.

Measures to Facilitate Labor

Brief potty breaks, coupled with encouraging the bitch to lie down on the opposite side from her previous position when she returns to the whelping box, are the most effective ways to facilitate speedy, uneventful delivery of the entire litter. The change in position and activity help move the puppies down the uterine horns and sometimes improve the puppies' position for entering the birth canal before the bitch is exhausted and the puppies weaken.

Walk the bitch on-lead and carry a towel just in case a puppy slips out. Exercise the bitch in a well-lit area, or be sure to carry a bright lantern at night—it is difficult to hold a flashlight and assist the bitch at the same time. If she starts to deliver a puppy, help her by standing close enough to offer physical support and hold the collar while pressing firmly on her arched topline each time she strains with the contraction. This provides balance and stability so that she does not fear falling over and fight the contraction.

When a portion of the puppy emerges from the vulva, let her complete the contraction and expel the puppy. Using the towel, grasp the presenting part and gently ease the puppy out of the bitch toward her belly so that it does not drop roughly to the ground; continue this pressure to encourage delivery of the placenta at the same time. While racing back to the house, wrap the puppy in the towel, with the head downward; quickly free the head from the membrane and clear the nasal passages. The umbilical cord can be clamped once everyone has returned to the house.

Several measures can facilitate delivery in the whelping box. Make the bitch changes position frequently; turn her from one side to the other every 15 minutes or so. If a puppy is lodged in a transverse position at the opening of the birth canal, this change in position facilitates a change of presentation to one that allows the puppy to enter the canal. Do not force the bitch to lie down if she wants to sit or to stand. Her contractions in these positions are often even more effective. When the bitch is lying on her side, she can bear down more strongly with her feet braced in a corner or against the breeder's legs if sitting in the box.

Pituitary oxypitocin (POP) is a hormone that stimulates uterine contractions. Pitocin has no effect at all if one or more of the biochemical components that stimulate normal contractions—such as calcium—are absent.

Pitocin is never used early in the game when the bitch is still fresh and having strong and effective contractions and the puppies are near the opening of the birth canal. Later puppies must work their way down the uterine horns, the bitch becomes tired and relaxes with the nursing puppies, and the contractions become less frequent and less forceful. Late in the delivery, when only one or two puppies are expected, is the time that pitocin is most beneficial. If more than 3 hours have passed without a puppy or signs of active labor, contact the veterinarian.

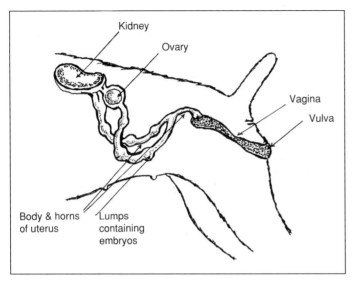

Figure 23-5: *The bicornuate uterus.*

It is a fairly common practice for veterinarians to give experienced dog breeders several syringes with pre-measured doses of pitocin to have on hand for whelping. This privilege must be earned! The veterinarian must have confidence in the breeder's experience, responsibility, and judgment. The veterinarian should be contacted each time the breeder feels that pitocin may be indicated so that the veterinarian can validate the need or, perhaps, decide that the bitch should be examined to determine whether a Cesarean section is advisable. If a puppy is lodged across the opening of the birth canal, pitocin will not only fail to bring it down but also in large, repeated doses can rupture the uterus, as well as causing fetal anoxia and partial or complete placental separation.

A standing position will allow maximum benefit from the very powerful pitocin-induced contractions, so take the bitch outside immediately after giving the medication—it acts within minutes and lasts only 10–15 minutes. Taking the bitch outside may allow the bitch to give in to the "need to defecate." Several effective pitocin-induced contractions bring the next puppy into the birth canal or expel a placenta that is blocking the way.

Fluid Intake and Nourishment

The bitch should be encouraged to drink and—if at all possible—eat something. Most refuse to eat anything during labor and delivery. Nevertheless, nourishment raises the blood sugar and gives the bitch extra strength and pep to complete the task.

Have small balls of raw hamburger or boiled, boneless chicken ready when the bitch goes into labor and allow them to warm to room temperature. The balls should be tossed near the bitch's hindquarters shortly after the time of delivery. The instinct to eat the placenta prompts even the most finicky bitch to gobble up the offering.

Prior to labor, dissolve 1 tablespoon of NutriCal® in a tablespoon of hot water, then mix with 1 cup of Pedialyte®. Offer this to the bitch between the delivery of each pup. NutriCal® contains glucose, which is absorbed directly from the stomach and reaches the bloodstream within 5 minutes, providing instant energy, and simultaneously provides additional fluids. The bitch becomes quite weary toward the end of delivering a litter, especially if it is a large one. Additional NutriCal® prior to the delivery of the last couple of predicted puppies may give her the extra energy needed to push out those puppies without resorting to pitocin.

Since adequate fluid intake aids an effective delivery, Pedialyte® will help maintain electrolyte balance during the enormous physical effort and stress of labor and delivery. If the bitch is reluctant to drink the NutriCal® mixture, try replacing it with a hard-boiled egg yolk, or chicken or liver broth in several cups of unflavored Pedialyte®; ideally, she should consume between 2 and 4 cups during delivery.

Delivery and Care of the Puppies

Sequence and Presentation

Canines, as well as other mammals that normally have multiple births, have a bicornuate (Y-shaped) uterus. Puppies are arranged in rows like peas in a pod, although the number in each horn may not be the same. A study by van der Weyden and associates found that 75% of the time, the first-born puppy is from the horn with the greater number of puppies. There is a tendency (78.2%) for the puppies to be born from alternating horns.[2]

In dogs, both head-first and feet-first presentations are normal. Jones and Joshua reported that 40% of the puppies in their study arrived feet first; van der Weyden and associates reported that 43.8% arrived feet first.[3] The feet-first presentation rarely causes any problems, although the breeder must sometimes give assistance to free the head and start clearing the lungs as soon as possible. The greatest concern is that the puppy may attempt to breathe before the head is free and may aspirate (inhale) amniotic fluid; the tell-tale sign is a gurgling sound or "snuffiness" when the puppy is held close to the ear.

Delivery

The Puppy

Delivery is usually preceded by a spurt of amniotic fluid when the sac breaks or tears as the puppy enters and passes

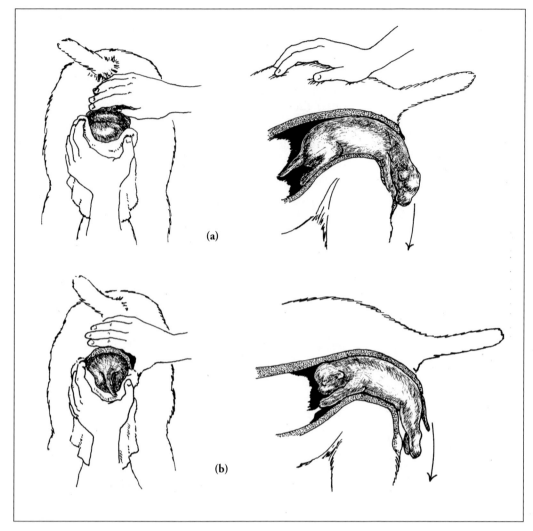

Figure 23-6: *Manual extraction of a puppy:*
(**a**) Anterior presentation. (**b**) Posterior presentation.

down the birth canal. The puppy descends slowly with each contraction and the perineum bulges, indicating the presence of the head or feet.

If the puppy is not expelled with several contractions after the presenting part appears, grasp the body gently but firmly with a towel and ease the puppy downward with each contraction toward the mother's belly, not directly outward. If just the legs are within reach, grasp only one leg. Tilt the shoulders or pelvis and try moving the puppy from side to side to free it. It sometimes helps to "grease" the puppy with KY® jelly (a watersoluble lubricant) on the sterile glove, reaching inside as far as possible.

When you are unable to free a puppy with the bitch in the whelping box and an assistant is available, stand the bitch on any floor that provides secure footing (or take her outdoors). It may be helpful if the front feet are significantly elevated to take advantage of gravity; additional lubrication may

also be helpful. The assistant holds the collar to give support and stability and pushes down on the top of the back with each contraction. Grasp the puppy with a towel and apply slow, steady traction in a downward direction with each contraction (if she has any) while pushing up and back on the perineum with the other hand.

Contact the veterinarian immediately if these efforts do not free the puppy within a few minutes. Sometimes, the veterinarian can "talk" the breeder through the delivery by explaining how to manipulate the puppy to free it and, if necessary, decide how long to try before bringing the bitch to the clinic.

As the puppy emerges, the typical Weimaraner mother frenziedly licks the fluid and bites at the cord. Encourage the dam to focus on the puppy and not the cord, a cord that is severed before the delivery of the after-birth may retract inside the bitch and impede expulsion of the next puppy.

If necessary, break the membrane covering the head. Encourage the mother to do the rest of the cleaning to stimulate bonding. The most important thing to remember is not to be in a hurry to do anything more than carefully break the membrane over the puppy's head as soon as the head or entire body is free.

If breathing and moving vigorously, the puppy may safely remain attached to the cord, and the wriggling stimulates delivery of the placenta. Minimize tension on the cord as much as possible. Experts disagree about whether or not such tension can cause a hernia unless there is a pre-existing umbilical weakness; however, there is little question that cord tension can make the difference between a minor hernia that

Figure 23-7: *Labor and delivery—Nanny's story.*

(a) In the first stage of labor, Nanny curls up, tight muscles indicating the discomfort of contractions that are dilating the cervix; the contractions can be felt by placing a hand on the bitch's abdomen.

(b) Panting and shivering, Nanny checks her rear nervously before her breeder encourages her to get up and change sides.

(c) The sharp arch in the back is typical of the second stage of labor, as the puppy enters the birth canal and the stronger contractions are visible.

(d) Nanny relaxes as the contraction passes and pants from exertion and anxiety.

(e) Nanny's tail arches during a contraction, and she pushes with her hind feet and groans as she bears down. The vulva begins to bulge as the puppy nears the exit.

(f) Pressure within the birth canal breaks the fetal sac, releasing a spurt of amniotic fluid mixed with blood. Bracing and pushing with her hind legs, Nanny bears down with the contraction.

(g) The presenting part appears.

(h) Halfway out, it can be seen that this is a posterior presentation.

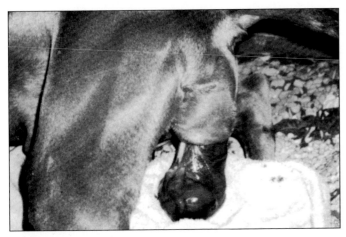

(i) Still in the sack but almost out, the puppy drops onto a towel that will absorb the remaining amniotic fluid.

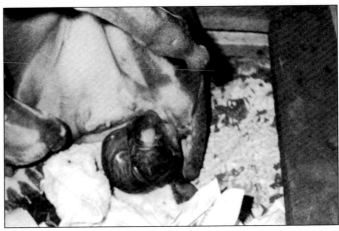

(j) Nanny reaches toward the puppy to break the sac. At this point, many breeders assist the bitch because it is vital to free the head for the puppy to take its first breath.

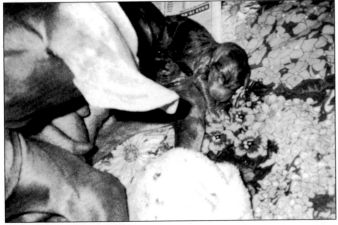

(k) Sac broken and puppy breathing, the cord remains intact as this unusual Weimaraner mother waits quietly for the placenta to be delivered.

(l) Cleansed and partially dry, the newborn begins searching for nourishment, and bonding begins.

(m) Still touching her firstborn, Nanny's tightly curled posture suggests another puppy may be on its way. With the birth canal stretched by the first puppy, subsequent deliveries are usually easier.

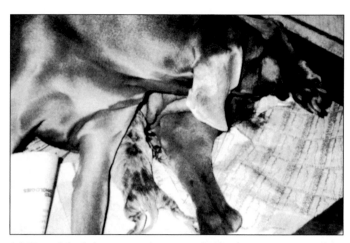

(n) Nanny's body language indicates another birth is imminent, and the second puppy soon arrives.

(o) Nanny rests her leg on the pig rail to allow access to the rear nipples. With less perceptive mothers, the leg can be elevated with a roll of paper towels.

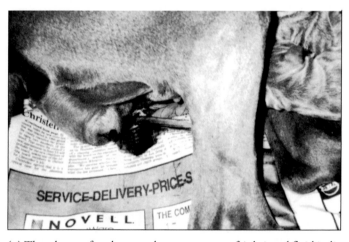

(p) Three hours after the second puppy, a spurt of red-tinged fluid indicates another puppy has entered the birth canal.

(q) With this unusually calm mother, the breeder allows the puppies to remain as the third one crowns. Nevertheless, the incubator is within reach, and the breeder is ready to snatch the puppies to safety if Nanny begins to thrash around with delivery—the cause of most newborn injuries.

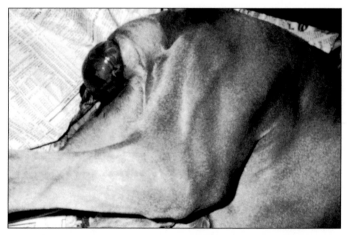

(r) With the birth canal stretched by the earlier puppies, Nanny does not need to bear down with this easy, headfirst delivery. A bitch, especially a tiring one, may benefit from additional leverage if someone will sit or stand in the box and allow her to brace her feet against their legs.

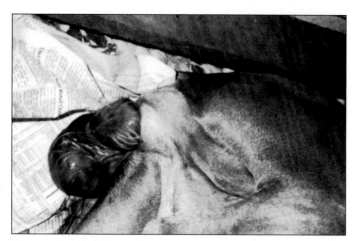

(s) Now, the shoulders.

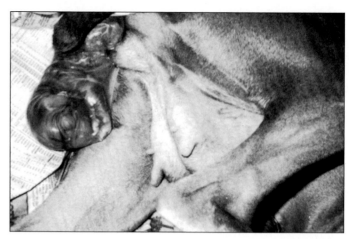

(t) All but the hind legs.

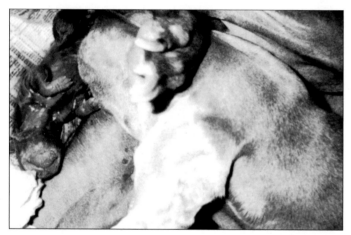

(u) Nanny reaches to remove the membrane, licking the puppy to stimulate breathing.

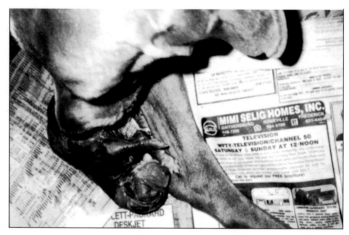

(v) The puppy remained limp and failed to breathe, and the breeder stepped in to help. It took 4 or 5 minutes of vigorous stimulation before the puppy was safely breathing.

(w) Coat dried, the puppy's pink nose indicates it is out of immediate danger. Such problems are not unusual with long intervals between puppies, and without help, this puppy would have died.

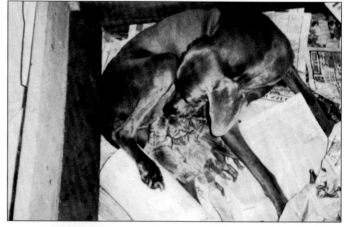

(x) Now there are three. Note Nanny's leg resting on a roll of paper towels. Nanny's next puppy did not come as easily, and her story is continued under "Complications of Whelping."

closes spontaneously within a few months and one that requires surgical repair.

Clamp the cord with forceps about an inch from the puppy's body, place the second set of forceps an inch farther, and shred the cord with your fingers. If the mother is too active to permit this, hold the cord with your thumb and forefinger about an inch from the puppy's body and encourage her to bite the cord. Then, concentrate on the puppy's breathing as described in "Immediate Care of the Puppy."

The Afterbirth

Although the immediate welfare of the puppy is the primary concern, it is possible to combine it with delivery of the placenta (afterbirth) if things are going smoothly. Whenever possible (and here is where an assistant is valuable), try to deliver the placenta with each puppy.

Ideally, the placenta simply slips out with the puppy. If the placenta is not delivered within a few minutes, grasp the cord with a piece of paper towel and attempt to ease the afterbirth out with firm, steady pressure. If the cord appears to be shredding, grasp it closer to the vulva. The trick is to maintain steady, light tension and pull gently toward the abdomen with each contraction.

Although undelivered placentas usually slip out later to be quietly eaten by the bitch, it is important to keep a count of each one delivered for many reasons:

- Undelivered placentas impede the delivery of later puppies

- When palpating for puppies toward the end of whelping, it is difficult to differentiate between puppies and placentas; if all placentas are accounted for, the mass is obviously a puppy

- If not delivered at all, placentas may be a source of later infection

Some literature recommends letting the bitch eat the afterbirth, which contains important hormones, but some advises against it. In reality, the bitch usually manages to eat it several despite efforts to stop her, but eating too many placentas has a laxative effect. The bitch can be distracted with a hamburger ball while the breeder removes the afterbirth.

Immediate Care of the Puppy

If the bitch lies quietly, the puppy may remain attached to the cord while breaking the membrane to free the head and stimulate breathing.

Shred the cord immediately if the puppy is having respiratory difficulty or does not appear to be alive. Wrap the

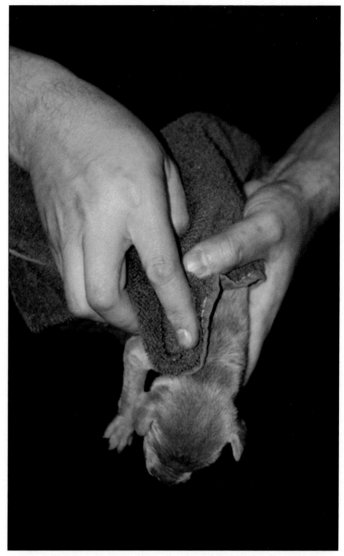

Figure 23-8: *If the puppy does not immediately begin breathing,* a quick, firm pinch of the sensitive upper lip area (above the mouth and right below the nose) will often facilitate the initial gasp. If the puppy does not begin breathing or breathing is irregular, encourage vocalization by holding the head downward, and massage vigorously with a terrycloth towel. The rubbing not only stimulates circulation, but assists in draining of fluid from the lungs. Wipe away any fluid that appears to prevent the puppy from expelling the liquid. A few robust cries indicate that the puppy has probably cleared the fluid and established a respiration pattern.

puppy in a towel for a secure grip, tilt the head downward to aid fluid drainage, and stick a finger down the throat to stimulate a gag reflex to initiate breathing. Wipe the mucus from the mouth and nostrils, and as soon as the puppy breathes, wipe away any bubbles on the nostrils. This procedure may need to be repeated. After the mucus is cleared from the puppy's mouth, concentrate on the breathing. Supporting

Figure 23-9: *"Swinging" a puppy.*

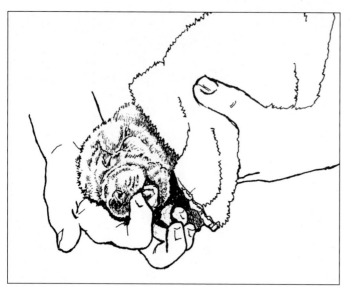

(a) Clear any fluid from the puppy's nose and mouth, wrap the puppy in a towel, and hold firmly with the head downward. Stand with the legs straddled, inserting an index finger into the mouth to stimulate the gag reflex and open the airway; provide additional support to the head and neck.

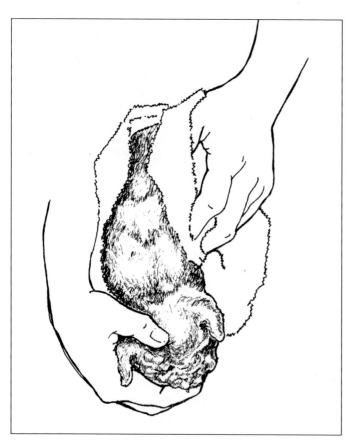

(b) Keeping a very secure grasp with both hands, supporting the head, hold the puppy at arm's length and swing hard, in a downward arc between the straddled legs. Repeat three times. Attempt to stimulate the gag reflex again and immediately wipe away any fluid from the mouth and nose. If no response, alternate with artificial respiration.

the puppy on the breeder's legs, with the head pointing downward, rub vigorously with a rough towel to stimulate breathing and circulation, as well as to get the puppy warm and dry. Use a paper towel to blot any fluid that drains out, and keep the airway clear. If bubbling sounds can be heard when holding the puppy's chest to your ear, try "swinging" the puppy, which is an effective way to clear the deeper respiratory passages. With the puppy wrapped in a towel, insert an index finger into the mouth and support the head with one hand while holding the body firmly with the other. With the puppy at arm's length, swing it in a downward arc. Remove any fluid from the nose and mouth with a paper towel after one or two swings.

Amniotic fluid is normally clear and colorless, and greenish black discoloration of the fluid or stains on the puppy's coat are caused by meconium (the tarry, blackish stool of the newborn), which indicates that some has been expelled during descent through the birth canal. When stained fluid precedes or accompanies expulsion from the birth canal, the puppy may have prolonged difficulty breathing if any meconium, which has a thick, tarry consistency similar to crude oil, got into the lungs. Check the color of the tongue frequently. If it is not a healthy pink, take action immediately. Rub the puppy briskly, head downward, with a rough towel. Whenever a puppy is not breathing strongly and regularly, do not hesitate to pinch the loose neck skin hard enough to make the puppy squeak. Each squeak indicates a vigorous inhalation that expands the lungs and circulates oxygenated blood to the brain.

A crying puppy is a live one!

Resuscitative measures often may get a very still and apparently dead puppy going. Check the gag reflex and the color of the tongue. As long as the tongue is pink and the body warm, there is a good chance of saving the puppy. Clear the nose and mouth of fluid. Cradling the puppy as shown in Figure 23-10, cup a hand over the nose and mouth and puff gently twice to inflate the lungs and expand the ribcage. Press rhythmically on the rib cage 15 times to circulate the oxygen. Repeat this procedure for as long as the tongue is pink; many a puppy that would have been given up for lost starts to breathe with this help. These instructions are not intended to replace formal instruction on canine CPR and artificial respiration, which are suggested for all dog owners, and can be obtained through most local Red Cross offices.

When the puppy is breathing strongly, trim the cord to about an inch. The cord circulation ceases shortly after birth, and umbilical bleeding is rarely a problem. Nevertheless, when time allows, remember to tie the cord as close to the

Figure 23-10: *Every breeder should take a Canine First Aid and CPR class.* If rough rubbing or swinging does not stimulate breathing (and result-ant vocalization), begin artificial respiration. **(a)** Cup the hand around the muzzle and give two gentle puffs, watching for the lungs to expand. **(b)** Follow with 7–10 quick, light compressions to circulate the oxygenated blood. Continue alternating with rough rubbing every few minutes and artificial respiration as long as there is color to the tongue and warmth to the body.

abdomen as possible—dental floss works very well for this. Even if it is a few hours after birth, it is thought that this may prevent small "bubble" hernias later (see Figure 28-8). Swab the umbilical stump with Betadine® or alcohol.

Management

Between Puppies

As soon as the puppy is breathing strongly, check the weight and identify it in one of the ways described below. Records should include the time of delivery, gender, iden-tification, placenta delivered or not, and general condition. Slip some dry newspapers under the bitch, and place the puppy with the mother for its first meal.

If the puppy was not delivered in the whelping box and the mother has still not accepted the box, use her interest in the puppy to coax her into the box and lie down with the new arrival. If necessary, place the bitch in the box and gen-tly but firmly force her to lie down. Give the new mother reassurance, and encourage her to clean the puppy as shown in Figure 23-12. While the puppy nurses, persuade the bitch to eat and drink by presenting her with food and water while she is lying in the whelping box.

When no further arrivals appear imminent after the puppy has nursed, transfer the puppy to the warmed incu-bator (the bitch should get up and follow), and change the newspapers. With everything under control, it is time to put a lead on the mother and get busy walking to stimu-late contractions.

Figure 23-11: *Resuscitating the stillborn pup.* If initial efforts at artifi-cial respiration do not produce an immediate response, the breathing reflex may be stimulated by pinching or pricking the upper lip of the neonate with a needle; inserting a rectal thermometer into the rectum has also produced a breathing response. These efforts should be alternated with the procedures outlined in Figure 23-8 through Figure 23-10.

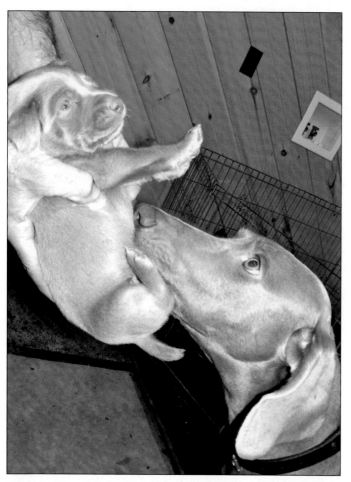

Figure 23-12: *To acquaint the mother with her new duties* and aid the blossoming of maternal instinct, encourage her to clean the puppy by presenting the parts that need her attention. This will be repeated during the first several weeks before and after the puppies nurse. Cleaning of the ano-genital areas is necessary to stimulate the elimination reflex in newborn puppies.

Walk for 4–5 minutes, return to the whelping box, reversing the mother's position, and let the mother continue getting acquainted with her offspring. One or two nursing puppies will also aid in stimulating contractions.

Intervals between puppies grow longer as whelping progresses. Take the bitch for a 5-minute potty break every 20–30 minutes until the next puppy arrives. If unproductive labor continues, using a sterile glove, apply some K-Y® lubricant just inside the vulva; encourage the bitch to assume a different position, such as sitting or standing to hopefully move the puppy to a more favorable position in the birth canal. If these efforts fail, and no puppies are delivered within an hour, contact the vet for guidance. It is also good to consult with the vet if labor appears to have ceased for several hours, and it is known that there are additional pups.

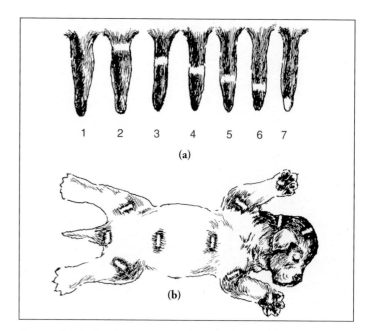

Figure 23-13: *Patch patterns of identification.*

Figure 23-14: *Colorful potholder loops* are flexible and inexpensive, offering eight colors in each package. Nylon loops are more durable than rayon loops.

When the next puppy appears to be coming, the first should be quietly placed in the incubator to avoid accidental injury while the mother is occupied with the delivery. After the newcomer is safely delivered, the first may be returned to the mother while the newest arrival is dried, weighed, identified, and placed at the breast.

Identification

All gray puppies look alike, and unless each puppy is clearly identified, there is no way to keep track of individual condition, vigor, and growth. Even white markings are not foolproof because small ones are easily overlooked while the puppy is wet or may show up several days later. As novices soon discover, nail polish and iodine rarely last 24 hours.

Weimaraner breeders have worked out a variety of marking methods, and the choice is a matter of personal preference.

Cutting a patch of the newborn Weimaraner's hair with scissors leaves an area of distinctly darker gray. Varying the location of the patches is an excellent way to identify each puppy.

One patch pattern is to cut the hair on the tail near the base. The next puppy of the same gender is marked a little farther from the base. Before tail docking, each puppy is identified with a colored collar made of pot holder loops or yarn.

Another pattern uses patches on different parts of the body—top of the head, withers, middle back, tail base, right and left shoulders, and so forth. These patches last until the hair grows out. If renewed before disappearing, they prevent later mixups if the colored collars come off.

The stretchable nylon loops used to weave pot holders make excellent little collars. Most hobby shops sell packages in a rainbow of colors.

Collars of colored yarn are popular and can be put on any time after whelping. They must be checked daily and changed every few days because puppies rapidly outgrow each one.

When the puppies are large enough, they can be identified with small collars. Many breeders use cat collars, punching extra holes and taping long ends. The QuickKlip® collars are safer and easier to use. The adjustable length (from 4 to 9 inches) can be made smaller than cat collars, there are no ends to worry about, and few puppies outgrow them before 7 weeks.

Figure 23-15: *Fetal malpresentations.*

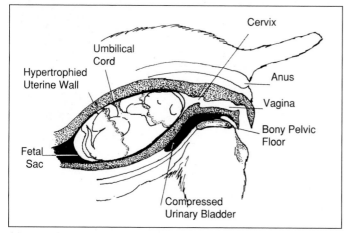

(a) Ventral position.

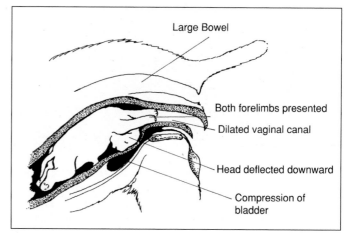

(b) Downward flexion of head and neck.

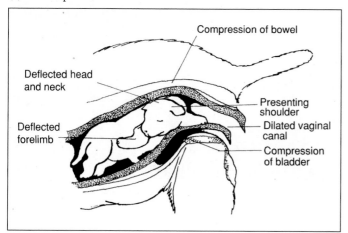

(c) Head and foreleg laterally deflected.

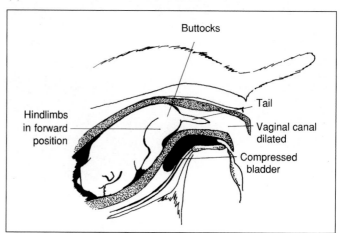

(d) True breech with tail and buttocks presenting.

Complications of Whelping

Visiting the Clinic

If problems occur and veterinary services are necessary, try to persuade the veterinarian to make a house call initially. Traveling stresses the bitch, usually stops contractions, and may interfere with maternal bonding. Also, moving the bitch and puppies can be logistically challenging.

If a trip is unavoidable, be sure to protect the car upholstery with large pieces of plastic. It is best to have a second person to monitor the bitch and puppies during the trip. Take along towels and everything else needed to deliver a puppy en route as well as the heated incubator to transport the litter as well as any new arrivals. In addition, take some-

thing to read and eat, which helps to pass the time while waiting at the clinic should the breeder be prohibited from accompanying the bitch during examination or treatment. If possible, avoid entering the clinic by requesting the bitch be examined outside in a less threatening environment.

One possible danger is the possibility of picking up an infection at the clinic. The bitch may carry organisms home on her feet and breasts from the sick dog that just left the waiting room or examining table. On returning home, immediately bathe the perineal area and breasts with diluted antibacterial soap, dipping the feet into the solution, as well. Rinse her thoroughly. If possible, finish with an all-over rinse because any remaining soap may discourage the puppies from nursing and could make the puppies sick.

Figure 23-16: *Complications of labor and delivery—Nanny's story continues.*

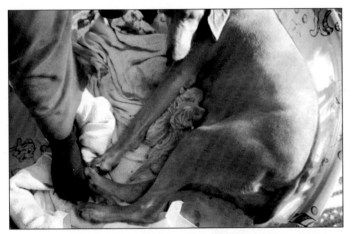

(a) Nanny was moved to a new whelping box (a small child's plastic wading pool) to give her better back support during her contractions. Nanny's breeder provided additional support by placing her foot in a convenient position for the bitch to brace her paws against, aiding the strength of the contractions. In spite of several strong contractions, no puppy was delivered.

(b) Nanny was taken outdoors in the hope that exercise would aid her labor or shift the puppy's position in the birth canal. The upright, couching position of elimination may sometimes encourage delivery. Since no additional puppies appeared, the veterinarian was once again called; to avoid the chance of stopping Nanny's labor, he made a house call.

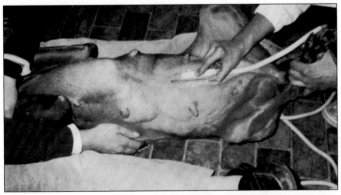

(c) After a shot of pitocin failed, the vet decided to take her to the clinic for a sonogram. The sonogram is a non-invasive procedure that may indicate the presence and vigor of any remaining living puppies through the fetal heartbeat. In this case, no life could be detected, and it was determined that there were several dead puppies present.

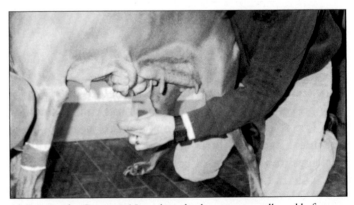

(d) Prior to the Cesarean, Nanny's vital colostrum was collected before any anesthesia or antiseptic wash was used. One final, but unsuccessful, attempt was made by the vet to remove the pup manually by lifting Nanny's front end and allowing gravity to assist. Nanny came through the surgery without any complications.

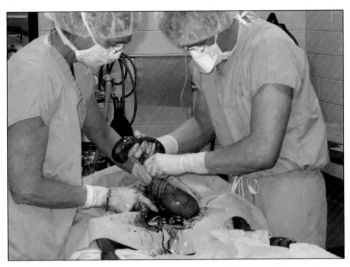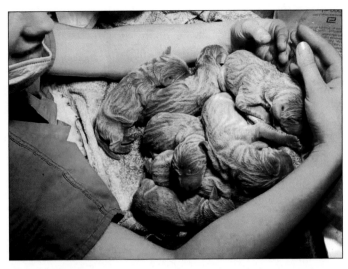

Figure 23-17: *A well-timed C-section may be the best solution* for an aging dam or a bitch with a past history of complicated deliveries. After the consideration of the mother's health, the second most important factor is the timing of the procedure. Since breeding dates are often spread over several days, the actual fertilization date is impossible to determine; proper timing of a Cesarean-section greatly enhances the survival rates of the litter. It is wisest to wait until the labor commences on its own as long as fetal monitoring indicates the pups are vigorous. This gives the bitch the opportunity to naturally birth if possible, but be prepared to intervene under the following conditions: if fetal monitoring indicates distress, more than three hours pass between delivery of puppies, if a puppy is obviously malpresented or the dam is in distress. If labor fails to commence within one or two days after the calculated due date, and a sonogram or x-ray confirms the pregnancy, begin progesterone testing immediately as test results usually take at least one full day.

Abnormal Labor

Abnormal labor—dystocia—is the most frequent complication of whelping. Maternal causes include pelvic malformations, pelvic fractures, poor muscle tone, hormonal imbalance, and insufficient calcium; fetal causes include being oversized and having an abnormal presentation. The effects of age, obesity, and number of litters have not been established, although they probably play a role. Fortunately, the most common cause of dystocia is simple exhaustion after an unusually large puppy or toward the end of a large litter. Often, a period of rest and some nourishment for energy, followed by pitocin, often do the trick.

Dystocia from poor muscle tone is uncommon in younger dogs that have maintained good condition through regular training and exercise, although a large litter may challenge an older matron or a less fit younger dog.

Sometimes, a malpresenting puppy can be manually manipulated into a position that permits normal delivery; if not, a Cesarean may be unavoidable.

If the bitch has already had a large litter and an X-ray confirms one remaining puppy, several factors must be considered. If the last puppy is confirmed dead, it will probably be naturally expelled within 24 hours; if, however, the puppy is viable, veterinary supervision and patience may be the wisest course. Potential complications from surgery may jeopardize the bitch's welfare and survival of the other puppies. If there are multiple puppies remaining, reasons for an immediate Cesarean may include (a) if not delivered naturally, multiple live or dead puppies must be removed anyway, and (b) one live puppy usually covers the expense.

Cesarean Delivery
Preoperative Care

While the veterinarian is setting up for the procedure, collect some colostrum. After washing the breasts with clear water, milk the colostrum into a small container such as a shot glass and transfer to a larger container for storage. Most anesthetics are transmitted through the milk, which is the last thing Cesarean-delivered puppies need.

Care of the Puppies

The breeder's help is usually needed (and expected) to care for the puppies as they are delivered in rapid succession, and nearby friends rally willingly if notified that help is needed. The anesthetic often makes puppies very sleepy and depresses their breathing, and on occasion Cesarean puppies may have additional fluid in their lungs. The combination of handicaps means that the puppies require constant observation and intensive stimulation to keep them breathing.

Clear the respiratory passage, dry, and stimulate each puppy as in a normal delivery. Each cord must be clamped before it is cut from the placenta to prevent excessive blood loss. At the earliest opportunity after lusty cries indicate a proper breathing pattern, attempt to stimulate elimination and give each puppy 1 cc of colostrum one drop at a time.

Maintain a steady temperature on both the top and the bottom of the puppy. Observe the puppies at all times. It is not unusual for a puppy to simply stop breathing without warning. The advantage of being at the veterinarian's is access to Dofram, which stimulates breathing. Panting and gasping are signs of respiratory distress. Keep rubbing and pinching to stimulate breathing. Remember, every squeak of protest indicates a vigorous inhalation that expands lungs, increases lung capacity, and promotes absorption of fluid. Check the color of the tongue frequently. If it is not bright pink despite vigorous stimulation, tell the veterinarian, who may give a medication to counteract the anesthetic.

The mother should never be spayed at this time unless it is the only way to control hemorrhage and save her life. The stress of additional blood loss and continued anesthesia is the most common cause of maternal mortality.

Table 23-1: *Guidelines for breeding after a Cesarean delivery.*

Reason for Cesarean	How to Avoid Repeating
Too few puppies (one or two) to initiate labor	Insure maximum conception by motivating ovulation closely and by multiple matings Try a different stud
Oversized puppies	Breed to a different sire Decrease prenatal caloric intake Discontinue heartworm preventive during pregnancy
Abnormal position of puppy obstructs birth canal	Breed again Isolated incident that will probably not occur again
Absence of labor (at or prior to estimated delivery):	Likely mis-estimate of delivery date, wait longer before initiating C-section; consider progesterone testing to determine delivery date
Absence of labor (well after estimated delivery)	None – high risk of repeat cesarean

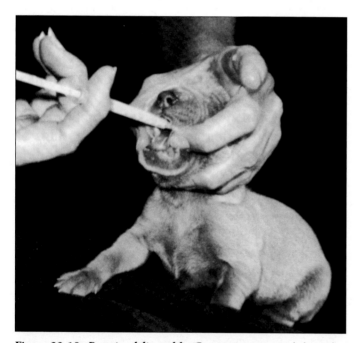

Figure 23-18: *Puppies delivered by Cesarean section* and those that have been revived or have "snuffling" or crackling sounds during respiration should not be allowed to nurse; the puppy will likely not be strong enough to nurse, and if he does, he will likely aspirate fluid. Keep these puppies in the incubator and provide 1 cc of Pedialyte® diluted 50/50 with colostrum every 30 minutes, one drop at a time on the puppy's tongue, to provide fluid and nourishment for several hours to allow the puppy to gather strength and allow the lungs to clear.

Postoperative Care

As soon as the mother is breathing well and semiconscious, put the puppies with her to promote bonding. Older barbituate-based anesthetics often resulted in frenzied anesthesia recovery and a bitch and puppies that were sluggish and "spacey" for several days. It is now common practice to use one of many excellent newer sedatives (i.e., Propofol®) combined with isoflourine gas, which result in a calmer anesthesia recovery, allowing the bitch to bond more quickly with her puppies, as well as reducing potential injuries. Do not be surprised if a maiden bitch is confused and puzzled about the presence of the squirming newcomers and needs diligent, hands-on encouragement to settle down and assume her maternal duties. Bitches that have had puppies before usually respond to them quickly. If the mother does not show a positive reaction, smear the puppies with some of her vaginal discharge to stimulate the instinct to clean them.

During recovery from anesthesia, the bitch should be turned frequently. Pinching the ears and pads stimulates breathing and speeds recovery from the anesthetic. Antibiotics are usually started immediately after surgery. Do not leave the clinic until the bitch has fully recovered from the anesthetic and is able to walk out on her own.

Due to the bitch's lethargy and lack of coordination during the first 24 hours after a C-section, it is necessary that the puppies receive assistance with feeding and elimination. Use the pontoon system to ensure that all nipples get used to prevent mastitis. Additionally, C-section puppies are less vigorous than their naturally born littermates and need extra assistance in nursing. The pontoon system reduces competition from stronger littermates. C-section puppies may appear to be nursing, but their weakened condition may prevent them from nursing vigorously and long enough to provide their needs; during the first 24 hours dilute Pedialyte® and the collected colostrum 50/50 and feed the weakest puppies 1 cc by dropper every hour or after each nursing period. Other puppies should be supplemented each nursing period with 1 cc of Pedialyte® administered directly on the tongue one drop at a time.

During this time, one set of puppies should be nursing at all times, while the others are in the incubator. Because of the mother's sluggishness due to recovery, before and after each nursing period, the breeder should wipe each puppy's genital area with a tissue or paper towel to stimulate urination. The now-warm, dampened paper towel can then be used to wipe the anal area to stimulate defecation. A repeated failure to elicit urination and defecation indicates a puppy that needs the attention of a veterinarian.

Future Breeding Plans

The question whether a bitch may ever be bred again after a Cesarean section must be carefully weighed, and Table 23-1 offers some guidelines. However, most Weimaraner bitches will have normal vaginal deliveries with subsequent litters. Whether or not the breeder plans to use the bitch again, spaying should be postponed whenever possible until the quality of the litter has been properly evaluated and the bitch has completely recovered from the pregnancy. Too often, breeders motivated by convenience or potential financial savings choose to spay during the C-section; however, the dam's weakened condition may contribute to possible complications (such as infection or reduced milk) and sadly, too often, possible mortality; a bitch should always be in the best of the health and fitness before any elective surgery.

Figure 23-19: *Mother and puppies need constant vigilance after a Cesarean section.* To reduce complications, the dam should be encouraged to take potty breaks, and her position should be alternated from side to side each time she returns to the whelping box. Until the anesthesia is completely out of the bitch's system, all puppies need constant monitoring and nutritional supplementation. The arrow indicates the incision site; although it may be sensitive, it is conveniently protected from the rooting of puppies by breasts full of milk. A clean washcloth (which must be changed frequently) can be folded into the crevice to protect the puppies if the incision oozes and to offer additional traction for the nursing puppies.

Figure 24-1: *"Early Roman Period."* First-time breeders are sometimes alarmed by the apparently deformed muzzle typical of the newborn Weimaraner puppy. Photograph by William Wegman.

CHAPTER 24

THE NEWBORN PERIOD

The first 4 days after whelping are critical, for this is when the greatest number of puppies is lost. Statistics vary widely, but one study reported that of 2,711 puppies born alive (on average, 56% of a litter is stillborn), 23.8% died within 2 weeks. Puppy mortality from birth to weaning ranges from 11%–34%. Mosier states, "Puppy mortality survey results indicate that a 60% reduction can be expected in the highest average puppy mortality with appropriate health care management."[1]

The mother and babies must be monitored closely for the first 4 days to identify developing complications while it is still possible to reverse deterioration, which is very rapid in puppies. Health issues in the dam quickly affect the puppies, so when any problem appears within the family, all must be examined carefully to treat or prevent problems. By the end of the 4th day, the puppies should be stabilized and the mother settled down to maternity routines. During this period, if there is nobody to watch the puppies while the breeder takes a nap or does essential chores, it is safest to place the dam in a crate and the litter in the incubator for a few hours.

Care of the Puppies

The "Pontoon System"

The "pontoon system" is an effective method of monitoring puppies for the first 4 days. The litter is divided into two groups that are rotated whenever they finish nursing. With a litter of four or more, the system ensures that smaller, weaker puppies have a better opportunity to nurse, and it helps the exhausted breeder identify the ones that need special help. Individually placing each puppy at the breast is the best if not the only way to be certain that each is vigorous and nursing well. Frequent observation often gives several hours'

advance warning of trouble and time to do something about it. Any puppy that does not latch on strongly, show enthusiasm for milk, and suck properly is a puppy that may be in distress in a few hours.

Divide the litter according to size and vigor—the small guys and the big bears. The small guys can be given extra attention and assistance. Their weaker attachment to the nipple is less likely to be disturbed when there is less competition and difference in strength. When the big bears are on, the small ones can safely cuddle up in the incubator without risk of crawling into a cold corner.

Most Weimaraner bitches are unwilling to change position at all during the first few days after whelping. Even after being taken outdoors, they return to the same position, lying on the same side, when they get back into the whelping box. As a result, puppies do not have access to both rows of teats. To stimulate both sides and ensure a better supply of milk, first let the little guys nurse when the teats are full; then let the big bears work for the rest, and then make the bitch lie down on the opposite side. Bitches that are accustomed to the routine soon learn to roll over at a touch on their legs.

Figure 24-2: *If mom is not available,* a healthy puppy will latch on to almost anything.

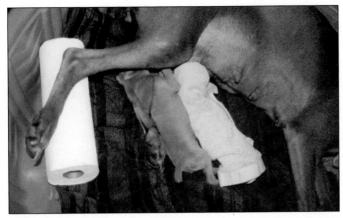

Figure 24-3: ***Weak puppies*** will have more success with individual nursing time without competition. They may find it easier to nurse while supported in a sideways position. Note that a roll of paper towels supports the bitch's hind leg to make the rearmost teat, often the fullest, more accessible.

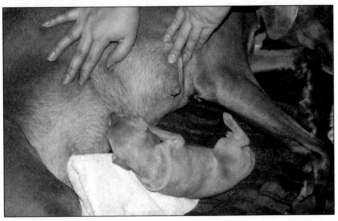

Figure 24-4: ***A less vigorous puppy may just need help*** latching on; try gently pulling the nipple outward and upward for easier access. A challenged pup may need this help frequently until he is able to manage on his own without support.

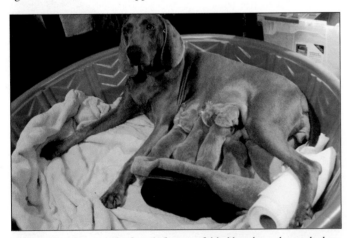

Figure 24-5: ***During the first 48 hours,*** a folded hand towel over the bottom row of nipples will give better traction and support and ensure that the puppies nurse off the top row. The bitch can then be turned on the other side, and the second set of puppies will nurse the other row. An additional rolled towel, anchored in place by a brick wrapped in a sock, provides additional support to help the puppies stay attached while nursing.

Nursing

As soon as the placenta is delivered and the dried puppy is breathing strongly, it should have the first lesson in nursing. Start the puppy on an easy teat, preferably one with a well-shaped nipple that is bursting with milk. Give the puppy a special time, 5–10 minutes, with the mother. When placing the puppy to nurse, never force the mouth open. Always allow the puppy to scoop up the nipple while you touch the side of the mouth to stimulate the sucking reflex. It helps if the teat has had a small amount of milk manually expressed first to tempt the novice nurser.

Once started, the puppies normally manage quite well, moving the alternate rear legs to slide along their abdomens, seeking warmth and nourishment. Although slow and weak, they move their heads from side to side to locate a nipple; if they are especially weak, it helps to gently stabilize the head of the nursing puppy to help them maintain an attachment.

Make sure the puppies, especially if there are less than four, nurse on all of the teats. Encourage them to use the back ones as well. The easiest way to do this is to insert a half roll of paper towels between the bitch's back legs. As long as the legs can be wedged open with the paper toweling, the puppies will be very content, and the mother will be so much more comfortable with those teats well nursed.

Puppies need good traction when nursing, something to push against with their hind legs. A brick that is covered with a sock works well—the brick should be removed when the bitch leaves the box and repositioned when she returns. When their hind legs are braced, they can "knead" the breasts more effectively with their little front paws, stimulating the release of milk.

When satiated (or too weak), puppies may lie quietly with the nipple in their mouths. To evaluate the condition, check for suction by gently trying to pull the puppy away. If sleeping, the little one will immediately begin sucking vigorously; however, a puppy that can be pulled off easily is probably not getting milk and needs help. It is sometimes helpful to place a weak puppy between two strong ones, preferably at the second or third teat. Their vigorous nursing stimulates the milk flow, enabling the weaker puppy to get more food with less effort; also begin supplementing this puppy with 1–2 cc of Pedialyte® every hour until vigor returns.

If the puppy is unable to suck or has no idea what to do, give some of the mother's colostrum to "prime the pump." Colostrum may be expressed into a shot glass by milking the breast in a squeezing fashion. Draw the colostrum into an eyedropper or insulin syringe and express one drop at a time on the back of the puppy's tongue.

Figure 24-6: ***These puppies definitely "got milk."*** When a puppy is nursing strongly, a low "glugging" noise can usually be heard. Good luck getting these guys off the nipple, whereas a weak puppy, which may or may not be getting an adequate supply of milk, can be easily pulled off. A weaker puppy can be placed between two of these stronger puppies and will have an easier time nursing as the milk flows more easily from the well-stimulated nipples on either side.

Supplement each puppy with at least 2 cc of the dam's milk or Pedialyte® every 2 hours during the first 24 hours to ensure that each has a source of energy for nursing. Newborn deaths are often a simple matter of inadequate caloric intake for energy to nurse strongly. Continue to supplement each needy puppy until it nurses vigorously—weak puppies may need help for several days.

Struggle to save that small one. Size at whelping is influenced by many things and totally unrelated to adult size, so make every effort to make sure that the little one has the best fighting chance, and it will probably be a fighter. Watch it closely, give fluid supplements, keep it warm, give it the choicest spot when nursing, and pamper it in every way.

Elimination

Newborn puppies cannot eliminate without external stimulation of the genitalia and anus until about 16–18 days old. When the groups are changed, present each puppy, tummy up, to the mother to clean and stimulate elimination (see Figure 23-12). This wakes the puppy up, leaves room for a little more food, and stirs the appetite; it will also go a long way toward preventing the possibility of staph infections and reducing odor. If the mother is too tired, disinterested, or not available, the breeder must do the job. Using a baby wipe or paper towel, simple massage usually stimulates prompt urination. Holding the tail out seems to stimulate stool elimination. Gently stroke the anal area with a moist towel for several minutes; even with stimulation, it sometimes takes a few minutes for the intestines to expel the stool. One caution, however; many nursing mothers consider it their duty to keep the whelping area clean and feel compelled to dispose of used wipes; therefore, they must be discarded in a Weimaraner-proof container—no easy task!

A puppy that is constipated (rare) is characterized by loss of appetite, crying, and a tight abdomen. Cut an infant glycerine suppository into lengthwise quarters, insert in the anus, wait a few minutes, and stimulate elimination. Wash the anal area thoroughly to remove traces of the suppository and monitor elimination for several bowel movements because the mothers despise the taste of the glycerine and sometimes refuse to clean the puppy for some time.

Concerns and Complications

Temperature

For the first 3 weeks, newborn puppies lack the ability to regulate their own body temperature and so must be provided with a warm and constant environment.

Newborn puppies are highly susceptible to hypothermia (subnormal body temperature), which may quickly progress to death. Chilled puppies usually cry and rapidly lose their appetite and vigor. As chilling progresses, the crying stops, activity decreases, and muscles become limp. The puppy's digestive tract slows, the digestive enzymes stop functioning, and milk and colostrum cannot be digested. With a chilled puppy, to avoid digestive distress, start the puppy out on Pedialyte® flavored with colostrum.

The mothers sometimes shove them aside, as if they were already dead. Puppies do not feel cold to the touch until their temperature is very low; if hypothermia is suspected, check their temperature. Normal temperature at birth is 96°F, progressing to about 100°F at 7 days. Care must be taken when taking the temperature of a newborn; a drop of olive oil is preferred to KY® lubricant on the thermometer, and the thermometer should be inserted no more than ¹/₄ inch. The body temperature must be raised gradually to avoid additional complications, by wrapping the puppy in a blanket surrounded by hot water bottles. Do not use an electric pad. Supplement with gentle massage and change the puppy's position often; frequent human contact seems to improve the will to recover and survival rates. Continue these measures until the rectal temperature reaches at least 96°F. As the temperature rises, puppies become more active and usually do quite well.

A whelping area that is too hot can be just a deadly as one that is too cold. Generally, a temperature of 75°F is ideal, however, giving the dam and her puppies a choice of finding the "just right" temperature will result in a bitch that is more willing to remain with her pups and allow the pups to seek out the spot in which they are most comfortable as well. With the pontoon system, remember that the puppies that are not nursing should be given the chance to find the most comfortable temperature as well. Puppies can be easily overheated by simply placing a lamp directly over or a pad in the bottom of the container, heating the entire area too warmly. It is preferable to place a safe offset heat source, creating a temperature gradient within acceptable ranges across the whelping area and holding boxes. These areas should be maintained at a constant temperature from below as well as above to avoid chilling the puppies with a cold floor; drafts can be the sneak thief of heat and must be carefully guarded against.

Puppies that are too warm generally cry frequently, pant, are reluctant to nurse, and often display redness in membranes and distal areas such as the webbing of the toes and

Figure 24-8: *That just right temperature* is indicated when puppies are scattered but maintain comforting contact. Puppies that are too chilly will all huddle together, indicating the need for more warmth. Puppies that are too warm will be spaced farther apart.

the flaps of the ears. Unless the pups are severely overheated, symptoms generally dissipate as soon as the temperature is returned to acceptable ranges.

Trauma and Suffocation

Trauma is a frequent cause of newborn deaths (37% in one report). Bite wounds, either deliberate or accidental when carrying the puppy, are usually inflicted by mothers that are nervous and frightened; puppies are also too often crushed by a dam leaping in or out of the whelping box. For this reason privacy, supervision, and quiet are so important during and following whelping.[2] Weimaraner bitches tend to be disturbed by every suspicious outside noise. They jump up, send puppies flying in every direction, and check every window to identify the source. Just as the puppies have recovered from the shock and crawled into a cozy pile, the mother jumps back into the box, upsetting the puppies all over again. Once the bitch gets a little expertise and confidence, this happens less frequently. It may help to move the whelping box to a more secluded room for the first few weeks. The only other measure is to drown out the alarming noises with one that is less threatening, such as a loud radio or television.

Puppies crawl everywhere. Having a pig rail in the whelping box decreases the incidence of crushed puppies. They also love to crawl into

Figure 24-7: *This puppy is about to lose his place at the milk bar...* if only his mother had been encouraged to clean him before he began to nurse. Puppies will nurse more vigorously and have more room for extra milk if the bladder and bowel are emptied before feeding.

little spaces and hide, so be careful that there is no way they can get under the bedding material. Be sure it is stretched tightly beneath the edges of the whelping box and that there are no holes or folds. The bitch is not always aware that the lump under the blanket is a puppy. If the little one does not squeal loudly enough for her to realize she is lying on it, the puppy may be crushed or suffocated.

The various ways Weimaraner bitches avoid lying on their puppies illustrate their strong maternal concern as well as their problem-solving traits. Old Countess arrived at what is probably the most efficient solution. She circled the whelping box, pushing all of the puppies into the center, chose her spot and lay down, and then nuzzled the puppies back to her side. Her granddaughter Madchen had no difficulty during the day; at night, she refused to lie down after changing her position. She would stand over the puppies and give a high-pitched whine guaranteed to wake the soundest sleeper until her owner got up, moved the puppies aside while she got comfortably settled, and then placed the puppies where they could nurse. Madchen had a talent for training owners!

Umbilical Infection

The umbilical cord dries up and drops off shortly after birth. Check the umbilicus several times for signs of redness or pus; several treatments with few drops of hydrogen peroxide diluted to half strength or a very weak Betadine® solution applied with a Q-tip® are usually all that is necessary to clear up minor infections.

Eye Infection

When presenting the puppy to the dam for nursing, observe the eyes for a grape-like, bulging appearance; usually just one eye will be affected. Without treatment, there is the potential for loss of vision. The breeder can apply a warm compress to soften the engorged area and tweak the corner of the eyelid closest to the muzzle to allow the pus to drain. A veterinary consult is recommended, as antibiotics appropriate for neonates are often necessary.

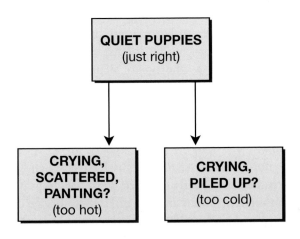

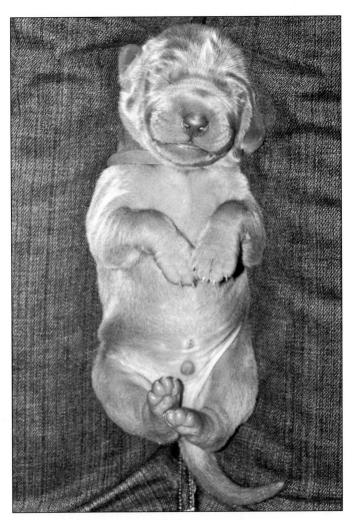

Figure 24-9: *Happiness is a warm lap....* The umbilical stump has already dropped off this day-old puppy.

Fading Puppy Syndrome

The most common bacteria that causes neonatal septicemia—the medical term for fading puppy syndrome—is *Streptococcus,* although occasionally *Staphylococcus* and other organisms have been identified. Infected bitches can transmit the organism (a) when the puppy passes through the birth canal, (b) through the milk, or (c) when licking the navel. Affected puppies are vigorous and nurse well after birth, but about 12–18 hours later, they suddenly fade away quietly. The highest onset occurs at 3–4 days, but deaths may occur up to 8 days. The only warning sign is persistent crying, and if alert, the breeder might identify the only other symptoms—abdominal tenderness on palpation and a temperature of 102°F–103°F. Untreated, puppies usually die within 12 hours after onset of symptoms. Prompt antibiotic treatment, as well as fluid replacement, of both puppies and dam is vital; puppies that survive 36 hours after onset usually recover.[3]

Shaky puppy

Hypomyelinogenesis is the failure of myelin sheath surrounding the nerves to properly develop; as a result, affected puppies lack coordination and muscular control. This condition usually begins to become apparent between 1 and 2 weeks of age (although earlier and later development have been reported). Puppies display tremors in the hindlegs first and a constant bobbing motion. Severely affected puppies will have difficulty nursing because the shaking often causes them to move backward. These puppies need supplementation. Affected puppies tend to get worse before they get better, but will generally improve, most often appearing normal by 2–4 months. As adults, they may or may not display varying degrees of the earlier symptoms. More detail on the care of these puppies is available through the WCA website (www.weimclubamerica.org/health/index.html).

Many times, the breeder is the only witness to these problems since these puppies can usually go on to lead normal lives, competing in many athletic events, including agility, obedience, and field. The breeder, however, should never forget and in spite of their unaffected appearance, these puppies should always be placed only as non-breeding stock.

Care of the Mother

Postpartal Checkup

The postpartal (after parturition/giving birth) period begins after the birth of the last puppy. When it appears that the last puppy has been whelped, if the veterinarian will make a house call, a visit at this time will allow the bitch to be examined for additional puppies and put the breeder's mind at rest. If everything appears normal, the bitch will likely be given a large dose of pitocin to expel retained placental material; the pitocin also contracts the uterine muscles to decrease bleeding and stimulate the flow of milk.

Postpartal Complications

Observation

Soon after whelping, the bitch's temperature rises to 102.5°F–103°F for 2–3 days before returning to the canine normal of 101°F–102°F. The temperature should be checked and recorded once a day if it remains within normal limits, more frequently if elevated.

During and shortly after whelping, the vaginal discharge is a mixture of blood and amniotic fluid. The blackish green fluid, which will permanently discolor flooring or fabric, is from meconium-stained amniotic fluid, which fortunately clears up shortly after whelping. This changes to a scanty, pinkish, odorless discharge that stops gradually in about 10 days. Keep a record of the discharge and bring any variations,

Figure 24-10: *Once the puppies have arrived,* the alarm clock will become the exhausted breeder's most reliable assistant to ensure that puppies are rotated regularly. The pontoon system allows the breeder to quickly identify weaker puppies and begin supplementation.

such as persistent bright blood, clots, foul odor, or pus, to the veterinarian's attention.

An elevated temperature is often the earliest sign of impending complications. In addition, anything that affects the mother's health also affects the puppies, and the first sign of illness in the mother may be her sick puppies. Do not waste time with indecision if the mother or any of the puppies become ill or listless within the first 48 hours. Consult the veterinarian immediately.

Eclampsia

Also called puerperal tetany, hypocalcemic tetany, and lactation tetany, eclampsia is caused by an insufficient level of blood calcium owing to pregnancy and lactation. The onset, which ranges from late pregnancy to early lactation, is characterized by nervousness, restlessness, anxiety, or chattering of the teeth. Progressive symptoms include dilated pupils, temperature up to 106.5°F, stiff gait, loss of muscular coordination, muscular spasms, and convulsions. The bitch usually dies unless given prompt veterinary treatment; however, if treatment is quickly initiated, the prognosis is very good.

Metritis

The bitch is at risk for developing metritis (bacterial uterine infection) after whelping. Retained placentas and dead puppies, as well as dystocia, are predisposing factors. The onset may or may not be accompanied by an elevated temperature as well as the typical depression and loss of appetite. In addition, any abnormality of temperature or discharge that lasts longer than 1 day should be brought to the veterinarian's attention.

Acid milk

The normal pH of canine milk is 7.1 (very slightly alkaline). Test the pH regularly by expressing a few drops of milk onto litmus paper (litmus and other pH indicators are carried by most pharmacies). Acid milk is not palatable to puppies;

the puppies begin to avoid the nipples with sour-tasting milk, and diminished use compounds the problem. If the pH appears to be a little high, manually express the contents of the nipple, wait an hour or two, and then present a puppy to the breast.

Mastitis

A bacterial infection of the mammary glands, mastitis is one of the most common postpartal complications. Be sure the puppies are nursing from the nipples between the front and rear legs, where problems are most common. The ones at the rear have small nipples, and puppies have difficulty maintaining strong suction, especially right after whelping, when the nipples are very hard. The nipples in front sometimes are inverted, which predisposes bitches to mastitis.

Attempt to work the inverted nipples out before whelping, and once started, a vigorously nursing puppy can finish the job. If a nipple appears hot, hard, and unused, strip the milk from the affected nipples, encourage the bitch to drink plenty of fluids, and ensure that puppies nurse evenly from all nipples in the future; if the puppies begin to lose vigor or nursing enthusiasm, or the condition does not improve, the bitch will need veterinary treatment. Any antibiotics given the bitch will be ingested by the puppies through her milk; be sure that treatments used are safe for nursing puppies.

Foster Mothers

Should the unthinkable happen and the mother is lost or unable to care for the litter, make every effort to locate a healthy foster mother (never one from the pound) for orphan litters. Veterinarians sometimes know of bitches that have just lost litters or a local organization that coordinates this. Bitches whose puppies have just been weaned are usually delighted to adopt another litter, although they may not have enough milk to feed the puppies without help. One Weimaraner raised two litters in separate whelping boxes, leaving her own puppies periodically to care for the orphans.

Experienced Weimaraner matrons often exhibit an intense desire to nurture all puppies (even young of other species), and they can be of priceless help in keeping orphan puppies warm, clean, and loved. Some even develop a little milk if at just the right point of their estrous cycle.

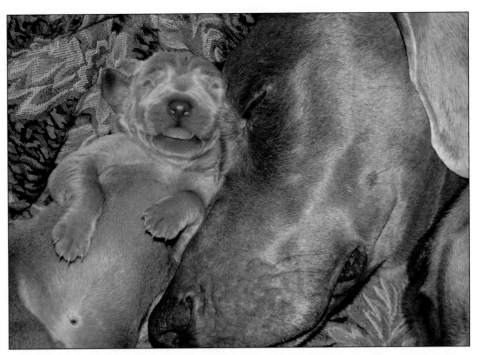

Figure 24-11: *Mom is it!* For the first 72 hours, the dam is the whole world for these puppies. Their lives depend on her continued good health and undivided attention. The breeder needs to pay as much heed to the bitch's well-being as to the puppies', providing exercise and support as well as monitoring her appetite, temperature, and attitude for changes that may indicate possible complications.

The old matrons also enjoy helping other bitches raise their puppies, and the mothers rarely object to "grandma" getting into the whelping box to help clean the puppies. The older bitches seem to believe that the mothers are not doing the best possible job, and the inexperienced ones seem to benefit from lessons on how to clean a puppy properly.

Fluid Intake and Nourishment

Many bitches refuse to drink for the first few days after whelping, and fluid intake should be monitored; an inadequate intake leads to dehydration of the bitch, decreased production of milk, and consequent dehydration of the puppies. A tablespoon of NutriCal, diluted in ½ cup of Pedialyte, four or five times a day provides fluid and restores energy. Keep a bowl of fresh water a short distance from the whelping box and offer a drink each time the puppies are changed.

Do not be alarmed if the exhausted new mother has little or no interest in food for a day or so after whelping. She may be experiencing intestinal discomfort and diarrhea from cleaning herself, cleaning the puppies, or eating afterbirth. Offer her 12 cups of fat-free cottage cheese, boiled chicken (with the fat removed), and 15–20 cc of Kaopectate® to relieve the discomfort.

Once the bitch feels more comfortable and recovers from the ordeal of whelping, her appetite becomes insatiable—indeed, she may never recover a maidenly appetite. While

Figure 24-12: ***When the birth mother of this litter in Australia*** was killed by a snake, Judy, the resident Smithfield terrier, took over a litter of 8 Weimaraner pups for Ron and Monique Cash of Silbersee Weimaraners. By the time the puppies were eight weeks old they were already larger than their surrogate mother, but Judy shows that even a small breed bitch can keep these puppies in line and meet the physical and emotional needs of a foster litter.

nursing, the mother's food and fluid intake is from two to four times greater.[4]

Breeders who have used the commercial pregnancy and lactation formulas (usually the puppy formula of the bitch's current food) without any supplements report little or no weight loss, generous milk production, and vigorous puppies. Although lactation formulas are nutritionally complete, most breeders find it necessary to tempt the bitch's appetite with high-protein treats, such as hard boiled eggs, hamburger, or even canned rations of the bitch's current kibble.

Maternal Behavior

For the first 2–3 days after whelping, the typical Weimaraner mother curls around the puppies, sometimes with a near-catatonic rigidity. Occasionally, a bitch will even refuse to allow known family members access to the puppies. Break this pattern by encouraging her to leave the whelping box for tempting snacks and to go outside for frequent exercise breaks. Upon her return, place her in a crate with a treat in a separate room while supplementing, weighing, and handling the pup-

pies. If possible, give her another opportunity for exercise outside before returning her to the box, with the puppies safely arranged in the center. Fortunately, this hormone-induced overprotective response rarely lasts more than a few days.

Occasionally, a new Weimaraner mother experiences a conflict between loyalties. Murphy, for example, had a problem. Her half-awake owner became aware of Murphy standing at the bedroom doorway, looking at the bed where she always slept—a responsibility she took very seriously. Then, the owner heard the click, click, click of Murphy's nails on the tile floor and the rustle of newspaper as she returned to the whelping box in the next room.

Almost immediately, she returned to the bedroom door, then back to her puppies, then to the bedroom, and back again. Murphy was torn between two weighty responsibilities—caring for her new puppies and caring for her owner.

Figure 24-13: ***Every new mother could use some help.*** It is not uncommon for another trusted household bitch to help care for the litter; the new mother (on the left) was reluctant to clean her puppies, so the housemate (on the right) assisted in the maternal duties. Dr. Judith Braun of von Hubertus kennel in Germany uses an inflated children's pool as a whelping box. The large size accommodates the comfort of the extended family while Judith supervises and encourages the less-than-enthusiastic dam. This also provides an opportunity to get the puppies accustomed to human contact and expose them to neural stimulation.

Suddenly, a puppy shrieked, the sounds of doggy paws neared, and Murphy landed on the bed with the puppy. Her solution to the conflict was to move the puppies to the bed where she could take care of everyone. Her owner picked up a blanket and pillow and prepared for an uncomfortable night on the floor next to the whelping box.

Although it is rare with Weimaraners, a bitch—especially a maiden—sometimes rejects her puppies. The most common cause is the complete lack of bonding that occurs through Cesarean delivery; other causes include confusion, stress, illness, and a long, difficult labor.

To encourage bonding and milk production, place the mother in a crate beside the whelping box—the sound of puppies stimulates reflex milk production. Breeders have discovered that a towel warmed in the dryer and placed over the mother's teats for about 5 minutes will also stimulate milk production. While she lies in the crate, put some of her milk on a puppy to encourage interest and licking as the puppy nurses; hold her down by force if necessary. After feeding the puppies, put the mother back in the crate for half an hour or so. Put a favorite blanket or very comfortable covering in the whelping box. Take her for a short walk and then enter the whelping box with no puppies present. Present the puppies one at a time; using the pontoon system may help the dam feel a bit less overwhelmed. When bonding occurs, she will cry to be let out and voluntarily get into the whelping box. Move the puppies so she can lie down, and adjust them so they can nurse. Bonding usually occurs within

Figure 24-15: *The first signs of dehydration* can be identified by inserting a little finger in the puppy's mouth over the tongue. The mouth should feel moist and slippery; a dehydrated puppy will feel dry, pasty, or sticky. A gradual increase of fluids, such as 1–2 cc per hour of Pedialyte, is recommended to avoid more serious complications.

24 hours. If there are any doubts about her total acceptance, put her back in the crate whenever she cannot be supervised.

Once the mothering instinct is stimulated, Weimaraners rapidly develop into great mothers, and subsequent litters are greeted with confidence and competence. They typically exhibit a strong desire to mother all puppies, even the young of other species. Matrons often demonstrate the "auntie" role typical of wild canines and help raise the litters of other bitches. If the other bitch trusts them, they lie down in the whelping box to clean puppies and keep them warm.

For a breed with such a well-developed protective instinct, Weimaraner mothers are surprisingly trusting and tolerant, rarely showing resentment when family members handle the puppies. By the time the puppies are a few weeks old, they usually permit strangers to approach the whelping box and handle the puppies without protest. The breeder must be sensitive to the bitch and use good judgment about this, however.

Tails and Dewclaws

An attractively docked tail of the correct length is an asset to all Weimaraners. Conversely, a poorly docked tail can disfigure an otherwise outstanding animal. If the tail is cut too short, of course, there is no remedy; if cut too long, the tail may be redocked, but the procedure is not without risk. The tail may not be carried with the same happy confidence as before redocking, and there is significant risk of developing a banana tail, which is more unsightly than a happily carried 9-inch tail.

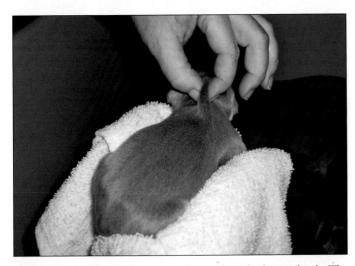

Figure 24-14: *The pinch test* is used to evaluate hydration levels. The skin on the back of the neck above the shoulders is gently pinched, tent-like, between the thumb and forefinger. If the skin is slow to return to its original position and the puppy is not nursing properly, it is at risk. Supplementation should begin immediately (refer to *Raising the Litter*) and continue until the skin responds normally and the puppy shows a strong sucking response.

Age for Procedure

If the puppies are vigorous, Weimaraner tails are routinely docked and dewclaws removed on the 3rd day after whelping. We have found, however, that fewer errors of tail length are made if docking is deferred until the puppies are 5 days old. Regardless of age, puppies should weigh well over a pound and be obviously vigorous. If any puppies in the litter have been ill (diarrhea) or died of fading puppy syndrome or other infection, docking should be deferred.

Breeders usually defer docking the tails of suspected long-haired puppies until they are 7–9 days old. The tails of long-haired Weimaraners should be either docked only two or three vertebrae or not docked at all. In a mixed-coated litter, longhairs are almost impossible to identify until they are 7–9 days old, and even then, mistakes are made. Litters in which some puppies have been docked at 4 days and others between 7 and 9 days exhibited no observable differences in healing or tail carriage.

The neural paths to the conscious areas of the newborn puppy's brain are non-functional, and tail docking and dewclaw removal are done without anesthesia up to 14 days of age. In addition, the blood vessels and nerves to the tail of the newborn are poorly developed, and there is little risk of hemorrhage.

Preparations

Measuring the Tail

The instructions in standard tail-docking tables in veterinary references specify the fractions to be removed. One reference, for example, gives the following directions: German Shorthaired Pointer, leave two-fifths; Vizsla, leave two-thirds; Weimaraner, leave three-fifths. The difference between the German Shorthaired Pointer and the Weimaraner is puzzling because the standards for both breeds call for a 6-inch tail at maturity. The real problem with all such tables is that they are based on the assumption that all puppies have the same number of tail vertebrae, but this varies considerably in Weimaraners.

To consistently dock Weimaraner tails to the correct length, each must be individually measured and marked as shown in Figure 24-18. A general guideline is that on almost every occasion, at least one-half of the puppy's tail length will be removed. Slightly too long is preferable to too short; remember that the proportions may be deceiving in tiny, newborn puppies. Most veterinarians are appreciative if the breeder marks the tails for them before arriving at the clinic.

An Orderly Departure

Start with all of the puppies in the incubator and return each to the mother in the whelping box after marking its tail so it can have a last-minute meal. If the incubator is warmed with water bottles, add fresh, warm water. During inclement weather, do not forget to take along extra new 8-hour ThermaCare® heating pads (inserted in a sock) in case of unexpected delays. Place a clean towel or paper in the incubator (for more than five puppies, prepare a second incubator). Transfer the puppies to the warmed incubator. Cover the incubator with a towel when transporting to protect the puppies from drafts and chilling and take several extra clean towels or a large blanket to cover the veterinarian's table. If the veterinarian's office is some distance from home or there is a possibility of the puppies going more than 2 hours without a meal, it is wisest to take the bitch along in case an unexpected delay occurs. She will then be able to give the puppies a nourishing meal as soon as the procedure is complete to facilitate a more rapid recovery.

Figure 24-16: *Undocked tails vary in length.*

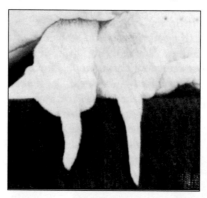 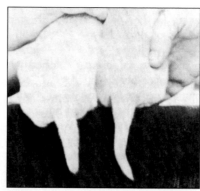

(a) Note the abrupt narrowing of the tail on the right.

(b) Kinked tails are not uncommon.

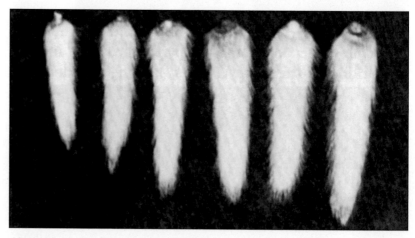

(c) Each tail must be individually measured, before going to the veterinarian, to determine the correct amount to remove. As a general rule, at least one-half of the tail should be removed.

A nonchalant departure minimizes the mother's distress. Take her outdoors for some exercise. By this time, she should be accustomed to seeing the puppies in the incubator while she goes outdoors. Avoid letting her see the empty whelping box upon her return and place her in a familiar crate in another room. She may fuss about the separation from her puppies, but with luck, she will not realize the puppies have been taken from the house. If possible, someone should remain at home with her.

If the incubator will fit, the safest place during travel is on the floor on the passenger side, where the puppies are easily observed. Shield from hot or cold drafts. The most common problem while transporting is that the covered incubator can overheat; if the car is heated, the lid of the incubator should be removed. Overheated puppies indicate discomfort by screaming and panting, with gums that are bright red. Be sure that the lid or sides provide ventilation and that there is an area to which the puppies can move that is away from the heat source.

The Procedures

The following equipment is used for both procedures: tourniquet (8-inch piece of stretch gauze or rubber tube), sharp, curved surgical scissors, container of Betadine® solution, a coagulant (such as Kwik-Stop® gel or silver nitrate sticks), Kelly® forceps, and 40 absorbable sutures on a pre-threaded curved cutting (skin) needle.

Start with the dewclaw removal as it is less traumatic and gives a good indication of the puppy's vigor and ability to tolerate the more stressful docking. The quality of the puppy's cries may be the first indication of health problems such as diaphragmatic hernia, cardiac abnormalities, or impending pneumonia.

The tail-docking procedure shown in Figure 24-20 has been consistently successful with Weimaraners. The following procedures have been tried and been proven unsatisfactory with this breed: puppy-tail clamp with no sutures; surgical glue instead of sutures; and "banding and drop off," a technique used for sheep.

Postoperative Care

While at the clinic, continue to monitor the puppies after docking for blood loss and shock. Be sure the incubator is warm and reheat the hot water bottles if necessary. Keep the car temperature comfortable; do not let it become overheated or too cold. If the dam is waiting in the car, let the puppies nurse before leaving for home.

Ask the veterinarian for some pediatric amoxicillin to have on hand in case of complications, such as infection or loose stools.

Upon arriving home, place the smallest or weakest puppies with the mother immediately. Present each one for her to stimulate elimination, being careful to discourage vigorous licking of the tail. Once these puppies have been fed, allow the others to nurse.

Infections are minimized by changing the bedding several times a day, even if it is not noticeably soiled. Some postoperative inflammation (heat and redness) is normal for the first 4–5 days. Check for the foul odor typical of infections with a sniff. Treat any infection by dipping the puppy's tail into a shot glass filled with fresh hydrogen peroxide or a very dilute Betadine® solution several times a day.

The absorbable sutures drop out in 3–5 days. Do not remove the scabs—this tears the fragile new scar tissue. Should the scab drop off too soon, while the wound appears bright red, apply a drop of antibiotic cream.

Continue to monitor the puppies' weight daily. Most show no gain for a day or two but then resume steady growth. Very rarely, a puppy has weight loss and may need supplemental feeding until it regains its former vigor.

Figure 24-17: *Comfort the puppy after the surgery.* Postpone tail surgery if **(a)** the puppy is frail or weighs less than 1 pound, **(b)** the puppy is suspected of being a longhaired Weimaraner, or **(c)** the sound of the cries during dewclaw surgery indicates a possible diaphragmatic hernia or heart defect.

Figure 24-18: *Measuring tails before going to the vet.*

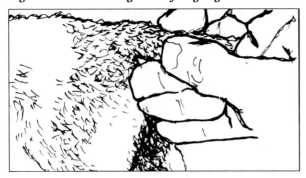

(a) Grasp the base of the tail between the thumb and forefinger, then slowly slide them toward the tip until you feel the taper point (where the tail suddenly becomes thinner).

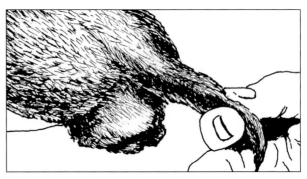

(b) Slide your fingers down at least one more vertebra so that both thumb and forefinger are holding the tail below the taper.

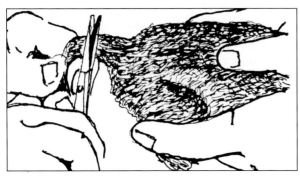

(c) Carefully clip the hairs over the taper point with sharp manicure scissors, so that a straight, clear line is visible, usually about 1¼ inches from the base.

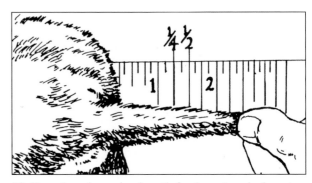

(d) Place the ruler under the tail, firmly against the base, just above the anus. Be sure the tail is straight out and in line with the back.

(e) Incorrect tail length is usually caused by pulling the tail downward over the ruler in this manner.

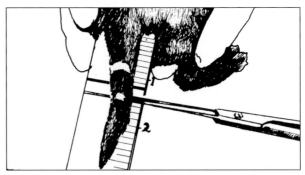

(f) With the tail stretched flat on the ruler, cut a second, straight, clear line at 1½ inches.

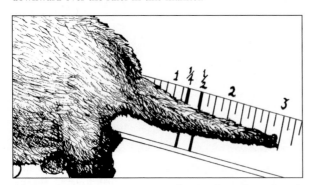

(g) It is sometimes necessary to deviate from the 1½-inch maximum length (delayed docking, croup angle, tails extra short or extra long), but be sure that the second mark does not exceed half of the tail's length.

(h) Be sure that the 1½-inch (second) mark completely covers the vulva or scrotal sac. If not, adjust the second mark so they are covered.

Figure 24-19: *At the vet's: removing the dewclaws*

(a) Clip the protruding dewclaw (first joint), removing no more skin than necessary.

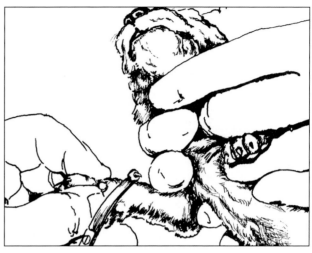

(b) Push the skin from below the cut toward the elbow so the second joint pops up, and clip at the joint. (Caution: Probing too deeply may damage tendons and nerves.)

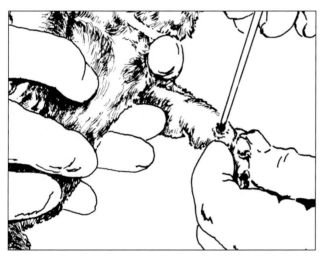

(c) Cauterize the area with Kwik-Stop® gel or silver nitrate sticks—sutures are unnecessary because so little skin is removed.

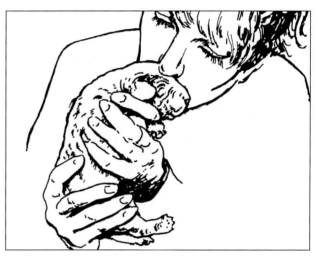

(d) Comfort the puppy. See below for reasons to postpone further surgery.

Postpone the final tail surgery if:
- the puppy is frail or weighs less than 1 pound
- the sound of the cries during dewclaw surgery indicates a possible diaphragmatic hernia or heart defect
- there is excessive blood loss during dewclaw removal
- the puppy is suspected of being long haired; surgery should be deferred until the status is determined

Figure 24-20: *Docking tails.*

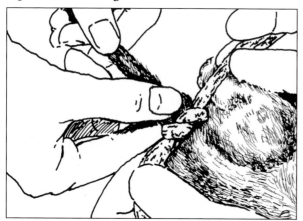

(a) Push the skin toward the base of the tail while an assistant applies the tourniquet beyond the excess skin. After docking, this extra skin will ensure that the tail's tip is loosely covered.

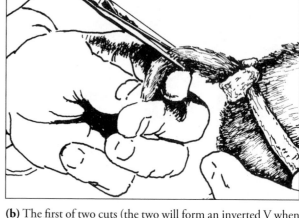

(b) The first of two cuts (the two will form an inverted V when viewed from the side) is made by cutting the skin at a downward angle from the 1½-inch mark toward the 1¼-inch mark. The cut should fall between the two markings, and it should not sever the bone.

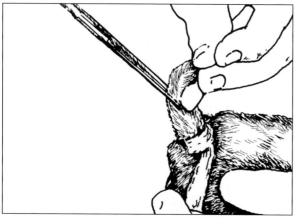

(c) The second cut is made from below the tail, starting at the same distance as the first cut, also not severing the bone. This final cut should be adjusted to meet the first cut, forming a V. If necessary, snip any remaining skin.

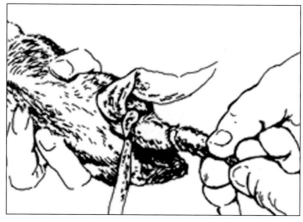

(d) With an assistant holding the puppy, grasp the outstretched tail firmly between thumb and forefinger. A quick twist is usually all that is needed to break the bone between vertebrae.

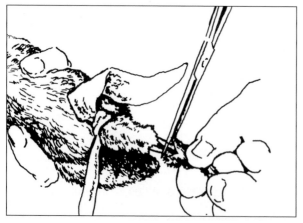

(e) Pull the tail firmly to separate the segments and to create enough space to snip the connecting tissue with the scissors.

(f) To ensure ample skin over the tail tip, remove one additional complete vertebra with sharp scissors (hooked suture removal scissors are best).

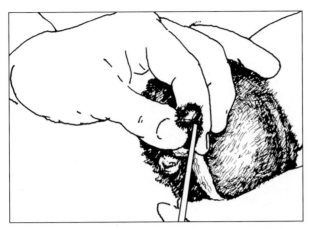

(g) Use tweezers to carefully remove any bone fragments, which would later cause discomfort or irritation.

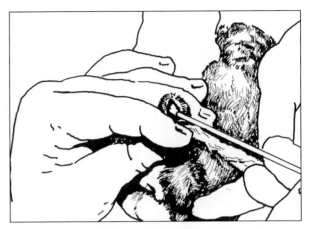

(h) To minimize bleeding, thoroughly swab the inside of the V-shaped skin pocket with Kwik-Stop® gel.

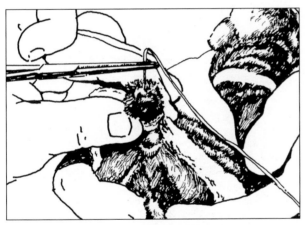

(i) Suture the flaps, stitching from top to bottom, crossing over and up. Tie with a double square knot. Cut the sutures to 1 inch or less to prevent removal by the mother.

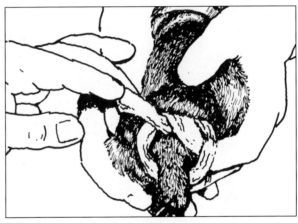

(j) Carefully loosen the tourniquet and massage the area for several minutes to stimulate circulation. If necessary, re-cauterize.

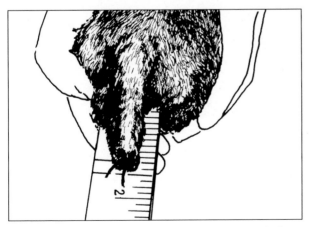

(k) With the tail flat on a ruler placed firmly against the base, just above the anus, recheck the length. Tails measuring between 1¼ and 1½ inches at docking are almost always the correct length.

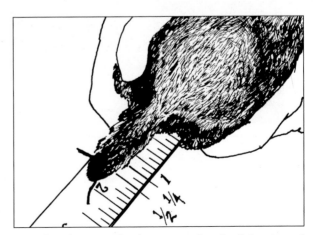

(l) Unless the reason for the excessive length of the pictured tail is intentional (such as an older puppy), it should be redocked at this time.

Figure 25-1: *Mother's Day,* by William Wegman.

CHAPTER 25

RAISING THE LITTER

Puppies grow at a phenomenal rate. This chapter discusses care and management of the dam and the simple physical management of puppies—keeping track of weight, being sure they all get enough to eat, weaning, and some of the early emotional and physical developmental needs as well.

Growth and Development

Weight at whelping is not always a reliable clue to a Weimaraner's size at maturity. The maximum size at maturity is limited by genetics. When the genes say "that's all," no amount of extra calories, protein, or vitamins can overcome that limit, and all that is accomplished by stuffing the puppy is to make it as fat as a Christmas goose, which may be detrimental to health and structural soundness. However, insufficient nutrients or illness can prevent a puppy from achieving its genetic size potential. Fortunately, puppies are astonishingly resilient. The most dramatic example is a litter that had severe salmonella infection and devastating weight loss; the best evidence that the potential genetic size was achieved is that all grew as tall as their 25-inch dam and 27-inch sire.

Many factors influence the growth and development of puppies. Some of the factors to consider when wondering whether they are the "right" size and weight include prenatal environment, gestational age, and developmental pattern of the ancestors.

Size at whelping is influenced by position in the uterus and placental nourishment. Close monitoring with supplemental feeding during the first 72 hours ensures that the smaller, weaker puppies get off to a solid start.

Gestational age is the time from the day of fertilization, not the day of whelping. A puppy born 58 days after conception is, in fact, 5 days younger than one born 63 days after conception. Between serial ovulation and multiple matings, the conceptual age of littermates often varies. The less mature puppies can be identified at whelping by brighter pink ears and feet as a result of less hair; later, their eyes open 1 or more days after some littermates. The "older" puppies tend to be stronger and nurse more vigorously, pushing "younger" littermates away from nipples and further increasing their advantage by

more rapid growth. The younger puppies often need extra help well after the first 72 hours, but with continued vigilance and supplemental feedings, they eventually catch up.

A tremendous range of normal growth and development is demonstrated by different Weimaraner strains. For example, Strain A may be characterized by large size at whelping and very rapid growth, whereas Strain B may be characterized by small size at whelping and slow growth; yet, both strains eventually mature at similar heights.

Figure 25-2: *A good rule of thumb* is that a young puppy should weigh no more in pounds than its age in weeks plus 1. Lucy, at 4 1/2 weeks, weighs in at 5 1/2 pounds—just right. Although roly-poly butterballs are the stereotypic "healthy puppy" vision, overweight puppies are prone to developmental disorders and injury, as well as slowed physical development.

Figure 25-3: *Stimulate brain development.* As early as the first few days, place puppies on new and different surfaces. Very mild stress during the first 3 weeks has been reported to increase the number of brain cells and the interconnections between brains cells in puppies. Since adult intelligence is the result of a combination of heredity and environment, careful management of the environment during the first 12 weeks will have a significant impact on the dog's future. Photograph by William Wegman.

Feeding Puppies

From Birth to 2 Weeks

Hand Feeding

Puppies have a much greater chance of survival if they have some of the dam's colostrum, which contains antibodies against common infectious diseases. If a bitch is too ill to allow the puppies to nurse or violently refuses to let the puppies nurse, milk as much of the colostrum as possible into a shot glass, transfer it to a larger container diluted 50/50 with unflavored Pedialyte®, and divide it between the puppies.

Although "mother's milk is best," breeders often hand feed newborn puppies for many reasons other than an orphan litter. After a Cesarean delivery, there is always a possibility that the mother will either reject the puppies or fail to develop enough milk during the first few days after surgery. Later, the breeder may have to step in if the bitch becomes ill.

Finally, with a large litter (the general rule is more puppies than teats on one side—all need a spot when the mother lies on either side), the breeder should consider supplementing each puppy at least three times a day with unflavored Pedialyte® after nursing. Weaker puppies and those not showing a consistent, measurable weight gain will be addressed below.

The conventional rule of thumb for Weimaraner growth is that a puppy should gain a pound a week. The limitations of this are clearly demonstrated by the wide range of growth of the five litters in Table 25-1. Although the litters from which the table was compiled are related to most major bloodlines, they are not a valid cross section of the breed because of the small sample size.

Nevertheless, the weights document the amazing variation typical of the breed: birth weights ranged from 10 to 24 ounces; 7-week weights ranged from 9 to 13 pounds; mature heights and weights are all within the standard, with little correlation to size at 7 weeks.

Table 25-1. *Weekly weight (in pounds) of five sample litters.*

	Litter	Birth	1 Week	2 Weeks	3 Weeks	4 Weeks	5 Weeks	6 Weeks	7 Weeks
Weight Range by Litter	1	1.12–1.25	1.50–1.67	2.00–2.87	2.50–3.25	3.75–4.50	5.50–6.25	7.75–9.25	9.75–11.75
	3	1.25–1.50	1.50–1.75	2.25–2.75	3.00–3.75	4.25–5.00	5.75–8.00	6.62–8.87	9.00–12.00
	2	1.00–1.25	1.25–1.75	2.25–2.75	3.25–4.25	4.50–5.00	6.00–7.75	8.00–10.50	9.00–12.00
	4	0.62–0.75	1.00–1.50	2.00–2.75	3.00–3.75	4.37–5.62	6.00–7.25	8.00–10.25	10.25–13.12
	5	0.62–0.87	1.12–1.50	1.87–2.50	2.87–3.50	3.87–5.00	5.50–7.00	7.50–9.37	9.25–12.50
Weight Range—All Litters		0.62–1.50	1.00–1.75	1.87–2.87	2.50–4.25	3.75–5.62	5.50–8.00	6.62–10.25	9.00–13.12
Weight Gain Range			0.12–1.00	0.50–1.25	0.62–1.50	0.75–1.87	1.37–3.25	1.12–3.00	1.25–3.87
Weight Median		1.00	1.37	2.37	3.37	4.62	6.75	8.50	11.00
Weight Gain Median			0.50	0.87	1.00	1.25	2.25	2.00	2.50
Weight Equivalents	0.12 = ⅛ pound = 2 ounces		0.37 = ⅜ pound = 6 ounces		0.25 = ¼ pound = 4 ounces		0.50 = ½ pound = 8 ounces		
	0.62 = ⅝ pound = 10 ounces		0.87 = ⅞ pound = 14 ounces		0.75 = ¾ pound = 12 ounces				

Sample: Stud A sired Litters 1 and 2; Stud B sired Litters 3–5. Litter 1 was hand raised. Litter 4 was delivered by Cesarean.

Formulas

Powdered and liquid puppy formulas are available from veterinarians and pet supply stores; some breeders feel goat's milk is a satisfactory canine milk substitute as well. The author has discovered that commercial powdered formulas diluted to manufacturer's instructions are usually too rich for newborn puppies and highly favors diluting the formula by half again with Pedialyte®. During the first 3–6 days, the newborn's need for calorie intake is not as great as the need for maintaining fluid balance. However, any supplementation should always be offered after the puppy's attempts at nursing to take best advantage of mother's milk.

For feeding, any fluid given should be at room temperature, especially during the first week. Unused portions poured from the container should be given to the mother or discarded—never returned to the refrigerator for a later feeding.

Once the container for powdered formula is opened, the manufacturer warns that it must not only be refrigerated, but also the unused amount must be discarded a month after opening. Both liquid and powdered products have a limited shelf life, so check the expiration dates on each container before purchase.

The breeder should consult the veterinarian for the total amount to feed a puppy that is completely dependent on supplementation.

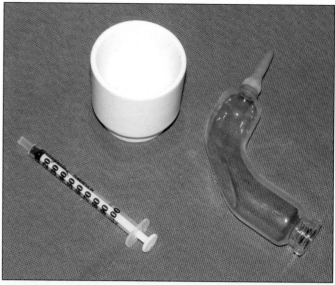

Figure 25-5. *A better idea.* The 1-cc syringe (needle removed) is recommended for supplementation during the first week; its limited capacity allows drop-by-drop feeding and minimizes the potential for fluid aspiration. The shot glass makes it easy to collect, mix, and draw the solution. During the first day, the preferred ratio is 50/50 colostrum and Pedialyte® (brand name is recommended over generics). For older puppies, the Foster and Smith bottle is more efficient for formula diluted half and half with Pedialyte®.

Techniques

While this chapter will discuss three different feeding techniques, the author strongly prefers the syringe method as the easiest and safest, especially for the weary breeder at 3 am. Before beginning any feeding procedure, the puppy's airways should be checked to ensure that there are no gurgling noises from the lungs and that the nasal passages are free of formula or milk. Hold the puppy head downward with a paper towel as a blotter at its nose to determine whether any fluid is draining from the nasal passages.

A puppy with gurgling noises or fluid draining from the lungs should have the airway and lungs clear before any attempt at nutrition is made; the syringe method is preferred for supplementing these challenged pups. To avoid the potential for illness resulting from bacterial contamination, it is essential that all feeding equipment be thoroughly cleaned and completely dried between feedings.

Syringe. The safest technique, under all conditions, for feeding newborn puppies is with a 1-cc insulin syringe (needle discarded) because it is so very easy to control the rate, even when half asleep. Holding the mouth open with the thumb and index finger, place a drop at a time on the

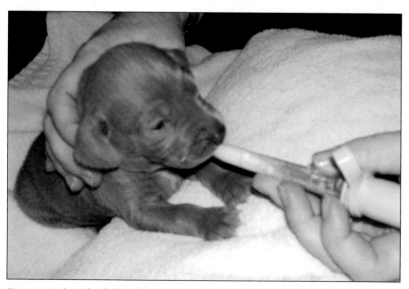

Figure 25-4. *A bad idea.* The Foster and Smith bottle or a 1-cc syringe are preferred over this infant medicine dropper or an eye dropper. One hard suck from the puppy and formula may end up in the lungs, potentially leading to fatal aspiration pneumonia. However, this puppy is shown in the most favorable position for bottle feeding; the rolled towel or pillow on the table (also covered with a towel for traction) simulates the mother's belly. This position allows the puppy to knead with its front paws while reaching out for the nipple.

Figure 25-6: *If the dam is unable to nurse* or if puppies are being supplemented, they must be stimulated to eliminate before being fed and, if at all possible, after feeding as well. While it promotes identification and bonding and is the most natural behavior, if the dam is unable or unwilling to perform this function, refer to *Whelping* for hints and advice.

center back of the puppy's tongue. As soon as the puppy swallows, give it another 1–2 drops. Under all circumstances, avoid allowing the puppy to suck the liquid from the syringe. A newborn puppy receives adequate nourishment with nursing and a supplement of 1–3 cc Pedialyte®/colostrum every 1–2 hours, based on the puppy's desire.

Tube feeding. The most timesaving technique for puppies is tube feeding (gastric gavage), in which a syringe is used to inject formula through a tube that has been inserted through the puppy's mouth into the stomach. Tube feeding should not be used to supplement nursing puppies. When tube feeding is deemed necessary as the sole source of nutrition for a puppy, the technique should be taught by a veterinarian and done under supervision until the breeder is comfortable and competent with the procedure. Illustrations and directions are provided only to acquaint the breeder with the technique and are not intended to provide instruction for this procedure.

Begin by assembling the equipment: 10- to 20-cc syringe, flexible plastic Number 10 catheter, towel, small glass of water, adhesive tape, and soft towels. Weigh the puppy and calculate the amount of formula as recommended by the veterinarian; warm the formula to 95°F–100°F (warm but

not hot when dropped on the wrist). Placing the tube next to the puppy, measure the distance from the last rib to the puppy's mouth, and mark the tube with a piece of tape; the tube must be re-measured each day to compensate for growth. Fill the syringe, and lay it within easy reach. Place the puppy on the towel, head extended but not raised. Moisten the tube by dipping the tip in the formula. Holding the tube near the tape so that it arcs, gently insert the tube in the puppy's mouth. The tube slides down surprisingly easily when following the arc. To be sure the tube has not entered the puppy's lungs, place the end in the glass of water; if the water bubbles, remove the tube and try again. Attach the syringe and gently inject the formula. Have the mother clean the puppy or stimulate elimination with a piece of cotton slightly moistened with warm water. Thoroughly wash and rinse the equipment and store in a covered container until the next feeding. Tube feeding is safe and easy with a weak puppy that has difficulty nursing.

With a normal, vigorous puppy, however, an assistant is mandatory—one to hold the tube securely in place in the squirming, cartwheeling, uncooperative subject while the other injects the formula. The more strong and active the puppy, the greater the danger of the tube slipping out of the stomach and curling at the back of the throat, where most of the formula, injected under pressure, will go directly into the lungs. If the puppy does not die instantly, it usually does so within hours.

Bottle feeding. Those who believe that feeding a puppy with a baby bottle should be the easiest and most logical technique are in for a rude surprise. The problems boil down to size of the nipple and the size of the aperture. The cheap nipples for the cute little bottles sold by many pet stores might work with a Chihuahua or kitten, but never a Weimaraner. Standard human baby nipples are too large and firm for the puppy to maintain effective suction, but in a pinch the nipples for premature babies are the only ones that come close to being the right size and being soft enough for a newborn Weimaraner. The fun really starts when trying to get the crosscut opening the right size. Weak puppies exhaust their limited energy reserves if the hole is too small, so it is enlarged. When the big bear grabs hold with a lusty suck, it gets too much milk too fast and develops pneumonia from all the milk in its lungs. The final disadvantage of bottle feeding is that it is very time consuming, and it can take over 2 hours to feed a litter of eight, finishing one feeding just in time to begin the next. The syringe method is preferred during the first days to maintain the puppies' hydration and strength; then, every effort should be made to have the mother resume her nursing duties. If the dam is still unable or unwilling to nurse, the puppies will quickly outgrow this method, and Dr. Foster's Favorite Feeding Bottle® (www.drsfostersmith.com) is then preferred to provide con-

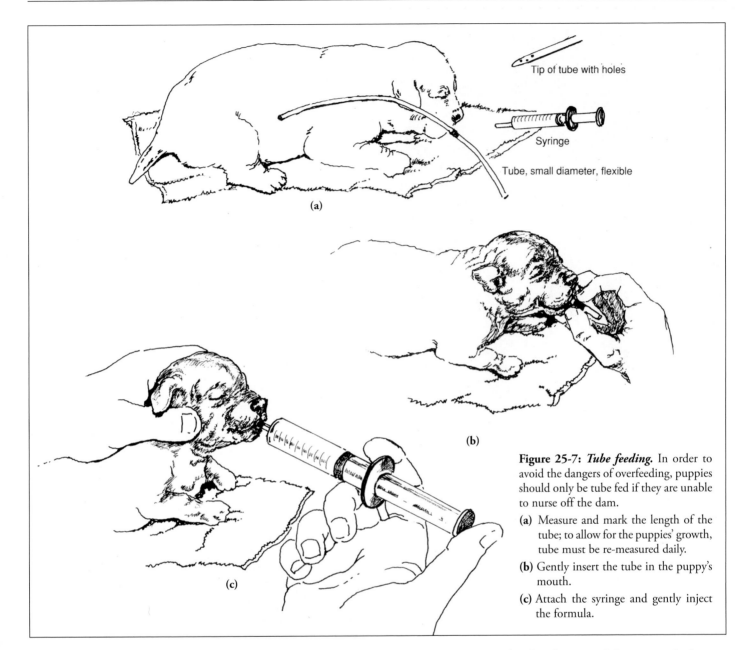

Tip of tube with holes

Syringe

Tube, small diameter, flexible

(a)

(b)

(c)

Figure 25-7: *Tube feeding.* In order to avoid the dangers of overfeeding, puppies should only be tube fed if they are unable to nurse off the dam.

(a) Measure and mark the length of the tube; to allow for the puppies' growth, tube must be re-measured daily.

(b) Gently insert the tube in the puppy's mouth.

(c) Attach the syringe and gently inject the formula.

trol while managing the larger volumes of liquid required by the rapidly growing puppies.

After the first 24 hours, diarrhea in a very young puppy is characterized by a foamy yellow projectile stool. Although it is difficult to identify with a good mother, a tell-tale odor and dehydration should create suspicion of diarrhea even if the puppy appears to be nursing vigorously. Refer to *The Newborn Period* for methods for determining dehydration. Under these conditions, additional supplementation formula (other than Pedialyte®) may aggravate the problem. A fresh fecal sample should be rushed to the vet for evaluation for the presence of intestinal parasites or protozoan infections. Use an insulin syringe (needle removed) to give 1 cc of unflavored Kaopectate® for a 12-ounce puppy, washing the medication down with up to 1–2 cc Pedialyte®. Repeat Keopectate® again in 3 hours. If unresolved and the puppy is

not nursing vigorously after the second dose, consult the veterinarian.

If all is well for mother and pups after the post-partal check-up, the pontoon system in *The Newborn Period* will help ensure early observation of potential problems in the puppies' health, as well as adequate nursing and protection from the less experienced dam's possibly stepping on the pups; it also begins the process of developing sound mental health through handling. Since nursing stimulates milk production, in preparation for weaning, provide supplemental feeding just before nursing. The partially satiated puppies will nurse less, decreasing the stimulus for the dam to produce milk. This "introductory period" also reduces the potential for digestive upset when the weaning process begins.

Figure 25-8: *Young explorers.* From 3–5 weeks, find a safe place in the house where each puppy can explore, one at a time. Puppies have little fear at this age and should easily accept new experiences, such as strange noises, going from light to dark, and changing floor textures. During these special excursions, the observant breeder will learn much about the pup's personality, courage, and learning potential, identifying those needing remedial opportunities and those naturally bold adventurers.

From 2 to 5 Weeks

During this time frame, the whole world begins to open for the young puppies; early in this period their eyes and ears begin to function. *Ages and Stages* provides information vital to understanding these changes and provides opportunities that will help puppies develop to their fullest potential. Early in this phase the dam provides both nutrition and emotional development, whereas after weaning, her greatest contribution will be supporting the puppies' mental and emotional growth; she is invaluable in teaching them canine etiquette and protocol.

Begin to condition puppies to loud noises as soon as their ears begin to function at 21 days. Start while they are nursing by lightly tapping on a metal bowl with a wooden spoon. Introduce many different types of sounds, ranging from deep to sharp, starting with the bowl and hand clapping and working up to a vacuum cleaner and gunfire. Start with noises soft and distant and gradually increase the loudness or sharpness, but stop when sensitivity or nervousness is noticed. Refer to *Starting the Gun Dog* for advanced noise education.

Management of Mother

About 2–3 weeks after whelping, the bitch begins to produce tremendous quantities of milk. The accompanying enlargement of the breasts—called the "second bag"—causes permanent residual breast enlargement. With early weaning, bitches often return to the show ring with little sign that they have had puppies.

Preparing for Weaning

The very young puppy's tongue is curled to provide the best suction during nursing; a puppy cannot be fully weaned until the tongue has flattened to allow lapping of food. This is a highly variable developmental stage and may vary by as much as a week within puppies in the same litter; however, the breeder can help prepare the mother and the puppies in advance.

In preparation for weaning, providing a supplemental feeding just before nursing decreases the stimulus to produce large quantities of milk and reduces the potential for digestive upset in the weaning puppies.

When the puppies start to cut teeth toward the end of the 3rd week, Weimaraner mothers begin to spend less time in the whelping box, and they become progressively more amenable to weaning. The weaning schedule can be started at either 3 or 4 weeks. Puppies can be completely weaned by 4 weeks and should be weaned no later than 5 weeks.

Figure 25-9: *When the weather is fine* and as soon as the puppies' eyes and ears are open and they are reasonably steady on their feet, allow each a few minutes in clean, fresh grass for a bit of fresh air and sunshine.

During the weaning process, the bitch should only be allowed to be with the puppies during supervised periods to prevent excessive nursing. Nursing periods should be closely regulated, permitted only for short periods after the puppies have consumed supplemental feeding. The number of nursing periods is reduced through the weaning process. If the bitch is removed from earshot, the puppy's crying will be less likely to stimulate additional milk production.

Do not be surprised if a bitch suddenly regurgitates her food in an instinctive attempt to assist in the weaning process. Some bitches may be comforted by "mothering" a few of the puppies' toys during this time. She also will need to have plenty of human contact and attention.

The sooner the weaning process is completed, the sooner she can return to her litter and begin educating her puppies in the rules of being a dog. After the bitch is completely dry, she should be allowed to be with the puppies several times a day for play and discipline and can accompany them on walks and adventures; however, she should not be left with them unsupervised in a pen or kennel for extended periods. Although their presence may stimulate minor milk production (excessive nursing can produce an entire new bag), most bitches have little desire to let the weaned puppies nurse, preferring to leap away and play tag and avoid their needle-sharp teeth.

Figure 25-11. *A puppy should be held* in this manner to have toenails clipped, ears cleaned, and medicine given. Weimaraner puppy nails grow at a phenomenal rate and should be trimmed at least once a week with an ordinary nail clipper or small manicure scissors. Unless the needle-sharp nails are kept trimmed, they scratch the dam's breasts, often causing open sores. At this time, also check the nose for formula or discharge and the skin for lesions.

When weaning, during the first 4 or 5 days, check the breasts 3 or 4 times a day for heat, redness, and hardness, especially those between the rear legs. If any breasts appear excessively full or hot to the touch, three or four strokes should express some milk, relieve the pressure, and ensure the bitch's comfort; it is important to express only enough milk to relieve the pressure and not enough to encourage additional milk production. Check the bitch's temperature daily; a veterinarian may sometimes suggest a low dose of antibiotics as a preventive measure for the bitch's comfort. It is important to only express enough milk to relieve the heat and fullness and not enough to cause possible mastitis.

Puppy Feeding

Puppy ration. The gradual transition from milk to solid food shown in Table 25-3 is easy and comfortable for all. Puppies have no difficulty digesting the commercial puppy rations by the time they are 4 weeks old. Soak the dry food

Figure 25-10: *Begin weaning* on a one-to-one basis. This puppy's tongue has not yet flattened enough to allow efficient eating, so he is not yet ready to begin eating out of a ground-level bowl with his littermates. Supplemental feedings in preparation for weaning make the process easier by reducing the dam's milk while teaching the pup to accept the new food.

Table 25-3: *Puppies' transition and weaning schedule.*

Age (Days)	Ration	Technique
14	Formula (milk)*	Puppy big enough to feed with a 2-cc syringe Feed five times a day if planning to show mother again
17	Formula and rice cereal*	Add a small amount of rice cereal (rice based seems to cause less digestive upset) to milk, let stand to thicken, and adjust consistency
		Feed with a 5-cc syringe, placing mixture on side of the tongue to encourage lapping
20	Formula, rice cereal, and 100% strained-meat baby food*	Can lap thin mixture from small, elevated saucer
		Add enough meat to give ration more color and flavor
23	Formula, commercial puppy ration, and strained meat*	Pre-soak puppy ration until mushy Use ration instead of rice cereal to thicken formula to consistency puppy can lap
26	Formula (75%) and puppy ration (25%)*	Add water, if necessary, for consistency puppy can easily manage
		Optional; cottage cheese for flavor
29	Formula (50%) and puppy ration (50%)	Sometime during the 4th week remove supplemental nursing
32	Formula (25%) and puppy ration (75%)	
35	Puppy ration (100%)	Use either scheduled feedings of moist food or free-fed dry food

*These rations are offered as a supplemental feeding *before* nursing.

thoroughly with warm water. There is surprising variation in the rate at which the rations absorb water. Puppy Eukanuba™ practically melts immediately, whereas the regular Iams™ puppy ration must be first broken into smaller pieces in a blender, crushed with a rolling pin, or soaked overnight in the refrigerator. Always use water when a moister consistency is desired; milk alters the nutrient balance of the formula.

Never substitute cow's milk for the milk formula! Puppies cannot digest it until they are many months older. When receiving calls about diarrhea in a puppy under 4 months old, the first question asked by the veterinary clinic is whether the puppy has been given cow's milk because 9 out of 10 times that is the cause.

Except for those dams interrupting a show career, early weaning should not occur until after 3¹/₂ weeks.

Transition to dish. By 3 weeks, the tongue has flattened enough that the puppy may lap thickened food from a dish. To evaluate whether or not the puppy is prepared to transition, let it lick or suck some food from a finger, and lead its mouth into food. Touching the side of the mouth with a finger dipped in food stimulates the sucking reflex. Each puppy must be fed individually. Elevating the shallow food dish on bricks minimizes the 3¹/₂-week-old puppy's

tendency to climb into the food, and placing it in a corner minimizes distractions.

The introduction of solid foods is a great time for puppies to develop a pleasurable association between the show stance and food, and 4 weeks is not too soon to start. In addition to being far easier to train for show, puppies started this way pose beautifully when taking 7-week photographs. Figure 25-15 shows how this can be accomplished.

Group feeding. Even if the puppies have not been started with individual supplemental meals from a dish, there is no special trick to teaching 4- to 5-week-olds to eat. Usually, all that is needed is to place the food in the whelping box and whistle or cluck to wake them. Most dive right into the food as soon as they scent it, and you can move the stragglers to the bowl for a sniff. If any still fail to catch on, use the technique described above. Divide puppies into feeding groups by strength and boldness to ensure all puppies receive appropriate nutrition; it is important to monitor feeding habits and weight gain during this time.

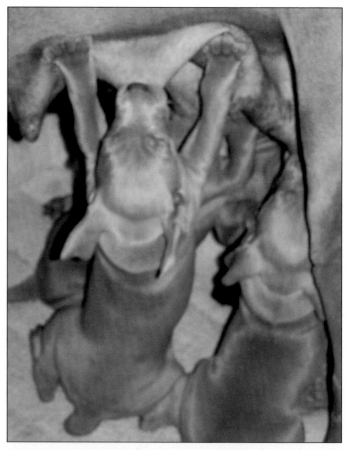

Figure 25-12: *Saggy baggies.* Allowing the bitch to nurse her puppies after a sensible weaning date often creates permanent enlargement and a sagging underline, especially if the puppies are allowed to nurse while the bitch is standing.

Mother's Weaning Schedule*

3–4 Weeks	Start puppies on heavy supplemental feeding
	Change from lactation ration to regular ration
	Allow contact with puppies only 12 hours a day
4 Weeks	Start weaning
Day 1	³/₄ amount of regular ration, limit water
Day 2	¹/₂ regular ration
Day 3	¹/₄ regular ration
Day 4	NO FOOD, 2 CUPS WATER
	Totally isolate from puppies (cries stimulate milk production)
Day 5	¹/₄ regular ration
Day 6	¹/₂ regular ration, continue until milk has dried

*During this period, provide the dam with plenty of emotional support, extra attention, and distracting activities.

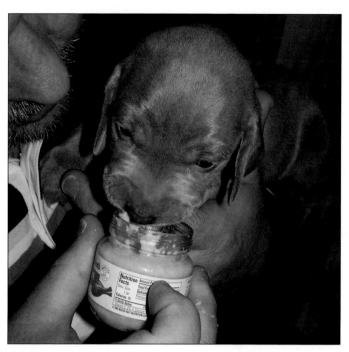

Figure 25-14. *Good stuff!* It is usually easier for puppies to begin by licking strained meat off the fingers. This puppy would rather go straight to the source, however, and is ready to move to the bowl. Strained meat baby food is an ideal first food after mother's milk.

Bowls. The most important aspect is a steady bowl that will not turn over during the mad rush of feeding puppies. A great puppy pan is now available; its raised center leaves a circular trough around the edge, allowing the puppies to consume every crumb while discouraging them from walking into the bowl. This arrangement prevents gluttons from hog-ging the food by lying in the middle of the bowl and helps ensure each pup gets its share. It also minimizes the amount of clean-up needed after mealtime as pups stay cleaner and the stainless steel pan can be easily washed in the dishwasher.

The clean-up. After eating, the puppies are liberally coated with food. The mothers are delighted to lick them clean, and wipes can be used to finish the job. Check the nostrils and gently and carefully remove gobs of food with a toothpick. Q-tips® are too large to be effective and tend to push the food farther into the nose. The clean-up is important because dried food causes chapping and cracks in the skin that often develop into serious skin problems, such as staph infections.

Water. When transitioning from weaning formula to dry food, water should be made available, and the puppies should be monitored for signs of dehydration (loose skin on the back of the neck holds a ridge when pinched) and consti-

Figure 25-13: *Back to the show ring.* If the puppies are weaned early (3¹/₂ to 4 weeks) the bitch is able to retain her championship form. Although Given has no milk (as several of her puppies have discovered), she can provide valuable social lessons before the puppies go to their new homes. Given returned to the show ring and successfully competed as a special after the birth of this litter.

pation. As soon as the puppies are regularly eating dry food, water should be available at all times.

Worming. Intestinal parasites can be quite insidious, even though the dam was wormed prior to breeding and no other infected dogs have been on the premises.

Many a breeder is surprised and shamed to have an entire litter of puppies diagnosed with intestinal parasites; it is not uncommon for the stress of pregnancy, whelping, and lactation to release encysted parasites back into the mother's system despite the most sanitary housing conditions. The parasites then infect the puppies through the milk and close contact with the dam, who is exposed again as she cleans her puppies. Pyrantel™ panmoate, a non-toxic canine anti-helminthic, as found in Nemex 2, has proven to be effective in the treatment of hooks and round worms and is gentle enough to use in puppies as young as 3 weeks with veteri-

nary approval; however, if there are no signs of poor stools or loss of weight, it is best to wait until 4 1/2 weeks, just before weaning. Plan to repeat the process 2 weeks later, when the puppies are completely weaned. Although it is very safe, it is necessary to have an accurate weight for each puppy in order to get the appropriate dosage.

Worming the dam should be postponed until after the puppies are completely weaned in order to avoid an excess exposure of medication to the puppies through her milk.

Unexplained loose stools with negative fecal exams could be indicative of a protozoan infection, such as Coccidiosis or Giardia, which are more difficult to identify; for this reason, fecal evaluations should be done on fresh stool samples.

Figure 25-15: *First lessons.* Get the young puppy used to being handled and touched. This familiarity is important to dogs in all venues of competition, especially conformation and field, but also for general husbandry, such as vet exams and grooming.

(a) Place in a show stance and push the tail; check testicles.

(b) Lift and handle each foot.

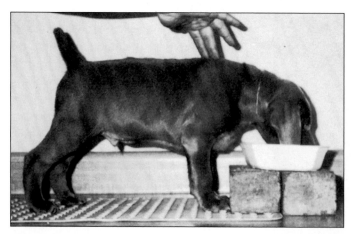

(c) Touch the back and rock the shoulders.

(d) Raise the dish, and behold a future champion.

From 5 to 7 Weeks

The two basic feeding methods—scheduled meals and free-feeding—are effective, and the choice is a matter of personal preference. Some breeders use a combination of free-feeding while at work and moist food several times a day and for training.

Meals should be scheduled 4 times a day at regular intervals, from the first chore in the morning to the last thing before going to bed. By establishing a regular routine for feeding and "exercise," pups will be well on the road to being housetrained; if location and weather permit, feeding the litter outside as often as possible, in a designated area, will also support good early toilet habits, since the puppies will be able to relieve themselves as soon as they eat. The colored collars will help you to keep track of which puppy has performed the necessary ritual in order to return inside. When offering food, make a consistent sound—a clucking noise or "zzzz." Puppies will quickly associate the sound with the soon-to-be offered food. Later on, this same sound can be used to get the dog's attention or lift flagging spirits when competing. As the puppies approach the time to go to their new homes, around the 7th week, meals can be reduced to 3 times a day.

To start puppies on the free-feeding method, begin with supplemental meals of moistened food in the 4th week, but also mount a dry-food dispenser for chicks on the side of the whelping box. The puppies will discover the container and begin to nibble the dry food with progressive ease as their teeth grow. By the middle of the 5th week, they no longer need a moistened ration. If a breeder must be gone for an extended period during the day, free-feeding can supplement the regularly scheduled meals. Free-feeding all meals does have a few disadvantages. It is very difficult to keep track of which puppies are getting enough nutrition. It also makes it nearly impossible to begin the housetraining process. Providing sufficient water becomes a challenge. The food cannot be kept moistened to encourage the puppies to eat sufficient amounts of food; additionally, bacterial growth can occur in moistened food left out for long periods.

Make every effort to maintain the puppies on the same food throughout the weaning process and until they go to their new homes. Plan to send a generous amount of food home with the new owners, and give them the name of the food ahead of time. Diarrhea is a natural result of changing

Figure 25-16: ***It is not enough*** to raise a litter of puppies that are well fed and not sick: physical development is important for the pup to learn balance, coordination, and control. Plan walks at regular intervals during the day, especially after meals, to encourage good housetraining habits. By dividing the puppies into smaller groups during these walks, they can begin to learn important skills while exploring the world outside, as well as learning to come when called and not to jump on people. Maria rewards the puppies with treats for coming and uses an empty watering can to gently bump the young ones and prevent them from achieving the inappropriate physical contact they are seeking.

diet and/or water supply and sometimes occurs as the result of the maturing digestive system. A dose of 20 cc of Kaopectate® for an 8- to 10-pound puppy should be followed by an equal amount of Pedialyte®; repeat within 2 hours up to 3 times. If the puppy does not respond, consult the veterinarian for other potential causes, such as parasites.

General Management

Preventing Contagious Diseases

While disease prevention is obviously important in raising healthy puppies, the breeder needs to also keep in mind mental heath. Most diseases, such as distemper and kennel cough, are less common today than in years past. Parvo represents the single greatest threat to a litter. A few reasonable precautions can allow the breeder to more confidently balance the fine line between meeting the emotional needs of maturing puppies and protecting their mental and physical health.

- Change clothing and shoes when returning from contact with strange dogs such as at shows, training classes, and so forth

Figure 25-17: (a) ***BOORRING!!*** This pen will not contain these puppies for long (right after the picture was taken the pen fell over and the puppies escaped to find more interesting pursuits). **(b)** ***Better.*** Visitors are invited to sit inside the exercise pen to socialize with the puppies. Variety is important: young and old, men and women (men with beards and mustaches), varied apparel (glasses and hats especially). While in a group, the bolder puppies will encourage less-bold puppies to enjoy the experience.

Figure 25-18: ***Best.*** Puppies are divided into groups according to temperament and physical development to play in a safe area. A crate with an inviting mat promotes early crate training. Toys should be rotated regularly to encourage interaction of littermates and pick-up-and-carry behavior. The concrete can be hosed clean several times a day, while varying surfaces offer climbing and footing opportunities as well as resting areas off the occasionally irritating hard surface. Fresh water is available at all times; the bucket is secured so it cannot be pushed over. Strong fencing, with a sturdy gate and lock, discourages escapist behavior as well as providing protection from intruders (human or animal). A sunshade protects from direct sun and heat. Puppies are fed in this area and are then immediately taken for a short walk to a grassy area to eliminate, promoting house training. Frequent walks outside the pen encourage exploration and socialization. Regular excursions, such as car rides and visits away from home, are also necessary to promote emotional maturation and are as important as physical development (especially between the ages of 6−8 weeks, just before they leave for their new homes). *Ages and Stages* discusses this further.

- Until puppies have had their first Parvo vaccine, be sure visitors have not been exposed to dogs that may be ill

- As an extra precaution, have visitors wash their hands and leave their shoes outside before handling the very young puppies

Room to Grow

By the time puppies are weaned, the whelping box seems to get smaller every day, and providing a safe area for exercise and play taxes a breeder's ingenuity. Possible solutions are limited by climate and time of year. Unless the weather is inclement, the puppies should be outdoors or on a screened porch several hours a day for some sunshine.

A permanently fenced dog area, just for puppies, within a larger fenced yard is ideal in some ways, but a portable exercise pen allows flexibility. Outdoors, it can be moved to a fresh area of lawn every day, and when the sun becomes too hot, it can be covered or moved to the shade. It can even be moved indoors, protecting the floor with newspapers. A plastic dog crate, with the door removed, can be left in the pen to provide an inviting sleeping den to begin crate and house training.

If outdoor concrete runs are used, be sure to provide plenty of alternate surfaces. The Weimaraner's short coat provides little protection from abrasions during rough play. Alternate surfaces provide the opportunity to experience different footings, as well as the chance to climb up and down.

Puppies can be turned loose in the larger backyard if it is fenced and if they are supervised the entire time. It takes only a short time to realize just how much trouble inquisitive puppies can find, even in a relatively confined area.

Everything must be tested with the mouth—the redwood shelf on the barbecue, the plastic chair cushion, the bag of fertilizer to be spread tomorrow, and the lawnmower, as well as every flower, bush, and tree. They can go under gates, get into crawl spaces, and find hazards never imagined. Remember that what would be a sufficient confinement for an adult dog may not contain tiny curious puppies.

After 5 weeks or so the exhausted breeder may find it is easier to just put puppies in an exercise pen and wait for them to go to new homes. But physical development is important to growing puppies so that they learn coordination and balance at an early age. Learning to walk on slippery floors and not slide into the wall from trying to turn too quickly are important lessons. The irregular surface and feel of grass and gravel are very different from the level, textured blankets of the whelping box. Learning to climb up on a small box uses different muscles and balance than wrestling with littermates. The exercise pen should not be a barren containment and elimination area; ideally, it should be a clean, cheerful place with lots to do. Instead of having guests lift the puppy out of the pen (never ever by the scruff of the neck!), make the pen more inviting by having guests join the puppies by sitting on the ground or on a stool at their level in the pen. If some puppies are significantly bolder or stronger than their littermates, be sure to separate out the weaker from the stronger, so no one gets intimidated. A boring, dirty exercise pen is just an encouragement for puppies to discover how to escape to the more interesting world on the other side of the wire, which is certainly a bad habit new owners will not appreciate. Physical development is closely tied to emotional development and will be more thoroughly discussed in *Ages and Stages.*

Figure 25-19: *A routine vet check* before going to their new home; at this time, puppies get a full health exam, their first shot, and weighing for worming medication. Refer to *Puppy Health Assessment*. This adventure can be valuable, combining a positive first veterinary experience with a fun trip in the car with littermates. Using the colored collars as identification, the entire litter can be microchipped at this time, as well. This allows the breeder to register the chips originally and then provide the paperwork to transfer the chip registration when the pup goes to its new home, not only ensuring that the pup is microchipped, but that the chip is actually registered. At the time of examination, request an individual health certificate for each pup's owner using the collar for identification. Plan on feeding puppies on their return rather than before the trip to avoid accidents and carsickness.

Figure 25-20: ***Well before the puppy departs,*** promote bonding through several visits by the new owners. If there are children involved, have them begin learning about puppy care and writing pledge letters to the parents and the breeder, as discussed in *Picking the Perfect Puppy.* If at all feasible, encourage new owners to select a name for the puppy so the breeder can begin using it as soon as possible.

This chapter concludes with the puppies going to their new homes and, when combined with the information in the chapters from *Whelping* to *Picking the Perfect Puppy,* should provide the breeder with enough information to raise a litter of physically and mentally gifted babies. Even products of generations of careful selection for desire and performance can be ruined by a sterile early puppyhood, so if a breeder is unable to provide the opportunities outlined in these chapters, they should first consider whether they are truly prepared to breed a litter at all. Should events circumvent the best-laid plans, consider allowing puppies to go to new homes, along with the information provided in these later chapters, as early as 7 weeks (where allowed), in order to allow the new owners to provide this enrichment and avoid the waste of the wealth of opportunities afforded during this highly impressionable, once-in-a-lifetime, 5- to 8-week learning period.

Figure 25-21: ***Allow puppies to explore*** on their own as well as to learn limits. Dana is about to discover that landscaping mulch is not as much fun to chew on as it might seem. The breeder has provided the supervised puppies with the opportunity to chew on some mulch and gravel that have been liberally sprayed with a deterrent; at the same time, a verbal or physical correction may also be offered. This lesson may prevent expensive veterinary calls or surgery or even death at a future date by preventing the ingestion of such common landscaping materials, especially rocks and gravel. Weim owners should be aware that in addition to potential blockages, cocoa mulch is also toxic and should never be used in areas to which dogs have access.

THE RULES OF 7s

By the time a puppy is 7 weeks old, he or she should have:

- Been on 7 different types of surfaces—carpets, concrete, wood, vinyl, grass, dirt, gravel, wood chips, etc.

- Played with 7 different types of objects—big balls, small balls, soft fabric toys, fuzzy toys, squeaky toys, paper or cardboard items, metal items, sticks or hose pieces, etc.

- Been in 7 different locations—front yard, back yard, basement, kitchen, car, garage, laundry room, bathroom, etc.

- Met and played with 7 new people—children, older adults, someone with a cane or walking stick, someone in a wheelchair or walker, etc.

- Been exposed to 7 different challenges—climb on a box, climb off a box, go through a tunnel, climb steps, climb over obstacles, play hide and seek, go in and out of a doorway, run around a fence, etc.

- Eaten from 7 different containers—metal, plastic, cardboard, glass, china, pie plate, pan, etc.

- Eaten in 7 different locations—crate, yard, kitchen, basement, laundry room, living room, bathroom, etc.

Courtesy of *Another Piece of the Puzzle: Puppy Development,* by Pat Hastings and Erin Ann Rouse, 2004.

Figure 25-22: *Beware the dam* that sneaks in a few extra meals for her pups. If given the opportunity, most bitches will allow puppies to nurse, which complicates the weaning process and is detrimental to the dam's return to athletic competition or show ring form. These puppies, bred and whelped in Australia, retain their tails since docking is prohibited in that country. On one author's recent trip to Australia, she found not one breeder pleased with the restrictions and results of the legislation. American Weimaraner enthusiasts must be constantly on the alert for animal rights groups that would ban tail docking and dewclaw removal here in this country. Such actions usually begin with a ban in a single community and spread quickly across the country as additional communities and states fall like dominoes; unwavering vigilance is required. Courtesy of Melanie, Weimaraner Club of New South Wales 2006 Calendar.

Figure 26-1: *Mom's Boy,* by William Wegman (2006).

CHAPTER 26

AGES AND STAGES

by Patricia Riley

No matter how many litters a breeder has whelped, most find there are no cut-and-dried days or weeks to mark the transition from one developmental period to another. Each puppy is an individual, and there are differences between breeds, as well as puppies within a litter. For Weimaraners, observable events are predictors of upcoming events in the puppies' lives and usually occur in a predictable chronological process.

The critical stages of development are a series of age-related canine phases in which specific tasks must be accomplished before progressing to the next stage. An understanding of the stages enables the breeder and owner to enhance each puppy's learning experience and stability of temperament. After much consultation with breeders of medium and large sporting breeds and testing many of these litters (see *Testing Natural Aptitude*), the authors have found the following ages and stages to be most appropriate for the Weimaraner.

It should be recognized that while the first stage is clearly defined by the opening of the ears and eyes, the following stages may show greater variability, and that variance may increase with age. These ages should be used as a general guideline to development and are not necessarily cut in stone.

Stage One: Birth through Hearing

Birth to 21 Days

Mom Is It: Survival and Transition

Stage Two: Hearing through Weaning

3rd Week to End of the 5th Week

I Am a Dog: Learning to Be Part of the Pack

Stage Three: Weaning to New Homes

6th Week to End of 8th Week

First Impressions: Individuality and Early Socialization

Stage Four: New Homes to Teething

2nd Month to End of 5th Month

A Whole New World: A New Pack Leader and Advanced Socialization

Stage Five: Teething to Adolescence

5th Month through End of 10th Month

Age of Cutting: Exploration and Relaxed Review

Stage Six: Adolescence to Sexual Maturity

10th Month through 16th Month

On-the-Job Training: Joining the Dog/Human Team

Stage Seven: Sexual Maturity to Senior Years

16th Month to 10 Years

Adulthood: Cooperative Self-sufficiency

Stage Eight: The Golden Silver Years

10 Years up to 18 Years

Graceful Retirement and Mentoring

Figure 26-2: *Little Big Head,* by William Wegman.

Stage One: *Birth through Hearing*

Birth to 21 days

Mom Is It: Survival and Transition

The first critical stage of puppyhood occurs between whelping and 3 weeks (21 days) old. The basic task during this time is simply survival. Refer to *Whelping* and *The Newborn Period* for more information. Stage One is characterized by total dependency on the mother or substitute mother. Initially, the puppy functions entirely on reflexes. The brain is immature, and only minimal neurological pathways exist. For example, excretion occurs only in a reflex response to maternal stimulation. The tail docking and dewclaw removal, done at 3–7 days, leave little, if any, emotional after-effects because memory pathways simply do not exist. During the first 21 days, development of neural pathways proceeds at a rapid pace and is often evident in the twitching of extremities, which is perfectly normal but occasionally alarming to first-time breeders, who fear the puppies are having seizures. True learning is considered negligible at this stage. The eyes open between the 11th and 15th days after whelping—the 13th day on average.

The last week of Stage One (14–21 days) is often called the transition period as nerve pathways throughout the body, eyes, and ears and motor coordination are developing at a phenomenal pace. Once the puppy can hear, learning occurs at a rapid rate.

Stage One puppies are considered incapable of learning, but more than 20 years ago, unbeknownst to each other, both authors began the practice of holding puppies as often as possible. While watching television, for example, each puppy was held for 5–10 minutes, with the human touching the puppy all over its body, allowing the pup to sniff, nuzzle, and lick and to fall asleep on its back. Initially, the objective was simply to teach the males to relax while on their backs so the testicles could be palpated and the earliest date of observation noted, but the females also had almost as much attention. Upon comparing notes, we later observed that litters that received this early handling had unusually stable temperaments.

Dr. Carmen Battaglia's recent work, *Developing High Achievers,* supports this process. His research showed that stimulating puppies between 3 and 16 days, with mild stress, resulted in adult dogs that were better able to cope with stress and had higher problem-solving ability. However, excessive stress has proved to be detrimental to development, so this is definitely not a case of more is better.

The breeder's main responsibilities at this stage are to keep the mother healthy and happy and to keep the litter warm, eating, and eliminating with normal stools. Each puppy should be monitored to ensure that it is thriving. Refer to *Raising the Litter* for tips on managing the whelps at this age. During the last week of Stage One, known as the transition period, the authors recommend the following to support healthy development in neonate puppies:

a) Before being set to the mother to nurse, stroke the anogenital area of each puppy with a warm, moistened paper towel to stimulate elimination. This will help deter the dam from unnecessary cleaning, which may disrupt successful nursing.

b) From 3–16 days, consider "prestressing" puppies daily using Dr. Battaglia's suggestions in *Developing High Achievers;* the cool weighing scale can be substituted for the cold towel for the 3–5 seconds that it takes to weigh puppies each day.

c) From birth onward, rock puppies individually while holding them snugly against the breeder's chest so the puppy can hear the human heartbeat; alternate this with lowering the puppy to the lap to encourage continued relaxation while it is lying on its back in a less "cuddled" position.

Figure 26-3: *At 10 days old,* these pups are getting the chance to experience fresh, clean grass on a warm, sunny day. Very mild stress such as changes in surface texture and temperature may stimulate increased brain growth and neuron production. *Field Stones,* by William Wegman.

Figure 26-4: *Tail cropping and dewclaw removal* usually leaves little physical or emotional trauma when done at 3–6 days. Puppies should be allowed to nurse immediately afterward and should be carefully monitored after surgery for any signs of stress. Note the unique colored collars on Mariah's puppies, which were provided at birth. These allow the development and socialization of each puppy to be monitored and tracked from the first day (refer to Figure 23-14). Puppies given sufficient human contact even from the first days will adapt to the human bond more readily; puppies that show discomfort when held or stroked (especially at this early age) should be given additional attention. Photograph by Bonnie Lane.

Figure 26-5: *Cradle,* by William Wegman.

Stage Two: *Hearing through Weaning*

Beginning of 3rd Week to the End of 5th Week

I Am a Dog: Learning to Be Part of the Pack

The second critical stage of puppyhood occurs with the onset of hearing and ending when the puppies are weaned; this phase is heralded by the first bark. The task of this stage is for the puppy to identify itself as a canine (species identification). Although canine-human bonding is the task of Stage Three, the foundation is laid in Stage Two. The breeder's responsibilities during this stage are to ensure that puppies learn to interact appropriately with each other and to provide beginning environmental enrichment. Before the weaning process, the breeder will provide the foundation for puppies to develop healthy human interaction with positive experiences, especially through appropriate tactile and auditory stimulation.

Three to 5 weeks is characterized by rapid learning, and positive and negative experiences at this age may have lifelong consequences. Canine socialization is learned through playing with littermates. The dam provides love, entertainment, nourishment, and discipline. Mimicking the disciplinary behavior of the dam—a growl, rolling the puppy off its feet, giving it a shake by the loose skin of the neck—is often an effective way to communicate disapproval to older pup-

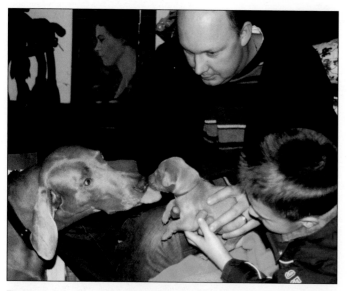

Figure 26-6: *Stage Two is not too early* to have visitors handle and admire puppies, laying a foundation for developing positive human relationships. A dam's stable temperament will set a good example for the pups even at this early age; conversely, a dam that is fearful of people or new experiences can also affect her puppies, and her influence should be limited by weaning puppies as early as possible and providing a positive role model through a mentor.

pies. During Stage Two, the temperament of the dam influences the temperaments of the puppies. If the dam is lacking in essential emotional aspects, e.g., she is shy with people or noise, minimize her interaction with the puppies as soon as they are weaned; consider substituting a bitch with more desirable traits as a mentor during this time.

This is also an ideal time to begin introducing other species with which a favorable relationship is desired, such as cats or rabbits that might be family pets in the puppies' future households.

In short, the dog is learning how to be a dog during this time. Puppies without these learning opportunities frequently do not understand how to interact appropriately with other dogs, missing the nuances of communication or protocol. As adults they are often social outcasts; they might show over-exuberance or excessive dominance or submission with other dogs. The breeder with a singleton litter must make special efforts to ensure this puppy learns good canine communication skills through interaction with another litter or mild-mannered adults.

Social Hierarchy

In general, inappropriate dominance within the litter does not develop until after 7 weeks and is not usually regarded as a problem in Stage Two; however, it does occur often enough with Weimaraners that the breeder should be alert for developing problems. The identifying colored collars are the only possible way to recognize the evolving hierarchy within the litter. Any puppy that seems too submissive to another one should be removed from the litter several times a day, played with separately, and given plenty of opportunities for independent exploration. Taking this time and effort with a puppy saves months of later work on socialization and development of self-confidence.

During this period, puppies begin wrestling and playing with each other, pouncing and stalking, growling and biting. During these interactions, puppies begin to learn a vital lesson in bite inhibition, learning to temper the pressure applied. The puppy learns that if he bites too hard, his playmate will yelp and move away, ending the interaction. This lesson will be useful during the next stage in teaching the puppy to inhibit his biting instinct when interacting with people. Puppies learn to submit to discipline and aggression and that exposing the belly and throat ends the unpleasant encounter.

Learning Opportunities

A breeder can enhance Stage Two environmental learning in many ways. In fact, the lessons are limited only by the breeder's time and imagination. The puppy's mind is a blank page, and the early experiences are not forgotten. A gentle, controlled introduction to changes at this time develops puppies that regard the world as their oyster. If the whelping box

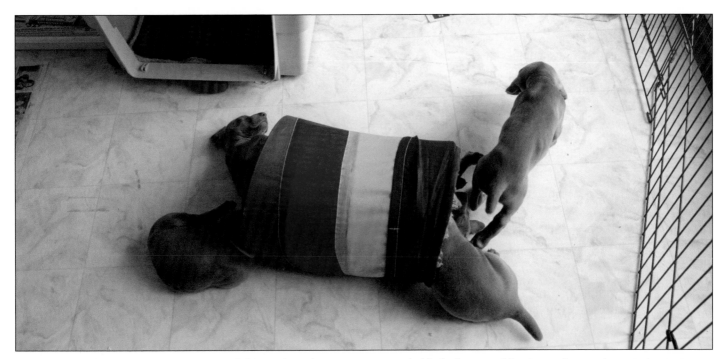

Figure 26-7: *Early exposure to environmental changes* through various toys, tunnels, blocks, boxes, and flooring surfaces teaches puppies acceptance and flexibility. Provide play objects that are appropriate to the size and age of the puppies; toys designed for cats (without catnip) and young puppies (such as the Pet Stages line) are usually good choices. Over-large or heavy toys may encourage the undesirable habit of tearing and destroying instead of carrying. A crate (door removed) with soft bedding is also available for the puppies; this begins the process of crate training as the pups become accustomed to sleeping in this cozy den. Photograph by Jay Fleming.

is in the basement or a secluded bedroom, the puppies cannot hear or see much of their surroundings. Puppies that are raised in isolation, away from noises and other environmental stimuli, have a very difficult time adjusting to everyday situations. This early sensory deprivation may cause a Weimaraner puppy to grow into a nervous, neurotic adult. The optimum place to whelp and raise Weimaraners is in the kitchen or family room, a marvelous source of environmental sights, sounds, and scents. Being in an area central to family activities encourages the much-needed handling of puppies as well; even holding puppies while watching television is a simple way to enhance human bonding.

The presence of many appropriately sized toys in the playpen (no matter how many times they must be washed) is valuable. Try hanging things such as a plastic pop bottle from the top of the whelping box to get the puppies accustomed to touches and bumps from overhead objects. Some breeders use mobiles for infants' cribs in the whelping box; you should use

Figure 26-8: *Stage Two is such a fun age!* Puppies are becoming mobile and active. This age is the beginning of social interaction and hierarchy. **(a)** At 5 weeks, pups display the early stalking and eye contact that are the hereditary hardwiring of hunting behaviors and social interaction. Photograph by Janet Meyer. **(b)** As this stage draws to an end, it is beneficial to divide the litter into play groups to avoid puppies bullying less dominant siblings. Photograph by Roman Braun.

only tough ones that puppies cannot demolish and with pieces they can not swallow. Overhead articles are excellent preparation for field training; puppies that have this experience are bolder when encountering any obstacle. Puppies need the early opportunity to pick up and carry objects at this age to fully develop the retrieving instinct later on.

Provide tactile experiences with a variety of textures in the whelping box—newspapers, blankets, towels, linoleum, carpet, and rubber mats have tactile differences. From the puppies' perspective, stairs can be intimidating obstacles, and negotiating stairs is a learning task that all puppies must eventually accomplish. A cinder block not only feels different but also introduces climbing, and stair steps are not nearly as awesome to puppies that have climbed all over a concrete block.

The desire to get out of the whelping box may appear as early as 3 weeks, and success follows eventually. Breeders often keep track of age and identity of the first ones to figure

Figure 26-10: *Children's wading pools* are becoming popular whelping boxes, but are difficult to divide into a sleeping and potty area. That's all right, make note of the first puppy to accomplish escaping the whelping box—often, this turns out to be the boldest or smartest pup in the litter. As pups learn to exit, also note who is able to return without assistance and who demands help; once personalities have been identified, a rolled blanket well secured around the bottom edge will allow pups to re-enter without assistance, encouraging cleanliness while giving the breeder a break.

it out. Escape requires some ingenuity and agility, and the first ones often prove to be the smartest and boldest when later tested.

When the pups are about 4 weeks old, divide the whelping box into a sleeping area and "potty" area, if possible. Cover one-half with newspapers and the other with a blanket held in place by a 2 × 4. The instinct to avoid soiling the place where they sleep leads puppies to eliminate on the newspaper, giving them an early start toward housebreaking. If the whelping area is too small to separate in this manner, place a crate with an oversized mat (too large to be pulled out of the crate) and line the remaining area with paper to encourage elimination outside the crate. During this time, it is important to pick up soiled papers immediately; puppies that become accustomed to playing in waste will be more difficult to housetrain. For the breeders' convenience in minimizing housekeeping, whenever possible feed puppies outside or take puppies to an outside exercise area immediately after eating to encourage cleanliness and appropriate toilet habits.

Make a lot of noise when the puppies are eating. Bang! Crash! Instead of fearing gunshots or the noise at indoor shows, these puppies are "turned on" because of the early association of noise with pleasure.

Make a clucking noise—the kind used to encourage a horse—when calling the puppies to eat and right after setting the bowl down. If the association is made from the earliest

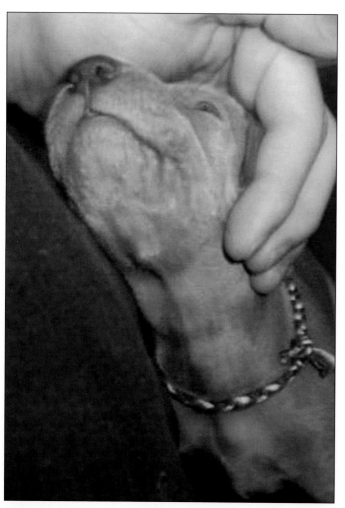

Figure 26-9: *This puppy has clearly connected* with a human as part of his world. Such early positive experiences with human hand and body contact bode well for this pup's future ability to accept leadership and training. Photograph by Shirley Nilsson.

Figure 26-11: *The boldest of Janet's Stage Three pups* (note the jauntily carried tail in the foreground) encourage less-bold littermates to explore and gain confidence. Once the reticent pups learn that such exploration can be fun they will be more willing to go out on their own. Photograph by Janet Meyer.

Socialization

Socialization with humans is of critical importance during this stage. Puppies that do not bond with humans have not had effective early socialization, and those that reach the age of 10 weeks without sufficient human contact begin to lose the potential to respond. Picking them up to move, worm, crate, or give a shot is not enough. Puppies whose only human contact consists of a reaching hand (often followed by an unpleasant experience) become hand-shy.

If isolated from human contact, puppies become dog-oriented—the so-called kennel syndrome. Weimaraners appear much more susceptible to this than many other breeds. It is impossible to raise a normal Weimaraner without giving it individual attention on a regular, one-to-one basis during Stage Three. With a Weimaraner puppy, fear of humans comes easily, as early as 5–6 weeks if the puppy has had little human contact.

There is a striking difference in emotional stability between a Weimaraner puppy with early sensory deprivation and an orphaned puppy that received a great deal of handling and love. Nine times out of 10, orphan puppies are much more responsive and better adjusted than ones raised in isolation, despite the lack of any maternal influence.

Contact with and handling by both men and women are important. Puppies that have received Stage Two and Three socialization exclusively by humans of one gender show a marked preference for either men or women throughout their lives. Leaving the television set on when away from home helps to get puppies accustomed to the sound of voices. In a household that does not include both men and women, this also gets the puppies used to both types of voices and minimizes later preference. At this time, be sure that puppies are exposed to people wearing hats, glasses, and coats.

stages of weaning, it becomes a subliminal Pavlovian response, and later this sound can be used on occasions in which a happy response is needed. The clucking sound, with its positive associations, just turns a Weimaraner on. The tail goes up and the stride lengthens without spoiling the front action, which is especially useful in the show ring. The Weimaraner just feels better because subliminally it anticipates being fed.

Stage Three: *Weaning to New Homes*
Beginning of 6th Week to End of 8th Week

First Impressions: Individuality and Early Socialization

The third critical stage of puppyhood begins after the puppies are weaned through going to the new homes. The learning task of this stage is human/canine bonding and learning to interact with the larger world. This is perhaps the most exciting stage of raising a litter. The yarn collars are replaced with "real" collars, signaling the shift from babies to youngsters. Puppies begin to develop their personalities. As they learn through experimentation, they create entertainment, providing a stage for visitors to share the fun.

Stage Three is also characterized by loving dependency. The learning potential during this stage is phenomenal and is too often is not used to its fullest potential. *Raising the Litter* and *Testing Natural Aptitude* provide a wealth of information on promoting development during this once-in-a-lifetime, highly impressionable age of 6–8 weeks.

Figure 26-12: *Hand-shy puppies start here.* Never pick puppies up by the loose skin on their necks; rather, be sure to use both hands to support the front and rear. Photograph by Brian Meaney.

Figure 26-13: *The movements, smells, and sounds of babies* are a unique and invaluable experience for a puppy. If a willing parent allows, provide puppies with closely supervised interaction with an infant. Photograph by Dorothy Derr.

Having a variety of visitors will familiarize puppies with different behavior and and movements, such as those made by children of all ages, as well as elderly adults. Pleasurable experiences with children are valuable and can establish a positive lifetime pattern. Unpleasant experiences, of course, can establish a negative pattern. It is usually best to allow only responsible older children to sit in the exercise pen with the puppies and to supervise them closely. Smaller children or children who are playing should remain outside the pen, allowing puppies to hear and observe the different behavior, sounds, and odors of children, which are completely different from that of adults. Such exposure is necessary if puppies are going to a home with youngsters, but it is just as valuable even for puppies going to homes with older or no children.

Puppies will also benefit from exposure to elderly adults and those with disabilities; both groups present a different manner of movement and behavior. This can teach the young puppy that while people may be different, they can all be the source of pleasant experiences.

Some common sense must be used, of course. Ask if the visitors have had any contact with sick dogs before letting them touch the puppies. If, for example, a prospective buyer is making daily trips to the pound (which can be a hotbed of contagious diseases) to find a lost dog or if someone has or has recently had a sick dog at home, visits and contact with the puppies should be denied.

Leaning Opportunities

Testing Natural Aptitude presents a series of learning opportunities developed over the past 25 years, oriented for the period from $4\,^1/_2$–$7\,^1/_2$ weeks. The foundations for these tests are centered on this stage, from 5–8 weeks, of rapid physical and mental growth. The progression of the evaluations will not only reveal the potential of a puppy but will benefit each puppy in its emotional and mental growth and preparation for its new home. The authors recommend that every effort be made to complete and repeat these evaluations throughout the first four stages of the puppies' lives to enhance the full genetic potential of every puppy.

By 5–6 weeks, the puppies are old enough to go out in good weather. Ideally, during this time puppies should be divided into groups based on temperament and size to minimize excessive oppression or bullying and to encourage individual exploration and development. Permanent puppy yards are wonderful, but play pens made by joining several exercise

26-14: *Puppies are encouraged to explore* under human supervision or a trusted canine mentor. **(a)** German methods mimic the behavior of wild canids; an aunt keeps a watchful eye on the litter as they explore and play. **(b)** When a "teachable moment" arises, mother Lena and her sister Battina converge to impart a valuable lesson in acceptable canine protocol. The offender displays submission while a littermate charges in to see what is going on.

pens can be moved to a fresh spot on the lawn whenever necessary. Both should be full of toys and obstacles for learning experiences. When the puppies become accustomed to being outdoors, they can be turned loose in a larger fenced yard whenever the breeder has time to supervise their play to ensure they do not get into trouble. Allowing the litter to accompany older dogs on a short walk outside the kennel area gives the breeder the opportunity to make many observations about the personality and potential of each puppy as it explores new surroundings. A good time to give the puppies an extended play and socialization period is just before bringing them indoors. The tired litter will then sleep peacefully for several hours.

By 4 to 6 weeks, most Weimaraner puppies begin to cry and fuss before they soil the whelping box. Taking them outdoors during this phase reinforces this behavior and provides a marvelous (and highly appreciated) start toward housebreaking. Removing drinking water at about 8 pm reduces the number of times puppies wake up to urinate during the night. If puppies are taken outdoors to eliminate at 10 or 11 pm, they often sleep until 3 am. If the breeder is a light sleeper and hears the puppies wake up, they may be taken outdoors before they soil the whelping box. They usually settle down quickly and then sleep until daylight. By the time puppies go to new homes at 7 to 8 weeks, they are almost housebroken and may even sleep through the night.

To ensure the subliminal connection, continue to use the clucking noise when providing food. Also continue exposing the puppy to loud noises at this time.

Puppies should be introduced to crates by weaning time so that they begin to develop self-identity and so they see the crate as a pleasant place to sleep. The companionship reinforces the feeling of security and helps a smooth transition to individual crating. A plastic dog crate with the door removed is an excellent portable indoor/outdoor doghouse in puppy pens. Bring a crate into the family room; leave the door open when puppies can be supervised, and close it at other times.

Stage Three puppies can easily be imprinted for swimming using the technique described in *Testing Natural Aptitude.* Lessons in swimming pools should include teaching the puppy where to find the steps and how to climb in and out of the water.

This is also the time to work diligently on exchanging toys for treats to reduce the potential for resource guarding. The puppy learns to accept that people can take an object away; a treat or toy is offered in exchange to encourage the puppy's willing cooperation and to reward appropriate behavior.

Expert opinions disagree on the "perfect" moment for puppies to go to new homes, varying from the 49th day until 10 or 12 weeks. However, the experience of the authors and the consensus among most authorities is that 7 to 8 weeks is a golden opportunity. By 8 weeks, puppies have had adequate worming and initial inoculations to be at least minimally

protected. Additionally, some areas prohibit the sale and/or shipping of puppies younger than 8 weeks. If not separated at 7 or 8 weeks, dependency bonds with the dam and littermates strengthen, and the potential for bonding with humans weakens. If a puppy is removed from a litter prior to 7 weeks, bonding with humans is enhanced and canine identification is weakened. Such puppies often show marked fear or aggression toward other canines unless they have continued contact with other dogs. Puppies that have been isolated from other dogs from the age of 3 to 4 weeks exhibit an extreme lack of canine identification by having little sexual interest in other dogs.

Figure 26-15: *Cuddling and slowly rocking* until the puppy relaxes and submits to the attention has proven to be an instrumental tool in helping the fearful or hyperactive puppy realize that humans are not only a part of its life but that such interactions can be pleasant and rewarding. While especially important for the tense, frightened, or overly aggressive, all puppies (as well as their humans) will benefit from an opportunity like this. This puppy demonstrates his complete trust and comfort with humans. He is ready to go to a new home and establish a relationship with a new pack leader.

Stage Four:
New Homes to Teething

2 to 5 Months

A Whole New World:
A New Pack Leader and Advanced
Socialization

Stage Four sees the puppy going to its new home at the beginning of the 9th week and ends just as the puppy begins cutting its adult teeth at approximately 4 to 5 months. During this stage, the puppy begins to generalize the idea of human leadership and broadens its socialization skills and experiences.

The new owner repeats the socialization process of Stage 3 in a new context. This experience helps the puppy generalize the concepts of socialization. People are friendly and fun wherever they are found, and the new pack leader will protect the pup from harm just as the first pack leader did. The commonly accepted concept of a fear period during this time might occur in an under-socialized pup but is rarely noticeable in the Weim puppy provided with the foundation described here. Should the breeder not have provided the best foundation, it is not too late; the dedicated owner can simply start with the experiences described in these chapters, starting at the beginning. This period is the golden opportunity for the new owner to imprint the puppy with all the basics of future desired behaviors.

Figure 26-16: *Leaving for a new home.* Love me, hold me, as I leave all that I have ever known and embark on a journey to a whole new world.

The pup has joined a new pack and should learn that all the conduct rules of his previous pack still apply; occasionally, difficulties may crop up during the transition period. If the new owner feels that behavior problems are occurring, NOW is the time to seek assistance. Do not delay and hope that the puppy will grow out of it. It is much easier to resolve situations with a young, malleable puppy than a resistant adolescent or hard-

Figure 26-17: *The right place.* **(a)** These lucky German pups are learning early the meaning of "place" with the help of their dam and mentor. **(b)** The owners of these pups will feel fortunate as this early training helps the puppy generalize the meaning of "place" in a new home.

ened adult. *Weimaraner Kindergarten* will provide an excellent foundation for either the family companion or the future competition partner. While establishing a new pack order, avoid giving the puppy commands that cannot be enforced, and profusely reward correct behaviors to help the pup make the transition.

Puppies remaining with a breeder during this time are at high risk for missing out on the opportunity to learn self-identification and generalization. Breeders must use extra diligence during this time to ensure proper emotional development if keeping more than one puppy. After the hectic weeks of raising a litter, it is easy to want to take a break and hope that the puppies will keep each other company and stay out of trouble. Nothing could be farther from the truth. Two puppies will get in more than twice the trouble if left unsupervised. Even worse, it is easier for the pups to bond with each other, missing out on the one-on-one human socialization necessary for success and so vital at this specific age for learning to live in their new world. It takes considerable commitment on the part of the owner and many hours of individual time and attention to develop and maintain the socialization and human bonding that will allow the Weimaraner puppy to become a great partner. For this same reason, the purchase of two puppies of this age (even if from different litters) at the same time is highly discouraged; it is simply too easy for the puppies to bond with each other instead of with humans.

Figure 26-18: *A big buddy...*be sure a large, soft, and indestructible pal is waiting to comfort the lonely new arrival. Photograph by William Wegman.

Figure 26-19: *Double trouble.* Without tremendous commitment, two puppies of the same age in a single household will not only get into more than twice as much trouble but will rarely develop to their full potential, as they will invariably bond more closely with each other than with their human companions. An older mentoring dog can benefit the puppy; however, the owners still must invest adequate individual time to develop strong human bonding. Photograph by William Wegman.

Figure 26-20: *Swimming is a good low-impact exercise* for growing joints and bones. A capable swimming companion will allow the puppy to take advantage of the tendency to mimic and minimize any natural reluctance or fears associated with this age. During this stage, shared swimming reinforces love of water with repetition and positive experiences. Not only will swimming bolster the sometimes flagging confidence of the stage, it is also good for emotional growth and gives the pup more opportunities to participate in activities with his owner. This is the time to gently reinforce past skills and desirable habits by plenty of exposure to a well-behaved mentor.

challenges are simply the result of the puppy's trying to soothe the itching and discomfort of emerging teeth. Toward the end of the period, destructive chewing is more often associated with attempts to "claim" desirable objects. Be sure that suitable chew toys are always available, and remove from temptation all inappropriate items. A rule of thumb is that the more valued or irreplaceable an object, the likelier it is to become an object of attention.

At this age, the puppy becomes mature enough to respond to more structured, intensive training. Good behavior and habits should be rewarded; bad habits should be prevented or corrected. Because the puppy now has a longer attention span, the trainer can be tempted to be more demanding. Independence increases and willful defiance may or may not be observed. Repeat the lessons of Stage Four, but with a more supportive and positive overtone. Puppies need support as they yo-yo between fearfulness and confidence.

Stage Five: *Teething to Adolescence*

Beginning of 5 Months tthrough 10 Months

Age of Cutting: Exploration and Relaxed Review

The fifth critical stage of puppyhood begins with the eruption of the adult teeth at approximately 4 to 5 months; its end is characterized by the puppy's entering adolescence at approximately 7 to 8 months. During this phase, puppies not only begin cutting their teeth, but begin cutting the apron strings as well; the learning task of this stage is independence, but the road is a circuitous one, full of detours and back tracks.

Stage Five is characterized by the puppy's first attempts to assert his own will. The loving, dependent puppy appears and disappears, frequently replaced by a mischievous and sometimes destructive character. In the early stages, many of the

Figure 26-21: *Fun matches and kids' shows* are another great place to get rewarding experiences now that the vaccination series is completed. While this is a good stage to provide a wide variety of new experiences, be prepared to be supportive and reward desirable behavior. If the pup shows reticence or a tendency to be frightened, allow the pup to approach at his own speed and then reward his boldness. Look for events where the pup can attend without competing so he can become accustomed to the noise and commotion and be rewarded for meeting new people without any pressure to perform as in serious competition.

Figure 26-22: *Make things really easy* and avoid the pressure of responsibility during this stage. Balance rewards and discipline carefully. Work on generalizing concepts; this is the time to review previously learned behavior in a setting where the puppy cannot make mistakes or poor choices. For example, use strong, wild birds that cannot be caught if the puppy flushes the birds; the birds will do the teaching without the owner needing to make a correction. Photograph by R. Moon.

Puppies at this age are learning important lessons regarding independence as well as cooperation; however, unpredictable is the best description of puppies at this stage. This phase is highly variable, dependent on established early training, bloodlines, and personality. The future trainability and success of the dog will, to a large degree, depend on the foundation that has been prepared up to this point. The puppy that has not learned foundational work will require a great deal more effort in order to learn the lessons that came so easily in the earlier stages, mentally as well as physically. No longer is the pup the blue-eyed baby bundle; rather, the former pup is now a gangly 45-pound adolescent with ideas of his own. All of a sudden, the puppy that used to come running when called seems to be deaf, or even runs away when called; the puppy that was doing so well on sit or stay suddenly seems to have completely forgotten these words! Occasionally, a pup, most often one that has been provided with a solid foundation, may appear to sail through this period with hardly a bobble.

The owner can prevent the development of an overly submissive or challenging attitude during this period by avoiding the opportunity for a puppy to "get away with" being disobedient. During this time, for example, practice the "come" command only when your puppy is on lead or in a confined area the puppy cannot escape from should he choose to ignore the command. If the puppy is at a distance, do not ask him to let go of a treasured object; be ready to offer a worthwhile substitute. Gently but firmly enforce commands, and be ready to return to a previous training level; go back to kindergarten and ensure that the puppy ends on a successful note.

To make this period even more confounding, puppies sometimes go through a secondary "fear imprint period" during this phase as well. While in general this is a good time to take advantage of new socialization opportunities, it is especially important to avoid frightening experiences for puppies that begin to show fear responses to new experiences. The puppy should be allowed to approach such situations at her own speed, but coddling and cajoling should be avoided so that the fear response is not inadvertently reinforced.

Do not despair! Puppies do outgrow this stage; patience during this stage will be greatly rewarded when the puppy returns in a few weeks to the cheerful, cooperative nature typical of the Weimaraner.

Figure 26-23: *Pups must learn their place* in the human social hierarchy before they are adolescents. Teaching children how to correctly offer treats to a pup also teaches the pup that humans, even though smaller and weaker, can control food and desirable objects. Refer to *Getting Off to the Right Start* and *Kindergarten Puppy Training*.

Stage Six: *Adolescence to Sexual Maturity*
10 to 16 Months

On-the-Job Training: Joining the Dog-Human Team

The old-school idea of waiting until the dog is 6 months old or more before beginning training will lead the Weimaraner owner who has waited until this point to regret procrastinating. The sincere desire to do things its own way begins to emerge, while the dog's physical development gives it the ability to succeed. Without a well-built foundation, the owner will be seriously challenged during this phase.

Do not think that the problems of an out-of-control adolescent will be resolved simply by spaying or neutering it at this age. In order to mature into a properly muscled and healthy adult, the Weimaraner still needs an additional 6 to 8 months to reach full physical and emotional maturity. Spaying or neutering at this age could result in an increased tendency for injuries, hip dysplasia, and incontinence in future years. The typical Weimaraner bitch will not come into her first season until sometime after her first birthday; males, however, are certainly capable of siring a litter as young as 7 months, these are more "accidents" than serious efforts. It is unusual to see behavioral problems related to sexual behavior before 12 months. When considering spaying or neutering the dog prior to sexual maturity, read Dr. Zink's article, "Early Spay-Neuter Considerations for the Canine Athlete" (2005).

Additionally, some breeders might have financial penalties for early spaying or neutering of dogs placed as competition or breeding prospects. Behavioral problems at this age generally require behavioral modification rather than physiological modification; the only solution is a new management plan. Refer to the breeder to address concerns at this time, or consider consulting a professional trainer or certified behaviorist knowledgeable about Weimaraners.

Fear and dominance behaviors can be easily reinforced at this stage. Look for some erratic behavior as surging hormones cause confusion. Previously familiar people and places could suddenly seem threatening to a young dog whose emerging sense of territoriality and protectiveness combines with the desire to establish adult social status. It is important to practice exchanging toys and food during this stage to minimize resource guarding; any object that elicits excessive possessiveness should be completely removed. It is particularly important that fears be dealt with compassionately but firmly. The owner who caters to fears takes a risk that the Weimaraner will think that fearful behavior is desirable. If the dog shows a strong fear response, leave the area and let the dog become accustomed to the fearful object or action in smaller steps through habituation rather than stimulus flooding. If swimming has been neglected up to this point, it is not a good time to teach a pup to swim. Because water fear can easily become permanently ingrained, wait for the pup to emerge from this particular stage or use completely inductive methods, such as a mentor or habituation.

Figure 26-24: *Do not let the dog forget previously learned behaviors* that should now be routine now. Even though he is house trained and can be trusted to not chew things, routinely practice crating to be sure he does not forget to respect the crate and restraint. Regular teeth and ear exams ensure that the dog remains accustomed to the procedure. Go over the dog nose to tail, including the feet and belly. Although nails need less frequent trimming in adults than in pups, keep the dog in practice.

Figure 26-25: *Now that the pup is approaching adulthood,* he must learn patience and the routine necessary at competitive events. An older, tolerant, and experienced canine companion on the stakeout or in the crating area will set a good example and keep the pup from stressing over his owner's absence. At some field events, noncompeting dogs are allowed to run the course or swim in water areas after competition is completed. A walkabout at the conformation show also will also provide a chance to see and enjoy the sights. Photograph by Gene LaFollette.

Figure 26-26: *Good social and obedience skills* are necessary at this stage to give the dog the opportunity to meet the increased need for exercise. Weimaraners of this age should be meeting a variety of other species and learning appropriate responses. Getty challenged this Axis deer from a neighboring exotic game ranch. Encouraged by this first encounter, a subsequent engagement resulted in Getty's being badly gored by the deer. Although Getty is now a field champion and remains intensely competitive as a field trial dog, she now ignores the ranch's livestock and visiting exotic game. Photograph by Nelwyn Clack.

to evaluate the dog's mental state on that particular day, especially in the early part of this stage. Once a foundation has been built, challenges can be added to test the dog's understanding of exercises in circumstances in which desirable responses can be enforced and undesirable behaviors prevented. Rewards are particularly important at this stage as the pup's desire to work for his owner's approval may wax and wane during this time. Most Weims really do love to work with their humans, so reinforce willing cooperation. In contrast, passive or active defiance can often be nipped in the bud: refuse to take the bait and remove the Weim from the opportunity to earn rewards. Let the reluctant student watch from a nearby crate while another dog gets to work and earn rewards. Use the Weim's tendency to mimic the behavior of other dogs and use mentors to reinforce desirable behaviors.

Rules must be made very clear at this time because the dog has the strength and experience to exert his own will. Consistency is critical at this time. For example, young male dogs (and some bitches) about this age will begin to raise a leg to mark, if given the slightest opportunity. However, should an owner prefer that a dog (such as a service dog) not mark, such behavior can be prevented if the dog is never given the opportunity to begin this behavior. Starting with the very young dog (when house training begins), simply use areas such as flat grass that lack vertical objects that tempt marking. Avoid allowing the dog to observe other males raising a leg to mark until the dog has passed through this stage. Most of the time, a dog that has reached full sexual maturity (12–18 months) without establishing this habit will begin marking if he is regularly exposed to marking males and when initial attempts to do so are not corrected.

This is a good time to begin adding complexity and polish, along with a healthy dose of fun, shared activities to the dog's repertoire. Pressure and expectations can gradually be increased, but be sure to go back and review easy material on a regular basis. Start training sessions with a review

Figure 26-27: *The right amount of exercise* is important to maintain an even keel in the adolescent pup, but do not overdo it. Some pups seem to be in a perpetual state of awkwardness, so be cautious that exercise does not stress growing bones and joints. Exercise the mind as well as the body by going to new areas; take advantage of weather changes for additional variety, but use common sense regarding temperatures or threatening weather. Avoid developing bad habits. Use strong-flying wild birds to reinforce the idea that birds cannot be caught. Avoid situations where the dog is likely to disobey a command that cannot be enforced. Photograph by Gene LaFollette.

Figure 26-28: *Regardless of the dog's previous accomplishments,* constant maintenance training is required to hold that competitive edge. After almost a year out of the bird field, her excitement is about to cause Emma to sin. Mary has come prepared with a check cord and is ready to steady Emma and remind her of the appropriate behavior. Consistency is critical to keeping the dog's performance level high.

Stage Seven:
Sexual Maturity to Senior Years
16–18 Months to 10 Years

Adult: Cooperative Self-sufficiency

Adulthood in Weimaraners can also be known as post-adolescence or advanced puppyhood and has been known to last until the muzzle turns from gray to silver. In her heart of hearts, every gray dog we have known, every Weim, longs to remain a puppy forever.... In all seriousness, the athletic nature of this breed allows most Weims to maintain an active working lifestyle for longer than many other breeds. Because this period spans so many years and there is great variety between individuals, this stage can actually be divided into two sub-stages: early and late adulthood.

Early Adulthood

The early years can be considered the prime competition years, and the concerns are those of any active dog. The years of early adulthood are probably the most competitive. All the hard work of building a strong foundation pays off now. Enjoy!!!! Keep the dog fit and be watchful for signs of illness and injury. Maintain a healthy diet and appropriate exercise if there is an off season. Frequently, Weimaraners are inveterate beggars and easy keepers; the owner must be vigilant to maintain an appropriate weight on the dog. Obesity adversely affects health as well as performance.

This is the stage when most Weimaraners make their reproductive contribution. A healthy bitch can usually be considered for breeding after 2 years and up to 6 or 7 years. *Breeding Basics, Mating Games,* and *Prenatal Care* will provide invaluable information on managing the brood bitch. Even if a male is not presently being used as an active stud,

consider collecting and storing semen at this time. The semen contribution will be larger and healthier, and, unfortunately, there is the possibility of injury or illness during the dog's lifetime, which could prevent natural breedings in the future. The only limit to the storage of semen is financial. For more information on determining whether the dog is stud-worthy, how to manage his career, and how to collect the semen, refer to *Breeding Basics* and *Mating Games.*

Late Adulthood

Most dogs have achieved their laurels by 5 years, so what to do for the remaining years? Consider that the Weim has become accustomed to traveling to training and competition on a regular basis after all these years. To the dog, this has become a way of life. Imagine the mental stress on a dog that is suddenly relegated to staying at home while the youngsters go to training classes and weekend competitions. The Weimaraner is such an athletic and versatile breed that no Weim should ever be bored. Keeping the dangers of a bored Weimaraner firmly in mind, *The Most Versatile Breed* explores new fields of interest to pursue after the original goals have been met. As the Weim matures toward the late adult years, look for low-impact sports, such as retrieving, swimming, and tracking, to introduce a new hobby. To keep the dog active and involved as he approaches his senior years, look for classes in almost every venue. Veterans' classes are sometimes offered for dogs older than 7 years; agility offers preferred classes with lower jump heights and slower time

Figure 26-29: *The irony of competitive dog events* is that many times the dog is ready to retire from competition by the time he reaches his physical prime at about 5 or 6. JC had "done it all" and then discovered non-regular competitive sports such as disk competition and high jumping. At his last competition, JC came in 2nd to the greyhound that would ultimately hold the Guinness World Record for the high jump.

Figure 26-30: *Consider getting a larger crate* for the mature dog; the crate should allow the dog to comfortably lie flat and to sit and stand with the head fully erect. This accommodation may help prevent neck and spinal problems in future years.

requirements. Many retired competition dogs will make an ideal entry as the junior handler learns the ropes. As long as the older dog is able to pace himself, he can make a great training partner for the younger dog also, being not only a good role model, but a steadying influence on the sometimes over-eager youngster. Many a retired field dog is the perfect teacher to help the young dog learn range, steadiness, and honor (see Figure 13-1). Maintaining involvement keeps the adult Weim emotionally happy, which can prevent behavioral and physical health problems.

The latter years of adulthood for the single-dog family are a good time to consider a puppy to extend the active years. The dog is young enough to enjoy company and increased activity, but not so old as to be inadvertently injured by obstreperous play.

For the few Weims that respected the electronic fence in their younger years, this is a not-uncommon age at which to find that the dog develops a disregard for electronic fencing in order to pursue his own interests and goals. The mature dog has had the opportunity to learn that he can simply grit his teeth and bull through the momentary discomfort to satisfy his desires on the other side of the fence.

When the dog turns 5, consider getting a crate that is a size larger, especially for dogs that spend a lot of time in a crate, so that the dog can sit and stand with its head completely erect. This might help prevent neck and spine disorders in the senior dog.

Bloat is a significant health threat during this stage, as the incidence of bloat increases with age. For individuals or bloodlines prone to bloat, be especially vigilant. Reduce stress whenever possible; for example, try to get a house sitter for the older Weim instead of boarding it at a facility. Most importantly, divide meals into at least twice-daily feedings. Restrict food and water before exercise; after feeding a moistened evening meal, restrict food and exercise. Refer to *Best of Health* for additional tips.

Change to a senior food when the dog begins to show signs of decreased activity and slower metabolism; this will help protect aging kidneys. This is also a good time to

begin supplements to reduce the potential for arthritis. There is a tendency to gain weight with declining activity and reduced metabolism, so be more observant and work hard to maintain the dog's exercise routine. At this time, the dog may begin to show a decreased need for exercise or less desire to participate in certain more-demanding activities. Respect the dog's choice.

Since AAHA now recommends most vaccines be boosted every 3 years, many dogs are not going in annually for a routine physical. All dogs older than of 5 or 6 years should get a regular physical at least once a year, and preferably twice a year. If you have an insurance policy for your dog, be sure to use it! Although eye problems are rare, the ears, kidney, heart, and thyroid should be evaluated regularly; catching problems early might keep them manageable. Regular grooming should include a thorough ear check, as incipient ear infections or mites can produce excessive head shaking, which can lead to hematomas on the ear. Consult your veterinarian and use discretion with vaccines as the dog approaches the senior years. For the more mature dog, the risk of year-round flea, tick, and heartworm treatments should be weighed against the potential exposure to these health threats. Consider discontinuing treatments during the winter months in areas where exposure to fleas, ticks, and mosquitoes is virtually zero. Older stud dogs, if used infrequently, need a sperm count and prostate check twice a year.

Figure 26-31: *An experienced, retired show dog* makes a great partner for the aspiring junior handler. The dog is settled and knows the routine, so it is easier for the junior to learn handling and to make the best impression; in return, the dog enjoys the excitement and attention of being back in the limelight again. Futurity and sporting-group winner Funny Valentine mentored 16-year-old Susan Wise in her early years; in turn, Susan eventually became chair of Junior Showmanship for the WCA. Her encouragement and timely advice has been greatly appreciated by many aspiring juniors in today's dog show world.

Stage Eight: *The Golden Silver Years*

10 to 18 Years

Graceful Retirement and Mentoring

The senior dog has given his best years. Respect his commitment by maintaining your commitment to him. Continue to keep him involved, not relegated to the bed in the family room or the farthest kennel; provide some special time each day to give the older dog individual attention so that he still feels he is a valued member of the family.

Encourage regular exercise but respect the dog's decision regarding physical limitations. Consider a second (or third) career, such as therapy work, to allow the use of all those trained skills and to keep the dog socially and mentally involved. Make sure the senior receives plenty of appreciation, praise, and attention. Do not let him just fade into the woodwork.

Monitor the older dog's weight on a regular basis through routine visual examination as well as the scale. Older dogs can sometimes have difficulty maintaining

Figure 26-33: *While other sensory skills may be compromised* by age, the sense of smell is usually one of the last to diminish in the Weimaraner. At 11 years, Hogan is getting her first tracking lesson after a successful career in the obedience and conformation ring. The low physical demands and mental stimulation of a sport like tracking can provide a new lease on life for the senior dog.

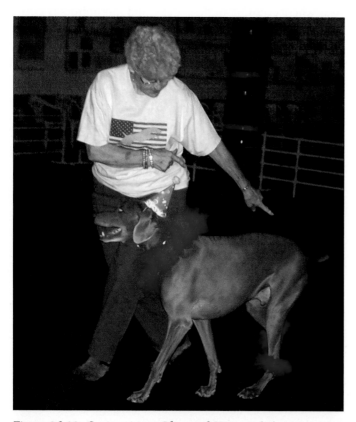

Figure 26-32: *Senior citizen Blitz and Nira* regularly visit nursing homes and schools to participate in musical freestyle obedience demonstrations. Older dogs love once again being the center of attention, and the chance to show off all his training keeps an older dog like Blitz mentally involved and physically active while providing an enjoyable show for children and the elderly.

weight because of reduced appetite related to dental or health issues; rapid or unexplained weight loss and sudden changes in appetite could indicate a serious illness. Conversely, it is also common to see reduced muscle mass in the senior dog. If caloric intake is not monitored in relation to activity, it is likely the older dog will gain weight, which could be detrimental to his comfort and health.

By 10 years, a special diet designed for the senior dog (not a weight-control diet) is necessary to help maintain weight and condition and to meet the unique dietary needs of the older dog.

The senior dog also needs to have free access to plenty of water during the day; however, nighttime accidents can be minimized by restricting water availability after 6 or 7 pm. Attention to such small details helps the older dog maintain dignity as well as health. For the incontinent dog (most commonly late-adult spayed bitches, especially those spayed prior to sexual maturity), an exercise pen can be placed on top of a waterproof liner and covered with blankets that can be easily washed. This gives the older dog room to stretch her legs and move around to find the most comfortable position for longer times when the owner is not available to respond to her more frequent need to go out.

Arthritis is not uncommon in the oldest Weims; if the dog is not already on a preventive supplement for arthritis, begin one now. Provide soft, comfortable bedding (indoors and out) at ground level to reduce the likelihood of injury by jumping onto or off of higher surfaces, such as beds or furniture. Protect the dog from extremes of the elements, as older dogs are more prone to heat or cold injury.

Figure 26-34: *Discourage jumping* by providing ramps or steps to higher places and offering very comfortable, soft bedding at ground level. Italian show champion Cindy, who has retired to a new career as a therapy dog, prefers to relax on her soft, snuggly ball awaiting her owner's return. Although the pace has slowed down, remembering to keep the dog active in less-demanding activities can add quality time for both the owner and the dog. These senior years can provide many golden memories as the family companion ages from silver to gray. Photograph by Telma Tucci.

If regular vet checks are not already a part of the routine, by the time a dog is 10 or 11 years old they are a necessity. While the Weim is generally healthy and problems like cataracts and hearing issues are uncommon until the dogs are quite elderly, routine checks of the blood, heart, kidneys, and thyroid should be requested from the veterinarian, especially if you have a health insurance plan. Be familiar with the dog's habits; small changes might indicate health changes. While it does not mean running to the vet every week, small signs such as increased thirst, confusion, reluctance to move, lameness, changes in appetite, edema, and the sudden appearance of lumps, especially hard lumps, can be early indicators of problems and should be checked. Catching such things early could prevent small problems from becoming serious. Frequent or painful urination, shortness of breath, any type of seizure, and sudden abdominal distention merit immediate veterinary attention.

Protect the canine senior citizen from unwanted attention from status-seeking or overly boisterous younger dogs. Enforce respect for the older dogs; do not allow younger dogs to bully the older dog either physically or mentally. Provide an area to which the old dog can escape when things get too rowdy to suit his taste or when he feels the need for a quiet nap.

The senior years may lack the frenetic activity of the younger years of intense competition, but there is no reason the senior Weimaraner cannot continue to fulfill the task for which he has been bred for hundreds of years—being a faithful companion and trusted, active member of the family. *Old as Well as Gray* celebrates the achievements of older Weimaraners and discusses the senior years in more detail.

Figure 26-35: *The mentor.* An older dog that is not in poor health or too frail to tolerate the physical roughhousing of a puppy may enjoy the company of a new companion. Many breeders find that the timing works well to keep a grand-pup of a favored stud or dam. Older dogs often thrive, gaining years of quality life, on the responsibility of mentoring a young pup. Photograph courtesy of Weimaraner Klub e.V.

Figure 27-1: *Anna and Able,* 8-week-old German pups, surprised everyone when they simply waded into a small stream and began swimming much like ducklings as they followed the only mother duck in sight. Make every effort to arrange a situation in which the puppy is led to believe that he is entering the water of his own volition. Weimaraners that are hurriedly forced to enter the water—those that are dropped, dragged, or tossed—most often develop a lifelong distaste for swimming. Photograph by Virginia Alexander.

CHAPTER 27

TESTING NATURAL APTITUDE

When provided with a loving, stimulating environment during their early weeks, Weimaraners make more effort than any other breed to go the extra mile to be a responsive companion. As a breeder, use the act of raising a litter as a privilege to influence and mold these babies into the best-adjusted and trainable puppies they can be before leaving home.

The tests described in popular dog literature were primarily developed by guide-dog breeders and are most effective with working breeds. Such tests have not been of notable value with sporting breeds because they do not evaluate the qualities most desired in hunting dogs.

The opportunities described in this chapter are based on the authors' years of experience and observation of puppies for the traits most desired in Weimaraners—pointing, retrieving, and use of nose. They also evaluate boldness, initiative, and self-confidence as well as learning and problem-solving aptitudes. The most recent version of this material was evaluated with 27 litters of other sporting dogs (Gordon Setters, Irish Setters, Labrador Retrievers, Golden Retrievers, Vizslas, and Curly Coated Retrievers) to add significance and to round out the variety of responses as well as to act as a control group.

The procedures and scoring at $4\,^1/_2$, $6\,^1/_2$, and $7\,^1/_2$ weeks are given in tables. Preparation and all other supplemental information are given in the text.

As most adults know, it is much easier for the young to learn new skills, not the least of which is the concept of "learning to learn." Progress at this age is rapid, and regardless of the responses, which provide valuable insight into the character, temperament, and natural abilities of the puppies, presenting a range of options and opportunities under controlled circumstances increases the aptitude to learn and perform tasks in the future. So regardless of its scores, each puppy will benefit from these experiences. Recording the results of the observations, according to the collar color, will provide a record of its pattern of development as the puppy matures.

In the "Nest"

For observation to be valid, puppies must be clearly and easily identified and remain with the same identification until they go to their new homes (see *Whelping* for identification methods). Begin making observations and keeping notes as the litter is whelped and weighed. Although the nest observations cannot be scored, puppies can be compared

Figure 27-2: *A rare opportunity* for the breeder to savor the wonder of each tiny life and contemplate the awesome responsibility of developing the innate abilities of each puppy for the future that lies ahead. When the puppy is 1 to 2 days old, carefully support it with both hands and turn each puppy upside down to observe its response. Photograph by Marek Bejna.

with their littermates, making adjustments for weight and other physical factors. Many times, a breeder can identify puppies that can benefit from special attention at this early age. The important thing is to note general patterns of consistent or unusual behavior.

By the 21st day, the breeder who spends extra time and makes daily observations has a "feel" for each puppy's vigor and temperament potential. Such observations require no experience, which is one reason first-time breeders sometimes make more accurate evaluations of puppies than an expert who first sees them for formal testing and then only for a brief time. Many conscientious breeders feel it is necessary to have an outside "professional" come to evaluate a litter and provide written unbiased test results for the new owners. Often, in order to ensure that the testing is untainted, many professional evaluators often discourage the breeder from providing the puppies with earlier enrichment experiences such as those outlined here. The authors, however, feel that the benefit from these experiences far outweighs the information provided from an isolated, single "raw" test. While such unbiased testing may provide much useful information, even the most novice breeder should listen to the small voice inside, based on 7 weeks of familiarization, when evaluating her own litter. The breeder's goal for every litter should be to provide the most well-socialized, responsive, and successful puppies possible. The experiences outlined below are designed specifically to provide precocious Weimaraner puppies that develop mentally more quickly than many pointing breeds, with a good foundation for learning and future relationships in preparation for leaving for their new homes.

Hands-on response. When taking the birth weight, hold the puppy in both hands and observe its first behavior. Is it nervous, tight to touch, wound up? Does it resist in a willful way, struggle for a long time, or settle down after a brief struggle? Is it stiff and ill at ease or totally relaxed and trusting? (Do not confuse relaxation with exhaustion.) How long does it take for it to relax and trust? Who takes the longest? Who never has a problem? Who has learned there is no need for concern at the next weigh-in?

When the puppies are 1 to 2 days old, again hold each puppy to observe its behavior. Turn each upside down, carefully supporting it with both hands. How hard does the puppy struggle to right itself? Note the gradations and rank within the litter—hardest, easiest, and how long. Watch for extremes.

Neurological observations. Observe the entire litter while they are nursing, and rank the puppies according to their natural and neurological coordination, making allowances for any that had a difficult birth. Can it hold on and nurse alone, or does it need a prop? Can the puppy nurse immediately, or does it need assistance? Does it hold the head stable and stay upright? How much does the head wobble? Does the puppy push each hind leg alternately, which is nor-

Figure 27-3: *All safe and sound.* After all puppies have arrived, observe them while nursing, and rank the litter according to their strength and neurological coordination, making allowances for any that had a difficult birth. Photograph by William Wegman.

Figure 27-4: *Pavarotti Pups.* Puppies that are very vocal at birth usually settle down within the first few days. Weimaraners that remain vocal after 3 weeks (when they begin hearing) most often tend to practice their talent well into adulthood. Photograph by William Wegman.

mal, or show the early sign of syringomyelia by pushing with both legs simultaneously like a frog? (All puppies frog kick, but those with syringomyelia rarely push with alternate hind legs.) When turned upside down, how long does the puppy take to turn upright and begin to crawl?

Activity level. Using the pontoon system *(Prenatal Care),* when returning the puppies to their mother, place each puppy at the mother's rear toes, and observe how quickly each one crawls along the leg to locate the nipple. Be sure to record exceptional responses according to the puppy's collar color.

Figure 27-5: *Loners.* Take special note of the puppy that chooses to avoid littermates. These loners are often longhaired or will need extra socialization. Photograph by William Wegman.

Just before the puppies' eyes open, place each puppy near the center of the mother's back and observe how long it takes to circle the mother and locate a nipple. Does it exhibit obvious use of the nose? If uncertain, try squirting some of the mother's milk and make a trail for the puppy to follow.

Can the puppy just go backward or backward and then forward? Those who go backward for longer usually go forward fastest.

Evaluate the puppy walking on a surface that offers good and poor traction. Who is first to support its body weight and walk? (Fat puppies tend to take longer to support themselves.)

When the puppies are walking well, place each on a slippery surface, like a kitchen counter. How long does the puppy take to stand tall on the new surface? Is it willing to stand up and walk?

Gender differences. Even at this early stage, female Weimaraners tend to be more precocious than males, displaying more coordination at an earlier age; also, larger puppies are often slower to develop coordination than their smaller littermates, regardless of sex. Therefore, the larger pup or a male that displays coordination equal to or exceeding female or smaller littermates should receive additional credit.

Vocalization. The amount of noise a puppy makes is often a clue to its adult character. Does the puppy constantly make noise, even while nursing? Does it complain to let the mother know when it is hungry or uncomfortable? Does the puppy make noise when there is nothing to complain about? Which is the first to make a distinct bark? Which is the quietest? Does a normally quiet puppy cry when moved away from mother or simply find the way back?

Nursing etiquette. Nursing manners are often the first expression of mature personality, be it bold or passive. Does the puppy consistently change nipples, knocking others away? This could be a bullying type or a smart one. Do any prefer a specific nipple and relocate to the same one when pushed off? Does the puppy object to being pushed off a nipple—fight, hang on as long as possible, or find another immediately if displaced? Some puppies are very passive. Most puppies have no nursing pattern, finding any convenient nipple, feeding until full, and falling off. Is any puppy always the last to get a nipple? However, do not be overly concerned about smaller puppies: although brute force rules at the nipple, persistence and cunning are worth noting as well.

Loners. Do any puppies have a pattern of not sleeping with others, and does this persist after the 21st day? If so, this could be a sign of either unusual independence or passiveness, and the behavior must be weighed with other observations. The puppy might also be longhaired and merely avoiding the uncomfortable warmth of littermates.

Figure 27-6: *An uptight puppy,* by William Wegman.

Figure 27-7: *Relaxed and trusting,* by William Wegman.

4¹/₂ Weeks

Weaning. By 3 weeks, the curled tongue has started to flatten, allowing puppies to lap thickened food from a dish. When evaluating, feed each puppy individually. This is easiest on a grooming table or on a towel placed on the kitchen table. The only other preparation for the test is to have a supply of strained baby veal or beef.

Sound responsiveness and sound association. These two observations are made simultaneously, but the puppies' responses are recorded separately (a) for the speed of their responsiveness to noise and (b) for the ability to associate a specific sound with something pleasurable.

As soon as the ears are open (at around 21 days), begin making a clicking noise (like clucking to a horse) while the puppies eat so they begin to associate the sound with food. Repeat this for several days to determine which puppies are most alert to sound stimuli. Observe which learn to associate a special noise with something pleasant.

Sound sensitivity. Begin conditioning the puppies to loud noises as soon as they can hear. Give special attention to any that are sensitive to noise, because to some degree this

Table 27-1: *4¹/₂ weeks.*

Objective	Procedure	Scoring
Weaning *Evaluate physical maturation* *Evaluate early learning aptitude*	Make clicking noise before showing food Let the puppy lick or suck some food from a finger Smear food on saucer rim. Lead puppy's mouth into food, touching the side of the mouth to stimulate tongue flattening	1 Laps eagerly from finger and saucer 2 Laps eagerly from finger, has trouble with saucer 3 Laps from finger, no interest in saucer 4 Refuses to eat at all, tries to spit out
Sound Responsiveness *Evaluate hearing*	Wait until the entire litter is asleep, preferably spread out so all have a similar opportunity to hear noise Begin making clicking noise, slowly at first, then faster and louder until the whole litter is awake Stand no farther than 3 feet from puppies with face at puppies' eye level	1 Awakened immediately by noise 2 Awakened by littermate movement, then responds to noise 3 Awakened by littermates' movement, no response to noise
Sound Association *Observe learned response to sounds*	Done at same time using same procedure as *Sound Responsiveness*	1 Circles, becomes aware of person, and approaches 2 Circles, looking for something associated with noise 3 No reaction, follows littermates
Sound Sensitivity *Observe sensitivity to loud noises*	Wait until the entire litter is eagerly eating Begin softly to beat on pan, counting slowly to 5 between beats Gradually increase volume until first puppy shows a flinching response	1 Keeps on eating 2 Looks up, returns to eating 3 Shrinks, turns around, holds ground but never settles 4 Stops eating and gets as far from noise as possible
Dominance Response *Acceptance of human control* *Assess stress level*	Place puppy on side Place hands on neck and chest, gently holding puppy down Hold for one full minute (less if totally panicked)—no speaking but may reassure with stroking of fingers	1 Resents being placed on side, but once there, gives trusting response 2 Struggles, resents restraint, then accepts and relaxes 3 Fights restraint, then accepts but remains tense 4 Continues to fight and/or vocalizes 5 Tries to bite persistently or panics
Cuddling Test *Evaluate human bonding potential*	Noting time, sit down in a comfortable chair and cradle puppy against chest, turned to side so puppy can hear heartbeat, being certain puppy is securely supported under rump Rock puppy slowly back and forth—no vocal or stroking reassurance Note length of time it takes for puppy to relax completely—maximum time, 5 minutes	1 Immediately trusting response, licking face, wagging tail, demonstrating pleasure of bodily contact 2 Response to contact not as intense, pleasure not as strong, but accepts contact readily 3 Struggles, tense, eventually accepts restraint, but constantly looks around and never relaxes, may tremble 4 Struggles, protests restraint, tries to jump down, may take a brief rest before resuming fight

is a learned behavior. The less sensitive a puppy is, the better its chances are of not being gun-shy. A surprising number of novice owners overlook the importance of a gradual introduction to gunshots as part of field training.

Dominance response. Puppies should be placed on a familiar surface such as a blanket or towel (see Figure 27-9 for additional information).

Cuddling. When taking the puppy away from its littermates, be sure to lift it carefully from the playpen from under the shoulders and rear—the response varies if all puppies are not picked up in this uniform way. Be sure puppy eliminates

before beginning the evaluation. Use no vocal or other sound stimulus during the test, and the environment should be as quiet as possible—no TV, traffic, and so forth.

Any puppies that do not accept cuddling need individual attention several times a day, unless the only problem was a need to eliminate. Surprisingly, most respond to special attention and show improvement when re-evaluated, indicating that to some degree human bonding is a learned behavior. Giving special loving attention from 4 to 7 weeks can make the difference between a puppy that becomes a normal, loving companion and one that has difficulty adapting.

Figure 27-8: *Weaning.* By 3 weeks, a puppy's curled tongue starts to flatten, and it can begin weaning with an enticing taste of strained 100% beef chicken or veal baby food.

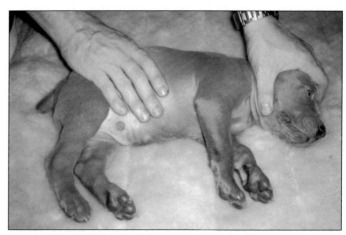

Figure 27-9: *Dominance response.* A puppy's response to physical restraint may indicate a future willingness (or unwillingness) to trust and respond to human leadership. This puppy shows a completely relaxed response to being restrained in a new location away from its littermates.

Figure 27-10: *Cuddling.* One of the special aspects of raising puppies is the opportunity to cuddle them. While most Weimaraner puppies instinctively enjoy snuggling with humans, those that are initially reluctant eventually learn to savor the experience. Theo, photographed here at 2 and 8 weeks, shows that in spite of phenomenal growth, once the puppy learns to enjoy the experience, he will never outgrow the desire to cuddle, even when he outgrows the lap as an adult.

6¹/₂ Weeks

Water love. When puppies are imprinted with a pleasant first encounter with water (not being sprayed with a hose), love of water is usually lifelong. Imprinted puppies are better swimmers and typically enter the water with an eager leap. Such enthusiasm surprises owners who believe their Weimaraner is going swimming for the first time, and of course, they attribute it to instinctive behavior rather than the breeder's bathtub.

It is important that the puppies have their first distemper measles shot several days prior to this experience because they should not be stressed or chilled immediately after immunizations.

Be sure that the bathroom is warmed ahead of time and that the water is also comfortably warm. Completely cover the tub's bottom with rubber bath mats, the kind with suction to prevent moving; there simply is no satisfactory substitute for the mats. Have a generous supply of assistants and warm bath towels for drying and cuddling the puppies. Since most puppies will attempt to drink the water, rinse the tub thoroughly to be sure there is no soap or cleansers in the water. Drinking water is an indicator of the puppy's comfort level; do not correct puppies for this.

This experience involves several phases. The first step is water imprinting, which involves getting only the puppy's legs and lower chest wet in shallow water. Before adding water for the swimming phase, repeat Phase 1 with puppies that did not accept the shallow water comfortably. Any that are frightened during this second opportunity should not go on to the swimming phase; repeat the shallow-water experience with those puppies in another week or so.

Phase 2 is swimming imprinting. Support and nonstop verbal reassurance are critical. Never remove the supporting hand entirely. Frequently, puppies of this age that are swimming with ease suddenly stop moving their legs and sink, turning a positive experience into a negative one.

The dry-and-cuddle phase should take at least 10 minutes because the cuddling, combined with praise and close body contact, is a vital part of the total imprinting experience. The puppies should return to a warm whelping box, and the breeder should take precautions to prevent chilling for at least 3 hours.

After this experience, water love can be reinforced in summer weather by providing a half-filled wading pool for the puppies to play in as well as other pleasant water experiences, such as adding toys or a bag of ice cubes to the pool water.

Figure 27-11: *Water love.* Imprinting water love and swimming is divided into three phases; never progress to the second phase until the puppy is comfortable with the first. Each experience should always end with the reassuring warmth and cuddling of the third phase.

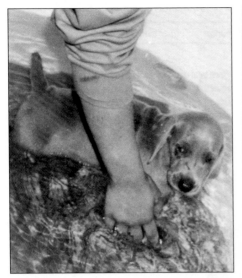

(a) Phase 1: Secure footing and water that reaches no farther than the chest teaches the puppy that water is not dangerous, while the breeder stimulates the puppy's playfulness and curiosity with a moving hand and gently moving water. Do not advance to Phase 2 if the puppy shows fear—i.e., the tail is tucked or the puppy refuses to move.

(b) Phase 2: Once more, water has been added to the tub. Always use one hand to support the puppy's chest during his swimming efforts to prevent the fun from suddenly turning frightening. Swimming one lap—down and back—is enough.

(c) Phase 3: "Such a wonderful puppy." Snuggling next to a human heart, until the puppy is completely dry and relaxed, completes a lifelong imprint that swimming is fun.

Crate. This may be a good time to put new colored nylon loops on all puppies so that each puppy is easy to distinguish inside the crate. If enough crates are available, all puppies can be evaluated at the same time.

Pick up and carry. At 3–4 weeks, enrich the puppies' environment with objects that stimulate the pick-up response as soon as teeth are in and pups start weaning.

This simple, individual observation should be made in an environment that the puppy has already explored. For the article, use a soft, furry object—an old wig, fur-lined glove (inside out), sheepskin, or rabbit skin—that the puppy has never seen before.

The few Weimaraner puppies that have failed to pick up and carry articles were raised in a sterile environment, with little socialization and few play objects. Puppies of several other pointing breeds, however, often showed little evidence of the pick-up-and-carry instinct even when given generous socialization and an interesting environment.

Be sure to differentiate between stalking behavior—also highly desirable—and the pick-up-and-carry response. Puppies that stalk and pounce before picking up the article receive a 1+ rating, as this trait is a strong indication of exceptional hunting potential. Any puppy that consistently fails to pick up and carry an article will need a great deal of additional attention to develop retrieving skills.

Scent aptitude (indoor). Prepare a couple of different treats ahead of time in case one does not appeal to the puppy. Nearly all puppies will respond to turkey or chicken hot dogs sliced very thinly and then in quarters; soft cat treats (which can be broken into small pieces) usually work as well. Any treat that is soft, quickly eaten, and odorous will work. If a particular puppy does not show great interest in the bribes at the beginning, try different treats until the puppy is highly motivated. An assistant makes this exercise much easier.

Puppies should have previously played in the area so there are no new environmental distractions, and the exercise must be done before feeding to be sure they are hungry. The only other equipment needed is a good-sized stuffed chair or any other object that can keep the puppy from seeing the hidden treat in the final step.

Give the puppy 5 minutes to find the hidden treat— this is also a problem-solving learning experience. If the puppy appears bored, try a different treat. It is vital to end with a successful find, even if it is necessary to go back and place the article in plain sight.

After this experience, avoid any further structured scent-finding games until the following week.

Meet the bird. This is the puppies' first contact with birds and should be done with a freshly killed or frozen quail—the small Coturnix® quail are ideal—or a pheasant

Figure 27-12: ***This simple and fun evaluation*** reveals nose-oriented and food-motivated puppies. Since many dogs have difficulty with the concept of a scent source above head level, these puppies show not only strong scent-detection ability but problem-solving skills as well by locating the opened can of treats on the high table. Such a puppy shows early promise for success in a field or working home.

skin with ample feathers. Pigeons are too heavy for 6-week-old Weimaraners to pick up, and some puppies find their scent and tight feathers offensive. Puppies are rough on freshly killed birds, so purchase at least one bird for every three or four puppies. Any excess birds can be frozen for the next litter or training session.

There is always at least one puppy in the litter that will pick up the bird and begin to carry it around, and soon the rest of the litter will be in full chase. Often, puppies catch and carry or drag the bird by a head, wing, or tail. Some have difficulty finding a part of the bird to pick up and carry easily. Holding out a wing or head to grab helps. As a last alternative, if no birds can be secured, a toy, scented with commercial bird scent, may be substituted.

This is one of the most interesting experiences to observe because it triggers the bird-hunting instinct. Oddly, the mechanism seems to be the feel or taste of feathers rather than sight or scent that does the trick, and the puppy's response is marked, as if someone flicked a light switch. Puppies that have been imprinted this way have a lasting, positive attitude toward stalking and carrying feathered creatures.

Table 27-2: *6¹/₂ weeks.*

Objective	Procedure	Scoring
Water Love *Imprint water love and swimming*	**Phase One** With mat on the bottom, fill tub with 3 to 5 inches of warm water Begin with boldest puppy Carefully lower puppy into water while giving lots of vocal encouragement Gently slap water to create movement and coax puppy to explore the tub; do not correct puppy for drinking water If badly frightened, adding a littermate that has already shown a positive reaction to water gives reassurance; if a littermate shows insufficient motivation, allow dam to join puppy in the tub Remove puppy, dry feet, and return puppy to littermates **Phase Two** Add warm water, increasing depth so puppies must swim Lower puppy into water while supporting chest with hand and giving vocal reassurance Allow puppy to swim the length of the tub and back, gradually decreasing support if the puppy indicates confidence and strong swimming ability, but always keeping hand under puppy in case it stops swimming **Phase Three** Dry thoroughly, cuddle until dry, then return to litter	1 Immediate positive response to shallow water, shows enough self-confidence to swim without support 2 Immediate positive response to shallow water, swims with confidence while supported 3 Positive response to shallow water, enthusiastic but "sink and splash" swimming style 4 Positive response to shallow water, strong fear response to deep water 5 Fear response to shallow water until littermate added 6 Fear response to shallow water even with littermate 7 Interest in mother's milk overcomes fear of water when dam is placed in the tub with the puppy 8 Fear response to shallow water even with mother present
Crate (with Company) *Evaluate acceptance of confinement with company*	Place two puppies in crate with toys Leave 10 minutes Repeat next day with different companion	1 Relaxed resignation, goes to sleep or plays 2 Objects vocally briefly before settling down 3 Objects vocally, restless, eventually accepts confinement 4 Objects vocally, tries to get out entire time 5 Panics
Crate (Alone) *Evaluate acceptance of confinement when alone*	Place one puppy in crate for 5 minutes, then give company for about 20 minutes Repeat the next day, increasing time alone to 15 minutes, and the following day to 30 minutes	1 Relaxed resignation, goes to sleep or plays 2 Objects vocally briefly before settling down 3 Objects vocally, restless, eventually accepts confinement 4 Objects vocally, actively tries to find way out, never relaxes 5 Exhibits stress—continuous barking, digging, biting at door 6 Panics, urinates, salivates

Figure 27-13: *Crate alone.* When puppies are crated individually for the first time at 6¹/₂ weeks, anxiety will be reduced if the crates initially face one another. The authors suggest doing this to minimize stress even in adult dogs.

Figure 27-14: *Pick up and carry.* For pick up and carry, select a toy the puppy finds desirable and that is a suitable size for the puppy to carry. A wig, preferably of human hair, is often an effective article to awaken the retrieving instinct of a Weimaraner of any age.

Table 27-2: 6¹/₂ weeks. *(continued)*

Objective	Procedure	Scoring
Pick Up and Carry *Observe pick-up-and-carry instinct* *Reinforce instinct*	Shake object enticingly and drop in front of puppy to pick up and carry around If not picked up: (a) place on a string to simulate live prey (b) bring out another puppy to demonstrate pick-up and stimulate copying behavior (c) check puppy's health and repeat next day (d) repeat for several days using different objects	**1** Picks up object immediately **2** Picks up object after teasing **3** Picks up object after watching another puppy **4** Picks up object but never carries **5** Never picks up object
Scent Aptitude (Indoor) *Scenting aptitude* *Attention span*	Hold puppy in lap, not more than 6 feet from large chair Introduce puppy to treat Allow the puppy to watch while assistant places treat on floor not more than 3 feet away and allow it to eat Hold in lap, allow puppy to watch while assistant lays scent track by finger walking to chair, and leave treat Release to track, increasing distance if successful If puppy does not follow track, try placing extra treat at halfway point Repeat for a successful ending	**1** Finds treat under chair on first try **2** Finds treat under chair, takes longer to find **3** Does not find it under chair but finds it at shorter distance; finds it under chair on second try **4** Finds it at short distance but appears to find it by sight rather than scent **5** Never makes attempt to search for treat
Meet the Bird *Instinctive response to feathered game* *Imprint with sight, scent, and feel of birds*	Tease whole litter with a freshly killed or thawed quail Remove all puppies, and give each puppy an opportunity to show interest individually. For puppies that are less interested, select two or three puppies, including at least one that tried to grab bird initially, and place others in a pen where they can watch Place bird on the ground to allow the most aggressive puppy to pick it up and run off with it As next puppy chases and tries to grab bird, take the bird from the first puppy, which is removed from test Let the second puppy run with the bird until the third puppy tries to steal it Continue letting each puppy run with the bird to entice another to steal it, then remove teaser from the game until each has had an opportunity to learn the taste and feel of feathers	**1** Strongly possessive of bird, protests removal **2** Strong determination to keep bird **3** Grabs bird but gives it up without strong protest **4** Takes bird from littermate but only interested in object possession **5** Picks up bird, drops immediately **6** Total refusal to pick up bird **7** Avoidance or suspicion of bird

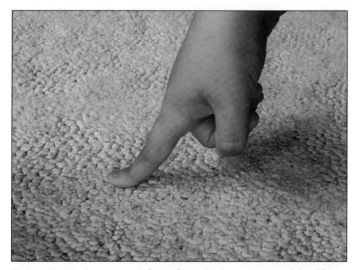

Figure 27-15: *Scent aptitude, indoors.* To lay a scent track by "finger walking," rub your fingertips on the odorous treat, then make a "track" by dragging your fingers along the floor's surface; let your fingers do the talking to the nose of the puppy following the walking trail. Photograph by Christopher Millan.

Figure 27-16: *Meet the bird.* Every litter will have at least one puppy eager to grab and possess this fascinating new object. Less-eager puppies will then want to possess the bird and try to snatch it away, thus creating a favorable experience for the taste and feel of feathers.

7¹⁄₂ Weeks

Stairs. Like children, puppies have a strong fear of falling, and going up or down stairs requires considerable courage. Stairs have proven to be the best way to evaluate self-confidence as well as physical coordination and balance. Puppies that score well on this consistently grow into adults that show boldness, initiative, and good problem-solving skills.

The ideal stairway is one with carpeted risers of average height or less and steps that are deep enough for the puppy to sit comfortably. Outside cement stairs also work well because of the good traction. Varnished hardwood stairs should be avoided, as should stairs with open backs.

Scent aptitude (outdoor). A helper, a crate, and a crate cover are required. Prepare the treats as in the indoor scenting, and be sure the puppies are hungry. Use whichever treats the puppy preferred at 6¹⁄₂ weeks first, but have alternatives at hand.

Each puppy must be familiar with the outdoor location, which should be secluded and away from littermates and other distractions. The area should include something, such as a bush, that can be used to hide the treats from sight; alternatively, use any large object that is not like the one used for the indoors. Wind should be low to average to provide the best opportunity for the puppies.

Allow the puppy 5 minutes to find the hidden treat. If the puppy is reluctant to move away from you, get up and walk with the puppy to encourage forward progress; stop and wait if the puppy begins to move forward on its own. If the puppy is having difficulty because he keeps returning to you, try getting up and walking past the scent cone of the hidden treat, watching the puppy for a response. End with success, even if it is necessary to go back to a simple sight find. Stop while the puppy is still happy and pleased with itself. With the most successful puppies, try increasing the distance (in small steps) and changing the location. Always end with a successful find.

Results are affected by the puppies' maturity level, which determines attention span and distractability. If a puppy shows a poor response, try different bait, such as a new food item or a favorite toy, or repeat the indoor scent testing. Try to stimulate interest with teasing, and compare with other responses.

Stalk and point. A short fishing rod (with or without a spinning reel) and a bird wing are the only equipment needed. Because puppies begin by sight pointing, however, a piece of cloth or plastic is almost as effective as a wing. If available, a small, live, harnessed quail may also be used to increase enthusiasm. Tie the wing (or toy or harnessed quail) securely to the end of the nylon fishing line, which has low visibility and does not distract the puppy's attention from the wing. When flipping the wing or bird in front of the puppy, the keys to success are ensuring the puppy does not catch the object and dropping the object suddenly in front of the puppy. Sometimes it is necessary to repeat the flipping process for several minutes to take the edge off the excitement before the tiring puppy realizes the wing cannot be caught and begins to stalk or point.

Figure 27-17: *Outdoor stairs* with solid steps and indoor stairs with low risers with closed backs are best for beginners. A bold long-haired puppy leads his less-confident littermate up these stone steps at breeder Rainer Münter's home in Canada.

The puppies' introduction to the rod and wing is a learning experience for all Weimaraner puppies. Any puppy that fails to give a good response should be given daily practice, trying different "birds"—a rag, piece of plastic, fur, or fresher wing. Allowing the puppies to observe their littermates strengthens desire. This is one enrichment opportunity that should be afforded to each puppy repeatedly, for short intervals every few days, until the puppies go to their new homes.

While an early strong display of pointing is always preferable, the pointing instinct does vary in strength and age of appearance. Therefore, do not totally write off a puppy that shows little interest in pointing birds at 7 weeks. Puppies that have shown desirable stalking behavior but very little enthusiasm for pointing may suddenly "wake up" at a later age. With Weimaraners, boldness, independence, desire to carry objects, and stalking behavior are often more accurate indications of a potentially outstanding hunting dog.

'Go fetch.' Use a familiar indoor location such as a long hallway or small room to minimize the distractions and exploratory options. Gather an assortment of appealing, highly visible objects, such as toys, small balls, and bird wings (nothing edible). Tease the puppy to see which article puppy wants most—the more the puppy desires the article, the more revealing will be its willingness or unwillingness to give it up. 'Go fetch,' as with stalk and point, should be repeated regularly with puppies as often as possible until they leave for new homes.

At 7½ weeks, puppies have relatively poor peripheral vision and often lose sight of the article. Keep the article low and within the puppy's visual field by rolling or sliding it along the floor.

Note the puppy's response if the article's fall is not marked, and repeat at a shorter distance if the puppy seems confused. Keep throwing the article until certain the puppy has seen it fall and is aware of the location.

If the puppy makes no movement toward the article, go back to teasing until the puppy takes the article, then praise the puppy and end the game. Place the puppy in a crate to observe other puppies retrieve, then provide another opportunity after it has watched other puppies retrieve and receive praise. If the puppy demonstrates little natural aptitude, it should get extra credit for copycat learning ability and the desire to please.

Most Weimaraners have some natural retrieving desire, more than many other pointing breeds. Imprinting at an early age is essential or the natural desire may be lost. However, Weimaraners typically love retrieving as a game, especially if started at an early age and reinforced with frequent practice and praise. With Weimaraners, learned or copycat retrieving is often as strong as the purely instinctive reflex response of the retrieving breeds.

'Walkies.' The puppies should have been wearing their new buckle-type collars in addition to the identifying colored nylon loops for several days now. After they have had 1–2 days to get used to the collar, attach a 1-foot rope with a knot to the collar. Allow each puppy, one at a time, to wear the rope while playing with the others; after 10–20 minutes, switch the rope to a different puppy until all the puppies have had the chance to be harassed as littermates tug and bite at the dragging rope. Never leave a puppy unsupervised with the rope attached. During this experience the tester should never drag the puppy; rather, kneel down and coax the puppy forward if necessary. If coaxing fails to produce the desired response, try following the puppy wherever it wishes to go.

For valid results, the evaluation must be done in a familiar area, out of view of the other puppies and before starting the lead-training technique described in *Ages and Stages*.

'Tough Pup.' Nobody enjoys hurting puppies, but breeders must identify overly sensitive puppies, too sensitive to ever be useful for hunting. Observe the range of response within litter, and be sure to give each puppy a treat and lots of love when finished. A hunting dog must be willing to go through potentially painful cover and terrain. Sometimes the difference between a good hunting dog and a great one (all things being equal) is simply a difference in sensitivity to physical pain. Although the desire to please and passion to hunt should outweigh physical discomfort, some dogs simply have a very low pain threshold. Overly sensitive dogs may quit on sharp rocks, go around the thorny thicket, or trot down a road. They may also refuse to retrieve game that falls in places associated with pain.

At the other extreme are Weimaraners with an extremely high pain threshold, an almost total lack of pain response. These dogs can hunt with severe injuries. On the whole, this is highly desirable, but such dogs must be controlled entirely by voice and desire to please—they certainly do not mind physical corrections. Most Weimaraner puppies and good field dogs fall between these two extremes.

As an alternative, especially if hunting toughness is not an issue, record the puppies' responses to vaccinations. This is, however, much less reliable because the pain stimulus is more variable, depending on how or where the vaccines are injected. Generally, any puppy that is consistently overly dramatic about painful stimuli should be noted.

Table 27-3: *7¹/₂ weeks.*

Objective	Procedure	Scoring
Stairs *Self-confidence* *Assess physical coordination and balance* *Evaluate human bonding*	Place puppy several steps below the person at the top of the stairs Call puppy, offering treats to coax up the stairs If puppy does not move, place puppy one step from the top and coax up one step After each successful trip up, move one step lower Test willingness to go down stairs using small segments of stairs If necessary, allow puppy to accompany successful littermate, retest	1 Goes willingly up and down the stairs 2 Goes willingly up, only goes down after learning 3 Goes down and up after learning 4 Only goes up and down a few steps even after learning 5 Never goes either up or down without company of littermate 6 Never goes up or down the stairs at all
Scent Aptitude (Outdoors) *Nose quality, willingness to learn, desire to please, memory and learning from previous (indoor) scent experience*	Bending over, offer treats to find which each puppy likes best Place treat on ground 2–3 feet in front of puppy; helper releases and allows puppy to find and eat treat. Repeat procedure, increasing distance while dragging treat along ground for 5–6 feet Repeat procedure, except this time cover the puppy's eyes so he does not see treat placed on ground; increase distance (not to exceed 10 feet) Move to a new location at least at least 10 feet upwind and repeat the unseen drag Release puppy and observe tracking behavior to locate treat Increase distance only if puppy shows aptitude and desire If unsuccessful, repeat scent drag at shorter distance If still unsuccessful, repeat last successful test to conclude evaluation	1 Adores game, immediate success at longer tracking distances 2 Immediate success at prescribed distances 3 Demonstrates tracking to hidden object 4 Success only when assisted by walking toward scent cone 5 Success only when assisted by walking through scent cone 6 Sight find only 7 Success only with random activity 8 Repeated efforts do not increase interest or success
Stalk and Point *Evaluate pointing instinct*	Initially, puppies are not allowed to watch others; attract the puppy's attention by flipping the wing in front of its nose; test and tease into chasing solid point Once the puppy decides to chase, flip the wing from one side to the other until the puppy realizes the wing cannot be caught, tires, and begins to pounce, stalk, or point If puppy shows no individual interest, bring in a previously tested "birdy" littermate as an example and to compete for the wing For a more accurate evaluation and for the puppy's enrichment, repeat the process with a live quail in a harness or on a string	1 Alert interest and quick stalking response with flash point 2 Alert interest and walking stalk with flash point 3 Alert interest, stalks and pounces with no flash point 4 Strong chase and desire, but no stalking or pointing 5 Brief chase, short attention span 6 Chases only when competing with littermates, little individual initiative 7 No interest or pursuit 8 Avoidance of bird
'Go Fetch' *Evaluate retrieving instinct* *Assess ability to combine retrieving with pick up and carry*	Tease the puppy with a favorite article Kneel, restrain the puppy while making certain it is watching, and toss the article 1 foot away Release; let the puppy start toward the article When puppy picks up article, back up 3–4 feet to encourage return, getting down to its eye level and calling coaxingly Repeat, tossing article about 5 feet	1 Immediate direct retrieve and willing delivery 2 Goes immediately to article and picks up, but needs coaxing to return 3 Goes immediately to article and runs off with it 4 Retrieves article after observing others 5 Goes to article but refuses to pick it up 6 Refuses to go to article
'Walkies' *Response to restraint*	Attach lead to collar and pick up lead Begin walking, coaxing puppy to come along No penalty for puppy that holds lead in mouth while walking with tester. Maximum length of test is 5 minutes (presumes puppy has had pre-conditioning described in "walkies" text)	1 Accompanies cheerfully 2 Initial resistance, then follows willingly 3 Strong resistance to lead, then follows with occasional resistance 4 Strong resistance to following, but willing to move in its own direction with person following 5 Fights lead entire time 6 Panics
'Tough Pup' *Assess pain threshold*	Place puppy on grooming table or crate or hold firmly Pinch the tip of one ear, or the webbing between toes; slowly increase the pressure, and count slowly until puppy shows a response	1 Longest time, pulls head or foot away 2 Moderate time, pulls away 3 Brief time, pulls away 4 Brief time, pulls away and yips or bites

Figure 27-18: *Stairs.* Climbing stairs is hard work for a tiny puppy. Do not expect the puppy to climb the entire flight of steps up to a landing on the first try; start with just a few stairs in the beginning.

Figure 27-19: *Scent aptitude, outdoors.* The scent track is laid by dragging a tasty treat along the ground and hiding it out of sight. The puppy follows the tantalizing scent and is rewarded with a treat.

Figure 27-20: *Stalk and point.* For some puppies, the initial response to the wing suddenly falling from above is a slow (deliberate), creeping stalk (often concluding with a pounce).

Figure 27-21: *Stalk and point.* When a harnessed quail flutters down, the same puppy is more likely to point instead of stalk. At this age either response, pointing or stalking, is favorable.

Figure 27-22: *Walkies.* If a cheerful voice cannot coax the balky puppy to accompany the evaluator, see if the puppy will allow the person to follow where it leads.

Figure 27-23: *Tough pup.* It is important to identify puppies with very high or low pain thresholds. Those with low pain tolerance will likely be averse to heavy vegetative cover, and those with a very high tolerance will need a strong leader to elicit compliance. The puppy's willingness to forgive the injury may also be indicative of trainability.

Star Search:
Special Tests for Special Talents

The above observations of general physical and mental traits are useful regardless of what type of home the puppy will be going to. However, in some cases it may be useful to identify pups with exceptional aptitude in certain areas. Traits deserving of special observation include

- ★ **Courage:** strong natural nerve combined with extensive socialization. This is the puppy perceived as bold and independent, the one constantly following its nose into potential trouble or unexpected places.

- ★ **Attention:** able to give individual focus to a task for long periods. Comparatively, this Weim puppy continues on its "mission" despite distraction long after its littermates have gone off on other pursuits.

- ★ **Native Talent:** a natural, genetic ability and desire or enjoyment in using that ability, combined with the physical soundness to perform the task.

While the overall soundness of structure is important to the longevity of life, service, and performance, talent is not dependent on outer beauty and may even overcome physical limitations.

For the most demanding activities, the natural traits listed above may even override the dog's desire to please the handler, creating a dog that may ignore the handler in pursuit of its own objectives or one that may disregard its own physical condition and literally work its heart out unless it is closely monitored. The dog with courage, attention, and native talent provides the raw material; it is then up to the trainer to provide the necessary direction and opportunity to excel in the chosen field, whether it is field trials, Search and Rescue, and or other demanding endeavors.

Scent Detection:
Narcotics, Explosives, and Search and Rescue

The most common test for scent-detection dogs is very simple and simultaneously evaluates focus, natural ability, and, to a minor extent, courage. Any dog that will be used for scent detection (Search and Rescue, narcotics, explosives, etc.) must first and foremost have strong nerve. These dogs will be expected to perform their work at the highest caliber, often under trying conditions of noise, physical challenges, and

Figure 27-24: ***The scent-detection candidate*** watches the first couple of times the toy is tossed into the higher cover. Subsequently, Bella is evaluated on her persistence and hunt desire when the toy is tossed without her having seen it thrown.

stress. If the dog is unable to focus and perform under these conditions, then all the talent in the world is useless.

Pups that have already shown strong nerves and scent detection and retrieving skills and are under consideration for a "star search" are taken to an area with moderately challenging ground cover. Pups are tested individually. As the puppy watches, a highly desired toy is tossed a short distance—just far enough to be out of the puppy's sight, maybe 3 or 4 feet—into the cover and the puppy is allowed to fetch the toy. Because puppies have limited peripheral vision, at first it is especially important that the toy be tossed directly ahead to ensure the puppy has seen the object being tossed into the cover. After a few repetitions, the puppy should easily understand the game.

The puppy watches as the toy is tossed back into the cover; the puppy is turned in a circle in order to break his visual mark. Does the puppy understand to go and look for the toy after his concentration has been interrupted? Does the puppy plunge eagerly into the cover? Throw the toy in different spots and at different distances. Does the puppy search in a hectic manner or with focused intensity? Is the area covered thoroughly, or does the puppy cover the same area over and over, leaving some places unsearched? Does the puppy show willingness to range farther away in his search? While the pup is evaluated for persistence in searching, his desire to keep possession of the ball or toy or his willingness to bring it back to initiate the game again is noted; either may be acceptable, depending on the training technique of the evaluator. The pup who finds the toy and neither possesses nor returns the toy is faulted.

Since the trait being evaluated is the desire to search for the toy for the sake of finding and possessing or returning the toy, no other reward, such as a treat, is offered. Ideally, the game can be continued until the puppy shows marked tiredness while still showing a mental willingness to continue; quit while the pup still wants to keep going. Young puppies may tire after a couple of tosses into dense cover; give bonus points for the puppy eager to continue after a short rest. Should a puppy show extreme hunt drive combined with excellent nose skills, it may be necessary to "fool" the puppy by not actually throwing the ball so that persistence can be truly evaluated; how long will the puppy search when the object cannot be found? (If this is done, once the evaluator is satisfied that the puppy shows persistence, the toy should be tossed where the puppy can find it so its persistence is rewarded.) In real-life searches, dogs are often expected to search areas for long periods of time when there is no scent source present. There is no specific length of time that makes a dog a candidate for scent-detection work; rather, it is a subjective comparison of candidates. When comparing puppies, the ability to focus longer and strength of desire are more highly desired than physical endurance at this age. Ideally, the test should be performed more than once because of the potential for variation in test conditions and the puppies' development.

Natural Preference: Air Scent or Ground Scent

It is not difficult to determine whether a dog has a strong natural preference for one scenting style (air scenting or ground scenting) over the other. It will be easier to train a puppy for tracking if it has a natural inclination to work ground scent as opposed to air scent. This does not mean that the dog that prefers to air scent cannot be trained to track, but all things being equal, why not work with the dog's own natural preference? Conversely, training a bird dog will progress more smoothly if the dog's natural inclination is to air scent.

An open area is needed with a good vegetative cover appropriate to the size and age of the dog—for small puppies, even short grass will do. Additionally, some sort of cover for the handler to hide behind, such as a building or dense bush, is needed. While an assistant holds the puppy, a person the puppy is attached to plays momentarily with the puppy to engage its attention and ensure the puppy is familiar with the person's scent. The assistant turns so the puppy will not see the playmate walk a short distance away and hide behind the object. The assistant sets the puppy on the ground where the person was last standing. Observe the pup for a natural inclination to drop its head to the ground to search for the ground scent trail of the missing playmate or to lift its head in an attempt to catch an air scent. Set up this exercise so that the wind will not be blowing the air scent directly from the playmate to the puppy; rather, there should be at least a slight cross wind so the puppy must move from its original location; the puppy that immediately catches the person's air scent will typically move in that direction instead of having the opportunity to choose whether to air scent or ground scent. The observation should be made several times, in different areas, to see whether the behavior shows a pattern.

Bird Dogs: Field Trial Competitor or Personal Gun Dog

While it is extremely difficult to identify a pup at this age that has the athleticism necessary for a top-notch field dog, some additional tests will help discover those with that extra degree of prey drive and scenting talent that often separates the personal gun dog from the field trial competitor. The more easily modified traits of courage and attention should in the hunting dog prospect take a back seat to a highly evolved natural skill in use of nose. We are looking for the pup with a highly developed natural desire and ability to locate prey. Without this

Figure 27-25: *The field trial candidate* may be revealed with this test for the nose and desire to locate and possess game. The tracks need to be laid far enough apart to prevent distraction by competing scent trails. The evaluation starts in low, easy cover, but challenges the puppy to break heavier cover to locate the prey. The puppy's behavior once he possesses the prey is also part of the evaluation. Photograph by Nicholas Millan.

Figure 27-26: *Another field trial candidate test.* **(a)** The puppy that immediately and confidently begins following the line of the scent drag without the need of a decoy bird, redirection, or the company of a person and **(b)** slows only to break cover to locate the prey is the ideal candidate. **(c)** Retrieving the prey imprints the taste and feel of the feathers, triggering the sense of empowerment and control. The puppy is praised and encouraged to possess and display his prize. A long line attached to the bird prevents the puppy from acquiring bad habits. Older puppies should be further evaluated, retrieving the prey on longer, more complex drags. Photograph by Marek Bejna.

overwhelming talent, the dog is less likely to withstand the pressure of breaking to wing and shot and still maintain the range and style necessary for the highest-caliber field trial performance. While they are very important talents in the hunting dog, trainability, pointing, and retrieving have been evaluated earlier in the chapter; here, superior scenting ability coupled with the native cunning to localize the scent even in the most difficult conditions is the most highly coveted trait. Later, these talents, when combined with the highest level of physical conditioning and drive, will define the difference between the average hunting companion and the true trial competitor, where "no find," even after a great run, means "no placement."

Set the scene. In order to offer a fair test, select an area that has low cover, such as a mowed lawn, and that is rarely traveled to reduce conflicting confusing scent. The area needs to be large enough to provide at least 20 feet between tracks, so that each pup can have a "clean" track to provide the basis for a fair comparison between pups. An assistant is necessary, as are two identical highly desirable objects with a distinctive scent, preferably quail. If birds are not available, commercial bird scents may be used to scent a toy. In a pinch, any strong odor will do, such as smelly cheese or hot dogs, but only as a last resort (just do not expect the food items to be returned to the evaluator).

Puppies that have not been tested need to be confined away from the testing area where they cannot hear or view the proceedings. Be sure that puppies have eliminated before testing and that they have not been fed a large meal. Give the pups a chance to explore a nearby area to become accustomed to the scents and conditions, but do not contaminate the area in which the evaluation will occur. If the weather is severe, testing can be accomplished in a large, empty building, but only if absolutely necessary.

Use light-colored plant stakes to mark starting points ahead of time. Put them approximately 20–30 feet apart to ensure that there is enough space to test all puppies and to prevent ending up with conflicting trails. Choose a location that will allow approximately 15–25 feet for each track, with a place to hide the bird (tuft of grass, small bush) at the end. Try to select an area where the wind is relatively still and distractions are minimal.

An assistant will exercise the puppy away from the testing area while the track is being laid. If using quail, allow it to thaw completely and even age for a half day or so wrapped in a paper towel in a closed plastic bag; the stronger the odor of the object, the better. If using a toy, put the toy wrapped in a paper towel

Figure 27-27: *Prey drive is a genetic gift and hard to teach—take this one home.* Photograph by Colleen Dugan.

liberally spiced with commercial bird scent for hours and place in a closed plastic bag. Remove the quail (or toy or treat) from the bag and attach a string. Rub the quail (or toy or food) on the ground around the starting stake and drag it along the ground to the desired cover area. If the bird is not very smelly or the puppies are very young, return it along the same path to the marker, then turn around and walk the trail for a third time. Deposit the bird behind the cover. If using an object other than a bird (toy or food), use the scented paper towel to press the scent onto the vegetation around the starting stake.

Bring the puppy (with a clearly identifiable collar) to the starting stake, calmly place the unleashed puppy on the starting pad, and give him every opportunity to fill his nose with the scent left at the stake by gently restraining and stroking. Do not force the puppy's nose to the ground; if the odor has not attracted the pup's notice, ruffle the grass with the fingers to draw his attention. Show the puppy the second bird (or identical object), and encourage the puppy to grab or attempt to play with the object by teasing. Drag it just a step or two along the track and then make the bird magically disappear by tossing it to the assistant, who immediately places it in a plastic bag (preferred) or tucks it securely in a closed pocket to minimize the scent of the remaining bird as much as possible.

If the puppy does not immediately begin to track toward the hidden bird, the tester may choose to walk a couple of steps in the right direction. If the puppy seems to lack confidence, the tester may choose to follow behind as the puppy progresses; however, the puppy that confidently tracks on its own is preferred. Noise may distract a young puppy, so keep encouragement and discussions to a minimum while the assistant silently takes notes on the puppy's response. Great praise and excitement are very appropriate, however, when the puppy locates and grabs his prize. As long as the puppy is not trying to eat or dissect the bird, allow him to keep the bird and parade around with it, in order to savor the scent and feel of feathers and to imprint the experience indelibly in his mind. The string attached to the object can be used to prevent the pup from carrying the prize to an inaccessible location without your having to have the unpleasant experience of chasing or grabbing the puppy.

Figure 27-28: ***Give extra points for natural ability and job focus.*** **(a)** This 10-week-old puppy is willing by trial and error to work out a way to cart off a 5-lb. duck. **(b)** This same pup demonstrates his genetically programmed prey drive creates a commitment to finding and possessing the bird. When conducting this test, be sure to use a bird that is just on the verge of being too large; a bird that is too small can be easily eaten—an undesirable lesson. Photographs by Colleen Dugan.

Frozen Birds

Freezing. Dry the feathers carefully to minimize frost accumulation. Wrap the bird in paper towels and freeze in a tightly sealed freezer bag.

Thawing. When removing the bird, knock off as much frost as possible and shake out the paper towel. Set aside for at least an hour to thaw feathers. Alternatively, place both bird and towel on a plate and microwave both for $1/2$–1 minute for quail or 2–3 minutes for pigeon, which is enough to warm and fluff the feathers appealingly and to release the scent without really thawing the body of the bird.

Using. Rewrap the bird in the microwaved paper towel (keeping the towel for extra scent marking) and replace everything in a plastic bag to minimize the human scent when carrying it. Because the bird's body remains frozen, puppies cannot seriously maul the bird and acquire undesirable habits. With luck, the birds may remain intact enough to dry the feathers and refreeze for another day.

Figure 27-29: *Mine!* Gretta, displaying her strong desire to maintain possession of the bird, earns extra points. If they are not quickly captured, often the most promising puppies may carry the prize under a bush or nearby vehicle; this perhaps may be the only time in which a growl is not a punishable offense, as it indicates the intense desire and courage needed for future success as a competitive field dog.

The most optimal response is the puppy that immediately begins to track and independently follows the trail to the bird. The ideal puppy would grab the bird and proudly display his treasure and is most often unwilling to it surrender it immediately. The puppy that repeatedly retraces the trail but eventually finds and grabs the dead bird is also given high marks. A puppy that remains interested but needs the tester to walk some distance toward or even past the bird in order to find it should be retested later on a fresh trail. If the puppy fails to make contact with the game, double lay the track (without the puppy watching) by dragging the bird along the exact same track, and restart the puppy immediately to end with success; retest this pup later. A puppy that shows only momentary interest in the trail before wandering off or any puppy that is frightened to be left without its littermates is not a strong candidate for consideration. Such a puppy should have additional scenting opportunities and should be returned to puppy kindergarten (see *Weimaraner Kindergarten*).

Summarizing the Results

Completing each of the experiences even once will greatly increase the mental capacity of puppies that participate. Each puppy, no matter how it scores, will be influenced by the mental enrichment, establishing new learning pathways. Remember that these are simply observations of how the puppy responds; never at any time is the puppy corrected for its response. Also, each puppy ends with a positive experience at the end of each opportunity. Although puppies may be ranked by their individual responses, there is no way to rank them by overall performance on all of the tests. More important than scores, the experiences serve as a tool for identifying each puppy's strengths and weaknesses, which helps the breeder match each with the most suitable owners. The observations also identify areas in which puppies can be helped to make marked improvement with extra attention, changing early weakness to later success.

Throughout the litter's growth, the puppies have had many chances to develop optimal talents and aptitudes and the breeder knows each individual very well. Puppies with exceptional early natural aptitude can be noted as highly promising candidates for breeding and more demanding careers. Although puppies with optimal responses to the first experiences are thrilling, any puppy that demonstrates progressive improvement through repeated opportunities or observation of other puppies until reaching the same level of performance should not be penalized for a slow start, because learning and problem-solving aptitudes are also critical breed traits. If time allows, these experiences can be offered several times while the puppies are waiting to go to their new homes. If a puppy offers less than optimal responses or lacks any desirable response at all, these opportunities should be repeated on a one-to-one basis whenever time allows. Immeasurable factors such as a difference in conceptual age or a pattern of slower growth and development could mask exceptional but later-developing natural ability. The important point is that the puppy should demonstrate learning ability and trust and responsiveness to human leadership.

Overall, the only trait that is a cause for concern is a puppy that consistently demonstrates a poor ability to learn or is fearful of new experiences. Nevertheless, work with human infants has revealed that if neurological and physiological irregularities are identified well before 3 years, amazing progress can be made to overcome their effects. As with human toddlers, Weimaraner puppies are amazingly responsive to positive early learning opportunities.

Figure 27-30: *Natural courage.* German puppies get off to an early start. Eight-week-old Duncan von Hubertus learns to jump on command. His willingness and trainability at this young age revealed Duncan's likely future as an outstanding hunting companion and won him a new home in America.

Figure 27-31: *The early observations* in this chapter will help a breeder match the puppies' natural character and abilities with an appropriate home. The Star Search tests may help identify puppies with exceptional aptitude for more demanding futures. It is the authors' hope that every breeder will appreciate the evaluation tools in this chapter and will use them to help select puppies, at an early age, that may most contribute to their future breeding goals. Here, Dante vom Forsthaus Gehegemühle is shown retrieving a hare over a ditch during a hunt test in Nordrhine West-falen, Germany. Dante's ability to perform these demanding exercises is the result of beginning with the basic ingredients, a puppy with the right genetic and mental foundation, combined with an owner prepared and committed to providing the necessary environment and training. Such testing will ensure that Weimaraners continue to exercise the skills for which they have been selected for more than a century—a valued partner and companion for the hunter and his family. Photograph by Angelika Joswig.

Figure 28-1: ***Good health is essential to the active life*** most Weimaraners prefer, ensuring long life. Here, CH Moonshine's Premium Slate, VCD2, MX, MXJ, NJP, JH, NRD, VX3, and his owner, Randy Reed, are competing in the Outdoor Channel's ECO Challenge. Slate's success in his many endeavors endeared him to many admirers. This multi-talented dog not only enjoyed fame throughout his lifetime in movies and advertisements, he shared his joy for living wherever he went. He was particularly welcomed at Ronald McDonald House events, where his special gift brought comfort and happiness to many children. Randy's last words about his relationship with Slate were, "I will never forget the joy of this journey! It is the memories that can never be taken away. The memories will always make me proud when I see his pictures with a smile on my face." Every breeder should strive to provide each owner with a canine companion with such potential. Photograph by Randy Reed.

CHAPTER 28

PUPPY HEALTH ASSESSMENT

Every breeder's goal is a well socialized and healthy puppy, but sometimes things go wrong. When they do, it helps to understand what happened and whether recurrences can be prevented. This chapter describes some of the problems that may occur before the puppy is 7 weeks old. See *Best of Health* for immunization and worming information.

Veterinary Examination

A veterinary examination of the litter at 6 weeks provides a preliminary screening before making the final evaluation of each puppy's potential. Bring along a stool specimen—a random sampling fresh from several puppies. If any puppies have loose stools, the specimen should also be checked for parasites, especially *Giardia*.

The health examination includes the following: temperature; weight (worming medication); mouth and gums (infection); teeth (bite and alignment); ears (infection); eyes (eyelid disorders); maxillary glands (enlargement, indicating infection); heart (murmurs, irregular rhythm); lungs (respiratory infection); abdomen (unusual masses, umbilical and diaphragmatic hernia); genitals (vaginitis, cryptorchidism).

While at the clinic, each puppy receives the first immunization. Individual dosages of a worming product are premeasured and given several days later to avoid compounding the immediate stress of the vaccination.

The breeder should obtain individual health certificates for his or her records, and a copy should be given to puppy buyers.

Sometimes Hereditary, Sometimes Not

Discovering a congenital disorder is always a distressing experience, especially for novices who are totally unprepared for a "flaw" in their perfectly planned purebred line. Experienced breeders have learned that sooner or later something (some say everything) shows up. Many congenital disorders can be identified before puppies are 7 weeks old and placed with new owners. They range from those that are definitely hereditary with a known mode of transmission to those that are definitely not.

The first clue that a disorder may be hereditary is that it recurs in several litters of related dogs. Related dogs, however, are often exposed to the same environment, and the familial pattern may reflect common environmental factors—climate, diet, stress, vaccinations, toxic plants, chemicals, and so forth. Furthermore, some abnormalities can be caused by hereditary factors and by environmental factors. In every case, careful investigation of all possibilities is imperative.

Cleft Palate

Cleft palates and lips are considered hereditary. Here, human genetic studies clarify the difficulty of identifying hereditary relationships. Of the 153 different human syndromes associated with cleft palates and lips, 79 are caused by single-gene inheritance; the 79 syndromes account for only 5% of the total cases.[1]

Figure 28-2: *Manni, a relaxed and healthy puppy.* Photograph by William Wegman.

Figure 28-3: *It is sometimes possible to palpate testicles* in a newborn puppy or just before the tail docking, where the tiny testicles can be felt like small peas moving within the abdomen. Males in which the testicles can be located at this early age can usually be considered non-carriers for cryptochidism and monorchidism. Photograph by Gene LaFollette.

Figure 28-4: *Locating the testicles in an older puppy* is easier if the relaxed puppy is held in a vertical position in the lap. Applying gentle downward pressure encourages the testicles to move closer to the scrotal sac. Since the left testicle usually descends first, it might be cause for additional attention if the right testicle appears first. Photograph by Shirley Nilsson.

Occasional cleft palates and lips occur in many breeds, and most are probably accidents of embryonic development or exposure to one of many teratogenic agents. Even when familial clustering is observed, the possibility of a common environmental factor must be considered. Overall, the incidence in Weimaraners is so low that breeders should not be unduly concerned when one crops up. Affected puppies can be identified shortly after birth because they cannot nurse, and they should be euthanized.

Cryptorchidism

Cryptorchidism is the failure of one or both testicles to descend into the scrotal sac; there is monolateral (only one testicle descends) and bilateral (neither testicle descends) cryptorchidism. The incidence of cryptorchidism is difficult to establish, and estimates range from 0.8 to 9.8%.[2] While it is common to refer to a dog with only one descended testicle as a monorchid, despite this commonly accepted usage, true monorchidism is defined by Willis and Merck as the presence of only one testicle in the body, whether it is descended or undescended. While monolateral cryptorchidism is not that uncommon, true monorchidism is very rare.

Cryptorchidism is a hereditary trait, but the specific mode of inheritance remains frustratingly elusive and controversial. Although no formal research has been done in dogs, the authors have both followed several generations of studs with confirmed early descent of testicles (by 34 weeks) and have observed a significant decrease of cryptorchidism, supporting the hypothesis that delayed descent may be a form of cryptorchidism.

At whelping, the tiny testicles are normally located near the penile sheath, but it requires a highly discerning touch to feel them. Male puppies can be palpated prior to the dewclaw and tail-docking procedure; if testicles can be felt near the penile sheath at this time, the chances of having undescended testicles at maturity are remote. If they have not descended into the scrotal sac by 8 weeks, the probability of descent decreases sharply, although final descent has been reported as late as 11 months.

Breeders and owners are justifiably distressed by the "disappearing" testicle, when a male that had both testicles descended into the scrotal sac before 8 weeks suddenly has only one a few days or weeks later. Until the inguinal ring closes, puppies can draw the testicles back into the abdominal cavity, usually when excited or stressed, such as by unaccompanied air travel to a new home or a visit to the veterinarian.

A monorchid or cryptorchid puppy is basically healthy and makes an excellent pet, particularly for owners who prefer a neutered dog. Although the puppy cannot compete in shows and should never be used for breeding, he can participate in AKC performance events. Because it is a disqualifying fault, a monorchid or cryptorchid dog is ineligible for WCA ratings unless it has been neutered.

Veterinarians often recommend early removal of undescended testicles, warning of the risk of cancer. Testicular tumors are rare in both normal and cryptorchid dogs, and about 90% of the tumors are benign.[3] We know of only a few Weimaraners diagnosed with testicular tumors, and all had two normal, descended testicles. Recent information also indicates that early sterilization may have a negative impact on the skeletal and muscular development of the canine athlete, leaving it more prone to injury or disorders such as hip dysplasia.[4] If the testicles are not properly descended at 1 year, the dog is then physically larger and more able to withstand the stress of the major surgery required for this procedure, which is more complex and invasive than a routine neuter.

Early Eye Infections

Just before the eyes open, sometimes earlier, puppies can develop swelling (resembling a small grape) around the unopened eyes. This is caused by infections, that occur for no apparent reason. Prompt treatment is vital to prevent permanent damage to the eye from pressure as well as infection.

Figure 28-5: *Observe puppies for the development of grape-like swelling* beneath unopened eyes, which indicates an infection. The usual treatment is to apply warm, moist compresses over the eye for several minutes to soften the crusty matter, which is then gently removed. Massage the swollen eyelid gently, stroking toward the nose, helping drain excess fluid and relieve the pressure. Photograph by Gene LaFollette.

Figure 28-6: *Eyelash abnormalities.*

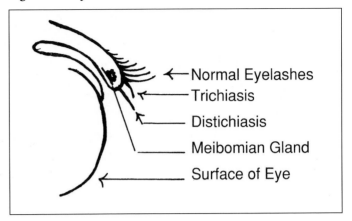

Have the veterinarian check the puppy as soon as possible. The usual treatment is to apply warm, moist compresses over the eye for several minutes to soften the crusty matter, which is then gently removed. Massage the swollen eyelid gently, stroking toward the nose, to express the pus and relieve the pressure. Be sure to avoid allowing the compresses or any expressed material to cross-contaminate the healthy eye; wash hands frequently. When no more pus can be expressed, apply some ophthalmic antibiotic ointment, which is provided by the veterinarian. The infections usually clear up quickly when the eyes open completely; however, random, inappropriate, or unsupervised use of antibiotics can be risky with such very young puppies. **Be sure to distinguish that the ointment is designated for use in the eyes; it is not hard to confuse the words otic and ophthalmic on the tiny bottles used to dispense these medications.**

Eyelid Disorders

Entropion and Ectropion

Entropion is an inward rotation of the eyelid (and eyelashes) that is characterized by watery eyes, blinking, conjunctivitis, sensitivity to sunlight, pain, and inflammation. Ectropion is the reverse—drooping or sagging of the lower eyelid that is characterized by excessive drying of the cornea with overflow of tears. Chronic conjunctivitis and the collection of debris in the eye aggravate the problem, and surgical correction is often necessary if the symptoms are severe and persistent. Both disorders may be either a congenital genetic trait or an acquired problem, secondary to injuries or chronic conjunctivitis. Several reports state that entropion appears to be inherited as a dominant with incomplete penetrance; no specific mode of inheritance is reported in literature on ectropion.[5]

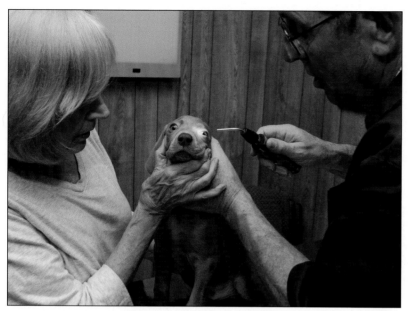

Figure 28-7: *Check puppies very carefully for eyelashes* that indicate potential problems. A veterinarian will use high-powered magnification to observe the fine, almost colorless eyelashes of distichiasis, which are not uncommon in Weimaraners, but rarely cause any complications; however, the coarse, bristly type is often accompanied by watery, irritated eyes and often require surgery. Photograph by Gene LaFollette.

tion shared by other breeders, the pattern of heredity for fine lashes seems consistent with a dominant gene with incomplete and variable penetrance. The incidence of coarse lashes was more common in the early years of the breed in the United States; prudent breeders usually chose to sterilize these animals, and the prevalence of this problem has been greatly reduced today. The occurrence is too low to observe any pattern, although this very rarity suggests that the two types may not be genetically linked and that the coarse type may be recessive.

All puppies should be carefully examined for distichiasis by a veterinarian at 7 weeks and again by the breeder (especially those puppies with watery eyes or irritation) in the final litter evaluation. The fine, almost colorless eyelashes of trichiasis and distichiasis can be seen only with a magnifying glass and very bright light. Although sunlight is best, a bright white reflective light works almost as well.

Trichiasis (trĭ-kî'-â-sis)

The term for normal eyelashes that grow inward against the cornea, causing chronic eye inflammation, is trichiasis. It is considered a probable genetic disorder, although the mode of inheritance has not been reported in the literature. It is also possible that it may be acquired through chronic irritation.

Distichiasis (dis'-tĭ-kî'-â-sis)

The term for the extra eyelashes that emerge from the Meibomian glands along the posterior margin of the eyelid—from one to 10 hairs may emerge from a single gland—is distichiasis (see Figure 28-5). Like other eyelid disorders, distichiasis may be either hereditary or acquired through chronic eye irritation. The age of onset ranges from a few weeks to 10 years.

The literature makes no distinction between the very soft, fine, colorless lashes that are very difficult to detect and the obvious coarse, stiff, bristly type; the latter are less common and easier to identify, and sometimes appear in complete rows of extra lashes. The symptoms of eye irritation, sensitivity to light, excessive tearing, and corneal ulcers occur with coarse lashes, but the fine type rarely causes any irritation. If the lashes cause corneal damage or obvious discomfort, they should be removed by electrolysis or by surgical excision of the affected glands.

The fine-lash type of distichiasis is prevalent in Weimaraners, but the coarse-lash type is associated with only a few strains. Between our own observations and informa-

Acceptable Surgical Procedures
and the AKC Show Dog

Be prepared to resist if a veterinarian insists on sterilization of prospective show stock due to certain defects or before performing certain procedures.

(Minutes from the October 1993 AKC Board meeting)

Surgical Procedures. The Board approved the publication of a list of procedures that, undertaken to restore the health of a dog, would not in and of themselves affect a dog's show eligibility. Such procedures would include but not be limited to:

1. The repair of broken legs, even if such procedures involve the insertion of pins, plates, or wires.
2. The removal of damaged cartilage.
3. The repair of ligaments that have ruptured or been torn.
4. Caesarean sections.
5. The repair of umbilical hernias.
6. The removal of tumors or cysts.
7. Gastric torsion/bloat surgery.
8. Splenic torsion surgery.
9. Tonsillectomy.
10. Correction of "Cherry Eye" (which involves the gland of the nictitating membrane).
11. Debarking.
12. The removal of dewclaws if a regular practice in the breed.

Refer to Rules Applying to Dog Shows (Amended Jan 2006) Chapter 11, Section 8, paragraph 7, pp. 46–47, for the current explanation and list of disallowed procedures.

The German Weimaraner Club's policy on distichiasis is that dogs with mild symptoms that do not require surgery are accepted in the studbook, but dogs that require surgery are excluded. This commonsense compromise minimizes perpetuating the trait until more is known about the mode of inheritance.

Evaluation

All four eyelid problems (entropion, ectropion, trichiasis, distichiasis) are believed to be hereditary, but all are also known to be acquired. This presents a particular problem with Weimaraners because after 8 weeks most puppies are active outdoors and are exposed to the irritants that may cause the acquired type. If any disorder appears before the age of 7–8 weeks, it should be considered a genetic problem. The puppy should be retained for further observation or placed without papers, with limited registration, or with a spay/neuter agreement. Problems that appear later, however, are probably acquired.

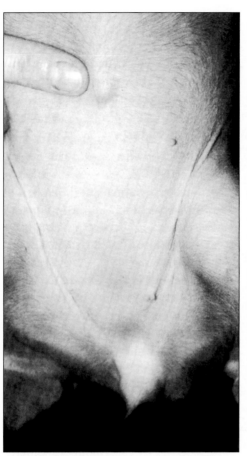

Figure 28-8: *Small umbilical bubbles* that are often mistaken for hernias are caused by a minor subcutaneous accumulation of fluid from the cord, often resulting from an improperly tied cord at birth. These are not true hernias, and treatment is rarely needed, as they usually resolve over time.

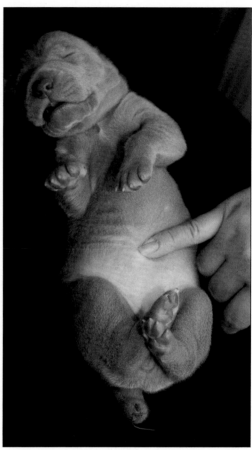

Figure 28-9: *If the tip of the little finger* cannot be totally inserted into the bubble, the opening usually closes spontaneously, with no need for surgery. These small outies are rarely noticeable in the adult and are more often the result of umbilical traction than genetic in origin.

Adults should also be checked for eyelid disorders, if only to begin keeping records. Interpretation of the findings is difficult as most adult Weimaraners have 1 to 2 abnormal eyelashes. Other problems are occasionally identified, such as in one bitch whose red, watering eye was caused by a wart (which was easily removed) on the nictitating membrane.

Swimmer Syndrome

Swimmers are puppies that move by sliding forward on a flattened sternum. They occur most frequently in breeds characterized by short legs and wide chests, such as the Bulldog, Basset Hound, and Scottish Terrier, in which the incidence appears unrelated to litter size and the onset usually occurs by the 1st or 2nd week. In longlegged breeds, swimmers are most likely to appear in small or singleton litters in which the puppies quickly become obese from too much milk and lack of competition for food; the chest flattening may be observed within a few days after birth.

The puppies have difficulty supporting their weight because the wide, flat sternum forces the forelegs apart. Improvement is usually prompt when a carpet or rubber mat is placed in the whelping box. With improved traction, puppies can support their weight more easily, which in turn encourages greater activity. Not surprisingly, once puppies are on their feet and getting more exercise, their chests gradually return to a normal contour, with no apparent residual effects.

Most authorities consider this an environmental disorder. Breeders should keep a record of the incidence, but at this time, there is no evidence that it is a hereditary problem. The puppies may be placed as show and breeding prospects, but on occasion these pups may lack depth of chest and move wider in the front than desired.

Hernias

Umbilical

A congenital hernia is a soft, skin-covered protrusion of the intestine through a weakness in the abdominal wall at the umbilicus. Umbilical hernias may be caused by excessive traction on the umbilical cord at whelping, which is probably the most common cause in Weimaraners. Many authorities report a familial tendency and suggest that umbilical hernias are a polygenic, recessive trait.[6] However, they may also be caused by teratogens such as corticosteroids, so evaluate the possible causes very carefully.

Small, fluid-filled bubbles at the umbilicus are often mistaken for hernias. These can be minimized by tying the cords, even if it is done several hours after whelping. No further intervention is necessary.

If the tip of the little finger cannot be inserted well into the depression, the hernia usually closes spontaneously within 6 months. Hernias larger than a fingertip may still close on their own, so potential repair should be delayed until further evaluation. Surgical repair for larger hernias (2–3 fingertips) should be deferred until the puppy is at least 3 months old. During surgery for a larger hernia, the veterinarian should also check for diaphragmatic hernias.

Unless hernias are a recognized problem in a line, most breeders consider puppies with hernias that close without intervention, and even those up to 1–2 fingertips that are repaired surgically, if they are otherwise excellent individuals, to still be breed worthy.

Diaphragmatic

A diaphragmatic hernia is an opening in the diaphragm, usually with the protrusion of the intestines into the thoracic cavity. Diaphragmatic hernias may be congenital or secondary to a traumatic abdominal injury, such as a fall, a kick (horse or human), or a car accident (see *Best of Health*).

Puppies with congenital diaphragmatic hernias are usually stillborn or die shortly after birth, and often the death may be blamed on other causes, such as the mother lying on the puppy. The symptoms are subtle and rarely noticed. The puppy may not nurse well or may always sleep with its head propped up on something to help it breathe. Veterinarians sometimes pick up the characteristic, slightly different vocal quality at tail-docking time. Affected puppies often have a soft spot in the abdominal muscle just below the end of sternum that can be felt with gentle palpation. Puppies with congenital diaphragmatic hernias rarely survive to adulthood.

A genetic cause has been positively implicated in all species; studies have not identified the mode of heredity, and suggestions range from simple recessive to polygenic recessive to simple dominant with incomplete penetrance.[7]

Teratogenic agents have also been implicated, however, such as quinine, phenmetrazine, and Vitamin A deficiency.

Omphaloceles (om'-fal-ô-sçl)

Dog fanciers speak of a puppy born with "a wide open hernia." The correct term is omphalocele, which is a congenital herniation of the abdominal organs into the umbilical cord.

Omphaloceles must be surgically closed immediately after birth. The puppies are often vigorous, however, and breeders often try to save them—or at least have them humanely euthanized. Apply sterile gauze soaked in saline, wrap with an elastic bandage in an effort to contain the intestines within the body cavity, and rush to the veterinarian. The prognosis is poor because this condition usually occurs in conjunction with other congenital disorders.

A familial tendency has been observed in Weimaraners. However, do not condemn the parents hastily, because omphaloceles can be produced in experimental animals by exposure to low oxygen pressure, folic acid deficiency, and tryptan blue. Should the condition occur on more than one occasion, with different combinations of bloodlines, the animal should be removed from breeding stock.

Cardiac Abnormalities

About 22 different congenital cardiac abnormalities have been identified in canines. The incidence ranges from 0.68% to 4.7% in different studies.[8]

Symptoms of cardiac abnormalities depend on the severity of the defect. They range from sudden neonatal death to difficult breathing, slow growth, or lack of vigor. Puppies may show no signs at all until the demands of increased size or physical activity exceed the cardiac reserves.

Hereditary congenital cardiac defects are multifactorial genetic traits—that is, their expression is influenced by environmental factors.[9] Only two broad generalizations can be made about genetic causes of cardiac abnormalities in dogs: (a) the incidence is higher in purebred dogs than in crossbreds; and (b) the incidence of specific disorders in some breeds is higher than in the general population of purebred dogs.

Cardiac defects have been produced in experimental animals by many teratogenic agents, including the following: Vitamin A, folic acid, and riboflavin plus galactoflavin deficiency; oxygen insufficiency; aspirin; and many other drugs or chemicals. So many teratogenic agents have been implicated that defects in littermates cannot be regarded as definitive evidence of hereditary factors.[10]

There are too many disorders and potential causes to automatically condemn the parents of a puppy with a cardiac abnormality as carriers of a hereditary disorder. Analysis of prenatal health records and multigenerational pedigrees might provide clues but could not realistically include a large enough sample to be considered conclusive evidence. It is prudent to avoid repeating any breeding that produces progeny with cardiac defects and, probably, to avoid similar crosses with related dogs. If cardiac defects occur in several litters from different bloodline combinations, a genetic relationship must be suspected.

Puppies with serious cardiac disorders can be detected by a veterinarian, and this is the primary reason for routinely examining all puppies at 6 weeks. Even if there are no symptoms, their life expectancy is poor. They should not be sold, and in general, humane euthanasia is best.

On occasion, "innocent heart murmurs" are detected at the 6-week veterinary examination. Many times conscientious breeders, placing these puppies in non-competitive homes, have been happy to discover that these "innocent murmurs" resolve by maturity and are absent in the adult dog.

Pancreatic Disorders

Weimaraner breeders have observed a pancreatic disorder that has such a consistent pattern among related dogs that most assume it is hereditary. However, there is no literature on the disorder, and Weimaraner fanciers have not collected records to attempt any systematic study. Because of this, there is understandable confusion about the so-called hereditary pancreatitis. To clarify the problem and to emphasize the danger of assuming that every Weimaraner with a pancreatic disorder has the hereditary type, it seems best to begin with a general description of the functions of the pancreas and what pancreatitis is.

The pancreas has two distinct and separate functions:

- To produce pancreatic juice (contains many enzymes needed to digest fats, proteins, and carbohydrates), which is secreted directly into the intestines through a tiny duct
- To produce insulin, which is secreted into the bloodstream (insufficient insulin produces *diabetes mellitus*)

Pancreatitis is any inflammation of the pancreas. The causes include infectious disease, toxic agents, and parasites, which may produce either transient inflammation or residual impairment. Pancreatitis rarely affects the insulin-producing cells of the pancreas.

The clinical presentation of the pancreatic disorder observed in Weimaraners is similar to that described in juvenile atrophy of the pancreas (also called pancreatic hypoplasia), but no literature on the disorder itself mentions a

genetic linkage. The characteristic symptoms are related to an insufficiency of pancreatic juice and an impaired ability to digest food.

- Loss of weight or failure to grow despite a ravenous appetite
- Stool eating because of insatiable hunger
- Frequent soft, fluffy, pale, foul-smelling stools, often containing undigested food
- Absence of trypsin in the stool confirms diagnosis

In Weimaraners, symptoms may be observed as early as 6–7 weeks. Puppies are the same size as littermates at birth but fall quickly behind; by 3 months, affected puppies may be half the size of littermates. The hereditary type must be suspected if:

- The onset is so early that growth is stunted
- Oral pancreatic enzymes do not produce a complete remission of symptoms with normal growth

The prognosis is poor, and puppies tend to pursue a progressive downhill course, leading to death.

Sadly, because of the gradual, delayed onset, puppies are often sold before the symptoms are recognized. The disorder has broken the hearts of many new owners, and it certainly merits research to at least help identify affected puppies at an earlier age.

Acquired pancreatitis with pancreatic insufficiency can develop at any age, and the causes include roundworms and parvovirus. If the onset occurs before 6 months, it is difficult to differentiate the acquired type from the genetic; however, any that develops after 6 months should be considered an acquired disorder.

In general, dogs have a near-normal life expectancy when maintained on oral pancreatic enzyme preparations such as Viokase. If the inflammation is transient, dogs often recover completely, and the enzymes can be gradually tapered off and discontinued after a few weeks or months; further, they can usually be managed through dietary adjustment and veterinary monitoring.

Spinal Dysraphism and Syringomyelia

Once thought to occur only in Weimaraners, rare cases of spinal dysraphism and syringomyelia have been identified in several other breeds. Both terms describe congenital developmental abnormalities of the spinal cord that usually occur simultaneously: spinal dysraphism is characterized by the failure of the dorsal and ventral halves of the spinal cord

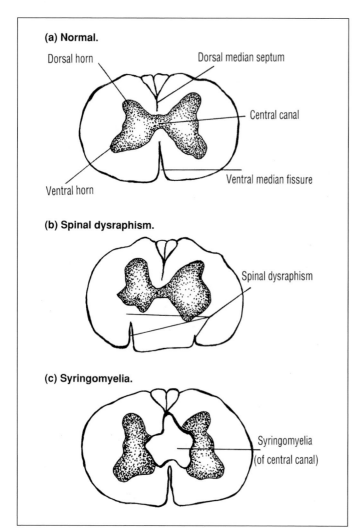

(a) Normal.

Dorsal horn

Dorsal median septum

Central canal

Ventral horn

Ventral median fissure

(b) Spinal dysraphism.

Spinal dysraphism

(c) Syringomyelia.

Syringomyelia
(of central canal)

Figure 28-10: *Cross section of the spinal cord.*

to fuse during embryonic development; syringomyelia is characterized by cavities within the spinal cord that may or may not be filled with fluid, and it is part of the spinal dysraphism syndrome.

Unlike most veterinary researchers, Dr. Donald Draper (Iowa State University College of Veterinary Medicine) began his study of the suspected hereditary disorder by ruling out teratogenic agents such as "slow viruses, febrile responses during gestation, potato blight." Nevertheless, the prevalence in the breed, the wide geographic distribution, and research support the genetic basis; realistically, Weimaraner breeders must regard it as hereditary. Although still inconclusive, the evidence strongly suggests that the hereditary mechanism is a codominant gene with reduced penetrance.[11]

The hereditary mechanism is a very complex one. Draper confirmed the genetic dominance of the trait by experimentally breeding dysraphic Weimaraners to individuals of breeds

in which the disorder is unknown, producing symptomatic puppies in the first generation.

It is, therefore, clear that both parents of a dysraphic puppy need not be carriers; one must be a carrier, and the other could be a carrier.[12]

If it is a dominant gene, why do two nonsymptomatic, apparently normal parents produce symptomatic puppies? Because of the variable penetrance, there is a wide range of genetic expression from severely affected dogs to those that appear completely normal.

Shelton (see *Notes*) classified her research population according to severity of symptoms. Classification is difficult, especially with those that have extremely subtle signs. Most nonsymptomatic carriers can be identified by neurological examination, and the findings are more reliable if the examiner has experience with dysraphia. Diagnosis of nonsymptomatic carriers is based on two neurological examinations with interpretations by more than one observer; the examination must demonstrate at least two neurological abnormalities in order for the dog to be considered a non-symptomatic carrier.[13]

Some severely affected puppies may be stillborn or die a few hours after birth. In puppies that survive, one may see the following clinical signs in the days following birth:

- When nursing, severely affected puppies may appear to push with both hind legs simultaneously—"frog kick"—and are unable to move the hind legs in the normal alternating sequence. In some puppies, this becomes accentuated as myelination of the nerve fibers progresses.

- When suspended in the air, equinovarus (an inward rotation of the hock and foot with the paw flexed) occurs in 90%–95% of severely affected puppies.[14]

Breeders often refer to dysraphic puppies as "hoppers" because of the characteristic bunny-hop gait, which involves moving both hind legs simultaneously. However, until the age of 6 weeks, normal puppies often hop at a trot or gallop because of immature muscular coordination, especially in deep grass. Dysraphic puppies hop at a walk. In addition, they usually stand in a characteristic crouching posture or with the rear legs overextended and far apart.

The symptoms of spinal dysraphism are not progressive, and the condition observed at 7 weeks will remain stable throughout the dog's lifetime. Most puppies are put to sleep when the diagnosis is made. However, those that have been raised for study appear to enjoy near-normal health, and many that we knew enjoyed happy, healthy lives well into

Figure 28-11: *Neurological examination.*

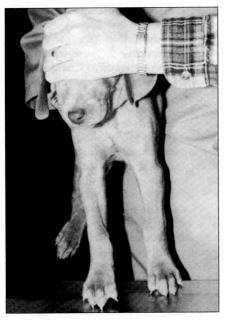

(a) Tactile placing reflex, front. With the eyes covered, the puppy is slowly moved toward the table so that one or both forelegs or pasterns touch the edge. The puppy's normal response is to lift the legs immediately and place the feet on the supporting surface.

(b) Tactile placing reflex, rear. The puppy is slowly moved toward the table so that one or both rear legs touch the edge. The puppy's normal response is to lift the legs immediately and place the feet on the supporting surface.

(c) Rear thrust reflex. Holding the puppy under the elbows and around the shoulders, slowly lower it until the rear feet touch the table. The puppy's normal response is for both rear legs to stiffen and thrust against the surface.

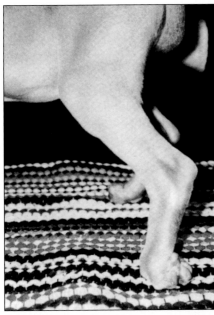

(d) Knuckling (proprioceptive) reflex. While standing on a surface with good traction, the puppy's rear paw is placed in a flexed position. The normal response is to return the paw to the usual digitigrade position within 13 seconds.

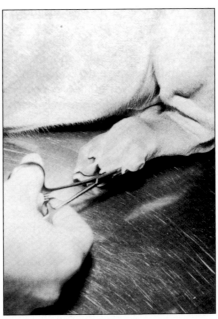

(e) Toepinch (flexor) reflex. Using a forceps, gently pinch the webbing between one of the rear toes. The normal response is for the puppy to withdraw the foot immediately. The puppy may or may not show evidence of pain.

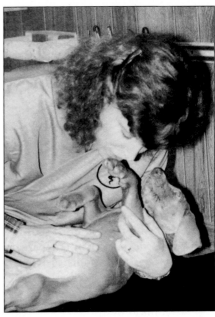

(f) Righting reflex. On a surface with good traction, lay the puppy on its back. The normal response is for the puppy to roll to the side and stand up.

their teens. Happily, while this condition was prevalent in the past, because of the efforts of Dr. Draper, the support of the WCA, and the diligence of breeders, reported occurrences are significantly reduced for the modern American Weimaraner.

Traumatic injuries to the spinal cord (such as those caused by a bitch landing on a puppy when jumping into the whelping box) can produce puppies with the clinical symptoms of dysraphia. Positive diagnosis can be made only by microscopic examination of the spinal cord. This should always be done with a puppy that has been put to sleep. A positive report leaves no room for doubt or denial; on the other hand, a negative report lightens the heart.

The earliest known producers of spinal dysraphism were, unfortunately, bred extensively before the disorder was understood, and they appear in most Weimaraner pedigrees. Because of the incomplete penetrance, dysraphia can go undetected for several generations before cropping up unexpectedly.

When dysraphism is suspected, please, consult a veterinary neurologist for an accurate diagnosis. Because neurological examination can detect about 90% of the nonsymptomatic carriers, it is certainly worthwhile having the parents of dysraphic progeny examined because of the possibility that one of them is not a carrier. Through identifying carriers by examining producers and littermates of affected puppies, there has been tremendous progress toward reducing the incidence even while continuing to use carriers in breeding programs. When dysraphism occurs, the outlook is far from hopeless, and this is one disorder that breeders can detect before selling the puppies.

Epilepsy

Hippocrates observed the familial nature of epilepsy. A great deal has been learned since then. Epilepsy is not a disease but rather a symptom of many different disorders and diseases that produce seizures. The following are examples of things that produce seizures:

Trauma (including birth)	Brain tumor
Hypoglycemia	Encephalitis
Hypocalcemia	Heavy metal ingestion
Hypoxia	Poisons and toxins
Liver disease	Electric shock
Vitamin D overdose	Kidney disease

In dogs, studies of the heredity of epilepsy are inconclusive, contradictory, and confusing. Nicholas and Tizard, two leading authorities on veterinary genetics, do not even mention epilepsy. Of two recent books on dog genetics, Robinson covers the subject in one paragraph, mentioning

several studies, but Willis provides an excellent, lengthy overview and describes the research in greater detail. In the end, however, all studies boil down to Hippocrates's observation of a familial relationship, with nothing conclusive about the mode of inheritance in dogs.[15]

Recently, the study of heredity in canine epilepsy has been further complicated by seizures associated with immunizations, which occur from 7–14 days after vaccination. Changing to a conservative vaccine program usually eliminates the vaccine-related seizures in subsequent litters. To date, the incidence of seizures is most commonly attributed as a symptom of injury, toxins, or a complicating ailment.

Hemophilia

Hemophilia A (classic hemophilia) is caused by a deficiency of clotting factor VIII. It has been reported in most popular breeds as well as mongrels, cats, horses, cattle, and humans, and it is a sex-linked genetic disorder of the X chromosome in all species. Robinson suggests that there is a mutational hot spot on the X chromosome.[16]

In 1967, Kaneko, Cordy, and Carlson reported that three of four Weimaraner puppies born from an accidental brother–sister mating had prolonged bleeding after tail docking; two died immediately after of massive acute hemorrhage, with two more dying later on. The report went on to state, "The whereabouts of the sire of these puppies is unknown, and the dam died on the 2nd day after acquisition of chronic suppurative metritis with rupture." The third puppy "died on the 8th day after a plasma transfusion." The fourth puppy "clinically was dehydrated and … died following 48 hours of acute illness."[17] The chronology of events is confusing because none of the deaths is linked to the number of days after whelping or tail docking. The report did not mention that other bleeding disorders (such as erlichiosis, which reached the United States about 1962) had been ruled out.

The report concluded that the puppies had hemophilia A, and since then every list of hereditary disorders in specific breeds includes hemophilia under Weimaraners. We have not only never heard of a single Weimaraner with hemophilia, we also have never been able to find anybody else who has reported it. The cases could be the result of a spontaneous mutation in one of the parents that proved fatal before it could be passed on. Another possibility is that the mother had undiagnosed erlichiosis or another bleeding disorder. For now, it seems safe to conclude that—despite the authoritative lists—hemophilia does not occur in Weimaraners. However, a new mutation could occur at any time, and failure to initiate a breeding control program immediately would be tragic.

Keep an Open Mind

Breeders should assess every puppy for congenital disorders and attempt whenever possible to determine whether the cause is genetic or acquired through teratogenic agents. Disorders such as cardiac abnormalities are not compatible with good health or longevity, and affected puppies should be euthanized. Other disorders such as cryptorchidism and umbilical hernia are usually compatible with a long, healthy life with or without minor surgery.

When a congenital defect does occur, assess the things to which the bitch has been exposed while carrying the litter before blaming the stud or condemning the bitch. Most disorders are isolated cases with little hereditary significance. If, however, the same disorder appears when the parent is bred to several dogs of varying bloodlines or the same disorder appears in several generations, a genetic linkage must be suspected.

The unthinking assumption that every congenital disorder has a hereditary basis is extremely dangerous. Priceless bloodlines (not to mention breeders' morale and reputations) can be destroyed while an unidentified teratogenic agent continues to prey on unsuspecting victims. Keep detailed records, watch for patterns, and consider the possibility of environmental causes as well as hereditary factors when congenital disorders occur.

Figure 28-12: *More than anything* a Weimaraner wants to be working with or for their owners. A complete health assessment before placing puppies in their new homes ensures that owners with expectations of serious athletic adventures are not disappointed. MACH Silverstar's Annie Get Your Gun, VCD1, NRD, VX2, displays the typical athletic nature of the Weimaraner while she and her owner compete in agility.

Figure 29-1: *I'm All Ears.* 2005. Photograph by Gene LaFollette.

CHAPTER 29

PICKING THE PERFECT PUPPY

Most people would like the pick-of-the-litter puppy; some will settle for nothing less. However, the best puppy in some litters may merely be the least faulty of a very poor lot, whereas the last choice in an exceptional litter may merely be slightly less outstanding than its best-in-show sibling. The real question is how to select the perfect puppy.

One of a breeder's most challenging responsibilities is to assess the litter accurately and honestly and to identify the perfect puppy for each prospective owner. The breeder's tools for initial selection are testing natural aptitude and the health assessment, as discussed in Chapters 27 and 28. The health assessment is a must for all puppies, regardless of their future prospects as a competitor or companion, and natural aptitude tests focus on evaluating a puppy's potential for additional activities such as the field, obedience, and agility. While structural soundness is important in all areas of competition, in the conformation ring the dog will be judged solely on how closely it approaches the written standard (see Appendix A). The aim of this chapter is to help identify the puppies with the greatest potential to most closely adhere to that standard of structural perfection. Additional tools discussed in this chapter are photography, hands-on structural evaluation, and floor-level observation of gait. Information is gathered and weighed for a final summary and decisions regarding placement of each puppy. And, lastly, suggestions are provided to the prospective purchaser on evaluating the breeder's potential for providing the perfect puppy.

What Is the Perfect Puppy?

The perfect puppy is the one that best meets the owner's hopes and expectations, and every healthy puppy in the litter should be someone's perfect puppy. The best one for the hunter is unlikely to be the best choice for an elderly couple, a handicapped person, or a Search-and-Rescue enthusiast. Even the show breeder may pass over the puppy with better overall structure and choose a puppy that is better in one specific trait that is especially desired in their breeding program—for example, exceptional shoulders. The perfect puppy is physically and mentally healthy, conditioned from birth to develop every aptitude needed to become a perfect companion. From this point on, the puppy's future is in the hands of the new owner, who must have a plan for success.

Figure 29-2: *Which one is the pick of the litter?* All of these puppies became champions, but which would best meet the needs of a family or the prospective breeder? This chapter helps identify the puppy with the best conformation prospects. *Testing Natural Aptitude* will help pinpoint special talents or abilities and discover the natural character and instincts to best match each puppy with the needs and desires of his future home; for every healthy puppy, there should be a perfect home, and the perfect puppy may not be the same for each prospective owner. Photograph by Lisa Sponsler.

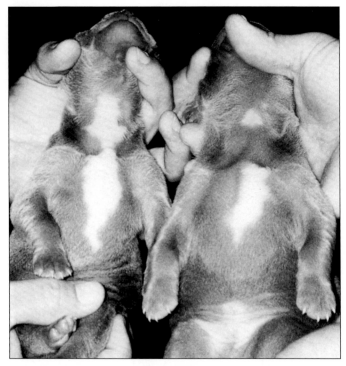

Figure 29-3: *An early easy choice.* These 7-day-old puppies should not be considered for a show home or conformation breeding program. While excessive white is penalized in the show ring, an otherwise healthy puppy would not be hampered by such markings in performance competition events such as field, obedience, or agility.

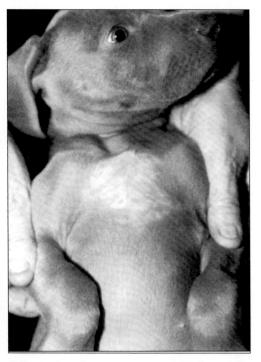

Figure 29-4: *If the Weimaraner carries the ticking allele,* gray hairs begin to appear within white markings at a few weeks. The amount of ticking is highly variable. At a minimum, it obscures the extent of the white; at most (in the adult), the area covered by the marking appears to be solid gray speckled with white. **(a)** A "headlight" at whelping. **(b)** By 6 weeks, the white was no longer glaring, and by maturity, gray hairs had almost completely camouflaged the marking.

Some Obvious Decisions

What's on the Outside?

Certain puppies may already indicate their availability for selection because of cosmetic faults that have very little to do with their basic good health and capabilities as a fine companion or hunter: for example, monorchidism, Doberman markings, or excessive white. Since they are usually the first to be spoken for placement in companion/pet homes, early decisions regarding these puppies lightens the task of selecting the perfect show- and breeding-quality youngsters.

Decisions regarding excessive white markings are not difficult. Puppies with blazes that include white on the neck and the entire front are glaringly obvious candidates for pet homes. It should be noted, however, that a great number of today's top-level field trial competitors have what would be considered excessive white markings for the conformation ring.

All things being equal, the Weimaraner without white on the chest is usually preferred for the conformation ring, but all things are not always equal. Many of the breed's great winners and producers contributed their outstanding qualities because breeders did not discard them as show prospects merely because white markings appeared to be larger than allowed by the standard when the pup was very young. The tricky decisions come with medium to large spots in the center of the chest—will they or will they not be too large at maturity?

Decisions should be deferred until the puppy is older. Chest spots usually remain the same size as at birth, while the rest of the puppy grows around the white. In other words, the marking that looks like a headlight on the newborn may be the size of a silver dollar on the adult. Blazes tend to grow in length—not width—and sometimes end up between the dog's forelegs, out of sight. Unless the toe-nail is also white, white markings on the toes will, without fail, minimize—usually to non-existence—with age.

To compound the difficulty of making decisions, some chest markings become camouflaged by partially filling in with gray hairs. White on the throat tends to decrease or disappear by maturity, whereas white on the abdomen and penile sheath typically makes a grand entrance at the age of 3 to 6 months.

Doberman (or Dobe) markings appear at various ages, ranging from shortly after whelping to 4 months. They are most easily seen in very bright light; sometimes, these markings totally disappear by 7 weeks. However, if such markings are ever observed, the breeder should be aware that the puppy is homozygous for the trait and will pass this recessive gene to all progeny.

What Is on the Inside?

Although this chapter deals with what to look for on

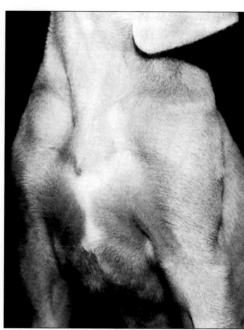

Figure 29-5: *The skin over the center of the forechest hardly grows at all.* **(a)** At 2 weeks, the white marking covers a large portion of the puppy's chest; however, as the puppy grows, the marking will often remain the same size. **(b)** At 3 months, the marking is a little longer, but the total area is almost unchanged, appearing proportionately smaller as the puppy grows.

the outside of the puppy, that winning edge in the show ring may be found on the inside. Success in conformation competition is more than just not having any disqualifying faults, and it is even more than a matter of sound conformation and outstanding movement. Being a top-level competitor takes a dog with style and a winning attitude. A shy, nervous, or sulky dog simply is not going to be the one that catches the favorable eye of the judge. Often, it is a dog that has less outstanding movement but has that confident "Hey! Look at ME!" attitude, that is unruffled by the noise and chaos, and that has a self-assured, sparkling personality that makes an impression that grabs the judge's eye and simply will not let the judge look anywhere else. A puppy that is timid or overly noise-shy is going to have a tough time making that kind of winning impression.

A dog that is always willing to eat and eager for whatever treat is offered is a dog that will work well in the show ring, will be easier to train, and is unlikely to go off its feed while on the road. All things being equal, the puppy that has more "food motivation" should be the easier puppy to work with.

Taking the Perfect Puppy Picture

Photography is a valuable aid in the assessment of physical structure. Some traits that may be observed include front and rear angulation, shoulder placement, topline, croup angle, and overall balance. Photographs should be taken at

7–8 weeks, when most Weimaraners have the approximate proportions that they will have at maturity—no matter what they look like in between. Photographs taken at 5–6 weeks are misleading, especially for length of leg and shoulder angulation. Avoid photographing puppies after 9 weeks. Rely on the 7- to 8-week silhouette as the best indicator of their mature balance and proportions.

The Digital Age

The advent of the commonly available camera allowed breeders to send pictures to prospective buyers; but perhaps more important, early puppy pictures allowed the modern breeder to keep a record over the decades of the trends, patterns, and progress of a breeding program. Advantages, however, were limited by the delay of taking the pictures and getting them developed.

You never knew for sure if you got a "good" picture until the film came back a week or two later. Imagine the frustration of taking pictures of a litter of 10 puppies only to find the angle of the table was completely wrong, or perhaps worst of all, that the identifying colored collar was out of the picture in every single photo! Then, along came the Polaroid! Photos could be viewed "almost" immediately. And even if the colored collar was forgotten, the information could be written right on the photo. Problems could be identified and rectified right away; the breeder was practically guaranteed to be able to get the photos needed. Film, however, was expensive, and there was no way to make copies (until the advent of the Xerox copier, and those wouldn't become publicly available for a while). Progress has once again, progressed. Today, digital pictures can be viewed instantly, allowing any problems to be corrected on the spot. Prints, as many as needed, can be produced immediately. Even better, the photos can be viewed and compared on screen and e-mailed anywhere in the world. Photos can be permanently stored without loss of quality over time, in a very small space. Even a relatively inexpensive digital camera will suffice for the quality of photos needed by most breeders. And perhaps best of all, since the photos are digital, the breeder can take as many as needed because the cost of film is no longer a factor.

No system for identifying puppies for pictures is foolproof; however, one practice has proven to be most reliable to avoid the "mystery puppy syndrome." Place the colored collar, or ID sign, directly in front of the puppy's front feet. Also, for the final picture in each series, have the puppy sitting facing the camera; this not only provides a photo of the puppy's front and expression, but also indicates that the next series of photos will be a different puppy. Most digital cameras allow the photographer to imprint a "title" and date on each photo; the photographer has to remember to change it for each puppy and ensure that the imprint does not obscure the puppy.

Getting Organized

Withhold food and limit water for 5 hours before photographing to ensure that puppies are hungry and that profiles are not distorted by full tummies. Puppies are more cooperative when baited, so have a generous supply and variety of tidbits available—liver, hot dogs, and cheese. Bait should be in large "lumps" so the puppy can gnaw on the bait without eating the entire treat or biting the gloved hand or fingers of the handler. At least one should prove irresistible to the fussy ones, and at least one should be unpalatable enough to obtain cooperation from the ones that "attack" fingers holding goodies.

The puppies may be stacked on a grooming table, dog crate, picnic table, or any other arrangement that is comfortable. Grooming tables are popular because of the built-in easy-traction top, but be sure to take off the grooming arm and cover the metal rim with non-reflective tape or fabric. A Size 400 or 500 fiberglass dog crate covered with a mat for traction is hard to beat, and of course, every dog owner has at least one. For those who have both, the choice may depend on the height of the person stacking the puppies: tall people sometimes find stooping over a low crate awkward; short people may not want their faces appearing just over the puppy's back on every picture. A picnic table works surprisingly well because the perfect level for 7- to 8-week-old puppies is for the photographer to kneel at the opposite end and rest the camera on the table. The separate boards on the table give good traction and consistent placement if the hind legs are placed strategically on a crack for support and the front legs are adjusted.

The ideal surface for posing puppies, however, is a one-piece, easy-to-grip, dark welcome mat with a brush-like surface. Rolls of non-slip textured vinyl shelf liners, in dark colors, are now readily available. They make a superior surface for photographing puppies because the tacky, but unusual, surface offers confident footing; they can be conveniently draped over most well-situated surfaces in any location, and they are compact and water and stain resistant.

This unfamiliar texture—the mystery surface—encourages puppies to stand tall and still without frightening them, often mesmerizing them for about 12 seconds, which is usually enough time to snap that first picture, which often turns out to be the best.

For uniform distance and angle, the posing surface should be marked with

Figure 29-6: ***When selecting the perfect puppy,*** if the coat feels thicker and appears to have a marcel, as on this pup's ear, it may be a longhair; this variation can occur unexpectedly in a litter of purebred shorthaired pups. Despite being a recognized aspect of the Weimaraner's heritage, at this time the United States is the only country in the world that disqualifies the longhair from competing in conformation; however, longhairs may be AKC registered and are eligible to compete in all other venues. Longhairs have competed successfully throughout the world in conformation at the highest levels; so a breeder with an outstanding longhaired pup may wish to consider a home for it in a foreign county. See Chapter 5, *Coat, Markings, and Color,* for identifying the longhair at an early age. **(a)** Cassie (Abisha Cassey van Boom tot Boom) at 8 weeks; **(b)** the mature Cassie working the field. Photographs courtesy of Ina van Ringen, Netherlands.

Figure 29-7: *Evaluating topline.* **(a)** For proper evaluation of topline, angulation and forechest, slowly coax the puppy forward with the bait until the head and shoulders are well over the front feet. **(b)** A hot dog held in a black gloved hand will not detract from the view of the puppy but will properly position the puppy for evaluation. The mystery surface offers secure footing while the surprising, unfamiliar texture stimulates a good pose.

strips of tape—one for the line along which to place the side closest to the photographer, the other for placing the front feet (placement of rear feet varies with puppy's structure). The photographer should sit on a low stool in order to get the correct angle and prevent foreshortening of the puppies legs. A tripod ensures consistent distance, focus, and stability. It is important to maintain the same distance and angle so that each puppy can be equally evaluated.

Have the designated puppy photographer review this section before the session begins, showing examples of desired poses—head and neck angle, straight topline, tail set, and parallel leg placement. Getting good photographs is so much easier if the photographer is also a dog show enthusiast and can tell the poser whether a leg must be moved, the head raised or lowered, and so forth.

How To Do It Right

If planning to take pictures from a low table or crate and a tripod is not available, the photographer must sit on a low stool, elbows on knees for support, so there is a horizontal line from the camera to the top of the puppy's feet (see Figure 29-8).

Figure 29-8: *For that perfect picture,* if a tripod is not available, the photographer must sit on a low stool, elbows on knees for support, so there is a horizontal line from the camera to the top of the puppy's feet.

The ideal setup is to pose puppies in front of a dark background. Inside, hang a piece of black fabric on the wall; outside, look for a dark background, such as a large evergreen or dark wall. The person posing the puppies should also wear solid-colored, dark clothing; using black-gloved hands to offer bait and hold up the tail reduces clutter and distraction in the photograph. However, standing puppies in front of any contrasting solid-colored background showing only the helpers' hands provides clear profiles. Taking photographs indoors ensures uniform lighting, comfortable temperature, and fewer distractions.

If desired, prepare a sign with date, ID, age, litter information, and gender. When organized, wake the puppy and place the collar in clear view near the mark for the puppy's front feet (for 35 mm or digital, add an identifying sign). Then, quickly stack the puppy on the mystery surface, and snap the picture.

The first photographs usually reveal problems with the setup and must be repeated. Check for distance, angle, lighting, background, and posing problems. Take the first shots with a puppy that is already considered an unlikely show prospect while finding solutions and practicing the routine because the first picture of each puppy often ends up being the best pose.

Common Problems and Mistakes

Puppy cooperation varies greatly, but the best pictures are obtained with hungry puppies that have had the training described in *Raising the Litter* and *Showing the Weimaraner*. These puppies usually stand quite still when hearing a clicking noise, and their tails can be stroked into a good angle.

The most difficult part of posing puppies is getting the correct angles of the neck and head for evaluation of forechest, neck placement, and shoulder layback. The neck should be at a 45° angle, and the head should be forward.

When bait must be used to get a good pose, get the body positioned and start with food-scented fingers to guide the puppy's head and shoulders into the desired position. Progressive measures include offering bait to encourage a forward lean, pushing back slightly with the bait to position head, with the shoulders directly over the front feet. If the puppy leans back, push on the tail until the puppy is just right.

Review of the Photographs

Place all the photos of each puppy on a dark surface or on a screen to determine the best shot. Note whether a particular fault appears consistently. If it does, take another photograph and try to eliminate the fault through better stacking. If the fault persists, the problem is not with posing the puppy. Make a final examination of your best shot with a magnifying glass to identify any flaws. Evaluate the puppy's conformation from the photos available, giving special atten-

Figure 29-9: *Happy Legs*®, or a similar set up, is a new tool that may help ensure consistency in stacking the inexperienced puppies by placing their feet on small blocks. This procedure allows more uniform position and angle of all the pups, making comparing conformation of the litter easier. The small blocks encourage the pups to be more cooperative. The black background behind the black-attired assistant minimizes visual distraction while her black-gloved hands deftly bait the puppy's head into the proper position and adjust the tail. Avoid the "mystery puppy syndrome" by double checking that each puppy's set of photos is clearly identified by an ending face-on shot (to capture expression) with the colored identification collar clearly displayed before proceeding to the next puppy.

tion to which puppy took seven shots to look great and which one achieved success with a single shot.

Choose the best photo of each puppy and have each of them photocopied on one page. There is no need to worry about an expensive color copy for personal records; economical black-and-white copies can be made from our silver puppy silhouetted against a black background. Also, make an enlargement of the best photo of each puppy, which sometimes reveals subtle structural flaws. An enlarged color photocopy presented to each owner often motivates an extra effort in obedience and show training, providing a reminder during the awkward growth stages that his or her hoped-for show champion will usually mature back into that picture-perfect puppy.

Individual Hands-on Evaluation

At 7–8 weeks, the conformation of each puppy should be formally evaluated. Although the hands-on examination can be done by one person, it is easier if someone takes notes while the other goes over each puppy. Comparisons are easier if the puppies are still identified by the different-colored

Figure 29-10: *Almost, but...*

1. This is a pretty puppy picture that is visually misleading. Take special note that more than half of the posing surface is visible, indicating that the shortened leg length of this subject is not genetic but due to photographer error (too high a camera angle). However, this photograph has been taken from the right distance to include as much of the puppy as possible without chopping off body parts.

2. The body of the puppy is posed in proper balance. The shoulders are almost directly above the front feet. This total silhouette, displaying correct front and rear angulation, can be achieved by gently coaxing the head of the puppy forward with bait, then slowly forcing the puppy's head back toward the shoulders as it eats the treat. This photograph was snapped at the exact moment the puppy's feet were directly beneath the shoulders.

3. The background drape should be raised to above the handler's head and shoulders so that the puppy's head, tail, and topline can be viewed with more clarity. With the drape higher, the handler's head could be removed from the photo with a touch of a black marking pen or, if taken with a digital camera, you can crop out the handler.

4. The low-glare drape beneath the table is dark enough to call no attention to its presence; however, the shine from the rim of the posing surface is distracting, and with bad luck, the next flash from the camera could reflect the light with spectacular results. Cover any metallic surface with black electrical tape.

5. The hard, matted surface of the grooming table allows a clear view of the puppy's correct pasterns and feet. If a soft blanket were used, the puppy's feet would most certainly disappear. Note that when displayed on this hard surface, the colored identification collar is clearly visible.

6. Watch those gloved hands. The handler has eliminated a portion of the puppy's tail. The arms should be completely covered so that there is no break between the beginning of the gloves and the end of the handler's dark sleeve. Gloves should be of a thick enough material to allow for dexterity while providing protection for the handler's hand—those puppy teeth hurt.

7. Photographic success is greatly increased by the help of a photographer who understands dog structure and is able to capture the subject at just the right moment.

collars they have worn since birth and then are divided into groups—the obvious pets, the boys, and the girls.

Head

The pronounced occipital bumps that are so common in Weimaraner puppies usually develop later, but they sometimes appear as early as 7 weeks. These bumps are not a concern. Nowadays, they rarely persist into adulthood, and even then, they should be regarded as more typical than faulty.

Ears

At birth the ears are tiny flaps of skin pasted tightly to the skull. However, by 8–12 weeks, the ears are almost the size they will be at maturity, appearing entirely out of proportion to the puppy's size.

Eyes

Use a magnifying glass and a bright light to make a final check for eyelash abnormalities (see discussion in *Health*

Figure 29-11: *Pronounced occipital bumps* sometimes appear at 7 weeks but usually develop many weeks later. These are not a concern because not only are they rare in adult American Weimaraners, they also are not faulty.

Figure 29-12: *Common problems in photographing puppies:* production by CH Ladenburg Arco v. Reiteralm, BROM, and Fancy's Cinnamon Girl (Fay Ray).

(a) Problem: Photographer at incorrect level.

(1) Too high.

(2) Too low.

(3) Just right.

(b) Problem: Getting attention.

  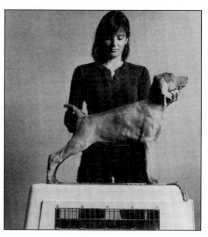

(1) "This is just too exciting."

(2) Supporting firmly, swing back and forth 10 times.

(3) Mesmerized cooperation lasts for about 2 minutes.

(c) Problem: Rocking back.

 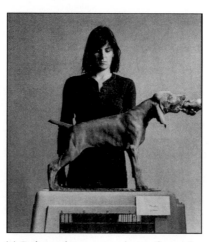 

(1) "I'll stand still, but I don't like this!"

(2) Bribe with a treat, and coax forward.

(3) Tease, using bait to bring head into position.

Figure 29-12 (continued)

(d) Problem: Fighting restraint.

(1) "I will not; you can't make me!"

(2) Escape controlled, with sympathetic assistance.

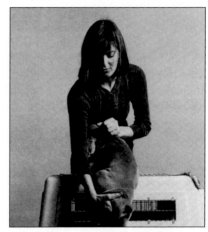

(3) Hand on back of neck clarifies who's boss.

(e) Problem: Arching back.

(1) "I'm scared. I don't like you pushing on my tail!"

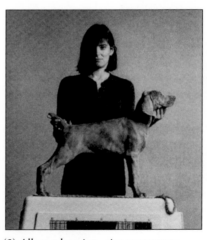

(2) Allow relaxation, give reassurance.

(3) Encourage with food.

(f) Problem: Needs to go outside.

(1) "I want the goodie, but I can't stand still!"

(2) Take out, cuddle, and reassure.

(3) That's better!

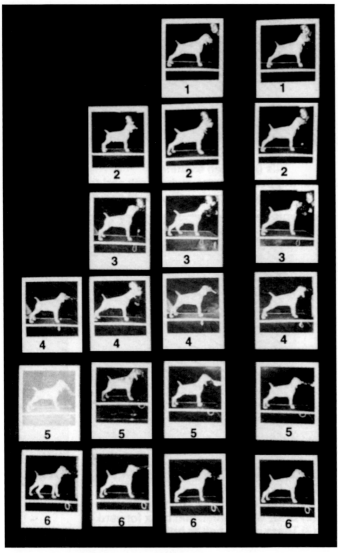

Figure 29-13: ***Place the photographs*** on a dark surface and study the puppies' conformation carefully. Make a special note that Puppy 1 looked great on the first shot, while Puppy 6 needed seven.

A severely overshot bite at an early age, as seen in Figure 29-15(b), may create health problems, as the lower canines may cause injury to the puppy's palate. In these cases a veterinarian should be consulted for solutions such as filing or removing the non-permanent teeth to prevent further injury. Most often, maturity and the arrival of permanent teeth usually resolve the problem; however, these animals should not be included in a breeding program.

Figure 29-14: *Ears and wrinkles.*

(a) By 8 weeks, a Weimaraner puppy's ears have almost reached mature size; the loose skin and wrinkles are typical of this puppy's dam line.

Assessment). A few lashes of the soft, non-irritating variety should be noted but not unduly penalized.

Bites

Place a finger inside the puppy's mouth and feel along the front to measure the space between the upper and lower incisors. The upper incisors should be in front of the lower ones. A bite that is as much as ¼ inch overshot—where the upper jaw extends past the lower jaw—at 7–8 weeks will usually be a normal scissors bite at maturity. An even bite without any space between the incisors is often undershot—where the lower jaw extends past the upper jaw—at maturity. A slightly undershot bite is typically severely undershot at maturity.

(b) As can be seen, she grew into her ears and wrinkles.

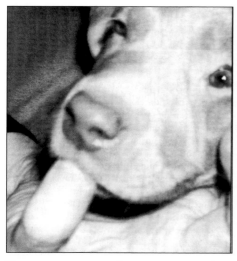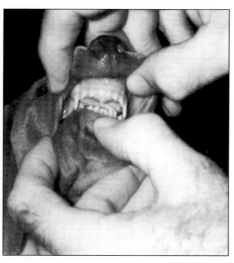

Figure 29-15: *Bite evaluation.* **(a)** Place a finger inside the puppy's mouth and feel along the front to measure the space between the upper and lower incisors, as well as checking for wry mouth. **(b)** This much overbite (over 1 inch) at 7 weeks is too much, and the puppy should be placed as a pet.

Weimaraner breeders have long recognized that puppies with level bites, sometimes even tight scissors bites, at 7 weeks had a higher incidence of undershot bites than those with a greater overbite. When breeders realized that most Weimaraner puppies with noticeably overshot bites at 7 weeks had perfect scissors bites by about 1 year, they stopped culling these puppies as non-breeding quality. The incidence of undershot bites has greatly decreased since puppies with mildly overshot bites have been incorporated into many bloodlines. Therefore, many breeders consider a slightly overshot bite in puppies not only common but also desirable.

Be sure to check the alignment of the incisors and note whether or not the lower jaw is in alignment with the upper jaw. Wry bites—right-to-left misalignment—occur occasionally. The few identified with this condition at an early age tend to show no improvement.

Although Weimaraners with severely overshot bites at maturity have been reported, this is not a common breed problem; undershot bites, however, are not rare. The Weimaraner's bite is usually mature and stable at 11 or 12 months; however, good bites that have gone undershot or wry as late as 3 years have been reported.

The Weimaraner's lower jaw grows at a slower rate than the upper jaw, reaching its mature size by about 10–12 months and occasionally growing past the upper jaw, which had stopped growing earlier. However, the rare Weimaraners that go undershot at 2 or even 3 years indicate that a correct scissors bite at 1 year does not always guarantee it will not change.

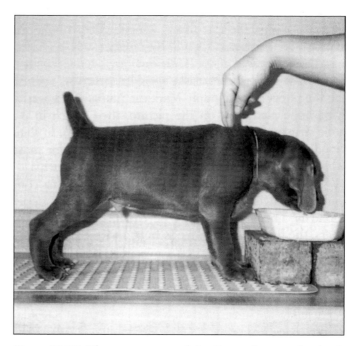

Figure 29-17: *The measurement of the distance* between the shoulder blades changes with the puppy's positioning. For standardized results, have the puppy stand with head lowered to eat, the front feet directly under the shoulders, and the front feet about 4 inches apart. To measure, place your fingers between the blades.

Figure 29-16: *No amount of stretching with bait* added length to this 6-week-old puppy's neck. If the neck is still short at 8 weeks, it will probably remain short.

Figure 29-18: *Verifying shoulder structure.*

(a) Palpate the bones and mark guide points on the photograph.

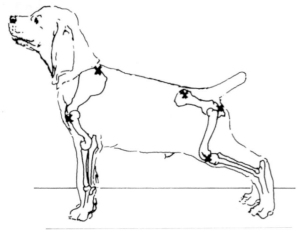

(b) Sketching in the bone placement clearly illustrates shoulder structure. Height is measured from the withers to the heel; length is measured from the point of the shoulder to the tip of the pelvis.

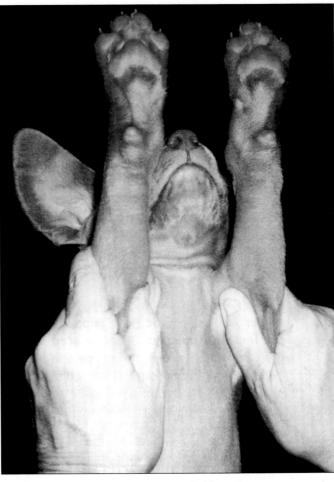

Figure 29-19: *When the elbows are held in this position,* neither pastern shows a tendency to twist out (it is not uncommon to have only one pastern turning out), and this puppy should have a straight front as an adult. Twisting or looseness at the pastern joint forewarns of an east-west front at maturity. Also note that a white "frosting" on the back of the pastern is common and acceptable in the breed.

Necks

Short necks are easily discovered when several photographs using different bait levels verify the condition. There is usually a bunching around the shoulders, which often seem loaded. Be aware that neck length at 7 weeks varies in different bloodlines, and it does not always indicate length at maturity. Recheck length at 12 weeks.

Shoulders

The measurement of the distance between the shoulder blades changes with the puppy's positioning. For standardized results, have the puppy stand with head lowered to eat, the front feet directly under the shoulders, and the front feet about 4 inches apart. To measure, place your fingers between the blades. The width ranges from two to four fingers and varies widely between bloodlines and between litters. Identify the average width for the litter, which will probably be average for the bloodline. The extremes will be either wider or narrower.

When in doubt about the shoulder structure, try tracing the puppy's photograph. Mark the points of the underlying bone placement on the picture, then sketch in the bone structure on the tracing (see Figure 29-18). In some bloodlines, shoulder layback improves later, but for most, what you see at 7–8 weeks will be the same at maturity.

When checking shoulder layback, be sure to compare the length of the shoulder blade with the upper forearm. The length should be equal, but in Weimaraners, the upper forearm tends to be shorter.

Fronts

Lateral deviation of the pasterns can be accurately judged with the puppy totally relaxed and upside down on the lap or a table. Grasp the elbows, twisting outward and away from the chest, extending the forelegs straight forward. Pasterns that are directly in line with the elbows usually remain straight and firm in the adult, whereas deviated ones that twist outward are a reliable warning of a true east-west front at maturity. No amount of chest development will correct this problem.

A different type of east-west front is seen in a puppy with an immature, narrow front, which stands east-west when posed. The problem here is that the chest is too narrow to hold the elbows in correct alignment. Before deciding it has no show potential, try placing it in a sitting position so that the curve of the ribs forces the elbows out. If the front is straight and no twisting of the pasterns can be observed in this position, the puppy will probably have a straight front at maturity. However, it will probably not win much until it has mature chest spring at 2–3 years. Such puppies often move exceptionally well in front, and because so many Weimaraners tend toward wide chests and out-at-the-elbows movement, these narrow-chested youngsters can be of considerable value in a breeding program.

A perfect front forewarns that mature rib spring and shoulder muscles may force the elbows out, causing the front to become too wide and producing numerous faults of movement. When assessing a young Weimaraner, the critical features are the straightness of the pasterns and the position of the front legs when the dog is in a sitting position, which forces the elbows out and approximates their placement with mature chest development. Correct front movement is another promising sign of a good front assembly.

Feet and Pasterns

While the puppy is learning to walk, the feet are typically rather splayed, and poor feet up to 6 weeks is normal. By the time puppies acquire coordination, the feet should improve if the nails are kept trimmed.

Feet usually become splayed during the stress of teething but should return to their earlier quality. Puppies that spend too much time in a concrete run, however, frequently develop permanently splayed feet. Too much crate time with insufficient exercise and sunlight is known to do the same. (When evaluating the breeding potential of a mature dog

Figure 29-20: *A helpful trick in assessing fronts.* **(a)** This puppy appears to have a hopelessly east-west front because of the narrow chest. **(b)** When sitting, the chest width forces the elbows out and approximates the elbow placement at mature chest development. Puppies like this rarely take points from the puppy class, but they should win consistently by the age of 2 or 3 years.

Figure 29-21: *As the puppy continues to develop* after 8 weeks, the chest appears more narrow; beware the front that is too perfect at 12 weeks. With mature chest width at 2 years, this puppy will be out at the elbows.

Figure 29-22: *At teething (about 4–5 months),* the puppy's chest often lags far behind growth of other parts of the body and is affectionately known as the "chestless wonder" stage.

(a) The underdeveloped chest allows the inward rotation of the elbows, resulting in the puppy standing east-west.

(b) When sitting, however, her front looks as nice as it did at 7 weeks and shows how it will look when she is full grown.

with poor feet, a check of the dog's history may disclose that the fault is not necessarily genetic.)

Accurate evaluation of feet and pasterns can be tricky; they are so sensitive to transient health problems that changes for the worse are a surprisingly accurate barometer of the puppy's state of health. Shipping stress, for example, can affect feet and pasterns quite dramatically. Several puppies were shipped to one author for final evaluation and placement in show homes. The author was shocked that the breeder considered the puppy in Figure 29-25 a show prospect because of weak pasterns and splayed feet. The breeder assured her that the puppy had excellent feet and pasterns when placed on the plane, and sure enough, the puppy was back to normal before 3 days had passed. This phenomenon has also been observed after immunizations and worming, as well as several days before a puppy becomes sick.

Hindquarters and Angulation

The best test for strength of the hindquarters at 7 weeks is to raise the puppy's rear by picking up the tail and dropping it while the puppy is distracted by food to see if the rear is strong or weak.

Figure 29-23: *A front that drops this true* at 8 weeks is a breeder's dream. This type of front stays better than most while growing, and youngsters often start winning points from the puppy class.

Figure 29-24: *Puppies this wide in front* at 7 weeks go only one way at maturity—wider!

Figure 29-25: *Shipping stress can affect feet and pasterns quite dramatically.*

(a) This picture of weak pasterns and splayed feet was taken shortly after the puppy's arrival.

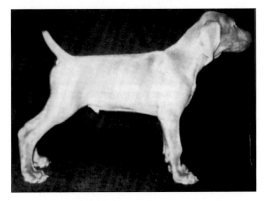

(b) Within 3 days, the puppy was back to normal.

Rears fall into one of four categories: bandy legged (out at the hocks), too narrow, cow-hocked, and just right. Bandy-legged rears usually tighten and mature into dogs that stand squarely. They often do not have as much rear end drive and tend to have a "swishy" movement. Narrow rears usually remain narrow, and at maturity, the dog may single track or cross over.

When rating cow hocks (that is, rear weakness), the degree of angulation must be taken into consideration.

1. Puppies with little rear angulation (straight stifles)—rare nowadays but common in the 1950s—undergo little change as adults. If a rear with little angulation is cow-hocked at 7–8 weeks, do not expect much improvement.

2. Moderately angled rears desirably drop straight and strong. If moderately weak, the puppy may remain cow-hocked, but there is a possibility of improvement.

Over-angulated rears are less consistent, but they tend to be weaker as puppies and get worse during periods of rapid growth. Such rears normally strengthen to some degree, especially if the puppy has ample opportunity for self-exercise in a sunlit, fenced yard. With mature muscle development, these rears often undergo remarkable improvement. An over-angulated puppy with a strong rear at 7–8 weeks should have an outstanding rear as an adult.

Even the best rear can be ruined by too much time in a crate. If the puppy is crated all day while the owners work, it should be loose all night. A good rule of thumb is a maximum of 9 hours per day in a crate.

Figure 29-26: *Group feeding is a good time to compare rears.* While the puppies are distracted by the food, the breeder can gently lift the puppy's rear by the tail and let the rear feet fall naturally. Defer final evaluation of over-angulated rears until later, as they normally strengthen with time.

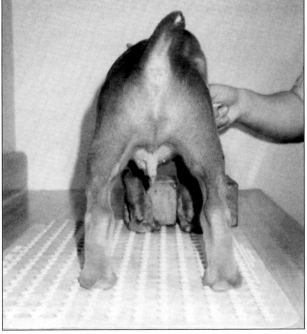

Figure 29-27: *The best test for good hindquarters* is to pick the puppy up by the tail—while distracted by food on a table—and drop the hindquarters into a stacked position. Rears can be classified as weak (cow hocked), strong, or bandy legged.

Conversely, too much exercise—such as jogging with the owner or early field conditioning—can also ruin a good rear. The ideal situation is to provide puppies with the opportunity for self-exercise in a fenced yard. They run and play enough to develop muscle strength and coordination but rarely stress their vulnerable joints or injure themselves by wild leaping without human encouragement.

Toplines and Tail Sets

Many puppies arch their backs when worried about a strange situation (or when they need to eliminate). Careful observation and photographs help to identify whether the roach is transient or a structural fault.

Also observe the topline when the puppy moves. It should remain level as in Figure 29-29.

The angle of the croup determines the tail set, and the angle observed at 7 weeks normally remains unchanged. When changes do occur, the tail set becomes lower—never higher. The change is usually minor, although rare Weimaraners have developed remarkably low tail sets between 11 and 14 months.

Size and Substance

Novices are typically attracted by the biggest puppy and consider the smallest one a runt. Experienced Weimaraner breeders know that early large size is often more indicative of a coarse, loose adult than mature size. Smaller puppies usually grow as big—or bigger—and they tend to have cleaner lines with smoother, tighter shoulders.

The best clue to adult size is the average size of the parents and grandparents and their littermates, although in gen-

Figure 29-29: *An excellent topline in spite of rocking back.* If the puppy were leaning forward correctly, with the feet directly under the shoulders, the true topline and forechest could be more accurately evaluated. However, if left undocked, this tail set high on the croup, would very likely curl over the back as in Figure 4-28 in *The Weimaraner Standard*.

eral, there is always a drift toward the breed average. Experienced breeders know better than to make any predictions about adult size. A good example is a litter with four bitches—three small ones like peas in a pod with identical weekly weights and one very big one that resembled the mother's litter sister at that age. At maturity, two of the smaller ones were a fraction over 23 inches, like their mother, but the third was a fraction under 26 inches, like their grand-

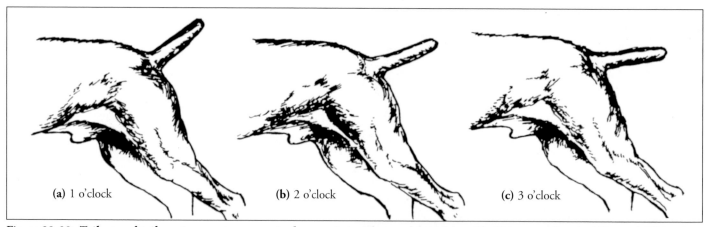

Figure 29-28: *Tail set and tail carriage are two separate characteristics.* The set of the tail (see *The Weimaraner Standard*, Figure 4-25) is a conformation trait and little can be done to change it. The carriage of the tail usually reflects the dog's attitude and temperament. A confident, happy Weim will usually carry the tail between 1 and 2 o'clock as in (a) and (b) above; when moving, the tail will often drop to 3 o'clock. With a tail set very high on the croup, it is not unusual to see a confident dog carry the tail as high as 12 o'clock (sometimes called a "gay" or "terrier" tail); a very low tail carriage many times results from a lack of confidence. However a "banana" tail (see *The Weimaraner Standard*, Figure 4-26) often occurs as a result of bone splinters or the skin being drawn too tightly over the tail tip during the docking procedure; in this case, it is important to notice the tail set rather than judge only the tail carriage.

(a) 1 o'clock   **(b)** 2 o'clock   **(c)** 3 o'clock

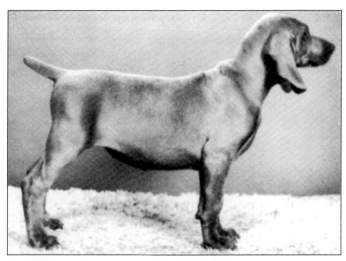

Figure 29-30: *The soft topline,* exaggerated by the short front legs and lack of breed type, would positively indicate this is a companion/pet puppy, compared with today's show-world Weimaraners. But in the early 1960s, sound movement, front and rear, propelled this puppy to a show-championship. (Breeders should always save a few pictures like this to keep them humble.)

Figure 29-31: *The "Pot Belly" test* reveals the true strength or weakness of the top line and is predictive of the adult appearance. After a full meal, two seemingly similar pups from the same litter are evaluated with full tummies. **(a)** Overfeeding exposes a possible problem with this topline. **(b)** A strong topline looks good under the same conditions.

mother. The big bitch also measured in at just under 26 inches, an inch taller than the aunt she resembled at 7 weeks.

Excess skin is similar to large size and is a growth pattern typical of rapid maturation. These puppies are usually large and should be shown as soon as they are competitive and before they become coarse.

Growth Patterns

Growth patterns vary between strains. The most common growth pattern follows a consistent sequence: (a) rear legs, (b) body and chest, (c) front legs, and (d) head. Growth may cease briefly before the sequence is repeated, giving a few days or weeks during which the puppy is in balance; then again, there may be no pause.

Large-boned Weimaraner males are most often high in the rear. Smaller-boned males tend to finish out without as many awkward phases. Many bitches never undergo these wildly awkward stages and tend to mature in a more consistent, predictable pattern. When changes do occur, the greatest variation is in the depth of chest and croup angle. Front and rear angulation, as well as topline in smaller-boned males and females, tends to show little change from the 7-week silhouette.

The greatest changes occur at teething, which often throws off the total balance of the dog. The feet and pasterns appear to be particularly stressed at this time. Worry on the owner's part over poor feet too often leads to over-exercise. If the young dog is roaded, negative gaiting patterns (side-winding, paddling, pacing) are often permanently acquired.

Assessing Movement

How to

Choose an area that is flat, dry, and narrow enough to force the puppy to move in a relatively straight line and that allows eye-level observation of movement. A cement driveway or freestanding kennel run of some length is an excellent setting for evaluation of gait. No valid observations can be made in tall grass or on hot pavement.

Unlike the hands-on examination, evaluating movement needs at least one but preferably two assistants. The puppy will be called back and forth between two of the team, and at some point, the breeder or other expert must be off to the side to observe side movement. Everyone can help tabulate the results for front, rear, and side movement.

Ideally, the puppy will trot back and forth between two people when called, allowing observation of front and rear movement, but few puppies are that cooperative. Sometimes, the best results are obtained by waking puppies from a sound sleep or waiting until they are thoroughly tired before attempting this type of testing. Most puppies are much too lively when starting to evaluate gait, they bound, hop, and jump everywhere, and even movement experts cannot evaluate the gait of a galloping puppy. Treats are often useful here, but it is important to have a puppy that is not so enthusiastic it runs instead of trots to the caller.

If the puppy responds only to the breeder, it is time to bring out the mother for help. A mother that walks quietly on lead often helps her puppies show off to their best advantage. With mama on lead, an assistant can walk back and forth between two observers. Some puppies will only follow the mother, which makes it impossible to observe front movement. When trotting beside the dam, most puppies twist to watch her, which produces gait faults that are unrelated to structure. More valid observations can be made if the puppy will cooperate and allow the assistant to be in the middle while trotting along calmly on the other side.

Another possibility is that one of the assistants has more experience than the breeder and that the breeder has had the time to lead train the puppies. For example, the puppy in

Figure 29-33: *Heavy-boned puppies* sometimes have "oversized suits."

Figure 29-32: *Comparing substance.*

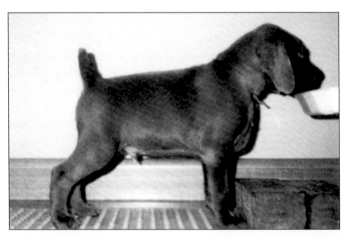

(a) A puppy with this much substance at 5 weeks will probably be loose and coarse at maturity, but final judgment should be deferred until 3 months.

(b) A similar amount of substance at 9 weeks is desirable.

Figure 29-39 moved smoothly on lead for the breeder, allowing the expert an excellent opportunity to evaluate its gait.

Patience and more patience is the key to success in evaluating gait. The observers must wait until the puppy reaches the state between wild enthusiasm and fatigue, during which valid observations can be made. The observers must be attuned to each puppy to figure out measures that will achieve cooperation. For some, a treat does the trick, whereas others perform best with mother's help.

Predicting Adult Gait

The Weimaraner that moves well is the Weimaraner that most often wins. Evaluating the gait of Weimaraner puppies at 7–8 weeks is complicated by the breed's typical late-developing coordination. The problem is that decisions must often be made at 7–8, weeks when most puppies leave home. Gait evaluation at 10–12 weeks is and always will be more accurate with this breed. Nevertheless, observations over many years and litters have been of considerable value, especially if the breeder is wise enough to get down on the puppies' level to get an accurate view of the coming-and-going movement.

When evaluating gait at 7–8 weeks, several points have shown themselves to be consistently true.

- If the movement is straight and fluid at an early age, it stays good; faults that develop later are either human-made or the result of trauma

- Consistent side-winding and elbow hooking rarely improve

Figure 29-34: *Light-boned puppies often exhibit a fairly even pattern of development.*

(a) At 5¹/₂ weeks, this puppy's shoulders appear straight and the forechest nonexistent.

(b) At 8 weeks, the puppy exhibits proportions that it will probably have as an adult: the topline settles, the forechest exhibits a mature profile, the shoulders are more laid back, and the forelegs lengthen. Note that rear angulation, tail set, and depth of chest are unchanged.

(c) At 3 months, the chest growth lags but the rest remains unchanged.

• Over-angulated rears, if weak, usually improve with mature development

Front Movement

With front movement, watch for persistent sidewinding as well as elbow hooking. Unlike puppy paddling and general front end looseness (which tend to be outgrown), sidewinding and elbow hooking rarely improve with maturation.

Side Movement

At 6 weeks, most Weimaraner puppies are not coordinated enough to evaluate movement from the side, typically hopping and skipping every few strides at the trot. By 10 weeks, however, many have enough coordination to observe for rear drive and front reach.

The side gait evaluation presents little problem, especially if the puppy is carrying a prized object with head held high and legs fully extended. Providing puppies with an opportunity to chase and retrieve balls or furry objects is also a superlative way of judging side extension, reach, and all-over balance in a trot. It is hard to get puppies to do this individually unless they are carrying something.

Rear Movement

Rear movement falls into one of three basic types:

• Too wide: This puppy usually needs more time to develop balance and coordination and should not be declared faulty until retested in several weeks

• Too close: If the tracks are close or converge, this puppy could have gaiting problems at maturity unless tracking improves in a few weeks

• Just right: Well-balanced puppies that gait properly are usually more mature and can be identified by feet that travel in parallel lines

Casual Observation– Another Evaluation Technique

Although breeders use it all the time, surprisingly few consider casual observation an important evaluation tool. Most breeder observations are made at a subconscious level, and when these observations are confirmed later, they may be ascribed to ESP or "instinct." Casual observations, made while the puppies are moving naturally and without restriction or control, are not only a valid evaluation tool but also often the most important one for a true and total assessment, since puppies may be less than cooperative during a formal evaluation. It is not unusual even for first-time breeders to identify the best puppy in the litter, especially if there is a range of quality. After all, they have lovingly observed the lit-

Figure 29-35: *At 4½ months, this pup demonstrates generally even growth.* Don't be alarmed or dismiss a show prospect, however, for less pleasing development patterns (especially between 3 and 5 months); consult the breeder, as some bloodlines exhibit an uneven growth pattern. Teaching the young puppy to "stand-stay" early is a valuable lesson for field, show, and obedience prospects, as well as giving the breeder a better opportunity to truly evaluate a young pup's structural balance and conformation at varying ages. With this setup, small, magnetized wooden blocks help establish a correct, steady stance; a moved foot leaves the pup with a paw hanging in mid-air and an unnerving loss of balance. This commercially available Happy Legs® kit comes in a folding magnetized base with four adjustable magnetized "stilts;" similar training tools can also be built at home.

ter over many weeks, watched their movement at play, and seen a puppy pause in a show stance. Keeping a brightly colored collar on each puppy from birth makes it possible to easily identify individuals even while they are playing in groups and to track each puppy's development over time.

Watch for eye-catching balance, attitude, style, and coordination. When viewed at ground level, look for straight, true movement as the puppy is casually trotting coming and going. Puppies that have pleasing balance at an early age tend to have that quality as adults. Observation of natural movement, stance, and attitude remains the best way to identify puppies with special potential—the rare ones with great style, charisma, and showmanship. It is also a good way to identify puppies that may have obvious conformation flaws but that sometimes finish more quickly than sounder siblings because of their "look at me, I'm the best!" attitude.

Putting It All Together

The time has come for decisions. The structural qualities of each puppy have been studied from many perspectives. The breeder has come to know the individual character through temperament and aptitude testing—from the bold one that wants to see the far side of the hill to the cuddler that just wants to be loved. The veterinary examination has identified any puppies that have undesirable hereditary traits that can be detected at an early age and that should not be bred. Conformation has been analyzed in many ways. The hands-on evaluation of each part (head, rears, and so

forth) has identified specific structural strengths and weaknesses. Photography has shown how the parts fit together when standing still, and movement analysis has indicated how they fit when in motion. Finally, observation has revealed the puppy with exceptional dynamic balance, natural poise, and charisma.

The fallacy of ranking an entire litter—one, two, three, four—should be obvious by now. It is difficult enough after separating puppies into the categories of obvious pets (nonbreeding), boys, and girls.

When ranking the conformation of puppies in a litter of uniformly good quality (always a joy), the breeder can be reduced to nitpicking. In this situation, extra help is needed to stack the finalists on the table at the same time. Who has the best front, the best rear, the best topline, or the best feet? There are always some minor differences.

Evaluate the litter as a whole for traits that appear in most, whether faults or virtues. If you observe a trend toward moderate or too little angulation, for example, one of the traits to consider in potential mates for these puppies would be prepotency for greater angulation. On the other hand, if all have straight, strong toplines, they will probably be prepotent for strong toplines, and this trait would not be a concern when selecting a mate.

Finally, it is time to ask, "Which puppy do I want to keep? Which puppy comes closest to my visualization of the perfect Weimaraner? Which puppy fulfills the goals of this particular mating?" For example, a breeder's goal was to improve shoulder layback without compromising soundness.

Figure 29-36: *Because of the interaction between rear angulation and rear strength,* the breeder's final evaluation takes both into consideration. In fact, an experienced breeder does not need a rearview photo unless the puppy deviates from the norm.

(a) A puppy with under-angulation that matches front to rear will move with a reasonable but unspectacular gait. When mature, this pup's lack of overall angulation will probably be fine coming and going, but in today's show ring his side gait will not make him a standout. A pup that is under-angulated AND cow-hocked is unlikely to improve.

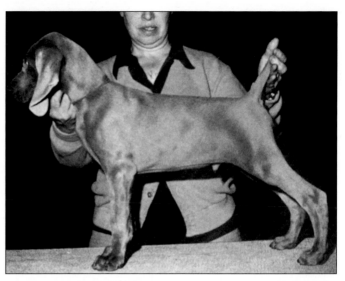

(b) A puppy with an over-angulated rear can be expected to be cow-hocked to some extent. These rears always improve, although the degree of improvement is unpredictable. Again, the front and rear angulation is balanced, and—if sound—this youngster has the potential for spectacular side movement.

If the litter is of uniformly good quality and all have better shoulders than the dam, the choice is simple. More often, quality is not absolutely uniform, and the breeder may face a variety of choices.

1. If all the puppies have adequate shoulder angulation like the dam but none is an improvement over her, the breeder has two choices: (a) keep the best puppy and hope for improvement in the next generation, or (b) face the fact that if no progress is shown, it may be best not to keep any of the puppies and to try the mother with a different stud. A good compromise in this situation might be to place the two best puppy bitches on co-ownerships, with the option of choosing the sire for a breeding and a puppy from that litter.

2. On the other hand, if the litter shows significant improvement for the desired trait, keep the two best puppies for at least a few more months.

3. The possibility does exist, however, that time will prove the 7- to 8-week evaluation for the desired trait was inaccurate; the original goal was realized but on a different time schedule than the one the breeder is familiar with. One of the most common variations in growth patterns is the time it takes to evaluate shoulders.

Sometimes, the breeder's choices are rough. What if the puppy that has exactly the hoped-for shoulders also has the

(c) The most damning combination is unbalanced angulation. This puppy's straight front shoulders and over-angulated rear may produce attractive side movement in the ring, but will likely exhibit paddling and crabbing coming and going. The converse (over-angulated front and straight rear) will also produce gaiting flaws. Balanced or not, excessive angulation, front or rear, has consistently proven to result in poor stamina in the field.

worst topline in generations? In terms of show-ring success, this would not be the breeder's pick of the litter; in terms of improving the long-term quality of the line and breeding the perfect Weimaraner, that puppy may be a key producer. If good toplines are typical of the bloodlines of both parents, with luck, the bad topline may be a fluke.

Assessing puppies is, at best, an educated guess at what the puppy will grow into. Experience with preceding generations is invaluable, which is why photographs and detailed records (health and performance as well as structure) become more valuable over the years in developing a long-term plan,

Figure 29-37: *To evaluate movement,* set up an exercise pen in a long, narrow configuration as shown. With all the puppies except the one being evaluated inside, the puppy under consideration will display its natural movement as it moves around the exterior of the pen. A change of position will allow observation of not only the coming and going movement, but also topline, extension, and side gait. Be sure to make all observations from ground level (seated on the ground or a low stool), rather than standing, to get the most accurate view.

Figure 29-38: *With a single puppy to evaluate,* have one skilled observer off to the side to assess side movement, extension, and topline, while two others call the puppy back and forth, appraising movement coming and going. Everyone should be at ground level to get the best view. The observers can make notes and then rotate positions to view the puppy from all sides.

as discussed in *Breeding Basics.* A detailed assessment can improve the probability of identifying a future great—it is, however, never a certainty.

Figure 29-39: *A mother that walks quietly* on lead often helps her puppies show off to their best advantage.

To a Good and Loving Home

For every healthy puppy there should be a perfect home…. But more goes into finding the perfect puppy than just looking in the "Dogs" section in the newspaper or a trip to the local pet shop. Pet shops are a good source for supplies, and newspapers make useful crate liners, but they are the last place to find the perfect puppy. AKC, WCA, NAVHDA, and many other organizations discussed in this book offer events designed to test and evaluate the appearance and abilities of Weimaraners, and these are the ideal place to find the ideal breeder of the perfect puppy. Many communities boast one or more all-breed or special-interest clubs for dog activities. Local Weimaraner specialty clubs can be located on the WCA website (www.weimclubamerica.org/about/alphaclubs.html). Try to attend a meeting or a sponsored event to get to meet the people and their dogs.

Matchmaker

So what attributes should a potential buyer look for in a breeder? After all, a puppy buyer can plan to have a strong bond with the breeder for 12–15 years to come. A breeder is a source of information about the parents and potential of that adorable puppy, and he or she has a wealth of knowledge to solve frustrations and answer questions. So, look for a person who inspires a sense of comfort and confidence, someone who is easy to talk to.

Responsible breeders are continually seeking out new knowledge about their dogs and their care and training; they

Figure 29-40: *This much reach at 5 weeks is rare.* Neurological maturation varies in different bloodlines. As a general rule, do not fault a puppy that does not trot or show notable extension before 10 weeks of age.

Figure 29-41: *For the "acid test" of side movement,* have the puppy carry something special. This 12-week-old puppy gaits with head high and shows off his eye-catching reach. Note how much more a ground-level photograph reveals.

Figure 29-42: *A littermate exhibits his maximum reach* under the same conditions. Although his reach and extension were not his strongest features, this pup would go on to finish his bench championship based on his overall sound conformation and would earn his MH due to his excellent nose.

should have membership in the WCA, which requires its members to agree to a Code of Ethics, which can be viewed at www.weimclubamerica.org. They will be testing their dogs against a standard of performance (in hunt tests, tracking tests, and the like) or competing against other dogs (at conformation shows or trials), constantly seeking to improve their dogs and their breeding program. Several ways in which a breeder—or prospective purchaser—can do this is to attend seminars and to be an active member of a local all-breed or special interest club (WCA, obedience, field, etc.).

It is not snobbish to look for titles on the parents of the prospective puppy. After all, this is one of the best ways of verifying through testing the dog's instinct, trainability, and temperament, traits that will hopefully be passed on to their offspring. Nor is it a conceit to look for OFA certifications, such as hip, thyroid, or eye clearances; this is another sign that a breeder is seeking to produce sounder, healthier dogs. OFA certifications (hips are a must) can be verified on the OFA website at www.offa.org using the dog's registered name or AKC registration number.

Expect the breeder to ask LOTS of questions! After all, they have invested a great deal of time, money, and heart into producing a litter of puppies. Is it unreasonable to want to try to ensure that the puppies are going to the best home possible? To the breeder, the process is much like finding adoptive homes for their children or grandchildren. They may ask questions about the prospective residence. Is the residence fenced? What are the number and ages of family members? What are the number and types of current pets? Previous pets owned? Planned feeding program? Family activities? Maybe even a reference from a veterinarian! A breeder who does not ask questions to help determine which puppy is the best match for a prospective family should arouse suspicion.

When discussing the potential home life of the puppy, be honest with the breeder. Most breeders will have puppies that they hope will go to competition homes, where the puppies will provide the opportunity to test the results of the breeding program. If looking for a competition prospect, say so! Allow the breeder the opportunity to provide a puppy with the best chance of success in that particular field of interest; do not plan on getting a "better deal" and hope to "get lucky"! Even a litter with the most star-studded pedigree may have puppies, those with physical or mental traits that would limit their success in competition, that are better suited for non-competitive homes. If you are not planning to compete, such a puppy may be better suited for the family lifestyle. Why pay for parts that are not needed?

It is not unusual to be put on a waiting list. Many responsible breeders produce only one or two litters a year, some even less. So it is possible that the perfect puppy may have several potential homes or that the "right" puppy is not in the current litter. This is a case where patience pays off. Do not be impa-

Figure 29-43: *Stand the puppies side by side, dropping the front and rear.* Notice how the use of black gloves and background when posing for pictures minimize distractions in the photograph.

(a) Compare the rears.

(b) Compare the fronts and feet.

tient; rather, appreciate the effort the breeder makes in matching puppies with the best home for both the puppy and the purchaser. If a breeder does not have, or is not expecting to have, the right puppy in a reasonable time, they may be able to refer you to another breeder of equal merit.

A responsible breeder will want to place puppies after 7 weeks, and sometimes later; releasing puppies prior to 7 weeks should be a warning sign. In some states, it is illegal to sell a puppy before 8 weeks. Prior to 7 weeks, puppies are still learning a great deal from their mother and littermates—important canine protocol and behavior that will enhance the chances of the puppy becoming a physically and mentally sound adult, able to interact responsibly in a human environment.

A prospective puppy owner should expect to be able to meet the dam of the litter. If she is unavailable, find out why, and be a bit wary. Meeting the mother can tell a lot about a puppy, since she has a large influence on the puppies' attitudes and temperaments. Her appearance will reveal much about the care provided to dogs on the premise; although she may be thin from caring for her puppies, she should have a happy attitude and otherwise healthy appearance. While she may be protective of her puppies, she should be friendly and tractable when she does not feel her puppies need protection. Puppies will imitate both the good and bad examples she sets for them. She often makes an indelible impression on the future temperament and character of the puppies well before they go to their new homes.

Do not be surprised if the sire is not available. Many breeders will use a stud dog from a different area when seeking the perfect addition to a breeding program; however, they should be able to discuss the attributes of the dog and why he was chosen. If the breeder owns the stud dog and he is on the premises, ask to meet him as well; after all, half the puppy's genes are from him!

Responsible breeders offer guarantees against certain genetic health issues (hips, eyes, heart, etc.). All puppies should have been examined by a veterinarian prior to going to their new home, as this provides an opportunity to identify any underlying health defects, such as a heart murmur or extra eyelashes, as well as to accurately weigh and worm all puppies. At a minimum, the purchaser should have 2 business days to take the puppy to a veterinarian of their choice for a complete health check—and do not pass up this opportunity!

The breeder should have a shot record available and may also have a recommended vaccination protocol. In some cases, the health guarantees in the contract may be voided if the vaccine protocol is not followed.

On the subject of contracts...

Do not be surprised if a breeder has a contract that both parties sign. A very common aspect of a contract is a re-homing clause. After all of the investment on the part of the breeder, it does not seem unwarranted that they would want to ensure that the puppy/dog goes to an appropriate home if the original owner can no longer keep a puppy. Also, do not

Figure 29-44: *The dam should always be available to meet the purchaser.* Her condition and behavior may reveal much about the puppies' future temperaments. Titles can demonstrate that conscientious breeders have tested their stock to ensure that they have the traits that make a Weimaraner representative of the breed. CH Nani's Jagmar Sweet Dividends, VCD2, MH, MX, MXJ, NSD, NRD, VX4, BROM, has earned a bench championship to show that she meets the conformation standard, an obedience title (CDX) to show that she is trainable and biddable, agility titles (MX, MXJ) to show her athleticism and desire to work with her master, and field title and ratings (MH, NSD, NRD) to show that she has the nose and instinct of a Weimaraner. Additionally, Diva, the proud mother of 10 champions, has also proven that she passes these traits on to her offspring, as she is the highest VX-rated BROM in America. Photograph by Terrie Borman.

be surprised by a spay/neuter clause or a limited registration for puppies purchased as pet or companion. These are two tools that a responsible breeder uses to ensure that dogs that have disqualifying faults or other traits that should not be passed on will not be bred in the future. A limited registration allows the puppy to compete in most AKC activities; however, any offspring from the puppy are ineligible for AKC registration. Should a puppy develop beyond its original expectations, the breeder may later convert a limited registration to a full registration.

A great way to gain access to a top-quality show, field, or breeding prospect is to agree to a co-ownership with a breeder/mentor. This tool allows the breeder to maintain a connection to top-quality puppies they feel have the best potential. Co-ownerships frequently have an expiration clause, such as when the dog finishes agreed-upon training

Figure 29-45: *While one should expect to meet the dam of a litter*, do not be concerned if the sire is not available; when choosing the sire for a litter, a wise breeder has looked for a dog with outstanding conformation and temperament that have been proven through testing and competition, with the requisite health certifications. Often, this means a stud dog that may be far away from home. Although the sire may not be available to meet, the breeder should be able to provide pictures, pedigree, and an explanation why this dog was selected as the father of the litter. A dog such as Am/Can CH Orion's Jaeger v. Reiteralm, CD, TD, MH, SD, RDX, BROM, CGC, has proven his character, soundness, and versatility with titles in tracking (TD), obedience (CD), field (MH, SD, RDX), and conformation (CH); an added bonus is that he is also a registered therapy dog and personal service dog, which indicates his outstanding temperament. The icing on the cake is that Jaeger is the top-rated VX BROM male, indicating his ability as a proven sire. Photograph by Tereen Zimmerman.

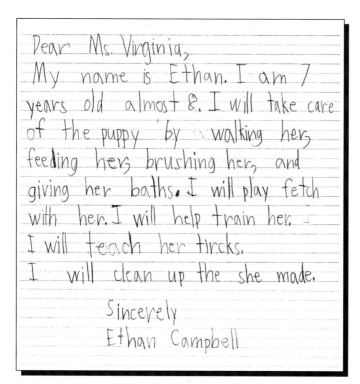

Dear Ms. Virginia,
My name is Ethan. I am 7
years old almost 8. I will take care
of the puppy by walking her,
feeding her, brushing her, and
giving her baths. I will play fetch
with her. I will help train her.
I will teach her tircks.
I will clean up the she made.

Sincerely
Ethan Campbell

Figure 29-46: *A child's pledge,* presented with a handshake, reminds even young children that if the agreement is broken, the breeder has the right to find a new, loving home for the puppy. Such a pledge makes even young children aware of the obligations of ownership.

or competition. These arrangements are also popular because they allow for the opportunity to pool time, experience, and financial resources to invest in the development of a pup with great potential.

Be wary if a breeder encourages or even allows two puppies to go to the same home. It is very difficult to provide the time and attention needed for two puppies in the same home. Without sufficient individual attention, such puppies are far more likely to bond closely to each other than to their human family and rarely meet their full potential as companions.

Be doubly wary of a breeder who allows a purchaser to come by and pick up a puppy on a first meeting, without previous contact or agreements, for cash only (no checks please!), without asking many questions, or even requesting that the purchasers consider their decision overnight.

If there are children in the household, some breeders have a special contract just for the youngsters. At the first visit, the breeder may supply reading material as well as other resources (local library or the AKC website www.akc.org) on the responsibilities of puppy ownership. Children may then be encouraged to go home and write out a pledge, including a description of their responsibilities and duties of caring for the new puppy. This author makes a small ceremony of the signing—a review of the contract and a handshake impress many children with the obligations of puppy ownership.

This ensures that the children understand that if these promises are not kept, the breeder has the right, even obligation, to find a new home for the puppy, where it will be loved and cared for.

All in all, finding the perfect puppy is not going to be like a trip to the mall to find the perfect Christmas present. It will likely take some time and a bit of research and study. Then, too, many new Weimaraner owners find themselves bitten by "the bug" of competition, whether it is show, field, obedience, or one of the myriad other activities that Weimaraners inspire their owners to become involved in. The time and patience spent investigating will repay itself with 12–15 years of dividends, as the carefully researched breeder, like a grandparent, will provide not only a wealth of knowledge and support, but may become a friend and mentor for the lifetime of that perfect puppy.

Figure 29-47: *Youngsters are encouraged* to visit, name their puppy, learn about pet care, and prepare a pledge note while waiting until the puppy is old enough to go to its new home.

FINAL CHECKLIST

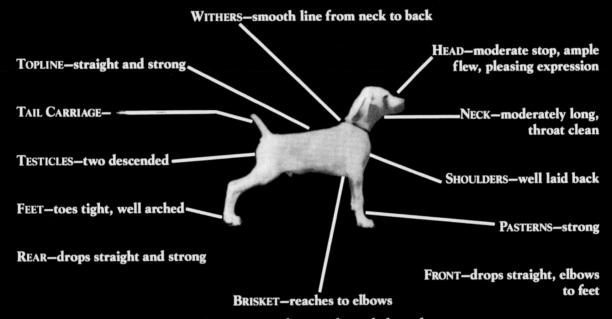

WITHERS—smooth line from neck to back

TOPLINE—straight and strong

TAIL CARRIAGE—

TESTICLES—two descended

FEET—toes tight, well arched

REAR—drops straight and strong

HEAD—moderate stop, ample flew, pleasing expression

NECK—moderately long, throat clean

SHOULDERS—well laid back

PASTERNS—strong

FRONT—drops straight, elbows to feet

BRISKET—reaches to elbows

ANGULATION—front and rear balanced

TOTAL IMPRESSION—well-proportioned, eye-pleasing

NOTE IN RECORDS
EYELASHES—if any, note number and type
EARS—length and set
TEETH—scissors bite or slightly overshot
SHOULDERS—finger width in relation to littermates
COAT—texture and shade
SIZE, BONE, AND SUBSTANCE—compare with littermates
MOVEMENT—record front, rear and side action
VETERINARY EXAMINATION—findings, good and bad
APTITUDE AND TEMPERAMENT TESTING RESULTS

Figure 30-1: *CH Aria's Allegra of Colsidex* (CH Colsidex Nani Follow A Dream × CH Top Hats Spitfire). Bred by Cheryl Orr and Christopher Buckley; owned by Judy Colan, Elaine Meader, and Joyce Kealoha.

CH Aria's Allegra of Colsidex

In the show ring, Fergie did it all. She finished with three 5-point majors, including the National Specialty at 13 months and Best Bitch in Futurity. After winning the Futurity, she went to Stan Flowers to be campaigned. Less than 1 month after going to Stan, she won her first Best in Show. In a little more than 18 months with Stan, she made breed history by breaking all records for the breed: 27 Best in Shows (the previous record, 15 Best in Shows, was held by CH Greymist's Silver Cloud), 77 Group 1s, 48 Group 2s, 27 Group 3s, 13 Group 4s, 211 Best of Breeds, and eight Specialty wins, including Best of Breed at the 1997 National Specialty. Her record of winning or placing in the porting group 82% of the time is eclipsed only by her seven-times-removed grandsire Val Knight Ranck. In 1959, he was the No. 1 Weimaraner and No. 2 Sporting Dog. She was bred only once and produced three champions: CH Colsidex Seabreeze Bet The Farm, TD, BROM; CH Colsidex The Farm Carbon Copy (Futurity winner); and CH Colsidex Celebrity of Camelot. Fergie never met a stranger; she loved and greeted everyone as long-lost friends. She was a great ambassador for the breed.

CHAPTER 30

BEST IN SHOW

by Nick Ambulos

The Best in Show

The all-breed Best in Show ribbon is the ultimate dream of show fanciers. Although the thrill of breeding or owning a winner comes to only a few, all Weimaraner fanciers enjoy the reflected glory each time another achieves this dream.

The Weimaraner got off to a slow start—indeed, there were many years where there was no Best in Show winner. Now, Weimaraners are gaining recognition in the sporting group as top contenders for group and Best in Show honors where their athleticism, remarkable coat, and showmanship are catching the eye and nod of more judges in the Best in Show ring.

Best in Show winners exert an extraordinary influence on their breed. Fanciers tend to modify their personal image of "The Perfect Weimaraner" and their interpretation of the standard toward that of the judges. As a result, many become popular producers and their offspring perpetuate their impact on breed type; of the Best in Show winners whose stories appear in this chapter, the reader might also notice many of these same names appearing on the BROM roles.

Although there are several systems of ranking show dogs, show entries have grown and conditions have changed so much that there is no valid way to evaluate achievements that span more than six decades; therefore, no comparison of these great Weimaraners is attempted, and their show records are given in a simple, uniform style. Old issues of *The Weimaraner Magazine* will allow the tracking of the career of a Best in Show winner from the novice breaking onto the show scene to the last hurrah before retirement. The Pictorial History, Volumes 1–3, available through the WCA, will also provide additional details on the careers of these memorable representatives of the Weimaraner breed. This chapter shares the stories of many of the Weimaraners that have won one of dogdom's most coveted awards—the red, white, and blue rosette for an all-breed Best in Show. Information was gleaned from breed literature, owners, breeders, fans, and personal experience. By grouping the stories of these winners chronologically, the reader can see how time has influenced changes in style and type in the breed.

Figure 30-2: *CH Burt v. d. Harrasburg, Import, BROM, HOF* (Arco v. d. Fitzen × Asta v. Bruckberg). Bred by Max Baumler; owned by Franz Sachse. Photograph courtesy of the WCA.

One of the goals of this chapter is to correct the common misconception that show Weimaraners miss out on the pleasures of a family life. The Weimaraners highlighted in this chapter are and were beloved companions, and their stories are for everyone who dreams of breeding, owning, or showing a Best in Show winner.

Their Stories

CH Burt v. d. Harrasburg, Import, BROM, HOF

CH Burt v. d. Harrasburg was the third of the famous Harrasburg B litter to arrive from Germany. When his owner, Frans Sachse, was stationed in Alaska, Burt staunchly retrieved birds from frigid arctic waters.

Burt became the first Weimaraner (and only import) to win an American all-breed Best in Show. The military sent Sachse to Alaska in 1952, and Burt competed only once

Figure 30-3: *CH Deal's Sporting True Aim II, BROM, HOF* (CH Bert v. d. Harrasburg, Import, SDX, BROM × CH Grafmar's Dove, CD, BROM). Bred by Mr. and Mrs. Elvin Deal; owned by Mrs. Grace Crafts. Photograph courtesy of the WCA.

that year (April) at the Alaskan Kennel Club—the territory's only show—where he went all the way to Best in Show. Because of Alaska's territorial status and the few entries at the show, many believed that the honor exceeded the achievement, and some Weimaraner literature states that CH Deal's Sporting True Aim II, BROM, is the breed's first American Best in Show winner. Nevertheless, Burt was among the best of his generation, winning the 1951 and 1954 National Specialties.

Burt is the sire of 19 champions, including CH Silver Blue Lucifer, winner of the 1952 National Specialty. He is the grandsire of Best in Show winner CH Grave's Rogue.

CH Deal's Sporting True Aim II, BROM, HOF

CH Deal's Sporting True Aim II was sired by CH Bert v. d. Harrasburg (the litter brother of Burt), who thrilled field-trial enthusiasts by becoming the first Weimaraner to win all-breed stakes.

True Aim became the breed's second Best in Show winner at Framingham, Massachusetts, in 1953—the first in the continental United States and the first American-bred. In addition, True Aim won the breed at Westminster in 1952 and 1953.

The sire of 23 champions—including Best in Show winner CH Ann's Rickey Boy, CD, BROM—True Aim set a record that solidly established him in American bloodlines. His record number of champions was soon surpassed by his sons—eastern-based Rickey Boy (28) and western-based CH Debar's Platinum Specter, BROM (29).

CH von Gaiberg's Ord

CH von Gaiberg's Ord, the breed's third Best in Show winner, was a grandson of CH Deal's Sporting True Aim II, BROM. Owned by Alexander Newton, Ord swept the Weimaraner world in 1957 with a brief but brilliant career. Under the guidance of Harry Sangster, the California-bred dog began the year by invading the East and winning the breed at Westminster. That summer, Ord won the 1957 National Specialty. In August 1957, Ord went Best in Show at Santa Cruz under Charles Siever; a second Best in Show made Ord the breed's first multiple Best in Show winner.

The sire of five champions, Ord's influence lives on, primarily through the offspring of his BROM son and daughter, CH Verdemar's Cosak and CH von Gaiberg's Kate Schwenden, CD, NRD. Bred to each other, the half-brother–half-sister mating produced the 1967 Westminster winner, CH von Gaiberg's Amy Schwenden, 1969 National Specialty winner, CH von Gaiberg's Alf Schwenden, and CH von Gaiberg's Anna Schwenden, BROM, the foundation of the well-known Valmar line.

Figure 30-4: *CH von Gaiberg's Ord* (CH Debar's Platinum Specter, BROM × CH von Gaiberg's Esta, BROM). Bred by Homer Carr; owned by Alexander Newton.

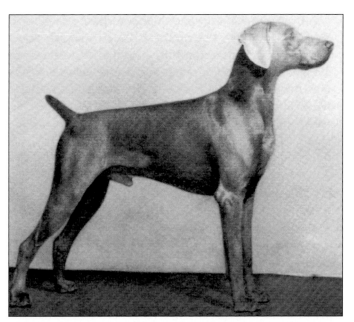

Figure 30-5: *CH Ann's Rickey Boy, CD, BROM, HOF* (CH Deal's Sporting True Aim II, BROM × CH Ann's Sidney Sue, CD). Bred and owned by Ann Kepler. Photograph courtesy of the WCA.

CH Ann's Rickey Boy, CD, BROM, HOF

In the early 1950s, CH Ann's Rickey Boy and Ann Kepler became the breed's first breeder-owner-handler team. Their extensive travels (primarily in the East, Midwest, and South) set a new precedent, and they even went north of the border for a Canadian championship. In those days of benched shows, Rickey and Ann were goodwill ambassadors for the breed, for few could resist their friendly charm. Rickey established a record 155 breed wins, and he ranked in the Top 10 Weimaraners, the Top 10 sporting dogs, and the Top 10 of all breeds. During his career, Rickey also achieved two American-Bred Best in Shows, which were commonly awarded at that time. At last, in 1958, they got the big one, the all-breed Best in Show, and Rickey retired.

Rickey would be considered a great dog on the strength of his show career alone. However, it is in the stud department that Rickey really left his mark; he is the sire of 28 champions and the sire of two group winners. The number of champions in whose pedigree he appears in is impossible to calculate, but their legions include many other entries in this chapter, including Best in Show Am/Can CH Shadowmar Barhaus Dorilio, BROM, HOF; CH Sir Eric von Sieben, BROM, HOF; CH The Rajah's Magic v. d. Reiteralm, BROM, HOF; CH Erbenhof Touch of Class, BROM; CH Nani's Visa v. d. Reiteralm, BROM, HOF; and CH Valmar's Pollyanna, BROM, HOF.

Rickey belonged to the entire Kepler family, and his retirement meant that Ann's husband Kep had a full-time hunting dog. In Pennsylvania's pheasant country, Rickey hunted for Kep, friends, and neighbors to the ripe old age of 15. He taught his descendants to point and honor, for he was a sire of all-around Weimaraners. Rickey sired 28 champions.

At that time, dog fanciers believed that only professional handlers could show dogs, and Ann was the breed's first successful amateur handler. Ann later became a professional handler, but she encouraged novices to show their own Weimaraners, generously donating her time and sharing her skills to help them. Soon, many open Weimaraner classes were filled with amateur owner-handlers, with Ann coaching from the sidelines. She encouraged others to help newcomers, especially junior handlers. One of the notable junior handlers taught by Ann is her daughter, Peggy Kepler Roush, who has carried on the tradition of sharing her skills with amateur handlers.

CH Gourmet's Sardar, BROM, HOF

CH Gourmet's Sardar became the breed's fifth Best in Show winner in the late 1950s. His admirer, Marie Seidelman, wrote, "I shall always remember his proud, flashy appearance and every inch a gentleman. He loved the crowds, the applause, the excitement of being in the ring."[1]

Bred by Erma Muster, Fritz was the smallest puppy of the litter and was sold as a pet. For one reason or another, the home did not work out, nor did subsequent ones. The

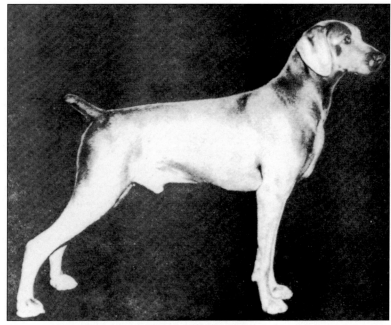

Figure 30-6: *CH Gourmet's Sardar, BROM, HOF* (CH Dok of Fairway × CH Silver Linda v. Feldstrom, UD). Bred and owned by Erma E. Muster. Photograph courtesy of the WCA.

Figure 30-7: *CH Val Knight Ranck, BROM, HOF* (CH Count von Houghton, SD, BROM × CH Brenda's Gray Shadow, CD, BROM). Bred by Wesley Ranck; owned by John M. Boehne.

third time Fritz returned, Erma decided the dark-gray was fated to be her dog, and his fine show career proved the wisdom of her decision.

Handled by Dick Cooper to 115 breed wins, Fritz went on to many group placements as well as three American and two Canadian Best in Show wins (1958–1961). He captured the breed at Westminster in 1958 and 1960 (he was the top-winning Weimaraner in those years) and at the Chicago International in 1959, 1960, and 1962, and he also captured the 1960 National Specialty. Fritz is a BROM sire of 14 champions.

CH Val Knight Ranck, BROM, HOF

CH Val Knight Ranck dominated the breed ring for three years in spite of his limited showing. Competing only 115 times, Val won an amazing 114 Breeds, from which he went on to a phenomenal 101 Group placements. Of the 41 times Val won the Sporting Group and competed for Best in Show, he walked off with the coveted red, white, and blue rosette nine times, which remained the breed Best in Show record for more than 30 years. He won the 1959 National Specialty, and in 1962 became the first of three Weimaraners to win the sporting-group win at Westminster and brought breed prestige to a new high. As the constant household companion of the Boehnes, who drove him to most of the shows, Val rarely campaigned far from home. In those days, group trophies were huge and of solid silver. Val's collection of tea services and Revere bowls filled the Boehne's huge 20 × 30–foot basement, and a whimsical sign on the door read, "This way to the poorhouse!"

Val's charismatic showmanship is legendary. As with all great show dogs, Val knew why he was in the ring. He posed without a hand or lead touching him. Frozen in his show stance and moving only his eyes to watch the judge, Val drew laughter from the crowd with a "woof" to distract the judge when he or she was examining the other dogs. A solidly built, flashy, light silver dog, Val was the first of the great-moving Weimaraners, with a gait described as "flowing perfection."

Incredibly, Val was first sold as a $75 pet. When his elderly owners found Val too lively a companion, they returned him to his breeder, Dr. Wesley Ranck. He resold Val to John M. Boehne for $100. To Dr. Ranck, a well-known veterinarian and breeder, Val was too different from the prevalent Weimaraner type to be a good show dog. To professional handler Tom Crowe, Val's unique traits—short body, powerful well-angulated rear, clean, elegant neck, and small, tight feet—stamped him as the epitome of the sporting-breed type, with qualities that sporting judges prized. It is not surprising that Val, with his far reaching movement, extreme extension, and compact body type, would create quite a stir—traits that were quite unusual for the time but that modern exhibitors now highly prize.

As a sire, Val did not disappoint his fans. Val stood at Stud to only 15 bitches. He sired 34 champions, including six group winners, and he held the breed record for as a sire of champions for several years he was surpassed by his own son. Mere numbers, however, do not begin to convey Val's impact on the breed: he was a pivotal sire, marking the beginning of the modern American Weimaraner.

CH Grave's Rogue

CH Grave's Rogue became the breed's seventh Best in Show winner. Famous for his free-flowing, driving gait, Rogue won the 1961 National Specialty, and he was the top-winning Weimaraner that year.

The primary interest of Rogue's Seattle-based owner, Eldon McCormack, was hunting, and he had little interest in standing Rogue at stud. In addition, it was very difficult to ship bitches to Seattle at that time. Appreciating the dog's gait and valuable pedigree, Dorothy (Dot) Remensnyder persuaded McCormack to send Rogue to her Shadowmar Kennel in upstate New York, where he sired several litters.

While with Dot, Rogue was shown at Westminster. Although he did not win the breed, he captured many fans, including Virginia (Ginny) Alexander, who described him as a dog with beautiful shoulders, powerful rear movement, and an outgoing, happy personality. Rogue was a sound dog, who never stopped with a foot (and a very good foot at that) out of place. "He was such a gorgeous animal," Ginny said, "with such true movement that I decided immediately that I had to have something out of him."

Figure 30-8: *CH Grave's Rogue* (CH Catalano's Burt × CH Grave's Princess Auger). Bred by R. Graves; owned by Eldon McCormack. Photograph courtesy of the WCA.

When Norman LeBoeuf bred the outstanding producer Shadowmar Valentress, BROM (a daughter of Best in Show winner CH Val Knight Ranck, BROM) to Rogue, Ginny seized the opportunity to buy a puppy, who became the breed's top-producing dam of 20 champions—CH Norman's Rona v. d. Reiteralm, NSD, SD, V, BROM. Rona is the dam of the Best in Show winner CH Ronamax Rajah v. d. Reiteralm, BROM and Dual CH Ronamax Rufus v. d. Reiteralm, CD, SDX, RDX, VX. She is the granddam of the Best in Show winners CH Rajah's Alexander v. d. Reiteralm (1971 National Specialty) and CH The Rajah's Magic v. d. Reiteralm, BROM (1976 and 1977 National Specialties).

Rogue contributed a strong foundation to Diane Swanson's Green Acres line; he sired CH Eldomac Rona of Green Acres (dam of CH Rona's Rogue of Green Acres, CD, NRD, V, BROM), CH Green Acres

Silbergrau Faun, CDX, BROM, and other Green Acres champions. Although he sired few litters, Rogue's outstanding qualities—excellent shoulder layback, correct gait, beautiful head, and strong hunting desire—live on in the breed.

CH Shadowmar Barthaus Dorilio, BROM, HOF

Marge Bartelli Wilson wrote that few suspected that the arrival of CH Shadowmar Little Kate at the Burbank Airport for a breeding to CH von Gaiberg's Nordsee Ponto marked the genesis of a legend—CH Shadowmar Barthaus Dorilio, BROM. Katie remained at Barthaus after the breeding, and Marge raised the litter.

The litter was an interesting line-breeding on CH Deal's Sporting True Aim II, BROM, through his sons CH Debar's Platinum Specter, BROM, and CH Ann's Rickey Boy, CD, BROM. Marge pointed out, however, that the Harrasburg combination was coincidental; their real objective was a line-breeding on the German Weimaraners behind Ponto's dam (Bora v. Nordseekoog, Import) and Kate's grandsire (CH Flott v. Haimberg, Import, SDX, RDX, BROM).

Marge described Dorilio as a sweet, even-tempered puppy who joined his excited littermates in pointing penned pheasants and ducks, and Marge suspected he would be a pleasure to live with. Dot Remensnyder, Kate's owner, chose Dor as her pick of the litter, and he left for Dot's New York home.

Figure 30-9: *CH Shadowmar Barthaus Dorilio, BROM, HOF* (CH von Gaiburg's Nordsee Ponto × CH Shadowmar Little Kate). Bred by Dorothy Remensnyder and Marjorie Bartelli Wilson; owned by Dorothy Remensnyder.

Figure 30-10: *CH Gwinner's Sportwheel, BROM* (CH Gwinner's Pinwheel, BROM × Brun Hilde Schmidt). Bred by Wesley O. Denison; owned by Tony P. and Beatrice S. Gwinner. Photograph courtesy of the WCA.

CH Gwinner's Sportwheel, BROM

CH Gwinner's Sportwheel was an arrogant dog. When the powerful, big-moving Weimaraner swept around the ring, he seemed to be saying, "Get out of my way or I'll knock you down!" Cocking his leg over the Best of Breed sign, then showering it with dirt with a backward kick, Sport proclaimed his supremacy in the clearest canine manner. Show business aside, Sport was a most congenial dog.

Like most Weimaraner fanciers, Tony and Gabby Gwinner began by owning a beloved pet, and Gabby enjoyed obedience competition. One thing led to another, and the Gwinners purchased their foundation bitch, CH Quicksilver Lady, CD, who produced CH Cati v. d. Gretchenhof, the mother of CH Gwinner's Pinwheel, BROM.

Pinwheel's show career was spectacular—winning the 1961 Western Futurity, ranking first on the 1963 and 1964 Top 10 Weimaraners, and winning the 1964 Westminster Best of Breed. Pinwheel's success helped the Gwinners decide to become professional handlers. They loved the gypsy life of handlers and attributed their happiness to Pinwheel.

As the Gwinners prepared to retire Pinwheel, a handsome Pinwheel son named Gwinner's Sportwheel joined their family. For almost a decade, the inseparable threesome of Gabby, Tony, and Sport were a familiar sight to all western exhibitors.

During his show career, Sport took home 255 Best of Breed ribbons, including the 1966 National Specialty and 1970 Westminster breed. Sport was the top-winning Weimaraner in 1966, the first year he campaigned as a special. The WCA began publishing a Top 10 list in 1967, and Sport ranked first in 1967 and 1968 and second in 1969 and 1970. Often asked when the formidable dog would retire and give someone else a chance, Tony always replied, "As soon as another Weimaraner can beat him consistently."

The duo's great day came on June 22, 1969, at the Five Valley Kennel Club, when Roy M. Cowan gave the nod to Tony and Sport as his Best in Show choice. Sport retired in 1971, when Tony began showing his son, CH Lemans Flashing Silver Wheel, the group-caliber youngster Tony had been waiting for.

A BROM sire of 16 champions, Sportwheel's outstanding progeny include Best in Show and 1972 National Specialty winner CH Lemans Flashing Silver Wheel, as well as the Futurity winner Kamsou Desert Dreamdust (1974). Sport sired the following BROM producers: Collier's Wheel of Joy; CH Dreamwheel's Heather; CH Kamsou Sterling Smoke, CD, NRD, NSD, V; Sportwheel's Bubchen Harmon; and Tempest of Westcliff.

Browsing through a show catalog, the name Dorilio (on a Golden Retriever) caught Dot's fancy. Although she discovered the word meant "the golden one," Dot's decision to use the name anyway proved surprisingly prophetic.

Dor's first indication of greatness was winning his junior Futurity class. Although not flashy, Dor was a sound and well-balanced dark-gray dog with excellent shoulders and an expressive head. Under Dot's capable handling, Dorilio finished easily and competed 93 times as a special. Dot Remensnyder became the breed's second breeder-owner to handle a Weimaraner to an all-breed Best in Show (1963) and the first to do it twice. Like his grandsire Rickey Boy, Dor spent his retirement years as a household pet and companion hunting dog.

Dor sired 33 champions (including Dual CH Halann's Checkmate Tamara, CD, SDX, NRD), only one short of equaling Val Knight Ranck's record. He, too, is a pivotal sire, appearing in most American pedigrees.

The Interlude

From 1952 through 1963, eight Weimaraners won the show world's highest honor; from 1957 through 1963, at least one Weimaraner per year had a Best in Show win, and the breed appeared solidly established as big-league contenders. Suddenly, the breed entered a strange hiatus, and no Weimaraner won a Best in Show for six years, which both puzzled and troubled breeders and exhibitors.

Nevertheless, Weimaraners continued to win and place in the sporting group, and in 1965, CH Gronbach's Aladdin, CD, BROM, captured first place in the sporting group at Westminster. The Best in Show jinx was finally broken by CH Gwinner's Sportwheel, BROM, in 1969.

CH Ronamax Rajah
v. d. Reiteralm, BROM, HOF

Rajah finished his championship in a spectacular fashion. Handled by Peggy Kepler Roush, Rajah's debut brought a best in sweepstakes, a five-point major, and his first Best of Breed at the 1969 Pittsburgh Specialty. The following day, Rajah won another five points and Best of Breed and placed second in the Sporting Group. A few weekends later, with Stan Flowers handling, Rajah won the central Futurity, two more five-point majors, and two more Best of Breed wins. Thus, Rajah's record for two show weekends in 1969 gave him 20 points, four Best of Breed wins (two specialties), and a Group 2, which placed him on the list of the breed's top winners of 1969. Strong and sound, many compared Rajah's fluid gait and dynamic style to Val's. While being campaigned, Rajah was the personal companion of Stan Flowers, and the bond was obvious as they swept around the ring.

His record was second to his grandsire Val Knight Ranck, and it stood for 15 years, until surpassed by his granddaughter CH Valmar's Pollyanna, BROM.

Rajah was the breed's first sire of more than 100 champions (119 champions from 51 litters), including the Best in Show and National Specialty winners CH Rajah's Alexander v. d. Reiteralm (1971 National Specialty) and CH The Rajah's Magic v. d. Reiteralm (1976 and 1977 National Specialties).

Rajah died as he lived—in style. Ginny's tale of what happened was reprinted in many dog magazines. Rajah's problems began when, with advancing age, more and more outstanding bitches were presented to him for service. Although never at public stud, our geriatric Romeo attended to each of his visitors with a growing, rather than a declining enthusiasm. Girls were now at the top of his list over birds and cats!

Rather suddenly, however, while Rajah was servicing the beautiful Nani's Cascade v. d. Reiteralm, he lost consciousness. A quick veterinary monitor of his heart suggested that he be permanently retired from further action at 13 years young. A careful daily scrutiny was taken of the three bitches sharing sharing the Alexanders' home with him, to be sure that none tempted his weakening heart or allowed his steady plodding gait to accelerate.

Weeks passed; Nani's Cascade v. d. Reiteralm, his last-serviced bitch, seemed barren (she whelped a litter of eight), and in short, things were very dull at home. Early one morning in April, while the Alexanders were out in the barn preparing horses for a local field trial, Rajah's moment came. He slipped out the front door and there she was. A HUGE BLONDE AMAZON OF A GREAT DANE BITCH…in heat. She left him a message. HE KNEW HER WELL; she was a regular visitor to the stable out back, where her owner's hunter was kept. SHE NEEDED HIM—and he knew just where she might be waiting. HE DIED AT A FULL GALLOP ON HIS WAY TO THE BARN. IT WAS QUICK, AND HIS OLD GRAY HEAD WAS AS HIGH AS HIS HOPES FOR THE DAY.

What a way to go!

CH Rajah's Alexander v. d. Reiteralm

The grapevine buzzed after the 1971 National Specialty. Did you hear about Rajah's son? Will he be even greater than his sire? Later, they asked, whatever happened to Alexander?

CH Rajah's Alexander v. d. Reiteralm, handled by Peggy Roush, became a celebrity overnight at 15 months. He won the 1971 Eastern Futurity and the five-point major at the Pittsburgh Specialty on 6 August. The following day, at the National Specialty (held in conjunction with the Beaver County Kennel Club show), Frederick W. Wencker gave the five-point major and Best of Breed to Alexander. An hour later, Mrs. R. Gilman Smith-Brown (who had given the points to Alexander the preceding day) judged the sporting group (it included the Springer Spaniel CH Salilyn's Adamant James, all-breed record holder for Best in Show wins), and she gave the nod to Alexander as the best in the sporting group.

Figure 30-11: *CH Ronamax Rajah v. d. Reiteralm, BROM, HOF* (CH Maximillian v. d. Reiteralm, NSD, BROM × CH Norman's Rona v. d. Reiteralm, SD, NRD, V, BROM). Bred by Virginia Alexander and Saundra Watson; owned by Virginia Alexander and C. Joseph Rymer.

Figure 30-12: *CH Rajah's Alexander v. d. Reiteralm* (CH Ronamax Rajah v. d. Reiteralm, BROM × Elken's Party Gal v. d. Reiteralm, BROM). Bred by Virginia Alexander and Gail Miller; owned by William M. Osborne, Jr. Photograph courtesy of the WCA.

Alexander began to show fatigue, and his fans feared that the showy youngster would fold during Best in Show judging, which followed immediately. Nevertheless, the top specials in the show had already been defeated in the sporting group, and Helen Schulz (WCA liaison to Germany for many years) saw only the Great Dane as a serious rival. "When the judge announced Rajah's Alexander v. d. Reiteralm as the Best in Show selected from 1349 dogs, we did not laugh, we all cried," she wrote. "This was one of the highlights in my life."[2]

The following day, Alexander took a third 5-point major to finish his championship. The large entry at the Beaver County show earned Alexander so many points for his Best in Show win that he ranked fourth on the Top 10 list of 1971.

After each win, Alexander's owner, Bill Osborne, kept saying, "I cannot believe it. I cannot take any more. This is the biggest day of my life."[3] Indeed, it would be impossible to surpass such an achievement, and Osborne retired Alexander after one weekend of spectacular glory! Osborne's work required him to travel constantly, and Alexander was his inseparable companion.

CH Lemans Flashing Silver Wheel

Those who cheer for the runt of a litter will be heartened by the story of CH Lemans Flashing Silver Wheel, better known as Dusty. Charles and Elizabeth Prewett bred CH Weimar Castle Jabetwheel to top-winning CH Gwinner's Sportwheel in 1969 for the first of two breedings that produced six champions. They must have been pleased when the litter of five males and two bitches was auspiciously whelped on the Fourth of July—grandfather Pinwheel's birthday. Dusty, the runt, of course, was immediately written off as pet quality. He not only lacked size but also had (horrors!) a blaze on his chest.

Little Dusty was duly sold to a boy who gave him the proud name Lemans Flashing Silver Wheel. He was soon sleeping on the bed, and the mother found this, as well as the puppy's happy vitality, unacceptable. The Prewetts realized that this would not be a congenial home, and they bought Dusty back. Unwilling to subject the puppy to another change, they decided to keep him, and Dusty grew up happily with his bigger brothers CH Monteverde's Beauwheel and CH Monteverde's Woodenwheel. Although Dusty remained smaller and lighter-boned than his bigger brothers, he could hardly be considered the runt at his mature height of 27 inches.

Handled by Tony Gwinner, Dusty took his first points and Best of Breed from the American-bred class in the fall of 1970 at Roseburg, Oregon. He followed this up with three 5-point majors in one sensational weekend in Arizona.

In addition to the driving gait and showmanship that made his sire such a great special, the clean-cut Dusty was flawlessly sound and never put a foot down wrong. Dusty headed the Weimaraner Top 10 list in 1971 and 1972 and ranked third in 1973. During his banner year, Dusty won the 1972 National Specialty and went Best in Show in October under Frank Haze Burch at the Heart of the Plains Kennel Club.

The Prewett Weimaraners were all house-dogs and part of the family, proving it is possible to have a congenial household with more than one male. A typical Weimaraner, Dusty brought his owners many chuckles. When Elizabeth found him taking a nap in the bathtub, she took a picture to prove it.

Bred sparingly, Dusty sired several fine champions, including Star-N-Wesmar's Gypsy Wheel, NSD, a group and specialty-show winner. Dusty is the sire of Star-N-Suede of Quail Run, NRD, NSD, who ranked second on the 1973 Top 10 derby list and who sired Dual CH Windsong's Bayside Barnaby, NRD, SDX, V.

Figure 30-13: *CH Lemans Flashing Silver Wheel* (CH Gwinner's Sportwheel, BROM × CH Weimar Castle's Jabetwheel, CD, BROM). Bred and owned by Charles and Elizabeth Prewett.

CH Chat-a-Wey Charley v. d. Reiteralm

Charley's mother, CH Rona's Sea Sprite v. d. Reiteralm, was at the top of the BROM lists in the earliest years; she believed in quality, not quantity, producing only eight puppies, but six of these pups would become champions. Charley and his sister CH Springdale's Rhea hold the distinction of being the only Best in Show littermates. Charley was placed as a show prospect with Ralph and Billie Leffew. Charley became the family companion, babysitter, and protector. Starting his show career somewhat later than his sisters, Charley began to catch up in 1972, ranking 10th on the Top 10 Weimaraner list. Charley had the sound, beautiful elegance and clean lines of his sire, Medicine Man, and Charley's strong, true movement and style made him a top special. In 1973, the only full year Charley campaigned, he headed the Top 10 list, winning the breed at Westminster, as well as the 1973 National Specialty. He went Best in Show at Mad River Kennel Club on 13 May under Louis Kleinhans.

Success did not spoil Charley. He contentedly retired to his primary career as the companion of the Leffew family.

CH W.C.'s The Dutchman of Dauntmar, BROM

A Best in Show win eluded CH Doug's Dauntless von Dor during his impressive show career. As Daunt's name rose higher and higher on the BROM list, with progeny winning

futurities and ranking in the Top 10, everyone began asking, will he sire a Best in Show winner? Dutchman did it!

Dutchman is the first Best in Show winner with the combination of bloodlines that has proven so successful—the cross between Dor's son Daunt and Val's grandson Rajah (Dutchman's dam is a Rajah daughter)—blending the best qualities of both. During the early 1970s, the Weimaraner began the transition from extremes of size and type to the smooth, clean lines, eye-pleasing balance, improved overall soundness, and sweeping movement that became the breed's hallmark in the 1980s.

Dutchman's magnificent balance drew the eyes of judges and spectators, and his elegance, sound movement, and superb, clean, well-laid-back shoulders kept them there. He ranked on the Weimaraner Top 10 in 1973, 1974, 1975, and 1977 (ranking 4th, 2nd, 3rd, and 10th). In 1974, his greatest year, Dutchman had three Best in Show wins.

Dutchman is the sire of 12 champions, including the Best in Show winner CH W.C.'s The Dynamic Dagowheel, 1972 National Specialty winner CH Kamsou Jack the Ripper, CD, SD, RD, VX, BROM, and the excellent producer CH Kamsou Dutch Treat, BROM.

Figure 30-14: *CH Chat-a-Wey Charley v. d. Reiteralm* (CH Seneca's Medicine Man, BROM × CH Rona's Sea Sprite v. d. Reiteralm, BROM). Bred by Gayle R. Eckenrode; owned by Ralph and Billie Leffew. Photograph courtesy of the WCA.

Figure 30-15: *CH W.C.'s The Dutchman of Dauntmar, BROM* (CH Doug's Dauntless von Dor, BROM × CH Heather's Baroness v. Dauntmar, BROM). Bred by Frank L. Sousa; owned by Mr. and Mrs. Louis A. Pardo.

CH Springdale Rhea v. d. Reiteralm, CD, HOF

The breed had consistently produced outstanding bitches, and it seemed unjust that the Best in Show wins always went to the boys. When would the breed produce a bitch that could win a Best in Show and an owner with the determination to pursue the dream?

Rhea's special magic was evident from the beginning. When stacked for the first time, Rhea stood like a statue in the pose that would captivate so many, as if hearing the future applause. From the first litter bred by Gayle Eckenrode Prescott, a talented junior handler, the gentle, loving little bitch was sent to Susan Orth in California, who provided a most special show home.

The legend began the weekend Rhea won a five-point major and Best of Opposite Sex at Ventura (her first show) and a second 5-point major and Best Bitch in the 1971 Western Futurity the following day at the Santa Barbara show. Sound and stylish, Rhea and handler Frank Housky dominated western competition. Then, teaming up with Stan Flowers, Rhea proved just as unbeatable in eastern competition.

Rhea became the breed's first bitch to win a Best in Show on 10 August 1974 at Jefferson City Kennel Club under Connie Bosold. She followed this up with another Best in Show at the Golden Gate Kennel Club in San Francisco and

a third Best in Show win in 1976. Rhea and her brother CH Chat-a-Wey Charley v. d. Reiteralm are the breed's first littermates to win an all-breed Best in Show.

During her career, Rhea ranked in the Weimaraner Top 10 from 1972 to 1976 (ranking 4th, 2nd, 1st, 1st, and 3rd). Rhea won the Sporting Group at two of the nation's most prestigious shows (the Chicago International and Santa Barbara). The amazing little lady also won the breed at Westminster for an unprecedented three consecutive years (1974–1976).

Maternity did not slow down Rhea's career. Only a few months after her only litter in October 1972 (sired by CH Maximilian v. d. Reiteralm, NSD, BROM), Rhea was back in the show ring, looking as trim as ever. Her litter of four produced three champions, and through her son CH Springdale's Tyr II, CD, Rhea is the granddam of Best in Show winner CH Star-N-Love Song v. Reiteralm, BROM.

Of all adjectives, "exquisite" seems the one that best describes Rhea. She was feminine perfection; she loved people, shows, and applause. Until Rhea came along, everyone believed that only a big Weimaraner could be a successful special; Rhea proved that "big enough" is just right when everything else is. She set a precedent for awarding a Best in Show to Weimaraner bitches; she won hearts and set records. "She made you catch your breath, she made your heart stand still, and if you ever saw her, you will never forget."[4]

CH Sir Eric von Sieben, BROM, HOF

CH Sir Eric von Sieben is from the first of two litters produced by CH Chaskar's Suddenly It's Rainy, BROM, and CH Doug's Dauntless von Dor, BROM. Even in the litter of seven, six of which finished, Eric's flashy stylishness stood out.

A great showman, the dog-show environment literally "turned Eric on." The greater the noise, the crowd, and the chaos, the higher he became, and indoor shows were his particular cup of tea. He knew he was the greatest and told other dogs to keep out of his way. Eric was usually handled by his teenaged breeder/owner, Helene Burkholder, with professional handler Patti Long helping out only occasionally.

Eric compiled an impressive show record, ranking on the Weimaraner Top 10 in 1974, 1975, and 1976 (ranking 3rd, 2nd, and 5th). He became the second Best in Show winner for Daunt on 30 May 1976 at the Memphis Kennel Club under Mrs. John B. Patterson.

Helene described Eric as "the sweetest, best tempered and loving pet around. The grandchildren in the family used to pull his ears and poke his eyes, which he accepted for pure

Figure 30-16: *CH Springdale Rhea v. d. Reiteralm, CD, HOF* (CH Seneca's Medicine Man, BROM × CH Rona's Sea Sprite v. d. Reiteralm, BROM). Bred by Gayle Eckenrode Prescott; owned by Susan Orth.

CH The Rajah's Magic v. d. Reiteralm, BROM, HOF

Her yellow puppy collar suggested the song "Yellow Bird," which became the well-known call name of CH The Rajah's Magic v. d. Reiteralm, BROM. She was from the first of two "magic" litters produced by CH Brandy's Blizz v. d. Reiteralm, BROM, and Rajah, which produced 11 champions, including CH Rajah's Magic Show v. d. Reiteralm, winner of the 1974 Eastern Futurity.

Yellow Bird seemed special from the start, and Ginny Alexander decided to try to finish her lovely bitch in spectacular style, keeping her home until ready to win the big shows. The gamble paid off, and indeed, she finished with three 5-point majors at specialty shows

Handled exclusively by Peggy Roush, the tall, sound, smooth-moving bitch went on to a remarkable specials career. Yellow Bird ranked on the Top 10 Weimaraner list in 1976, 1977, and 1978 (ranking 1st, 2nd, and 9th). On 31 July 1976, Yellow Bird became the breed's second Best in Show bitch at the Penn Ridge Kennel Club. As though making up for the years of male domination, the big, stunning bitch repeated her cousin Rhea's triumphs by winning the 1976 and 1977 National Specialties. Yellow Bird adored Peggy, and when it came time to retire, Ginny gave her a forever home in the hills of Pennsylvania with Peggy.

The mating of Yellow Bird to CH Sir Eric von Sieben produced the breed's first litter from Best in Show winners, and their sons—CH Ann's Magic v. d. Reiteralm, BROM, and CH Reiteralm's Rio Fonte Saudade, NRD, BROM—are among the breed's top sires. The dam of 10 champions, Yel-

love of the little ones." Eric was crazy about birds and was an enthusiastic retriever on land and in water. When he was 15 years old, Helene commented, "His muzzle is gray and eyes are not clear. But every once in a while I'll see him strutting across the backyard parading in front of a stray dog, and I actually do a double take. The spirit is still there, and it makes him look young on occasion."

Soundness, balance, style, and good movement best describe Eric and his progeny. Eric is the sire of 44 champions, including the Best in Show winners CH Erbenhof Touch of Class, BROM, and CH Valmar's Pollyanna, BROM, as well as Dual CH Redhill's Chief Geronimo, SDX, NRD, V. Four of Eric's sons are sires of more than 20 champions, and it is clear that the full story of his influence on the breed is still unfolding.

Figure 30-17: *CH Sir Eric von Sieben, BROM, HOF* (CH Doug's Dauntless von Dor, BROM × CH Chaskar's Suddenly It's Rainy, BROM). Bred and owned by Helene M. Burkholder.

Figure 30-18: *CH The Rajah's Magic v. d. Reiteralm, BROM, HOF*
(CH Ronamax Rajah v. d. Reiteralm, BROM × CH Brandy's Blizz v. d. Reiteralm, BROM). Bred by Virginia Alexander and Gail Muller; owned by Virginia Alexander.

low Bird's outstanding beauty and flawless movement live on in many top winners now being shown.

CH Colsidex Standing Ovation, BROM, HOF

Judy Colan had specific goals when she bred Pixie (CH Colsidex Dauntless Applause, NSD, BROM) to Doc (CH Seneca's Medicine Man, BROM). The product of half-brother and half-sister breeding of Dorilio progeny, Pixie had the smoothly balanced conformation and the sweet, amiable temperament characteristic of Dor's descendants. Judy hoped to retain Pixie's conformation and temperament, which won specialty shows and group placements, and to obtain the showmanship and higher tail set characteristic of Doc's progeny.

At 6 weeks, it seemed that Doc's fire had bypassed Joga, and Judy sold him to an old friend who simply wanted a nice pet. When Joga was about 10 months old, Judy decided to show him in a nearby match. He had never been lead trained or stacked in a show pose, but as soon as he stepped in the ring, Joga became a show dog! He won the match group, besting 150 other sporting dogs.

A few months later, Judy began showing Joga, and he finished a month later. At Christmas, John Moakler gave Judy full ownership, saying that Joga was what she had been breeding for and that she should own him.

Joga had an international show career. In 1977, he finished his Canadian championship in three shows with two group wins and his first all-breed Best in Show, as well as enough points to be the top-winning Canadian Weimaraner for the year. The following year, 1978, Joga won the first Canadian National Specialty and his second Canadian Best in Show.

In the United States, Joga won his first Best in Show on 16 July 1977 at the Champlain Valley Kennel Club under Mrs. Maynard Drury, becoming the breed's third breeder-owner-handler team to achieve this dream. Joga ranked on the Weimaraner Top 10 list from 1975 through 1978 (ranking 5th, 2nd, 1st, and 2nd), and he retired after winning the breed at Westminster in 1979. Joga came out of retirement to win the 1981 National Specialty from the veterans class. His four breed wins in 1981 brought two group wins, two placements, and the No. 8 spot on the Top 10. In 1982, the amazing veteran parlayed two breed wins to two Best in Shows and No. 5 on the Top 10. The great 10-year-old trouper won the 1984 National Specialty.

Statistics fail to convey Joga's perfection of soundness, line, and balance or the thrilling showmanship and bond between a dog and handler. They also fail to describe his private personality. Judy wrote, "He remained the same easygoing, loving dog he had been as a pup. Content to curl up on the sofa or stand with his head in your lap, he was totally unaware of all his accomplishments."

Joga is the breed's second leading sire with 143 champions, including the American Best in Show winners CH Harline's Ballet; CH Nani's Hawaiian Punch, BROM; and CH Greywind's Jack Frost, CD, SD, V, BROM (1986 and 1990 National Specialties); as well as the 1982 National Specialty winner CH Hoot Hollow's Roy's Rob Roy, CD, BROM.

CH Erbenhof Touch of Class, BROM

CH Erbenhof Touch of Class, better known as T.C., is the breed's third Best in Show winning bitch. Judy Mitchell had a hunch that breeding CH Stolz Nebel von Sieben back to her sire, Eric, would produce something special, and she was right! She placed the promising puppy in co-ownership with Wiley Greene.

Wiley handled T.C. throughout her show career that, although brief, took them from Louisiana to California. Her soundness, sweetness, and fluid, flowing movement indeed gave her that special "touch of class." T.C. finished her championship easily, with a three-point major from the 6- to 9-month puppy class and back-to-back four-point majors at 12 months. Lightly campaigned by co-owner and handler Wiley Green in 1977, T.C. ranked sixth on the breed's Top 10. On the day T.C. was 21 months old (20 November 1977), Nicholas Kay presented her with Best in Show at the Texarkana Kennel Club.

Figure 30-19: *CH Colsidex Standing Ovation, BROM, HOF* (CH Seneca's Medicine Man, BROM × CH Colsidex Dauntless Applause, NSD, BROM). Bred and owned by Judy Colan.

On his way home from a show circuit, Tony Gwinner visited Ron and Gina Columbo to select the stud-fee puppy, and he delivered "the Dago" to Adelene Pardo. The youngster was later purchased by Mrs. Cheryl Cheek and was handled by Adelene throughout his career.

Dago was a big dog in every way, with sweeping style and grand showmanship so characteristic of the Gwinner dogs in his pedigree. When given a ring big enough to "do his thing," Adelene could really open up with the big, flashy dog on a loose lead for a crowd-pleasing performance. During 1978, 1979, and 1980, Dago ranked on the breed's Top 10 (ranking 1st, 1st, and 2nd). His first of two Best in Show wins came in October 1978 under Judge Derek Rayne.

Dago's champion progeny include the group-placing special CH Tapfer's Traum von Rahan, CD, NSD, NRD, V, best dog in the 1982 Southern Futurity.

CH W.C.'s Starwarwheel of Ranah

Amazingly, the breed's next Best in Show winner was another Ripper son, also handled by Adelene Pardo. For Ripper's second litter, her owners chose the fine sire CH Jar-Em's Rhinestone Cowboy, BROM. Delighted with Dago from Ripper's first litter, Adelene purchased Starwar when he was 7 months old.

During 1979 and 1980, Adelene campaigned both Starwar and Dago, entering them on alternate days. Although

T.C. was sweet, lovable, prim, and proper and definitely a lady. Susan wrote, "When bedtime came, she was always the first one to bed. T.C. always started her nights at the end of the bed, and then somehow always ended up between us, sometimes even with her head on the pillows. Her most special trait was the way she held a rubber ball in her mouth, arched her neck up, and came up to you with a yodel or 'woo-woo' sound. She did this when she was happy or excited."

T.C. was a loving mother. She was always willing to share her achievements and did not mind when neighbors came to admire her puppies. The dam of field-rated and obedience-titled progeny, T.C. is a BROM producer of five champions.

CH W.C.'s The Dynamic Dagowheel

Dago's dam—CH Kamsou Riptide, BROM—waited until the age of 5 years before beginning her spectacular career as a producer of 11 champions. For the sire of her first litter, the Columbos and the Souths chose the multiple Best in Show winner CH W.C.'s Dutchman of Dauntmar, and the litter of six produced four champions, including the 1979 National Specialty winner CH Kamsou Jack the Ripper, CD, SD, RD, VX.

Figure 30-20: *CH Erbenhof Touch of Class, BROM* (CH Sir Eric von Sieben, BROM × CH Stolz Nebel von Sieben). Bred by Judy Mitchell; owned by Wiley D. Greene.

Figure 30-21: *CH W.C.'s The Dynamic Dagowheel* (CH W.C.'s The Dutchman of Dauntmar, BROM × CH Kamsou Riptide, BROM). Bred by Ronald Columbo and Kamsou Kennels; owned by Mrs. Cheryl Cheek.

and campaigned only one more year, Visa led the Weimaraner Top 10 list in 1980 and 1981. Three more Best in Show wins in 1981 brought her total to five, and she retired after only 18 months of showing.

Visa was only 2 years old when she launched a second career of motherhood. From two litters that produced 10 puppies, both sired by Ovation, nine became champions. Their accomplishments have not been disappointing. Her Futurity winners are CH Nani's Hawaiian Punch, BROM (1984); and CH Nani's Colsidex Hula Cooler, NRD, SDX (1984); her maturity winner is CH Nani's Apple-Sass, BROM (1985). Punch went on to become the breed's youngest Best in Show male.

Although unable to have more puppies herself, Visa's loving disposition made her an ideal foster mother. She never let a new litter go unattended (no matter who the natural mother was), keeping a constant vigil outside the whelping room door. Visitors always mistook Visa for the puppies' dam because she gave them such a warm welcome and showed off the puppies with obvious maternal pride.

CH Star-N-Love Song v. Reiteralm, BROM

It is almost impossible for Hawaiian Weimaraners to rank on the breed's Top 10 simply because there are not many dog

they competed in only half as many shows, both ranked on the breed's Top 10 those years—Starwar ranked 5th in 1979 and 3rd in 1980. He went Best in Show in 1979 at the Cen-Tex Kennel Club under Mildred Bergen.

CH Nani's Visa v. d. Reiteralm, BROM, HOF

Visa made breed history in a big way, winning her first Best in Show at 9 months from the puppy class! Moreover, she had three different handlers that day, from the puppy class to Best in Show competition. Never putting a foot down wrong or presenting an unattractive stance, Visa went on to finish her championship by the time she was 10 months old, handled to nine of her points by friends who had been sitting at the ringside. She could win with no particular assistance from a handler.

Fanciers are somewhat skeptical about spectacular puppies, for they often continue to grow, and grow, sometimes becoming too large or coarse. Visa, however, did not disappoint her fans. She remained charmingly feminine in every way. Like all great specials, Visa had showmanship and unique ring presence. With the poise of a Miss America, she waited for the audience to admire her and return her love.

Visa won the 1980 Eastern Futurity and a second Best in Show that year. Amateur-handled by Smokey Medeiros

Figure 30-22: *CH W.C.'s Starwarwheel of Ranah* (CH Jar-Em's Rhinestone Cowboy, BROM × CH Kamsou Riptide, BROM). Bred by Ron and Gina Columbo and Kamsou Kennels; owned by Adelene Pardo.

Figure 30-23: *CH Nani's Visa v. d. Reiteralm, BROM, HOF* (CH Reiteralm's Rio Fonte Saudade, NRD, BROM × CH Nani's Soul Sister, BROM). Bred by Christine O. Medeiros and Roi Ann Olson; owned by Christine O. Medeiros.

shows on the Islands. The 4-month rabies quarantine effectively limits competition in and from the continental U.S. This does not, however, mean that group competition on the Islands is not stiff. Dogs from rabies-free England, Australia, and New Zealand do not have to go through quarantine, and many outstanding individuals have been brought to Hawaii.

Nancy Mednick was among the pioneers of the 1970s who began to bring mainland Weimaraners to the Islands to encourage interest in the breed and to develop a breed club. With only two all-breed shows on the Islands at the time, it could take most of a dog's life merely to finish a championship. Nancy imported the finished champions CH Halann's Erik von Arimar, CD; and CH Swinger's Sweet.

Cindy Victory—the skillful junior handler-owner of CH von Sieben's Royal Flush, CD, NSD, V, BROM—purchased Lovey as a puppy from her breeder, Barbara Nicks, and showed Lovey to her championship. Realizing that she would have little time for Lovey when she started college, Cindy sold the 2-year-old bitch to Nancy Mednick.

Sound and showy, Lovey became Hawaii's top-winning sporting dog from 1978 through 1981 and was ranked third in 1982; she ranked on the Hawaiian all-breed Top 10 list (6th, 3rd, 4th, 2nd, and 10th) for five consecutive years. Her first Best in Show win came on 15 June 1980 at Orchid Island Dog Fanciers Club. Just to prove that 7 years is not over the hill, Lovey strutted off with another Best in Show rosette on 27 September 1981 at the Windward Hawaiian Dog Fanciers.

Bred by Cindy to Royal Flush, Lovey's first litter produced CH V. L. Constant Commotion. From three litters sired by CH Star-N-Tsuru Tani Majitsu, CD, Lovey produced four champions: Haiku Tsuru-Tani Kyoku-Jin, CD; Haiku Misty Morn, NRD, NSD; Haiku Tsuru-Tani Summer Lady; and Haiku Mele Ka'I O Iemi, CD; OTCH Haiku Solar Eclipse, UDT (from the same breeding) became the third Hawaiian Weimaraner to earn a UD.

CH Innomine Foxy Chime's Chance, NSD, NRD, V

Foxy, (CH Rowdy's Royal Foxmist, TD) had reached the age of 11 without siring a litter, and by that time there was considerable speculation about whether he could. Nevertheless, Marianne saw some special qualities in the fine old champion that looked like a special match for Chime (CH Monomax Vesper Bell of Joy, NRD). Marianne wrote, "Foxy knew how, he just wanted a chance, and Chance is what we got."

Foxy had reached the age of 11 without siring a litter, and by that time there was considerable speculation about whether he could. Nevertheless, Marianne saw some special qualities in the fine old champion that looked like a special match for Chime (CH Monomax Vesper Bell of Joy, NRD).

Figure 30-24: *CH Star-N-Love Song v. Reiteralm, BROM* (CH Springdale's Tyr II, CD × CH Star-N-Charmen Cher, CD). Bred by Barbara Nicks; owned by Nancy Mednick.

Marianne wrote, "Foxy knew how, he just wanted a chance, and Chance is what we got."

Like many breeders, Marianne wanted a bitch for the next generation, but "sometimes, when you don't get what you want, you're better off without it." Things did not go smoothly, and Marianne ended up with an astronomical bill for the Cesarean and only one male puppy.

But, what a puppy! It is easy to imagine how he was pampered and fussed over. No wonder he considered himself hot stuff in the show ring. Chance had "the ability to communicate to judge and spectator that he chose to grace them with his presence. Or maybe I should call it arrogance."

This attitude plus soundness and balance is what puts a Weimaraner in the Top 10 in any year and put Chance on the list from 1982 to 1984 (ranking 3rd, 2nd, and 9th). His big days came near the end of 1983 when he went Best in Show at Delaware Ohio Kennel Club (30 October) and

Figure 30-25: *CH Innomine Foxy Chime's Chance, NSD, NRD, V* (CH Rowdy's Royal Foxmist, TD × CH Monomoy Vesper Bell of Joy, NRD). Bred and owned by Marianne Reder.

Chenango Valley Kennel Club (8 December). Chance polished off an already shining career by winning the 1985 National Specialty.

At home, Chance is a typical Weimaraner with many of the breed mannerisms, such as the cat-like use of his paw to demand attention, cocking his head when you are not communicating well, and using his internal clock to give ample warning that dinnertime is nearing. His intense curiosity keeps him in the middle of every activity. Marianne concludes, "I feel especially lucky to have bred and to own Chance, but I wouldn't love him any less if he hadn't been a top-winning dog."

CH Harline's Ballet

For their very first litter, Alan and Susan Line selected Ovation for CH Dofo's Cristel v. Hoot Hollow, producing CH Harline's Ballet—Ovation's first Best in Show winner. Susan handled Ballet, a beautifully sound and elegant bitch, throughout her impressive career.

Ballet campaigned for only 18 months during 1982 and 1983. She was best known for her driving movement that became most spectacular in the larger group ring. Ballet's first Best in Show win came on 30 October 1983 at the Faith City Kennel Club under Maxine Beam, and her second came only 8 days later at Tri State Kennel Club under Melbourne Downing. At the Tri State show, Ballet defeated 1,391 dogs, including the Best in Show winner of the 1984 Westminster Kennel Club show. This lovely lady retired at the height of her success. On her last circuit, she won six consecutive breeds and five group ribbons, including a 1st. She was the top-winning bitch in 1982 (4th in the breed's Top 10); in 1983, she was first on the breed's Top 10 and was ranked in the Top 20 Sporting Dogs.

CH Nani's Hawaiian Punch, BROM

Multiple Best in Show winners are not so common that mating them to each other is an everyday event. Everyone, naturally, had great expectations for the first litter from multiple Best in Show winners Visa and Ovation, and they were not disappointed.

Only slightly less precocious than his dam, Visa, Punch became a group winner at 11 months and had three specialty wins by 13 months old. His Best in Show came at 15 months on 26 May 1984 at Illinois Capitol Kennel Club under James R. White, becoming the breed's youngest male Best in Show winner. To nobody's surprise, he also won the 1984 Southern Futurity. Punch won the breed at the AKC Centennial in 1984. He retired at the Purina Invitational (competitors all in the Top 10 of their breeds), where he went Best of Breed and Group 2nd. Amateur-handled by Smokey Medeiros and campaigned for only 2 years, Punch ranked in the Weimaraner Top 10 in 1984 and 1985 (1st and 2nd).

Given the sobriquet "Perfect Punch," not for his show achievements but for a very quiet, uncomplaining disposition, Punch never misbehaved or seemed to do anything wrong. His manners in the show ring were flawless. He would stand in a show pose for several minutes, without being touched by his handler, and he gaited as if he had no need of anyone on the other end of the lead. Punch is the sire of 36 champions.

CH Windemeire's Silber Streifen, BROM

Sandy Jaremczuk bred and showed Jar-Em's Rhinestone Cowboy, BROM (better known as Bronk), the sire of CH Windemeire's Silber Streifen. This fine sire of 16 champions not only sired Best in Show winner CH Starwarwheel of Ranah but also Dual CH Silverbrand Rafferty v. Jar-Em, NRD, VX.

When Sandy evaluated the puppies in the litter sired by Bronk out of Norm and Mary Jensen's Essence von Tadellos, she found them of excellent quality and unexpectedly uniform in type for an outcross breeding. She was tempted to buy one, but prudence and a full kennel overcame temptation.

About 6 weeks later, the Jensens brought Streak to a show where Sandy was stewarding. Prudence lost. "I knew

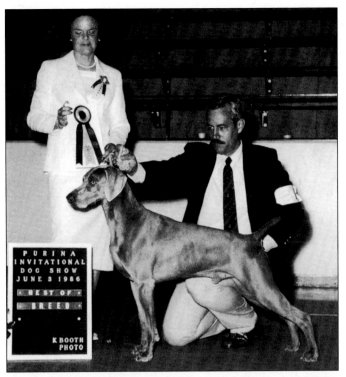

Figure 30-27: *CH Nani's Hawaiian Punch, BROM* (CH Colsidex Standing Ovation, BROM × CH Nani's Visa v. d. Reiteralm, BROM). Bred by Christine Medeiros and Betty Olson; owned by Donna Edwards and Christine Medeiros.

right then that I had to have that puppy!" wrote Sandy. "Even at three months, he was a show dog—extremely animated, alertly interested in everything going on at the show. And could he move!" That evening, Sandy tried to buy the puppy. The Jensens thought they wanted to keep Streak for show, but they thought they might sell him, which they finally did a few months later.

Show training began, and by the first shows, the experienced amateur handler—that is, Sandy—began having unaccustomed butterflies in her stomach. She knew deep down that "Mr. Clown" would humiliate her before one and all. Streak, however, responded to the competitive atmosphere once inside the ring, and he settled right down to the business of showing. Unless, of course, the judge said, "good boy," which always mandated a thank-you kiss.

In only 8 brief weeks of showing, Streak finished his championship with four majors and his first group placement. A few months later, Elaine Meader became Streak's co-owner, and Stan Flowers began campaigning him.

Streak spent the next 18 months of showing with Stan. The Great Day came on 16 June 1984; the place was Rapid City Kennel Club in Casper, Wyoming. Sandy described the thrill of a Best in Show win quite aptly when she wrote, "When Stan called me and said, 'Your dog just took a BIS'— I think I was speechless for the first time of my life."[5]

Figure 30-26: *CH Harline's Ballet* (CH Colsidex Standing Ovation, BROM × CH Dofo's Cristel v. Hoot Hollow). Bred and owned by Alan and Susan Line.

Figure 30-28: *CH Windemeire's Silber Streifen, BROM* (CH Jar-Em's Rhinestone Cowboy, BROM × Essence von Tadellos). Bred by Norm and Mary Jensen; owned by Elaine Meader and Sandra Jaremczuk.

Streak retired from intensive campaigning for about 6 months, but it is hard to keep an exciting special at home on the sofa. In May 1986, Streak teamed up with Bob Burns, who showed him for 2 more years. Streak ranked on the Weimaraner Top 10 in 1984, 1985, 1986, and 1987 (3rd, 3rd, 5th, and 2nd).

Streak's puppies are now competing, and he is the sire of 11 champions.

CH Valmar's Pollyanna, BROM, HOF

Joan Valdez described Polly as "that once in a lifetime show dog that everyone hopes for and rarely manages to come up with." She is perfection when stacked and in motion, and she has all the showmanship so necessary in a great special.

Polly is the fourth generation of Valmar breeding, all handled by Joan throughout their careers. Joan chose the Best in Show winner CH Sir Eric von Sieben for the lovely Serenade, and the success of the combination was evident as Polly and her sister Pepsi Challenge began to dominate the southwestern shows in sweepstakes and puppy classes. Polly finished first, at 14 months.

Not to be outdone by her sister, who won the 1982 Central Futurity, Polly won best in the Western Futurity 2 weeks later. On the same day, Polly launched her amazing career as a special by winning the breed, besting 80 entries and going on to a Group 1. She captured the 1983 Maturity, confirming her domination over the best of her generation.

During the years that followed, Polly continued her winning ways and has only rarely been defeated for Best of Breed. On 27 May 1985, Polly captured that greatest honor, the all-breed Best in Show at San Gabriel Valley Kennel Club show, topping an entry of 2,028. Less than a month later on 22 June, she did it again at the San Mateo Kennel Club show. Lest people think she was slowing down at the ripe age of 5 years, Polly captured her third Best in Show at Santa Ana Valley on 27 April 1986 with an entry of 2,421.

Polly ranked in the Top 10 Weimaraner list from 1982 through 1986 (9th, 3rd, 3rd, 1st, and 2nd), as well as the all-breed lists of 1984 and 1985. When the statistics were compiled for her banner year 1985, Polly ranked 4th among all sporting breeds and 23rd among all breeds, defeating more than 16,000 dogs that year—breaking the record of her

Figure 30-29: *CH Valmar's Pollyanna, BROM, HOF* (CH Sir Eric von Sieben, BROM × CH Valmar Serenade v. Wustenwind, BROM). Bred and owned by Joan Valdez.

great-grandsire Rajah and setting one that will be difficult to equal. Although she officially retired in 1986, Polly gave an encore performance to add Best of Breed at the 1987 National Specialty to her long list of honors. Polly is the dam of 10 champions.

CH Greywind's Jack Frost, CD, SD, V, BROM, HOF

Greywind's Jack Frost, better known as Brae, is the third generation of Weimaraners bred by John and Ellen Grevatt. Their first litter produced CH Greywind's Sea Breeze, UD, NSD, V, who sired CH Greywind's Ashley Frost, CD. Handled by Ellen, Ashley won the 1979 Eastern Futurity and went on to become a multiple breed and specialty-show winner with group placements.

Bred to Ovation, Ashley's first litter (four males, three females) produced three champions—Greywind's Texas Ranger, NSD, Greywind's November Frost, and Greywind's Jack Frost. November Frost, a multiple group winner, ranked in the 1983 and 1984 Weimaraner Top 10 lists (10th and 4th).

Although Brae finished his championship at 10 months with three spectacular majors from the puppy class, he stayed home to mature while November Frost was being specialed. Brae finally matured and began his specials career in 1985.

With an auspicious beginning for 1986, Brae won the breed and Group 3 at the Westminster show. He repeated his Westminster breed wins in 1987 and 1988, tying Rhea's record of three consecutive years.

Brae's Big Day came at the 1986 National Specialty, which was held in conjunction with the Santa Maria Kennel Club show on 19 July 1986. Brae won the specialty, and excitement mounted as he won the sporting group. Could he go all the way? There were tears in many eyes as Barbara Heller awarded the Best in Show ribbon, trophy, and bouquet of roses to Ellen and Brae for a well-deserved win.

Brae ranked on the breed's Top 10 list in 1985, 1986, 1987, 1988, and 1989 (7th, 1st, 1st, 5th, and 9th) and among the top sporting dogs of 1986, winning three Best in Shows and the 1990 National Specialty.

Ellen described Brae as "very easy going and laid back. He sleeps in our bed every night and is a very devoted dog. He is not at all aggressive toward other dogs, and gets along well with other males. Brae gives hugs and kisses and loves to play ball—he is a great retriever. He has a special frog squeak toy he plays with and will not destroy. He is very birdy and loves to run in the fields and find birds." Brae is the sire of 59 champions.

CH Silverkist Davie Lee

"Davie Lee was special from the moment he was born," wrote Donna Mayfield. She went on to describe the long, fear-filled hours preceding his birth.

Figure 30-30: *CH Greywind's Jack Frost, CD, SD, V, BROM, HOF* (CH Colsidex Standing Ovation, BROM × CH Greywind's Ashley Frost, CD). Bred and owned by Ellen J. and John B. Grevatt.

Bred to CH Valmar's Jazzman, CH Silverkist Andrea Jennie had her first puppy, Silverkist Dana Lynn, about 3 pm on Sunday afternoon. Sending visitors home, Donna settled down to wait for the rest of the puppies. The clock ticked off the hours, but no more puppies appeared. Donna finally located her veterinarian at a party, but because Jennie showed no signs of labor or distress, he did not examine her until about 9 pm. An x-ray revealed only one unborn puppy. The veterinarian gave Jennie some pitocin and sent Donna home with an additional dose to give if the first produced no results. Donna, who had never given any injection before, bravely gave Jennie the second dose about 11:30 pm. Jennie continued to rest, contentedly nursing her single puppy. Sick at heart, Donna went to bed at 2 am, still watching Jennie in the whelping box in her bedroom. If the pitocin produced no results, she was to bring Jennie to the clinic in the morning so the dead puppy could be surgically removed. About a half-hour later, Jennie delivered a huge male, twice the size of the bitch. As Donna began to lay aside the dead puppy, it wiggled and then squeaked. Davie Lee was welcomed with tears of joy.

At the 1980 Western Futurity, Davie Lee won the intermediate class. He finished his championship easily by March 1981 and later finished a Mexican championship. Amateur handled by his friend Tiena Darrow, Davie Lee won the 1983 National Specialty, where the huge ring let him show his true movement, driving gait, and showmanship to advantage.

The Big Day came on 26 April 1987 at the Orange Coast Weimaraner Club Specialty held in conjunction with the Santa Ana Valley Kennel Club show. Davie Lee won the specialty from the veterans class, then the sporting group. Nearly 8 years old, the big dog had plenty of stamina and continued to cruise around the ring with style; Joy Davidson awarded him the well-deserved red, white, and blue Best in Show rosette.

CH Debar's Song of the South

The 8-week-old puppy that left the litter to live with Carl and Susan Cobb left with only a "show name." Carl, a teacher, had a contest for his young students, "Name the Dog;" the winning name was "Hank", after country singer, Hank Williams. Early on, Hank was handled by Carl. While a pup, Hank was entered in a local shooting ratings and earned a Novice Shooting Dog title on his first attempt. Having done so well, Hank and Carl entered a bench show in Fisherville, Virginia. At this time, Hank met Karen Ashe. It was a partnership that would make magic. Hank and Karen were on the show circuit for a brief but fruitful time. In less than 1 year of showing, after earning his championship, they achieved 15 Best of Breeds, one National Specialty, five group placements, two 1st placements, three 3rd placements, and one Eastern Futurity in 1987. Hank's only Best in Show came on a lark. Carl entered Hank in a show

Figure 30-31: *CH Silverkist Davie Lee* (CH Valmar's Jazzman, CD, NRD, NSD, BROM × CH Silverkist Andrea Jennie). Bred and owned by Donna M. Mayfield.

locally in West Virginia, asking a friend to casually show him. No one expected anything, and lo and behold, they went Best in Show. Susan had decided that they were going to have a family vacation in Myrtle Beach. Carl had other plans. He took Hank to the National Specialty in Columbus, Ohio, while Susan took the family to the beach. Hank went on to win the National Specialty! Carl then drove through the night to get back to the family at the beach. Fearing to walk through the door, Carl opened it, threw Hank's bouquet of roses through the door and meekly asked if they could come in. After it was safe to enter, Carl presented to Susan the silver-plated tea service that Hank had won. All was forgiven. At the young age of 2½ years old, Hank gracefully retired to the status of beloved friend and family member. He spent his remaining days going to school with his dad and producing seven show champions.

CH Silversmith Dawn v. Greystoke

Dawn was bred by Elena and Allen Smith, Silversmith Kennel (CH Hoot Hollow's Roy's Rob Roy, BROM × CH Silversmith Omni v. Reiteralm, CD, TD, RD, NSD, VX, BROM). She was owned and campaigned by Irv and Dawn Boshears of California and handled by Glen Lycan, PHA. Dawn was one of a number of quality champions from the two breedings of her parents. She was a Top 10 show dog for 2 years. Her show record consists of 143 breed wins (four specialties); 84 group placements (21 firsts, 22 seconds, 26 thirds, 15 fourths); and three Best in Shows. At the completion of her specials campaign, beautiful and elegant showgirl Dawn was bred once to Best in Show CH Valmar Smokey City Ultra Easy, BROM and had a litter of five pups; several finished their championships. Elena's pup from that litter was CH Silversmith PazleeGreystoke, JH, NSD, NRD, V, BROM (who died at 15). Dawn's great grand-pup, CH Pike's Peak Annie Get Your Gun was a Top 10 Weimaraner for 2007 and 2008.

CH Nani's Wood-Win, BROM

CH Nani's Wood-Win was the only puppy to be born alive from a premature litter from two maturity-winning parents. He was born weighing just 5 ounces, completely without hair, and was not expected to live. His breeder, Chris Medeiros-Grisell, kept him for his first 6 months before she was confident enough to place him. At that time, T. Owen Forbes was looking for one last promising youngster to show before he retired. Owen teamed up with Dr. and Mrs. Sam F. Burke, Jr., and acquired "Woody" from Chris. Woody finished his show championship easily before he was 12 months old and picked up a group win along the way. He won

Figure 30-32: *CH Debar's Song of the South* (CH Bama Belle's Mountain Man × Rochel's Debar Devil May Care). Bred by Virginia Johnson; owned by Carl and Susan Cobb.

his Futurity in 1988. He became one of the breed's top show dogs, and with limited showing garnered 136 Breed wins, including two specialties, 89 group placements (28 firsts, 20 seconds, 22 thirds, and 19 fourths) and two Best in Shows. Woody was the WCA's 1989 No. 1 Show Dog. Woody was retired at the end of 1989 along with Owen and became Owen's close companion.

CH Valmar Smokey City Ultra Easy, JH, NSD, BROM, HOF

Easy was a "stud fee" puppy selected by Joan Valdez for Tom Wilson, and what a choice it was! During his show career, Easy traveled with his best companion Peggy Roush, who guided him to three consecutive Pedigree Awards, an all-breed Best in Show, and multiple group placements. But on one of the rare occasions he was shown by his owner, Easy demonstrated that a great dog can make a great handler by winning the Best of Breed title at the first WCA Winter Specialty.

Some of Easy's more memorable achievements include No. 2 Weimaraner, Pedigree Award Winner, 1987; No. 1

Weimaraner, Pedigree Award Winner, 1988; No. 1 Weimaraner, Pedigree Award Winner, 1989; Best of Breed, WCA's First Winter Specialty; No. 1 WCA Top Producing Sire 1990, 1991, 1992, 1993, 1994 and 1995; No. 2 WCA Top Producing Sire 1996; and No. 1 All-Time Top Producing Sire.

While he had great success in the ring, his most profound contribution was as a stud dog. Easy became the all-time top-producing Weimaraner dog in 2007, when a frozen semen "daughter" was finished by Steve Siegel. This grand total of 148 champions makes him the top-producing Weimaraner stud to date.

His fantastic record also establishes him as the second AKC top-producing stud of all breeds. Upon completing his show career, Easy's intelligent and biddable personality allowed him to be Tom's constant companion, earning him free reign of the farm while at home and when traveling. Had time been available from conformation and stud duties, it is very likely that Easy's career may have well surpassed his Junior Hunter title, as he also demonstrated real talent as a field dog and hunting companion.

CH Bing's Southern Sass, CD, NSD, NRD, V

Out of a litter of six champions, Sass started her show career as a puppy, achieving her championship at an early age, then her versatile rating. Her wonderful ring presence, strong topline, and good front assembly made her an eye-

Figure 30-33: *CH Silversmith Dawn V Greystoke* (CH Hoothollow's Roy's Rob Roy, CD, BROM × CH Silversmith Omni V Reiteralm, CD, TD, NSD, RD, VX, BROM). Bred by Elena and Allen Smith; owned by Irvin and Shawn Boshears.

Figure 30-34: *CH Nani's Wood-Win, BROM* (CH Nani's Kona Gust, CD, BROM × CH Nani's Apple-Sass, BROM). Bred by Christine Medeiros; owned by Dr. and Mrs. Sam F. Burke, Jr.

Figure 30-35: *CH Valmar Smokey City Ultra Easy, JH, NSD, BROM* (CH Smokey City Easy Does It × CH Valmar's Serenade v. Wustenwind, BROM). Bred by Joan Valdez; owned by Tom Wilson and Don Grenier.

catching special. She was very sweet and fun-loving and enjoyed life to the fullest. Shown only a few times as a special, her Best in Show was the bright star in her crown.

CH Adam von Arras

Adam, along with his dam CH Mistywoods Miriam v. Arras, were of unparalleled importance in the life of longtime Weimaraner lover Pat Miller of Cedar Rapids, Iowa. Pat had yearned for a dog like Adam, who would allow her to win the elusive Best in Show. Adam did that under the able hand of Stan Flowers! Multiple group winning and group placing and No. 1 Weimaraner for a time, Adam was handled by David Gray and Stan Flowers. Adam made many dreams come to pass for Pat. He was bred to another Best in Show winner, BIS/BISS CH Nani's Win'k of an Eye, VCD1, JH, NRD, V, BROM.

CH Harline's WF Rockefeller, BROM

Wally capped a wonderful year in 1990 by finishing No. 1 in the WCA ratings. His show career included more than 100 group placements, including 30 Group 1s and three all-breed Best in Shows. Wally was also the Best of Breed winner at Westminster in 1991 and 1992. Wally produced at least 17 champions, including two all-breed Best in Show winners, as well as Futurity and group placing offspring. Susan, Wally's breeder, owner, and handler, considered Wally the world's best traveling companion and friend.

CH Wolfstadt's First Frost, NSD, BROM

Wolfstadt's First Frost was nicknamed Willie by his owners/breeders, Jeanne and Lance Wolfe, Bill by his specials career handler, Ellen Grevatt; and Mr. Bill by his professional holder, John Grevatt. Willie was from an outstanding litter of six champions out of CH Parmar's Prima von Wolfstadt, sired by CH Greywind's Jack Frost. His siblings were Bliss, owned by Audrey Meinke; Autumn, owned/handled by Diane Cordero; Alice, owned by Richard Trochia; Shadow, owned by Philip Berger; and Claudia, owned by veterinarian Dr. Harry Millar. All were handled to their championships by their owner-breeders. This litter was consistently in the limelight from 1987 through 1991 with major championship points, sweepstakes wins, Futurity wins and placements, specialty bests, Best of Breeds, group placements, and group wins. The highlight of their accomplishments was Willie's Best in Show at Framingham Kennel Club on 2 June 1991. Willie completed his championship at the tender age of 11 months. His points, which included three majors, were garnered from the puppy and bred-by-exhibitor classes, handled by Lance. After a short hiatus for obedience and field training, Willie continued his winning ways under Lance's tutelage, winning Best Dog at the 1988 Futurity, numerous Best of Breeds and group placements, and three Group 1s. This chapter of his show career culminated with the title of Best Dog at the 1989 Maturity. At this time, he was turned over to his father's owner, Ellen Grevatt, for a 1-year specials

Figure 30-36: *CH Bing's Southern Sass, CD, NSD, NRD, V* (CH Bing's Southern Saga Del Oro, CD, NSD, NRD, V, BROM × CH Bing's Tatiana v Windsong, NSD, NRD, V, BROM). Bred by Jean White; owned by Jean White.

Figure 30-38: *CH Adam von Arras* (CH Stardust Orion Reiteralm × CH Mistywoods Miriam v. Arras). Bred and owned by Pat and Max Miller.

Figure 30-37: *CH Harline's W.F. Rockefeller, BROM* (CH Nani's Scirroco of Mattrace, BROM × CH Harline's Hurrah, BROM). Bred by Vicki Roye, Susan Line, and Brenda Walton; owned by Alan and Susan Line.

career. Ellen handled him to Top 10 status and his Best in Show. Selectively offered as stud, Willie produced 18 champions that include two Best in Show winners, Am/Can CH Greywind's High Flying Cloud, JH, TD, V, BROM (Ben) and CH Silvermont's Green Mountain Boy (Yuppie). His son Ben produced Best in Show winner CH Greywind's Snow Cloud, JH (Sea Bee). This extended the consecutive generations of Best in Show dogs started by CH Colsidex Standing Ovation to five. Retiring while in his prime, Willie moved with his owners to a Pennsylvania farm, where he was the canine ruler, grouse and pheasant hunter, and best and most loyal companion until his passing at the age of 12.

CH W.F. Mattrace Harline Roquelle

Kelly was whelped from the third and last repeat of CH Nani's Scirroco of Mattrace, CD, BROM, and CH Harline's Hurrah, BROM. Her siblings include CH Harline's WF Rockefeller, No. 1 Weimaraner, multiple Best in Show winner and Best of Opposite Sex at the National Specialty; CH Mattrace's Harline Roquette, multiple-group-placing bitch and Best of Opposite Sex at the National Specialty as well as other champions. Kelly won multiple Best in Shows, many Group 1s, and many, many group placements. Her easy, ground-covering side gait made her a favorite. She had a 'never-say-die' attitude and great showmanship, although she did have her own agenda on many occasions. Kelly was bred by Vicki Roye, Susan Line, and Brenda Walton. She had one litter; both of the puppies from this litter finished, and one daughter, CH Harline Mattrace Rolling Stone, went on to be a Top 10 bitch and multiple group winner. This bitch in turn was the dam of CH Harline Mattrace BB King and CH Mattrace Harline ByeByeBirdie, who won the 12–18 class at the National Specialty, going reserve winners' bitch the day before; she went on to have multiple group placements.

Am/Can CH Norman's Greywind Phoebe Snow, JH, HOF

Phoebe always had it all. She thought very highly of herself. Right from the beginning, she knew she was "special." She started her show career the day she turned 6 months old by going Winners' Bitch and Best of Winners at her first show. When she finished her championship, she stayed home to mature and start working on her Junior Hunter title and qualified at her first Hunt Test. Phoebe started her specials career in January 1992, with owner/handler Ellen Grevatt holding the lead. In June, she went to Stan Flowers, and the rest is history. A little more than 3 years after receiving her first points, Phoebe broke the record for Best in Shows for a Weimaraner. Not content to settle for breaking the 32-year-old record, she went on to win a total of 14 all-breed Best in Shows. Phoebe and Stan were truly a great team, and the special bond between the two was evident every time they entered the ring together. Phoebe

Figure 30-40: *CH W.F. Mattrace Harline Roquelle* (CH Nani's Scirroco of Mattrace, CD, BROM × CH Harline's Hurrah, BROM). Bred by Vicki Roye, Susan Line, and Brenda Walton; owned by Jack and Vicki Roye.

proved that a Weimaraner can work both the field as well as the sporting group by earning her Junior Hunter title. As a producer, she would carry on the versatile Greywind heritage when she returned home to become a mother. She produced a Best in Show son with CH Greywind's High Flying Cloud, TD, JH, V, BROM, who was the sire of BIS/BISS CH Greywind's Snow Cloud, JH. Phoebe was truly a gift, not only for her owners but because she opened the door for other Weimaraners that followed her, to be acknowledged in the sporting group and Best in Show ring.

Am/Can CH Norman's Smokey City Heat Wave, JH, BROM, HOF

Owned by Ronna Katzin and Tom Wilson, Allie displayed the versatile heritage of the Weimaraner. While she was a far-ranging and gifted hunting dog, when placed in the capable hands of Peggy Roush, she would blossom into an outstanding show dog as well. The year 1990 would end with Allie as the WCA's No. 1 Weimaraner (Best of Breed points) and recipient of the KalKan Pedigree Award. Things would only get better; 1991 would see her as the No. 1 Weimaraner in both Canada and the United States (all systems), as well as the winner of the WCA National Specialty and the Canadian National Specialty. Allie repeated her win at the WCA National Specialty in 1992. Her career included an all breed Best in Show (1992), 143 Best of Breeds, 15 Group 1s, and 53 group placements. She is the dam of 13 champions, earning the title of WCA's Top Producing Dam in 1996.

Figure 30-39: *CH Wolfstadt's First Frost, NSD, BROM* (CH Greywind's Jack Frost × CH Parmar's Prima von Wolfstadt). Bred and owned by Jeanne and Lance Wolfe.

Figure 30-41: *Am/Can CH Norman's Greywind Phoebe Snow, JH* (Am./Bda. CH Greywind's Jack Frost, CD, SD, V, CGC, BROM, HOF × CH Norman's Easybrae Katie, BROM). Bred by Norman F. LeBoeuf; owned by Mrs. Jack L. Billhardt and Ellen J. Grevatt.

Within a month, she had back-to-back Best in Show and Maturity wins. In her career, she had back-to-back National Specialty wins, 76 Group 1s and so many group placements, Sweepstakes, and Specialty wins that it's difficult to keep track of. She made it to No. 11 in the country in the all-breed standings and broke all breed records to date. She retired in 1995 after securing a group placement at Westminster and her 15th Best in Show. She had only one litter, which produced nine pups, five of which became champions.

CH Silvermont's Green Mountain Boy, BROM

CH Silvermont's Green Mountain Boy, better known as Yuppie, was bred by Valerie Berberich in snowy Vermont; he went to live with his co-owners Dorothy and George Heinze when he was 18 months old. He finished his championship the following year, going Best of Breed his first time as a special. He continued to win his Canadian championship in four shows as well as his Bermuda championship in three days at the World Con-

CH Greymist's Silver Cloud, BROM

CH Greymist's Silver Cloud, Lily was born 24 February 1991, the last of a litter of 7. She showed very early promise and never went through a 'gawky' stage. She was entered in her first show at 7 months and was shown by her novice owner/handler. The first time in the ring, she went Best in Show over specials for a four-point major. She finished her championship at 14 months of age and at 16 months was Best in Futurity, receiving an Award of Merit at the National Specialty, again while being shown by her novice owner/handler. It was apparent that Lily was much better than I, so I gave in to Keith Pautz's request to show her for me. Lily knew only me as her handler, but soon she and Keith became the "dream team." Within a couple of months of part-time handling by Keith, she won her first Best of Breed. Within 2 months, she won Best of Breed every day at a four-day circuit and placed in the group three times on the same circuit.

Figure 30-42: *Am/Can CH Norman's Smokey City Heat Wave, JH, BROM, HOF* (Am/Can Valmar Smokey City Ultra Easy, JH, NSD, BROM × CH Norman's Frostroy Colleen, BROM). Bred by Norman LeBoeuf; owned by Tom Wilson and Ronna Katzin.

Figure 30-43: *CH Greymist's Silver Cloud* (CH Silversmith's Ez Payment Plan, CD, JH × CH Sunmist Silver Shadow, CD, JH). Bred by R. and J. Shelby; owned by J. Shelby, K. Pautz, and R. Shelby.

CH Wilwins Alice in Wonderland

Ken and Connie Williams used to joke around and say that if they could get the pretty look of their foundation bitch Jodi and the great side movement of their male Hollywood, they could have a Best in Show winner. That combination not only gave them one Best in Show winner, but two, the first being Emma. Emma did not have a very auspicious beginning as third pick in a litter of five. She was sold on a co-ownership to her new parents with the understanding that she first was their pet but that if she turned out nicely, the Williams could finish her championship. Unfortunately, when her litter was 6 months old, we lost the first- and second-pick puppies in her litter, one to a rare but deadly disease; the other was lost and never found by a family who had been puppy-sitting him. Since the other two puppies in the litter had been sold as pets and were now fixed, that left only Emma from her litter to be shown. She debuted in the show ring when she was 13 months old and finished quickly over six weekends with three majors and a Best of Breed. Emma started her serious campaign in April 1994 and won her first Best in Show shortly after at the Santa Ana Valley Kennel Club on 1 May 1994 under Mr. Freeman Claus. She went on to win a second Best in Show the next year at the Burbank Kennel Club on

gress of Kennel Club Shows held in Bermuda in 1992, winning three Best of Breeds and three group placements. With limited campaigning as a special by his handler Gale Young, Yuppie had spectacular success with 92 Best of Breeds and 15 group placements, including winning the group six times. At the National Specialty, in 1994, he was Best of Opposite Sex under Michelle Billing. The big day came under George Bragaw at the Mid-Coast Kennel Club of Maine, when he went Best in Show. During 1992, 1993, and 1994, Yuppie was in the breed's Top 10. He sired the 1997 Western Maturity winner as well as both field and show champions. Yuppie had infinite patience in the ring and the stamina to never wear down, no matter how long he was in the ring. He would virtually glide around the ring on a slack lead and would walk into a 'stack' and hold it for minutes on end. He continued to win as a veteran, his last win coming the day he retired at age 11. Around the house, he was the sofa dog, reserved and relaxed, as well as a BROM producer of 10 show champions.

Figure 30-44: *CH Silvermont's Green Mountain Boy, BROM* (CH Wolfstadt's First Frost, BROM × CH Silvermont's Covered Bridget). Bred by Valerie H. Berberich; owned by Dorothy and George Heinze.

Figure 30-45: *CH Wilwins Alice in Wonderland* (CH Harline's Hollywood, BROM × CH Casa Perry's Prime Diamond, BROM). Bred by Ken and Connie Williams and Patricia Bruno; owned by Dennis and Marcia Forsyth and Ken and Connie Williams.

22 July 1995 under Mrs. Carol Esterkin. Emma was also the winner of Best Bitch at the 1994 Western Futurity and Best Bitch at the 1995 Southern Maturity. Emma retired from campaigning the weekend of the WCA National the end of September 1995. Even though she was campaigned for only 9 months in 1994 and 9 months in 1995, she was ranked No. 4 and No. 7, respectively, in all-breed points those years. Emma is the dam of four champions, three sired by CH Mattrace Harline Key Largo, BROM, including her Best in Show winning son CH Wilwins Flash Fire, BROM and the Winners Dog at the 1998 National CH Wilwins Wild Fire. Emma was breeder/owner handled by Connie Williams her entire career.

CH Camelot's Matinee Idol

Brando is a dog one would have to live with to truly appreciate! He was easy-going, loving, sensitive to his owner's feelings, and intelligent. Brando made the Top 10 list for three consecutive years; he was both a Futurity and Maturity winner, group winner, and Best in Show winner. Brando went Best in Show at the 2000 Westminster Kennel Club show, at 7½ years young! His puppies have his wonderful temperament, with soundness of mind as well as body. He produces get that is true to the Weimaraner Standard. Brando produced more than 30 champions, Futurity and Maturity winners, and Best of Breed winners. His gentle nature is missed by all who knew him.

CH LD's Merry Melodies

LD's Merry Melodies, "Hope" had an excellent top line and was a smooth mover. Judges would often comment that she was one of the best Weimaraners they had seen in a long time. Hope was the top Weimaraner in the state of Florida for more than 3 years, placing in the Top 10 in the country during that same period. Hope went Best in Show on 12 November 1995, handled by Ron Hahn. Hope was bred once and produced four champions out of a litter of eight.

Am/Can CH BIS/BISS Nani's Win'k of an Eye, HOF, JH, VCD1, NRD, VX, BROM

"Flirt" finished her champion from the puppy class with a major at 7 months and her second major at 8 months, also going Best of Breed over 15 specials. In the Top 10 for 5 years, her appearances were as an 8-month-old puppy and as a veteran! One of her most prestigious wins was Best in Specialty Show at the Yankee Weimaraner Club with the National Specialty, from the Veteran Class. As she made

Figure 30-46: *CH Camelot's Matinee Idol* (CH Nani's Southern Cross, BROM × CH Camelot's Halley's Comet, BROM). Bred by Susan Thomas and C. and E. Waterman-Storer; owned by Susan Thomas.

Figure 30-47: *CH LD's Merry Melodies* (CH Nani's Careless Caper O'Lani × CH Moonshine's Adora). Bred by D. Walsh and L. Miner; owned by Rachel D. Olsen and Lani N. Miner.

wind's Playn the Game, JH, NSD, BROM, HOF, produced four champions. She was the Top Producing Dam for 1998.

CH Ultimas Stetson v. Hufmeister, CD, BROM

Stetson was bought unseen as a puppy for his novice owner Teresa Hill to show. He began winning matches at 4 months of age, finishing his championship with four majors. Stetson was turned over to Rusty Howard for his specials career. Stetson won the central Futurity at the Nationals and then went on to win his Maturity in 1995. Stetson was ranked No. 1 Weimaraner in 1995 with several Group 1s and placements and four Best in Shows and was the National Specialty winner in 1996.

Stetson, known for his outstanding movement, showmanship, and headpiece was chosen by many breeders as a sire. He produced 40 champions, including Maturity winners CH Rosaic's Gala Baraka, CD, JH, NSD, NRD, V; CH Valmar's Summer Rain, BROM; and CH Hufmeisters Well Decorated, group winner and Top 10 in 2004.

CH Valmar's Apache Rebel, BROM

Rebel is an all-breed Best in Show, Specialty, and 1995 National Specialty Best of Breed winner. He was ranked on the Top 10 show list for three years (1993–1995). Rebel is

the last lap, the crowd was on its feet, applauding and yelling. Her breeder-handler said later, "I needed a Flexi to keep up with her." Her show record speaks for itself—in 2 years, she had 47 group placements, with 12 Group 1s, 132 Best of Breeds, and 16 specialty awards. She had an Award of Merit at Westminster and three National Awards of Merit—including one from the Veteran Class. Flirt was the first Weimaraner to go Best in Show while holding an AKC hunting title, and the only all-breed Best in Show Weimaraner to hold a WCA Versatile Excellent rating. By virtue of earning her Companion Dog, Tracking Dog, Novice Ability, and Novice Agility Jumper, Flirt earned the Versatile Companion Dog title—only the second Weimaraner to do so and the only Best in Show Weimaraner to do so.

Flirt was also a Top Producer. Her first litter from BIS/BISS CH Adam von Arras produced two champions; her second litter from BISS CH Baht N Grey-

Figure 30-48: *Am/Can BIS/BISS CH Nani's Win'k of an Eye, JH, VCD1, NRD, VX, BROM* (CH Nani's Baht a Pack a Trouble, CD, JH, V, BROM × CH Nani's Kookaburra, BROM). Bred by Christine Grisell; owned by Dr. Dana Massey and Pat Miller.

Figure 30-49: *CH Ultimas Stetson v. Hufmeister, CD, BROM* (CH Colsidex Nani Reprint, JH, SD, BROM × CH Ultima's Sadie Hawkins, BROM). Bred by Ann H. and Peter Loop; owned by Thomas and Teresa Hill.

CH Windwalker's Graeagle, CD, JH, NRD, V, BROM

Grady was truly a champion, not only in the show ring, but also in his attitude, abilities, and personality. He was willing and able to do anything, and he loved people and attention. Grady was on the Top Producer list for 7 years and rated No. 1 in 2000 and 2002. Shown throughout his career by Keith Pautz, he had three Best in Shows and nine Specialty wins, along with many Sporting Group wins and placements, and was Best Dog in the Western Maturity in 1996.

Grady has produced 85 show champions to date, including Futurity winner CH OB's A Night to Remember and Maturity winner AM/Can CH Swan Creek's Emerald Queen, and another Top Producer and winner, CH Silversmith's Ethan Allen, JH, BROM. Many of these dogs have multiple versatile titles in field, agility, obedience, and tracking, including CH Rockville's Truman Greystone, VCD2, TDX, MH, MX, MXJ, SDX, RDX, VX5, NAVHDA UT1.

CH Wilwins Do It to Me

Sadie, like her older sister Emma, had a fairly short show career. We started showing her in the classes at the 1994 Western Futurity weekend when she was 13 months old; she

well balanced, of medium size, with nice shoulder layback, a good topline, and a wonderful temperament, with loads of personality. He is known for his strong, ground-covering gait and beautiful headpiece. He has produced sound, well-balanced offspring, which include Specialty, group, Futurity, and Maturity winners. His top-producing BROM offspring include CH Valmar's Unanimous Decision, BROM; CH Valmar's Urban Cowboy, BROM; and CH Valmar's Grayshar Burgundy, BROM.

Rebel retired at the age of 6 from the show ring, and after being away for a year his owners decided it would be fun to support their specialties with a veteran. At the age of 8, he went Best of Breed several times from the Veteran class. Rebel was a "Once in a Life Time Special," he was always so up at dog shows. As Andy Linton once said, "Rebel would salute us wherever we set clapping without breaking gait." At home, he was named Saint Rebel by his good friend Vicki Ruiz he was so laid back and a joy to be around.

Figure 30-50: *CH Valmar's Apache Rebel, BROM* (CH Top Hat's Top Gun, BROM × CH Valmar's Starling, BROM). Bred by Joan Valdez and Terry Cumins; owned by Rachel Aguilar and Joan Valdez.

Figure 30-51: CH Windwalker's Graeagle, CD, JH, NRD, V, BROM (CH Nani's 'N Tophat's Backlash, CD, NSD, V, BROM × CH Windwalker's Gemborie, BROM). Bred and owned by Arlene and Phil Marshrey.

Am/Can CH Greywind's High Flying Cloud, TD, JH, V, BROM

Greywind's High Flying Cloud, "Ben" was easily shown to his championship by owner/handler Linda Snyder. Once Ben was finished, his breeder–co-owner, Ellen Grevatt, showed him to No. 2 and No. 3 Weimaraner in 1996 and 1997 and finished his short, successful career with numerous specialty wins, Best of Opposite at Westminster at 22 months of age, and two Best in Shows.

Ben was the youngest dog in the history of the breed to be certified for his tracking title (TD) at the age of 3 months and easily earned this title his first time out at the age of 6 months, 3 days! At 5 months, he earned his NAVHDA title and soon after earned his Junior Hunter title, all owner-handled by Linda.

Ben's wonderful, loving temperament has been passed on to his get. Ben has sired litters from the East to West coasts, with his get attaining numerous versatile titles, including three Futurity winners. He shared his home with five other males, and they spent many hours a day running the acreage there. He will always have a special place in the hearts of those who knew him.

won back-to-back five-point majors, finishing not long after. She started her specials career in October 1995 after her older sister Emma's retirement. Her specials career lasted only 16 months, ending in January 1997. Sadie won her Best in Show on 5 October 1996 under Mr. Vincent Grosso. Sadie was also breeder/owner handled for her entire career by Connie Williams. Sadly, we never had the opportunity to breed Sadie.

CH Wismar's Slow Gin Fizz

Ginny went Best in Show at the Augusta Kennel Club show on 9 November 1996 under Judge Ms. Corky Gauger. Ginny finished 1996 as No. 1 Weimaraner by breed points and is the 1996 Pedigree winner. She also finished No. 2 Weimaraner by all breed points. The icing on the cake was her Best of Breed win at the 1997 Westminster Kennel Club show under Judge Col. Jerry Weiss. She attained these wins throughout her career with her owner, then junior handler, Susan Wise. After her retirement from the conformation ring, she became one of the few Best in Show bitches to produce a Best in Show daughter, CH Wismar's With a Twist. Good girl, Ginny!

Figure 30-52: *CH Wilwims Do It to Me* (CH Harline's Hollywood, BROM × CH Casa Perry's Prime Diamond, BROM). Bred by Ken and Connie Williams and Patricia Bruno; owned by Egidio and Carrie Della Ripa and Ken and Connie Williams.

Figure 30-53: *CH Wismar's Slow Gin Fizz* (CH Valmar's Smokey City Ultra Easy, JH, BROM × CH Wismar's Mint Julep, BROM). Bred by Barbara Wise and Linda Springthorpe; owned by Barbara and Susan Wise.

1997 at the Hilton Head Island, South Carolina, all-breed show. That same year he was ranked No. 2 Weimaraner all systems at just 1½ years old. In 1998, he received an award of merit at the Westminster Kennel Club Dog Show and went on to win Best Dog at the Southern Maturity. Roscoe's next Best in Show came in the fall of 1998 at the Stone City Kennel Club, handled by Stan Flowers. The following month he went Best in Show, again handled by Stan Flowers, at the Granite City Kennel Club. His ranking at the end of 1998 was No. 1, all systems. Roscoe continues to be ranked in the ALL-TIME show dog list. For the duration of his show career, Roscoe has remained on the Top 10 Show lists. Roscoe is also the first stud dog in breed history to sire the Best of Breed, Best of Opposite Sex, and Best of Winners at a National Specialty. He was the Top Producer in 2003 and has been on the Top Producers list for 2000–2004.

CH Smokycity D'Nunder Lazer Beam, BROM

Sydney started showing promise early on in her career. Her exceptional movement and outstanding breed type was hard to miss in the ring. Along with her handler Bob Dou-

Am/Can CH Carousels Roscoe T Picotrane, BROM

Roscoe completed his American Championship at 9 months of age, with three majors. At 11 months of age, he won his first Best in Specialty show under breeder Judge Michael Shoreman. During the 1997 National Specialty week in Perry, Georgia, Roscoe went Best in Futurity. He also received an Award of Merit at that National. During the following years, he received several awards of merit at National Specialties. At the 1999 National, he went Best of Opposite Sex. He is also undefeated in the stud dog class at every National he entered. Handled by Rusty Howard, Roscoe won his first Best in Show in November

Figure 30-54: *Am/Can CH Greywind's High Flying Cloud, TD, JH, V, BROM* (CH Wolfstadt's First Frost, NSD, BROM × CH Greywind's Snow Bird). Bred by Patricia Crowley and Ellen Grevatt; owned by Linda and William Snyder.

Figure 30-55: *Am/Can CH Carousels Roscoe T Picotrane, BROM* (CH Jax's von Major × Am/Can CH Kasamar Rocks The Carousel). Bred by Bill and Pat Van Camp; owned by Bill and Pat Van Camp and Quinn and Mia Truckenbrod.

had moved to Hawaii for a short time, and after a breeding with Cricket in 1995, produced six puppies, all with fabulous temperaments. The high quality of the litter was apparent almost as soon as they put their feet on the ground. Four finished their championships (two bitches in California).

Karla's friend, Daryle Oliveira, who had established his own line 'Ekahi' (No. 1 in Hawaiian), was a frequent visitor to Jokar as the litter grew. He surprised everyone by purchasing "pink collar." Sadie finished her championship in five shows at only 10 months of age. At 11 months of age, her first weekend as a special, she was awarded a Best of Breed and a Futurity 2. She was handled exclusively in Hawaii by her co-owner, Daryle Oliveira. Sadie was sent to California for part of the summer in 1997. Just off the plane, she won back-to-back Best of Breeds at Shoreline DFA of Orange County and Long Beach Kennel Club, defeating the No. 1 Weimaraner in the country on both days.

ble, she was winning breeds and group placements from the puppy classes.

In 1998, she was the No. 1 Weimaraner and Pedigree winner and was No. 2 in all breed competition. The year 1999 was fantastic for Sydney and Bob, when she won the WCA National Specialty, the first of her three all-breed Best in Shows, No. 1 both systems, and when she was the breed winner at the Westminster Kennel Club show. Sydney and Bob were a great team to watch, both in and out of the ring. Bred to CH Smokey City El Nino, JH, she was the dam of Best in Show winner Am/Can CH Smokeycity Hail Mary, who, like Sydney, was expertly campaigned by Bob Double. To date, Sydney is the dam of 10 champions.

CH Jokar's N 'Ekahi RC Prelude

Although Sadie was whelped in Hawaii, she is really a California gal, coming from two California-bred top producers. Karla Payne had first seen Sadie's sire "Remy" at the Venture shows. As luck would have it, Remy

Figure 30-56: *CH Smokycity D'Nunder Lazer Beam, BROM* (Am/Can/Au CH Divani Loads a Trouble × CH Smokey City Ex Elegance). Bred by Tom Wilson and Jennifer Miller-Howard; owned by Tom Wilson, Bob Double, and Anne Cullen-Tormey.

Figure 30-57: *CH Jokar's N 'Ekahi RC Prelude* (CH Top Hat's Dorian Gray, BROM × CH Valmar's Gallorette v. Jokar, BROM). Bred by Karla Payne; owned by Daryle Oliviera and Karla Payne.

Wise. "Willie" won three Group 1s and a Best in Show at Blennerhasset Kennel Club on her weekend in West Virginia. She continued her winning ways by taking Best Bitch in Maturity at the Western Futurity/Maturity in August 1999 while on her way to the WCA's Top 10 list for that same year. The Best of Breed winner at the 2000 Westminster Kennel Club show, Willie and her record speak for her.

CH Nani's Smart Aleck, JH, NRD, V, BROM

CH Nani's Smart Aleck, JH, NRD, V, BROM, was owned by Christine Grisell and Suzy Casper. He was the result of eight generations of Nani's breeding. He was a standout in a successful litter that produced not only winners but also Top Producers. He finished his championship with three 5-point majors from the puppy class and many Best in Sweepstakes. He was a joyous puppy in the show ring and gave no end of laughter for the spectators, much to Chris's horror and embarrassment.

"Aleck" completed his Junior Hunter as a puppy and remained a loyal hunting companion. He also had field trial placements and his Novice Retrieving Dog.

As an adult, he was the supreme show dog! He would step into his stack perfectly, without a hand on him, and could gait around the ring with no help from his handlers, stopping in perfect poise. He never had a down day, win or lose.

She was also awarded a Group 4 at Long Beach. Sadie is only the second Weimaraner to win a Best in Show in Hawaii. This was on 19 April 1998. Shown only eight times in 1998, Sadie accumulated enough wins to be the No. 1 Sporting Dog and the No. 7 All Breed for Hawaii. That year, she was also ranked among the Top 20 Weimaraners nationally—no small feat for a Weim from Hawaii. This resulted in an invitation to the first Top 20 Invitational, held at the 2000 National Specialty.

Sadie and her half-brother (also out of Cricket), CH Jokar's Falstaff v. d. Strand, CD, have greatly boosted Cricket's ranking on the BROM list. This is notable because there are currently only 18 all-breed shows and four specialties per year (2003). The only puppy of these two half-siblings, CH 'Ekahi N Jokar Solo Performanz, is being shown and is ranked among Hawaii's Top 10 sporting dogs.

CH Wismar's With a Twist

No one should have been surprised that this daughter of Best in Show winner CH Wismar's Slow Gin Fizz would follow in her mother's pawprints. Like her mother, Wilhemina was handled exclusively by her breeder and best friend, Susan

Figure 30-58: *CH Wismar's With a Twist* (Am/Can CH Silberschoen's Lucky Strike × CH Wismar's Slow Gin Fizz). Bred by Barbara and Susan Wise; owned by Marcia Greene and Barbara Wise.

Figure 30-59: *CH Nani's Smart Aleck, JH, NRD, V, BROM* (CH Midnite Magic von HolyHaus × CH Nani's Knocker, CDX, TD, JH, SD, VX, BROM). Bred and owned by Christine Grisell and Susan Casper.

prestigious wins was Best in Specialty Show at the Louisville Weimaraner Club Specialty, in conjunction with the Futurity/Maturity in a very large entry of 177. Her show record speaks for itself—ranked as high as No. 1, in 2 years of specialing she had 77 group placements with 15 Group 4s, 34 Group 3s, 23 Group 2s, and 5 Group 1s, along with 15 awards at Specialty shows. She earned two National Awards of Merit and finished her career with 212 Best of Breeds.

Am/Can CH Greywind's Snow Cloud, JH

Greywind's Snow Cloud, "Seabee," was a substantial, elegant dog. He was known for his breathtaking movement and magnificent head. Seabee finished his Junior Hunter title easily at one year and unfortunately was killed in a tragic accident at the age of 5, before he could pursue more titles. He was birdy and wanted to please; he ran for hours every day on the acreage where he lived.

Linda Snyder exclusively owner-handled Seabee to numerous specialty wins, multiple group

Aleck went Best in Show at the Southern Indiana Kennel Club Dog Show on 4 June 2000 under AKC Judge Tim Catterson. The win we were most proud of came on 17 May 2000, when he was the winner of the Inaugural WCA Top 20 Invitational.

He also excelled as a sire of champions; he was the Top Producing Stud Dog in 2001. He has winning offspring all over the world and sired many Futurity and Maturity winners.

CH Win'Weim Shootin' High Brass

"Brassy" is Win'Weim's first owner-breeder-handled Champion. Brassy was Reserve Winners Bitch at the WCA Nationals in 1997 from the puppy class, and it was all fun after that win! Earning three majors, going Best of Opposite Sex in very tough competition at three specialty shows before she was 14 months old, she continued her winning ways. Besides her Best in Show, probably one of her most

Figure 30-60: *CH Win'Weim Shootin High Brass* (CH Nani's Concert Master, SH, BROM × CH SmokyCityEZ Win'd Bnth R Wings, NSD, NRD, V, BROM). Bred by Dr. Dana Massey; owned by Dr. Dana Massey and Pat Miller.

Figure 30-61: *Am/Can CH Greywind's Snow Cloud, JH* (CH Greywind's High Flying Cloud, JH, TD, V, BROM × CH Norman's Greywind Phoebe Snow). Bred by Ellen Grevatt and Mrs. Jack Billhardt; owned by Linda A. Snyder, Ellen Grevatt, and Mrs. Jack Billhardt.

placements, several group wins, and ultimately in the summer of 2000, to his Best in Show. Seabee was also ranked No. 5 Weimaraner in both 1999 and 2000. In July 2000, Seabee earned his Canadian Championship and placed in the group every day, including a Group 1. This trip earned him the title of No. 1 Weimaraner in Canada in 2000.

Seabee will never be forgotten by those who knew him, especially Linda and Bill, with whom he lived—he never spent a night away from Linda his entire life.

CH Smokycity Riverboat Gambler

CH Smokycity Riverboat Gambler, known as Rhett, was truly the Clark Gable of Weimaraners. He was bold yet elegant, a stallion of a male, yet had eyes that looked into your soul, powerful but with a soft heart for all. He was a movie-star personality to his friends and family and, in the ring, he was a showboat. Rhett lived up to his name in every situation and fulfilled every dream asked of him. Rhett began his show career at 11 months with a Best of

Winners and Award of Merit at the 1999 WCA Nationals. Like any good movie star in the making, Rhett left his home with Tom Wilson at Smoky City Kennels and moved to California with his sponsor and co-owners, J. Logan and Ron Goularte, Crescent Kennels. He was campaigned nationally by his best friend and handler, Keith Pautz, from 2000 to 2003.

Rhett's support team of J., Tom, and Keith, along with Rhett's fans, family, and co-breeder-owner, Kelly Photopoulos, enjoyed Rhett's successes, wins, honors, and records. At Rhett's retirement show, the 2003 Garden at Westminster, Rhett won Best in Breed from distinguished Judge Michelle Billings. Once again, Rhett took center stage, this time at his farewell. He returned to his east coast home with Tom Wilson to continue his stud career. He sired the WCA 2002 National Specialty winner, his daughter, Smokycity Simpatico. In addition to his stud duties, Rhett traveled to many hospitals and convalescent centers as a therapy companion. During Tom Wilson's struggle with terminal illness, it was said that Rhett kept Tom going. Thus, Rhett walked into a new role with deep compassion and a tenderness that spirits embrace during times of deep struggle. Rhett was always there with Tom and always fulfilled all that was asked of him. Rhett understood the human side of personalities that few humans know. Rhett is the Weimaraner for all seasons. His show record includes: 2001 WCA National Specialty Winner, Best of Breed Westminster 2003,

Figure 30-62: *CH Smokycity Riverboat Gambler* (Am/Can CH Silberschoens Lucky Strike, BROM × CH SmokyCity Sumthn T Talkabout, BROM). Bred by Tom Wilson and Kelly Photopoulos; owned by J. Logan and Tom Wilson.

sire of 2002 WCA National Specialty Winner, No. 1 Weimaraner 2001, all-breed Best in Show, Multiple Specialty Best in Show, 45 Group 1s, and No. 1 Male in 2002, all-breed system.

CH Reiteralm's High Flutin' Chloe

Chloe's dam "Rosie" (CH Stoneybrook Rose of Reiteralm, NSD) was 6 years old and had missed on two breedings. Sharon Cooper followed Ginny Alexander's suggestion that she try once more and take Rosie to "Rio" (CH Northwoods River to Graytsky, JH, SD, NRD, V), a young dog that had caught her eye. As fate would have it, a star was born. Rio's owner, Michael Anderson, was to show Chloe, and, when she was 7 months old, he went to see her and noted that Chloe was a natural even then. Michael quickly piloted Chloe to her championship, and it became evident that she was special indeed. Chloe's captivating ring presence and effortless ground-covering gait became her hallmark.

Rusty Howard was engaged to show Chloe at her Maturity at the 2000 National Specialty. Rusty started handling Chloe just 3 weeks prior. Their first weekend out, Chloe won a supported entry of 65 at Old Dominion Kennel Club and

Figure 30-63: *CH Reiteralm's High Flutin' Chloe* (CH Northwoods River to Graytsky, JH, SD, NRD, V × CH Stoneybrook Rose of Reiteralm, NSD). Bred by Sharon Cooper; owned by Amy Anderson, Sharon Cooper, and John Croft.

went Best of Breed Group 2 at Baltimore County Kennel Club; she won her first Specialty (Delaware Valley Weimaraner Club) the following week at the Trenton Kennel Club. Chloe launched her record-breaking career 9 days later in St. Louis by winning her Maturity and going Best of Breed at both the Regional Specialty and the National Specialty. Chloe went on to an all-breed Best in Show at Tidewater Kennel Club of Virginia in 2001. She set the all-time record for Breed Points in a single year (2,117 points in 2001), set the record for most specialties won in a single year (nine in 2001), won consecutive Best of Breeds at the Westminster Kennel Club show (2000 and 2001), was two-time Pedigree Award winner for being No. 1 in Breed (2000 and 2001), was No. 1 All System in 2000, was National Specialty JAM in 2001, and was the winner of the WCA Top 20 Invitational in 2001.

CH Wilwins Flash Fire, BROM

Flash was that puppy that just caught your eye and heart and dared you not to keep him. He had his trials while growing up; our vet made more than a few dollars stitching him up many times as he "crashed" his way through his youth. He debuted in the show ring when he was 14 months old, finishing entirely from the bred-by class in only four weekends. He went on that same year to win Best Dog at the Southern Futurity after not being able to compete in the Western because he had sliced his pad open the week before. Flash never had a "real" campaign, as the Williamses were busy with a new business and could not devote the time or money to campaign him seriously. Flash was shown off and on over the next few years by several different handlers (owners Ken and Connie and friends Robert Grant, Sonda Peterson, and Pamela Lambie). The judges seemed to find him no matter who was at the end of the lead; each of his three Group 1s were won with a different handler. After being out of the ring for almost a year, they decided to bring him out for our local Southland Specialty in July 2001. They hired their very good friend and professional handler Pamela Lambie to show him as they had already made commitments to show other dogs there. The Williamses had Pam show him a couple of weekends before the Specialty to practice with him. He won three of the four breeds he was in and then won the Specialty under breeder-Judge Dr. Dana Massey. Flash went on to win his Best in Show the next day, 6 July 2001, under Mr. Gerald Schwartz. They sadly lost Flash to an intestinal blockage in April 2004 when he was

Figure 30-64: *CH Wilwins Flash Fire, BROM* (CH Mattrace Harline Key Largo, BROM × CH Wilwins Alice In Wonderland). Bred by Dennis and Marcia Forsyth and Ken and Connie Williams; owned by Ken and Connie Williams.

owner and popular mentor to all, passed away. In Carole's memory, and in honor of her particular support of breeder-owner-handlers, her friends have established a special award, "Best Bred By Exhibitor," to be presented at the WCA's National Specialty for at least the next 10 years.

Am/Can CH Smokeycity Hail Mary

Along with Bob Double, and continuing in the footsteps of her mother, Sydney (CH Smokycity D'Nunder Lazer Beam), "Mary" made her mark in the dog show world. Mary has earned six all-breed Best in Shows, 2004 WCA National Specialty Best of Breed, No. 1 Weimaraner both systems for 2003 and 2004, and Best of Breed winner at the Westminster Kennel Club show; she holds the record for 12 independent specialty wins. Mary completed her Canadian championship, went Best of Breed at the Canadian National specialty, and won an all-breed Best in Show in a memorable whirlwind 24 hours! Mary finished 2004 as the No. 6 Sporting Dog in the country. In 2005, Mary's show career spanned just 1 short month, due to the unexpected death of

only 8 years old. Flash was bred to only eight bitches in his life, producing 16 champions (with at least one more to finish soon), including Futurity, Maturity, Specialty, and group winners, thereby easily earning his BROM.

CH Tri-D's Grand Finale

"Allie" won numerous groups, Specialty Shows, WCA Top 20 Invitational, Eukanuba AKC Classic Sporting Group, the coveted Best in Show at the Augusta Kennel Club, and last but not least, the Pedigree Award in 2002. During her show career, Allie was co-owned by Carole Donaldson and Michael Parker, MD, and handled by Carole until 2001, when she was co-owned by Carole Donaldson and Cecilia Ruggles and handled by Scott Sommers. Allie's record speaks for itself. During her career, Allie earned 109 Best of Breeds, 51 group placements (17 Group 1s), and a Best in Show at the Augusta Kennel Club, on 12 April 2002 under Linda Stebbins-Hurlebaus. Having been bred twice, Allie has earned the title BROM, to date, with eight champions out of CH Bluhaven's Get'm While Th'r Hot and CH Tri-D's Invincible. One of Allie's last appearances was at the 2006 WCA National Specialty, where she won the Veteran Bitch class. Sadly, a short week later, Carole Donaldson, Allie's beloved

Figure 30-65: *CH Tri-D's Grand Finale* (CH Bluhaven's All Electric × CH Tri-D's Go With The Flow). Bred by Carole Donaldson and M. Klaas; owned by Cecelia Ruggles and Carole Donaldson.

Figure 30-66: *Am/Can CH Smokeycity Hail Mary* (CH Smokey City El Nino, JH, BROM × CH Smoky City D'Nunder Lazer Beam, BROM). Bred by Tom Wilson, Monika Hood, and Anne Cullen-Tormey; owned by Cindy Cassidy, Tom Wilson, Jennifer Martin, and Anne Cullen-Tormey.

her devoted friend and handler, Bob Double. Despite this, she remained in the WCA Top 10 in both breed and all-breed points for the year. She is the dam of nine champions to date. Her progeny have won multiple groups, Futurities, a bred by Best in Show, and an all-breed Best in Show.

CH ShoMar's Dustivelvet High Time

Confident and outgoing from the beginning, Ruff commanded everyone's attention. Often, it seemed he was the only puppy in the litter. When Mary Clark inquired about a male puppy, there was no question that Ruff had to be the one. Ruff flew to Dallas to meet his new family at 3 months of age. Upon landing, he loudly proclaimed his low opinion of the service in the cargo hold to all within earshot. His complaints continued on the drive to the Clark's home in New Mexico, thus earning him the name "Ruff." Today, whether at home or on the road, Ruff is a complete gentleman who enjoys meeting new people, especially children.

A wonderful showman who began his career at 8 months old, Ruff finished his championship when he was 10 months old. His first weekend out as a young special, Ruff garnered a Group 3 in tough competition at the Denver shows. He won the senior Futurity class at the Central Futurity and later won Best Dog in Maturity at the Western. Ruff has appeared on the breed's Top 10 from 2001 through 2005. He was No.

1 male in 2003 and 2004. Ruff's first all-breed Best in Show was his gift to the Clarks on their 45th wedding anniversary. He went on to earn three consecutive all-breed Best in Shows that week. Ruff's record includes five all-breed Best in Shows, numerous Best in Specialty Sweepstakes, 25 Group 1s, and numerous Group 2s, 3rds, and 4ths.

Bred sparingly, Ruff has sired a number of young champions, with many others close to finishing.

CH K-Line's Smokycity N'Style

The stars were perfectly aligned on that cold, clear winter night in Phoenix, Arizona, when Caroline Katzin, Weim whelper extraordinaire, first set her eyes on Alexis. Caroline later said, "I knew at first sight that she was destined for a great show career. Alexis had a special presence, and an aura of greatness that I have never experienced before." Ronna Katzin and Tom Wilson had scoured the continent for many months to find the perfect breeding partner for Alexis's dam, Ariel (CH Smokey City K-Line Tradewins, BROM). Ariel had an impressive show record, having won the 1998 National Specialty, the Western Futurity and Maturity, numerous Best in Specialty Sweepstakes, and countless group placements. The hand of destiny led them to the ideal choice of sire, Canadian and U.S. Champion Echobar's Forged in Fire, who complemented Ariel's unparalleled movement and grace with

Figure 30-67: *CH ShoMar Dustivelvet High Time* (Am/Br CH Pan/Am CH Int. CH ShoMar's I Don't Giveadamn, CD, CGC, TDI × CH ShoMar's Touch The Future, CD, JH). Bred by Charlene Scalzott; owned by Mary Clark and Charlene Scalzott.

Figure 30-68: *CH K-Line's Smokycity N'Style* (CH Echobar's Forged in Fire × BISS CH Smokey City K-Line Tradewins, BROM). Bred and owned by Ronna Katzin and Tom Wilson.

a mystically perfect top line and tail set. And, as they say, the rest is history.

Alexis is a multiple Best in Show and Best in Specialty Sweepstakes winner. She won the 2003 Western Maturity and the prestigious WCA National Specialty Top 20 Invitational in 2005. Alexis has followed in the paws of her grandparents, CH Norman's Smokey City Heat Wave, JH, NRD, V, BROM, twice National Specialty winner, top producing dam in 1996, and Best in Show winner, as well as CH Smokey City EZ Moonstone, JH, on the maternal side and CH Baht N Greywind Play the Game, NSD, BROM, and CH Arokats Echobar a Dime a Dance on the paternal side.

Alexis is an extraordinary show dog, a born leader, cosmopolitan (she understands five languages, and including Mandarin Chinese), imposing but incredibly graceful. She loves to travel and enjoys classical guitar music and long walks on the beach with her family. Her favorite sports are ultimate Frisbee and wrestling with her littermate Alex.

CH Greydove 'Ekahi IslandGal

Tita is the third Weimaraner to receive Best in Show status in Hawaii and the second owner-handled by Daryle Oliveira. She is also the first Australian-bred Weimaraner to receive this honor in the U.S.

Not wanting to deal with the quarantine situation between the mainland U.S. and Hawaii, he looked to the Australian breeders. After a 2-year search, he found a breeding that was line-bred on Am/Can/Au Grd CH Divani Loads a Trouble, using two recent U.S. imports, Am/Aust CH Colsidex Grauhund Just Jeans and Am/Au CH Nani N Greydove Milenium Bug. Daryle thought the pedigree showed a lot of promise, and as he had already been communicating with Val Peters and Narelle Goold of Greydove Kennels, he made the inquiry, and they selected the bitch puppy for him.

Tita received her Best in Show, when she was only 17 months old, on 17 April 2005 at the Windward Hawaiian Dog Fanciers Association show, held in Kaneohe, Hawaii. She had received the Group 1 win from Mr. Houston Clark and the Best in Show nod from Mr. Roger R. Hartinger.

CH Colsidex Seabreeze Perfect Fit

Marge has been nothing short of exciting. Winners Bitch, from the 6–9 Puppy Class, at the 2004 National Specialty and finishing with another five-point Specialty win at 11 months of age, Best Bitch in Futurity in 2005, and her first Best in Show the same weekend. At the 2006 National

Figure 30-69: *CH Greydove 'Ekahi IslandGal* (Au Grd CH Waldiese Ndout Aboutit, TD × Aust CH Greydove Nice N Easy). Bred by Greydove Kennels (Australia); owned by Daryle Oliveira and Val Peters.

Figure 30-70: ***CH Colsidex Seabreeze Perfect Fit*** (CH Colsidex The Farm Top of the Mark, BROM × CH Seabreeze Colsidex Perfect Timing, JH). Bred by Judy Colan, Marge Davis, and Debra McCray; owned by Ellen Charles, Alessandra Folz, and Judy Colan. Marge was owner-handled to this prestigious and memorable Group 1 placement at the 2008 Westminster dog show.

Specialty, she was Best Bitch in Maturity as well as Best of Breed at the National Specialty. She ended 2006 as No. 1 Weimaraner. The year 2007 brought more triumphs for Marge: she was winner of the Top 20 competition at the National and earned her second National Specialty win. She was winner of the Sporting Group at the Eukanuba Classic. The year 2008 brought excitement to the Weimaraner world ,with Marge winning the Sporting Group at Westminster Kennel Club. She made breed history when she won the National Specialty for the third time in 2008, breaking the record for Best in Shows that was set by her great grandmother, Fergie. To date, Marge's record reflects 36 Best in Shows, 142 Group 1s, 81 Group 2s, 38 Group 3s, 17 Group 4s, 3 National Specialty wins, 389 Best of Breeds, No. 1 Weimaraner (2006–2008), and No. 3 Sporting Dog (2007 and 2008).

Am/Can CH Bowbent Carousel Hidden Gem

Jade entered the show ring at the 2003 Weimaraner Club National Specialty in Rhode Island at the age of 6 months, 5 days. Winning the huge class, breeder-handled by Angela McClure, Jade went on to Winner's Bitch and Best of Win-

ners. This spectacular win set a breed record for the youngest ever to win at a National Specialty. Jade went on to finish her American championship just after turning 8 months old. Along the way, she picked up several Best in Sweepstakes. Also competing in Canada at the same time, she finished her Canadian championship, taking Best of Breed over specials. Several sporting puppy groups were also won during her campaign to Canadian champion. In 2004, Jade, handled by Rusty Howard, won the WCA's Eastern Futurity.

Jade's specials career, which would be limited to one year of campaigning, began in January 2005, again handled by Rusty Howard. She began the year going opposite sex at the Eukanuba Invitational. Numerous Best of Breeds were won, and her first Best in Specialty was won in February. At year end, Jade tied the club record of 12 Specialties won in 1 year. Jade also received an Award of Merit at the Westminster Kennel Club show. In October 2005, at the Palisades Kennel Club, Jade won the Sporting Group under Christina Hubbell. Later that day, she went Best in Show under Terry DePietro, all handled by Rusty. At the end of 2005, Jade was the No. 1 in Best of Breed points, beating more than 2,177 Weimaraners. Her show points (12,977) were another major accomplishment in one short year of campaigning, and Jade ranked No. 10 on the all-time Weimaraner show list. At the end of 2005, Jade was No. 1 all systems and the No. 13 sporting dog in the U.S.

Figure 30-71: ***Am/Can CH Bowbent Carousel Hidden Gem*** (Am/Can CH Carousels Roscoe T Picotrane, BROM × Am/Can CH Bowbent N Donmar's Goldrush). Bred by Ross and Angela McClure; owned by Bill and Pat Van Camp and Angela McClure.

Figure 30-72: *CH Bzyfeet American Idol* (CH Silversmith Ethan Allen, JH, NSD × CH Valmar Bzyfeet Good Luck Charm). Bred by Vicki Ruiz, Connie Williams, and Sandy Koch; owned by Vicki Ruiz and Connie Williams.

CH Bzyfeet American Idol

Clay is not a close line-bred dog but a product of a combination of kennels that when brought together produced a lovely package of looks, movement, and temperament, a testament to all the fine kennel names in his pedigree. Clay was a show dog from the start, strutting around even as a small puppy, daring you to not look. He finished easily from the Bred-by class in November 2004 at 11 months old and went on to win Best Dog in the Western Futurity in 2005 and Best Dog at the Western Maturity in 2006. As of this writing, Clay has been out on the campaign trail for only 8 months and is quickly surpassing all our expectations. Clay is one of those dogs we all hope for but seldom get. He is a dream to live with, being the perfect laid-back, bed-warming, condo dog for his mom, Vicki Ruiz, babysitter to her youngest grandchildren, who like to dress him in a tutu (he wishes Vicki would not tell people that; he claims it is embarrassing!). Yet, he still goes into the show ring and gives 110% to his handler and co-owner Connie Williams. He lives to please his two "moms." Clay's get are just starting to be old enough to show, and we have high hopes

that they will do even better than their father. Clay won his first Best in Show on 5 August 2006 under Dr. Robert Moore, followed by his second the next day under Mr. Jerry Watson.

CH GraytSky Win'Weim It's My Prague-ative

"Dagmar's" favorite place is in the show ring or at the window watching little animals. She earned her two 5-point majors when she was 6½ months old with Eileen Hackett and then went on to earn Best of Breeds from the classes to finish with breeder/owner/handler Michael Anderson. She sat on the sidelines for 6 months watching her two littermate brothers break into the Top 10 lists. A meeting with Susan Line the week of Westminster created a match made in heaven. With Susan on the lead, Dagmar's climb up the Top 10 list was steady and sure, getting her to No. 3 Weimaraner All Breed in less than 3 months! Dagmar was on the move; she won six Best in Specialty Shows, 101 Best of Breeds, seven Group 1s, 15 Group 2s, 13 Group 3s and seven Group 4s before going Best in Show—all in 14 months of showing! Besides her Best in Show, probably one of the most prestigious wins was Best in Maturity at the Southern Maturity in 2005, with her friend Eileen again at the lead. In addition, Dagmar was honored with the First Award of Merit at Westminster Kennel Club, First Select at the AKC/Eukanuba

Figure 30-73: *CH GraytSky Win'Weim It's My Prague-ative* (Am/Can BISS CH Ashmore's Win'Weim Royal Flush, JH, BROM × CH BISS GraytSky's StellaLuna, BROM). Bred by Amy and Michael Anderson and Dr. Dana Massey; owned by Dr. Dana Massey and Amy and Michael Anderson.

Figure 30-74: *CH Smokycity Devil May Care* (CH Smokycity True Grit × Smokycity Ez Time Will Tell). Bred by Tom Wilson; owned by Tom Wilson and Jennifer Martin.

Figure 30-75: *CH Moonshines on the War Path* (CH Mysterybrooks Captivator × CH Moonshine's Magic Pocahontas). Bred by Marlene Judd and Judy Donnelly; owned by Mara Doherty, Marlene Judd, Nancie Mages, and Kimberly Halcom.

National Championship, Award of Merit at the WCA Nationals, plus Judges Select at the Top 20 in 2006.

CH Smokycity Devil May Care, NSD

The first time that Jennifer Martin saw Dharma, she knew there was something special about her. She had gone to Tom Wilson's to evaluate a litter of puppies, with no intention of bringing any home. Not surprisingly, Jennifer was soon driving home with Dharma on her lap, trying to figure out what she was going to tell her husband!

Dharma was a "high-maintenance" puppy—into everything and afraid of nothing. She started her show career by winning the breed out of the 9- to 12-month puppy class and finishing with four majors.

Her first Group 1 was at the prestigious Morris and Essex Dog Show, and she kept going from there. To date, she has four all-breed Best in Shows, two Sporting Dog Best in Shows, nine Best in Specialty Sweepstakes, Best in Match, 47 Group 1s, and many additional group placements. Since her retirement from the show ring, she has completed her Novice Shooting Dog and two legs of her Junior Hunter. While impressive, the most important thing about Dharma is that she did it all with an owner-handler who had never done any of this before. She is truly a once-in-a-lifetime dog that has accomplished more than Jennifer could have ever dreamt, and she did it on her own. At the end of the day, she is Jennifer's loyal friend and companion that she adores; the rest is just icing on the cake.

Dharma was sired by CH Smokeycity True Grit and by dam Smokycity E.Z. TimeWill Tell, a frozen-semen daughter of Am/Can CH Valmar Smokey City Ultra Easy, JH, NSD, BROM.

CH Moonshines on the War Path

"Tillie" was bred by Marlene Judd and daughter Judy Donnelly. She is owned by Mara Doherty, Marlene Judd, Nancie Mages, and Kimberly Halcom. Tillie is the granddaughter of BIS Am/Can CH Carousels Roscoe T Picotrane and BIS CH LD's Merry Melodies. Before completing her championship, she won several Best in Specialty Sweepstakes. Tillie finished at the Northern Illinois Weimaraner Club Specialty when she was 10 months old. Her specials career started when she was young, competing with top mature specials and going breed over top-ranked dogs. In 2006, Tillie went Best Opposite Sex at the Eukanuba Invitational in Long Beach, California. Tillie is a multiple Specialty winning bitch. On 22 April 2007, at the Fond Du Lac Kennel Club in Wisconsin, she won the group with tough competition under Connie Gerstner Miller. That same day, under Beth Speich, Tillie went Best in Show, a breeder's dream come true. We wish Marlene could have lived to see the spectacular win, but we feel Marlene was there in spirit.

Figure 30-76: *CH Unity Juscanis Surely Temple* (CH Seabreeze Colsidex Sands of Time, RN, JH, BROM × CH Am/Can/Braz Gr CH Juscanis Mater Ad Colsidex, BROM) Bred by Greg McLogan, K. Schwab, and A. Folz; owned by Lauren Austin, Greg McLogan, and Amy Tourond.

Figure 30-77: *CH Smokycity Silhouette DBL UR Pleasure* (BISS CH Nani's Indecent Exposure, JH, NAJ, V, BROM × BIS/BISS CH Smokeycity Hail Mary). Bred by C. Cassidy, T. Wilson, J. Martin, and A. Cullen-Tormey; owned by Cindy and Bruce Cassidy

CH Unity Juscanis Surely Temple

Crush's debut came when she was handled by her owner, Lauren Austin, winning Best of Breed over multiple specials when she was 6 months old. Along the way to her championship, she won two back-to-back Best in Sweepstakes on the January circuit before finishing with a four-point major win at the Chattahoochee Specialty. In 2007, Crush was shown on a limited basis during the first half of the year by her breeder, Greg McLogan. With Greg, Crush won three Specialties, nine group placements, including two Group 1s, an Award of Merit at the National Specialty, as well as Best Bitch in the Central Maturity. In July 2007, Crush went on the road with Rusty Howard. In just 6 weeks, Crush won seven group placements, including four Group 1s and a Best in Specialty Show. It was during this short time with Rusty that Crush achieved her first all-breed Best in Show at the Lexington Kennel Club. A few days later she did it again, winning her second all-breed Best in Show at the Mid-Kentucky Kennel Club. Shown only three more weekends in 2007, she won three more group placements and two more Best in Specialty Shows. Crush quickly became more than her owner had ever anticipated for her first show dog. Exhibiting outstanding breed type, movement, and that look-

at-me attitude, she is without any doubt "that once in-a-life-time dog" that everyone dreams of having. In limited showing, Crush ended 2007 ranked No. 5 Weimaraner all breed and No. 4 in breed points.

CH Smokycity Silhouette DBL UR Pleasure

Wrigley is easy to live with, intelligent, fun-loving, and a beautiful girl. She started showing when she was 7 months old. In her first weekend out, while being shown in the classes by Eileen Hackett, she earned a three-point major at the Cincinnati Weimaraner Club. She finished her championship, having earned four majors just a few days past her first birthday. She started her specials career at 14 months old with Keith Pautz; her first weekend out, she got a group placement. Since then, she has earned multiple Best in Specialty Sweepstakes and Group 1s and two Best in Show. Even at her young age, we knew she had a lot of promise and the best is yet to come. She is living up to the legacy of her winning parents, sire BISS CH Nani's Indecent Exposure, JH, NAJ, V, BROM, and dam BIS/BISS CH Smokeycity Hail Mary.

Figure 30-78: *CH Monterra's Best Bet, MH* (CH Win Weim Gratsky Cowboy Boots, JH × CH Windchymes Spirit Dancer, JH, SD, NRD, V). Bred by Liz Krupinski; owned by Liz Krupinski and Tim Bintner.

CH Monterra's Best Bet, MH

CH Monterra's Best Bet is America's first Best in Show, Master Hunter Weimaraner. Stoli earned his Senior Hunter title two weeks before his second birthday and exactly on his second birthday he earned a Best in Show. He continued with his hunt work and earned his Master Hunter title before his third birthday in five straight tests, a truly stellar accomplishment!

At a young age, Stoli instinctively understood holding his game and honoring other dogs, which may be due to his pheasant hunting trips, which started when he was six months old. He sailed through his junior hunter in four consecutive tests, even honoring his junior brace mates. While not flawless, he finished his senior hunter title in five tests, but pretty good for a dog not yet 2 years old. Even, more impressively Stoli earned his Master Hunter title in five straight tests, including four qualifications in one weekend.

Stoli's kind, intelligent expression and silliness endear him to all who he meets. He is a joy to live with and shares his life with three humans, two Weimaraners, and three Vizslas. He is easygoing and has that wonderful Weimaraner sense of humor.

Stoli was trained and started in field and show by his owner Liz, but an unexpected medical condition cut their competition time short. Proving his ease with people, Stoli was easily handled by Connie Williams in the 2007 western futurity and won best dog. Friend Tad Walden continued training and handled Stoli for the Best in Show and SH. He also won second place with Stoli in the 2008 southern maturity and in early 2009 earned his Master Hunter. Stoli is co-owned with Liz's spouse Tim Bintner.

CH Nani's Tsurutani Honor Bound, JH

CH Nani's Tsurutani Honor Bound, JH, was the result of line-breeding a CH Nani's Southern Cross granddaughter, CH Nani's Jagmar Sweet Dividends, VCD2, MH, MX, MXJ, NSD, NRD, VX4, BROM, to a very promising unproven young sire, CH Nani's Indecent Exposure, JH, NAJ, V, BROM, who was a CH Nani's Southern Cross grandson.

Bounder made his mark early in the breed ring, winning his first major during a Specialty weekend at just 6 months of age and his second major during the Southern Futurity/Maturity weekend at 7 months of age. Once Bounder finished his Championship, he traveled to Hawaii to finish growing up with his co-owner Karen Taniguchi and sired his first litter out of BIS CH Greydove's 'Ekahi Island Gal. The resulting litter has produced four U.S. champions to date and a son with an Australian Best in Show, earned before he was 1 year old.

In 2006, Bounder returned to the U.S. for the National Specialty, where he rewarded his co-owner's decision to make the trip by going Best of Opposite Sex at the National Specialty under Carl Liepmann. Carl's comments regarding Bounder were, "Strong on the down and back and equally powerful on the go around, he was macho all of the way."

Figure 30-79: *CH Nani's Tsurutani Honor Bound, JH* (CH Nani's Indecent Exposure, JH, NAJ, V, BROM × CH Nani's Jagmar Sweet Dividends, VCD2, MH, MX, MXJ, NSD, NRD, VX4, BROM). Bred by Teresa Borman and Christine Grisell; owned by Karen Taniguchi and Christine Grisell.

He returned to the States to be specialed by co-owner Chris Grisell in 2007. During that year, he earned several Group 1s and Best in Specialty wins and ended the year in the Top 10 List for both Show and Breed.

Bounder returned to Hawaii in early 2008 and continued his winning ways, culminating in a Best in Show win at the Windward Hawaiian Dog Fanciers under Judge Dorothy Mac-Donald, expertly handled by Daryl Oliveira.

Bounder is a very balanced dog with a solid topline, a forward free flowing gait, and a stable temperament, which he has passed on to his offspring.

CH Harline Win'Weim It's My 2nd Martini

"Olive" is owned by Susan Line and Dana Massey, bred by Susan Line, Dana Massey, and Michael Anderson, and is always shown by Susan Line. Olive goes everywhere with Susan who refers to Olive as her "purse." Olive is a multiple-group winner who finished her championship with four majors from the BBE. She received a first award of merit at the prestigious AKC Eukanuba Championship show in Long Beach, CA, in 2008. A promising youngster just starting her career—Olive was 20 months old at her first Best in Show under Judge Robert Shreve after winning the group under the legendary Miss Virginia Lyne. Olive made her entry onto the 2009 Top Weimaraners in the U.S. as the No. 1 Weimaraner in All Breed competition. As the old saying goes, this "Olive" did not fall far from the tree! Her sire is "Streak" National CH Nani's Indecent Exposure, JH, NA, V, BROM. Not only was Streak a National Specialty Winner, but he was a Top Twenty Winner, Best in Futurity, Best in Maturity, Pedigree Top Producing Sire, Best of Breed at Eukanuba, and multiple group and specialty show winner. Her dam is "Dagmar" CH GraytSky Win'Weim It's My Prague-ative. Dagmar is an All-Breed Best in Show winner, seven-time Best in Specialty winner—including the WCA Winter Specialty, with AOMs at the WCA Nationals, Eukanuba, and Westminster.

Figure 30-80: *CH Harline Win'Weim It's My 2nd Martini* (CH Nani's Indecent Exposure, JH, NA, V, BROM × CH GraytSky Win'Weim It's My Prague-ative). Bred by Susan Line, Dana Massey, and Michael Anderson; owned by Susan Line and Dana Massey.

Figure 30-80: *She's got high hopes!* The winsome 28-week-old puppy is CH Zara's ZZ Zinderella, NSD. Bred and owned by Carole Richards and Jack McCourt. Photograph by Jack McCourt and Carole Richards.

Figure 31-1: *Tom and Desi Hansen with National Field Champions all trained and handled by Tom.* Left to right, NFC FC Kipbirtzel's Texas Kid with Al Forsyth, 1979 and 1980; NFC FC AFC Laine's Thor v Time Bomb with Gorden Hansen, 1981; NFC DC Jafwin's One and Only with Bruce Crowthers, 1982; NAFC FC AFC DC's Hons Tobie v Sieger with Virgil and Trudy Jennings, 1982 and 1983; NFC FC Outdoors Boots with Shirley Hansen, 1983; NFC FC Birtzel's Lay Back Zach with Milly Showers, 1984.

CHAPTER 31

BEST IN FIELD

by Sharon Sturm

The field trial evolved from a friendly day of shooting to a friendly competition to find out who had the "best" and most versatile hunting companion. These early events were almost exclusively patterned after the German hunting evaluations with hunters on foot, carrying their own gun, and shooting for themselves whatever birds were found. These competitions grew more popular and rules emerged to level the playing field. The rules were also changed to accommodate the emerging professionals who were handling dogs for those who were unable to either walk the long courses or whose marksmanship was less than adequate to test the dog's retrieving skills. Although field trials today can be extremely competitive the spirit of friendly competition can still be found. Refer to *Weimaraners Afield* and *Starting the Gun Dog* for more information on the training and trials themselves.

This chapter is a celebration of significant events, people and dogs who have marked the history of the Weimaraner in the bird fields of the United States. For a complete list of Field Champions, please refer to the Appendix.

The WCA National Field Trial

The NFC

The first WCA National Field Trial was held at a New Jersey game farm in November 1950. Twenty-three entries from all over the country gathered to run in the open all-age and open derby stakes. All entrants had to demonstrate water retrieving ability and had to place in regional qualifying trials (a prerequisite until 1968).

In a history of the WCA National Field Trial written for the 1984 program, John Lennon, the WCA's historian, set the scene of the first National field trial held in 1950:

"Although organizational and physical variations in the conduct of the National have evolved over the years, perhaps the greatest difference between the first one and those held only a few years subsequently was in philosophy. Judge Evelyn Monte, in her report to the American Field on the 1950 National, described the philosophy of that event: '...this was no effort of the part of the Weimaraner fanciers to promote their dogs as adversaries for pointer and setter field trial contenders. The trial was run just as

Figure 31-2: *Early influence.* Helen Schultz (German liaison for the WCA), Joseph Albanese, and Gilbert Wehmann (early Presidents of WCA) helped develop early Weimaraner field trials to mirror the German hunting experience and tests of the parent club in Germany. Handling their own dogs, hunters walked the course and (hopefully) shot their own birds.

the dogs are used in the field, as close shooting dogs.' Thus, the running of the first trial was designed to simulate natural hunting conditions. To that end, handlers walked and carried shotguns during the running; birds were shot by the handlers on the back course, as well as in the bird field to demonstrate the dog's retrieving ability, and, at the conclusion of the field work, double water retrieves for all-age dogs and single ones for the derbies were an integral part of the judges' evaluation of the winners."

Many features of the first National gradually changed. Shooting on the back course was eliminated and official gunners were added. In 1953 the all-age stakes were expanded to one-hour heats and handlers were allowed the option of horseback handling. Over time, these changes significantly impacted the style of the dogs running, favoring wider-ranging dogs and giving the foot-sore professional handlers a break.

After the 1951–1954 Nationals were held in the Midwest, the WCA adopted the practice of rotating locations—East, Midwest, West—a practice still followed with the National specialty show. After rotating to Ardmore, Oklahoma, in 1968 and 1971, the WCA chose Oklahoma's lovely Lake Murray grounds as the permanent site of the National field trial held the first week of December.

Another critical change occurred in 1968, when WCA field events were first run under AKC regulations. Until then, national, regional, and local trials followed American Field regulations. Instead of cumulative points, American Field recognizes specific events as championship stakes and awards the title to winners if their performance is of championship quality. Thus winners can hold several American Field championship titles. Winners of more than one championship stake indicated this with a numeral followed by a slash—for example, 7/Fld. CH Fritz von Wehmann aus Rockledge. In the tradition of this event the winner is still named the National Field Trial Champion.

Over the years, new stakes have been added to showcase the Amateur all-age dogs, the Derbies and the Futurity. The National Field Futurity (the last of the four sectionals held as part of the WCA's Field Futurity program) is sandwiched between the National Field Championship (NFC) and the National Amateur Field Championship (NAFC). After the conclusion of the NAFC, the final stake, the National Open Derby, is run according to AKC Derby rules. The Weimaraner Foundation Fund (see *The Weimaraner Club of America*) awards the first- and second-placing dogs a scholarship for continued field trial training to encourage promising young dogs to continue to the next level.

Figure 31-3: *Enter the professional handler.* The professional handler, such as Chet Cummings, compensated for the owner who was either unable to walk the long courses or whose marksmanship was inadequate to demonstrate the dogs' retrieving skills. Officially allowed in competition in 1953, a horse allowed the professional to handle many more dogs in a single trial. Since the mounted handler afforded the dog better contact at greater distances, the use of the horse resulted in the Weimaraner's straying away from the original roots of the close and thorough hunting dog of our German ancestors.

Figure 31-4: *During the early years of the Nationals,* the dog wagon and the gallery were offered a much clearer view since the closer hunting dogs kept the gallery tightly bunched as they paralleled the action. In the early 1950s the handler walked and was required to take the shot himself if the opportunity presented itself. In modern days a continuous course and increasing range means the gallery must maintain a respectful distance behind the judges and may get only a few brief glimpses of the brace after the breakaway. Radios are necessary to maintain contact between the stake manager and the dog wagon to arrange the drop-off and pick-up as the braces change after the one-hour heats.

Today, these WCA National stakes, unlike many events, are run on a continuous course. That is, the first brace casts from the line. When the brace has run for the designated time, the dogs are picked up and a new brace begins from that point, rather than returning to the original starting line. A dog wagon transports the dogs in each upcoming brace to their starting point and picks up the dogs that have completed their run. The handlers for all the braces ride along as part of the gallery until it is time to run their dog. It is no longer required to pass a water test before entering a trial. In order to complete an AKC Field Trial Championship the dog must pass a water test or NRD. The top-winning dogs of today's NFC and NAFC must cast quickly and far, show steadiness to wing shot, and fall with blanks used on the course, and demonstrate a full retrieve only in a callback. Although the goal of sportsmanship and competition is still the same, the times have indeed changed from nearly 60 years ago, when the dog's owner walked the course, shooting and receiving to hand whatever birds his dog pointed.

Figure 31-5: *The gallery has a good view* of the running at the 1959 National.

WCA National Field Championship Historical Highlights

1950 Inaugural National Field Trial held (American Field regulations) Open all-age and open derby stakes (handlers on foot)

1952 Amateur derby and amateur all-age stakes added

1953 All-age stakes extended to 1-hour heats, first-year optional horseback handling allowed

1955 Water retrieving as a requirement to enter the Nationals eliminated

1956 First field futurity held

1961 Last year amateur derby held

1968 Change Field Championship from American Field to AKC rules

1974 First year the WFF provided training scholarships to the 1st and 2nd placements in the National Derby (See WFF in Chapter 3)

1975 Derby or Open Stake (Amateur, Limited, or All-Age) placement requirement added to enter the Championship Stake

1986 Field futurities added to the three sectional Classic events

1999 Only Open Stake (Amateur, Limited, or All-Age) placements accepted to enter the National Championship

2006 Field trial headquarters erected on the Lake Murray grounds, partially funded by the WFF and dedicated to Dub Emde

Figure 31-6: *Major stakes are often sponsored by well-known dog food companies.* Standing atop her 1995 National Amateur's Field Champion prize, NFC NAFC FC AFC Outdoors Magic Misty expresses her opinion that this is one of the most popular awards at the WCA's National event among dogs and handlers alike.

Figure 31-7: Owner Gilbert Wehmann (former WCA President) with *FC Fritz von Wehmann aus Rockledge, RDX, SDX, HOF* (CH Cuno v. d. Harasburg, Import × Pinky of Rocklege) on the left. Archrival FC Grafmar Kings Aid (DC Palladin Perseus × Grafmar's Reward) on the right.

Top Winners

The top winner of WCA National Field and National Amateur Field Championships is pretty much a dead heat between two memorable campaigners. One must be impressed by the fact that three of the breed's four top winners of National events are dual champions.

FC Fritz von Wehmann aus Rockledge, RDX, SDX, HOF

One of the most recognized campaigners at National events was FC Fritz von Wehmann aus Rockledge, RDX, SDX, HOF, owned by Gil Wehmann (1963–1965 WCA president) and trained and handled by Chet Cummings. Fritz started his WCA roll in style by winning the open and amateur derby stakes in 1953. He took the open all-age stakes in 1956 and 1957 and the amateur all-age titles in 1958 and 1960. Then, to cinch his record, he again won the open title in 1961 at the age of 9 years.

DC AFC Top Deaugh, MH, NRD SDX, VX, HOF

DC AFC Top Deaugh, MH, NRD, SDX, VX, HOF owned by Charlie Williams is one of the breed's most durable campaigners, ranking on the Top 10 field list for five consecutive years: 1987–1991 (6, 9, 6, 6, 6). Topper swept the national amateur all-age championship for four consecutive years (1988–1991), trained and handled by his owner, Charlie Williams. For good measure, he captured the 1991 open all-age title, just a few weeks before his 10th birthday.

DC Palladian Perseus, HOF

DC Palladian Perseus, HOF began his illustrious career by winning the open derby (1951). Just one year later, the talented dog owned by O.W. Ogilvie followed up by winning the amateur all-age stake in 1952, the open in 1954, and the amateur again in 1955 and 1956.

DC AFC Othen's Princess Pretty, NRD, SDX, VX

In fourth place for national honors and first place for bitches, was DC AFC Othen's Princess Pretty, NRD, SDX, VX, who won the open and amateur championships in 1973, and repeated her sweep in 1974 for a total of four national titles (1973, 1974 top 10). She was trained by Ken Jellings and handled in amateur stakes by her owner Tom Glennon. She is still the only Weimaraner to capture both all-age stakes for two consecutive years.

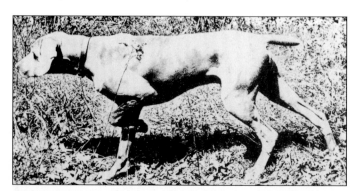

Figure 31-8: *DC Palladian Perseus, HOF* (Ricki of Rocklege × CH Debar's Platinum Pallas). Bred by Mrs. Donald Bullock; owned by O.W. Olgilvie. Photograph courtesy of the Weimaraner Club of America.

Figure 31-9: *DC AFC Top Deaugh, MH, NRD SDX, VX, HOF,* one of the breed's most durable campaigners, won more National Championships than any other field or dual champion; taking home the silver for the National Amateur Field Championship from 1988–1991, and topping it off by winning the National Field Championship as well in 1991 Field Trial chairman, Patrick Petriangelo (middle left) presents owner/breeder Charlie Williams (far right), his wife Sue (middle right), and handler Tom Hansen (far left) with Topper's trophies at the National Field Trial in 1991.

Four outstanding males have each won three national titles

FC AFC Alger's May Day, NRD, SDX, HOF: 1948 open all-age; 1978, 1979 amateur all-age; 1974 derby Top 10 (1); 1977–1981, 1983 top 10 (1, 1, 4, 1, 1, 8)

FC AFC High Ridge Jesse von Horn, HOF: 97 NFC, and 98 NFC, 98 NAFC and was the top field all-age gun dog for an unprecedented five consecutive years.

FC Kipbirtzel's Texas Kid, NRD, SDX: 1979, 1980 open all-age; 1980 amateur all-age; 1978–1982 top 10 (7, 1, 2, 6, 6)

FC Von Whitcomb's Tor, RDX, SDX: 1962 and 1965 amateur all-age, 1965 open all-age

Figure 31-10: *DC AFC Othen's Princess Pretty, NRD, SDX, VX* (CH Val's Veto v. d. Reiteralm, NSD × CH Othen's Velvet Venus, BROM). Bred by Duncan Othen; owned by Tom and Irene Glennon. Princess not only captured the national open all-age and amateur all-age stakes in 1973 but also repeated her sweep of both stakes in 1974. Princess, handled by Ken Jellings in the National Stakes and by her owner, Tom Glennon, in the Amateur, is the only Weimaraner to win both the National All-Age and the Amateur in two consecutive years.

Fifteen dogs have won two national titles

Bitsu von Basha, HOF: 51 NFC, 52 NFC

Deal's Upland Fantasy: 53 NFC, 53 NAFC

FC Grafmar's King's Aide: 59 NFC, 59 NAFC

CH Gerri v Fabian, HOF: 55 NFC, 58 NFC

FC Mac von Whitcomb: 61 NAFC, 63 NFC

Schultzie's Gretchen von Bach: 66 NAFC, 68 NAFC

DC Pine Grove Farm's Brunhilde, HOF: 64 NAFC, 67 NFC

FC Unserhund v Seiger, HOF: 75 NFC, 76 NFC

FC AFC DC's Hon's Tobie v Seiger: 82 NAFC, 83 NAFC

FC Lay Back Nick Chopper, SDX, HOF: 88 NFC, 90 NFC

FC AFC Hoglund's Tiger von Thor: 93 NFC, 94 NAFC

FC AFC Outdoors Magic Misty: 94 NFC, 95 NAFC

DC Snake Breaks Saga v. Reiteralm, CD, MH, RDX, VX2: 99 NFC, 02 NAFC

FC AFC Scooby Doo's Treeline Storm, CDX, NRD, V: 00 NFC, 03 NAFC

FC AFC Grau Geist Lil's Gust v. Westend, CD, RE, MH, SDX, RDX, VX: 02 NFC, 05 NAFC

FC AFC Sasha's Nogoodnic: 07 NFC, 07 NAFC

Table 31-1: *All-Age Gun Dog of the Year*

	Dog	Owner
2008	FC Axel's Bleu Bayou of Reiteralm	S. Tsantes and S. Parkowski
2007	NFC NAFC FC AFC Dietz's Sasha Nogoodnic	P. Dietz
2006	FC AFC Windancers Jota v. Reiteralm	B. Wayson and V. Alexander
2005	NFC NAFC FC AFC Grau Geist Lil's Gust v. Westend	D. and C. Gould
2004	NAFC FC AFC Gould's Jus Call Me TJ	D. and C. Gould
2003	NFC FC AFC Grau Geist Lil's Gust v. Westend	D. and M. Meifert
2002	NFC FC AFC Grau Geist Lil's Gust v. Westend	D. and M. Meifert
2001	2xNFC NAFC FC AFC High Ridge Jesse Von Horn	J. Goldstein
2000	2xNFC NAFC FC AFC High Ridge Jesse Von Horn	J. Goldstein
1999	NFC NAFC FC AFC High Ridge Jesse Von Horn	J. Goldstein
1998	NFC FC AFC High Ridge Jesse Von Horn	J. Goldstein
1997	FC High Ridge Jesse Von Horn	J. Goldstein
1996	FC AFC Outdoors Dakota	J. Cushing
1995	Outdoors Wingfield Duffy	D. Coller
1994	NAFC FC AFC Snake Breaks Sgt Schultz	S. Reynolds
1993	FC AFC Outdoors Tony Lama	G. and S. Hansen
1992	FC AFC Outdoors Tony Lama	G. and S. Hansen
1991	FC AFC Outdoors Tony Lama	G. and S. Hansen
1990	FC Falke Von Horn	M. Horn
1989	FC Grendel Von Horn	M. Bjornsen
1988	FC Mile Hi Casper v. Gip	V. Hess

Figure 31-11: *2xNFC NAFC FC AFC High Ridge Jesse von Horn* (FC Grey Wynn Bad to the Bone × FC Ida Augusta Von Horn), 97 NFC, 98 NFC, and 98 NAFC and was the top field all-age gun dog for an unprecedented five consecutive years.

Figure 31-12: *NFC 2NAFC FC AFC Alger's May Day* (FC Unserhund v Sieger × BL's Sabrina v Staub) was crowned top field all-age gun dog 4 years.

Table 31-1: *All-Age Gun Dog of the Year (continued)*

	Dog	Owner
1987	FC AFC Baja's Zephyr	B. and G. Hansen
1986	DC AFC Lady Athena of Camelot	S. Thomas, G. Studeny, C. Crosby
1985	Edith Ann Von Horn	M. Horn
1984	FC Ambrose	A. Forsyth
1984	FC Gandalf's Indian Summer	D. and T. Lyons
1983	Ambrose	A. Forsyth
1982	FC DC's Hans Tobie Von Sieger	V. Jennings
1981	FC AFC Alger's May Day	J. and P. Alger
1980	FC AFC Alger's May Day	J. and P. Alger
1979	FC Kipbirtzel's Texas Kid	A. Forsyth
1978	FC AFC Alger's May Day	J. and P. Alger
1977	FC Alger's May Day	J. and P. Alger
1976	FC Strevlyn's Storm Trysail	J. Sterling
1975	FC Ichabod	B. Windon
1974	DC Lilith v Hirschhorn	H. Hirschhorn
1973	DC Othen's Princess Pretty	T. and I. Glennon
1972	Unserhund von Sieger	W. and A. McGinty
1971	FC Heizar's Chief Oshkosh	H. Danforth
1970	FC Lady Baron's Win-ee	J. Babb
1969	FC Lady Baron's Win-ee	J. Babb

Figure 31-13: *NFC NAFC FC AFC Grau Geist Lil's Gust v. Westend* (NFC FC AFC Westend's Li'l Sage Rider × NFC FC AFC Graugeist Lilith von Legs) topped the list of all-age gun dogs for 3 years.

Figure 31-14: *NFC FC AFC Edith Ann Von Horn* (FC Weinerschnitzel's Bad News × Gandalf Fleiginde Nonne) is the dam or granddam of the top all-age gun dog on eight occasions.

The Weimaraner at Field Trials

The Weimaraner began competing in field trials under the American Field and converted to the AKC rules in 1968. Although the obvious and ultimate goal has remained the same, the complexion of the field trial has changed over the years, just as most dog sports have (such as conformation and obedience). Travel is much easier now but access to land is more restricted. Laws regarding wildlife have also impacted the conduct of field trials.

In the early years while competing under American Field rules, the Weim was respected as the gentleman's gun dog. Conversion to AKC rules and competition with the pointing specialists left a bit of tarnish on the gleaming silver dog's reputation in the field. However, as the years have progressed the Weimaraner continues to gain a reputation as a dog not to be dismissed out of hand. More and more Weims are gaining their Field Championship and

Figure 31-15: *The Winter Specialty heralds the beginning of the Ardmore week events.* CH Nani's Emma von Derr winning Best of Breed from the Veterans Class at the 2001 Winter Specialty. Emma was owned and handled by the late Dorothy Derr, greatly admired Executive Secretary of the WCA.

National Championship Callbacks

Figure 31-16: *National Championship callbacks then and now:* from haywagons in 1959 to digital cameras operating from custom-built SUVs in 2008.

Amateur Field Championship, with wins at the all-breed trials. Oddly enough, while the top dogs at the WCA National Field Trials are often the most competitive at Weimaraner and all-breed field trials throughout the year, there are some exceptions. The WCA began keeping a list of the top 10 field dogs in 1969. This list recognizes the dogs that are consistently top performers throughout the year.

The National Field Trial is an important social event as well! In recognition of the dual nature of the Weimaraner, since 1989 the Winter Specialty segues into the National Field Trial. Fanciers and field trialers alike, many who have not seen each other in the past year, have a chance to mingle, cheer for the winners of the conformation show, receive the running order for each of the stakes, and exchange preparations for the upcoming trial while enjoying food and drink from the lavish buffet. The National/Field Trial begins as the first brace casts off promptly at 8 am the next morning. Each stake allows a gallery to follow. Borrow or rent a horse. Not a rider? Try the hay wagon in fair weather. The gallery and hay wagon provide a chance to see some of the top dogs run and to discuss the finer points of training and trialing with knowledgeable folks, as well as meeting those new to the sport.

After the conclusion of the last brace of the day, more social events are planned for each evening; one of the most popular is the Texas Tequila Party and most recently the "Winner's Banquet." Traditionally, the winners of the previous year's National Championships plan and host this event.

The stakes are run in a specified order: National Field Championship, Futurity, Amateur, and Derby. Although it is typical that the trial concludes on the following Saturday with the running of the Derby, the unpredictable nature of the weather and the number of entries have resulted in the trial concluding as late as Sunday. Irrespective of the timing of the stakes the National Raffle and Awards banquet is always held on Friday evening. The awards are presented for the National Field Trial champion, the Futurity Winners, and the National Amateur champion. The Charlie Williams Award is presented for outstanding sportsmanship and contributions to the Weimaraner breed. The last presentation is the infamous Armadillo Award for the dog with the most memorable encounters during the previous week.

December 2004 Schedule of Events at Ardmore, Oklahoma

Thursday December 2:   Board Meeting

Friday, December 3:   Board Meeting continues
                                                  Welcome Party
                                            Winter Specialty Show

Saturday, December 4:   National Championship begins
          Winner's Party (hosted by last year's winners)

Sunday, December 5:   Continue National Championship

Monday, December 6:   Final braces for National Championship
                    Callbacks for National Championship
          Cincinnati Chili Party (In honor of Fred Melcher)

Tuesday, December 7:   Field Futurity begins
                 Maria's Garden—Ladies' Night Out

Wednesday, December 8:   Run final braces Field Futurity
                    Amateur Championship begins
                Amateur Party (hosted by the Pros)

Thursday, December 9:   Continue Amateur Championship
                Stephanie's Boutique—Ladies' Night Out

Friday, December 10:   Final braces for Amateur Championship
                 Callbacks for Amateur Championship
         National Awards Banquet Lake Murray Lodge

Saturday, December 11:   National Derby begins
                  Awards when Derby is completed

Figure 31-17: *A birdless dog is not a winning dog....* In the case of the continuous championship courses at Ardmore, an ATV allows bird planters, unsung heroes such as Ron Hudson and his cohort Joe Fingerlin, to efficiently "salt" the course, ensuring that the big running dogs are given the best chance to show bird work that will catch the judge's eye. Refer to the Appendix for John Rabidou's article, "Give the Dogs a Chance," to learn how bird planting techniques can affect dog performance.

Figure 31-18: *A last-minute polish* for the stunning silver trophies to be presented at the Friday evening National Field Trial Banquet.

Figure 31-21: *Spirited Calcuttas* are held which allow spectators to "bid" on the dogs that they favor to win in the derby and amateur stakes.

Figure 31-19: *Fanciers check their "stretch" of tickets.* Raffles are held at the Winter Specialty and the Awards Banquet to benefit the WOOF Fund.

Figure 31-22: *Coffee and conversation* can be found in the WCA's new "garage." A recent addition to the amenities at the Ardmore grounds, named in honor of Dub Emde, serves as a warmer substitute for the historic hay wagon. New technology, such as cell phones, allows spectators to keep abreast of events as the braces run.

Figure 31-20: *A family affair.* Many young handlers get their first taste while riding the course with a parent at the National Field Trial.

Figure 31-23: *The Armadillo Award.* A fun-spirited presentation awarded each year to the dog with the most memorable armadillo contact during the National Field Trial.

Figure 31-24: *The Charlie Williams Award* is presented annually for outstanding contributions to the field Weimaraner. It represents the dedication and sportsmanship that was Charlie's hallmark. Ever willing to help others advance their dog's performance and consistently endeavoring to improve the breed, Charlie influenced not only the breed but uncounted Weimaraner owners outside the field trial as well. Between 1969 and 1978, Charlie ran 16-week field dog training classes in Colorado, and later free weekend seminars around the country, to teach people to train their field dogs. Roy Pelton receives the 2007 Award from Charlie Williams's beloved wife, Sue Williams. Previous winners include Joe Fingerlin (2004), Eugene Green (2005), and Virginia Alexander (2006). In 2008, this award was presented to Shirley and Gorden Hansen (2008).

Figure 31-25: *Dub Emde and his wife Tommie enjoy the Lake Murray grounds with Shirley Hanson.* In 1968, the Weimaraner Club of America discovered Ardmore, Oklahoma, and a love affair with Lake Murray began as the ideal place to run the WCA National Field Trials. Dub, self-appointed ambassador, was there to lend a hand at every field trial on the grounds regardless of the breed affiliation, not just the Brittanies he loved so much. Regardless of what was needed, from birds to water, Dub would get it; from official gunner to road repair, Dub would do it. And rather than just "maintain" the status quo, each year the grounds improved as a result of Dub's efforts. Since his passing in March 2005, the Dub Emde Memorial Building was dedicated on the Lake Murray grounds; its shelter and hospitality are a fitting tribute to one who always gave more than he took.

Noteworthy Bloodlines and Kennels

Andicks: Dick and Andrea Pearson
Ardreem: Linda Frisbee
Arimarlisa: Jackie Isabell and Lisa McClintock
Aztec's: Tom and Eileen Ingala
Birtzel's: Roy Pelton
Blitzkrieg: Lance Fargo
Borg's: David and Nancy Borg
Briarmeadows: Eugene and Doris Green
Camelot: Sue Thomas
Caprocks: Kevin and Vicki Jar
Cherrystone: Pam Cherry
Daroca: Rosemary Carlson
Davison: Alan and Marcia Davison
Deaugh: Charlie and Susan Williams
Elden: Dan Richmond
Erbenhof: Judy Mitchell
Flatlands: Larry Walsh
Gandalfs: Danny and Tina Lyons
Goulds: David and Cathy Gould
Grafmar: Margaret Horn
Grau Geist: Dick and Mary Wilber
Grayshadow: Dave Carriveanu
GRB's: Gina Bosio
Grey Wynns: Ken Miller
High Ridge: John Goldstein
Jafwins: Frank and Jennifer Sexton

Jax: Jack Potter
Knights: Holly and Randy McKnight
Layback: Kay Love
Legends: Joseph Stroup
Let's Go: Philip and Elizabeth Letzo
Markee: Tom and Tina Markee
Mile High: William and Jackie McClure
Newbury: Bob and Kay Snyder
Nimrod's: Harry Hirschhorn
Nordsee: Marg Wilson
Northern Lights: Mark Beaven
Norton Creek: Earl and Margit Worsham
On-The-Rise: Bill and Patti Kuehnhold
Othen's: Duncan Othen
Otter Creek: Barbara Auerback
Outdoors: Gorden and Shirley Hansen
Ozark: Joel Hatch
Palomar: Paul and Mary Lester
Pecan Creek: Mike Freeman
Quest Found: David Turbin
Redhill: Ted and Lorie Jarmie
Regen: Judi Voris, Anne Tyson and Shirley Nilsson
Reiteralm: Virginia and Mark Alexander
Richmark: Cecil and June Beaven
Rockledge: Leon Arpin
S and S: Stanford and Mary Schemnitz

Saga's: Mary and Jeff Brown
Sanbar: Sandy West
Shadowmar: Dorothy Remensnyder
Silver Blue: Ray Lumpkin
Silver Rain: Leslie Like
Silvershot: Judy Balog
Sirius: Richard and Helene Moore
Smokey City: Tom Wilson
Snake Breaks: Steve Reynolds
Starfire: Lynn Berryman
Stoneangel: Pat and Barb Pietrangelo
Texmara: Gene and Barb Dagenhart
Tri D's: Bill and Carole Donaldson
Von Harwil's: Joanne Hardy
Von Horn: Marilyn Horn
Von Knopf: Don and Lou Button
Von Luchbach: Dan and Cindy Long
Von Wehmann: Gil Wehmann
Von Weiner: Diane Vater
Von Whitcomb: Whit Overholtzer
Wayback's: Wayne and Beverly Cowgill
Weinerschnitzel: Shirley Paulsen
Westend: Myron and Debra Meifert
Windancer: Jay and Dubose Fleming
Winstars: Ray Bowman
Zdon: Stanley and Doreen Zdon
Zum Ziel: Nicholas and Aline Scharpf

Amateur Owners Handlers and Breeders of Note

Figure 31-26: *Ted and Lori Jarmie* bred under the Redhill kennel name, producing many top field trial and show winners through the 1960s and 1970s. Ted and Lori were both show judges and Ted judged the National Championship several times. FC AFC Greta v. Kollerplatz SDX (CH Alf v Luckner × Gretchen of Lakeland's Star). Bred by Herbert D. Hoon; owned by Ted and Lorie Jarmie. Redhill's foundation dam, Greta was the first bitch to hold both the AKC and American Field championships. From three litters, she produced show and field champions and is the double granddam of DC Redhill's Fanny Jo, SDX.

Figure 31-27: *The Overholtzers* became involved with Weimaraners in the 1960s, and the Von Whitcomb Weimaraners earned multiple wins in the National Open and Amateur Championships. Whit's dogs also won in Weimaraner and all-breed trials on the West Coast. The Overholtzers' children frequently handled the dogs in retrieving tests as well as tracking.

Figure 31-28: *Bob and Kay Snyder* were active in the 1960s and 1970s breeding and trialing with Ken Jellings as their handler under the Newbury kennel name. Newbury dogs won six National Field Futurities and four National Derbies. They also carded many wins and placements in the Mid-America and Eastern Classics. Their breedings were based on the bloodlines of FC Fritz v. Wehmann and FC Duke v. Gunston.

Figure 31-29: *Charlie Williams* started with Weimaraners in the early 1950s, and his dog Patty was one of the first to get AKC field points. When he bred Charlie's Angel II to Weiner-schnitzel's McDuff he founded the "Deaugh" prefix, which has continued to produce foundation breeding stock. Some of his other noted dogs were 1985 NFC FC Super Deaugh, SDX, NRD, NFC; 4xNAFC DC AFC Top Deaugh, MH, VX, SDX, NRD; 2xNFC FC Lay Back Nick Chopper, SDX, NRD. Charlie's advice to breeders: breed the dog to meet the standard; don't lower the standard to meet the dog. Charlie was also well known on the field trial circuit for what he always carried in his saddle bags: candy to be shared with all who rode in the gallery.

Figure 31-30: *Shirley Paulsen* began breeding her line of Weiner Schnitzel Weimaraners in the late 1960s. Shirley started with a male named Michael Weiner Schnitzel and two bitches with prominent field trial bloodlines. Several dogs of the Weiner Schnitzel line are on the top-producing field sire and dam lists today and are found in the pedigrees of recent and present field trial winners. Weiner Schnitzel's McDuff (foreground) and Mister Plywood as Derby dogs with breeder/owner/handler Shirley Paulson.

Figure 31-31: *Marilyn Horn,* of New Jersey, won the 1991 Eastern Classic with FC Grendel Von Horn. She has been breeding successfully for many years with her Von Horn line of field winners. Von Horn dogs have won five National Championships and two National Amateur Championships plus many placements in the Classics. Marilyn supports the field trial Weim with her well-planned breeding program, but she also contributes to the breed through her mentoring activities, as well as her detailed recordkeeping of field bloodlines and their performance.

Figure 31-32: *Cecil and June Beaven* of Canada won the 50th WCA National Amateur Championship with NAFC AFC Northern Light's This Buds ForU, handled by their son Mark Beaven. Field trials are a family affair for the Richmark Kennel. They are regular fixtures and always welcomed for their contribution to field trial operations (June specializes in helping run the breed calcuttas with her spicy humor and good spirits). Having a highly selective breeding program, the Beavens are noted for their support of their new puppy owners and aspiring breeders.

Figure 31-33: Eugene Green and Tom Hansen (handler) are congratulated for winning the 2001 National Field Trial Championship with Eugene's homebred NFC FC Briarmeadow Buck. Known as "Mr. Ardmore" or occasionally "Grandfather Weimaraner," Eugene Greene is perhaps one of the longest continuously and still currently active Weimaraner field trial competitors today. His efforts have been indispensable in the continuing improvements to the Ardmore grounds for the National Field Trial. His ability to bring Texas hospitality to Ardmore for this national event guarantees that Eugene Green is fondly regarded by all.

Figure 31-34: *Dick and Mary Wilber,* of Lubbock, Texas, have run a "non-kennel" kennel for more than 25 years, since all of their dogs are in-home companions and personal gun dogs, as well as field trial competitors. Producing fewer than one litter a year, they have still established bloodlines that have provided an excellent genetic base for many contemporary field trial winners. To their credit, they have 19 Field Champions, with many more close to finishing and two National Champions, of which one was also a National Amateur Champion. A family portrait of foundation dogs of Grau Geist (top clockwise): Qizef von Nimrod's Lil CD (No. 12 top field-producing dam), FC AFC Grau Geist Marlene, NFC FC AFC Grau Geist's Lilith von Legs (No. 6 top field-producing dam), and FC AFC Qizef's Grau Geist Gruppe B.

Figure 31-35: *Gorden and Shirley Hansen* have been breeding under the Outdoors kennel name since the 1970s and have finished many Field Champions under the prefix. Gorden has handled three dogs to their National Amateur Field Championships, and the Hansens have recently garnered a Dual Championship from their breeding program. They have the distinction of being the breeders and owners of FC AFC Outdoors Tony Lama, the breed's top-producing dam of field champions. Gorden and Shirley recently began training and handling Weimaraners professionally. A few of the offspring from the Outdoors line: Gorden Hansen with Outdoors Reno; Nicolle Vincze with FC Outdoors Twister; Shirley Hansen with FC Outdoors Sport; David Routhier with DC Outdoors Life of Riley and Outdoors Princess; and John Vincze with FC Gould V Three Remington.

Figure 31-36: *Until her untimely death, Lue Button* was a staunch supporter and mentor of the versatile Weimaraner, as well as an award-winning author of books on tracking and Search and Rescue. She made significant contributions in research on the use and abilities of K9 scent detection. Most people remember Lue most fondly for her kindness and mentoring of those new to the world of dog sports.

Figure 31-37: *The Zdons.* Field trialing is truly a family adventure, with everyone participating in every aspect of trialing as owners, breeders, trainers, and handlers. They recently made a splash in the Weimaraner field trial circuit with Gould's Just Git R Done v Zdon, by winning all three of the major stakes at the 2009 Eastern Classic, trained and handled by the same amateur owner-handler in all of the stakes, Although they are relative newcomers to the Weimaraner field trial circuit, they have quickly gained the respect and admiration of their fellow competitors. AFC Grey Wynn's Xena Von Zdon, JH, their talented foundation bitch, is behind most of the stock they are currently running.

Figure 31-38: *The Beginning of Reiteralm.* Author, Virginia Alexander at age 13, with her first purebred dog, Jenny. Virginia led Jenny to earn the first Utility and Utility Dog Tracking titles on a Dalmation; in those days, when you paid the $3 entry fee for the conformation classes, the entry for junior handling and obedience were free. Ironically, Virginia's first experience in training field dogs was with Jenny as she taught the Dalmatian to earn her keep by pointing game and retrieving ducks that her father shot. Jenny's prolonged and eventually fatal renal disease also led Virginia to a career studying, and later teaching, physiology and genetics. Eventually Virginia and her cat-loving husband, Mark, imported Bella v. d. Reiteralm from Germany, adopting Weimaraners as "their" breed, and founding the Reiteralm Kennel name. Fifty years later, Bella's German influence is seen in the pedigrees of 66 of the 71 Best in Show dogs since her arrival in the United States. Bella's Reiteralm bloodlines have earned six National Field Trial Championships and produced 25 Dual Champion.

Figure 31-40: *David and Cathy Gould,* based in Northern California, are avid amateur field trialers who have developed a very successful breeding program stemming largely in recent years from the many talented offspring of their homebred bitch, NAFC FC AFC Gould's Jus' Call Me TJ. Currently tied for 2nd top-producing field trial dam with six FCs and two AFCs, she is also the mother of 3 National Field Champions: FC NFC Gould's Wicked Runner (2003), NFC FC AFC Gould's GRB's Little Chular, NSD (2006), and NFC FC Gould's Farwest Lunatic (2008). With such consistent performances, it seems likely the future holds more outstanding field dogs as the offspring of the current Gould program pass on their talents.

Figure 31-39: *Early experiences are needed* to cement the power behind the proven field trial pedigree of these nine hopeful pups. The Weimaraner is often a late-maturing pointing dog. Despite this, early opportunities, from 5 weeks on, are critically important for each pup

to reach its greatest potential. Successful field breeders have discovered that the most promising prospects come from litters where each pup has had one-on-one experiences to realize the power of his nose (such as the German practice of tracking the breeder hiding in tall grass), coupled with the earliest possible exposure to wild birds (to balance developing prey drive with the understanding that birds should be stalked and pointed as soon as possible since they cannot be caught). Most importantly, these field outings encourage confidence and promote independence. Maximizing genetic potential also involves selecting owners who are willing to invest in continuing the development process, after the initial 8 weeks of imprinting by the breeder, through a fun-filled and enriching environment (refer to *Starting the Gun Dog*). Photograph courtesy of William Wegman.

Homage to the Professional Handlers

It could arguably be said that without the dedication of professional Weimaraner field trial handlers, the Weimaraner would not be as successful in field competition as they are.

Not just because of their success in competition, but because professional handlers understand that Weimaraners are not oddly colored English or German Shorthaired Pointers. Professional handlers are willing to accept that the training methods used on many pointing dogs are not always the most effective with the high IQ and personality of the Weimaraner. And not only are they par excellence in the skills of training dogs, but many of these truly remarkable professionals have been willing to share their knowledge and have impacted not only the dogs they handled, but their owners as well.

Figure 31-42: *Ken Jellings* launched his career by taking his first Weimaraner, FC Ranger's Revenge, to win the 1964 National Field Trial. An auspicious beginning, this tall lanky Marine would go on to train and handle one of the longest series of winners the breed had seen in many years. During the course of his 30-year professional career, Ken trained and finished 46 FCs, eight of which were also Dual Champions, five National Champions, uncountable regional all-age and derby wins, as well as many Futurity and Derby Champions. Although closely associated with Bob and Kay Snyder's Newbury Kennel, Ken dominated the field trial scene, in his own name, during the 1960s and 1970s, handling dogs from many bloodlines. A number of bench champion owners discovered that Ken's flexible and positive training methods made it possible to earn a coveted Dual Champion. Ken has left an indelible mark on the field trial Weimaraner world because he was always available as a judge and mentor for almost any field activity or event.

Figure 31-41: *Chet Cummings* became a Weimaraner legend in the 1950s as the first professional trainer to take the Gray Ghost to wins in field trials. Chet won the inaugural WCA National Open with Ricki of Rockledge in 1950. He went on to handle seven winners of the National Championships in the 1950s and early 1960s. He also piloted the Weimaraner Crested Glade Warrior to the title in the inaugural running of the National German Pointing Dog Championship in 1955. Perhaps his most notable successes occurred while handling FC Fritz von Wehmann aus Rockledge, RDX, SDX, HOF, to five National Championships.

Figure 31-43: *Larry Walsh,* of Eastern Washington, started training and handling in the early 1980s. He was most helpful to all those he met, teaching them to train and handle their own dogs in competition. Ever ready to share a helpful hint, Larry was a true sportsman, finding his greatest satisfaction through the successes of those people and dogs he taught. He will be sadly missed by all those who were lucky enough to have known this multifaceted and jovial sportsman.

Figure 31-44: *Mary and Tim Hildago* campaigned all four of DC Wynwood's Rain on the Rise (top left with owner Bill Kuehnhold) offspring to their Field Championships: FC Storm Warning on the Rise (with Patty Keuhnhold, top right), DC Dust Storm on the Rise (with Mary, bottom left), FC AFC Davison's Orion on the Rise, MH, and FC Lightning Strikes on the Rise (both with Tim, bottom right). The team of Tim and Mary, based at their centrally located Oklahoma ranch, can be found competing coast to coast to present the Weimaraner in Weimaraner-only as well as all-breed trials.

Figure 31-45: *Roy Pelton* started trialing in the early 1970s after successfully training and handling his own DC Birtzel von Staub. Roy finished many Field Champions and trained and handled the unforgettable Hall of Fame NFC FC Unserhund V. Seiger to two National wins. Unser and his get dominated wins at the National-level trials in the late 1970s and 1980s. Unser's name can be found in the background of many of today's competitive field dogs. Roy also appreciated the show dog that was well put together and had a special knack for gently tutoring the field-talented Bench Champion into a Dual Champion. Retired from active trialing for more than 15 years, Roy continues to support the WCA Nationals each year—a convivial host to the judges and welcome source of advice, encouragement, and counsel to handlers.

Figure 31-46: ***Tom Hansen*** turned professional trainer and handler in 1975. In 1977, he won his first National with New Worlds Wild Hunter and went on to win a still-standing record 15 National Championships (of the last 24), establishing himself as a legend in the breed. For more than two decades, Tom and his wife Desi traveled from coast to coast every year to support Weimaraner field trials. He trained in Washington State in the summer and in Stillwater, OK, in the fall. His young dogs won eight Futurities, and his owners won at least 10 National Amateur titles. Tom was always interesting to be around, ever willing to help when needed. See Figure 31-1 of this chapter for more highlights of his amazing career.

Figure 31-47 *Scott Beyer* started with his dad, who was a highly respected and successful field trainer with GSPs and Gordon Setters; Scott added Weimaraners to his string of dogs in the early 1990s. He won the National twice with FC High Ridge Jessie V. Horn and maintained Jessie at the top of the WCA National open all-age field dog standings from 1997–2001. Quiet, with a gentle hand for his dogs, he was a true competitor and carded several National Futurity wins. Devoted to his family, Scott's move to Florida to help his father's game farm was a real loss to Weimaraner field trialers. Known for being as patient with people as he was to his dogs, he continued to mentor those who were willing to travel to see him.

Figure 31-48: ***Steve Reynolds*** and his two favorite "training partners," Sgt Schultz and Rudi, along with their field futurity-winning and Field Champion offspring. Having been raised with Weims, and devoting his professional career to Weims only, Steve is particularly familiar with the breed because his father was responsible for importing several of the earliest hunting Weimaraners from Germany to the U.S. Hunting with Weimaraners "since he was old enough to walk," Steve quickly became known for his quiet and gentle way with dogs, as well as his consistent success. In fewer than the 14 years that Steve has been a professional, he has finished titles on more than 30 dogs, including almost 30 National Field Trial winners and placers.

Figure 31-49: *Dan and Cindy Long* present Gray Shadows Field Laureate after winning the 2002 National Derby Championship. Located in Ohio, this team offers an unusual combination of services for the dual-minded Weimaraner owner. The centrally located kennel gives them access to field trials and conformation shows across the country. Both Dan and Cindy are talented handlers in the field; Cindy, however, brings an additional dimension as a successful show handler with multiple Futurity and Maturity wins, as well as National Specialty and Best in Show victories to her credit.

Figure 31-50: *Mike Mullineaux* and FC Axel's Bleu Bayou v Reiteralm, the 2008 WCA Top Gun Dog of the Year. After considerable success running German Shorthaired Pointers and Vizslas on the East Coast, in the last few years Mike has established himself as a top contender with Weims at all-breed trials. A retired Army dog trainer and knowledgeable behaviorist, he has helped his clients obtain top gun dog ratings. With Mike's support and coaching, owner Stephanie Tsantes contributed to Bleu's success by handling her dog in the amateur stakes.

Figure 31-51: Deborah and Myron Meifert with some of the successful field champion offspring of NFC FC AFC Westends Lil Sage Rider, HOF. The Meiferts started out as a hunting-hobby kennel under the Westend name; they arrived with a bang 15 years ago when Sage Ryder hit the field trial circuit. The Meiferts have recently turned professional and continue their winning ways while still offering advice and support to those with dogs who have their bloodlines. NFC Ryder has produced a lengthy list of successful offspring carrying the Westend name, and is currently the top field-producing sire. Left to right are Field Champions Goulds V Three Remington, Grau Geist Bold Rebel Sol, Goulds GRB's Little Chular, Grau Geist Cowboy Take Me Away, Grau Geist Lil's Gust v Westend, Grau Geist Lil's Femme Nikita, and Windancer's Jota V Reiteralm.

These six women have competed and succeeded at the Nationals, at the highest level of competition, in a field typically dominated by men.

Figure 31-52: *Barbara Heller* was the first woman handler to win a Weimaraner Club of America National Title. In 1964, DC Pine Grove Farm's Brunehilda, HOF, and Barbara won the National Amateur Field Championship. Mrs. Heller was an early advocate of the dual Weimaraner; she was equally at home in the conformation ring as in the field and she expected her dogs to not only meet the breed standard but to be a polished field dog as well. While Chet Cummings frequently handled Brunehilda, either Barbara or her husband Herbert handled the dog in the amateur stakes. After the death of her husband, she went on to become a well-respected judge in the breed and group and was tapped to judge the Sporting Group at Westminster Kennel Club's prestigious show.

Figure 31-53: *Jackie McClure* won the 1981 National Amateur Field Championship with FC AFC Weinerschnitzel Gipsi McDuff, becoming the first woman to breed, train, and handle to a WCA national field title. While Jackie was a welcome source of advice and willing mentor to anyone who asked for help, it was rare that Jackie trained or handled dogs other than her own. The carefully cultivated bloodlines Jackie, Shirley Paulsen, and Charlie Williams created, known by the Weinerschnitzel and Deaugh names, have gone on to provide foundation stock for many of today's field-trial-winning bloodlines.

Figure 31-54: *Twenty years later, Mary Brown* would pilot DC Snake Breaks Saga v Reiteralm, CD, MH, RDX, VX2, to the 2002 National Amateur Field Championship. Steve Reynolds handled Saga to the 1999 National Field Championship when Saga was just 3 years old. Mary continued to develop Saga's versatility and competed with Saga in retrieving, obedience, and field. To date, Saga is the only NFC to hold a WCA versatilty rating of VX2. Saga's success is just beginning to be told. Presently the sire of five FCs, his upcoming offspring give promise to many more field winning progeny.

Figure 31-55: *Diane Vater* was the first, and so far the only person, to handle the same dog to win all four Field Futurities (including the National Field Futurity) with NFC NAFC FC AFC ScoobyDoo's Treeline Storm, CDX. Scooby and Diane would add the icing on the cake when the two-year-old Scooby also won the National Field Trial Championship that same year. Diane's background as an obedience trainer and her passion for fieldwork were good starting points. She turned pro in the late 90s. Add her high energy level, penchant for hard work, and a great training partner and scout in her husband Chuck Cooper, and the result has been phenomenal success by any measure. Competing in field trials across the country, Scooby's offspring have provided Diane and Chuck with a nearly continuous parade of trips to the winner's circle.

Figure 31-56: *Pam Dietz and her sister-in-law, JoAnne Hardy,* reflect the spirit of the true amateur sportswoman, enjoying the entire experience of training and field trialing. Together, they have shared many years of triumphs and disasters in competition in field and show events with the Harwil bloodlines. Pam and NFC NAFC FC AFC Sasha's Nogoodnic revel among the masses of silver-plate trophies reflecting Sasha's successes at the 2007 WCA National Field Championship in Ardmore and the Mid-America. Sasha became the first dog since 1991 to win both the NFC (handled by Diane Vater) and NAFC (handled by Pam) in the same year. A year of success was capped by a well-earned ranking of WCA's No. 1 Gun Dog of the year. Not long after this photo, Sasha delivered a healthy litter of 10 pups in a unique artificial insemination by two sires FC Jax's Waybac Tyler and FC Grau Geist Lil's Caprock Rev.

Figure 31-57: *Gina Bosio gave the Weimaraner Field Trial scene notice* when on a cold February day in 2001 the novice who had trained and handled her year-old puppy, Chular, to 1st place in Open Derby and Open Walking Derby. Later that year, they would win the Field Futurity and Open Derby at both the Mid-America and the Nationals in Ardmore. The highlight of Chular's field career would culminate with her win at the 2006 National Championship. Gina continued her field-trial winning ways with two other dogs, GRB's Mia Dolce Vita and GRB's Hearty Burgundy. Gina's four Field Futurity and National Championship wins with owner handled and trained dogs has gained great respect and admiration from her peers. Most will agree that it is Gina's teamwork and rapport with her dogs that is truly exceptional; however, Gina gives Chular most of the credit, saying Chular always "runs with her whole heart. Giving everything she has and more."

Figure 31-58: *Record-breaking five Field Champions from one litter* sired by NAFC FC AFC Snake Breaks Sgt. Schultz out of FC Briarmeadow Sunshine Abigail. Left to right, FC Reiteralms Snake Breaks Dot Com; FC AFC Winstar's Diamond Lil; Dam FC Briarmeadow Sunshine Abigail; FC Windancer Izzy von Reiteralm; FC Snake Breaks Wanted in Idaho; sitting in front, FC Snake Breaks Run Wild Idaho.

Figure 31-60: *Pin-up pup.* Saga's Blitzkreig v Reiteralm began his career by working his way through bird-dog school, posing as a pin-up for owner Lance Fargo's Coastal Printing. When a serious injury placed a temporary hold on his field career, Blitz went back to modeling while recovering from surgery to remove a large portion of one lung before once again returning to the field to finish his championship.

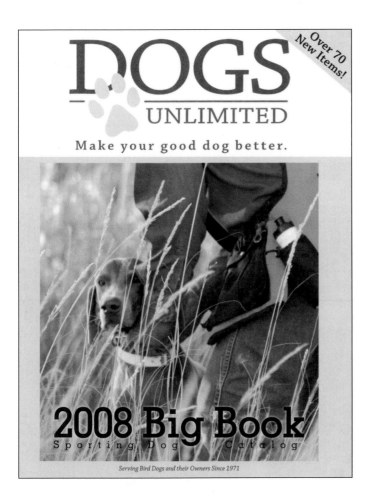
Figure 31-59: *Workin' Weims.* Retirement has led to an even busier schedule for NAFC FC Robynski Deaugh Davison. After a career as a top Field Trial dog, the National Amateur Field Trial win in 2001, and field trial producer (No. 8 Top-Producing Field Trial Sire with seven field-trial-titled offspring), Robie moved on to a new career, testing and modeling the field equipment for the Davison's newly purchased company, Dogs Unlimited.

Top-Producing Sires

Name	Field Champions	Amateur Field Champions	Dual Champions	Show
FC AFC NFC Westend's Li'l Sage Rider, CD, SH, NSD, NRD, V	17	4	1	1
FC AFC Andick's Big Time Jake	16	5		1
NFC FC Unserhund Von Sieger, SDX, HOF	13	5	1	2
FC AFC NAFC Snake Breaks Sgt Schultz, HOF	12	2	2	2
NFC FC AFC Laine's Thor Von Time Bomb, SDX, HOF	6	4		1
FC AFC NAFC Northern Light's This Budsforu	6	2	1TC	1
Weiner Schnitzel's McDuff, NSD	6	2		1
FC NAFC Robynski Deaugh Davison, JH	6	1		
FC Grey Wynn Bad to the Bone	5	5		
FC NFC Lay Back Nick Chopper, SDX, HOF	5	3		
NFC FC Shenandoah Drummer Boy, RD	5	1	1	2
FC Outdoors Rising Sun	5		1	1
DC NFC NAFC AFC Snake Break's Saga V Reiteralm, CD, MH, RDX, VX2	5			1
FC NAFC NFC AFC High Ridge Jesse Von Horn, HOF	4	3		
NFC FCH Birtzel's Lay Back Zach	4	2		
FC AFC Stormcrow's Deaugh Blitzen, SH	4	2		
CH Redhill's Satellite, SDX	4		1	6
NFC NAFC AFC Von Whitcomb's Tor, SDX, RDX	4			1
NFC FC Ranger's Revenge	4			
NFC NAFC FC AFC Grau Geist Lil's Gust V Westend, MH, CD, RE, SDX, RDX, VX	3	2		
FC Weiner Schnitzel's Bad News	3	2		
DC Halann's the Judge V Reiteralm, BROM, SDX, RDX	3	1	1	8
FC Newbury Gustave	3	1	1	1
NFC AFC Hoglunds Tiger Von Thor	3	1		
CH Maximilian Vom Der Reiteralm, NSD, BROM, HOF	3		2	62
FC Elsmere's Baron Aus Wehmann	3		1	5
CH Axel Reiteralm of Weimar's Joy, CD, JH, RD, NSD, VX (Import)	3			7
CH Mckenna's Dirk	3			1
DC NFC AFC The Sundance Kid, CD, NRD, VX	3			
FC AFC Falke Von Horn	2	2		
FC Gould's Thunder Und Blitz, JH	2	2		
CH Von Sieben's Smart N Special, NSD, BROM, HOF	2	1	2	28
DC Birtzel's Johnny Reb, NSD, RD, VX	2	1		1
FC AFC Mile Hi Caspar V Gip	2	1		
DC AFC NFC NAFC Top Deaugh, MH, SDX, NRD, VX, HOF	2	1		
FC Outdoors Fritz's Duke	2	1		
Box River Big Chili	2	1		
DC AFC VC Magnum Gunnar Silvershot, MH, SDX, RDX, VX, BROM	2		2	9
CH Eichenhof's Ginger Man, BROM	2		2	8
CH Ludwig Von Dottlyle	2		2	5
Wolfgang Von Sachsengang, JH, CD, NSD, NRD, V	2		2	3
CH Valmar's Jazzman, CD, NSD, NRD, V, BROM	2		1	80
Braunhilde's Silver Blaze, NRD	2		1	3
DC NFC AFC Gents Silver Smoke, CDX, RDX, VX	2		1	2
Texmara's Jeb the Great, SD, NRD	2		1	2
Lucky Deaugh	2		1	1
NFC NAFC FC Fritz V Wehmann Aus Rockledge, SDX, RDX, HOF	2			3
DC Zandor Vom Lechsteinhof, CD	2			
FC AFC Ruburn's Duser Bruiser	2			
FC Duser's Amazin Ace	2			
FC NFC Briarmeadow Buck	2			
FC NFC AFC Scooby Doo's Treeline Storm, CDX, NRD, V	2			

Order of precedence was determined in the following order: # FC, # of AFC, # DC, # of CH, and date of appearance in the AKC stud book (oldest to newest).

Top-Producing Sires of Field Trial Champions

Figure 31-61: No. 1 Top-Producing sire of Field Champions *NFC FC AFC Westends Lil Sage Rider, CD, SD, NSD, NRD, V, HOF* (FC AFC Falke Von Horn × Westends Desert Star). Owned by Myron and Debra Meifert. Run, style, desire, the heart of a true champion are a few words that describe the leading sire of Weimaraner field champions, NFC FC AFC Westend's Lil Sage Rider. This tough little dog from Oregon had many judges sitting big in the saddle, watching his fine performances, which earned him a spot on the Top 10 Field Trial Dog lists: Derby in 1994 and 1995 and All-Age Gun Dog 1996, 1997, and 1998; he continued his winning ways by taking the National Field Championship in 1996. But the mark of a truly prepotent sire is the quality of his get and Ryder's kids have more than measured up. The sire of four National Field Champions and one National Amateur Field Champion, Ryder's get won eight of the WCA's field futurities between 1998 and 2004. Ryder has produced 17 field champions, four amateur Field Champions, and one Dual Champion.

Figure 31-62: No. 2 Top-Producing sire of Field Champions *FC AFC Andick's Big Time Jake* (NAFC FC AFC DC's Hons Tobi Von Sieger, SDX, NRD × FC Rosa Andick Luxembourg). Owned by Virgil and Trudy Jennings.

Figure 31-64: No. 4 Top-Producing sire of Field Champions *NAFC FC AFC Snake Breaks Sgt Schultz* (2x NAFC FC Lay Back Nick Chopper, SDX × Baby Deaugh, SH, SD, NRD). Owned by Steve Reynolds.

Figure 31-63: No. 3 Top-Producing sire *FC Unserhund Von Sieger, SDX,* 75 NFC, 76 NFC. (FC Shenandoah Drummer Boy, RD × Aumar's Mona). Owned by William and Adele McGinty.

Figure 31-65: No. 5 Top-Producing sire of Field Champions *NFC FC AFC Laine's Thor Von Time Bomb, SDX* (Brought-Mars Time Bomb V Tor × Mikesell's V Maggie). Owned by Gorden and Shirley Hansen.

Figure 31-66: No. 6 Top-Producing sire of Field Champions *NAFC FC AFC Northern Light's This Budsforu* (NAFC FC AFC Gray's Ghost Hunter, JH × FC AFC Richmark Hot Tamale, JH). Owned by Cecil Beaven.

No. 7 Top-Producing sire of Field Champions *Weiner Schnitzel's McDuff, NSD* (FC Michael Weinerschnitzel, SDX, NRD × Taylor's Heidi). (See Figure 31-30). Owned by Shirley Paulsen.

Figure 31-67: No. 8 Top-Producing sire of Field Champions *NAFC FC Robynski Deaugh Davison, JH* (FC AFC Andick's Big Time Jake × Prairie Deaugh, MH, SDX, NRD). Owned by Alan and Marcia Davison.

Figure 31-68: No. 9 Top-Producing sire of Field Champions *FC Grey Wynn Bad To The Bone* (FC AFC Andick's Big Time Jake × Cadney Dellie Con Mac). Owned by Ken Miller.

Figure 31-69: No. 10 Top-Producing sire of Field Champions NFC FC Lay Back Nick Chopper, SDX (FC AFC Mile Hi Casper Von Gip × Gandalf Lay Back LC Smith). Owned by Charles and Susan Williams.

Figure 31-70: No. 11 Top-Producing sire of Field Champions *FC Shenandoah Drummer Boy, RD* (FC McKee's Silver King × Van Heidi's Ginger Snap). Owned by Ivan and Pam Lawyer.

Figure 31-71: No. 12 Top-Producing sire of Field Champions *FC Outdoors Rising Sun* (FC AFC Andick's Big Time Jake × FC AFC Outdoors Tony Lama). Owned by Patrick Thiel.

Figure 31-72: No. 13 Top-Producing sire of Field Champions *DC NFC NAFC AFC Snake Break's Saga Von Reiteralm, CD, MH, RDX, VX2* (NAFC FC AFC Snake Break's Sgt Schultz × FC Arimarlisa's Rudi Von Reiteralm). Owned by Jeff and Mary Brown.

Figure 31-73: No. 14 Top-Producing sire of Field Champions *NFC NAFC FC AFC High Ridge Jesse Von Horn* (FC Grey Wynn Bad to the Bone × FC Ida Augusta Von Horn). Owned by John Goldstein.

Figure 31-74: No. 15 Top-Producing sire of Field Champions *NFC FC Birtzel's Lay Back Zach* (Weiner Schnitzel's McDuff × Britzel's Lookaway Dixieland). Owned by Millie Showers.

Figure 31-75: No. 16 Top-Producing sire of Field Champions *FC AFC Stormcrow's Deaugh Blitzen, SH* (DC NFD NAFC AFC Top Deaugh, MH, SDX, NRD × Prairie Deaugh, MH, SDX, NRD). Owned by Chuck Cooper.

Figure 31-76: No. 17 Top-Producing sire of Field Champions *CH Redhill's Satellite, SDX* (FC Elsmere's Baron Aus Wehmann × FC AFC Greta Von Kollerpaltz, SDX). Owned by Ted and Lori Jarmie.

Figure 31-77: No. 18 Top-Producing sire of Field Champions *FC AFC Von Whitcomb's Tor, SDX, RDX* (Joch Von Whitcomb, CD, TD × Berry's Heidi Der Bratt, CD). Owned by Whitcomb Overholtzer.

Top-Producing Dams

Name	Field Champions	Amateur Field Champions	Dual Champions	Show
FC AFC Outdoors Tony Lama, HOF	8	2		
NAFC FC AFC Gould's Jus Call Me Tj	7	4		
Treeline's Lyza Jayne	6	2		
FC AFC NFC Grau Geist's Lilith Von Legs, NRD, V	6	1		
Weimaracres Kipbirtzel, SDX, NRD	5	2	1	1
NFC FC AFC Edith Ann Von Horn, SDX, NRD, HOF	5	2		
DC Wynwood's Rain on the Rise, SDX, NRD, VX	5	1	1	3
Weiner Schnitzel Seme Scoot	5	1		
FC Briarmeadow Sunshine Abigail	5	1		
Gandalf's Fleiginde Nonne, SD, NRD	4	3		
Cocoa Von Shorian	4			
Qizef Von Nimrod's Lil, CD, RDX, SD, V	3	2		
NFC FC AFC Outdoors Boots	3	2		
FC AFC Qizef's Grau Geist Marlene	3	2		
FC AFC Richmark Diamond	3	2		
FC AFC Markee's Rumor Has It, JH	3	2		
Deaugh Daze, SH	3	1	1	1
FC Arimarlisa's Rudi V Reiteralm	3	1	1	1
Prairie Deaugh, MH, SDX, NRD	3	1		
Fairview's Arrow	3			
FC Windchymes	3			
CAN CH Reiteralm's Absolute Point, JH, NSD	3			
Bk's Sabrina Von Staub, NSD, NRD	2	2		
FC AFC Markee's Shelby Centerfold, SH, NSD	2	2		
Outdoors Gould's Electricity	2	2		
CH Redhill's Song Girl, CD, NSD, NRD, BROM	2	1	2	7
TC AFC Regen's Summer Blaze, RE, VCD3, UDX2, SDX, RDX, MH, MX, MXJ, VX6, BROM	2	1	1TC	5
NAFC FC Weiner Schnitzel's Gipsi McDuff, NRD, SD, V	2	1		1
Mikesell's Von Maggie	2	1		
Orkan's Dutchess v. d. Reiteralm	2	1		
Sharp's Lady Genevieve	2	1		
Westend's Desert Star	2	1		
FC Grau Geist's True Love Ways, RD	2	1		
CH Arimar's Desert Diana, NSD, NRD, V, BROM	2		2	5
DC Sirius Really Rosie, CDX, JH, RD, VX2, BROM	2		2	4
Schaden's Kuhl Luca V Ardreem, CD	2		2	3
CH Kristof's Proud Heritage, NSD	2			3
FC AFC Greta Von Kollerplatz, SDX	2			2
FC Outdoors Twister	2		1	1
Aumar's Mona	2			
Darwin's Dakota Belle	2			
Dawnell's Silver Satin	2			
Deal's Game Huntress	2			
FC AFC Sandcast Sandy Rose	2			
FC Denab Von Andick	2			
FC AFC Outdoors Shawnee	2			
V Hennerich's Zephyr V Horrido, JH, NSD, NRD	2			
Grau Geist's Lil's Grau Haus Maus	2			

Order of precedence was determined in the following order: # FC, # of AFC, # DC, # of CH, and date of appearance in the AKC stud book (oldest to newest).

Top-Producing Dams of Field Trial Champions

Figure 31-78: No. 1 Top-Producing dam of Field Champions *FC AFC Outdoor's Tony Lama, HOF* (NFC FC AFC Laine's Thor Von Time Bomb, SDX × NFC FC AFC Outdoor's Boots). Owned by Gorden and Shirley Hansen. The Top-Producing FC dam for more than 13 years, Tony is not only the mother of eight FCs and two AFC's, she is also the only dam to produce an unprecedented seven Field Futurity winners. Although an exceptional producer, motherhood did not deter her from a successful career in the field. She was the WCA's top all-age gun dog for 3 consecutive years, from 1991–1993. The loving care, training and handling of Gorden and Shirley Hansen helped Tony produce an unusually long and successful field career as well, winning an all-age gun dog stake at an all-breed trial when Tony was 13 years old. Tony continued to enjoy her position as top dog from the passenger's seat of the Hansen's truck until her passing at the age of 17. In recognition of her incredible career and contributions to the breed, Tony Lama was inducted into the WCA Hall of Fame in 2009.

Figure 31-79: No. 2 Top-Producing dam of Field Champions *NAFC FC AFC Gould's Jus Call Me TJ* (FC Gould's Thunder Und Blitz, JH × Outdoors Gould's Electricity). Owned by David and Cathy Gould.

Figure 31-81: No. 4 Top-Producing dam of Field Champions *NFC FC AFC Grau Geist's Lilith Von Legs, NRD* (Mile Hi Bandit Von Gip × FC AFC Qizef's Grau Geist Marlene). Owned by Dick and Mary Wilber.

Figure 31-80: No. 3 Top-Producing dam of Field Champions *Treeline's Lyza Jane* (FC Outdoors Rising Sun × FC Windchymes). Owned by Jack Potter.

Figure 31-82: No. 5 Top-Producing dam of Field Champions *Weimaracres Kipbirtzel, SDX, NRD* (CH Birtzels Happy Von Reiteralm × Biene Vom Haischbachtal, CD, SDX, NRD). Owned by Dorothy Pelton.

Figure 31-83: No. 6 Top-Producing dam of Field Champions *NFC FC AFC Edith Ann Von Horn, SDX, NRD* (FC Weiner Schnitzel's Bad News × Gandalf's Fleiginde Nonne, SD, NRD). Owned by Marilyn Horn.

Figure 31-84: No. 7 Top-Producing dam of Field Champions *DC Wynwood's Rain on the Rise, SDX, NRD* (CH Valmar Smokey City Ultra Easy, JH, NSD × CH Vanoah's Glory Hallelujah, NSD, NRD). Owned by Bill and Patty Kuehnhold and Greg and Sharon Hartmann.

Figure 31-85: No. 8 Top-Producing dam of Field Champions *Weiner Schnitzel Seme Scoot* (Michael Weiner Schnitzel, CD, RD, SDX × Baby Doe Von Touber). Owned by Shirely Paulsen.

Figure 31-86: No. 9 Top-Producing dam of Field Champions *FC Briarmeadow Sunshine Abigail* (FC Outdoors Rising Sun × FC Windchymes). Owned by Ray Bowman.

Figure 31-87: No. 10 Top-Producing dam of Field Champions *Gandalf's Fliegende Nonne, SD, NRD* with DC The Sundance Kid (FC Unserhund Von Sieger, SDX × DC AFC Shadowmar Arthemis Impeda, CDX, SDX, RDX). Owned by Marilyn Horn.

No. 11 Top-producing dam of field champions *Cocoa Von Sorian* (Vi Mar's Sportenhoff's × Gretchal Von Leemhuis). Owned by Tom Taylor.

Figure 31-88: No. 12 Top-Producing dam of Field Champions *Qizef Von Nimrod's Lil, CD, RDX, SD* (Baikiel Von Nimrod's Eks Crook × DC Lilith Von Hirschhorn, CDX, TD, RDX, SDX). Owned by Dick and Mary Wilber.

Figure 31-89: No. 13 Top-Producing dam of Field Champions *NFC FC AFC Outdoors Boots* (Weiner Schnitzel's McDuff, NSD × Weiner Schnitzel's Seme Scoot). Owned by Gorden and Shirley Hansen.

Figure 31-90: No. 14 Top-Producing dam of Field Champions *FC AFC Qizef's Grau Geist Marlene* (NFC FC Birtzel's Lay Back Zach × Quizef Von Nimrod's Lil, CD, RDX, SD). Owned by Dick and Mary Wilber.

Figure 31-91: No. 15 Top-Producing dam of Field Champions *FC AFC Richmark Diamond* (FC Newbury Silver Knight × Autumn Robin). Owned by Cecil and June Beaven.

Figure 31-92: No. 16 Top-Producing dam of Field Champions *FC AFC Markee's Rumor Has It, JH* (FC Grey Wynn Bad to the Bone × FC AFC Markee's Shelby Centerfold, SH, NSD). Owned by Tom and Tina Markee.

Figure 31-93: No. 17 Top-Producing dam of Field Champions *Deaugh Daze, SH.* (Weiner Schnitzel's McDuff, NSD × Charlie's Angel II, SDX). Owned by Charles and Susan Williams.

Figure 31-94: No. 18 Top-Producing dam of Field Champions *FC Arimarlisa's Rudi Von Reiteralm* (FC AFC Andick's Big Time Jake × CH Woodspur's Blue Chip). Owned by Steven Reynolds and Virginia Alexander.

A Champion of the Heart

CH Lightfoot Whisper the Wind, JH, NRD, NSD, HOF
"Windy"

From the beginning, breeder Debbie Moody knew Windy was a special pup. Earl Worsham was an experienced Weimaraner owner and would provide Windy with all the advantages a typical Weimaraner appreciates. Only fate would know that they would each provide the other with much, much more.

Windy earned her bench championship easily, and her natural birdiness and drive made the WCA Novice Shooting Dog title a breeze as well. Windy's future was bright and hopeful. When Windy showed no interest in the quail one weekend, Earl and his wife knew that something must be terribly wrong. After several consultations and weeks of treatment with no improvement, a trip was scheduled to the University of Georgia for more extensive testing; Windy was diagnosed with an advanced case of an unusual fungal infection called blastomycosis.

The veterinarians offered treatment and the Worshams agreed to do all they could for Windy. But Windy had the heart of a champion, and she made the decision to never give up. The treatment was long and painful and not without setbacks. Complications resulted in the removal of both of Windy's eyes, but that seemed to do the trick, and Windy soon began a remarkable recovery. A week later she went home with her family.

Windy immediately set the standard; she didn't want any special treatment, and the Worshams agreed. Windy's true heart became apparent as life returned to "normal." Long walks through the mountainous Worsham property saw Windy casting to the front as she quickly learned to compensate for her loss of sight with her other senses. Soon Windy returned to swimming. Not long after that Windy made it clear she still had a passion to retrieve.

On August 21, 1988, a bare 6 months after Windy's illness, her recovery was "official" when she earned the WCA's Novice Retrieving Dog rating. With her amazing nose, she found the fallen bird and, using her keen hearing, completed the 20- to 40-yard retrieve returning to her handler standing within a marked 12-foot circle; when she repeated this performance for the water retrieve, there was not a dry eye in the gallery. In her daily life, Windy continued to refuse to allow her physical "limitations" to set limits on her life. She loved to hunt and Earl obliged. In the spring of 1989 Earl and Windy earned their Junior Hunter title in four consecutive tests. The two demonstrated true teamwork; Earl would maintain verbal contact to allow Windy to determine just how far to range, allowing Windy to confidently and efficiently locate the wily quail by scent alone, surely a feat never before achieved by a sightless dog.

Windy continued to live her life, refusing to be treated as "handicapped." Whether she was ever frightened by her circumstances, we will never know. She reigned over her domain with confidence and assurance until she peacefully passed away in Earl's arms when she was 12. She was judged a conformation champion based on her physical attributes, but as a champion of the heart, she was honored in 2005 by her induction into the Weimaraner Club of America Hall of Fame.

What the Future Holds

Field trials of today have altered in many ways since their inception. In the early days, trials attempted to imitate as much as possible a day's hunt afoot and to reward mannerly, well-rounded, bird-hunting dogs working in close partnership with their owner. Over time, field trials have changed to reward qualities of ambitious range, maximum groundspeed, intense desire, and high style on bird work with a significantly reduced emphasis on both retrieving capability and polish. Within the breed, there are strong advocates both for and against the way in which field trialing has developed. However, whichever version is preferred, it remains that Weimaraners competing in field trials throughout history have proven themselves in the vast majority to be top-notch real-life hunting companions.

For a newcomer, the field trial world can be dauntin—professional handlers and serious amateur competitors pulling big rigs with several horses and up to dozens of dogs on their stakeouts, horseback handling and a second horseback mounted scout often a necessity to best showcase and handle a dog, and a competitive atmosphere—but fortunately the field trial community is typically very welcoming and supportive of new arrivals, particularly those willing to pitch in and support the host club with the multitude of jobs needing to be done at every trial, everything from filling bird bags for the birdplanters to flipping burgers in the hospitality tent. Many local Weimaraner clubs wisely offer juvenile amateur walking stakes as well as some walking gun dog stakes as a way to accommodate new participants, who may not be comfortable on a horse. Some clubs even offer seminars on basic horsemanship and bird-planting. When taken one step at a time, the journey from promising puppy to Field Trial Champion can be both an achievable dream and also a thrilling adventure.

On a broader scale, in recent times there have arisen significant new challenges affecting anyone involved with bird dog training and competition. Population growth has limited the availability of training, trialing, and hunting grounds, animal-rights activist groups are attempting to thwart hunting-related activities of all kinds, and urbanization has reduced the number of people able to keep horses, flocks of homing pigeons, or gamebirds. In response to these challenges, professional trainers may play even a greater role in the development of hunting and trialing dogs than they previously have; private shooting preserves are already increasing in number to provide new access sites for training and trialing. This trend may continue. Recently, political action has begun to rebuff the positions taken by animal-rights lobbying groups. How these factors will play out over time remain unclear, but it behooves the entire community of field trialers to be particularly respectful and appreciative of private property owners with regard to land access and use, to ensure that the transport, housing, care, and dispatch of game birds used in field events are done humanely, and to always have the health, well-being, and safety of the horses and dogs involved in the sport be of foremost concern.

—Shirley Nilsson

Figure 31-95: *The chain gang* waiting for the fog to clear at a field trial. Photograph by Shirley Nilsson.

Diesel

OBEDIENCE

FIELD

TRACKING

SHOW

TC CT Regen's Rip Stop, VCD3, UDX4, MH, SDX, RDX, VX6 (NAFC FC AFC Northern Lights This BudsForU × TC AFC Regen's Summer Blaze, VCD3, UDX2, RA, MX, MXJ, MH, SDX, RDX, VX6). Bred by Judith Voris and Shirley Nilssen; owned by Anne Tyson and Judith Voris.

By finishing his Tracking Championship in May 2009, Diesel became the breed's first quadruple AKC Champion (read about his mother, Ruby, the first Triple Champion Weimaraner on the overleaf of The Weimaraner Club of America, at the end of this chapter). In many respects, Diesel's career in obedience, field, conformation, and tracking has been nothing short of phenomenal. He started with a bang, finishing his OTCH at 3 years of age, spending 2003–2009 on the breed's Top 10 obedience list (3 years as No. 1). He set a new record for lifetime OTCH points before he turned 4 and has earned more than 30 High in Trial wins and nearly 20 High Combined awards. See *The Obedient Weimaraner* for more on Diesel's obedience career.

While he loves all activities, he lives to hunt. Diesel began his field career with a 2nd in his field futurity as a 9-month-old with his novice owner/handler. He then earned a maximum score of 112 points on the NAVHDA Natural Ability test. Later that year, he went on to win the Mid-America Classic Derby. He proved equally talented as a broke dog by winning the Western Classic Amateur Gun Dog in 2006, placing fourth at the National Amateur Championship in 2008, earning perfect 10s on his last leg of Master Hunter and his CKC Field Dog Excellent tests, and garnering multiple placements in all-breed field trials.

A deep-nosed and very serious tracker, Diesel completed his VST test in 22 minutes, complete with interference by two different squirrels. The second squirrel ran right across his path within 30 yards of the final article. True to form, he was able to re-focus and get right back on task.

It is worth mentioning that Diesel and Anne have trained and competed at the highest levels in all of these venues concurrently! Diesel has started the quest for his fifth Championship, the MACH, and has already earned a few Double Qs and some MACH points. Will Diesel become the first Weim to earn the VCCH (OTCH, CT, MACH), and maybe even AKC's first VCCH TC? Stay tuned!

CHAPTER 32

THE BEST OF THE BEST: DUAL AND TRIPLE CHAMPIONS

The road to the Dual or Triple Championship is not a simple one. Owners are constantly faced with conflicts of time and training. The road begins with quality conformation, exceptional field aptitude, and the requisite biddable and enthusiastic temperament, but from there the difficulty of competing in multiple venues is staggering. Youngsters in field and performance events training risk injuries that could endanger the chances of a show championship. If not started early in field, however, young hopefuls miss their chances for puppy and derby points and the priceless early experience that goes with them. The sometimes sun-bleached and field-worn coat of the heavily muscled, hard-fit field trial dog might have difficulty catching the eye of the judge when in the ring with more stylish cousins that routinely compete in conformation. When competing in both arenas simultaneously, the conditioning necessary for a competitive field dog often makes it difficult to maintain the elegant and smooth silhouette desirable in conformation.

The mystery of the declining occurrence of the Dual Champion in recent years may be as basic as the conformation trends of the differing venues. The successful field dog must be able to gallop for long periods in the field. As a result, it is more likely to have a more moderately angled front and rear. These dogs also tend to be on the smaller end of the height standard for the breed. The dogs who are currently catching the judge's eye in the conformation ring, however, are tending to have a more angulated front and rear, as well as having more size and substance. As a result, in today's conformation ring, the competitive field dog may find it difficult to gain the required majors, even though the dogs are well within the breed standard.

This is not to imply that field dogs cannot win in the ring (or, conversely, that a "breed" dog cannot compete in the field). Among some, the opinion is that the Weimaraner is simply not a "dual" breed, that the show lines and field lines are too far apart. But perhaps the facts show a different story. Of the 70 dual champions, 17 have won the title of National Champion (of any stake) at the WCA's yearly National Field event, and more than a half dozen have done it more than once! DC Top Deaugh won the national Amateur All-Age Championship 4 years in a row! Three duals have been accorded the honor of WCA All-Age Gun Dog of the Year, (DC Lady Athena of Camelot, DC Lilith von Hirschorn and DC Othen's Princess Pretty), and many have been ranked among the WCA's Top 10 field lists.

Building the foundation for serious versatile competition usually begins at the youngest of ages. It involves not merely learning the exercises but creating the positive attitude and socialization to compete in the variety of venues and circumstances the dog and handler will face. The accrual of points for each of the championships may take years to acquire. A high level of performance must be maintained which requires a delicate balance between the dog's cooperation and independence, competition and training, down time and the conflicts of peaking performance for high exposure events in a variety of activities. All in all, the process is a complicated dance to the tune of time marching on.

The handler must find the time and money to compete in the various venues while juggling the calendar, not just to find time to train, but to actually compete!

Figure 32-1: *Who knows what the future holds?* Building a foundation for the potential multiple champion begins with planning, such as planning the breeding, the first experiences, the right owner, the training program, the career. Who knows what can happen when the details align with good fortune? But while we make plans, can anyone really tell which puppy holds the seeds of potential for the next dual or triple champion? Photograph by William Wegman.

The coveted designation of DC, or Dual Champion, is not awarded to a dog "just" for earning two championships, but rather a dog that has earned both a field championship and a bench (conformation) championship. The first dual champion Weimaraner was DC Palladian Perseus; his FC was earned under the American Field rules. The 1968 transition from American Field rules to AKC Field Trial Regulations created a second "first" dual champion when Staubich von Risen RD, SDX became the first Weimaraner to earn both a Bench Championship and a Field Championship under the new system.

The even more rarified Triple Champion (TC) is reserved for the dog who earns a bench championship, a field championship, AND a companion dog event championship (obedience, tracking, or agility). To date, only two Weimaraners have earned this amazing honor. The first was TC AFC Regen's Summer Blaze, UDX2, MH, MX, MXJ, VCD3, RE, SDX, RDX, VX6, in 2005. Not only was she incredibly talented (she earned more than 50 titles in the U.S. and Canada), but she proved that it was not just a fluke by passing on her talent to her children, becoming the WCA's first dam to be awarded both the Field Register of Merit (FROM) and BROM. In 2008, the Weimaraner world was graced with not only the second Triple Champion, but the

first time ever (of any breed) mother/son triple champion combination with Ruby's son, TC Regen's Rip Stop, VCD3, UDX3, TDX, MH, AX, RDX, SDX, VX5. Diesel continued his success by earning Champion Tracker in 2009, making him the first Weimaraner to earn four AKC championships, achieved by only a few other dogs of any breed.

In 2001, the AKC introduced the Versatile Companion Championship (VCCH) to be awarded to the dog who earns a championship in each of the companion dog events: obedience, tracking and agility. To date, only two dogs of any breed have earned this title. This of course begs a few questions…. When will a Weimaraner earn this title? When will a dog earn both the TC AND a VCD? Is there a dog out there with the intelligence, soundness, and ability to earn a championship on the bench, in the bird and tracking field, as well as the obedience and agility rings? Will this special dog be matched with an equally special owner with the talent, time, and determination required for such a campaign? If any breed of dog can, the Weimaraner, with its heritage of working closely with and for a human partner, is certainly a candidate!

The following pages celebrate these exceptional dogs and highlights some of their accomplishments.

Figure 32-2: *TC AFC Regen's Summer Blaze VCD3, UDX2, RE MH, MX, MXJ, VX6, BROM, FROM* (CH Jak's Repeat Offender × AM/CAN CH Skyhi's EZ Magical Reign, JH, UD, SD, NRD, VX, BROM). Bred by David and Nina Sherrer and Judi Voris; owned by Shirley Nilsson and Judi Voris and trained and handled by Shirley. Ruby is the breed's first TC, earning her bench championship in 2000 with three majors. Ruby began by claiming her bench championship in 2000 with three majors. Her FC followed in 2001, and she finished off her TC with her OC in 2005. With just nine offspring placed in competition homes, Ruby is well established as a producer who has left a mark on the breed and is the breed's first dam to earn both the FROM and BROM. Ruby was not only the first TC Weimaraner, she is the only Weimaraner to have produced offspring that earned Show (5), Field (3), Obedience (2), and Tracking (1), Championships, including Diesel, the dog who earned all four of those, and three MH offspring. Ruby's offspring additionally earned Canadian Show (3), Obedience (3), Agility (1), and Tracking (1), Championships, and all three of her offspring who took the NAVHDA NA test earned perfect scores. Ruby is the first Weimaraner to have been designated by both the BROM and the FROM for the achievements of her progeny. While a wonderful working dog and producer, Ruby's true passion was real-life hunting, and despite a strong working bond, Ruby would drop Shirley like a hot potato if Shirley's husband Sly reached for a shotgun and headed for the truck.

Dual and Triple Champions by Decade

1960s

DC Baron von Randolph D
DC Baroness of Magmar (S603991) B
DC Birtzel von Staub (SA183899) D
DC Bruno Auger Silver Duke (S628817) D
DC DV's Laughing Girl (S891356) B
DC Halann's The Judge v. Reiteralm (SA633347) D
DC Halann's Checkmate Tamara (SA573048) B
2xNAFC 2XNFC FC DC Othen's Princess Pretty V (SA681659) B
NFC FC DC Palladian Perseus (S374207) D
DC Paron's Bingo (9SA296514) B
DC Patmar's Silver Countess (S442643) B
DC Pine Grove Farm's Brunhilde (SA102502) B
DC Schmidt's Countess Kristine (SA17097) B
NFC FC DC Sportabout's Boeser Bengel (SA475602) D
DC Staubich's von Risen (S545265) D
DC Von Gaiberg's Cosak (S454334) D
DC Whidbey's Baron (S870685) D
DC Zandor Von Lechsteinhof (S381760) D

1970s

DC Arimar's Ivan (SB3693851) D
DC Arimar's Lovely Lyric (SB656562) B
DC Birtzel's Johnny Reb (SB735425) D
DC Crook 'N' Nanny's Silver Titan (SA807162) D
DC Eldan's Mohave Sundancer (SA456458) D
DC Firebird's Second Chance (SB867034) B
DC AFC Gents Silver Smoke (SA807575) D
DC AFC Gradaus Katrinka (SA989907) B
NFC DC AFC Jafwin's One and Only (SC400928) B
DC Jafwin's the Goodbye Girl (SC385925) B
DC Kristof's Classic Venture (SC445564) D
DC Lady Rebecca of Camelot (SC100741) B
DC AFC Landbee's Liberty Flyer (SB740885) D
DC AFC Lilith Von Hirschhorn (SA764285) B
DC AFC Marbil's Baron von Josephus (SB632544) D
DC Ozark's Buckeye Rebel (SB688150) D
DC Prinz Rolf von Kiry (SB061331) D
DC Redhill's Chief Geronimo (SC 505813) D
DC Redhill's Fanny Jo (SB137448) B
DC Ronamax Rufus v. Reiteralm (SA945638) D
DC AFC Shadowmar Artemis Impenda (SB712027) B

DC Show Me Silver Shadow (SB879081) D
DC Silverbrand Rafferty V Jar-Em (SC282383) D
DC Takusan's Sonic Boom (SC671181) D
DC Weimaracres Sunny Boy (SA798866) D
DC Whidbey's Jake (SA837744) D
DC Whidbey's Samantha (SC008721) B
DC Windsong's Bayside Barnaby (SB19401) D
DC Winnie von Ostfriesland (SA934154) B

1980s

DC AFC Bayer's Silver Mr V Reiteralm (SF670391) D
DC Jo-Ron's Silber Eich (SF803620) D
DC AFC Lady Athena of Camelot (SC993906) B
4xNAFC NFC DC AFC Top Deaugh (SD390684) D
DC Tri-D's Sterling Silver (SE903423) D
DC Valmar's Valiant Knight (SSE116082) D
DC Watchpoint's Foreshadow (SD358081) D

1990s

DC Ardreem's Southern Maverick (SN10614505) D
DC Ardreem's Wolf Von Betelgeuse (SM85735105) D
DC Camelot's Desert Fox (SN31835901) D
DC Exuma Hyatt of Norton Cr (SN27280505) D
DC NAFC AFC Knight's Ti-Ki Toi (SG028056) D
VC DC AFC Magnum Gunnar Silvershot (SN1575888) D
DC Mile Hi Murphy (SM95025303) D
DC Sir Anthony Jake of Sanbar (SN44779208) D
DC The Sundance Kid (SD701356) D
DC AFC Tri-D's Clean Sweep v Y-Me (SF847916) B
DC Von Weiner's Withheld (SN10695707) D
DC Wynwood's Rain on the Rise (SM92226706) B

2000s

DC Dust Storm on the Rise (SN65498402) D
DC Outdoors Life of Riley (SN73959506) D
TC Regen's Rip Stop (SN18329814) D
TC Regen's Summer Blaze (SN37831703) B
DC NFC Sirius Mostly Mongo (SN83681301) D
DC Sirius Peppermint Schnapps (SN55132401) B
DC Sirius Really Rosie (SN17587907) B
NFC NAFC DC AFC Snake Break's Saga v Reiteralm (SN40290901) D
DC Windwalker's Heart of Gold (SN37780301) B

The Dual Champions that Produced the Most Bench Champions

Figure 32-3: *DC Valmar's Valiant Knight, CD, NRD, VX, BROM* (CH Valmar's Jazzman, CD, NSD, NRDV, BROM × CH Valmar's Pollyanna, BROM). Bred by Joan Valdez; owned by Gorden Hansen and Joan Valdez. The sire of an impressive 26 show champions, Val was considered to be the product of a complete "show line" breeding, but after completing his show career, co-owner Gorden Hansen persuaded Joan Valdez to give Val the opportunity to shine in the bird field as well. As a result, Val earned the rare distinction of being ranked in the Top 10 Show Dogs (1986), as well as the Top 10 All-Age Gun Dogs (1988).

Figure 32-4: *DC Windwalker's Heart of Gold, BROM* (CH Windwalker's Hills of Shiloh, CD, JH, SDX, NRD, VX × Ghostwalker Storm Cloud). Bred by Don Ella Hatch; owned by Philip and Arlene Marshrey. Scarlett is the dam of seven show champions and has passed on her sound conformation and love of the field to her offspring. Happiest when running in the field, Scarlett's field career was littered with many "near misses" at major events, as her independent nature kept everyone on the edge of their seat up to the last call-back.

Figure 32-5: *The magical 6- to 12-week period is very important* in developing the dual potential in a puppy. While a talented pup can still be successful, it will take much more effort to regain the opportunities of this stage if this time is squandered. Refer to *Ages and Stages* and *Testing Natural Aptitude* for ideas. Photograph by William Wegman.

The Dual Champions that Produced the Most Field Champions

Figure 32-6: *DC NFC AFC NAFC Snake Break's Saga V Reiteralm, CD, MH, RDX, VX2* (FC AFC NAFC Snake Breaks Sgt Schultz × FC Arimarlisa's Rudi V Reiteralm). Bred by Steve Reynolds and Virginia Alexander; owned by Mary and Jeffrey Brown. Saga is the sire of five FC, with several more youngsters who are major field and bench pointed. Saga was a two-time National Field Trial Champion, and at the time of his first win in 1999 was the youngest dog to win. Three years later, handled by his owner, Mary Brown, Saga would become the National Amateur Field Trial Champion. Some might consider Saga a weekend field warrior because he accompanies Mary to work each day and spends his time as a therapy dog working with mentally challenged adults. A truly versatile Weimaraner, Saga is the only top-producing DC with a VX2. Photograph by Gene LaFollette.

Figure 32-7: (a) *DC Wynwood's Rain on the Rise, SDX, NRD, VX* (AM/CAN CH Valmar Smokey City Ultra Easy, JH, NSD, BROM × CH Vanoah's Glory Hallelujah, NSD, NRD, V, BROM). Bred by Brenda Martz; owned by W. and P. Kuehnhold and S. Hartman. Rainy is the dam of five FC and one AFC as well as three show champions, including a DC, making her the No. 7 Top-Producing field dam. Her offspring's talents are not limited to U.S. shores. Two of her children traveled to the Netherlands and earned International Show Championships, as well as top ratings in field competition. The daughter of a Best in Show winner and a show champion personal gun dog, Rainy, and her progeny, prove that the heart of a hunting dog beats strongly in many of our show lines. **(b)** *DC Dust Storm on the Rise, JH, BROM.* Rainy's son, by VC DC AFC Magnum Gunnar Silvershot, MH, SDX, RDX, VX, BROM, after an impressive field trial career handled by Tim Hidalgo (see Figure 31-44), now spends his retirement as the personal pheasant dog of his owner David Borg. Not only handsome and talented, he is also the sire of five show champions.

The Dual Champion Firsts with American Field, AKC, and WCA

Figure 32-8: *DC Palladian Perseus* (FC Ricki of Rocklege × CH Debar's Platinum Pallas). Bred by Mrs. Donald Bullock; owned by O. W. Ogilvie. Perseus was the first Weimaraner to earn both an AKC Bench Championship and an FTC (under American Field rules). A dominant influence at Weimaraner field trials in the 1950s, he won the Open Derby at the WCA National Field Trial in 1951, the Amateur All-Age three times (1952, 1955, 1956), and the Open All-Age in 1954.

Figure 32-9: *DC Tri-D's Sterling Silver, NSD, BROM* (CH Eb's You Otta See Me Now, JH, SD, NRD, V × CH Tri D's Bain De Soleil, NRD, BROM). Bred by Carole Donaldson; owned by Donald M. Coller. Sam is the only Weimaraner to sweep the WCA's Futurity and Maturity program; in 1988 he won the Southern Bench Futurity and National Field Futurity, and then in 1989, he won the Southern Maturity. Fulfilling the intentions of the WCA's futurity program, Dusty completed his DC in 1991.

Figure 32-10: *DC Staubich von Risen, RD, SDX* (Bruno v. Brombachtal, import × Sola de Fortuna). Bred by Waldwinkel Kennels; owned by Carl Lindstrom. Dusty is the first Weimaraner to earn both the AKC Bench Championship and the AKC Field Championship. Dusty's journey to DC was not typical. She began life as a hunting companion and didn't even begin field trialing until the age of 4. She entered her first conformation show at the age of 6. Bred once to DC Zandor v. Lechsteinhof, she produced a show champion and a field champion.

The First Dual Champion Sire and Dam of a Dual Champion

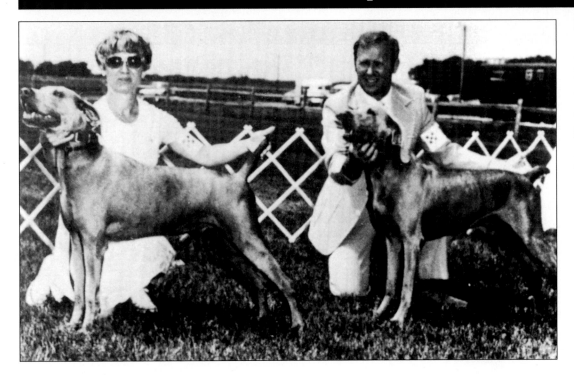

Figure 32-11: *DC AFC Gent's Silver Smoke, CDX, RDX, VX* (left) (Ladivs Silver Gent × Johnny Ginny). Bred by Mildred Ferguson; owned by Al and Eleanor Miller. Smokey sired the first second-generation dual champion Weimaraner DC Show Me Silver Shadow, NRD, SD, VX (right) (Gents Silver Smoke × Top-ofields Second Bonnie). Bred by Al Miller; owned by Al and Suzy Miller.

Figure 32-12: (a) *DC Redhill's Fanny Jo, SDX, BROM* (CH Redhill's Satellite × CH Redhill's Fanfare). Bred and owned by Ted and Lori Jarmie. Fanny Jo is the first DC BROM dam and the first mother-son DC producer. The lovely, elegant Fanny Jo finished her show title with ease and is a multiple breed winner. She won the 1973 field futurity and national open derby stake, finished her field title in two consecutive weekends with two majors at 3¹/₂ years of age, and ranked in the WCA Top 10 field list in 1980. **(b)** *DC Redhill's Chief Geronimo, SD, NRD, V,* Fanny Jo's son by Best in Show winner CH Eric von Seiben, continued to hunt for his owner, Judy Mihlik, for many years after his retirement from competition; he sired an FC son.

The First Producer of Two Dual Champions

Desert Diana was bred to Eichenhof's Gingerman to become the first dam of two DCs, DC Arimar's Lovely Lyric and DC Arimar's Ivan

Figure 32-13: *CH Arimar's Desert Diana, NSD, BROM* (CH Doug's Dauntless von Dor × CH Halaan's Schonste Madchen, CD, NRD, NSD, V, BROM). Bred by Tom and Jackie Isabell; owned by Tom and Jackie Isabell. Group placing and futurity winning Deedee became the breed's first dam of two DCs when bred to CH Eichenhof's Ginger Man BROM. She also has five show champions to her credit.

Figure 32-14: *DC Arimar's Ivan, CD, NSD, VX, BROM* (CH Eichenhof's Ginger Man BROM × CH Arimar's Desert Diana, NSD, BROM.) Bred and owned by Tom and Jackie Isabell. Ivan is Diana's son from her second breeding to CH Eichenhof's Ginger Man, BROM. For more than a decade, Ivan's 23 show offspring held the record for a DC.

Figure 32-16: *DC Arimar's Lovely Lyric, CD, SDX, RD, VX* (CH Eichenhof 's Ginger Man, BROM × CH Arimar's Desert Diana, NSD, BROM). Bred by Tom and Jackie Isabell; owned by J. and I. Bahde, Jr. Lyric became the breed's youngest DC at the time by finishing her FC at the age of 34 months.

Figure 32-15: *DC Takusan's Sonic Boom, NSD, NRD, V* (CH Halaan's the Judge, SDX, RDX × DC Arimar's Lovely Lyric, CD, SDX, RD, VX). Bred by Jean Bahde; owned by Bill and Jenny Straub. The product of a rare DC to DC breeding, Boomer fulfilled his promise as a young dog. Unfortunately, Boomer died a few months after completing his DC, ending hopes of a third-generation DC.

Figure 32-17: *DC Halann's The Judge v. Reiteralm, SDX, RDX* (CH Maximilian Vom der Reiteralm, NSD, BROM × Manning's Westwood Ladybird, BROM). Bred by C. and M. Mannings; owned by Virginia Alexander. A broken leg at 5 months of age didn't stop the Judge from becoming a Dual. For more than 20 years, he also led the list of DC field producers with one DC, three FCs, one AFC, and eight show champions.

The first Dual Champion–Dual Champion breeding to produce a Dual Champion

DC Halann's The Judge v. Reiteralm was bred to DC Arimar's Lovely Lyric to produce DC Takusan's Sonic Boom

Duals that highlighted the early years of Susan Thomas' Camelot

Figure 32-18: DC Lady Rebecca of Camelot, CDX, SDX, NRD, VX, BROM (Sue's Sir Lancelot, UD, RD, NSD, V × Lady Guinevere of Ekselo). Bred by G. Thomas and E. Oleske; owned by Susan Thomas. Amateur owner trained and handled, Rebecca is the first DC dam to produce a second-generation DC daughter, DC Lady Athena of Camelot. Rebecca ranked on the WCA's Top 10 field and obedience lists in 1979 and 1980.

Figure 32-19: *DC AFC Lady Athena of Camelot, NRD* (CH Colsidex Kg Arthur of Camelot, CD, SD, RD, VX, BROM× DC Lady Rebecca of Camelot, CDX, SDX, NRD, VX, BROM). Bred by S. Thomas, C. Studney, and C. Crosby; owned by Susan Thomas. Amateur owner trained and handled, Athena is the first second-generation DC motherdaughter combination and was on theWCA Top 10 field lists for three consecutive years, including No. 1 in 1986.

Duals that launched the professional field career of Dan Long

Figure 32-20: DC AFC Tri-D's Clean Sweep V Y-Me, SDX, NRD, V (CH Tri D's Wingfield's Ottowo, JH × CH Tri D's Good as Gold, JH, NRD). Bred by C. and B. Donaldson; owned by C. Schuch and C. Donaldson. A talented performer from Carole Donaldson's ever successful Tri-D dual breeding program, Gina excelled with her great nose and dependable prey drive to serve as Dan's best instructor and mentor. Gina finished with an amateur 5-point major at an all-breed trial at Kildeer Plains; with Dan in the saddle, she also won an Eastern Classic.

Figure 32-21: DC AFC Bayer's Silver Mr v. Reiteralm, NSD, NRD, VX (CH Reiteralm's Rio Fonte Saudade, BROM × CH Ladenburg Bessie v. Reiteralm, CD, BROM). Bred by Virginia Alexander; owned by J. and B. Bayer and Virginia Alexander. The product of a German mother and a sire from the first breeding of two Best in Show winners, Coors quickly obtained his show title well before he ever saw a bird. In quick succession, Dan Long was able to obtain his field and amateur field championships with 5-point wins at both the Mid-America and Eastern Classics. In memory of Coors' untimely death, the Weimaraner Club of the Washington D.C. Area (WCWDCA) offers an annual trophy to their top field dog.

The first Dual Champion dam to produce 2 Dual Champions
DC Sirius Really Rosie produced DC Sirius Peppermint Schnapps and DC Sirius Mostly Mongo

Figure 32-22: ***DC Sirius Really Rosie, CDX, JH, RD, VX2, BROM*** (Texmara's Jeb the Great, SD, NRD × CH Sirius Sweet Samantha). Bred by Helene and Richard Moore and B. Dagenhart; owned by Helene and Richard Moore. In addition to earning the AKC's DC and WCA's VX2 rating, Rosie and her littermates would earn the NAVHDA NA Breeder's award, a first for the Moores, as well as for Weimaraners; Rosie then produced litters that resulted in the Moores' second and third NAVHDA breeders' awards. Four of her pups also earned bench CHs as well.

Figure 32-24: ***DC Sirius Peppermint Schnapps, NRD, VX*** (VC DC AFC Magnum Gunnar Silvershot, MH, SDX, RDX, VX, BROM × DC Sirius Really Rosie, CDX, JH, RD, VX2, BROM). Bred and owned by Helene and Richard Moore. Pepper completed her field championships with handler Diane Vater. Pepper enjoys her retirement with her owner-breeders in sunny Florida and has traded hunting quail for chasing seagulls.

Figure 32-23: ***DC NFC Sirius Mostly Mongo, JH, NRD, VX*** (FC AFC NFC Westends Lil Sage Rider, CD, SH, NSD, NRD, V × DC Sirius Really Rosie, CDX, JH, RD, VX2, BROM). Bred and owned by Helene and Richard Moore. To prove that beauty is as beauty does, Mongo not only earned his bench CH, he won the 2002 National Field Futurity and in 2005 became the NFC. Currently, Mongo is still a strong presence on the field trial circuit under the skilled handling of Diane Vater.

Figure 32-25: ***Puppies can benefit from adult role models*** from their earliest days. A calm, confident and talented adult can help build a strong foundation for the promising DC candidate providing a stable emotional example for the youngster to copy while experiencing many aspects of a future career. Photograph by William Wegman.

Full-sibling Dual Champions

Figure 32-26: *DC Ardreem Wolf Von Betelgeuse, JH, SDX, NRD, VX* and *DC Ardreem's Southern Maverick, V,* (Wolfgang Von Sachsengang, JH, CD, NSD, NRD, V × Schaden's Kuhl Luca V Ardreem, CD). Bred by Linda Frisbee; owned by Linda Frisbee (Wolf), A. Dumbleton and Linda Frisbee (Maverick). These two handsome dogs were siblings from repeat breedings and were trained and handled by their breeder throughout their careers. Linda is an inspirational example of the special thrill of training, handling, and winning with a dog you have bred yourself.

Figure 32-27: *These two talented girls are the first DC Weimaraners from the same litter* (CH Von Siebens Smart N Special, NSD, BROM × CH Redhills Song Girl, CD, NSD, NRD, BROM). Bred by F. and J. Sexton. **(a)** DC Jafwin's the Goodbye Girl, SDX, NRD. Owned by L. and H. Weesner. In addition to earning her DC, Nina would earn a spot on both the WCA's Top 10 field and bench lists, with sporting group placements to her name. **(b)** *DC AFC NFC Jafwin's One and Only, SD, NRD, VX.* Owned by S. and B. Crouther. Not to be outdone by her littermate, she not only won the National All-Age Championship at Ardmore in 1982, she continued to remain on the WCA's Top 10 field list from 1982–1984 and again in 1986. (See their parents in Figures 32-40 and 32-41.)

Dual Champion Winners of National Field Events

Figure 32-28: *DC NFC NAFC AFC Top Deaugh, MH, NRD, SDX, VX, HOF* (Weiner Schnitzel's McDuff, NSD × Charlie's Angel II). Bred, owned, and handled by Charles G. Williams to win four National Amateur Championships from 1988–1991. Top Deaugh was handled by Tom Hansen to the 1991 Open All-Age Championship and a fifth national title.

Figure 32-29: *DC NFC NAFC FC Othen's Princess Pretty, NRD, SX, VX* (CH Val's Veto v. d. Reiteralm × CH Othen's Velvet Venus). Bred by Duncan Othen; owned by Tom and Irene Glennon. Handled by Ken Jellings and her owner Tom, Princess won the NFC and NAFC in 1973 and 1974. To date, no other dog has won both the Open and Amateur Championships in back-to-back years.

Dual Champion Winners of National Field Events

Open All-Age

1954 DC Palladian Perseus

1967 DC Pine Grove Farm's Brunhilde*

1972 DC Sportabout's Boeser Bengel, DCS, RD, SDX, VX

1973 DC Othen's Princess Pretty, NRD, SDX, VX

1974 DC Othen's Princess Pretty, NRD, SDX, VX

1982 DC Jafwin's One and Only, NRD, SD, VX

1987 DX The Sundance Kid, CD, NRD, VX

1991 DC Top Deaugh, MH, NRD, SDX, VX

1999 DC Snake Break's Saga V Reiteralm, CD, MH, RDX, VX2

2005 DC Sirius Mostly Mongo, JH, NRD, VX

Amateur All-Age

1952 DC Palladian Perseus

1955 DC Palladian Perseus

1956 DC Palladian Perseus

1964 DC Pine Grove Farm's Brunhilde

1970 DC Eldan's Mojave Sundancer*

1973 DC Othen's Princess Pretty, NRD, SDX, VX

1974 DC Othen's Princess Pretty, NRD, SDX, VX

1975 DC Gent's Silver smoke, RDX, SDX, VX

1988 DC Top Deaugh, MH, NRD, SDX, VX

1989 DC Top Deaugh, MH, NRD, SDX, VX

1990 DC Top Deaugh, MH, NRD, SDX, VX

1991 DC Top Deaugh, MH, NRD, SDX, VX

1993 DC Knight's Tiki Toi, NSD

2002 DC Snake Break's Saga V Reiteralm, CD, MH, RDX, VX2

Open Derby

1951 DC Palladian Perseus

1973 DC Redhill's Fanny Jo, SDX, BROM

Field Futurity

1973 DC Redhill's Fanny Jo, SDX, BROM

1975 DX Ozark's Buckeye Rebel, RDX, SD, VX

1988 DC Tri-D's Sterling Silver, NSD

2002 DC Sirius Mostly Mongo, JH, NRD, VX

*Placed first, championship withheld

Figure 32-30: *DC NFC AFC The Sundance Kid, CD, NRD, VX* (Mikesell's Von Baronwheel × Ildebrannfugle's Donna Marie). Bred by Adelaide Davis; owned by Marilee Horn. Purchased as an adult by Marilee, Sunny was handled by Tom Hansen to the 1987 NFC. He is also the sire of 1992 NFC FC Rynmichael Sir Knight von Horn and grandsire of 1997–1998 NFC and 1998 NAFC FC High Ridge Jessie von Horn.

Figure 32-32: *DC NFC Sportabout's Boeser Bengal, CDX, SDX, RD, VX* (CH Cuedes Silver Dust × Hildegarde Xiv). Bred by C. Schilbach; owned by Jerome and Jo Molitor. Before winning the 1972 NFC, Boeser, handled by his amateur owners, was a 1969 WCA Top 10 Show dog, winning multiple Sporting Group placements, including a Group I. Boeser was also the sire of five bench champions.

Figure 32-31: *DC NAFC FC Pine Grove Farm's Brunhilde* (FC Elsmere's Baron Aus Wehmann × Dulcimers Way Up Susiana). Bred and owned by Herbert and Barbara Heller. Brunhilde won the 1964 NAFC, handled by her owner, Barbara Heller, and then ventured into the conformation ring with noted Weimaraner matriarch Anne Kepler. Completing her CH, she returned to the bird field in 1967. Handled by Chet Cummings, Brunhilde took first place at the Open All-Age Championship.

Figure 32-33: *DC NAFC AFC Knight's Ti-Ki Toi, CD, JH, SDX, RD, VX* (S and S's Shot of Tequila × Lyonesse Ginger Star Knight). Bred by Randall and Holly McKnight; owned by Holly McKnight. Toi was as much at home in the show ring (Group placements) as he was in the field (1993 NAFC), winning before the age of 3. Owner-handled throughout his career, he would earn multiple WCA National Field Trial placements. He passed on his talents as the sire of four CHs and a field futurity winning FC, as well as many other versatile titled offspring.

Versatile Dual Champions from show and field line crosses

Figure 32-34: *DC Camelot's Desert Fox, SH, SDX, NRD, VX* (CH Camelots Life of Riley × Lady Kelsy of Camelot). Bred by Susan Thomas and Bill Moran; owned by R. Derrick Hart. Handled by breeder Susan Thomas, Desert Fox quickly completed his show title with specialty and futurity wins. He sired multiple futurity and maturity winners, as well as four bench champions. After being successfully piloted to his field title by Diane Vater, Fox became the pampered weekend hunting buddy of Derrick Hart.

Figure 32-36: *DC Outdoors Life of Riley, CD, JH, SDX, RDX, VX2* (CH Greymists Xactly Right, JH, NRD, V × FC Outdoors Twister). Bred by Michelle and Samantha Stillion; owned by Anne Taguchi and David Routnier. Grandson of a Best in Show winner and son of a well-known top-producing FC, Riley was a busy boy. He joyfully completed his field and show titles with impressive wins. He then continued to compete, owner-handled, gaining WCA's top retrieving and shooting ratings, and swiftly acquired his VX2 at a very early age.

Figure 32-35: *DC Exuma's Hyatt of Norton Cr, JH* (FCH Outdoors Rising Sun × CH Tri-D's Little Nookie V Daroca, JH). Bred by C. and A. Jacobsen and Rosemary Carlson; owned by Margit Worsham. The show line–field line cross is the typical pedigree of many Weimaraner dual champions. While it seems that a DC cross should improve the odds, it appears that the hunting genes run deep in nearly all Weimaraners.

Figure 32-37: *DC Sir Anthony's Jake of Sanbar, NAJ, NJP, VX* (NFC AFC NAFC Snake Break's Saga v. Reiteralm, CD, MH, RDX, VX2 × CH Sanbar's Send Me No Flowers). Bred by Saundra and Polly West; owned by Anthony and Patricia Bailey. With Steve Reynolds handling, Jake quickly completed his FC. At 10 years of age, he earned his multiple jumper agility titles in record time. A year later, Jake's smooth, spirited, but totally correct gaiting at the 2009 Nationals was memorable.

Leading Producers of Dual Champions and Multiple Show Winners

Figure 32-38: *Maximallian v. d. Reiteralm, NSD, BROM* (CH Val Knight Ranck, BROM × Bella v. d. Reiteralm, BROM). Bred and owned by Virginia Alexander. The first Weimaraner to sire two DCs, way back in the 1970s, Max was a happy genetic mix produced from a half-German father and a completely unrelated imported German mother. Maximilian, the over-the-hill dog who made good (see Figure 34-31), can be found in the pedigrees of 59 Best in Show winners and more than 75% of the WCA National Specialty winners born after him. A multiple field winner himself, he still stands as the only Weimaraner to produce multiple DCs and Multiple Best in Show winners.

Figure 32-39: *A talented pair in their own right,* both sporting group winners and WCA Top 10 show dogs, their talented offspring would include two DC littermates (see Figure 32-28). **(a)** *CH Redhill's Song Girl, CD, NSD, NRD, BROM* (CH Kams Rauchessen of Redhill × Wiewandt's Nova, CDX, NRD). Owned and handled by Jennifer Sexton. She was a WCA Top 10 show dog for several years. Her talented offspring earned seven CH, two FCs and one AFC. **(b)** *CH Von Seiben's Smart and Special, NSD, BROM, HOF* (CH Eric Von Sieben, BROM × CH Reichtenstadt's Royal Flush.) Amateur-handled by owner Lynne Burns throughout his career. Sieben made the WCA Top 10 show dog lists for 4 years and earned more than 100 breed wins and many group placements, as well as Best of Opposite Sex at the 1976 National Specialty. Sieben also sired 28 show champion offspring.

Producers of Two DC and Show Winners

		DC	FC/AFC	Show	Total
Sires	CH Maximilian v. Reiteralm, CD, BROM, HOF	2	3	62	67
	CH Von Seiben's Smart and Special, CD, NSD, BROM, HOF	2	3	28	33
	FC AFC NAFC Snake Break's Sgt Schultz, HOF	2	14	2	18
	DC AFC VC Magnum Gunnar Silvershot, MH, SDX, RDX, VX, BROM	2	2	9	13
	CH Eichenhof's Ginger Man, BROM	2	2	8	12
	CH Ludwig's von Dottlyle	2	2	5	9
	Wolfgang von Sachsengang, CD, JH, NSD, RD, NRD, V	2	2	3	7
Dams	CH Redhill's Song Girl, NRD, NSD, BROM	2	3	7	12
	CH Arimar's Desert Diana, NRD, NSD, V, BROM	2	2	5	9
	DC Sirius Really Rosie, CDX, JH, RD, VX2, BROM	2	2	4	8
	Schaden's Kuhl Luca v. Ardreem, CD	2	2	3	7

Harry Hirschhorn and his International Winning Dual Champions

Figure 32-40: *DC Ronamax Rufus v. Reiteralm, CD, RDX, SDX, VX* (CH Maximilian Von Der Reiteralm, NSD, BROM × CH Norman's Rona v. d. Reiteralm, NRD, SD, V, BROM). Bred by Virginia Alexander; owned by Harry Hirschhorn and Virginia Alexander. Rufus earned bench titles in the U.S., Canada, Panama, and the Dominican Republic and is a full brother to 14 AKC show champions, out of a dam who is still our breed's top producer 40 years later. Rufus was the first American-bred Weimaraner to qualify for the prestigious VGP in Austria. His son, NZ Aust CH Arimar's Rolf v. d. Reiteralm, would further contribute multiple Best in Show winners and improved field performance in England, New Zealand, and Australia.

Figure 32-41: *Intl DC and AKC DC AFC Lilith Von Hirschhorn, CDX, TD, RDX, SDX, VX* (Braunhildes Silver Blaze × Crook N Nannys Tosca). Bred by Marie Seidelman; owned by Harry Hirschhorn. Lilith is the only Weim to earn both the AKC DC and the FCI Dual International Championship. She also earned bench championships in Canada, Mexico, Bermuda, Panama and the Dominican Republic and CDs and TDs in Canada and Bermuda. She is the first Weim to earn a NAVHDA UD rating. Lilith earned more than 35 titles in all, in addition to making the WCA's Top 10 field list for 3 years. She still holds the Weimaraner record for titles earned in the most countries 40 years later.

Two Duals that sparked the professional field career of Diane Vater

Figure 32-42: *DC Joron Silber Eich, UD, TD, MH, SDX, RDX, VX3, UD* (CH Bama Belles Mountain Man, BROM × Greysport Duchess of Grace). Bred by R. and J. Good; owned by Diane Vater, and R. and J. Good. Moose was a prepotent sire of show champions and versatile hunters, including multiple offspring with titles on both ends of their names. A VX3 himself, Moose was one of the most versatile campaigners in the early 1990s and earned himself a Hall of Fame nomination in 2008. To quote owner/trainer/handler Diane Vater, "Moose gave me a jumpstart with his mistakes and victories and helped me learn the ropes."

Figure 32-43: *DC Von Weiner's Withheld, CDX, MH, SD, RDX, VX2* (DC Tri D's Sterling Silver, NSD, BROM × CH Sirius Octrude Von Weiner, CDX, TD, SH, SDX, RD, VX2). Bred and owned by Diane Vater. Blue's trainability and desire to win added a VX2 to his many accomplishments in the late 1990s. A DC sire himself, out of a dual, he had the needed genetic components to produce 12 offspring earning more than 25 titles, including three bench champions and an OTCH. Blue is the sire of the 2003 National Derby winner Howard's Dusty Breeze and OTCH VX4 daughter Regen's State of the Art.

What's a Dual to Do?

Retirement, or the passing of the competition season, doesn't change the DC's love for the hunt. While many activities will keep the dog and hunter active and happy, Judy Balog and Gunnar decided to go green and support wildlife preservation by assisting in the capture, banding, and release of game birds. Gunnar pinpoints the bird's location while Judy carefully approaches with a net. The woodcock is captured and carefully banded so that game managers can track the birds, aiding in population and habitat management. Once the banding is completed, the uninjured bird is released. Photographs by Craig Koshyk.

VC DC AFC Magnum Gunnar Silvershot, MH, SDX, RDX, VX, BROM
(CH Green Acres Good Grief Colby, CD × CH Dustivelvet's Spring Rain). Bred by Kathleen Elkins; owned by Judy Balog.

Figure 33-1: *CH Norman's Rona v. d. Reiteralm, SD, NRD, V, HOF.* Bred by Norman LeBeouf; owned by Virginia Alexander and Saundra Watson. Dam of 20 champions.

Fresh out of the field after earning her Shooting Dog rating the week before, Rona stands proudly beside her young son, Rajah, at his debut at the Pittsburg Specialty more than 40 years ago. Rona went Best of Opposite Sex to her son Rajah, who had just taken Best of Breed, beating 22 specials his first time in the show ring. (Read more about Rajah in Chapter 34, *A Blueprint of Quality: The Sires.*)

While en route to her show championship, Rona went Winners' Bitch at Westminster, but Rona would not allow herself to be limited to being just a beauty queen. For many years, she was the only Top-Producing BROM bitch with a Versatile rating; however, her true contribution to the breed occurred in the whelping box. She was the first Weimaraner to earn the Kennel Review Diamond Award (20 or more champions for a bitch) and the only Diamond Award dam of any breed to produce a Diamond Award Sire (Ronamax Rajah v. d. Reiteralm with 118 champions). In addition to her 20 AKC champions, she produced five more champions in other countries. Her offspring include National Specialty and Futurity winners, as well as a Best in Show and a Dual Champion (DC Ronamax Rufus v. d. Reiteralm CD, RDX, SDX, VX, NAHVDA UT). Rona's daughter, CH Rona's Sea Sprite v. d. Reiteralm, left a mark on the breed as well. She was a Top-Producing BROM dam, the only bitch to produce two littermates that would win both Best in Show and the National Specialty (see Chapter 30, *Best in Show,* for CH Springdale Rhea v. d. Reiteralm, CD, and CH Chat A Wey Charley v. d. Reiteralm). Of the 65 dams of 10 or more champions, Rona appears in the pedigree of 43. Of the 70 sires of 20 or more champions, Rona appears in the pedigree of 42. When reviewing the 2007 WCA list of All-Time No. 1 show dogs, Rona appears in the pedigree of 27 of the Top 30 and at least 20 Dual Champions. Even after 35+ years, Rona's record of 20 Bench champions, including one Dual Champion, at a time when shows were much more limited than today, still stands. She left an impressive legacy.

Rona lived happily at Reiteralm as the Chief of Hospitality and Head Disciplinarian for more than 15 years.

CHAPTER 33

OUR FOUNDATION OF THE FUTURE: THE DAMS

by Terrie Borman

It seems unjust, somehow, that most of the honor, prestige, and credit for outstanding progeny goes to the sires. Nevertheless, every breeder knows that the brood bitch is the heart of a breeding program, with frequent references to "the foundation bitch of _____ kennel."

The sires must strut their stuff in the show ring and run their hearts out in the field to impress the owners of bitches, the breeders. The breeders review what is available, appraise their bitches, and select the sires. The reputations of great sires are made by great bitches; great bitches are developed by great breeders.

This chapter pays tribute to some of the Top-Producing Dams of the breed, with their photographs, brief summaries, and breeding—note the scattering of WCA ratings indicating field aptitude in many so-called pure show bloodlines. The criterion for inclusion here is simple: they are dams of 10 or more AKC champions. Admittedly, this arbitrary figure rules out the inclusion of some of the breed's most influential producers.

The Weimaraner's popularity has waxed and waned over the years, and during the "Crazy Years" of the 1960s, quality did indeed suffer. However, the breed has made great progress in returning to quality over quantity. In February 1985, Tom Wilson, then-President of the WCA, presented some impressive figures regarding the quality of the modern Weimaraner. In 1984, 172 Weimaraners earned a Bench championship, or one of every 26 Weimaraners registered; in contrast, the Poodle, which registered more than 90,000 dogs that year, finished 185 Bench champions, or one of 485 dogs registered.

Research for the Top-Producing Dams began with the 1984 BROM list, but eventually required investigating a variety of sources, including the updated BROM list (a yeoman's effort led by Sandy West), the Bremar pedigree service, and decades of *Weimaraner Magazine.*

Later, owners submitted information and photographs when their records indicated that bitches qualified. All contradictions were resolved using the highest figure from the various sources. While it is possible that other dams might have produced more than 10 champions in past years, this list compiles our best research efforts. With the support of many people who dug through dusty old boxes and the assistance of Colleen Dugan's technical magic, this chapter brings photographs and biographies of almost every bitch on the list, an amazing accomplishment given the fact that some of the dogs are from the 1950s

The 65 dams featured in this chapter belong to an elite group of producers, and their owners are among the most astute and fortunate of breeders. The influence of these top producers can best be measured by the fact that they appear in the pedigrees of so many Weimaraners of the 1990s and 2000s, although it might be necessary to extend the pedigrees for quite a few more generations to find them.

The list is presented by number of qualifying progeny, and then presented in the biographical section alphabetically for ease of reference.

Figure 33-2: *Mothers react to puppies with loving interest.* Photograph by William Wegman.

Top Producers: Dams

Rank		Year of Birth	Champions
1	CH Norman's Rona v. d. Reiteralm, SD, NRD, V, HOF (SA335719)	1965	20
2	CH Smokey City Jedda Arokat (SF317673)	1988	17
3	CH Grayshar Easy Impression, NSD (SM85565803)	1991	17
4	Kristof's Tnt Jessica (SB697989)	1974	16
5	CH Camelot's Constellation, TD, NSD, V (SM84072801)	1991	16
6	AM/CAN CH Reichtenstadt's Cameo (SA958459)	1971	15
7	CH Bing's Galactica Von Konsul, CDX, SD, NRD (SC497283)	1978	15
8	CH Nani's Cobbie Cuddler, HOF (SD519237)	1982	15
9	CH Kris-Miss Shadow, CD (SA232932)	1963	13
10	AM/CAN CH Nani's Ariana v. d. Reiteralm (SB292617)	1973	13
11	CH Silversmith Omni V Reiteralm, CD, TD, RD, NSD, VX (SD065945)	1980	13
12	CH Jarem's Casino Roulette (SF507879)	1989	13
13	CH Norman's Frostyroy Colleen (SD880940)	1983	13
14	AM/CAN CH Norman's Smokey City Heat Wave, JH, HOF (SF200181)	1988	13
15	CH Elken's Sherri (SA192000)	1963	12
16	AM/CAN CH Colsidex Dauntless Applause, NSD, HOF (SB67661)	1971	12
17	CH Nani's Soul Sensation (SB853718)	1975	12
18	CH Nani's Soul Sister (SC41035)	1976	12
19	CH Nani's Cascade v. d. Reiteralm (SC677945)	1979	12
20	CH Tophat's Aria, CD, NSD, V (SE222169)	1985	12
21	CH Valmar's Grayshar Burgundy (SN15647305)	1994	12
22	Bella Von Der Reiteralm [German import], CD, HOF (SA46575)	1957	11
23	CH Brandy's Blizz v. d. Reiteralm (SA716371)	1969	11
24	CH Brandybuck's Lady Jennifer, CD, TD, V (SA916561)	1970	11
25	CH Kamsou Riptide (SA935517)	1971	11
26	CH Starbuck's California Dove, NSD (SB636338)	1974	11
27	CH Jamspirit Complikate, CDX, RDX, SDX, VX (SB475607)	1974	11
28	CH Kamsou Dutch Treat (SC107577)	1976	11
29	CH Lady Sarah of Camelot, NSD (SD008550)	1980	11
30	CH Valmar's Serendipity (SD616938)	1982	11
31	CH Forshado Nani's Crystal Vision (SE593519)	1986	11
32	CH Casa Perry's Prime Diamond (SE685064)	1986	11
33	CH Valmar's Evening Sonata (SF084951)	1987	11

Top Producers: Dams

Rank		Year of Birth	Champions
34	AM/CAN CH Bremar Freedom Hills Isis, NSD (SF103796)	1987	11
35	CH Camelot's Halley's Comet (SF625469)	1989	11
36	CH Windwalker's Moment in time, JH, NSD (SN01578306)	1992	11
37	CH Valmar's Night N Gale (SM96145302)	1992	11
38	AM/CN/INT CH Moonshine's Gray Brocade, CD, NSD, V (SN09893701)	1993	11
39	CH Silversmith Lady Gracie, JH, NSD, NRD, V (SN17586510)	1994	11
40	AM/CAN CH Skyhi's Northern Dare to Dream (SN26158201)	1995	11
41	CH Graytsky's StellaLuna (SN75519401)	2000	11
42	CH Chaskar's Suddenly It's Rainy (SA798422)	1969	10
43	CH Wetobe's Ballerina Ribbons, CD (SA917930)	1970	10
44	CH Rajah's Sass of Gray Brigade, CDX, TD, NSD, VX (SB70780)	1971	10
45	BIS CH The Rajah's Magic von Reiteralm, HOF (SB450137 6-78)	1973	10
46	CH Colsidex Symphony (SB718598)	1975	10
47	BIS CH Valmar's Pollyanna, HOF (SD151423)	1981	10
48	CH Warheit's Silver Sensation, CD, NSD, V (SD220093)	1981	10
49	CH Bing's Tatiana V Windsong, CD, NSD, NRD, V (SD497906)	1982	10
50	CH Silversmith Indigo V Kristof, CD, NRD, V (SD456431)	1982	10
51	CH Harline's Hurrah (SD672430)	1982	10
52	CH Arokat's the Bremar Headline (SD912700)	1983	10
53	CH Lightfoot's Oceana V Atlantis, JH, NSD, RD, V (SE305483)	1985	10
54	CH Winfield Queen Cleo Starbuck (SE122878)	1984	10
55	CH Vanoah's Glory Hallelujah, NSD, NRD, V (SE027191)	1984	10
56	CH Windwalkers Sunrise Jubilee, CD, JH, NSD, V (SE732035)	1986	10
57	CH Valmar's Starling (SE817453)	1986	10
58	CH Nani's Perfect Cadence, CD, JH, V (SM9095370)	1991	10
59	CH Smokey City Ez Wind B'Nth R Wing, NSD, NRD, V (SM97825003)	1992	10
60	Telmar Hot Topic of Rushland (SN26861902)	1995	10
61	CH Tophat's Fantome Shallyn Debut (SN24467913)	1995	10
62	BIS CH Smokycity D'Nunder Lazer Beam (SN39272402)	1996	10
63	CH Nani's Nobodie's Patsie, JH (SN47195602)	1997	10
64	CH Nani's Jagmar Sweet Dividends, VCD2, CDX, TD, MH, MX, MXJ, NSD, NRD, VX4 (SN68261701)	1999	10
65	CH Silver Cloud's Grand Contessa (SR12290802)*	2003	10

* It was the hope of the authors to be able to include biographies and photographs for all top-producing Weimaraners, but those who were added as this book went to print were not able to be showcased. We include their names here in appreciation of their merit.

Figure 33-3: *CH Arokat's the Bremar Headline* (CH Rajah's Mr Magic v. d. Reiteralm × Am/Can CH Arimar's Prelude to Arokat, BROM). Bred by John and Diane Archibald; owned by Alan and Pam Patunoff. Dam of 10 champions.

CH Arokat's the Bremar Headline

Canadian-bred Ishtar was the foundation of Bremar. She was a half-sister through her dam to Am/Can CH Arokat's Legionnaire, BROM, sire of CH Nani's Southern Cross, BROM and CH Nani's Kookabura, BROM. Breeders have had nice success in combining their progeny down the generations.

Ishtar finished in nine shows and won her Futurity. Bred twice, she produced five champions in each litter. Her first litter by Am/Can CH Bremar Johannes, BROM, contained the Maturity winner CH Bremar Guinevere.

Her second litter by CH Colsidex Nani Reprint, BROM, was memorable, and has bred on, particularly when the daughters were bred to CH Nani's Southern Cross, BROM. This litter contained the Futurity winner, Am/Can CH Bremar Extra Extra, CD; Am/Can CH Bremar Arokat's Perfect Foil, CD, NSD, NRD, BROM, a Futurity winner who finished at a National specialty; the multispecialty winner, Am/Can CH Bremar Freedom Hills Isis, BROM, who finished by winning Breed from the classes at Westminster and is the dam of Am/Can CH Bremar Maker's Mark, BROM.

Truly, Ishtar was a wonderful brood bitch whose influence is felt to this day.

Bella v. d. Reiteralm, CD, HOF
(German Import)

Ginny Alexander's careful search for a special German bitch paid dividends when she acquired three-year-old Bella from the German Reiteralm Kennels. With Ginny handling, Bella won 11 points before an emergency hysterectomy ended

her show career. Bella is best known, however, as the foundation of the Reiteralm line. Bella's 11 champions (from 13 puppies in two litters sired by CH Val Knight Ranck, BROM, HOF) stood as a breed record for many years, and her seven champions in a single year stood as an all-breed record for Kennel Review as late as the early 1980s. When the Orthopedic Foundation for Animals (OFA) initially organized at the University of Pennsylvania (before settling in the Midwest), Dr. Wayne Riser x-rayed and evaluated Bella's hips. At the age of 10, she earned an excellent rating and was the 13th Weimaraner to receive an OFA number. Her German heritage of hunting talent, structural soundness, and trainable temperament placed her stamp on the quality of the modern America Weimaraner. Her most significant contributions were passed to current generations through her son CH Maximilian v. d. Reiteralm, BROM, HOF. Max held the breed record of 62 champion offspring until surpassed by his own son, CH Ronamax Rajah v. d. Reiteralm, BROM, HOF. Rajah held the Phillips system annual show record for 15 years until surpassed by his granddaughter BIS CH Valmar's Pollyanna, BROM, HOF. Bella's legacy to the breed included legions of show champions and working field dogs. Of the dams of 10 or more champions, Bella appears in the pedigree of 45; of the sires of 20 or more champions, she appears in the pedigree of 44. Bella is the ancestress of 58 Best in Show winners, as well as an amazing 24 Dual Champions. Bella's influence on the modern American Weimaraner is undeniable.

Figure 33-4: *Bella v. d. Reiteralm, CD, HOF* (Germany) (Greif v. d. Harrasburg, HZ1, G2, MSW × Blanka v. Steeg W, V). Bred by Allan Lubic; owned by Virginia Alexander. Dam of 11 champions.

Figure 33-5: *BISS CH Bing's Galactica Von Konsul, CDX, NSD, NRD, V* (Mex BISS CH Bing's Konsul Von Krisdaunt, CDX, BROM × Bac's Aurora Elisa). Bred by B. Mac; owned by Jean White. Dam of 15 champions.

BISS CH Bing's Galactica Von Konsul, CDX, SD, NRD, V

Gala was out of a litter of five females. This litter produced three champions, four Companion Dogs, two Companion Dogs Excellent, one Utility Dog, two Novice Retrieving Dogs and two Novice Shooting Dogs. Gala won groups from the classes and started her specials career at slightly more than 1 year old. She had no trouble running from the breed ring to the obedience ring and then to the group ring, placing in both the group and obedience ring on the same days. She ended the year, 1981, the No. 2 WCA Show Dog and achieved her Companion Dog, Companion Dog Excellent, Novice Retrieving Dog, and Novice Shooting Dog during the same time. Gala had her first litter when she was 4 years old, and from three litters, she produced 15 champions. She was the WCA's Top-Producing Dam in 1985.

BISS CH Bing's Tatiana V Windsong, CD, NSD, NRD, V

Tia finished her championship in great style, including 13 points, three majors, one Best of Breed over a special and a Group 1 in four days. She had several other Best of Breeds over specials and group placements in limited specialing. Tia acquired her ratings and Companion Dog with ease and lots of enthusiasm. Bred only twice, she produced 10 champions, including a Best in Show Bitch (CH Bing's Southern Sass, CD) and multiple Futurity/Maturity winners.

Retiring from the show ring and whelping box, she spent her remaining years making new friends and greeting old ones as she sailed the seas each summer. Showing her expertise in retrieving, she learned to keep the ball from going overboard on the sailboat—most of the time. She loved many and was loved by many more.

Figure 33-6: *BISS CH Bing's Tatiana V Windsong, CD, NSD, NRD, V* (CH Bing's Razzmatazz Von Konsul, CD, BROM × BISS CH Bing's Glactica Von Konsul, CDX, SD, NRD, V, BROM). Bred and owned by Jean White. Dam of 10 champions.

Figure 33-7: *CH Brandybuck's Lady Jennifer, CD, TD, V* (Lisa's Brandybuck Von Dorval, CD × Cricket's Princess Kim). Bred by Charles Churchill; owned by Sally and Gordon Harris. Dam of 11 champions.

CH Brandybuck's Lady Jennifer, CD, TD, V

Jenny began her show career when she was 7 months old with a Best in Sweepstakes at the Weimaraner Association of Pittsburgh's 1971 Specialty Show over an entry of 42. She seemed to enjoy dog shows, and spectators adored her ground-covering gait.

Figure 33-8: *CH Brandy's Blizz v. d. Reiteralm* (CH Doug's Dauntless Von Dor, BROM × CH Elken's Brandy v. d. Reiteralm, BROM). Bred by Gail Muller and Virginia Alexander; owned by Virginia Alexander. Dam of 11 champions.

A versatile lady, Jenny passed her outstanding talents to her progeny, producing a total of 11 champions—two from CH Seneca's Medicine Man, BROM, and nine from CH Reichenstadt's Majestic, BROM. In addition to winning Bests of Breed and group placements and competing in field trials, Jenny's offspring shared her versatile talents, and her champions hold the following titles and ratings: nine hold obedience titles (4 Companion Dogs, 5 Companion Dog Excellents); six hold tracking titles (6 Tracking Dogs); three hold shooting ratings (4 Novice Shooting Dogs, 1 Shooting Dogs, 1 Shooting Dog Excellents); three hold retrieving ratings (1 Novice Retrieving Dog, 2 Retrieving Dogs); and six hold versatility ratings (1 Versatile, 5 Versatile Excellent).

CH Brandy's Blizz v. d. Reiteralm

Linebred to CH Ronomax Rajah v. d. Reiteralm, BROM, HOF, Blizz (the third generation of BROM dams) produced 11 "magic" champions, including the Futurity winner CH Rajah's Magic Show v. d. Reiteralm (1974). She is best known as the dam of Best in Show and two-time national specialty winner (1976–1977) CH The Rajah's Magic v. d. Reiteralm, BROM, HOF, who is the dam of the Top-Producing Sires CH Ann's Magic v. d. Reiteralm, BROM, and CH Reiteralm's Rio Fonte Saudade, NRD, BROM. Blizz also produced two BROM daughters, CH The Rajah's Magic v. d. Reiteralm, HOF, and Gartensteol Magic Reiteralm.

Am/Can CH Bremar Freedom Hills Isis, NSD

Isis was a charismatic show dog with a beautiful ground-covering gait. She would never, ever quit showing, no matter how long she had to show or what the conditions were. Isis finished by winning Best of Breed from the classes at Westminster. She won at the Yankee WC Specialty when it was held with the Nationals with a ringside volunteer as her handler. She won the Nutmeg WC Specialty after two litters. She won the Pittsburgh Specialty in a huge entry after a lengthy competition. Health and financial reasons prevented her from being shown often, but those who saw her in the ring remember her to this day.

Isis was the dam of 11 champions, including the Maturity winner CH Bremar's Homarc Taylor, sired by CH Nani's Southern Cross. Her daughter, CH Bremar's Troll at Sveorice, sired by CH Smokey City Ultra Easy, produced a Canadian Best in Show winner, Can CH Sveorice Iron Man Gunner, who made the Top 10 Canadian Sporting Dog list. Isis has bred on, principally through her son by CH Nani's Southern Cross, Am/Can CH Bremar Maker's Mark, BROM. She is the grandmother and great-grandmother of Specialty, Futurity, Maturity, and Top 10 Weimaraners.

Figure 33-9: *Am/Can CH Bremar Freedom Hills Isis, NSD* (Am/Can CH Colsidex Nani Reprint, JH, SD, BROM × CH Arokat's the Bremar Headline, BROM). Bred and owned by Alan and Pam Patunoff. Dam of 11 champions.

Figure 33-10: *CH Camelot's Constellation , TD, NSD, V* (CH Valmar Smokey City Ultra Easy, BROM, HOF × CH Camelot's Halley's Comet). Bred by Susan Thomas; owned by Charlene Scalzott. Dam of 16 champions.

Figure 33-11: *CH Camelot's Halley's Comet* (CH Colsidex Nani Reprint, SD, BROM × CH Lady Sarah of Camelot, NSD, BROM). Bred by Susan Thomas; owned by Susan Thomas, Clare Waterman, and Eileen Storer. Dam of 11 champions.

CH Camelot's Constellation, TD, NSD, V

CH Camelot's Constellation, "Connie," came to ShoMar when she was almost 4 years old to add some new blood to the ShoMar line. She couldn't have made a better contribution! The dam of 16 champions, Connie's get have distinguished themselves in the Futurity/Maturity and in the Group ring, as well as in the field. Many also hold obedience titles.

Connie was "in charge" at ShoMar from the moment she arrived. Always haughty yet always playful, Connie's spirit and sense of humor live on in her get. Born to the role of motherhood, Connie mothered everyone and everything — even a tiny kitten! Her first litter at ShoMar, sired by CH ShoMar's Instant Replay, JH, NRD, V, BROM, produced four Champions in a litter of five. One puppy from this litter, CH ShoMar's Touch The Future, JH, CD, is a Group winner who went on to produce BIS BISS CH ShoMar Dustivelvet High Time.

Later in life, Connie met and instantly bonded with Karin Bakken. The feeling was mutual, and soon Connie went to live with Karin, who spoiled her in the manner she insisted upon.

CH Camelot's Halley's Comet

CH Camelot's Halley Comet, BROM was out of two-time No. 1 Top-Producing Dam CH Lady Sarah of Camelot, NSD, BROM. She was a Futurity winner and a Specialty winner. Halley was a wonderful producer and was the dam of 11 champions. Most noteworthy were Best in Show winner CH Camelot's Matinee Idol, BROM (by CH Nani's

Figure 33-12: *CH Casa Perry's Prime Diamond* (CH Valmar's Xtra Copy × CH Kristof's Midnight Lace). Bred by Phyllis Reilly and Patrick Bruno; owned by Connie Williams and Patricia Bruno. Dam of 11 champions.

Southern Cross, BROM), who is also a Top-Producing Sire with 29 champions to date. From the same litter Halley produced CH Woodrose Starfall of Camelot, CD, NSD, V, who went on to be a Group winner.

Figure 33-13: *CH Chaskar's Suddenly It's Rainy* (Kams Redhill Resolute × Klicka Magna). Bred by Newton England, Jr.; owned by Helene Burkholder. Dam of 10 champions.

CH Casa Perry's Prime Diamond

CH Casa Perry's Prime Diamond, BROM, was the dam of 11 Champions for Wilwin Kennel. Jodi was the WCA 1995 Top-Producing Dam with five Champions that year.

CH Chaskar's Suddenly it's Rainy

From her litter of seven puppies, sired by CH Doug's Dauntless Von Dor, Rainy produced her first six champions, all shown to their championships by Rainy's junior handler-owner, Helene Burkholder. Helene's pick of this litter, CH Sir Eric Von Sieben, BROM, is a Best in Show winner and Top-Producing Sire.

Through Eric and her BROM daughter, CH Hidden Heather Von Seiben, CD, NRD, SD, V, Rainy is solidly represented in American bloodlines. Rainy is the grand dam of DC Redhill's Chief Geromino, NRD, SDX, V, and the Best in Show winners CH Erbenhof Touch of Class, BROM, and CH Valmar's Pollyanna, BROM (1987 National Specialty).

Am/Can CH Colsidex Dauntless Applause, NSD, HOF

Judy Colan wrote that Pixie "was a joy, easy to live with, intelligent, birdy, and beautiful." Lightly specialed, Pixie had 22 Best of Breed wins (four specialties) and two group placements.

Pixie's first litter, sired by CH Seneca's Medicine Man, BROM, HOF, produced three champions, including the multiple Best in Show and National Specialty winner (1981 and 1984) CH Colsidex Standing Ovation, BROM, HOF ,and Group-placing CH Colsidex Medicine Show, BROM.

Figure 33-14: *CH Colsidex Dauntless Applause, NSD, HOF* (CH Doug's Dauntless Von Dor, BROM, HOF × Shadowmar Winema Von Elken). Bred and owned by Judy Colan. Dam of 12 champions.

Figure 33-15: *CH Colsidex Symphony* (CH Woodhill's Grayhawk, CD, BROM × CH Colsidex Dauntless Applause, NSD, BROM, HOF). Bred by Judy Colan; owned by Michele and George Govette. Dam of 10 champions.

Bred to CH Woodhill's Grayhawk, CD, BROM, Pixie produced three champions; bred back to her son Ovation, she produced six champions in several litters.

Pixie is the dam of three Futurity winners: CH Colsidex Medicine Show, BROM (1975); CH Colsidex Roschel's Premiere (1977); and CH Colsidex The Farm's Act One, NRD, NSD, V (1977). She is the dam of six BROM producers: CH Colsidex Standing Ovation, HOF, CH Colsidex Medicine Show, CH Colsidex Symphony, CH Colsidex Simply Smashing, NSD, CH Colsidex Ingenue, CD, SD, and field-pointed CH Colsidex Kg Arthur of Camelot, NRD, SD, V.

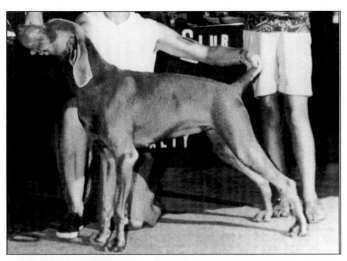

Figure 33-16: *CH Elken's Sherri* (CH Elken's Vanguard, BROM × Elken's Merry Tess). Bred by Jo and Elaine Cox; owned by Elaine Cox, Somervell Linthicum Jr., and Lyle Alexander. Dam of 12 champions.

Figure 33-17: *CH Forshado Nani's Crystal Vision* (CH Nani's Kona Gust, CD, TDV, BROM × CH Nani's Crystal Key, BROM). Bred by Mary Bewig and Susan Hutchings; owned by Christine Medeiros and Mary Bewig. Dam of 11 champions.

CH Colsidex Symphony

In Pepper's all-too-brief show career, she was handled exclusively by Michele Govette (Deerpath Kennel). She won the prestigious Pittsburgh Specialty Sweeps under breeder-Judge Jeannie O'Danielle and finished at 14 months old. After capturing several Best of Breed wins, Pepper retired for maternity with impressive success. She is the dam of 10 champions, including Am/Aust CH Deerpath's Charlemagne, a multiple Best in Show and a leading sire in Australia during the mid-1980s. His name appears in many Aussie pedigrees today. "Charlie" was the Grand Sire to CH Divani's Load of Trouble D'Laser, a great tribute and legacy to his fabulous dam, CH Colsidex Symphony, BROM.

CH Elken's Sherri

One of the great show bitches of the 1960s, the group and specialty winning Sherri gathered her honors under the skilled guidance of Jo Cox. Sherri came out of retirement occasionally to win the brood bitch and veteran bitch classes at specialties for her junior handlers/co-owners Somervell Linthicum, Jr., and Lyle Alexander, who fought for the privilege of taking her into the ring. It really did not matter who held her lead; head and tail high, Sherri knew how to turn in a winning performance.

Sherri combined her show career with maternity and produced 12 champions, 10 sired by CH Maximilian v. d. Reiteralm, NSD, BROM, HOF. The Sherri-Max "nick" resulted in BROM producer CH Elken's Brandy v. d. Reiteralm and three futurity winners: CH Shadowmar Wileen v. d. Reiteralm (1967), CH Elken's Juliana v. d. Reiteralm (1967), and CH Elken's Missy v. d. Reiteralm (1968).

CH Forshado Nani's Crystal Vision

CH Forshado Nani's Crystal Vision was a stud fee puppy. Weezie finished her championship with multiple Best of Breeds over specials. She did this having overcome a broken foot at 8 months of age and having a screw inserted to put it together. Weezie was a truly outstanding producer and can be seen in most of today's pedigrees. Weezie's 11 champion offspring were sired by three different studs: CH Arokat's Legionnaire, BROM; CH Nani's Ringside Rumor, CD, BROM; and CH Colsidex Standing Ovation, SD, JH, BROM; and produced the 1993 Top-Producing Dam, CH Nani's Kookaburra, BROM. Her most famous offspring was CH Nani's Southern Cross—the No. 4 Top Producing Sire of all time.

Figure 33-18: *CH Grayshar Easy Impression, NSD* (Am/Can CH Valmar Smokey City Ultra Easy, JH, BROM × Am/Can CH Greysport Touch Of Grace, TD, BROM). Bred and owned by Sharon J. Hartmann. Dam of 17 champions.

CH Grayshar Easy Impression, NSD

CH Grayshar Easy Impression was a tremendous producer and is currently the No. 2 all time Top-Producing Dam, with 17 Champions. She was the WCA's 1997 Top-Producing Dam and has Maturity and Futurity winning offspring. When bred to Am/Nat CH Valmar's Apache Rebel, BROM, she produced CH Grayshar's Reason To Believe, NSD, BROM, who was a Futurity and Maturity Winner and also received a JAOM at our National Specialty.

CH GraytSky's StellaLuna

Stella's high-spirited attitude, athleticism and beautiful breed type made her a joy to show and she completed her championship earning the AKC Bred by Exhibitor Medallion. Stella garnered Futurity and Maturity placements and 3 Best in Specialty Show, again owner handled. Her most important contribution, however, was as a producer. Stella was the 2004 WCA Top-Producing Dam and was tied for Pedigree Top Sporting-Breed Producer. Stella's three litters, sired by Am/Can CH Ashmore Win'Weim's Royal Flush, JH, BROM (2X), and CH Colsidex Nani Reprint, JH, BROM, have produced have produced 11 champions to date. Especially noteworthy among her get are: CH Grayt-Sky Win' Weim Affair in Times Square, "Broadway," who won three five-point majors in 24 hours to complete his AKC Championship at six-and-a-half months old, Best in Match, and 3 Best in Specialty Show; Am/Can/Aust CH GraytSky's Smokin' in Havana, "Mac," multiple group and 3 Best in Specialty Show, Top 10 All Systems; CH GraytSky Win It's My

Figure 33-19: *CH GraytSky's StellaLuna* (BIS CH Nani's Smart Aleck, JH, NRD, NSD, V, BROM × CH Nani N' GraytSky's Harvest Moon). Bred and owned by Amy and Michael Anderson. Dam of 11 champions.

Figure 33-20: *CH Harline's Hurrah* (CH Colsidex Standing Ovation, BROM × CH Dofo's Cristal V Hoot Hollow). Bred by Alan and Susan Line and Owen Forbes; owned by Alan and Susan Line. Dam of 10 champions.

Prague-Ative, "Dagmar," Best in Match, multiple group and 7 Best in Specialty Show, Top 10 All Systems, All Breed Best in Show; and CH GraytSky Anson Royal Flush Blush, "Rose," group winner, Canadian Best Puppy in Show, Top 10 All Systems.

CH Harline's Hurrah

CH Harline's Hurrah, BROM, finished her championship with three majors including a Best in Specialty Show win over seven specials. Bridget produced 15 puppies by CH Nani's Scirroco of Mattrace, CD, BROM, in her lifetime. Ten completed their championships and two more were pointed. She had several noteworthy offspring including multiple All-Breed Best in Show CH Harline's W F Rockefeller, who was the No. 1 Weimaraner in 1990; multiple All-Breed Best in Show CH WF Mattrace Harline Roquelle, who was on the Top 10 list for three years; and CH Mattrace Harline Roquette, who went Best of Opposite Sex at the WCA National Specialty and was a Group-placing show dog.

CH Jamspirit Complikate, CDX, RDX, SDX, VX

In the mid-1990s, Cheer and her owner-breeder Sami Simons explored all aspects of Weimaraner versatility—show, field, ratings, and obedience—simultaneously, and they proved a winning team. Cheer finished with five majors by her first birthday. Lightly specialed, Cheer has 20 breed wins (including a specialty), two group seconds, and three thirds. As for versatility, those Excellents in obedience, retrieving, and shooting leave nothing to add.

Figure 33-21: *CH JamSpirit CompliKate, CDX, RDX, SDX, VX* (CH JamSpirit Revolution, NRD, NSD, V, BROM × CH Sandvold's JamSpirit v. Creasy, CD, NRD, V, BROM). Bred and owned by L.K. (Sami) Simons. Dam of 11 champions.

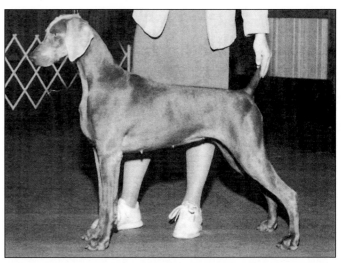

Figure 33-22: *CH Jarem's Casino Roulette* (CH Windemeire's Silber Striefen, BROM × Woodcreek's for Your Eyes Only, BROM). Bred by Sandra Jaremczuk; owned by Sandra Jaremczuk and Randy Hall. Dam of 13 champions.

Cheer passed her winning style and versatility to her puppies, and her 11 champions hold many obedience titles as well as shooting, retrieving, and versatile ratings. Bred to CH Colsidex Kg Arthur of Camelot, NRD, SD, V, BROM, Cheer produced four champions; bred to DC Arimar's Ivan, CD, NSD, SD, V, BROM, she produced seven champions, including OTCH pointed CH JamSpirit Evenstar, UDT, RDX, SD, VX. Cheer is the dam of two Futurity winners (both by Ivan): group-winning CH JamSpirit Evolution, CD, RDX, SDX, VX, BROM (1979) and CH Jam-Spirit Helmsman, CDX, TD, RD, NSD, VX (1982).

CH Jarem's Casino Roulette

From the time Nellie was 4 weeks old, she stood out over the rest of her siblings and we quickly decided she was the one to keep. Nellie was late maturing and was not seriously shown until she was 13 months old. She won her first two times out, picking up both majors and a Best of Breed over Specials. She completed her championship in less than 6 weeks, winning six of the eight shows she entered and picking up one more major. Shown briefly as a special, she won 10 Best of Breeds and five Best of Opposite Sex. However, her greatest accomplishment was her ability to produce. Bred to CH Arnstadt's Wotan Van Doblin, TD, CD, JH, VX, Nellie produced six Champion offspring and a multiple HIT OTCH son. The sire of her next litter was CH Nani's South-

Figure 33-23: *CH Kamsou Riptide* (CH Gwinner's Arco Wheel, BROM × CH Kamsou Redhill Remembrance). Bred by Kamsou Kennels; owned by Gina Columbo and Kamsou Kennels. Dam of 11 champions.

ern Cross, BROM, HOF, which produced four champions. The following year, she was bred to CH Sunmist Travel N Style, which produced one champion and one Junior Hunter. Her final litter was sired by CH Hope's Thunder Jack of Diamonds, JH, which produced two champion offspring, one of which is also an OTCH, with multiple High in Trials, a Junior Hunter and a Versatile Excellent Rating. Nellie was truly a breeder's dream come true.

CH Kamsou Riptide

Following a distinguished show career with multiple group placements in 1974 and 1975, Ripper was older than five when she began motherhood. Her record of three Best in Show winners from three different sires will be difficult to equal. CH WC's The Dynamic Dagowheel, a multiple Best in Show winner (sired by CH WC's The Dutchman of Dauntmar, BROM) led the breed's Top 10 list in 1978 and 1979. CH WC's Starwheel of Ranah (sired by CH Jarem's Rhinestone Cowboy, BROM) went Best in Show at 17 months. Am/Aust CH Ranah's Bold Ruler v Reiteralm (sired by CH Reiteralm's Rio Fonte Saudade, NRD, BROM) is a multiple Best in Show winner in Australia. Winner of the 1979 National Specialty, the group-winning CH Kamsou Jack the Ripper, CD, RD, SD, VX, BROM, won Gun Dog and All-Age stakes before his untimely death. Ripper's four BROM daughters are carrying on her tradition of quality: CH Kamsou's Dutch Treat; CH Ranah's Carry Me Back, CD, TD, NRD, SD, VX; CH Ranah's Totally Hot, NSD; and CH Ranah's Continental Wirlaway.

CH Kamsou Dutch Treat

CH Kamsou Dutch Treat, BROM, is synonymous with Warheit Weimaraners, Gayle Taber, and a product of the original Ranah Weimaraners, Gina and Ron Columbo. This funny, fat, bundle of gray puppy arrived in Texas after a nearly 2-year wait. Her sire was three-time Best in Show CH W. C.'s The Dutchman of Dauntmar and her dam the beautifully elegant Top Producer CH Kamsou Riptide, BROM.

Along with Goodie came many firsts for Warheit, an astounding accomplishment on Goodie's part. Some of those firsts include Gayle Tabor's first show dog, first Futurity class winner, (Junior Central Futurity, 1977), first Champion, and from Goodie's first litter, her first Futurity winner, CH Ranah's Rajah v. d. Reiteralm (Western Futurity, 1980), sired by CH Ronamax Rajah v. d. Reiteralm, BROM. Most important, Goodie was her first Top Producing BROM and from Goodie have come so many more Weimaraners in all these categories.

Goodie has left her mark on numerous other breeding programs, including Image Weimaraners, Cindy James-Moore, with Goodie's great-grandson Best in Futurity CH Warheit's High Caliber, CD, NSD, NRD, BROM, Gayle's first male BROM.

The dog world has been good to Gayle; through Goodie and all her produce, she has become more knowledgeable and have met and made many lifelong friends.

Goodie will always be FIRST in her heart and memories.

CH Kris-Miss Shadow, CD

Karla South wrote, "We had never been to a dog show and did not select Kris by the recommended methods. Somehow, Kris was meant to leave a legacy of greatness." Never specialed, Kris won the veteran class at the 1975 National Specialty at the age of 12.

Bred twice to CH Warhorse Billy of Redhill, CD, BROM, and once to CH Gretchenhof Silver Thor, NRD, Kris produced the group winners CH Kams Rauchessen of Redhill, BROM (Canadian Best in Show); and CH Wotan Von RiMar. Her Futurity winners Rauchessen and CH Oliver's Valkyrie of Redhill (by Billy) swept the honors at the 1966 Western Futurity, and Kams Dusty Twilight (by Thor) won in 1970. Kris held the

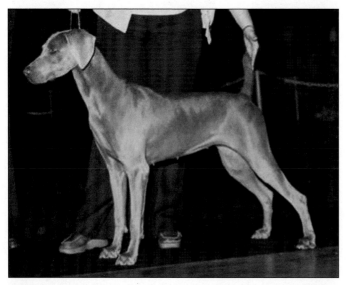

Figure 33-24: *CH Kamsou Dutch Treat* (CH W. C.'s The Dutchman of Dauntmar, BROM × CH Kamsou Riptide, BROM). Bred by Gina and Ron Columbo; owned by Gayle Taber. Dam of 11 champions.

Figure 33-25: *CH Kris-Miss Shadow, CD* (Monarch of Long Beach × Dutchess Amber). Bred by J. L. McMurray; owned by Karla and Martin South. Dam of 13 champions.

Figure 33-26: *Kristoff's TNT Jessica* (Kamsou's Seawind Thunderhead × Ann's Rose Tiara von Kristof). Bred and owned by Sharon Krube. Dam of 16 champions.

Figure 33-27: *CH Lady Sarah of Camelot, NSD* (CH Colsidex Kg Arthur of Camelot, BROM × DC Lady Rebecca of Camelot, BROM). Bred and owned by Sue Thomas. Dam of 11 champions.

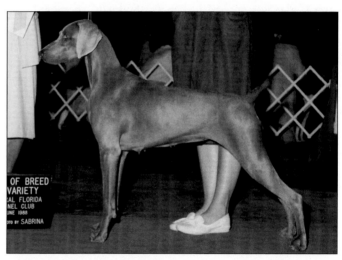

Figure 33-28: *CH Lightfoot's Oceana V Atlantis, JH, NSD, RD, V* (CH EB's You Otta See Me Now, JH, SD, V, BROM × CH Skytop's Misty Blue, CD, TD, NSD, VX, BROM). Bred by Deborah Jo Moody; owned by Ginger D. Spreen. Dam of 10 champions.

breed record of 13 champions for many years. Through her BROM daughter CH Kams Rauchigalen of Redhill, CD, and her other top-producing progeny, many American Weimaraners owe at least a little of their qualities to this fine bitch.

Kristof's TNT Jessica

Jessie never got her championship, but because of her great temperament, intelligence, and good health, she was bred to CH Kristof's Kitsap Coho, CH Sir Eric Von Sieben, and CH Kristof's Royal Crusader. Last records show 16 champions (four with Coho, three with Eric, and nine with Cruser). Jessie attained the BROM in July 1980. She was listed as a Top Producer in the February 1981 Kennel Review Magazine and was awarded in 1982 the Schlintz Top Producers Silver Certificate. She was the dam of the 1980 Best Bitch in Western Futurity and Best Bitch in Central Futurity. Jessie was known also for her tremendous ear size.

CH Lady Sarah of Camelot, NSD

A Top 10 Derby dog with a field major, CH Lady Sarah of Camelot earned her BROM with her first two litters. Sarah was the WCA's No. 1 Top-Producing Dam twice. Like her Dual Champion mother and Dual Champion sister, Sarah was a beautiful Best of Breed winner and a competitive field bitch. The years were kind to Sarah; at the age of 13 she received an Award of Merit at the National Specialty. She was the dam of 11 champions, who have won both Field and Bench Futurities as well as field trials. Sarah's daughter won the Eastern Field Futurity, handled by breeder-owner

Sue Thomas. She is the dam of CH Camelot's Halley's Comet, BROM (sired by Am/Can CH Colsidex Nani Reprint, JH, SD, BROM), who also went on to be a Top Producer for Camelot. Sarah lived contentedly to a respectable age of 16 1/2 years.

CH Lightfoot's Oceana V Atlantis, JH, NSD, RD, V

CH Lightfoot's Oceana V Atlantis, JH, NSD, RD, V, BROM, was specially chosen for Ginger Speen by her mother, Carole Donaldson, Tri-D Weimaraners, and friend, Helen Remaley, Skytop Weimaraners. Ginger shares that through their guidance, "Oshi and I both learned and experienced so much together, making friends and memories everywhere we traveled." Oshi proved to be the perfect companion and foundation dam of Atlantis Weimaraners. Her sweet personality and versatility was passed on to her progeny. She produced 10 bench champions, establishing her as a WCA Top-Producing Dam. Many of her pups earned AKC Hunt Test and obedience titles in addition to WCA Shooting Dog and Retrieving Dog rating titles. Her daughter, CH Atlantis You've Got The Look, JH, SD, NRD, V, was a group competitor and WCA Specialty and Maturity winner. Oshi was an absolute joy to own and a true ambassador to the breed. To this day Ginger is thankful to Debbie Moody, for sharing this wonderful girl with her.

Am/Can CH Moonshine's Gray Brocade, CD, NSD, V

Am/Can CH Moonshine's Gray Brocade, CD, NSD, V, BROM, came to the Taylor family at 11 months old from breeder Marlene Judd of Moonshine Weimaraners. Two weeks later Cadee was entered in her first Specialty Show and won Best in Sweepstakes. The next day at the All-Breed Show she won her first major. She finished in six weekends of showing at age 13 months. Five months later, she won her first two group placements. Cadee was a group winner, finished her Canadian Championship in three days, went Best in Specialty Show from the classes at the WCA National Specialty in 1996, and placed in her Futurity and Maturity. She came out of retirement at age 11 and won a Best in Specialty Show from the Veteran class. She produced 11 champions and was the WCA's 1999 Top Producer. Cadee was bred to BIS BISS National CH Ultima's Stetson V Hufmeister, CD, BROM, and produced five champions, including one who was a multiple group placer in the U.S. and Canada. Cadee's second breeding was to BIS BISS CH Wind-

Figure 33-30: *CH Nani's Ariana v. d. Reiteralm* (CH Maximilian v. d. Reiteralm, NSD, BROM, HOF × CH Nani's Silver Sparkle). Bred by Carl Pospsil and Smokey Medeiros; owned by Christine Medeiros. Dam of 13 champions.

walker's Graeagle, CD, JH, NRD, V, BROM, and produced six champions. This litter produced multi-titled and winning progeny, including a Futurity winner, Best in Specialty Show , Sporting Dog Spectacular Group 1 winner in Canada, and numerous performance titles.

Am/Can CH Nani's Ariana v. d. Reiteralm

Gumby finished in only six brief weeks of showing and retired to become the reigning Nani matriarch. The dam of 13 champions, Gumby produced CH Nani's Windward Makimilio from CH Landbee's Upland Danny Boy. She is best known, however, for the "soul" litter with CH Brandy's Rebel v. d. Reiteralm, NRD, BROM, which produced consistently impressive soundness and beauty, and for her BROM daughters from that cross—CH Nani's Soul Sensation and CH Nani's Soul Sister.

Figure 33-29: *Am/Can CH Moonshine's Gray Brocade, CD, NSD, V* (CH Moonshines' Go Silverwind × CH Moonshine's Alpha Centauri). Bred by Marlene and Judy Judd; owned by Barbara and Jesse Taylor. Dam of 11 champions.

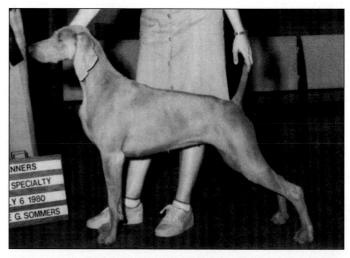

Figure 33-31: *CH Nani's Cascade v. d. Reiteralm* (CH Ann's Magic v. d. Reiteralm, BROM × CH Nani's Soul Sensation, BROM). Bred and owned by Christine Medeiros. Dam of 12 champions.

CH Nani's Cascade v. d. Reiteralm

Cadey finished her championship with two 5-point majors at specialty shows and went on to become a third-generation producer of 12 or more champions.

In four litters by four different sires, Cadey produced 12 champions. Her outstanding progeny include the following: CH Nani's Weejun Reiteralm; CH Nani's Grey Gucci; CH Nani's Stride Rite Reiteralm, NSD; CH Nani's Rising Sun; and Nani's Footnotes to Dawn, CDX—10th on the breed's Top 10 obedience list in 1985. Cadey's BROM daughters CH Nani's Cobbie Cuddler and CH Nani's Ananas of Silvermont carry on the Nani tradition of top-producing bitches in the United States; her daughter Nani's Helga of Bromhund, is the dam of 10 Australian champions, including two all-breed Best in Show winners.

CH Nani's Cobbie Cuddler, HOF

Cuddles finished her championship with two five-point majors at specialty shows. She then began her important career as a producer and is the fourth generation of Nani Producers in this chapter. From three litters sired by Am/Can CH Colsidex Standing Ovation, BROM, HOF, Cuddles produced 15 champions that include group and specialty winners. She is the dam of the Futurity winner CH Nani's Scirroco of Mattrace, BROM (1985), and four Maturity winners: CH Nani's Island Breeze (1986), CH Nani's Valley Girl (1986), CH Nani's Kona Gust, CD, BROM (1986), and CH Colsidex Nani Reprint, JH, SD, BROM, HOF (1988). After finishing his championship and siring litters in the United States, Am/NZ CH Nani's Totally Awesome, BROM, went to New Zealand, where he proved to be an influential sire.

Figure 33-32: *CH Nani's Cobbie Cuddler, HOF* (CH Nani's Master Charge, NRD, NSD, V, BROM, HOF × CH Nani's Cascade v. d. Reiteralm, BROM). Bred and owned by Christine Medeiros. Dam of 15 champions.

Figure 33-33: *CH Nani's Jagmar Sweet Dividends, VCD2, CDX, TD, MH, MX, MXJ, NSD, NRD, CGC, VX4* (CH Nani's Concert Master, SH, BROM × CH Nani's Sweet Investment, CD, BROM). Bred by Claire Durivage and Christine Grisell; owned by Teresa Borman and Christine Grisell. Dam of 10 champions.

CH Nani's Jagmar Sweet Dividends, VCD2, CDX, TD, MH, MX, MXJ, NSD, NRD, VX4

CH Nani's Jagmar Sweet Dividends, VCD2, CDX, TD, MH, MX, MXJ, NSD, NRD, VX4, BROM, finished her bench championship easily and then focused on performance work. With her novice owner, Diva proceeded to excel in everything she tried, earning numerous obedience, hunt, agility, tracking, and versatility titles and an all-breed obedience High in Trial award. In 2004, Diva took time off from performance competition to have two litters sired by CH Nani's Indecent Exposure, JH, NAJ, V, BROM, and found yet another area where she excelled. Of the 12 resulting offspring, a record-setting 10 finished their U.S. Championship in one year, earning Diva the 2005 Top-Producing Dam award and making her the sixth generation of No. 1 Top Producers. Several offspring finished their championships with five-point majors earned during Futurity/Maturity weekends, and one went Winners Bitch at the 2005 National Specialty (CH Nani's Sophisticated Lady, MH, NA, NAJ, SDX, VX). Her progeny include a son (CH Nani's Tsurutani Honor Bound, JH) who is a Best in Show winner, Top 10 Show Dog and the Best of Opposite Sex winner at the 2006 WCA Nationals and another son (AUS Grand CH/CH Nani's Sovereign Cross Check, JH) in Australia who is a multiple Best in Show winner. They are also following in their mother's performance footsteps, where several have earned advanced hunt, agility, tracking, retrieving, and Versatile Excellent titles.

Figure 33-34: *CH Nani's Nobodies Patsie, JH* (CH Midnite Magic von HolyHaus × CH Nani's Knocker, CDX, TD, JH, SD, VX, BROM). Bred by Christine Grisell and Susan Casper; owned by Christine Grisell and Mary Grabow-Fenchek. Dam of 10 champions.

Figure 33-35: *CH Nani's Perfect Cadence, CD, JH, V* (CH Nani's Baht a Pack a Trouble, CD, JH, V, BROM × CH Nani's Kookaburra, BROM). Bred by Christine Grisell; owned by Christine Grisell and Kari Chaney. Dam of 10 champions.

CH Nani's Nobodies Patsie, JH

CH Nani's Nobodies Patsie, JH, BROM, was a littermate to CH Nani's Smart Aleck, JH, NRD, V, BROM. While Aleck was being specialed, Patsie decided to make her mark in the whelping room. Patsie's first litter of two was an AI litter sired by CH Nani's Southern Cross, BROM, and both offspring won their Maturities. Her champion daughter from that litter went on to produce a National Specialty winner and a Futurity and Maturity winner. Patsie had two additional litters with two different sires. A total of 10 champions were produced, exemplifying the consistency of her progeny, and she was the Top-Producing Dam in 2003.

CH Nani's Perfect Cadence, CD, JH, V

When CH Nani's Perfect Cadence, CD, JH, V, BROM, became available at 10 months of age, her breeder gladly purchased her back. What a great decision that turned out to be, as Cadey went on to be a wonderful producer. She started by easily finishing her championship and was a Best in Specialty Show winner. Cadey then went on to produce 10 champions and was the Top-Producing Dam in 1997. One of her sons, CH Nani's Concert Master, SH, BROM, was the Top Producing Sire for 1999. Following her litters, Cadey tried her hand at performance events with her co-owner and readily earned her Companion Dog, Junior Hunter, and Versatility titles.

Figure 33-36: *CH Nani's Soul Sensation* (CH Brandy's Rebel v. d. Reiteralm, NRD, BROM × CH Nani's Araina v. d. Reiteralm, BROM). Bred by Christine Medeiros and Judith Lundbeck; owned by Christine Medeiros. Dam of 12 champions.

CH Nani's Soul Sensation

Bertha is from the first Nani "soul" litter produced with Rebel and Ariana. During her outstanding show career, Bertha ranked on the Top 10 Weimaraner lists in 1977 and 1978 (ranking 4th and 5th). The dam of only two litters, both sired by CH Ann's Magic v. d. Reiteralm, BROM,

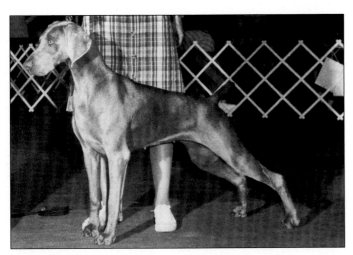

Figure 33-37: *CH Nani's Soul Sister* (CH Brandy's Rebel v. d. Reiteralm, NRD, BROM × CH Nani's Araina v. d. Reiteralm, BROM). Bred by Christine Medeiros and Judith Lundbeck; owned by Christine Medeiros. Dam of 12 champions.

Figure 33-38: *CH Norman's Frostyroy Colleen* (CH Greywind's Jack Frost, BROM, HOF × Doblens Sirene Sunrise). Bred and owned by Norman LeBoeuf. Dam of 13 champions.

she produced 16 puppies. Bertha is the dam of 12 champions, including the Maturity winner CH Nani's Jubilee Jill of Ranah (1982), and the Top Producer CH Nani's Cascade v. d. Reiteralm, BROM.

CH Nani's Soul Sister

A repeat of the Nani "soul" breeding of Ariana and Rebel produced Sis, who finished with many Best of Breed wins from the classes over Specials. Sis quickly proved to be an outstanding producer. Her litter, sired by CH Nani's Silver Slate, NRD, NSD, produced three champions, including CH Nani's Raising Ned at Charmony, a Top Producer in Brazil. Bred to CH Reiteralm's Rio Fonte Saudade, NRD, BROM, Sis produced nine champions, including the breed's youngest Best in Show winner, CH Nani's Visa v. d. Reiteralm, BROM (Futurity 1980). The Sis-Rio combination also produced the following: CH Nani's Master Charge, NRD, NSD, V, BROM, HOF (top-winning Weimaraner of 1982), CH Nani's Cartel, CD, NRD, NSD (1985 Top 10), CH Nani's Carte Blanche, BROM (top winner of groups and specialties in Hawaii), CH Nani's Ann of Enchantment, BROM, and Nani's Spirit-O-Moonshine, CD, BROM.

CH Norman's Frostyroy Colleen

CH Normans Frostyroy Colleen was the dam of 13 champions for the Norman's kennel. Colleen's offspring include two Futurity winners, group winners and the "Pedigree's Best of the Best of Breed Award" winner. When bred to Am/Can CH Valmar Smokey City Ultra Easy, JH, NSD, BROM, HOF, Colleen produced BIS Am/Can CH Norman's Smokey City Heat Wave, BROM, who was the 1990 and 1991 No. 1 Show Dog and the 1991 and 1992 National

Specialty winner. The same litter also produced Am/Can CH Norman's Smokey City Chill Fact'r, JH, NRD, BROM, as well as Futurity winner CH Norman's EZ Platinum.

Am/Can CH Norman's Smokey City Heat Wave, JH, HOF

In the very capable hands of Peggy Rousch, Am/Can CH Norman's Smokey City Heat Wave, JH, BROM, HOF, was the No. 1 Weimaraner in the U.S.. in 1990 and 1991 and in Canada in 1991. She won the WCA National Specialty in

Figure 33-39: *Am/Can CH Norman's Smokey City Heat Wave, JH, HOF* (Am/Can CH Valmar Smokey City Ultra Easy, JH, BROM, HOF × CH Norman's Frostyroy Colleen, BROM). Bred by Norman LeBoeuf; owned by Tom Wilson and Ronna Katzin. Dam of 13 champions.

1991 and 1992, along with the Canadian National Specialty in 1991. Her career included an all-breed Best in Show, 143 Best of Breeds, 15 Group wins, and 53 group placements. She was the dam of 13 champions, five by CH Nani's Sanbar Ringside Rumor, JH, BROM, and eight by CH Smokey City Ez Moonstone, JH, NRD, BROM. Her most noteworthy offspring was CH Smokey City El Nino, JH, BROM, who is the sire of 64 champions to date.

BIS CH The Rajah's Magic v. d. Reiteralm, HOF

Upon the conclusion of her spectacular show career, Best in Show winner CH The Rajah's Magic v. d. Reiteralm (Yellow Bird) retired to live with her handler, Peggy Roush. Yellow Bird was first bred to Best in Show winner CH Eric Von Sieben, BROM, producing the breed's first litter from two Best in Show winners. This litter would produce the BROM brothers CH Ann's Magic vd Reiteralm (39 champions) and CH Reiteralm's Rio Fonte Saudade (44 champions); these two studs appear in the pedigrees of 85% of the Best in Show Winners since their birth. Eric's son CH Von Sieben's Smart 'n Special, NSD, BROM, sired her second litter which produced six champions, including Silberholm Ricky v Reiteralm, BROM (14 champions). Yellow Bird is one of only three bitches that were able to combine both show and whelping box careers and as a result make both the Best in Show list as well as the Top-Producing Dams list. In recognition of her contributions to the breed, she was inducted into the Weimaraner Club of America's Hall of Fame in 2004.

CH Rajah's Sass of Gray Brigade, CDX, TD, NSD, VX

CH Rajah's Sass of Gray Brigade, CDX, TD, NSD, VX, BROM, was a consistent producer with 10 champion offspring to her credit. When bred to CH Chatawey's Rumor V. Reiteralm, BROM, Sassy produced five champions for the Wismar Kennel and another four champions under the Wismar Kennel, when bred to CH High Fields Heir Major and CH Maximilian von der Reiteralm, NSD, BROM. Her offspring also earned several performance titles, including six who earned their Tracking Dog title.

Am/Can CH Reichenstadt's Cameo

Cami began her impressive show career as Southland Weimaraner Club's top-winning puppy in 1972, and she went on to become a multiple group winner. Linebred to CH Kam-

Figure 33-40: *BIS CH The Rajah's Magic v. d. Reiteralm, HOF* (BIS CH Ronamax Rajah v. d. Reiteralm, BROM, HOF × CH Brandy's Blizz v. d. Reiteralm, BROM). Bred by Virginia Alexander and Gail Muller; owned by Virginia Alexander. Dam of 10 champions.

Figure 33-41: *CH Rajahs Sass of Gray Brigade, CDX, TD, NSD, VX* (CH Ronamax Rajah v. d. Reiteralm, BROM, HOF × Harris Rebel Of Vicksburg). Bred by T. G. Harris Jr.; owned by Barbara and John Wise. Dam of 10 champions.

Figure 33-42: *Am/Can CH Reichenstant's Cameo* (CH Doug's Dauntless von Dor, BROM, HOF × CH Kams Rauchigalan of Redhill, CD, BROM). Bred by Richard Slater; owned by Maurice and Colleen Kertz. Dam of 15 champions.

Figure 33-43: *CH Silversmith Indigo V Kristof, CD, NRD, V* (CH Kristof's Royal Crusader, BROM × CH Wismar's April Silversmith, CDX, TD, RD, NSD, VX, BROM). Bred by Allen and Elena Smith; owned by Marcia Snyder and Elena Smith (Lamberson). Dam of 10 champions.

Figure 33-44: *CH Silversmith Lady Gracie, JH, NSD, NRD, V* (CH Cameo's Island Hunter, JH, NSD, NRD, V, BROM × CH Telmar's Gayna Silversmith, JH, SD, NRD, V, BROM). Bred by Elena Smith Lamberson; owned by Tracy Brabham and Elena Smith Lamberson. Dam of 11 champions.

sou Whirlpool, CH Kamsou Sterling Smoke, CD, NRD, NSD, V, BROM, and CH Reichenstadt's Majestic, BROM, Cami is the impressive dam of 15 champions, including group winning CH Reichenstadt's Kona v. Arenas, BROM. Cami's BROM daughters are Kona, CH Arena's Wine and Mink, and CH Kandans Jai Alai v. Arenas.

CH Silversmith Indigo V Kristof, CD, NRD, V

Poppy was one of five champion littermates. She was shown to her championship with ease as she had wonderful conformation and flashy movement. She was a multiple Best of Breed and Best of Opposite Sex winner over specials from the classes and placed twice in the Sporting Group. She was bred to CH Jarem's Rhinestone Cowboy, BROM; BIS Am/Can CH Valmar's Smokey City Easy Does It, JH, BROM; and CH Silversmith Omni Roy, CD, RD, NSD, V, BROM; producing 10 champions, including Futurity and Maturity, Best of Breed winners, and group placers. When the Snyders moved to London, Poppy went to live with Sam and Margie Williams in New Mexico and died at age 15.

CH Silversmith Lady Gracie, JH, NSD, NRD, V

Beautiful and showy, CH Silversmith Lady Gracie, JH, NSD, NRD, V, BROM, finished her Championship from the Bred by Exhibitor class and then went to live with 13-year-old Tracy Brabham, who showed her in Juniors all the way to

Figure 33-45: *CH Silversmith Omni V Reiteralm, CD, TD, RD, NSD, VX* (CH Reiteralm's Rio Fonte Saudade, NRD, BROM × CH Robin's Song v. Reiteralm). Bred by Rebecca Harris and Virginia Alexander; owned by Elena and Allen Smith. Dam of 13 champions.

Westminster. Gracie won the Southern Maturity handled by Alessandra Folz. Tracy showed her to many Best of Breeds, several Group wins, Specialty wins, an all-breed Veteran Best in Show, and Award of Merit at the Nationals from the veteran class. She was bred twice to CH Windwalker Graeagle, JH, CD, BROM, and produced 11 champions, including several Futurity, Maturity, specialty, and group winners.

CH Silversmith Omni V Reiteralm, CD, TD, RD, NSD, VX

Feebee was the foundation bitch of Silversmith Kennel. She was an eye-catching, gorgeous bitch, extremely versatile, and novice owner-handled to all her titles. She finished at the Weimaraner Club of South Florida Specialty, went Best of Breed the next day over seven champions, and won junior bitch from a class of 25 at the WCA's largest Futurity. Feebee was bred to four stud dogs: CH Silversmith Harbor Pilot; CH Hoot Hollows Roy's Rob, CD, BROM; FC Weick's Tidewater Sil-

Figure 33-46: *Am/Can CH Skyhi's Northern Dare to Dream* (Am/Can CH Skyhi's Electric Sensation × Am/Can CH Skyhi's Ez Magical Reign, JH, UD, SD, NRD, VX, BROM). Bred by Judith Voris, David Sherrer, and Nina Hancock; owned by Judy Edinger, Shannon Edinger, and Kerry Edinger. Dam of 11 champions.

Figure 33-47: *CH Smokey City Jedda Arokat* (Am/Can CH Arokat's Legionnaire, BROM × Smokey City's Split Decision). Bred by Tom Wilson and E. Frye; owned by Tom Wilson. Dam of 17 champions.

versmith, UD, RDX, SDX, VX; and the last to her beautiful young grandson, CH Indigo's Patriot Silversmith, JH, NRD, NSD, V. From these litters she produced 13 champions. Feebee herself was beautifully line-bred and was prepotent for lovely type, soundness, and birdiness, and her puppies have tremendous showmanship. Her progeny include the following: Best in Show, multiple group and specialty winner CH Silversmith Dawn v. Greystoke, best in Futurity and best in Maturity, CH Silversmith Omni Roy, CD, JH, RD, NSD, VS, BROM, and the first American-bred Weimaraner champion to win Best in Show in Germany, CH Silversmith Harbor Pistol.

Am/Can CH Skyhi's Northern Dare to Dream

Am/Can CH Skyhi's Northern Dare to Dream, BROM, show career included multiple group wins and placements, two specialty Best of Opposite Sex, and multiple Best Junior Handler awards with her young owner-handlers. In 2005 at the WWWC specialty, Dream received a Judges' Award of Merit at 10 years of age. Dream was bred twice to CH Valmars Unanimous Decision, BROM, and Isle Vue Kennels Reg. was born. Of 14 puppies, 11 are AKC champions and six are also Canadian champions. CH Isle Vue Cocktails & Dreams, RN, OAJ, followed in her footsteps and was awarded Best of Opposite Sex at the WWWC 2005 Specialty. The Best in Specialty Show winning bitch CH IsleVue Dare to Love Lucy had a distinguished specials career and ranked in the top five in 2004. Many of Dream's offspring hold performance titles in the field, obedience, agility, and one is a certified Delta Therapy Dog. Dream's effortless movement and outstanding show presence can be seen in her Isle Vue progeny.

CH Smokey City Jedda Arokat

CH Smokey City Jedda Arokat, BROM, was sold as a pet and bought back when she was 10 months old; in hindsight, it was a fortuitous decision. Jedda was bred exclusively to CH Valmar Smokey City Ultra Easy, and the resulting litters produced 17 champions. She is the second-highest Producing Dam to date. Jedda was also the WCA's Top-Producing Dam in 1993, with seven champions finished that year. Of her 17 champions, an impressive six won either their Futurity or Maturity, and one won both her Futurity and Maturity. Some of her progeny have become influential producers in breed history, including her son CH Smokey City Ez Moonstone, JH, NRD, V, BROM, the sire of 24 champions; her grandson, CH Smokey City El Nino, JH, BROM, who went on to sire 64 champions; her daughter, WinWeim's foundation bitch, CH Smokycity Ez Win'd BNTH R Wing, NRD, NSD, BROM, the dam of 10 champions; and her granddaughter, Multi-BIS CH Smoky City D'Nunder Lazer Beam, the dam of 10 champions.

Figure 33-48: *CH Smokey City EZ Win'd B'nth R Wings, NSD, NRD V,* (Am/Can CH Valmar's Smokey City Ultra Easy, JH, BROM, HOF × CH Smokey City Jedda Arokat, BROM). Bred by Tom Wilson; owned by Dana Massey. Dam of 10 champions.

Figure 33-49: *BIS CH Smokycity D'Nunder Lazer Beam* (Am/Can/Grand Aust CH Divani Loads A' Trouble, BROM × CH Smokey City E Z Elegance). Bred by Tom Wilson and Jennifer Miller owned by Monika Hood, Anne Cullen-Tormey, and Tom Wilson. Dam of 10 champions.

CH Smokey City EZ Win'd B'nth R Wings, NSD, NRD, V

CH Smokey City Ez Win'd B'nth R Wings, NRD, NSD, BROM, produced BROM champions from one litter out of National/AKC CH BISS Nani's Southern Cross, BROM, HOF. Wings other champions were from two litters out of CH BISS Nani's Concert Master, SH, BROM. Her get include multiple Best in Specialty Show and AKC All-Breed Best in Show winner CH Win'Weim's Shootin' High Brass, three BROM bitches, and multiple international champions, Companion Dog, Tracking Dog, Novice Agility, Novice Agility Jumper, and Open Agility titled get, and a Versatile Companion Dog 1. Her grand-get include Junior Hunter, Senior Hunter, All-Breed High in Trial, Best in Futurity, and Best in Maturity. On her last day with Dana, she played with her human grandchildren, ran in the field, chased an annoying Sheltie, helped trim the gate for Christmas, curled up on the front porch to go to sleep, and never woke up. She was Dana's soulmate—and foundation bitch.

BIS CH Smokycity D'Nunder Lazer Beam

CH Smokycity D'Nunder Lazer Beam, BROM, completed her championship at 9 months of age, winning the Breed over Top 10 Specials, winning group placements, and was the 12th in All-Breed standings in only 6 months of showing. Along with Bob Double in 1999, Sydney won the Breed at the WCA National Specialty, was Best Bitch in the Eastern Maturity, and won the first of her three All-Breed Best in Shows. Syd-

ney also won the Breed at the Westminster Kennel Club dog show, was the No. 1 Weimaraner for both systems, and the Pedigree winner for 1999. Bred to CH Smokey City El Nino (Logan), she produced some of the top-winning dogs in recent times. These include CH Smokey City Hail Mary, who was a multiple Best in Show winner and won both the American and Canadian National Specialty in the same year; CH Smoky City True Grit, who was a multiple group winner and a Futurity and

Figure 33-50: *CH Starbuck's California Dove, NSD* (CH Valmar's Creco Schwenden × CH Halann's Star of Rajah, BROM). Bred by Henrietta (Rusty) Jenrette; owned by Rusty Jenrette and Florence W. Coons. Dam of 11 champions.

Figure 33-51: *CH Top Hat's Aria, CD, NSD, V* (CH Valmar's Rio Bravo × CH Valmar's Theme Song). Bred by Debbie and Jim Hopkins; owned by Cheryl Orr and Debra Hopkins. Dam of 12 champions.

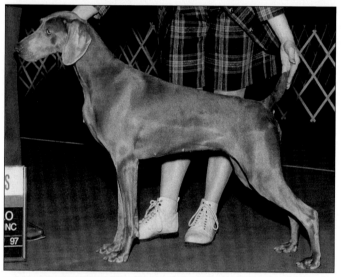

Figure 33-52: *Telmar Hot Topic of Rushland* (CH Aria's Aladdin of Telmar × Telmar H H Entertainer). Bred by Ann Marie Marcoux; owned by Joyce Tetla and Tom Wilson. Dam of 10 champions.

Figure 33-53: *CH Top Hat's Fantome Shallyn Debut* (CH Windwalkers Graeagle, CD, JH, NRD, V, BROM × CH Top Hat's Dubtant, BROM). Bred by F. Farr and D. Hopkins; owned by Debra Hopkins. Dam of 10 champions.

Maturity winner; and CH Smoky City Like a Rollin Stone, who finished with three 5-point Specialty wins before his first birthday and was a Futurity winner.

CH Starbucks California Dove, NSD

Rusty Jenrette struck gold when she bred this outstanding bitch—a fifth-generation BROM dam. To validate her belief in back-crossing to an outstanding grandsire, Rusty bred Dove to CH Ronamax Rajah v. d. Reiteralm, BROM, HOF, a combination that produced her 11 champions, including Futurity winner CH Starbuck's Quailtrac Pixie (1978). Pixie went on to become a group winner and the top-winning Weimaraner bitch in 1980. The lightly specialed CH Starbuck's Desert Rajah, CD, was a multiple specialty and group winner.

Telmar Hot Topic of Rushland

Telmar Hot Topic of Rushland, BROM, produced 10 champion offspring for the Smokycity kennel. Bred to CH Smokey City El Nino, JH, BROM, she produced eight American champions and one Dutch champion, including a Best Bitch in Maturity winner. She then produced two more champions by Am/Can CH Valmar Smokey City Ultra Easy, JH, NSD, BROM, HOF.

CH Top Hat's Aria, CD, NSD, V

CH Top Hat's Aria, CD, NSD, V, BROM, was her breeder's first homebred litter and first champion. Pippa is the producer of 12 champion progeny and was WCA's Top-Producing Bitch for 1989 and 1992. Pippa's owner, Cheryl Orr, novice-handled her to her championship. Pippa was bred to CH Nani's N Top Hat's Backlash, CD, NSD, V, and produced seven champions, including two Top 10 progeny, "Bogie" CH Top Hat's Top Gun, BROM (sire of WCA Top 10 BIS/BISS CH Valmar's Apache Rebel, BROM) and "Bria" BISS CH Top Hat's Spit Fire, who was Junior-handled to her WCA Top 10 and qualified for Juniors for the prestigious Westminster Kennel Club Show. Bria is also the dam of the Top Show bitch, CH Aria's Alegra of Colsidex with 27 Best in Shows. Another offspring, CH Top Hat's Warlord, was a group winner and 1990 Western Maturity winner, finishing his career on the WCA Top 20.

CH Top Hat's Fantome Shallyn Debut

CH Top Hat's Fantome Shallyn Debut, BROM, was from the first litter produced by CH Windwalker's Graeagle, CD, JH, NRD, V, BROM. She came back to us when she was 2 years old, too much Weimaraner for her owner to handle! Piper was WCA's 2002 Top-Producing Bitch, while her litter sister, CH Top Hat's Fantome of the Heart,

Figure 33-54: *CH Valmar's Evening Sonata* (CH Bama Belle's Mountain Man, BROM × CH Valmar's Pollyanna, BROM, HOF). Bred and owned by Joan H. Valdez. Dam of 11 champions.

Figure 33-55: *CH Valmar's Grayshar Burgundy* (BIS CH Valmar's Apache Rebel, BROM × CH Grayshar Easy Impression, BROM). Bred by Sharon Hartmann; owned by Rachel M. Aguilar and Joan H. Valdez. Dam of 12 champions.

BROM, was Top Producer for 1999. Piper produced 10 champions. From her first litter by CH Top Hat's Outrageous Fortune, she produced CH Top Hat's West Side Story, UD, JH, NRD, NSD, VX. Her second litter by CH Nambe N Zara's Zackly Right, CDX, OA, OAJ, NAP, NSD, V, produced CH Top Hat's Why Ask Y, JH, NRD, NSD, who showed great promise in the field and was pointed when he was taken to the Rainbow Bridge much too early. Piper's last litter by CH Carousels Roscoe T. Picotrane, BROM, produced several wonderful babies, including CH Top Hat's Down On The Corner, who won four Best in Specialty Show. Piper's daughter, CH Top Hat's Bad Moon Rising, CDX, RE, OA, OAJ, NAP, NSD, VX, continues her career as a multiple-High in Trial Obedience and High in Rally Trail competitor.

CH Valmar's Evening Sonata

CH Valmar's Evening Sonata, BROM is a typical, sound bitch with a sweet, bubbly personality. Sony began her show career at 8 months of age, by winning a five-point major from the puppy class and then went on to win Best of Breed over seven specials (including the No. 1 Top 10 Weimaraner). Sony's second major was also from the puppy class. After finishing her championship, Sony was specialed for the remainder of the year, capturing 22 Best of Breeds and three group placements. The highlight of that year came when she won Best in Western Futurity in 1989. As a producer, Sony is the dam of 11 champion offspring, which includes Top Producers CH Valmar's Night N Gale, BROM, and CH Valmar's Ez Jazz Time, NSD, NA, BROM.

Figure 33-56: *CH Valmar's Night N Gale* (CH Nani's N Top Hat's Backlash, BROM × CH Valmar's Evening Sonata, BROM). Bred and owned by Joan H. Valdez. Dam of 11 champions.

CH Valmar's Grayshar Burgundy

CH Valmar's Grayshar Burgundy, BROM, is a graceful, elegant bitch with beautiful eye-catching side movement. Her temperament is extremely sound and loving. Burgie finished her championship with ease with three major wins and won the Southland Specialty her first time out as a special. Burgie is the dam of 12 champion offspring whose records include Best of Breed wins, specialty wins, group wins, and Maturity wins. She is the dam of Top-Producing CH Greyoaks Valmar Lady Madonna, BROM.

Figure 33-57: *BIS CH Valmar's Pollyanna, HOF* (CH Sir Eric von Sieben, BROM, HOF × CH Valmar's Serenade v Wustenwind, BROM, HOF). Bred and owned by Joan Valdez. Dam of 10 champions.

Figure 33-58: *CH Valmar's Serendipity* (CH Hoot Hollow's Roy's Rob Roy, BROM × CH Valmar Serenade V Wustenwind, BROM, HOF). Bred by Joan H. Valdez; owned by Joan H. Valdez and Lynne L. Nelson. Dam of 11 champions.

CH Valmar's Night N Gale

CH Valmar's Night N Gale, BROM, was a typical, sound, elegant bitch with a sweet, outgoing personality. Gala finished her championship quickly with back-to-back five-point major wins and went on to win the 1994 Western Maturity. Shown on a limited basis as a Special, Gala was a multiple Best of Breed winner, including a Specialty Best of Breed win in her debut as a Special. Gala is the dam of 11 champion offspring, including Top Producers, CH Valmar's Unanimous Decision, BROM; CH Valmar's Urban Cowboy, BROM; and CH Valmar's Summer Rain, BROM.

BIS CH Valmar's Pollyanna, HOF

Polly interrupted her record-setting show career (she won "Best in Show") in 1984 to produce a litter sired by her grandsire, CH Valmar's Jazzman, CD, NRD, NSD, V, BROM, HOF. The time off for maternity hardly slowed down her 1984 show career, for she appeared on the Top 10 breed and sporting lists for the year. The litter produced DC Valmar's Valiant Knight, CD, NRD, VX, BROM, the first of Polly's 10 champions. His show accomplishments include Best Dog in the 1985 Western Futurity and 1986 Western Maturity, with his sister CH Valmar's Victoria, CDX, capturing Best Bitch in the Maturity. His unique distinction is ranking not only on the Top 10 show list, but also the Top 10 field list in 1986, later finishing in field to become a dual champion.

Polly's other outstanding progeny include CH Valmar's Evening Sonata, BROM (sired by CH BAMA Belle's Mountain Man), winner of the 1989 Western Futurity, and CH Valmar's Silver Dove, BROM (sired by CH Valmar's Xtra Copy, BROM), Best Bitch in the 1989 Western Maturity.

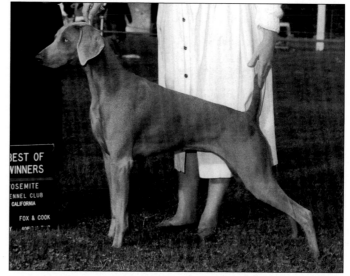

Figure 33-59: *CH Valmar's Starling* (CH Valmar's Xtra Copy, BROM × BIS CH Valmar's Pollyanna, BROM, HOF). Bred by Joan H. Valdez; owned by Joan H. Valdez and Terry Burian. Dam of 10 champions.

CH Valmar's Serendipity

CH Valmar's Serendipity, BROM, was an extremely sound, elegant bitch with excellent shoulders and topline. Sera is the half-sister to CH Valmar's Pollyanna, BROM, HOF. Sera is the dam of 11 champion offspring and was the WCA Top-Producing Dam in 1986, with five finishing that year. Among Sera's offspring are top winning and producing CH Valmar's Xtra Copy, BROM; CH Valmar Xtra Aura V Watchpoint, BROM; CH Valmar's Harvest Moon, BROM; and CH Valmar's Yours Truly, BROM, the No. 1 Show Dog.

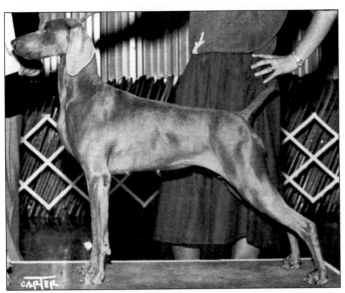

Figure 33-60: *CH Vanoah's Glory Hallelujah, NSD, NRD, V* (CH Von Luchbach's Clazy × Laura's Lady Kay). Bred by James Killingsworth; owned by Brenda Martz and Cindy Victory-Kimball. Dam of 10 champions.

Figure 33-61: *CH Wetobe's Ballerina Ribbons, CD* (CH Doug's Dauntless Von Dor, BROM, HOF × CH Wetobe Ballerina Deb, CD, NRD, V, BROM). Bred by Maureen Barnett; owned by Marylou Schnegelberger. Dam of 10 champions.

CH Valmar's Starling

CH Valmar's Starling, BROM, was a sweet, good-natured individual. Katy finished her championship easily from puppy class competition. Katy is the dam of 10 champions, including Best in Show and National Specialty winner CH Valmar's Apache Rebel, BROM (sire of 32 champions), and Futurity-Maturity winner CH Valmar's Streak O Luck, CDX. She was co-owned by Joan Valdez and Terry Burian. In addition, Katy's littermate, CH Valmar's Silver Dove, BROM, is the dam of Top-Producing sire CH Top Hat's Dorian Gray, BROM (sire of 34 champions).

CH Vanoah's Glory Hallelujah, NSD, NRD, V

CH Vanoah's Glory Hallelujah, NSD, NRD, V, BROM, was the dam of 10 champions. She produced six champions by CH Nani's Wood Win, BROM, and four champions by Am/Can CH Valmar Smokey City Ultra Easy, JH, NSD, BROM, HOF, including DC Wynwood's Rain on the Rise, SDX, NRD, V who was also a Field Futurity winner.

CH Warheits Silver Sensation, CD, NSD, V

CH Warheit's Silver Sensation, CD, NSD, V BROM (CH Ronamax Rajah v. d. Reiteralm, BROM × CH Kamsou Dutch Treat, HOF, BROM). Bred by Gayle Taber and Gina Columbo, and owned by Debbie Mills. Cessie was an extremely well bred bitch whose parents, CH Ronamax Rajah v. d. Reiteralm and CH Kamsou Dutch Treat, were both noted producers. She followed in their footsteps and was the dam of ten Champions for the Wymill Kennel. When bred to CH Kristof's Royal Crusader, BROM she produced two

Figure 33-62: *CH Windwalker's Moment in Time, JH, NSD* (CH Long Run's Silver Smoke, BROM × CH Windwalker's Sunrise Jubilee, CD, JH, NSD, V, BROM). Bred and owned by Phil and Arlene Marshrey. Dam of 11 champions.

Champions and when bred to Silberholm Ricky V Reiteralm, BROM she produced eight Champions.

CH Wetobe's Ballerina Ribbons, CD

Marylou Schegelberger purchased Ribbons as a foundation brood bitch, and her show career, with three majors (ranking 4th, 4th, and 5th) and a Group 3 her first time out as a special, proved the wisdom of Marylou's choice. Many of Ribbon's 10 champions were handled by their breeder, including the specialty-winning, group-placing CH Hoot Hollow's Ruddy Duck, NSD, BROM, and the breed-win-

ning, field-placing CH Hoot Hollow's Ruffed Grouse. The group-winning bitch, CH Hoot Hollow's Fox Feather, had a distinguished specials career and was the top-winning Weimaraner bitch in 1979. CH Hoot Hollow's Bumper Rabbit, a daughter, is a BROM Producer.

CH Windwalker's Moment in Time, JH, NSD

CH Windwalker's Moment in Time, JH, NSD, BROM, was Best Bitch in the 1995 Western Maturity when she was shown by her amateur owner. Shana was "the Princess," who acted sweet and innocent, and who ruled with a velvet paw. Shana was a good hunting dog but thought obedience was silly and always had something up her sleeve. She produced 11 show champions, seven from a litter of nine with CH Gaul's Jazz v. Reiteralm, BROM. She was on the Top Producer list for 1996 and 1997. Her pups inherited her sweet personality and talent.

Figure 33-63: *CH Windwalker's Sunrise Jubilee, CD, JH, NSD, V* (DC Valmar's Valiant Knight, CD, NSD, NRD, VX, BROM × CH Nordsee's Yonda Dawn, CD). Bred and owned by Phil and Arlene Marshrey. Dam of 10 champions.

CH Windwalker's Sunrise Jubilee, CD, JH, NSD, V

CH Windwalker's Sunrise Jubilee, CD, JH, NSD, V, BROM, was the foundation bitch of Windwalker Weimaraners. Sunny produced 10 show champions, including 1990 Best in Western Futurity, CH Long Run's Windwalker Alpha; Best Bitch in 1991 Western Maturity, CH Windwalker's Gemborie, BROM; and Best Bitch in 1995 Western Maturity, CH Windwalker's Moment in Time, JH, NSD, BROM. Seven of these champions were from two breedings with CH Long Runs Silver Smoke, BROM, who was Best Dog in the 1983 Western Futurity. Sunny is also Grand Dam of BIS CH Windwalker's Graeagle, CD, JH, NRD, V, BROM, who was the 1996 Western Maturity winner. In the show ring, Sunny's wins included Best Puppy, several Best of Breeds, and a Group 3 with limited showing. She was tied for WCA Top-Producing Dam in 1991. Sunny was a great companion around the house, kept the other dogs in order, and the corner of the couch warm. She had good hunting instincts and a willingness to learn, which she passed on to her pups.

CH Winfield Queen Cleo Starbuck

Cleo had that combination of elegance along with substance that breeders strive for. Along with her sound conformation and smooth movement, these characteristics were passed on to her offspring, 10 of which won their championships. Cleo finished with four 4-point majors. She was a WCA Top-Producing Dam with four offspring becoming champions in 1991. Two of Cleo's sons have earned the Versatile Excellent Rating title: CH Starbuck Katakam Silvr Saber, CDX, TD, JH, RD, NSD, VX, CGE, and CH Starbuck's Son of a Gun, MH, TDX, VX, CGE, TDI. She had a sweet and loving personality that she also passed down to her children.

Figure 33-64: *CH Winfield Queen Cleo Starbuck* (CH Bing's Razzmatazz von Konsul, CD, BROM × CH Harline Jazabel Winfield). Bred by Nancy Dever and Cora Appleton; owned by Henrietta Jenrette. Dam of 10 champions.

Figure 33-65: *No matter where in the world* the puppies are born, the role of the dam is a vitally important one in raising a litter to its full potential. Abba's calm nature and confident role model set an excellent example for her puppies. Photograph by Sherry Bixler.

Working Moms

Figure 33-66: *The genetic blueprint* for structure and performance must be reinforced with an environment rich in opportunities in order for the inherited temperament and abilities to be optimally expressed. This highly rated long-haired German hunting bitch encourages her pups early boldness and field skills while allowing them to learn through their own exploration. Photograph by Hans Schmidt, Germany.

Figure 34-1: *BIS Am/Can CH Valmar Smokey City Ultra Easy, JH, NSD, HOF* (Am/Can CH Smokey City's Easy Does It, NSD, NRD, V, BROM × CH Valmar Serenade V Wustenwind, BROM). Bred by Joan Valdez; owned by Tom and MaryAnn Wilson. Sire of 148 champions. CH Valmar Smokey City Ultra Easy, JH, NSD, BROM, HOF, was a "stud fee" puppy selected by Joan Valdez for Tom Wilson…and what a choice it was! Easy was shown by Peggy Roush to three consecutive Pedigree Awards, an all breed Best in Show, and multiple group placements. Shown by Tom, Easy won Best of Breed at the first WCA Winter Specialty. Easy's outstanding show career (1 Best in Show, 8 Group 1s, and 216 Best of Breeds) gave him a lot of exposure, and he was in high demand as a stud dog. Even as a young dog he established himself early as a prepotent stud, and history would prove he nicked well with bitches from a variety of bloodlines. In addition to passing on his conformation and style in the show ring, he also had a tendency to pass on his "Easy" temperament and biddability. Easy was always welcome at any gathering for his happy, friendly attitude and gained a reputation as a real "party dog." He was the top-producing sire for 5 consecutive years from 1990 to 1995. Easy became the all-time top-producing Weimaraner dog in 2007, when Steve Siegel handled CH SmokeyCity Wildest Dream, a frozen semen "get," to his final championship points. Upon completing his show career, Easy was the constant companion of Tom Wilson, traveling everywhere that Tom did. While his offspring would stand out mostly in the show ring, Easy himself possessed a great deal of native talent as a hunting dog. Victor Wojciak trained and handled Easy in field competition, where he effortlessly obtained his Novice Shooting Dog rating and Junior Hunter title. While Easy did not have the opportunity to spend as much time in the field as his talented justified, his daughter, DC Wynwood's Rain on the Rise, SDX, NRD, VX (out of CH Vanoah's Glory Hallelujah, NSD, NRD, V, BROM), would prove his offspring possessed his birdiness as well as his conformation and temperament; Easy's field potential would be passed on to successive generations, as Rainy became the No. 6 top-producing field trial dam. Read more about Easy in *Best in Show.* Photograph by Harry Giglio.

CHAPTER 34

A BLUEPRINT OF QUALITY: THE SIRES

by Terrie Borman

As highly as breeders prize the gals, where would they be without the guys? The sires in this chapter stole the hearts of many breeders and went on to vindicate the breeder's judgment. It is no coincidence that all are champions, most Best of Breed winners. Of the 70 sires, 19 have won a Best in Show, and two are Dual Champions.

The Weimaraner's popularity has waxed and waned over the years, and while during the "Crazy Years" of the 1960s quality did indeed suffer, the breed has made great progress in returning to quality over quantity. In 2007, 6,932 Weimaraners were registered. In that same year, 196 earned a bench championship, or 1 champion for every 36 dogs registered. These are excellent results for Weimaraner breeders, compared with other popular sporting breeds, such as the Labrador (the most popular breed in the U.S. that year) with 1 champion for every 541 dogs registered and the Golden Retriever (No. 4 in popularity), with 1 in 158.

Additionally, at least three Weimaraner sires have produced well over 100 champions: Am/Can CH Valmar Smokey City Ultra Easy, JH, NSD (148 champions), and Am/Can CH Colsidex Standing Ovation (147 champions) rank among the all-time most successful sires of all breeds. And then there is CH Ronamax Rajah v. d. Reiteralm (118 champions), way back in the 1960s, holding a respectable standing even without benefit of the current technology of frozen semen.

This chapter pays tribute to some of the top-producing sires of the breed. As with the dams, the criterion for inclusion is based on the number of champion progeny: all are sires of 20 or more AKC champions before the end of 2008, an impressive list of 70 dogs.

Again, the information was compiled from a variety of sources, including the BROM lists, WCA records, the Bremar pedigree service, and owners' records. If a sire has been overlooked, it is sincerely regretted.

The top producers are presented in alphabetical order for ease of reference.

Figure 34-2: ***Fathers regard puppies with aloof dignity,*** wary of those sharp teeth. Photograph by William Wegman.

Top Producers: Sires

Rank		Year of Birth	Champions
1	BIS Am/Can CH Valmar Smokey City Ultra Easy, JH, NSD, HOF (SD915356)	1983	148
2	BIS Am/Can CH Colsidex Standing Ovation, HOF (SB508707)	1974	147
3	BIS CH Ronamax Rajah v. d. Reiteralm, HOF (SA593379)	1969	118
4	CH Nani's Southern Cross, HOF (SF232694)	1988	89
5	BIS CH Windwalker's Graeagle, CD, JH, NRD, V (SN13511104)	1994	87
6	CH Valmar's Jazzman, CD, NSD, NRD, V, HOF (SB992716)	1976	75
7	Am/Can CH Colsidex Nani Reprint, JH, SD, HOF (SE521833)	1987	72
8	CH Camelot's Go for the Gold (SN83520702)	2001	66
9	BIS Am/Can CH Carousel's Roscoe T Picotrane (SN32573801)	1996	64
10	CH Smokey City El Nino, JH (SN30478201)	1995	64
11	BIS CH Greywind's Jack Frost, CD, SD, V, HOF (SD351698)	1981	64
12	CH Maximilian Von Der Reiteralm, NSD, HOF (SA148632)	1965	62
13	CH Nani's Concert Master, SH (SN19725606)	1994	59
14	CH Doug's Dauntless Von Dor, HOF (SA377534)	1967	52
15	CH Bing's Razzmatazz Von Konsul CD (SC888004)	1980	52
16	CH Bama Belle's Mountain Man (SD193291)	1981	51
17	BIS CH Nani's Smart Aleck, JH, NRD, V (SN47195601)	1997	51
18	CH Nani's Indecent Exposure, JH, NAJ, V (SN92630501)	2002	51
19	CH Colsidex the Farm Top of the Mark (SN56897103)	1998	49
20	CH Valmar's Xtra Copy (SE326452)	1985	47
21	BIS CH Sir Eric Von Sieben, HOF (SB79940)	1974	44
22	CH Reiteralm's Rio Fonte Saudade (SC374970)	1978	44
23	BIS CH Ultima's Stetson V Hufmeister, CD (SN04182107)	1993	40
24	CH Ann's Magic v. d. Reiteralm (SC368060)	1977	39
25	BIS CH Nani's Hawaiian Punch (SD756295)	1983	38
26	AM CAN CH Ashmore's Win' Weim Royal Flush, JH (SN55248001)	1998	38
27	CH Nani's N Tophat's Backlash, CD, NSD, V (SE621491)	1986	37
28	CH Colsidex Blueprint (SN03828403)	1992	36
29	BIS CH Val Knight Ranck, HOF (S850395)	1959	34
30	Am/Can CH Reichenstadt's Majestic, CD (SA814506)	1972	34
31	CH Nani's Baht a Pack a Trouble, CD, JH, V (SF185449)	1988	34
32	CH Silversmith Ez Payment Plan, CD, JH, SD, V (SF429879)	1988	34
33	CH Top Hat's Dorian Gray (SF489253)	1989	34
34	BIS Am/Can CH Shadowmar Barthaus Dorillio, HOF (SA33085)	1961	33
35	CH Baht N' Greywind Playn' the Game, NSD, HOF (SN00829603)	1992	33

Top Producers: Sires

Rank		Year of Birth	Champions
36	BIS Am/Can CH Greywind's High Flying Cloud, TD, JH, NSD, V (SN06662301)	1993	33
37	Am/Can CH Valmar's Unanimous Decision, NSD (SN41061302)	1997	32
38	CH Gaul's Jazz V Reiteralm (SG003605)	1990	32
39	BIS CH Valmar's Apache Rebel (SF785433)	1989	32
40	CH Debar's Platinum Specter (S478109)	1951	30
41	CH Von Sieben's Royal Flush, CD, NSD, V (SB681737)	1975	30
42	CH Kristof's Royal Crusader (SC386373)	1978	30
43	BIS CH Camelot's Matinee Idol (SM99995003)	1992	29
44	CH Silversmith Ethan Allen, JH, NSD (SN77088904)	2000	29
45	BIS CH Ann's Rickey Boy, CD, HOF (S537937)	1952	28
46	CH Von Sieben's Smart N Special, NSD (SB681990)	1975	28
47	Am/Can CH Nani's Master Charge, NSD, NRD, V, HOF (SC755210)	1979	28
48	Am/Can CH Silberschoen's Lucky Strike (SN35753001)	1995	28
49	BIS CH Bzyfeet American Idol (SR12958801)*	2003	28
50	Am/Can CH Seneca's Medicine Man, HOF (SA329679)	1967	27
51	AM CAN CH Bremar Maker's Mark (SN16542205)	1994	27
52	Am/Can CH Juriel's Space Ace (SB41062)	1974	26
53	CH Nani's Scirroco of Mattrace, CD (SE198777)	1984	26
54	DUAL CH Valmar's Valiant Knight, CD, NRD, VX (SE116082)	1984	26
55	CH Wismar's Jack Daniels (SE488048)	1985	26
56	CH Moonshine's Alpha Centauri (SM84531506)	1991	25
57	BIS Am/Can CH Deal's Sporting True Aim II, CD, HOF (S331069)	1949	24
58	CH Bing's Southern Saga Del Oro, CD, NSD, NRD, V (SD369060)	1981	24
59	CH Norman's Smoky City Chill Fact'r, JH, NRD, V (SF200182)	1988	24
60	CH Smokey City Ez Moonstone, JH, NRD, V (SG043174)	1990	24
61	DUAL CH Arimar's Ivan, CD, NSD, VX (SB393851)	1973	23
62	CH Ladenburg Arco von Reiteralm [Germany] (SE567939)	1985	23
63	CH Tri-D's Invincible, NSD (SM96589107)	1992	23
64	CH Bert v. d. Harrisburg, SDX [Germany] (S313378)	1947	22
65	Am/Can CH Hoot Hollow's Roy's Rob Roy, CD (SC759562)	1979	22
66	CH Eb's You Otta See Me Now, JH, SD, NRD, V (SD819842)	1983	22
67	BIS CH Smokycity Riverboat Gambler (SN56303005)*	1998	21
68	CH Warhorse Billy of Redhill, CD (SA2199)	1960	20
69	CH Nani's Sanbar Ringside Rumor, JH (SM88313402)	1991	20
70	CH Zara's on Zee Rampage (SN30508101)	1996	20

* It was the hope of the authors to be able to include biographies and photographs for all top-producing Weimaraners, but those who were added as this book went to print were not able to be showcased. We include their names here in appreciation of their merit.

Figure 34-3: *CH Ann's Magic v. d. Reiteralm* (CH Sir Eric von Seiben BROM × CH The Rajah's Magic v. d. Reiteralm, BROM). Bred and owned by Virginia Alexander. Sire of 39 champions.

Figure 34-4: *BIS Am/Can CH Ann's Rickey Boy CD, HOF* (CH Deal's Sporting True Aim II, BROM × CH Ann's Sidney Sue, CD). Bred and owned by Ann Kepler. Sire of 28 champions.

CH Ann's Magic v. d. Reiteralm

Guy is pictured here at 12 1/2 years of age. His alert stance is guaranteed due to the presence of a cat held within 6 feet of his nose. Guy was piloted to his title by Peggy Roush with three 5-point majors. As a young dog, Guy briefly enjoyed an exciting field career as a strong competitor at mixed-breed trails; however, his field success was cut short by a well-placed kick from a trainer's trial horse. Guy, a Kennel Review Sire of Distinction and the father of multiple Top 10, Field, Futurity and Maturity winners, thanks his many grand children for their consistent Best in Show wins and top-producing records. Sound and stylish and intensely birdy, Guy consistently passed these qualities to his progeny. His special contribution, however, comes from the highly complementary nick when his progeny are crossed with those from his litter brother CH Reiteralm's Rio Fonte Saudade, NRD, BROM, and the linebred descendents of Guy and Rio appear in the pedigrees of many of today's top winners and producers. A prepotent and enthusiastic stud dog, who sired his last litter shortly before his death at the age of 14 1/2, producing two more champions. Guy himself appears in the pedigrees of 45 of the 58 Best in Show winners since his birth; either Guy or Rio appears in 85% of Best in Show winner since their birth; more amazing, however, the combination of these two brothers, Guy and Rio, appear in 65% of these winning dogs.

BIS Am/Can CH Ann's Rickey Boy, CD, HOF

In the early 1950s, CH Ann's Rickey Boy and Ann Kepler became the breed's first breeder-owner-handler team. Their extensive travels (primarily in the East, Midwest, and South) set a new precedent, and they even went north of the border for a Canadian championship. In those days of benched shows, Rickey and Ann were goodwill ambassadors for the breed, for few could resist their friendly charm. Rickey established a record of 155 breed wins, and he ranked in the top 10 Weimaraners, the top 10 sporting dogs, and the top 10 of all breeds. During his career Rickey also achieved two American-Bred Best in Shows, which were commonly awarded at that time. At last, in 1958, they got the big one, the all-breed Best in Show, and Rickey retired.

Rickey would be considered a great dog on the strength of his show career alone. However, it is in the stud department that Rickey really left his mark; he is the sire of 28 champions and the sire of two Group winners. The number of champions in whose pedigree he appears in is impossible to calculate, but their legions include many other entries in this chapter, including BIS Am/Can CH Shadowmar Barhaus Dorilio, BROM, HOF; CH Sir Eric von Sieben, BROM, HOF; CH The Rajah's Magic v. d. Reiteralm, BROM, HOF; CH Erbenhof Touch of Class, BROM; CH Nani's Visa v. d.

Figure 34-5: *DC Arimar's Ivan, CD, NSD, VX* (CH Eichenhof's Ginger Man BROM × CH Arimar's Desert Diana, NSD, BROM). Bred by Tom and Jackie Isabell; owned by Jackie Isabell. Sire of 23 champions.

Figure 34-6: *Am/Can CH Ashmore's Win' Weim Royal Flush, JH* (CH Nani's Concert Master, SH, BROM × CH Colsidex the Farms Reflection). Bred by Tom, Teresa, and Ryan Sanders; owned by Dana Massey and Teresa Sanders. Sire of 38 champions.

Reiteralm, BROM, HOF; and CH Valmar's Pollyanna, BROM, HOF.

Rickey belonged to the entire Kepler family, and his retirement meant that Ann's husband, "Kep" had a full-time hunting dog. In Pennsylvania's pheasant country, Rickey hunted for Kep, friends, and neighbors to the ripe old age of 15. He taught his descendants to point and honor, for he was a sire of all-around Weimaraners.

At that time, dog fanciers believed that only professional handlers could show dogs, and Ann was the breed's first successful amateur handler. Ann later became a professional handler, but she encouraged novices to show their own Weimaraners, generously donating her time and sharing her skills to help them. Soon, many open Weimaraner classes were filled with amateur owner-handlers, with Ann coaching from the sidelines. She encouraged others to help newcomers, especially junior handlers. One of the notable junior handlers taught by Ann is her daughter, Peggy Kepler Roush, who has carried on the tradition of sharing her skills with amateur handlers as well.

DC Arimar's Ivan, CD, NSD, VX

Undefeated in regular classes, Ivan took his first major from the American-bred class. Shown twice in open class, he finished with back-to-back five-point majors and a Best of Breed. Specialed only occasionally and rarely outside the Phoenix area, the merry dog with the driving gait captured 21 breed wins (two specialties) and two Group 4s as well as the field and veteran dog classes at the 1980 National Specialty.

Someone said it was a fluke when Ivan's younger sister Takusan (DC Arimar's Lovely Lyric, CD, RD, SDX, VX) became the breed's youngest dual at 34 months. To prove it was not, Ivan started field training when he was almost 5 years old. When he finished with wins in both all-age and gun dog stakes, Ivan and his sister became the breed's first Dual siblings. Ivan competed only once after finishing his field championship, winning a limited gun dog stake over several national all-age championship winners.

Figure 34-7: *CH Baht N' Greywind Playn' the Game, NSD, HOF* (CH Greywind's the Snowman BROM × CH Baht's Cuttin Corners). Bred by Jill Watson; owned by Ellen Grevatt and Mrs. Jack L. Billhardt. Sire of 33 champions.

Figure 34-8: ***CH Bama Belle's Mountain Man*** (Am/Can CH Colsidex Standing Ovation, BROM × Bama Belle's Limited Edition). Bred by Patricia Teer; owned by Patricia Teer, Kelli Fallbach and Paul Averill. Sire of 51 champions.

Figure 34-9: ***CH Bert v. d. Harrasburg, SDX*** (Arco v. d. Filzen × Asta v Bruckberg). Bred by Max Baumler; owned by Mr. and Mrs. Elvin Deal. Sire of 22 champions.

Figure 34-10: ***CH Bing's Razzmatazz Von Konsul, CD*** (CH Bing's Konsul Von Krisdaunt, CDX, BROM × CH Bing's Picante Von Konsul, CD, BROM). Bred and owned by Jean White. Sire of 52 champions.

An all-around dog in every way, Ivan is the first Dual to become a BROM sire, still leading with 23 champions. Bred sparingly, only five bitches produced Ivan's champions, many of which earned field ratings, field points, and obedience titles, including OTCH CH JamSpirit Evenstar, UDT, RDX, SD, VX. Ivan sired three Futurity winners: CH I've a Dream of Arimar, CD, NSD, V (1976), group winning CH JamSpirit Evolution, CD, RDX, VX, BROM (1979), and CH JamSpirit Helmsman, CDX, TD, RD, NSD, VX (1982).

Ivan's BROM progeny are Evolution and CH Moonshadow of Beaver Lake, UD, NRD, NSD, VX—obedience Top 10 in 1985, 1986, and 1987 (ranking 5th, 1st, and 7th).

Am/Can CH Ashmore's Win' Weim Royal Flush, JH

How do you come up with a call name of 'Fred'? From a 12-year-old who loved Fred Flintstone! Yabba-Dabba-Do! Fred's AKC championship was earned at 10 months old, completely owner-handled by Dana Massey. His BROM was earned before he was 3 years old—out of two litters whose dams were CH Nani's Glitter Bug, JH, BROM, and CH Win'Weim JC's Cross Stitch, TD, CD, NRD, V, BROM. During a very limited specials career, he reached a Top 5 Weimaraner position in 3 months, before being retired. His offspring include AKC, Canadian, and Australian champion get and grand-get, AKC multiple Best in Specialty Show, Top 5, and Top 10 for several years. In addition, the versatility of his pups is evidenced in multiple Versatile Excellent ratings, Senior Hunter, and field-trial placements. As the sire of 13 champions in 2004, Fred was named Top-Producing Sire.

Figure 34-11: *BISS CH Bing's Southern Saga Del Oro, CD, NSD, NRD, V* (CH Bing's Razzmatazz Von Konsul, CD, BROM × CH Reichenstadt's Summer Magic, CD, SD, BROM). Bred by M. Wojcinski; owned by Jean White. Sire of 24 champions.

Figure 34-12: *Am/Can CH Bremar Maker's Mark* (CH Nani's Southern Cross BROM × Am/Can CH Bremar Freedom Hills Isis, NSD, BROM). Bred and owned by Alan and Pam Patunoff. Sire of 27 champions.

CH Baht N' Greywind Playn' the Game, NSD, HOF

CH Baht N' Greywind Playn' the Game, NSD, BROM, HOF, was the sire of 33 champions. Polo was the 1997 WCA Top-Producing Sire. He had several noteworthy offspring, with his most noteworthy being CH Ghostmar's Funny Valentine, NRD, BROM, and CH Nani's Concert Master, SH, BROM, who went on to be the WCA's 1999 Top-Producing Sire. When bred to CH Nani's Perfect Cadence, CD, NRD, V, BROM, the resulting litters produced 10 American champions.

CH Bama Belle's Mountain Man

CH Bama Belle's Mountain Man, BROM, owned by Patricia Teer, Kelli Fallbach, and Paul Averill, was the sire of 51 champions. Cowboy had several noteworthy offspring including CH DeBar Song of the South, who finished at 12 months with five majors and was a Futurity winner, a Top 10 Show Dog, a Best in Show Winner, a WCA National Specialty winner; and the Top 10 Show Dog CH Mountain Man's Cowbelle CD, JH, NSD, V. His daughter CH Valmar's Evening Sonata, BROM, went on to be the WCA's 1991 Top Producing Dam. Cowboy also produced offspring who excelled in performance, including the extremely versatile DC Jo-Ron's Silber Elch, TD, MH, UD, SDX, RDX, VX3.

CH Bert v. d. Harrasburg (Germany), SDX

Bert earned a reputation as an influential sire of the 1950s. Bert appears many times in most Weimaraner pedi-

grees. He finished in seven shows, amateur-handled by Elvin Deal. With 17 field trial victories, Bert brought new prestige to the breed by becoming the first to win an Open All-Age stake over Pointers and Setters and qualifying for the Sports Afield All-American Team. Bert passed his dual traits to his progeny. He sired the Best in Show winner CH Deal's Sporting True Aim II, BROM, and the 1953 National Open and Amateur All-Age championship winner Deal's Upland Fantasy. His BROM progeny are CH Deal's Sporting True Aim II, CD, and All-Age-placed CH Deal's Helmsman, CD.

CH Bing's Razzmatazz Von Konsul, CD

Razz is from the last litter (all five champions) sired by CH Bing's Konsul Von Krisdaunt, CDX, BROM, and whelped after Konsul's death. Razz finished his championship from the puppy class at 10 months, with two Best of Opposites over specials, and he finished his Companion Dog before the age of 2.

Razz is the sire of multiple group winners (some from the classes), including CH Bing's Southern Saga Del Oro, CD, NRD, NSD, V, BROM—breed Top 10 in 1984 and 1985 (ranking 5th and 6th). Many have field and versatile ratings as well as obedience titles. Razz sired the Futurity winners and group-placing CH Bing's Lagerfeld v. Windsong, NSD (1983) and CH Moonshadow's Hope for Rain, NRD, NSD, V (1987), as well as the Maturity winners CH Bing's Razzle Dazzle v. Warheit, NRD, NSD, V (1987), and Woodcreek H'rd it Thru T Grp'vin (1991). His BROM producers, in addition to Saga, are CH Bing's Razzberri v. Winfield, CH Winfield's Queen Cleo Starbuck, and CH Tatiana v. Windsong, NRD, NSD.

Figure 34-13: *CH Camelot's Go for the Gold* (CH SmokyCity Mob Boss, JH × CH Camelot's Plkadots N' Moonbeams). Bred by Susan Thomas; owned by Susan Thomas and Sharlene Craig. Sire of 66 champions.

Figure 34-14: *BIS CH Camelot's Matinee Idol* (CH Nani's Southern Cross, BROM × CH Camelot's Halley's Comet, BROM). Bred by Susan Thomas and C. and E. Waterman-Storer; owned by Susan Thomas. Sire of 29 champions.

CH Bing's Southern Saga Del Oro, CD, NSD, NRD, V

Saga was the epitome of a Top 10 Show Dog. He loved the excitement and attention and always led the Sporting Group, as his movement was ground-covering with excellent reach and drive. Saga had over 100 Best of Breed wins, including Best in Specialty, placements in the group over 25% of the time, including 15 Group 1s. His ratings were accomplished with much enthusiasm. He was as happy getting his Companion Dog as he was in the group ring. Saga was out of his sire's first litter and was the first of the five champions to finish. The sire of 24 champions out of seven litters, including a Best in Show (CH Bing's Southern Sass, CD) and multiple Best in Futurity and Maturity. Saga was a loyal, loving, and exciting dog that we will forever miss. He won a lot of friends for this breed.

Am/Can CH Bremar Maker's Mark

Am/Can CH Bremar Maker's Mark, BROM, was a dignified, well-mannered gentleman who much preferred home to the show ring. Roberto was a masculine dog who was blessed with a big, ground-covering gait like his dam.

Roberto has proven to be a breeders' dog whose grandkids are better than his kids. He has bred on through both his sons and his daughters. Notable are his littermate sons out of CH Sagenhaft Colsidex Whiz Kid. Am/Aust Grand CH Colsidex Grauhund Just Jeans is the first imported Australian Grand Champion, a multi-Best in Show winner and a leading sporting sire. CH Colsidex the Farm Top of the Mark, BROM, the sire of Futurity, Maturity, and Specialty winners is one of the dominant sires of his generation. Roberto's specialty-winning daughter, CH HiBourne's HiClass Lass, out of CH HiBourne's

Visions of Glory, CD, JH, has in turn produced a Specialty winner, CH HiBourne's Mountain Magic. Other kids and grandkids are Futurity and Maturity winners, as well as Top 10 contenders. It seems clear that the records of Roberto's descendents remain mainly to be written as time goes by.

CH Camelot's Go for the Gold

CH Camelot's Go for the Gold, BROM, is a medium-large male with an incredible personality and temperament, excelling

Figure 34-15: *BIS Am/Can CH Carousel's Roscoe T Picotrane* (CH Jax's Von Major × Am/Can CH Kasamar Rocks the Carousel). Bred by Bill and Pat Van Camp; owned by Bill and Pat Van Camp and Quinn and Mia Truckenbrod. Sire of 64 champions.

in both field instincts and show potential. His soundness in mind, body, and movement is outstanding. Hudson finished quickly and went on to be a competitive Special at less than 18 months of age. He is a Best of Breed Winner at both Westminster and the Eukanuba Classic, a Futurity and Group winner, and was also a Top 20 Invitational winner. Hudson's show name and winning attitude exemplifies the same spirit as his best buddy, Olympic gold medal winner Jim Craig (hockey). He is the sire of 66 champions to date, including Futurity and Maturity winners. He has produced several Top 10 Show dogs, including CH Silver Clouds Grand Contessa, a multiple group winner and Top 10 Show Dog for 3 years, and Am/Can CH Starlight's Olympic Record Holder. Hudson was the WCA Top Producing Sire in 2006 and 2007. He also has get with a Junior Hunter, Senior Hunter, and Master Hunter titles.

BIS CH Camelot's Matinee Idol

CH Camelot's Matinee Idol, BROM, was a dog one would have to live with to truly appreciate! Brando was easy going, loving, sensitive to human feelings, and intelligent. Brando won five majors from the puppy class, finishing with a specialty win at Delaware Valley WC over specials. He was a Futurity and Maturity winner and a Top 10 Show Dog for 3 consecutive years. Brando also thrilled us with a Best in Show win. His crowning achievement was a Best of Opposite Sex win at Westminster Kennel Club at 7 years young. Brando was the sire of 29 Champions, and his puppies inherited his wonderful temperament, with soundness of mind as well as body and are true to the Weimaraner Standard.

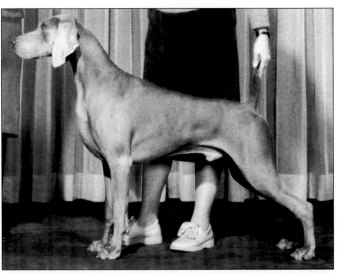

Figure 34-17: *Am/Can CH Colsidex Nani Reprint, JH, SD, HOF* (CH Colsidex Standing Ovation, BROM × CH Nani's Cobbie Cuddler, BROM). Bred by Judy Colan and Chris Medeiros; owned by Judy Colan. Sire of 72 champions.

BIS Am/Can CH Carousel's Roscoe T Picotrane

Am/Can CH Carousel's Roscoe T Picotrane, BROM, completed his championship by 9 months of age and was on the Top 10 list by 11 months of age. Roscoe completed his first year as a special ranked No. 2 with handler Rusty Howard. He has three Best in Shows on his record, and in 1998 Roscoe was the No. 1 Best of Breed and Show Dog.

Roscoe received his Bench Register of Merit at 4 years of age. To date, he is the sire of 64 bench champions. Roscoe is the first stud dog in the history of the breed to sire the Best of Breed (CH Dakotaridge Carousel's Ola Lola), Best of Opposite Sex (CH Barona Ba-Brown Nose), and Best of Winners (Bowbent Carousel Hidden Gem—the youngest winner in history at 6 months, 6 days old) at the same National Specialty (2003). Bowbent Carousel Hidden Gem went on to win her 2004 Futurity, was a multiple Best in Show winner and the No. 1 Best of Breed and Show Dog in 2005. Roscoe has sired several Futurity and Maturity winners, field titled and obedience champions. He was on the Top Producers list 1999 through 2004 and was the 2003 Top Producer.

CH Colsidex Blueprint

Carlos was an exceptional dog. He spent his time between his two co-owners' homes. When with Joe, he lived on a 40-foot sailboat and spent his days in Joe's office, sleeping under the desk. He was extremely athletic and loved to jog and pull Joe on roller blades. They once even won a race against two ponies pulling a cart. When living with Judy, he traveled to dog shows and was a multiple Specialty winner. He often went to work with Judy and earned many friends for the breed with his loving disposition while in her office at the vet clinic.

Figure 34-16: *CH Colsidex Blueprint* (Am/Can CH Colsidex Nani Reprint, JH, SD, BROM × CH Nani's Colsidex Crosstalk). Bred by Judy Colan; owned by Joe Dealteris and Judy Colan. Sire of 36 champions.

Figure 34-18: *BIS AM/Can CH Colsidex Standing Ovation, HOF* (CH Seneca's Medicine Man, BROM × CH Colsidex Dauntless Applause, NSD, BROM). Bred and owned by Judy Colan. Sire of 147 champions.

Figure 34-19: *CH Colsidex the Farm Top of the Mark* (CH Bremar Maker's Mark, BROM × CH Saganhaft Colsidex Whiz Kid). Bred by Judy Colan and Alessandra Folz; owned by Judy Colan. Sire of 49 champions.

Carlos never met a stranger, and his happy, outgoing temperament was passed on to his offspring. He sired 36 champions, which included Futurity and Maturity winners, group winners, field trial winners, and a High in Trial winner. His get include hunt test, obedience, and tracking titled dogs.

Am/Can CH Colsidex Nani Reprint, JH, SD, HOF

From his sire's last litter, Jack represents the qualities for which Joga was famous—clean, elegant lines and flawless movement with a reaching, driving gait. Jack began his show career at 6 months with a five-point specialty win. He finished with three majors from the Puppy class, and a Best of Breed over seven specials at 13 months. He went on to be a multiple Specialty winner, Group winner, and Maturity winner, as well as Westminster Best of Breed winner. He was in the Top 10 for several years and earned his Junior Hunter in four straight hunt tests.

Jack's real contribution to the breed was his ability as a sire. Sire of 72 champions, he is currently the No. 7 BROM Top Producer. His offspring have followed in his tradition, and Jack is a grandsire of over 250 champions. His offspring include a Best in Show winner, Futurity and Maturity winners, obedience title holders, hunt titles holders, and BROM top producers. He is the grandsire of the breed's all-time top Best in Show winner CHCH Colsidex Seabreeze Perfect Fit (36 Best in Shows). In addition to his American offspring, his frozen semen was used in Australia for one litter. That litter produced five Best in Show winners, which include the all-time top-winning Weimaraner in Australia, Aus/Gr CH Divani Just a Dash, with 42 Best in Shows. Dash's wins include the Sidney Royale

(the Westminster of Australia,) with an entry of over 5,000 dogs.

BIS Am/Can CH Colsidex Standing Ovation, HOF

A multiple Best in Show winner (see *Best in Show*), Joga was always breeder and owner handled. He won three Best in Shows in the U.S. and two Best in Shows in Canada. He was No. 1 Weimaraner in 1976 and 1977. Joga's reaching, driving gait and outstanding conformation made him a formidable contender in top competition. He was winner of the WCA National Specialty twice from the Veterans Class, at 8 and 10 years old.

The proof of any dog is in their get, and this is where he proved himself many times over. Joga was the sire of 147

Figure 34-20: *BIS Am/Can CH Deal's Sporting True Aim II, CD, HOF* (CH Bert v. d. Harrasburg, SDX, BROM × CH Grafmar's Dove, CD, BROM). Bred by Mr. and Mrs. Alvin Deal; owned by Mrs. Grace Crafts. Sire of 24 champions.

champions, which include Best in Show winners, Group winners, Specialty winners, and over 20 Futurity winners. Over 25 of his offspring are BROM Top Producers. He achieved the ranking of No. 1 All-Time BROM Sire in 1984 and for 24 years was the No. 1 All-Time BROM Sire, and is grandsire of over 600 champions. You can find Joga in almost every Top Winning and Top Producing pedigree. His ability to produce offspring who are also top producers has been passed on through several generations.

He was a very loving, devoted dog and easy to live with. Visitors could not believe that this dog who put his head in their lap to be petted was the same dog that showed his heart out in the ring. The minute he walked through the ring, he became a different dog, with a "Here I am, I am the best!" attitude.

CH Colsidex the Farm Top of the Mark

Despite an unfortunate experience of being attacked ringside at his second show, Cliffy finished with two Best of Breeds from the classes, including the Nutmeg Weimaraner Club Specialty. He was never shown as a Special, as being attacked ringside left him with an aversion for dog shows. He was an exceptionally beautiful dog that impressed all who came to visit, with his effortless ground-covering movement, sweet, loving temperament, and almost constantly wagging tail.

As a producer, he was prepotent for producing breed type and his effortless ground-covering gait. He is the sire of 49 champions that include multiple Best in Show winner and four time National Specialty Winner CH Colsidex Seabreeze Perfect Fit, No. 1 Weimaraner in 2006–2008 and No. 3 Sporting Dog in 2007 and 2008. He is also the sire of several other group winners, multiple Futurity and Maturity winners, agility, tracking, obedience, hunt test titled offspring, including a Master Hunter, who finished the title at 2 years of age. His real contribution to the breed is his ability to produce offspring that are also good producers. The 2006 and 2007

Figure 34-22: *CH Doug's Dauntless Von Dor, HOF* (CH Shadowmar Barthaus Dorillio × Norman's Nuther Nina). Bred by Doug Kline; owned by Frank Sousa. Sire of 52 champions.

Top-Producing Dams were both Cliffy daughters: 2006 Am/Can/Br CH Juscani's Mater Ad Colsidex, BROM, and 2007 CH Eb's N Seabreeze Sorcerers Stone, JH, BROM.

BIS Am/Can CH Deal's Sporting True Aim II, CD, HOF

True Aim (the breed's second Best in Show winner—see *Best in Show*) became the first to sire a second-generation Best in Show winner with CH Ann's Rickey Boy, CD, BROM—a feat not repeated until 1971 (CH Ronamax Rajah v. d. Reiteralm, BROM, sire of CH Rajah's Alexander v. d. Reiteralm).

True Aim sired the first Eastern Futurity winner Cindy (1957) and the 1955 National Specialty winner CH Atomic of Wolf Trap. Through his top-producing sons—eastern-based CH Anne's Rickey Boy and western-based CH Debar's Platinum Specter, BROM—True Aim shaped the breed from coast to coast.

CH Debar's Platinum Specter

Specter's show career included many breed (1955 Westminster) and Group wins. One of the foundation sires of Homer Carr's Gaiberg line, Specter is the sire of 30 champions, including the Best in Show winner CH Von Gaiberg's Ord and the BROM sire CH Verdemar's Ajax. Specter was Carr's personal hunting dog, and many fine field performers trace back to him.

Figure 34-21: *CH Debar's Platinum Specter* (BIS CH Deal's Sporting True Aim II, BROM × CH Grafmar's Dilly Dally, BROM). Bred by C. Paul Berry, Jr.; owned by Homer L. Carr. Sire of 30 champions.

Figure 34-23: *CH EB's You Otta See Me Now, JH, SD, NRD, V* (CH Redhill's Reflections, NSD, NRD, V, BROM × CH EB's Mystical Mushroom). Bred by Ed and Barbara Didjurgis; owned by Bill and Carole Donaldson. Sire of 22 champions.

Figure 34-24: *CH Gaul's Jazz V Reiteralm* (CH Ladenburg Arco Von Reiteralm, BROM × CH Fleur De Gaul Von Reiteralm, BROM). Bred by Christopher Gaul and Virginia Alexander; owned by Christopher Gaul. Sire of 32 champions.

CH Doug's Dauntless von Dor, HOF

Following his eastern Futurity win in 1967, Daunt ranked in the breed's Top 10 in 1968, 1969, and 1970 (ranking 6th, 1st, and 7th). Daunt's balance and clean lines appealed to many breeders, He nicked so well with bitches of different bloodlines that he brought a popular new uniformity to breed type in the 1970s.

Daunt sired the Best in Show winners CH W.C.'s the Dutchman of Dauntmar, BROM, and CH Sir Eric Von Sieben, BROM. He is the sire of three Futurity winners: CH Brandy's Rebel v. d. Reiteralm, NRD, BROM (1970); CH Valmar's Eclipse von Bergen, NRD, BROM (1971–1972 Top 10 derby); and CH Arimar's Desert Diana, NSD, BROM (1972), as well as CH Arimar's Desert Dream, NRD, SD, V (1972 field Futurity second).

The best evidence of Daunt's impact on the breed are his 17 (almost one-third of his champions) BROM progeny, including CH Colsidex Dauntless Applause, NSD; CH Brandy's Blizz v. d. Reiteralm; CH Dauntmar's Diana v. Green Acres, BROM; CH. Hidden Heather von Sieben, CD, NRD, SD, V; CH Hi Country's Blackwater Alert, NSD; CH Marbill's Firebrand Von Arimar, NRD, NSD, V; Am/Can CH Reichenstadt's Cameo; CH Reichenstadt's Royal Flush; CH Wetobe's Ballerina Ribbons, CD; CH Wetobe's Miss Daunt; CH Bing's Konsul Von Krisdaunt, CDX; and CH Nordsee's Ponto v. d. Reiteralm, NRD, NSD, V.

Daunt is the grandsire of four Dual Champions: Arimar's Ivan, CD, NSD, VX, BROM; Arimar's Lovely Lyric, CD, RD, SDX, VX; Marbil's Baron Von Josephus, RD, SDX, VX; and Redhill's Chief Geronimo, NRD, SDX, V. In addition, he is the great-grandsire of four Dual Champions: Jafwin's One and Only, NRD, SD, VX; Jafwin's the Goodbye Girl, NRD, SDX; Takusan's Sonic Boom, NRD, NSD, V; and Valmar's Valiant Knight, CD, NRD, VX, BROM.

CH EB's You Otta See Me Now, JH, SD, NRD, V

CH EB's You Otta See Me Now, JH, SD, NRD, V, BROM, earned AKC Top 10 show status in 1986 and was a multiple group placing and Specialty winning dog. Otto was Tri-D's most influential foundation stud dog. Many of his 24 titled progeny achieved AKC bench, field, obedience, and hunt test titles and WCA Futurity and Maturity winners, proving they were at home equally in the field as well as performing in the ring. He sired two Dual Champions in his lifetime. DC Tri-D's Sterling Silver, BROM, was the only Weimaraner in history to win the WCA 1988 Field and Bench Futurity and 1989 Maturity, and DC AFC Tri-D's Clean Sweep V, Y-ME, NSD, V, finished No. 5 on the 1994 Top 10 Gun Dog list. He also sired the youngest Weimaraner to achieve the title of AKC Junior Hunter at the age of 6 months, Tri-D's Wingfield's Dusty Otto, JH.

CH Gaul's Jazz V Reiteralm

Jazz earned his championship in three back-to-back weekends. His 14 Best in Show Specialty wins were unsurpassed

Figure 34-25: *BIS Am/Can CH Greywind's High Flying Cloud, TD, JH, NSD, V* (CH Wolfstadt's First Frost, NSD, BROM × CH Greywind's Snow Bird, NSD, BROM). Bred by P. Crowley and E. Grevatt; owned by Linda and William Snyder. Sire of 33 champions.

when he retired. Jazz was a Futurity and Maturity winner and for 2 years, 1993 and 1994, he was the best of the Best of Breed. During his show career, he earned 10 Group 1s along with a great many group placements, and went Best of Opposite Sex at the National Specialty. In 1998, he earned the WCA's Top-Producing Sire Award. Incredibly elegant, with movement that judges described as 'floating on air,' Jazz was a wonderful credit to his breed and a gentle, loving, and incredibly loved, loyal friend. His children, grandchildren, and great-grandchildren share in his superb qualities and have earned championships as well as titles in the field, obedience, tracking, and agility. To date, Jazz is the sire of 32 champions, including multiple group placer, CH Chatawey's Good Golly Miss Molly, CD, JH, RN, OA, OAJ, NAP, VX, BROM, multiple group placer, multiple Specialty Best of Breed winner, CH Chatawey-N-Pengles CEO D'Gaul, NSD, and multiple group placer, multiple Specialty Best of Breed winner, CH SeaMyst Grayt Slate von Gaul, JH, NSD who was Winner's Dog at the 2000 National Specialty.

BIS Am/Can CH Greywind's High Flying Cloud, TD, JH, NSD, V

BIS/BISS Am/Can CH Greywind's High Flying Cloud, TD, JH, NSD, V, BROM, was the sire of 33 champions. Not only was Ben a Best in Show and Best in Specialty winner himself, but when bred to BIS CH Norman's Greywind Phoebe Snow, JH, the resulting litter produced a Best in Show winner: CH Greywind's Snow Cloud, JH, who was also a Best in Specialty Show winner and a Top 10 Show Dog. His offspring were also excellent performance dogs with several having Versatile and Versatile Excellent ratings.

Figure 34-26: *BIS CH Greywind's Jack Frost, CD, SD, V, HOF* (CH Colsidex Standing Ovation, BROM × CH Greywind's Ashley Frost, CD). Bred and owned by Ellen J. and John B. Grevatt. Sire of 64 champions.

BIS CH Greywind's Jack Frost, CD, SD, V, HOF

A multiple Best in Show winner (see *Best in Show*), Brae proved to be an outstanding sire. In addition, his versatile progeny have earned field points, obedience titles, and field and versatility ratings, including a champion Master Hunter son, CH Greywind Frozen in Time, MH. Brae is the sire of 54 champions. One of those is Am/Can CH Norman's Greywind Phoebe Snow, JH, who broke a Best in Show record that stood for 32 years.

Brae is the sire of five Futurity winners: CH Norman's Frosty Morn, CD, NSD, V (1984); CH Breylin's Born to Run (1985); CH Silvermorn's Roger Rebel (1988); CH Wolfstadt's First Frost (1988); and Norman's Breasy Bubba (1991). First Frost went on to win the Maturity in 1989 and a Best in Show in 1991. Brae's BROM producers include CH Norman's Frostyroy Colleen, CH Woldstadt's First Frost, CH Norman's Greywind Robert Frost, CH Greywind's the Snowman, CH Greywind's Snowbird, CH Norman N Greywind's Bonnie Brae, CH Silvermont's Top Gun, CH Thorndorhylls How High Can I Go, and CH Weltmeister Ain't Misbehavin. He is also the sire of CH OTCH Eb's Red

Figure 34-27: *Am/Can CH Hoot Hollow's Roy's Rob Roy, CD* (Am/Can CH Colsidex Standing Ovation, BROM × CH Mardi's Gretchen Herr, CD). Bred by M. Schnegelberger; owned by Dorothy Roy. Sire of 22 champions.

Hot Seabreeze, UDX, JH, NRD, VX, the first champion OTCH in the breed. Brae truly left his mark on the Weimaraner breed.

Am/Can CH Hoot Hollow's Roy's Rob Roy, CD

Am/Can CH Hoot Hollow's Roy's Rob Roy, CD, BROM, was a WCA National Champion winner. He was bred sparingly but produced 22 champions and several noteworthy offspring. When bred to CH Silversmith Omni V Reiteralm, CD, TD, RD, NSD, VX, BROM, the resulting litter produced the following offspring: CH Silversmith Houston Rob Roy, NRD, who finished with five majors and was a Best of Breed winner, group placer, and 1st intermediate Futurity winner; CH Silversmith Sky Hi Zorba, TD, CD, NRD, V, who earned a Dog World award for his novice obedience scores while earning his Companion Dog with all firsts and finished his championship with four majors; CH Silversmith Omni Roy, NSD, who finished with four majors from the puppy class and was a Futurity and Maturity winner; CH Silversmith Dawn V Greystoke, who was a multiple group and specialty winner and Top 10 show dog; and CH Silversmith Deutsch Royal, who finished with four majors, was a 1st intermediate dog Futurity winner, and was a multiple Best in Show winner. Rob Roy also produced Valmar Serendipity, BROM, who was the WCA's 1986 Top-Producing Dam.

Am/Can CH Juriel's Space Ace

Sam began his show career with points at Westminster and ranked in the Top 10 for several years with multiple group and specialty wins. Exclusively owner handled, Bill Hammond

Figure 34-28: *Am/Can CH Juriel's Space Ace* (CH Seneca's Medicine Man, BROM × CH Sudden Splendore, BROM). Bred by Dorothy Driscoll; owned by William and Elizabeth Hammond. Sire of 26 champions.

Figure 34-29: *CH Kristof's Royal Crusader* (CH Von Seiben's Royal Flush, CD, NSD, BROM × Can CH Kristof's Amethyst, CD, BROM). Bred and owned by Sharon Krube. Sire of 30 champions.

and Sam were an unbeatable combination of class, style, and grace. His owners wrote, "Sam...was perfectly developed,

Figure 34-30: *CH Ladenburg Arco v Reiteralm* (Furst von Selztal × Fanni von der Lusshardt, BROM). Bred by Dr. Robert Shoeman III; owned by Virginia Alexander. Sire of 23 champions.

Figure 34-31: *CH Maximillan von der Reiteralm, NSD, HOF* (CH Val Knight Ranck, BROM × Bella v. d. Reiteralm, CD, BROM [Import]). Bred and owned by Virginia Alexander. Sire of 62 champions.

never going beyond the graceful balance we strive for in our dogs….This dog was a thrill to watch in the ring, with his graceful long reaching movement and fantastic rear drive."

The favorite pastime of the magnificent physical specimen was relaxing on the living-room davenport. His 26 champions include four BROM producers: CH Stabuck's Dolly Dynamite; CH Eb's Glory Be of Skytop, CDX, TD, RDX, SD, VX; CH Eb's Go Go of Xitation; and CH Eb's Gravel Gertie.

CH Kristof's Royal Crusader

CH Kristof's Royal Crusader, BROM, was the sire of 30 champions. When Cruser was bred to Kristof's TNT Jessica, BROM, the litters produced 10 champion offspring. Cruser's offspring garnered obedience titles and ratings. He also produced two BROM offspring: CH Kristof's Velvet Touch and CH Silversmith Indigo v Kristof, CD, NRD, V.

CH Ladenburg Arco v Reiteralm (Germany)

We thank breeder Dr. Robert Shoeman and Dr. Werner Petri, breed warden of the German Weimaraner Club, for allowing the A and B litters from Furst vom Selztal and Fanni von der Lusshardt to be whelped in America. To date, CH Ladenburg Arco v Reiteralm, BROM, remains the only 100% German dog to produce 23 show champions. But that is not all; the offspring of Arco and his BROM littermates Anni and Atilla (Alphie), and the B BROM littermates, Bryna and Bessie, excelled in every venue: top-producing stud and top show dog of the year, Maturity and Futurity winners, Best in Specialty Sweepstakes winners, Master Hunter, NAVHDA Natural Abil-

ity and UT prizes, multiple field placements, numerous WCA ratings, agility, tracking, and obedience titles (including several Utility Dogs), and a Dual Champion. His "marriage" to William Wegman's Fay Ray produced celebrities in unexpected venues, with multiple appearances on network talk shows and children's programming such as Sesame Street. Pictures of Arco's children were circulated internationally in museums, movies, books, and magazine covers. Many years have passed, but the legacy of this gift from Germany—trainability, versatility, and solid good health—still influences our breed today. Arco is photographed showing off just 2 years before his death at nearly 17 years young.

CH Maximilian von der Reiteralm, NSD, HOF

A storybook life. Placed as a pet, when a noted breeder examining Virginia Alexander's very first litter, declared Max to be too out of type. Max lived the first 5 years of his life as a generally ignored outside dog. Virginia, unable to see much but pity for the then over 126 lb Max, repurchased him with much difficulty in order to save his life. Over a year later, with a new coat of unbleached hair and a slim 76 lb profile, he finished his bench title quickly. Who knew that this over-stuffed, over-the-hill dog would turn into a clean necked, full-chested Prince Charming, that when stacked looked just like a silver Doberman Pinscher.

Figure 34-32: *CH Moonshine's Alpha Centauri* (CH Moonshine von Siegfried, BROM × CH Moonshine's Magic Moment, BROM). Bred and owned by Marlene Judd and Judy (Judd) Donnelly. Sire of 25 champions.

Figure 34-33: *CH Nani's Baht a Pack a Trouble, CD, JH, V* (CH Valmar's Xtra Copy, BROM × CH Nani's Poison Ivy, BROM). Bred by Jill Watson and Christine Grisell; owned by Laura Haverstick and Christine Grisell. Sire of 34 champions.

Figure 34-34: *CH Nani's Concert Master, SH* (CH Nani's Perfect Cadence, CD, JH, BROM × CH Baht N' Greywind Playn' the Game, NSD, BROM). Bred by Christine Grisell and Kari Chaney; owned by Christine Grisell. Sire of 59 champions.

With paired genes for most of his structural phenotype, Max's get were also consistently "out of type;" a genetic surprise, considering that he was out of half German sire, from a totally unrelated imported German mother.

In conformation and temperament, Max could be counted on to give you Max, which came with high prey drive, tiny cat feet, and his specialty: well-angulated, correctly moving shoulders, a genetic combination that was to become a signature stamp for his pups, irregardless of the bridal choice. As time passed, when other outstanding similarly structured individuals were added to the genetic mix, Max's "out of type" silhouette, with its uncluttered extended movement, gained popularity among breeders and judges over the Labrador Retriever look that was prevalent throughout the 1950s and early 1960s.

Bred to 26 bitches, he produced 62 show champion offspring; a field winner himself, he is also the only Weimaraner stud to produce multiple Dual Champions and multiple Best in Show winners. His legacy can be seen even in his offspring today; during the past 35 years, Max appears in the pedigree of 32 of the No. 1 All-Time Winning show dogs (Phillips System). He is the ancestor of 75% of the National Specialty Winners born after him and all but 11 of the 70 Best in Show Weimaraners. So despite his less than promising start as an overweight aging Romeo, Max's all-around influence on the breed is undeniable.

CH Moonshine's Alpha Centauri

CH Moonshine's Alpha Centauri was bred and owned by Marlene Judd and Judy (Judd) Donnelly. Alpha loved showing; finishing at 18 months old, he was a certified therapy dog (TDI), registered service dog by Sunshine Independent Dog,

and a CGC (Canine Good Citizen) by AKC. Alpha produced 25 champions, including CH Moonshine's Magic Pocahontas, BROM, who produced a daughter, CH Moonshine's on the War Path, the first Best in Show for the Moonshine lineage. He was a loved family dog that enjoyed visiting with Marlene's grandchildren as well as going to dog shows and visiting with spectators. Alpha spent his "retirement" with Marlene, an LPN, at nursing homes and hospitals, visiting and spreading joy to all he encountered. Alpha, 1991–2003, and Marlene, 1936–2004, will be greatly missed by their Moonshine families.

CH Nani's Baht a Pack a Trouble, CD, JH, V

CH Nani's Baht a Pack a Trouble, CD, JH, V, BROM, is the sire of 34 champions to date, with some still being shown. Packer is the sire of All-Breed and Specialty Best in Show winners, Maturity winners, and field pointed, hunt test, and obedience title offspring. He produced very "high" drive, and many of his get needed to have a full time "job," enabling his offspring to excel at performance events with several earning Versatile and Versatile Excellent ratings. When bred to CH Nani's Kookaburra, BROM, the resulting litter had many influential offspring, including the WCA's 1997 Top-Producing Dam, CH Nani's Perfect Cadence, CD, JH, V, BROM, and WCA's 1998 Top-Producing Dam, Am/Can CH Nani's Win'k of An Eye, VCD1, JH, VX, BROM, who was also a Best in Show Winner.

CH Nani's Concert Master, SH

CH Nani's Concert Master, SH, BROM, started his show career by going Reserve Winners Dog at the Yankee Specialty the day before the National Specialty over 100 dogs from the 6- to 9-month class. He easily finished his championship from the puppy class and went on to be a Best in Specialty Show winner. Maestro was also a natural in the field and handily earned his Senior Hunter title. But his biggest accomplishment was as a sire. Maestro sired 59 champions and has many offspring still being shown. He was the Top-Producing Sire in 1999. His progeny include All-Breed and Specialty Best in Show winners, Maturity winners, and numerous offspring that have excelled in performance events, including offspring who are field trial pointed, hunt test titled, agility titled, tracking titled, Top 10 Obedience dogs, Obedience All-Breed High in Trial winners, and a National Obedience High in Trial winner. One of his most noteworthy offspring is CH Nani's Jagmar Sweet Dividends, VCD2, CDX, TD, MH, MX, MXJ, NSD, NRD, CGC, VX4, BROM, who accumulated all of her performance titles with her novice owner handler and was the 2005 Top-Producing Dam, with 10 offspring finishing their championship that year.

BIS CH Nani's Hawaiian Punch

The first Best in Show winner of Best in Show parents (see *Best in Show*), Punch passed his winning qualities to his progeny. He sired the Futurity winners CH Sandcreek's Sand Dancer (1987) and CH Nani's Leave 'Em Laughing (1991). Punch's Maturity winners are CH Sanbar's Diamonds are Forever (1986), multiple group winning CH Harline's Mauna Loa (1986), CH Nebula's Nuthin' but Blue Skies (1991), and CH Nani's Leave 'Em Laughing (1992).

Punch's BROM producers are CH Nani's Ananas of Silvermont and CH Tri-D's Sterling Silver, NSD, the first Weimaraner to win both bench and field futurities.

CH Nani's Indecent Exposure, JH, NAJ, V

CH Nani's Indecent Exposure, JH, NAJ, V, BROM, was out of a litter of two, sired by semen collected in 1986 and frozen. Streak had a successful show career, starting with a Specialty major win his first time in the ring at 6 months of age and finishing his championship at 12 months of age with a large five-point major during the Canfield, Ohio, Specialty

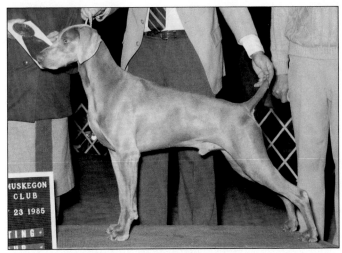

Figure 34-35: *BIS CH Nani's Hawaiian Punch* (CH Colsidex Standing Ovation, BROM × CH Nani's Visa v. d. Reiteralm, BROM). Bred by Chris Medeiros and Betty Oelesen; owned by Donnie Edwards and Chris Medeiros. Sire of 38 champions.

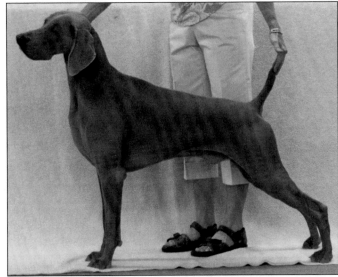

Figure 34-36: *CH Nani's Indecent Exposure, JH, NAJ, V* (Am/Can CH Colsidex Nani Reprin, JH, SD, BROM × CH Nani's Tattletale, JH, BROM). Bred by Christine Grisell; owned by Christine Grisell and Susan Casper. Sire of 51 champions.

weekend. He was the Best of Opposite Sex winner at the 2004 National Specialty at 1½ years and went on to win the 2005 National Specialty and the 2006 Top 20 Invitational. He was a Futurity and Maturity winner and was on the Top 10 list for three consecutive years. However, his most important accomplishments were earning his BROM well before his 3rd birthday and siring 19 champions in 2005, earning him the 2005 Top-Producing Sire award. He has multiple Best in Show winning offspring—CH Smokycity Silhouette Dbl Ur Pleasure, CH Nani's Tsurutani Honor Bound, and CH Harline Win'Weim It's My 2nd Martini—as well as a Top 20 Invitational Winner and Futurity and Maturity winning offspring, multiple group winning, and Top 10 Show offspring, as well as a son who went Best of Opposite Sex at the 2006 WCA Nationals, and a son in Australia who is a multiple Best in Show winner, and a son in Portugal who went Best in Show over 3,100 other dogs. His get have also completed many hunt, agility, tracking, retrieving, obedience, and Versatile Excellent titles.

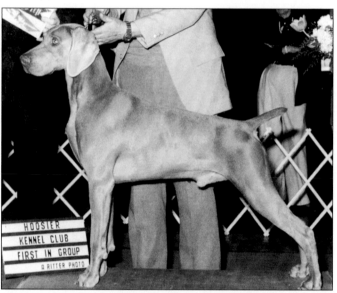

Figure 34-37: *CH Nani's Master Charge, NSD, NRD, V, HOF* (CH Rio Fonte Saudade, NRD, BROM × CH Nani's Soul Sister, BROM). Bred by Christine Medeiros and Roiann Morford; owned by Christine Medeiros and Betty Olson. Sire of 28 champions.

CH Nani's Master Charge, NSD, NRD, V, HOF

With only 9 months of campaigning, the multiple group and specialty show winning Clout headed the breed's Top 10 list in 1982. Clout's most important job, however, was being Christine's constant companion. He accompanied her to the Dairy Queen and the bank, where he was always well rewarded by the employees. An avid retriever, Clout was the perfect helper when it was time to unload the car after dog shows and shopping trips. "The greatest thing of all," wrote Christine, "is to watch the veteran dog play so gently with the young puppies."

A litter brother of the Best in Show winner CH Nani's Visa v. d. Reiteralm, BROM, Clout produces the style and showmanship that made both such outstanding specials. He is the sire of many group and specialty winners and the Maturity winner CH Sanbar's Just a Sample (1985). Nani's Footnotes to Dawn, CDX, had a High in Trial (199) and ranked 10th on

Figure 34-38: *CH Nani's Sanbar Ringside Rumor, JH* (CH Ann's Magic v. d. Reiteralm, BROM × CH Bryrwood Sanbar's Hot Ticket, BROM). Bred by Christine Grisell and Sandy West; owned by Suzette Jett and Christine Grisell. Sire of 20 champions.

Figure 34-39: *CH Nani's Scirroco of Mattrace, CD* (CH Colsidex Standing Ovation, BROM × CH Nani's Cobbie Cuddler, BROM). Bred by Christine Medeiros; owned by Vicki Roye. Sire of 26 champions.

Figure 34-40: *BIS CH Nani's Smart Aleck, JH, NRD, V* (CH Midnite Magic von HolyHaus × CH Nani's Knocker, CDX, TD, JH, SD, VX, BROM). Bred and owned by Christine Grisell and Susan Casper. Sire of 51 champions.

Figure 34-41: *CH Nani's Southern Cross, HOF* (CH Arokat's Legionnaire, BROM × CH Forshado Nani's Crystal Vision, BROM). Bred by Christine Medeiros-Grisell and Mary Bewig Stratil; owned by Christine Medeiros-Grisell. Sire of 89 champions.

the breed's Top 10 obedience list in 1985. Clout's son DC Watchpoint's Foreshadow, NRD, NSD, ranked eighth on the Top 10 field dog list in 1986, establishing Clout as a sire of performance ability as well as beauty. Clout is the sire of four BROM producers: CH Nani's Cobbie Cuddler; CH Sanbar's Mighty Movin' Molly; CH Silversmith Nani Rendezvous, CD, TD, RD, NSD, VX; and CH Nani's Northern Star.

CH Nani's Sanbar Ringside Rumor, JH

CH Nani's Sanbar Ringside Rumor, JH, BROM, was an exciting young dog, that proved his mettle early. Rumor went Best of Winners from the 6- to 9-month class in his first show, finished at 12 months, and won a Best in Specialty Show before he was 18 months old. He also earned his Junior Hunter title in four straight tries with four different handlers. By far, Rumor's most outstanding accomplishment was his progeny. He produced 20 champions in just seven litters, earning his BROM at 3 years of age. He also had a champion daughter that was a multiple group and Futurity winner.

CH Nani's Scirroco of Mattrace, CD

CH Nani's Scirroco of Mattrace, CD, BROM, was a very special dog in many ways and a great ambassador for the breed. Rocky sired a handful of litters, but they were full of quality. His get included Top 10 winners, group winners and placers, Futurity and Maturity winners, winners at National Specialty shows (i.e., Best of Opposite Sex, Winners Bitch,

etc.), and obedience titled dogs. The most well known were the Best in Show winning siblings CH WF Mattrace Harline Roquelle (Kelly) and CH Harline's WF Rockefeller, BROM. Both of these lovely animals were out of the great producing bitch CH Harline's Hurrah, BROM.

Especially nice is the fact that Rocky's offspring have bred on. For example, Rocky's son CH Harline's WF Rockefeller, BROM, was bred to the group placing Rocky daughter CH Donmar's Wind in the Willows, BROM, producing CH Mattrace Harline Key Largo, BROM, who has sired multiple Best in Show winners. Rockefeller also sired the dam of the top winning, top producing dog CH Carousel's Roscoe T Picotrane. Another Rocky grandson, also by Rockefeller, was CH Harline's Hollywood, who has sired multiple Best in Show winners.

BIS CH Nani's Smart Aleck, JH, NRD, V

CH Nani's Smart Aleck, JH, NRD, V, BROM, finished his championship with three 5-point majors from the puppy class. From there, Aleck went on to be an all-breed Best in Show winner, a multiple Best in Show Specialty winner, and the first Top 20 Invitational winner. He currently has 51 champions to his credit and was the Top-Producing Weimaraner and Top 5 All-Breed producer for 2001 with 22 champions. He has produced numerous offspring that have excelled in performance. They have earned hunt test, agility, tracking, and obedience titles and include several all-breed obedience High in Trial winners. Aleck has multiple progeny that have won futurities and maturities and was the sire of the 2004 Top-Producing Dam.

CH Nani's Southern Cross, HOF

CH Nani's Southern Cross was the youngest National Specialty winner in breed history, winning it at 16 months of age in 1989. Cross was both a Futurity and Maturity winner and was ranked in the Top 10 Show list. But his biggest contribution to the Weimaraner breed was as a sire, where he was the Top-Producing Sire in 1996 and 1998 and is currently ranked as the No. 4 all-time Top Producer. He has produced 89 champions, multiple Futurity and Maturity winners, and All-Breed and Specialty Best in Show winners. More importantly, Cross's get have also produced well, with his offspring producing 300 champions to date. Along with a daughter who was the 2000 Top-Producing Dam, Cross has two grandsons that were the 2001 and 2005 Top-Producing sires and two granddaughters that were the 2003 and 2005 Top-Producing Dams. His legacy is definitely living on through his offspring!

CH Nani's N Top Hat's Backlash, CD, NSD, V

CH Nani's N Top Hat's Backlash, CD, NSD, V, BROM, came to Top Hat Weimaraners to become our foundation stud dog and crossed excellently with our foundation Valmar bloodlines. Debra owner-handled Topper to his championship and group placements. He was quickly surpassed in the breed ring by his own Top 10 sons, CH Top Hat's Top Gun and CH Top Hat's Dorian Gray. From a very limited breeding program, Topper spent several years as the No. 10 WCA Top-Producing sire, again to be replaced by his last Top 10 son, BIS CH Windwalker's Graeagle, CD, JH, NRD, V, BROM. Topper sired 37 champions, one Best in Show winner, five WCA Top 10 dogs, and several Futurity and Maturity winners and BROM producers. With his limited progeny, Topper influenced breeding programs as far away as Australia and Japan. His 1992 WCA Top-Producing dam/Top 10 daughter, CH Top Hat's Spitfire, went on to produce BIS CH Aria's Allegra of Colsidex, who earned 27 Best in Show.

Am/Can CH Norman Smokey City Chill Fact'r, JH, NRD, V

Am/Can CH Normans' Smoky City Chill Fact'r, JH, NRD, V, BROM, was shown sparingly by Peggy Rousch, finishing his championship with three 5-point majors in very strong competition. Ice lived with Peggy during his specials career, and she recalls the story of a magazine photo shoot

Figure 34-42: *CH Nani's N Top Hat's Backlash, CD, NSD, V* (CH Nani's Kona Gust CD, TD, V, BROM × CH Nani's Apple-Sass, BROM). Bred by Christine Medeiros; owned by Debra Hopkins. Sire of 37 champions.

Figure 34-43: *Am/Can CH Norman Smokey City Chill Fact'r, JH, NRD, V* (Am/Can CH Valmar Smokey City Ultra Easy, JH, NSD, BROM × CH Norman's Frostroy Colleen, BROM). Bred by Norman LeBoeuf; owned by Tom Wilson. Sire of 24 champions.

with Ice and his sister Am/Can CH Norman's Smokey City Heat Wave (Allie). They were each to sit on a rock for the picture. Allie jumped right up, but Ice was just not going to jump up onto his rock. After several tries, Peggy finally decided to try them BOTH on the same rock. With his sister already sitting on the rock, Ice was happy to jump up! In 1990, Ice was the No. 1 Weimaraner in Canada, in 1991, he won the WCA Winter Specialty, in 1992, he was the Pedigree Award winner and the No. 1 Weimaraner, and in 1993 he was the second Top-Producing dog. Ice was the sire of 24 champions, many that achieved recognition for their field ability. Folllowing in his father's footsteps, Ice was the constant companion of Tom Wilson, traveling everywhere with him.

Am/Can CH Reichenstadt's Majestic, CD

CH Reichenstadt's Majestic, BROM, who was the son of CH Shadowmar Barthus Dorillio, BROM, and CH Kam's Rauchigalen of Redhill, CD, BROM, combined two strong East and West coast lines. Majestic is the sire of 34 champions, including group winning CH Shadowmar Leap Year Luv v Eb (Top 10 Weimaraner 1974 and 1975). He sired three Futurity winners: CH Shadowmar Tsungani CDX, NSD, V, BROM (1973); CH Graumeir's Aphrodite, NRD (1975); and CH Kamsou Altair (1975).

Majestic is the sire of seven BROM producers: CH Shadowmar Tsungani, CDX, NSD, V; CH Graumeir's Andromeda; CH Jagerhof's Midnight Magic CD, CH Reichenstadt's Kona v. Arenas; CH Reichenstadt's Summer Magic, CD, NSD, V; Reichenstadt's Amanda V Gab, CD; and CH Shadowmar Ace O' Butternut Hill.

CH Reiteralm's Rio Fonte Saudade

Finished undefeated from regular puppy classes, Rio began gathering points at 7 months—no surprise for a puppy from the breed's first litter produced by two Best in Show winners. He finished his championship in short order and by the age of 3 managed to qualify for BROM status. He is the sire of the multiple Best in Show winners CH Nani's Visa v. d. Reiteralm, BROM (Futurity winner, 1980), and Am/Aust CH Ranah's Bold Ruler v. Reiteralm (Australia). His second Futurity winner is CH Bayer's Ferdinand v. Reiteralm, CDX, NSD, V (1990). Rio's Maturity winners are CH Orion's Nova Von Reiteralm, JH, NRD, NSD, V, BROM (1982 Top 10), CH Nani's Cartel, CDX, NRD, NSD, V (1985 Top 10), field pointed CH ArimarLisa's Reiteralm Foxy, and DC AFC Bayer's Silver Mr V Reiteralm, NSD, NRD, VX (1991). Rio sired eight BROM producers: CH Nani's Visa von der Reiteralm, Am/Can CH Nani's Master Charge, NSD, NRD, V (sire of DC Watchpoint's Foreshadow, NRD, NSD), CH Nani's Ann of Enchantment; CH Nani's Carte Blanche, Nani's Continental Whirlaway, CH Nani's Spirit O Moonshine

Figure 34-44: *Am/Can CH Reichenstadt's Majestic, CD* (CH Shadowmar Barthaus Dorillio, BRP × CH Kams Rauchigalan of Redhill, CD, BROM). Bred by Richard Slater; owned by Richard Slater and Micahle Clark. Sire of 34 champions.

Figure 34-45: *CH Reiteralm's Rio Fonte Saudade* (CH Eric von Seiben, BROM × CH The Rajah's Magic v. d. Reiteralm, BROM). Bred and owned by Virginia Alexander. Sire of 44 champions.

CD, CH Orion's Vixen Von Reiteralm NSD NRD V, and CH Silversmith Omni v. Reiteralm, CD, TD, RD, NSD, VX (dam of the Best in Show winners CH Silversmith Dawn v. Greystoke and CH Silversmith Harbor Pistol—Germany). Either Rio, or his brother, Guy, appear in 85% of the pedigrees of the Best in Show Winners since their birth. Rio is one of the few sires to produce both multiple Best in Show winners as well as a Dual Champion.

BIS CH Ronamax Rajah v. d. Reiteralm, HOF

Co-owned and sponsored by Joseph Rymer, Rajah earned conformation honors that included four all breed Best in Show wins and the 1970 National Specialty. His Phillips System record, as show dog of the year, stood for 15 years, until surpassed by his grand-daughter CH Valmar's Pollyanna, BROM.

As a stud, Rajah dominated the breed for many years, becoming the first sire of over 100 champions. In the early 80s, both Rajah and his dam Rona were awarded the Kennel Review Diamond Certificate, given to the sires of 100 or more and dams of 20 or more champions, and to date, they are still the only mother and son of any breed to attain this prestigious honor. Bred to but a few carefully selected bitches, who produced 51 litters, in the days before the convenience of easy transportation and artificial insemination, the high percent-

Figure 34-47: *Am/Can CH Seneca's Medicine Man, HOF* (CH Gronbach's Aladdin, CD, BROM × CH Eilatan's Karlrise Seneca, CD, BROM). Bred and owned by William B. and Elizabeth Q. Hammond. Sire of 27 champions.

Figure 34-46: *BIS CH Ronamax Rajah v. d. Reiteralm, HOF* (CH Maximillian v. d. Reiteralm, NSD, BROM × CH Norman's Rona v. d. Reiteralm, NRD, SD, V, BROM). Bred by Virginia Alexander and Saundra Watson; owned by Virginia Alexander and C. Joseph Rymer. Sire of 118 champions.

age of Rajah's champion get is impressive and resulted from his ability to nick well with bitches of varying types and bloodlines. His offspring consistently demonstrated excellent movement and a sweet, willing temperament.

Rajah sired the Best in Show and National Specialty winners CH The Rajah's Magic v. d. Reiteralm, BROM (1976 and 1977), and CH Rajah's Alexander v. d. Reiteralm (1971) as well as the Westminster Best of Breed winner CH Halann's Rocket v. d. Reiteralm (1973).

Rajah's influence is still apparent today, as he appears in the pedigrees of 24 of the last 30 National Specialty winners. Since his own Best in Show in 1970, Rajah is found in the pedigrees of 51 other Best in Show winners. Nineteen of our breed's Dual Champions are descended from this versatile gentleman's hunting dog. A stud dog before the advent of AI and dedicated to his duties, Rajah sired a litter (which resulted in four championship get) shortly before his demise at the age of 13 (refer to *Best in Show* for the details of his final romantic encounter).

Am/Can CH Seneca's Medicine Man, HOF

Handled by his breeder/owner, Bill Hammond, Doc won over 200 Best of Breeds (including Westminster 1968 and 1971) and numerous specialties and group wins. The clean, elegant lines that made Doc so breathtaking also characterized his outstanding progeny.

His accomplishments as a sire are particularly spectacular, considering his limited use at stud. The Hammonds would only use Doc at stud if you brought the bitch to him. They would not keep a bitch following an unfortunate experience of a visiting bitch bloating while at their home. Due to his limited use, he only sired 27 champions. Of those 27 champions, Doc set a breed record when he became the first sire of three Best in Show winners. All three of these Best in Show winners were National Specialty winners, too: CH Chat-A-Wey Charley v. d. Reiteralm (1973), his littermate, CH Springdale Rhea v. d. Reiteralm, CD (1974 and 1975), and CH Colsidex Standing Ovation, BROM (1981 and 1984). He also sired Futurity winners, Rhea (1971), Charley (1971), and CH Colsidex Medicine Show, BROM (1975).

Doc is the sire of four BROM progeny, CH Colsidex Medicine Show, CH Colsidex Standing Ovation, CH Juriels Space Ace, and CH Normans Docval Heatheress.

BIS Am/Can CH Shadowmar Barthaus Dorillio, HOF

As his grandsire Rickey Boy had dueled with True Aim to become the breed's leading sire, so the Best in Show winners Dor and Val Knight Ranck, BROM, fought for the new record; like his sire, Dor lost by one (see *Best in Show*). Nevertheless, Dor became one of the most influential sires of the breed through his 33 champions, including the Futurity winners CH Doug's Dauntless Von Dor (1967) and DC Halann's Checkmate Tamara, CD, NRD, SDX.

Dor sired nine BROM producers: CH Dauntmar's Silver Splendoress; CH Doug's Dauntless von Dor; CH Eichenhof's Ginger Man, Ginger Dorco of Windage Farm; CH Moeller's Ambassador, CDX; CH Norman's Dorval von Martin; CH Rona's Rogue of Green Acres, CD, NRD, V; CH Reichenstadt's Majestic; and CH Shadowmar's Sue's Silver Belle.

Am/Can CH Silberschoen's Lucky Strike

Am/Can CH Silberschoen's Lucky Strike, BROM, was a multiple Best in Specialty Show winner and a Futurity winner. Frisco made the Top 10 Breed List for 1998 and Top Producers list for 1998, 1999 and 2000. He has produced 28 champions and Best in Show, multiple Best in Specialty Show and Futurity and Maturity winners. Five offspring have made the Top 10 lists, including two No. 1s. He has also produced two Best of Breeds and a Best of Opposite Sex winner at the prestigious Westminster show and the winner of the 2001 National Specialty, BIS CH Smokey City Riverboat Gambler, BROM.

CH Silversmith Ethan Allen, JH, NSD

"Ethan" was originally purchased from his breeders, Elena Smith Lamberson and Tracy Brabham, as a pet on a Limited registration. He was the last puppy left in his litter and his buyer had no intentions of showing him. As he grew though his owner, Pamela Cherry, saw that there was something special in his presence and in his movement while

Figure 34-48: *BIS Am/Can CH Shadowmar Barthaus Dorillio, HOF* (CH Von Gaiberg's Nordsee Ponto × CH Shadowmar Little Kate). Bred by Dorothy Remensnyder and Marjorie Bartelli Wiosom; owned by Dorothy Remensnyder. Sire of 33 champions.

Figure 34-49: *Am/Can CH Silberschoen's Lucky Strike* (CH Nani's Southern Cross, BROM × Can CH Silberschoen's Northern Dancer) Bred and owned by Maurice and Gladys Cote. Sire of 28 champions.

watching him run on the beach. At 5 months of age, his breeders saw him and lifted his limited registration. And so the journey began for both him and his owner.

He quickly finished his bench championship at just under 12 months of age with four Majors. At this time he took a hiatus from the show ring and obtained his Junior Hunter title in four consecutive tests, proving his natural bird ability with a novice owner/handler.

At just under 2 years of age his 'specials' career began, and he and Doug Carlson became known as a team. His powerful, effortless movement and reach and drive was noted by many who saw him. During his career he had many Sporting Group and Specialty wins.

He has produced 29 champions to date. Among those are multiple Best in Show winner CH Bzyfeet American Idol and Can CH Waltz State Fair V Silversmith, who was imported to the UK and was awarded his first Challenge Certificate and a Best of Breed over 130 dogs at the 2007 Darlington Championship. He has "nicked" well with a wide variety of bitches and in those litters has produced three Futurity and four Maturity winners, along with other Top 10 show dogs thus far in his young stud dog career.

Figure 34-50: *CH Silversmith Ethan Allen, JH, NSD* (CH Windwalker's Graeagle, CD, JH, NRD, V, BROM × CH Silversmith Lady Gracie, JH, NSD, V, BROM). Bred by Tracy Brabham and Elena Smith Lamberson; owned by Pamela Cherry. Sire of 29 champions.

He has several of his get in training for Senior and Master Hunter titles and is passing on his bird ability, water love, retrieve drive, and biddable temperament.

CH Silversmith's EZ Payment Plan, CD, JH, SD, V

CH Silversmith's EZ Payment Plan, CD, JH, SD, V, BROM, was a multiple Best of Breed winner, group placer, and the Best Dog in the 1990 Western Futurity. Cash produced 34 champions. His most noteworthy offspring was out of CH Sunmist Silver Shadow, JH, CD, BROM; CH Greymist's Silver Cloud, BROM, who was the WCAs 1995 No. 1 Show dog, earned 15 Best in Show awards, was a two time Nationals Specialty Best of Breed winner, and a Futurity/Maturity winner. At the time she retired she was the No. 1 All-Time Winning Weimaraner in recorded history.

BIS CH Sir Eric von Seiben, HOF

A Best in Show winner (see *Best in Show*), Eric sired the Best in Show winners CH Erbenhof Touch of Class, BROM, and CH Valmar's Pollyanna, BROM—a Futurity (1982), Maturity (1983), and National Specialty (1987) winner. Eric's other Futurity winners are CH Wismar's Regal Prince, CD, NRD, V (1978), and CH Valmar's Pepsi Challenge (1982).

Eric is the sire of eight BROM producers: CH Ann's Magic v. d. Reiteralm; CH Erbenhof's Bold Venture (1979 and 1980 Top 10); CH Erbenhof Touch of Class; CH Pic-a-Star's Trump v. d. Reiteralm, CD; CH Reiteralm's Rio Fonte Saudade, NRD; CH Von Sieben's Royal Flush, CD, NSD, V, (1977 Top 10); CH Von Sieben's Smart 'N' Special, NSD (1977, 1978, 1982 Top 10 and the breed's third sire of two Dual Champions); and CH Valmar's Pollyanna (dam of a Dual Champion).

One indication of Eric's remarkable influence on the breed is that five of his BROM progeny qualified for these chapters on the breed's top producers: Ann's Magic, Rio, Royal Flush, Smart 'N' Special, and Pollyanna. In addition, Eric's descendents display consistent quality in the field, beginning with his son DC Redhill's Chief Geronimo, NRD, SDX, V. He is the grandsire of four Dual Champions, including, Jafwin's One and Only, NRD, SD, VX (winner of the 1982 National All-Age Championship); Jafwin's The Goodbye Girl, NRD, SDX; and Valmar's Valiant Knight, CD, NRD, VX, BROM. The great grandsire of DC Watchpoints Foreshadow, NRD, NSD, the pattern of Eric's continued influence on the breed's dual aptitude will be interesting to follow.

CH Smokey City El Nino, JH

It was fitting that the final Allie-Monroe breeding produced only one male puppy, who was immediately given the

Figure 34-51: *CH Silversmith's EZ Payment Plan, CD, JH, SD, V* (Am/Can CH Valmar Smokey City Ultra Easy, JH, NSD, BROM × CH Silversmith Page V Reiteralm, NRD, NSD, V, BROM). Bred by Elena Smith; owned by Tony and Vicki Ruiz. Sire of 34 champions.

Figure 34-52: *BIS CH Sir Eric von Seiben, HOF* (CH Doug's Dauntless von Dor, BROM × CH Chaskar's Suddenly It's Rainy, BROM) Bred and owned by Helene M Burkholder. Sire of 44 champions.

Figure 34-53: *CH Smokey City El Nino, JH* (CH Smokey City Ez Moonstone, JH, NRD, V, BROM × CH Norman's Smokey City Heat Wave, JH, BROM). Bred by Tom Wilson and Kelly Photopoulos; owned by Kelly Photopoulos and Tom Wilson. Sire of 64 champions.

purple collar. Tom and Kelley knew that this dog was going to stay and was going to be the one to carry on for the great Smokey City sires in his pedigree—Chaz, Easy, and Ice. Logan's show career was unremarkable; he finished quickly and had a short career as a special with a few wins but nothing spectacular. However, his first breedings in his early stud dog career showed that his great success was going to be as a sire. To date, Logan has sired 64 champions and 12 Futurity or Maturity winners, including BIS CH Smokey City Hail Mary, CH Smoky City True Grit, CH Smokey City Mob Boss, and CH Von Luchbach N Wynwoods Shelly, and other multiple Futurity, Maturity, Group, and Best in Show winners. He is also the sire of Top 10 show dogs and Top 10 Derby field trial dogs.

The part of this wonderful dog that is unknown to many is his phenomenal temperament, which he passes on to his puppies. He was a great family dog, completely devoted to the children in his family, and an absolute pleasure to live with. He will always be much missed in our family.

CH Smokey City Ez Moonstone, JH, NRD, V

Monroe won his Futurity and Maturity, clearly showing his powerful reach and drive. Shown sparingly with Peggy Rousch, he achieved top breed wins and group placements. His wonderful temperament and desire to work were evident as he competed in "Juniors" competition with the capable Jennifer Miller Howard. When bred to "Allie" (CH Smokey City Heat Wave), he was the Top-Producing sire in 1993, and

Figure 34-54: *CH Smokey City Ez Moonstone, JH, NRD, V* (Am/Can CH Valmar Smokey City Ultra Easy, JH, NSD, BROM × CH Smokey City Jedda Arokat, BROM). Bred by Tom Wilson; owned by Tom Wilson, Diana Campbell and Kate Masters. Sire of 24 champions.

Figure 34-55: *CH Top Hat's Dorian Gray* (CH Nani N Tophat's Backlash, CD, NSD, V, BROM × CH Valmar's Silver Dove, BROM). Bred by Debra Hopkins; owned by S. Spielman. Sire of 34 champions.

several Futurity and Maturity winning get were produced as a result of this outstanding breeding. Monroe continued the tradition of his Top-Producing parents, No. 1 all-time Top-Producing sire, CH Valmar Smokey City Ultra Easy, and No. 2 all-time Top-Producing dam, Smokey City Jedda Arokat. Monroe is the sire of Smokey City El Nino, who also appears on this list, with 64 champions to date.

CH Top Hat's Dorian Gray

Remy first entered the show ring at a fun match when he was 3 months old and won his first Sporting Group that day. At 6 months old, Remy won the points his first three times out, including a major. He finished his championship at 13 months and soon had 18 Best of Breeds. Thereafter, Remy had an exciting show career, primarily with Keith Pautz, including 88 breed wins, 21 group placements, 7 Group 1s and two Best in Specialty Show. The WCA recognized Remy as the No. 6 Show Dog in 1991 and as No. 8 in 1993.

Remy sired 34 U.S. champions and many champions in Australia and New Zealand. His first puppy in Australia was Puppy of the Year, and several of his get "down under" are Best in Show and multiple Best in Show winners.

Remy was the ultimate showman, with his powerful, floating side movement and stunning profile. To talk about Remy as merely a sum of his accomplishments would be an incomplete portrait of him. Remy was "scary smart", mischievous, head-

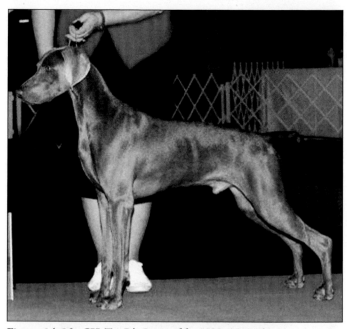

Figure 34-56: *CH Tri-D's Invincible, NSD* (CH Eb's You Otta See Me Now, JH × CH Tri-D's Bain De Soleil). Bred by Carole and Bill Donaldson; owned by Michael P. Parker, MD and Carole Donaldson. Sire of 23 champions.

strong, charismatic, and confident to the point of being arrogant. Remy was a once-in-a-lifetime dog, and we miss him every day.

CH Tri-D's Invincible, NSD

CH Tri-D's Invincible, NSD, BROM, was from the final breeding of CH Eb's You Otta See Me Now, JH × CH Tri-D's

Bain de Soleil. Carole Donaldson gave Vince to Michael Parker when he was a 3-month-old puppy, promising that this was a puppy that could "make him proud." She was right. Vince developed into a very sound, smooth-moving specimen of the breed and finished his championship in short order with back-to-back five-point majors. Following in his top producing sire's footsteps, Vince proved his greatest worth as a sire, stamping his signature traits on multiple offspring. To date, Vince is the sire of 23 champions.

BIS CH Ultimas Stetson V Hufmeister, CD

Stetson was bought unseen as a puppy for his novice owner Teresa Hill to show. He began winning matches at 4 months of age, finishing his championship with four majors, Stetson was turned over to Rusty Howard for his specials career. Winning the Central Futurity at the Nationals, then going on to win his Maturity in 1995. Stetson was ranked No. 1 Weimaraner in 1995, with several Group 1s and placements, four Best in Shows, and the National Specialty winner in 1996.

Stetson, known for his outstanding movement, showmanship and headpiece was chosen by many breeders as a sire. Stetson was the producer of 40 champions, including Maturity winners CH Rosaic's Gala Baraka, CD, JH, NSD, NRD, V; CH Valmar's Summer Rain, BROM; and CH Hufmeisters Well Decorated, Group winner, and Top 10 in 2004.

BIS CH Val Knight Ranck, HOF

Record-holding winner of nine Best in Shows (see *Best in Show*), Val also held the record as top-producing sire (32 champions) for many years, until he was surpassed by his son CH Maximilian v. d. Reiteralm, NSD, BROM (62 champions), who was surpassed in turn by his own son CH Ronamax Rajah v. d. Reiteralm, BROM (118 champions). Rajah's daughters, great and grand, when line bred back to Val's several times great-grandsons, CH Valmar Smokey City Ultra Easy (No. 4 top producer of all breeds with 148 champions) and CH Colsidex Standing Ovation (No. 5 all breeds with 147 champions), would contribute to the continuation of Val's dynasty of top producers.

Figure 34-58: *BIS CH Val Knight Ranck, HOF* (CH Count von Houghton, SD, BROM × CH Brenda's Gray Shadow, CD, BROM). Bred by Wesley Ranck; owned by John M. Boehne. Sire of 34 champions.

Figure 34-57: *BIS CH Ultimas Stetson V Hufmeister, CD* (Am/Can CH Colsidex Nani Reprint, JH, SD, BROM × CH Ultima's Sadie Hawkins, BROM). Bred by Ann H and Peter Loop; owned by Thomas and Teresa Hill. Sire of 40 champions.

Val sired the 1967 National Specialty winner CH Brandy's Twilight of Knight and the Futurity winner CH Val's Veto v. d. Reiteralm, NSD (1963), who would sire DC Othen's Princess Pretty, NRD, SDX, V, twice winner of both the National open all-age and the national amateur all-age championships (1973 and 1974). Val's multiple group winners are CH Rum Runner v. d. Reiteralm, CH Sandra Silver Knight, BROM, and CH Brandy's Twilight of Knight, BROM; other group winners are CH Verdemar's Bismark, CH Greggy v. Haimberg Ranck, and CH Bamby's v. d. Simba.

Standing at stud only 17 times, Val also sired five BROM producers: CH Eilatan's Valmist Comet; CH Maximilian v. d. Reiteralm, NSD; CH Sandra Silber Knight; Shadowmar Valentress; and CH Verdemar's Von Bradford, NSD. Val was able to make this lasting genetic contribution as the result of fortuitous circumstances as well as planning. He was the result of a breeding of two unrelated half-German show champion parents, and in hindsight, the closely monitored German breeding program granted him a pedigree and phenotype that would "nick" exceptionally well with the outcross German import Bella v. d. Reiteralm, CD, BROM, HOF. To future generations (most often from the Bella-Val offspring), he left a predictable genetic imprint that enabled fanciers to line breed back to him without incurring notable genetic penalty, fortunately carrying with it his stamp of modern type, good health, and birdiness. The strength of his legacy can be seen through the generations: Val appears in the pedigrees of 48 of the 65 Top-Producing dams (10 or more champions) and 51 of the 70 Top-Producing sires (20 or more champions). His type and fluid movement can be seen in his progeny even today as he appears in the pedigrees of 37 of the last 40 years of National Specialty winners and all but four of the Best in Show winners since his offspring hit the show circuit. Val also contributed greatly to the versatility of the modern Weimaraner, as can be seen from his remarkable appearance in the pedigrees of 37 Dual Champions.

BIS CH Valmar's Apache Rebel

Rebel is an All-Breed Best in Show, Specialty, and 1995 National Specialty Best of Breed winner. He was ranked in the Top 10 show list for 3 years (1993–1995). Rebel is well balanced, of medium size, with nice shoulder layback, a good topline, and a wonderful temperament, with loads of personality. He is known for his strong, ground-covering gait and beautiful headpiece. He has produced sound, well-balanced offspring, including specialty, group, Futurity, and Maturity winners. His top-producing BROM offspring include CH Valmar's Unanimous Decision, NSD, BROM; CH Valmar's

Urban Cowboy, BROM; and CH Valmar's Grayshar Burgundy, BROM.

Rebel retired at the age of 6 from the show ring, and after being away for a year his owners decided it would be fun to support their specialties with a veteran. At the age of 8 he went Best of Breed several times from the Veteran class. Rebel was a "Once in a Life Time Special", he was always so up at dog shows. As Andy Linton once said, "Rebel would

Figure 34-59: *BIS CH Valmar's Apache Rebel* (CH Top Hat's Top Gun, BROM × CH Valmar's Starling, BROM). Bred by Joan Valdez and Terry Cumins; owned by Rachel Aguilar and Joan Valdez. Sire of 32 champions.

Figure 34-60: *CH Valmar's Jazzman, CD, NSD, NRD, V, HOF* (CH Valmar's Chancelor v. Starbuck × CH Valmar's Elke Scwenden). Bred and owned by Joan Valdez. Sire of 75 champions.

Figure 34-61: *Am/Can CH Valmar's Unanimous Decision, NSD* (CH Valmar's Apache Rebel BROM × CH Valmar's Night N Gale, BROM). Bred by Joan H. Valdez; owned by Greg McLogan. Sire of 32 champions.

salute us wherever we sat clapping without breaking gait." At home, he was named Saint Rebel by his good friend Vicki Ruiz, he was so laid back and a joy to be around.

CH Valmar's Jazzman, CD, NSD, NRD, V, HOF

The winning qualities of the team of Jazz and Joan were evident when the breed-winning youngster won the 1977 Western Futurity; Jazz ranked among the Top 10 Weimaraners from 1978 to 1980. His 100 breed wins include three specialties and the 1980 National Specialty, with 23 group placements (four 1s, six 2s, six 3s, and seven 4s).

Jazz sired the Best in Show and 1983 National Specialty winner CH Silverkist Davie Lee. His group winning get include CH Harline's Jazzabel Winfield; CH Harline's Belushi; and CH Agbay's Touch of Class.

Jazz is the sire of four Futurity winners: CH Jafwin's All That Jazz (1981); CH Valma's Ditto Dorevlon (1984); DC Valmar's Valiant Knight, CD, NRD, VX, BROM (1985); and CH Valmar's Xtra Copy, BROM (1986). His Maturity winners are Valiant Knight (1986) and CH Valmar's Victoria, CDX (1986).

Jazz is the sire of versatile and field-rated Weimaraners, including FC Kristof Critic's Choice, NSD, and DC Valmar's Valiant Knight. He sired five BROM producers: CH The Farm's Country Air; CH Valmar's Serenade v. Wustenwind; DC Valmar's Valiant Knight, CD, NRD, VX; CH Valmar's Xtra Copy; and CH Valmar's Truly Yours.

Am/Can CH Valmar's Unanimous Decision, NSD

Dakota finished his championship with five majors, completely novice owner-handled. From May 1998 to August 2000, Dakota earned more than 100 breed wins and more than 35 group placements. He is a Futurity and Maturity winner and finished 1999 as No. 4 Weimaraner. He retired mid-2000 but maintained his Top 10 ranking that year.

True to the standard as a medium-sized dog with elegance and style, Dakota has stamped this into his get. As of this writing, he has 32 American champions, many Canadian champions, and several others nearly finished in both countries.

Dakota has made an impact as a stud dog, as evidenced by his daughter Am/Can CH Anson's Millennium Magic winning Best of Breed at the 2001 Weimaraner Association of Canada (WAC) National Specialty and his son, Am/Can CH Bartland's Gustav V Valmar going Best of Opposite. In 2003, a littermate to the 2001 WAC winner, Am/Can CH Anson's Mr. Millennium, went Best of Breed. To date, Dakota's top-winning daughter is Am/Can Islevue's Dare to Love Lucy, who was the 2004 No. 4 Weimaraner.

Figure 34-62: *DC Valmar's Valiant Knight, CD, NRD, VX* (CH Valmar's Jazzman, CD, NSD, NRD, V, BROM, HOF × CH Valmar's Pollyanna, BROM, HOF). Bred by Joan H. Valdez; owned by Gorden Hansen and Joan H. Valdez. Sire of 26 champions.

Dakota has become the inspiration for Unity Weimaraners. He is in the pedigree of all their dogs, and they look forward to seeing his children and grandchildren contribute to the breed in generations to follow.

DC Valmar's Valiant Knight, CD, NRD, VX

Val has the rare distinction of being a Dual Champion that was ranked Nationally on both the Top 10 show and field lists. He was the No. 4 Show Dog in the U.S. (All-Breed points) in 1986 and No. 7 All-Age Gun Dog in 1988. His show record includes 37 Best of Breeds, 11 group placements, Best Dog in the 1985 Western Futurity, and Best Dog in the 1986 Maturity. After accomplishing this, Val was given the opportunity to prove himself in the field with his co-owner, Gorden Hansen. Val again was very competitive, winning 22 field placements (6 1sts) in just 2 years of competition and finishing with two major wins! As a producer, Val is the sire of 26 show champions.

CH Valmar's Xtra Copy

Copy was a handsome, well-muscled, and very sound individual. He was campaigned as a Special in 1987 and was ranked nationally as No. 6 Show Dog (breed points) and No. 9 Show Dog (group points). He compiled 46 Best of Breed wins and multiple group placements during that year. Copy is a full brother to CH Valmar's Yours Truly, BROM, the No. 1 Top Show dog for 1988. As a producer, Copy is the sire of 47 champions, which includes top producers CH Valmar's Starling, BROM; CH Valmar's Silver Dove, BROM; CH Nani's Baht a Pack a Trouble, CD, JH, V, BROM; CH Casa Perry's Prime Diamond, BROM; CH Valmar's Rolls Royce, BROM; CH Green Acres Fancy Copy, BROM; and CH Innomine Sassy Cali Copy, BROM.

CH Von Sieben's Royal Flush, CD, NSD, V

In mid-1976, 18-month-old Royal finished his championship with a five-point major, capably handled by 16-year-old Cindy Victory. Royal and Cindy, with only limited showing, ranked 3rd on the 1977 Weimaraner Top 10. From 27 Breed wins (2 Best in Specialties), Royal went on to 14 group placements (three 1sts, six 2nds, three 3rds, and two 4ths). After retirement, Cindy added a CD and NSD to their achievements.

Royal's champion offspring include multiple group winners, and the many obedience titles and field ratings of his get established him as the sire of versatile Weimaraners. Royal sired five Futurity winners: CH Kristof's Royal Hanja (1979); CH Kristof's Royal Crusader, BROM (1979); CH Skytop's for Heaven Sake, NSD, BROM (1981); CH Von Luchbach's Royal Heir, NRD, NSD, V, BROM (1983); and CH Von Luchbach's I've Got It All (1983).

Royal sired six BROM producers: CH Kristof's Canadian Caper; CH Kristof's Royal Crusader; CH Skytop's Ace in the Hole v. Tri-D, NSD, NRD; CH Skytop's For Heaven Sake, NSD; CH Skytop's Misty Blue, CD, TD, NRD, NSD, VX; and CH Von Luchbach's Royal Heir, NRD, NSD, V.

Figure 34-63: *CH Valmar's Xtra Copy* (CH Valmar's Jazzman, CD, NSD, NRD, V, BROM, HOF × CH Valmar's Serendipity, BROM). Bred by Joan H. Valdez and Lynne L. Nelson; owned by Joan H. Valdez. Sire of 47 champions.

Figure 34-64: *CH Von Sieben's Royal Flush, CD, NSD, V* (CH Eric Von Sieben BROM × CH Reichenstadt's Royal Flush, BROM). Bred by Lorraine Burkholder; owned by Cindy Victory. Sire of 30 champions.

CH Von Sieben's Smart n Special, NSD

Amateur handled by Lynne Burns throughout his career, Sieben ranked in the breed's Top 10 in 1977, 1978, and 1979 (ranking 8th, 7th, and 10th). Because these statistics do not include the years Sieben was not extensively campaigned, the

incomplete record of those years shows 57 breed wins (5 Best in Specialties) and 15 group placements (three 1sts, five 2nds, two 3rds, and three 4ths)—the unofficial total is over 100 breed wins. The great-moving dog won Best of Opposite Sex at the 1976 National Specialty.

Sieben's Futurity winners are CH Clear Day's Special Feature, SD (1979), and CH Silberholm Herr Weltmeister (1981). Sieben is the breed's third sire of two Dual Champions—litter sister's Jafwin's One and Only, NRD, SD, VX (winner of the 1982 National All-Age Championship), and Jafwin's The Goodbye Girl, NRD, SDX. He sired the BROM producer Silberholm Rickey v. Reiteralm.

Figure 34-65: *CH Von Sieben's Smart 'N' Special, NSD* (CH Eric Von Sieben BROM × CH Reichenstadt's Royal Flush, BROM). Bred by Lorraine Burkholder; owned by Robert and Lynne Burns. Sire of 28 champions.

CH Warhorse Billy of Redhill, CD

One of the most influential sires of his generation, Billy upheld the image of Weimaraners as a dual breed and Redhill as a dual bloodline. A group winner himself, Billy sired the group and Canadian Best in Show winner CH Kams Rauchessen of Redhill, BROM, as well as other group winners. Billy's field talent (a winner of all-age stakes) appeared in his progeny, and they include many all-age winners and Top 10 field Weimaraners. Described as an unusually intelligent dog, Billy was a high-scoring obedience winner, a trait passed on to CH Redhill's Gretchen, UD, who made a perfect score of 200 and brought home many trophies for High in Trial.

Billy's Futurity winners are Margreta of Glenrose, CD (1965); CH Kams Rauchessen of Redhill, BROM (1966);

Figure 34-66: *CH Warhorse Billy of Redhill, CD* (CH Wolfsburg Lobo × Perry's Silver Czarina). Bred by Daryl S. and Brent Keener; owned by T. W. and Loretta Jarmie. Sire of 20 champions.

Figure 34-67: *BIS CH Windwalker's Graeagle, CD, JH, NRD, V* (CH Nani's 'N Tophat's Backlash, CD, NSD, V, BROM × CH Windwalker's Gemborie, BROM). Bred and owned by Arlene and Phil Marshrey. Sire of 87 champions.

and CH Oliver's Valkyrie of Redhill (1966). He sired three BROM producers: Rauchessen; CH Kams Rauchigalan of Redhill, CD; and CH Machig Dammerung of Redhill, CD.

The prepotency of Billy's sons and daughters ensured his place as the founder of one of the breed's most important dynasties.

BIS CH Windwalker's Graeagle, CD, JH, NRD, V

A truly versatile Weimaraner who loved people, Grady excelled in whatever he did. He was a true showman who loved the excitement of the show ring and was a pleasure to watch with his ring presence and strong movement. Winner of three Best in Shows and nine Specialties, along with many Sporting Group wins and placements, he was rated No. 1 Show Weimaraner and No. 9 Sporting Dog in 1997, winning the Pedigree Award. He was on the Top 10 show list from 1996 through 1999, and his show record in 1997 made him the top-winning male show dog in the history of the breed.

Grady was Top-Producing Weimaraner in 2000 and 2002. His sons and daughters have proven that they carry on his qualities and versatility by winning many Best of Breeds, Futurities, Maturities, Sweepstakes, and Sporting Groups, as well as qualifying for titles in field, agility, obedience, and tracking.

A handsome dog, solid gray, strong and athletic, sound in mind and body, intelligent, inquisitive with an excellent nose and good hunting instincts, Grady was everyone's friend and loved nothing better than a good 'howl.' He was a wonderful and loyal companion.

Figure 34-69: *CH Zara's on Zee Rampage, CGC* (CH Zara's Silver Stash, NSD, NRD, V × CH Zara's Boozey Floozey, NSD). Bred and owned by Carole Richards and Jack McCourt. Sire of 20 champions.

CH Wismar's Jack Daniels

CH Wismar's Jack Daniels, BROM, was a medium-sized solid gray dog who inherited his mom's flowing movement and showy personality. He finished his championship at 13 months with three majors. He started his specials career at 19 months. Jack was on the Top 10 Show list for 4 years in a row and was a group winner and a Best in Specialty winner. Jack was not just a show champion but was a great mentor and teacher, too; he was handled throughout his show career by his junior handler Susan Wise (the daughter of his breeders John and Barbara Wise) as he taught her the ropes of showmanship.

He spent his senior years ruling the Wise household from whatever high perch was available. Jack was the sire of 26 champions, including a Futurity winner.

CH Zara's on Zee Rampage, CGC

Page was a big-boned fellow we affectionately called Arnold Schwartzenpuppy.

He was a funny, outgoing guy with his own view of the world. He loved going to shows but did not like showing, although he finished his championship with two specialty majors. He always demonstrated his lifelong distain for the show ring by sitting ringside with his back facing the ring. He much preferred to interact with the people; it was better

Figure 34-68: *CH Wismar's Jack Daniels* (CH Wismar's Dry Martini × CH Wismar's Funny Valentine, TD, BROM). Bred and owned by Barbara Wise. Sire of 26 champions.

than watching the dogs. Extremely gregarious, he very seriously took on the role of convincing any nearby human that Weimaraners are the most wonderful dogs in the world.

Page was only bred to five different bitches, producing 20 champions. Within that select group of 20 are dogs whose versatility is shown by accomplishments that include a Best in Futurity, Master Hunter, and numerous agility, tracking, and obedience titles, and WCA ratings. Page was blessed with a wonderful temperament and consistently passed it on to his progeny.

Figure 34-70: *Chairman of the Board.* Photograph by Harry Giglio.

Dr. Werner Petri, Breeding and Testing Regulator 1976–1989. Weimaraner Klub e. V. President 1989–1999.

Figure 35-1: In this historic centenary photo, Dr. Petri officially opens the *breed show* (Zuchtschau), conducted on the grounds of the *castle* (Schloss Belvedere) in Weimar, Germany, 1997. The international fall weekend events, held in and around Weimar, celebrated 100 years of the Weimaraner in Germany.

On October 8, 2005, the Weimaraner world lost one of its most significant breed contributors. Dr. Werner Petri, President Emeritus of the Weimaraner Klub e.V., was struck and killed by a street trolley in his home town of Karlsruhe, Germany. He was only 69 years of age. He will always be revered as one of the finest experts on the Weimaraner breed. Dr. Petri was a man unfailingly prepared to share his vast and unique knowledge to assist other breed fanciers. He was not only an exceptional ambassador, holding vast experience with the breed in general and of the bloodlines as well.

While always a welcome judge in countries outside the Weimaraner's home, he was also a welcoming host to fanciers visiting Germany wishing to learn more about his treasured breed. One may also say that besides Major a.D. Herber, who saved the Weimaraner breed over the difficult times of the 1930s and 1940s, Dr. Werner Petri molded the Weimaraner to become the universal dog it represents today, finding the balance between the traditional characteristics necessary for a fine, healthy, hunting dog and the demands of the modern German household companion. He published many excellent articles in dog and hunting magazines. Two of his most significant works include a booklet titled *Der Weimaraner Vorstehhund* (the Weimaraner pointing dog) and the only book on the breed written in German, titled *Weimaraner Heute* (the Weimaraner Today). Dr. Petri's legacy to the Weimaraner, as a breeder for over 50 years and as an officer of the Weimaraner Klub e.V for over 23 years, will continue as long as there are Weimaraners hunting the fields for their owners. *Let us always preserve the last few drops of lead dog* (Leithund) *blood.* Photograph courtesy of Mimmi Erixon, Sweden. Reprinted from Deborah Andrews, *The Weimaraner Memory Book,* 2003.

CHAPTER 35

THE GERMAN WEIMARANER TODAY

by Deborah Andrews and Brigitta Guggolz

The AKC's classification of the Weimaraner as a pointer deprives the breed of opportunities to use the full spectrum of the hunting talents for which the breed was developed and continues to be strictly reinforced by selective breeding to fulfill the requirements of German hunters. Americans find it difficult to understand the Weimaraner's characteristic hunting style—the painstakingly methodical search, the tendency to track game, the joyous pursuit of rabbits and predatory animals—all traits that must be modified by training (often with difficulty) for the Weimaraner to compete successfully in field trials for pointing breeds.

Manfred Hölzel, author of *The German Pointing Dogs (Die deutschen Vorstehhunde),* describes some of the qualities a hunting dog must have to meet the needs of German hunters: "This dog cannot have the traits and characteristics of a wimp…. Its job is to retrieve ducks from icy swamps, to chase injured hares in the dead of winter in unfamiliar territory and retrieve them even through thick thorny underbrush. Its job is to chase a male buck of any size, grab it by the throat and pull it down, or if circumstances require, to defend its master."[1]

The German hunter lives by a code of ethics, strict conservation standards, and the maxim *A well-trained hunting dog is essential to the hunt.* During the hunt, the gun dog is an indispensable partner of the German hunter. It is illegal to hunt without a finished gun dog that can track wounded game of any species to enable the hunter to end its suffering as soon as possible.

This chapter clarifies the full spectrum of the Weimaraner's hunting talents, the conditions under which the breed developed, and the performance expected of the German Weimaraner today.

Hunting History, Laws, and Traditions

No other German activity is more steeped in centuries of tradition than the hunt. It has its own language, costumes, gastronomy, folklore, poetry, songs, music, instruments, and celebrated artists.

European developments immediately before A.D. 800 are considered the most significant influence on German hunting customs of today. During this period, the feudal sov-

Figure 35-2: *Best In Show Silver Punch Bowl, Australian Weimaraner Club 3rd Nationals in November 2005.* Presented in Memory of Dr. Werner Petri, President Emeritus of the Weimaraner Klub e. V. from his friends and admirers throughout the world. The puppy gracing the memorial trophy is the grandson of the Weimaraner awarded Best in Show by Dr. Petri at the first Australian National in 1995. Photograph courtesy of Judy Glover, Australia.

ereigns claimed the right to hunt as the sole prerogative of royalty. Hunting became a major court recreation, with elegant court protocol and ceremony.

By 1500, hunting was generally regarded as a sport for royal gentlemen. Customs added about this time included folklore, hunting songs, and poetry. Drive hunts, with game being driven into confined areas for shooting, became popular during the next three centuries. Elaborate hunting castles were erected in areas where game was plentiful. Today, many of these castles are preserved along with their trophies and artifacts.

Land, social, and religious reforms were widespread following the French Revolution (1789). The Napoleonic Wars

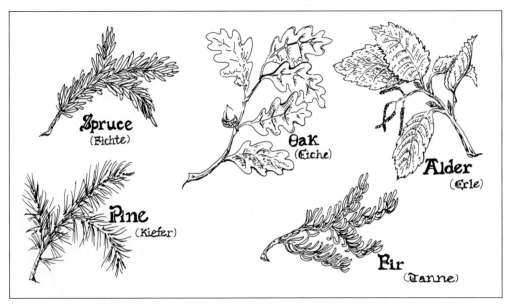

Figure 35-3: Native German trees that are proper for *branch signs* (Bruchzeichen).

ended feudal hunting rights, and title to much of the land passed to the common people. The revolts of 1848 brought further changes in hunting laws, which in turn resulted in the need for a new type of hunting dog.

Nineteenth century German hunters demanded that their dogs be capable of performing many functions. They were required to work equally well as pointers and retrievers in small-game hunting and also for tracking wounded big game. They had to be clever, displaying calmness in the presence of game, willingness to track and locate game, *give tongue* (Laut geben), point, retrieve, and work passionately in the water. Selective breeding adapted the ancient silver grey hound of Weimar to meet these new demands. The result of these practices became known as the *Weimaraner Pointer* (Weimaraner Vorstehhund). New combinations created other German versatile hunting breeds: German Shorthaired, Wirehaired, and Longhaired Pointers; Small and Large Münsterländer Pointers; Wirehaired Pointing Griffons; and Pudelpointers.

Extensive, almost uncontrolled, hunting by the new landowners nearly exterminated the big-game animals. In the early 20th century, European countries passed laws to improve game management. The innovations included game conservation, limited hunting seasons, and selective hunting to cull poor breeding stock.

Today, Germany is divided into local hunting districts. The right to hunt exclusively belongs to the owner of the land, who may pass it on. The lessor may be an individual, a community, a corporate body, or the state or federal government. Hunting seasons in Germany vary with each species of game. Regulations specify the type of weapon and ammunition and the method of hunting each type of animal. Poaching is a serious offence. The sound of a gunshot is likely to start the game warden's telephone jingling, as people call in from all over to report hunting. Merely walking in the woods with a gun or

letting a dog roam freely is reason for a fine.

Specific managerial responsibilities accompany the privileges of a lease. The lessee, e.g., the owner of the hunting rights, is responsible for predator control, which may include feral dogs and cats as well as varmints. The task of tracking and often killing these predators falls to the hunting dog. The lessee is required to provide a certified hunting dog to track the various types of wounded game, e.g., a blood tracking dog for cloven-hooved game, a dog certified for water work in the case of duck hunting. Financial liability for damage to surrounding crops by the game is an additional motivation for strict management.

The lessee insures that compliance with game laws is adhered to. Interestingly, taking too little game is as detrimental as taking too much, for overpopulation leads to damage of the forage and forces the game onto the farmlands. Hunting rights holders are bound by law to manage and conserve game. The law ensures an equitable balance is maintained between available feed and cover and crop damage is minimized. The basic instrument for management is called the *Annual Game Harvest Shooting Plan* (Abschussplan).

Figure 35-4: Deborah Andrews and Astor vom Kohlwald sport their sprigs of oak leaves earned during the blood-tracking portion of the Brauchbarkeitsprüfung.

German Names of Some Game Animals and Birds by Rank

Hochwild

Rotwild	Red deer *(Cervus elaphus):* the common deer of Europe and Asia; similar to but smaller than the wapiti or North American elk *(Cervus canadensis).*
Damwild	Fallow deer *(Dama dama):* a small European deer with palmated antlers; the near-black dorsal stripe is bordered by white spots, and the background color ranges from near black to yellow-brown.
Muffelwild	Mouflon *(Ovis ammon musimon):* a rare wild sheep introduced from Sardinia and Corsica.
Gamswild	Chamois *(Rupicapra rupicapra):* goat-like antelope of the Alps, Black Forest, and Vosges.
Schwarzwild	Wild boar *(Sus scrofa):* European wild pig; also called Sauen.
Elchwild	Moose *(Alces alces):* large deer of Europe and Asia resembling but smaller than the North American Moose *(Alces americana);* should not be confused with the wapiti or North American elk.
Auerwild	Capercaillie/Capercalizie *(Tetrao urogallus):* Old World grouse species found in hilly or mountainous, densely forested areas; one of the highest-ranking trophies and a capital game bird. Rare and endangered.
Adler	The golden eagle *(Steinadler/Aquila chrysaëtos)* of the Alps, and the white-tailed eagle *(Seaadler/Haliaeëtus albicilla)* of the coastal areas, and the ospray eagle *(Fischadler/Pandion haliaëtus):* are all protected endangered species.

Niederwild

Rehwild	Roe deer *(Capreolus capreolus):* a small deer of Europe and Asia with erect cylindrical, fork-shaped antlers. The species is noted for its nimbleness and grace; field roe prefer meadowlands, whereas the more plentiful forest roe prefer small woodlands.
Fuchs	Red fox *(Vulpes vulpes):* also classified as a predator.
Hase	European hare *(Lepus europaeus):* the most plentiful German game animal, hares in forests and fields; the young are born above ground, have fur, and can see at birth.
Kaninchen	Old World rabbit *(Oryctolagus cuniculus):* differs from hare in colony burrowing habit; born underground, young are blind and naked at birth; also called Karnickel.
Fasan	Pheasant *(Phasianus colchicus):* any bird of the family Phasianidae (order *Galliformes*) that is larger than a quail or partridge. Most pheasants—some 50 species in about 16 genera of the subfamily Phasianinae—are long-tailed birds of open woodlands and fields, where they feed in small flocks.
Wildenten	Wild ducks *(Anatinae):* in the Northern Hemisphere, common name for the mallard.
Rebhuhn	Partridge *(Perdrix perdrix):* medium-sized, stout-bodied European game bird; also called Feldhuhn.
Schnepfe	European woodcock *(Scolopax rusticola)* .
Bekassine	Wilson's snipe *(Gallinago gallinago):* small, slender bird with long, straight bill; resembles woodcock but distinguished by head markings, smaller body, and zigzag flight pattern.

This is only a partial listing of furred and feathered small game. The German Federal Hunting Law lists Elchwild and Bison as big game, even though the two species are no longer found in Germany.

Figure 35-5: Well-trained Weimaraners are always welcome in public eating areas and hotels. Photograph courtesy of Roman and Judith Braun, Germany.

Figure 35-6: *Special Reserved Table* (Stammtisch). Fenja zum Laubwald and Conny vom Hüseder Forsthaus demonstrate that the Weimaraner's love of dressing up and posing is not a U.S. exclusive. Photograph courtesy of Peter Hoppe, Germany.

When I joined the German Weimaraner Club in 1984, I learned that hunting customs are as important to the German hunters as the actual search for game. These customs have been handed down from father to son. One of the customs I am fond of is *Hunter's Luck* (Waidmannsheil) and *Hunter's Thanks* (Waidmannsdank). *Waidmannsheil* is a greeting exchanged when two hunters meet or separate, when a hunter joins a group at a drive or social hunt, and on similar occasions. The hunter replies with *Waidmannsheil* when speaking to a group or accepting congratulations for a successful shot. This term is also used in closing letters addressed to hunter friends, instead of *Sincerely Yours* or a similar expression. *Waidmannsdank* is an appropriate reply in a situation in which one would say thanks.

Branches, which are always broken from the tree, are used in many interesting as well as practical ways in the hunt. The *Ownership Branch* (Inbesitznahmebruch), a twig broken from a native German tree, is placed on each animal with the broken end pointing toward the head of males, the tip pointing toward the head of females. The *Last Bite* (Letzter Bissen), a small sprig from a native German tree, is placed crosswise in the mouth of all male cloven-hooved game or in the beak of the big species of the *grouse family* (Auerhahn) as a token of respect. The *Hunter's Branch* (Schuetzenbruch) is a similar sprig that has been dipped in the blood of the game after the kill. The branch is then placed on the blade of a hunting knife or on a hunting hat and presented to the successful hunter. The host of the hunt hails the successful hunter, saying *Waidmannsheil*, to which the recipient replies *Waidmannsdank*, and places the branch at the right side of his or her hat. When the game has been tracked down by a dog, the dog's handler presents the branch to the hunter. The hunter returns a piece of the branch to the dog handler, who in turn breaks off another piece and puts it in the dog's collar.

For example, I met this custom in a *Regional Utility Test* (Brauchbarkeitsprüfung or Brb). Everyone participating selects a number from a hat, signifying which blood track their dog will work. I had selected *track 1* (Fährte 1). This was a lucky track for us. It had rained hard the entire night before, and it was impossible to see any traces of blood on the leaves, bushes, or grass as we proceeded, so I had to trust Astor's nose. When the dog completes the track successfully, which we did, the judges gather around the handler and dog to offer *congratulations* (Waidmannsheil) and a sprig of an appropriate tree.

The *language of the hunt* (Waidmannssprache or Jägersprache) has a special term for almost everything associated with hunting. An animal's eyes are *lights* (they shine in the dark woods); its nose is a *wind catcher;* the white rump patch on a deer is a *mirror;* and a rabbit's tail is a *flower.* The usual fine for inappropriate use of the term *Waidmannssprache* is to purchase a round of drinks after the hunt. Many terms, such as those that designate large and small game, reflect the feudal origins of the hunting language. *Large animals* (Hochwild) refers to the game that could be hunted only by aristocracy; *small animals* (Niederwild) refers to game that could be hunted by others only when granted a license by the king. Within each group, the game has a hierarchical rank.

Game is often harvested with various types of *social drive hunts* (Gesellschaftsjagden), by invitation only, which are incomplete without buglers, who add spirit to the occasion as they signal instructions to the hunters and beaters with traditional hunting calls. The lessee (owner of the hunting rights) invites from 25 to 40 experienced hunters and hires an equal number of beaters. In the *circular drive hunt* (Kesseltreiben), which is primarily used for hare, the hunters form a circle about a half-mile in diameter, and at the sound of the horn, they begin to walk toward the center. The beaters precede the hunters, driving the game from the brush. When they come together in the center,

---

Additonal Breeding Requirements

- Dams and sires must be at least 18 months old.
- After the age of 8 years, dams may no longer be bred.
- The dam's first litter must have taken place before the age of 6 at the latest.
- Dams may only produce one litter per year.
- When puppies must be taken by Caesarean on two occasions, the dam is excluded from further breeding.
- A sire may be used for breeding a total of 5 times within 2 breeding periods.
- Parents, grandparents, or their respective brothers and sisters may only appear twice within the great-grandparents of the dogs proposed for breeding.
- The assessment of additional abilities and performances, such as *Rigorous Toward Predators* (Härtenachweis/HN), *Lost Game Retrieval on a Natural Blood Track* (Bringtreue/Btr), *Retrieving*

Reliability Examination (Verlorenbringer/Vbr), *Sound* (Laut), *Master's Performance Examination* (VGP), and *Blood Tracks* (Schweiss), are highly desired and provide valuable indications regarding the existence of positive hunting aptitudes.

- When dealing with dogs from foreign countries, there are two new Test Regulations (ZO):

  4.10 (p. 238): Prior to the use for breeding of Weimaraners registered in a foreign stud book, a thorough examination must be conducted, especially regarding the dog's origin and freedom from hereditary defects. Permission for breeding is granted by the breed regulator with mutual consent from the Board.

  8.3 (p. 240): JGHV-relevant test results of Weimaraners bred abroad can be entered into the club's stud book. This can only be accomplished under the conditions that their foreign pedigree is recognized by the JGHV, and the dogs are entered with the stud book number of their country of origin into the club's stud book.

Figure 35-7: *Line presentation of small game.* Every 10th piece of game is pulled out of the lines for counting purposes. Some of these hunters are blowing the traditional FürstPless horns; one is using the Parforce horn as they signal a successful hunt on the island of Baltrum/Ostfriesland, Germany. Photograph courtesy of Dr. Hans Schmidt, Germany.

Requirements for Breed Control and Litter Recording

1. Before a breeder and a chosen kennel name are accepted, the kennel facilities are inspected by the president of the individual Weimaraner club state group.

2. At least 6 weeks before the planned mating, the breeder has to apply for permission. If the mating complies to the required qualifications, the breed regulator gives his consent in writing.

3. Directly before the mating, the owners of the dogs envisaged for breeding have to check that all conditions for the planned breeding are fulfilled, e.g., control of tattoos/chips and breed permission papers.

4. The owners of the sire and dam confirm the mating on a special form (Deckschein).

5. The breed regulator has to be informed in writing of the mating within 10 days.

6. In case the bitch does not conceive, the breed regulator and the owner of the sire have to be informed accordingly.

7. Every breeder has to report the entire litter to the breed regulator within 10 days. This report has to include stillborn or perished puppies and mention the reason of their death.

8. The litter should, if possible, be at least 7 weeks old when it is inspected and tattooed or chipped, which must be done in the breeder's kennel with the bitch present.

9. During a visit by the inspector, the general condition of the puppies, their eyes, teeth, testicles, etc., are checked. The puppies must be vaccinated for distemper, hepatitis, leptospirosis, and parvovirus. Evidence of immunization must be shown, upon request, to the inspector.

10. Litters may be tattooed and inspected by members of the Weimaraner club board (including those board members of the various state groups) as well as breed regulators of clubs that are members of the JGHV.

11. A written report must be made out for each litter on the litter control form (Formblatt Wurfabnahme) and sent to the breed regulator.

12. The puppies may not leave the kennel before they are 8 full weeks old. The breeder has to send a list of the new puppy owners to the breed regulator (Wurfabgabe).

they will have caught most of the game. Several circles are formed during a day of hunting. At the conclusion of a social drive hunt, it is customary to exhibit game at a pre-designated spot in the hunting area. Game is displayed in rows, lying on its right side, according to the established rank. An appropriate hunting horn call is played for each category of game.

During the hunt, vigor is restored with hot soup and *clear liquor* (Schnaps). The hunt is concluded with a festive meal, usually served at a tavern on the forest's edge. The menu consists of dishes such as venison, schnitzel, red cabbage, and dumplings, washed down with a wonderful variety of beer and wine.

Owing to the diversity of wildlife, small- and large-game animals, as well as birds, may be encountered and shot in a single hunt. The meat belongs to the hunting rights holder,

although the hunter who shot the animal usually has first claim to buy it. The rest brings a good price at game stores and speciality restaurants featuring wild game on the menu. Nevertheless, such profit merely offsets a small portion of the expense of rental and hired beaters, plus food and drink for all hunters and beaters.

The German Weimaraner Club (Weimaraner Klub e. V.)

In Germany as in the United States, each breed has a parent breed club that is affiliated with a coordinating organization, but that is where the similarity ends. The German Weimaraner Club is affiliated with the following organizations:

Figure 35-8: *Importance of early exposure to shallow water* and feathered game.

(a) Puppies introduced to shallow water. Photograph courtesy of Gerhard Eiben, Germany.

(b) Tanja swims ahead of Banja and Carlo, thus enticing them to follow. Photograph courtesy of Brigitta Guggolz, Germany.

Figure 35-9: *Importance of early exposure to furred game.*

(a) Puppies introduced to a fresh hide. Photograph courtesy of Heinz Gräber, Germany.

(b) Puppy exposed to a dead fox. Photograph courtesy of Peter Koch, Germany.

Figure 35-10: *Figure 35-10: Golo vom Zehnthof displays style and intensity* on point. Photograph courtesy of Hans Halaber, Netherlands.

Figure 35-11: *Panu zum Laubwald named Piezl,* owned and handled by Steven Graham, North Plains, Oregon, went over to Germany to participate in the German evaluations.

- *The German Versatile Hunting Dog Association* (JGHV) coordinates interests and activities of the hunting breeds.
- *The German Dog Breed Association* (VDH) coordinates purebred dog clubs in Germany.
- *The Fédération Cynologique Internationale* (FCI) maintains jurisdiction in most European countries, and establishes uniform breed standards.[2]

The FCI is the world organization of cynology. It is currently made up of 82 member or partner countries (only one association per country—Germany is represented by the VDH). These organizations establish their own pedigrees and instruct judges. The FCI guarantees, within its organization, the mutual recognition of the pedigrees of the individual countries, as well as of the judges. The main task of the FCI is to describe the breed standards and to internationally fix breed regulations. It publishes breed descriptions in the official languages of the FCI, primarily English, German, French, and Spanish. (The USA, England, and Canada are not members of the FCI. However, agreements between the Kennel Clubs of these countries and the FCI exist.)

The German Weimaraner Club was founded in 1897. During the division of Germany, after World War II, the Weimaraner Club of West Germany was re-established on October 13, 1951, in Nienburg/Weser with its own stud book. Meanwhile, the Weimaraner population of East Germany was recorded in the German Shorthair Breed Book of the German Democratic Republic, just as during the Regime of the National Socialists in the 1930/1940s, when the entire Weimaraner population of Germany had to also be registered in the German Shorthair Breed Book. Major Herber remained continuously opposed to this situation.

After the reunification of Germany in 1990, the club expanded the number of state groups in 1991 to include two in former East Germany. The club has its headquarters at Fulda, where general membership meetings are held every 2 years. The membership is small, with strong bonds of friendship among the members, who refer to themselves as *the family.* Local Weimaraner activities are coordinated by 9 state groups that have a function similar to American local clubs.[3] Each state group has an elected chairman, who is a member of the extended executive committee of the national club. The state groups sponsor hunting tests in the spring and fall as well as other events.

The German Weimaraner Club's motto—*It is not the breed, but the breeder's selection that guarantees highest quality of conformation and best performance* (Nicht die Rasse, sondern die Zuchtauswahl aus ihr ist die Bürgschaft für höchste Form und beste Leistung)—clarifies the objectives and importance of the breeding regulations. The purpose of the performance tests is to identify Weimaraners that will perpetuate desirable qualities. Approval for breeding is granted when both parents meet the breed standard. The dog must possess certifiable hip results, achieve an acceptable performance during the fall breeding tests, and display good character and temperament traits.

Although American literature uses the term breed warden, Germans prefer the less pejorative term *breed regulator* (Zucht-und Prüfungswart), the official who is entrusted with responsibility for maintaining the breed's quality. The holder of this significant office, who must be a trusted and respected breed authority, is elected for 4 years at the general meeting held every 2 years at Fulda.

The breed regulator is responsible for the breeding. The keeper of the *stud dog records* (Zuchtbuchführer) is responsible for the stud book, e.g., the individual records of each Weimaraner.

A list of dogs is maintained that have qualified for breeding, which is periodically published in the club's magazine. The breed regulator may consider eliminating a sire and dam that have produced faulty puppies from being used again. The regulator usually consults with other members of the executive board to reach this decision.

Owing to the growing number of litters, it has become impossible for the breed regulator to perform all of the tasks. Many of the responsibilities are delegated to and shared by the presidents of the nine state groups

To qualify for breeding, every German Weimaraner must meet the minimum requirements, although exceptions may be granted by the executive committee.

- **Conformation/Coat Quality.** The Weimaraner must have a minimum conformation rating of good, approved by one judge and awarded at a club breed show.

- **Genetic Quality.** The Weimaraner must be free of the following faults, which are considered hereditary: poor temperament (excessive anxiety, nervousness, fear-biting, and water and gun-shyness); deformities of any kind; entropion and ectropion; diseases such as epilepsy; cryptorchidism; hip dysplasia; incorrect color and markings (a brown tint, too much white on the chest, white paws); and defective dentition (faulty bites, missing teeth, extra teeth etc.).

- **Hip Rating.** Required rating of HD B2 or better.

- **Soundness of Character.** Proven by passing the club's respective test, and the JGHV-hunting ability tests.

- **Working Ability.** With few exceptions, which will be clarified later, the Weimaraner must have passed the *Breeding Examination* (Verbands-Herbst-Zuchtprüfung [HZP]). Actually the dog must pass not only the HZP, but produce a minimum result of 6 working points in the following subjects: Search in the Field, Blind Retrieve in Densely Vegetated Water, and Search Behind Living Duck in Densely

Vegetated Water (without the retrieving part). Alternately, it must pass a VGP obtaining at least 3 (good) working points in the following subjects: Search in the Field and two Water Disciplines (without the retrieving part).

When owners of eligible bitches wish to breed them, they must notify the regulator. The breeders identify the stud they wish to use on the application form; if the mating is not approved, the regulator may suggest an alternative stud.

Other regulations are given in the list of Requirements for Breed Control and Litter Recording. It is against club regulations to sell a Weimaraner without its registration papers or to sell one for a profit. Breeders make every effort to sell their puppies to hunters, preferably owners who will make a commitment to fulfill the requirements for breeding eligibility.

Training Young Dogs
by Roman Braun and Dieter Dröge

To discuss this topic, it is necessary to travel some decades into the past. Until the 1960s, it was a well-adopted practice that a hunting dog should not be worked with before it was grown up or at least until the dentition was complete. Formal training and dressage were initiated when the puppy was at least 9 months of age. Traditionally, many of these pups grew up in kennels with a very limited amount of personal contact and infrequent possibilities to run and discover their environment. These dogs were brought to the *Natural Ability Examination* (Verbands-Jugend-Prüfung [VJP]) basically without any formal training. It was even considered wrong to do that. The idea was to test for natural abilities.

The disciplines have not changed since, with the exception of the test for *Rigorous Toward Predators* (Raubwildschärfe). It is eliminated from the rule book as part of the test.

Figure 35-12: *Puppies learn to explore from the earliest age.* (a) Päivi Schmidt takes these 6-week-old puppies out on walks through the forest with their mother. The practice encourages the puppies to explore as a group. Later, when older, the puppy will feel more confident exploring on its own. Reprinted with permission from Deborah Andrews, *The Weimaraner Memory Book,* 2003. (b) The wise German owner occasionally engages in a game of hide and seek while walking the individual pup. At some point, the pup will wander far enough afield to suddenly feel lost and vulnerable; if the owner waits patiently and quietly, the pup will discover that he can use his nose to find the way back to his owner hiding in the tall grass—certainly a valuable skill. This should be done rarely so as not to discourage the pup's range or independence.

 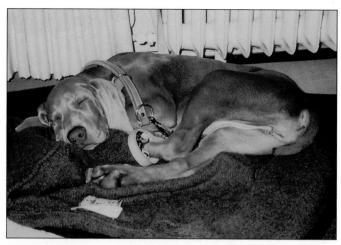

Figure 35-13: *Lessons learned from the mother.* (a) Britta's puppies learn their place lying on a comfortable mat with her. Photograph courtesy of Dr. Hans Schmidt, Germany. **(b)** Freya vom Uphuser Grashaus's early lessons have prepared her to stay in a special place in her new home. This is a common scene in the German home, to find the puppy tied to an upright radiator and lying on a comfortable cushion or hunting jacket. Photograph courtesy of owner Andre Buchsch, Germany.

Rigorous Toward Predators still exists, however, as a title the dog may receive in a true hunting situation by killing a fox or cat. The advantages of the system described are obvious: dogs that mentally survived the secluded life and despite all the difficulties of their childhood did well were without any doubt exceptional individuals.

Formal training was started after successful completion of the VJP. Training was based on absolute obedience and was often achieved using rough methods. Hunting dogs were considered working animals and were rarely seen as pets.

About 35 years ago, one of the first individuals to modify the system and propagate early puppy training in Germany, was the current *President Emeritus of the German Hunting Dog Association* (Jagdgebrauchshundverband [JGHV]), Heinrich Uhde. An important coincidence helped him to establish his puppy groups: an increasing number of town people with no space for a kennel started to hunt. Hunting dogs became more and more family companions and therefore a certain amount of obedience was essential from the beginning. It needs to be mentioned that early training inevitably masks some of the natural abilities. This holds true for both directions; *cooperation* (Führigkeit) and *obedience* (Gehorsam) are improved with increased "absolute obedience dressage," whereas sharpness on game is diminished and needs more time to develop. In my mind, the advantages far outweigh the disadvantages.

Early training starts as soon as the new owner receives the puppy from the breeder at 8 or 9 weeks of age. This is the time when the puppy learns to differentiate between good and bad. Needless to say, at this level "praise" dictates the language. Nevertheless, the puppy has to learn a few taboos right from the beginning. This starts with not "going to the bathroom" inside the house, chewing or climbing on furniture, etc. Everyone will find taboos that are important to them. Negative behavior must be corrected with a distinct "NO"!

During walks, it is important to discourage the puppy from eating all the nastiness that is found nowadays on the road. But, on the other hand, we do not discipline a young dog that brings presents even when they are gross! If the puppy grows up in a rural area, chasing of poultry, sheep, etc. must be corrected. This will help with future pointing training. Puppies need to go on long walks to be introduced to every imaginable situation. Contact with other dogs is as important as contact with strangers. The puppy is given reassurance when encountering a frightening situation, resulting in a positive outcome. These situations are key to modeling a youngster into a self-assured individual.

It is important to find safe space where the dog can run without a leash every day from the first moment we pick the puppy up. It is much more difficult to teach a puppy to follow us around once it is a half year old, has gained enough self-confidence, and thinks it does not need us any more. Most of us can easily catch an 8-week-old puppy running away; try this with a 4-month-old! At this age we have a major advantage on our side: almost all dogs feel insecure in a new environment. Playing hide and seek really helps to get the puppy's attention. While a young dog is discovering its environment, just keep on walking. At one point the puppy will realize it is alone, vulnerable, and without big daddy. This is the point when it becomes interesting! Often, puppies cry and start to run around without a concept. Just watch, don't call them. Allow the puppy to experience the situation and realize it has a nose to find you. Most young dogs first rely on their vision and get very nervous when they cannot see you. Taking advantage of this situation at a very early age is one of the best tools we have to make the dog focus on us. We are teaching the dog that whenever it might get lost in a hunting situation, it has the ability to find the way back to you. Believe it or not, there are superb hunting dogs of all different breeds

Figure 35-14: *Exposure to wild game.* The Weimaraner in Germany is expected to hunt fur as well as feathered game. Early acculturation imprints this natural instinct for the scent and texture of the fur of wild game. **(a)** The P-litter vom Vosstruben is introduced to a fresh wild boar. **(b)** A young, dead fox hanging from a rope stimulates the natural prey drive of the Weimaraner, further developing its instincts to benefit the hunter's needs.

with exceptional noses that when hunting too far away, have no clue how to find the way home. It is in your hands to develop this ability. It is a wonderful game and truly amazing how difficult it becomes to really hide. Every now and then, not seeing the young dog for some minutes can be scary, but that is the price we pay…

It is important for the young dog to learn to come when we call it. Coming back or finding us again is always a very positive situation, and the dog deserves to be treated very exuberantly with praise. The dog owner should also find a way to get the dog's attention; a certain noise, a distinct silent whistle, or the very popular clicker are all essential tools that work well. For me, noises I can make without a tool always work best. This leaves me not so dependent on the clicker, whistle, etc., which may have been forgotten at home.

I should mention that we always talk to our dogs quietly, and they understand gestures very well. A dog used to hearing quiet commands is more likely to obey when disobedient and hears our voices raised. It will know it is time to do what we ask of it.

Puppies need to be introduced to all kinds of dead animals, both fur and feather; hides and carcass of any game do a wonderful job. When they are young, dogs will sniff and even chew a little bit on hides, igniting their interest. Diversity is key; there are enough dogs that have trouble, for example, retrieving dove and other birds with loose feathers.

A dog confronted with dead animals as a puppy is less likely to have trouble when grown up. Breeders should already begin doing special exercises with the puppies to include the mother. Exposure to riding in a car, walks, shallow water, dead game, and gunfire are vital to sound development.

Another important aspect is contact with water. Many dogs feel uncomfortable going into water. We should take advantage of big puddles, small streams, and rivers, allowing the puppy to learn to cross, first with our help, and then alone.

When we want to expose the youngster to all these things, it is most likely we will need to travel by car. For dogs that have not traveled routinely early in life, this can be a stressful event. Riding in a vehicle should be practiced frequently. When used to travelling at an early age, dogs seldom experience problems with motion sickness. Upon returning home from our excursions, it is a good time to teach the puppy to stay alone for a while. In my opinion, a crate is a super tool for this purpose.

Due to the decreased population of *small game* (Niederwild) and the growing population of wild boar in Germany, blood tracking (Schweissarbeit) needs more emphasis in the training protocol than ever before. As soon as we find that our youngster uses its nose around the 10th–12th week, we start with some easy tracking work. We use about 100 cc of blood from a cloven-hooved animal to make a 100-yard track. The next morning, we will bring the puppy to the starting point on the long tracking lead. You would be surprised how interested most puppies are and how well they will work. At the end, they will find something they really like. We do this once a day for the first 3 or 4 days until the puppy knows the routine. After this initial phase, once a week is sufficient, otherwise, the dog might lose interest. A puppy started in this way has learned to follow a track slowly and learned the basics. This early exposure provides added benefits in other areas like the *hare track* (Hasenspur) or the *drag track* (Schleppen). Over time, we increase the distance and decrease the blood and/or start with the *tracking boot* (Färtenschuh).

Around the 12th week, the time has come for the first *obedience practice exercise* (Unterordnungsübung). We keep the sessions short yet very distinct and correct. These exercises include Sit and Down. We practice them several times a day with increasing length as the dog gets older. Also we should not forget to lead break the puppy. The dog has to walk next to us without pulling on the leash. If we cannot enforce this exercise with a simple collar, we should not be afraid to use a choke collar. The Down command is an immediate and deliberate action. There is never a fast enough response. It is a must: the dog immediately drops when we give him the Down command; otherwise, we need to enforce it by tossing the puppy on to the ground.

Walking with the dog on our left side, as we give the command, the dog is pushed immediately to the ground. At this stage, it is not important whether the dog gets to lay on its side or on its belly. Actually, most puppies will lay on their back to show total surrender. The puppy will learn the correct down position with daily practice.

A couple of points should be clarified as we discuss the Platz and Down commands. Before the 12th week, the puppy learns its *place* (Platz), a behavior which is reinforced at home in a relaxed environment. Many puppy owners use the "kennel" command when it is time for the dog to be in its place.

However, when teaching the Down, the puppy soon understands that this command is absolute. Often, the trill end of the whistle is introduced shortly after the puppy understands the Down.

When the puppy is a few months old (this will vary with the individual), we should introduce it to loud gun noise. Shooting a bird in front of the puppy is a wonderful experience, if the puppy makes the right connection. But, it is very unpredictable how it will react. A much safer way is to walk with the puppy to a rifle range, starting our walk from half a mile away until we get there. As soon as the puppy shows any sign of fear, we must play with it to reassure it that everything is ok. The next step is to ask a friend to shoot at some distance away and later right next to us. Often, dogs are more impressed by the clicking noise of the shell ejector than by the shot. The entire procedure of introducing loud gun noise may be supported by the breeder when shooting in the vicinity of the litter in the presence of their mother.

Many handlers make the fault of beginning the practice of calm behavior while the hunter is *staying by the stand* (Verhalten auf dem Stand) and *staying in place* (Ablegen), shortly before the VGP. I believe this should be accomplished during the first year. The advantage is obvious: the dog thinks of shooting in a pretty neutral way and is not hot when it hears a shot. The older dog, especially those that have already experienced duck hunts before being trained to stay down or at least to stay when a gun is fired, will take much more work.

As soon as all the *practice exercises* (Unterordnungsübungen) work sufficiently well, we can advance to the *forced retrieve* (Zwangsapport). I believe it is the only way to produce a 100% retriever. One important point the handler must understand is that the force does not imply pain or cruelty. A dog accepts any pressure as long as it understands what is being asked. We must stop whatever pressure we use immediately when the dog gives in. The better and quicker we are with this timing, the more successful we will be with dog training. I like to use my hand for the first lessons instead of a dummy. I give the command "Take it" (apport) and stick my flat hand into the dog's mouth. Usually, the dog will try to spit the hand out, but with gentle pressure, I will hold on to the dog's nose with my fingers. At the point when the dog stops fighting my hand for a second, I tell it to let go (aus) and pull my hand out of its mouth. I try to work on the forced retrieve several times per day for the first weeks but try to keep every session very short. I make sure to quit immediately when the dog does a good job. When it does something good, always praise the dog very intensively. We should never forget that we are dealing with a young dog that can handle pressure only to a very limited extent.

When the dog is used to the hand, I proceed with the next step. We use a light dummy with a soft and relatively thin mouthpiece or alternatively a stinky old sock that is filled with some soft material. After three days of training with the

Figure 35-15: *Tracking exercises for young dogs.* Photographs courtesy of Brigitta Guggolz, Germany.

(a) Tracking exercises on the long line.

(b) Puppy finds reward at the end of the track.

dummy, the average puppy should be able to hold the dummy for about 30 seconds and give out on command.

The next step involves learning to carry the dummy for some distance. When the dog does all these steps well, we will teach it to pick up the dummy from the ground. It is very important at this point for the dog to actively grab the dummy. It is not necessary to shove the dummy into its mouth any more. Some individuals refuse to take the dummy from the ground. Make the transition as smooth as possible. At first, you may need to place some bricks underneath the dummy to lift it off the ground.

Some dogs are very challenging and opposed to the dummy. For these situations, we need to find a weak point, e.g., pinching the ear, stepping on the toe, or using a choke collar. When the dog opens its mouth to say *ouch* (au), we stick the dummy into the mouth. All pressure stops immediately.

Things to remember...

- Right from the start, teach the puppy OK and NOT OK
- Teach the puppy to come to you and lead break it, both with treats and toys
- Let the puppy have contact with different types of dead game
- Introduce it to water
- Start early with the blood tracking on a special tracking lead
- Teach the Sitz (sit) by gently pushing the back end down with the hand
- Teach the Platz (down or place)
- Introduce the dog to gun and shot
- Teach forced retrieve gently

Figure 35-16: *The puppy learns to retrieve.*

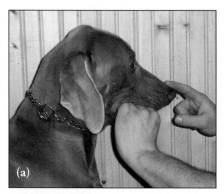
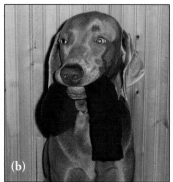

(a) Jett first learns to gently but firmly hold whatever is put in its mouth, in this case the trainer's hand. **(b)** Once the hold is mastered, the puppy begins to carry a retrieved object. A stinky sock is often easier than a dummy.

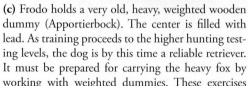

(c) Frodo holds a very old, heavy, weighted wooden dummy (Apportierbock). The center is filled with lead. As training proceeds to the higher hunting testing levels, the dog is by this time a reliable retriever. It must be prepared for carrying the heavy fox by working with weighted dummies. These exercises increase strength in the dog's head and neck muscles. Photograph courtesy of Gerhard Eiben, Wittmund, Germany. **(d)** The Oberländer Apportierbock is another version of the heavy wooden dummy. The weights may be changed on each end using different wooden or iron rings. Photograph courtesy of Deborah Andrews.

The handler needs to be exuberantly friendly and happy. The dog must understand, when it obeys our command, we praise and love him and when he refuses the command, it will hurt. A very small number of dogs are extremely difficult, e.g., terriers. The owner should ask a professional for advice before ruining the dog. Finally, I would like to mention that every dog will refuse at one point to retrieve on command. It is better to master this situation at home with a dummy where we can enforce the command, as opposed to a hunting or test situation. For dogs that have never failed or refused to retrieve, a set-up scenario must be created that forces them to fail. The set-up must be practiced in a controlled environment to be certain the dog is fully force-broken to retrieve. (Do not do this with a puppy!) If you have trouble with the force-retrieve, ask a professional for guidance!

To maintain control, always practice with the dog on a leash. Keep the sessions no longer than 10 minutes, but repeat them several times every day. Early puppy training is a critical endeavor. When done correctly, it can be a wonderful thing, but when inconsistent and harsh techniques are practiced, the consequences can ruin the dog for life.

This discussion does not claim to be complete; neither is it intended as training doctrine, but it demonstrates a real thread through a hunting dog's first year of life.

Figure 35-17: *Providing positive reinforcement in a frightening situation.* Photographs courtesy of Brigitta Guggolz, Germany.

(a) Puppy encounters frightening situation.

(b) Owner gives reassurance to puppy.

(c) Puppy accepts stranger.

Performance Examinations and Ratings

Standards and Regulations

A common American misconception is that the performance examinations—like the WCA rating tests—are exclusive to the German Weimaraner Club. In fact, the regulations and standards are established by the German Versatile Hunting Dog Association (JGHV) and sponsored by all the member clubs. Eligible dogs of all hunting breeds may only enter each kind of test twice in order to improve a qualifying score. There are exceptions, however, such as the Hegewald and International Tests. There are some variations of testing regulations in certain breed groups, but all hunting breeds require a qualifying score on specific performance examinations to become eligible for breeding.

There are usually three judges, one of which acts as senior judge. Each group is made up of four to five dogs taking the examination. No handler may enter more than two dogs in a trial. The judges make notes of the dog's performance during each test, giving a predicate (attribute) of excellent, very good, good, satisfactory, deficient, or insufficient. The predicate is used to establish a performance value. Only at the end of the test or after the performance is fully completed are

Figure 35-18: *Formblatt 1/Stand 2006/2.* Standard entry form.

Figure 35-19: *Water work series retrieving duck.*

(a) Dingo von der Schelmelach displays calm, confidence, and strength in a water retrieve of the duck. Dingo is owner handled by Michael Österle, Germany. Photograph by Brigitta Guggolz, Germany.

(b) Argon von Walhalla, a son of Dingo, proudly holds the duck gently but firmly, following a water search in order to present table-worthy game to his owner. Argon is owned by Deborah Andrews, USA. Photograph by Alexandra Barbero, Germany.

the exact values established on the basis of the predicate. For example, the predicate very good comprises the values 9, 10, and 11. During the test, the judges only speak of the predicate very good. After the work, the exact judgement number, e.g. 10, is decided. Later, after consultation with all judges in the group, the performance values are multiplied by the test's value factor, which weighs the importance and difficulty of the subject. The result of this computation is the judgement note. The judgment notes for each subject are added up for the total point score. Apprentice judges, having no vote, must attend two levels of each test before being accepted as a judge.

A *standard entry form* (Formblatt 1) is used for all tests. The top of the form lists six test groups: *Organization Youth, Fall Breeding, Usefulness Tests* (Verbands-Jugend, Herbstzucht, Gebrauchs); *Proof of Hunting After the Sho*t (Verbandsprüfung [VPS] nach dem Schuss); *Simulated Blood Tracking Test* (Verbandsschweissprüfung [VSwP]); and *Simulated Tracking Test Using the Tracking Boot* (Verbandsfährtenschuhprüfung [VFSP]), and the one being taken is marked. The examinations will be discussed in this order, followed by a section on supplementary tests and ratings.

Robert Shoeman estimated that of the Weimaraners whelped in Germany each year during 1978–1982, 60%–70% passed the spring tests and 50% the fall examinations. Due to more Weimaraners going to non-hunting owners, a development the club is trying by all means to stop, these percentages have deteriorated in the years up to 2000. Since then, one can state that the percentages have stabilized at around 52% for the spring and 35% for the fall examinations.

Natural Ability Examination

The Verbands-Jugend-Prüfung (VJP) is also known as the *Spring Youth Trial.* The examinations, which are held each spring, test natural hunting ability. Similar to the NAVHDA Natural Ability Test, the VJP assesses the development of inherent hunting abilities in the young dog. The development is brought about by exposure and guided experience, not by training.

Performance points are awarded in the following five tests or subjects: will to track, searching, pointing, use of nose, and cooperation. Great emphasis is placed on the VJP search. The young Weimaraner with the highest score in the test is awarded a *special search-champion* (Suchensieger) recognition for the trial. A favorable overall score is 70 points; however, if a dog gives an outstanding performance, it may be awarded additional points, and a higher score is possible.

In addition to the performance categories that are given a point score, the manner of hunting (type of voice can only be determined on furred game—hare or fox), gunfire tolerance, special characteristics (temperament), and physical deficiencies (dentition, eyes, testicles, and others) are assessed at the VJP. A dog exhibiting gun-shyness or sensitivity to gunfire will fail the test.

Each dog is tested individually and given several opportunities to demonstrate its abilities. Because it is natural for a young dog's performance to vary in different situations, the overall impression is the determining factor in the final judgement. Dogs can pass the test only if they receive a minimum predicate of deficient (2 points) for pointing and sufficient (3 points) in all other test categories.

Table 35-1: *Level No. 1: Natural Ability Examination (Verbands-Jugend-Prüfung [VJP])*

Test Subject/ Trait Demonstrated	Procedure and Description
1. Tracking (Hare) Willingness and desire, Concentration under difficulty, Manner of hunting (Sound) is noted	*Tracking* is tested on the fresh trail of a hare not visible to the dog. The handler is permitted to work the dog on a release cord up to 30 meters (about 30 yards) to enable the dog to better concentrate and to be sure it is working track correctly; then, the dog is released with a track command. The dog's natural will to track and its ability to stay on the track is evaluated. Willingness, sureness, and difficulties encountered are given greater consideration than the length of the track: willingness is demonstrated by excited anticipation, attacking the track with enthusiasm, persistence under difficult conditions, and calmly attempting to relocate the track if lost; sureness is demonstrated by the way the dog pushes the track forward with confidence and independence.
2. Use of Nose Sensitive, accurate scent discrimination	*Use of Nose* is evaluated during the Search, Pointing, and Tracking subjects. The fine nose is identified during the Search as the young dog finds game frequently, moves in carefully on game detected at some distance, briefly marking spots where game has been, and occasionally marking other bird scents (songbirds). Indications of losing, relocating, and crossing other tracks should be used when evaluating the nose. Wind, terrain, humidity, and barometric pressure all play a critical part in evaluating scent performance.
3. Search Desire to find game, Stamina and style	The emphasis of the Search is the will to find game (ingenuity). The Search demonstrates determination, hunting passion, and endurance. A dog that searches erratically, moves no faster than a trot, and repeatedly overruns game receives a maximum rating of good.
4. Pointing Indicate location of game, Intensity on point, Duration of point	The dog's inherited ability to indicate game, either standing or lying down, is evaluated. The pointing reflex is slow to develop in the versatile breeds, and it is not always demonstrated at the VJP, at the age of 12–15 months; therefore, the slightest indication of pointing is considered positive. A dog with strong intensity (outstretched neck and body, quivering muscles, etc.) scores higher than one that is relaxed and soft. A dog that points for 5 seconds or longer behind game that is not moving or flying without any influence from the handler is rated very good. Difficulties arising from game that is holding tightly, not moving or flying. Definite indications of blinking are a disqualification. Every indication of game is weighed and averaged for the final performance points. Running after flushed game is not faulted. If feathered game is not available, pointing can be evaluated on furred game and is given the same value.
5. Cooperation Teamwork, Attentiveness	*Cooperation* (Führigkeit) is a highly valued trait, and it is observed in all sections and rated by overall performance. Cooperation is demonstrated for example by awareness of the handler's location, changing directions with the handler, and checking location of handler after working out of sight. The natural tendency of the dog to work with the handler is evaluated, but never in the presence of game.
5.2 Obedience Reactions to commands	*Obedience* (Gehorsam) is also observed during the entire test. It is demonstrated by how the dog reacts to commands given by its handler. A dog that continues to avoid its handler or obstructing the test process cannot pass the examination.

Other Traits Evaluated

1. *Manner of Hunting* (Sound). The hunting sound rating distinguishes dogs that indicate the presence of game by barking or baying. It can be evaluated only on hare or fox. Sichtlaut and spurlaut are highly valued traits. The following ratings are found on Hunting Test Forms 3 and 5. A dog may be both spur- and sichtlaut:

spurlaut: gives sound when on scent track of game	*sichtlaut:* gives sound when game is in sight
fraglich: questionable, could not be determined	*stumm:* silent on track and in sight of game
waidlaut: barking while searching without the presence of game; aimless chasing and breaking off from track (highly undesirable trait)	

2. *Gunfire Tolerance.* To evaluate the reaction to gunfire during Search, at least two shots are fired at a minimum of 20-second intervals within 30–50 meters of the dog; if the response cannot be judged satisfactorily, the test is repeated after at least 30 minutes. The ideal behavior is either no response to the shot or an eager attempt to look for the game that was brought down. One of the following is noted on the form:

schussfest (shot stable): performance undisturbed by gunshots
leicht schussempfindlich (lightly gunsensitive): general intimidation but without interruption of search
schussempfindlich (moderately gunsensitive): seeks protection of handler but returns to search in less than 1 minute
stark schussempfindlich (severely gunsensitive): stops work, exhibits fear, but returns to search in more than 1 but less than 5 minutes
schussscheu (gunshy): shows fear and does not return to search within 5 minutes; runs off, out of handler's control

3. *Other Signs of Temperament and Physical Deficiencies.* Gunshy and handshy (displays fear of the handler) dogs are disqualified; other deficiencies of mental stability are looked for and recorded. The dog is examined for correct bite and dentition, freedom from eye defects, and number of testicles or number and alignment of nipples.

Führigkeit, the close bond of cooperation between the Weimaraner and its *handler* (Führer), is demonstrated by the dog's awareness of the handler's location by looking back frequently for a change of direction or command. This inherent trait, which must not be confused with obedience, is very highly regarded.

Manner of Hunting (Art des Jagens=Laut): Display of scent track loud, sight loud, questionable, silent or hunt loud are evaluated. This can only be done on hare or fox. However, to permit participation in a VSwP, where the certification of a loud is required, sight or scent track loud may also be noted on the deer. A dog displaying scent track loud is noted as very favorable.

Advanced Natural Ability and Breeding Examination

The Verbands Herbst Zucht Prüfung (HZP) is also known as the Fall Breeding Trial. The examinations, which are held each fall, test natural hunting ability and elementary trained skills, and assess the young dog's worthiness for use in breeding. The objectives are similar to those of the NAVHDA Utility Preparatory Test. After the VJP, the youngsters begin preparation for the HZP examinations, which are held in September.

Performance points are awarded in the following test subjects. The first seven subjects assess the Weimaraner's *nat-*

Figure 35-20: *Bringen von Fuchs über Hindernis.* Reprinted, with permission, from Manfred Hölzel, Die Deutschen Vorstehhunde, 1986.

Figure 35-22: *During the VGP examination,* Peter Reichert and Catja vom Kohlwald are observed by the judges as shots are fired nearby and as much noise and distractions as possible are made. Catja must remain in a down position, which means with the head on the ground between the forelegs. Photograph courtesy of the Weimaraner Klub e. V.

Figures 35-21: *These two photographs display the subject of retrieving the fox over a barrier* [Bringen von Fuchs Űber Hindernis]. Roland Maag places Jonas vom Forst on a down-stay, as he prepares to place the fox within the enclosure. The dog is sent over the barrier and must pick up the fox and return over the barrier, delivering to the handler. Photograph courtesy of the Weimaraner Klub e. V.

ural abilities (Anlagefächer); the next four categories assess *trained skills* (Abrichtefächer).[5] Reference to these test subjects may be found in the HZP Test Form in Table 35-3.

Similar to the VJP, a determination of manner of hunting, gunfire soundness, and mental behavior of the dog as well as physical defects must be assessed. A very favorable score is 180 points, although like the VJP, a higher score is possible for an outstanding performance.

Master Utility Examination

The Verbands Gebrauchs Prüfung (VGP) examination is an extremely difficult proof of hunting usefulness for which there is no American equivalent (the NAVHDA Utility Test has some similarities). The VGP may only be conducted in the fall. Only during the VGP, considered to be the master utility examination for a hunting dog, is the completed training of a hunting dog evaluated. It is important to emphasize that a dog entering this test must be fully finished in all trained subjects. The prime objectives of the VGP are to evaluate those dogs best suited for conservation hunting and to expose them to a variety of hunting situations.

The VGP includes four specialized groups and their respective test subjects. Obedience and cooperation are of utmost importance; performance points are awarded for the work of the dog and handler together and for the dog's desire, cooperation, and willingness to work. The dog is under test during the entire 2-day period, which includes breakfast, lunch, supper, and during the night.

If, for example, the dog picks a fight with another dog during lunch, the dog will fail the test for insufficient obedience. In Germany, Austria, Switzerland, France, the Netherlands, and other European countries, the well-rained hunting dog is indispensable.

Well-trained hunting dogs are expected to kill and retrieve foxes, martens, and other predators; retrieving the fox over a *barrier* (Bringen von Fuchs über Hindernis) dates back to the early 1900s. All dead foxes used in the test are required to have been examined for rabies. Dogs must have special training and practice to carry a fox, owing to its heavy weight (4–8 kg) and offensive smell.

Although the VGP is not mandatory to be eligible for breeding, it is granted high breeding value and considered one of the most important breeding tools. On a certified pedigree, the elite individuals who have passed the VGP have a special number to the right of the registration number. This number is recorded in the *German Versatile Hunting Dog Record Book* (Deutsches Gebrauchshund Stammbuch [DGStB]); which is used for recording performances, certifying, and publishing.

Figure 35-23: *Fenja vom Nestelberg retrieves the goose.* Photo courtesy of owners Thomas and Iris Feindt, Germany.

Figure 35-24: *Ceres vom Erlenhain looks proud* as she presents a red fox. Photograph courtesy of the Weimaraner Klub e. V.

Table 35-2: *Advanced Natural Ability and Breeding Examination (Verbands-Herbstzucht-Prüfung [HZP]).*

Regulations for the Association Breed Tests

A. *Generalities*	The priority of the HZP is the evaluation of the inherited natural tendencies of the young dog with respect to its suitability an future use for versatile hunting tasks and breeding.
	The preparation and training of the hunting dog in the field and water work should largely be completed at this time.
	To enter the HZP, a dog must not be born prior to October 1, two years before; e.g., to participate in the 2008 HZP, the dog's birth date must not have been prior to October 1, 2006.
	During the HZP, the following subjects are to be tested.

Test Subject/ Trait Demonstrated	Procedure and Description
1. Tracking (Hare) Willingness and desire. Concentration	The trait demonstrated and procedure are the same as in the VJP, although the performance must reflect greater maturity, experience, and training. It is left up to the organization conducting the HZP test whether to include Tracking (Hare) as a mandatory phase, which is published in the announcement.
2. Use of Nose Sensitive, accurate scent discrimination Scenting from great distances Intelligent use of the wind Ability to positively locate birds Find game	The trait demonstrated and procedure are the same as in the VJP, although the performance must reflect greater maturity, experience, and training. Use of the nose is carefully observed during the *Search, Tracking* (except drag tracks), and *Water Test.*
3. Search Good search pattern Stamina and style Gunfire soundness Desire to find game	The trait demonstrated and procedure are the same as in the VJP, although the performance must reflect greater maturity, experience, and training. The Weimaraner should be adjusting its search pattern to the prevailing wind and terrain. The greatest value is applied to the dog's will to find and demonstration of a good search pattern. The dog should exhibit endurance and is expected to range far enough to cover the area thoroughly. During the search the gunfire soundness is judged.
4. Pointing Intensity on point Duration of point	In general, these are older dogs and their performance reflects greater control. The manner in which the dog indicates location of the game (standing or lying down) should leave no doubt that game is present. A dog that points for 10 seconds or longer as the handler approaches within 5 yards is rated "very good". Any negative work, such as busting birds, should be counted. Definite indication of blinking is a disqualification. If feathered game is not available, pointing may be evaluated on furred game and is given the same value. The special difficulties when game moves or takes off have to be taken into consideration.
5. Cooperation Teamwork Attentivenes	Cooperation is evaluated in all phases. A dog that works for the handler with few commands, keeps eye contact with him, and displays a desire to please receives the highest score.
6. Desire to work	The desire to work is indicated during the entire examination by the dog's willingness to perform all test subjects. The dog should demonstrate a passion for work on land as well as in water.
7. Water Work Water love, desire, and stamina Willingness to swim How the dog takes to the work in the water Gunfire soundness	This subject has three phases: 1. Gunfire Soundness 2. Blind Retrieve in Densely Vegetated Water 3. Search Behind a Live Duck in Densely Vegetated Water **General Rules:** In order to allow the duck to make full use of flight possibilities, the area used for this work has to fulfill the following conditions: a minimum size of 2,500 m² (5/8 acre) of open water that partially is at least 6 meters wide and deep enough to force the dog to swim. In addition, the cover available has to amount to 500 m² (so that the duck may fully make use of flight possibilities). Dogs that fail in the Gunfire Soundness or the Blind Retrieve may not be tested with a live duck. The reason for this regulation: To work with an untrained, thus unreliable dog is regarded as cruelty to the duck. The ducks used must be fully mature mallards raised as if in the wild, i.e., sufficiently acquainted with cover and water. During the test, their pinion feathers are bound together by a paper ribbon to make them unable to fly.

Table 35-2: *Advanced Natural Ability and Breeding Examination (Verbands-Herbstzucht-Prüfung [HZP]), continued*

Test Subject/ Trait Demonstrated	Procedure and Description
Gunfire Soundness in the Water Display independent retrieve Willingness to swim Soundness to gunfire	A dead duck is thrown as far as possible into open water while the dog is watching. The dog is then commanded to retrieve. While the dog is swimming out to the duck, a shotgun is fired into the water in the direction of the duck. The dog MUST retrieve the duck independently. A dog that fails here may not be tested further at the water. *Reason, see above.* A dog that does not go into the water within approximately 1 minute of being given the first command may not be tested any further in Water Work.
Blind Retrieve in Densely Vegetated Water Ability to follow signals to locate game Willingness and ability to find shot game, as if during the hunt Search in difficult areas	A blind retrieve in densely vegetated water follows immediately after the gunfire soundness test in the water. A freshly shot duck is thrown out of the dog's sight in such a manner (island, opposite shore, reedy area) that the dog MUST be sent across open water into the cover. From a location, which is at least 30 meters from the duck, the handler is shown the approximate line in which the duck has fallen. From this location the dog should search for the duck independently; it must find and retrieve the game independently to hand. If the dog is sent only once and quickly locates and retrieves the duck, it receives a "very good" rating. A dog that does not retrieve a duck when located, by sight or scent, for the first time cannot pass the test. The handler may direct the dog with voice, hand signal, or whistle. He is allowed to call or throw a stone to encourage the dog to search; however, continuous support lessens the score. The retrieve of the duck is scored for the dog's pick up, carry (hold), and manner of delivering to hand; if the dog comes happily and willingly, sits quietly without command or with just a soft command and releases the duck calmly into the handler's hand, it will receive a "very good" score. If the dog drops the duck on the shore to shake, it receives a maximum rating of "good." Correction of the hold on the duck is allowed if, in the judges' opinion, the dog would not have lost the live duck; otherwise the correction is penalized. A dog which is not evaluated with at least the attribute "sufficient" may not be further tested with the live duck. *Reason, see above.*
Search Behind a Live Duck in Densely Vegetated Water Willingness to swim Perserverance for searching dense cover Strength of character	A duck will be released into heavy cover without marking the release site. This preparation may not be seen by the dog. After the release, the judges will lead the handler to a point within shotgun range from the respective release point of the duck and provide the direction taken. At this point the handler sends the dog to search. The dog should independently search and find the duck. The handler may direct and assist the dog during its work, however, constant influences will lower the attribute. The duck is shot in front of the dog as soon as it is driven out on open water (safety regulations must be strictly observed). During this test subject, only if and how the dog (as an expression of its attitude) conducts the search in the water, whether it wants to find and retrieve, and whether it does retrieve the duck at all, are rated; the **Manner of Retrieving** is an expression of skill learned through training—that is, the picking up, grip, and delivery are rated under this subject. A dead duck will be thrown into the water plus a hail shot, in case it was not possible to shoot a live duck. A dog must display an *independent* retrieve when first locating a duck shot in front of it, or that it has already gripped, or one that was tossed within sight. Otherwise, the dog cannot pass the test. If the dog breaks off after the shot, whether or not the duck was hit, and does not return to the water on command, it is **disqualified**. Evaluation of the Search and the Nose is done only when the dog cannot see the duck.

TESTS OF TRAINED SKILLS (ABRICHTEFÄCHER)

8. Feathered Game Drag Will to find fowl immediately (work the drag track) Desire to bring fowl (work back to handler) 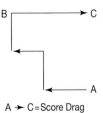 A ➤ C=Score Drag B ➤ C=Score Retrieve	The handlers may provide their own fresh animals for the dragtrack work (Schleppenarbeit). The drag is to be laid with a minimum length of 150 meters (approximately 200 steps) by a judge, immediately before testing the dog, on vegetated ground with the wind at its back, to include two obtuse angles. The distance between the individual drag tracks must be no less than 100 meters at all points. At the end of the drag a piece of fresh game of the same species, will be placed in the open (not covered or in a dip). The handler may choose which piece of game (dragged or carried) shall be placed. Then the judge continues to walk in the direction of the drag and hides, so he is not visible to the dog. He must lay the remaining game down openly in front of himself. He may not prevent the dog from picking up this piece of game. A recent ruling also allows for only one piece of game to be used, so that the one in front of the judge no longer "exists." The handler may choose one or two pieces of fresh game to be dragged. The dog may not see the laying of the drag. The handler may work the dog on a release cord for the first 20 meters (25 steps) of the drag, then the dog is released with a "fetch" command, and the handler must come to a stop. In the event that the dog returns without having located the game and does not independently take up the drag again, the handler may start it two more times. A dog that has found the game but does not retrieve may not be started again.

Table 35-2: *Advanced Natural Ability and Breeding Examination (Verbands-Herbstzucht-Prüfung [HZP]), continued*

Test Subject/ Trait Demonstrated	Procedure and Description
	According to the new retrieving regulations explained under **10. Manner of Retrieving,** the dog must, by using its nose, willingly and independently find, quickly pick up, and happily retrieve the bird. The dog's work on the trail and back is to be evaluated. Examination of the following performance areas is given exclusive evaluation. If and how the dog takes to its work, whether it has determination to find and retrieve, and whether it will deliver the game to the handler at all. Retrieving performance is an expression of the skills learned through training for example, the dog is evaluated on how it picks up, carries, and delivers to hand for the ***Manner of Retrieving.***
9. Furred Game Drag Same as *Feathered Game Drag*	Dead hares or rabbits (the two are never mixed) are used. Also in this instance, the handler may choose to work with two pieces or only one piece of game. The track distance is 300 meters (400 steps). Preparation and performance are the same as for the *Feathered Game Drag.*
10. Manner of Retrieving Trained skill in pick-up, carry, and delivery correct	Rated in all sections of the HZP that require retrieving (furred game, pheasant, and duck etc.). A correct delivery is demonstrated by coming to the handler happily and willingly, sitting without command or after a quiet word, and holding the game calmly until the "give" command. Eating, burying, or extreme hard-mouthing are reasons for disqualification. There is one very important new regulation for all retrieving subjects: All retrieving work for both the HZP and VGP MUST be performed independently without any corrective interference from the handler, especially when the dog is disobedient or makes mistakes. The handler may, however, praise his dog or try to get its attention as long as the dog's work is not interfered with. To better understand: If the dog picks up the duck and is not coming back to the handler but getting out of the water on the opposite shore (mistake), the handler may not interfere. If the dog picks up the game and is swimming back to the handler (correct), he may say something like "good dog."
11. Obedience Quick, willing response to voice, hand signal, and whistle	Cooperation is given by the dog to the handler; in contrast, obedience is demanded by the handler from the dog. Obedience is evaluated in all phases of the examination; however, obedience is not evaluated in the presence of game; obedience is evaluated during the search work by the way the dog responds to the handler's signals and commands. The dog shows that it is calm and under control in the presence of other dogs and handlers.

TESTS OF TRAINED SKILLS (ABRICHTEFÄCHER)

1. Manner of Hunting (Sound)	This is the same as in the VJP.
2. Gunfire Soundness	The rating is the same as in the VJP; the evaluation is done during the *Field Search* and before *Blind Retrieve in Densely Vegetated Water* and *Search Behind Live Duck in Densely Vegetated Water.* During the *Field Search* the reaction of the dog to gunfire is tested by a minimum of two shots being fired during the search when the dog is nearby (30 to 50 meters), with the time between each shot being at least 20 seconds. Very sensitive, gunshy, game-shy and handshy dogs cannot be awarded a passing score; however, they are to be completely tested.
3. Physical Attributes	General conformation and coat value are not part of any hunting test. They are judged at the "Zuchtschau." However, the dog's overall physical characteristics (eyes, teeth, expression, testicles, etc.) are examined and noted on the HZP Judges' Form.

Master's Performance Examination
(*Verbands-Gebrauchs-Prüfung [VGP]*)

Supplemental Examinations and Ratings

The supplemental examinations and ratings are conducted for most German versatile hunting breeds. They normally are held in the fall. The ratings are included on the German pedigree.

Rigorous Toward Predators/Härtenachweis

In Germany the authorized killing of predators and scavengers such as feral cats, dogs, raccoons, and martens normally falls under the tasks of the hunter with his gun. However, in situations in which the dog is already engaged in battle, so the predator cannot be shot, there is no legal violation. If the performance is witnessed by reliable observers, the dog can be registered by the JGHV in the appropriate instinctive natural toughness category.

Lost Game Retrieval on a Natural Blood Trail

The Verlorenbringen (Vbr) is a most valuable observation that best defines the dog's traits and qualifications for hunting. It may only be demonstrated during a hunt on natural blood trails of wounded hares or foxes (Verlorenbringen). The dog must fol-

Table 35-3: *Master Performance Examination (Verbands-Gebrauchs-Prüfung [VGP]).*

Test Subject/ Trait Demonstrated	Procedure and Description

I. *FOREST WORK (WALDARBEIT)*

1. Blood Tracking on Lead for Hoofed Game
Desire
Initiative
Calmness, confidence and concentration

Optional Free Tracking (Totverbeller or Totverweiser)

Correct behavior when locating game
Ability to guide handler to game

When applying for the examination, about 4 weeks ahead, the handler is required to declare the kind of track = overnight or day, and the style of tracking = [a] mandatory *pure leash work* (Riemenarbeit) only or [b] additional optional free tracking using either the *dead game barker* (Totverbeller) or the *dead game guide* (Totverweiser) method. During the examination itself, shortly before the subject begins, the handler must explain to the senior judge, in the case of the dead game guide, how he will recognize his dog has located, i.e., how the dog indicates that it has found the game and how it will lead him there.

The dead game at the end of the track can be any kind of cloven hoofed animal, such as fallow, red, or roe deer and wild boar.

The blood used is from fresh game (such as deer, wild boar or stag) or fresh domestic animals (such as cattle, sheep, or pigs or a mixture); no chemicals may be added as a preservative.

The simulated blood track is made by using either a blood dropper, so that drops fall, or by dabbing with a blood-soaked sponge. (The track layer uses a sponge, attached to a stick, soaked with blood. It is then "printed" on the ground, thus leaving particles of blood along the track.)

Not more than 1/4 liter (8.5 ounces) of blood may be used for the mandatory 400-meter track; not more than 1/8 liter (4.2 ounces) of blood may be used for the additional optional 200-meter track (total length with options is 600 meters).

Also a special *track shoe* (Fährtenschuh) may be used. Similar to using "snow shoes", the track shoe attaches to your foot and contains the hooves of cloven game extruding on the bottom plus a little container for blood.

The track age is from 2 to 5 hours for "day tracks" or at least 14 hours for "overnight tracks" (the factor of the latter on the result sheet being 8 compared to 5 for the day track, thus emphasizing the more difficult work on the overnight track).

The track runs from the game's position when shot in the direction the game ran and never doubles back; only one path is allowed in making the track.

Turns are made after approximately 100 and 300 meters.

For the dog performing leash work only, one wound bed is made at a suitable location, approximately 200 meters from where the track begins. The game is placed at the end of the 400-meter track.

For dogs performing optional free-tracking work, a second wound bed made at 400 meters is clearly marked, while the carcass is positioned at the 600-meter mark end.

Control signs must be placed in a way not visible to the handler.

2. Retrieving Fox Over the Barrier

This exercise (Bringen von Fuchs über Hindernis) is a very old practice, dating back to the early 1900s; owing to the weight and scent of the fox, this is a very difficult exercise.

The exercise is conducted during the forest work.

The obstacle can be a ditch or a hurdle: a ditch must be at least 80 cm deep and 1 meter wide, with steep edges; a hurdle must be 70–80 cm high and constructed so that the dog cannot become entangled between the rungs.

The dog must not be able to wade through, climb, or go around the barrier.

The judges direct the handler to have the dog lie down in front of the barrier at a minimum distance of 5 meters.

After having tossed the dead fox, which must weigh at least 7 pounds, into the pen or over the ditch; the handler sends the dog from its location to retrieve the fox.

As soon as the dog has been sent the first time, the handler may not approach the barrier from his location.

The dog jumps the barrier, picks up the fox, returns over the barrier, and delivers to hand.

Only two commands are given during the exercise: (a) to retrieve the fox and (b) to release it to hand.

There is a difference between the retrieve of "useful" (such as rabbits, hares, pheasants, duck, etc.) and "useless" game like the fox. The dog must retrieve "useful" game independently when first located. If it does not, it has failed and may not be sent again. The dog may however, be sent three times on drags with "useful" game as long as it has not discovered the game.

In the case of the fox, the dog may be sent two more times, even if it has found, but not retrieved, the "useless" game.

Sending the dog repeatedly (up to a total of three times is allowed) lowers the score.

3–5. The Furred Game Drag Tracks
Manner of working track and retrieve
Use of nose
Perseverance
Desire

Two furred game drags are made: one is tested with a fox (weighing at least 7 pounds); the other is tested with either hare or rabbit.

Depending on how the dog has been trained, the handler may decide whether one or two pieces of freshly killed animals of one kind are used for each drag track; the handler may provide fresh game in suitable condition for the exercises.

Table 35-3: *Master Performance Examination (Verbands-Gebrauchs-Prüfung [VGP]), continued.*

Test Subject/ Trait Demonstrated	Procedure and Description
	Walking in the direction of the wind, the tracklayer (one of the judges) carries one animal and drags the other on a cord from the spot (marked with hair from the game) where the game was shot, making two obtuseangle turns in the 300-meter track and at the end of the track detaches the piece of game from the cord and places it openly on the ground not in a dip or behind a tree.
	Then, the tracklayer continues in the same direction for a short distance and hides in cover. If he laid the drag with two animals, he lays the second one in front of himself and waits to observe the dog's behavior when it finds the game.
	The dog may retrieve either piece of game; an exceptional dog will try to retrieve both.
	Taking the dog to the beginning of the track (shown by the judge), the handler is permitted to work the dog up to 20 meters on a slip cord; he may also follow up to the 20 meters, even if he released the dog earlier.
	The handler may start the dog a maximum of three times, if it has not found the game.
	Any influence is considered as a new start and lowers the result.
	Dogs that bury or try to eat the game are not only disqualified for the exercise but excluded from further testing.
4–6. *Retrieving* (Bringen) **Retrieving the Fox** **Retrieving the Hare (Rabbit)**	In each phase (land and water) of the examination, the dog's training in retrieving is evaluated pick up, carry (hold), and give on feathered (duck, pheasant) and furred (fox, hare, rabbit) game. The correct pick up and carry are adjusted according to the type and weight of the game. The dog comes willingly and happily, sits quietly without command before the handler, and calmly releases the game on command. Errors include too strong or weak a grip; hard-mouthing is penalized.
7. *Independent Forest Search* (Stoebern) Perseverance, Passion Boldness	"Stoebern" means the use of the dog to drive game in dense vegetation. The search is conducted in brush, thickets, or young tree plots populated with game. The dog ranges a good distance to search the assigned area very thoroughly for 10 minutes. The judges observe the dog for the correct systematic, quartering search; running through the thicket in a haphazard pattern, and overrunning game are undesired behaviors. The type of hunting sound or voice, when locating game, is noted.
8. *Dense Forest Undergrowth Search* (Buschieren) Cooperation Calm, Purposeful Search	"Buschiere" means the dog searches in parts with young pole woods/timber, in low-growing cultures, or short-growing wood patches. The dog hunts in range of the gun (about 40 meters), taking advantage of wind and cover. The dog hunts in a purposeful and calm manner, so the handler can follow it easily. During "Buschieren," the handler must fire oneormore shots when instructed by the judges. The dog should be easily directed by its handler and work without loud commands. Much importance is placed on a good contact between the handler and the dog. If during the dense brush search, the dog has possibilities to show performances regarding the subjects; pointing, steadiness to fur and feather, steadiness to shot, and retrieving, these shall be considered by the judges for each of the relevant subjects.
II. *WATER WORK* (WASSERARBEIT)	
General Rules	The general rules and conditions for the water work section apply to both the HZP and the VGP. Besides the three water subjects of the HZP, the subject "Search in Densely Vegetated Water Without a Duck" is tested in addition. The order in the VGP is as follows: 1. Search in Densely Vegetated Water Without a Duck 2. Gunfire Soundness in Water 3. Blind Retrieve in Densely Vegetated Water 4. Search Behind a Live Duck (if not yet successfully passed during a prior examination like the HZP)
1. **Search in Densely Vegetated Water Without a Duck** Systematic search pattern Will to find Desire to work in water	No duck is released for this exercise. The dog shall enter the water at the handler's first command and search independently for about 10 minutes. The dog shall demonstrate its will to find game, desire to work in water, as well as thoroughly searching the entire area provided. A negative search is displayed by pottering in one area. The handler may assist the dog, but continuous help reduces the results.
2. **Gunfire Soundness**	Please refer to respective subject under the HZP.
3. **Blind Retrieve in Densely Vegetated Water**	Please refer to respective subject under the HZP.

Table 35-3: *Master Performance Examination (Verbands-Gebrauchs-Prüfung [VGP]), continued.*

Test Subject/ Trait Demonstrated	Procedure and Description
4. **Search Behind a Live Duck in Densely Vegetated Water**	Please refer to respective subject under the HZP. However, this subject will only be tested if the dog has not already successfully completed it in a prior examination like the HZP. Any successful result from prior examinations will be transferred to the VGP.
5. **Manner of Retrieving the Duck**	A correct delivery is demonstrated by coming to the handler happily and willingly, sitting without command or after a quiet word, and holding the game calmly until the "give" command. Eating, burying, or extreme hard-mouthing are disqualifications. Regarding all the other retrieving subjects, the rule that the dog must retrieve independently when the game is first located, without any correcting influence, applies here as well.
III. FIELD WORK (FELDARBEIT)	
General Rules	The field work is done in an area where small game is found in a typical hunting situation. Each dog shall be given several opportunities to display its abilities to find and handle partridges and pheasants, so the judges may fairly evaluate the dog's performance correctly. Much emphasis is placed on how the dog uses its nose.
1. **Use of Nose** Sensitive, accurate scent discrimination Scenting from great distances Intelligent use of the wind Ability to positively locate birds Finds game	The good use of the nose during the search is indicated by taking advantage of the wind, quick and finding of game, occasional marking of bird scent, quick pinpointing of running game, and indicating game from a distance.
2. **Search** Desire Stamina Cooperation	The will to find game is of greatest importance in this phase; proper search pattern is also considered. Furthermore, the search should be at a good pace, deliberate, and persistent. The search covers the area in a manner suggesting that nothing has been overlooked and at a tempo that fits the nose's finding ability. The dog should adapt to the area, the existing game, and the wind. The dog has the opportunity to work in good cover. Furthermore, the judges take into consideration the way in which the dog is willing to be handled and obeys commands (voice, hand or whistle signs) given by its handler.
3. **Pointing** Intensity	The dog should hold point behind game which does not move in a manner that allows the handler to approach and be able to shoot. If the game takes off, the dog may have no possibility to hold the point.
4. **Manners on Game** Ability to relocate and hold game	The dog exhibits good manners behind game by its ability to control its actions when game is located. When the dog locates the fresh scent of game that has just run away, it displays good follow-up ability by a slow, controlled pursuit of the track until it produces game for the handler to shoot.
5. **Bird Drag and Blind Retrieve** Willingness to find and retrieve game Independence	The bird drag is a substitute for search and retrieve of a crippled bird. The preparation of the track is done in a fashion similar to the fur drags; the drag is laid by a judge, using ground with good cover and moving in the direction of the wind; the track has two obtuseangle turns and a minimum length of 200 meters (250 steps). The blind retrieve is a substitute for the search and retrieve of a freshly shot bird that the dog did not see fall. Without the dog seeing the procedure, a bird is thrown into a covered area, so that the dog cannot know its position, but has to use its nose to find the bird. All exercises require that the dog finds the game willingly, quickly, and independently and that it happily brings the game to the handler without additional influences. Gunshyness, handshyness, extreme hard-mouthing, and eating or burying the game disqualify the dog.
IV. OBEDIENCE SPECIALTY GROUP (GEHORSAM)	
General Rules	Obedience is the foundation of correct performance and a precondition of any hunting usefulness of the dog.
1. **General Behavior: Obedience**	It is shown when the dog willingly follows the commands of its handler. It is displayed when the dog is quiet on lead, not pulling, and does not interfere with other handlers and hunters. Obedience is judged in all phases of the examination, and the dog is under judgement at all times during the 2-day VGP examination.

low the wound track of a hare or fox it has not formerly seen for at least 300 meters, find the animal, and retrieve it. The performance must be confirmed by at least one judge and one hunter as witnesses. The manner of hunting (sound) must be recorded. This qualification may not be applied for, if the dog displays a negative performance on other wound tracks during that day.

Retrieving Reliability Examination

The Bringtreueprüfung (Btr) examines the hunting dog's retrieving reliability. The dog must retrieve any game or animal of prey that it encounters accidentally without being influenced by its handler. A dead (cold) fox is set out in a wooded area, free of any other game, if possible, at 100 meters from the forest edge. Three judges must be present for this test. Small open patches should be available for the judges to observe the working dog, especially its behavior when encountering the fox. Two judges observe the dog's work in the wooded area and must make sure that, for example by using a high-seat, they are not seen or scented by the working dog. The third judge walks with the handler to observe that all regulations are met. The handler gives the dog the Search! (not Fetch!) command. No further commands may be given. The dog must find and retrieve the fox to hand within 20 minutes to pass the examination. The handler may walk up and down the road but cannot enter the wooded area and must display an absolutely quiet manner. During the 20-minute period, the dog may be silently re-sent as often as necessary to search in the forest.

The Retrieving Reliability Examinations are conducted from August until the end of April.

Armbruster Halt Award

The Halt Certificate (Armbruster Haltabzeichen [AH]) was originally established by Len F. B. Armbruster. He was not only an American but also the only one to achieve recognition as a successful breeder, trainer, and instructor of the Deutsch Drahthaar breed and its versatile use in Germany.

In 1957, Armbruster began to develop his thoughts that there must be a middle ground between the desires of breeders who wanted to produce the best utility dog, which at times was hard to handle, and the owner of the dog who wanted an easily handled dog possessing strong natural abilities. He came up with the idea of training the Halt. He was going to use this training to evaluate both the effectiveness of the breeding and handler control. His idea was to train the dog to stop on command and go down as a hare was flushed in the field. The obedience training was thought to show handling ability, cooperation of the dog, and good hunting ability at the same time. In 1970, the German Versatile Hunting Dog Association established the Armbruster Halt Award to be given to a dog in an Association test that would demonstrate the halt by stopping on command at the sight of a flushed hare, then come up on command to take the track and successfully track the hare. Haltabzeichen is the badge awarded to the dog trained to halt (stay). This is a badge worn with honor in Germany by those trainers whose dogs have mastered this skill.

Regional Utility Examination/Brauchbarkeitsprüfung

German law requires the hunting rights owner must provide a dog that is certified to track wounded game. The Brauchbarkeitsprüfung (Brb) is the district-oriented certification

Table 35-4: *Performance Results in Search and Water Work* (1988–2008).

	VJP			HZP						
Year	No. of Dogs	Middle Value for the Field Search	Variable %	No. of Dogs	Middle Value for the Field Search	Variable %	Middle Value for Water Work Without a Live Duck	Variable %	No. of Dogs	Middle Value for Water Work With a Live Duck	Variable %
1988	120	8.4	3.3	72	8.8	2.4	8.7	3.4	72	7.7	5.7
1989	141	8.7	2.8	89	9.3	1.2	9.2	2.8	89	8.5	5.8
1990	138	8.7	3.1	86	9.1	2.3	8.9	2.9	86	7.8	6.0
1991	162	8.7	3.0	91	9.0	3.0	8.6	3.8	91	8.5	5.3
1992	150	9.1	2.6	109	9.2	2.1	8.5	4.6	75	8.5	5.4
1993	177	8.8	3.5	123	9.3	2.2	8.5	4.4	83	9.0	2.9
1994	156	8.5	4.0	104	9.3	1.9	8.4	4.7	86	8.7	4.6
1995	225	8.8	3.0	160	9.2	2.3	8.4	4.7	125	9.1	3.8
1996	210	8.6	3.2	133	9.2	2.6	8.6	4.0	98	9.1	4.7
1997	205	8.9	3.1	149	9.1	2.3	8.6	4.1	126	9.0	4.7
1998	214	8.8	1.7	146	9.0	1.6	8.3	2.2	111	9.2	1.7
1999	249	8.3	4.1	171	9.0	2.6	8.4	5.1	166	8.9	5.1
2000	264	8.7	3.6	169	9.2	2.1	8.9	4.0	166	9.1	4.3
2001	200	8.8	3.2	141	8.8	3.4	8.5	4.1	138	8.8	3.8
2002	280	8.9	2.7	205	9.3	2.1	8.9	4.2	194	8.9	4.5
2003	290	8.9	2.8	202	9.1	2.8	8.8	3.5	194	9.4	3.5
2004	350	8.9	2.8	232	9.2	2.5	8.6	4.3	225	9.2	3.5
2005	297	9.0	2.6	200	9.4	1.9	8.7	3.9	194	9.0	4.5
2006	347	9.1	2.4	226	9.4	2.2	8.8	3.4	219	9.2	4.6
2007	309	8.9	3.5	196	9.3	2.7	8.8	5.2	187	9.1	5.2
2008	319	9.1	3.2	226	9.4	2.2	8.8	3.9	224	9.2	4.5
Average		8.8			9.2		8.7			8.9	

Data courtesy of Heinrich Giesemann, Weimaraner Klub e. V. Breeding Regulator.

examination to gain this proof. This test demands qualified tracking and various other aptitudes developed through skilful, dedicated training. Some dog handlers, not interested in breeding enter their dogs in this test.

The Regional Utility Examination only consists of subjects after the shot. It is similar to the VGP, but not as extensive. Its purpose is to prove the dog's usefulness to work as a reliable partner for tasks required during the hunt. This proof is also required to obtain the liability insurance.

Normally, it is organized by the regional hunting organizations (Landes- und Kreisjagdverbände). Since every state (Bundesland) has individual laws, the test regulations unfortunately vary accordingly. The primary subjects, however, can be summarized as follows:

Test Subjects/Procedure and Description

1. Obedience
    a. Overall Obedience
    b. Staying at the Stand
    c. Walking at heal
2. Shot Stability
    a. In the Field or Forest
    b. In the Water
3. Retrieving
    a. Furred Game Drag Track
    b. Feathered Game Drag Track
    c. Blind Retrieve of Feathered Game
4. Water Work
    a. Blind Retrieve of Duck in Dense Water
    b. Search behind Live Duck
5. Blood Tracking
    a. Overnight Track
    b. Day Track
    c. Staying by the Game (without mutilation outside the sight of the handler)

In order to achieve the certification, all dogs are required to pass the subjects under 1 and 2. The subjects under 3 to 5 can either be performed together or separately. This means that the tested dog may pass one of these subjects individually, for example; Blood Tracking. It is then allowed to work in a cloven-hooved game area and may be used accordingly during the hunt. However, it is not allowed to work during duck shooting. For this purpose, it would have to pass the corresponding Water Work subject as well.

For a more detailed description, please refer to corresponding subjects in the VGP.

Because of the regional variations in the examinations and their lack of bearing on breeding considerations, the Brb is not mentioned on the German pedigree.

Figure 35-25: *Head held high,* this longhaired Weimaraner retrieves the heavy fox. Photograph courtesy of Dr. Hans Schmidt, Germany.

Figure 35-26: *Tinka von der Wapelburg* working the blood track for wounded game. Courtesy of Gerhard Eiben, Germany.

Figure 35-27: *Three judges observe a Weimaraner* working a blood track during a VGP examination. Photograph courtesy of Deborah Andrews.

Figure 35-28: ***Dargo vom Blanken displays Totverbeller*** next to the *fallow buck* (Damhirsch). Dargo is renowned as a blood-tracking specialist. Owner Dr. Horst Klerke, Germany. Photograph courtesy of the Weimaraner Klub e.V.

Figure 35-30: ***Amboss vom Heldenhain*** displays his ability as a *dead game finder* (Totverweiser) after locating and dispatching the wounded *mouflon ram* (Muffelwidder). Amboss holds the *leather thong* (Bringsel) and returns to guide the handler to the game. Courtesy of David Secord, Michigan, USA.

Figure 35-29: ***The blood-tracking or searching after wounded game*** is the elementary ground rule or obligation of every hunter. Reprinted, with permission, from Manfred Hölzel, Die Deutschen Vorstehhunde, 1986.

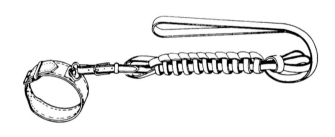

Figure 35-31: ***The proper blood-tracking collar and lead*** (Riemenarbeit). Reprinted, with permission, from Manfred Hölzel, Die Deutschen Vorstehhunde, 1986.

Local or district hunting organizations usually conduct training classes for the Brb from February through August. Because the test includes some areas of work tested in both the HZP and VGP, the Brb is an excellent way for the handler to assess the dog's readiness.

Simulated Blood-Tracking Examinations and Ratings

Preparation and Implementation

The blood tracking of wounded game (Schweissarbeit) is a prized Weimaraner aptitude of which most Americans are unaware. In its native land, the Weimaraner is used to track a variety of wounded game that is, wild boar, mouflon, chamois, and fox as well as roe, red, and fallow deer. Blood tracking is a multi-faceted discipline, a highly respected art requiring mas-

tery of technical skills, and is steeped in tradition and custom. The training is strenuous, requiring dogs that have been bred from generations of proven blood-tracking ability.

It takes a great deal of practice for both handler and dog to learn to work the track surely, eagerly, methodically, and as a team. The dog must discriminate between its objective and cross tracks from fresh game. The dog is given the experience of tracking the blood of many different game animals. The type of blood used in the tests varies with regulations and locale. Bits of liver, heart, or kidney from the game are sometimes added to the track to entice the dog to indicate the 2 wound beds.

The beginning of the simulated track, symbolic of where the game was shot, is prepared by clearing and sprinkling the area with blood and pelt hair. Other clearings are made along the track, called wound beds, simulating where the wounded

Figure 35-32: *Arimarlisa's Reiteralm Falco at a breed show,* a group of judges evaluate the conformation and coat quality of Falco, an American-bred longhair donated to the Weimaraner Club e. V. (Germany). Falco was trained and handled by Rainer Münter to qualify for the prestigious VGP title. Photograph courtesy of Deborah Andrews.

Figure 35-33: At the Zuchtschau, the judge completes a careful and thorough examination of the dog; a scribe reports the results which are included in the dog's permanent breeding records; the record includes such physical traits as the number of teeth, hair covering on the belly, and teats. At the conclusion of the judging, the results of each examination are read aloud. Reprinted with permission, from Deborah Andrews, *The Weimaraner Memory Book,* 2003.

animal may have lay down to rest. There are various methods to lay tracks: drop, pull a piece of lung and submerge it in the blood from time to time, the tracking boot (Fährtenschuh), etc. If the drop method is used, the blood is carried in a container that allows drops to fall as the track-maker lays a wandering path characteristic of wounded game. In this practice scenario of working the blood track, trees along the trail are marked with arrows to indicate turns, and bits of paper or thumb tacks to aid the handler's direction during the exercise. When the track is completed, the pelt is set down on a small clearing at the base of a tree and sprinkled with a little blood to simulate the dead animal. However, during an examination, no signs may be detected by the handler and no pelt is used. The actual dead game must be placed at the end of the track.

Besides the special blood-tracking tests of various specified lengths and ages conducted according to the JGHV rules as mentioned below, the simulated blood trails are also an integral part of the VGP and various Regional Utility Examinations.

The VGP examination, for example, contains blood-tracking work, for which there are three acceptable methods: Riemenarbeit, Totverbellen, and Totverweisen. The method the dog will use must be indicated on the entry form.

- *On-lead tracking* (Riemenarbeit) indicates that the dog works on a tracking lead (Riemen) that is about 30 feet long. The dog must also wear either a wide regulation tracking collar (Halsung) or a tracking harness, all other tracking equipment is prohibited. Each dog must work a mandatory 400-meter track on a lead for the VGP or the Brb. The exercise may include a day track (at least 2 to 5 hours) or an overnight track

Figure 35-34: *At a large Zuchtschau a best longhair and best shorthair* are selected among the 4 top winners (best longhaired dog and bitch, best shorthaired dog and bitch). The winners of the 1997 Weimaraner Klub e. V. Centenary show rest before the commemorative plaque presented to the city of Weimar by the German breed club honoring the Weimaraner's 100th Anniversary. *The Weimaraner Memory Book,* by Deborah Andrews, provides a detailed record of the historic centenary breed events held in 1997.

Figure 35-35: *Test with an object (Wesenstest Gegenstand = WG).* The examination consists of two parts. Photographs courtesy of Brigitta Guggolz, Germany.

(a) The dog under observation is tethered to a tree or wagon near a rucksack containing a piece of small game, e.g., rabbit. The test agitator approaches the dog to promote a protective response.

(b) The dog passes the test when it displays a natural protective behavior (result= WG 2), or avoids the person testing without showing specific fear (result=WG 1). The dog fails (result=WG 0) when it exhibits fright, fear biting, or aggressiveness.

(at least 14 hours). For the JGHV Blood-Tracking Test, the track is at least 1,000 meters long and aged 20 or 40 hours.

- An *Optional dead game bayer* (Totverbeller) must track off lead during the additional 200-meter portion of the track. Upon finding the dead animal, the dog must remain beside the game while barking loudly for a minimum of 10 minutes to bring the handler to the site.

- An *Optional dead game guide* (Totverweiser) must also track off lead for the additional 200-meters. Upon finding the dead animal, the dog must flip the 5-inch leather thong (Bringsel) attached to its collar into its mouth to communicate that it has

located the game. The dog must quickly return to and then guide the handler to the deer. The two optional methods are highly esteemed and add great value to the dog's hunting versatility.

Association Blood Tracking Examination

The Verbands Schweiss Prüfung (VSwP) is a separate blood-tracking test that is conducted by the JGHV and its member clubs. The manmade blood trail is a minimum of 1 kilometer (1,000 meters) long, using a ¼ liter of Wildschweiss: The literal translation of Schweiss is sweat or perspiration; in hunting language it means blood from game when it becomes visible. Cloven-hooved game is prescribed in preparation of this examination. The two levels of difficulty are based on the different ages of the tracks, a minimum of 20 or 40 hours old. Degrees of performance are rated: I = very good, no correction; II = good, 1 correction; III = passing, two corrections. A gun dog under test cannot pass when corrected a third time. It can conceivably pass more than one VSwP.

Breed Show/Zuchtschau

In addition to the hunting-performance categories, the Weimaraner's conformation, coat quality, and its soundness of character are assessed as prerequisites to qualify for breeding.

Breed Show/Conformation

Licensed conformation judges are recommended by the state groups and nominated by the German All-Breed Dog Association (Verband für das Deutsche Hundewesen [VDH]). Before nomination, the candidate must assist with judging at sanctioned shows, pass a test conducted by the VDH, and participate in the ongoing training program. To guarantee consistent assessment, the number of approved judges is kept small, and all continue formal training on a regular basis.

During a breed club show, a group of dogs is examined by one judge. Apprentices may assist with the judging, and their opinion may be solicited; however, the official rating is given by the approved judge.

In addition to passing the performance tests, Weimaraners must meet conformation standards to qualify for breeding (see the FCI standard in Appendix A).

To standardize conformation judging with other clubs affiliated with the VDH and FCI, some changes went into effect in November 1986. Conformation ratings are now given to Weimaraners that are at least 9 months old in a youth class and to those at least 15 months old in an adult class.

Every dog can be examined in the youth class and in the adult class one time, and each evaluation is entered on the pedigree. The ratings may be done only when the organization holding the event is in possession of the dog's pedigree, because the rating results are placed immediately on the pedigree when the dog is examined. Weimaraners must receive a minimum rating of good to qualify for breeding.

German and other European show championships are so different than American that there simply are no analogies, no basis for comparison. The FCI and show titles are explained in Chapter 34.

Examination for Character, Temperament, and Protection (Wesenstest)

The Weimaraner's protectiveness is a distinctive and highly valued breed characteristic. The objective is to evaluate the dog's strength of character and response to provocation.

Soundness of character (Wesensfestigkeit) is one of the most important breeding qualifications for Weimaraners. It is evaluated by observing the dog during various events such as hunting tests, breed shows, and a specific test developed for this purpose.

This examination consists of two parts:

1. *Test with an Object* (Wesenstest Gegenstand=WG)

In the first part, the behavior of the dog is evaluated when placed beside an object, e.g., a rucksack containing some type of small game such as a rabbit.

The dog passes the test when it displays a natural protective behavior (result=WG 2), or avoids the person testing without showing specific fear (result = WG 1). The dog fails (result = WG 0) when it exhibits fright, fear biting, or aggressiveness.

2. *Test with the Handler* (Wesenstest=WF)

During the second part, about 12 persons form a wide and later on a closed circle. During various sequences both in and outside the circle, the dog has to behave with self-assurance and neutral behavior toward strangers and show no fear or aggressiveness. The dog passes this part of the test (result=WF 1) when it meets each challenge in an unimpressed manner.

Any kind of uncertainty, fright, fear-biting, or aggressiveness against strangers is absolutely not desired, and the dog fails (result=WF 0) if it displays any of these traits.

Breeding permission is only granted if the dog has passed both parts of the test. It is excluded if it receives a rating of 0 in either portion.

This test may be repeated under special conditions.

Figure 35-36: *Test with the handler (Wesenstest = WF).* Photographs courtesy of Brigitta Guggolz, Germany.

(a) *Test with the handler in the circle (Wesenstest im Kreis=WF).* During the second part of the test for character, protection, and temperament, about 12 persons form a wide and later on a closed circle.

(b) *Test with the handler outside the circle (Wesenstest von aussen Kreis=WF).* During various sequences both in and outside the circle, the dog has to behave with self-assurance and neutral behavior toward strangers and show no fear or aggressiveness.

(c) *Test with the handler in the circle (Wesenstest im Kreis=WF).* The dog passes this part of the test (results=WF 1) when it meets each challenge in an unimpressed manner. Any kind of uncertainty, fright, fear-biting, or aggressiveness against strangers is absolutely not desired, and the dog fails (results=WF 0) if it displays any of these traits.

Figure 35-37: *An American wedding in Austria.* When American Weimaraner fanciers Sal and Laurie Casteneda chose to have their wedding in Austria, their friends Tanja and Ronja were honored to be their flower girls. June 7, 2002. Photograph courtesy of Brigitta Guggolz, Germany.

Understanding a German Pedigree

The *certified pedigree* (Ahnentafel) is also the Weimaraner's formal registration certificate. The first page of the pedigree states that the document is a certified pedigree only if it contains the official stamp and signature of the official in charge of the studbook. Beneath the club emblem, one may find the stamps of the FCI, VDH, and JGHV, without which the pedigree is not valid, as well as the club motto. Identification includes the following: registered name, whelping date, sex, coat type, color, markings, breeder, and registration number/year of birth.

The second and third pages provide the three-generation pedigree, with a key to the abbreviations in a fourth column. The multiple lines under each name provide an amazing amount of information referred to in the abbreviation descriptions.

Line 1 displays the registered name. Line 2 provides the registration number/year whelped, DGStB number, and possible small color/coat faults, e.g., little white stripe. Lines 3, 4, and

sometimes 5 contain the conformation, and coat quality and color, plus all the performance information.

The fourth page of the pedigree is used for many things.

- The first two lines on top of the page provide the date when the litter was inspected and tattooed and the name and function of the person who performed this service.

- The following four lines are reserved to record transfer of ownership.

- The pedigree is taken to all examinations and shows, and organizations sponsoring the events place an identifying stamp on the page, adding the date, test, score, and official signature by hand. The pedigree is returned to the owner on the same day.

- After the dog's hips have been X-rayed, usually following the VJP, the veterinarian forwards the X-ray to the practice of Dr. Stief, official veterinarian for the Weimaraner Klub e. V. (HD-Auswertungsstelle des Weimaraner Klub e.V.). The X-rays are evaluated for approval. After the dog's hips have been rated by the official veterinarian, the result is sent to the breed regulator. A copy is also provided to the veterinarian who took the X-ray, and a certification form is sent to the owner. The owner then has the veterinarian sign and date the stamp HD with the HD result on page 4 of the pedigree.

Table 35-5: *Litter Results from 1984–2008*

Year	Total number of puppies whelped (long + shorthaired)	Number of longhaired puppies whelped
1984	253	23
1986	287	27
1988	216	44
1990	222	70
1992	345	109
1994	407	151
1995	467	136
1996	441	109
1997	471	163
1998	541	151
1999	548	168
2000	499	146
2001	577	161
2002	606	132
2003	633	166
2004	573	167
2005	657	141
2006	656	161
2007	633	171
2008	567	139

Data courtesy of Heinrich Giesemann, Weimaraner Klub e. V. Breeding Regulator.

The German pedigree provides extensive information about the dog's heritage. The typical American pedigree, copied by the breeder on a commercial form, rarely gives more than names and champions and occasionally obedience and WCA ratings. For a fee, a certified AKC pedigree may be obtained, but it gives only names, AKC titles, and registration numbers. Additional information about the dog's qualities must be learned from the breeder, other individuals who have known them, and research in WCA literature.

Analysis of a typical German pedigree illustrates how much information is condensed on to the pedigree form. Armed with the abbreviations, a great deal can be learned from the sample pedigree about the ancestors of Paulette vom Vosstruben (Polly).

The conformation/coat rating is given in a consistent format style. For example, Odette vom Vosstruben is awarded the conformation/coat value of excellent (v/v=v). There are no long-haired Weimaraners in the pedigree.

Beginning with the Sire in Box 1 of our example, Balu vom Moosdobl was whelped during the breeding period 2002, which extended from October 1, 2002 to September 30, 2003. The name beginning with the letter B identifies him as one of the second litter bred by the Moosdobl kennel. His conformation and coat are rated in the consistent format. Balu received excellent (v/v=v); his color is deer-gray, and a glance at his parents and grandparents shows that all are acceptable shades gray. There is a number following Balu's registration number on Line 2, identifying him as one of the elite that have passed the extremely difficult VGP examination. Ideally, the club prefers that both parents qualify in this 2-day master hunting test. Polly's sire and dam have done so. This proof is stamped on the bottom of the first page of the pedigree (Aus VGP-geprüftem Eltern). It is interesting to note that every dog in Polly's three-generation pedigree has earned the VGP title. Some of these were earned in Austria = ÖVGP. Balu qualified in the VGP on a second examination with a score of G327/prize1. The initials ÜF indicate

he successfully completed the overnight blood track. Balu qualified in the test titled Rigorous Toward Predators, indicated by HN. He gives voice when trailing game that is within sight (sichtlaut). The abbreviation Sw I/ means Balu achieved an organization blood-tracking test with a prize one in a 20-hour blood track.

The dam, Odette vom Vosstruben, in Box 2, was whelped during the breeding period 2001/2002, from the 15th litter bred by Vosstruben kennel. Once again, you will

Figure 35-38: *Examples of a recent Weimaraner Klub e. V. three-Generation Pedigree/Registration* for Paulette vom Vosstruben. Courtesy of the Weimaraner Klub e. V.

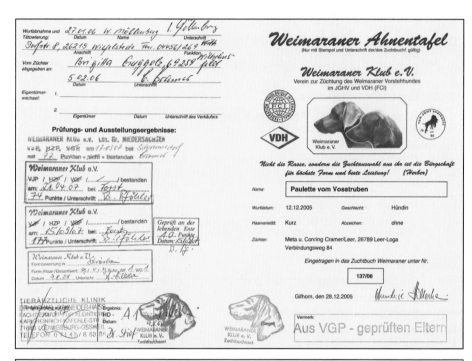

Abbreviations for German Hunting Pedigrees

Vater	Sire
Mutter	Dam
ZbNr	Breedbook Number
DGStB	Registered Number in the German Studbook or Hunting Dog Register (for recording performance, certifying and publishing) **Red number** recorded for successful completion of the **VGP**
CACIB	Certificat d'Aptitude au Championat International de Beaut *A Conformation Championship Certificate issued by the FCI International Breed Shows*
	The Weimaraner belongs to Group 7–Sporting Dogs. All entries for nominations must have proof of hunting test qualification
CACIT	Cetificat d'Aptitude au Championat International de Travail *A Working Championship Certificate issued by the FCI*

Dogs Appearing in Pedigree with Foreign Breed Book Registration:

DDR	Eingetragen im Zuchtbuch der Deutschen Demokratischen Republik (DDR)
CLP	Eingetragen im Zuchtbuch die Czech und Slovak Republiken.
ÖHZB	Eingetragen im Zuchtbuch Austria

Conformation/Coat Quality (Formwert/Haarwert)–
separate ratings indicated by a slash (/)
Examples:

v/sg	(vorzüglich) excellent/(sehr gut) very good
g/sg	(gut) good/(sehr gut) very good
ggd/ nggd	(genügend) sufficient/(nicht genügend) insufficient, not sufficient, or unsatisfactory
(J)	(Jugend) Youth conformation/coat rating from 9–15 months. This rating is no longer necessary. A dog under 15 months can also get a "v".

Color/Coat Type

mgr	(mausgrau) mouse gray (very dark gray)
sgr	(silbergrau) silver gray
hrgr	(helles rehgrau) light deer-gray
drgr	(dunkles rehgrau) dark deer-gray
K	(Kurzhaar) shorthair (SH)
L	(Langhaar) longhair (LH)
LK	(Langhaar) out of longhair × shorthair, or only shorthair parents.
LV	(Langhaarvererber) LH carrier. Not an officially recognized coat designation.
ST	(Stockhaar) Stockhaar is a product of longhair × shorthair. No an officially recognized coat designation.

Performance Tests/German Hunting Dog Association

JGHV	(Jagdgebrauchshundverband) German Hunting Dog Association
J	(Verbands-Jugend-Prüfung) Natural Ability Youth Test—followed by either (a) Point score (present style) or (b) Prize 1, 2, or 3 (old style)
H	(Verbands-Herbstzucht-Prüfung) Advanced Natural Ability or Fall Breeding Test—followed by point (or prize) rating
AZP	Breed Examination [dogs granted special permission to test when exceeding the maximum age of 24 months]—no longer applicable to Weimaraners.
G	(Verbands-Gebrauchs-Prüfung) 2-Day Master's Performance Examination—followed by prize rating: dogs passing the VGP receive a special number in the German Versatile Hunting Dog Register, which appears in red (rote Nummer) to the right of the regular registration number.

Supplemental Tests

Vbr.	(Verlorenbringernachweis) Lost Game Retrieval during a Natural Blood Trail Examination
Btr.	(Bringtreueprüfung) Retrieving Reliability Examination
sil	(sichtlaut) Gives voice when game sighted
st	(stumm) Does not give voice, silent
spl	(spurlaut) Gives voice when on game scent track

Wesenstest
Evaluation of soundness of temperment/character/protection

WG	(Gegenstand) Object
WF	(Kreis) Circle
Totverb.	(Totverbeller) Barks to guide handle to dead game
Totverw.	(Totverweiser) Carries leather thong in mouth to indicate dead game found at end of blood track, guides handler to game
AH	(Armbruster-Haltabzeichen) Armbruster Halt Award
HN	(Härtenachweis) (/) The justified killing of predatory game, feral cats, and raccoons, for the purpose of game protection is a duty of hunters with firearms. Provided a hunting dog caught and killed one of these predators before a shot was possible, is also considered an act of justified conservation hunting.
LN	(Lautjagernachweis) (/) During the VJP, HZP or VGP, if a gun dog barks on the track of a fox or hare, it earns the LN title. This title may also be earned during the hunt, or if the gun dog gives voice during the Stöbern = Search in the woods while performing in a VGP.

Lawinenhundprüfung
Dogs achieving this title are specially trained in Search and Rescue work to locate persons buried in avalanches. Very few Weimaraners have earned this prestigious title.

SchH1, 2, 3
(Schutzhundeprüfung/Stufe) Protection Dog Test
Stufe refers to the three grade levels in this test.

Bloodtracking

VSwP	(Verbands-Schweissprüfung) Association Blood-Tracking Examination Variations in abbreviations are found on the pedigree; all represent important differences.
SWI/, SWII/, SWIII/	Roman numeral represents prize 1, 2, or 3: slash (/) following numeral indicates track at least 20 hours old.
SW/I, SW/I, SW/II	Roman numeral represents prize 1, 2, or 3; slash (/) preceding numeral indicates track at least 40 hours old.
SWI/I	Roman numeral represents prize 1, 2, or 3; slash (/) between numerals indicates dog qualified on both 20- and 40-hour blood tracks.
SchwP	(Vereins-Schweissprüfung) Club Blood-Tracking Examination. Similar rating procedures apply. The dog does not need the proof of a Laut (sichtlaut or spurlaut), as it does for the Association Test.
ÜF	(Übernachtfärhte) A more difficult overnight blood track, aged over 14 hours
TF	(Tagfährte) Not an overnight blood track, aged over 2 to 5 hours
Schw.N	(Schweiss Natur) a real (natural) blood track
(Schw.N)	(Schweiss Natur am Schalenwild) a real blood track used for tracking a weak cloven-hooved game animal.

find a number following her registration number on Line 2, identifying her as one of the elite that have passed the extremely difficult VGP examination. The G310/2 ÜF on Line 4 indicates Odette received a Prize 2. She also completed an overnight blood track. Odette's conformation and coat quality are excellent and color deer-gray. All of her predecessors appear in various shades of gray. Odette gives voice when trailing game that is out of sight (spurlaut). This trait is highly valued by the Weimaraner breeder.

Two puppies from the P-Litter vom Vosstruben (Polly and Paula) confirmed their spur- and sichtlaut traits during an early VJP 2007, while two other littermates (Paco and Paul) earned their individual sichtlaut traits during the VJP 2007.

Going on to Box 3 of the paternal grand-sire, Falk von Aeskulap was from Aeskulap's 6th litter, which was whelped during the breeding period 1995/1996. His conformation was rated overall very good (sg). Falk achieved exceptional

Figure 35-40: *Infotan vom Zehnthof protects game* and the rucksack. Photograph courtesy of the Weimaraner Klub e. V.

scores after qualifying in three VGP examinations held in Austria (ÖVGP338/3c, ÖVGP397/1d, ÖVGP399/1a). He improved his score each time. He missed performing in the youth test and fall breeding test and was allowed to participate in the alternate breed test (AP). The AP is no longer conducted.

As we look at Box 6 of the maternal grand-dam, Freya vom Entenstrich was born during the breeding period 1995/1996. She qualified in two VJP examinations with scores of 71 and 74 points out of a maximum of 80 points, apparently improving her performance on the second try. She received 186 and 184 points out of a maximum of 198 points (without subject hare track) in the HZP. These are exceptional scores for both tests, resulting in the judges' writing special comments on the dog's score sheet. Freya earned a prize III in the organization blood-tracking test (SW III/). The roman numeral indicates the prize (1, 2, or 3); slash (/) between numerals indicates dog qualified on a 20-hour track. This test is further explained in the table titled Abbreviations on German Pedigrees.

Skipping to several other interesting items in the pedigree, Graf von der Kampfheide (Box 11) successfully passed the Verlorenbringen and Bringtreueprüfung ratings. He is also rated sicht- and spurlaut. Ben von der Wartelshöhe (Box 5) proved to give voice while hunting and passed the VGP earning 331 points/prize 1. He worked the last 200 meters of the overnight blood track off line, qualifying him as a dead game guide (Totverweiser). This noteworthy skill is an optional 200-meter part in addition to the 400-meter artificial blood-tracking subject; both are explained in the VGP table.

In all, German pedigrees indicate a great emphasis on the breed's working qualities. Although dog shows are not of much interest, conformation must meet minimum standards. All individuals on the pedigree are free of hip dysplasia and many other hereditary disorders.

Figure 35-39: *Commemorating a hunt from 50 years ago,* a proud hunter and his Weimaraner display a magnificent *red deer stag* (Rothirsch).

THE GERMAN HUNTING TRADITIONS AND HUNTING PRACTICES PAST TO PRESENT

Contributed by K. Wilhelm Döring and W. Krannich, Germany (2009)

1. The practical methods and forms of hunting have not really changed over the past 50 years.

2. Since 1936, Germany, Austria and parts of Northern Italy (South Tirol) have observed nearly the same hunting methods, identical hunting laws, and especially *hunting territorial structures* ("Reviersystem").

3. Overall, Germany has the strictest hunting laws worldwide pertaining to hunting in the wild.

4. The species of wild game animals that may be hunted has been restricted. Various species, in particular, birds of prey (e.g., buzzard and goshawk), as well as quail, partridge and jays, are completely removed from the possible hunting game list. The hunting quota has been drastically reduced through limiting the shooting seasons due to population reduction (e.g., hare).

5. Among wild animals subject to *big-game hunting* ("Hohe Jagd"), the population of wild boar has, in some German states, multiplied by 20 times. In this situation, the ecological hunting associations, respectively, the agriculture and the "Green" politicians, are planning to reduce this game increase by organized "police hunts" and feeding the "birth control pill" to the wild boars.

6. The fallow deer and red deer populations are being consciously and deliberately reduced in certain regions.

7. Sika deer (cervus Nippon) are managed only in selected areas.

8. Chamois deer are managed only in the medium mountains (e.g., Black Forest) and in the high mountain ranges (Alps).

9. Mouflon is only managed in selected habitats, that are particularly suitable.

10. The species of game, noted under points 6–9, have an established harvest plan, differentiating between male/female and youth and age categories. Age sub-categories additionally differentiate even further in terms of strength-condition, weight-/quality+, and age steps.

11. Currently, there is an increase in the number of small, private animal parks as recreational facilities. The parks are certified by Government officials applying strict guidelines. The facilities must meet species-appropriate requirements and undergo continuous, strictly enforced inspections.

12. Game reserves per se are generally not very widespread in Germany. There are certain National Parks, for example *Bavarian Forest* ("Bayrischer Wald"), *Keller Forest* ("Kellerwald"), and the coast of the *North* and *East Sea* ("Wattenmeer"), where nature has been put under special protection in general and hunting is forbidden or only allowed with special restricted permits. In rule, individual selection hunting on a case-by-case basis may be allowed.

13. The re-settlement of lynx and wolves as wild game is addressed in a specific effort, but they are under annual hunting protection.

14. European bison and moose are emigrating from the east and are well-liked by nature lovers and hunters. These animals may not be hunted.

15. Feeding of wild game is only allowed during severe hunger periods and under special provisions.

16. The German *hunting season* (Jagdzeit) is associated with the *baiting* (Kirrung) of wild boar. (The term "Kirrung" means to feed at certain locations in order to selectively hunt, therefore reducing overpopulation. It also prevents field damage to agricultural industry.)

17. Furthermore, the Federal Hunting Law permits "supplemental or spot feeding" (without hunting in a certain radius around the feeding stations and spatial distance from agricultural land) to reduce or completely eliminate the agricultural damages wild animals cause to the farming industry and to a lesser extent in Forestry management.

18. It is generally prohibited to abandon or capture wild game. Animal orphans, mostly caused by vehicular accidents, are often nursed by hunters or other nature lovers. The orphans are generally turned over to animal zoos or returned to wildlife after their recovery. This procedure has been in place for some time. It must be mentioned though, that the control of the species treatment in this case has become stricter. In certain known cases, treatment is specifically monitored by official organizations.

19. Generally, a shortage or depletion of wild game is not mentioned. Numbers of game animals are managed deliberately, because in densely populated Germany, only limited space is available.

20. Therefore, hunting types and methods have partly changed. Stationary hunts, individual hunts, and drive hunts are practiced more and more to hunt wild boar and now include red and roe deer. By using these methods, it is expected to hunt successfully with a minimum of effort required. It is especially true also, because the use of economic forestry management has changed its format. There is more and more natural growth with mostly young brush, and natural development. Hunting is becoming more difficult without dogs or drivers!!!

Figure 35-41: *A convenient seat is a must for the spectator* at a German Performance test. Unlike American events, where spectators may sometimes ride on horseback or assemble and wait at a headquarters site until their dog is called, spectators and handlers at the German events traditionally observe the testing of all the dogs from a convenient vantage point. This onlooker's walking stick conveniently converts to a perch, which with a little practice, provides a comfortable seat from which to watch the events. Reprinted, with permission, from Deborah Andrews, *The Weimaraner Memory Book,* 2003.

Conclusion

Understanding the special hunting conditions in the Weimaraner's native country clarifies the breed's versatility as well as the continued emphasis on performance examinations, which are required of all German hunting breeds. Clearly, bird hunting is only one aspect of the Weimaraner's hunting talents. Conformation is valued as an aspect that contributes to the breed's performance.

Many Americans regard the German control of breeding as ideal, but several things must be kept in perspective. Owing to Germany's smaller area and Weimaraner population, close supervision is realistically manageable. With an average of 80 to 90 litters per year (from breeding periods 2001 to 2008), an established tradition and the willingness of Germans to accept the decisions of the breed regulator for all breeding plans is understandable. It would be unrealistic to attempt a comparable program in the United States. In area to be supervised alone, no single breed regulator could manage the job. In addition, Americans have an established tradition of independence in the selection of sires and dams.

It is unfortunate, in many ways, that the AKC classified the Weimaraner as a pointing breed, rendering it ineligible to compete in retrieving trials and trailing hound trials. The interests and objectives of American Weimaraner fanciers are fragmented into show, obedience, tracking, retrieving, and field trials. Many American owners are successful in AKC tracking tests, which are open to all breeds. A few have successfully participated in Schutzhund work, a non-AKC examination for working dogs. Because the objectives of the NAVHDA tests are similar to those of the JGHV, many American Weimaraner fanciers are developing a greater interest in testing and hunting their dogs. The JGHV-affiliated German Drahthaar Group–North America organizes German breed tests throughout the U.S. and is open to other versatile gun dog breeds.

Figure 35-42: *The Weimaraner remains a valuable tool* in managing game throughout Europe today; in AKC venues the talents of the Weimaraner are limited to the bird field, but in Europe the Weimaraners abilities to track vermin, pests, and wounded game as well as retrieving smaller game are highly prized. This red stag provided a memorable hunt in Hungary. Left to right: David Secord, Peter Koch and Paul Misch. Photograph courtesy of David Secord.

Figure 36-1: ***Because so many great Weimaraners have come to and from America*** it was impossible to select a single dog to honor on the overleaf of this chapter. Instead, at the suggestion of William Wegman, we chose to salute the spirit of all the Weimaraner's who have traveled with us, sharing the special qualities of the grey ghost throughout the world. ***Puppies in suitcase,*** by William Wegman.

CHAPTER 36

THE INFLUENCE OF AMERICAN IMPORTS AND EXPORTS

by Patricia Riley

The earliest owners of the Weimaraner treasured their dogs for their talents and abilities; those same traits make the Weimaraner loved and admired today. The modern fancier has many advantages that the earliest breeders never dreamed of: the knowledge of genetics and the advent of world travel. With these tools fanciers around the world have access, not only to bloodlines, but to information as well. While the basic palette is the same—a medium-sized grey dog of prodigious hunting talent and a special bond with humans—Weimaraner admirers around the world find that the "perfect dog on the hill" can appear somewhat different if that hill is in a different country. This chapter will focus on American dogs that have been exported or imported and the impact these exchanges have had on American bloodlines, and conversely, the results of exporting American dogs to other countries.

The early Germans emphasized working ability over type, and as a result of different interpretations and the passage of time, the appearance of Weimaraners may vary, but those disparities are no greater between countries than within those countries with large enough populations to support a wide variety of bloodlines. However some basic differences do become apparent in obvious traits… for example, the set of the tail has had a strong influence on the silhouette of the dog; in America, a higher tail set may produce a winning appearance when the tail is docked, but that same attribute in another country may result in a tail that curls unattractively over the topline when left naturally intact (see Figure 4-28). Some faults considered insignificant one country may take on greater significance in another; the WCA standard allows up to four missing teeth before it is considered a major fault, whereas in Germany missing more than two teeth is a severe fault, resulting in a restriction of breeding privileges.

The American standard differs from other standards around the world in two significant aspects regarding the length and color of the Weimaraner coat. First, only the U.S. and (recently) Canadian standards, even mention the blue Weimaraner, as a disqualifying trait; it is apparently a uniquely North American issue. Second, since the Canadians have in recent years accepted the longhaired Weimaraner, the U.S. is apparently now the only country in the world that specifically disqualifies the trait.

In addition to differences in standards, the requirements for titles vary from country to country. Not only does the vision of what the perfect dog looks like differ, but how the dog looks when working differs as well. As an example, field trial competitors in Iceland accustomed to the dog flushing the bird would be surprised at a U.S. field trial where the dog must be steady until the handler flushes and shoots the bird, and finally releases the dog to retrieve. Obedience competitors

Figure 36-2: *Differences in standards may determine* where a dog will be most successful. A surprise from his short-haired parents, Maxi von der Reiteralm's longhair would disqualify him from conformation competition in the U.S., so he was given as a gift to Wolfgang Schypkowski. Maxi would go on to earn his working titles and breeding privileges, and to support the German breeding program by contributing fresh genetic material. Maxi and two hunting companions, with Wolfgang and the results of the day's hunt. Courtesy of the *Weimaraner Memory Book*, 2003.

Figure 36-3: *The standard of performance in the field also varies* from country to country. In Iceland, Silva (an American import out of two well-known FCs) establishes point on the well-camouflaged ptarmigan (a variety of cold weather grouse). After the hunter positions himself, the dog is commanded to flush the bird. The dog then retrieves the fallen bird to hand. In order to become a conformation champion, the Icelandic Weimaraner must also pass a hunting certification. In recent years, it has become imperative that all exhibitors are familiar with local laws regarding the docking of tails. In some countries, entry of docked-tailed dogs is forbidden, regardless of the reason for entry or for the docking. Conversely, when importing dogs from other countries, the buyer should ask if the pup will have its tail docked at the appropriate time.

traveling between England and the U.S. would find that the ideal heel position for the British competition ring, where the dog's head is in actual contact with the handler's leg, would earn quite a number of lost points for bumping or interfering in a U.S. ring. Agility exhibitors would find that although the equipment is the same, the design style of the courses are quite different from those typically found in the U.S.

In recent years it have become imperative that all exhibitors are familiar with local laws regarding the docking of tails, in some countries entry of docked tailed dogs is forbidden, regardless of the reason for entry or for the docking. Conversely when importing dogs from foreign countries the buyer should query if the pup will have its tail docked at the appropriate time.

Conformation Championship Titles
Basic Systems

Requirements for earning conformation championship titles differ in every country, but the most common are variations of two basic systems—points or challenge certificates.

FOREIGN KENNEL CLUBS

The address and additional information about kennel clubs for many foreign countries can be obtained through the AKC's website: **www.akc.org**

The point system is familiar to Americans—points are determined by the number of opponents defeated. Challenge certificates, more commonly seen elsewhere, are awarded only to dogs that, in the judge's opinion, are worthy of becoming champions, and are earned regardless of the number of dogs competing. Further complicating matters, some countries also require a Weimaraner to demonstrate field aptitude in addition to acquiring the necessary points or certificates in order to complete a conformation championship.

The Federation Cynologique Internationale (FCI)

The FCI, headquartered in Thuin, Belgium, is unique in its international jurisdiction over affiliated national kennel clubs in 84 countries; as such it is, like the AKC, a "club of clubs." The FCI does have a reciprocity agreement to recognize registrations of unaffiliated national kennel clubs such as the American Kennel Club and the Canadian Kennel Club. Unlike the AKC, the FCI is not a registry, but rather acts only as a records center for processing conformation and working titles earned though its affiliates. The FCI provides uniform breed standards and translations used by all FCI affiliates and keeps a list of internationally licensed judges. The FCI provides a registry of kennel names at the international level and provides an international calendar of events. From there, similarities decrease, and the relationships become complex. More information is available from the website *www.fci.be*

Although all affiliated national kennel clubs comply with basic FCI show regulations, each national club may also determine the requirements for championship titles in that country; thus, there are as many championships as there are

---

NATIONAL KENNEL CLUBS AFFILIATED WITH THE FCI
Federated Members

Argentina	Estonia	Lithuania	Republic Dominicana
Australia	Finland	Luxumburg	Republic of Korea
Austria	France	Macedonia	Romania
Azerbaijan	Georgia	Malaysia	Russia
Bahrain	Germany	Malta	San Marino
Belgium	Gibralter	Mexico	Serbia
Bolivia	Greece	Moldavia	Singapore
Brazil	Guatemala	Montenegro	Slovakia
Bulgaria	Honduras	Morocco	Slovenia
Byelorussia	Hong Kong	Monaco	South Africa
Chile	Hungary	Netherlands	Spain
China	Iceland	New Zealand	Sri Lanka
Colombia	India	Nicaragua	Sweden
Costa Rica	Indonesia	Norway	Switzerland
Croatia	Ireland	Panama	Taiwan
Cuba	Israel	Paraguay	Thailand
Cyprus	Italy	Peru	Ukraine
Czechia	Japan	Philippines	Uraguay
Denmark	Kazakhstan	Poland	Uzbekistan
Ecuador	Kyrgyzstan	Portugal	Venezuela
El Salvador	Latvia	Puerto Rico	

FCI RELATIONSHIPS WITH NATIONAL KENNEL CLUBS AND OTHER GERMAN ORGANIZATIONS

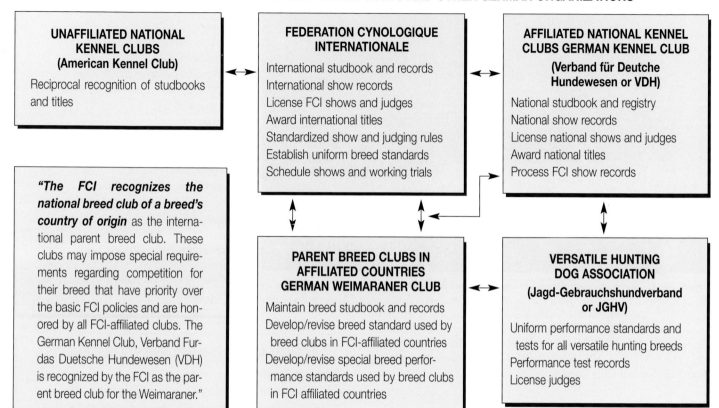

UNAFFILIATED NATIONAL KENNEL CLUBS
(American Kennel Club)

Reciprocal recognition of studbooks and titles

FEDERATION CYNOLOGIQUE INTERNATIONALE

International studbook and records
International show records
License FCI shows and judges
Award international titles
Standardized show and judging rules
Establish uniform breed standards
Schedule shows and working trials

AFFILIATED NATIONAL KENNEL CLUBS GERMAN KENNEL CLUB
(Verband für Deutche Hundewesen or VDH)

National studbook and registry
National show records
License national shows and judges
Award national titles
Process FCI show records

"The FCI recognizes the national breed club of a breed's country of origin as the international parent breed club. These clubs may impose special requirements regarding competition for their breed that have priority over the basic FCI policies and are honored by all FCI-affiliated clubs. The German Kennel Club, Verband Fur-das Duetsche Hundewesen (VDH) is recognized by the FCI as the parent breed club for the Weimaraner."

PARENT BREED CLUBS IN AFFILIATED COUNTRIES GERMAN WEIMARANER CLUB

Maintain breed studbook and records
Develop/revise breed standard used by breed clubs in FCI-affiliated countries
Develop/revise special breed performance standards used by breed clubs in FCI affiliated countries

VERSATILE HUNTING DOG ASSOCIATION
(Jagd-Gebrauchshundverband or JGHV)

Uniform performance standards and tests for all versatile hunting breeds
Performance test records
License judges

countries, all with slightly different requirements. While most countries have a certain minimum age at which a dog can compete, and all joint FCI-CACIB/CAC shows will comply with these restrictions, some countries have a different minimum age at which the dog can earn points towards the championships at CAC-only shows (refer to the FCI Show Regulations on the website). In Australia, puppies as young as three months may compete; however, challenge certificates can be earned only when the dog is a year or older. Luxembourg holds only two major CACIB shows each year and requires only two CACs for a championship. The most prestigious title awarded by the FCI is the International Champion, which requires a dog to earn two CACIBs under two different jduges in two different ocuntries, as well as a working qualification. In 1999, the FCI rules were changed to allow dogs in certain countries to earn a the title of International Champion by inviting foreign judges into the country to judge rather than sending the dog out. However, because there are many organizations other than the FCI around the world, whenever the title of International Champion appears before a dog's name, it would be worthwhile to inquire about the awarding organization and its requirements.

The FCI recognizes the national breed club of a breed's country as the club responsible for the standard of that breed. Among FCI affiliates, these enjoy a special position. The German Weimaraner Club, for example, may decide on amendments of the breed standard that are honored in all FCI-affiliated countries.

Just as there are other registries in the United States, such as the States Kennel Club, the United Kennel Club, and the International All-Breed Kennel Club, many countries have several large show-sponsoring organizations that are not affiliated with the FCI; exhibitors should inquire which registry is sponsoring the show. While living in Germany, Ben and Kelly Lovejoy entered Luger (Silversmith Harbor Pistol) in some German shows and he compiled an impressive show record in just 5 months, winning first prize in all-breed classes, titles as National and International Beauty Champion, and even an all-breed Best in Show. Only then did the Lovejoys discover that the DKZ (Deutsche Kynologische Zuchtgemeinshaft e. V.), which sponsored the shows was not an FCI affiliate. Undaunted, the Lovejoy's began entering Luger in FCI shows, and he finished his FCI title.

Attending a show or two in advance will give the exhibitor a chance to learn the ring protocol for the style of show. Americans might be quite surprised at how much less formal the ring judging may be in some countries.

The German Kennel Club
An FCI affiliated National Kennel Club

The Verband für das Deutsche Hundewesen (VDH), or German Kennel Club, has headquarters in Dortmund, where

Figure 36-4: *There are many show sponsoring organizations elsewhere,* just as there are in the U.S. After a blazing success in a series of shows, the Lovejoy's discovered Luger wasn't earning points towards the FCI title they hoped for. Luger would go on to become Int. Am. CH Silversmith Harbor Pistol (Am. CH Silversmith Harbor Pilot, CD, NSD, V × Am. CH Silversmith Omni v. Reiteralm, CD, TD, NSD, RD, VX, BROM). Bred by Elena and Allen Smith; owned by Ben and Kelly Lovejoy.

it maintains its national studbook. In addition to coordinating activities of parent breed clubs, it oversees group organizations such as the German Versatile Hunting Dog Association, better known as the JGHV. Like the AKC, the VDH licenses shows and judges, and processes show records; unlike the AKC, the VDH sends the list of CACIB earned at FCI international shows on to the FCI. Also refer to The German Weimaraner Today for more information on conformation and testing in Germany or visit *www.vdh.de*

Show Organization and Awards

Shows that are licensed by the VDH award certificates called Certificat d'Aptitude au Championnat (CAC), which may be applied toward the requirements of a German championship. The CAC is for national championships only; a CAC earned in the Netherlands, for example, may be applied only toward a championship in that country. Shows that are licensed by both FCI and VDH award Certificat d'Aptitude au Championat International de Beauté de la FCI (CACIB), which are applied toward the FCI title and the VDH title, and CACs. As in the United States, there are all-breed shows, with Group and Best in Show judging, and breed specialty shows. Thus, German Weimaraners may compete in the four different types of shows listed.

The judge's written evaluation of each dog is typed up by the ring secretary; the evaluation is forwarded with the show records, and a copy is given to the owner. At FCI international shows, each entry is rated as Excellent (Vorzuglich—V), Very

---

GERMAN SHOWS AND CLASSES

Shows

FCI/VDH licensed all-breed shows: award CACIB/CAC

VDH licensed all-breed shows: award CAC only

FCI/VDH licensed breed specialty shows: award CACIB/CAC

VDH licensed breed specialty shows: award CAC only

Classes (Divided by gender)

Jüngstenklasse (puppy): 6–9 months

Jugendklasse (youth): 9–18 months

Offenen Klasse (open): over 15 months

Sieger Klasse: FCI national affiliate or international championship

Gebrauchshundklasse (utility): holder of working certificate (offered only in sporting and working breeds; type of certificate specified by parent breed club)

GERMAN AND FCI CHAMPIONSHIP REQUIREMENTS

Types of Certificates

CAC (Certificat d'Aptitude au Championat): issued by FCI

CACIB (Certificat d'Aptitude au Championat International de Beaute): issued by FCI

CACIB (Certificat d'Aptitude au Championat International de Travail): issued by FCI

German Championships: any one of the following combinations of validated certificates, with at least 12 months between the dates of the first and the last certificates:

Four CACIBs

Three CACIB and one CAC at either an all-breed or a breed specialty show

Two CACIBs and two CACs at breed specialty shows

FCI Championships: the final (or qualifying) CACIB must be awarded at least 1 years and one day after the first. A dog must be at least 15 months old to compete for a CACIB/CAC; therefore, 27 months is the youngest age a championship could be finished.

1. International Beauty Champion (Championat International de Beaute/International Schönheits Champion)—all of the following:

   Four CACIBs under at least three different judges in at least three different countries

   One CACIB must be won in the country of the owner's residence or in the home country of the parent breed club

2. International Working Champion (Championat International de Travail/International Arbeitchampionat)—all of the following:

   Two CACITs under two different judges in at least two different countries

Good (Ser Gut—SG), Good (Gut—G), sufficient, disqualified or cannot be judged. Class placements through fourth place are awarded to entries that rated excellent.

Only winners of the open, intermediate, champion, and utility (working) classes may compete for the CACIB/CAC, which is awarded to the best dog and best bitch of each breed that, in the judge's opinion, is worthy of becoming a champion; individuals rated excellent are not necessarily worthy of a title.

As in AKC shows, reserve CACIBs and CACs may also be awarded in case the winner is subsequently disqualified for incorrect entry, owner, age, and so forth. If records later show

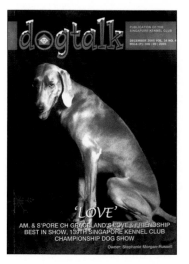

Figure 36-5: *AM and S'pore CH Graceland's Love and Friendship* (CH Bavarian Mist Flying Cloud, JH, NSD, NRD, V × CH Camelot's Jewel of Graceland, BROM). Bred by Stephanie Morgan-Russell and Susan Thomas; owned by Stephanie Morgan-Russell. Handled by Don Thames, Love earned her American Championship before moving with her owners to Singapore. The dog fancy is young in Singapore, but the participants are educated and dedicated. Love's first time out in Singapore at the end of 2004, she won Best in Show under New Zealand judge Keith Simmons. As in Europe, Sporting Dogs are called "Gun Dogs" in Singapore. Love won the Singapore Kennel Club's "Gun Dog of the Year" in 2005.

that the dog receiving the CACIB/CAC does not need the proposal to meet a championship requirement (say a French Champion competing for a German or FCI championship), the proposal is automatically passed on to the reserve winner. In some countries, four reserves can equal a CAC, but only one may be applied toward a title.

When the show records have been processed by the licensing organization, confirming correct eligibility, ownership, and so forth, verified certificates are sent to the FCI office to be processed to have CACIB cards issued. These are then sent back to the show organizer, which in turn, sends them to the owners. A verified CACIB may be applied toward titles in other affiliated national clubs.

Because verified certificates may be applied to several titles in several countries, owners must apply for the championship titles by submitting photocopies of the certified pedigree and the verified certificates to the national kennel club.

The FCI awards a special international working title, the equivalent of the CACIB on the work scene, called the CACIT, for hunting and working breeds that pass a utility test that is determined by its particular breed club as well as two CACIBs under two different judges in two different countries. There must be a time lapse of at least one year and one

Figure 36-7: *PR Int Pan Lat Am CH Graytsky's Int'l Dateline, CD, RE, NA, NAJ, V* (CH Ashmore's Win'Weim Royal Flush, JH, BROM × CH Graytsky's Stella Luna, BROM). Bred by Amy and Michael Anderson and Dana Massey; owned by Ramon and Eleanor Abarca. In recognition of the challenges some fanciers face in more isolated countries, FCI 1999 rule changes allow those fanciers in designated countries to earn International championship by competing in their home country under internationally certified judges rather than traveling to show under judges in foreign countries. Jett however, did enjoy traveling so in addition to earning her International Championship, she earned titles in AKC as well as bench championships in several other countries.

Figure 36-6: *Int Isr Cyp Rom Lux Pol Bul CH Camelot's Royal Flush* (CH Nani's Southern Cross, BROM × CH Camelot's Halley's Comet, BROM). Bred by Susan Thomas; owned by Ilana Bar-Tal. Junior European Winner 2004. Roy earned his FCI international Championship by earning four CACIB's under judges in at least three different countries. Roy certainly enjoyed traveling, earning, in addition to his International championship, bench championships in six other countries, accruing wins also as Central East European Winner Mediterranean Winner 2007, and Hungarian Club Winner 2008.

day between the dates of the two CACIBs and the utility examination. American owners of dogs competing for FCI titles may qualify for a waiver of the requirement of the time period of one year and one day time lapse. In summary, the title of International Beauty Champion for working breeds is gained by winning two CACIBs and a working qualification; the title of International Working Champion is obtained by winning two CACITs *and* a "very good" at an international FCI show.

FCI World, European, and National Championships

Many special championship titles are awarded annually by the FCI and affiliated national kennel clubs. The annual World Dog Show is held in a different FCI-affiliated country each year, and entrants compete for the coveted World Champion title (Weltsieger 20--) awarded in each breed.

An international all-breed show is held each spring at Dortmund's Westfalenhalle. After completion of the regular judging, each breed offers a class for all dogs that received a rating of excellent in the open, champion, intermerdiate, and utility classes. The winner is awarded the title European Champion Dortmund (Europaisieger Dortmund 20--) to distinguish it from similar titles awarded at other countries. In addition, all dogs rated excellent in the youth class (9–18 months) compete for the title European Youth Champion Dortmund (Europajugendsieger Dortmund 20--).

A national all-breed show is held each fall at Dortmund's Westfalenhalle. The procedure is identical, and the winners are awarded the titles of German National Champion (Deutscher Dundessieger 20--) and German National Youth Champion (Deutscher Dundesjugendsieger 20--).

Foreign Exchange

Thanks to the advent of convenient and (relatively) affordable international travel, it is becoming more common to see Weimaraners travel to compete in other countries; as well as the exchange of semen allows a stud dog to produce successful progeny around the world. Perhaps the most significant event in recent years has been the changes to the quarantine laws of many countries and the advent of an international "passport" for dogs traveling in the European Community. This section will focus on the influence or impact of "foreign exchange" in or from the United States. While it is certain that there are many more dogs that have contributed to the international scene that we are not aware of and are not represented in these pages, we regret that we have been limited to presenting only a few of the dogs that have come to our attention that have either been exported from the United States and had an impact in other countries and those imported dogs which have influenced bloodlines in the United States. As a result, it is not possible to list all of the dogs that have achieved success through "foreign exchange" efforts; rather this section is just an attempt to highlight some of the dogs that have come to our attention and acknowledge the similarities and differences of "the dog on the hill" when the hills are in different countries.

Figure 36-9: *2008 World Champion Best in Show Brace:* (front) Intrl Eur Itl Cro Am CH Nani's to Be or Not to Be, JH (CH Nani's Concert Master, SH, BROM × CH Nani's Nobodie's Patsie, JH, BROM). Bred by Chris Grisell; owned by Dario Raimondi Cominesi; (back) Am and Itl CH Nani's Outrage, JH (CH Nani's Indecent Exposure, JH, NAJ, V, BROM × CH Nani's Net Worth, JH, NJP, NSD, V). Bred by Chris Grisell; owned by Dario Raimondi Cominesi. Individually, these dogs are quite successful, (see Figures 36-72 and 36-73) but together they earned even more accolades, winning BIS at the European Champions Show in 2007, and BIS at the World Championship in 2008.

Figure 36-8: *2001 World Champion Sporting Group Winner CH Nani's James Robert* (CH Midnite Magic Von Holly Haus, BROM × CH Nani's Knockers, CDX, TD, NA, JH, SD, VX, BROM). Bred by Suzy Casper and Chris Grisell; owned by Paulina Walkowska. Robert was an older brother to Aleck (Nani's Smart Aleck) from the first breeding. He has had an exceptional show career and has set a high bar for Weimaraners in Europe.

Figure 36-10: *Exhibitors await judging of their class.* The German Zuchshau is much more casual outside the ring than most American shows. Dogs are often expected to wait patiently on a "platz" (down) command, without benefit of crates or ex-pens. Inside the ring can be equally casual where posing or stacking of the dog is discouraged. After judging, the results of each dog's individual examination is recorded for the dog's pedigree and breeding record and then announced, presenting the dogs by order of their grading. Although no championship points are granted, at such Zuchshaus the goal is to achieve a conformation rating that is required in order to be granted breeding privileges.

Germany

Germany is the native country of the beloved Weimaraner, and as such holds a special place in the hearts of Weimaraner fanciers. The United States has been truly fortunate to have established a valuable reciprocal relationship with both the German Weimaraner Club and many respected breeders in that country. Because of the established and continuing emphasis on the performance, American bloodlines have benefited from influxes of contemporary bloodlines to offer genetically and phenotypically strong stock. This exchange has been facilitated by good relations with our European friends but also by the minimal quarantine and international import-export restrictions between the two countries. This situation has resulted in continuing exchanges both to and from the United States to the Weimaraner's historic home.

Figure 36-11: *At the 75th Anniversary show in Austria,* the Weimaraner Ways trophy was presented by the author to Caruso vom Gstettenhof, bred by R. Broswimmer; owned by M. Kurz, the winner of the annual conformation championship which is similar to the WCA's National Specialty. Before dogs can enter this prestigious event, they must have qualifying credentials for temperament and field performance. Photograph courtesy of Dr. Werner Petri, *Weimaraner heute.*

German Littermates Succeed in America

Figure 36-12: *Casar vom Schelmelach, SH, SDX, NRD, NAVHDA, UTP2* (Butz vom Wiesengrund v=v,rgr, WG2, WF2, WF3, HD-B1, HN, AP103/163, FUW307/1a, ÖVGP326/3D, freundlich, ausgeglichenes, Wessen × Bella vom Wasen sg/sg=sg, mgr, rgr, WG1, WF2, HD-B1, J66, spl, HO, H172). The constant companion and therapy dog of Cynthia Picha, when time permitted they enjoyed the field. Casar is the only German import to prize in the NAVHDA UPT.

Figure 36-14: *Cora vom Schelmelach, MH, SD, NRD* (Butz vom Wiesengrund v=v,rgr, WG2, WF2, WF3, HD-B1, HN, AP103/163, FUW307/1a, ÖVGP326/3D, freundlich, ausgeglichenes, Wessen × Bella vom Wasen sg/sg=sg, mgr, rgr, WG1, WF2, HD-B1, J66, spl, HO, H172). Cora is the first and only German import to earn an AKC MH. Breedings to VC DC AFC Magnum Gunnar's Silvershot, MH, SDX, RDX, VX and DC NFC NAFC AFC Snake Breaks Saga v. Reiteralm, CD, MH, RDX, VX2, have earned Cora a pair of NAVHDA Natural Ability Breeder's Awards with their offspring earning 19 individual NAVHDA prizes.

Our Birgitta...

Figure 36-15: *Birgittta with her newest hunting companion Paulette vom Vosstruben, VJP77, HZP177, VGP 321/1, ÜF, WF1, WG1,* return from successfully tracking a small wild sow during a wild boar hunt in 2008. Photograph courtesy of Brigitta Guggolz.

Figure 36-13: *As an officer and member of the local and national German Weimaraner Club,* Birgitta Guggolz has gone well above and beyond the call of duty with her generous support to foreign Weimaraner fanciers. Welcomed assistance with the German language and customs is a given. A bouquet of roses at the airport is not a surprise. And neither is a sumptuous dinner party at her home, with notable guests that you feel privileged to meet. An avid huntress herself, Birgitta pauses beneath a display of the days hunt with her three hardworking partners: Arimarlisa Ronja v Reiteralm VJP61, WF2, Tanya vom Birkeneck VJP70, HZP176, VGP267/III, sil, WF4, and Bessie von Kohlwald ms4, VJP70, HZP180, Photograph courtesy of Debbie Andrews, *The Weimaraner Memory Book,* 2003.

An Enduring International Friendship

Figure 36-16: *Argon von Walhalla, HD-A2, sg/sg=sg, rgr, 63cm, WG2, WF1, J 76, spl, sil, H 175, G 321/1 ÜF, Btr, SwII/* (Dingo von der Schelmelach × Birke vom Erlenstoc). Bred by R. Jakob; Argon came to America to mature as a family dog. After a year, he returned to his German homeland to complete his formal training and breeding certifications. Testing completed with high marks, he was returned to his home in West Virginia to become the personal hunting dog of his forever owner Deborah Andrews. See Argon's expressive face at Figure 9-5. Photograph by Deborah Andrews.

Figure 36-18: *100 Years of Weimaraner History: The Weimaraner Memory Book,* by Deborah G. Andrews Commemorating 100 years of the Weimaraner Klub of Germany (1897–1997). English/German presentation with a wealth of illustrations. For more information visit *www.weimaraner100.com.*

Our Debbie...

Figure 36-17: *Debbie Andrews and Astor vom Kohlwald, v/sg", J 67 + 67, H 162 + 177, ms2, HD-frei, CACIB, CAC Stuttgart, NAVHDA Utility Prize II + III,* sport sprigs of oak leaves earned during the bloodtracking portion of the Brauchbarkeits-Prufing. While in Germany, Astor earned his German certifications, and once arriving in the U.S. Debbie gained many new friends for NAVHDA with Astor and qualified for the NAVHDA UT (see Figure 14-16). Photograph courtesy of Deborah Andrews.

Debbie Andrews has been the WCA liaison to Germany for more than a decade. Her many years of residence in Germany provides her with excellent qualifications. While living there, Debbie not only improved her German language skills, but became an active member of the German Weimaraner Club, competing and earning qualifications with her first Weimaraner, Astor vom Kohlwald. During this time, she met and became close friends with Birgitta Guggolz. Their shared interest in Weimaraners would later prove fortuitous as the two joined forces in 1997 to provide support to the large U.S. contingent that would arrive in the Germany to celebrate the Weimaraner Club's 100th birthday. While Debbie coordinated events stateside and provided volumes of information with translations to smooth the journey over, Birgitta organized field trips and social activities for visitors of many nationalities after their arrival. The events at and surrounding the Centennial are documented in Debbie Andrews *100 Years of Weimaraner History: The Weimaraner Memory Book* (see Figure 36-18). After the festivities concluded, Birgitta has continued to provide a welcoming committee for many visitors, and is considered by many American visitors to be "Germany's hostess with the mostess". Her flair for linguistics allows Birgitta's multicultural guests to share their ideas in spite of any possible language barriers. In the U.S., Debbie has continued to be a valued source of information and contacts for American Weimaraner enthusiasts, by helping maintain their German memberships as well as encouraging involvement in training Weimaraners as versatile hunting dogs.

100% German, but Born in the U.S.A.

Dr. Robert Shoeman, with the full permission of Dr. Werner Petri, the German Breed Club Warden, brought Furst vom Selztal (SG/SG, RGR J55, H164, SIL) and Fanni von der Lusshardt (HD-Frei) to the United States while working on a two-year research grant. With the help of German Breed Club Member, Virginia Alexander, both the A and B Litters produced offspring that widened the genetic scope of existing versatile bloodlines and resulted in three BROM sisters and two BROM brothers. Among them, they produced 59 titled progeny, many with titles both before and after their names.

Figure 36-21: *CH Ladenberg Arco v. Reiteralm, BROM* (A Litter), owned by Virginia Alexander.

Figure 36-19: *As a guest of Germany's Birgitta Guggolz,* Dr. and Mrs. Petri, and Virginia Alexander congratulate Dr. and Mrs. Shoeman on behalf of Fanni von der Lusshardt, the first German bitch to be awarded a WCA Breeder Register of Merit (BROM) pin for her successful and talented children from both her A and B litters born in the U.S..

Figure 36-22: *Ladenberg Anni v. Reiteralm, BROM* (A Litter), owned by Virginia Alexander.

Figure 36-20: *CH Ladenberg Bessi v. Reiteralm* (B Litter), owned by John and Debbie Bayer and Virginia Alexander.

Figure 36-23: (left to right) *CH Ladenberg Bryna v. Reiteralm, NRD, BROM* (B Litter), owned by Bill and Alice Smithers and Virginia Alexander and *CH Pic-a-Star's Atilla v Reiteralm, CDX, TD, NSD, NRD, VX, BROM* (A Litter), owned by Cynthia Picha and Virginia Alexander

German Foreign Exchange

Figure 36-24: *Bina von der Letzlinger Heidi* (Larry von der Wapelburg × Bonny vom Dusterntal) sg/sg=sg, HD81, HZP180, VGP315/1, SWII, WF-3, DGST, sil, ÜF, totverw, Schwp3). Bina arrived in the U.S. with her owner Dr. Roman Braun, while he was on a veterinary internship. At the suggestion of Dr. Werner Petri of the German Weimaraner Club, the Dutch import, Axel (see Figure 36-78) was selected for an American breeding.

Figure 36-25: *A family reunion* of those pups from the Bina-Axel cross that remained in the United States: Misty, Rio (see page 4), and Bina.

Figure 36-27: *Amor vom Grunenherz, JH, SDX* (Dargo vom Blanken × Amsel vom Forsthaus Gehegemühle). Bred by Klaus Gunther; owned by Aline Curran. Panzer's primary duties include working as a personal gun dog on upland birds, waterfowl, deer, hog and rabbit; additionally he trails wounded and retrieves fallen game for guests at a private game preserve. Panzer was a WCA Top 10 Derby and Gun Dog, and also uses his talents to volunteer as a certified Search and Rescue dog.

Figure 36-26: *After returning to Germany,* two of Bina's daughters went on to their own successful careers. (front) Axel's Lena von Hubertus sg=sg, rgr, WG2, WF1, HD-B2, AH, HN, LN, J60, sil, J71, spl, H176, G188/0, ÜF (Back) Benita von Hubertus, sg/sg=sg, rgr, WG2, WF1, HD-A2, AH, HN, LN, J79, spl, sil, H182, G262/0ÜF, G320/2ÜF (Arto vom Nollenwal × Bina).

Figure 36-28: *Fanny vom Siebenhauser, SH, SDX* (Cassius vom Münsterlander × Dunja vom Siebenhauser). Bred by Jurgen Rebers; owned by Aline Curran. Flair "earns her keep" trailing wounded game and retrieving at a private game preserve as well as Alines's personal gun dog for upland game birds, waterfowl, deer, hog, and rabbits. She also uses her talents as a certified Search and Rescue dog.

Friends Near and Far

American fanciers have also developed particularly close relationships with breeders in Canada and Australia. Ironically, this occurred in one case because we are such close neighbors, and in the other because we are so very far apart.

Our Friends Up North: Canada

The common heritage is reflected in the earliest breed club orientation when the Weimaraner Club of America represented both North American countries. The first WCA constitution established a system of regional clubs and organized Canadian Weimaraner activities began as a WCA regional club in June 1955. When Region 23 of the WCA disbanded, the Canadian Weimaraner Club, active since 1964, became the only national Weimaraner Club until 1971 when the Weimaraner Association of Canada was founded. The CWC disbanded in 1977, and the Canadian Kennel Club officially recognized the association as the only national Weimaraner club.

The earliest known Canadian Weimaraners were imported from the United States by Harry Kolthammer of British Colum-

bia, who raised the first litter in 1949. His dogs were not registered with Canadian organizations, and little more is known. The first Weimaraner was registered with the Canadian Kennel Club in 1948, owned by Mr. F. Bush of Moose Jaw, Saskatchewan. The second and third were owned by Matthew Starzer (WCA regional vice president) of Yorktown, Saskatchewan, who imported Ajax v. Reiningen from Germany in 1948. Benjamin and Helen Schultz of Niagara Falls, Ontario, registered the first Canadian-bred litter in 1949 – sired by Grafmar's Citation out of their Grafmar's Super Silver Dusty. The Schultzes become lifelong breed enthusiasts. They were active members of the Canadian Club as well as the WCA. Helen served for many years as WCA liaison to the German Weimaraner Club, traveling to Germany every year.

The Weimaraner Association of Canada (WAC) had their first meeting on May 18, 1971, at the home of Isabelle and Armand Kirby in Scarborough, ON. They had a Constitution a few years later and in 1977 the Canadian Kennel Club made the club official. The club continued to grow, and today it is truly a National club with representation across Canada.

Canadian show rules are a little different than AKC, requiring 10 points to be earned under three different judges and at least one 2-point win, either at the breed or group level. There are no "major" requirements and the rules for calculating the number of dogs competing are different as well. The ring procedures themselves are similar enough that most U.S. fanciers would be comfortable showing their dogs in the conformation ring.

Recently the CKC has implemented a Grand Champion program and the requirements are quite stringent, consisting of earning a minimum of 100 points that must include one Best in Show or a Best of Breed at a Breed National Specialty or a Best in Multiple Breed Specialty with at least five breeds represented; plus three Group Is or three Breed Specialty wins. Points are accumulated based on a point system for Group placements and Best of Breed wins. In addition, the dog must have been awarded a title from any CKC event other than conformation, or awarded a Canine Good Neighbour Certificate. Grand CH GraytSky Ansons Royal

Figure 36-29: *Am Can CH Hoot Hollow's Peter Rabbit, BROM* (CH Nani's Bubble Up Colsidex, BROM × CH Hoot Hollow's Gypsy Moth, NRD, BROM). Bred by Marylou Schnegelber; owned by Michael and Rosemary Shoreman. An early pioneer to hop across the border from the U.S. and take two Best in Shows in Canada.

Figure 36-30: *Am. Can. CH Davora's Bremar Notoriety* (CH Colsidex the Farm Top of the Mark, BROM × Am. Can. CH Davora's Bremar Magic Tricks). Bred and owned by Alan and Pam Patunoff, Devora Lynch, David Kuehl.

Figure 36-32: *CH Sveorice Iron Man Gunner, CD* (Am. Can. CH Silberschoen's Lucky Strike × Am. Can. CH Bremar's Troll at Sveroice). Bred by Marianne Svard; owned by Denise Gordeyko and Norma Jeanne Pohl.

Figure 36-31: *Am. Can. CH Davora' Bremar Magic Tricks,* (Can. CH Arokat's Echobar the Dancer × Am. Can. CH Arokat's Flirt in a Skirt). Bred by Devora Lynch, David Kuehl, Pam Bruce; owned by Alan and Pam Patunoff, Devora Lynch, and David Kuehl.

Figure 36-33: *CH Instar's Simplee Irresistible* (CH Cameo's Island Hunter, JH, NSD, NRD, V, BROM × AM CAN CH Wonwish Upon A Travel N' Star). Bred by Alice K. Ramon and Leeanne R. Mitchell; owned by Judith Goldman and Leeanne R. Mitchell.

Table 36-1: *Canadian Top Show Dogs*

G1	G2	G3	G4	BIS	Points		
22	30	26	23	5	6963	CH Davora's Bremar Notoriety	No. 1 2007, 2008, 2009
11	21	32	19	1	4793	CH Davora's Bremar Magic Tricks	No. 1 2005
18	21	24	26	1	3314	CH Sveorice Iron Man Gunner, CD	No. 1 2001, 2002
16	14	14	15	0	2770	CH Instar's Simplee Irresistible	No. 1 1997
15	11	11	7	1	2516	Gr CH Graytsky Ansons Royal Flush Blush*	
19	20	13	11	3	2503	CH Minalt All Wraped In Misletoe	
5	2	2	1	2	2309	CH Hoothollow's Peter Rabbit	No. 1 1989
1	4	13	17	0	2169	CH Arokat's Flirt In A Skirt	No. 1 1998, 1999
12	10	13	11	0	2038	CH Nani's Leith Kodak Moment	
8	6	8	9	0	1774	CH Weatherrun's Maggie Tee	No. 1 2004
6	9	4	8	0	1733	CH Davora's Devil's Paint Brush	No. 1 2003
4	9	14	12	0	1650	CH Silverseas Northern Lights	
3	7	3	11	0	1502	CH Ansons On The Rocks, CD	No. 1 2006
2	4	5	5	0	1315	CH Graushattns Carbon Copy	
2	5	5	3	0	1309	CH Silverisle's Summer Storm*	
0	2	6	6	0	1297	CH Arokat's Tutu Tango	No. 1 1992, 1993
2	0	0	0	1	1145	Normans Smokey City Heat Wave	No. 1 1991
7	6	12	7	1	1099	CH Greydove's Simply Charlotte	
1	4	4	7	0	1055	CH Wismar's Winstrae V Morrall	
1	3	2	5	0	1011	CH Ansons Mr Millenium, CD*	

*National Specialty Winner

Figure 36-34: *Grand CH GraytSky Ansons Royal Flush Blush* (AM CAN CH Ashmore's Win Weim Royal Flush, JH, BROM × CH Graytsky's Stella Luna, BROM). Bred by Amy Anderson, Michael Anderson, and Dana Massey; owned by Donna L. Alarie and Jan Lowe. The first Weimaraner to earn the newly minted designation of CKC Grand Champion.

Flush Blush, an American bred Canadian owned bitch, was the first Weimaraner to earn this honor.

The CKC and AKC standards for the Weimaraner conformation are quite similar, the most significant difference being that of the Long Hair. In 2007, the WAC finalized the new CKC standard for full inclusion of the Longhair. The original agreement with the CKC was to have the two coats shown as separate varieties with both going into the Group; at the 11th hour, the CKC changed this and stated that both varieties would be shown together, with only one Weimaraner going to the Group. Although it appears that many judges are unsure of what to do with this new variation, a number of Long Hairs have earned their Champions.

Also, the Canadians offer a great many more opportunities for puppies to compete in conformation, in addition to the regular classes, puppies also compete for Best Puppy in Breed, Group and Show; this may make a great early campaign for a young dog to gain show-ring experience. American exhibitors should be aware that there may be a significant difference between the entry deadlines between the U.S. and Canada.

WEIMARANERS NORTH OF THE BORDER

Weimaraner Association of Canada—www.weimaranercanada.org
Canadian Kennel Club—www.ckc.ca/en/

American Kennel Club registered dogs may exhibit in most Canadian events but are required to apply for an Event Registration Number (ERN) within 30 days of the first entry in a CKC show or awards may be cancelled. Also, dogs entering with an AKC number will have to pay an additional fee. Many American exhibitors have developed reciprocal associations with Canadian friends, exchanging dogs or lodging in order to compete on both sides of the border on a regular basis.

WCA programs such as the BROM are more difficult for Canadian breeders to obtain as most of the puppies born in Canada, stay in Canada. The majority of puppy owners are amenable to their beloved Weimaraner competing locally, but often do not want them gone for prolonged periods. let alone the expense and time commitment required by the breeder to obtain titles in both countries. With this in mind, Canadian-bred and owned BROM sires and dams deserve special recognition (see Table 36-2).

Withdrawal of Region 23's eligibility to host field trials under American Field rules began a marked decline in field trials in the region, and likely eventually contributed to the demise of the organization. However, the organization of NAVHDA events signaled a renewal of field activities in the 1970s and today field work and hunting are alive and thriving in Canada, with many people actively hunting their Weimaraners. NAVHDA is popular with the Weimaraners in Canada, performing well in that activity.

In addition to conformation shows and field trials and tests, the Canadian Kennel Club offers many activities that are generally familiar to American Weimaraner fanciers; obedience, agility, and tracking. The Weimaraner Association of Canada also offers ratings tests similar to the tests offered by their U.S. counterparts. But the devil being in the details, there are many differences in the rules; exhibitors would be well advised to read the rules carefully, and when possible attend events before entering.

Since the earliest years, the long border, coupled with minimal animal import restrictions in either country, has encouraged the free exchange of bloodlines. The resulting numerous dogs, have been successful both in competition, as well as producers, on both sides of the border with littermates that are equally successful in either country. Today, many Canadian fanciers travel freely across the border and many dedicated Weimaraner Breeders in Canada often title their dogs both in Canada and the United States. Many of the Weimaraner Association of Canada's (WAC's) members also hold membership in the Weimaraner Club of America (WCA), actively participating in events and programs offered by the organizations in both countries. Due to the vast expanse that is Canada, and the much smaller population base, events in Canada often involve considerable travel time; for this reason, Weimaraner owners in Canada are quite willing to travel south of the border to compete with their brethren in the U.S., and have done so quite successfully. It would be nearly impossible to document the extensive exchanges between the United States and our close allies on our northern border; pedigrees are so often intertwined that it would be very difficult, in some cases, to say whether a dog was "American-bred" or "Canadian-bred."

Figure 36-35: *AM/CAN CH Silberschoen's Lucky Strike, BROM* (CH Nani's Southern Cross, BROM × CAN CH Silberschoen's Northern Dancer). Bred and owned by Maurice and Gladys Cote (Canadian bred and owned; 28 U.S. Champions)

Figure 36-36: *Am Can CH Arokat's Legionnaire, BROM* (Am Can CH Colsidex Standing Ovation, BROM × Am Can CH Arimar's Prelude to Arokat, U.S. Imp, BROM). Bred and owned by Dianne and John Archibald (Canadian bred and owned; 12 U.S. champions)

Table 36-2: *Canadian Bred or Owned Dogs with a WCA Bench Register of Merit*

Canadian Bred and Owned BROM Sires	Points	Ch	Nom
Am/Can CH Arokat's Legionnaire	262	12	13
Am/Can CH Silberschoen's Lucky Strike	1,131	28	29
Canadian Bred and Owned BROM Dams			
CH Bowbent N Donmar's Goldrush	387	7	7
Am/Can CH Rudolph's Anson Summer Symphony	231	7	7
Am/Can CH Gramayre's Water Colours, NA	72	4	5
CH Weatherrun's Maggie Tee	56	5	5
Canadian Bred and U.S. Owned BROM Dams			
Am CH Nani's Jagmar Sweet Dividends, VCD2, MH, MX, MXJ, NSD, NRD, VX4	361	10	10
CH Arokat's the Bremar Headline*	267	10	10
CH Bremar Arokat's Perfect Foil, CD, NSD, NRD, V*	75	4	5
U.S. Bred and Canadian Owned BROM Dams			
CH Arokat's the Bremar Headline*	267	10	10
TC AFC Regen's Summer Blaze, VCD3, UDX2, MH, MX, MXJ, SDX, RDX, VX6	228	4	5
CH Regen's Fast N Furious JH, TD, NSD, V	168	4	5
CH Arokat's Tutu Tango CD, NSD, V*	139	8	8
Am/Can CH Nani's Sweet Investment, CD	114	4	5
Am/Can CH Arimar's Prelude to Arokat	71	5	6
CH Bowbent Venture Queens Fancy, JH, NSD, NRD, V	52	5	5

*National Specialty Winner

Figure 36-37: *CH Bowbent N Donmar's Goldrush, BROM* (CH Paragon- Harline Hullabaloo × Donmar's Breezy Sitka). Bred by Ross and Angela McClure and Donna Buscemi; owned by Ross and Angela McClure (Canadian bred and owned; 7 U.S. Champions).

Figure 36-38: *AM CH Nani's Jagmar Sweet Dividends, VCD2, MH, MX, MXJ, NSD, NRD, VX4, BROM* (CH Nani's Concert Master, SH, BROM × AM/CAN CH Nani's Sweet Investment, CD, BROM). Bred by Chris Grisell; owned by Terrie Borman and Chris Grisell (Canadian Bred, U.S. owned, 10 U.S. Champions). Photograph by Lisa Sponsler.

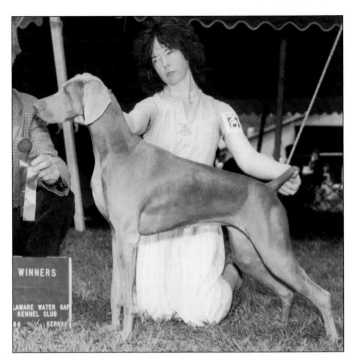

Figure 36-39: (a) *Am Can CH Arimar's Prelude to Arokat, (U.S. Imp), BROM* (Am Can CH Coldisdex Standing Ovation, BROM × CH I've a Dream of Arimar, CD, NSD, V). Bred by Jackie Isabell; owned by Dianne and John Archibald. (U.S. bred, Canadian owned, 5 U.S. champions) **(b)** *CH Arokat's the Bremer Headline* (CH Rajah's Mr Magic v. d. Reiteralm × AM CAN CH Arimar's Prelude to Arokat, BROM). Bred by John and Dianne Archibald; owned by Alan and Pam Patunoff. (U.S. bred, Canadian owned, 10 U.S. Champions). These two bitches, top show winners themselves, contributed a strong stamp on the type and movement of the Canadian Weimaraner and appear in the pedigrees of nearly all of the top Canadian winners and producers.

Figure 36-40: *BISS BIS Am/Can CH Bowbent Carousel Hidden Gem* (BIS/BISS Am/Can CH Carousel's Roscoe T. Picotrane, BROM × Am/Can CH Bowbent N'Donmar's Goldrush, BROM). Bred by Ross and Angela McClure; owned by Ross and Angela McClure and Bill and Pat Van Camp. Born and raised in Canada, but with owners on both sides of the border, Gem is a frequent campaigner in the U.S. as well. To keep things fair, she won the National Specialty in Canada, went Best in Show in the U.S. and was the WCA's 2005 No. 1 Show Dog.

Figure 36-41: *TC AFC Can CH Can MOTCH Can VCH Regen's Summer Blaze, VCD3, UDX2, RE, MH, MX, MXJ, SDX, RDX, VX6, BROM, FROM, Can FDX, Can AGX, Can TDX, NAVHDA UT1* (U.S. bred, Canadian owned; three U.S. Field Champions, four U.S. Show Champions). One of the most titled Weimaraners in breed history, she crossed the border routinely, and became the AKC's first Triple Champion Weimaraner (see Figure 3-1). Ruby was also the first dam honored to be named to both the WCA FROM and BROM lists.

Our Friends Down Under: Australia

Over the past couple of decades the relationship between the U.S. and Australian breeders have strengthened despite the immense distance between the two countries, resulting in more frequent exchanges of bloodlines and information. The advent of increased travel, e-mail, and chat groups, as well as artificial insemination, has allowed infusions of new stock to cross in both directions across the vast ocean. American fanciers visiting Australia may find that the "dog on the hill" in Australia bears a close resemblance to the one in the United States. While this chapter is focusing on Weimaraners exported from the United States, *Searching for Silver Grey* (2005) by Liz Harding and Debbie Ryan, provides a complete and detailed history of the Weimaraner in Australia with a new edition, *Silver-Grey* scheduled for release in 2010. Much of the information provided in this section was extracted from information compiled and contributed through the efforts of Liz Harding.

The first pair of Weimaraners arrived in Australia in July 1955—they were "Strawbridge Graf" and "Strawbridge Fidget" purchased from Major Robert Petty of North Devon, U.K. by Drs. Roma and Chris Christensen of New South Wales. The second pair followed within a few months and were also purchased from Major Petty by Matt Sproul of New South Wales—they were "Strawbridge Furst" and "Strawbridge Gypsy". Fidget and Furst were whelped on 8-18-1954—(Thunderjet (U.S.) × Cobra von Boberstrand (Imp. Germany)). Graf and Gypsy were whelped on 9-29-1954 (Bando v. Fohr (Imp. Germany) × Hella aus der Helmeute (Imp. Germany).

From 1955 to 1959 there were no other Weimaraners imported into Australia.

Well-known Australian gun dog show, field, and retrieving judge Mr. Jack Pontin of Victoria, purchased a bitch, Passau Silver Wraith, from the second Passau litter in 1957. In 1959, under his well-known Pointer and Retriever prefix Marnisse, he bred the first litter from a Passau progeny. Luckily for Mr. Pontin, Mr. R. F. Harris arrived in Victoria from the U.S., bringing with him his Weimaraner dog, Regal Wunder Columbian Duke (Imp. U.S.), whelped in 1954, (CH Rudolph aus der Wolfsriede × CH Billou's Azure Belle). Duke was the first American Weimaraner imported into Australia. Possibly this dog was bred by E. L. Regal and was a sibling of

> This chapter presented a great number of challenges with the many worthy dogs that could have been included as a result of their accomplishments in their own or other countries, a subject deserving of an entire book of its own. As a result we were forced to make difficult decisions, limiting the dogs presented here, regardless of nation, to those dogs that were imported to or exported from the United States.
>
> Our heartfelt thanks to Mrs. Harding in particular for her special contributions, providing, in her own words, a detailed history and description of the successes of American dogs imported to and exported from Australia and New Zealand.

Figure 36-42: *Searching for Silver Grey* (Ghostdog Productions, 2010) by Liz Harding and Debbie Ryan provides the Weimaraner enthusiast with the detailed history of the Weimaraner in Australia. An invaluable resource for pedigree research and a fascinating documentation of the development of the breed and well known bloodlines throughout the country. More information may be found at *www.ghostdog.com.au*. The dogs from upper right corner going clockwise are: Aust. CH Belgrigio Claudia, UD, TD (QC)(Silvahunter Kennel); Shayne Ramsay's bitch leased to Divani Kennels, Aust. CH Bromhund Ultra Sonic (Steve Ramsey, leased to Divani Kennels) with Aust. CH Divani Romancn With Trouble; Aust. CH Trupoint Rich Bitch (Silvahunter Kennels); Silverodhar Boy Ndoubt (J and S Boland) winner of 2005 Australian Weimaraner National Specialty; CH Bromhund No Nonsense (G. Russel); Grand Dual CH (Rt) Besko Th Red Baron (Besko Kennels); John Harding with Aust. DC (T) Waldwiese Quintessential. The stars are those of the Southern Cross (part of our Australian flag) which are now always featured on Australian Olympic uniforms. The two dogs on the top of the etching are the silver grey logo hand drawn by Dr. Lindsay Dyson. Image courtesy of Ghostdog Productions.

Regal Wunder aus Felsen, CD and Regal Wunder Randolf CD, (see *The Complete Weimaraner* by William Denlinger, pg 270). There are no photos of this dog, but we assume he would most probably have been similar in type to the Regal Weimaraner (see *Denlinger*, page 192).

From 1964 to 1967 there were 6 Weimaraners imported into Australia from the U.K.

In 1967, Mrs. Heterick of New South Wales purchased a dog from the U.S., Aust. CH Fritz von Singen (Imp.U.S.) (Hans von Stedimar × The Lady Sachet von Gordon). He was to play a major role in opening up the bloodlines of the Aus-

tralian Weimaraner, allowing breeders to move away from the strong British bloodlines and acquire some of the elegance of the American bloodlines. It had been approximately eight years since the first American import which had been used at stud only once.

In 1972, a German dog and bitch were imported into Australia by Gary Vize (Queensland) but these were taken by Mr. Vize to New Zealand for a few years where he bred them under the Spectral Prefix. These were the foundation of Longhair breeding in Australia and New Zealand.

Figure 36-43: *Eng. Sh. CH, NZ and Aust. CH Arimars Rolf v. d. Reiteralm (Imp. U.S.),* whelped 1-15-1979, (Am DC Ronamax Rufus Reiteralm, Can and Dominican CH International, CACI, CD, RDX, SDX, VX, NAVHDA [Prize3] × Am. CH I've a Dream of Arimar, CD, NSD, V). Bred by Jackie Isabell and Alice Morgan; owned by John and Rosemary Mayhew.

Figure 36-45: *Am. CH and Aust. CH Deerpath's Charlemagne (Imp. U.S.A).* (Am. CH Colsidex Medicine Show, BROM × Am. CH Colsidex Symphony, BROM). Bred by George and Michele Govette; owned by Eileen Huxtable.

Figure 36-44: *Aust CH Ranah's Bold Ruler v. d. Reiteralm* (Imp. U.S.), whelped 5-29-1979 (Am. CH Reiteralm's Rio Fonte Saudade, NRD, BROM × Am CH Kamsou Riptide, BROM). Bred by Ron Columbo and Kamsou Kennels; owned by Shirley Whitefield.

Figure 36-46: *Nani's Charmin for Ghostwind* (Imp. U.S.A.) (Am. CH Colsidex Big Spender × Am. CH Nani's Cascade v. d. Reiteralm, BROM). Bred by Chris Grisell; owned by Sue Shrigley (Ghostwind Kennels).

Figure 36-47: *Nani's Helga for Bromhund* (Imp. U.S.) (Am CH Colsidex Big Spender × Am CH Nani's Cascade v. d. Reiteralm, BROM). Bred by Chris Grisell; owned by John and Rosemary Mayhew in Queensland.

Figure 36-49: *Am. and Aust. CH Nani's Dis-Harmony* (CH Baht N' Greywind Playn' the Game, NSD, BROM × CH Nani's Perfect Cadence, CD, JH, V, BROM). Bred by Chris Grisell; owned by Val Peters.

Figure 36-48: *Am. and Aust. CH Traditions Tradewind Ke Nani* (Imp. U.S.) (Am. NZ CH Nani's Totally Awesome, BROM × CH Nani's Finesse, BROM). Bred by Chris Grisell; owned by Dianne Horner and Val Speck.

Figure 36-50: *Am and Aust CH Nani's Miss Chievous, JH* (CH Nani's Baht a Pack a Trouble, CD, JH, V, BROM × CH Nani's Valley Platinum Blonde, BROM). Bred by Christine Grisell; owned by Sue Shrigley.

From 1972 until 1978, 12 Weimaraners arrived from the U.K., 2 longhairs from New Zealand and a bitch from Germany.

In 1978, John and Rosemary Mayhew looked to the U.S. with a view of importing something that would both look good and carry good working ability. John and Rosemary, with the help of Virginia Alexander, Jacqueline Isabell, and Alice Morgan, negotiated the purchase of a dog, Arimars Rolf v. d. Reiteralm (Imp. U.S.), whelped 1-15-1979, (Int Can Dom CH Am DC Ronamax Rufus v. d. Reiteralm, CD, SDX, RDX, VX, NAVHDA UT3 × Am. CH I've a Dream of Arimar, CD). Tank was sent to Australia via England and

New Zealand. Tank became Eng. Sh. CH, NZ and Aust. CH Arimars Rolf v. d. Reiteralm (Imp. U.S.). Tank's immediate success as a sire created a strong desire for other American imports. He sired 68 show champions as well as numerous field and obedience champions. Tank's bloodlines not only improved the show stock but also improved the willingness to retrieve in and through water in the retrieving and field dogs. The Mayhew's also imported a dog from Germany in 1982, Salto vom Zehnthof.

1983 saw Shirley Whitefield of Quabana Kennels purchase a dog from the U.S., Aust CH Ranah's Bold Ruler v. d.

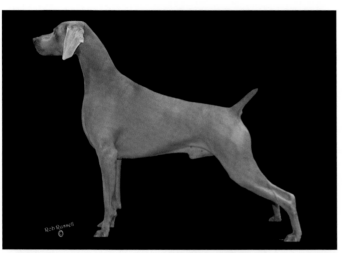

Figure 36-51: *Am. and Aust. CH Colsidex Grauhund Just Jeans, Imp. U.S.,* (Am. Can. CH Bremar Makers Mark, BROM × Am. CH Sagenhaft Colsidex Wiz Kid). Bred by Judy Colan and A. Folz; owned by Grauhund Kennels: Carol Wright and Shellie Marshall.

Figure 36-52: *Australian GR CH Endlich Lugar zum Feldjaeger (LH)* (Imp U.S.) (Quercus Skrunt (LH) × Alice vom Hollweder Wald (LH, Imp. Germany). Bred by Jeremy Freidberg; owned by Judy Glover.

Figure 36-53: *Am. CH/Aust. Gr. CH Nani's Sovereign Cross Check, JH, TD, Imp. U.S.,* (Am. CH Nani's Indecent Exposure, JH, NAJ, V, BROM × Am. CH Nani's Jagmar Sweet Dividends, VCD2, MH, MX, MXJ, NSD, NRD, VX4, BROM). Bred by Chris Grisell and Terrie Borman; owned by Carol Wright and Shellie Marshall.

Reiteralm (Imp. U.S.), whelped 5-29-1979, (Am CH Reiteralm's Rio Fonte Saudade, NRD, BROM × Am CH Kamsou Riptide, BROM). By 1984 others were keen to acquire the more refined look of the American Weimaraner. Eileen Huxtable of New South Wales imported Aust Am CH Deerpath's Charlemagne (Imp. U.S.) (Am CH Colsidex Medicine Show, BROM × Am CH Colsidex Symphony, BROM).

Later in 1984, two litter sisters arrived from Chris Grisell's Nani's; both were longhaired Weimaraners—Nani's Charmin for Ghostwind (Imp. U.S.) who went to Sue Shrigley of Ghostwind Kennels (then in Western Australia), and Nani's Helga for Bromhund (Imp. U.S.) who went to John and Rosemary Mayhew in Queensland (Am CH Colsidex Big Spender × Am CH Nani's Cascade v. d. Reiteralm BROM). Both bitches produced many champions and enhanced the longhair bloodline desired by those wanting to breed longhaired Weimaraners. John and Rosemary's Helga, bred to Tank, produced some extremely big winning show dogs and bitches such as Aust. CH Bromhund Graphic Art, Aust. CH Bromhund Galaxie, and Aust. CH Bromhund Ultra Sonic.

In 1985, Sue Shrigley imported a mature bitch from the U.S., Am. and Aust. CH Nani's Windward Gale (Imp. U.S.), whelped 11-29-1984, (Am CH Colsidex Standing Ovation, BROM × Am CH Nani's Cobbie Cuddler, BROM). Shirley Whitefield also imported a bitch from the U.S., Aust. CH Ranah's Jordach of Quabana (Imp. U.S.) (Am CH Nani's Topsider × AM CH Kamsou London Fog). She mated this bitch to her imported dog, she then sold the bitch to Maureen Wilkinson of Stolzjager kennels in Western Australia.

Toward the end of the 1980s, Dianne Horner and Val Speck of Divani Kennels in New South Wales imported Aust.

CH Traditions Tradewind Ke Nani (Imp. U.S.) (Am. NZ CH Nani's Totally Awesome × CH Nani's Finesse). Trad was a double grandson of the famous Am. Can. CH Colsidex Standing Ovation, BROM.

In the late 1980s, importing semen into Australia became the cheapest way of achieving the bloodlines that breeders wanted for their Australian bitches, many of whom now carried some American lines in their pedigrees. Divani Kennels imported semen from both Am. CH Norman's Double Bubble and Am. CH Nani's Baht a Pack A' Trouble, JH. Carol Wright of Grauhund Kennels in Victoria, imported semen from Am. CH Colsidex Nani Reprint, JH, SD, BROM. This semen was put to her home-bred bitch Aust. CH Grauhund It'n'abit and produced one of the most highly successful litters ever seen in Australia. A summary of some of the semen imported is listed at the end of this report. (We cannot at this stage know of all imported semen unless breeders are prepared to share their information, if some dogs have been overlooked, we apologize as it was not our intention to do so.)

During the 1990s, Jean Hutchison and Kathleen Kaggelis (now Rogers) of Queensland imported a dog from the U.S., Am. CH Von Luchbach's All Fired Up, NRD (Imp. U.S.) (whelped 1993, Am. Can. CH Valmar's Smokey City Ultra Easy, JH, BROM × Am. CH Von Luchbach's Magic Moment, NSD, NRD).

In 1997, Lynne Webster and Jessie Hughes of South Australia imported a dog from the U.S., Am. CH Hibourne Colsidex Showoff (Imp. U.S.), whelped 7-17-93, exited quarantine 1-5-1998, (Am. CH Colsidex Standing Ovation, BROM × Am. CH Hibourne Quest for Glory JH, NSD, RD, VX, BROM). Unfortunately Bryce sired very few litters in Australia and a dog kept from this litter by Jessie and Lynne has only just recently passed away. 1998–1999 saw Greydove Kennels of New South Wales (Val Peters and Narelle Gould) purchase a beautiful American girl, Am. CH Nani's Disharmony, Imp. U.S., (Am. CH Baht N Greywind Playn the Game, NSD, BROM × Am CH Nani's Perfect Cadence, CD, JH, V, BROM) and then again in 2000, Aust. and Am. CH Nani N Greydove Milenium Bug, Imp. U.S., (Am. Can. CH Ashmore WinWeim Royal Flush, JH, BROM × Am. CH Nani's Glitter Bug, JH, BROM) who after a successful career in Australia went to the U.K.

In 1998–1999, Shirley Whitefield again imported a dog from the U.S., Am. Aust. CH Black Forest Clark Gable, Imp. U.S., (whelped 8-4-1996, Am. CH Black Forest Dorian's Halston, BROM × Am. CH Silverwind Tinseltown Tornado, BROM). Sue Shrigley of Ghostwind Kennels also imported a bitch from the U.S., Am. CH Nani's Miss Chievous, JH, Imp. U.S., (whelped 2-7-1994, Am. Can. CH Valmar's Smokey City Ultra Easy, JH × Nani's Valley Platinum Blonde, BROM).

In the 10 years between 1990 and 2000 seven Weimaraners were imported into Australia from the U.K.

In 2000, Carol Wright traveled to the States and chose a puppy that would go on to be another one of the most influential sires in Australian history, Gr. CH and Am. CH Colsidex Grauhund Just Jeans, Imp. U.S., (Am. Can. CH Bremar Makers Markm, BROM × Am. CH Sagenhaft Colsidex Wiz Kid), bred by Judy Colan. Levi was a multiple Best Exhibit in Show All-Breeds winner and a multiple Specialty Best in Show winner, producing many champions, Grand Champions, and Dual Champions. He is the only Weimaraner in the history of the breed to produce 10 Grand Champions.

At about this time, Greydove Kennels also imported Am. CH Jokar's RC Promise, Imp. U.S., (Am. CH Tophats Dorian Gray, BROM × Am. CH Valmar's Gallorette v. Jokar).

In 2004, Greydove imported Am. Aust. CH PewterRun Greydove Black Magic, Imp. U.S., (Am.CH Camelot's Go For

the Gold, BROM × Am. CH Silversmith PewterRun Betsy Ross, BROM), an ultimate show dog who won many All Breeds Best in Shows, Best of Breeds at several Royal Shows and is sire of several Australian and American Champions.

During 2005, Judy Glover of Feldjager Kennels in Queensland, imported a longhaired Weimaraner from the U.S., Aust. CH Endlich Lugar zum Feldjaeger, Imp. U.S., (Quercus Skrunt (LH) × Alice vom Hollweder Wald [LH – Imp. Germany]). This longhaired boy has again enhanced the

Figure 36-54: *Am/Aust CH Ekahi Greydove Quicksilver,* Imp. U.S., (Am. CH Nani's Tsurutani Honor Bound, JH × Am. CH Greydove Ekahi Island Gal, BROM (Imp. Aust.). Bred and owned by Daryle Oliveira and Val Peters.

Figure 36-55: *Aust Gr. CH. Am/Can CH Graytsky's Smokin In Havana, Imp. U.S.* (whelped 1-30-03, Am Can. CH Ashmore's Winweim Royal Flush, JH, BROM × Am. CH Graytsky's Stella Luna, BROM). Bred and owned by Amy Anderson.

Figure 36-56: *Aust. Gr. CH Am. Can CH Divani Loads a Trouble* (AI). Lazer was whelped on 2-19-1991. (Am. CH Nani's Baht a Pack a Trouble, CD, JH, V, BROM [U.S.] × Aust. CH Divani Enter Thstar). Bred and owned by Diane Horner and Val Speck. Lazer holds a unique position, being born out of the first AI litter of Weimaraners in Australia. At the age of 6, after an extremely successful career at home, Lazer visited North America, taking away two bench Championships and leaving behind a legacy in his daughter BIS Am CH Smokey City D'Nunder Lazer Beam, who would become WCA's No. 1 show dog; as did his granddaughter, BIS Am. CH Smokey City's Hail Mary.

longhair gene pool. Late in 2005, Carol Wright of Grauhund Kennels imported a dog from Nani's Kennels, Gr. CH Am. CH Nani's Sovereign Cross Check, JH, TD, Imp. U.S., (Am. CH Nani's Indecent Exposure, JH × Am. CH Nani's Jagmar Sweet Dividends, VCD2, MH, MX, MXJ, NSD, NRD, VX4, BROM.) He is a multiple Best Exhibit in Show Winner and Specialty Winner. Boomer went BIS at the Canberra Royal Show in 2009 under Mike Shoreman of Canada.

Also late in 2006, Greydove Kennels imported a dog and bitch, as babies, from the same litter from Hawaii, Aust. CH Greydove Ekahi Surfer Girl, Imp. U.S., and Am. Aust. CH Ekahi Greydove Quicksilver, Imp. U.S., (Am. CH Nani's Tsurutani Honor Bound, JH × Am. CH Greydove Ekahi Islandgal, Imp. Aust. Jett, the boy, was Best Puppy in Show at the Sydney Royal in 2007; at 13 months he became an All Breeds Best in Show winner in Australia, and is now a Best in Specialty Show winner in the U.S., after he was exported back to the States as a mature dog.

Also late in 2006, Sue Shrigley of Ghostwind Kennels in Tasmania, imported a dog on lease, and in partnership with American breeder, Amy Anderson of Graytsky's Weimaraners. This mature dog, Aust Gr. CH. Am/Can CH Graytsky's Smokin in Havana, Imp. U.S., (whelped 1-30-03, Am Can. CH Ashmore's Winweim Royal Flush, JH, BROM × Am. CH Graytsky's Stella Luna, BROM), made a huge impact on the Australian dog world, and in the two years he was in Australia, he won many Best Exhibit in Shows, All Breeds, plus Specialty Shows and a Best Exhibit in Show at a Royal Show. He was

shown in Australia for Sue by Russell Little (who is now a partner in Ghostwind). Mac was shown through to his Australian Grand Championship in only two years—a pretty impressive record. He has left many progeny behind in Australia including dogs and bitches who in 2009 were well on their way to their Grand Championships plus one Dual Champion bred by Waldwiese Kennels and owned by Silvahunter Kennels.

Knowing that Mac would be returning to the States, Sue Shrigley acquired another dog with bloodlines that would work in with her Ghostwind bitches lines; her latest dog is Aust. BIS Aust. and Am. CH Wagers's Casino Winning Streak, Imp U.S., (Am CH Graytsky's Southern Fire × CH Wager's Casino Magic). He, too, is making his mark on Australian soil. Lainie Knox of Ashlaren Weimaraners in New South Wales also recently imported a male from Canada, Am. Can. Aust. CH Davora Bremar Mark of Ashlaren, Imp. Canada, (Am. CH Colsidex The Farm Top of the Mark, BROM, Imp. U.S. × Am. Can. CH Davor's Bremar Magic Tricks). Mark won the WCA National Maturity in 2008; and he has easily gained his Australian title and has show-winning progeny on the ground.

Finally, there have been two dogs who have been exported from Australia and who have returned home after making their mark on the Weimaraner world: Lazer and Oska. While they really have simply returned, they do in fact appear in the Australian Kennel Club records as being imports.

The first of the dogs is Divani Kennels' (Di Horner and Val Speck) Aust. Gr. CH Am. Can CH Divani Loads a Trouble [AI]. Lazer was whelped on 2-19-1991. (Am. CH Nani's Baht a Pack a Trouble, JH [U.S.] × Aust. CH Divani Enter Thstar). Lazer visited the U.S. and Canada in 1997. In 31 days he obtained two championship titles, including three 5-point majors. Lazer had a wonderful temperament that allowed him to be taken overseas and extensively campaigned in such a short time, plus remain in quarantine after his return to Australia, happily awaiting the day he would return to Di, Val, and Bruce.

More recently, Lainie Knox and her daughter, Rachael, (Ashlaren Weimaraners) sent their beautiful homebred dog to Europe to reside for a couple of years with Paulina Walkowska of Imperium Star Weimaraners (Poland). Oska has returned to Australia as Aust. Eur Lux Ger Fin Pol Ltu Slv Lv CH Ashlaren Caipiroska (Gr. CH Divani Just a Dash × Gr. CH NZ CH Ashlaren Crepe Suzette)—a really fantastic effort!

Another Weimaraner is expected to arrive in Australia from the States in 2010, Greydove Kennels Rissana Hillwoods's Perfect Harmony at Greydove (Imp. U.S.) (Am. CH Nani's Indecent Exposure, JH, NAJ, V, BROM × Am. CH Colsidex Seabreeze Perfect Fit). Greydove Kennels now have their prefix registered in the United States and occasionally import and export dogs and bitches to both countries.

From 2001 until 2010 there have been four Weimaraners imported to Australia from the U.K.; one from Sweden and three from Canada. There have been many exports and imports to and from New Zealand over the past 30 or so years. Access to bloodlines in both countries has become quite easy in recent years. Imports range from New Zealand, such as those from Spectral in the early 1970s, Rifleman and Weissenberg in the 1980s and 1990s through to the recent Carnmellis and Greyflyte stock. In 2006, Cyd Welsh of Greyflyte Kennels, sent her American-bred dog over to be campaigned through to his Australian show title Aust NZ. Am. CH Tri-D's Greyflyte Grand Slam, Imp. NZ (whelped 4-15-2003, Am. CH Tri-D's Invincible, NSD, BROM × Am. CH Tri-D's Grand Finale, BROM). There are also many Australian dogs and bitches that have been sent to New Zealand from the following Australian prefixes to gain their New Zealand show title and returned to Australia: Ashlaren, Bromhund, Divani, Ghostwind, Grauhund, Graustrum, and Greydove are just a few who appear in both records.

The Australian chapter is far from over; there will be many, many imports and semen from all over the world arriving in the future. In personal correspondence Liz Harding said, "The wonderful thing about this huge blend of both European and American Weimaraners over the years has been their wonderful quality—strength without coarseness, elegance without fineness; health and temperament, but most definitely, they have not become a fad which keeps the rehouse/rescue factor to the bare minimum." For the complete history of the Weimaraner in Australia, refer to Harding and Ryan's *Searching for Silver Grey* (2005) and *Silver-Grey*.

Figure 36-57: *Aust NZ. Am. CH Tri-D's Greyflyte Grand Slam,* Imp. NZ, (whelped 4-15 -2003, Am. CH Tri-D's Invincible, NSD, BROM × Am. CH Tri-D's Grand Finale, BROM). Carole Donaldson, Michael Parker and Cecelia Ruggles; owned by Cyd Welsh.

This chapter has addressed Artificial Insemination in only a general sense, and not specific litters or breedings. However, AI has played a role in the breeding programs of many Australian breeders; in recognition of this, a list of known AI shipments to Australia is provided. Currently there is no system for tracking imports and exports of semen, so it is regretful that some shipments might have been overlooked.

Am. CH Arokat's Echobar Riverdance

Am. CH Colsidex Nani Reprint, JH, SD, BROM

Eb's YoShida Da

Eng. CH Gunalt Harris Tweed

Eng. CH Hansom Portman of Gunalt

Can. CH Hoot Hollows Peter Rabbit, BROM (bred in the U.S.), semen imported from Canada.

Am. CH Nani's Baht a Pack A'Trouble CD, JH, V, BROM

Am. Can. CH Nani's Choir Boy

Am. CH Nani's Class Clown

Am. CH Nani's Concert Master, SH, BROM

Am. CH Nani's Indecent Exposure, JH, NAJ, V, BROM

Am. CH Nani's Smart Aleck, JH, NRD, V, BROM

Am. NZ CH Nani's Totally Awesome, BROM

Am. CH Norman's Double Bubble, BROM

Am. CH Orion's Jaeger V Reiteralm, TD, CD, MH, SD, RDX, VX3, BROM

Eng. CH Pondridge Practical Joker (Long Hair)

Am. CH Smokey City EZ Moonstone, JH, NRD, V, BROM

Am. CH Tophat's Big Wave Surfer

Am. CH Tophat's Dorian Gray, BROM

Am. CH Tophat's Surfin' Safari

Am. CH Tophat's Top Gun, BROM

Am. CH Valmar's Apache Rebel, BROM

Am. CH Valmar's EZ Jazz Time, CD, OA, SD, VX, BROM

Am. CH Valmar's Sage v Wustenwind, NSD, NRD, V, BROM

Am. CH Valmar's Unanimous Decision, NSD, BROM

Am. CH Valmar's Xtra Copy, BROM

Am. CH Wismar's Jack Daniels, BROM

Central and South American Connections

Figure 36-58: *Int, Cen Am, Lat Am, ElS, Hon, Nic Gua Cos Am CH Silversmith Flying Eagle, RN, BROM* (CH Windwalker's Graeagle, JH, CD, NRD, V, BROM × CH Silversmith Lady Gracie, JH, NSD, NRD, V, BROM). Bred by Elena Smith Lamberson and Tracy Brabham Duff; owned by Steph Meyers (Costa Rico).

Figure 36-61: *CH Colsidex Nani Follow A Dream* (CH Colsidex Standing Ovation, BROM × CH Forshadow Nani's Crystal Vision, BROM). Bred by Judy Colan and Chris Grisell; owned by Jose Maria Lorenzo (Argentina).

Figure 36-59: *Chi Arg Urg Lat Am. Am and Car Am CH Nani's von Obst Gringo* (CH Nani's Indecent Exposure, JH, NAJ, V, BROM × CH Nani's Evrybody Luvs Sombody, JH, BROM). Bred by Chris Grisell and Sarah Mae Barker; owned by Pablo Berrios (Chile).

Figure 36-62: *Chi Lat Am Int CH Nani's Ad-Lib* (Am. CH and Aust. Gr. CH Nani's Sovereign Crosscheck, JH, TD × CH Nani's Tattletail, JH, BROM). Bred by Chris Grisell; owned by Pablo Berrios (Chile).

Figure 36-60: *Am CH BrNtlMster CH. Br Gr CH PanAm CH Int CH. Camelot's Country Parson* (CH Orions Quest for Camelot, CD, JH, V × CH Camelot's Femme Fatale). Bred by Susan Thomas; owned by Ingrid Heins (Brazil).

Figure 36-63: *Int BrNtlMster. Bra. BraGr. PanAm. Am CH Ultima's Winston Supreme* (CH Colsidex Nani Reprint, JH, SD, BROM × CH Ultima's Sadie Hawkins Bred by Ann Loop; owned by Ingrid Heins (Brazil).

American Weimaraners in United Kingdom

Fig 36-64: *Eng. Sh. CH NZ CH Aust. CH Arimar's Rolf v. d. Reiteralm (Imp. USA).* (Int Can Dom CH Am DC Ronamax Rufus v. d. Reiteralm, CD, SDX, RDX, VX, NAVHDA UT3 × Am. CH I've a Dream of Arimar, CD, NSD, V). Bred by J. Isabell and A. J. Morgan; owned by John and Rosemary Mayhew.

Figure 36-67: *NZ Am CH Nani's Totally Awesome* (Am CH Colsidex Standing Ovation, BROM × Am CH Nani's Cobbie Cuddler, BROM). Bred by Chris Grisell; owned by G. and S. Wilcox. (England). A short-time visitor before moving on to Australia and New Zealand, this dog's greatest mark is perhaps left by his son Sh CH Flimmoric Fanclub.

Figure 36-65: *Eng CH Kamsou Moonraker von Bismark* (Am CH Kams Tempest × Am CH Kams Dusty Moonshine). Bred by Kamsou Kennels and Edith Huntley; owned by Richard and Jane George (England). This long-term resident of the U.K. sired 14 litters and produced nine champions.

Figure 36-66: *Breeding Weimaraners since 1976, Pasty and Stephen Hollings,* under the Gunnalt Kennel name, have been frequent and consistent producers of champion show Weimaraners. As the result of strict quarantine laws, import and export of American dogs (even semen) to the U.K. is quite limited.

Figure 36-68: *The Essential Weimaraner* by Patsy Hollings provides a history of the Weimaraner. An International Championship Show judge, Patsy Hollings is also a world recognized breeder, owner, and handler of the Gunalt Kennel in England.

Our Italian Friends

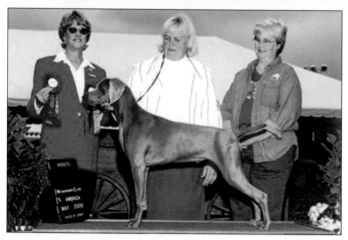

Figure 36-69: *CH Willie's Juliet von Reiteralm, JH, NSD.* After taking Best of Winners at the 2000 WCA National Specialty handled by co-breeder Sandy West, then obtaining her CH, JH, and hip clearance, Julie was bred to an OFA Excellent Champion Master Hunter. Once Julie was confirmed to be in whelp, Virginia and Lynn Berryman presented her as a gift to Telma Tucci and the Italian Weimaraner club.

Figure 36-72: *Intrl Eur Itl Cro Am CH Nani's to Be or Not to Be, JH* (see Figure 36-9) 2007 Top Italian Producer, 2007 Best Brace in Show European Championship, 2008 Best Brace in Show World Championship 2009.

Figure 36-70: *Homarc's Phoenix Ascending* (CH Homarc's Silver Smoke × CH Homarc's Mark of Zara). Owned by Telma Tucci. A pioneer among the modern Weimaraner breeder's in Italy, Telma Tucci imported Phoenix. Telma and Phoenix (a registered therapy dog) earned many Best of Breeds as an early ambassador for the Weimaraner in the conformation ring.

Figure 36-73: *Am and Itl CH Nani's Outrage, JH* (see Figure 36-9) 2008 Top Italian Producer, 2007 Best Brace in Show European Championship Show, 2008 and 2009 Best Brace in Show World Championship Show 2009.

Figure 36-71: *The Weimaraner Club of Italy's member's welcomed* and greeted new Weimaraner owners with a doggy picnic held at the more than 200-year-old summer home of Telma Tucci. Hospitality and memorable fun activities were provided during a puppy field training and grading seminar held by Virginia Alexander.

Imports and Exports from the Netherlands

Figure 36-74: *Multi Ch. Nani's Clay Pigeon, W.'09, JH, NSD* (CH Bzyfeet American Idol, BROM × CH Nani's Sophisticated Lady, MH, NA, NAJ, SDX, VX). Bred by Chris Grisell; owned by Leonor Honing and Chris Grisell. Homer easily earned his American CH and then moved to the Netherlands where he added five new country championships to his name, an Open International Working and Beauty Championship as well as taking best male at a Crufts qualifying show. Homer returned to his native land in 2009 where he won his Futurity class and took an Award of Merit at the WCA National Specialty.

Figure 36-76: *Dutch CH Sanbar's Coach v. Sagenhaft* (CH Colsidex Blueprint, BROM × CH Sanbar's Diva Von Sagenhaft, CDX, NRD, V, BROM). Bred by James and Billie Thompson; owned by Martina De gruijter. Coach was imported to the Netherlands when he was four months old. He earned his Europe Junior Championship at just nine months of age at his very first show and went on to handily earn his Dutch Championship. He is the sire of four Dutch Champions, with his most noteworthy offspring out of the U.S. imported Dutch CH Nani's Georgette.

Figure 36-77: *Dutch CH Grayshar's Hella von Furst Pless* (Astor vom Kohlwald (Ger) × CH Grayshar Easy Impression, NSD, BROM). Bred by Gregg and Sharon Hartmann; owned by Jan and Carla Vrek. Hella won Best of Breed at the celebratory Dutch Weimaraner Club championship Breed Match in 1997.

Figure 36-75: *De Weimaraner* is written by pioneer Dutch breeder and judge, J.A.M. Deckers MDR (with additional contributors). This second edition of the book was published in October 2001 and contains 624 pages, colour and black and white photos, including a full update on Weimaraners bred in and imported to the Netherlands, new chapters on Dutch, German and Austrian field trials, the FCI, English and AKC breed standard in Dutch, English and German, a chapter on the aging Weimaraner and a new chapter on Dutch and FCI field trials. The book was published by the Dutch Weimaraner Club and is still available at *www.weimaraners.nl/weimaranerboek*

Imports and Exports from the Netherlands

Figure 36-78: *CH Axel Reiteralm of Weimar's Joy, CD, JH, RD, VX, NAVHDA NA 111, VX* (Dargo vom Blanken, sg/sg=sg, v/sg=v, rgr, WF3, VJP69, HZP178, VGP308/1, HN, SchwP2h, 600/2, Schwp2/, SW111/, SchwN × Lux CH Grayshar Windsong on the Rise). Since Axel's arrival in America more than 30 of his children can be individually credited with AKC field wins or placements without even considering the records of his sons: Czar, Sampson, and Bleu Bayou. As a result of Axel's high prey drive and natural bidability, records show that during the last 10 years his children have earned well over 80 titles in obedience, field, and tracking most owner-trained and -handled. Currently, Axel can be credited with siring nine show champions in America and Canada. Owner Virginia Alexander will be forever grateful to Jur and Yvonne Decker of the Netherlands for sharing their best with America.

Figure 36-79: *Int, Lux, Dut, Ger (VDH) CH The Rise and Grayshar Royal Heir, JVP50, HZP, 136, VGPIII-277, WSII-303, VGP II-383, CQN* (CH Grayshar's Royal Valor × DC Wynwood's Rain on the Rise, SDX, RDX, VX). Bred by Patti and Bill Kuehnhold and Gregg and Sharon Hartmann; owned by Rob and Els Theel. European Champion 96, VDH Europasieger 96, Clubwinner 99 (=overall Winner of the club show of Vereniging de Weimarse Staande Hond), Belgian Schoonheidskampioen 2000. In the Netherlands Roy accomplished many hunting ratings: Voorjaarsveldwerk (spring trial) -Goed (jeugd), -KNJV-B Diploma (retrieving test), -all WSH club trials (retrieving tests) + therefore given the Predikaat.

Figure 36-80: *Windy* (far right) is the sister of Roy (Figure 36-79) and mother of Axel (Figure 36-78). (Far left) *Int. Sh CH Dazzling Dewdrop of Weimar's Joy, JW'03, HZP, Feld & Wasserprüfung, VGP, Lux Sh CH, Dan. Sh CH, HD-A* (Sh CH Gunalt's Wharfe at Rockleyan × Autumn Breeze of Weimar's Joy). *Autumn Breeze of Weimar's Joy, JW '98, Lux Youth Sh CH, VJP, HZP, Feld & Wasserprüfung, VGP Dutch Veteran Sh. CH, HD-A,* (Dargo von Blanken VJP, HZP, VGP × Grayshar Windsong on the Rise). *Bright Rain 'n Gale of Weimar's Joy, Feld & Wasserprüfung, VGP, HD-A,* (Forgun's Fifty Five × Grayshar Windsong on the Rise), *Lux Sh CH, Grayshar Windsong on the Rise VJP, HZP, Feld & Wasserprüfung, VGP HD-A,* (CH Grayshar's Royal Valor × DC Wynwood's Rain on the Rise, SDX, NRD, VX).

Exports to Spain and Portugal

Figure 36-81: *INT, AM and CAR, POR, SPA, ARG, LUX, GIB, BEL CH Soul Coast Mark's Promise* (Multi CH Juscanis Mens Legis Ad Colsidex × Multi CH Soul Coast New Age Dinkie). Bred by Andre Lucas; owned by João and Rute Soares. Goya loves to show and it is obvious. He started his career at an early age with successes as a puppy and as an adult. His travels earned him eight bench championships, including an International championship. Not satisfied to be "just" a winner, Goya was Portugal's Best Dog in Group and 5th Best Dog of All Breeds in 2004, as well as a World Winner in 2005. In addition to passing on his love of travel, he passed on his good looks too; read about his daughter Gracie in Figure 36-91.

Figure 36-82: *Span FC Legend's Mani v. d. Reiteralm, VJP, HZP190, VGP336* (VC DC AFC Magnum Gunnar Silvershot, MH, SDX, RDX, VX, BROM, FROM × Cora von der Schelmelach, MH, SD, NRD, Import). Bred by Virginia Alexander and Joseph Stroup; owned by Oliver Zügel. The product of a German mother and a American VC DC sire, Mani's field work earned him the cover of Sept 2003 Perros de Caza; the article discusses Mani's performance: "Mani impressed the judges and spectators by displaying a systematic and thorough field search pattern, covering the terrain from edge to edge. He was awarded a rating of "Excellent" in pointing, guiding, and steadiness to shot and fall. The dream of every dog trainer is to achieve the maximum possible 336 point score in the German Master Hunting Exam (VGP) which demonstrates the perfection of the dog's usefulness in every hunting situation. Very few dogs achieve maximum scores. Mani ended up being one of three to accomplish this goal, in what is the most complete and rigorous examination for versatile hunting dogs in the world." Mani would eventually become an international jetsetter, traveling to hunt and compete throughout Europe and South America.

Figure 36-83: *Am CH, Ptg CH, Spn CH, Lux CH, Gib CH Bella N Silhouette's Heart Throb* (CH Nani's Indecent Exposure, JH, NAJ, V, BROM × CH Silhouette All That Jazz, JH, NSD). Bred by Charlotte Haney; owned by João and Rute Soares, Casa de Juno Lisbon Winner 2006 and 2007, Oporto Winner 2007. (5) All Breeds Best in Show Winner, (6) All Breeds Reserve Best in Show Winner, (24) Best in Group, and multiple Group placements. All Breeds Best Dog of the year in Portugal 2006 and 2007 (by the Portuguese Kennel Club), represented Portugal at the 1st Edition of the Eukanuba World Challenge in Long Beach, CA. Best Opposite Sex at AKC/Eukanuba National Championship 2007

Figure 36-84: *Int Isr Gre Cyp Bul Yug Rom Spn Lux Swi Pol Cro CH Grayshar's Honor Bound* (CH Valmar's Apache Rebel, BROM × CH Grayshar Easy Impression, NSD, BROM). Bred by Sharon Hartman; owned by Ilana Bar-Tal. The winner of eight all breed BIS and five Reserve BIS, Zippo was also Junior European Winner 1999, Vice World Winner 2000, European Winner 2001 and 2004, and World Winner 2006.

Figure 36-85: *FCI CH Grayshar Eleanor V Reiteralm, NAJ, NAP, NJP, NRD, CD, HIT* (CH Grayshar Diesel Von Rob Roy, JH × CH Grayshar Silke V Valmar). Bred by Gregg and Sharon Hartmann; owned by Dr. Noa Safra. Eleanor was bred in the U.S. and exported to Israel as a puppy. In 2002, Eleanor's owner returned to the U.S. to continue her veterinary studies. In their spare time, Eleanor and Noa enjoyed competing in AKC agility and obedience.

Figure 36-86: *Int Isr Swi Lux Gre Cyp CH Camelot's Dorian Gray* (CH Nani's Southern Cross, BROM × CH Camelot's Halley's Comet, BROM). Bred by Susan Thomas; owned by Ilana Bar-Tal, Israel. Gray earned five all breed BIS as well as four reserve BIS, and was declared the Central European Champion and Vice World Winner in 1995, and the European Winner 1997 and 1999, and Vice World Winner 1995.

Figure 36-87: *If at all possible,* plan on visiting the interested breeder in their home country well before the proposed sale, or at least make liberal use of e-mail, photos, videos, and phone calls. This will not only allow the stateside breeder to determine what type of dog will best compliment the proposed breeding program, but that the new owner is responsible and knowledgeable with a proven track record. The development of the Reynisson's breeding program will help illustrate how well such relationship can work. Iceland has a very small and restricted gene pool, the Reynisson family competes in conformation, field, and junior showmanship in many countries under FCI and Icelandic Kennel Club rules, and they enjoying the bountiful opportunites to hunt game for the table.

An International Breeding Program

A compilation of suggestions from experienced breeders have produced some thoughts to consider when working with breeders in foreign countries.

Weimaraner breeders today have not only the opportunity to exchange bloodlines but a great responsibility when doing so. By considering the needs of the breeder in a foreign country, American breeders can enrich their gene pool by sending semen, leasing or selling quality stock. Many of the original exports, in the 1950s and 1960s, were pet puppies, traveling with their owners, who were willing (in many cases) to risk quarantine, but most often with little consideration on how the individual could improve or harm the breed as a whole. While it may be less expensive to send over a young puppy, it may, in the long term, be a false economy; the pup may not develop as anticipated, or may not prove to be a reliable producer. Artificial insemination may profit the breeder in the short term, but without a long term plan, may not be of the greatest benefit to the continuing program of either the stud owner, or the foreign breeder. Instead consider a long range program involving proven adult animals. But such a plan requires, well, planning.

If at all possible, visit the country well before hand; second best would be extensive e-mail exchange of photographs, videos and written judges' commentaries. Use this time to exchange evaluations of the strengths and weaknesses of each others' programs, and to gain hands on familiarity with each country's standard and style. Most importantly this will allow the breeder insight to the new owner's responsibility, knowledge, and track record, and if they are willing and able to accomplish competitive expectations. The new owner is assured they have a knowledgeable mentor in exchange. Far too many breeders have had promising pups disappear once they leave the U.S.; if there is any doubt, find a stateside home for that precious pup.

Sending only superior animals that will help improve the genetic pool without introducing undesirable genetic baggage, advancing the long term health and development of the breeder's program, will also enhance the U.S. breeder's reputation. Therefore, export only a dog that would be worthy of consideration in the breeder's own program. If a puppy or young dog has been identified as having a desirable genetic contribution based on the pedigree, keep, train and compete with the animal long enough to establish it's *bona fides*—health clearances, temperament, type, trainability, and talent that are worthy of duplication and as complimentary as expected. Usually this means finishing a championship (or at least well pointed) and earning additional performance titles.

Figure 36-88: *Schattenbergs Spice V Reiteralm, JH, NSD* (CH Axel Reiteralm of Weimar's Joy, CD, JH, RD, NSD, VX × Sanbar's Ms-kitty von Reiteralm). Bred by Virginia Alexander; owned by Selma Gudnadottir. A proven brood matron, Spice, generously donated by geneticist Jackie Isabell, was the first Weimaraner to participate in the Reynissons' new program. At the time of export, Spice already titled in the field and conformation pointed and was also the dam of multiple show champions. Spice's pedigree included a proven imported Dutch sire, and a maternal granddam of solid bench championship lines with a Hall of Fame Field Champion maternal grandsire. It proved to be the perfect cup of tea for the fledgling Icelandic breeding program, demanding the duality of show quality conformation and solid field talent. The two litters Spice would produce in Iceland have proven to be pivotal in the development of solid working and conformation bloodlines for the Reynissons'.

If sending a stud dog, remember to collect and store several artificial inseminations before the change of ownership. This will allow the original breeder continued access to a superior dog's genetic contribution, but establishing the dog's conformation and performance credentials in another country may even enhance the dog's desirability as a sire at home. A breeder in another country may wish to consider importing an established sibling of well-known sire, if unable to purchase the most desired stud.

Plan on a continuing mentorship and on-going relationships, with personal visits or at least frequent e-mails. Consider the likelihood and future willingness of sending another Weimaraner of the opposite sex with complimenting bloodlines. If a foreign breeder already has a favored stud, a bitch may be another step in a long term program. Just as with a stud, the bitch's credentials should be well established. Maiden bitches will be able to provide a longer breeding career; however, her value remains to be proven, and could potentially be a disappointment. Although breeders are often extremely reluctant to part with a proven matron bitch, their prepotency is already known, as well as the likelihood of a favorable nick with a particular stud. If planning multiple lit-

Figure 36-89: *Silva SGT Schultz Rider* (NFC FC Grau Geist Lil's Caprock Rev × FC Snake Breaks Run Wild Idaho). Bred by Roger Schlachter; owned by the Reynissons'. When working with breeders from elsewhere, it is important to select dogs that will meet the specific needs of the new owner. The small population of Weimaraners in Iceland demands true versatility. Silva was chosen because her bloodlines indicated she would improve scenting skills and staunch pointing in the Reynissons' lines. Silva was the first Weimaraner to place at an Icelandic field trial where the ptarmigan is the common game found at trials and prized for the table. The plan proved successful; as when bred back into mainly show lines, Silva's pups have won group placements in the conformation ring and have exceeded their mother in the field placements and wins.

Figure 36-90: *CH Kasamar Antares* (FC AFC Davison's Orion on the Rise, MH × CH Bluhaven's Diamon Lil, JH, NRD, V). Bred by Karen Sanvold and Marilyn Stokes; owned by the Reynissons'. Sired by a field trial champion (of straight field trial lines) with a dam who was a show champion (of straight show lines), Taso was donated by Karen Sandvold, Marilyn Stokes, and Holly McKnight as a gift to the Icelandic Kennel Club, and was completely unrelated to any of the dogs previously sent. He had already earned his Bench CH (with a Group Placement), qualifications toward his JH, and rated OFA Excellent. Since arriving at his new home he has earned his Icelandic conformation title totally junior handled, and is working on his final field rating in order to complete his International FCI Championship.

Figure 36-91: *Int, Por, Irs, Spa Gib Ntl Int CH Casa de Juno Amazing Grace* (Multi CH Soul Coast Mark's Promise × Gunalt Ingenious) A true product of the Jet Age...Gracie loves to travel, and has along the way, according to her owners, become the most titled bitch of all time in Europe, with 19 all-breed BIS. Her travels began early as the daughter of an English bitch and an Brazilian sire imported to Portugal. Gracie has traveled back to the U.S. to be bred to an American stud and passed her traveling genes on to two of her children who have gone BIS, one in Portugal and the other in Hungary. She and her breeders demonstrate the value of the knowledgeable exchange of bloodlines regardless on nationality.

ters from the same bitch, it is wisest to use different sires for each litter, even if the first breeding is considered highly successful; artificial inseminations from differing complimentary sires will allow more options to return back to the bitch in future generations, improve flaws that may unexpectedly arise, as well as offer genetic diversity in limited gene pools.

The greatest flexibility for both the exporter and importer is to consider leasing rather than purchasing animals. This allows the foreign breeder the chance to increase genetic diversity and more options to improve flaws or reinforce strengths by leasing different animals over a long term. When the lease has been fulfilled the dog returns to the U.S. with an international reputation, and perhaps an array of conformation and performance titles earned with the lessee who in turn, benefits from the dog's contribution to their own and other local breeding programs. If lessee has stored semen during the lease, the contribution may continue well into in the future. If the original owner collected semen before sending off the well insured international Casanova, they will still be able to include him in their own breeding program while he is away.

The Intricacies of International Travel

Traveling between countries

American Weimaraner fanciers who decide to enter the world of international competition or importing and exporting of stock need to become familiar with not only the United States Department of Agriculture regulations, but also the import and export regulations of the countries they wish to visit. While the European Union (E.U.) has resulted in "some" consistency of regulations among those countries, there are still variations. The American Consulate in the destination country would be a good starting point for anyone wishing to travel with, import or export a dog.

All dogs shipped as cargo or traveling on airlines are required to have a health certificate; for international travel the veterinarian issuing the certificate must be approved by the Department of Agriculture. The vet providing this service should be a good source of tips and information regarding international travel; they will also be able to tell if it is necessary to acquire an additional certification from the respective Department of Agriculture and/or the consulate of the receiving country (do not rely solely on the airlines to provide accurate information regarding paperwork that may be required upon arrival in the destination country). While it is necessary to plan well ahead of time, health certificates are only valid for a limited period, so make sure you do not get this done too early.

One of the greatest deterrents to international travel has consistently been the quarantine regulations and their wide variations. Under the Pet Travel Scheme (PETS) many E.U. countries have dispensed with quarantines for dogs with appropriate health and vaccination records; and in most cases dogs can travel freely though E.U. countries as long as they have a European Pet Passport. Preparations to qualify for a Passport can be lengthy; those planning to travel to the E.U. may need to begin making preparations as much as nine months in advance. At least through 2010, however, the United Kingdom (Ireland has its own regulations) remains the most notable exception, with the strictest regulations and quarantines of any country; dogs from certain "listed" countries may move in and out of the U.K. as long as they have the required documentation and have not been to any country not "listed" in the preceding six months. Any dog which has been, or even passed through an unlisted country must endure a 6-month facility quarantine (for which reservations must be made in advance).

Figure 36-92: *Int PR, Lat Am, Car, Am CH Kaceem's Karibbean Kaper, CDX, OA, V* (CH Smokey City EZ Moonstone, JH, NRD, V, BROM × Am. and Can. CH Kaceem's Flash Dancer). Bred by Kate Masters; owned by Eleanor Abarca, Puerto Rico. Dog fanciers in Puerto Rico, a U.S. territory, have unique opportunities. They are able to participate in AKC activities, while also enjoying access to many FCI venues. Kaper went Winners Bitch at the World Dog show held in Puerto Rico. Other familiar organizations such as USDAA (United States Dog Agility Association) are also available.

Figure 36-93: *Int, PR, Lat Am, Car, Am CH Graytsky's Moon Shadow, CDX, RE, OA, OAJ, NAP, NJP, V* (CH Nani's Smart Aleck, JH, NRD, V, BROM × CH Nani N'Graytsky's Harvest Moon). Bred by Amy and Michael Anderson and Patricia Crowley; owned by Eleanor and Ramon Abarca, Puerto Rico. While WCA opportunities are fewer, there are abundant opportunities to compete in other venues. The ability to compete in AKC activities does allow Puerto Rican fanciers to still earn versatility tiles competing in AKC activities.

Many other countries outside the E.U. also have quarantine periods which range from 120 days (Guam and Norway) to 14 days (Japan), while 30 days is a common time frame for countries such as Australia and New Zealand. Again in many cases, reservations for quarantine space must be made in advance at a licensed quarantine facility. A few countries (such as Norway and Ireland) also require an in-home quarantine period after the facility quarantine.

When planning air travel, shop all the airlines to find the most direct flight possible; non-stop is always preferable. When shipping a dog abroad, it might best to travel to the nearest major international airport ahead of time to get the animal on a non-stop flight and avoid having the dog transferred between airlines or flights. The regulations for crates for international travel are slightly different than for travel within the United States; review the regulations to be sure the crate meets the added requirements (such as ventilation on all four sides of the crate rather than the required three sides common in domestic travel).

Always inquire what the fare would be if the dog were shipped as cargo (unaccompanied) versus being shipped as accompanied cargo or flying in cabin with a passenger. Prices for these services may vary by several hundred dollars; on occasion it may be more cost effective (and enjoyable) to fly over with the dog as accompanied baggage or in cabin.

The regulations for travel, both within and without the United States are constantly changing. Check with both the U.S. State Department and the embassy in your destination country for assistance; frequently a visit to the country's consulate as well as the Department of Agriculture is required to complete the paperwork, which usually has a short deadline. Alternatively, if the idea of international travel seems overly daunting, consider an international pet transportation service that will not only help meet compliance regulations, but also help plan and arrange the trip. While this service may save many headaches, as well as providing a resource if things do not go as planned, this service usually comes with a hefty charge. Consult with others, and get strong references for whatever agency is being considered.

Refer to *Life with Weimaraners* for additional travel tips.

Figure 36-94: *Aust Am CH Greydove Ekahi Island Gal, BROM* (Aust GrCH Waldiese N dout About It, CD × Aust CH Greydove Nice N EZ). Bred by Greydove Kennels; owned by Daryle Oliveria and Val Peters. Imported form Australia to Hawaii she quickly earned her U.S. CH and went on to earn an all breed BIS when she was just 17 months old. Tita has earned her BROM rating and is the dam of six champions.

Figure 36-95: *Aus Gr CH Divani Just a Dash (AI)* (Aust Gr Ch Am Ch Colsidex Grauhund Just Jeans (Imp USA) × Aust Ch Divani Vanity Fair). Bred and owned by D. Horner, V. Speck, and G. and L. Kellett. Dash has earned 35 All Breed Best in Show wins in Australia. His pedigree reflects his breeder's consideration of the use of a mixture of resources, using artificial insemination and imports to combine with her own established lines to develop and progress toward her vision of the dog on the hill. Although Australian born and bred, only 11 of his 62 ancestors in a five-generation pedigree are Australian dogs.

Artificial Alternatives

The advent of improved artificial insemination and shipping practices has made the transportation of frozen semen a viable alternative to actually shipping animals for breeding purposes. When considering the potential for artificial insemination verify that the destination country allows the registration of dogs from AI, and that the owner of the receiving bitch is knowledgeable regarding inspection and registration of such

Figure 36-96: *CH Nani's Tsurutani Honor Bound, JH* (CH Nani's Indecent Exposure, JH, NAJ, V, BROM × CH Nani's Jagmar Sweet Dividends, VCD2, MH, MXJ, MX, NSD, NRD, VX4, BROM). Bred by Teresa Borman and Chris Grisell; owned by Karen Taniguchi and Chris Grisell. Bounder went to Hawaii after finishing his championship stateside, he then earned his BIS handled by Daryle Olveria. Returning stateside on two different occasions, Bounder went Best of Opposite Sex at the 2006 and 2009 WCA National Specilty.

offspring. When shipping semen abroad, there are still quite often very strict regulations. When shipping individually, there may be limits on the number of vials/straws of semen that may be included in a single shipment, as well as providing health clearances similar to a health certificate for a live animal. Some semen storage facility have international connections as well, possibly providing routine shipping connections with their counterparts which may be a convenient and less expensive alternative for shipping semen to or from overseas, saving the breeder a great deal of difficulties. These specialists, and storage facilities are knowledgeable in the specialized regulations that may allow the shipment to proceed through customs without opening the actual container for inspection (which may be a critical factor in timeliness and maintaining proper temperatures), as well as the required return shipment of the container and any hazardous material clearances that may be required. Additionally, specialized companies and storage facilities can coordinate bulk shipments which may be more cost effective and subject to different regulations that may be more favorable to insuring the viability of the semen on arrival. With a little sleuthing a breeder may find that very large conformation circuit shows routinely host semen collection services; these companies often have international connections to provide storage in several countries.

International shipments of semen absolutely require significant time to plan ahead. It is virtually impossible to ship the frozen semen in a timely manner once the bitch has come into season. Send the semen ahead of time and pay the month or so storage fee with the overseas storage facility while waiting for the most propitious moment. Carefully consider using fresh chilled semen for overseas breedings—the chances of success may be reduced due to the extended shipping time.

It is best to take the bitch to the destination storage facility for implantation. Otherwise a second transportation of the semen is required, not only increasing costs, but risking the quality and viability of the frozen semen. Since overseas shipments of frozen semen can be expensive, be sure that all agreements are settled well ahead of the desired breeding time, particularly regarding who will pay the costs of shipping (all shipping, if multiple shipments are required). The stud owner should be adamant about not signing the release for the semen until payment is in hand (not in the mail).

Weims Around the World

The option of shipping semen for artificial insemination opens many doors for Weim fanciers around the world to explore many options that have not been previously available. While these opportunities may seem an easy way to open new genetic doors for areas with limited gene pools, a wise breeder will open the door slowly and carefully. Participating in such international exchanges should be considered a privilege as well as a responsibility; the fancier should carefully consider what a dog has to contribute to another country. A creative and dedicated breeder may consider many options that allow the greatest flexibility. International artificial insemination is certainly one option, but also consider collecting and maintaining the semen of a special dog here in the U.S. before exchanging, leasing, or selling the dog to a great home in another country to spread genetic diversity. In return, the breeder may gain international reputation and titles, in addition to contributing to genetic diversity. Breeding basics will provide a foundation, but perhaps equally as important as the opportunity to exchange genetic material is the chance for fanciers to exchange ideas and information, and explore the philosophy and practices of breeding, raising, training, and testing Weimaraners. With forethought and consideration, this type of exchange can strengthen not only the ties between fanciers but contribute to the overall health, type, and talents of Weimaraners on many far away hills around the world.

Figure 36-97: *The dog on the hill…may every breeder be blessed with their own vision.* Photograph by Barney Riley.

Figure A-1: *CH Colsidex Seabreeze Perfect Fit* (CH Colsidex The Farm Top of the Mark, BROM × CH Seabreeze Colsidex Perfect Timing, JH). Bred by Judy Colan, Marge Davis, Debra McCray; owned by Ellen Charles, Alessandra Folz, and Judy Colan. The product of a line breeding of the top winners and producers from the Colsidex and Seabreeze lines, Marge (named for her co-breeder Marge Davis) is every breeder's dream. Winners Bitch from the 6–9 Puppy class at the 2004 National Specialty and on to Best Bitch in Futurity in 2005 and her first Best in Show at the same show. She broke all records for the breed including her grandmother's, CH Arias Allegra of Colsidex, of 27 Best in Shows. Marge retired with No. 1 Weimaraner for 3 years, No. 3 Sporting Dog in 2007 and 2008, and Sporting Group Is at both the 2007 Eukanuba Classic and 2008 Westminster Kennel Club Show, a record-breaking 36 Best in Shows, as well as an unprecedented consecutive 4 National Specialty wins. Marge achieved every one of these accolades under the talented handling and conditioning of her co-owner Alessandra Folz.

WEIMARANER STANDARDS

AKC Weimaraner Breed Standard

Sporting Group

General Appearance

A medium-sized gray dog, with fine aristocratic features. He should present a picture of grace, speed, stamina, alertness and balance. Above all, the dog's conformation must indicate the ability to work with great speed and endurance in the field.

Height

Height at the withers: dogs, 25 to 27 inches; bitches, 23 to 25 inches. One inch over or under the specified height of each sex is allowable but should be penalized. Dogs measuring less than 24 inches or more than 28 inches and bitches measuring less than 22 inches or more than 26 inches shall be disqualified.

Head

Moderately long and aristocratic, with moderate stop and slight median line extending back over the forehead. Rather prominent occipital bone and trumpets well set back, beginning at the back of the eye sockets. Measurement from tip of nose to stop equals that from stop to occipital bone. The flews should be straight, delicate at the nostrils. Skin drawn tightly. Neck clean-cut and moderately long. Expression kind, keen and intelligent. Ears—Long and lobular, slightly folded and set high. The ear when drawn snugly alongside the jaw should end approximately 2 inches from the point of the nose. Eyes--In shades of light amber, gray or blue-gray, set well enough apart to indicate good disposition and intelligence. When dilated under excitement the eyes may appear almost black. Teeth—Well set, strong and even; well-developed and proportionate to jaw with correct scissors bite, the upper teeth protruding slightly over the lower teeth but not more than 1/16 of an inch. Complete dentition is greatly to be desired. Nose—Gray. Lips and Gums—Pinkish flesh shades.

Body

The back should be moderate in length, set in a straight line, strong, and should slope slightly from the withers. The chest should be well developed and deep with shoulders well laid back. Ribs well sprung and long. Abdomen firmly held; moderately tucked-up flank. The brisket should extend to the elbow.

Coat and Color

Short, smooth and sleek, solid color, in shades of mouse-gray to silver-gray, usually blending to lighter shades on the head and ears. A small white marking on the chest is permitted, but should be penalized on any other portion of the body. White spots resulting from injury should not be penalized. A distinctly long coat is a disqualification. A distinctly blue or black coat is a disqualification.

Forelegs

Straight and strong, with the measurement from the elbow to the ground approximately equaling the distance from the elbow to the top of the withers.

Hindquarters

Well-angulated stifles and straight hocks. Musculation well developed.

Feet

Firm and compact, webbed, toes well arched, pads closed and thick, nails short and gray or amber in color. Dewclaws—Should be removed.

Tail

Docked. At maturity it should measure approximately 6 inches with a tendency to be light rather than heavy and should be carried in a manner expressing confidence and sound temperament. A non-docked tail shall be penalized.

Gait

The gait should be effortless and should indicate smooth coordination. When seen from the rear, the hind feet should be parallel to the front feet. When viewed from the side, the topline should remain strong and level.

Temperament

The temperament should be friendly, fearless, alert and obedient.

Faults

Minor Faults: Tail too short or too long. Pink nose.

Major Faults: Doggy bitches. Bitchy dogs. Improper muscular condition. Badly affected teeth. More than four teeth missing. Back too long or too short. Faulty coat. Neck too short, thick or throaty. Low-set tail. Elbows in or out. Feet east and west. Poor gait. Poor feet. Cowhocks. Faulty backs, either roached or sway. Badly overshot, or undershot bite. Snipy muzzle. Short ears.

Very Serious Faults: White, other than a spot on the chest. Eyes other than gray, blue-gray or light amber. Black mottled mouth. Non-docked tail. Dogs exhibiting strong fear, shyness or extreme nervousness.

Disqualifications

Deviation in height of more than one inch from standard either way. A distinctly long coat. A distinctly blue or black coat.

Approved December 14, 1971

The Canadian Kennel Club Weimaraner standard can be found at:

www.ckc.ca/en/Portals/0/pdf/breeds/WIA.pdf

Figure A-2: *Early exposure to game is vital* in developing the puppies prey-drive and natural hunting abilities. Photographs courtesy of Michaela Czeslik, "A-litter," Kennel von Unstrut, Germany.

German Weimaraner Breed Standard

FCI-Standard N° 99/13. 02. 2002/GB

Weimaraner

Translation: C. Seidler.

Origin: Germany.

Date of publication of the original valid standard: 27.02.1990.

Utilization: Versatile hunting dog, pointing dog.

Classification F.C.I.: Group 7, Continental Pointing Dogs.

Section 1.1 Continental Pointing, Dogs, Type «Braque».
With working trial.

Brief Historical Summary

There are numerous theories regarding the origin of the Weimaraner Pointing Dog. Only so much is certain: That the Weimaraner, which at that time still contained a great deal of liam hound blood («Leithund») was already kept at the Weimar court in the first third of the 19th century.

In the middle of the century, before pure breeding was started, breeding was mainly in the hands of professional hunters and game keepers in central Germany, mostly in the regions round Weimar and in Thuringia. As the days of the liam hounds passed, the dogs were crossed with the «Hühnerhund» and breeding was continued with this cross. From about 1890 on, the breed was produced according to a plan and regarded as suitable for registration in a stud book. Apart from the short-haired Weimaraner, a long-haired variety occurred, if only singly, since the turn of the century. Since being admitted to the stud book, the Weimaraner has been pure bred, remaining mostly free from crosses with any other breeds, in particular, Pointers. Therefore the Weimaraner is likely to be the oldest German «pointing» breed, which has been pure bred for about a hundred years.

General Appearance

Medium to large size hunting dog. Functional working type, pleasing in shape, sinewy and very muscular. Difference in type between dogs and bitches easily distinguished.

Important Proportions

Length of body to height at withers approximately 12: 11.

Proportions of the head: From tip of nose to stop slightly longer than from stop to occiput.

Forequarters: Distance from elbow to mid-pastern and distance from elbow to point of withers about equal.

Behaviour/Temperament: Versatile, easily trained steady and passionate hunting dog. Persevering in systematic search, yet not too lively. Remarkable ability to pick up scent. Ready to seize game and other prey; he is a good watchdog, without aggressiveness however. Reliable pointing dog and worker in water. Remarkable inclination to work after the shot.

Head

Cranial Region

Skull: In balance with size of body and facial region. Broader in dogs than bitches, yet in both, the relationship between width of cranial region to total length of head must be in good proportion. Median groove on forehead. Slightly to moderately protruding occipital bone. Zygomatic arches easily traceable behind the eyes.

Stop: Extremely slight.

Facial Region

Nose: Nose leather large, protruding over the underjaw. Dark flesh colour, merging gradually into gray towards the rear.

Muzzle: Long and, specially in the male, powerful, appearing almost angular. Region of canines and carnassial teeth equally strong. Bridge of nose straight, often slightly arched, never with a concave curve.

Flews: Moderately deep, flesh coloured, as are the gums. Slight labial corner.

Jaws/Teeth: Jaws strong; teeth complete, regular and strong. Top and bottom incisors closely touching (scissor bite).

Cheeks: Muscular, clearly defined. Definitely «clean» head.

Eyes: Amber colour, dark to pale, with intelligent expression. Sky-blue in puppies. Round, set barely slanting. Lids well fitting.

Leathers: Lobular, broad and fairly long, just reaching to corner of mouth. Set on high and narrow, forming a rounded off point at tip. In alterness, turned slightly forward, folded.

Neck

Noble appearance and carriage. Upper line arched in profile. Muscular, nearly round, not too short, clean. Becoming stronger towards the shoulders and merging harmoniously into the topline and chest.

Body

Topline: From the arched neckline, over the well defined withers the topline merges gradually into the relatively long, firm back.

Withers: Well defined.

Back: Firm and muscular, without a dip. Not running up towards the rear. A slightly longer back, a breed characteristic, is not a fault.

Croup: Pelvis long and moderately sloped.

Chest: Strong but not unduly broad, with sufficient depth to reach almost to elbows and of sufficient length. Well sprung without being barrel-shaped and with long ribs. Forechest well developed.

Underline and Belly: Rising slightly, but belly not tucked up.
Tail: Set on slightly lower than with other similar breeds. Tail strong and well coated. Carried hanging down in repose. When alert or working, carried level or higher.

Limbs

Forequarters

General: High on leg, sinewy, straight and parallel, but not standing wide.

Shoulders: Long and sloping. Well fitting, strongly muscled. Well angulated shoulder joint.

Upper arm: Sloping, sufficiently long and strong.

Elbows: Free and lying parallel to median plane of body. Turned neither in nor out.

Forearm: Long, straight and vertical.

Pastern joint: Strong and taut.

Pastern: Sinewy, slightly sloping.

Front feet: Firm and strong. Standing straight in relation to median plane of body. Toes arched. Longer middle toes are a breed characteristic and therefore not a fault. Nails light to dark gray. Pads well pigmented, coarse.

Hindquarters

General: High on leg, sinewy i.e. well muscled. Standing parallel, turning neither in nor out.

Upper thigh: Sufficiently long, strong and well muscled.

Stifle: Strong and taut.

Lower thigh: Long with clearly visible tendons.

Hock joint: Strong and taut.

Hock: Sinewy, almost vertical in position.

Hind feet: Tight and firm, without dewclaws, otherwise like front feet.

Gait/Movement

Movement in all gaits is ground covering and smooth. Hind and front legs set parallel to each other. Gallop long and flat. Back remains level when trotting. Pacing is undesirable.

Skin

Strong. Well but not too tight fitting.

Coat

Hair

Short-haired: Short (but longer and thicker than with most comparable breeds), strong, very dense, smooth lying topcoat. Without or with only very sparse undercoat.

Long-haired: Soft, long topcoat with or without undercoat. Smooth or slightly wavy. Long flowing hair at ear set on. Velvety hair is permissible on tips of leathers. Length of coat on flanks 3–5 cm. On lower side of neck, forechest and belly, generally somewhat longer.

Good feathering and breeching, yet less long towards ground. Tail with good flag. Hair between toes. Hair on head less long. A type of coat similar to a double-coat (Stockhaar) with medium length, dense, close fitting topcoat, thick undercoat and moderately developed feathering and breeching, sometimes occurs in dogs of mixed ancestry.

Colour

Silver, roe or mouse grey, as well as shades of these colours. Head and leathers generally slightly paler. Only small white markings on chest and toes permitted. Sometimes a more or less defined trace occurs along the back. Dog with definite reddish-yellow marking («Brand») may only be given the classification « good ». Brown marking is a serious fault.

Size and Weight

Height at the withers

Dogs: 59–70 cm (ideal measurement 62–67 cm).

Bitches: 57–65 cm (ideal measurement 59–63 cm).

Weight

Dogs: about 30–40 kg.

Bitches: about 25–35 kg.

Faults

Any departure from the foregoing points should be considered a fault and the seriousness with which the fault should be regarded should be in exact proportion to its degree.

Serious Faults

Clear deviation from type. Untypical sexual characteristics.

Gross deviations from size and proportions.

Facial region: Gross deviations e.g. too strong flews, short or pointed muzzle.

Jaws and teeth: Lack of more than two PM1 or M3.

Eyes: slight faults, above all slight and unilateral faults in eyelids.

Leathers: Definitely short or long, not folded.

Throatiness (dewlap), great deviation in neck shape and muscle.

Back: Definite sway or roach back. Rump higher than withers.

Chest, belly: Barrel shaped chest. Insufficient depth or length of chest. Tucked up belly.

Gross anomalies in stance i.e. lack of angulation, out at elbows, splay feet.

Pronounced bow legs or cow hocks.

Bad movement in different gaits, also lack of free forward movement or drive, pacing.

Serious deficencies i.e. skin very fine or very coarse.

Mixture of coat varieties defined in the standard.

Lack of feathering on belly or leathers (leather ears). Widely spread woolly coat in the short-haired Weimaraner or curly or sparse feathering in the long-haired variety.

Departure from shades of gray, such as yellow or brownish. Tan marking («Brand»).

Strong departure from correct height or weight (e.g. more than 2 cm from measurements given in the standard).

Slight deficiency in temperament.

Other serious faults.

Eliminating Faults

Faulty temperament, i.e. shy or nervous.

Completely untypical, above all too heavy or too light in build.

Completely unbalanced.

Absolutely untypical, e.g. bulldog - type head.

Facial region: Absolutely untypical i.e. distinctly concave nasal bridge.

Jaws and teeth: Overshot, undershot, missing further teeth other than quoted.

Eyes: Entropion, ectropion.

Leathers: Absolutely untypical, i.e. stand-off.

Particularly pronounced dewlap.

Back: Severe sway or roach back. Definitely overbuilt at croup.

Chest, belly: Markedly barrel shaped or malformed chest.

Legs rickety or malformed.

Chronic lameness.

Totally restricted movement.

Skin defects and malformations.

Partial or total hair loss.

White markings other than on chest and feet.

Colour other than gray. Widespread brown marking.

Definitely over-or undersized.

Other malformation. Illnesses which must be considered hereditary, i.e. epilepsy.

The compilers can, naturally, not list all faults which occur, the above are to be regarded as examples.

Any dog clearly showing physical or behavioural abnormalities shall be disqualified.

N.B.: Male animals should have two apparently normal testicles fully descended into the scrotum.

Figure A-3: *Pick of the litter.* Photograph by Virginia Alexander.

Figure B-1: *MacBeth,* by William Wegman

WCA PROGRAMS

Ratings

For the most current rules and procedures for hosting a ratings test please refer to the WCA website www.weimclubamerica.org

In order to qualify for a rating the dog's owner must be a member of the WCA.

Shooting Ratings

NSD-Novice Shooting Dog

The purpose of this classification is to determine whether young or inexperienced dogs have field and hunting aptitude.

A. Range and Performance

1. The dog must have the DESIRE TO HUNT and the ability to range out to a practical hunting distance. He is not required to work in a systematic manner.

B. Point and Shot

1. Dogs to be run in braces, if possible.

2. Dogs must point (flash point accepted) and a .22 blank (no crimps) will be fired by handler on bird contact. Gun shy dog cannot pass, catching or chasing will not be penalized.

3. Birds should be planted in a manner to allow visibility of the dog for the judges (Novice Dog only). Flags, ribbons, etc. shall not be used to indicate the location of the bird.

C. Recognized game birds "preferred" or pigeons, a minimum of three (3) birds per brace shall be used. Flight of bird shall not be impaired by caging, hobbling, wing clipping, brailing or any other manner.

D. Dogs are to be run for a total of 20 minutes. If birdfield is used, no more or less than eight (8) minutes permitted in birdfield.

E. Dogs are to be run on a pass-fail basis, and must pass in all the following categories to qualify:

1. Desire to hunt.
2. Boldness.
3. Initiative and search.
4. Point.
5. Reasonable obedience to handlers commands.
6. Gun shy dogs cannot pass.

SD—Shooting Dog

This rating is to establish that a dog of any age has definite hunting ability, bird sense, and show some field training.

A. Range and Performance

1. Dogs to be run in braces, if possible, and must show a keen desire to hunt, be bold and independent, have a fast and yet attractive style of running, and demonstrate not only intelligence in seeking objectives, but also ability to find game.

B. Point and Shot

1. Shooting Dogs must point and must not flush the bird before the handler makes an honest effort to flush bird, if the dog then breaks and catches or flushes the bird, this will be deemed an acceptable performance. If the bird flushes wild due to no fault of the dog, the judges may allow the dog to re-demonstrate pointing ability. Also see Section V Item C.

2. Dog need not be steady to wing and shot.

3. A dog encountering its bracemate on point must honor. Failure of a dog to honor when it sees its bracemate on point must be penalized, and a dog that steals its bracemate's point shall be disqualified. Dog may be held after establishing an honor.

4. Dog interfered with on point will be allowed to re-demonstrate ability.

5. Retrieve

   a. The dog must make a direct retrieve of all birds. Delivery to hand is not required but the bird must be brought to within reach of the handler. Serious hard mouthing can disqualify the dog, if the bird is examined and found seriously damaged by both judges.

C. Recognized game birds, a minimum of three (3) birds per brace shall be used. Flight of bird shall not be impaired by caging, hobbling, wing clipping, brailing or any other manner.

D. Dogs are to be run for a total of 30 minutes. If bird field is used, no more or less than eight (8) minutes permitted in bird field.

E. .22 caliber blanks, or larger, shall be fired on "back course" contact with birds (no .22 caliber crimps allowed).

F. Dogs are to be run on a pass-fail basis, and must pass in all the following categories to qualify:

1. Keen desire to hunt.

2. Boldness and independence.

3. Cover ground quickly in an attractive style.

4. Seek objectives.

5. Locate and point game.

6. Retrieve.

7. Reasonable obedience to handlers commands.

8. Gun shy dogs cannot pass.

SDX—Shooting Dog Excellent

This is the top award offered under the field ratings and dogs qualifying must be finished, fully broken bird dogs.

A. Range and Performance

1. Their field work should show the class and style expected of top Weimaraners. As some of these dogs may be field trial dogs, their range may vary between All Age Dogs and Gun Dogs. Each dog should be judged accordingly and on an individual basis, with neither being penalized as long as they remain under the control of the handler.

B. Point and Shot

1. Dogs shall be run in braces, if possible. The stake shall be a retrieving stake, with all the manners associated with that type of stake.

2. The dog must find a bird and establish a staunch point.

3. A dog encountering its bracemate on point must honor. Failure of a dog to honor when it sees its bracemate on point must be penalized, and a dog that steals its bracemate's point shall be disqualified. Honoring dog cannot be physically restrained.

4. A reasonable move of a dog to mark a bird flushed after point is acceptable; but this shall not excuse a break or a delayed chase: Dog may be collared out of the area if applicable to the situation.

5. Retrieve

   a. The dog must make a direct retrieve of all birds. Delivery to hand is required. Serious hard mouthing can disqualify the dog, if the bird is examined and found seriously damaged by both judges.

C. Recognized game birds, a minimum of three (3) birds per brace shall be used. Flight of bird shall not be impaired by caging, hobbling, wing clipping, brailing or any other manner.

Figure B-2: *Callbacks at Ardmore.* Photograph by Rodney Moon.

Retrieving Dog

A. Requirements for dogs competing for RD shall be as follows:

1. Land Retrieve

   a. The dog is required to retrieve a wide-spaced (approximately 60 degree angle) double with the first fall at approximately 50 yards, and the second fall at approximately (but not less than) 20 yards, one bird will be shot.

   b. Caliber of gun shall be 20 gauge or larger or .22 caliber blank.

2. Water Retrieve

   a. The dog is required to retrieve a wide-spaced (approximately 60 degree angle) double through eight (8) decoys, with the falls being at distances of approximately 50 yards on the first fall through decoy, and 20 yards on the second fall.

   b. Dog must enter water promptly.

B. Scoring—All scoring is on a pass/fail basis according to the official result forms.

C. Procedures

1. Handler MUST release from, and MUST remain within the circle, and dog MUST retrieve TO HAND in all retrieving tests.

2. No dog may be sent to retrieve until the last bird has hit the ground/water and the handler has been directed to send dog by judges.

3. The dog shall be steady on the line (controlled break allowed). Touch to release permitted, but restraint not permitted. Controlled break allowed means "Voice and/or hand signal may be used to stop dog, however, dog must have all four feet inside the circle to be defined as being under control."

4. Handler must remain within the circle until the retrieve is completed. Dog must deliver bird to circle with at least the dog's front feet in the circle in all retrieving tests.

5. Disqualifications

   a. Hardmouthing (both Judges must declare bird as unfit.

   b. Excessive delay of over two (2) minutes to enter or reenter the water.

   c. Loses interest, wanders around aimlessly, or up and down water edge.

   d. Refuses handler commands to handle, over five (5) times.

   e. Lift their leg on every bush, etc.

   f. Performance so bad, judge would not take hunting.

Figure B-3: *Silver.* Photograph by Cindilla Trent.

Versatile Ratings

I.   Schedule of Available Versatile Points

A. Bench Champion	8
Ten Bench Points (includes major win)	6
Five Bench Points	4
Bench Pointed	2
B. Obedience Trial Champion	10
UDX	8
UD	6
CDX	4
CD	2
C. Field Champion, AFC or MH	10
Senior Hunter, SDX or 1st place in AA/GD Retrieving Stake	6
Junior Hunter, SD or 4 Field Points	4
NSD or 1 Field Point	2
D. RDX	6
RD	4
NRD	2
E. Champion Tracker (CT)	10
Variable Surface Tracking (VST)	8
Tracking Dog Excellent (TDX)	6
Tracking Dog (TD)	4
F. Master Agility Champion	10
Master Agility Excellent (MX) or MXJ	8
Agility Excellent (AX) or AXJ	6
Agility Excellent Preferred (AXP) or AJP	5
Open Agility (OA) or OAJ	4
Open Agility Preferred (OAP) or OJP	3
Novice Agility (NA) or NAJ	2
Novice Agility Preferred (NAP) or NJP	1

II. Requirements for Award of Versatile "V"

    A. Twelve (12) versatile points minimum total.

    B. Above Twelve (12) points must be obtained from at least three (3) of the above six (6) groups.

    C. Points are not accumulative in any one group (i.e., a UD entitles a dog to six (6) points. His CDX and CD cannot be added.)

III. Requirements for Award of Versatile Excellent "VX"

    A. Eighteen (18) points minimum total

    B. Above eighteen (18) points may be obtained from three (3) of the above six (6) groups and must include a Bench Champion, Field Champion, Amateur Field Champion, Obedience Trial Champion, Master Agility Champion or Champion Tracker.

    OR

    Above eighteen (18) points may be obtained from at least four (4) of the six (6) groups.

C. Points are not accumulative in any one group.

IV. Requirements for Award of Versatile Excellent 2 (VX2)

    A. Twenty four (24) points minimum total.

    B. Above twenty-four (24) points must be obtained from at least four (4) of the above six (6) groups.

    C. Points are not accumulative in any one group.

V. Requirements for Award of Versatile Excellent 3 (VX3)–VX7

    A. Must meet the requirements of Versatile Excellent 2 (VX2)

    B. Minimum total points required:

        VX3 30 Points

        VX4 36 Points

        VX5 42 Points

        VX6 48 Points

        VX7 54 Points

VI. Procedure for Awarding Versatile Titles

    A. 0The National Office will automatically award Versatile through Versatile Excellent 7 ratings to dogs with the appropriate titles to qualify. WCA members owning dogs with field or bench points that qualify the dog for a title will contact the National Office in writing to apply. The Office will request any copies of the awards, and/or certificates needed.

Figure B-4: Photograph by Creative Indulgence Photography

Figure B-5: *CH Colsidex Standing Ovation* has been the leading BROM sire for over 24 years. A familiar site at ringside, Judy and Joga are portrayed as so many will always remember them, but also capture the spirit of the special bond between owners and their Weimaraners.

Registers of Merit

Bench Register of Merit

The Bench Register of Merit (BROM) is the WCA program designed to recognize sires and dams of successful offspring. Points are earned towards this designation each time a puppy achieves certain titles or accomplishments in a variety of competitive events. As a result new names are added to the list, and the position of a dog on the lists, are constantly changing. The current lists of BROM sires and dams may be found at www.wcaadmin.com

The efforts of Sandy West currently allow the points earned by a particular dog to be looked up at www.wcaadmin.com/listoffspring.aspx

The rules and point schedule for the BROM program:

WCA BROM

1. In order for a sire to become eligible for the BROM designation, the following requirements must be met:

   a. His point total must be 100 or more.

   b. The points must be earned by 10 or more progeny.

   c. 8 of those progeny must achieve the AKC title of CHAMPION.

2. In order for a bitch to become eligible for the BROM designation the following requirements must be met:

   a. Her point total must be 50 or more.

   b. The points must be earned by 5 or more progeny.

c. 4 of those progeny must achieve the AKC title of CHAMPION.

3. BROM points may be earned by offspring PROVIDED that in conformation, the offspring (either sex), has also won at least a Reserve Winners at a major (3 or more) point show.

   a. Show BROM points:

Show points	3 pt.	4 pt.	5 pt.
BOB from Specials	3	4	5
BOS from Specials	2	3	4
*BOB from Classes	2	2	2
*BOS from Classes	1	1	1
Winners Dog or Bitch or Best of Winners for Additional Points	1	2	3

NOTE: Major points must be awarded to sex of BOS for either BOS category to qualify.

The class dog (either sex) who wins BOB or BOS will earn as many points as the dog going BOB or BOS from specials. GROUP PLACEMENTS NOT CONSIDERED.

Championship	5 pts.
Best Dog/Bitch in Bench Futurity	5 pts.
Best in Show	10 pts.
Best Dog/Bitch in Maturity	5 pts.

Weimaraner Club of America Rules and Policies Revised December, 2009 b. Obedience, Tracking, Hunt Tests and Agility BROM points.

CD	4 pts.		UDX2	4 pts.
CDX	4 pts.		UDX3	4 pts.
UD	4 pts.		UDX4	4 pts.
UDX	4 pts.		OTCH	6 pts.
TD	4 pts.		VST	4 pts.
TDX	4 pts.		CT	0 pts.

(CT awarded by virtue of earning the other tracking titles.)

JH	4 pts.		MH	4 pts.
SH	4 pts.			
NAP	2 pts.		NJP	2 pts.
OAP	2 pts.		OJP	2 pts.
AXP	2 pts.		AJP	2 pts.
MXP	2 pts.		MJP	2 pts.
NA	4 pts.		NAJ	4 pts.
OA	4 pts.		OAJ	4 pts.
AX	4 pts.		AXJ	4 pts.
MX	4 pts.		MXJ	4 pts.
MACH	6 pts.		MACH3	6 pts.
MACH2	6 pts.		MACH4	6 pts.

The above points are to be awarded to the sire and dam EACH time one of his or her progeny achieves a title.

c. Field BROM points.

1st Place in a 2 or more point regular AKC derby or the National Field Futurity (may be counted once by any progeny) 3 pts.

All Age or Gun Dog Stake

2 point stake	3 pts.	4 point stake	5 pts.
3 point stake	4 pts.	5 point stake	6 pts.
FC (AKC)	6 pts.	AFC	6 pts.

National WCA Championship
(in addition to points earned from the stake)   6 pts.

National Amateur WCA Championship
(in addition to points earned from the stake)   6 pts.

d. WCA Rating Title BROM points

NSD	2 pts.	NRD	2 pts.
SD	2 pts.	RD	2 pts.
SDX	2 pts.	RDX	2 pts.

e. DC, TC and Versatile titles are awarded by virtue of earning other titles, no additional BROM points are given.

Figure B-6: *Hopefuls.* Photograph by Doreen Zdon.

Field Register of Merit

The Field Register of Merit (FROM) was designed by Sandra West to recognize those sires and dams producing consistently competitive field offspring with limited credit for conformation successes. This long a-waited program has recently come to fruition led by the gallant efforts of Sandy West; the initial list of eligible sires and dams is still being researched. Current rules can be found at the WCA website *www.wcaadmin.com*

As with the BROM, the list of dogs, their points and rankings are constantly changing. A complete current list of FROM sires and dams and their points and ranking can be found here *www.wcaadmin.com*

FROM Rules and Awards

FROM Rules

1. An individual dog will be nominated to earn FROM points for his parents providing he meets the minimum requirement. The minimum requirement is a Senior Hunt title or above; or 1st or 2nd in a major pointed broke dog stake; or a win in a major pointed juvenile stake.

2. FROM points earned in all breed stakes will be doubled.

3. Open and amateur stakes count equally.

4. Only AKC and WCA events are counted.

5. Only first place wins in field trial stakes are counted except for field futurities and national championships in which all 4 placements are counted.

Sires: Requirements for FROM Award

1. Must have 60 FROM points or more

2. FROM points have to be earned by at least 5 nominated progeny

3. Must have at least 4 Field Champions, Amateur Field Champions and/or Master Hunters. Any combination of these titles will be accepted. National Field Champion and/or National Amateur Field Champion can be counted as well.

Dams: Requirements for FROM Award

1. Must have 40 FROM points or more.

2. FROM points have to be earned by at least 3 nominated progeny

3. Must have at least 2 Field Champions, Amateur Field Champions and/or Master Hunters. Any combination of these titles will be accepted. National Field Champion and/or National Amateur Field Champion can be counted as well.

Annual Top Producing Sire and Dam Award

A top producing FROM sire and dam award will be given annually at the National Field Trial banquet. The awards will be given to the sire and dam who have earned the most FROM points for the preceding year. The awards will be of the caliber given to the top producing show sire and dam.

FROM Point Schedule

First Place in:

Puppy Stakes (Amateur and Open)

1 point stake	1 FROM point
2 point stake	2 FROM point
3 point stake	3 FROM points
4 point stake	4 FROM points
5 point stake	5 FROM points

In addition to stake points the following would be awarded:
Sectional Puppy Stake Win 1 FROM point

Derby Stakes (Amateur and Open)

1 point stake	1 FROM point
2 point stake	2 FROM points
3 point stake	3 FROM points
4 point stake	4 FROM points
5 point stake	5 FROM points

In addition to stake points the following would be awarded :
Sectional/National Derby Stake Win 2 FROM point

All Age, Gun Dog, Limited Gun Dog (Amateur and Open)

1 point stake	2 FROM point
2 point stake	3 FROM points
3 point stake	4 FROM points
4 point stake	5 FROM points
5 point stake	6 FROM points

In addition to stake points the following would be awarded :
Sectional (All Age or Gun Dog) Stake Win 2 FROM point

WCA Field Futurity (Sectionals and Nationals)

1st Place	5 FROM points
2nd Place	4 FROM points
3rd Place	3 FROM points
4th Place	2 FROM point

WCA National Field Championship

1st Place	6 FROM points
2nd Place	4 FROM points
3rd Place	2 FROM points
4th Place	1 FROM point

WCA National Amateur Field Championship

1st Place	6 FROM points
2nd Place	4 FROM points
3rd Place	2 FROM points
4th Place	1 FROM point

AKC Hunt Titles

Master Hunter	6 FROM points
Senior Hunter	4 FROM points
Junior Hunter	2 FROM points

WCA Ratings Titles

SDX/RDX	3 FROM points
SD/RD	2 FROM points
NRD/NSD	1 FROM point

WCA Bench Futurity

Best Dog/Bitch	5 FROM Points
AKC Field Championship	6 FROM Points
AKC Amateur Field Championship	6 FROM Points
AKC Bench Championship	5 FROM points

(Providing nominee has earned a minimum of 4 FROM points)

Figure B-7: *Dessa.* Photograph by Oleg Popov.

Snow bunny. Just weeks before the new *Weimaraner Ways* was to go to print, the East Coast of the United States was hit by a record snowfall. Colleen Dugan, whose skills as a photographer and reproduction artist have contributed immensely to the images in this book, was held captive by the weather, along with her Weimaraner-friend, Gertie. The images that follow were taken by Colleen that first snowbound day. While we can appreciate the effort and success it takes to earn a title of recognition, one of the qualities that truly endears our canine companions to us is their ability to frolic—even in the most taxing of circumstances.

BENCH EVENTS

Because the primary use of these lists is for pedigree research, all known titles and ratings are given, *whether or not the dog actually held them on the date of the win.*

National Specialty Show

1948: CH Ymar's Alaric, CD, BROM
(Silver Knight × Quincy's Penny, CDX)

1949: CH Ymar's Alaric, CD, BROM
(Silver Knight × Quincy's Penny, CDX)

1950: CH Klarbert's Ador
(Grafmar's Ador, CD, BROM × Grafmar's Happy Day, BROM)

1951: CH Burt v. d. Harrasburg, Import, BROM
(Arco v. d. Filzen × Asta v. Bruckberg)

1952: CH Silver Blue Lucifer
(CH Burt v. d. Harrasburg, Import, BROM × Silver Blue Lolita, BROM)

1953: SPECIALTY CANCELLED

1954: CH Burt v. d. Harrasburg, Import, BROM
(Arco v. d. Filzen × Asta v. Bruckberg)

1955: CH Atomic of Wolftrap
(CH Deal's Sporting True Aim II, BROM × Tenneck, Import)

1956: CH Valkon Von Houghton
(CH Count Von Houghton, SD, BROM × Cita Valkyr)

1957: CH Von Gailberg's Ord
(CH Debar's Platinum Specter, BROM × CH Von Gailberg's Esta, BROM)

1958: CH Grau Begleiter, CDX, NRD
(Grau Fremdenfuhrer, CD × Rosenkavalier das Vielchen)

1959: CH Val Knight Ranck, BROM
(CH Count Von Houghton, SD, BROM × CH Brenda's Gray Shadow, CD, BROM)

1960: CH Gourmet's Sardar, BROM
(CH Dok of Fairway × CH Silver Linda v. Feldstrom, UD)

1961: CH Grave's Rogue
(CH Catalano's Burt × CH Grave's Princess v. Auger)

1962: CH Elge of Belle Creek
(Ricki of Rocklege × Constant Germaine)

1963: CH Baron Von Hugh, SD
(CH Flottheim's Hansie × Gwynned's Silver Gretel)

1964: CH Mar-Car's Frakker Von Amweg
(CH Joel Von Frakker, Jr. × Agnes Von Frakker)

1965: CH Gretchenhof Silver Thor, NRD
(CH Hans v. d. Gretchenhof, CD, BROM × CH Silver Dust XVI, CD)

1966: CH Gwinner's Sportwheel, BROM
(CH Gwinner's Pinwheel, BROM × Brun Hilde Schmidt)

1967: CH Brandy's Twilight of Knight
(CH Val Knight Ranck, BROM × Lady Brandywine II, CD)

1968: CH Windage Farms Maco Scuddahoo
(CH Norman's Dorval Von Martin, BROM × CH Eilatan's Valmist Comet, BROM)

1969: CH Von Gaiberg's Alf Schwenden
(CH Verdemar's Cosak, BROM × CH Von Gaiberg's Kate Schwenden, CD, NRD, BROM)

1970: CH Ronamax Rajah v. d. Reiteralm, BROM
(CH Maximilian v. d. Reiteralm, NSD, BROM × CH Norman's Rona v. d. Reiteralm, NRD, SD, V, BROM)

1971: CH Rajah's Alexander v. d. Reiteralm
(CH Ronamax Rajah v. d. Reiteralm, BROM × Elken's Party Gal v. d. Reiteralm, BROM)

1972: CH Lemans Flashing Silver Wheel
(CH Gwinner's Sportwheel, BROM × CH Weimar Castle's Jabetwheel, CD, BROM)

1973: CH Chat-A-Wey Charley v. d. Reiteralm
(CH Senecca's Medicine Man, BROM × CH Rona's Sea Sprite v. d. Reiteralm, BROM)

1974: CH Springdale Rhea v. d. Reiteralm, CD
(CH Seneca's Medicine Man, BROM × CH Rona's Sea Sprite v. d. Reiteralm, BROM)

1975: CH Springdale Rhea v. d. Reiteralm, CD
(CH Seneca's Medicine Man, BROM × CH Rona's Sea Sprite v. d. Reiteralm, BROM)

1976: CH The Rajah's Magic v. d. Reiteralm, BROM
(CH Ronamax Rajah v. d. Reiteralm, BROM × CH Brandy's Blizz v. d. Reiteralm, BROM)

1977: CH The Rajah's Magic v. d. Reiteralm, BROM
(CH Ronamax Rajah v. d. Reiteralm, BROM × CH Brandy's Blizz v. d. Reiteralm, BROM)

1978: CH Blackwater Mack v. d. Reiteralm, ROM
(CH Maximilian v. d. Reiteralm, NSD, BROM × CH Hi Country's Blackwater Alert, NSD, BROM)

1979: CH Kamsou Jack the Ripper, CD, RD, SD, VX, BROM
(CH W.C.'s the Dutchman of Dauntmar, BROM × CH Kamsou Riptide, BROM)

1980: CH Valmar's Jazzman, CD, NRD, NSD, V, BROM
(CH Valmar's Chancelor v. Starbuck × CH Valmar's Elke Schwenden)

1981: CH Colsidex Standing Ovation, BROM
(CH Seneca's Medicine Man, BROM ×
CH Colsidex Dauntless Applause, NSD, BROM)

1982: CH Hoot Hollow's Roy's Rob Roy, CD, BROM
(CH Colsidex Standing Ovation, BROM ×
CH Mardi's Gretchen Heer)

1983: CH Silverkist Davie Lee
(CH Valmar's Jazzman, CD, NRD, NSD, V, BROM ×
CH Silverkist Andrea Jennie)

1984: CH Colsidex Standing Ovation, BROM
(CH Seneca's Medicine Man, BROM ×
CH Colsidex Dauntless Applause, NSD, BROM)

1985: CH Innomine Foxy Chimes Chance, NRD, NSD, V
(CH Rowdy's Royal Foxmist, TD ×
CH Monomoy Vesper Bell of Joy, NRD)

1986: CH Greywind's Jack Frost, CD, SD, V, BROM
(CH Colsidex Standing Ovation, BROM ×
CH Greywind's Ashley Frost, CD)

1987: CH Valmar's Pollyanna, BROM
(CH Sir Eric Von Sieben, BROM × CH Valmar Serenade v. Wustenwind, BROM)

1988: CH DeBar's Song of the South, NSD
(CH Bama Belle's Mountain Man, BROM ×
Roschel's DeBar Devil May Care)

1989: CH Nani's Southern Cross, BROM
(CH Arokat's Legionnaire ×
CH Foreshado Nani's Crystal Vision, BROM)

1990: CH Greywind's Jack Frost, CD, SD, V, BROM
(CH Colsidex Standing Ovation, BROM ×
CH Greywind's Ashley Frost, CD)

1991: CH Norman's Smokey City Heat Wave
(CH Valmar Smokey City Ultra Easy, NSD, BROM ×
CH Norman's Frostroy Colleen, BROM)

1992: CH Norman's Smokey City Heat Wave
(CH Valmar Smokey City Ultra Easy, BROM ×
CH Norman's Frostyroy Colleen, BROM

1993: CH Greymist's Silver Cloud
(CH Silversmith EZ Payment Plan ×
CH Sunmist Silver Shadow)

1994: CH Greymist's Silver Cloud
(CH Silversmith EZ Payment Plan ×
CH Sunmist Silver Shadow)

1995: BIS CH Valmar's Apache Rebel
(CH Tophat's Top Gun × CH Valmar's Starling)

1996: CH Ultimas Stetson v. Hufmeister
(CH Colsidex Nani Reprint, JH × CH Ultima's Sadie Hawkins)

1997: CH Aria's Allegra of Colsidex
(Colsidex Nani Follow A Dream × CH TopHat's Spitfire)

1998: CH Smokey City K-Line Tradewins
(CH Smokey City E Z Moonstone, JH ×
CH Norman's Smokey City Heat Wave, JH)

1999: SmokyCity D'Nunder Lazer Beam
(CH Divani Loads A'Trouble × CH Smokey City EZ Elegance)

2000: CH Reiteralm's Hi'Flutin' Chloe
(CH Northwoods River to GraytSky, JH, SD, NRD, V ×
CH Stoneybrook Rose of Reiteralm, NSD)

2001: CH Smokey City Riverboat Gambler
(Am/Can CH Silberschoen's Lucky Strike, BROM ×
CH SmokyCity Sumthn T Talkabout, BROM)

2002: CH SmokyCity Simpatico
(CH Smokey City Riverboat Gambler ×
SmokyCity Mayd in America)

2003: CH DakotaRidge Carousels Ola, Lola!
(CH Carousels Roscoe T Picotrane × Kasamar Morning Star)

2004: CH SmokyCity Hail Mary
(CH Smokey City El Nino, JH ×
CH SmokyCity D'Nunder Lazer Beam)

2005: CH Nani's Indecent Exposure, JH
(CH Colisdex Nani Reprint, JH × CH Nani's Tattletail, JH)

2006: CH Colsidex Seabreeze Perfect Fit
(CH Colsidex The Farm Top of the Mark, BROM ×
CH Seabreeze Colsidex Perfect Timing, JH)

2007: CH Colsidex Seabreeze Perfect Fit
(CH Colsidex The Farm Top of the Mark, BROM ×
CH Seabreeze Colsidex Perfect Timing, JH)

2008: CH Colsidex Seabreeze Perfect Fit
(CH Colsidex The Farm Top of the Mark, BROM ×
CH Seabreeze Colsidex Perfect Timing, JH)

2009: CH Colsidex Seabreeze Perfect Fit
(CH Colsidex The Farm Top of the Mark, BROM ×
CH Seabreeze Colsidex Perfect Timing, JH)

Winter Specialty

1989: CH Valmar Smokey City Ultra Easy, JH, NSD, BROM
(AM/CAN CH Smokey City's Easy Doesit, NSD, NRD, V
BROM × CH Valmar Serenade V Wustenwin, BROM)

1990: CH Gauner's Amity von Reiteralm
(CH Ladenburg Arco Von Reiteralm, BROM ×
Halann's Tasha V Reiteralm)

1991: Am/Can CH Norman Smoky City Chill Fact'r, JH, NRD, BROM
(AM/CAN CH Valmar Smokey City Ultra Easy, JH, NSD,
BROM × CH Norman's Frostyroy Colleen, BROM)

1992: CH W.F. Mattrace Harline Roquelle
(CH Nani's Sirroco of Mattrace, CD, BROM ×
CH Harline's Hurrah, BROM)

1993: CH Warheit's High Caliber, NSD NRD V
(CH Woodcreek Thats the Way U Do It, CDX, NSD, V ×
CH Warheit's Razz to Riches, CD, NSD, NRD, V, BROM)

1994: CH Von Luchbach's Perfect Copy
(CH Valmar Smokey City Ultra Easy, JH ×
CH Von Luchbach's Magic Moment, NSD, NRD)

1995: CH Nani N Win Bone 'a Contention
(CH Nani's Baht a Pack a Trouble, CD, JH, V, BROM ×
CH Nani's Apple Cobbler, JH)

1996: CH Mattrace Harline Rolling Stone
(CH Sanbar's Here Comes Tomorrow ×
CH WF Mattrace Harline Roquelle)

1997: CH Image's Leap To Conclusions Topw'n
(CH Weltmeister Living Daylites, BROM ×
CH Image's Hearts a Fire, JH, CD, BROM)

1998: Cancelled

1999: CH Bing's Double Trouble
(CH Bing's Comet × AM/CAN CH Bing's Razzmajyk
V Arnstadt, CD, TD, JH, NRD, NSD, VX, BROM)

2000: AM/CAN CH Carousel's Roscoe T Picotrane, BROM
(CH Jax's Von Major, NSD ×
AM/CAN CH Kasamar Rocks The Carousel)

2001: CH Nani's Emma von Derr
(CH Nani's Baht a Pack a Trouble, CD, JH, V, BROM ×
CH Nani's Kookaburra, BROM)

2002: CH Graytsky's Stella Luna, BROM
(CH Nani's Smart Aleck, JH, NRD, V, BROM ×
CH Nani N'Graytsky's Harvest Moon)

2003: CH Eb's N Seabreeze Sorcerers Stone, JH, BROM
(CH Colsidex The Farm Top Of the Mark, BROM ×
CH Eb's Autumn Stardust)

2004: CH Smoky City True Grit, BROM
(CH Smokey City El Nino, JH, BROM ×
CH Smoky City D'Nunder Lazer Beam, BROM)

2005: CH GraytSky-Win It's My Prague-Ative
(AM/CAN CH Ashmore's Win Weim Royal Flush, JH, BROM
× CH Graytsky's Stella Luna, BROM)

2006: CH HM Milhaven's Alexandria
(CH Camelot's Go For the Gold, BROM ×
CH Milhaven's Kiss N Tell, BROM)

2007: CH Seabreeze Colsidex Snow Angel, JH, NSD
(AM/CAN CH Colsidex Nani Reprint, JH, SD, BROM ×
CH Eb's N Seabreeze Sorcerers Stone, JH, BROM)

2008: CH Nani's Say It Isn't So
(CH Nani's Indecent Exposure, BROM, JH, NAJ, V ×
CH Nani's Evrybody Luvs Sumbody, JH, BROM)

2009: CH Harline Win'Weim It's My 2nd Martini
(CH Nani's Indecent Exposure, JH, NAJ, V, BROM ×
CH GraytSky Win It's-My-Prague-Ative)

Bench Futurity

1957: **Eastern BIF: Cindy**
(CH Deal's Sporting True Aim II, BROM ×
Kottner's Platinum Juno, CD)

BOS: Russell's Baron Von Kris Kraft
(CH Craft's Chrysolite ×
Russell's Chetlo Von Helda)

Central BIF: CH Freya Von Houghton
(CH Count Von Houghton, SD, BROM ×
CH Anneliese v. Frakker, BROM)

BOS: George Von Frakker
(CH Count Von Houghton, SD, BROM ×
CH Anneliese v. Frakker, BROM)

Western BIF: Arno v. d. Gretchenhof
(CH Hans v. d. Gretchenhof, CD, BROM ×
Silver Christina)

BOS: Barba v. Heckenweg
(CH Johnson's Arco v. d. Auger ×
CH Hoffmar's Dietzi v. d. Berg)

1958: **Eastern BIF: CH Norman's Springfield Johanna**
(CH Ann's Rickey Boy, Jr. ×
CH Ann's Merrylande Bounce)

BOS: CH Ann's Silver Knight
(CH Ann's Rickey Boy, Jr. ×
CH Ann's Pattie Grey Missie)

Central Biff: CH Rudolph Von Frakker
(CH Count Von Houghton, SD, BROM ×
CH Anneliese v. Frakker, BROM)

BOS: CH Asta Von Ranck
(CH Count Von Houghton, SD, BROM ×
CH Brenda's Gray Shadow, CD, BROM)

Western BIF: Grave's Silver Lance
(CH Catalano's Burt ×
CH Grave's Princess v. Auger)

BOS: CH Cilly v. d. Gretchenhof
(CH Hans v. d. Gretchenhof, CD, BROM ×
CH Quicksilver Lady, CD)

1959: **Eastern BIF: Shadowmar Obenauf**
(CH Durmar's Nokomis ×
CH Shadowmar Little Kate)

BOS: CH Norman's Nifty Nina, BROM
(CH Ann's Rickey Boy, Jr. ×
CH Ann's Merrylande Bounce)

Central BIF: Vernaitch's Spiker v. Lane, NRD
(FC Nelson's Dok-A-Lane, NRD, SDX ×
Vernaitch's Larkado, RD, SDX)

BOS: Vernaitch's Princess Merry
(FC Nelson's Dok-A-Lane, NRD, SDX ×
Vernaitch's Larkado, RD, SDX)

Western BIF: Gretchenhof's Destiny
(CH Hans v. d. Gretchenhof, CD, BROM ×
Sussan Von Linden)

BOS: Dawnell's Pixie A.D.C. Brun
(CH Sil-Val's Modeloat, CDX ×
Dawnell's Silver Satin, CD)

1960: **Eastern BIF: CH Heidi Houghton v. Ranck**
(CH Count Von Houghton, SD, BROM ×
CH Brenda's Gray Shadow, CD, BROM)

BOS: Gretchenhof's Eagle
(CH Crax v. d. Gretchenhof ×
Gretchenhof's Tinker Belle)

Central: COMBINED WITH EASTERN

Western BIF: CH Gwinner's Pinwheel, BROM
(CH Johnson's Arco v. d. Auger ×
CH Cati v. d. Gretchenhof)

BOS: Mistimorne's Mabeso
(Erick Von Braun × Kelton's Fraulein Heidi)

1961: **Eastern BIF: King of Marshall's Folly**
(CH Gert v. d. Alten Eiche, Import ×
CH Roxy Von Ranck, CD)

BOS: Cindy Von Houghton
(FC Count Von Houghton, SD, BROM ×
Trudel von aus der Grau)

Central: COMBINED WITH EASTERN

Western BIF: Dyck Von Dottlyle
(FC Johann Von Keitel × Madela of Blue Heights)

BOS: CH Kristi Von Dottlyle, CD
(CH Johann Von Keitel × Madela of Blue Heights)

1962: **Eastern BIF: CH Linden's Dien O'Grindelwald**
(CH Count Von Houghton, SD, BROM ×
CH Gourmet's Pamala)

BOS: CH Linden's Sarda Von Houghton
(CH Count Von Houghton, SD, BROM ×
CH Gourmet's Pamala)

Central: COMBINED WITH EASTERN

Western BIF: CH Merryhart Reflection
(CH Crax v. d. Gretchenhof ×
CH Adel Regina Von Lolligag)

BOS: CH Gwinner's Thigpenwheel
(CH Gwinner's Pinwheel, BROM ×
Thigpen's Northern Lights)

1963: **Eastern BIF: CH Val's Veto v. d. Reiteralm, NSD**
(CH Val Knight Ranck, BROM ×
Bella v. d. Reiteralm, Import, CD, BROM)

BOS: CH Gronbach's Bewitching, CD, BROM
(CH Ann's Rickey Boy, CD, BROM ×
CH Norman's Nifty Nina, BROM)

Central: COMBINED WITH EASTERN

Western BIF: CH Jan's Radar
(FC Ludwig Von Weisenhof ×
CH Leer's Jan Tomerlin, RDX, SDX)

BOS: Gwinner's Kit K Boodlewheel
(CH Ann's Rickey Boy, CD, BROM ×
CH Cati v. d. Gretchenhof)

1964: **Eastern BIF: CH Gronbach's Ace of Cumberland**
(CH Gronbach's Aladdin, CD, BROM ×
CH Ilka of Red Rock, BROM)

BOS: CH Burmar's Lienka
(CH Elge of Belle Creek × Abbi Von Toulaire, CD)

Central: COMBINED WITH EASTERN

Western BIF: CH Dart Von Dottlyle, CD
(CH Gary Von Dottlyle, CD ×
CH Merryhart Reflection)

BOS: Deka Von Dottlyle
(CH Gary Von Dottlyle, CD × Asta Von Anaheim)

1965: **Eastern BIF: Marcar's Felicity Von Amweg**
(CH Mar-Car's Frakker Von Amweg ×
Sarah Von Amweg, CD)

BOS: CH Xeno of Desi's Flashbacks, CD, NSD, V
(CH Hasibar's Flash of Silver ×
Sully's Desiree Von Richard, CD, RDX, SDX, V)

Central: COMBINED WITH EASTERN

Western BIF: Deric Von Dottlyle
(CH Gary Von Dottlyle, CD × Queen Von See)

BOS: Margreta of Glenrose, CD
(CH Warhorse Billy of Redhill, CD, BROM ×
Darby's Silver Gretchen)

1966: **Eastern BIF: Monomoy Bewitching Too**
(CH Gronbach's Aladdin, CD, BROM, ×
CH Gronbach's Bewitching, CD)

**BOS: CH Halann's Gustav v. d. Reiteralm,
CDX, RD, SD, V**
(CH Verdemar's Von Bradford, NSD, BROM ×
Halann's Woodland Reverie)

Central BIF: CH Othen's Velvet Venus
(CH Valhalla's Gray Majesty, BROM ×
Velvet Wendy of Kirkwood)

BOS: CH Othen's Fighten Titan
(CH Valhalla's Gray Majesty, BROM ×
Velvet Wendy of Kirkwood)

Western BIF: CH Kams Rauchessen of Redhill, BROM
(CH Warhorse Billy of Redhill, CD, BROM ×
CH Kris-Miss Shadow, CD, BROM)

BOS: CH Oliver's Valkyrie of Redhill
(CH Warhorse Billy of Redhill, CD, BROM ×
CH Kris-Miss Shadow, CD, BROM)

1967: **Eastern BIF: CH Doug's Dauntless Von Dor, BROM**
(CH Shadowmar Barthaus Dorilio, BROM ×
Norman's Nuther Nina)

BOS: CH Shadowmar Wileen v. d. Reiteralm
(CH Maximilian v. d. Reiteralm, NSD, BROM ×
CH Shadowmar Sue's Silver Belle)

Central BIF: CH Elken's Juliana v. d. Reiteralm
(CH Maximilian v. d. Reiteralm, NSD, BROM ×
CH Elken's Sherri, BROM)

BOS: Twilight Storm
(CH Brandy's Twilight of Knight ×
Mournful Moe's Patty)

Western BIF: CH Halann's Silver Spook, SD,
(CH Verdemar's Von Bradford, NSD, BROM ×
CH Halann's Woodland Pixie, BROM)

**BOS: CH Halann's Schonste Madchen,
CD, NRD, NSD, V, BROM**
(CH Verdemar's Von Bradford, NSD, BROM ×
CH Halann's Woodland Pixie, BROM:

1968: **Eastern BIF: CH Rona's Lorelei v. d. Reiteralm**
(CH Val's Viking v. d. Reiteralm × CH Norman's
Rona v. d. Reiteralm, NRD, SD, V, BROM)

BOS: CH H. H. Stonewall v. d. Reiteralm
(CH Maximilian v. d. Reiteralm, NSD, BROM ×
Collier's Wheel of Joy, BROM)

Central BIF: CH Seneca's Sudden Storm
(CH Gronbach's Aladdin, CD, BRM ×
CH Eilatan's Karlrise Seneca, CD, BROM)

BOS: CH Elken's Missy v. d. Reiteralm
(CH Maximilian v. d. Reiteralm, NSD, BROM ×
CH Elken's Sherri, BROM)

Western BIF: Frantz Von Dottlyle, CD
(CH Dart Von Dottlyle, CD × Kari Von Dottlyle)

BOS: CH Redhill's Emissary
(Von Ryan of Blackwine ×
CH Redhill's Gretchen, UD)

1969: **Eastern BIF: CH Johmar Minor Magic**
(CH Shadowmar Chickasaw, BROM ×
CH Johmar Minor Miracle)

BOS: CH Tannenhof's Silver Heather
(FC Elsemere's Braon ×
CH Flottheim's Gretchen)

Central BIF: CH Ronamax Rajah v. d. Reiteralm, BROM
(CH Maximilian v. d. Reiteralm, NSD,
BROM × CH Norman's Rona v. d. Reiteralm,
NRD, SD, V, BROM)

BOS: CH Dunwishin Rina v. d. Reiteralm
(CH Maximilian v. d. Reiteralm, NSD,
BROM × CH Norman's Rona v. d. Reiteralm,
NRD, SD, V, BROM)

Western BIF: Dusty's Dolly v. d. Reiteralm
(CH Gretchenhof Silver Thor, NRD ×
CH Elken's Brandy v. d. Reiteralm, BROM)

BOS: Asgard's Dante Schwenden
(CH Verdemar's Von Bradford, NSD, BROM ×
CH Von Gaiberg's Kate Schwenden, CD,
NRD, BROM)

1970: **Eaastern BIF: Greypoint's Silver Jude**
(Saed's State Trooper × Burmar's Holly's Dolly, CD)

BOS: CH Ronamax Rebecca v. d. Reiteralm
(CH Maximilian v. d. Reiteralm, NSD, BROM
× CH Norman's Rona v. d. Reiteralm, NRD,
SD, V, BROM)

Central BIF: Seaton's Herr Fritz Von Auburn
(CH Norman's Dorval Von Martin, BROM ×
Othen's Dor Venus)

BOS: CH Ronamax Robin v. d. Reiteralm
(CH Maximilian v. d. Reiteralm, NSD, BROM
× CH Norman's Rona v. d. Reiteralm, NRD,
SD, V, BROM)

Western BIF: CH Brandy's Rebel v. d. Reiteralm, NRD, BROM
(CH Doug's Dauntless Von Dor, BROM ×
CH Elken's Brandy v. d. Reiteralm, BROM)

BOS: Kams Dusty Twilight
(CH Gretchenhof Silver Thor, NRD ×
CH Kris-Miss Shadow, CD, BROM)

1971: **Eaastern BIF: CH Rajah's Alexander v. d. Reiteralm**
(CH Ronamax Rajah v. d. Reiteralm, BROM ×
Elken's Party Gal v. d. Reiteralm, BROM)

BOS: CH Chat-A-Wey's Slate v. d. Reiteralm
(CH Seneca's Medicine Man, BROM ×
CH Rona's Sea Sprite v. d. Reiteralm, BROM)

Central BIF: CH Bubchen's Princess Tana
(CH Sportwheel's Bubchen Harmon, BROM ×
CH Z's Silver Princess, CD)

BOS: CH Gustav Von Duncan
(CH Monomoy Jack of Diamonds, CD, NRD,
NSD, BROM × CH Gretchen Lucille v. Duncan)

Western BIF: CH Valmar's Eclipse Von Bergen, NRD, BROM
(CH Doug's Dauntless Von Dor, BROM ×
CH Von Gaiberg's Anna Schwenden, BROM)

BOS: CH Springdale Rhea v. d. Reiteralm, CD
(CH Seneca's Medicine Man, BROM ×
CH Rona's Sea Sprite v. d. Reiteralm, BROM)

1972: **Eastern BIF: CH Shadowmar Excalibur, CD, NRD, SD, V, BROM**
(CH Valhalla's Diamond Eagle ×
Shadowmar Oyaneh Aghenha)

BOS: The Farms Maxine v. d. Reiteralm, CD
(CH Maximilian v. d. Reiteralm, NSD, BROM ×
Woodsprite v. d. Reiteralm)

Central BIF: CH Ross' Bonnie Lad Jock, CD, TD, NSD, V
(CH Monomoy Jack of Diamonds, CD, NRD,
NSD, BROM × Ross' Bonnie Lass Jennie,
NRD, NSD)

BOS: CH Halann's Star of Rajah, BROM
(CH Ronamax Rajah v. d. Reiteralm, BROM ×
CH Halann's Heidi Von Bradford, BROM)

Western BIF: Short Acres Max Marsu
(CH Monteverde's Woodenwheel ×
CH Dreamwheel's Heather, BROM)

BOS: CH Arimar's Desert Diana, NSD, BROM
(CH Dough's Dauntless Von Dor, BROM ×
CH Halann's Schonste Madchen, CD, NRD,
NSD, V, BROM)

1973: **Eastern BIF: CH Shadowmar Tsungani, CDX, NSD, V, BROM**
(CH Reichenstadt's Majestic, BROM ×
CH Dauntmar's Silver Splendoress, BROM)

BOS: Shadowmar Prince Valiant
(CH Valhalla's Diamond Eagle ×
Shadowmar Oyaneh Aghenha)

Central BIF: CH Krook-A-Nanny's Silver Sue
(CH Birtzel's Happy v. Reiteralm, NRD, V. ×
CH Crook 'N' Nanny's Rogue, SD)

BOS: CH Kleefield's Ivan Sportwheel
(CH Sportwheel's Bubchen Harmon, BROM ×
Nordsee's Iridescent Ivy, BROM)

Western BIF: CH Asgard's True Grit
(CH Asgard's Sun of a Gun ×
Grete Lijakkwe of Asgard)

BOS: CH Rebel's Rona Too v. d. Reiteralm, SD
(CH Brandy's Rebel v. d. Reiteralm, NRD, BROM × CH Norman's Rona v. d. Reiteralm, NRD, SD, V, BROM)

1974: Eastern BIF: CH Rajah's Magic Show v. d. Reiteralm
(CH Ronamax Rajah v. d. Reiteralm, BROM × CH Brandy's Blizz v. d. Reiteralm, BROM)

BOS: Arimar's Tana Von Donar
(CH Eichenhof's Ginger Man, BROM × CH Arimar's Desert Diana, NSD, BROM)

Central BIF: Maju's Silver Satan
(CH Woodhill's Gray Hawk, CD, BROM × Maju's Silvermist Von Birtzel)

BOS: CH Chrismar's Bit-O-Honey
(CH Karlek's King George × Chrismar's Katrina Von Shade)

Western BIF: Daybreak of Silver Dawn, SDX
(Silver Dawn's Allister × Greta Von Hartford, NRD)

BOS: Kamsou Desert Dreamdust
(CH Gwinner's Sportwheel, BROM × Kams Desertwind, NRD, NSD)

1975: Eastern BIF: CH Graumeir's Aphrodite, NRD
(CH Reichenstadt's Majestic, BROM × CH Reichenstadt's Mystic Charm)

BOS: CH Colsidex Medicine Show, BROM
(CH Seneca's Medicine Man, BROM × CH Colsidex Dauntless Applause, NSD, BROM)

Central BIF: Beau's Grayangel Sugarfoot
(Elken's Beau Jac × Chet's Von Silver Damon)

BOS: CH Stainless Steel Euripides
(CH Shadowmar Excalibur, CD, NRD, SD, V, BROM × CH Fur-N-Feather's Arethousa, CD, BROM)

Western BIF: CH Von Allendorf's Maximilian, CD, NRD, NSD, V
(CH Bama Belle's Beau Gest, CD, BROM × Rebel's Robyn v. Allendorf)

BOS: CY Kamsou Altair
(CH Reichenstadt's Majestic, BROM × CH Kams Dusty Moonshine)

1976: Eastern BIF: CH Sanbar's Virginia Dare, CD, RD, NSD, V
(CH JamSpirit Revolution, NRD, NSD, V, BROM × CH Sandvold's Barbry West, CD)

BOS: Winterwind's Silver Smoke
(CH Silver Lake Knight Errant × Winterwind's Kondor Glory)

Central BIF: CH Daroca's Foxy v. Reiteralm
(CH Chatawey's Rumor v. d. Reiteralm, BROM × CH Halann's Christi v. Reiteralm, CD, BROM)

BOS: CH Star-N-Potyr Romeo
(CH Springdale's Tyr II, CD × CH Star-N-Love Potion, CD, BROM)

Western BIF: CH Hel-Len Tale of Casey Jones
(CH Kandan's Tale of Samson, NRD, NSD, V × CH Hel-Len Anna Versary)

BOS: CH I've a Dream of Arimar, CD, NSD, V
(DC Arimar's Ivan, CD, NSD, VS, BROM × CH Arimar's Desert Dream, NRD, SD, V)

1977: **Eastern BIF: CH Wismar's Secret Success,
CD, TD, RDX, NSD**
(CH Chataway's Rumor v. d. Reiteralm, BROM
× CH Rajah's Sass of Gray Brigade, CDX, TD,
NSD, V, BROM)

BOS: CH Colsidex Roschel's Premiere
(CH Colsidex Standing Ovation, BROM ×
CH Colsidex Dauntless Applause, NSD, BROM)

Central BIF: CH Silver Lake Ra v. d. Reiteralm
(CH Ronamax Rajah v. d. Reiteralm, BROM ×
CH Silver Lake Mistral)

BOS: Durandal Pickwick
(CH Shadowmar Chickasaw, BROM ×
CH Durandal's Lucy)

Western BF: CH the Farm's Act One
(CH Colsidex Standing Ovation, BROM ×
CH Colsidex Dauntless Applause, NSD, BROM)

**BOS: CH Valmar's Jazzman,
CD, NRD, NSD, V, BROM**
(CH Valmar's Chancelor v. Starbuck ×
CH Valmar's Elke Schwenden)

1978: **Eaastern BIF: CH Nordicstar-N-Sagitta**
(CH Star-N-Potyr Romeo × CH Nordicwheel's
Boo 'N' Arrow, CD, NSD, V, BROM)

**BOS: CH Wismar's Regal Prince,
CD, TD, RDX, NSD, V**
(CH Sir Eric Von Sieben, BROM × CH Rajah's
Sass of Gray Brigade, CDX, TD, NSD, V, BROM)

Central BIF: Frolichgeist Tobias Rex
(CH Green Acres Cardi Curtain Call ×
CH Cal Von Nimrod's Rad)

BOS: CH Starbuck's Quailtrac Pixie
(CH Ronamax Rajah v. d. Reiteralm, BROM ×
CH Starbuck's California Dove, NSD, BROM)

Western Bif: CH Kachina's Night Spirit, UDT, NSD, VX
(CH Colsidex Standing Ovation, BROM ×
CH Bama Belle's Kachina, CD, TDX, V)

**BOS: CH Sargent's Indian Summer,
CD, NRD, NSD, V**
(CH Kamsou Seawind Cirrus ×
CH Von Alga's Flaming Wheel, CD)

1979: **Eastern BIF: CH Greywind's Ashley Frost, CD**
(CH Greywind's Sea Breeze, UD, NSD, V ×
Grey Point's Sea Call)

BOS: Reiteralm's Ruben Special
(DC Ronamax Rufus v. d. Reiteralm, CD,
RDX, SDX, VX × Vedvick's Sally v. d. Reiteralm,
NRD, NSD)

Central BIF: CH Kristof's Royal Hanja
(CH Von Sieben's Royal Flush, CD, NSD,
V, BROM × Kristof's Amethyst, BROM)

**BOS: CH JamSpirit Evolution,
CD, RDX, SDX, VX, BROM**
(DC Arimar's Ivan, CD, NSD, VX, BROM ×
CH JamSpirit CompliKate, CDX, RDX, SDX,
VX, BROM)

Western BIF: CH Clear Day's Special Feature, DS
(CH Von Sieben's Smart 'N' Special, NSD, BROM
× CH Redhill's Clear Day, NRD, SD, V)

BOS: CH Kristof's Royal Crusader, BROM
(CH Von Sieben's Royal Flush, CD, NSD, V,
BROM × Kristof's Amethyst, BROM)

1980: **Eastern BIF: CH Nani's Visa v. d. Reiteralm, BROM**
(CH Reiteralm's Rio Fonte Saudade, NRD,
BROM × CH Nani's Soul Sister, BROM)

BOS: CH Colsidex Smashing Finale, BROM
(CH Colsidex Standing Ovationa, BROM ×
CH Colsidex Simply Smashing, NSD, BROM)

**Central BIF: CH Hoot Hollow's Roy's Rob Roy,
CD, BROM**
(CH Colsidex Standing Ovation, BROM ×
CH Mardi's Gretchen Heer)

BOS: CH Kristof's Winsome Whirl
(CH Kristof's Royal Crusader, BROM ×
Kristof's T.N.T. Jessica, BROM)

**Western BIF: CH Ranah's Rajah v. d. Reiteralm,
NRD, NSD, V**
(CH Ronamax Rajah v. d. Reiteralm, BROM ×
CH Kamsou Dutch Treat, BROM)

BOS: CH Kristof's Winsome Wish
(CH Kristof's Royal Crusader, BROM ×
Kristof's T.N.T. Jessica, BROM)

1981: Eastern BIF: Shomar Talisman of DeBar
(CH Blackwater Mack v. d. Reiteralm, BROM ×
Reichenstadt's Amanda v. Gab, CD, BROM)

**BOS: CH Walhalla's Zara v. Hoch Essen,
CD, NRD, NSD, V, BROM**
(CH Colsidex Standing Ovation, BROM ×
CH Walhalla's J.C. Fricka, CD, NSD, V, BROM)

**Central BIF: CH Skytop's for Heaven Sake,
NSD, BROM**
(CH Von Sieben's Royal Flush, CD, NSD, V,
BROM × CH Eb's Glory Be of Skytop, CDX,
TD, RDX, SD, VX, BROM)

BOS: CH Silverholm Herr Weltmeister
(CH Von Sieben's Smart 'N' Special, NSD, BROM
× CH Moonshadow's Arimar Beta, NSD)

**Western BIF: CH Green Acres Cardi Carrousel,
TDX, BROM**
(CH the Farm's Country Air, BROM ×
CH Green Acres Cardi Show Stopper)

BOS: CH Jafwin's All that Jazz
(CH Valmar's Jazzman, CD, NRD, NSD, V,
BROM × CH Jafwin's T for Texas, NRD, NSD)

1982: Eastern BIF: CH DeBar's Debutante v. Reiteralm
(CH Ranah's Rajah v. d. Reiteralm, NRD, NSD,
V × Pewter's Fancy Me v. Reiteralm, CD, TD)

BOS: CH Hoot Hollow's Shadowhawk
(CH Colsidex Standing Ovation, BROM ×
CH Mardi's Gretchen Heer)

Central BIF: CH Valmar's Pepsi Challenge
(CH Sir Eric Von Sieben, BROM ×
CH Valmar Serenade v. Wustenwind, BROM)

**BOS: CH JamSpirit Helmsman,
CDX, TD, RD, NSD, VX**
(DC Arimar's Ivan, CD, NSD, VX, BROM ×
CH JamSpirit CompliKate, CDX, RDX, SDX,
VX, BROM)

Western BIF: CH Valmar's Pollyanna, BROM
(CH Sir Eric Von Sieben, BROM ×
CH Valmar Serenade v. Wustenwind, BROM)

BOS: Redhill's Spellbinder
(CH Redhill's Reflections, NRD, NSD, V, BROM
× CH Redhill's Lola Montez)

Southern BIF: Weick's No Nonsense v. Wismar
(CH Wismar's Dry Martini ×
CH Wismar's Haas und Pfeffer, CD, NRD, NSD)

**BOS: CH Tapfer's Traum Von Ranah,
CD, NRD, NSD, V**
(CH W.C.'s the Dynamic Dagowheel ×
CH Ranah's Totally Hot, NSD, BROM)

1983: Eastern BIF: CH Colacorta's Argentina Mist
(CH Colsidex Standing Ovation, BROM ×
CH Skytop's Alcachofa Belle, NSD)

**BOS: CH Eco's Magic Murphy v. Reiteralm,
UD, RD, NSD, VX**
(CH Hoot Hollow's Roy's Rob Roy, CD,
BROM × CH April Lady v. Reiteralm, BROM)

Central BIF: CH Bing's Lagerfeld v. Windsong, NSD
(CH Bing's Razzmatazz Von Konsul, CD,
BROM × CH Bing's Galactica Von Konsul,
CDX, NRD, NSD, V, BROM)

BOS: CH Von Luchbach's I've Got it All
(CH Von Sieben's Royal Flush, CD, NSD,
V, BROM × CH Skytop's for Heaven Sake,
NSD, BROM)

**Western BIF: CH AZ Gold's Sassi Chassis,
NRD, NSD, V, BROM**
(CH Del Oro Stoch v. Reichenstadt, NSD, NRD,
V × CH Schattenburg's Lady Love, NRD, NSD, V)

BOS: CH Long Run's Silver Smoke
(CH Nordsee's Eric Von Long Run, NRD,
NSD, V × Grandeur's Flashy Dancer)

Southern BIF: CH Silversmith Harbor Pilot, CD, NSD, V
(CH Kristof's Royal Crusader, BROM ×
CH Wismar's April Silversmith, CDX, TD,
RD, NSD, VX, BROM)

**BOS: CH Von Luchbach's Royal Heir,
NRD, NSD, V, BROM**
(CH Von Sieben's Royal Flush, CD, NSD,
V, BROM × CH Skytop's for Heaven Sake,
NSD, BROM)

**1984: Eaastern BIF: CH Nani's Colisidex Hula Cooler,
NRD, SDX**
(CH Colsidex Standing Ovation, BROM ×
CH Nani's Visa v. d. Reiteralm, BROM)

BOS: CH Norman's Frosty Morn, CD, NSD, V
(CH Greywind's Jack Frost, CD, SD, V, BROM
× Doblen's Sirene Sunrise)

Central BIF: Heritage Hills Gabriel
(CH Hoot Hollow's Roy's Rob Roy, CD, BROM
× CH Shadowmar Butternut Hill Echo, BROM)

BOS: Innomine Deuce Dennis Domino
(CH JamSpirit Evolution, CD, RDX, SDX,
VX, BROM × CH Monomoy Vesper Bell of Joy,
NRD)

Western BIF: CH the Farm's Princess Leia
(CH Colsidex Standing Ovation, BROM ×
CH Green Acres Cardi Bluegrass)

BOS: CH Valmar's Ditto Docrevlon
(CH Valmar's Jazzman, CD, NRD, NSD, V,
BROM × CH Silberholm's Tina Del Oro)

Southern BIF: CH Nani's Hawaiian Punch, BROM
(CH Colsidex Standing Ovation, BROM ×
CH Nani's Visa v. d. Reiteralm, BROM)

BOS: CH Arokat's the Bremar Headline, BROM
(CH Rajah's Mr. Magic v. d. Reiteralm ×
CH Arimar's Prelude to Arokat, BROM)

1985: Eastern BIF: CH Lodi's Nani Nacho
(CH Colsidex Standing Ovation, BROM ×
CH Nani's Ann of Enchantment, BROM)

BOS: CH Breylin's Born to run
(CH Greywind's Jack Frost, CD, SD, V, BROM
× Arokat's Cloud Nine)

Central BIF: CH Wyvern's Schuyler of Wismar
(Wismar's Silver Spun Ramses ×
Wismar's Misty Morning's Song)

BOS: CH ArimarLisa's Reiteralm Adagio
(CH Ann's Magic v. d. Reiteralm, BROM ×
CH Arimar's Reiteralm Scherzo)

Western BIF: CH Feathercap's Echo of Victory
(CH Kristof's Canadian Caper, BROM ×
CH Long Run's Firebrand)

**BOS: DC Valmar's Valiant Knight,
CD, NRD, VX, BROM**
(CH Valmar's Jazzman, CD, NRD, NSD,
V, BROM × CH Valmar's Pollyanna, BROM)

**Southern BIF: CH ShoMar's Designer Genes,
NRD, NSD, V**
(CH Nani's Colsidex Coke Is it ×
CH ShoMar Celebration v. Orion)

**BOS: CH Nani's Scirroco of Mattrace,
CD, BROM**
(CH Colsidex Standing Ovation, BROM ×
CH Nani's Cobbie Cuddler, BROM)

**1986: Eastern BIF: CH Dixie Rose v. Reiteralm,
CDX, TD, JH, RD, NSD, VX**
(CH Nani's Stride Rite Reiteralm, NSD ×
Rio's Elsa v. d. Reiteralm)

BOS: CH Arokat the Farm's Attache
(CH Roschel's DeBar Ace of Hearts ×
CH Arokat the Farm's Carbon Copy, CD)

Central BIF: CH Stardust Orion Reiteralm
(CH Nani's Stride Rite Reiteralm, NSD ×
Lady Chances Shadow)

BOS: CH Graystone's Tiara Tess
(CH Hidden Acres Tank Von Mart ×
CH Graystone Stainless Steel AG)

Western BIF: CH Kristof's High Roller
(CH Valmar's Rio Bravo ×
CH Kristof's Winsome Whirl)

BOS: CH Valmar's Xtra Copy, BROM
(CH Valmar's Jazzman, CD, NRD, NSD, V,
BROM × CH Valmar's Serendipity, BROM)

**Southern BIF: CH Silversmith Omni Roy,
CD, JH, RD, NSD, VX, BROM**
(CH Hoot Hollow's Roy's Rob Roy, CD, BROM
× CH Silversmith Omni v. Reiteralm, CD, TD,
RD, NSD, VX, BROM)

BOS: CH Starbuck's Naughty Nell
(CH Ranah's Full Tilt v. Lamar × CH Bluline's
Harlow v. Starbuck)

1987: Eastern BIF: CH DeBar's Song of the South, NSD
(CH Bama Belle's Mountain Man, BROM ×
Roschel's DeBar Devil May Care)

BOS: CH Wismar's Cassatta Cabe
(Wismar's Silver Apparition ×
CH Wismar's Misty Morning's Song)

Central BIF: CH Sandcreek's Sand Dancer
(CH Nani's Hawaiian Punch, BROM ×
CH Sanbar's Mighty Movin' Molly, BROM)

BOS: CH Maju's V'lvet Hammer Reiteralm
(CH Graystone's Sunsational Zoar ×
CH Nani's Aigner v. Reiteralm)

**Western BIF: CH Moonshadow's Hope for Rain,
NRD, NSD, V**
(CH Bing's Razzmatazz Von Konsul, CD,
BROM × CH Moonshadow's Evensong,
CD, TD, RD, NSD, VX, BROM)

BOS: CH Bing's Best Seller v. Wynmar
(CH Bing's Southern Saga Del Oro, CD, NRD,
NSD, V, BROM × CH Bing's Chloe v. Windsong)

Southern BIF: CH Wismar-Stonecreek C Me Strut
(CH Wyvern's Schuhler of Wismar ×
CH Stonecreek Image of Wismar)

BOS: CH Indigo's Bleu Silversmih, CD
(CH Valmar Smokey City Ultra Easy, NSD,
BROM × CH Silversmith Indigo v. Kristof,
CD, NRD, V, BROM)

1988: Eastern BIF: CH Bing's Witch Upon a Star
(CH Bing's Southern Saga Del Oro, CD, NRD,
NSD, V, BROM × CH Bing's Galactica Von
Konsul, CDX, NRD, NSD, V, BROM)

BOS: CH Wolfstadt's First Frost
(CH Greywind's Jack Frost, CD, SD, V, BROM
× CH Parmar's Prima Von Wolfstadt, BROM)

Central BIF: CH Silvermont's Reggae Rebel
(CH Greywind's Jack Frost, CD, SD, V, BROM
× CH Nani's Ananas of Silvermont, BROM)

BOS: CH Norman's EZ Platinum
(CH Valmar Smokey City Ultra Easy, NSD,
BROM × CH Norman's Frostroy Colleen, BROM)

Western BIF: CH Nani's Wood-Win, BROM
(CH Nani's Kona Gust, CD, BROM ×
CH Nani's Apple-Sass, BROM)

BOS: CH Colsidex Liberty Belle, NRD, SD, V
(CH Nani's Kona Gust, CD, BROM ×
CH Nani's Colsidex Hula Cooler, NRD, SDX)

Southern BIF: DC Tri-D's Sterline Silver, NSD
(CH Eb's You Otta See Me Now, JH, NRD,
SD, BROM × CH Tri-D's Bain de Soleil,
NRD, BROM)

BOS: CH Homarc's Easy Asis
(CH Valmar Smokey City Ultra Easy, NSD,
BROM × CH Winfield Homarc Ashley)

1989: Eastern BIF: CH Greywind's Show Flurrie
(CH Colsidex Nani Reprint, SD, BROM ×
Greywind's Frost Warning)

BOS: CH Bremar Extra Extra, TD
(CH Colsidex Nani Reprint, SD, BROM ×
CH Arokat's the Bremar Headline, BROM)

Central BIF: CH Bremar Arokat's Perfect Foil
(CH Colsidex Nani Reprint, SD, BROM ×
CH Arokat's the Bremar Headline, BROM)

BOS: CH Von Mystic's Aroused Insight, CD, NSD, V
(CH Von Mystic's Aroused Interest, CDX, NSD, NRD, V × Wismar's Starlight Dancer)

Western BIF: CH Valmar's Evening Sonata
(CH Bama Belle's Mountain Man, BROM × CH Valmar's Pollyanna, BROM)

BOS: CH Danan'n SkyHi's Flash Dancer
(CH Von Luchbach's Clazy × CH Kristof's Velvet Touch)

Southern BIF: CH Nani's Apple Cobbler
(CH Nani's Kona Gust, CD, BROM × CH Nani's Apple-Sass, BROM)

BOS: CH Nani's Southern Cross, BROM
(CH Arokat's Legionnaire × CH Foreshado Nani's Crystal Vision, BROM)

1990: Eastern BIF: CH Bayer's Ferdinand v. Reiteralm, CD
(CH Reiteralm's Rio Fonte Saudade, NRD, BROM × CH Ladenburg Bessie Von Reiteralm, Import)

BOS: CH Camelot's Halley's Comet
(CH Colsidex Nani Reprint, SD, BROM × CH Lady Sarah of Camelot, NSD, BROM)

Central BIF: Innomine Sassy Nada Copy
(CH Valmar's Xtra Copy, BROM × CH Innomine Dixie Sassy Sara)

BOS: Wismar's Chevas Regal
(CH Wyvern's Schuyler of Wismar × CH Wismar's Funny Valentine, TD)

Western BIF: CH Long Run's Windwalker Alpha
(CH Long Run's Silver Smoke × CH Windwalker's Sunrise Jubilee, BROM)

BOS: CH Silversmith EZ Payment Plan
(CH Valmar Smokey City Ultra Easy, NSD, BROM × CH Silversmith Page v. Reiteralm)

Southern BIF: Wingfield's Family Affair Tri-D
(CH Tri-D's Wingfield Ottotwo, JH × CH Tri-D's Wingfield Dusty Otto, JH)

BOS: CH Norman's Double Bubble
(CH Nani's Bubble Up Colsidex × CH Norman's Frostroy Colleen, BROM)

1991: Eastern BIF: CH Bryrwood Colsidex Hot Stuff
(CH Colsidex Nani Reprint, SD, BROM × CH the Farm's Ride Sally Ride, CD, RD, NSD, V, BROM)

BOS: Norman's Braeasy Bubba
(CH Greywind's Jack Frost, CD, SD, V, BROM × CH Norman's Easybrae Katie)

Central BIF: CH Moonshadow's Masterpiece
(CH Bing's Best Seller v. Wynmar × CH Moonshadow's Hush Puppy, NSD, NRD, V)

BOS: Fair Wind'w Wedding Belle
(CH Greywind's the Snowman × CH Wolfstadt's Bliss of Greywind)

Western BIF: CH Sanbar's Baht a Season Ticket
(CH Nani's Baht a Pack a Trouble × CH Nani's Sheer Elegance)

BOS: Top Hat's Entrepreneur
(CH Valmar's Xtra Copy, BROM × CH Top Hat's Tootsie)

Southern BIF: CH Nani's Leave 'Em Laughing
(CH Nani's Hawaiian Punch, BROM × CH Nani's Kookaburra)

BOS: Donmar's Briana of Mattrace
(CH Nani's Sciroco of Mattrace, CD, BROM × CH Donmar Esprit v. Reiteralm)

1992: Eastern BIF: CH Baron Marke of Camelot
(CH Valmar Smokey City Ultra Easy, NSD, BROM × CH Camelot's Halley's Comet)

BOS: Windward's Perfect Harmony
(CH Silver Heirloom Coke Classic × CH Wagner's Kiss Me Kate, JH)

Central BIF: CH Warheit's High Caliber
(CH Woodcreek's That's the Way U Do it × CH Warheit's Razz to Riches)

BOS: Peachtree's Cassiopeia
(CH Nani's Southern Cross, BROM × CH StoneCreek Magic of Wismar)

Western BIF: CH Valmar's EZ Jazz Time
(CH Valmar Smokey City Ultra Easy, NSD, BROM × CH Valmar's Evening Sonata)

BOS: CH Greymist's Silver Cloud
(CH Silversmith EZ Payment Plan × CH Sunmist's Silver Shadow)

Southern BIF: Smokey City EZ Moonstone
(CH Valmar Smokey City Ultra Easy, NSD, BROM × CH Smokey City Jedda Arokat)

BOS: CH Arokat's Tutu Tango
(CH Nani's Southern Cross, BROM × CH Bremar Arokat's Perfect Foil)

1993: Eastern BD: Starbuck's Katakam Fireworks
(CH Katakam's Firestarter, CD × CH Starbuck's Naughty Nell)

BB: Evergrey's Chelsea of Lorien
(CH Wolfstadt's First Frost × CH Evergrey's Buterfly Dancer)

Central BD: Roschel's Double Impact
(CH Nani's Southern Cross, BROM × CH Roschel's Panache)

BB: Ultima's AH 'Sum Artemis
(CH Colsidex Nani Reprint × CH Al's Georgia Girl)

Southern BD: Weick's Maximillian of Wismar
(CH Wismar's Jack Daniels × CH Weick's Silver Dollar v. Wyvern)

BB: Liberty's Gone with the Wind
(CH Wolfstadt's First Frost × CH Hoot Hollow's Liberty Rabbit)

Western BD: CH Valmar's Streak O Luck
(CH Silversmith EZ Payment Plan × CH Valmar's Starling)

BB: Bing's Razzmajyk v. Arnstadt, TD
(CH Bing's Razzmatazz Von Konsul, CD, BROM × CH Doblen's ZZ Top Bad Girl, TD, JH)

1994: Eastern BD: CH Camelot's Matinee Idol
(CH Nani's Southern Cross × CH Camelot's Halley's Comet)

BB: Ultima's Lil Ms Firecracker
(CH Colsidex Nani Reprint × CH Ultima's Sadie Hawkins

Central BD: CH Ultima's Stetson v. Hufmeister
(CH Colsidex Nani Reprint × CH Ultima's Sadie Hawkins)

BB: Wismar's Delta v Morral
(CH Valmar Smokey City Ultra Easy, JH, NSD, BROM × CH Wismar Mint Julep)

Western BD: Thundering Hot Blis v. Tapfer
(CH Jak's Repeat Offender × CH Brynwood's Some Like it Hot, CD)

BB: CH Wilwins Alice in Wonderland
(CH Harline's Hollywood × CH Casa Perry's Prime Diamond)

Southern BD: Tapfer's One Hot Promise
(CH Jak's Repeat Offender × CH Bryrwood's Some Like it Hot, CD)

BB: CH Smoky City Harbor West Xact Cut
(CH Sanbar Nani Ringside Rumor × CH Norman's Smokey City Heat Wave)

1995: Eastern BD: Pennywood's Tell Tale Heart
(CH Silvermont's Top Gun × CH Fair Wind's Ice Maiden v. Penywd, JH)

BB: CH Aria's Allegra of Colsidex
(CH Colsidex Nani Follow a Dream × CH Top Hat's Spitfire)

Central BD: CH Smokey City EZ Toll E Radical, JH
(CH Valmar Smokey City Ultra Easy, JH, NSD, BROM × Keystone Smokey City Emmy)

BB: Larkols Fair Blows the Wind
(CH Nani's Southern Cross × Larkols Evening Mist)

Western BD: **CH Valmar's Sage v. Wustenwind**
(CH Valmar's EZ Jazz Time ×
CH Valmar's Top Flight)

BB: **Reiteralm's Windstar of Orion**
(CH Freedom Hill's Bremar Perseus ×
CH Orion's Vixen von Reiteralm)

Southern BD: **Mattrace'S Bosun Hemingway**
(CH Harline's W F Rockefeller ×
CH Donmar's Wind in the Willows)

BB: **CH Von Luchbach's Perfect Copy**
(CH Valmar Smokey City, NSD, BROM, JH ×
CH Von Luchbach's Magic Moment)

1996: Eastern BD: **CH Liberty's Master of the Game, JH**
(CH Baht N'Greywind Playn' the Game × CH
Thondor Hylls Miss Liberty)

BB: **ArimarLisa Rona von Reiteralm**
(CH Nani's Rudy Valley v. Reiteralm ×
CH Reiteralm's Hi-Octaine Emmy)

Central BD: **Northwood's Rommel Do'Dl Gsty**
(CH Baht N'Greywind Playn' the Game ×
CH Greyhawk Sage v. Silversmith, CD, JH)

BB: **Sagenhaft Flight of the Nike**
(CH Colsidex Blueprint ×
CH Sanbar's Diva von Sagenhaft)

Western BD: **Colsidex the Farm's Magic Man**
(CH Colsidex Blueprint ×
CH the Farm's Made in the USA)

BB: **CH Sagenhaft Colsidex Whiz Kid**
(CH Colsidex Blueprint ×
CH Sanbar's Diva von Sagenhaft)

Southern BD: **CH Kaceem's Smokey City Hi Voltage**
(CH Colsidex Blueprint ×
CH Kaceem's Smokey City Electra)

BB: **CH Mattrace Harline Rolling Stone**
(CH Sanbar's Here Comes Tomorrow ×
CH WF Mattrace Harline Roquelle)

1997: Eastern BD: **CH Silberschoen's Lucky Strike**
(CH Nani's Southern Cross ×
Silberschoen's Northern Dancer)

BB: **CH Smoky City Harbor West Tornado**
(CH Smokey city EZ Moonstone, JH ×
CH Norman's Smokey City Heat Wave, JH)

Central BD: **CH Wilwins Flash Fire**
(CH Mattrace harline Key Largo ×
CH Wilwins Alice in Wonderland)

BB: **CH Grayshar's Reason to Believe**
(CH Valmar's Apache Rebel ×
CH Grayshar Easy Impression)

Western BD: **CH Echobar Arokat's Ashcrof Touche**
(Arokat's Ashcrof Green Hornet ×
CH Arokat's Tutu Tango)

BB: **CH SmokeyCity K-Line Tradewins**
(CH Smokey City EZ Moonstone, JH ×
CH Norman's Smokey City Heat Wave, JH)

Southern BD: **CH Carousel Roscoe T Picotrane**
(CH Jax's von Major ×
CH Kasamar Rocks the Carousel)

BB: **Liberty's Angel O'er Graytsky**
(CH Liberty's Zane Gray ×
CH Thondor Hylls Miss Liberty)

1998: Eastern BD: **Nani's Greywind Music Man**
(CH Baht N'Greywind Playn' the Game ×
CH Nani's Perfect Cadence)

BB: **CH Norman's Liberty Cloud Dancer, JH**
(CH Greywind's High Flying Cloud, TD, JH ×
Norman's Ashley Germaine, JH)

Central BD: **Quantrel's Bottom of the Ninth**
(CH Greywind's High Flying Cloud, TD, JH ×
CH Quantrel's Quick Silver)

BB: **CH SmokyCity D'Nunder Lazer Beam**
(CH Divani Loads a Trouble ×
CH Smokey City EZ Elegance)

Western BD: **CH Valmar's Unanimous Decision**
(CH Valmar's Apache Rebel ×
CH Valmar's Night N Gale)

BB: **Graystar's Winning Streak**
(CH Valmar's Streak O Luck ×
CH Docaci's Black Forest Sapphire)

Southern BD: **Seabreeze For Better or Worse, CD**
(CH Wismar Lockport Otis Jackson ×
CH Seabreeze Sweet Pat-Tootie)

BB: **Zara's Winsome Zephyr**
(CH Weltmeister Living Daylites ×
CH Zara's Jezebel)

1999: Eastern BD: **Bavarian Mist Flying Cloud**
(CH Greywind's High Flying Cloud, TD, JH ×
Bavarian Misty N Zara's Ivana, JH)

BB: **Scchattenberg She Got it All**
(CH Valmar's Apache Rebel ×
CH Smokey City Somth'n Easy)

Central BD: **Echobar's Forged in Fire**
(CH Baht N'Greywind Playn' the Game ×
CH Arokat's Echobar a Dime a Dance)

BB: **Echobar's Wild Fire**
(CH Baht N'Greywind Playn' the Game ×
CH Arokat's Echobar a Dime a Dance)

Western BD: **Greyoaks Valmars Trav'ln Man**
(CH Valmar's Apache Rebel ×
CH Smokey City Smoketh'n Easy)

BB: **CH Wilwins Just Cruzin'**
(CH Wilwins Flash Fire ×
CH Wilwins Did You Hear)

Southern BD: **Graybar N Zara's Damn Itz Good**
(CH Shomar's Instant Replay ×
CH Zara's Milady in Gray, OA, OAJ)

BB: **Indigo's Courgette Silversmith**
(CH Hallmar Zorba's Rapid Refund, CD, SH ×
CH Cameo's Indigo Silversmith, JH)

2000: Eastern BD: **Graycord's Legend of the Fall**
(CH Pennywood's Ziggy Stardust ×
Graycord's Autumn Sunset)

BB: **Griselda's Freya von Valor**
(CH Watchpoint's Exclusive Copy ×
CH Griselda's Smoky Maia)

Central BD: CH Peridot's Welcome To Oz
(CH Carousels Roscoe T Picotrane ×
CH Peridot's Debut of Emma K)

BB: CH Silversmith's Touch of Class
(CH Windwalkers Graeagle ×
CH Wilversmith Lady Gracie)

Western BD: Winstrae's the Mighty Fraser
(CH Brittania Caballero De Plata ×
Bestebret Kaithness Kirsty)

BB: CH Swan Creek's Emerald Queen
(CH Windwalker's Graeagle, CD, JH ×
CH Moonshine's Gray Brodade, CD)

Southern BD: CH Smokey City Riverboat Gambler
(CH Silberschoen's Lucky Strike ×
CH Smokey City Sumthn T Talk About)

BB: Moonshine Mint Julep
(CH Spicer's Lexus × CH Moonshine's Fina Rich)

2001: Eastern BD: CH Liberty's All in One
(CH Liberty's Zane Grey, NRD, NSD, V ×
CH Norman's Liberty Cloud Dancer, JH, NSD)

BB: Scribbles Jitterbug N Swing
(CH Northwoods River To GraytSky, JH, SD,
NRD, V × CH Tory's Scribble Silversmith, JH)

Central BD: CH Silhouette's Wise Guy
(CH Nani's Smart Aleck, JH, NRD, V, BROM ×
CH Nani's Putting on the Ritz, JH)

BB: CH Smoky City Expectation
(CH Smokey City El Nino, JH, BROM ×
Telmar Hot Topic of Rushland, BROM)

Western BD: CH Anson's Mr. Millenium, D, NSD, V
(CH Valmar's Unanimous Decision, NSD,
BROM × CH Rudolphs Anson Summer
Symphony, BROM)

BB: CH Valmar's Golden Nugget
(CH Urban Cowboy BROM ×
CH Valmar's Over the Rainbow)

Southern BD: CH Smokycity Broadway Limited, JH, NSD
(CH Smoky City Change of Luck ×
CH SmokyCity Lightning Banshee, JH)

BB: Starbuck's Tribute to Bailey
(CH Watchpoint's Exclusive Copy, BROM ×
CH Starbuck's Rowan Lady, BROM)

2002   Eastern BD: CH Sunnydell's Perseus, UDX, RN
(CH Nani's Smart Aleck, JH, NRD, V ×
Amity's Alula Borealis, CD, JH, OA, NAJ, RA,
NSD, NRD, V, BROM)

BB: CH Stardust 'N' Echobar's Legal Tender, NSD
(CH Echobar's Forged in Fire × CH Norman's
'N' Greywinds Bonnie Brae, BROM)

Central BD: CH Greyoaks Valmar Foxx Hunter
(CH Silberschoen's Lucky Strike, BROM ×
CH Valmar's Grayshar Burgundy, BROM)

BB: CH Globemaster N'Zara's All Too Active
(CH Zara's on Zee Rampage, BROM ×
CH Tophat's Fantome of the Heart)

Western BD: CH Bravo's Rudy Charisma, NA NAJ,
(CH Nani's Smart Aleck, JH, NRD, V ×
Bravo Mattrace Ritz Café, CD, OA, NAJ, V)

BB: CH Dakotaridge Carousels Ola Lola!
(CH Carousels Roscoe T Picotrane, BROM ×
Kasamar Morning Star, BROM)

Southern BD: CH Camelot's Go For the Gold, BROM
(CH SmokyCity Mob Boss, JH, BROM ×
CH Camelot's Polkadots N'Moonbeams)

BB: CH Ob's a Night To Remember
(CH Windwalkers Graeagle, CD, JH, V, BROM
× CH OB's Valentine v. Reiteralm, NSD)

2003   Eastern BD: CH SmokyCity in Your Dreams
(CH Valmar Smokey City Ultra Easy, JH, NSD,
BROM × CH Arokat's True Lies)

BB: CH Quantrel's Ramblin' Brook, RE
(CH Arokat's Echobar Riverdance ×
Quantrels Tie Breaker)

Central BD: CH SmokyCity True Grit
(CH Smokey City El Nino, JH, BROM ×
CH SmokyCity D'Nunder Lazer Beam, BROM)

**BB: CH Zephyr N'Zara's Winjamin'Lizzy, JH,
NA, NAJ, OAP, NJP, RE, NSD, NRD, V**
(CH Carousels Roscoe T Picotrane, BROM ×
CH Zephyr N'Zara's WinJammer, JH, OA, OAJ,
AXP, AJP, NFP, RE, NSD, NRD, VX ,BROM)

Western BD: CH Valmar's Hot Streak CDX NSD
(CH Valmar Streak O Luck, CDX ×
CH Valmar's Tropicana, JH, SD)

BB: CH Graceland's San Francisco Dai, NSD
(CH Bavarian Mist Flying Cloud, NRD, NSD, V
× CH Camelot's Jewel of Graceland, BROM)

Southern BD: CH Bowbent Majestic Endeavour
(CH Carousels Roscoe T Picotrane, BROM ×
CH Bowbent N Donmar's Goldrush, BROM)

BB: Grea-N-Ghostmar Pink Champagne
(CH Grayluv's Cupid of Caspers × CH Dress Me
Up's All Tricked Out, BROM)

2004   Eastern BD: CH Ghostmar N' Grea's Smooth Move
(CH Tri-D's Supernatural, BROM ×
CH Ghostmar's Grea Mya, NSD, BROM)

BB: CH Bowbent Carousel Hidden Gem
(CH Carousels Roscoe T Picotrane, BROM ×
CH Bowbent N' Donmar's Goldrush, BROM)

**Central BD: CH Nani's Indecent Exposure,
JH, NAJ, V, BROM**
(CH Colsidex Nani's Reprint, JH, SD, BROM ×
CH Nani's Tattletail, JH, NSD, BROM)

**BB: CH Jewel's Devine Secrets,
JH, RN, NSD, NRD, V**
(CH Greybrooks Smoke on the Water, NSD,
NRD, V × Indigo's Jewel v. Silversmith, JH, NA,
NAJ, NAP, OJP, NSD, V)

Western BD: CH Bowbent Carousel Meltn Glacier
(CH Carousels Roscoe T Picotrane, BROM ×
CH Bowbent N Donmar's Goldrush, BROM)

BB: CH Ghostmar'N Grea Osso Smooth, JH, NSD
(CH Tri-D's Supernatural, BROM ×
CH Ghostmar's Grea Mya, NSD, BROM)

Southern BD: CH Ghostmars Grea Marksman, JH, NSD
(CH Colsidex the Farm Top of the Mark,
BROM × CH Ghostmar's Grea Mya, NSD,
BROM)

BB: Moonshine's Secret Ingredient
(CH Colsidex the Farm Top of the Mark,
BROM × CH Moonshine's Velvet Intrigue)

2005   Eastern BD: CH Liberty's the Right Stuff
(CH Colsidex the Farm Top of the Mark,
BROM × CH Liberty's This I Remember)

BB: CH Hallmar's Double Indemnity, JH, SD
(CH Smokey City El Nino, JH, BROM ×
CH Hallmar's Manjula, SH, RN, NRD, SDX,
V, BROM)

Central BD: CH SmokyCity Like a Rollin Stone
(CH Smokey City El Nino, JH ×
CH SmokyCity D'Nunder Lazer Beam, BROM)

BB: CH Colsidex Seabreeze Perfect Fit
(CH Colsidex the Farm Top of the Mark × CH
Seabreeze Colsidex Perfect Timing, JH)

Western BD: CH Bzyfeet American Idol
(CH Silversmith Ethan Allen, JH, NSD, BROM
× CH Bzyfeet Good Luck Charm)

BB: CH Unity's Anson My Pants
(CH Valmar's Unanimous Decision, NSD
BROM × CH Anson's Shasta Daisy)

Southern BD: CH Greybrook-Win-Weim Trail-Blazer, NRD, NSD, V
(CH Win'Weim-Greybrook Win'k-At-Danger,
CD, NRD, NSD, V × CH Greybrook-
Win'Weim Fire-In-Th'-Sky)

BB: CH Hallmar's Jurisprudence, SH, NRD, SDX, V
(CH Smokey City El Nino, JH, BROM × CH
Hallmar's Manjula, SH, RN, SDX, NRD, V,
BROM)

2006   Eastern BD: CH Northwoods a River Runs Through It, NSD
(CH Silversmith Ethan Allen, JH, NSD, BROM
× CH Northwood's Brooke v. Reiteralm.

BB: CH Telmar's Limited Edition
(CH Graytsky's Smokin' in Havana ×
Telmar HiBournes Fantasy

Central BD: CH WinWeim N Nani Paparazzi
(CH Nani's Indecent Exposure, JH, NAJ, V ×
CH Nani's Shutterbug, BROM)

BB: CH Starwood's Emma v. Donnergeist
(CH Starwoods Handsome as Ever ×
CH Starwoods Western Sky v. Valmar)

Western BD: CH Star Synchronous Rotation, MH, NRD, V
(CH Camelot's Go For the Gold ×
CH Star Wilwin Figure Skater, JH, NSD)

BB: CH Star Ursa Minor
(CH Camelot's Go For the Gold, BROM ×
CH Star Wilwin Figure Skater, JH, NSD)

Southern BD: CH Starlights Olympic Record Holder
(CH Camelot's Go For the Gold, BROM ×
CH Camelot's Rising Star)

BB: Carizma N Bing's Celebration JH
(CH WilWin's Flash Fire, BROM × CH Bing 'N
Carizma Solitaire, CDX, JH, RE, SD, NRD, VX)

**2007: Eastern BD: CH Bivinsfrslnd Lord of the Isles,
CD, RN, MX, MXJ, XF, NRD, VX**
(CH SmokyCity True Grit, BROM ×
CH Frieslands Bivins Lisl, CDX RA, JH, OA,
MXJ, NF, NSD, NRD, VX2, BROM)

BB: CH SmokeyCity Fallen Angel
(CH Smokycity Like a Rollin Stone ×
SmokyCity EZ Time Will Tell)

**Central BD: CH Ashcrof Mack's One For the Money,
RN, JH, NRD, V**
(CH Northwoods A River Runs Through It,
NSD, BROM × CH Ashcrof's Bertha' the Blues)

BB: CH Nani's Foxrun Sneak a Peek, JH, NSD
(CH Nani's Indecent Exposure, JH, NAJ, V,
BROM × CH Nani's Ashmore Why Not)

Western BD: CH Monterra's Best Bet, MH
(CH Win'Weim-GraytSky Cowboy Boots ×
CH Winchymes Spirit Dancer)

BB: CH GraytSky's Chiao Soho
(CH Nani's Indecent Exposure, JH, NAJ, V,
BROM × CH GraytSky's NY State of Mind)

**Southern BD: CH GraytSky's Stratus Sphere,
CD, RA, TD, V**
(CH Bzyfeet American Idol, BROM × CH Grayt-
Sky WinWeim Yankee Stuck N TX, BROM)

BB: CH Sandolar Seabreeze Smokenmirors
(CH Seabreeze Colsidex Sands of Time, RN, JH,
BROM × CH Seabreeze Colsidex Sand Cliff)

**2008: Eastern BD: CH Pike's Peak Silversmith Summit,
JH, NSD**
(CH Silversmith Ethan Allen, JH, NSD, BROM
× CH Pewterrunsilversmith P.P.Smoke, NA, NAJ)

BB: CH Wismar's Bombay Sapphire
(CH Wismar's Manhattan ×
CH Wismar's Pink Lady, BROM)

Central BD: CH Unity's Golden Boy
(CH Colsidex Big Spender ×
CH Seabreeze Colsidex Sand Cliff)

BB: CH Camelot's Pretty Woman
(CH Camelot's Marathon Man, BROM ×
CH Silver Clouds Grand Contessa, BROM)

Western BD: CH Diamond MK Get Your Kicks
(CH Silverado Kamikaze ×
CH Nani's Diamondmk Pink Sunrise, BROM)

BB: CH Ola Lola's Dulce Americana
(CH Bzyfeet American Idol, BROM ×
CH Dakotaridge Carousels Ola, Lola!)

Southern BD: CH Camelot's You've Got It
(CH Camelot's Playboy to the Stars ×
CH Camelot's the Good Life, JH)

BB: CH Ghostmar Grea's Mosquito Flyer, JH
(CH Wing's Dakota Flyer, CDX, RE, SH, NRD,
VX × CH Ghostmar's Grea Mark v. X'Lence)

2009: Eastern BD: CH Camelot's Knockin' on Heaven's Door
(CH Camelot's Main Attraction ×
CH Camelot's Happy Times)

BB: Bvnfrslnd SandolarSeabreze Seasprite
(CH Seabreeze Colsidex Sands of Time, RN, JH,
BROM × CH Bivins Cassandra Tunket Lady,
JH, NRD, V)

Central BD: CH Wayback's Strategic Vision
(CH Country Star's Magpie C E O ×
CH Seabreeze Ordr of the Phoenix)

BB: CH Nani's GraytSky Bewitched, NSD
(CH SmokeyCity Nanis DBL Silhouette ×
CH GraytSky WinWeim Yankee Stuck N TX,
BROM)

Western BD: CH Rosewin Anson's Cervelo
(CH Bzyfeet American Idol, BROM ×
CH GraytSky Ansons Royal Flush Blush)

BB: CH Rosewin Classic Schwin of Anson
(CH Bzyfeet American Idol, BROM ×
CH GraytSky Ansons Royal Flush Blush)

Southern BD: CH Image's Quick Greens
(CH Image's in Hot Pursuit of Warheit, JH ×
CH Image's it's a Cinch)

BB: CH Bravo Milhaven's Masterpiece
(CH Bzyfeet American Idol, BROM ×
CH Milhaven's Kiss "N" Tell, BROM)

Maturity

1982: National BD: CH Jar'Em's Frochlichgeist Chips, CD
(CH Frochlichgeist Yankee Clipper ×
Ranah's Delite of Jar-Em, CD)

BB: CH Nani's Jubilee Jill of Ranah
(CH Ann's Magic v. d. Reiteralm, BROM ×
CH Nani's Soul Sensation, BROM)

1983: National BD: CH Reichenstadt's Simon Peter
(CH Redhill's Reflections, NRD, NSD, V, BROM
× CH Reichenstadt's Kona v. Arenas, BROM)

BB: CH Valmar's Pollyanna, BROM
(CH Sir Eric Von Sieben, BROM ×
CH Valmar Serenade v. Wustenwind, BROM)

1984: National BD: CH Roschel's DeBar Ace of Hearts
(CH Blackwater Mack v. d. Reiteralm, BROM ×
Roschel's Razzmatazz)

BB: CH Ruffian's Country Time
(CH Bama Belle's Mountain Man, BROM ×
CH Ibie's Ambition Ruffian, NSD)

1985: National BD: CH Sanbar's Just a Sample
(CH Nani's Master Charge, NRD, NSD, V,
BROM × CH Sanbar's Mighty Star Loma, BROM)

BB: CH Nani's Apple-Sass, BROM
(CH Colsidex Standing Ovation, BROM ×
CH Nani's Visa v. d. Reiteralm, BROM)

1986: Eastern BD: CH Arokat the Farm's Atache
(CH Roschel's DeBar Ace of Hearts ×
CH Arokat the Farm's Carbon Copy, CD)

BB: CH Harline's Mauna Loa
(CH Nani's Hawaiian Punch, BROM ×
CH Dofo's Cristel v. Hoot Hollow, BROM)

Central BD: CH Sanbar's Diamonds Are Forever
(CH Nani's Hawaiian Punch, BROM ×
CH Sanbar's Mighty Star Loma, BROM)

BB: CH Nani's Island Breeze
(CH Colsidex Standing Ovation, BROM ×
CH Nani's Cobbie Cuddler, BROM)

**Western BD: DC Valmar's Valiant Knight,
CD, NRD, VX, BROM**
(CH Valmar's Jazzman, CD, NRD, NSD, V,
BROM × CH Valmar's Pollyanna, BROM)

BB: CH Valmar's Victoria, CDX
(CH Valmar's Jazzman, CD, NRD, NSD, V,
BROM × CH Valmar's Pollyanna, BROM)

Southern BD: CH Nani's Kona Gust, CD, BROM
(CH Colsidex Standing Ovation, BROM ×
CH Nani's Cobbie Cuddler, BROM)

BB: CH Nani's Valley Girl
(CH Colsidex Standing Ovation, BROM ×
CH Nani's Cobbie Cuddler, BROM)

1987: Eastern BD: CH Bing's Southern Knight v. Rex, NSD
(CH Bing's Southern Saga Del Oro, CD, NRD,
NSD, V, BROM × CH Bing's Tatiana v. Wind-
song, NRD, NSD, V, BROM)

**BB: CH Bing's Razzle Dazzle v. Warheit,
NRD, NSD, V**
(CH Bing's Rassmatazz Von Konsul, CD, BROM
× CH Warheit's a Mist of Deja-Vu, NSD, BROM)

Central BD: CH Country Star's Take Five
(CH Colsidex Standing Ovation ×
Hoot Hollow's Sea Frost, NSD, BROM)

BB: Kinder Anmut, NSD
(CH JamSpirit Helmsman, CDX, TD, RD,
NSD, VX, × CH Moonshadow's Evensong, CD,
TD, RD, NSD, VX, BROM)

Western BD: CH Q-Bert Von Prunehead
(CH Jafwin's Starbuck NRD, NSD ×
CH Valmar's Razzmajazz)

**BB: Bing's Southern Song Von Rex,
NSD, NRD, V**
(CH Bing's Southern Saga Del Oro, CD, NRD,
NSD, V, BROM × CH Bing's Tatiana v. Wind-
song, NRD, NSD, V, BROM)

**Southern BD: CH Silversmith Omni Roy,
CD, JH, RD, NSD, VX, BROM**
(CH Hoot Hollow's Roy's Rob Roy, CD, BROM
× CH Silversmith Omni v. Reiteralm, CD, TD,
RD, NSD, VX, BROM)

BB: Bremar Guinivere
(CH Bremar Johannes, CD, NSD, BROM ×
CH Arokat's the Bremar Headline, BROM)

1988: Eastern BD: CH Traho 'N'Tomar's Algonquin, NSD
(CH Rommel's Gray Panzer × Tomar's Tapanzee)

BB: CH Rainbow's-N-Heavenly Crystal
(Silberholm Rickey v. Reiteralm, BROM ×
CH Frau Gretchen Von Vienna, BROM)

**Central BD: CH Smokey City Ultra EZ Rhythm,
NRD, NSD, V**
(CH Valmar Smokey City Ultra Easy, NSD,
BROM × CH Silversmith Indigo v. Kristof, CD,
NRD, V, BROM)

**BB: CH Von Mystic's Aroused Intrigue,
CD, NRD**
(CH Von Mystic's Aroused Interest, CDX,
NRD, NSD, V × Jusmarlen's Hydee Honey)

Western BD: CH Colsidex Nani Reprint, SD, BROM
(CH Colsidex Standing Ovation, BROM ×
CH Nani's Cobbie Cuddler, BROM)

BB: CH Donmar Espirit v. Reiteralm, NSD
(CH Winterun Kurbis v. Reiteralm ×
Donmar Francesca v. Reiteralm, NSD)

Southern BD: CH Foreshadow's Boss of Bull Run
(CH Nani's Kona Gust, CD, BROM ×
CH Nani's Crystal Key)

BB: CH Nani's Whistle in the Wind
(CH Nani's Kona Gust, CD, BROM ×
CH Nani's Apple-Sass, BROM)

1989: Eastern BD: CH Wolfstadt's First Frost
(CH Greywind's Jack Frost, CD, SD, V, BROM
× CH Parmar's Prima Von Wolfstadt, BROM)

BB: CH Mountain Man's Cowbelle
(CH Bama Belle's Mountain Man, BROM ×
CH Bama Belle's Spice Nottingham, NSD,
NRD, V, BROM)

Central BD: Tradition's Nebula Tornado
(CH Nani's Rising Sun × CH Nani's Finesse)

BB: CH Wismar's Miss Liberty Bell v. Debar
(CH Wyvern's Schuyler of Wismar ×
CH Arokat the Farm's Showoff)

Western BD: CH Harline's W.F. Rockfeller
(CH Nani's Scirroco of Mattrace, CD, BROM ×
CH Harline's Hurrah, BROM)

BB: CH Valmar's Silver Dove, BROM
(CH Valmar's Xtra Copy, BROM ×
CH Valmar's Pollyanna, BROM)

Southern BD: DC Tri-D's Sterling Silver, NSD
(CH Eb's You Otta See Me Now, JH, NRD,
SD, BROM × CH Tri-D's Baiin de Soleil,
NRD, BROM)

BB: CH Ultima's Sadie Hawkins
(CH Bama Belle's Mountain Man, BROM ×
CH Eb's Y's and Wherefores, BROM)

1990: Eastern BD: CH Nani's Southern Cross, BROM
(CH Arokat's Legionnaire ×
CH Foreshado Nani's Crystal Vision, BROM)

BB: CH Bryrwood the Farms Hot Streak
(CH Colsidex Nani Reprint, BROM ×
CH the Farm's Ride Sally Ride, CD, RD, NSD,
V, BROM)

Central BD: CH Nebula's Nothin' But Blue Skies
(CH Nani's Hawaiian Punch, BROM ×
CH Hope's Diamond Mist)

BB: CH Harbor West Shado v. Reiteralm, CD
(CH Ladenburg Arco Von Reiteralm, Import,
BROM × Machu v. d. Reiteralm)

Western BD: CH Tophat's Warlord
(CH Nani's N Tophat's Backlach ×
CH Tophat's Aria, CD)

BB: CH Arokat the Farm's Small Talk
(CH Colsidex Nani Reprint, SD, BROM ×
CH Arokat's All Dressed Up)

Southern BD: CH Nani's Baht a Pack a Trouble
(CH Valmar's Xtra Copy, BROM ×
CH Nani's Poison Ivy, BROM)

BB: CH Atlantis You've Got the Look
(CH Skytop's Ace in the Hole v. Tri-D, BROM ×
CH Lightfoot's Oceana v. Atlantis, JH, BROM)

1991: Eastern BD: CH Wismar's Chevas Regal
(CH Wyvern's Schuyler of Wismar ×
CH Wismar's Funny Valentine, TD)

BB: Shomar's Georgia on My Mind
(CH ShoMar's Front Page Story ×
CH SoMar's Uptown Girl)

Central BD: Tophat's Double Take
(CH Nani's N Tophat's Backlash ×
CH Valmar's Silver Dove, BROM)

BB: Woodcreek H'rd it Thru T Grp'vin
(CH Bing's Razzmatazz Von Konsul, CD, BROM
× CH Woodcreek's People Get Ready)

Western BD: CH Valmar's Grand Slam
(CH Nani's Wood-Win, BROM ×
CH Valmar's Serendipity, BROM)

BB: Windwalker's Gemborie
(CH Long Run's Silver Smoke ×
CH Windwalker's Sunrise Jubilee, BROM)

Southern BD: CH Bayer's Silver Mr v. Reiteralm
(CH Reiteralm's Rio Fonte Saudale, NRD,
BROM × CH Ladenburg Bessie Von Reiteralm,
Import)

BB: CH Shomar's Caught in the Rapture
(CH SmoMar's Front Page Story ×
CH ShoMar's Uptown Girl)

1992: Eastern BD: CH Nani's Rudi Valley v. Reiteralm
(CH Nani's Southern Cross, BROM ×
CH Nani's Valley Girl)

BB: CH ShoMar's Too Hot to Handle
(CH ShoMar's the Jazz Singer ×
CH ShoMar's Uptown Girl, JH)

Central BD: CH Gaul's Jazz v. Reiteralm
(CH Ladenburg Arco Von Reiteralm, Import,
BROM × CH Fleur De Gaul Von Reiteralm)

BB: CH Bremar Heritage Hills Aria
(CH Colsidex Nani Reprint, SD, BROM ×
CH Bremar Bartered Bride)

**Western BD: CH Orion's Nova Von Reiteralm,
NRD, NSD, V.**
(CH Reiteralm's Rio Fonte Saudade, NRD, BROM
× CH Ladenburg's Bryna v. Reiteralm, Import)

BB: CH Valmar Terra's Cherokee Indian
(CH Top Hat's Top Gun × CH Valmar's Starling)

Southern BD: CH Nani's Leave 'Em Laughing
(CH Nani's Hawaiian Punch, BROM ×
CH Nani's Kookaburra)

BB: CH Bryrwood Colsidex Hot Stuff
(CH Colsidex Nani Reprint, SD, BROM ×
CH the Farm's Ride Sally Ride, CD, RD,
NSD, V, BROM)

1993: Eastern BD: Smokey City EZ Opal
(CH Valmar Smokey City Ultra Easy, NSD,
BROM × CH Smokey City Jedda Arokat)

BB: CH Kuwati Lady v. Reiteralm
(CH Ann's Magic v. d. Reiteralm, BROM ×
CH Gauner's Amity Von Reiteralm)

Central BD: Smokey City EZ Moonstone
(CH Valmar Smokey City Ultra Easy, NSD,
BROM × CH Smokey City Easy Moonstone)

BB: Warheit's Hopes High Flight
(CH Woodcreek's That's the Way U Do it ×
CH Warheit's Razz to Riches)

Western BD: CH Valmar's EZ Jazz Time
(CH Valmar's Smokey City Ultra Easy, NSD,
BROM × CH Valmar's Evening Sonata)

BB: CH Greymist's Silver Cloud
(CH Silversmith EZ Payment Plan ×
CH Sunmist Silver Shadow, CD)

Southern BD: CD Moonshine's Alpha Centauri
(CH Moonshine's Von Siegfried ×
CH Moonshine's Magic Moment)

BB: Greywind's Farrier's Pride
(CH Silvermont's Top Gun ×
CH Greywind's Snow Bird)

1994:   Eastern BD: LD's Irish Jig
(CH Donmar's Whirlwind v. Mattrace, JH ×
CH Moonshine's Adora)

BB: Smokey City EZ Lady
(CH Valmar Smokey City Ultra Easy ×
CH Smokey city Jedda Arokat)

Central BD: Roschel's Double Impact
(CH Nani's Southern Cross ×
CH Roeschel's Panache)

BB: CH Smokey City's Easy Goer
(CH Valmar Smokey City Ultra Easy ×
CH Smokey City Jedda Arokat)

Southern BD: CH Vikter's Smooth Move
(CH Valmar Smokey City Ultra Easy ×
CH Von Luchbach Trivial Pursuit)

BB: Smokey City's EZ Elegance
(CH Valmar Smokey City Ultra Easy ×
CH Smokey City Jedda Arokat)

Western BD: CH Valmar's Streak O'Luck
(CH Silversmith EZ Payment Plan, CD, JH ×
CH Valmar's Starling)

BB: CH Valmar's Night N' Gale
(CH Nani's N Tophat's Backlash ×
CH Valmar's Evening Sonata)

1995:   Eastern BD: CH Camelot's Matinee idol
(CH Nani's Southern Cross ×
CH Camelot's Halley's Comet)

BB: Ultima's Mississippi Queen
(CH Colsidex Nani Reprint ×
CH Ultima's Sadie Hawkins)

Central BD: Smokey city EZ Express Mail
(CH Valmar Smokey City Ultra Easy, JH ×
CH Smokey City Jedda Arokat)

BB: CH Wismar's Delta v. Morrall
(CH Valmar Smokey City Ultra Easy, JH ×
CH Wismar's Mint Julep)

Southern BD: CH Ultima's Stetson V. Hufmeister
(CH Colsidex Nani Reprint, JH ×
CH Ultima's Sadie Hawkins)

BB: CH Wilwins Alice in Wonderland
(CH Harline's Hollywood ×
CH Casa Perry's Prime Diamond)

Western BD: CH Skyhi's Electric Sensation
(Skyhi's Special Edition ×
CH Skyhi's Flash Dancin Rose)

BB: CH Windwalker's Moment in Time
(CH Long Run's Silver Smoke ×
CH Windwalker's Sunrise Jubilee)

1996: Eastern BD: CH Rosaics Gala Baraka
(CH Ultimas Stetson v. Hufmeister ×
CH Freedom Hills Bremar Galatia)

BB: Bremar's Homarc Taylor
(CH Nani's Southern Cross ×
CH Bremar Freedom Hills Isis)

Central BD: CH Liverty's Love Em And Leave Em
(CH Silvermont's Top Gun ×
CH Hoot Hollow's Liberty Rabbit)

BB: CH Nani's Outshine's 'Em All
(CH Valmar's Heat of the Night ×
CH Nani's Emma von Derr)

Southern BD: CH Nani's Blitz Grauschatten
(CH Nani's Baht a Pack a Trouble, JH ×
CH Nani's Apple Cobbler)

BB: Sanbar's Stella v. Reiteralm
(CH Bayer's Ferdinand v. Reiteralm, CDX ×
CH Sanbar's Lovett v. Reiteralm)

Western BD: CH Windwalker's Graeagle, JH
(CH Nani's N TopHat's Backlash, CD ×
CH Windwalker's Gemborie)

BB: CH Zara N Nambe's One in a Zillion
(CH SmokyCity Greystok Nokursoxof ×
CH Zara's Taupe Tempest, CDX)

1997: Eastern BD: CH Bryrwood's Diamond in the Rough
(CH Colsidex Blueprint ×
CH Bryrwood Colsidex Hot Stuff, CD, JH)

BB: CH Mattrace harline Rolling Stone
(CH Sanbar's Here Comes Tomorrow ×
CH WF Mattrace Harline Roquelle)

Central BD: CH Woodcreek's Raisin the Roof, CD, NA
(CH Von Mystic's Aroused Impulse ×
CH Wood Creek Hrd it Thru T'Grp'vin)

BB: CH Seabreeze Honky Tonk Angel, JH
(CH Wismar Lockport Otis Jackson ×
CH Seabreeze Sweet Pat-Tootie)

Southern BD: CH CJ's ShoMar Venture Capital
(CH ShoMar's the Jazz Singer ×
CH ShoMar's Caught in the Rapture, JH)

BB: Silversmith Lady Gracie
(CH Cameo's Island Hunter, JH ×
CH Telmar's Gayna Silversmith, JH)

Western BD: CH M and M's El Capitan, JH
(CH Silvermont's Green Mtn Boy ×
CH M and M's Sassaberry Cream, CD)

BB: CH Valmar's Summer Rain
(CH Ultima's Stetson v. Hufmeister ×
CH Valmar's Night N' Gale)

1998: Eastern BD: CH ShoMar's I Don't Giveadamn, CD
(CH Camelot's Matinee Idol ×
CH ShoMar's Joyful Noise, TD)

BB: CH Arokat's Little White Lie
(CH Roschel's Double Impact ×
CH Arokat's Scandal, CD)

Central BD: CH Smokey City Famous Seamus
(CH Sanbar's Austin City Limits ×
CH Smokey City EZ Wynwood Mirage)

BB: CH Grayshar's Reason to Believe
(CH Valmar's Apache Rebel ×
CH Grayshar's Easy Impression)

Southern BD: CH Carousel's Roscoe T Picotrane
(CH Jax's von Major ×
CH Kasamar Rocks the Carousel)

BB: Ranah's Cross' Out of the Grey
(CH Nani's Southern Cross ×
CH Ranah's Promises To Keep)

Western BD: CH Wilwin's Flash Fire
(CH Mattrace harline Key Largo ×
CH Wilwin's Alice in Wonderland)

BB: CH Smokey City K-Line Tradewins
(CH Smokey City EZ Moonstone ×
CH Norman's Smokey City Heat Wave)

1999: Eastern BD: CH Seabreeze For Better or Worse
(CH Wismar Lockport Otis Jackson ×
CH Seabreeze Sweet Pat-Tootie)

BB: CH SmokyCity D'Nunder Lazer Beam
(CH Divani Lods A'Trouble ×
CH Smokey City EZ Elegance)

Central BD: CH Kasamar Galahad, SD, NRD, V
(CH Renegade Bleu v. Kasamar ×
Kasamar Viva Rae)

BB: CH Sassafras Lucy's Lovely Rita
(CH Nani's Concert Master ×
CH Smokey City EZ Lady)

Southern BD: CH Valmar's Ultimate Design
(CH Valmar's Apache Rebel ×
CH Valmar's Night N'Gale)

BB: Starbuck's Fleur De Gaul
(CH Gaul's Jazz v. Reiteralm ×
CH Starbuck's Rowan Lady)

Western BD: CH Valmar's Unanimous Decision
(CH Valmar's Apache Rebel ×
CH Valmar's Night N'Gale)

BB: CH Wismar's With a Twist
(CH Silverschoen's Lucky Strike ×
CH Wismar's Slow Gin Fizz)

2000: Eastern BD: CH Starbuck's Stars N Stripes
(CH Watchpoint's Excluzive Copy ×
Starbuck's Katakam Joyride)

BB: CH Greybrook Mistywd D'Vus D'Lila
(CH Nani's Concert Master ×
CH Win'Weim Greybrook Nani's Cross)

Central BD: CH Echobar's Forged in Fire
(CH Baht 'N'Greywind Playn' the Game ×
CH Arokat's Echobar a Dime a Dance)

BB: Reiteralm's Hi-Flutin' Chloe
(CH Northwoods River to GraytSky, JH,
SD, NRD, V × CH Stoneybrook Rose of
Reiteralm NSD)

Southern BD: CH Jamspirit Monogram
(CH Vanity Visionary, JH ×
CH Woodcreek Dollars And Diamonds)

BB: CH Northwood's Rina von Reiteralm
(CH Nani's Rudy Valley v. Reiteralm ×
CH Greyhawk Save v. Silversmith)

Western BD: CH Orions Smokejumper
(CH Wilwins Flash Fire ×
CH Reiteralm Windstar of Orion)

BB: CH Orion's Madison v. Reiteralm
(CH Wilwins Flash Fire ×
CH Reiteralm Windstar of Orion)

2001: Eastern BD: CH Maxlhof Valhalla's Believer
(CH Ghostmar's Funny Valentine ×
CH Valhalla's Fair Bianca)

BB: CH Camelot's Platinum Charisma
(CH Camelot's I Did I My Way ×
CH Camelot's Whidbey Island)

Central BD: Nani's Tsurutani Phantom Jet
(CH Nani's Smart Aleck × CH Nani's Chris-Cross)

BB: CH Nani's Net Worth
(CH Nani's ConcertMaster ×
CH Nani's Good Time v. Hollyhaus)

Southern BD: CH Peridot's Jager Der Zeitgeist
(CH Carousel'f Roscoe T Picotrane ×
CH Peridot's Debut of Emma K)

BB: CH Kasamar Leibschen v. Carousel
(CH Carousels Roscoe T Picotrane ×
CH Kasamar Topaz)

Western BD: CH Valmar's Greyoaks Hey Jude
(CH Valmar's Urban Cowboy ×
CH Valmar's Grayshar Burgundy)

BB: Smokycity Keepin' the Faith
(CH SmokyCity Harborwest Boomrang ×
CH SmokyCity Tot'l Shades of EZ)

2002: Eastern BD: Liberty's All in One
(CH Liberty's Zane Gray ×
CH Norman's Liberty Cloud Dancer)

BB: Hufmeisters Well Decorated
(CH Ultimas Stetson v. Hufmeister ×
CH Wismar Hufmeister Tia Maria)

Central BD: Nani's Grey-Al Wavewalker
(CH Nani's Concert Master ×
CH Nani's Good Time v. Hollyhaus)

BB: CH Nani's Tattletail, JH
(CH Nani's Southern Cross ×
Nani's Nobodies Patsie, JH)

Southern BD: CH Nani's Cross Examine
(CH Nani's Southern Cross ×
CH Nani's Nobodyies Patsie, JH)

BB: SmokyCity Horseshoe Curve
(CH SmokyCity Change of Luck ×
CH SmokyCity Lightening Banshee, JH)

Western BD: CH Bravo's Rudy Charisma
(CH Nani's Smart Aleck, JH, NRD, V ×
Bravo Mattrace Ritz Café, NA, NAJ)

BB: CH Dakotaridge Carousels Ola, Lola!
(CH Carousels Roscoe T Picotrane ×
Kasamar Morning Star)

2003: Eastern BD: Liberty's Good Will Hunting
(CH Colsidex the Farm Top of the Mark ×
CH Liberty's This I Remember)

BB: CH Dakotaridge Carousels Ola, Lola!
(CH Carousels Roscoe T Picotrane ×
Kasamar Morning Star)

Central BD: CH Chatawey's Awesome Secret
(CH Windwalkers Graeagle ×
CH Chatawey's My Golly Miss Molly)

BB: Elite JC's Turbonium
(CH JC's Neiman-Marcus ×
JC's Cake Batter in a Bowl)

Southern BD: Moonshine Hallmark of Xlence
(CH Moonshine's Alpha Centauri ×
Starbuck's Jillian)

BB: Wismar's Royal Highness
(CH Wismar's Gin Ricky Reiteralm ×
CH Wismar's Brandy Cobbler)

Western BD: CH K-Line SmokyCity N'The Chips
(CH Echobars Forged in Fire ×
CH Smokey City K-Line Tradewins)

BB: CH K-Line SmokyCity N'Style
(CH Echobars Forged in Fire ×
CH Smokey City K-Line Tradewins)

2004: Eastern BD: CH SmokyCity True Grit
(CH Smokey City El Nino, JH ×
CH SmokyCity D'Nunder Lazer Beam)

BB: CH Zephyr N'Zara;s Winjammin'Lizzy
(CH Carousels Roscoe T Picotrane ×
CH Zaphyr N'Zara's Winjammer)

Central BD: CH Valmar's Hot Streak, CD
(CH Valmar's Streak O'Luck, CDX ×
CH Valmar's Tropicana, JH)

BB: Moonshine's on the Warpath
(CH Mystery Brook's Captivator ×
CH Moonshine's Magic Pocahantas)

Southern BD: Silverstar Thunder in the Mist
(CH Smokey City El Nino, JH ×
CH Silverstar Mist Nthe Smokies, CD, TD)

BB: CH Davora's Bremar Magic Tricks
(Arokat's Echobar the Dancer ×
CH Arokat's Flirt in a Skirt)

Western BD: CH Wilwins Star Marathon Man
(CH Bremar Maker's Mark ×
CH Wilwins Just Cruzin')

BB: CH Anson's Raspberry Tarte
(CH Echobar Arokat's Ashcrof Touche ×
Rudolphs Anson Summer Symphony)

2005: Eastern BD: CH Starwood's Handsome As Ever
(CH Wilwins Flashfire ×
CH Starwood's Martha Stewart)

BB: CH HiBournes Mountain Magic
(CH Rosiac Mountain Man's Image, CD, JH ×
HiBournes HiClass Lass, JH)

Central BD: CH Nani's Indecent Exposure, JH
(CH Colsidex Nani Reprint, JH ×
CH Nani's Tattletail, JH)

BB: CH Nani's Legal Brief, JH
(CH Colsidex Nani Reprint, JH ×
CH Nani's Tattletail, JH)

Southern BD: CH Bowbent Carousel Meltn Glacier
(CH Carousels Roscoe T Picotrane ×
CH Bowbent N Donmar's Goldrush)

BB: CH GraytSky-Win It's-My-Prague-Ative
(CH Ashmore's Win Weim Royal Flush, JH ×
CH GraytSky's StellaLuna)

**Western BD: CH GraytSky Win'eim AffairIn-
TimesSquare**
(CH Ashmoor Win'Weim Royal Flush, JH ×
CH GraytSky's Stella Luna)

BB: CH Swan Creek's Winter Solstice
(CH Colsidex the Farm Top of the Mark ×
Am/Can CH Swan Creek's Mirage)

2006: Eastern BD: CH Camelot's Easy Rider
(CH Camelot's Up to Par ×
CH Camelot's Star Attraction)

BB: CH Smokycity Devil May Care
(CH Smokycity True Grit ×
Smokycity EZ Time Will Tell)

Central BD: CH Greybrook-Win-Weim Trail-Blazer, NRD
(CH Win'Weim-Greybrook Wink-at-Danger,
NRD × CH GreyBrook-Win'Weim Fire-in-th' Sky)

BB: CH Colsidex Seabreeze Perfect Fit
(CH Colsidex the Farm Top of the Mark, BROM
× CH Seabreze Colsidex Perfect Timing, JH)

Southern BD: CH Sussex Peterbilt Special
(CH Smokycity El Nino, JH, BROM ×
CH Top Hat's Jessica)

BB: CH Unity's Anson My Pants
(Am/Can CH Valmar's Unanimous Decision,
NSD, BROM × CH Ansons Shasta Daisy)

{Appendix C: Bench Events 833}

Western BD: CH Bzyfeet American Idol
(CH Silversmith Ethan Allen, JH, NSD ×
CH Valmar Bzyfeet Goodluck Charm)

BB: Camelot's Just Dynamite
(DC Camelot's Desert Fox, SH, SDX, NRD, VX
× CH Camelot's in a Heartbeat, JH)

**2007:   Eastern BD: CH Kristen's Center Stage of Ranah,
JH, NSD**
(CH Ranah's Knifewing ×
CH Kristen's Always in Focus, BROM)

**BB: CH Bivins Cassandra Tunket Lady,
JH, NRD, V**
(CH Camelot's Go For the Gold, BROM ×
CH Frieslands Bivins Lisl, CDX RA, JH, OA,
MXJ, NF, NSD, NRD, VX2, BROM)

**Central BD: CH Northwoods A River Runs Through
It, NSD, BROM**
(CH Silversmith Ethan Allen, JH, NSD, BROM
× CH Northwoods Brooke v. Reiteralm)

BB: CH Unity's Juscanis Surely Temple
(CH Seabreeze Colsidex Sands of Time, RN, JH,
BROM × CH Juscanis Mater Ad Colsidex, BROM)

**Western BD: CH Star Synchronous Rotation,
MH, SDX, RD, VX**
(CH Camelot's Go For the Gold, BROM ×
CH Star Wilwin Figure Skater, JH, NSD, NRD,
V, BROM, FROM)

BB: CH GraytSky Ansons Royal Flush Blush
(CH Ashmore's Win Weim Royal Flush, JH,
BROM × CH GraytSky's StellaLuna, BROM)

Southern BD: CH Win'Weim N Nani Paparazzi
(CH Nani's Indecent Exposure, JH, NAJ, V,
BROM × CH Nani's Shutterbug, BROM)

BB: CH Cherrystone Ghost Crab
(CH Silversmith Ethan Allen, JH, NSD, BROM
× CH Cherystone Perl of Sagenhaft, MH, SDX,
NRD, VX, BROM)

2008:   Eastern BD: CH Davora Bremar Mark of Ashlaren
(CH Colsidex the Farm Top of the Mark, BROM
× CH Davora's Bremar Magic Tricks)

BB: CH Smokeycity Silhouette DBL Ur Pleasure
(CH Nani's Indecent Exposure, JH, NAJ, V,
BROM × CH SmokyCity Hail Mary, BROM)

Central BD: CH Seabreeze Colsidex N Silhouette
(CH Colsidex Nani Reprint, JH, SD, BROM ×
CH Eb's N Seabreeze Sorcerer's Stone, JH, BROM)

BB: CH Ob's Especially Amazing Grace
(CH Silversmith Ethan Allen, JH, NSD, BROM
× CH Ob's Playin With the Big Boys)

Western BD: Monterra's Desert Star
(CH Win'Weim-GraytSky Cowboy Boots, JH ×
CH Windchymes Spirit Dancer, SH, SD, NRD, V)

BB: CH Aldemar's Red Hot Southern Belle
(CH Bzyfeet American Idol, BROM ×
Aldemar's Over the Rainbow)

Southern BD: CH GraytSky's Stratus Sphere, CD, TD, V
(CH Bzyfeet American Idol, BROM × CH Grayt-
Sky WinWeim Yankee Stuck N TX, BROM)

BB: CH Nani's Foxrun Sneak A Peek, JH, NSD
(CH Nani's Indecent Exposure, JH, NAJ, V,
BROM × CH Nani's Ashmore Why Not)

2009:   Eastern BD: CH Nani's Crosswinds First Look
(CH Nani's Indecent Exposure, JH, NAJ, V,
BROM × CH Nani's Evrybody Luvs Sumbody,
JH, BROM)

BB: CH Harline Win'Weim it's My 2nd Martini
(CH Nani's Indecent Exposure, JH, NAJ, V,
BROM × CH GraytSky-Win it's-My-Prague-
Ative, BROM)

Central BD: CH Smokycity Lord of the Rings
(CH Camelot's Go For the Gold, BROM ×
CH SmokyCity Hail Mary, BROM)

BB: CH Bowbent Carousel Midnight Sun
(CH Carousels Roscoe T Picotrane, BROM ×
CH Bowbent Carousel Hidden Gem)

Western BD: CH Eden's Horatio
(CH Greybrook-Win-Weim Trail-Blazer, NSD,
NRD, V × CH Nike N Eden's Nina Ricci, JH,
NSD, NRD, V)

BB: CH Nani's Hellena Handbasket, JH, NSD
(CH Nani's Indecent Exposure, JH, NAJ, V,
BROM × CH Nani's Evrybody Luvs Sumbody,
JH, BROM)

Southern BD: CH Win'Weim's It's My Grey Goose
(CH Nani's Indecent Exposure, JH, NAJ, V,
BROM × CH GraytSky-Win it's-My-Prague-
Ative, BROM)

BB: CH Ghostmar Grea's Mosquito Flyer, JH
(CH Wing's Dakota Flyer, CDX, RE, SH, NRD,
VX × CH Ghostmar's Grea Mark v. X'Lence)

Figure D-1: *Good girl.* Photograph by Leslie Like.

FIELD EVENTS

Because the primary use of these lists is for pedigree research, all known titles except amateur field championships and ratings are given, whether or not the dog actually held them on the date of the win. An asterisk (*) indicates that the championship title was withheld, though the individual won first place.

National Open All-Age Championship

1950: Ricki of Rocklege
(CH Decker's Misty Marvel × Silver Blue Lark)

1951: Bitsu Von Basha
(CH Grafmar's Jupiter, UDT × Super Silver's Dusty)

1952: Bitsu Von Basha
(CH Grafmar's Jupiter, UDT × Super Silver's Dusty)

1953: Deal's Upland Fantasy
(CH Bert v. d. Harrasburg, Import, SDX, BROM ×
Asta v. d. Murwitz, Import)

1954: Dual CH Palladian Perseus
(Ricki of Rocklege × CH Debar's Platinum Pallas)

1955: FC Gerri Von Fabien, CD
(Fabien, RDX, SDX × Afra v. Norwald)

1956: FC Fritz von Wehmann aus Rocklege, RDX, SDX
(CH Cuno v. d. Harrasburg, Import × Pinky of Rocklege)

1957: FC Fritz von Wehmann aus Rocklege, RDX, SDX*
(CH Cuno v. d. Harrasburg, Import × Pinky of Rocklege)

1958: FC Gerri Von Fabien, CD
(Fabien, RDX, SDX × Afra v. Norwald)

1959: FC Grafmar's King's Aide, SD
(DC Palladian Perseus × Grafmar's Reward)

1960: FC Oliver Von Schoenhausen
(FC Ludwig Von Weisenhof × Chesanine's Hela)

1961: FC Fritz von Wehmann aus Rocklege, RDX, SDX
(CH Cuno v. d. Harrasburg, Import × Pinky of Rocklege)

1962: FC Zouave's Miss Cuca, RD, SDX
(Von Gailberg's Zouave × Von Gaiberg's Yogi)

1963: FC Mac Von Whitcomb, RDX, SDX*
(Karl Von Weisenhof × Lisa Von Iba)

1964: FC Ranger's Revenge, CD
(FC Ranger v. Lechsteinhof × Asta's Knight Ridge)

1965: FC Von Whitcomb's Tor, RDX, SDX*
(Jock Von Whitcomb, CD, TD × Berry's Heidi Der Bratt, CD)

1966: FC Duke Von Gunston, RDX, SDX
(Sirius of Beaconsfield × Cocoa Von Shorian)

1967: DC Pine Grove Farm's Brunhilde*
(FC Elsmere's Baron × Dulcimer's Way Up Susiana)

1968: FC Von Whitcomb's Hurry, RD
(FC Von Whitcomb's Tor, RDX, SDX ×
Dawnell's Silver Satin, CD)

1969: FC Shenandoah Drummer Boy, RD
(FC McKee's Silver King, RD ×Von Heidi's Ginger Snap)

1970: FC Newbury Renegade Lady, RDX
(FC Duke Von Gunston, RDX, SDX × Cocoa Von Shorian)

1971: Suebirtzel's Mr. Lucky
(Staub Von Suebirtzel, CD × Summer's Gay Image)

1972: DC Sportabout's Boeser Bengel, CDX, RD, SDX, VX
(CH Cuede's Silver Dust, CD Brom ×
CH Hildegarde, XIV, CD, BROM)

1973: DC Othen's Princess Pretty, NRD, SDX, VX
(CH Val's Veto v. d. Reiteralm, NSD ×
CH Othen's Velvet Venus, BROM)

1974: DC Othen's Princess Pretty, NRD, SDX, VX
(CH Val's Veto v. d. Reiteralm, NSD ×
CH Othen's Velvet Venus, BROM)

1975: FC Unserhund v. Sieger, SDX
(FC Shenandoah Drummer Boy, RD × Fairview's Arrow)

1976: FC Unserhund v. Sieger, SDX
(FC Shenandoah Drummer Boy, RD × Fairview's Arrow)

1977: New World's Wild Hunter, CD, NRD, SD*
(Willie v. Mitt × Bella v. d. Zwei Vogel)

1978: FC Alger's May Day, NRD, SDX
(FC Unserhund v. Sieger, SDX ×
B.K.'s Sabrina v. Staub NRD, NSD)

1979: FC Kipbirtzel's Texas Kid, NRD, SDX
(FC Unserhund v. Sieger, SDX ×
Weimaracres Kipbirtzel, NRD, SDX)

1980: FC Kipbirtzel's Texas Kid, NRD, SDX
(FC Unserhund v. Sieger, SDX ×
Weimaracres Kipbirtzel, NRD, SDX)

1981: FC Laine's Thor Von Time Bomb, SDX
(Brought Mar's Time Bomb v. Tor × Mikesell's Von Maggie)

1982: DC Jafwin's One and Only, NRD, SD, VX
(CH Von Sieben's Smart 'N' Special NSD, BROM ×
CH Redhill's Song Girl, CD, NRD, NSD, V, BROM)

1983: FC Outdoor's Boots
(Weiner Schnitzel's McDuff, NSD × Weinerschnitzel's Seme Scoot)

1984: FC Birtzel's Lay Back Zach, NSD
(Weiner Schnitzels McDuff, NSD × Birtzel's Lookaway Dixieland)

1985: FC Super Deaugh, NRD, SDX
(Weiner Schnitzel's McDuff, NSD × Weinerschnitzel's Seme Scoot)

1986: FC Edith Ann Von Horn, NRD, SDX
(FC Weinerschnitzel's Bad News, NSD × Gandalf Fliegende Nonne, CD, NRD, SDX, V)

1987: DC The Sundance Kid, CD, NRD, VX
(Mikesell's Von Baronwheel, NRD × Ildebrannfugle's Donna Marie)

1988: FC Lay Back Nick Chopper, SDX
(FC Mile Hi Caspar v. Gip × Gandalf Lay Back LC Smith)

1989: WITHHELD

1990: FC Lay Back Nick Chopper, SDX
(FC Mile Hi Caspar v. Gip × Gandalf Lay Back LC Smith)

1991: DC Top Deaugh, MH, NRD, SDX, VX
(Weiner Schnitzel's McDuff, NSD × Charlie's Angel II)

1992: Rynmichael Sir Knight Von Horn
(Dual CH The Sundance Kid, CD, NRD, VX × FC Edith Ann Von Horn, NRD, SDX)

1993: FC Hoglund's Tiger Von Thor
(FC Laine's Thor Von Time Bomb, SDX × FC Edith Ann Von Horn, NRD, SDX)

1994: Outdoors Magic Misty
(FC/AFC Andick's Big Time Jake × FC/AFC Outdoors Tony Lama)

1995: FC/AFC Grau Geist's Lilith von Legs
(Mile Hi Bandit v. Gip × FC/AFC Qizef's Grau Geist Marlene)

1996: FC Westend's Li'l Sage Rider, JH
(FC/AFC Falke von Horn × Westend's Desert Star)

1997: FC High Ridge Jesse von Horn
(FC Grey Wynn Bad To The Bone × FC Ida Augusta von Horn)

1998: NFC/FC/AFC High Ridge Jesse von Horn
(FC Grey Wynn Bad To The Bone × FC Ida Augusta von Horn)

1999: FC Snake Breaks Saga v. Reiteralm
(NAFC/FC/AFC Snake Breaks Sgt. Schultz × ArimarLisa's Rudi v. Reiteralm)

2000: Scooby Doo's Treeline Storm
(FC/AFC Stormcrow's Deaugh Blitzen, SH × Treeline's Lyza Jayne)

2001: FC Briarmeadows Buck
(FC/AFC Andick's Big Time Jake × FC Windchyme)

2002: FC/AFC Grau Geist Lil's Gust v. Westend, NSD, NRD
(NFC/FC/AFC Westend's Li'l Sage Rider, CD, SH, NSD, NRD, V × NFC/FC/AFC Grau Geist Lilith von Legs, NRD, V)

2003: Gould's Wicked Runner
(NFC/FC/AFC Westend's Li'l Sage Rider, CD, SH, NSD, NRD, V × FC/AFC Gould's Jus Call Me TJ)

2004: FC Von Weiner Smokn' Winds Holiday, NSD
(FC Grau Geist Lil's Caprock Rev × Countess Anastasia v. Weiner)

2005: DC Sirius Mostly Mongo, JH, NRD, VX
(NFC/FC/AFC Westend's Lil Sage Rider, CD, SH, NRD, V × DC Sirius Really Rosie, CDX, JH, RD, VX)

2006: FC/AFC Gould's GRB's Little Chular
(NFC/FC/AFC Westend's Li'l Sage Rider, CD, SH, NSD, NRD, V × NAFC/FC/AFC Gould's Jus Call Me TJ)

2007: FC Dietz's Sasha Nogoodnic
(Von Harwil's Boris Badenof × FC Dietzs Liesle Weapon v. Harwil)

2008: FC Gould's Farwest Lunatic
(NFC FC Briarmeadows Buck × NAFC FC AFC Gould's Jus Call Me TJ)

2009: Erbenhof SnS Boogie Woogie Bo
(NFC NAFC AFC Scooby Doo's Treeline Storm, CDX, NRD, V × Erbenhof S and S Razzmatazz, JH, AX, AJX, NSD, NRD, V)

Figure D-2: *Championship callbacks.* Photograph by Rodney Moon.

National Amateur All-Age Championship

1952: DC Palladian Perseus
(Ricki of Rocklege × CH Debar's Platinum Pallas)

1953: Deal's Upland Fantasy
(CH Bert v. d. Harrasburg, Import, SDX, BROM ×
Asta v. d. Murwitz, Import)

1954: Leo's Blue Dawn
(Silver Blue Leo × Super's Silver Dawn)

1955: DC Palladian Perseus
(Ricki of Rocklege × CH Debar's Platinum Pallas)

1956: DC Palladian Perseus
(Ricki of Rocklege × CH Debar's Platinum Pallas)

1957: Dan's Ricki of Rocklege
(Ricki of Rocklege × Burgerl v. d. Alten Eiche, SDX)

1958: FC Fritz von Wehmann aus Rocklege, RDX, SDX
(CH Cuno v. d. Harrasburg, Import × Pinky of Rocklege)

1959: FC Grafmar's King's Aide, SD
(DC Palladian Perseus × Grafmar's Reward)

1960: FC Fritz von Wehmann aus Rocklege, RDX, SDX
(CH Cuno v. d. Harrasburg, Import × Pinky of Rocklege)

1961: FC Mac Von Whitcomb, RDX, SDX
(Karl Von Weisenhof × Lisa Von Ilba)

1962: FC Von Whitcomb's Tor, RDX, SDX
(Joch Von Whitcomb, CD, TD × Berry's Heidi Der Bratt, CD)

1963: Von Whitcomb's Tess*
(Joch Von Whitcomb, CD, TD × Terry's Heidi Der Bratt CD)

1964: DC Pine Grove Farm's Brunhilde
(FC Elsmere's Baron × Dulcimer's Way-up Susiana)

1965: FC Von Whitcomb's Tor, RDX, SDX
(Joch Von Whitcomb, CD, TD × Berry's Heidi Der Bratt, CD)

1966: Schultzie's Gretchen v. Bach, SDX*
(FC Johann Von Keitel × Kensita's Ador Vantam)

1967: Schultzie's Blitz v. Bach, SDX
(FC Johann Von Keitel × Kensita's Ador Vantam)

1968: Schultzie's Gretchen v. Back, SDX
(FC Johann Von Keitel × Kensita's Ador Vantam)

1969: FC Von Whitcomb's Tornado, RD
(FC Von Whitcomb's Tor, RDX, SDX × Dawnell's Silver Satin, CD)

1970: DC Eldan's Mohave Sundaner*
(CH Mike Silver Blaze × CH Von Zel's Aphrodite)

1971: FC Elder's Soren Ludwig, RD, SDX*
(Tyrone of Glen Hill Acres × Dusseldorf Liebchen Velvet)

1972: FC Miller's Silver Jill, NRD, SDX
(CH King's Aide Rex × Princess Rum Von Gelt)

1973: DC Othen's Princess Pretty, NRD, SDX, VX
(CH Val's Veto v. d. Reiteralm, NSD ×
CH Othen's Velvet Venus, BROM

1974: DC Othen's Princess Pretty, NRD, SDX, VX
(CH Val's Veto v. d. Reiteralm, NSD × CH Othen's Velvet
Venus, BROM

1975: DC Gent's Silver Smoke, RDX, SDX, VX
(Ladiv's Silver Gent × Johnny Ginny)

1976: FC Fran's Dee Dee Von Heiser, RDX
(FC Newbury Gustave, RDX × Tina Marie Von Gunston)

1977: WITHHELD

1978: FC Alger's May Day, NRD, SDX
(FC Unserhund v. Sieger, SDX ×
B.K.'s Sabrina v. Staub, NRD, NSD)

1979: FC Alger's May Day, NRD, SRX
(FC Unserhund v. Sieger, SDX ×
B.K.'s Sabrina v. Staub, NRD, NSD)

1980: FC Kipbirtzel's Texas Kid, NRD, SDX
(FC Unserhund v. Sieger, SDX ×
Weimaracres Kipbirtzel, NRD, SDX)

1981: FC Weinersnitzel's Gipsi McDuff, NRD, SD, V
(Weiner Schnitzel's McDuff, NSD × Weinerschnitzel's Seme Scoot)

1982: FC D.C.'s Hons Tobie Von Sieger, NRD, SDX
(FC Unserhund v. Sieger, SDX ×
B.K.'s Sabrina v. Staub, NRD, NSD)

1983: FC D.C.'s Hons Tobie Von Sieger, NRD, SDX
(FC Unserhund v. Sieger, SDX ×
B.K.'s Sabrina v. Staub, NRD, NSD)

1984: FC Birtzel's Good Friday, SDX
(FC Unserhund v. Sieger, SDX ×
Weimaracres Kipbirtzel, NRD, SDX)

1985: FC Ambrose
(Golden Colorado's Smoke × Titan's Chiquita)

1986: FC Egon Blitzkrieg v. Horn, CD, NRD, SD, V
(FC Weinerschnitzel's Bad News, NSD ×
Gandalf Fliegende Nonne CD, NRD, SDX, V)

1987: WITHHELD

1988: DC Top Deaugh, MH, NRD, SDX, VX
(Weiner Schnitzel's McDuff, NSD, × Charlie's Angel II)

1989: DC Top Deaugh, MH, NRD, SDX, VX
(Weiner Schnitzel's McDuff, NSD, × Charlie's Angel II)

1990: DC Top Deaugh, MH, NRD, SDX, VX
(Weiner Schnitzel's McDuff, NSD, × Charlie's Angel II)

1991: DC Top Deaugh, MH, NRD, SDX, VX
(Weiner Schnitzel's McDuff, NSD, × Charlie's Angel II)

1992: FC Outdoors Starfire
(FC Outdoors Fritz's Duke × FC Outdoors Boots)

1993: Dual CH Knight's Ti-ki Toi, NSD,
(S and S's Shot of Tequila, JH ×
Lyonesse Ginger Star Knight, JH, RDX, SDX, V)

1994: NFC/FC Hoglund's Tiger Von Thor
(NFC/FC/AFC Laine's Thor von Time Bomb × NFC/FC/AFC
Edith Ann von Horn)

1995: NFC/FC Outdoors Magic Misty
(FC/AFC Andick's Big Time Jake × FC/AFC Outdoors Tony Lama)

1996: FC/AFC Snake Breaks Sgt. Schultz
(2xNFC/FC Lay Back Nick Chopper × Baby Deaugh, SH)

1997: FC/AFC Gray's Ghost Hunter, JH
(CH Sir Karol von Zop Of Camelot × Outdoors Whirlwind v.
Aldemar)

1998: NFC/FC/AFC High Ridge Jesse von Horn
(FC Grey Wynn Bad To The Bone × FC Ida Augusta von Horn)

1999: Nothern Lights ThisBudsForU
(NAFC/FC/AFC Gray's Ghost Hunter, JH ×
FC/AFC Richmark Diamond)

2000: FC/AFC Silverstreak's One Lucky Dude
(FC/AFC Richmark Bo Brandy × FC Outdoors Raya de Plata)

2001: FC Robynski Deaugh Davison
(FC/AFC Andick's Big Time Jake × Prairie Deaugh)

2002: NFC/DC/AFC Snake Breaks Saga v. Reiteralm
(NAFC/FC/AFC Snke Breaks Sgt. Schultz ×
FC ArimarLisa's Rudi v. Reiterlam)

2003: NFC/FC/AFC Scooby Doo's Treeline Storm, CDX
(FC/AFC Stormcrow's Deaugh Blitzen, SDX, NRD ×
Treeline's Lyza Jayne)

2004: FC/AFC Gould's Jus Call Me TJ
(FC Goulds Thunder Und Blitz, JH × Outdoors Gould's Electricity)

2005: NFC/FC/AFC Grau Geist Lil's Gust v. Westend, CD, RN, MH, SDX, RDX, VX, CGC
(NFC/FC/AFC Westend's Lil Sage Rider, SH, NSD, NRD ×
NFC/FC/AFC Grau Geist's Lilith von Legs, NRD, V)

2006: Aztec's American Pie
(NAFC/FC/AFC Northernlights This BudsForU ×
Grau Geist's True Love Ways, NRD)

2007: FC Dietz's Sasha Nogoodnic
(Von Harwil's Boris Badenof × FC Dietzs Liesle Weapon v. Harwil)

2008: NAFC AFC Aztec's American Pie, JH, SDX
(NFC FC AFC Northernlights This Buds4U ×
FC Grau Geist True Love Ways)

2009: FC Questfound Bottle Rocket
(NAFC FC AFC Northernlight's This BudsForU ×
Questfound Stormline Zoe)

National Open Derby

1950: Y'mar's Dawn
(Grafmar's Bright Dorleson × Quincy's Penny, CDX)

1951: DC Palladian Perseus
(Ricki of Rocklege × Ch Debar's Platinum Pallas)

1952: Crested Glade Warrior, SDX
(Bitsu Von Basha × Deal's Sporting Chance)

1953: FC Fritz von Wehmann aus Rocklege, RDX, SDX
(Ch Cuno v. d. Harrasburg, Import × Pinky of Rocklege)

1954: Heinrick v. Nyl-Acker
(Bitsu Von Basha × Gretel v. Gruener Wald)

1955: FC Michael Von Zuppenhauser
(Ell Dew's Hasso v. Capbar × Vida v. Lechsteinhof)

1956: Maggie's Mighty Mark, SDX
(CH Ludwig Von Dottlyle × CH Fallbrook Merry Maggie)

1957: CH Spook Von Zuppenhauser
(FC Michael Von Zuppenhauser × Mame v. Lechsteinhof)

1958: FC Duke Von Gunston, RDX, SDX
(Sirius of Beaconsfield × Cocoa Von Shorian)

1959: FC Elsemere's Baron
(FC Fritz von Wehmann aus Rocklege, RDX, SDX ×
Regal Wunder Velletri)

1960: FC Jus Jill, RDX, SDX
(FC Duke Von Gunston, RDX, SDX × Cocoa Von Shorian)

1961: Baron Der Shonnes Broshunder
(FC Duke Von Gunston, RDX, SDX × Susan of Hilltop)

1962: Trena Von Braustein
(Baron of Rosebay Acres × Hilda Von Braustein)

Figure D-3: *Ardmore lakeside.* Photograph by Ann Tyson.

1963: **Weary Lueger**
(Vegas Lueger × Shannon's Silver Shamrock)

1964: **CH Ric-B Silver Tempest, NRD, NSD**
(CH Warhorse Billy of Redhill, CD, BROM ×
CH Miss BB Von Zwei Vogel, NRD, BROM)

1965: **FC Newbury Gustave, RDX**
(FC Shenandoah Drummer Boy, RD × Richard's Silver Heidi)

1966: **WITHHELD**

1967: **Hickory Hill Adina**
(FC Ranger's Revenge, CD × Ruhnke's Schatzi Von Feicht)

1968: **FC Heizar's Chief Oshkosh**
(FC Ranger's Revenge, CD × Heidi Von Heinrich)

1969: **FC Kelshawn Smoke v. d. Reiteralm**
(FC Elsmere's Baron × Wildcat v. d. Reiteralm)

1970: **FC Newbury Buck**
(FC Shenandoah Drummer Boy, RD × Blue Pine's Aumar's Sue)

1971: **Newbury Silver Shadow, NRD**
(FC Newbury Gustave, RDX × Ranger Silver Liesl)

1972: **J.T. Willy Boy, RDX**
(Trena's Michigan Morgan × Dandee Duchess)

1973: **DC Redhill's Fanny Jo, SDX, BROM**
(CH Redhill's Satellite, SDX × FC Redhill's Fanfare, RD)

1974: **FC Redhill's Merlin v. Jaegerhof, NRD, SDX**
(CH McKenna's Dirk ×
CH Redhill's Jo-Val v. Jaegerhof, NRD, NSD, V)

1975: **WITHHELD**

1976: **Weimaracres Gin-N-Tonic, SD**
(DC Weimaracres Sunny Boy, RDX, SDX, VX ×
Weimaracres Cherokee, SD)

1977: **FC Weinersnitzel's Gipsi McDuff, NRD, SD, V**
(Weiner Schnitzel's McDull, NSD × Weinerschnitzel's Seme Scoot)

1978: **Well's Silver Sages Clipper**
(Suebirtzel's Mr. Lucky × Silver Dawn's Aurora)

1979: **Dressel's Haus Von Ruff-Traud**
(Retsel's Ruffneck v. Harrasburg, NRD × D.C's Traudl Von Dressel)

1980: **Newbury Dandy Dan**
(FC Alger's May Day, NRD, SDX ×
FC Fran's Dee Dee Von Heiser, RDX)

1981: **FC Mile Hi Bullet v. Gip**
(DC Birtzel's Johnny Reb, RD, NSD, VX ×
FC Weinersnitzel's Gipsi McDuff, NRD, SD, V)

1982: **CH Nordsee's Yoda, NRD**
(CH Redhill's Reflections, NRD, NSD, V, BROM ×
CH Medallion Nordsee Little Lil, CD, NSD, V)

1983: **Bongen's Blitzkrieger, NRD, SDX**
(DC Gent's Silver Smoke, RDX, SDX, VX ×
Bongen's Klein Teufelchen, NRD, NSD)

1984: **Palimar's Ancient Mariner**
(FC Birtzel's Lay Back Zach, NSD ×
FC Birtzel's Good Friday, SDX)

1985: **Tex's Dakoda Thunder**
(FC Kipbirtzel's Texas Kid, NRD, SDX × Inga Blue Bell)

1986: **FC Lay Back Nick Chopper, SDX**
(FC Mile Hi Casper v. Gip × Gandalf Lay Back LC Smith)

1987: **FC Outdoors Scooter Pie**
(FC Outdoors Fritz's Duke × FC Outdoors Boots)

1988: **Grau Rauch's Barbarisch**
(FC Andick's Big Time Jake × Gray Angel Grau Rauch, RD, SD)

1989: **Ricochet Deaugh, NRD**
(FC Lay Back Nick Chopper, SDX × Deaugh Daze, CD, NRD)

1990: **WITHHELD**

1991: **Prairie Deaugh**
(FC Lay Back Nick Chopper, SDX × Baby Deaugh)

1992: **Stoneangel's Devil Deaugh**
(Lucky Deaugh × Deaugh Daze, CD, NRD)

1993: **K-Don's Carpe Diem Mit-Mir**
(FC Zach's Grau Geist Gruppe B × Dumel's Lady Sunshine J)

1994: **Von Oben's Eclipse in the Knight**
(NFC/FC Rynmichel Sir Knight von Horn ×
Celys Texas Kool Runnin Jynx)

1995: **Misselthwaites Daisy May**
(Duser's Amazin Ace × Misselthwaites Maggie May)

1996: **Robynski Deaugh Davison**
(FC/AFC Andick's Big Time Jake × Prairie Deaugh)

1997: **Ale N' Quail Sir Graystoke, JH, NSD**
(FC/AFC Gray's Ghost Hunter, JH ×
Von Weiner's Sugar Dale, CD, JH)

1998: **Ayla of Norton Creek**
(FC Duser's Amazin Ace × Lanes Hannah Of Harley Dee)

1999: **Stoneangels Devil in Disguise**
(FC Outdoors Rising Sun × FC Stoneangel's Devil Deaugh)

2000: **Howard's Charming Chelsea**
(FC Ruburn's Duser Bruiser ×
FC Howard's Ottercreek Belle, JH, SDX)

2001: **Gould's GRB's Little Chular**
(NFC/FC/AFC Westend's Li'l Sage Rider ×
FC Gould's Jus Call Me TJ)

2002: **Grayshadows Field Laureate**
(FC Gray Shadow Ghost Buster × S And S's Lid'l Lacy Lu, JH)

2003: **Howard's Dusty Breeze**
(DC Von Weiner's Withheld, CDX, MH, SD, RDX, VX × FC
Howard's Ottercreek Belle, JH, SDX)

2004: **Mojo's Little Jo of Westend, NSD**
(NFC/FC/AFC Grau Geist Lil's Gust v. Westend, CD, MH,
SDX, RDX, VX × Flatlands Two Time Mojave)

2005: **Buck's Blue Boy**
(NFC Briarmeadow Buck × Bailey Bin of Norton Creek)

2006: **Izzywindancer Lilbit of Cheer**
(FC/AFC Ruburn's Duser Bruiser × FC Windancer Izzy v. Reiteralm, NRD)

2007: **Grau Geist's Shelter Belt Echo**
(Grau Geist's Freon Freeze × Grau Geist's Rising Star v. Maus)

2008: **Erbenhof Luci Lawless**
(Erbenhof John Wayne × Erbenhof Battenburg),

2009: **Grau Geist's Hidden in Plane Sight**
(FC Outdoors Sport, NRD ×
Grau Geist's Rising Star v. Maus, NSD)

Figure D-4: *Oops!* Photography by Rodney Moon.

Field Futurity
Only One Futurity a Year from 1956–1985

1956: Nationals: **Maggie's Merry Missie**
(CH Ludwig v. Dottlyle ×
CH Fallbrook Merry Maggie)

1957: Nationals: **CH Jomar's Rock and Roll**
(FC Gerri Von Fabien, CD ×
CH Jomar's Pixie of Sylvan Glen)

1958: Nationals: **Von Whitcomb's Sky King**
(Joch Von Whitcomb, CD, TD ×
Dawnell's Silver Satin, CD)

1959: Nationals: **FC Elsemere's Baron**
(FC Fritz von Wehmann aus Rocklege, RDX,
SDX, × Regal Wunder Velletri)

1960: Nationals: **Siegfried's Sugar Foot**
(Graybar's Blitz × Silver Buff)

1961: Nationals: **Baron Der Shonnes Groshunder**
(FC Duke Von Gunston, RDX, SDX ×
Susan of Hilltop)

1962: Nationals: **Lakota Tag Von Lou**
(FC Oliver Von Schoenhausen ×
Darwin's Dakota Belle, RDX)

1963: Nationals: **Weary Lueger**
(Vegas Lueger × Shannon's Silver Shamrock)

1964: Nationals: **FC Von Whitcomb's Hurry, RD**
(FC Von Whitcomb's Tor, RDX, SDX, ×
Dawnell's Silver Satin, CD)

1965: Nationals: **Heidi Von Heinrich**
(Tomalor's Scotch × Dove Aura O. Egerness)

1966: Nationals: **FC Redhill's Constellation**
(FC Elsemere's Baron ×
FC Greta Von Kollerplatz, SDX)

1967: Nationals: **Newbury Smoke, NRD**
(Blue Pine's Elken's Bucky ×
Blue Pine's Aumar's Sue)

1968: Nationals: **FC Heizar's Chief Oshkosh**
(FC Ranger's Revenge, CD ×
Heidi Von Heinrich)

1969: Nationals: **Newbury Katrina, RD**
(FC Shenandoah Drummer Boy, RD ×
Aumar's Mona)

1970: Nationals: **FC Spatlese Bismark's Baron, TD, RDX**
(Stoddard's Silver Baron × Hein's Honey Girl, NRD)

1971: Nationals: **Ollie's Storm Warning, NRD**
(DC Birtzel Von Staub ×
CH Othen's Blazing Beauty)

1972: Nationals: **FC Newbury Penelope**
(Newbury Duke Von Knopf, CD, NRD ×
FC Newbury Renegade Lady, RDX)

1973: Nationals: **DC Redhill's Fanny Jo, SDX, BROM**
(CH Redhill's Satellite, SDX ×
FC Redhill's Fanfare, RD)

1974: Nationals: **CH Orkan's Tejas v. d. Reiteralm,
NRD, NSD**
(CH Maximilian v. d. Reiteralm, NSD, BROM
× DC Halann's Checkmatge Tamara, CD,
NRD, SDX)

1975: Nationals: **DC Ozark's Buckeye Rebel, RDX, SD, VX**
(FC Lechsteinholf's Ozark Pete, RDX, SDX ×
Pinochle Keno Kate)

1976: Nationals: **Gretchen of Southwind**
(FC Unserhund v. Sieger, SDX × Fairview's Arrow)

1977: Nationals: **Solar Energy**
(Mister Plywood, SDX ×
Weinerschnitzel's Seme Scoot)

1978: Nationals: **FC Whidbey's Sweet Rosie O'Grady**
(Mister Plywood, SDX ×
Weinerschnitzel's Seme Scoot)

1979: Nationals: **Birtzel's Cool Hand Luke**
(DC Ozark's Buckeye Rebel, RDX, SD, VX ×
FC Strevelyn's Storm Trysail)

1980: Nationals: **Newbury Dandy Dan**
(FC Alger's May Day, NRD, SDX ×
FC Fran's Dee Dee Von Heiser, RDX)

1981: Nationals: **FC Outdoors Shallico**
(FC Laine's Thor Von Time Bomb, SDX ×
FC Sandcast Sandy Rose)

1982: Nationals: **Galadriel Von Floppenears, NSD**
(FC Laine's Thor Von Time Bomb, SDX ×
Mys T's Invincible)

1983: Nationals: **Von Knopf's Frolicsome Freda, NSD**
(FC Mile Hi Bullet v. Gip × Mys T's Invincible)

1984: Nationals: **Palimar's Ancient Mariner**
(FC Birtzel's Lay Back Zach, NSD ×
FC Birtzel's Good Friday, SDX)

1985: Nationals: **Caljak Dolly**
(CH Nordsee's Warlord, NSD ×
Caljak's Antoniet of Sandcast)

1986: Nationals: **Newbury Andick Final Victory**
(2xNAFC/FC/AFC DCs Hons Tobie v. Sieger ×
FC Rosa Andick Luxembourg)

Midwest: Newbury Andick Final Victory
(2xNAFC/FC/AFC DCs Hons Tobie v. Sieger ×
FC Rosa Andick Luxembourg)

Eastern: Lady Jill of Camelot
(CH Tortuga's Canterbury Tales ×
CH Lady Sarah of Camelot)

Western: Grendel Von Horn
(FC AFC Falke von Horn ×
Gandalf's Fliegene Nonne)

1987: **Nationals: Birtzel's Kiz Harp**
(Birtzel's Lookaway Dixieland × Birtzel's Scatman)

Midwest: Richmark Diamond
(FC Newbury Silver Knight × Autumn Robin)

Eastern: Richmark Diamond
(FC Newbury Silver Knight × Autumn Robin)

Western: Hoglund's Tiger von Thor
(FC Laine's Thor Von Time Bomb, SDX ×
FC Edith Ann Von Horn, NRD, SDX)

1988: **Nationals: CH Tri-D'S Sterling Silver**
(CH Eb's You Otta See Me Now, JH, NRD, SD,
BROM × CH Tri-D's Baiin de Soleil, NRD, BROM)

Midwest: Outdoors Starfire
(Outdoors Fritz's Duke ×
NFC FC AFC Outdoors Boots)

Eastern: Outdoors Starfire
(Outdoors Fritz's Duke ×
NFC FC AFC Outdoors Boots)

Western: Outdoors Starfire
(Outdoors Fritz's Duke ×
NFC FC AFC Outdoors Boots)

1989: **Nationals: Lea Knopf Corral**
(Poll's Smart Smoke × Daisy von Knopf)

Midwest: Ida Augusta von Horn
(FC DC The Sundance Kid, VX ×
FC Edith Ann Von Horn, SDX)

Eastern: Ida Augusta von Horn
(FC DC The Sundance Kid, VX ×
FC Edith Ann Von Horn, SDX)

Western: Ida Augusta von Horn
(FC DC The Sundance Kid, VX ×
FC Edith Ann Von Horn, SDX)

1990: **Nationals: Outdoors Urban Terrorist**
(FC Andick's Big Time Jake ×
FC Outdoors Tony Lama)

Midwest: Outdoors Urban Terrorist
(FC Andick's Big Time Jake ×
FC Outdoors Tony Lama)

Eastern: Outdoors Urban Terrorist
(FC Andick's Big Time Jake ×
FC Outdoors Tony Lama)

Western: Holly of Brookmont
(2xNFC FC Lay Back Nick Chopper ×
CH Brendy of Brookmont)

1991: **Nationals: Richmark Bo Brandy**
(FC Andick's Big Time Jake ×
FC Richmark Diamond)

Midwest: Grau Geist's Lilith von Legs
(Mile Hi Bandit von Gip ×
FC AFC Qizef's Grau Geist Marlene)

Eastern: Grau Geist's Lilith von Legs
(Mile Hi Bandit von Gip ×
FC AFC Qizef's Grau Geist Marlene)

Western: Rynmichel Sir Knight von Horn
(FC CH The Sundance Kid, VX ×
FC Edith Ann Von Horn, SDX)

1992: **Nationals: Outdoors Rising Sun**
(FC/AFC Andick's Big Time Jake ×
FC/AFC Outdoors Tony Lama)

Midwest: Outdoors Raya de Plata
(FC Andicks Big Time Jake ×
FC Outdoors Tony Lama)

Eastern: Sky-Gen Feebe von Horn
(FC AFC Grendal von Horn ×
FC Dumels Crystal Lakes)

Western: Andick's Outdoors Sam
(FC Andicks Big Time Jake ×
FC Outdoors Tony Lama)

1993: **Nationals: Grau Geist's River City Dixie**
(Box River Big Chili ×
FC/AFC Qizef's Grau Geist Marlene)

Midwest: Outdoors Game Bandit
(FC Andicks Big Time Jake ×
FC Outdoors Tony Lama)

Eastern: Wynwood's Rain on the Rise
(CH Valmar Smokey City Ultra Easy, JH,
BROM × CH Vanoahs Glory Hallelujah)

Western: Outdoors Speedy
(FC Andicks Big Time Jake ×
FC Outdoors Tony Lama)

1994: **Nationals: Von Oben's Baron**
(NFC/FC Rynmichel Sir Knight von Horn ×
Celys Texas Kool Runnin Jynx)

Midwest: Dunes Outdoors Yo-Yo
(NFC FC Rynmichael Sir Knight von Horn ×
Outdoors April Patty)

Eastern: Wingfield's Dan D Jake
(FC Andicks Big Time Jake ×
Tri-D's Darracott's Lady)

Western: Lane's Scarlett O'Hara
(FC Hoglunds Tiger von Thor ×
FC Outdoors Urban Terrorist)

1995: **Nationals: Briarmeadow Sunshine Abigail**
(FC Outdoors Rising Sun × FC Windchyme)

Midwest: Briarmeadow Shadow
(FC Outdoors Rising Sun × FC Windchyme)

Eastern: Briarmeadow Shadow
(FC Outdoors Rising Sun × FC Windchyme)

Western: Ryanmichael Veron von Mac
(FC Outdoors Rising Sun × FC Windchyme)

1996: **Nationals: Markee's Rumor Has It, JH**
(FC Grey Wynn Bad To The Bone ×
FC/AFC Markee's Shelby Centerfold, SH)

Midwest: **Briarmeadows Buck**
(FC Andicks Big Time Jake × FC Wyndchyme)

Eastern: **Markee's Rumor Has It, JH**
(FC Grey Wynn Bad To The Bone ×
FC/AFC Markee's Shelby Centerfold, SH)

Western: **V Hennerichs Blitzen v. Himmel**
(CH Wilsons Baron of Westend ×
Westend's Desert Star)

1997:   Nationals: **Briarmeadows Discovery**
(FC Outdoors Rising Sun × FC Windchyme)

Midwest: **Knight's Gnarly Carly**
(NAFC DC AFC Knight's Ti-Ki Toi, CD, JH ×
Von Obens Eclipse in the Knight)

Eastern: **Briarmeadows Jagrhund**
(FC Outdoors Rising Sun × FC Windchyme)

Western: **Briarmeadows Jagrhund**
(FC Outdoors Rising Sun × FC Windchyme)

1998:   Nationals: **Grau Geist Lil's Caprock Rev**
(NFC/FC Westend's Li'l Sage Rider ×
NFC/FC/AFC Grau Geist's Lilith von Legs)

Midwest: **Grau Geist Lil's Caprock Rev**
(NFC/FC Westend's Li'l Sage Rider ×
NFC/FC/AFC Grau Geist's Lilith von Legs)

Eastern: **Reiteralm Sandbar Snake Break**
(NAFC FC AFC Snake Breaks Sgt Schultz ×
FC Arimarlisa's Rudi V Reiteralm)

Western: **Snake Breaks Fritz v. Reiteralm**
(NAFC/FC/AFC Snake Breaks Sgt. Schultz ×
FC Arimarlisa Rudi v. Reiteralm)

1999:   Nationals: **Von Harwil's Miss B Havin**
(FC Grey Wynn Bad To The Bone ×
FC/AFC Von Harwil's Slick Willie)

Midwest: **Hunter's Shooting Star**
(2xNFC NAFC Fc AFC High Ridge Jesse von
Horn × Shelby's Shooting Star)

Eastern: **Sandbar Windancer v. Reiteralm**
(NAFC FC AFC Snake Breaks Sgt Schultz ×
CH Sanbar's Send Me No Flowers)

Western: **Sandbar Windancer v. Reiteralm**
(NAFC FC AFC Snake Breaks Sgt Schultz ×
CH Sanbar's Send Me No Flowers)

2000:   Nationals: **Scooby Doo's Treeline Storm**
(FC/AFC Stormcrow's Deaugh Blitzen, SH ×
Treeline's Lyza Jayne)

Midwest: **Scooby Doo's Treeline Storm**
(FC/AFC Stormcrow's Deaugh Blitzen, SH ×
Treeline's Lyza Jayne)

Eastern: **Scooby Doo's Treeline Storm**
(FC/AFC Stormcrow's Deaugh Blitzen, SH ×
Treeline's Lyza Jayne)

Western: **Scooby Doo's Treeline Storm**
(FC/AFC Stormcrow's Deaugh Blitzen, SH ×
Treeline's Lyza Jayne)

2001:   Nationals: **Gould's GRB's Little Chular**
(NFC/FC/AFC Westend's Li'l Sage Rider ×
FC Gould's Jus Call Me TJ)

Midwest: **Goulds's GRB's Little Chular**
(NFC/FC/AFC Westend's Li'l Sage Rider, CD,
SH, NSD, NRD, V × NAFC/FC/AFC Gould's
Jus Call Me TJ)

Eastern: **Rocket of Norton Creek**
(DC Exuma's Hyatt of Norton Cr ×
FC Ayla of Norton Creek)

Western: **Peach of Norton Creek**
(DC Exuma's Hyatt of Norton Cr ×
FC Ayla of Norton Creek)

2002:   Nationals: **Sirius Mostly Mongo**
(NFC/FC/AFC Westend's Li'l Sage Rider,
CD, SH, NSD, NRD, V × DC Sirius Really
Rosie, CDX, JS, RD, VX)

Midwest: **Sirius Mostly Mongo**
(NFC/FC/AFC Westend's Li'l Sage Rider,
CD, SH, NSD, NRD, V × DC Sirius Really
Rosie, CDX, JS, RD, VX)

Eastern: **Axel's Sampson v. Reiteralm**
(CH Axel Reiteralm Of Weimars Joy, JH ×
Knight's Sanbar Lone Coyote, JH)

Western: **Westend's Lil Texas Ranger**
(NFC FC AFC Westend's Li'l Sage Rider ×
Westends' Let'er Buck)

2003:   Nationals: **Aztec's Midnight Shift**
(NAFC/AFC Northernlights This BudsForU ×
Grau Geists True Love Ways, NRD)

Midwest: **Outdoors Sport**
(NFC FC Briarmeadow Buck ×
FC Outdoors Twister)

Eastern: **Grayshadows Field Laureate**
(FC Gray Shadow Ghost Buster ×
S And S's Lid'l Lacy Lu, JH)

Western: **Wingfield's Just Jessie**
(DC Von Weiner's Withheld ×
FC Howard's Ottercreek Belle)

2004:   Nationals: **Questfound Bottle Rocket**
(NAFC/FC/AFC NorthernLights This BudsForU
× Questfound Stormline Zoe)

Midwest: **Grau Geist's Rising Star v. Maus**
(NFC FC AFC Westend's Li'l Sage Rider ×
Grau Geist Lil's Haus Maus)

Eastern: **Saga's Blitzkrieg v. Reiteralm**
(DC NFC NAFC AFC Snake Breaks Saga V Reiteralm, MH CD × Reiteralm Absolute Point, JH)

Western: **Gould's Farwest Lunatic**
(NFC FC Briarmeadow Buck ×
NAFC FC AFC Gould's Jus Call Me TJ)

2005:   Nationals: **Buck's Blue Boy**
(NFC Briarmeadow Buck ×
Bailey Bin of Norton Creek)

Midwest: **Buck's Blue Boy**
(NFC Briarmeadow Buck ×
Bailey Bin of Norton Creek)

Eastern: **Grayshadow Fasnjaeger**
(Von Luchbach MRH Scout ×
Grayshadows Mighty Heidi)

Western: Buck's Blue Boy
(NFC Briarmeadow Buck ×
Bailey Bin of Norton Creek)

2006: **Nationals: Gould's GRB's Mia Dolce Vita**
(NFC/NAFC/FC/AFC Grau Geist Lil's Gus v.
Westend, CD, RA, MH, SDX, RDX, VX ×
NAFC/FC/AFC Gould's Jus Call Me TJ)

Midwest: Leatherneck's Uncle Sam
(NFC NAFC FC AFC Scooby Doo's Treeline
Storm × Erbernhof Chere Petite Fille)

Eastern: Izzy's Tilla the Hon Windancer
(FC AFC Ruburn's Duser Bruiser ×
FC Windancer Izzy v Reiteralm)

Western: GRB's Hearty Burgundy
(NFC FC Von Weiner Smokn' Winds Holiday ×
NFC FC AFC Gould's GRB's Little Chular)

2007: **Nationals: Caprock Rev's Ollie Hot N' Tot**
(FC Grau Geist Lil's Caprock Rev ×
FC/AFC Jax's Treeline Blitzin Tilly)

Midwest: Waybac's Ahwawego
(FC Jax's Waybac Tyler ×
Grau Geist's Remembr The Alamo)

Eastern: Rokridges Raging Cajun
(FC Jax's Third Times a Charm ×
Grayshadow's Willow)

Western: Outdoors Hans Solo
(FC Grau Geist Lil's Caprock Rev ×
Outdoors Reno)

2008: **Nationals: Erbenhof SNS Boogie Woogie Bo**
(NFC NAFC FC AFC Scooby Doo's Treeline
Storm × Erbenhof S and S Razzmatazz,JH)

Midwest: Erbenhof SNS Jezz E. Bell
(NFC NAFC FC AFC Scooby Doo's Treeline
Storm × Erbenhof S and S Razzmatazz,JH)

Eastern: Erbenhof SNS Jezz E. Bell
(NFC NAFC FC AFC Scooby Doo's Treeline
Storm × Erbenhof S and S Razzmatazz,JH)

Western: Westend's Jagdfreund
(NFC NAFC AFC Grau Geist Lil's Gust v
Westend × Outdoors Gabrielle von Buck)

2009: **Nationals: Grau Geist's Buk Naked Tiger Lily**
(GRB's Hearty Burgundy ×
Grau Geist's Buck Naked)

Midwest: Not Enough Entries—Cancelled

Eastern: WestWeims California Lady Jane
(Buck's Blue Boy ×
FC AFC Gould's Outlaw Jessie Jane)

Western: WestWeims California Lady Jane
(Buck's Blue Boy ×
FC AFC Gould's Outlaw Jessie Jane)

Figure D-5: *Break away at Ardmore.* Photograph by Leslie Like.

Figure E-1: *The Connector,* by William Wegman

THE CHAMPIONS ARE...

Photos of each of the champions for Agility, Obedience, Tracking, and NAVHDA may be found in their respective chapters; however, in this appendix we have taken the opportunity to also include those dogs whose championships were too recent to otherwise be included.

And the AKC Agility Champions are...

MACH August Grub Grau, NSD, NRD, V
(Badboy's Little Boy-Buddie × Hill's Maggie Mae Sunshine)
Bred by Kathryn Hills; owned by Jennifer Dec and Jim Fleming.

MACH5 Chloe's Blue Velvet
(Cal's Choctaw × Coleman's Blue Velvet)
Bred by Dale G. Coleman; owned by Gene and Lori Barbee.

MACH GrayQuest Repeat Performance, VCD2, RN, JH, SD, NRD, VX3
(Deiter Schweinhund Sprocket × Coleman's Blue Velvet)
Bred by Dale G. Coleman; owned by Lori Barbee.

CH MACH3 Jamspirit Nobility, JH, NRD, VX2
(CH Vanity Visionary, MX, MXJ, JH, CD, NJP, VX2, NRD, NSD, BROM × CH DaBeck's Future Classic)
Bred by Sami Simons and Melissa Chandler; owned by Melissa Chandler.

MACH Jet, CDX, RA, OF
(unknown x unknown) Bred by Unknown. Owned by Chris Forster.

CH MACH2 Lechsteinhof 's Silver Lady, CDX, RN
(Lechsteinhof's Silver Smoke × Oakview's Grey Ghost)
Bred by unknown; owned by Kimberly Budd.

MACH Princess Fallon of Amber Glen, CD, NAP, NJP
(unknown × unknown) Bred by unknown; owned by Sheila Cook.

CH MACH6 Regen's GrayQuest Rock Candy, VCD2, RN, TDX, MXF, RD, NSD, VX3
(CH Rockville's Truman Greystone, VCD2, TDX, MH, MX, MXJ, SDX, RDX, VX5 × CH MACH Regen's Hot Chili Pepper, VCD3, MH, SDX, RDX, VX5) Bred by Judi Voris and Shirley Nilsson; owned by Lori Barbee and Judi Voris.

CH MACH Regen's Hot Chili Pepper, VCD3, MH, RDX, SDX, VX5
(CH Valmar's Apache Rebel, BROM × CH Regen's Summer Triumph)
Bred and owned by Judi Voris.

Am/Can CH MACH2 Regen's Rocket Launcher, VCD2, TDX, AX, MXJ, SD, VX4
(CH Rockville's Truman Greystone, VCD2, TDX, MH, MX, MXJ, SDX, RDX, VX5 × CH MACH Regen's Hot Chili Pepper, VCD3, SH, SDX, RDX, VX5)
Bred by Judi Voris and Shirley Nilsson; owned by Steve and Laurie Jenks.

CH MACH Silverstar's Annie Get Your Gun, VCD1, NF, NRD, VX2
(CH Valmar's Sage v Wustenwind, NSD, NRD, V, BROM × CH Green Acres Gift of Lace n' Gus, CD)
Bred by Renee Romberg; owned by Renee Romberg.

MACH Wesley II, NF
(Dawn's Twinkle Toes × Brian's Shotgun Annie)
Bred by unknown; owned by R. McFadden

MACH4 Wanric Trevor Tracks, CDX, RA, AXP, AJP, NF, RD, NSD, VX
(Brutus × Tilly May Delight)
Bred by Darlene Williams; owned by Wanda Gunter.

WSOTC Agility Trials, 7/11/09
©2009 Creative Indulgence, all rights reserved

Figure E-2: *Am/Can CH MACH2 Regen's Rocket Launcher, VCD2, TDX, AX, MXJ, SD, VX4* (CH Rockville's Truman Greystone, VCD2, TDX, MH, MX, MXJ, SDX, RDX, VX5 × CH MACH Regen's Hot Chili Pepper, VCD3, SH, SDX, RDX, VX5). Bred by Voris and Shirley Nilsson; owned by Steve and Laurie Jenks. Booster truly lived up to his name as he and handler Steve rocketed through the classes and gathered points for his first and second MACHs. In the Dance of Dog Agility, Steve and Booster outshine even Fred Astair and Ginger Rogers. Booster's and his littermates are truly model the versatile Weimaraner (see Figure 20-1) but Booster's forte seems to be agility. In 2007, Booster captured the AKC National Invitational 24″ class. 2009 was perhaps an even more auspicious year in some respects, he was not only crowned WCA National Agility Champion and Top 10 list, his 2009 performance at the AKC National Invitational earned him second place, but with an astonishing 5 clean runs and placements in each run! Photograph used by permission of Creative Indulgence Photography.

Figure E-3: *MACH2 Jet, CDX, RA, OF* (unknown × unknown). Bred by unknown; owned by Chris Forster. Jet came to Chris at 5 months old, from a family that no longer had time for her. She had no crate training, wasn't house broken, and suffered from separation anxiety. Arriving at her new home she entered the family room, picked the furthest dog bed and plopped into it. Chris and Jet started together in Nov A dog, beginning in both obedience and agility right away. At 2 1/2 years old, Jet debuted in obedience at the WCA Nationals in Frankenmuth, MI. Jet earned her CD with three 1st placements and a top score of 195.5; graduating to Open she earned a 1st place with a score of 191.5. In agility, Jet consistently takes 1st and 2nd, getting the multipliers with clean fast runs. Jet's biddable, eager, smart, and funny temperament has made this a journey Chris will never forget, "She has taught me so much. I will always own a Weimaraner because of her."

Figure E-4: *Valor's Etheldreda Regina, CD, RN, AX, AXJ, MXP2, MJP2, PAX, NF* (CH Watchpoint's Excluzive Copy × Isolde's Silver Mint Julep) Bred by Susan and Dale Brumfield; owned by Alan Spearman, Mary Edmonds and Susan Brumfield. Audrey is the first Weimaraner to earn the AKC PAX title. The Preferred Agility Excellent title is awarded to a dog achieving 20 double qualifying scores obtained from the Preferred Excellent B Standard Agility class and the Preferred Excellent B Jumpers With Weaves class (Q's earned on the same day at the same trial). There is no time point requirement, however, and the jumps are 4" lower than the standard classes. This gives older dogs the opportunity to continue to compete, as well as a chance for slow maturing or inexperienced dogs (or handlers) the chance to gain valuable experience in a less demanding venue.

Figure E-5: *CH MACH Silverstar's Annie Get Your Gun, NF, VCD1, NRD, VX2* (CH Valmar's Sage v. Wustenwind, NSD, NRD, V, BROM × CH Green Acres Gift of Lace 'n Gus, CD) Bred and owned by Renee Romberg. Renee claims her involvement in agility stated on a whim, in order to earn the Versatile Companion Dog title (VCD). Since she had never even been to agility trial before that time Annie and Renee, learned together along the way. And they both must have learned pretty well. Renee says she never imagined the exciting journey would lead to Annie becoming the 10th Weimaraner to earn a Master Agility Championship. But Renee says the best part has been the many great friends they have made along the way and the fun she and Annie had together, as a team. "I couldn't have asked for a better partner."

And the Champion Trackers are...

**CT Ardreem's Oberon Phantasm,
VCD2, RE, JH, SDX, RDX, VX2**
(CH Ricochets Banner Flying on the Rise ×
Ardreem's Elenor Rigby, JH)
Bred by Lin Frisbee; owned by Gretchen and Stewart Stephenson.

CT Beau's Li'l Bird Dawg, CD
(Scott's Lucky Silver Ghost × Scott's Smoky Sable)
Bred by Sheryl Scott; owned by Beth Schofield.

CT CC's Amaz'n Rainy's Gabriele, CD, RN
(Amaz'N Gra'Z Second Chance, NA, NAJ, CD, JH, NSD ×
Cc's Rainy Daze Sweet Desire)
Bred by Chris Conklin; owned by Linda Swanson and Chris Conklin.

CT Pewter Run's Diamond in the Sky, JH, NRD, VX
(CH Pewterun Greydove Blackmagic × CH PewterRun's Kiss Me Kate)
Bred by Paul and Sharon Manning; owned by Linda Swanson and
Christine Conklin.

CT Pewter Run's Papermoon
(CH Carousels Roscoe T Picotrane × CH Silversmith's Touch of Class)
Bred by Sharon and Paul Manning; owned by Ruth A. Vaughan,
Mark G. Erdle and Sharon Manning

**TC CT Regen's Rip Stop,
VCD2, UDX4, MH, AX, RDX, SDX, VX6**
(FC AFC NAFC Northern Lights This BudsForU ×
TC AFC Regen's Summer Blaze, RE, VCD3, UDX2, TDX, SDX,
RDX, MH, MX, MXJ, VX6, BROM)
Bred by Judith Voris and Shirley Nilssen; owned by Anne Tyson
and Judi Voris.

CH CT Sandstorm's a Lady of the Lake
(CH Seabreeze Colsidex Windy Cliff, TD, NSD, V × CH Arnstadt's
Silvershot Arietta, MH, TD, SDX, NRD, VX, NAVHDA NA)
Bred by Sandra L. Hoesel; owned by Sandra L. Hoesel and Craig
W. Schrameyer.

Figure E-6: *CT Ardreem's Oberon Phantasm, VCD2, RE, SH, RDX, SDX, VX3, CGC, TDI-A* (CH Ricochets Banner Flying on the Rise × Ardreem's Elenor Rigby, JH). Bred by Lin Frisbee; owned by Gretchen and Stewart Stephenson. Obie greets every morning with excitement to get the day going; always up for training he often pesters owner, Gretchen into working him. As a puppy, he escaped from his crate to follow the track Gretchen was working, with another dog, to find her. After earning his TD at just over a year old, tracking went on the backburner to pursue other activities. After earning hunting, retrieving, obedience and agility titles, it was time to concentrate on tracking again. Obie always wants to be correct before making a decision, so though he moves quickly when he is sure, he takes his time solving a problem. His thorough nature allowed Obie to earn his TDX and VST titles a little over 6 months apart. Gretchen said, "Words can't express the joy I felt when Obie found the final article on his VST track." Since earning his CT title, Obie has returned to his true love, hunting, and has added the Senior Hunter title to his credit and is in the fields working on his Master Hunter title. Photo Credit Ed Presnall.

Figure E-7: *CT Beau's Li'l Bird Dawg VCD1, CDX, OJP, RE, V* (Scott's Lucky Silver Ghost × Scott's Smokey Sable). Bred by Sheryl Scott; owned by Beth Schofield. Birdie started formal tracking lessons at the age of 12 weeks, with mentor Terry McGauley, who also works with Bullitt County Search and Rescue in Kentucky. Once his great tracking ability, was recognized, Birdie's AKC tracking training provided a valuable cornerstone for Search and Rescue training. It is very exciting and rewarding to know something that started out as fun has turned into something that can benefit the community as well. While Birdie also trained in obedience and agility, it was obvious that his first love is tracking. He received his CT title on November 4, 2007. He is a very loving and social dog who is also a certified therapy dog and Hospice volunteer.

Figure E-8: *CT PewterRun's Diamond in the Sky, JH, NRD, VX, NAVDHA NA II* (CH Pewterun Greydove Blackmagic × CH PewterRun's Kiss Me Kate, BROM) Bred by Paul and Sharon Manning. Owned by Linda Swanson and Christine Conklin. Kya is a prime example of the Versatile Weimaraner! Her natural talent and extreme intelligence has allowed her to excel in every venue she, Linda and Chris have participated in, including passing the VST test to become the 7th Champion Tracker Weimaraner. Kya then spent 5 weeks in field training to polish her skills as a finished gundog…and promptly earned 2 legs towards her Master Hunter title in the first two tests entered. She has been so busy with her performance career that she has had limited ring time, but still has garnered a BOB and 5 conformation points and will be working towards finishing in 2010, along with earning her MH title.

Figure E-9: *CT Pewter Run's Paper Moon, VCD 2, AXJ, RE, VX* (CH Carousel's Roscoe T. Picotrane × CH Silversmith's Touch of Class) Bred by Sharon and Paul Manning; owned by Ruth Vaughan, Mark Erdle and Sharon Manning. Truman shows that the natural versatile talents and biddable nature of a well bred Weimaraner make them a good choice for a first time competition partner; Truman has earned 18 titles so far in obedience, tracking, agility, rally, and WCA ratings. Having passed the VST in November, 2008, (the 4th Weim, and one of only about 200 dogs all-breeds, to earn this coveted title) Truman and Ruth experienced a "dream come true" by participating in the 2009 AKC Tracking Invitational. While he loves to track, having earned the highest tracking titles, Truman and Ruth are now working on the AKC UD and Excellent Agility titles. When not competing Truman loves hiking in the Adirondacks, as well as long walks in the woods closer to their upstate New York home. Photograph by Wendi Pencille, Horsefeathers Photography.

Figure E-10: *CH CT SandStorm's a Lady of the Lake* (CH Seabreeze Colsidex Windy Cliff × CH Arnstadt Silvershot Arietta, MH, TD, SDX, NRD, VX, NAVHDA NA) Bred by Sandra L. Hoesel; owned by Sandra L. Hoesel and Craig W. Schrameyer. On April 6, 2008, "Lady" SandStorm's a Lady of the Lake TDX passed the AKC Variable Surface Tracking test making her the third Weimaraner in the USA to garner such a prestigious title and add the CT in front of her name. Lady was the breed's first AKC Bench Champion and AKC Champion Tracker. Lady started her tracking career as a prodigy, earning her TD at 6 months + 1 day, and her TDX at 11 months, both on the first try. She is a tracking fiend and proved it that day; despite her young age (less than 3 years old) and in spite of moderate sustained winds and a 3.5 hour aged track our girl methodically worked thru the difficult scenting conditions, and thrilled her owner and the gallery when she indicated article #4 after 57 minutes. With the highest Tracking titles achieved, Lady is heading to the fields to hunt rather than track.

And the Obedience Champions are...

OTCH Brought Mar's Samantha P. Smog, UDTX, SDX, RDX, VX, HOF
(CH AFC Brought-Mars Game Bandit v. Tor
× Madchen's Blu Phantom
Bred by Mr. and Mrs. William C. Yarborough; owned by Wentworth and Irene Brown.

CH OTCH Eb's Redhot Seabreeze, UDX, JH, NA, NRD, VX, CGC, HOF
(CH Greywind's Jack Frost, CD × CH Seabreeze Autumn Piper, CD
Bred by Karen Lewis, Marge Davis and Barbara Didjurgis; owned by Sherry Cooper and Marge Davis.

OTCH Freder's Gray Velvet v. Elsax, UDT, JH, RDX, VX,
(CH Reichenstadt's Axel v. Gab, CD, TD × Elsa Von Brandt
Bred by Lisa Dillon Sackbauer; owned by Stephanos and Jeanne Popovits.

OTCH Haiku Solar Eclipse, UDT
(CH Star-N-Tsuru-Tani Majitsu ×
CH Star-N-Love Song v. d. Reiteralm
Bred by Nancy Mednick;; owned and handled by Marty Fast.

OTCH Heidi v. Falkenberg, UDT
(Kurt's Krazy Kriss × Ranah's Royal Lady Priscilla
Bred by Unknown; owned by Booth and Anna Kelley.

OTCH Jar Em's Lightning Storm, UDX7, JH, NRD, VX
(CH Arnstadt's Wotan von Doblen, CD, TD, JH
× CH Jarem's Casino Roulette
Bred by Sandra L. Jaremczuk; owned by Randy Scharich.

OTCH CH Jar-em's Special Sporting Clay, UDX5, JH, VX
(CH Hope's Thunder Jack of Diamonds, JH
× CH Jar Em's Casino Roulette
Bred by Sandra L. Jaremczuk; owned by Randy Scharich

TC CT Regen's Rip Stop, VCD3, UDX4, MH, SDX, RDX, VX6
(NAFC FC AFC Northern Lights This BudsForU ×
TC AFC Regen's Summer Blaze, VCD3, MH, MX, MXJ, RE, SDX, RDX, VX6
Bred by Judy Voris and Shirley Nilsson; owned by Anne Tyson and Shirley Nilsson

OTCH Regen's State of the Art, VCD2, UDX2, RE, MH, TDX, SDX, RDX, VX4
(DC Von Weiner's Withheld, MH × TC AFC Regen's Summer Blaze, VCD3, MH, MX, MXJ, RE, SDX, RDX, VX6)
Bred by Shirley Nilsson and Judi Voris; owned by Shirley Nilsson

TC AFC Regen's Summer Blaze, VCD3, UDX2, RE, TDX, MH, MX, MXJ, SDX, RDX, VX6
(CH Jak's Repeat Offender ×
CH Skyhi's EZ Magical Reign, UD, JH, SD, RD, VX
Bred by David and Nina Sherrer and Judi Voris; owned by Shirley Nilsson and Judi Voris

Figure E-11: *OTCH Regen's State of the Art, VCD2, UDX2, RE, MH, TDX, SDX, RDX, VX4* (DC Von Weiner's Withheld, MH × TC AFC Regen's Summer Blaze, VCD3, MH, MX, MXJ, RE, SDX, RDX, VX6). Bred by Shirley Nilsson and Judi Voris; owned by Shirley Nilsson. Eve is enthusiasm itself. A prodigy in obedience, Eve began by earning her Companion Dog obedience title in 3 straight legs at 6 months old. She went on to earn her OTCH as a 3 year old and has won many HIT awards including HIT at the WCA National Obedience trial with top scores in competition of 199 in both the Open and Utility classes. A natural afield, Eve has run broke with high style on both wild and planted birds since she was 5 months of age. She earned a perfect score of 112 on her NAVHDA NA test and, at 11 months old, earned her Retrieving Dog Excellent and Shooting Dog Excellent titles. A month later Eve earned her CKC Field Dog Excellent title in three consecutive tests with a top score of 99 out of 100. She completed her Master Hunter title at just 2 years of age. Eve wrote herself into the record books by becoming the first Weimaraner to earn CKC Urban Tracking Dog Excellent and Tracking Champion titles.

And the Field Champions are....

The list of Field champions was compiled from the most reliable sources available; however, some of these records are not as complete for Field Champions as for other types of championships. We regret that there may be some worthy dogs who have been inadvertently omitted or that information may be incomplete for some dogs.

FC Acee Duecee of Brookmont	(SF399940)
NFC NAFC FC AFC Algers May Day	(SB425379)
FC Andicks Big Time Jake	(SE399546)
FC Andicks Outdoor Sam	(SF958645)
FC Another Top Deaugh	(SN10746101)
FC Archibald Von Karlshugel	(SA621800)
DC Ardreem Wolf Von Betelgeuse	(SM85735105)
DC Ardreems Southern Maverick	(SN10614505)
FC Arimarlisas Rudi V Reiteralm	(SN19878203)
DC Arimars Ivan	(SB393851)
DC Arimars Lovely Lyric	(SB656562)
FC Axel's Bleu Bayou of Reiteralm	(SR10142108)
FC Axels Czar Von Reiteralm	(SN63415805)
FC Axel's Sampson V Reiteralm	(SN84173902)
FC Ayla of Norton Creek	(SN43727003)
2xNAFC AFC FC Aztec's American Pie	(SN87500605)
FC Aztec's Midnight Shift	(SN87500606)
FC Bahamm Von Andick	(SB667720)
FC AFC Bajas Zephyr	(SD262586)
DC Baron V Randoplh	(S905503)
DC Baroness of Magmar	(S603991)
DC Bayers Silver Mr V Reiteralm	(SF670391)
FC Bea's Ultra Blitz von Ludwig	(SA468838)
DC Birtzel V Staub	(SA193899)
FC Birtzel's Aberfelda Duke	(SB522011)
NAFC FC Birtzels Good Friday	(SC433954)
DC Birtzels Johnny Reb	(SB735425)
NFC FC Birtzels Lay Back Zach	(SC734272)
FC Bj's Zib Von Der Harrasburg	(SB576650)
FC Borg's Canis Major on the Rise	(SN83073307)
FC Braunhilde's Moon Maid	(SA715834)
NFC FC Briarmeadow Buck	(SN24332702)
FC Briarmeadow Shadow	(SN10371901)
FC Briarmeadow Sunshine Abigail	(SN10371906)
DC Bruno Auger Silver Duke	(S628817)
FC Buck's Blue Boy	(SR15375506)
DC Camelots Desert Fox	(SN31835901)
FC Cameo's Schnikelfriz	(SB540389)
FC Chapter Two V Saga	(SR23295401)
FC Christopher Von Tauber	
DC Crook N Nannys Silver Titan	(SA807162)
FC AFC Davison Orion on the Rise	(SN44241002)

NAFC FC AFC Dcs Hons Tobie Von Sieger	(SB998258)
FC Denab Von Andick	(SB948470)
FC Dietzs Liesle Weapon von Harwil	(SN32488003)
FC AFC Duchess Allimonds	(SF733423)
FC Duke Von Gunston	(S856520)
FC Dummels Crystal Lakes of Erin	(S E225887)
FC Dusers Amazin Ace	(SM89524801)
DC Dust Storm on the Rise, JH	(SN65498402)
FC Dutchess Rita Von Turner	(SA882183)
DC Dv's Laughing Girl	(S891356)
NFC FC AFC Edith Ann Von Horn	(SD146467)
AFC Egon Blitz von Horn	(SD179934)
DC Eldan's Mohave Sundancer	(SA456458)
FC Elder's Soren Ludwig	(SA559558)
AFC Elke von Neu Berlin	(SA822495)
FC Elsmere's Baron Aus Wehmann	(S933199)
DC Exumas Hyatt of Norton Cr	(SN27280505)
FC Fairviews Sassy Secret	(SE701159)
FC AFC Falke Von Horn	(SD784157)
DC Firebird's Second Chance	(SB867034)
FC Flatlands Isadora Von Horn	(SF061987)
FC AFC Fran's Dee Dee Von Heiser	(SA774805)
FC Fritz V Wehmann Aus Rockledge	(S529353)
FC Gandalf of Eskelo II	(SB515896)
FC AFC Gandalfs Indian Summer	(SC647546)
FCH Gemma Von Andick	(SD126219)
DC Gents Silver Smoke	(SA807575)
FC Gitaway Fella Lee Heidelberg	(SA922335)
FC AFC Gould's Cascade Shasta	(SN43076204)
NFC FC Gould's Farwest Lunatic	(SN91962705)
NFC FC AFC Gould's Grb's Little Chular	(SN71717305)
NAFC FC AFC Gould's Jus Call Me Tj	(SN27128501)
FC Gould's Jus Git R Done V Zdon	(SR26816304)
FC AFC Gould's Outlaw Jessie	(SR18329814)
FC Gould's Thunder Und Blitz	(SM82193303)
FC Gould's V Three Remington	(SN71717304)
NFC FC Gould's Wicked Runner	(SN71717303)
DC AFC Gradaus Katrinka	(SA989907)
FC Grafmars Kings Aide	
FC Grau Geist Cowboy Take Me Away	(SN72711202)
FC Grau Geist Lils Caprock Rev	(SN43134202)
FC Grau Geist Lil's Femme Nikita	(SN52247903)

NFC NAFC FC AFC Grau Geist Lils Gust V Westend
(SN43134201)

FC Grau Geist's Bold Rebel Sol (SR00724401)

FC AFC Grau Geists Chili Salsa (SM90458806)

NFC FC AFC Grau Geists Lilth Von Legs (SF597730)

FC Grau Geist's Red Chili Pepper (SM90458804)

FC Grau Geist's Tascosa Valley (SN52247901)

FC Grau Geists True Love Ways (SN43134204)

FC Grau Geist's Valley High (SN33203702)

FC Gray Shadow Ghost Buster (SN38256905)

FC Grayfires Hawkeye (SE779539)

FC AFC Grays Ghost Hunter (SM84689505)

FC Grayshadows Field Laureate (SN83766703)

FC AFC Grendel Von Horn (SE271372)

FC AFC Greta Von Kollerplatz (S887903)

FC Grey Wynn Bad to the Bone (SM89697701)

FC AFC Grey Wynn Gypsy Jewel (SN53197510)

DC Halanns Checkmate Tamara (SA573048)

DC Halann's The Judge v. Reiteralm (SA633347)

FC Helene of Wingwood (SA897776)

2xNFC NAFC FC AFC High Ridge Jesse Von Horn
(SN14665002)

NFC FC AFC Hoglunds Tiger Von Thor (SE407664)

FC Howard's Max-a-million Major (SN65648607)

FC AFC Hunters Shooting Star (SN54498705)

FC Ichabod (SA904517)

FC Ida Augusta Von Horn (SF012938)

NFC DC Jafwin's One and Only (SC400928)

DC Jafwin's the Goodbye Girl (SC385925)

FC Jake VII (SB380580)

FC Jax's Third Times a Charm (SR02758207)

FC AFC Jax's Treeline Blitzin Tilly (SN78110803)

FC Jax's Waybac Tyler (SN78110804)

DC Jo-rons Silber Eich (SF803620)

FC AFC Kachinas Outdoors Bucko (SD635583)

FC Kachinas Rain Drop (SC158024)

FC Kaiser Von Reiteralm (SC381420)

FC K-Don's Carpe Diem Mit Mir (SM99490203)

FC Kelshawn Smoke v. d. Reiteralm (SA693785)

FC Killcreek's Geist V Blitz (SF198878)

FC Killcreeks Sturmisch Herzen (SM88715203)

FC Kip Von Suspam (S901644)

2xNFC FC AFC Kipbirtzel's Texas Kid (SN33731126)

FC Knights Gnarly Carly V Toi (SN33731126)

DC NAFC Knights Ti-ki Toi (SG028056)

FC Kristel Dawn V Reiteralm (SC376825)

DC Kristof's Classic Venture (SC445564)

FC Kristof's Critics Choice (SD105445)

FC Kristof's Western Ryder (SD425337)

FC AFC Krystal Elena Von Horn (SD165976)

DC Lady Athena of Camelot (SC993906)

DC Lady Rebecca of Camelot (SC100741)

NFC FC AFC Laines Thor Von Time Bomb (SB690201)

DC AFC Landbees Liberty Flyer (SB740885)

FC Landbees Upland Pro (S740537)

FC Lane's Freilaufer Rugerhund (SN05539304)

2xNFC FC Lay Back Nick Chopper (SE485222)

FC Leatherneck's Chesty Puller (SR19766505)

FC AFC Lechsteinhof's Ozaark Pete (SA995841)

FC Lechsteinhof's Silver Cloud (SC293259)

FC Lightning Strikes on the Rise (SN44241006)

DC Lilith Von Hirschhorn (SA764285)

FC Lil-ryders Grau Geists Gator (SN43134206)

FC Llennoco's Brunhilde (SB285875)

FC Ludwig V Weisenhof

FC Mac V Whitcomb (S 822613)

VC DC AFC Magnum Gunnar Silvershot (SN15758808)

DC Marbils Baron Von Josephus (SB632544)

FC AFC Markee's Dear John (SN53492308)

FC Markee's High Ridge Hunter (SN53492302)

FC AFC Markee's Lay Back Lizy Borden (SN02032001)

FC AFC Markee's Rumor Has It (SN18449303)

FC Markee's Shelby Centerfold (SE576386)

FC McKee's Silver King (SA71412)

CH AFC Meg Hidlegarde Altman (SA852097)

FC Michael Weinerschnitzl (SB131234)

FC Mile Hi Bullet V Gip (SC915659)

FC AFC Mile Hi Caspar V Gip (SD738843)

DC Mile Hi Murphy (SM95025303)

FC Mit Mir's Earthquake (SN44845006)

FC Mojo's Little Jo of Westend (SR04623902)

FC Nani's Baron v. d. Reiteralm (SB806395)

FC AFC Newbury Buck (SA685996)

FC Newbury Gustave (SA263067)

FC Newbury's Mister Moses (SB968560)

FC AFC Newbury's Penelope (SB058212)

FC Newbury Renegade Lady (SA287804)

FC Newbury Silver Knight (SC962574)

NAFC FC Northernlights This Budsforu (SN19948801)

FC Nottingham's Max (SB479081)

FC Oliver Von Schoenhousen

FC Othen's Artemis Belle Breeze (SC252940)

DC Othens Princess Pretty (SA681659)

FC Otter Creek Pip Squeak (SN41286806)

FC Outdoors Bingo Girl (SN35533601)

NFC FC AFC Outdoors Boots (SC794487)

FC AFC Outdoors Dakota (SF990029)

FC Outdoors Fritzs Duke (SE569706)

FC Outdoors Game Bandit (SM96758002)

DC Outdoors Life of Riley (SN73959506)

NFC FC AFC Outdoors Magic Misty (SF540228)

FC Outdoor's Raya De Plata (SF952840)

FC Outdoors Rising Sun (SM79363401)

FC Outdoors Scooter Pie (SE710315)

FC Outdoors Shallico (SC964043)

FC AFC Outdoors Shawnee (SF908464)

FC Outdoors Sir Tahoe (SC931239)

FC Outdoors Sport (SN86321503)

FC Outdoors Starfire (SE744372)

FC AFC Outdoors Tony Lama (SE324346)

FC Outdoors Twister (SN43478501)

FC Outdoors Urban Terrorist (SF517424)

FC Outdoors Wingfield Duffy (SM96758005)

DC Ozarks Buckeye Rebel (SB688150)

DC Palladian Perseus (S374207)

FC Parmer's Gray Baron (SB689497)

DC Paron's Bingo (SA296514)

DC Patmar's Silver Countess (S442643)

FC Pecancreek Reflection of Tia (SN93288101)

FC Pecan Creek Star Rider (SN93288107)

FC Peterson's Snow Bird (SA905905)

DC Pine Grove Farms Brunhilde (SA102502)

DC Prinz Rolf V Kiry (SB61331)

FC AFC Qizefs Grau Geist Marlene (SE655419)

FC Questfound Bottle Rocket (SR04384902)

FC Ranger's Izquieroa Zapata (SA623955)

FC Ranger's Revenge (SA55516)

DC Redhill's Chief Geronimo (SC505813)

FC Redhill's Constellation

FC Redhill's Fanfare (SA264619)

DC Redhill's Fanny Jo (SB137448)

FC Redhill's General Nuisance (SC199260)

FC Redhill's Maxmillian

FC Redhill's Merlin V Jaegerhof (SB364184)

TC CT Regens Rip Stop (SN91227601)

OTCH FC AFC Regens Rip Tide (SN91227605)

TC AFC Regens Summer Blaze (SN37831703)

FC Reiteralms Sandbar Snake Break (SN40290909)

FC Reiteralms Snake Break-dot-com (SN71159305)

FC AFC Richmark Bo Brandy (SF716398)

FC Richmark Diamond (SE421818)

FC AFC Richmark Hot Tamale (SM89524806)

FC Robynski Deaugh Davison (SN27194204)

DC Ronamax Rufus v. d. Reiteralm (SA945638)

FC Rosa Andick Luxembourg (SD197184)

FC Royalstons Scout V Reiteralm (SR02674405)

FC AFC Ruburns Duser Bruiser (SN05911207)

FC Runyon's Silver Certificate (SB933262)

NFC FC Rynmichel Sir Knight Von Horn (SF714593)

FC S and S's Jagermeister (SM98011802)

FC Saga's Blitzkrieg V Reiteralm (SR06906003)

FC Saga's J. P. Getty Von Reiteralm (SR23295405)

FC Sandcast Sandy Rose (SC464780)

DC Schmidt's Countess Kristine (SA17097)

FC Schnitzel Von Trommier (SA680254)

NFC NAFC FC AFC Scooby Doos Treeline Storm
(SN59758808)

FC Seevogel Sabre V Reiteralm (SA783048)

DC AFC Shadowmar Artemis Impenda (SB712027)

AFC Shadowmar's Hunter Jake (SB305504)

FC Shannendoah Drummer Boy (SA185101)

DC Show Me Silver Shadow (SB879081)

FC Silver Rain's Bull Rider (SR06619501)

DC Silverbrand Rafferty V Jarem (SC282383)

DC Sir Anthonys Jake of Sanbar (SN44779208)

FC Sir Heidelburg Redhill (SB131462)

NFC DC Sirius Mostly Mongo (SN83681301)

DC Sirius Peppermint Schnapps (SN55132401)

DC Sirius Really Rosie (SN17587907)

AFC Skipper von Grau Cinderella (SA432652)

FC Snake Breaks No Quarter (SR30558301)

FC Snake Breaks Run Wild Idaho (SN71159302)

NFC NAFC DC AFC Snake Breaks Saga V Reiteralm
(SN40290901)

NAFC FC AFC Snake Breaks Sgt. Schultz (SG039407)

FC Snake Break's Wanted In Idaho (SN71159303)

FC Snakebreak Hogan V Reiteralm (SN40290904)

FC Spatlese Bismark Baron (SA631363)

DC Sportabouts Boeser Bengel (SA475602)

FC Starbuck a Covey In the Hand (SN40838403)

FC Starfire Sleet on the Rise (SN44241004)

FC Starfire's First Cent V Saga (SN80166603)

DC Staubich Von Risen (S545265)

FC Stoneangels Devil Deaugh (SM95025301)

FC Stoneangel's Devil In Disguise (SN52805701)

FC Storm Warning on the Rise (SN44241003)

FC AFC Stormcrows Deaugh Blitzen, SH (SN10746103)

FC Strevelyn's Storm Trysail (SB570997)

FC Summer Von Der Reiteralm (SC915624)
NFC FC Super Deaugh (SC524149)
FC AFC T Zs Kaitlin of Silverbrooke (SF525884)
DC Takusan's Sonic Boom (SC671181)
NFC DC The Sundance Kid (SD701356)
NFC 3xNAFC DC AFC Top Deaugh (SD390684)
DC Tri-D's Clean Sweep V Y-me (SF847916)
DC Tri-D's Sterling Silver (SE903423)
FC AFC Tzs High Flyer Bie Markee (SN53492306)
NFC FC Unserhund Von Sieger (SA547651)
FC Unserhund's Star Vom Arrow (SB944413)
FC AFC Upwind Party Doll (SN50442512)
FC V Hennerich's Hochwald Gretel Don (SN54449507)
FC V Hennerichs Hochwald Hansel (SN54449506)
DC Valmars Valiant Knight (SE116082)
FC Vikkis Explorer Von Knopf (SD536052)
DC Von Gaiberg's Cosak (S454334)
FC Von Harwil's Miss B Havin (SN54270005)
FC Von Harwils Slick Willie (SN06401602)
FC Von Waldons Aphrodisia (SB086666)
NFC FC Von Weiner Smokn' Winds Holiday
(SN76873407)
DC Von Weiners Withheld (SN10695707)
FC Von Whitcoms Hurry (SA211657)
FC Von Witcombs Tor (S995100)
DC Watchpoints Foreshadow (SD358081)

FC Webbdant's Pied Piper (SB799660)
FC Weick's Tidewater Silversmith (SC635908)
DC Weimaracres Sunny Boy (SA798866)
FC Weinerschnitzels Bad News (SB983829)
FC Weinersnitzels Gipsi Mcduff (SB988242)
FC Westends Desert Moon (SN30625104)
NFC FC AFC Westends Lil Sage Rider (SM90779002)
DC Whidbey's Jake (SA837744)
FC Whidbeys Sweet Rosie O'grady (SC328565)
DC Whidbey's Baron (S870685))
DC Whidbey's Samantha (SC008721)
FC Windancer Izzy Von Reiteralm (SN71159309)
FC AFC Windancers Jota V Reiteralm (SN77197901)
FC Windchyme (SF585750)
DC Windsong's Bayside Barnaby (SB819401)
DC Windwalkers Heart of Gold (SN37780301)
FC Wingfield's Jade of Jaxs (SR02758204)
DC Winnie Von Ostfriesland (SA934154)
FC AFC Winstar's Diamond Lil (SN71159301)
AFC Wyndjammr's Silver Fawn (SD450178)
FC Wynd N Fyres Rocky Star (SC960897)
FC Wyndom Garth the Great (SN48357808)
DC Wynwoods Rain on the Rise (SM92226706)
FC Young's Velvet Danny (SA485769)
FC AFC Zachs Grau Geist Gruppe (SE655418)
DC Zandor Vom Lechsteinhof (S381760)
FC Zouave's Miss Cuca

Figure E-12: *Clean find.* Photograph by Leslie Like.

And the Dual Champions are....

The list of Dual Champions was compiled from the most reliable sources available; however, some of these records are not as complete for Dual Champions as for other types of championships. We regret that there may be some worthy dogs who have been inadvertently omitted or that information may be incomplete for some dogs.

DC Ardreem Wolf Von Betelgeuse, JH, SDX, NRD, VX
(Wolfgang Von Sachsengang, JH, CD, NSD, NRD, V ×
Schaden's Kuhl Luca V Ardreem, CD)
Bred and owned by Linda Frisbe

DC Ardreem's Southern Maverick, V
(Wolfgang Von Sachsengang, JH, CD, NSD, NRD, V ×
Schaden's Kuhl Luca V Ardreem, CD)
Bred by Linda Frisbee; owned by A. Dumbleton and Linda Frisbee.

DC Arimar's Ivan, CD, NSD, VX, BROM
(CH Eichenhof's Ginger Man, BROM ×
CH Arimar's Desert Diana, NSD, BROM)
Bred and owned by Tom and Jackie Isabell.

DC Arimar's Lovely Lyric, CD, SDX, RD, VX
(CH Eichenhof's Ginger Man, BROM ×
CH Arimar's Desert Diana, NSD, BROM)
Bred by Tom and Jackie Isabell; owned by J. and I. Bahde, Jr.

DC Baron V Randoplh, UDT
(Sire × Dam)
Bred by Ralph Davis; owned by Earl Collins

DC Baroness of Magmar, RDX, SDX
(Anton of Bon Ton × Treffa Von Waldheim)
Bred by H. H. Magil; owned by Raymond and Bety Blunk

DC AFC Bayer's Silver Mr v. Reiteralm, NSD, NRD, VX
(CH Reiteralm's Rio Fonte Saudade, BROM ×
CH Ladenburg Bessie v. Reiteralm, CD, BROM)
Bred by Virginia Alexander; owned by J. and B. Bayer and
Virginia Alexander

DC Birtzel Von Staub
(Staub V Suebirtzel × Jo Ann's Duchess)
Bred and owned by Roy Pelton

DC Birtzel's Johnny Reb, NSD, RD,VX
(FCH Unserhund Von Sieger SDX ×
Weimaracres Kipbirtzel SDX NRD)
Bred by Dorothy H. Pelton; owned by John A. Stving

DC Bruno Auger Silver Duke
(Deal's Otto V Auger × Bruno's Silver Susie)
Bred by Unknown; owned by Unknown.

DC Camelot's Desert Fox, SH, SDX, NRD, VX
(CH Camelots Life of Riley × Lady Kelsy of Camelot)
Bred by Susan Thomas and Bill Moran; owned by R. Derrick
Hart.

DC Crook N Nannys Silver Titan, CD, NRD, VX
(CH Crook N Nanny's Silver Thor, RDX, SDX, VX ×
Most Misty Lady of Dawn).
Bred by G. Most; owned by R. and B. Zabransky

DC Dust Storm on the Rise, JH, BROM.
(VC DC AFC Magnum Gunnar
(Silvershot, MH, SDX, RDX, VX, BROM ×
DC Wynwood's Rain on the Rise, SDX, NRD, VX).
Bred by G. and S. Hartman and W. and P. Kuehold; owned by
David and Nancy Borg.

DC Dv's Laughing Girl
(Nelson's Chance × Zela Von Brunner).
Owned by M. and M. Opperman

DC Eldan's Mohave Sundancer
(CH Redhill's Satellite, SDX × CH Von Zel's Aphrodite).
Bred and owned by Dan and Ethel Richmond

DC Exuma's Hyatt of Norton Cr, JH
(FC Outdoors Rising Sun ×
CH Tri-D's Little Nookie V Daroca, JH)
Bred by C. and A. Jacobsen and Rosemary Carlson; owned by
Margit Worsham.

DC Firebird's Second Chance
(Firebird's Courageous Kahn × Stylish Maid, BROM)
Bred by R. and M. Bjornsen; owned by R. M. Mills.

DC AFC Gent's Silver Smoke, CDX, RDX, VX
(Ladivs Silver Gent × Johnny Ginny).
Bred by Mildred Ferguson; owned by Al and Eleanor Miller.

DC AFC Gradaus Katrinka, CD, SDX, RD, VX
(Romira's Contraband D × Trish Von Emmers)
Bred by R. and D. Spearly; owned by E. and R. Hedrick

DC Halanns Checkmate Tamara, CD, SDX, NRD
(AM/CAN CH Shadowmar Barthaus Dorillio, BROM ×
CH Halann's Brandy Von Bradford)
Bred by H. Bushman; owned by L. and J. Irwin

DC Halann's The Judge v. Reiteralm, SDX, RDX
(CH Maximilian Vom der Reiteralm, NSD, BROM ×
Manning's Westwood Ladybird, BROM).
Bred by C. and M. Mannings; owned by Virginia Alexander.

NFC DC AFC Jafwin's One and Only, SD,NRD,VX
(CH Von Siebens Smart N Special, NSD, BROM ×
CH Redhill's Song Girl, CD, NSD, NRD, BROM)
Bred by F. and J. Sexton; owned by S. and B. Crouther

DC Jafwin's the Goodbye Girl
(CH Von Siebens Smart N Special, NSD, BROM ×
CH Redhill's Song Girl, CD, NSD, NRD, BROM)
Bred by F. and J. Sexton; owned by L. and H. Weesner

DC Joron Silber Eich, UD, TD, MH, SDX, RDX, VX3, UD
(CH Bama Belles Mountain Man, BROM ×
Greysport Duchess of Grace)
Bred by R. and J. Good; owned by Diane Vater, R. and J. Good.

DC NAFC AFC Knight's Ti-Ki Toi, CD, JH, SDX , RD, VX
(S and S's Shot of Tequila × Lyonesse Ginger Star Knight)
Bred by Randall and Holly McKnight; owned by Holly McKnight.

DC Kristof's Classic Venture, NSD
(CH Kristof's Kitsap Coho BROM × Ann's Tiffany Von Kristof
BROM)
Bred by A and S Kruebbe, Owned by Larry Walsh.

DC AFC Lady Athena of Camelot, NRD
(CH Colsidex Kg Arthur of Camelot, CD, SD, RD, VX,
BROM × DC Lady Rebecca of Camelot, CDX, SDX, NRD,
VX, BROM)
Bred by S. Thomas, C. Studney, and C. Crosby; owned by
Susan Thomas.

DC Lady Rebecca of Camelot, CDX, SDX, NRD, VX, BROM
(Sue's Sir Lancelot, UD, RD, NSD, V ×
Lady Guinevere of Ekselo).
Bred by G. Thomas and E. Oleske; owned by Susan Thomas.

DC AFC Landbees Liberty Flyer
(Sire × Dam)
Owned by J. Johnson

Intl DC and AKC DC AFC Lilith Von Hirschhorn, CDX, TD, RDX, SDX, VX
(Braunhildes Silver Blaze × Crook N Nannys Tosca)
Bred by Marie Seidelman; owned by Harry Hirschhorn.

DC Ludwig Von Weisenhof
(CH Ludwig Von Dottlyle × Silver Blue Lupe)
Bred by George Wyse; owned by Dr. James Oliver

VC DC AFC Magnum Gunnar Silvershot, MH, SDX, RDX, VX, BROM
(CH Green Acres Good Grief Colby, CD ×
CH Dustivelvet's Spring Rain)
Bred by Kathleen Elkins, owned by Judy Balog.

DC Marbils Baron Von Josephus, NSD, NRD,VX
(CH Archduke Von Brombachtal, BROM ×
CH Marbil's Firebrand V Arimar, NSD, NRD, V, BROM)
Bred by W. and M. Parrilli; owned by L. and C. Kinght.

DC Mile Hi Murphy, JH, SD, RDX, VX
(Lucky Deaugh D Lucky × Augusta Da Grossoscasa)
Bred by Susan Williams; owned by Joan and Fred Cowley

DC NFC NAFC FC Othen's Princess Pretty, NRD, SX, VX
(CH Val's Veto v. d. Reiteralm × CH Othens Velvet Venus).
Bred by Duncan Othen; owned by Tom and Irene Glennon.

DC Outdoors Life of Riley, CD, JH, SDX, RDX, VX2
(CH Greymists Xactly Right, JH, NRD, V ×
FC Outdoors Twister)
Bred by Michelle and Samantha Stillion; owned by Anne Taguchi and David Routnier.

DC Ozarks Buckeye Rebel, RDX, SD, VX
(FC Lechsteinhof's Ozark Pete, RDX, SDX ×
Pinochle Keno Kate)
Bred by Donald Howerton; owned by James Brown

DC Palladian Perseus
(FC Ricki of Rocklege × CH Debar's Platinum Pallas)
Bred by Mrs. Donald Bullock; owned by O. W. Olgilvie.

DC Paron's Bingo, SDX, RDX, VX
(CH Landbee's Upland Sabre, BROM × Paron's Joe Annie)
Bred by Unknown; owned by J. Paron.

DC Patmar's Silver Countess, RD
(CH Enno v. d. Burg, BROM × CH Silver Blue Loarco, CD)

DC NAFC FC Pine Grove Farm's Brunhilde
(FC Elsmere's Baron Aus Wehmann ×
Dulcimers Way Up Susiana)
Bred and owned by Herbert and Barbara Heller.

DC Prinz Rolf Von Kiry, NSD, RD, VX
(Bierman's Von Hansel × Gretel Von Widicus)
Bred by Unknown; owned by J. and A. Kiry

DC Redhill's Chief Geronimo
(CH Sir Eric von Seiben × DC Redhill's Fanny Jo, SDX, BROM)
Bred by Ted and Lorie Jarmie; owned by John and Judy Mihlik

DC Redhill's Fanny Jo, SDX, BROM
(CH Redhill's Satellite × CH Redhill's Fanfare)
Bred and owned by Ted and Lori Jarmie.

TC AFC Regen's Summer Blaze, VCD3, UDX2, RE, MH, MX, MXJ, VX6, BROM, FROM,
(CH Jak's Repeat Offender × AM/CAN CH Skyhi's EZ Magical Reign, JH, UD, SD, NRD, VX, BROM)
Bred by David and Nina Sherrer and Judi Voris; owned by Shirley Nilsson and Judi Voris

TC CT Regen's Rip Stop, VCD3, UDX4, MH, SDX, RDX, VX6
(NAFC FC AFC Northern Lights This BudsForU ×
TC AFC Regen's Summer Blaze, VCD3, UDX2, RA, MX, MXJ, MH, SDX, RDX, VX6)
Bred by Judith Voris and Shirley Nilssen; owned by Anne Tyson and Judi Voris

DC Ronamax Rufus v. Reiteralm, CD, RDX, SDX, VX
(CH Maximilian Vom Der Reiteralm, NSD, BROM ×
CH Norman's Rona v. d. Reiteralm, NRD, SD, V, BROM)
Bred by Virginia Alexander; owned by Harry Hirschhorn and Virginia Alexander.

DC Schmidt's Countess Kristine, CD
(CH Count Von Houghton, SDX × CH Cedar Lane Siglinde)
Bred by G. Schmidt; owned by Joe Albanese

DC AFC CH Shadowmar Arthemis Impeda, CDX, SDX, RDX, VX
(CH Shadowmar Excalibur, CD, SD, NRD, V, BROM ×
CH Dauntmar's Silver Splendoress, BROM)
Bred by D. Remensnyder; owned by K. Lyons.

DC Show Me Silver Shadow, NRD, SD, VX,
(Gents Silver Smoke × Top-ofields Second Bonnie).
Bred by Al Miller; owned by Al and Suzy Miller

DC Silverbrand Raferty V Jar-Em, NRD, VX
(CH Jar Em's Rhinestone Cowboy, BROM ×
CH Pattianne Von Sieben)
Bred by Sandra Jaremczuk; owned by David McConathy.

DC Sir Anthony's Jake of Sanbar, NAJ, NJP, VX
(NFC AFC NAFC Snake Break's Saga v. Reiteralm, CD, MH, RDX, VX2 × CH Sanbar's Send Me No Flowers)
Bred by Saundra and Polly West; owned by Anthony and Patricia Bailey.

DC NFC Sirius Mostly Mongo, JH, NRD, VX
(FC AFC NFC Westends Lil Sage Rider, CD, SH, NSD, NRD, V × DC Sirius Really Rosie, CDX, JH, RD, VX2, BROM).
Bred and owned by Helene and Richard Moore.

DC Sirius Peppermint Schnapps, NRD, VX
(VC DC AFC Magnum Gunnar Silvershot, MH, SDX, RDX, VX, BROM × DC Sirius Really Rosie, CDX, JH, RD, VX2, BROM)
Bred and owned by Helene and Richard Moore.

DC Sirius Really Rosie, CDX, JH, RD, VX2, BROM
(Texmara's Jeb the Great, SD, NRD × CH Sirius Sweet Samantha)
Bred by Helene and Richard Moore and B. Dagenhart; owned by Helene and Richard Moore.

DC NFC AFC NAFC Snake Break's Saga V Reiteralm, CD, MH, RDX, VX2
(FC AFC NAFC Snake Breaks Sgt Schultz ×
FC Arimarlisa's Rudi V Reiteralm)
Bred by Steve Reynolds and Virginia Alexander; owned by Mary and Jeffrey Brown.

DC NFC Sportabout's Boeser Bengal, CDX, SDX, RD, VX.
(CH Cuedes Silver Dust × Hildegarde Xiv)
Bred by C. Schilbach; owned by Jerome and Jo Molitor.

DC Staubich von Risen, RD, SDX
(Bruno v. Brombachtal [import] × Sola de Fortuna).
Bred by Waldwinkel Kennels; owned by Carl Lindstrom.

DC Takusan's Sonic Boom, NSD, NRD, V
(CH Halann's The Judge v. Reiteralm, SDX, RDX ×
DC Arimar's Lovely Lyric, CD, SDX, RD, VX)
Bred by Jean Bahde; owned by Bill and Jenny Straub.

DC NFC AFC The Sundance Kid, CD, NRD, VX
(Mikesell's Von Baronwheel × Ildebrannfugle's Donna Marie).
Bred by Adelaide Davis; owned by Marilee Horn.

DC AFC Tri- D's Clean Sweep V Y-Me, SDX, NRD, V,
(CH Tri D's Wingfield's Ottowo, JH ×
CH Tri-D's Good as Gold, JH, NRD)
Bred by C. and B. Donaldson; owned by C. Schuch and C. Donaldson.

DC Tri-D's Sterling Silver, NSD, BROM
(CH Eb's You Otta See Me Now, JH, SD, NRD, V ×
CH Tri D's Bain De Soleil, NRD, BROM)
Bred by Carole Donaldson; owned by Donald M. Coller.

DC NFC NAFC AFC Top Deaugh, MH, NRD, SDX, VX, HOF
(Weiner Schnitzel's McDuff, NSD × Charlie's Angel II)
Bred and owned by Charles G. Williams.

DC Valmar's Valiant Knight, CD, NRD, VX, BROM
(CH Valmar's Jazzman, CD, NSD, NRDV, BROM ×
CH Valmar's Pollyanna, BROM)
Bred by JoanValdez; owned by Gorden Hansen and Joan Valdez.

DC Von Gaiberg's Cosak
(CH Boris Von Der Teufelsposse × CH Debar's Platinum Zephir)
Bred by Unknown; owned by Unknown.

DC Von Weiner's Withheld, CDX, MH, SD, RDX, VX2
(DC Tri D's Sterling Silver, NSD, BROM ×
CH Sirius Octrude Von Weiner, CDX, TD, SH, SDX, RD, VX2).
Bred and owned by Diane Vater.

DC Watchpoints Foreshadow, NSD, NRD
(CH Nani's Master Charge, NSD, NRD, V, BROM ×
Watchpoint's Allya)
Bred by M. Straitil and D. Rosenblatt; owned by M Straiil and D. Grenier.

DC Weimaracres Sunny Boy, SDX, RDX, VX
(FCH Shenandoah Drummer Boy, RD ×
Die Jaegerine Aus Tor Wheel)
Bred by Ivan Lawyer; owned by Gene Teasley.

DC Whidbey's Jake, RD, VX
(El Tigre Marado × Lady Morado)
Bred and owned by Adelaide Davis.

DC Whidbey's Baron, CD, SDX
(CH Ludwig Von Dottlyle × CH Whidbey's Lady Day)
Bred and owned by Adelaide Davis.

DC Whidbey's Samantha
(Mikesell's Von Whitcomb × Flywheel's Misty Lady)
Bred by S. and C. Pitchard; owned by A. Davis.

DC Windsong's Bayside Barnaby, SDX, NRD, V
(Star N Suede Of Quail Run × CH Star N Jerichos Angellic)
Bred by M. Baldwin; owned by J. Staymates and M. Baldwin.

DC Windwalker's Heart of Gold, BROM
(CH Windwalker's Hills of Shiloh, CD, JH, SDX, NRD, VX ×
Ghostwalker Storm Cloud)
Bred by Don Ella Hatch; owned by Philip and Arlene Marshrey.

DC Winnie Von Ostfriesland
(CH Landbee's Upland Tiger × Queen Von Ostfriesland)
Bred by Unknown; owned by R. and S. Smit.

DC Wynwood's Rain on the Rise, SDX, NRD, VX,
(AM/CAN CH Valmar Smokey City Ultra Easy, JH, NSD, BROM
× CH Vanoah's Glory Hallelujah, NSD, NRD, V, BROM).
Bred by Brenda Martz; owned by W. and P. Kuehnhold and S. Hartman.

DC Zandor Vom Lechsteinhof, CD
(Denador of Grafmar × Frika Vom Lechsteinhof)
Bred by Col. James Moorhead; owned by Ivan Carlson.

Figure E-13: *The First Best in Show Master Hunter Weimaraner: CH Monterra's Best Bet, MH.* (AM/CN/INT CH Win'Weim Graytsky Cowboy Boots, JH × CH Windchymes Spirit Dancer, RA, SH, NSD, NRD, V). Bred by Liz Krupinski; owned by Liz Krupinski and Tim Bintner. Stoli earned his Senior Hunter title two weeks before his second birthday and exactly on his second birthday he earned a Best in Show. He continued with his hunt work and earned his Master Hunter title before his third birthday in five straight tests, a truly stellar accomplishment! Photograph by Gene LaFollette.

And the Master Hunters are....

The list of Master Hunters was compiled from the most reliable sources available; however, some of these records are not as complete for Master Hunters as for other types of accomplishments. We regret that there may be some worthy dogs who have been inadvertently omitted or that information may be incomplete for some dogs.

CH Adonai's Twenty-One Gun Salute, MH, SDX, NRD, VX
Owned by Kay Walker

CH Amity Greysea's Dune Whitetip, CD, MH, NSD, VX
Owned by William and Ann Zinger and Lynn Baker

FC Another Top Deaugh, MH, SDX
Owned by Susan Williams

CH Arnstadt Silvershot Arrieta, TD, MH, SDX, NRD, VX
Owned by Sandra Hoesel and Elizabeth Raiman

Baht's Top Gun Salute, MH, SDX, RDX, V, NA1
Owned by Allison M. Stamides

CH Baron Sparks in the Mist, CD, TD, MH, SDX, RDX, VX3
Owned by Jack and Mable Scullion

Bing's Donner, CD ,TD, MH, SDX
Owned by Sandra Hoesel and Jean White

CH Blazin' Love von Reiteralm, MH, SDX, NRD, VX, BROM
Owned by Tim Easter and Barbara Jacobs

Blue Velvet Ashley, MH
Owned by Clint Shaffer

Camerons Outdoor Eagle Scout, MH, SDX, RD
Owned by Cristine Sue Cameron

Cassandra Ansehnlich Dhondt, MH
Owned by Virginia and Mike Dhondt

CH Cherystone Perl of Sagenhaft, MH, SDX, NRD, VX, BROM
Owned by Pamela and Christian Cherry

Cora Von Der Schelmelach, MH, SD, NRD (Germany)
Owned by Virginia Alexander and Joseph Stroup

CH Creekside N Zara's Renne, MH, NRD, VX
Owned by Ken R. Koebel

FC/AFC Davison's Orion on the Rise, MH
Owned by Alan O. Davison

Emily's Wild Bill Grayshadow, MH
Owned by David S. and Emily J. Gibbs

Ezekiel Melchizedek Thunder, MH
Owned by Robert and Mary Barth

Furstpless Galan V Reiteralm, MH
Owned by Luis and Brenda Bonilla and Deborah Andrews

Gauls Derich von Reiteralm, MH
Owned by Luis Bonilla and Virginia Alexander

Ghostwalker's Wind Rider, VCD1, MH, AX, AXJ, SDX, RD, VX
Owned by Cydney Hansen

CH Graceland's Bavarian Dream, MH, SD
Owned by Liz Krupinski and Stephanie Morgan-Russell

NFC/NAFC/FC/AFC Grau Geist Lil's Gust v. Westend, CD, RE, MH, SDX, RD, VX, FROM
Owned by David and Cathy Gould

CH Grauschattens Ghostly Encore, CDX, RN, MH, OA, OAJ, SDX, RDX, VX3
Owned by Mary Beth Hall

CH Grayangel Benjamin, MH, SDX, RD, VX
Owned by Glenn and Karen Hummel

Grayangel Big Time Trouble, MH
Owned by Bernard Rossi and Grayangel Kennels

Grayangel Buck Stops Here, MH
Owned by Bernard Rossi and Grayangel Kennel

CH Grayangel Crystal II, MH, NRD, VX
Owned by Grayangel Kennel and Bill and Judy Anderson

CH Grayangel Dixiebell Boregard, MH, SDX, NRD, VX
Owned by Bradley S. Jeffrey and Mary Karen Mayo

CH Grayangel Good Bet, MH, SDX, NRD, VX
Owned by Mary Karen Mayo and Bradley S Jeffrey

CH Grayangel Jan Von Ruprecht, MH, NSD, NRD, VX, FROM
Owned by Don and Agnes Gunn and Grayangel Kennels

Am/Can CH Grayangel Little Zephanja, MH, SD, NRD, VX
Owned by Michelle Nowacki and Grayangel Kennels

Grayfires Yankee Doodle, MH
Owned by Leonard and Judythe Coffman

CH Grayshar's Odessa Spirit, MH, SD, RD, VX, BROM
Owned by Oleg Popov, Sharon Hartmann, and Karen Aubrey

CH Greywind Frozen in Time, MH
Owned by Ellen J. and John B. Grevatt

CH Hallmar's Directed Verdict, CDX, RE, MH, SDX, NRD, VX2
Owned by Linda Garrett and Mary Ann and William Hall

Herr Von Beau Regard, MH, SDX, RD
Owned by Joe B. Stringer

CH Hope's Rolling Thunder, MH, SDX, NRD, VX
Owned by Joseph Anthony Pyka

CH Indabas First Addition, MH, SD, UT2
Owned by Kim Harter

DC Jo-Ron's Silber Elch, UD, TD, MH, SDX, RDX, VX3
Owned by Diane Vater and R. and J. Good

VC Luke der Humdinger, CDX, MH, SDX, RDX, V, NA2, UT1
Owned by Rahl Hoeptner

CH M and M's Rocky Mountain Ranger, CDX, MH, SDX, NRD, VX
Owned by Marilyn Fields

CH M and M's Sassaberry Cream, CDX, MH, SDX, RD, VX
Owned by Marilyn Fields

VC DC AFC Magnum Gunnar Silvershot, MH, SDX, RDX, BROM, FROM, NA1, UPT1, UT1
Owned by Judy Balog

Maiweims Kwabena Zorie, MH, SDX, NRD
Owned by Kimball Anderson and Debbie Ozner-Anderson

Maximus Sparticus Agustus, MH
Owned by Robert Barth

BIS CH Monterra's Best Bet, MH
Owned by Elizabeth Krupinski and Timothy Bintner

CH Nani's Jagmar Sweet Dividends,
VCD2, MH, MX, MXJ, NSD, NRD, VX4, BROM
Owned by Teresa L. Borman and Christine Grisell

Nani's N Tsuru-Tani Echo, MH, SD
Owned by Susan Covault and Steve Deboer

CH Nani's Sophisticated Lady, MH, NA, NAJ, SDX, VX
Owned by Ross and Rosi Adams and Chris Grisell

Nix Blaze Orange Jaeger, MH, SDX, RD
Owned by Steven T Porter and Michel B Porter

CH Orion's Jaeger V Reiteralm,
CD, TD, MH, SD, RDX, VX3, BROM
Owned by Stephanie Horner and Alice Smithers

Prairie Deaugh, MH, SDX, NRD
Owned by Susan Williams

CH QuikSilvr's Magic StarChaser, CD, RE, MH, SDX, RDX, VX2
Owned by Babetta Breuhaus

CH Regen's Fast Buck, CD, TD, MH, SD, RDX, VX3
Owned by Holly Palmer and Shirley Nilsson

Am/Can CH MACH Regen's Hot Chili Pepper,
VCD3, MH, SDX, RDX, VX5
Owned by Judith Voris and Shirley Nilsson

CH Regen's Moonstruck, UD, RE, MH, NA, NAJ, SD, RDX, VX3
Owned by Pat Gannon

TC CT Regen's Rip Stop,
VCD3, UDX5, OM1, MH, SDX, RDX, VX6, NA1
Owned by Anne Tyson and Judith Voris

OTCH Regen's State of the Art,
VCD2, UDX2, RE, TDX, MH, SDX, RDX, VX4, NA1
Owned by Shirley Nilsson and Judith Voris

TC AFC Regen's Summer Blaze, VCD3, UDX2, RE, MH, MX,
MXJ, SDX, RDX, VX6, BROM, FROM, UT1
Owned by Shirley Nilsson and Judith Voris

Remsso's Rocky Mountain Utah, MH, SDX, NRD
Owned by John and Mary Cernak

CH Rockville's Truman Greystone,
VCD2, TDX, MH, MX, MXJ, SDX, RDX, VX5, UT1
Owned by Frank Sommer

Sandbar Echoin' Cowboy Colt, MH, SDX, RDX
Owned by Dawn Gritzinger

Sigmund Karmel Von Hallmar, MH, SDX, NRD
Owned by Mary Ann Hall

CH Silver Rain Touch of Silversmith, MH, SDX
Owned by Elena Smith Lamberson

CH Silversmith Harbor Cruise, CD, MH, NA, SDX, RDX, VX2
Owned by William Hall

Silversmith's Maximum Tide, MH, SDX, RDX
Owned by Brian Gray and Carolyn A Mehl

VC Skeeter's Tannerbaum, MH, SDX, RDX, NA1, UT1
Owned by Teresa A. and Gerald W. Gertiser II

CH Smokey Topaz Winstar Zephyr, MH, NSD, NRD, VX
Owned by Deborah D. and James W. Ebert

NFC/NAFC/DC/AFC Snake Breaks Saga v Reiteralm,
CD, MH, RDX, VX2, FROM
Owned by Mary and Jeffrey Brown

Spectrum Once in a Blue Moon, CD, MH, NA1
Owned by Anne Taguchi

CH Star Camelot Knight of Orion, MH, NSD, NRD, VX
Owned by Pamela Chavez-Hutson and Trish Zeimantz

CH Star Lightyears Beyond, CDX, RN, MH, SDX, NRD, VX2
Owned by Dona Tanaka and Louise Brady

CH Star Synchronous Rotation, MH, SDX, RD, VX
Owned by Louise Brady and Candice Gerson

CH Starbuck's Son Of a Gun, TDX, MH, VX2
Owned by Maxine Grossinger

Steele's Mian Beata, MH, SDX, RDX, V, NA1, UT1
Owned by Michael Hall

Steele's Precious Gem, MH, SDX, RD, NA1, UT1
Owned by Donald K. Steele

Steele's Titanium Gun, MH, SDX, RDX, V, NA1, UT1
Owned by Donald K. Steele

CH Sundown Jager von Reiteralm, MH, SDX, RD, VX
Owned by David A. Stingl

Terri's Silbern Geist, CDX, MH, SD, RDX, V
Owned by Terri Sandvik and Betty Culbreth

DC NFC 4xNAFC AFC Top Deaugh, MH, SDX, NRD, VX, HOF
Owned by Charles G. Williams

Top Deaugh Too, MH, SDX, NRD
Owned by Susan Williams

CH Top Hat's Stevie Nicks, CD, RN, MH, SDX, RD, VX2
Owned by Sue McMahan and Debra L. Hopkins

Uplands Rrmi Max's 1st Chance, MH
Owned by Sean H. Heimburg

Can CH Victor Von Nimrod's Reiter, CDX, MH, SDX, RDX, V
Owned by Harry J Hirschhorn

DC Von Weiner's Withheld, CDX, MH, SD, RDX, VX2
Owned by Diane Vater

Weimshadow Cross The Rockies, CD, MH, NSD, NRD, V, NA1
Owned by Jack and Mable Scullion and Sally Jo Hoaglund

VC FC AFC Windancers Jota v. Reiteralm, MH, SDX, RDX, UT1
Owned by Brian Wayson and Virgina Alexander

CH Windwalkers Midnight Star,
CDX, RN, MH, SDX, NRD, VX2
Owned by Rick and Debbie Maher

CH Windwalker's Princess Chester, CD, RN, MH, VX
Owned by Rick and Debbie Maher

FC Wyndom Garth the Great, MH, SDX, NRD
Owned by John J. and Mary A. Cernak

And the NAVHDA VC Champions are...

VC Luke der Humdinger,
CDX, MH, SDX, RDX, NA2, UT1,
(Kugel vom Blum × Jill die Humdinger)
Bred by Herb and Annette Hoeptner; owned by Rahl Hoeptner.

DC VC Magnum Gunnar Silvershot,
MH, SDX, RDX, NA1, UPT1, UT1
(CH Green Acres Good Grief Colby, CD ×
CH Dustivelvet's Spring Rain)
Bred by Kathleen Elkins and Mary Clark; owned by Judy Balog.

VC Skeeter's Tannerbaum, MH, SDX, RDX, NA1, UT1
(Gray Shadow Ghostbuster × McLeod's Unser Shatze)
Bred by Karla McLeod; owned by Gerald Gertiser, II.

VC FC AFC Windancers Jota v. Reiteralm,
MH, SDX, RDX, UT1
(NFC/FC/AFC Westend's Li'l Sage Rider, CD, SH ×
FC Reiteralms Sandbar Snake Break)
Bred by Sandy West and Virginia Alexander; owned by Brian
Wayson and Virginia Alexander.

Figure E-14: *VC FC AFC Windancers Jota v. Reiteralm, MH, SDX, RDX, UT1*

Type	Name	Test Dt	Pts
IT	**Windancers Jota v. Reiteralm**	**9/17/09**	**200**
UT	Silvershot's Lil 'Tom Boy	8/16/09	201
UT	**Silvershot's Mirage v. Reiteralm**	**8/29/09**	**204**
NA	Axel's Dogwood Hill Smok'n v. Reiteralm	3/29/09	110
NA	**Fairhaven's Daring to Dream**	**4/26/09**	**112**
NA	Kick Em Up Rocco of Uplandfarm Lodge	9/12/09	105
NA	**Mani's Una von Reiteralm**	**11/15/09**	**112**
NA	My Goodness My "Gunnar" Von Zdon	9/12/09	110
NA	**Nani's Versa Artus von Rauhnacht**	**9/27/09**	**112**
NA	Regen's Light My Fire	12/6/09	108
NA	Riley's Baby Girl Prissy ZZ	4/5/09	106
NA	Shadowpoint's Camden Briggs	5/9/09	107
NA	**Shadowpoint's Ruby Tuesday**	**8/30/09**	**112**
NA	**Shadowpoint's Sterling Sir Symon**	**5/10/09**	**112**
NA	Shadowpoint's Summer Daisy	5/9/09	108
NA	Shomar's Do it Again	11/6/09	105
NA	**Silvershot's Artful Dodger**	**5/30/09**	**112**
NA	**Silvershot's Jett Legend**	**4/18/09**	**112**
NA	**Silvershot's Monster Point**	**4/18/09**	**112**
NA	**Silvershot's Pine Ridge Gertie**	**5/2/09**	**112**
NA	**Silvershot's Pocket Rocket**	**6/14/09**	**112**
NA	**Silvershot's Victoria Secret**	**7/17/09**	**112**
NA	**Westendsheidipolitz**	**4/18/09**	**112**
NA	Westweims 6-Gun Wyatt Earp	6/21/09	110
NA	**Zauberhaft's Celestial Storm Tracker**	**10/3/09**	**112**
NA	Zauberhaft Victoria's Secret Storm	10/3/09	101

It was a banner year for NAVHDA Weimaraners, with a whopping 23 NA Prize I's and 2 UT Prize I's (and qualifying for next year's Invitational Test), not to mention a new VC. Unfortunately the results were not available until too late to be included in the NAVHDA chapter (see Chapter 14), it was impossible to resist recognizing these outstanding dogs here in the appendix (maximum scores in bold type).

Old Dog Makes Good

Start with a new baby puppy owner named Brian Wayson who just wanted a pet but promised his breeders that he would compete in the Field Futurity, "No matter what."

The First Act: Enter Jota: a pup with the genetics and prey drive that foretold something special

The Second Act: Steve Reynolds and Dave Pomfret providing the outstanding training, steadying, and handling that helped Jota quickly complete both field titles and rise rapidly to national attention. In 2006, Brian's "Best Pal" and "Pet Dog" became the WCA's No. 1 All-Age Gun Dog!

The Third Act: 2007–2009: Jota and Brian teamed up, traveled, had fun, made mistakes, but learned as they went along and in the process earned an MH, SDX, and RDX.

Intermission: retirement—not quite!

Guided by veteran trainer Alan Burkhardt, an aging but water-loving Jota earned a UT Prize 1 to qualify for the most grueling and demanding land and water test of a total hunting dog offered in America—the NAVHDA International Championship Competition

Epilogue: Competing with 87 other qualified dogs from all of the sporting and retrieving breeds and in spite of nearing 10 years of age, Jota excelled and won a VC to become the 4th Weimaraner to win this honor in the 20+ year history of the NAVHDA Championship. Making this accomplishment even sweeter to Jota's breeders Sandy West and Virginia Alexander, is the fact that Brian more than kept his promise to run Jota in the Field Futurity—no matter what. With love and commitment he gave his "young-old dog" the opportunity to break all Weimaraner performance records at the NAVHDA invitational with a perfect score of 200!

Figure F-1: *Stacked,* by Williams Wegman

ARTICLES OF INTEREST

Cannula Treatment of Hematoma of the Weimaraner Ear

Hemtomas of the ear are a relatively common problem in Weimaraners and other breeds with pendulous ear leathers. The problem is usually not very painful for the dog but is a real nuisance due to recurrence even with aggressive means of control by veterinary surgeons. Some of the treatment techniques can be reviewed at various internet sites. One that provides photos of the results of surgical treatment and discusses the role for cannulation of the hematoma, an approach that will be described later in this article, can be found at: *http://www.marvistavet.com/html/aural_hematoma.html*

The hematoma can occur as the result of head shaking and ear scratching secondary to an infection in the ear. Shaking the head due to worrisome insects can also cause damage to the small blood vessels in the ear; bleeding beneath the skin occurs, resulting in the hematoma beneath the skin of the ear. This usually occurs on the inside of the earflap. In the photo (see Figure F-1), there is no hematoma but the dotted line is placed to show the usual location and extent of the subcutaneous swelling that occurs with the hematoma. The swollen area is soft and yields to gentle pressure. Palpation usually does not cause any pain. Pain may be a sign of a more serious problem, such as an infection involving the entire ear or inflammation secondary to an insect bite.

Figure F-2: *There is no hematoma shown* but the dotted line is placed to show the usual location and extent of the subcutaneous swelling that occurs with the hematoma.

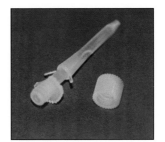

Figure F-3: *The simplest and least bothersome to the dog* is use of the Larson Teat Tube. This is a small, sterile, plastic device that is just rigid enough to allow placement and to stay in place but still soft enough to be adapted to use for maintaining drainage of the blood and serum from the ear.

Various techniques have been described for resolution of the problem but the simplest and least bothersome to the dog is use of the Larson Teat Tube. This is a small sterile plastic device that is just rigid enough to allow placement and to stay in place, but still soft enough to be adapted to use for maintaining drainage of the blood and serum from the ear. The Larson Teat Tube can be ordered through a few online sources and from some of the canine veterinary supply houses. They are usually used in bovine veterinary practice to insert in a cow's teat to allow drainage of infection when an infection of the udder occurs. In the cow, these infections usually cause blockage of the milk draining from the infected teat and the teat tube was designed to permit drainage and to hold open the infected milk duct. The same effect applies to the use of the teat tube in the ear hematoma. The opening made through the skin is held open by the teat tube for two to three weeks until all of the serous blood has drained from the ear and the walls of the hematoma have collapsed and started to stick together. This latter effect will serve to prevent recurrence of the problem. Although no technique will prevent recurrence in all cases, this technique is by far the simplest and easiest to repeat if necessary.

There is a small cap on the end of the tube that is removed to allow the serous liquefied blood to drain through the opening in the tube. If the opening becomes closed with a small blood clot, the fluid will still drain around the outside of the tube. In Figure F-2, note the tiny wings that stick out of the side of the teat tube. These are relatively soft but rigid enough to prevent the tube from sliding out of the ear. They are also soft enough to allow the tube to be pulled out of the ear with minimal discomfort when all drainage has stopped. The plastic of the teat tube is relatively soft and will allow a portion of the flange to be cut off with a small sharp knife or scalpel. Cutting off one side of this flange allows the tube to lie flat

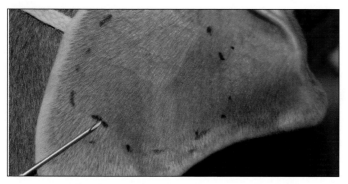

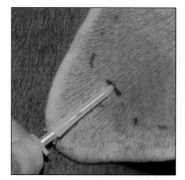

Figure F-4: *The object of the process is to insert the needle* to aspirate most of the fluid and then insert the teat tube through the same hole in the lowest point at the bottom of the hematoma to allow gravity to aid in drainage.

Figure F-5: *Insertion of the teat tube using a clean technique* with careful hand washing, and washing the ear with surgical soap and water, are usually all that is required.

against the side of the ear. Figure F-2 shows the appearance of the tube after removal of a portion of the flange. Other items needed for successful placement of the teat tube is a large needle and a syringe of 10 cc capacity or greater. The needle needs to be an 18-gauge or larger, such as 16- or 14-gauge. Needles this size may be available at your local farm store. The object of the process is to insert the needle to aspirate most of the fluid and then insert the teat tube through the same hole in the lowest point at the bottom of the hematoma. This will allow gravity to help drain the fluid from the ear. A small scalpel blade, such as a size 15 or size 11, can be used to make a small slit at the lowest point of the hematoma. Figure F-3 illustrates the location where the needle will be placed relative to the hematoma or the location of the tiny slit, if using a scalpel. Once the needle has been placed in the hematoma and most but not all of the fluid drained out, the teat tube can be forced into the pocket of the hematoma through the hole made by the needle. Leaving a small amount of fluid in the hematoma after aspiration with the needle will make placement of the teat tube an easier process. If the hole presents resistance to placing the teat tube in the opening, a slight slicing motion with the tip of the needle can enlarge the opening. Figure 3 illustrates the location for insertion of the needle to drain the fluid. Figure 4(a) demonstrates the relationship of the teat tube to the opening and the angle to be used to position the tube inside the pocket of the hematoma. Once inserted, the tube needs to be turned slightly to allow the flat side that you created to lie against the ear. Figure F-4(b) illustrates the final appearance after correct insertion of the tube up to the flange. At this point in the procedure, any fluid remaining in the hematoma will be draining out. Have towel available to collect the blood from the hematoma during the procedure. The procedure is a bit messy because there is no good way to catch the fluid as you drain the hematoma and the fluid continues to drain from the ear. Drainage for a few days will require the dog to be isolated from your best furniture. Roughhousing with kennel mates should be limited to prevent premature removal.

Sterile technique is not necessary for the placement procedure. Insertion of the teat tube using a clean technique with careful hand washing and washing the ear with surgical soap and water are usually all that is required. A dressing over the ear and around the head will usually be more worrisome for the dog than just leaving the area open and allowing it to drain freely. Some gentle washing each day with soap and warm water will remove any crust from dried serum that can accumulate for a few days after teat tube placement. Trying to keep the area too clean will even be a detriment to a successful procedure since a little irritation from some bacteria will help the walls of the collapsed hematoma seal together. After the tube has been in for two to three weeks and there is no further drainage, the tube can be pulled out. Anticipate that there will be a small amount of bleeding when the tube is removed; the process of removal should cause some discomfort but this is usually minimal. This technique is not new and is relatively simple when compared to the more complex surgical procedures used to resolve this problem as seen on the internet site mentioned in the first paragraph. The cosmetic result for the dog is usually much better than the surgical procedures described in the veterinary literature. Leaving the hematoma alone without treatment is acceptable; this may result in the deformity known as cauliflower ear that is seen in bipedal boxers who have hematomas secondary to boxing matches.

Figure F-6: *Dr. Ted Grissell,* of Nani's Weimaraners, Indiana, has been active in Weimaraners for over 20 years. Dr. Grisell, a practicing board certified (human) surgeon at the time, learned this procedure from his wife, Chris, who learned it from a farmer in North Dakota 35 years ago. Because this technique has produced excellent results in the subsequent years, Ted continues to share this information with dog enthusiasts of several breeds.

Canine Leptospirosis

This article is intended to provide owners of Weimaraner dogs with information on the nature, management and prevention of the infectious disease, canine leptospirosis. Canine leptospirosis is a long-standing and still-evolving disease. It is important that Weimaraner breeders and fanciers are knowledgeable of this condition.

What Is Canine Leptospirosis and How Does My Dog Get the Disease?

Canine leptospirosis is a bacterial disease caused by several pathogenic Leptospira species. Historically, the organisms that were most often associated with canine leptospirosis were L. canicola and L. icterohaemorrhagiae. These are just two of the nearly 200 serovars or varieties of Leptospira. Most recently, the serovars grippotyphosa, pomona, bratislava, and icterohaemorrhagiae were identified as the most common causative agents of canine leptospirosis.

Dogs can contract the disease in several ways. One way is to have contact with reservoir hosts. A reservoir host is an animal that remains infected with leptospirosis and continues to shed the organism in its environment, often for months. Leptospires are shed in the urine of infected animals. Dogs can become infected when infected urine, water and other objects come in contact with the dog's mucous membranes, abraded skin or water-softened skin. Leptospira organisms can remain infective in urine, water or soil for months. Any dog that is involved in hunting activities, swimming in streams or ponds and/or that runs in parks or back yards where there are Leptospira reservoir hosts or contaminated water or soil could be exposed to the disease. Dogs also can become infected by eating infected tissue from reservoir hosts. Additionally, dogs that consume leptospirosis-infected deer or rabbit tissue could become infected even though deer and rabbits are not normal reservoirs for the leptospirosis organisms.

What Will Happen to My Dog if it Gets Leptospirosis?

The signs of disease will depend on several factors, including the virulence of the leptospirosis organism, how the dog was exposed, the dog's immune status and overall health, and possibly the amount of the organism. Young dogs seem to be more harshly affected than adults. Acute and/or subacute forms of the disease occur. Dogs that are severely affected will first exhibit a fever, shivering, and muscle tenderness. Thereafter, vomiting, dehydration, rapid breathing and a rapid irregular pulse can be observed. Widespread vascular defects may be seen including blood in the vomitus and stools, bloody nose and numerous petechial hemorrhages on the skin and mucous membranes. Some acutely affected dogs will exhibit icterus or yellowing of the mucous membranes.

Subacute infections are milder. The most common signs include vomiting, unusual drowsiness or stupor, not wanting to eat, frequent urination, and excessive drinking. Other signs that may be seen include pinpoint red spots in the skin, stiff or painful joints, muscle pain and yellowing of the skin. Your veterinarian may observe fever, eye abnormalities, tenderness of the abdomen or back, and pain sensitivity near the kidneys.

How Can Leptospirosis be Diagnosed and Confirmed?

Your veterinarian will use a combination of history, clinical signs and various diagnostic tests to diagnose leptospirosis. Because leptospirosis often presents as a severe renal or liver disease, blood chemistries are run to determine the condition of the kidneys and liver. If leptospirosis is suspected, it is accepted practice to run a microscopic agglutination serological test to determine which Leptospira serovar(s) is involved. The results of this test are often negative if the test was performed at the beginning of the infection. It is therefore important to run the test again several weeks later particularly if other findings are supportive of a leptospirosis infection. Other tests that can be performed include blood and urine cultures, immunofluorescent staining of tissues, and the polymerase chain reaction testing of urine.

What Can be Done to Treat a Dog if It Gets Leptospirosis?

Leptospirosis is caused by a bacterial organism; therefore the usual treatment involves the use of antibiotics. Treatment with ampicillin or penicillin G for up to two weeks is usually recommended. Subsequently, it is recommended to use doxycycline for another two weeks to decrease the shedding of the leptospirosis organisms in the urine. Dogs that have serious or acute leptospirosis infections should receive intravenous fluid treatment and nutritional support.

What Can be Done to Prevent Canine Leptospirosis?

The protocol for vaccination for leptospirosis will vary, depending on the home environment and activities of the dog. Dogs that have little exposure to the outdoors, rodents, or wild animals might not need immunization. However, many Weimaraners are vaccinated for leptospirosis. Dogs that spend a lot of time outside, particularly any dogs that are used extensively for hunting or water tests, should be immunized against leptospirosis. Suburban dogs that are let out to run in parks or backyards where they can be exposed to rodents, wild animals, or urine contaminated soil or water also should be immunized against leptospirosis. Currently there are at least two commercial vaccines available for leptospirosis immunization. Both of these products are marketed as protective against the four common serovars: ictero-haemorrhagie, canicola, pomona and grippotyphosa. Both commercial vaccines are bacterins; therefore the duration of the immunity is not long. The usual recommended protocol is to administer the vaccine separate from other vaccines and in two doses, three to four weeks apart. This should be followed by an annual booster. Dogs that are hunted extensively in areas where leptospirosis can be prevalent should receive a booster more frequently (every six to eight months).

Some owners will be concerned about possible reactions to the leptospirosis vaccine. If they know that their dog reacts to the vaccine, then they have several choices. They can opt not to vaccinate and risk the possibility of infection. They can notify their veterinarian of their dog's reaction to the vaccine. The veterinarian can pretreat the dog with antihistamines or other similar agents prior to immunization to prevent or minimize the anaphylactic shock reaction to the vaccine.

It is equally important to manage dogs so that their contact with leptospirosis reservoir hosts or contaminated sites is eliminated or minimized.

Can I or My Family and Friends Get Leptospirosis?

It is critically important that owners understand that leptospirosis is a zoonotic disease. This means that adult humans and children can contract the disease leptospirosis from an infected dog or other infected animal. All proper precautions should be taken by owners and members of their family if their dog becomes infected with leptospirosis. Protective gloves and clothing should be worn when around dogs infected with leptospirosis. Owners should thoroughly disinfect any area in which the dog was housed or present in their home.

Because leptospirosis is a zoonotic disease, owners of dogs that have been diagnosed with leptospirosis may be concerned about whether they can or should take their dog home from the veterinary hospital. If the dog is properly treated and managed, a dog can continue to live a relatively normal life in the owner's home, if they are willing to accept the long-term responsibility of strict management and control to reduce the potential of passing on the infection to other dogs and family members.

The owner must understand that when a dog is correctly diagnosed with lepto the disease can persist for a long period, as much as six months or longer. It is therefore important that children or adults who are immunosuppressed not have contact with the recovering dog for at least a month after it returns home. Owners should restrict where the dog urinates and not allow other dogs access to that area. For six months, the recovering dog should not be allowed to participate in any events where there are other dogs.

Suggested Reading Material

Brown K. Presecott JF. Leptospirosis in the family dog: a public health perspective. *Canadian Medical Association Journal.* 2008, 178:397–398.

Guptill LF. Canine leptospirosis update. *Proceedings North American Veterinary Conference.* 2009 (January), 644–646.

Greene CE. *Infectious Diseases of the Dog and Cat.* Third Edition. Saunders-Elsevier, 2006, pp. 402–417.

Langstrom CE, Heuter KJ. Leptospirosis-A re-emerging zoonotic disease. *Veterinary Clinics of North America: Small Animal Practice.* 2003, 33: 791–807.

Moore GE, Guptill LF, Glickman NW, Caldanaro RJ, et al. Canine leptospirosis, United States, 2002–2004. *Emerging Infectious Diseases.* 2006, 12: 501–503.

Sessions JK, Greene CE. Canine leptospirosis: Epidemiology, pathogenesis, and diagnosis. *The Compendium: continuing education for the practicing veterinarian.* 2004, 26: 606–623.

Sessions JK, Greene CE. Canine leptospirosis: treatment, prevention, and zoonosis. *The Compendium: continuing education for the practicing veterinarian.* 2004, 26: 700–706.

Ward MP, Glickman LT, Guptill LF. Prevalence of and risk factors for leptospirosis among dogs in the United States and Canada: 677 cases (1970–1998). *JAMVA.* 2002, 220: 53–58.

Ward MP, Guptill LF, Prahl A, Wu C-C. Serovar specific prevalence and risk factors for leptospirosis among dogs: 90 cases (1997–2002). *JAVMA.* 2004, 224: 1958–1963.

Figure F-7: *Dr. Donald Draper* has been a constant source of veterinary support to Weimaraner owners for over 30 years. In the 1960s, Dr. Draper led pivotal research which allowed the identification of carriers and near eradication of spinal dysraphism (hoppers) in Weimaraners (refer to *The Best of Health* and his article in the *Bibliography*). Dr. Draper, Professor and Dean, Department of Biomedical Sciences, College of VeterinaryMedicine at Iowa State University, continues to enjoy hunting over his own GreyGhost, Radar.

Do It Right and Give the Dogs a Chance

By John Rabidou
Weimaraner Club of America Magazine, August 1972

Birdplanting is often the most under-rated and overlooked task in conducting a class field trial. The art of birdplanting—and it is an art—is often given casual attention in the conduct of our field trials. It is often delegated to the least experienced and knowledgeable members of the field trial committee or club. Often these persons, new to the sport, are handed of birds and directed to "go plant these." The results can be disastrous to the quality of performance achieved by the contestants. Obviously this is unfair to both the dogs, their owners and handlers, and to the sport of field trialing.

The quality of birdplanting is especially important in our single course trials with half hour stakes. Typically, these are highly artificial circumstances in which to test the capabilities of contestants. All contestants run over more of less the same area and have but 30 minutes to demonstrate all abilities. This is a very minimal time for even the most knowledgeable judges to evaluate an individual dog's actual capabilities. Proper birdplanting is one of the ingredients of a class trial that can enhance the chances of all contestants demonstrating their capabilities.

Before discussing birdplanting further, it is important to distinguish between two types of birdplanting—birdfield situations and back course situations. Here we will concern ourselves primarily with the back course variety because, contrary to some opinions, this is the most difficult and most often handled incorrectly.

We must concern ourselves with the location of our "plants" and the manner in which the actual plant is made. If planting game birds on a back course is to be of any value, game must be "find-able." Thus the bird planter should seek to maximize the possibility of game contact for each contestant that has the tools (nose, etc.) to find birds and that has searched intelligently. However, game contact is not enough. It should be as close as possible to the type that one experiences when hunting native game, but not the horse-track finds so often seen. What has the judge really learned about a contestant's ability when he finds birds a few yards either side of the horse track? The closer the bird work can be to that found in natural conditions, the better the test will be.

The ability to locate your "plants" in likely, natural places is critical. This requires keen insight into many circumstances. Some of these are: scenting conditions, topographic features, cover conditions, configuration of objectives, and the type of stake involved.

Assuming that all dogs in a given stake will run over the same course, the bird planter must continuously be assessing the course ahead for likely places to make his plants. He must be looking ahead of him and keeping the above factors in

Figure F-8: *John Rabidou* is the secretary of the National German Shorthaired Pointer Association and field trial chairman of the Four Lakes GSPC, Madison, WI, which places special emphasis on training the bird planters for its trials.

mind, placing his three or four birds for the next brace in spots where competent bird dogs would be expected to go in search of game.

We have all seen trials where brace after brace went birdless and then suddenly, dogs begin to find tons of birds. Scenting conditions are obviously unpredictable and uncontrollable and can change dramatically. Factors such as direction and intensity of the wind, heat, humidity, atmospheric pressure, and so forth, affect this mysterious variable. However, intelligent planning can help alleviate even the worst scenting conditions.

Make your plants so as to maximize the chances of a dog coming into the area into the wind. Of course, we can not predict the dog's movement, but dogs with "bird smarts" will tend to approach most objectives on the downwind side. Use objectives where the logical flow of the course will bring the good mobbing dog into the wind to find the birds.

Windy, blustery weather causes spookiness in most birds. Under these circumstances, they will run and/or flush more often. So put them down "tighter."

Choose your trial weekend when you can expect favorable conditions, that is, not too early in the fall or too late in the spring.

Depressions, gullies, dead furrows and knolls all produce erratic air currents from dead calm areas to swirling air to "off wind" air movement. Never put a bird in a depression with no air circulation. The same holds true for dead furrows. Both of these are often tempting because they harbor cover heavy enough to hold a bird. If a bird is sitting in a depression with no air circulation, there is no movement of his body scent and the likelihood of his being found is very small. Place your birds where the breeze can move the scent.

Figure F-9: *Callbacks.* Tim prepares a pheasant at the 2007 National Open Gun Dog callbacks. For each dog in the callbacks a single bird is dizzied and placed and then the individual dog is immediately brought in to locate and point. The bird will be flushed by the handler allowing the accompanying gunners to shoot—the dog must demonstrate steadiness to wing and shot, as well as the retrieve to hand...all required of a WCA National Champion.

It is difficult to speak generically about cover as each field trial or training ground presents a new set of cover conditions. However, generally speaking, make your plants in cover where you would be most likely to find birds if you were hunting this area, and within the logical limits of the course. Locate your plants to maximize scent movement and to keep the birds from running. This usually means placing them in a clump of grass, brush, briars, etc. that is exposed on all sides, or at least on the up and down wind sides. This will permit air to move to and through the cover. These exposed objectives, if not so exposed that they won't hold the bird, tend to reduce excessive running of birds because most "sane birds" do not wander out into the open when it is avoidable.

Use objectives that are really objectives. Choose spots where a bird dog should go to seek game. Of course, this is often difficult or impossible on some grounds. On these grounds, the bird planter must also be imaginative. Be sure to spread your plants out throughout the entire course. Contestants should hunt and expect to find game on the entire course wherever possible. Rotate the use of your objectives. Don't plant a bird in the same bush hedgerow, or whatever, for every brace. Vary your plants by using as many objectives as available throughout the entire course.

The birdplanter should also be mindful of the type of stake for which he is planting – gundog, all age, puppy, etc. The depth and width of the planting should be adjusted to accommodate the average dog expected in the stake. Of course, some will be wider, others closer, but by working for the mean you will serve the best interests of the greatest number of participants. The common fault is planting too close to the center of the course. This is done either because of ignorance or because the birdplanter is more concerned with keeping up with the gallery than doing a competent job of planting. The planter must be prepared to sacrifice his self-interest in watching as much of the stake as possible. If he does his job conscientiously, he won't have time for "galleryizing."

Beyond proper locations of the plant, it is also imperative that the bird be planted in a manner that maximizes the chances that he will pin, flush, and sly well. The amount of dizzying that is necessary varies from bird to bird—cocks typically require more than hens, especially spring hens that are laying and can stand very little rough treatment. The immediate health of the bird will also affect its ability to withstand stress. The longer it stays in a crate without food, water, and exercise, the weaker will be its condition. So the birdplanter must be sensitive to each bird's overall condition as he prepares to plant him.

Figure F-10: *Birdfield.* Wendy goes out between the braces running at a hunt test to "salt" the bird field and insure that game birds will be available when the brace arrives. These birds are planted on foot, just prior to the dogs entering the area. Using the proper technique for planting birds for different requirements will improve the dog's chances to turn in a good performance.

By planting, we mean dropping the bird off the horse (do not get off the horse and leave your scent) in a slightly dizzied state, just dizzied enough to prevent his flying off prior to being found and to allow placement in the given objective.

Dizzying is best accomplished by placing both hands around the body of the bird and slightly in front of the wings. Then hold the bird in a head-low position and begin a rapid circular movement with a lot of wrist action. This maximizes the spin of the bird's head relative to the body. This "relative spin" (lots of head spin—little body spin) produces abrupt dizziness, but do not overdo it because you could kill or cripple the bird. With experience, you will be able to judge an individual bird's ability to take it.

Basically, you want just enough dizziness to allow you to successfully drop the bird in the objective and then to ride off without flushing it. The bird must be fully awake and capable of movement when the dog and/or handler return to flush it. The above technique, if properly employed, yields a bird that is alert and ready to fly. Remember, if you are going to err, do it on the side of too little rather than too much spin.

Planting birds in a birdfield is much simpler. There is little locational problems as you merely spread them out within the confines of the birdfield. Speaking of confines, make your birdfields big enough so that a dog must hunt a little to cover it and so that the bracemates can get apart in their hunting efforts. In determining where to locate your birdfield, if there are options available, consider the aforementioned variables of terrain, cover, wind conditions, etc.

The actual planting of the birds should be done in a different manner than when planting a back course. Here the bird should be planted on foot just prior to the time the dogs enter the birdfield, but not so close that birdplanters and dogs are there simultaneously.

Rather than dizzy the bird, make the plant in the following fashion. First take the bird by both legs and rub the under side of its body on the grass of cover that will be used. This will help ensure that the bird's scent is strong in the area, stronger than other scents such as the bird's planter. Remember that the bird is strongly scented under his wings as you rub him on the cover. This is why it is often difficult to find birds immediately after they have flown—they are "wind washed."

Pull the bird's head gently around and under one wing. Then spread a slit between two centrally located flight feathers and pull the head into the slit. Close the feathers around the neck close to the base of the head. Then place the bird on its side in the desired plant location with the side the head is on under the bird. Position the bird so that it can see nothing. Hold your hand gently on top of the bird for a few seconds because it might struggle for a few moments. With your free hand, push the cover lightly over the bird. When all attempts at movement have stopped, remove the hand that is holding the bird and exit cautiously.

Why is this technique preferable? Because as soon as the handler disturbs the bird by poking it with his toe, it will roll over, the head will be free from the wing, and it is ready for full flight, unimpaired by dizziness. Furthermore the action of disturbing the bird from this position occurs rapidly and tends to spook the bird into immediate flight rather than running.

Obviously, birds will not remain in this position for long periods and occasionally you will find a bird you just cannot hold with this technique. However, if you time your plants just prior to the entry of the dog into the birdfield, there is usually no problem.

Selection of an experienced end knowledgeable bird dog enthusiast to plant your trail is critical to the quality of performance achieved in your stakes. The same holds true for your individual training endeavors. Your planter must understand all the vagaries of topography, weather, and dogs that make bird planting a most difficult art to master.

Figure F-11: *Field trial.* The birds Pam plants can make the difference in the quality of the dogs' work on the back course at a field trial. Being on horseback allows birds to be planted over a wider area and minimizes the presence of human scent. Bird planting should not be relegated to the newest, least experienced member of the club, but rather it is a labor which must be provided by a dedicated assistant with knowledge of the rules as well as how dog's work scent under the influence of wind, terrain and vegetation.

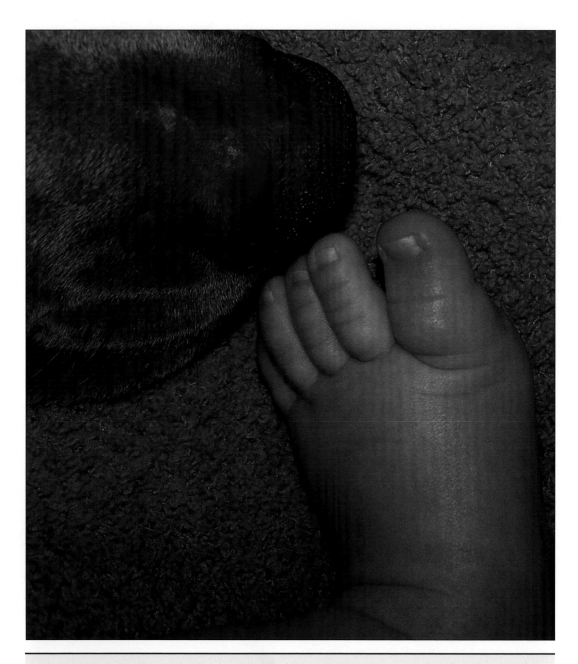

Give the household dog(s) the chance to meet the new packmate before ever coming home by allowing the dogs to smell blankets or clothing that have the baby's scent on them. Play audio tapes of baby noises during pregnancy so the new sounds will become familiar ones. When mother and baby come home, allow the dogs (one at a time if multiple dogs) under supervision to sniff the baby all over, explaining in a positive and happy tone, "This is the new puppy we are going to keep." Try to maintain a regular routine, and involve the dogs in baby activities, especially walk times. New parenting is difficult but try to provide as much attention to the dog(s) as before the baby, so the dog does not feel overlooked; it won't be long before the dog has a new best friend. Photograph by Jen Redmond.

FOOTNOTES

Chapter 1: In the Beginning

1. Ludwig Beckmann, *Geschitchte und Beschribung der Rassen des Hundes,* 2 vols. (Braunschweig, Germany: Vieweg, 1894; Reprint, Mürlenbach, W. Germany: Kynos Verlag Helga Flieg, 1983), 1:171. Translation by Deborah Andrews

2. John Cummings, *The Hound and the Hawk: The Art of Medieval Hunting* (London: Weidenfeld and Nicolson, 1988), 15.

3. Ibid., 21.

4. Ibid., 28.

5. Andre Harmand, Les Braques (Paris: DeVecci, 1983), 72; Pierre Bontier and Jean le Verrier, *The Canarian; or Book of the Conquest and Conversion of the Canarains in the Year 1402* (London: The Hakluyt Society, 1872).

6. "Is This a Weimaraner?" *Weimaraner Magazine,* February 1949, 14.

7. Richard Strebel, *Die Deutsche Hunde und Ihre Abstammung* (Munich: Ertel, 1905), quoted in William Denlinger, The Complete Weimaraner (Richmond, VA: Denlingers, 1954), 24–25.

8. Denlinger, *Weimaraner,* 37.

9. Ibid., 36.

10. "Minutes of the Meeting of the Board of Governors of The Weimaraner Club of America Held on 8 May 1950 at 10 am at the Hotel Ambassador, New York City" (Photocopy typescript).

11. Beckmann, *Geschichte,* 1:297.

12. The stocky Spanish Pointer has a pronounced median line on the skull, also typical of the Weimaraner. The typical colors are orange and white and liver and white; weight 55–65 pounds; height 20–24 inches; stocky, pronounced median line on skull. Bonnie Wilcox and Chris Walkowicz, *Atlas of Dog Breeds of the World* (Neptune City, NJ: TFH Publications, 1989), 655–656.

13. Beckmann, *Geschichte,* 1:306–307.

14. August, Stroese, *Unser Hund* (Neudamm, Germany: Neumann, 1902), quoted in Denlinger, Weimaraner, 25.

15. Beckmann, *Geschichte,* 1:169.

16. Denlinger, *Weimaraner,* 25. Although most Weimaraner literature cites this passage from Fama, none identify the original source.

17. Robert a.d. Herber, *Deutsche Waidwerk,* No. 22, 1 September 1939, quoted in Denlinger, Weimaraner, 26,28.

18. Ibid., 28–29.

19. Ibid., 29.

20. Ibid., 29, 31.

21. Ibid., 32.

Chapter 2: America's Wonder Dog

1. Werner, Petri, *Der Weimaraner Vorsthhund,* rev. ed. (Karlsruhe, W. Ger:N.p., 1984), 20.

2. Jack Denton Scott, *The Weimaraner* (Louisville, KY: Fawcett-Dearing, 1952), 11–12.

3. Jack Denton Scott, "The Gray Ghost Arrives," *Field and Stream,* October 1947, reprinted in *Weimaraner,* by Scott, 14–20.

4. Scott, *Weimaraner,* 12.

5. "The Versatile Weimaraner," *Life,* 12 June 1950, 89.

6. Alastair, MacBain, "The Smartest Dogs in the World," *True,* September 1949, reprinted in *Weimaraner* by Scott, 30–33.

7. Weimaraner, Scott, 30.

8. Ibid., 11,148; "The Best in Dogdom," *Argosy,* July 1949, reprinted in *Weimaraner,* by Scott, 29, "A Fortune in Dogflesh,: *The American Legion,* n.d. reprinted in Weimaraner, by Scott, 44.

9. Jackie Isabell, "Casar Von Gaiberg: The Weimaraner of a Different Color" (Tempe, AZ, November, 1986, Typescript), 3–4. The information about Casar Von Gaiberg is from this unpublished paper, which is primarily based in the "Minutes of Meeting of Board of Governors of the Weimaraner Club of America Held on 8 May 1950 at 10 a.m. at the Hotel Ambassador, New York City" (Photocopy typescript).

10. Homer L. Carr, "The Blue Weimaraner" (Santa Monica, CA, 8 July 1957, Photocopy), 2–3.

11. Petri, *Vorstehund,* 20. Tranlsation by Deborah Andrews.

12. Scott, *Weimaraner,* 131.

13. Ibid.

14. Tom Wilson, "State of the Club & the Breed," *Weimaraner Magazine,* February, 1985, 6.

Chapter 4: The Weimaraner Standard

1. American Kennel Club, *Rules Applying to Dog Shows,* amended ed. (New York: American Kennel Club, 2006), Chapter 11, Section 8A, 47.

2. Leon Fradley, Whiteney, *How to Breed Dogs,* 3rd ed. (New York-Howell Books, 1971), 297–298.

3. "Minutes of the Meeting of the Board of Directors of the Weimaraner Club of America," *Weimaraner Magazine,* March 1986, 50,

4. American Kennel Club, *Rules Applying to Dog Shows,* Chapter 11, Section 8, 45–48.

Chapter 5: Color, Markings and Coat

1. Clarence C. Little, *The Inheritance of Coat Color in Dogs* (Ithaca, NY: Comstock Publishing, 1957), 132.

2. Leon Fradley Whitney, *How to Breed Dogs,* 3rd ed. (New York: Howell Books, 1971), 154,155,157.

3. Little, *Coat Color,* 31–32; H. Pope, "Revision des Erbfaktorenschemas für die aus Loh und Schwarz Zusammergestzte Grunfärbung bei Hundid Sowid Aufdeckung Paralleier Verhältnisse bei Kaninchen," *Zeitschrift für Tierzüchtung und Zuchtungsbiologie,* 100 (1983): 252–265.

4. N.A. Iljin, "Wolf-Dog Genetics," *Journal of Genetics,* 42 (1941): 366–368: Eugene A. Carver, "Coat Color Genetics of the German Shepherd Dog," *Journal of Heredity,* 75 (1984): 251.

5. Iljin, "Wolf-Dog," 366–368.

6. Wally Finch, "Longhairs," *National Dog* (Aust.) July 1988, 46.

Chapter 9: Life With Weimaraners

1. Arizona Humane Society
2. *"Touring With Towser"* is available for $1.50 prepaid through Quaker Professional Services, 585 Hawthorne Ct., Galesburg, IL 64101.

Chapter 10: Best of Health

1. Morris Animal Foundation, "Bloat Update," *Weimaraner Magazine,* October 1987, 40–41
2. ASPCA Animal Poison Control Center in Urbana, IL
3. Roger Yeary, "Herbicides," in *Current Veterinary Therapy IX: Small Animal Practice,* ed. Robert W. Kirk (Philadelphia: Saunders, 1986) 153–156.
4. E. A. Corley and P.M. Hogan. "Trends in Hip Dysplasia Control: Analysis of Radiographs Submitted to the Orthopedic Foundation for Animals, 1974 to 1984," *Journal of American Veterinary Medical Association,* 187 (1985): 805–809; E. A. Corley "Hip Dysplasia: A Report for Orthopedic Foundation for Animals," *Seminars in Veterinary Medicine and Surgery (Small Animal),* 2 (1987) 141–151.
5. Malcolm B. Willis, *Genetics of the Dog* (London: H.F. & G. Witherby, 1989), 148.
6. W. H. Riser, "The Dog as Model for the study of Hip Dysplasia," *Veterinary Pathology* 12 (1975): 235, 321.
7. Ibid, 318.
8. Ibid, 317.
9. Ibid, 247, 319.
10. Ibid, 246–247.
11. Ibid, 253, 256.
12. Ibid, 246; Willis, *Genetics,* 157–160.
13. Riser, "Hip Dysplasia," 246–248.
14. D.G. Lewis, "Cervical Spondylomyelopathy ('Wobbler Syndrome') in the Dog: A Study Based on 224 Cases," *Journal of Small Animal Practice,* 30 (1989): 658.
15. H. Preston Hoskins, J. V. Lacroix, and Karl Mayer, eds., *Canine Medicine,* 2nd ed. (Santa Barbara: American Veterinary Publications, 1959), 18.

Chapter 11: Old as Well as Gray

1. S. Arnold et al., "Urinary Incontinence Spayed bitches: Prevalence and Breed disposition," *Schweizer Archiv für Tierheilkunde,* 131 (1989): 259.
2. The contributor asked not to be identified. Kent Dannen gives a beautifully written discussion of the theological aspects in "Do Dogs Go to Heaven?" *Pure-Bred Dogs/American Kennel Gazette,* December 1987, 42–44.

Chapter 13: Weimaraners Afield

1. *NAVHDA: Aims–Programs–Test Rules,* rev. ed. (Arlington Heights, IL: North American Versatile Hunting Dog Association, 2007), 1.
2. American Kennel Club, *Field Trial Rules and Standard Procedures for Pointing Breeds.* Rev. ed. (New York, NY: American Kennel Club, 2006), Chapter 14, Section 2, 21.
3. American Kennel Club, *Field Trial Rules and Standard Procedures for Pointing Breeds.* Rev. ed. (New York, NY: American Kennel Club, 2006), Chapter 14, Section 7, 23–25.
4. American Kennel Club, *Field Trial Rules and Standard Procedures for Pointing Breeds.* Rev. ed. (New York, NY: American Kennel Club, 2006), Chapter 14, Section 7, 25

Chapter 21: Mating Games

1. Melissa F. Goodman, "Reproductive Physiology—Understanding the Bitch's Cycle," *ICG News,* 5(1991): 3.
2. Ibid., 1.

3. Ibid.
4. Ibid., 3.
5. Ibid., 5.

Chapter 23: Whelping

1. D. Edward Jones and Joan O. Joshua, *Reproductive Clinical Problems in the Dog* (Boston: Wright PSG, 1982). 62.
2. G.C. van der Weyden et al., "the Intra-Uterine Position of Canine Foetuses and their Sequence of Expulsion at Birth," *Journal of Small Animal Practice,* 22 (1981): 509.
3. Ibid., Jones and Joshua, *Problems,* 74.

Chapter 24: The Newborn Period

1. James E. Mosier, "Neonate Survival," *Purebred Dogs/American Kennel Gazette,* May 1990, 84.
2. Cheri A. Johnson and Janet A. Grace, "Care of Newborn Puppies and Kittens," *Forum,* 6 (1987): 15–16.
3. H. Preston Hoskins, J.V. Lacroix, and Karl Mayer, eds., *Canine Medicine,* 2nd edition (Santa Barbara: American Veterinary Publications, 1959) 747–748.
4. Johnson and Grace, *"Newborn,"* 11.

Chapter 28: Health Assessment

1. James J. Nora and F. Clarke Fraser, *Medical Genetics: Principles and Practice,* 2nd edition. (Philadelphia: Lea & Febiger, 1981), 309.
2. Donald D. Draper, "Cryptorchidism in the Dog," *Weimaraner Magazine,* May 1979, 14.
3. John S. Reif and Robert S. Brodey, "The Relationship Between Cryptorchidism and Canine Testicular Neoplasia," *Journal of the American Veterinary Medical Association,* 155 (December 1975): 2005, 2010.
4. Chris Zink, "Early Spay-Neuter Considerations for the Canine Athlete One Veterinarian's Opinion," www.canine-sports.com/SpayNeuter.html HYPERLINK "http://www.canine-sports.com/biograph.html" 2005.
5. C. W. Foley, J. F. Lasley, and G.D. Osweiler, *Abnormalities of Companion Animals: Analysis of Heritability* (Ames: Iowa State University Press, 1979), 69–71; K.C. Barnett, "Comparative Aspects of Canine Hereditary Eye Disease," *Advances in Veterinary Science and Comparative Medicine,* 20 (1976): 43.
6. Frederick B. Hutt, *Genetics for Dog Breeders* (San Francisco: W.H. Freeman, 1979), 163–164; M. W. Fox, "Inherited Inguinal Hernia and Midline Defects in the Dog," *Journal of the American Veterinary Medical Association,* 143 (1963): 602: J.M. Phillips and T. M. Felton, "Hereditary Umbilical Hernia in Dogs," *Journal of Heredity,* 30 (1939): 435.
7. Foley, Lasley, and Osweiler, *Abnormalities,* 139; Joseph Warkany, *Congenital Malformations* (Chicago: Year Book Medical Publishers, 1971), 752–753; Marca Burns and Margaret N. Fraser, *Genetics of the Dog* (Philadelphia: Lippincott, 1966), 89;H. Preston Hoskins, J.V. Lacroix, and Karl Mayer, eds., Canine Medicine, 2nd edition (Santa Barbara: American Veterinary Publications, 1959), 185.
8. Foley, Laskley, and Osweiler, *Abnormalities,* 55.
9. F. W. Nicholas, *Veterinary Genetics* (Oxford: Clarendon Press, 1987), 203–207.
10. Warkany, *Congenital,* 459–463, 470–472; D. F. Patterson, "Canine Congenital Heart Disease, Epidemiological Hypotheses," *Journal of Small Animal Practice,* 12 (1971): 208–281.
11. Mary E. Shelton, "A Possible Mode of Inheritance for Spinal Dysraphism in the Dog with a More Complete Description of the Clinical Syndrome": (Master's Thesis, Iowa State University, 1977), 47–48; Donald Draper, J.P. Kluge, and W.J. Miller, "Clinical and Pathological Aspects of Spinal Dysraphism in Dogs," In *Proceedings*

of the Twentieth World Veterinary Congress, Thessalonika, 1975 (Thessalonika, Greece: G. Papageorgeiou, 1975), 134.

12. Ibid., 137.

13. Shelton grouped the most severely affected dogs (A4) with those that had less sensory deficit (A3) for statistical analysis. A third group (A2) showed minimal but consistent neurological deficit. Those with minimal deficits to pinprick were designated A or Ne. Shelton, "Inheritance," 37–39, 52.

14. Ibid., 37,57–58.

15. Roy Robinson, *Genetics for Dog Breeders,* 2nd edition. (New York: Pergamon, 1990), 231; Malcolm B. Willis, *Genetics of the Dog* (London: H.F. & G Witherby, 1989), 180–187.

16. Robinson, *Genetics,* 242–243.

17. J.J. Kaneko, D. R. Cordy, and G. Carlson, G., "Canine Hemophilia Resembling Classic Hemophilia A," *Journal of American Veterinary Medical Association,* 150(1967): 15–21.

Chapter 35: The German Weimaraner Today

1. Manfred Hölzel, *Die Deutschen Vorstehhunde* (Mürlenbach, Germany: Kynos Verlag Helga Flieg, 1986), 245-246. Translation by Deborah Andrews.

2. The club's official name is Weimaraner Klub e.V.—the e.V. indicating that it is a registered member of the Association for the German Dogs Concern (Der Verband für das Deutsche Hundewesen e.V. [VDH]). The club is also a member of the German Versatile Hunting Dog Association (Jagd-Gebrauchsunverband [JGHV]) and the Fédération Cynologique Internationale (FCI). Germany and all European member countries use the FCI breed standards.

3. The nine Landesgruppen (LG) of the Weimaraner Klub e.V. are Niedersachsen, Bayern, Nord, Südwest, Nordrhein-Westfalen, Hessen, Rheinland-Pfalz/Saarland, Sachsen-Anhalt, and Thüringen.

4. *Schleppenarbeit* is defined as following a *Schleppe* (drag track) made with furred game (fox, rabbit, hare) or feathered game (pheasant, partridge, duck) and retrieving the game to hand. This is considered more of an obedience exercise than a test of nose. The dog must return with the game.

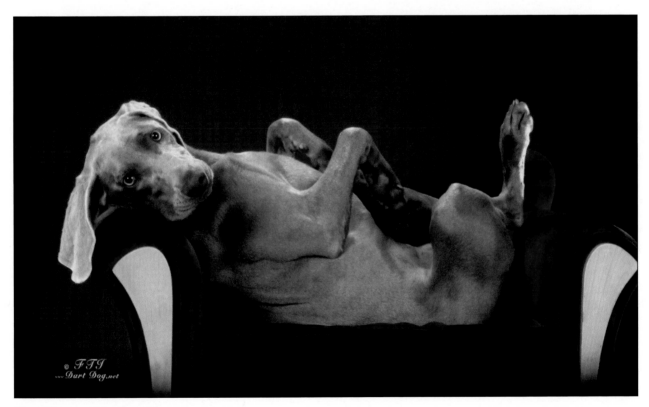

Uma. Photograph by Betty Hogan.

In the Groove, Dogs on Rocks (2009) by William Wegman.

Popular Dog Literature

Books

Adler, Judi. *The Audible Nose* (Sherwood, OR: self-published, 1995).

Aloff, Brenda. *Canine Body Language: A Photographic Guide Interpreting the Native Language of the Domestic Dog* (Wenatchee: Dogwise Publishing, 2005).

American Kennel Club. *The Complete Dog Book.* 16th ed. New York: Howell Books, 1979.

American Rescue Dog Association. *Search and Rescue Dogs—Training the K9 Hero* (New York, NY: Howell House Books, 1991,2002).

Anderson, Bobbie. *Building Blocks for Performance.* Loveland, CO; Alpine Publications. 2002.

Andrews, Deborah G., *The Weimaraner Memory Book,* (Cherry Hill: FurstPless, 2003)

Arnold, Terri. *Steppin' Up to Success With Terri Arnold* (Book 1-3): Freetown: Steppin Up Press, 1999.

Baird, Jack. *Weimaraners.* Jersey City, N.J.: TFH Publications, 1974.

Bambridge, Vicky. *The Weimaraner Today.* (Dorking: Ringpress Books, Interpet Publishing, 2000).

Barwig, Susan. *Schutzhund.* Englewood, Colo.: Barwig, 1978.

Bauman, Diane L. *Beyond Basic Dog Training.* New York: Howell Books, 1986.

Beckman, Ludwig. *Geschichte und Beschreibung der Rassen des Hundes.* 2 vols. Braunschweig, Ger.: Vieweg, 1894. Reprint. Mürlenbach, W. Ger.: Kynos Verlag Helga Flieg, 1983.

Brown, Wentworth, *Bring Your Nose Over Here* (In 2005 available only through Weimaraner Club of Northern Illinois 6971 N Tonty Ave, Chicago, IL 60646).

Bryson, Sandy. *Search Dog Training.* Pacific Grove, Calif.: Boxwood, 1984.

Bulanda, Susan, *Scenting on the Wind* (Sun City, AZ: Doral Publishing, 2002.

Burgoin, Gillian. *Guide to the Weimaraner.* Woodbridge, Eng.: Boydell Press, 1985.

Burns, Marca, and Fraser, Margaret N. *Genetics of the Dog.* Philadelphia: Lippincott, 1966.

Button, Lue. *Practical Scent Dog Training.* Loveland, Colo.: Alpine Publications, 1990.

Bylandt, Henri, Comte de. *Dogs of All Nations.* Deventer, Neth.: A.E. Kluwer, 1904.

Byron, Judy and Yunck, Adele. *Competition Obedience, A Balancing Act.* City: Jabby Productions. 1998.

Campbell, William E. *Behavior Problems in Dogs.* Santa Barbara: American Veterinary Publications, 1975.

Carlson, Delbert G., and Griffin, James M. *Dog Owner's Home Veterinary Handbook.* New York: Howell Books, 1980.

Coffman, Judythe. *A New Owner's Guide to Weimaraners.* (Neptune City: TFH Publications, 1999).

Cummins, John. The Hound and the Hawk: *The Art of Medieval Hunting.* London: Weidenfeld and Nicolson, 1988.

Davis, L. Wilson. *Go Find! Training Your Dog to Track.* New York: Howell Books, 1972.

Header, Dogs on Rocks (2009) by William Wegman.

Dearth, Jane. *The Rally Course Book, A Guide to AKC Rally Courses.* Loveland, CO: Alpine Publications, 2004.

Deckers, J.A.M. (red.) *De Weimaraner* (Langweer, the Netherlads WSH 2001).

Denlinger, William. *The Complete Weimaraner.* Richmond, VA.: Denlingers, 1954.

Dildei, Gottfried, *Tracking Video,* (Littleton, CO: Canine Training Systems, 1993).

Eliott, Rachel P. *The New Dogsteps.* New York: Howell Books, 1983.

Eldred, Susan and Eldred, Orrin, *Fascinating Scent,* (Honor, MI: Purlie Productions, 2004).

Forsyth, Robert, and Forsyth, Jane. *The Forsythe Guide to Successful Dog Showing.* New York: Howell Books, 1975.

Fox, Michael. *The Behavior of Wolves, Dogs, and Related Canids.* New York: Harper and Row, 1970.

Fox, Michael. *Understanding Your Dog.* New York: Coward, McCann, and Geoghegan, 1972.

Fox, Michael. *Between Animals and Man.* New York: Coward, McCann, and Geoghegan, 1976.

Fox, Sue. *Weimaraners, A Complete Pet Owners Manual.* (Hauppage: Barron's Educational Series, 2000).

Ganz, Sandy, and Boyd, Susan. *Tracking from the Ground Up.* St. Louis: Show-Me Publications, 1990.

Geier, Joyce, *Training for Tracklayers,* (Albuquerque, NM: Bishop Printing Company, 1991).

Gerritsen, Resi, and Haak, Ruud, *K9 Professional Tracking—A Complete Manual for Theory and Training* (Calgary, Alberta, Canada: Detseling Enterprises, Ltd., 2001).

Gorny, Boguslaw P., *Tracking for Search and Rescue Dogs* (Calgary, Alberta, Canada: Detseling Enterprises, Ltd, 2003).

Hammond, Shirley M., *Training the Disaster Search Dog* (Wenatchee, WA: Dogwise Publishing, 2005).

Handler, Barbara. *Successful Obedience Handling, Put Your Best Foot Forward in the Obedience Ring.* Loveland, CO: Alpine Publications, 2000.

Harding, Liz and Ryan, Debbie. *Searching for Silver-Grey—2005* (Melbourne: Ghostdog Productions, 2010).

Harding, Liz and Ryan, Debbie. *Silver-Grey* (Melbourne: Ghostdog Productions, 2010).

Harmand, Andre. *Les Braques.* Paris: DeVecci, 1983.

Harper, Lavonia. *Weimaraner, A Comprehensive Owner's Guide* (Allenhurst: Kennel Club Books, 2004).

Hart, Ernest. *This is the Weimaraner.* Jersey City, N.J.: TFH Publications, 1965.

Hill, Gene. *A Hunter's Fireside Book: Tales of Dogs, Ducks, Birds, and Guns.* Hermosa Beach, Calif.: M.C. Winchester, 1972.

Hollings, Patsy. *The Essential Weimaraner.* (New York:: Howell Book House, 1996).

Hölzel, Manfred. *Die Deutschen Vorstehhunde.* Mürlenbach, W. Ger.: Kynos Verlag Helga Flieg. 1986.

Hutt, Frederick B. *Genetics for Dog Breeders.* San Francisco: W.H. Freeman, 1979.

Isabell, Jackie. *Genetics: An Introduction for Dog Breeders.* Loveland, CO: Alpine Publications, 2002.

Jacobs, Jocelyn, DVM. *Performance Dog Nutrition.* (Sanford: Sno Shire Publications, 2005.

Jecs. Dawn. *Choose to Heel.* Puyallup, WA: Self-published, 1995.

Johnson, Glen R. *Tracking Dog—Theory and Methods.* Clark Mills, N.Y.: Arner Publications, 1975.

Kaldenbach, Jan, *K9 Scent Detection—My Favorite Judge Lives in a Kennel* (Calgary, Alberta, Canada:Detseling Enterprises, Ltd., 1998).

Koehler, William P. *The Koehler Method of Dog Training.* New York: Howell Books, 1962.

Kramer, Charles, L. *Agility Training for All Breeds.* Manhatton, Kans.: Cascade Press, 1987.

Kramer, Charles. *Rally–O the Style of Rally Obedience.* CITY: Fancee Publications, 2005.

Washed Up, Dogs on Rocks (2009) by William Wegman.

Krause, Carolyn, *Try Tracking!* (Wenatchee, WA: Dogwise Publishing, 2005).

Lee, Muriel P. *The Whelping and Rearing of Puppies: A Complete and Practical Guide.* Minneapolis: Plantin Press, 1983.

Little, Clarence C. *The Inheritance of Coat Color in Dogs.* Ithaca, N.Y.: Comstock Publishing, 1957.

Lyon, McDowell, *The Dog in Action.* New York: Howell Books, 1950.

Mayer, Diane. *Conquering Ring Nerves: A Step-by-Step Program for All Dog Sports.* New York: Howell Book House. 2004.

McConnell, Patricia B., *I'll Be Home Soon.* Black Earth, WI: Dog's Best Friend Ltd, 2000).

Merck, E., Line, Kahn, Cynthia, Line, Scott. *The Merck Veterinary Manual,* (Whitehouse Station: Merck, 2008).

Monks of New Skete. *How to be Your Dog's Best Friend.* Boston: Little, Brown, 1978.

Morgan, Diane. *Feeding Your Dog for Life.* (Sun City: Doral Publishing, 2002).

Morgan, Diane. *The Weimaraner.* (Neptune City: TFH Publications, 2004).

Mueller, Betty A, *About Track Laying—Guidelines for the Dog Tracking Enthusiasts* (Eliot, ME: Howlin Moon Press, 2001).

NAVHDA: *Aims—Programs—Test Rules.* Rev. ed. Toronto, Ohio: North American Versatile Hunting Dog Association, 1993.

Nicholas, Anna Katherine. *Weimaraners.* Jersey City, N.J.: TFH Publications, 1986.

Ottley, Matt. *What Faust Saw.* (New York: Dutton Children's Books, 1995).

Palika, Liz, *Consumer's Guide to Dog Food.* (New York: Howell Book House, 1996).

Patterson, Gary, *Tracking from the Beginning* (Engelwood, CO: Sirius Publishing, 1992).

Pearsall Margaret. *The Pearsall Guide to Successful Dog Training.* 3d. ed. New York: Howell Books, 1981.

Pearsall, Milo, and Vergruggen, Hugo. *Scent, Training to Track, Search, and Rescue.* Loveland, Colo.: Alpine Publications, 1982.

Pelar, Colleen. *Living With Kids and Dogs Without Losing Your Mind.* (Woodbridge: C&R Publishing, 2005).

Petri, Werner. *Der Weimaraner Vorstehhund.* Rev. ed. Karlsruhe, W. Ger.: N.p., 1984.

Pfaffenberger, Clarence. *The New Knowledge of Dog Behavior.* New York: Howell Books, 1963.

A Pictorial History of the Weimaraner. Rev. ed. Cincinnati: Weimaraner Club of America, 1982.

Prine, Virginia. *How Puppies Are Born.* New York: Howell Books, 1975.

Rebmann, Andy, and David, Edward, and Sorg, Marcella, *Cadaver Dog Handbook—Forensic Training and tactics for the Recovery of Human Remains* (New York, NY: CRC Press, 2000).

Riley, Patricia. *The Weimaraner, An Owner's Guide to a Happy Healthy Pet.* (Foster City: Howell Book House, 2000).

Riser, Wayne H., and Miller, Harry. *Canine Hip Dysplasia and How to Control It.* Philadelphia: Orthopedic Foundation for Animals, 1966.

Robinson, Roy. *Genetics for Dog Breeders.* 2nd ed. New York: Pergamon, 1990.

Rugaas, Turid. *On Talking Terms With Dogs.* (Wenatchee: Dogwise Publishing, 2005).

Sanders, William (Sil), *Enthusiastic Tracking—The Step by Step Training Handbook* (Stanwood, WA: Rime Publications, 1991).

Schoon, Adee and Haak, Ruud, *K9 Suspect Discrimination—Training and Practicing Scent Identification Line-Ups* (Calgary, Alberta, Canada: Detseling Enterprises, Ltd, 2002).

Scott, Jack Denton. *The Weimaraner.* Louisville, KY.: Fawcett-Dearing, 1952.

Self, Robert T. *Dogs Self-Trained, A Training Manual.* Galesburg, IL: R.T. and Associates, 1980.

Sendak, Maurice, and Margolis, Matthew. *Some Swell Pup: Or, Are You Sure You Want a Dog.* New York: Farrar, Straus and Giroux, 1976.

Smith, Cheryl. *Dog Friendly Gardens, Garden Friendly Dogs.* (Wenatchee: Dogwise Publishing, 2003)

Smith, Marsha and Busbyshell, Shalini. *Building a Bridge from Training to Testing.* West Chester, NY: Building a Bridge Publications, 2005.

Sternberg, Sue. *A Guide to the Inducive Retrieve.* Accord, NY: Roundout Valley Kennels, 1993.

Strebel, Richard. *Die Deutsche Hunde und Ihre Abstammung.* Munich: Ertel, 1905.

Stroese, August. *Unser Hund.* Neudamm, Ger.: J. Neumann, 1902.

Syrotuck, William G., *Scent and the Scenting Dog* (Westmoreland, NY: Arner Publications, 1972) Currently (Mechanicsburg, PA: Barkleigh Publications, 2000).

United States Department of Agriculture—Forest Service, *Fire Weather,* Agriculture Handbook 360 (USDA, 1977).

Tarrant, Bill. *The Best Way to Train Your Gun Dog: The Delmar Smith Method.* New York: McKay, 1977.

Wegman, William. *Dogs on Rocks.* (New York City: Marion Bolton Stroud Publisher, 2008).

Wehle, Robert G. *Wing & Shot.* Henderson, N.Y.: Country Press, 1964.

The Weimaraner Manual, rev. ed. Washington, D.C.: Weimaraner Club of the Washington, D.C., Area, 1983.

White, Steve, *Tracking* (Meridian, ID: Tawser Dog Videos, 2005).

Whitney, Leon Fradley. *How to Breed Dogs.* 3d ed. New York: Howell Books, 1971.

Wilcox, Bonnie, and Walkowicz, Chris. *Atlas of Dog Breeds of the World.* Neptune City, N.J.: TFH Publications, 1989.

Willis, Malcolm B. *Genetics of the Dog.* London: H.F. & G. Witherby, 1989.

Winterhelt, Sigbot, and Bailey, Edward. *The Training and Care of the Versatile Hunting Dog.* Toronto, Ohio: North American Versatile Hunting Dog Association, 1973.

Zink, Christine, DVM, *Dog Health and Nutrition for Dummies.* (New York: Hungry Minds, Inc., 2001).

Articles, Papers, Pamphlets

Alexander, Virginia. "Puppy Dog Tails." *Weimaraner Magazine,* February 1970, 17-19.

American Kennel Club. *Registration and Field Trail Rules and Standard Procedure for Pointing Breeds.* Amended ed. New York: American Kennel Club, 1985.

American Kennel Club. *Rules Applying to Registration and Dog Shows.* Amended ed. New York: American Kennel Club, 1989.

American Kennel Club. *Regulations for AKC Hunting Test for Pointing Breeds.* New York: American Kennel Club, 1986.

American Kennel Club. *Obedience Regulations.* Amended ed. New York: American Kennel Club, 1989.

Andrews, Debbie. "The Weimaraner Vorstehhund in Deutschland." *Weimaraner Magazine,* April 1986, 16-21

"The Best in Dogdom." Argosy, July 1949. Reprinted in *The Weimaraner,* by Jack Denton Scott, 20-30. Louisville, KY.: Fawcett-Dearing, 1952.

Brown, Ken. "A Tribute to Tammy." *Weimaraner Magazine,* January 1951, 14.

Burgoin, Gillian. "The Weimaraner." *Dogs Monthly,* July 1987, 11-17.

Carr, Homer L. "The Blue Weimaraner." Santa Monica, Calif. 8 July 1957. Photocopy.

Couto, C. Guillermo. "Immunodeficiency in Young Weimaraners." *Weimaraner Magazine,* September 1988, 9-10.

Dannen, Kent. "Do Dogs Go to Heaven." *Pure-Bred Dogs/American Kennel Gazette,* December 1987, 42-44.

"The Doggondest Dog!" Pageant, August, 1951. Reprinted in *The Weimaraner,* by Jack Denton Scott, 49-51. Louisville, KY.: Fawcett-Dearing, 1952.

Draper, Donald D. "Syringomyelia and Spinal Dysraphism in the Weimaraner." *Weimaraner Magazine,* November 1970, 2-6.

Draper, Donald D. "Cryptorchidism in the Dog" *Weimaraner Magazine,* May 1979, 13-15.

Finch, Wally. "Longhairs." *National Dog* [Aust.], July 1988, 46, 48.

"A Fortune in Dogflesh." *The American Legion Magazine,* n.d. Reprinted in *The Weimaraner,* by Jack Denton Scott, 43-44. Louisville, KY.: Fawcett-Dearing, 1952.

Hall, Elizabeth. "A Digest of Toxic Dangers." *Pure-Bred Dogs/American Kennel Gazette,* February 1981, 29-36.

Herber, Robert, a.d. *Deutsche Waidwerk,* No. 22, 1 September 1939. Reprinted translation in *The Weimaraner,* by William Denlinger, 26-32. Richmond, Va.: Denlingers, 1954,

"Is This a Weimaraner." *Weimaraner Magazine,* February 1949, 14.

Isabell, Jackie. "Cäsar Von Gaiberg: The Weimaraner of a Different Color." Tempe, Ariz., November 1986. Typescript.

Isabell, Jackie. "Exporting a Weimaraner to Down Under." *Pure-Bred Dogs/American Kennel Gazette,* May 1989, 38-41.

Isabell, Jackie. "Lost Dog: Diary of a Nightmare." *Weimaraner Magazine,* April 1991, 35-38; May 1991, 33-36.

Two Rail, Dogs on Rocks (2009) by William Wegman.

Isabell, Jacqueline R. "The Immunization Enigma." Tempe, Ariz., March, 1990, Typescript.

Johnson, Cheri A., and Grace, Janet A. "Care of Newborn Puppies and Kittens." *Forum, 6* (Number 1, 1986): 9-16.

Lyle, Jean M. "Bloat, Seizures, and Stained Teeth . . . Do North Americans Inflict Them Upon Their Dogs?" *Poodle Variety,* June-July 1987, 20, 22, 24.

MacBain, Alastair. "The Smartest Dogs in the World." True, September 1949. Reprinted in *The Weimaraner,* by Jack Denton Scott, 30-42. Louisville, KY.: Fawcett-Dearing, 1952.

Morris Animal Foundation. "Bloat Update." *Weimaraner Magazine,* October 1957 40-41.

Mosier, Jacob E. "Neonate Survival." *Pure-Bred Dogs/American Kennel Gazette,* May 1990, 84-90.

O'Kelley, Joyce. "Swimmers." *Showdogs,* September 1976, 40, 48.

Poole, Ellen. "Schnapps,' the Dog Who sees." *Weimaramer Magazine,* January 1951, 4, 6-7.

Schulze, Helen, "In Thirty-Six Hours from Unknown Puppy to Star in the Dog World." *Weimaraner Magazine,* September 1971, 6-7.

Scott, Jack Denton. "The Gray Ghost Arrives." Field and Stream, October 1974. Reprinted in *The Weimaraner,* by Jack Denton Scott, 14-20. Louisville, KY.: Fawcett-Dearing, 1952.

Scott, Jack Denton. "Is Enthusiasm a Crime." Weimaraner Magazine, February 1951. Reprinted in *The Weimaraner,* by Jack Denton Scott, 408-413. Louisville, KY.: Fawcett-Dearing, 1952.

Seidelman, Marie. "A Tribute to Int. Champion Gourmet's Sardar." *Weimaraner Magazine,* December 1967, 10.

Thau, Susan, "Wrestlemania." *Dog World,* September 1986 69-71.

"The Versatile Weimaraner." *Life,* 12 June 1950, 89.

Wilson, Tom. "State of the Club & the Breed." *Weimaraner Magazine,* February 1985, 6-8.

Veterinary and Other Professional Literature

Books

Christiansen, Ib J. *Reproduction in the Dog and Cat.* Philadelphia: Bailliere Tindall. 1984

Foley, C. W.; Lasley, J. F.; and Osweiler, G.D. *Abnormalities of Companion Animals: Analysis of Heritability.* Ames: Iowa State University Prress, 1979.

Arcade Game, Dogs on Rocks (2009) by William Wegman.

Fox, M. W. *Canine Pediatrics.* Springfield, IL: Charles C. Thomas, 1966.

Heinonen, O.P.; Sloan, D.; and Shapiro, S. *Birth Defects and Drugs in Pregnancy.* Little, Mass.: Publishing Sciences Group, 1977.

Hoskins, H. Preston: Lacroix, J. V.; and Mayer, Karl, eds. *Canine Medicine.* 2d ed. Santa Barbara: American Veterinary Publications, 1959.

Jones, D. Edward, and Joshua, Joan O. *Reproductive Clinical Problems in the Dog.* Boston: Wright PSG, 1982.

King, Robert C., ed. *Handbook of Genetics.* Vol. 4. *Vertebrates of Genetic Interest.* New York: Plenum Press, 1975.

Kingsbury, J.M. *Poisonous Plants of the United States and Canada.* Englewood Cliffs, N.J.: Prentice Hall, 1964.

Lampe, Kenneth F., and McCune, Mary Ann, *AMA Handbook of Poisonous and Injurious Plants.* Chicago: American Medical Association, 1985.

Magrane, William G. *Canine Ophthalmology.* 3d ed. Philadelphia: Lea & Febiger, 1977.

The Merck Veterinary Manual: A Handbook of Diagnosis, Therapy, and Disease Prevention, and Control for the Veterinarian. 6th ed. Rahway, N.J.: Merck, 1986.

Laid Back, Dogs on Rocks (2009) by William Wegman.

Nicholas, F. W. *Veterinary Genetics.* Oxford: Clarendon Press, 1987.

Nora, James J., and Fraser, F. Clarke. *Medical Genetics: Principles and Practice.* 2d ed. Philadelphia: Lea & Febiger, 1981.

Searle, Anthony Gilbert. *Comparative Genetics of Coat Colour in Mammals.* New York: Academic Press, 1968.

Shepard, T. H. *Catalog of Teratogenic Agents.* Baltimore: John Hopkins University Press, 1980.

Tizard, Ian R. *An Introduction to Veterinary Immunology.* Philadelphia: Saunders, 1977.

Warkany, Josef. *Congenital Malformations.* Chicago: Year Book Medical Publishers, 1971.

Articles and Papers

Arnold, S.; Arnold, P.; Hubler, M.; Casal, M.; and Rüsch, P. *"Urinary Incontinence in Spayed Bitches: Prevalence and Breed Disposition."* Schweizer Archiv für Tierheilkunde, 131 (1989): 259-263.

Barnett, K. C. "Comparative Aspects of Canine Hereditary Eye Disease." *Advances in Veterinary Science and Comparative Medicine,* 20 (1976): 39-67

Carmichael, L. E.; Joubert, J. C.; and Pollock, R. V. H. "A Modified Live Canine Parvovirus Vaccine. II. Immune Resonse." *Cornell Veterinarian,* 73 (1983); 13-29

Carmichael, Leland E., and Olin, John M. "Immunization Strategies in Puppies— Why Failures?" *The Compendium for Continuing Education for the Practicing Veterinarian,* 5 (1983): 1043-1052.

Carver, Eugene A. "Coat Color Genetics of the German Shepherd Dog." *Journal of Heredity,* 75 (1984): 247-252.

Corley, E. A. "Hip Dysplasia: A Report from the Orthopedic Foundation for Animals." *Seminars in Veterinary Medicine and Surgery (Small Animal),* 2 (1987): 141-151.

Corley, E. A., and Hogan, P. M. "Trends in Hip Dysplasia Control: Analysis of Radiographs Submited to the Orthopedic Foundation for Animals, 1974-1984." *Journal of the American Veterinary Medical Association,* 187 (1985): 805-809.

Draper, Donald D.; Kluge, J. P.; and Miller, W. J. "Clinical and Pathological Aspects of Spinal Dysraphism in Dogs." In *Proceedings of the Twentieth World Veterinary Congress, Thessalonika,* 1975, 134-137. Thessalonika, Greece: G. Papageorgeiou, 1975.

Farrow, Brian R. H. "Canine Distemper." In *Current Veterinary Therapy VII: Small Animal Practice,* edited by Robert W. Kirk, 1284-1286. Philadelphia: Saunders, 1980.

Fox, M. W. "Inherited Inguinal Hernia and Midline Defects in the Dog" *Journal of the American Veterinary Medical Association,* 143 (1963): 602-604.

Georgi, J. R.; Georgi, M. E.; Fahnestock, G. R.; and Theodorides, V. J. "Transmission and Control of Filaroides Hirthi Lungworm Infection in Dogs." *American Journal of Veterinary Research,* 40 (1979): 829-831.

Glickman, L. T., and Appel, M. J. "Parvovirus Infection and Distemper Vaccination." *Journal of the American Veterinary Medical Association,* 178 (1981): 1030-1031.

Goodman, Melissa F. "Reproductive Physiology—Understanding the Bitch's Cycle." *ICG News,* 5 (1991): 1, 3, 5.

Kaneko, J. J.; Cordy, D. R.; and Carlson, G. "Canine Hemophilia Resembling Classic Hemophilia A." *Journal of the American Veterinary Medical Assication,* 150 (1967): 15-21.

Kelly, John D. "Canine Heartworm Disease." *In Current Veterinary Therapy IX: Small Animal Practice,* edited by Robert W. Kirk, 326-335. Philadelphia: Saunders, 1986.

Klecka, Candace. "Canine Erlichiosis." *Texas Veterinary Medical Journal,* March-April 1984, 16-18.

Krakowka, S.; Olsen, R. G.; Axthelm, M. K.; Rice, J.; and Winters, K. "Canine Parvovirus Infection Potentiates Canine Distemper Encephalitis Attributable to Modified

Live-Virus Vaccine." *Journal of the American Veterinary Medical Association,* 180 (1982): 137-140.

Lawson, D. D. "Canine Distichiasis." *Journal of Small Animal Practice.* 14 (1972): 469-478.

Lewis, D. G. "Cervical Spondylomyelopathy ('Wobbler' Syndrome) in the Dog: A Study Based on 224 Cases." *Journal of Small Animal Practice,* 30 (1989): 657-665.

Martin, K. O. "Panel Report: Vices of Dogs." *Modern Veterinary Practice,* 60 (1979): 756, 758-759.

Mastro, J. M.; Axthelm, M.; Mathes, L. E.; Krakowka, S.; Ladiges, W.; and Olsen, R. G. "Repeated Suppression of Lymphocyte Blastogenesis Following Vaccinations of CPV-Immune Dogs with Modified-Live CPV Vaccubes," *Veterinary Microbiology,* 12 (1986): 201-211.

Pape, H. "Revision des Erbfaktorenschemas für die aus Loh un Schwarz Zusammengestzte Grundfärbung bei Hunden Sowid Aufdeckung Paralleier Verhältnisse bei Kaninchen." *Zeitschrift für Tierzüchtung und Züchtungsbiologie,* 100 (1983): 252-265.

Patterson, D. F. "Canine Congenital Heart Disease. Epidemiological Hypotheses." *Journal of Small Animal Practice,* 12 (1971): 263-287.

Phillips, J. M., and Felton, T. M. "Hereditary Umbilical Hernia in Dogs." *Journal of Heredity,* 30 (1939): 433-435.

Read, D. H., and Harrigonton, D. D. "Experimentally Induced Thiamine Deficiency in Beagle Dogs: Clinical Observations." *American Journal of Veterinary Research,* 42 (1981): 984-991.

Reif, John S., and Brodey, Robert S. "The Relationship Between Cryptorchidism and Canine Testicular Neoplasia." *Journal of the American Veterinary Medical Association,* 155 (1975): 2005-2010.

Riser, W. H. "The Dog as a Model for the Study of Hip Dysplasia." *Veterinary Pathology.* 12 (1975): 235-334.

Roberson, Edward L., and Cornelius, Larry M. "Gastrointestinal Parasitism" In *Current Veterinary Therapy VII: Small Animal Practice,* Edited by Robert W. Kirk, 935-948. Philadelphia: Saunders, 1980.

Ruhr, Lawrence P. "Ornamental Toxic Plans." In *Current Veterinary Theraphy IX: Small Animal Practice,* edited by Robert W. Kirk, 216-220. Philadelphia: Saunders, 1986.

Schneider, Norman R. "Teratogenesis and Mutagenesis." In *Current Veterinary Therapy VII: Small Animal Practice,* edited by Robert W. Kir, 161-171. Philadelphia: Saunders, 1980.

Shelton, Mary E. "A Possible Mode of Inheritance for Spinal Dysraphism in the Dog with a More Complete Description of the Clinical Syndrome." Master's Thesis, Iowa State University, 1977.

Siracusa, Linda D.; Russel, Liane B.; Eicher, Eva M.; Corrow, Dorcas J.; Copeland, Neal G.; and Jenkins, Nancy A. "Genetic Organization of the Agouti Region of the Mouse." *Genetics,* 117: 93-100.

Slater, E. A. "The Response to Measles and Distemper Virus in Immuno-Suppressed and Normal Dogs." *Journal of the American Veterinary Medical Association,* 156 (1970): 1762-1766.

Smythe, R. H. "The 'Fading' Syndrome in Newborn Puppies." *Veterinary "Record,* 75 (1963): 741.

Strombeck, Donald R. "Acute Gastric Dilation—Volvulus." In *Current Veterinary Therapy VII: Small Animal Practice,* edited by Robert W. Kirk, 896-901. Philadelphia: Saunders, 1980.

Tizard, Ian R. "Why Vaccines Fail." *Veterinary Reports,* 2 (1989): 2-3.

van der Weyden, G. C.; Taverne, M. A. M.; Okkens, A. C.; and Fontijne, P. "The Intra-Uterine Position of Canine Foetuses and Their Sequence of Expulsion at Birth." *Journal of Small Annimal Practice,* 22 (1981): 503-510.

Yeary, Robert A. "Herbicides." In *Current Veterinary Therapy IX: Small Animal Practice,* edited by Robert W. Kirk, 53-156. Philadelphia: Saunders, 1986.

2 p.m., Dogs on Rocks (2009) by William Wegman.

Catty, by William Wegman

INDEX OF DOG NAMES